The 50 States

The 50 States

Managing Editor, **R. Kent Rasmussen**

Contributors

Charles F. Bahmueller
Center for Civic Education
Calabasas, California

Rose Secrest
Signal Mountain, Tennessee

Carl L. Bankston III
Tulane University
New Orleans, Louisiana

R. Baird Shuman
University of Illinois
Urbana, Illinois

Kevin M. Mitchell
Glendale, California

Rowena Wildin
South Pasadena, California

Lauren M. Mitchell
Glendale, California

Michael Witkoski
Columbia, South Carolina

SALEM PRESS, INC.

PASADENA, CALIFORNIA   HACKENSACK, NEW JERSEY

Editor in Chief: Dawn P. Dawson

Managing Editor: R. Kent Rasmussen   *Copy Editor:* Lauren M. Mitchell
Research Supervisor: Jeffry Jensen   *Research Assistant:* Jeff Stephens
Acquisitions Editor: Mark Rehn   *Assistant Photo Editor:* Philip Bader
Production Editor: Joyce I. Buchea   *Layout:* William Zimmerman
Photograph Production: Yasmine Cordoba   *Design and Graphics:* James Hutson

Maps in this volume are adapted from Cartesia's MapArt™ Geopolitical Deluxe v2.0 (1998)

Library of Congress Cataloging-in-Publication Data

The 50 states / managing editor, R. Kent Rasmussen ; contributors, Charles Bahmueller . . . [et al.].
     p. cm.
Includes bibliographical references and index.
ISBN 0-89356-999-2 (alk. paper)
    1. U.S. states—Miscellanea. 2. United States—Miscellanea. I. Title: Fifty states. II. Rasmussen, R. Kent. III. Bahmueller, Charles F.

E180.A15 2000
973—dc21   00-026577

Third Printing

CONTENTS

Contents

Contents

Contents

Contents

Contents

Publisher's Note

This volume is designed to serve the needs of students and members of the public seeking basic and up-to-date information on individual states of the United States. One of its central objectives is to help users find the information they want as quickly and efficiently as possible. To this end, each state is the subject of its own chapter. Moreover, every chapter presents the same kinds of information, in the same formats, and in the same order. The chapters themselves are arranged alphabetically, by the states' names.

Each chapter in *The 50 States* opens with a profile listing basic data on population, geography, history, and other facts. This section is followed by a brief history of the state, emphasizing the events and forces that worked to make it what it is today. Additional historical details are provided in a time line, which is followed by study notes on both published books and resources on the World Wide Web.

Every chapter also contains a list of all the counties in the state, giving their populations and areas. Each county list is complemented by a map of the state showing the location of every county. Each chapter also has a list of the largest cities and towns of at least ten thousand residents, as well as a map of cities and towns. In addition to these maps, every chapter contains a map showing the state's major physical features.

The bulk of each chapter is made up of thirty-eight statistical tables. Drawing mostly on the latest federal government statistics, these tables emphasize current data on the subjects likely to be of greatest interest to readers. Moreover, the Editors have made every effort to present data in forms that can be readily understood. Many tables contain special features not found in government-published compilation statistics: figures showing how each state ranks in important statistic categories and figures showing each state's share of a national total. For example, the very first demographic table gives state and national population totals for selected years between 1970 and 1997, as well as each state's share of the national figure and its rank among all the states.

The tables offer comprehensive population data, including projections of each state's population growth through the year 2025. Other tables summarize such vital statistics as infant mortality rates; average lifespans; and marriage, divorce, and death rates. Economic data are provided in tables summarizing statistics on housing, land use, gross state products, personal income, and agricultural data. The book also offers statistics on state government revenue and expenditures. Political data include lists of all state governors, political makeups of state and federal legislators, and voter participation in presidential elections. Other tables offer data on transportation, recreation, crime, and law enforcement.

Appendices summarizing data on state population size, land area, and several other subjects can be found at the back of the volume. Users should be able to find most of the information they seek by simply turning to the chapters for the states that interest them. If they need additional help, they can refer to the subject index at the end of the volume.

While most of the information in this volume has been adapted from government resources, the Editors are grateful to the scholars who contributed the original essays that begin each chapter.

The 50 States

United States of America

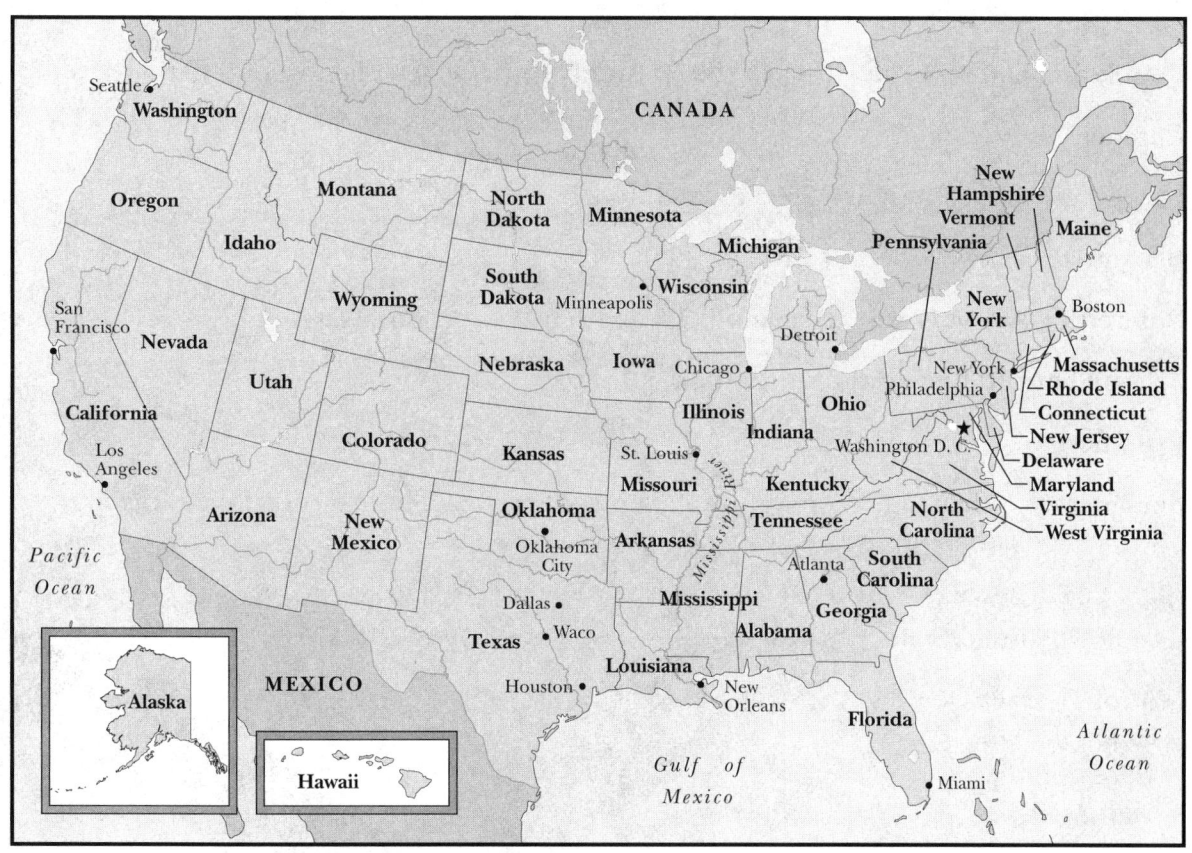

Alabama

Location: Southeastern continental United States

Area and rank: 50,750 square miles (131,443 square kilometers); 52,423 square miles (135,776 square kilometers) including water; twenty-eighth largest state in area

Coastline: 53 miles (85 kilometers)

Shoreline: 607 miles (977 kilometers)

Population and rank: 4,319,154 (1997); twenty-third largest state in population

Capital: Montgomery

Largest city: Birmingham (252,997 in 1998)

Became territory: March 3, 1817

Entered Union and rank: December 14, 1819; twenty-second state

Present constitution adopted: 1901

Counties: 67

State name: "Alabama" is thought to have come from a Choctaw word meaning "thicket-clearers" or "vegetation gatherers"

State nickname:
Yellowhammer State

Motto: *Audemus jura nostra defendere* (We dare defend our rights)

State flag: White field with crimson cross of Saint Andrew

Highest point: Cheaha Mountain — 2,405 feet (733 meters)

Dauphin Street in Alabama's second-largest city, Mobile. (Alabama Bureau of Tourism & Travel/Karim Shamsi Basha)

Lowest point: Gulf of Mexico — sea level

Highest recorded temperature: 112 degrees Fahrenheit (44 degrees Celsius) — Centerville, 1925

Lowest recorded temperature: −27 degrees Fahrenheit (−33 degrees Celsius) — New Market, 1966

State song: "Alabama"

State tree: Southern pine (longleaf)

State flower: Camellia

State bird: Yellowhammer

State fish: Tarpon (saltwater); largemouth bass (freshwater)

Alabama History

Alabama is in the southeastern part of the United States, between Mississippi to the west and Georgia and Florida to the east. Most of Alabama's southern border adjoins Florida, but a small portion of the state extends down to the Gulf of Mexico. The northern part of Alabama, just below Tennessee, is known as the Appalachian region. It is made up of high plateaus, ridges, valleys, and the high Talladega Mountains. The Piedmont Plateau, another rocky region, extends from the Talladega Mountains to the Georgia border. Until well into the twentieth century, many of the people in the highlands of Alabama lived the isolated lives of mountain and hill dwellers. The Interior Low Plateau region is the part of northern Alabama drained by the Tennessee River. Below the northern uplands, the Gulf Coastal Plains extend south to the Gulf of Mexico. The Gulf Coastal Plains include the Black Belt, a dark-soiled prairie.

The Tennessee River area and the Black Belt have rich soil. Together with Alabama's hot, humid climate, this has made these territories ideal for agriculture. As a result, agriculture tended to dominate the state's economic activities until the second half of the twentieth century. Worldwide demand for cotton in the nineteenth century led the state to specialize in cotton production. Since cotton was a crop that required a great deal of unskilled labor, this created a reliance on slavery that profoundly affected the state's history.

Early History. Before the arrival of the Europeans, Alabama was dominated by Native Americans known as the Mound Builders, after their ceremonial earth mounds. The best-known archaeological site of the Mound Builders in Alabama is at Moundville on the Black Warrior River in central Alabama. Moundville was a large and complex society, second in size and organization only to the Cahokia site of Mound Builder culture in Illinois. Both a populous town and a political and religious center, the Moundville community itself probably housed about one thousand people at its height and was surrounded by around ten thousand people living in the Black Warrior River Val-ley. This settlement lasted from about 1000 C.E. to about 1450.

In the eighteenth century, the Creeks were one of the largest and predominant Native American groups in Alabama. The Creek, who lived in villages of log houses, sided with the British against the Americans in both the Revolutionary War and the War of 1812. At war with the Americans, they were defeated by General Andrew Jackson, and by 1828 they agreed to give up all of their lands and move to Indian Territory in modern Oklahoma. Similarly, most of the Choctaw and the Chickasaw were removed from Alabama and the adjacent states. The Cherokee, who were spread throughout the Southeast, were also well represented in Alabama. In 1838 most of the Cherokee were also forced to relocate to Indian Territory.

Exploration and Colonization. Spanish explorers reached Alabama around 1519. The Spanish attempted to establish a settlement at Mobile Bay but soon deserted it, leaving cattle, hogs, and horses behind, all of which became part of local Native American ways of life. Two decades later, the French claimed much of Alabama as part of their vast Louisiana territory, and they built forts and trading posts. After France and Great Britain fought the French and Indian Wars (1754-1763), Alabama fell under the control of the British. The coastal area, including Mobile Bay, became part of West Florida. North of West Florida, all of Alabama was reserved by the British for the Native Americans.

During the American Revolution, Spain captured Mobile from the British, shutting the British out of Alabama. After the Revolution, West Florida became Spanish land, and interior Alabama was turned over to the new United States. After several years of border disputes, the United States and Spain finally agreed in 1795 that latitude thirty-one degrees north would be the boundary between U.S. land and West Florida; this would continue to be the boundary between Alabama and the Florida Panhandle. In 1798 the U.S. Congress formed the Mississippi Territory, made up of modern Mississippi and Alabama. The portion of the territory along the Mississippi River became the state of Mississippi in 1817, leaving Alabama as a new territory in its own right. Two years later, Alabama was admitted to the Union as the twenty-second state.

Slavery and Civil War. Alabama's rich soil led to an influx of settlers. Worldwide demand for cotton made this crop enormously profitable for a few wealthy landowners. Black slaves worked the cotton plantations, and between 1830 and 1860 the state's slave population grew by 270 percent, while the white population grew by only 170 percent. Although the big plantation owners made up only about 6 to 7 percent of Alabama's population, they were enormously influential and dominated the state's society. The majority of white Alabamians, especially in the hills and mountains, were small subsistence farmers.

Slavery became a contentious issue in the United States in the first half of the nineteenth century. As new territories entered the United States, many Northern leaders opposed the spread of slavery. The Southern political leadership, dominated by the plantation owners, saw slavery as essential to the Southern agri-

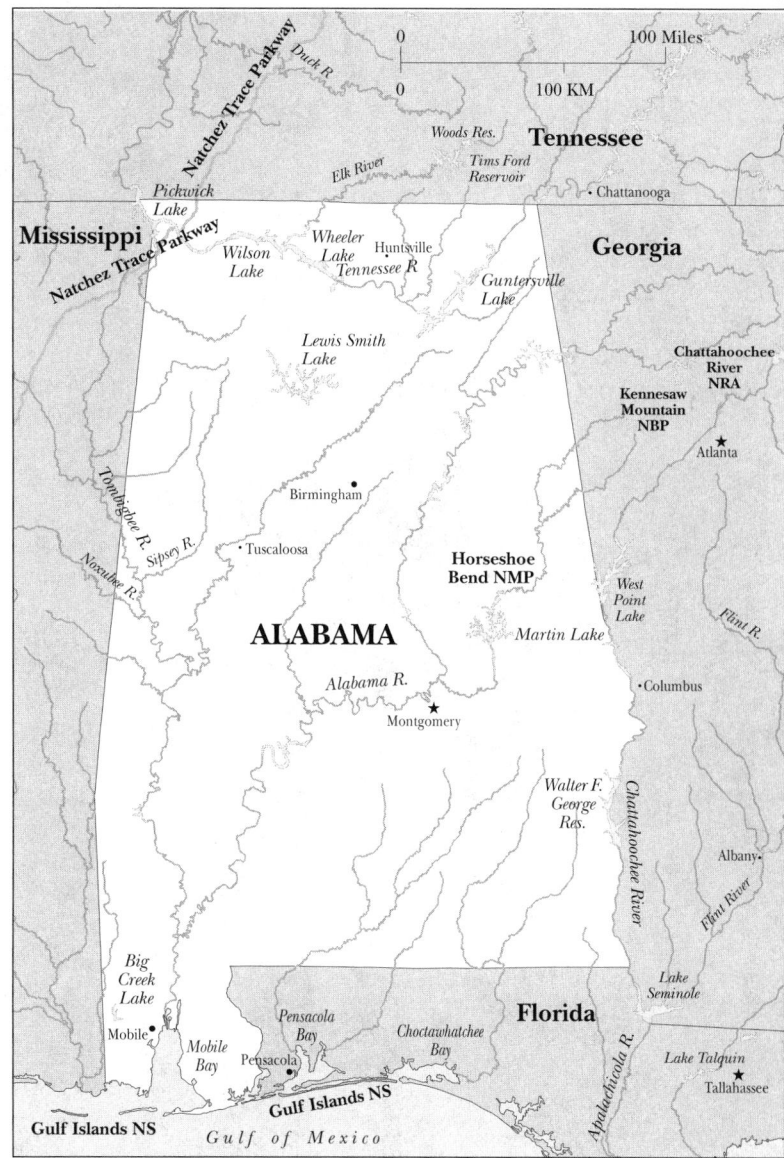

cultural way of life and feared falling under the control of the populous North. In 1861 Alabama joined other Southern states in seceding from the United States and forming the Confederate States of America. The bitter Civil War ensued. By 1865 Alabama and the other Southern states had been defeated and occupied by Northern troops.

With the end of the Civil War, Alabama's slaves received freedom. However, there were few economic opportunities for them, and most had to take jobs working as low-income agricultural la-

borers for white landowners. The American Missionary Association and the Federal Freedmen's Bureau helped to establish schools that formed a basis for future African American education. Although African Americans received the right to vote during Reconstruction, the period from after the Civil War to 1877, when Union troops withdrew from the South, relatively few Alabamian blacks were able to take positions of political leadership because of the former slaves' lack of education and experience. By 1874, white Southern

Democrats managed to take control of the state government. Throughout the nineteenth century, the white state government established legal segregation and restriction of the rights of African Americans.

The Civil Rights Era. During the 1950's and 1960's, African Americans in Alabama and other southern states began organizing to oppose segregation and racial discrimination. In 1955 Rosa Parks, a black citizen of Montgomery, Alabama, was arrested when she refused to give up her seat on a bus to a white passenger. In response, the Afri-

can American residents of Montgomery, under the leadership of the clergyman Dr. Martin Luther King, Jr., organized a boycott of the city's public transportation system. The successful boycott made King a national civil rights leader, and he went on to advocate desegregation campaigns and marches throughout the South.

Alabama Governor George Wallace, first elected in 1962, came to national prominence as a result of his opposition to integration. Wallace had experienced defeat in a first run for governor in 1959, when he refused the support of the Ku Klux Klan and ran a campaign of racial moderation. After that defeat, he became a staunch segregationist and attempted to block the integration of Alabama's schools and universities. On the basis of the national recognition brought by his segregationist policies, Wallace ran for president of the United States in 1968 as the candidate of the American Independent Party.

Although racial inequality continued to be a problem in Alabama, segregation became illegal, and black Alabamians achieved substantial social and political influence. From 1969 to 1970, the percentage of African American students attending integrated schools increased from 15 percent to 80 percent. In 1982, when George Wallace was elected to his third term as governor, he actively appealed to black voters and renounced his earlier racial positions.

Alabama's Industrialization. Alabama saw substantial industrialization over the course of the twentieth century. In 1907 United States Steel Corporation established a steel industry in Birmingham. Iron and steel became leading products of Alabama, concentrated mainly in the Birmingham area.

The port city of Mobile became a center of shipbuilding during World War I. Shipbuilding and ship repair continued to be important on the Alabama Gulf Coast, but the area around Mobile also began to produce paper and chemical products. The city of Huntsville became a focal point of U.S. government missile manufacturing and the aerospace industry after World

The somewhat whimsical Boll Weevil Monument in Enterprise recalls the important part cotton played in Alabama's history. (Alabama Bureau of Tourism & Travel/Dan Brothers)

War II. Cutbacks in federal government spending caused Huntsville to diversify its economy after the 1970's, and other high technology industries located there.

Despite the rapid industrialization, agriculture continued to be a major economic activity. However, most modern agricultural activities in Alabama are heavily mechanized and use relatively little labor. Cotton remains important, but many of the old cotton fields now produce peanuts, soybeans, corn, and other crops.

As Alabama has industrialized, its population has shifted from rural areas to urban areas. In 1990, 60 percent of the people in the state lived in places with more than 2,500 inhabitants. Birmingham was the largest concentration, with more than a quarter million people. African Americans, who lived almost entirely in rural areas in the early twentieth century, were heavily concentrated in larger cities in the southern and central parts of the state by 1990.

Carl L. Bankston III

Birmingham's Civil Rights Institute is a memorial to the city's central role in the Civil Rights movement. (Alabama Bureau of Tourism & Travel/Karim Shamsi Basha)

Alabama Time Line

700-1300	Mound Builders of the Mississippian culture build ceremonial mounds in the eastern part of North America, including Moundville in Alabama's Hale County.
1519	Spaniard Alonzo Alvárez de Piñeda sails into Mobile Bay.
July 2, 1540	Spanish explorer Hernando de Soto reaches Mobile, Alabama, while exploring southeastern North America.
1682	French explorer René-Robert Cavalier, sieur de La Salle, travels down the Mississippi to its mouth and claims all lands along the river in the name of France.
1712	French settlement and fort are established at Mobile, on the Gulf of Mexico.
1763	Great Britain takes control of Alabama and other parts of the Mississippi region after winning the French and Indian War.
Mar. 4, 1780	Spanish capture Mobile from the British during the American Revolution.
1799	American surveyor marks the thirty-first latitude as the boundary between Spanish West Florida and the United States.
1802	State of Georgia gives up its claims on most of the lands of modern Alabama.

(continued)

1805-1806	Choctaw, Chickasaw, and Cherokee lands are opened up to settlement by non-Native Americans.
Apr. 15, 1813	Spanish surrender Mobile to American forces; United States annexes part of Spanish West Florida, including the Alabama coast.
July, 1813	Creek Indian Wars begin between the United States and the Creeks.
Mar., 1817	Alabama is made a territory.
Dec. 14, 1819	Alabama becomes the twenty-second state of the Union.
1826	Alabama's capital is moved from St. Stephens to Tuscaloosa.
Sept. 27, 1830	Choctaws cede the rest of their lands to Alabama and are removed to Oklahoma.
1846	Alabama's general assembly votes to move the capital to Montgomery.
1856	Large-scale coal mining begins in Alabama when the Alabama Coal Mining Company establishes underground mines.
Jan. 11, 1861	Alabama convention votes to secede from the Union.
May 26, 1865	Last Confederate army unit surrenders, ending the Civil War.
1868	Alabama ratifies a new constitution, recognizing the right of blacks to vote; is then readmitted to the United States.
1871	Birmingham is founded.
1874	Conservative Democrats regain control of the Alabama state government.
Feb. 10, 1881	Booker T. Washington founds Tuskegee Institute (later Tuskegee University), a renowned African American center of higher education.
1901	New state constitution is ratified that effectively disenfranchises black Alabamians and greatly reduces the number of poor white voters.
1907	U.S. Steel Corporation establishes a steel industry in Birmingham.
1948	Democratic president Harry S Truman's support for civil rights prompts conservative southern Democrats to form Dixiecrat Party, which nominates Strom Thurmond for president.
1955-1956	Montgomery bus boycott follows refusal of seamstress Rosa Parks to give up her bus seat to a white passenger.
1963	George C. Wallace begins the first of his four terms as governor.
1965	Civil rights march from Montgomery to Selma calls national attention to the need for a national voting rights bill.
1982	George Wallace is elected with black support to his third term as governor.
1987	Guy Hunt becomes the first Republican governor since Reconstruction.
1991	Alabama's state universities are ordered by a federal district judge to hire more minority faculty members.

Notes for Further Study

Published Sources. *Alabama: The History of a Deep South State* (1994), by William Warren Rogers, Robert David Ward, Willia Rogers, and Leah R. Atkins, is an excellent history of Alabama. It is divided into three sections. The first ends with Alabama's Civil War defeat in 1865, the second covers the state from the end of the war to the 1920's, and the third covers Alabama to 1993. Allen Cronenberg's *Forth to the Mighty Conflict: Alabama and World War II* (1995) is an intriguing examination of the impact of World War II on the state and of the role played by Alabamians in this modern struggle. Some of the most interesting parts of the book concern the Tuskegee Army Air Field, where African American pilots learned to fly, and the prisoner-of-war camps for German soldiers in Alabama. Readers will find an in-depth look at the beginnings of the Civil Rights movement in *Alabama in Daybreak of Freedom: The Montgomery Bus Boycott* (1997), a documentary history assembled by editor Stewart Burns. Historian Glenn T. Eskew provides a look at another center of the Civil Rights movement in *But for Birmingham: The Local and National Movements in the Civil Rights Struggle* (1997), which describes the movement in Birmingham from the end of World War II onward. Marshall Frady's *Wallace* (1996) is a political biography of the controversial Alabama governor and U.S. presidential candidate George Wallace. Frady provides a detailed portrait of this complex individual, and he argues that Wallace's 1968 campaign for president helped to build a conservative working-class voting block that later contributed to the election of President Ronald Reagan.

Web Resources. The Alabama Department of Archives and History has a wide range of Internet links available (http://www.archives.state.al.us). This may be the best place on the Web to begin looking for information on any aspect of Alabama history or modern life in Alabama. For geographic information, there is a map of Alabama at the Auburn University Web site (http://www.eng.auburn.edu/alabama/map.html). Data on cities may be obtained by clicking at the appropriate places on this map. It also provides ready access to files on counties, emblems and symbols, historical resources, statistics, state agencies, and various political officials. Those interested in learning about their family connections to Alabama's Civil War history will want to look at the Alabama Civil War Roots home page (http://www.rootsweb.com/~alcwroot). The purpose of this page is to help people find their Alabama Civil War ancestors, on both the Union and Confederate sides. Another good resource on the Civil War in Alabama is the Alabama Civil War Regimental Histories page (http://www.tarleton.edu/~kjones/alregts.html), which offers brief histories of infantry and cavalry units raised in Alabama.

Counties

County	Sq. miles	1996 pop.	County	Sq. miles	1996 pop.
Autauga	596.0	40,061	DeKalb	778.0	57,165
Baldwin	1,596.5	123,023	Elmore	621.6	58,460
Barbour	885.0	26,475	Escambia	947.5	35,620
Bibb	622.4	18,142	Etowah	534.8	102,129
Blount	645.7	43,392	Fayette	627.8	17,944
Bullock	625.1	11,188	Franklin	635.7	29,253
Butler	776.9	21,530	Geneva	576.4	24,618
Calhoun	608.5	113,511	Greene	646.0	9,947
Chambers	597.4	36,748	Hale	643.8	16,288
Cherokee	553.2	21,170	Henry	562.0	15,232
Chilton	694.1	35,323	Houston	580.4	83,778
Choctaw	913.6	15,714	Jackson	1,078.8	50,428
Clarke	1,238.5	27,982	Jefferson	1,112.7	661,927
Clay	605.1	13,544	Lamar	604.9	15,591
Cleburne	560.2	13,445	Lauderdale	669.5	83,593
Coffee	679.2	41,910	Lawrence	693.4	33,037
Colbert	594.6	52,490	Lee	608.8	95,038
Conecuh	850.9	14,112	Limestone	568.1	59,844
Coosa	652.5	11,444	Lowndes	718.0	12,811
Covington	1,034.7	37,263	Macon	610.6	23,563
Crenshaw	609.6	13,514	Madison	805.0	270,309
Cullman	738.5	73,274	Marengo	977.1	23,430
Dale	561.1	49,167	Marion	741.5	30,718
Dallas	980.8	47,362	Marshall	567.1	79,159

(continued)

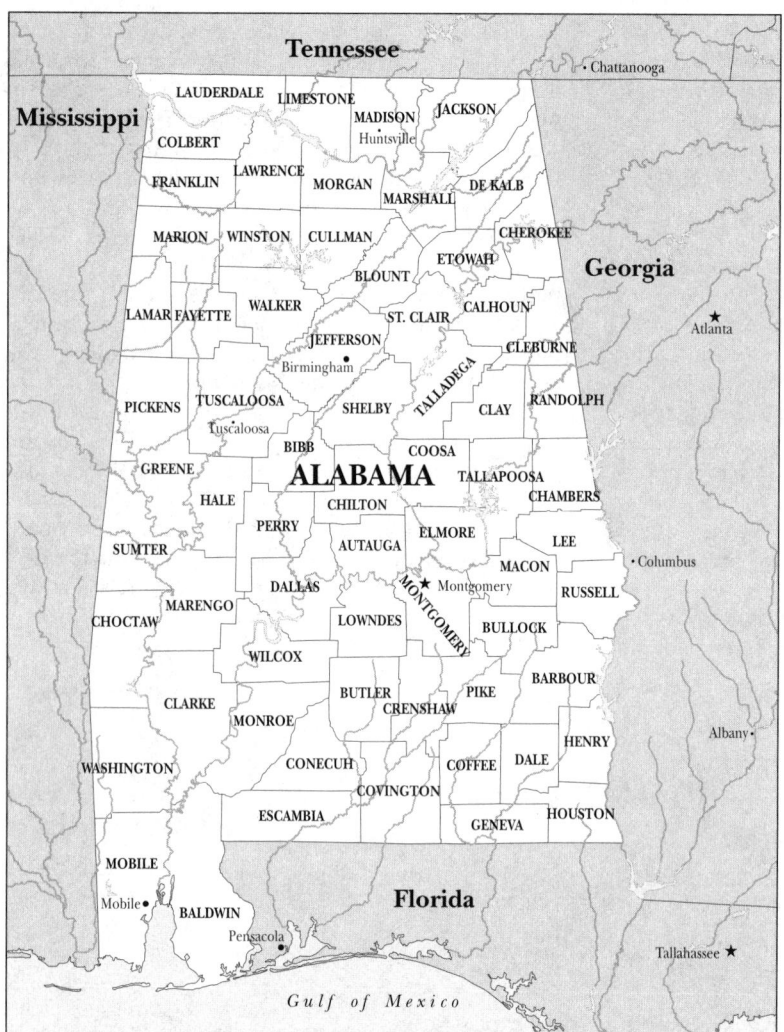

County	Sq. miles	1996 pop.
Mobile	1,233.4	395,952
Monroe	1,026.0	23,874
Montgomery	789.9	216,434
Morgan	582.2	106,942
Perry	719.5	12,717
Pickens	881.5	20,864
Pike	671.1	28,464
Randolph	581.1	20,073
Russell	641.1	51,439
Saint Clair	634.0	59,218
Shelby	794.9	130,165
Sumter	905.0	16,174
Talladega	739.6	76,369
Tallapoosa	718.0	39,810
Tuscaloosa	1,325.3	158,779
Walker	794.5	69,686
Washington	1,080.7	17,341
Wilcox	888.8	13,515
Winston	614.5	23,602

Source: U.S. Census Bureau; National
   Association of Counties.

Cities
With 10,000 or more residents

Rank	City	Population		Rank	City	Population
1	Birmingham	252,997		8	Decatur	54,694
2	Mobile	202,181		9	Gadsden	42,158
3	Montgomery	197,014		10	Auburn	40,425
4	Huntsville	175,979		11	Florence	39,098
5	Tuscaloosa	83,376		12	Prichard	32,610
6	Hoover	59,551		13	Bessemer	30,841
7	Dothan	57,069		14	City	27,353

After World War II, Huntsville became an aerospace and space technology hub; today it is home to the U.S. Space and Rocket Center. (Alabama Bureau of Tourism & Travel/Karim Shamsi Basha)

Rank	City	Population	Rank	City	Population
15	Prattville	25,769	26	Mountain Brook	18,497
16	Anniston	25,524	27	Talladega	17,449
17	Madison	25,400	28	Albertville	16,867
18	Opelika	24,490	29	Alexander City	16,024
19	Alabaster	23,760	30	Daphne	15,687
20	Homewood	22,452	31	Hueytown	14,978
21	Selma	22,037	32	Cullman	14,437
22	Vestavia Hills	21,838	33	Scottsboro	14,215
23	Enterprise	21,663	34	Pelham	14,146
24	Northport	20,247	35	Jasper	14,110
25	Athens	19,720	36	Troy	13,487

(continued)

Rank	City	Population
37	Eufaula	13,463
38	Saraland	12,976
39	Fairhope	12,734
40	Ozark	12,660
41	Fort Payne	12,648
42	Sylacauga	12,518
43	Hartselle	12,431
44	Trussville	11,516
45	Fairfield	11,183
46	Oxford	11,031
47	Tuskegee	10,989
48	Muscle Shoals	10,966
49	Millbrook	10,824
50	Leeds	10,750
51	Pell City	10,399
52	Jacksonville	10,053
53	Sheffield	10,001

Population figures are estimated for mid-1998.

Source: U.S. Bureau of the Census.

Index to Tables

NA = Reliable data are not available.

DEMOGRAPHICS

Resident state and national populations, 1970-1997

Population figures given in thousands

	State pop.	U.S. pop.	Share	Rank
1970	3,444	203,302	1.7%	21
1980	3,894	226,546	1.7%	22
1985	3,973	237,924	1.7%	22
1990	4,040	248,765	1.6%	22
1995	4,262	262,761	1.6%	23
1997	4,319	267,636	1.6%	23

Source: U.S. Bureau of the Census.

Resident population by age, 1997

Age group	Total population
Under 5 years	293,000
5 to 17 years	779,000
18 to 24 years	436,000
25 to 34 years	630,000
35 to 44 years	684,000
45 to 54 years	551,000
55 to 64 years	385,000
65 to 74 years	312,000
75 to 84 years	188,000
85 years and over	61,000
Portion of residents 65 and older	13.0%
National average	12.7%

Population figures are rounded to nearest thousand persons; figures include armed forces personnel stationed in state.
Source: U.S. Bureau of the Census.

Resident population by race, Hispanic origin, 1997

	State pop.	Share	U.S.
All residents	4,319,000	100.0%	100.0%
Hispanic white	34,000	0.8%	10.0%
non-Hispanic white	3,122,000	72.%	72.7%
African American	1,120,000	25.%	12.7%
Native American	15,000	0.4%	0.9%
Asian, Pacific Islander	28,000	0.7%	3.8%

Source: U.S. Bureau of the Census.

Projections of state population, 2000-2025

	Model A Uses interstate migration observed from 1975-1994	Model B Uses Bureau of Economic Analysis employment projections
Year	Population	Population
2000	4,451,000	4,436,000
2005	4,631,000	4,617,000
2010	4,798,000	4,802,000
2015	4,956,000	4,986,000
2020	5,100,000	5,162,000
2025	5,224,000	5,319,000

All population projections, including those for 2000, were calculated in 1997.
Source: U.S. Bureau of the Census, Population Paper Listings PPL-47.

VITAL STATISTICS

Average lifetime in years by race, 1989-1991

	State	U.S.	Rank
All residents	73.64	75.37	45
White residents	75.01	76.13	44
Black residents	69.23	69.16	21

Ranks are from longest-lived to least longest-lived. Ranks exclude Alaska, for which reliable data are not available. Rank for black residents is based on the 32 states for which reliable data are available.
Source: U.S. National Center for Health Statistics.

Infant mortality rates, 1980 and 1995

	State	U.S.
All residents		
1980	15.1	12.6
1995	9.8	7.6
White residents		
1980	11.6	11.0
1995	7.1	6.3
Black residents		
1980	21.6	21.4
1995	15.2	15.1

Figures represent deaths per 1,000 live births of resident infants under 1 year old, exclusive of fetal deaths; all-residents figures include other races not listed separately.
Source: U.S. National Center for Health Statistics.

Marriages and divorces

Marriages in 1996. 47,400
Rate per 1,000 population, 1995. . . . . 9.9
U.S. rate, 1995 . . . . 8.9
Rank among all states 15

Divorces in 1996 25,800
Rate per 1,000 population, 1995. . . . . 6.1
U.S. rate, 1995 . . . . 4.4
Rank among all states. 8

Rank is from highest to lowest in country.
Source: U.S. National Center for Health Statistics.

Death rates by leading causes, 1995
Deaths per 100,000 resident population

Cause	State	U.S.
Heart disease	314.2	280.7
Cancer	221.4	204.9
Cerebrovascular diseases	65.2	60.1
Accidents and adverse effects	52.5	35.5
Motor vehicle accidents	26.8	16.5
Chronic obstructive pulmonary diseases	39.5	39.2
Diabetes mellitus	27.3	22.6
HIV	9.2	NA
Suicide	13.2	11.9
Homicide	12.5	8.7
All causes	996.1	880.0

Rank in overall death rate among states	8

Figures exclude nonresidents who die in state. Causes of death follow International Classification of Diseases. Rank is from highest to lowest in country.
Source: U.S. National Center for Health Statistics.

ECONOMY

Gross state product, 1990-1996

In current dollars

	State product	Increase
1990	$71.1 billion	
1993	$83.0 billion	
1994	$89.3 billion	7.59%
1995	$95.0 billion	6.38%
1996	$99.2 billion	4.42%

Source: U.S. Bureau of Economic Analysis; *Survey of Current Business,* June, 1998.

Gross state product by industry, 1996

In billions

Farms, forestry, fisheries	$1.8
Construction	3.6
Manufacturing	21.0
Transportation, public utilities	8.8
Wholesale trade	6.0
Retail trade	9.5
Finance, insurance, real estate	10.6
Services	13.9
Government	14.0
State total	$90.7
Total U.S.	$6,923.8
State share	1.31%
Rank among states	25

Total figures include mining, not listed separately.
Source: U.S. Bureau of Economic Analysis; *Survey of Current Business,* June, 1998.

Personal income per capita, 1990 and 1997

In current dollars

	1990	1997
Per capita income	$15,231	$20,842
U.S. average	$19,188	$25,598
Rank among states	42	38

1997 data are preliminary.
Source: U.S. Bureau of Economic Analysis; *Survey of Current Business,* May, 1998.

Energy consumption, 1995

In trillions of British thermal units (BTU)

End-use sectors

Residential	331.5
Commercial	167.4
Industrial	974.8
Transportation	459.5

Sources of energy

Petroleum	559.6
Natural gas	330.9
Coal	826.9
Hydroelectric power	97.9
Nuclear electric power	221.2
Total state per capita consumption	455.3
Total U.S. per capita consumption	344.4
Rank among states	7
Total state energy consumption	1,933.3
Total U.S. energy consumption	90,547.4
State share of U.S. total	2.14%
Rank among states	17

Total figures include items not listed separately.
Source: U.S. Energy Information Administration; *State Energy Data Report.*

Nonfarm employment by sectors, 1997

Total	1,863,000
Construction	97,000
Manufacturing	380,000
Transportation, public utilities	91,000
Wholesale trade, retail trade	427,000
Finance, insurance, real estate	84,000
Services	428,000
Government	346,000

Figures are rounded to nearest thousand persons. Total includes mining, not listed separately.
Source: U.S. Bureau of Labor Statistics; *Employment and Earnings,* monthly.

Foreign exports, 1990-1997

In millions of dollars

Year	State	U.S.	State share
1990	2,834	394,045	0.72%
1996	5,170	624,767	0.83%
1997	5,932	688,896	0.86%

Source: U.S. Bureau of the Census; *U.S. Merchandise Trade,* series FT 900.

LAND USE

Federally owned land, 1996

	State	U.S.	State share
Total acres	32,678,000	2,271,343,000	1.44%
Federally owned	1,080,000	563,129,000	0.19%
Federal share	3.3%	24.8%	—

Areas are rounded to nearest thousand acres. Figures for
federally owned land do not include trust properties.

Source: U.S. General Services Administration; *Inventory Report
on Real Property Owned by the United States Throughout the
World,* annual.

Land use, 1992
In acres, rounded to nearest thousand

Total surface area	33,091,000
Federal land	921,000
Total nonfederal	31,192,000
Developed	2,046,000
Total rural	29,147,000
Cropland.	3,147,000
Pasture land	3,760,000
Range land	67,000
Forest land	20,968,000
Minor cover/use.	1,205,000

Total surface area figures include water area not shown
separately.

Source: U.S. Dept. of Agriculture; Soil Conservation Service;
Iowa State University, Statistical Laboratory; *Summary
Report, 1992 National Resources Inventory.*

Farms and crop acreage, 1997

	State	U.S.	Share	Rank
Farms (thousands)	45	2,058	2.19%	19
Acres (millions)	10	968	1.03%	31
Acres per farm	216	471	—	33
Acres planted	2,373	334,139	0.71%	31
Acres harvested	2,188	319,894	0.68%	31
Farm value (mill.)	$576	$108,805	0.53%	34

Numbers of farms are rounded to nearest thousand.

Source: U.S. Dept. of Agriculture; National Agricultural
Statistics Service.

GOVERNMENT AND FINANCE

Units of local government, 1997

	State	Total U.S.	Rank
All local governments	1,131	87,453	27
Counties	67	3,043	20
Municipalities	446	19,372	19
Townships	0	16,629	—
School districts	127	13,726	30
Special districts	491	34,683	23

County ranks are based on the 48 states with county
governments; township ranks are based on the 20 states
with township governments; school district ranks are based
on the 46 states with such districts.

Source: U.S. Bureau of the Census; *1997 Census of Governments,
Government Organization,* Series GC97(1).

State government revenue, 1996

Total revenue	$12,741 mill.
General revenue	10,894 mill.
Per capita.	2,541
U.S. per capita average	2,910
Rank among states.	40
Intergovernmental revenue	
Total	$3,347 mill.
From federal government	3,301 mill.
From local government	46 mill.
Charges and Miscellaneous	
Total	$2,290 mill.
Current charges	1,641 mill.
Misc. general revenue	649 mill.
Taxes	
Total	$5,258 mill.
General sales	1,439 mill.
Selective sales	1,335 mill.
License taxes	423 mill.
Individual income	1,578 mill.
Corporate income	218 mill.
Other	265 mill.
Insurance trust revenue	1,710 mill.

Total revenue figures include items not listed separately.

Source: U.S. Bureau of the Census.

State government expenditures, 1996

General expenditures

Intergovernmental	$3,077 mill.
Direct expenditures	7,915 mill.
Total	10,992 mill.

Selected direct expenditures

Education	$4,872 mill.
Public welfare	2,325 mill.
Health, hospital	1,330 mill.
Highways	881 mill.
Police	87 mill.
Corrections	220 mill.
Natural resources	174 mill.
Parks and recreation	8 mill.
Government administration	283 mill.
Interest on debt	217 mill.

Other

State per capita expenditures	$2,564
U.S. per capita average	2,854
Rank among states	35
Total state expenditures	12,127 mill.
Total U.S. expenditures	859,959 mill.

Totals include items not listed separately.
Source: U.S. Bureau of the Census.

POLITICS

Governors since statehood

D = Democrat; R = Republican; O = other;
(r) resigned; (d) died in office; (i) removed from office

William W. Bibb (O)	(d)	1819-1820
Thomas Bibb (O)		1820-1821
Israel Pickens (O)		1821-1825
John Murphy (D)		1825-1829
Gabriel Moore (D)	(r)	1829-1831
Samuel B. Moore (D)		1831
John Gayle (D)		1831-1835
Clement C. Clay (D)	(r)	1835-1837
Hugh McVay (D)		1837
Arthur P. Bagby (D)		1837-1841
Benjamin Fitzpatrick (D)		1841-1845
Joshua L. Martin (O)		1845-1847
Reuben Chapman (D)		1847-1849
Henry W. Collier (D)		1849-1853
John A. Winston (D)		1853-1857
Andrew B. Moore (D)		1857-1861
John G. Shorter (D)		1861-1863
Thomas H. Watts (D)	(i)	1863-1865
Lewis E. Parsons		1865
Robert M. Patton		1865-1868
William H. Smith (R)		1868-1870
Robert B. Lindsay (D)		1870-1872
David P. Lewis (R)		1872-1874
George S. Houston (D)		1874-1878
Rufus W. Cobb (D)		1878-1882
Edward A. O'Neal (D)		1882-1886
Thomas Seay (D)		1886-1890
Thomas G. Jones (D)		1890-1894
William C. Oates (D)		1894-1896
Joseph F. Johnston (D)		1896-1900
William D. Jelks (D)		1900
William J. Samford (D)	(d)	1900-1901
William D. Jelks (D)		1901-1907
Braxton B. Comer (D)		1907-1911
Emmet O'Neal (D)		1911-1915
Charles Henderson (D)		1915-1919
Thomas E. Kilby (D)		1919-1923
William W. Brandon (D)		1923-1927
(David) Bibb Graves (D)		1927-1931
Benjamin M. Miller (D)		1931-1935
(David) Bibb Graves (D)		1935-1939
Frank M. Dixon (D)		1939-1943
Chauncey M. Sparks (D)		1943-1947
James E. Folsom (D)		1947-1951
(Seth) Gordon Persons (D)		1951-1955
James E. Folsom (D)		1955-1959
John M. Patterson (D)		1959-1963
George C. Wallace, Jr. (D)		1963-1967
Lurleen B. Wallace (D)	(d)	1967-1968
Albert P. Brewer (D)		1968-1971
George C. Wallace, Jr. (D)		1971-1979
Forrest ("Fob") H. James (D)		1979-1983
George C. Wallace, Jr. (D)		1983-1987
Guy Hunt (R)		1987-1993
James E. Folsom (D)		1993-1995
Forrest ("Fob") H. James (D)		1995-1999
Don Siegelman (D)		1999-

Composition of state legislature, 1990-1998

	Democrats	Republicans
State House (105 seats)		
1990	82	23
1992	82	23
1994	74	31
1996	72	33
1998	69	36
State Senate (35 seats)		
1990	28	7
1992	27	8
1994	23	12
1996	22	12
1998	23	12

Figures for total seats may include independents and minor party members.

Source: Council of State Governments; *State Elective Officials and the Legislatures.*

Composition of congressional delegations, 1989-1999

	Dem	Rep	Total
House of Representatives			
101st Congress, 1989			
State delegates	4	2	6
Total U.S.	259	174	433
102d Congress, 1991			
State delegates	5	2	7
Total U.S.	267	167	434
103d Congress, 1993			
State delegates	4	3	7
Total U.S.	258	176	434
104th Congress, 1995			
State delegates	2	5	7
Total U.S.	197	236	433
105th Congress, 1997			
State delegates	2	5	7
Total U.S.	206	228	434
106th Congress, 1999			
State delegates	2	5	7
Total U.S.	211	222	433

	Dem	Rep	Total
Senate			
101st Congress, 1989			
State delegates	2	0	2
Total U.S.	55	45	100
102d Congress, 1991			
State delegates	2	0	2
Total U.S.	56	44	100
103d Congress, 1993			
State delegates	2	0	2
Total U.S.	57	43	100
104th Congress, 1995			
State delegates	0	2	2
Total U.S.	46	53	99
105th Congress, 1997			
State delegates	0	2	2
Total U.S.	45	55	100
106th Congress, 1999			
State delegates	0	2	2
Total U.S.	45	54	99

Figures are for starts of first sessions. Figure for U.S. Representatives for 101st Congress does not include Alabama and Indiana, which had vacancies. Figures for total U.S. Representatives for 102d, 103d, and 106th Congresses do not include Vermont, which had 1 Independent-Socialist. Figure for U.S. Representatives for 104th Congress does not include Vermont, which had 1 Independent-Socialist, and California, which had 1 vacancy. Figure for U.S. Representatives for 105th Congress does not include New York, which had 1 vacancy. Figure for U.S. Senators for 104th Congress does not include Oregon, which had 1 vacancy. Figure for U.S. Senators for 106th Congress does not include New Hampshire, which had 1 Independent.

Source: U.S. Congress; *Congressional Directory,* biennial.

Voter participation in presidential elections, 1992 and 1996

	1992	1996
State voting age pop.	3,080,000	3,218,000
Total U.S. voting age pop.	189,524,000	196,509,000
State share of U.S. total	1.6%	1.6%
Rank among states	21	21
Percent of state casting vote	54.8	50.4
Percent of U.S. total voting	55.1	49.0
Rank among states	30	24

Source: U.S. Bureau of the Census.

HEALTH AND MEDICAL CARE

Medicare, 1997

	Recipients	Payments
State	660,000	$3,583 mill.
Total U.S.	37,514,000	$206,064 mill.
State share	1.76%	1.74%
Rank among states	19	18

Recipient figures are rounded to nearest thousand persons.
    Ranks are from highest to lowest.
Source: U.S. Health Care Financing Administration.

Medicaid, 1996

	Recipients	Payments
State	546,000	$1,461 mill.
Total U.S.	35,028,000	$121,419 mill.
State share	1.56%	1.20%
Rank among states	20	24

Recipient figures are rounded to nearest thousand persons.
    Payment figures for fiscal year reflect federal and state
    contribution payments. Ranks are from highest to lowest.
Source: U.S. Health Care Financing Administration.

Health insurance coverage, 1996

	State	U.S.
Total persons covered	3,726,000	225,070,000
Total persons not covered	550,000	41,716,000
Part not covered	12.9%	15.6%
Rank among states	28	—
Children not covered	144,000	10,554,000
Part not covered	12.8%	14.8%
Rank among states	23	—

Ranks are from most to fewest uninsured. Population figures
    are rounded to nearest thousand persons.
Source: U.S. Bureau of the Census.

AIDS, syphilis, tuberculosis, and measles cases, 1997

Cases	U.S.	State	Share
AIDS	58,443	570	0.98%
Syphilis	8,550	410	4.80%
Tuberculosis	18,534	416	2.24%
Measles	148,000	NA	NA

Measles figures are rounded to nearest thousand cases.
Source: U.S. Centers for Disease Control and Prevention.

HOUSING

Homeownership rates, 1985-1997

	1985	1990	1997
State	70.4%	68.4%	71.3%
Total U.S.	63.9%	63.9%	65.7%
Rank among states	10	19	13

Source: U.S. Bureau of the Census.

Home sales, 1990 and 1997
In thousands of units

Existing home sales	1990	1997	Change
State sales	61.1	82.2	21.1
Total U.S. sales	3,560	4,730	1,170
State share of U.S. total	1.72%	1.74%	0.02%
Rank among states	22	21	—

Source: National Association of Realtors; *Real Estate Outlook: Market Trends and Insights.*

EDUCATION

Public school enrollment, 1995

State K-8 enrollment	539,000
Total U.S. K-8 enrollment	32,341,000
State share of total U.S.	1.67%
State 9-12 enrollment	207,000
Total U.S. 9-12 enrollment	12,500,000
State share of U.S. total	1.66%
State public school enroll. rate	95.8%
Overall U.S. rate.	91.6%
Rank among states	6

Enrollment figures (which include unclassified students) are rounded to nearest thousand pupils in fall term; kindergarten (K)-8 grade enrollment figures include some prekindergarten students. Enrollment rate is based on percentage of persons 5-17 years old. Rank is from highest to lowest.

Source: U.S. National Center for Education Statistics.

Public college finances, 1996

State FTE enrollment	177,400
Total U.S. FTE enrollment	8,268,800
State share of total U.S.	2.15%
Rank among states.	15
State and local appropriations	$681,200,000
Total U.S. state and local appropriations.	$39,699 mill.
State share of total U.S.	1.72%
Rank among states.	21
State net tuition revenues.	$406,700,000
Total U.S. net tuition	$18,348,100,000
State share of total U.S.	2.22%
Rank among states.	16

FTE=Full-time equivalent; credit and noncredit enrollment including summer session in academic year ending in 1996.

Enrollments are rounded to nearest thousand students. Net tuition revenues exclude appropriation to students attending in-state public institutions. Rankings are from highest shares to lowest.

Source: Research Associates of Washington.

TRANSPORTATION AND TRAVEL

Highway mileage, 1996

Interstate	904
Other arterial.	8,748
Collector roads	22,473
Local roads	63,378
Urban roads.	20,116
Rural roads	73,224
Total state	93,340
U.S. total	3,933,985
State share	2.4%
Rank among states.	17

Source: U.S. Federal Highway Administration.

Motor vehicle registrations and driver licenses, 1996
In thousands

Vehicle registrations	State	U.S.	Share	Rank
Autos, trucks, buses	3,324	206,365	1.61%	22
Autos only	1,746	128,439	1.36%	26
Motorcycles	36	3,832	0.94%	32
Driver licenses	3,138	179,539	1.75%	22

Figures do not include vehicles owned by military services.
Source: U.S. Federal Highway Administration; *Highway Statistics; Selected Highway Statistics and Charts.*

Domestic travel expenditures, 1995
Spending by U.S. residents on overnight trips and day trips of at least 100 miles

Total expenditures in state	$4,092 mill.
Total expenditures in U.S.	$360,314 mill.
State share of total U.S.	1.14%
Rank among states.	28

Source: Travel Industry Association of America.

CRIME AND LAW ENFORCEMENT

State and local police officers, 1996

Local police	6,484
State police	581
Sheriffs	1,963
Total	9,767
Officers per 10,000 residents	23
U.S. average	25
Rank among states	21

Figures cover full-time sworn officers; totals include special police not shown separately.
Source: U.S. Bureau of Justice Statistics; *Census of State and Local Law Enforcement Agencies, 1996.*

Crime rates, 1996

Rates per 100,000 resident population

Violent crimes	*State*	*U.S.*
Total violent	565	634
Murder	10.4	7.4
Forcible rape	32.7	36.1
Robbery	167	202
Aggravated assault	356	388
Property crimes		
Total property	4,255	4,445
Burglary	1,002	943
Larceny/theft	2,887	2,976
Motor vehicle theft	366	526
Totals	4,820	5,079

Source: U.S. Federal Bureau of Investigation; *Crime in the United States,* annual.

State prison populations, 1980-1996

	State	*U.S.*	*State share*
1980	6,543	305,458	2.14%
1990	15,665	708,393	2.21%
1996	21,760	1,025,624	2.12%

Figures exclude prisoners in federal penitentiaries.
Source: U.S. Bureau of Justice Statistics.

Alaska

Location: Northwest of Canada

Area and rank: 570,374 square miles (1,477,267 square kilometers); 656,424 square miles (1,700,138 square kilometers) including water; largest state in area

Coastline: 5,580 miles (8,978 kilometers)

Shoreline: 31,383 miles (50,495 kilometers)

Population and rank: 609,311 (1997); forty-eighth state in population

Capital: Juneau

Largest city: Anchorage (254,982 people in 1998)

Alaska's largest city, Anchorage has four times as many residents as the state's next two largest cities, Fairbanks and Juneau, combined. (PhotoDisc)

Became territory:
August 24, 1912

Entered Union and rank: January 3, 1959; forty-ninth state

Present constitution adopted: April 24, 1956

Boroughs: 16

State name: "Alaska" comes from an Aleut word meaning "great land" or "that which the sea breaks against"

State nicknames: The Last Frontier; Land of the Midnight Sun

Motto: North to the Future

State flag: Blue field with eight gold stars forming Ursa Major and the North Star

Highest point: Mount McKinley — 20,320 feet (6,194 meters)

Lowest point: Pacific Ocean — sea level

Highest recorded temperature: 100 degrees Fahrenheit (38 degrees Celsius) — Fort Yukon, 1915

Lowest recorded temperature: −80 degrees Fahrenheit (−62 degrees Celsius) — Prospect Creek, 1971

State song: "Alaska's Flag"

State tree: Sitka spruce

State flower: Forget-me-not

State bird: Willow ptarmigan

State fish: King salmon

National parks: Bering Land Bridge, Denali, Gates of the Arctic, Glacier Bay, Katmai, Kenai Fjords, Kobuk Valley, Lake Clark, Wrangell-St. Elias

Alaska History

Alaska must be described in terms of absolutes and superlatives. When it was admitted to the Union in 1959, it became the first state outside the forty-eight contiguous states. It is the northernmost state, and remarkably, it is also the westernmost and easternmost state, extending from 130 degrees west longitude, across the 180 degree meridian, to 172 degrees east longitude. Its length runs from Barrow in the Arctic at 72 degrees north to the southernmost point in the Aleutian Islands, where its latitude is 52 degrees north, giving it greater latitude than the entire forty-eight contiguous states and almost as much in range of longitude. Alaska lies geographically in four time zones, although, for practical purposes, two official time zones have been established.

Alaska is the only state that borders the Arctic Ocean and extends into the Arctic Circle. It lies closest to Asia of any of the states, its western extreme on Little Diomede Island being just two miles from the Russian island of Big Diomede. On the east and north, its border with Canada is the longest of any state. The shortest air routes between the United States and Asia are directly over Alaska, which has the largest oil and natural gas reserves in the United States. With a land mass of 570,374 square miles, it is the largest state, more than twice the size of Texas. Alaska has the largest glaciers and the most volcanoes of any U.S. state. With 1.1 persons per square mile, it has the lowest population density in the United States. Alaska's Mount McKinley, at 20,320 feet, is the highest point on the North American continent.

Early History. Alaska's earliest inhabitants were the Tingit-Haidas and members of the Athabascan Tribes. The Aleuts and Eskimos, or Inuits, crossed the Bering Strait from Russia more than four thousand years ago and settled along the coast, surviving largely by fishing and hunting. These migrants were likely Asians who came to the region when what is now Alaska was linked to mainland Asia by a land bridge. By 1750, some seventy thousand na-

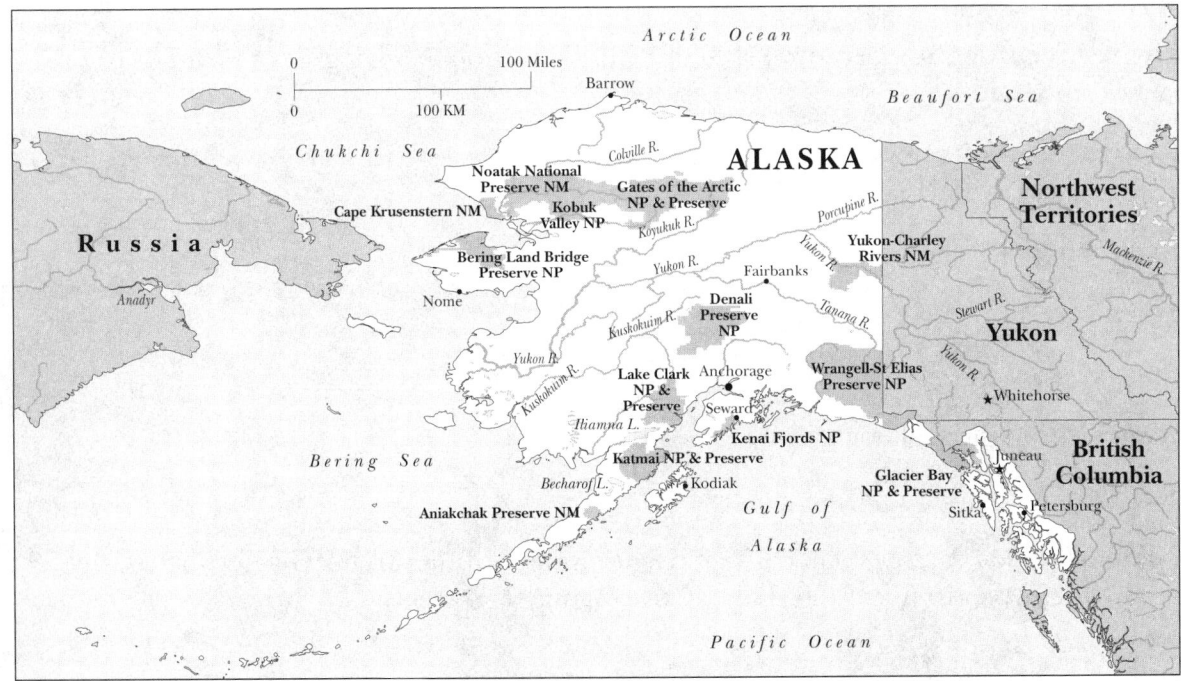

tive Inuits lived in Alaska, and that number has not significantly changed. Aleuts were driven from the Aleutian Islands by the Russians in the eighteenth and nineteenth centuries and by the American military forces during World War II.

The earliest incursions by westerners occurred in 1741, when Vitus Bering, a Dane supported in his ventures by Russia, sailed to Alaska. Grigori Sheilikhov established the first settlement on Kodiak Island in 1784. The fur business, important and lucrative in early Alaska, thrived with the establishment in 1799 of the Russian-American Company. It controlled the fur trade from its headquarters in Archangel, present-day Sitka.

The discovery of gold in 1898 drew prospectors from all over the world in one of the last great gold rushes. (Alaska Division of Tourism)

Russia owned Alaska until 1867, when President Andrew Johnson's secretary of state, William H. Seward, negotiated its purchase by the United States for $7.2 million. Although the U.S. Senate approved this purchase enthusiastically, buying this little-known area, which most people considered a frozen wasteland, was unpopular and known as "Seward's Folly." This "folly" paid off handsomely when a major gold strike was made near Juneau in 1880, unleashing a later gold rush to the region and stimulating the exploration of Alaska for its mineral wealth.

In 1896 gold was discovered in Canada's Klondike, and, in 1898, at Fairbanks, causing another gold rush. Fish canneries built in the southeastern part of the area in the 1880's and 1890's imported workers from the United States. American traders moving to Alaska in search of riches established a route along the Yukon, the fourth longest river in the northern hemisphere.

Steps Toward Statehood. As Alaska became more viable economically, Congress viewed it with increased interest. In 1884 Alaska was made a judicial district, with Sitka as its capital. In 1906 it was permitted one elected delegate in the United States House of Representatives. The region was granted territorial status in 1912, and Juneau was declared its capital. Its political powers, however, were limited. Statehood was first proposed in Congress in 1916 but was rejected. In 1946, however, Alaskans, in a referendum, approved statehood. Ten years later, a state constitution was adopted. On January 3, 1959, Alaska was admitted to the Union as the forty-ninth state.

When statehood was first proposed for Alaska in 1916, the state was extremely isolated from the rest of the country. Many U.S. citizens had gone there to work during last half of the nineteenth century, but communication and transportation were limited. With the advent of radios and telephones, these problems began to fade, although it was many years before telephone communication with the "lower 48," as the United States mainland was called, was perfected. Almost simultaneously with better telephone communication came the development of air transportation, which had evolved rapidly during World War I and was, by the 1920's, becoming a major factor in transportation worldwide.

Alaska's enormous spaces made it an ideal venue for private aircraft. During the late 1920's and the 1930's, many Alaskans owned private planes, shrinking perceptibly the time they needed to cover the state's huge expanses. Commercial aircraft began to serve Alaska's major cities, and Anchorage became a refueling stop for planes flying from the United States and Canada to Asia.

These factors eliminated some of the earlier objections to statehood. Also, because the Japanese attacked and eventually occupied some of the Aleutian Islands during World War II, Americans became increasingly aware of Alaska's defensive importance.

Alaska's Economy. From its earliest days, Alaska had a stable economy. While the mainland U.S. struggled economically during the Great Depression of the 1930's, Alaska was undergoing an economic rebirth brought on largely by gold mining. Alaska had thriving copper mines as well. As revenues increased, the territorial government built much-needed roads, whose construction employed thousands of workers, many of whom came to Alaska and remained there as permanent residents.

World War II had a profound effect on the Alaskan economy. With Japan's invasion of the Aleutian Islands in 1942, the United States deployed about 200,000 military personnel to Alaska, where major military installations were built at Adak, Anchorage, Fairbanks, Kodiak, and Sitka. The Alcan highway was completed, creating a road link among Alaska's major cities.

Throughout the 1950's, military construction in Alaska continued at a brisk pace. This activity brought both construction workers and military personnel to the area in large numbers. Many, impressed by Alaska's grandeur and economic opportunities, remained there when the work that originally brought them to Alaska was completed.

In 1957 huge oil deposits were discovered in Alaska's Kenai Peninsula, and shortly thereafter other vast fields were found at Prudhoe Bay. Despite the harsh climate and great distances involved, the eight-hundred-mile long Trans-Alaska oil pipeline was completed in 1977. Alaska became so oil-rich that it was able to finance a giant expansion and still give each of its citizens more than one thousand dollars a year as a cash bonus for several years. It had no need for a state income tax.

The oil boom waned during the 1980's and by the mid-1980's was virtually over. The state by this time had attracted many new residents who viewed Alaska as the land of opportunity. Its population increased by 36.8 percent between 1980 and 1990, reaching just over 550,000 in 1990. The 1997 population registered a more than 10 percent increase, having grown to almost 610,000.

Following the oil boom, Alaska struggled to attract tourist dollars. It also began establishing trade with such Asian countries as South Korea, Taiwan, and Japan, although

Completion of the Trans-Alaska oil pipeline in 1977 raised Alaska to an unprecedented level of prosperity. (Digital Stock)

the slowing of the Asian economies in 1998 and 1999 temporarily stalled some of these efforts. Alaska's abundance of many resources that Asia does not have makes trade enviable. Natural gas development became vigorously pursued within the state, which also did a great deal to increase the amount of metal mining done within it boundaries. Alaska has deposits of every known mineral except bauxite.

The Threat of Oil Spills. Environmentalists were concerned about the building of the Trans-Alaska Oil Pipeline because portions of it were laid in areas with geological faults. However, the pipelines have been fashioned to resist the earthquakes that are common in fault areas. A severe earthquake in 1964, followed by a tsunami, a huge tidal wave, devastated much of coastal Alaska, doing considerable damage in Anchorage, Kodiak, Seward, and Valdez. At this time, there was no pipeline that might rupture. The potential for destruction of the pipeline is slight, but still a cause for concern.

In 1989 a huge supertanker, the *Exxon Valdez*, foundered in Prince William Sound and spilled more than 240,000 barrels of oil into the surrounding water. The result was catastrophic: The impact on commercial fishing was so negative that many who fished for a living were forced out of business. The wholesale destruction of wildlife in the area would take years to recover completely. If any good came out of the *Exxon Valdez* disaster, it is that the shipping of oil on supertankers became more strenuously regulated. Many new tankers have double hulls so that if the outside hull is punctured, the oil will not leak into the ocean.

R. Baird Shuman

Alaska Time Line

c. 10,000 B.C.E.   Human habitation of the area toward the end of the last Ice Age has been documented.

c. 650 C.E.   Aleuts and Eskimos separate; Eskimos divide into Yupic and Inupiaq.

c. 1000 C.E.   Eskimos migrate from Alaska to Greenland.

1741   Vitus Bering lands off Kayak Island.

1774-1792   Spanish explore Alaska's west coast.

1778   British captain James Cook surveys Alaska coast.

1784   Russian Grigori Sheilikhov establishes Russian settlement near present-day Kodiak.

1791   British captain George Vancouver charts southeastern Alaska.

1799   Czar Paul I charters Russian-American Company.

1802   Tlingit Indians attack Russian-American Company, killing 408.

1823   Father Ivan Veniaminov works among the Aleuts.

1824-1825   Boundaries of Russian settlement in Alaska are fixed.

Mar. 30, 1867   United States purchases Alaska from Russia for $7.2 million.

1876   First Protestant mission in Alaska is established at Wrangell.

1878   First salmon cannery is built at Klawock.

1880   Gold is discovered at Juneau.

1884   Alaska becomes a judicial district with the capital at Sitka; native land rights are preserved and laws of Oregon are enforced.

(continued)

1891	Sheldon Jackson introduces reindeer into Alaska to compensate for near-extinction of whales and walrus.
1892	Alaskan gold rush begins, continuing for twenty years.
1900	United States Congress reforms Alaska's civil government and makes Juneau the capital.
1906	Alaska is permitted to elect one delegate to the United States House of Representatives.
1911	Alaska signs international agreement to restrict seal hunting off Pribilof and other islands.
Aug. 24, 1912	Alaska is granted territorial status.
1913	Women receive voting rights.
1916	Alaskan statehood is first proposed in Congress.
1917	University of Alaska is founded.
1923	Alaska Railroad is completed, connecting Anchorage and Seward with Fairbanks.
1923	Alaska Agricultural College and School of Mines opens.
1924	Lieutenant Carl Ben Eielson flies first airmail.
1931	Federal Building is completed in Juneau.
1935	Matanuska agricultural colony is established under New Deal.
1942	Japanese bomb Dutch Harbor.
June 7, 1942	Japan invades and occupies Kiska and Attu in the Aleutian Islands.
Nov. 20, 1942	Alcan Highway, running from Great Falls, Montana, to Fairbanks, is completed.
1943	United States recaptures Aleutians from the Japanese.
1945	Racial discrimination in public accommodations is ruled illegal.
1946	Alaskans approve statehood in statewide referendum.
1952	First pulp and paper mill is built outside Ketchikan.
1955	Eklutna Power Project opens near Palmer.
1955	Military fuel pipeline opens between Haines and Fairbanks.
April 24, 1956	Alaskans adopt state constitution.
1957	Oil is discovered on Kenai Peninsula.
Jan. 3, 1959	Alaska is granted statehood.
1963	Alaska's first oil refinery opens.
Mar. 27, 1964	Most severe earthquake in North America's history strikes; tsunamis devastate Anchorage, Kodiak, Seward, and Valdez.
Aug. 14-15, 1967	Record floods damage Fairbanks.
1971	Alaska Native Land Claims Settlement Bill is enacted.
1977	Trans-Alaska Pipeline is completed.
1981	Alaska National Interest Lands Conservation bill is enacted.
1988	Forest fires destroy over two million acres.

1988	Border between Alaska and eastern Soviet Union opens.
Mar. 24, 1989	*Exxon Valdez* spills 240,000 barrels of oil into Prince William Sound.
1996	Exxon Corporation pays Alaska $900 million for clean-up following *Exxon Valdez* oil spill.
1997	Congress passes bill to phase out largest factory trawlers for bottom fishing on the Bering Sea.
1997	Alaska ranks among the top three states in per-pupil expenditures for public education.
1998	Federal budget gives Alaska pollock processors $100 million.
1999	Alaska and Canada sign pact to protect endangered salmon species.

Notes for Further Study

Published Sources. Robert Hedin and Gary Holt-haus's *The Great Land: Reflections on Alaska* (1994) offers comprehensive overviews of the state. George W. Rogers, in *Change in Alaska: People, Petroleum, Politics* (1970), considers what the oil discoveries at Kenai Peninsula and Prudhoe mean to the state and is especially useful read in conjunction with Robert B. Weeden's *Messages from Earth: Nature and Human Prospect in Alaska* (1992) and Craig A. and Katherine M. Doherty's *The Alaska Pipeline* (1998). Bryan Cooper's *Alaska: The Last Frontier* (1973) also focuses on the effect the petroleum discoveries of the late 1960's and early 1970's had upon the ecology and economy of Alaska. Jeff Wheelwright's *Degrees of Disaster: Prince William Sound: How Nature Reels and Rebounds* (1994) considers the aftermath of the *Exxon Valdez* oil spill.

The contributors to *Contemporary Alaskan Native Economies* (1986), edited by Steve J. Langdon, consider the subsistence economies of the Eskimos, Aleuts, and other native residents of Alaska's circumpolar regions, and the contributors to *Developing America's Northern Frontier* (1987), edited by Theodore Lane, discuss how development affected both Alaska's and Canada's far north. In *Going up in Flames: The Promises and Pledges of Alaska Statehood Under Attack* (1990), edited by Malcolm B. Roberts for the Commonwealth North Federal State Relations Committee, various experts discuss the failure of many of the pledges made in the development of Alaskan industry.

Owen K. Mason, William J. Neal, and Orrin H. Pilkey consider threats to the Alaskan coastline in *Living with the Coast of Alaska* (1997). David S. Case considers how native Alaskans adapt to American laws in *Alaska Natives and American Laws* (1997). The Alaska Craftsman Home Program published *Northern Comfort: Advanced Cold Climate Home Building Techniques* (1995) that explores building techniques suitable to Alaska's harsh climate. Theodore Lane considers the special climatic conditions of Alaska and how to cope with them in *Developing America's Northern Frontier* (1987). Carole Marsh's *Alaska Timeline: A Chronology of Alaska History, Mystery, Trivia, Legend, Lore, and More* (1992) is aimed at the juvenile market and is a worthwhile study. Kathleen Thompson's *Alaska* (1988) is also written with juveniles in mind.

Web Resources. The government Web site (http://www.state.ak.us) and tourist Web site (http://www.commerce.state.ak.us/tourism) are good starting points that lead to other pertinent Web sites. Those planning outdoor activities in the state should consult the Alaska Adventures Web site (http://www.alaskaadventures.com). Bike tours are advertised on Alaska Bike Tours' Web site (http://www.alaskabike.com). Fishing enthusiasts will find information on the *Alaska Angler*'s Web site (http://www.alaskaangler.com), on the Alaska Fly Fisher's Web site (http://www.akflyfishers.org), and on Alaska Halibut's Web site (http://www.alaskahalibut.com). The Whale Watching Web site (http://www.juneauwhalewatching.com) covers whale watching thoroughly. Alaska national parklands are described on the National Parklands Web site (http://www.nps.gov/akso), while guides to state parks are found on the Alaska Parks Web site (http://www.alaskaparks.com).

The Matanuska experiment begun in 1935 as a New Deal initiative brought midwesterners to Alaska to farm, taking advantage of summer days that were almost twenty-four hours long. The project is reviewed on the Matanuska Web site (http://www.matanuske.com). For scientific information about Alaska's Arctic regions, the Arctic Research Consortium's Web site (http://www.arcus.org) is helpful. The Eskimo Web site (http://www.eskimo.com) provides information about the history and present status of Alaska's native population.

Counties

County	Sq. miles	1996 pop.
Aleutians East	6,984.8	2,304
Anchorage	1,697.6	250,505
Bristol Bay	519.2	1,322
Denali	NA	2,043
Fairbanks North Star	7,362.4	84,061
Haines	2,357.0	2,170
Juneau	2,593.6	29,756
Kenai Peninsula	16,078.9	47,131
Ketchikan Gateway	1,219.6	14,517

County	Sq. miles	1996 pop.
Kodiak Island	6,462.6	15,082
Lake and Peninsula	23,632.3	1,701
Matanuska-Susitna	24,693.6	52,500
North Slope	87,860.5	7,110
Northwest Arctic	35,862.5	6,552
Sitka	2,881.5	8,510
Yakutat		827

Alaska's counties are called boroughs.
Source: U.S. Census Bureau; National Association of Counties.

Cities
With 10,000 or more residents

Rank	City	Population
1	Anchorage	254,982
2	Fairbanks	33,295

Rank	City	Population
3	Juneau	30,191

Population figures are estimated for mid-1998.
Source: U.S. Bureau of the Census.

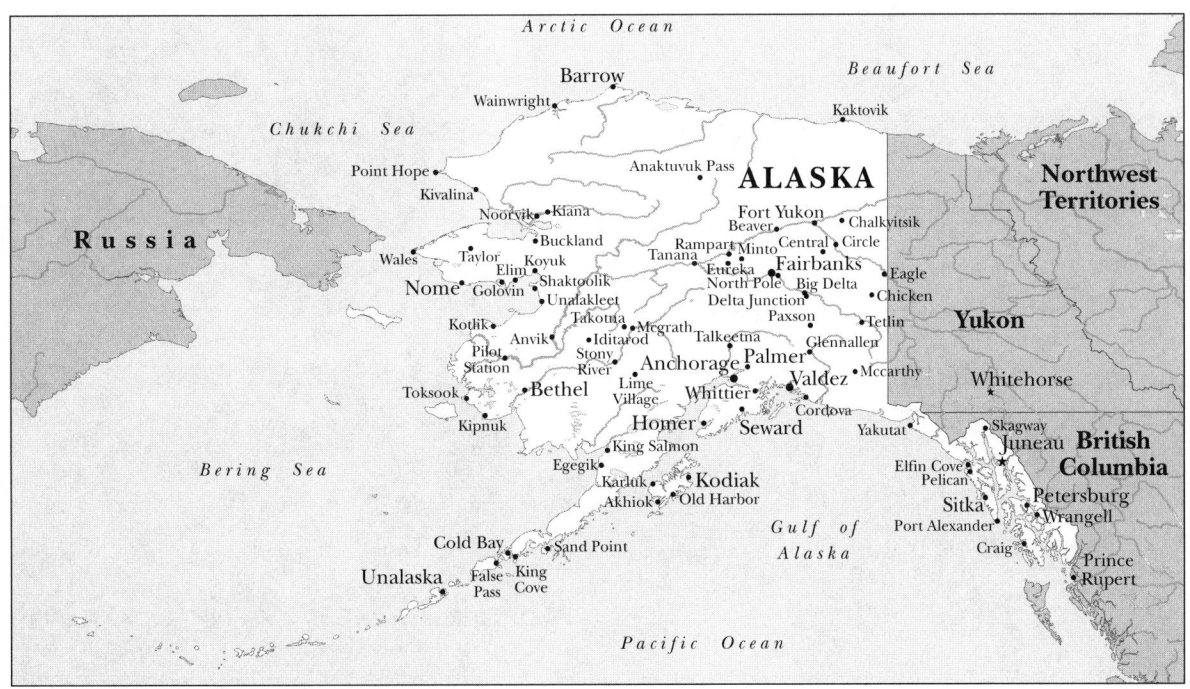

Rising to an altitude of 20,320 feet, Mount McKinley is the tallest mountain in North America. (PhotoDisc)

ALASKA

Arctic Ocean

Beaufort Sea

Chukchi Sea

Barrow
Wainwright
Kaktovik

Point Hope
Kivalina
Anaktuvuk Pass

Noorvik • Kiana

Russia

Wales
Taylor
Elim
Koyuk
Buckland

Nome
Golovin
Shaktoolik
Unalakleet

Kotlik
Takotna

Pilot
Station
Anvik
Stony
River

Toksook
Bethel

Kipnuk

Bering Sea

Cold Bay
Sand Point

Unalaska
False
Pass
King
Cove

Pacific Ocean

Fort Yukon
Beaver
Chalkvitsik

Rampart Minto
Central
Circle

Tanana
Eureka
Fairbanks
Eagle

North Pole
Big Delta
Chicken

Delta Junction
Paxson
Tetlin

Iditarod
Megrath
Talkeetna
Glennallen

Anchorage
Palmer
Mccarthy

Lime
Village
Whittier
Valdez

Homer
Cordova

King Salmon
Seward
Yakutat

Egegik

Karluk
Kodiak
Akhiok
Old Harbor

Gulf of
Alaska

Northwest
Territories

Yukon

Whitehorse

British
Columbia

Skagway
Juneau

Elfin Cove
Pelican

Sitka
Petersburg
Wrangell

Port Alexander
Craig

Prince
Rupert

Index to Tables

NA = Reliable data are not available.

DEMOGRAPHICS

Resident state and national populations, 1970-1997

Population figures given in thousands

	State pop.	U.S. pop.	Share	Rank
1970	303	203,302	0.1%	50
1980	402	226,546	0.2%	50
1985	532	237,924	0.2%	48
1990	550	248,765	0.2%	49
1995	602	262,761	0.2%	48
1997	609	267,636	0.2%	48

Source: U.S. Bureau of the Census.

Resident population by age, 1997

Age group	Total population
Under 5 years	49,000
5 to 17 years	139,000
18 to 24 years	67,000
25 to 34 years	80,000
35 to 44 years	114,000
45 to 54 years	86,000
55 to 64 years	42,000
65 to 74 years	21,000
75 to 84 years	9,000
85 years and over	2,000
Portion of residents 65 and older	5.3%
National average	12.7%

Population figures are rounded to nearest thousand persons;
figures include armed forces personnel stationed in state.
Source: U.S. Bureau of the Census.

Resident population by race, Hispanic origin, 1997

	State pop.	Share	U.S.
All residents	609,000	100.0%	100.0%
Hispanic white	19,000	3.1%	10.0%
Non-Hispanic white	443,000	72.7%	72.7%
African American	24,000	3.9%	12.7%
Native American	97,000	15.9%	0.9%
Asian, Pacific Islander	27,000	4.4%	3.8%

Source: U.S. Bureau of the Census.

Projections of state population, 2000-2025

	Model A Uses interstate migration observed from 1975-1994	Model B Uses Bureau of Economic Analysis employment projections
Year	Population	Population
2000	653,000	632,000
2005	700,000	659,000
2010	745,000	690,000
2015	791,000	728,000
2020	838,000	773,000
2025	885,000	825,000

All population projections, including those for 2000, were calculated in 1997.
Source: U.S. Bureau of the Census, Population Paper Listings PPL-47.

VITAL STATISTICS

Marriages and divorces

Marriages in 1996 5,400
Rate per 1,000 population, 1995. . . . . 9.0
U.S. rate, 1995 . . . . 8.9
Rank among all states 19

Divorces in 1996 2,800
Rate per 1,000 population, 1995. . . . . 5.0
U.S. rate, 1995 . . . . 4.4
Rank among all states 18

Rank is from highest to lowest in country.
Source: U.S. National Center for Health Statistics.

Infant mortality rates, 1980 and 1995

	State	U.S.
All residents		
1980	12.3	11.0
1995	7.7	7.6
White residents		
1980	9.4	11.0
1995	6.1	6.3
Black residents		
1980	19.5	21.4
1995	NA	15.1

Figures represent deaths per 1,000 live births of resident infants under 1 year old, exclusive of fetal deaths; all-residents figures include other races not listed separately.
Source: U.S. National Center for Health Statistics.

Death rates by leading causes, 1995
Deaths per 100,000 resident population

Cause	State	U.S.
Heart disease	90.6	280.7
Cancer	95.1	204.9
Cerebrovascular diseases	24.0	60.1
Accidents and adverse effects	56.2	35.5
Motor vehicle accidents	16.1	16.5
Chronic obstructive pulmonary diseases	17.7	39.2
Diabetes mellitus	9.3	22.6
HIV	5.0	NA
Suicide	17.1	11.9
Homicide	8.9	8.7
All causes	423.0	880.0
Rank in overall death rate among states		50

Figures exclude nonresidents who die in state. Causes of death follow International Classification of Diseases. Rank is from highest to lowest in country.
Source: U.S. National Center for Health Statistics.

ECONOMY

Gross state product, 1990-1996
In current dollars

	State product	Increase
1990	$25.4 billion	
1993	$22.5 billion	
1994	$21.9 billion	−2.67%
1995	$23.7 billion	8.22%
1996	$24.2 billion	2.11%

Source: U.S. Bureau of Economic Analysis; Survey of Current Business, June, 1998.

Gross state product by industry, 1996
In billions

Farms, forestry, fisheries	$0.3
Construction	0.8
Manufacturing	1.1
Transportation, public utilities	3.5
Wholesale trade	0.7
Retail trade	1.5
Finance, insurance, real estate	2.3
Services	2.5
Government	4.3
State total	$21.4
Total U.S.	$6,923.8
State share	0.31%
Rank among states	45

Total figures include mining, not listed separately.
Source: U.S. Bureau of Economic Analysis; Survey of Current Business, June, 1998.

Personal income per capita, 1990 and 1997
In current dollars

	1990	1997
Per capita income	$21,097	$25,305
U.S. average	$19,188	$25,598
Rank among states	9	19

1997 data are preliminary.
Source: U.S. Bureau of Economic Analysis; Survey of Current Business, May, 1998.

Energy consumption, 1995
In trillions of British thermal units (BTU)

End-use sectors

Residential	49.5
Commercial	62.7
Industrial	404.9
Transportation	169.3

Sources of energy

Petroleum	222.2
Natural gas	432.8
Coal	12.9
Hydroelectric power	14.1
Nuclear electric power	0
Total state per capita consumption	1,139.1
Total U.S. per capita consumption	344.4
Rank among states	1
Total state energy consumption	686.3
Total U.S. energy consumption	90,547.4
State share of U.S. total	0.76%
Rank among states	35

Total figures include items not listed separately.
Source: U.S. Energy Information Administration; State Energy Data Report.

Nonfarm employment by sectors, 1997

Total	268,000
Construction	13,000
Manufacturing	15,000
Transportation, public utilities	24,000
Wholesale trade, retail trade	56,000
Finance, insurance, real estate	12,000
Services	65,000
Government	73,000

Figures are rounded to nearest thousand persons. Total includes mining, not listed separately.'
Source: U.S. Bureau of Labor Statistics; Employment and Earnings, monthly.

Foreign exports, 1990-1997
In millions of dollars

Year	State	U.S.	State share
1990	2,850	394,045	0.72%
1996	2,879	624,767	0.46%
1997	2,721	688,896	0.39%

Source: U.S. Bureau of the Census; U.S. Merchandise Trade, series FT 900.

LAND USE

Federally owned land, 1996

	State	U.S.	State share
Total acres	365,482,000	2,271,343,000	16.09%
Federally owned	171,788,000	563,129,000	30.51%
Federal share	47.0%	24.8%	—

Areas are rounded to nearest thousand acres. Figures for federally owned land do not include trust properties.
Source: U.S. General Services Administration; *Inventory Report on Real Property Owned by the United States Throughout the World,* annual.

Farms and crop acreage, 1997

	State	U.S.	Share	Rank
Farms (thousands)	1	2,058	0.05%	49
Acres (millions)	1	968	0.10%	44
Acres per farm	1,804	471	—	6
Acres planted	NA	334,139	NA	—
Acres harvested	NA	319,894	NA	—
Farm value (mill.)	NA	$108,805	NA	—

Numbers of farms are rounded to nearest thousand.
Source: U.S. Dept. of Agriculture; National Agricultural Statistics Service.

GOVERNMENT AND FINANCE

Units of local government, 1997

	State	Total U.S.	Rank
All local governments	175	87,453	48
Counties	12	3,043	44
Municipalities	149	19,372	37
Townships	0	16,629	—
School districts	0	13,726	—
Special districts	14	34,683	50

County ranks are based on the 48 states with county governments; township ranks are based on the 20 states with township governments; school district ranks are based on the 46 states with such districts.
Source: U.S. Bureau of the Census; *1997 Census of Governments, Government Organization,* Series GC97(1).

State government revenue, 1996

Total revenue . . . . $8,254 mill.
General revenue . . . . 6,819 mill.
Per capita 11,272
U.S. per capita average 2,910
Rank among states 1

Intergovernmental revenue
Total . . . . $1,017 mill.
From federal government . . . . 1,012 mill.
From local government. . . . . 5 mill.

Charges and Miscellaneous
Total . . . . $4,283 mill.
Current charges . . . . 294 mill.
Misc. general revenue . . . . 3,988 mill.

Taxes
Total . . . . $1,519 mill.
General sales . . . . NA
Selective sales . . . . 99 mill.
License taxes. . . . . 79 mill.
Individual income . . . . NA
Corporate income . . . . 326 mill.
Other . . . . 1,015 mill.
Insurance trust revenue . . . . 1,418 mill.

Total revenue figures include items not listed separately.
Source: U.S. Bureau of the Census.

State government expenditures, 1996

General expenditures
Intergovernmental . . . . $1,058 mill.
Direct expenditures . . . . 4,047 mill.
Total. 5,105 mill.

Selected direct expenditures
Education . . . . $1,236 mill.
Public welfare. . . . . 713 mill.
Health, hospital . . . . 191 mill.
Highways . . . . 623 mill.
Police. . . . . 53 mill.
Corrections. . . . . 150 mill.
Natural resources. . . . . 267 mill.
Parks and recreation. . . . . 15 mill.
Government administration . . . . 294 mill.
Interest on debt . . . . 240 mill.

Other
State per capita expenditures $8,438
U.S. per capita average 2,854
Rank among states 1
Total state expenditures . . . . 5,630 mill.
Total U.S. expenditures . . . . 859,959 mill.

Totals include items not listed separately.
Source: U.S. Bureau of the Census.

POLITICS

Governors since statehood

D = Democrat; R = Republican; O = other;
(r) resigned; (d) died in office; (i) removed from office

William A. Egan (D) 1959-1966
Walter J. Hickel (R). . . . . (r) 1966-1969
Keith H. Miller (R) 1969-1970
William A. Egan (D) 1970-1974
Jay S. Hammond (R) 1974-1982
William Sheffield (D). 1982-1986
Steve Cowper (D) 1986-1990
Walter J. Hickel (O) 1990-1994
Tony Knowles (D) 1994-

Composition of state legislature, 1990-1998

	Democrats	Republicans
State House (40 seats)		
1990	23	17
1992	20	18
1994	17	22
1996	16	24
1998	14	26
State Senate (20 seats)		
1990	10	10
1992	10	10
1994	8	12
1996	7	13
1998	5	15

Figures for total seats may include independents and minor party members.

Source: Council of State Governments; *State Elective Officials and the Legislatures.*

Composition of congressional delegations, 1989-1999

	Dem	Rep	Total
House of Representatives			
101st Congress, 1989			
State delegates	0	1	1
Total U.S.	259	174	433
102d Congress, 1991			
State delegates	0	1	1
Total U.S.	267	167	434
103d Congress, 1993			
State delegates	0	1	1
Total U.S.	258	176	434
104th Congress, 1995			
State delegates	0	1	1
Total U.S.	197	236	433
105th Congress, 1997			
State delegates	0	1	1
Total U.S.	206	228	434
106th Congress, 1999			
State delegates	0	1	1
Total U.S.	211	222	433
Senate			
101st Congress, 1989			
State delegates	0	2	2
Total U.S.	55	45	100
102d Congress, 1991			
State delegates	0	2	2
Total U.S.	56	44	100
103d Congress, 1993			
State delegates	0	2	2
Total U.S.	57	43	100
104th Congress, 1995			
State delegates	0	2	2
Total U.S.	46	53	99
105th Congress, 1997			
State delegates	0	2	2
Total U.S.	45	55	100
106th Congress, 1999			
State delegates	0	2	2
Total U.S.	45	54	99

Figures are for starts of first sessions. Figure for U.S. Representatives for 101st Congress does not include Alabama and Indiana, which had vacancies. Figures for total U.S. Representatives for 102d, 103d, and 106th Congresses do not include Vermont, which had 1 Independent-Socialist. Figure for U.S. Representatives for 104th Congress does not include Vermont, which had 1 Independent-Socialist, and California, which had 1 vacancy. Figure for U.S. Representatives for 105th Congress does not include New York, which had 1 vacancy. Figure for U.S. Senators for 104th Congress does not include Oregon, which had 1 vacancy. Figure for U.S. Senators for 106th Congress does not include New Hampshire, which had 1 Independent.

Source: U.S. Congress; *Congressional Directory*, biennial.

Voter participation in presidential elections, 1992 and 1996

	1992	1996
State voting age pop.	405,000	425,000
Total U.S. voting age pop.	189,524,000	196,509,000
State share of U.S. total	0.2%	0.2%
Rank among states	49	49
Percent of state casting vote	63.8	56.6
Percent of U.S. total voting	55.1	49.0
Rank among states	13	11

Source: U.S. Bureau of the Census.

Health insurance coverage, 1996

	State	U.S.
Total persons covered	569,000	225,070,000
Total persons not covered	89,000	41,716,000
Part not covered	13.5%	15.6%
Rank among states	24	—
Children not covered	27,000	10,554,000
Part not covered	11.6%	14.8%
Rank among states	25	—

Ranks are from most to fewest uninsured. Population figures are rounded to nearest thousand persons.
Source: U.S. Bureau of the Census.

HEALTH AND MEDICAL CARE

Medicare, 1997

	Recipients	Payments
State	37,000	$163 mill.
Total U.S.	37,514,000	$206,064 mill.
State share	0.001%	0.08%
Rank among states	50	50

Recipient figures are rounded to nearest thousand persons. Ranks are from highest to lowest.
Source: U.S. Health Care Financing Administration.

AIDS, syphilis, tuberculosis, and measles cases, 1997

Cases	U.S.	State	Share
AIDS	58,443	52	0.09%
Syphilis	8,550	1	0.01%
Tuberculosis	18,534	78	0.42%
Measles	148,000	NA	NA

Measles figures are rounded to nearest thousand cases.
Source: U.S. Centers for Disease Control and Prevention.

Medicaid, 1996

	Recipients	Payments
State	69,000	$278 mill.
Total U.S.	35,028,000	$121,419 mill.
State share	0.20%	0.23%
Rank among states	47	47

Recipient figures are rounded to nearest thousand persons. Payment figures for fiscal year reflect federal and state contribution payments. Ranks are from highest to lowest.
Source: U.S. Health Care Financing Administration.

HOUSING

Homeownership rates, 1985-1997

	1985	1990	1997
State	61.2%	58.4%	67.2%
Total U.S.	63.9%	63.9%	65.7%
Rank among states	43	46	32

Source: U.S. Bureau of the Census.

EDUCATION

Public school enrollment, 1995

State K-8 enrollment	93,000
Total U.S. K-8 enrollment	32,341,000
State share of total U.S.	0.29%
State 9-12 enrollment.	34,000
Total U.S. 9-12 enrollment	12,500,000
State share of U.S. total	0.27%
State public school enroll. rate	94.8%
Overall U.S. rate.	91.6%
Rank among states.	13

Enrollment figures (which include unclassified students) are rounded to nearest thousand pupils in fall term; kindergarten (K)-8 grade figures include some prekindergarten students. Enrollment rate is based on percentage of persons 5-17 years old. Rank is from highest to lowest.
Source: U.S. National Center for Education Statistics.

Public college finances, 1996

State FTE enrollment.	17,400
Total U.S. FTE enrollment	8,268,800
State share of total U.S.	0.21%
Rank among states.	49
State and local appropriations	$155,800,000
Total U.S. state and local appropriations.	$39,699 mill.
State share of total U.S.	0.39%
Rank among states.	42
State net tuition revenues	$38,800,000
Total U.S. net tuition	$18,348,100,000
State share of total U.S.	0.21%
Rank among states.	49

FTE=Full-time equivalent; credit and noncredit enrollment including summer session in academic year ending in 1996.
Enrollments are rounded to nearest thousand students. Appropriations and tuitions are rounded to nearest million dollars; net tuition revenues exclude appropriation to students attending in-state public institutions. Rankings are from highest shares to lowest.
Source: Research Associates of Washington.

Modern dogsledders recall Alaska's rugged past in Anchorage's annual Winter Festival. (Anchorage Convention & Visitors Bureau/Grant Klotz)

TRANSPORTATION AND TRAVEL

Highway mileage, 1996

Interstate	1,086
Other arterial	1,512
Collector roads	2,982
Local roads	7,904
Urban roads	1,795
Rural roads	11,460
Total state	13,255
U.S. total	3,933,985
State share	0.3%
Rank among states	47

Source: U.S. Federal Highway Administration.

Motor vehicle registrations and driver licenses, 1996

In thousands

Vehicle registrations	State	U.S.	Share	Rank
Autos, trucks, buses	531	206,365	0.26%	49
Autos only	226	128,439	0.18%	50
Motorcycles	13	3,832	0.34%	49
Driver licenses	440	179,539	0.25%	49

Figures do not include vehicles owned by military services.
Source: U.S. Federal Highway Administration; *Highway Statistics; Selected Highway Statistics and Charts.*

Domestic travel expenditures, 1995

Spending by U.S. residents on overnight trips and day trips of at least 100 miles

Total expenditures in state	$1,157 mill.
Total expenditures in U.S.	$360,314 mill.
State share of total U.S.	0.32%
Rank among states	45

Source: Travel Industry Association of America.

CRIME AND LAW ENFORCEMENT

State and local police officers, 1996

Local police	740
State police	290
Sheriffs	0
Total	1,254
Officers per 10,000 residents	21
U.S. average	25
Rank among states	30

Figures cover full-time sworn officers; totals include special police not shown separately.
Source: U.S. Bureau of Justice Statistics; *Census of State and Local Law Enforcement Agencies, 1996.*

Crime rates, 1996

Rates per 100,000 resident population

Violent crimes	State	U.S.
Total violent	728	634
Murder	7.4	7.4
Forcible rape	65.6	36.1
Robbery	117	202
Aggravated assault	538	388
Property crimes		
Total property	4,723	4,445
Burglary	843	943
Larceny/theft	3,387	2,976
Motor vehicle theft	493	526
Totals	5,450	5,079

Source: U.S. Federal Bureau of Investigation; *Crime in the United States,* annual.

State prison populations, 1980-1996

	State	U.S.	State share
1980	822	305,458	0.27%
1990	2,622	708,393	0.37%
1996	3,716	1,025,624	0.36%

Figures exclude prisoners in federal penitentiaries.
Source: U.S. Bureau of Justice Statistics.

Arizona

Location: Southwestern continental United States

Area and rank: 114,000 square miles (295,249 square kilometers); 114,006 square miles (295,276 square kilometers) including water; sixth largest state in area

Population and rank: 4,554,966 (1997); twenty-first largest state in population

Capital: Phoenix

Largest city: Phoenix (1,198,064 people in 1998)

Became territory: February 24, 1863

Entered Union and rank: February 14, 1912; forty-eighth state

Present constitution adopted: 1911

Counties: 15

State name: "Arizona" derives from the American Indian "Arizonac," which means "little spring" or "young spring"

State nickname: Grand Canyon State

Motto: *Ditat Deus* (God enriches)

State flag: Blue field on bottom half; thirteen red and yellow rays and a copper star on top half

Highest point: Humphreys Peak — 12,633 feet (3,851 meters)

Lowest point: Colorado River — 70 feet (21 meters)

Arizona's second-largest city, Tucson originated as a mission station in 1692. (PhotoDisc)

Highest recorded temperature: 127 degrees Fahrenheit (53 degrees Celsius) — Parker, 1905

Lowest recorded temperature: −40 degrees Fahrenheit (−40 degrees Celsius) — Hawley Lake, 1971

State song: "Arizona March Song"

State tree: Palo Verde

State flower: Flower of saguaro cactus

State bird: Cactus wren

State fish: Arizona trout

National parks: Grand Canyon, Petrified Forest

Arizona History

Arizona's arid climate and southwest location combined to play influential roles in its history. Lack of rain has placed water at the center of Arizona's concerns, because without water, economic development is impossible. In the 1850's, the federal government even imported camels for a route through Arizona. The state was later than others in developing, with a population of barely forty thousand in 1880. On the other hand, the completion of a number of significant dams before and after World War II provided copious water and electric power, and the state's warm winters attract millions of new arrivals.

Early History. American Indians are believed to have inhabited Arizona for thousands of years, probably as early as 25,000 B.C.E. First to have settled were the Anasazi, ancestors of today's Pueblo, Hohokam, and Mogollon peoples. Not long before the entrance of Europeans to the region, the Navajos and Apaches arrived. In the sixteenth century, Spanish and Native Americans came in contact with each other. A succession of Spanish expeditions arrived, headed by priests such as Franciscan friar Marcos de Niza, who came in 1539 searching for the fabled Seven Cities of Cibola. Other adventurers arrived, such as Francisco Vásquez de Coronado, who explored the region from 1540 to 1542. More explorers entered the region later in the century searching for precious metals.

In the next century a number of priests came in search of American Indian souls to save and began erecting missions. Perhaps the most illustrious was Father Eusebio Francisco Kino, a Jesuit mathematics professor of German origin, who went to Mexico in 1680. Kino thoroughly explored the region, covering twenty thousand square miles and finding an overland route to California. Kino also founded several missions, including San Xavier del Bac Mission, located near Tucson, established in 1692. It is the only surviving Mexican Baroque church in the United States.

In the eighteenth century Spanish activity continued. In 1776, when the American colonies declared independence from Britain, Spanish cleric Father Francisco Silvestre Vélez de Escalante undertook important explorations of the Colorado River region. The previous year, Tucson had been founded when a fortress, Old Pueblo, was constructed there. In succeeding years, Spanish troops were busy dealing with hostile American Indians. In the 1780's they conquered the Yumas, and in 1790 negotiations with the Apaches resulted in a peace lasting until 1822. Peace with the Navahos after their military defeat in 1806 lasted thirteen years.

American involvement in the region began in the 1820's, when traders and trappers entered the territory. From 1828, trapper, scout, and soldier Kit Carson used Taos, New Mexico, as a base for expeditions, which in some cases traveled through Arizona. Another famous trapper and scout, Pauline Weaver, arrived in 1830 and was active more than thirty years later when he led gold-hunting parties. In these years modern Arizona was part of Mexico, which gained independence from Spain after its War of Independence, begun in 1810.

From Spanish to American Rule. Arizona passed from Mexican to American hands as a consequence of the Mexican-American War (1846-1848). The terms of the Treaty of Guadalupe Hidalgo called for Mexico to cede all lands north of the Gila River, which runs through southern Arizona. Thus Arizona became part of New Mexico, which, in 1850, became a territory after its annexation to the United States.

The Gila River border proved problematic, however, when plans for a transcontinental railroad were being drawn up, since the best route ran south of the river. Accordingly, an American diplomat, James Gadsden, American Minister to Mexico, negotiated transfer of the required land. In 1853, by the terms of the Gadsden Purchase, Mexico agreed to sell a strip of territory along its northern border between Texas and California for $10 million.

Arizona was still part of New Mexico when the Civil War broke out. In 1861, when Southern President Jefferson Davis declared New Mexico part of the Confederacy, Kit Carson was asked to raise a force to defend the territory against invasion.

When the Confederacy sent troops to the region in 1862, the only Civil War battle on Arizona soil occurred, resulting in Union victory. Thereafter, claims of the Confederacy to the region rang hollow. To ensure its status, however, Congress made Arizona a separate territory in 1863. Prescott was the new territory's first capital, though the site changed from one place to another until Phoenix became the permanent capital in 1889.

Native American Relations. During the Civil War, the area was nearly emptied of European settlers. Yet after the war, when miners and ranchers returned, American Indian attacks became a serious matter. In 1864 Kit Carson led a successful campaign against the Navahos. The defeated Indians were then required to trek, many of them on foot, to Bosque Redondo, New Mexico, some 250 miles away. The event became known as the Long Walk. They remained there until 1868, when they made the Long Walk Home.

The Apaches, however, remained hostile and active in Arizona. With such leaders as Cochise, Mangas Coloradas, and Geronimo, the Apaches were a formidable threat, attacking not only ranches but also towns and even forts. Not until 1886 did the last raiding party led by Geronimo surrender to federal forces.

Despite problems with Native Americans, much economic progress was made. Mining made great strides in the 1870's, and after 1886 grazing prospered despite frequent range wars between cattle and sheep ranchers. In the 1880's copper was discovered near Bisbee, in the southeast. Eventually copper became an important state resource. Settlement of the territory was assisted by several congressional acts, such as the Homestead Act (1862), which gave land to settlers but required them to de-

velop it to make good their claims. A tremendous boost to the state's development occurred when the first transcontinental railroad appeared in 1880. Six years later, track for a second railroad was laid in northern Arizona. Population, which was a dismal 9,658 in 1870, jumped to more than 40,000 ten years later and reached 88,000 in 1890. At the close of the century, it was 123,000, and in 1910, just prior to statehood, it passed 200,000.

From Territory to Statehood. With the American Indian menace behind them, Arizonans of the 1890's agitated for statehood. Not until 1910, however, could Congress be persuaded to pass enabling legislation. Accordingly, a constitution was adopted. Like those of other western states, it provided for the initiative and referendum and allowed recall of public officials. This provision included recall of judges by voters, but President William Howard Taft strongly objected and refused to agree to Arizona statehood unless it was removed. He believed that judicial independence, essential for constitutional government, would be fatally compromised by such a provision. The offending provision was therefore deleted. Upon attaining statehood, however, voters restored the provision.

The constitution provides for a governor elected for no more than two four-year terms. Four other executive branch officials are elected—a secretary of state, attorney general, treasurer, and superintendent of public instruction. These officials form a line of succession if a governor dies, resigns, or is removed from office; they, too, are limited to two four-year terms. Members of the bicameral legislature can be elected to a maximum of four two-year terms. The state's supreme court justices are appointed by the governor to six-year terms, at the end of which voters decide whether to retain them.

The recall provision was most notably used in 1988 to remove a sitting governor.

Social and Economic Progress. By the time Arizona achieved statehood, it had begun the process of advancing from an extraction to a manufacturing economy. With the emergence of labor unions in mines, labor strife became familiar. Among militant labor organizers were the Marxist International Workers of the World (IWW). A notorious event in the state's labor history involving the IWW was the "Bisbee deportation" of July 12, 1917, during World War I. In this incident, some two thousand persons, most of them copper miners called out on strike by the IWW, were arrested by armed civilians, headed by the sheriff. Those who refused to abandon the strike, nearly 1,200 men, were loaded onto cattle cars and taken across the New Mexico border. There, they were unloaded in the desert, where they spent two unsheltered days before U.S. troops arrived. Hundreds of civil suits were filed afterwards and settled out of court.

Apache leaders Geronimo (center left with arms on knees) and Nana (to Geronimo's right) negotiating with General George Crook (second from right with white hat) confer around 1886 in one of several attempts to end the region's Apache wars. (Library of Congress)

Located in the northwestern corner of Arizona, the Grand Canyon is a deep gorge cut by the Colorado River that stretches about 280 miles. (PhotoDisc)

Along with those of neighboring states, the U.S. entrance into World War I gave a significant, though temporary, boost to Arizona's economy, when the prices of minerals skyrocketed. During the two decades following the war, the federal government continued planning and constructing a series of dams and reservoirs that eventually would be of tremendous value to the state's economy by enabling irrigation, cheap power, and flood control. The Roosevelt Dam had been constructed prior to statehood. After the war, further projects included the Coolidge Dam on the Upper Gila River in south central Arizona, other dams on the Verde and Salt Rivers, and the great Hoover Dam, one of the century's great engineering projects, on the Arizona-Nevada border. In 1922 the Colorado River Compact devised a scheme for water sharing among seven states, including Arizona. As further irrigation became possible, agriculture prospered.

The Depression years of the 1930's, however, were as difficult for Arizona as for the rest of the nation.

World War II and Postwar Developments. The state's economy rebounded through federal spending during World War II, when numerous air bases were opened due to the state's ideal flying weather. After the war the boom continued. Between 1940 and 1960, population nearly tripled, reaching 1.3 million. Adequate water supplies allowed manufacturing to expand, especially after 1963, when the U.S. Supreme Court awarded the state rights to 2.8 million acre feet of water a year from the Colorado River. By then, Arizona's extraction economy had been transformed by industrialization.

By the 1990's the state had undergone a second transformation. Manufacturing accounted for only 12 percent of its income, though high-tech industries were making their mark. Agriculture was just 2 percent and mining a scant 1 percent of state income. The lion's share was now taken up by services, including a thriving tourist industry. Society had also been transformed by a postwar flight from the eastern and midwestern "rust belt" to the warmer climate and economic opportunities of the Southwest. From a raw frontier territory at the start of the century, Arizona had become a prosperous modern, postindustrial society, with a rich and colorful past and a confident future.

Charles F. Bahmueller

Arizona Time Line

500-1450	Hohokam Indians flourish; build more than two hundred miles of canals for water for irrigation and domestic use.
c. 1000	Cochise Indians settle near present-day Bisbee.
1526	Don José de Basconales crosses part of Arizona.
1536	Explorer Alvar Núñez Cabeza de Vaca crosses part of southwest Arizona.
1539	Franciscan friar Marcos de Niza explores in Arizona, searching for rich Seven Cities of Cibola.
1540	Francisco Vásquez de Coronado explores Arizona region.
1581-1583	Spanish expeditions through Arizona find precious metals.
1620	Franciscan missionaries appeal to Hopi Indians.
1680	Father Eusebio Francisco Kino begins missionary work.
1692	Father Kino founds San Xavier del Bac Mission.
1752	First white settlement is founded by Spanish at Tubac.
1776	Tuscon is founded as Spanish fort.
1776	Father Francisco Silvestre Vélez de Escalante explores Colorado River region.
1782	Spanish military forces conquer Yuma Indians.
1804-1806	Navaho Indians are defeated by Spanish military; peace endures for thirteen years.
1821	Arizona becomes province of Mexico; Santa Fe Trail opens.
1824	American traders begin exploring Apache territory.
1827	Mexican Republic expels Franciscans, ending missionary era.
1830	American trapper and scout Pauline Weaver begins Arizona travels.
Dec. 17, 1846	Mormon battalion occupies Tuscon; raises U.S. flag on road from Santa Fe to the Pacific.
1848	Mexico cedes all land north of Gila River to United States in Treaty of Guadalupe Hidalgo.
Sept. 9, 1850	Territory of New Mexico, which includes Arizona, is established.
1853	Gadsden Purchase makes southern Arizona U.S. land.
1860	First newspaper, the *Weekly Arizonan*, begins publication.
1860	Apache chief Cochise leads raids on settlers.
1861	Southern president Jefferson Davis declares Arizona a Confederate territory.
1862	Sole civil war battle in Arizona fought at Picacho Peak, near Tucson; results in Union victory.

Feb. 24, 1863	Union president Abraham Lincoln creates Arizona Territory; Prescott is made capital.
1863	Navahos are forced to walk 250 miles from Arizona to Fort Sumner, New Mexico, after military defeat.
1866	First public schools open, in Prescott and Tuscon.
1867	Treaty establishing Navaho Reservation is signed.
Apr. 30, 1871	Grant Camp Massacre occurs, in which 108 Apaches are killed by whites.
1875	First copper is mined at Clifton.
1879	Tombstone is founded after gold is discovered.
1880	First railroad crosses state.
Oct. 26, 1881	Gunfight at the O.K. Corral, among Wyatt Earp, Doc Holliday, and others, takes place in Tombstone.
1883	Santa Fe Railroad crosses northern region of Arizona.
1886	Geronimo's Apaches surrender to federal troops.
1907	Arizona is nation's leading copper producer.
1911	Roosevelt Dam is dedicated.
Feb. 14, 1912	Arizona becomes forty-eighth state.
1919	Grand Canyon National Park is established.
1928	Coolidge Dam is dedicated.
1936	Boulder (now Hoover) Dam, on Arizona-Nevada border, is completed.
1942	Almost eighteen thousand Japanese Americans are interned in Poston.
1948	Arizona Indians win right to vote.
1963	U.S. Supreme Court gives Arizona Colorado River water rights.
1963	Judge Lorna Lockwood becomes first female state supreme court chief justice.
1969	Navajo Community College, the first college on an Indian reservation, opens in Tsaile.
1974	Construction begins on Central Arizona Project, designed to assure Arizona sufficient water.
1991	Central Arizona Project is completed.
1997	Arizona's population is estimated at 4,554,966.

Notes for Further Study

Published Sources. Among books useful for an understanding of government in Arizona are David R. Berman's *Arizona Politics & Government: The Quest for Autonomy, Democracy, and Development* (1998) and Gerald E. Hansen and Douglas A. Brown's *Arizona: Its Constitution and Government* (1993). There is also an annually updated yearbook series, *Arizona Yearbook: A Guide to Government in the Grand Canyon State.* On Arizona's geography, see Malcolm L. Comeaux, *Arizona: A Geography* (1982); for place names, there is Will Croft Barnes's *Arizona Place Names* (1988); for a historical atlas, one should consult Henry Pickering Walker's *Historical Atlas of Arizona* (1987).

For natural history, an excellent source is *The Smithsonian Guide to Natural America: The Southwest—New Mexico and Arizona* (1995). For an overview of Arizona history, see Robert Wozinicki's *History of Arizona* (1987); Donald Gawronski's *An Introduction to Arizona and Government* (1988); and Thomas G. Aylesworth, et al., *The West: Arizona, Nevada, Utah* (1995). Travelers should consult Marshall Trimble's *Roadside History of Arizona* (1986). Studies on Native Americans include W. E. Coffer's *Sipapu: The Story of the Indians of Arizona and New Mexico* (1986). Regarding individual tribes, Ruth Underhill studies *The Papago and Pima Indians of Arizona* (1990), and Franck C. Lockwood examines *The Apache Indians* (1987). Ancient Indian culture is explored in James J. Reid and Stephanie Whittlesey's *The Archeology of Ancient Arizona* (1997).

Web Resources. The official state of Arizona Web site (http://www.state.az.us) is a good starting place for information on the state. Arizona Online (http://www.azonline.net/gover), a site with government links, is useful. The governor's site (http://governor .state.az.us/dept/gita.html) and the State of Arizona Legislative Information System (http://www.u.arizona.edu/~knr/azlinks.html) offer resources on the political workings in the state. For questions regarding Arizona law see Fine Law (http://finelaw.com/11stategov/az/state.htm).

Extensive links on Arizona history may be found at http://www.rr.gmcs.k12.us/arizona.htm. Other good links to Arizona history sites are a Scottsdale site (http:// www.scottsdale.org.curriculum/Chaney/chaneyfinal .html) and a Prescott site (http://prescott.org/history .htm). For a taste of the state's varied ethnic history, see The Promise of Gold Mountain: Tucson's Chinese Heritage (http://www.library.arizona.edu.promise). The Arizona state historical society maintains information on library archives on Arizona history (http://wwwazstarnet.com/~azhist/library.htm). The archaeology of ancient Arizona may be explored (http://www .uapress.arizona.edu/samples/sam1013.htm), and the Arizona Military Museum site (http://www.azng.com/museum.htm) is a good research tool.

Information on Arizona's Native Americans is found at numerous sites, such as the list of the state's tribes and those in each state of the Union (http://members .tripod.com/~MGO/Indian.html). Information on individual tribes may also be researched, such as the Hohokum Indians in Arizona (http://biology.uoregon .edu/Biology_www/Online_), the Hopi (http://www.carizona.com/nativeland/hopi.html), and the Camp Verde Yavapai Apache (http://carizona.com/nativeland/campverde.html). A specialized site that may be of interest deals with public policy questions as they relate to Native Americans (http://www.ou.edu/special/albertctr/archives.Natv.htm).

Counties

County	Sq. miles	1996 pop.
Apache	11,205.7	69,087
Cochise	6,170.0	110,358
Coconino	18,619.1	112,260
Gila	4,768.1	47,338
Graham	4,629.6	30,780
Greenlee	1,847.1	9,330
La Paz	4,499.6	14,497
Maricopa	9,204.0	2,611,327
Mohave	13,312.4	126,294
Navajo	9,953.8	92,086
Pima	9,187.0	767,873
Pinal	5,370.0	135,376
Santa Cruz	1,237.7	36,952
Yavapai	8,123.5	139,368
Yuma	5,514.4	125,142

Source: U.S. Census Bureau; National Association of Counties.

This statue of Arizona's late seventeenth century missionary pioneer and explorer Eusebio Francisco Kino stands in the national capitol building in Washington, D.C. (Library of Congress)

Cities
With 10,000 or more residents

Rank	City	Population
1	Phoenix	1,198,064
2	Tucson	460,466
3	Mesa	360,076
4	Scottsdale	195,394
5	Glendale	193,482
6	Tempe	167,622
7	Chandler	160,329
8	Gilbert	88,840
9	Peoria	87,048
10	Yuma	62,433
11	Flagstaff	56,657
12	Lake Havasu City	40,495
13	Sierra Vista	38,068
14	Prescott	34,129
15	Bullhead City	28,152
16	Avondale	27,580
17	Casa Grande	23,003

Rank	City	Population
18	Nogales	22,042
19	Oro Valley	21,411
20	Apache Junction	21,235
21	Fountain Hills	19,159
22	Prescott Valley	18,873
23	Kingman	18,369
24	Goodyear	15,262
25	Douglas	15,208
26	Surprise	14,849
27	Paradise Valley	14,544
28	SanLuis	12,149
29	Payson	11,978
30	Florence	11,911
31	Winslow	10,684

Population figures are estimated for mid-1998.
Source: U.S. Bureau of the Census.

Index to Tables

NA = Reliable data are not available.

DEMOGRAPHICS

Resident state and national populations, 1970-1997

Population figures given in thousands

	State pop.	U.S. pop.	Share	Rank
1970	1,775	203,302	0.9%	33
1980	2,718	226,546	1.2%	29
1985	3,184	237,924	1.3%	28
1990	3,665	248,765	1.5%	24
1995	4,308	262,761	1.6%	22
1997	4,555	267,636	1.7%	21

Source: U.S. Bureau of the Census.

Resident population by age, 1997

Age group	Total population
Under 5 years	374,000
5 to 17 years	904,000
18 to 24 years	425,000
25 to 34 years	649,000
35 to 44 years	703,000
45 to 54 years	536,000
55 to 64 years	361,000
65 to 74 years	335,000
75 to 84 years	208,000
85 years and over	59,000
Portion of residents 65 and older	13.2%
National average	12.7%

Population figures are rounded to nearest thousand persons;
figures include armed forces personnel stationed in state.
Source: U.S. Bureau of the Census.

Resident population by race, Hispanic origin, 1997

	State pop.	Share	U.S.
All residents	4,555,000	100.0%	100.0%
Hispanic white	933,000	20.5%	10.0%
non-Hispanic white	3,113,000	68.3%	72.7%
African American	161,000	3.5%	12.7%
Native American	255,000	5.6%	0.9%
Asian, Pacific Islander	93,000	2.0%	3.8%

Source: U.S. Bureau of the Census.

Projections of state population, 2000-2025

	Model A Uses interstate migration observed from 1975-1994	Model B Uses Bureau of Economic Analysis employment projections
Year	Population	Population
2000	4,798,000	4,838,000
2005	5,230,000	5,432,000
2010	5,522,000	6,025,000
2015	5,808,000	6,620,000
2020	6,111,000	7,193,000
2025	6,412,000	7,729,000

All population projections, including those for 2000, were
calculated in 1997.
Source: U.S. Bureau of the Census, Population Paper Listings
PPL-47.

VITAL STATISTICS

Average lifetime in years by race, 1989-1991

	State	U.S.	Rank
All residents	76.10	75.37	22
White residents	76.42	76.13	22
Black residents	70.84	69.16	7

Ranks are from longest-lived to least longest-lived. Ranks
exclude Alaska, for which reliable data are not available.
Rank for black residents is based on the 32 states for which
reliable data are available.
Source: U.S. National Center for Health Statistics.

Infant mortality rates, 1980 and 1995

	State	U.S.
All residents		
1980	12.4	12.6
1995	7.5	7.6
White residents		
1980	11.8	11.0
1995	7.2	6.3
Black residents		
1980	18.4	21.4
1995	17.0	15.1

Figures represent deaths per 1,000 live births of resident
infants under 1 year old, exclusive of fetal deaths; all-
residents figures include other races not listed separately.
Source: U.S. National Center for Health Statistics.

Marriages and divorces

Marriages in 1996. 39,200
Rate per 1,000 population, 1995 . . . . 9.2
U.S. rate, 1995 . . . . 8.9
Rank among all states 17

Divorces in 1996 25,800
Rate per 1,000 population, 1995 . . . . 6.6
U.S. rate, 1995 . . . . 4.4
Rank among all states. 5

Rank is from highest to lowest in country.
Source: U.S. National Center for Health Statistics.

Death rates by leading causes, 1995
Deaths per 100,000 resident population

Cause	State	U.S.
Heart disease	242.6	280.7
Cancer	190.1	204.9
Cerebrovascular diseases	51.8	60.1
Accidents and adverse effects	47.0	35.5
Motor vehicle accidents	23.5	16.5
Chronic obstructive pulmonary diseases	48.3	39.2
Diabetes mellitus	19.5	22.6
HIV	11.5	NA
Suicide	19.1	11.9
Homicide	12.7	8.7
All causes	837.9	880.0

Rank in overall death rate among states	34

Figures exclude nonresidents who die in state. Causes of
death follow International Classification of Diseases. Rank
is from highest to lowest in country.
Source: U.S. National Center for Health Statistics.

ECONOMY

Gross state product, 1990-1996
In current dollars

	State product	Increase
1990	$68.5 billion	
1993	$85.0 billion	
1994	$95.4 billion	12.24%
1995	$104.0 billion	9.01%
1996	$111.5 billion	7.21%

Source: U.S. Bureau of Economic Analysis; Survey of Current Business, June, 1998.

Gross state product by industry, 1996
In billions

Farms, forestry, fisheries	$1.7
Construction	5.6
Manufacturing.	16.8
Transportation, public utilities.	8.2
Wholesale trade.	6.7
Retail trade	11.4
Finance, insurance, real estate	18.3
Services	19.6
Government	13.0
State total	$102.6
Total U.S.	$6,923.8
State share	1.48%
Rank among states.	24

Total figures include mining, not listed separately.
Source: U.S. Bureau of Economic Analysis; Survey of Current Business, June, 1998.

Personal income per capita, 1990 and 1997
In current dollars

	1990	1997
Per capita income	$16,640	$22,364
U.S. average	$19,188	$25,598
Rank among states	35	35

1997 data are preliminary.
Source: U.S. Bureau of Economic Analysis; Survey of Current Business, May, 1998.

Energy consumption, 1995
In trillions of British thermal units (BTU)

End-use sectors

Residential	234.2
Commercial	226.9
Industrial	223.2
Transportation	378.0

Sources of energy

Petroleum	409.1
Natural gas	124.3
Coal	342.4
Hydroelectric power.	87.3
Nuclear electric power	287.6
Total state per capita consumption	246.0
Total U.S. per capita consumption	344.4
Rank among states.	45
Total state energy consumption	1,058.9
Total U.S. energy consumption	90,547.4
State share of U.S. total	1.17%
Rank among states.	28

Total figures include items not listed separately.
Source: U.S. Energy Information Administration; State Energy Data Report.

Nonfarm employment by sectors, 1997

Total	1,977,000
Construction.	131,000
Manufacturing.	207,000
Transportation, public utilities.	96,000
Wholesale trade, retail trade	481,000
Finance, insurance, real estate	127,000
Services	599,000
Government	324,000

Figures are rounded to nearest thousand persons. Total includes mining, not listed separately.
Source: U.S. Bureau of Labor Statistics; Employment and Earnings, monthly.

Foreign exports, 1990-1997
In millions of dollars

Year	State	U.S.	State share
1990	3,729	394,045	0.95%
1996	10,503	624,767	1.68%
1997	13,820	688,896	2.01%

Source: U.S. Bureau of the Census; U.S. Merchandise Trade, series FT 900.

LAND USE

Federally owned land, 1996

	State	U.S.	State share
Total acres	72,688,000	2,271,343,000	3.20%
Federally owned	31,337,000	563,129,000	5.56%
Federal share	43.1%	24.8%	—

Areas are rounded to nearest thousand acres. Figures for
federally owned land do not include trust properties.
Source: U.S. General Services Administration; *Inventory Report
on Real Property Owned by the United States Throughout the
World,* annual.

Land use, 1992
In acres, rounded to nearest thousand

Total surface area	72,960,000
Federal land	30,280,000
Total nonfederal	42,408,000
Developed	1,404,000
Total rural	41,004,000
Cropland	1,198,000
Pasture land	76,000
Range land	32,227,000
Forest land	4,718,000
Minor cover/use	2,785,000

Total surface area figures include water area not shown
separately.
Source: U.S. Dept. of Agriculture; Soil Conservation Service;
Iowa State University, Statistical Laboratory; *Summary
Report, 1992 National Resources Inventory.*

Farms and crop acreage, 1997

	State	U.S.	Share	Rank
Farms (thousands)	8	2,058	0.39%	40
Acres (millions)	35	968	3.62%	8
Acres per farm	4,720	471	—	1
Acres planted	808	334,139	0.24%	38
Acres harvested	800	319,894	0.25%	38
Farm value (mill.)	$1,232	$108,805	1.13%	30

Numbers of farms are rounded to nearest thousand.
Source: U.S. Dept. of Agriculture; National Agricultural
Statistics Service.

GOVERNMENT AND FINANCE

Units of local government, 1997

	State	Total U.S.	Rank
All local governments	637	87,453	40
Counties	15	3,043	42
Municipalities	87	19,372	41
Townships	0	16,629	—
School districts	231	13,726	23
Special districts	304	34,683	37

County ranks are based on the 48 states with county
governments; township ranks are based on the 20 states
with township governments; school district ranks are based
on the 46 states with such districts.
Source: U.S. Bureau of the Census; *1997 Census of Governments,
Government Organization,* Series GC97(1).

State government revenue, 1996

Total revenue	$12,594 mill.
General revenue	10,867 mill.
Per capita	2,451
U.S. per capita average	2,910
Rank among states	45
Intergovernmental revenue	
Total	$3,105 mill.
From federal government	2,767 mill.
From local government	338 mill.
Charges and Miscellaneous	
Total	$1,352 mill.
Current charges	666 mill.
Misc. general revenue	686 mill.
Taxes	
Total	$6,409 mill.
General sales	2,720 mill.
Selective sales	938 mill.
License taxes	391 mill.
Individual income	1,494 mill.
Corporate income	448 mill.
Other	418 mill.
Insurance trust revenue	1,706 mill.

Total revenue figures include items not listed separately.
Source: U.S. Bureau of the Census.

State government expenditures, 1996

General expenditures
Intergovernmental . . . . $4,255 mill.
Direct expenditures . . . . 6,563 mill.
Total . . . . 10,818 mill.

Selected direct expenditures
Education . . . . $3,788 mill.
Public welfare. . . . . 2,605 mill.
Health, hospital . . . . 600 mill.
Highways . . . . 1,143 mill.
Police . . . . 120 mill.
Corrections . . . . 499 mill.
Natural resources. . . . . 169 mill.
Parks and recreation. . . . . 29 mill.
Government administration . . . . 335 mill.
Interest on debt . . . . 181 mill.

Other
State per capita expenditures $2,440
U.S. per capita average 2,854
Rank among states. 44
Total state expenditures . . . . 11,898 mill.
Total U.S. expenditures . . . . 859,959 mill.

Totals include items not listed separately.
Source: U.S. Bureau of the Census.

POLITICS

Governors
D = Democrat; R = Republican; O = other;
(r) resigned; (d) died in office; (i) removed from office

George W. P. Hunt (D) 1912-1917
Thomas E. Campbell (R) . . . . (i) 1917
George W. P. Hunt (D) 1917-1919
Thomas E. Campbell (R). 1919-1923
George W. P. Hunt (D) 1923-1929
John C. Phillips (R) 1929-1931
George W. P. Hunt (D) 1931-1933
Benjamin B. Moeur (D) 1933-1937
Rawghlie C. Stanford (D) 1937-1939
Robert T. Jones (D). 1939-1941
Sidney P. Osborn (D) . . . . (d) 1941-1948
Daniel E. Garvey (D) 1948-1951
(John) Howard Pyle (R) 1951-1955
Ernest W. McFarland (D) 1955-1959
Paul J. Fannin (R) 1959-1965
Samuel P. Goddard, Jr. (D). 1965-1967
John R. (Jack) Williams (R) 1967-1975
Raul H. Castro (D) . . . . (r) 1975-1977

Wesley Bolin (D) . . . . (d) 1977-1978
Bruce Babbitt (D) 1978-1987
Evan Mecham (R) 1987-1988
Rose Mofford (R). 1988-1991
Fife Symington (R) . . . . (r) 1991-1997
Jane Dee Hull (R) 1997-

Composition of state legislature, 1990-1998

	Democrats	Republicans
State House (60 seats)		
1990	27	33
1992	25	35
1994	22	38
1996	22	38
1998	20	40
State Senate (30 seats)		
1990	17	13
1992	12	18
1994	11	19
1996	12	18
1998	14	16

Figures for total seats may include independents and minor party members.
Source: Council of State Governments; *State Elective Officials and the Legislatures.*

Composition of congressional delegations, 1989-1999

	Dem	Rep	Total
House of Representatives			
101st Congress, 1989			
State delegates	1	4	5
Total U.S.	259	174	433
102d Congress, 1991			
State delegates	1	4	5
Total U.S.	267	167	434
103d Congress, 1993			
State delegates	3	3	6
Total U.S.	258	176	434
104th Congress, 1995			
State delegates	1	5	6
Total U.S.	197	236	433
105th Congress, 1997			
State delegates	1	5	6
Total U.S.	206	228	434

	Dem	Rep	Total
106th Congress, 1999			
State delegates	1	5	6
Total U.S.	211	222	433
Senate			
101st Congress, 1989			
State delegates	1	1	2
Total U.S.	55	45	100
102d Congress, 1991			
State delegates	1	1	2
Total U.S.	56	44	100
103d Congress, 1993			
State delegates	1	1	2
Total U.S.	57	43	100
104th Congress, 1995			
State delegates	0	2	2
Total U.S.	46	53	99
105th Congress, 1997			
State delegates	0	2	2
Total U.S.	45	55	100
106th Congress, 1999			
State delegates	0	2	2
Total U.S.	45	54	99

Figures are for starts of first sessions. Figure for U.S. Representatives for 101st Congress does not include Alabama and Indiana, which had vacancies. Figures for total U.S. Representatives for 102d, 103d, and 106th Congresses do not include Vermont, which had 1 Independent-Socialist. Figure for U.S. Representatives for 104th Congress does not include Vermont, which had 1 Independent-Socialist, and California, which had 1 vacancy. Figure for U.S. Representatives for 105th Congress does not include New York, which had 1 vacancy. Figure for U.S. Senators for 104th Congress does not include Oregon, which had 1 vacancy. Figure for U.S. Senators for 106th Con-gress does not include New Hampshire, which had 1 Independent.
Source: U.S. Congress; *Congressional Directory,* biennial.

Voter participation in presidential elections, 1992 and 1996

	1992	1996
State voting age pop.	2,812,000	3,094,000
Total U.S. voting age pop.	189,524,000	196,509,000
State share of U.S. total	1.5%	1.6%
Rank among states	23	23
Percent of state casting vote	52.9	64.5
Percent of U.S. total voting	55.1	49.0
Rank among states	36	1

Source: U.S. Bureau of the Census.

HEALTH AND MEDICAL CARE

Medicare, 1997

	Recipients	Payments
State	632,000	$3,211 mill.
Total U.S.	37,514,000	$206,064 mill.
State share	1.68%	1.56%
Rank among states	21	20

Recipient figures are rounded to nearest thousand persons. Ranks are from highest to lowest.
Source: U.S. Health Care Financing Administration.

Medicaid, 1996

	Recipients	Payments
State	528,000	$211 mill.
Total U.S.	35,028,000	$121,419 mill.
State share	1.51%	0.17%
Rank among states	21	49

Recipient figures are rounded to nearest thousand persons. Payment figures for fiscal year reflect federal and state contribution payments. Ranks are from highest to lowest.
Source: U.S. Health Care Financing Administration.

Health insurance coverage, 1996

	State	U.S.
Total persons covered	3,642,000	225,070,000
Total persons not covered	1,159,000	41,716,000
Part not covered	24.1%	15.6%
Rank among states	2	—
Children not covered	357,000	10,554,000
Part not covered	25.0%	14.8%
Rank among states	1	—

Ranks are from most to fewest uninsured. Population figures are rounded to nearest thousand persons.
Source: U.S. Bureau of the Census.

AIDS, syphilis, tuberculosis, and measles cases, 1997

Cases	U.S.	State	Share
AIDS	58,443	448	0.77%
Syphilis	8,550	132	1.54%
Tuberculosis	18,534	272	1.47%
Measles	148,000	5,000	3.38%

Measles figures are rounded to nearest thousand cases.
Source: U.S. Centers for Disease Control and Prevention.

HOUSING

Homeownership rates, 1985-1997

	1985	1990	1997
State	64.7%	64.5%	63.0%
Total U.S.	63.9%	63.9%	65.7%
Rank among states	36	36	41

Source: U.S. Bureau of the Census.

Home sales, 1990 and 1997
In thousands of units

Existing home sales	1990	1997	Change
State sales	86.3	135.1	48.8
Total U.S. sales	3,560	4,730	1,170
State share of U.S. total	2.42%	2.86%	0.43%
Rank among states	14	12	—

Source: National Association of Realtors; *Real Estate Outlook: Market Trends and Insights.*

EDUCATION

Public school enrollment, 1995

State K-8 enrollment	549,000
Total U.S. K-8 enrollment	32,341,000
State share of total U.S.	1.70%
State 9-12 enrollment	195,000
Total U.S. 9-12 enrollment	12,500,000
State share of U.S. total	1.56%
State public school enroll. rate	93.5%
Overall U.S. rate	91.6%
Rank among states	17

Enrollment figures (which include unclassified students) are rounded to nearest thousand pupils in fall term; kindergarten (K)-8 grade enrollment figures include some prekindergarten students. Enrollment rate is based on percentage of persons 5-17 years old. Rank is from highest to lowest.
Source: U.S. National Center for Education Statistics.

Public college finances, 1996

State FTE enrollment	161,900
Total U.S. FTE enrollment	8,268,800
State share of total U.S.	1.96%
Rank among states	17
State and local appropriations	$761 mill.
Total U.S. state and local appropriations	$39,699 mill.
State share of total U.S.	1.92%
Rank among states	17
State net tuition revenues	$346,800,000
Total U.S. net tuition	$18,348,100,000
State share of total U.S.	1.89%
Rank among states	21

FTE=Full-time equivalent; credit and noncredit enrollment including summer session in academic year ending in 1996.
Enrollments are rounded to nearest thousand students. Net tuition revenues exclude appropriation to students attending in-state public institutions. Rankings are from highest shares to lowest.
Source: Research Associates of Washington.

TRANSPORTATION AND TRAVEL

Highway mileage, 1996

Interstate	1,169
Other arterial	4,838
Collector roads	10,303
Local roads	40,334
Urban roads	16,233
Rural roads	38,662
Total state	54,895
U.S. total	3,933,985
State share	1.4%
Rank among states	35

Source: U.S. Federal Highway Administration.

Motor vehicle registrations and driver licenses, 1996

In thousands

Vehicle registrations	State	U.S.	Share	Rank
Autos, trucks, buses	2,983	206,365	1.45%	25
Autos only	1,750	128,439	1.36%	25
Motorcycles	71	3,832	1.85%	19
Driver licenses	2,727	179,539	1.52%	25

Figures do not include vehicles owned by military services.
Source: U.S. Federal Highway Administration; *Highway Statistics; Selected Highway Statistics and Charts.*

Domestic travel expenditures, 1995

Spending by U.S. residents on overnight trips and day trips of at least 100 miles

Total expenditures in state	$6,333 mill.
Total expenditures in U.S.	$360,314 mill.
State share of total U.S.	1.76%
Rank among states.	19

Source: Travel Industry Association of America.

CRIME AND LAW ENFORCEMENT

State and local police officers, 1996

Local police	6,967
State police	952
Sheriffs	1,563
Total	10,088
Officers per 10,000 residents	23
U.S. average	25
Rank among states.	21

Figures cover full-time sworn officers; totals include special police not shown separately.
Source: U.S. Bureau of Justice Statistics; *Census of State and Local Law Enforcement Agencies, 1996.*

Crime rates, 1996

Rates per 100,000 resident population

Violent crimes	State	U.S.
Total violent	632	634
Murder	8.5	7.4
Forcible rape	31.2	36.1
Robbery	168	202
Aggravated assault	424	388
Property crimes		
Total property	6,436	4,445
Burglary	1,256	943
Larceny/theft	4,253	2,976
Motor vehicle theft	927	526
Totals	7,067	5,079

Source: U.S. Federal Bureau of Investigation; *Crime in the United States,* annual.

State prison populations, 1980-1996

	State	U.S.	State share
1980	4,372	305,458	1.43%
1990	14,261	708,393	2.01%
1996	22,493	1,025,624	2.19%

Figures exclude prisoners in federal penitentiaries.
Source: U.S. Bureau of Justice Statistics.

Arkansas

Location: Southern continental United States

Area and rank: 52,075 square miles (134,875 square kilometers); 53,182 square miles (137,741 square kilometers) including water; twenty-seventh largest state in area

Population and rank: 2,522,819 (1997); thirty-third largest state in population

Capital: Little Rock

Largest city: Little Rock (175,303 people in 1998)

State capitol building in Little Rock. (A. C. Haralson/Arkansas Department of Parks & Tourism)

Became territory:
March 2, 1819

Entered Union and rank: June 15, 1836; twenty-fifth state

Present constitution adopted: 1874

Counties: 75

State name: "Arkansas" comes from a Quapaw Indian word

State nickname: The Natural State

Motto: *Regnat populus* (The people rule)

State flag: "Arkansas" and four blue stars on white diamond surrounded by blue bars with twenty-five white stars, over red field

Highest point: Magazine Mountain — 2,753 feet (839 meters)

Lowest point: Ouachita River — 55 feet (17 meters)

Highest recorded temperature: 120 degrees Fahrenheit (49 degrees Celsius) — Ozark, 1936

Lowest recorded temperature: −29 degrees Fahrenheit (−34 degrees Celsius) — Pond, 1905

State song: "Arkansas"

State tree: Pine

State flower: Apple Blossom

State bird: Mockingbird

National park: Hot Springs

Arkansas History

The history of Arkansas was greatly influenced by the natural division of the area into northwestern highlands and southeastern lowlands. Running through these two regions as it flows in a southeasterly direction to meet the Mississippi River, the Arkansas River has also been of major importance in the area's history. As long as ten thousand years ago, hunters and gatherers wandered the land surrounding the Arkansas River, attracted by the abundant wildlife. About one thousand years ago, bluff dwellers and mound builders grew crops in the area's fertile soil. By the time Europeans arrived in the New World, the primary groups of Native Americans inhabiting the area were the Osage, in Missouri and northwestern Arkansas; the Caddo, in Louisiana and southwestern Arkansas; and the Quapaw, along the Arkansas River. All three groups were forced into Oklahoma by the middle of the nineteenth century.

Exploration and Settlement. The first Europeans to reach the area were led northwest from Florida by Spanish explorer Hernando de Soto in 1541. A French expedition led by Jacques Marquette and Louis Jolliet reached the area in 1673 by traveling south from Michigan. In 1682 a similar expedition was led by René-Robert Cavalier, sieur de La Salle. La Salle claimed the entire valley of the Mississippi River, including all of Arkansas, for France. This enormous area was named Louisiana in honor of King Louis XIV of France.

Despite La Salle's claim to the area, European settlement of the area began modestly. In 1686 French explorer Henri de Tonti established Arkansas Post, the first permanent European settlement in the area, near the point where the Arkansas River meets the Mississippi River. Starting with a population of six residents, Arkansas Post grew to become the largest city in Arkansas until the nineteenth century. In 1722 French explorer Bernard de la Harpe led an expedition along the Arkansas River and named a natural rock formation Little Rock. Nearly a century later, a city of the same name was founded there.

The Road to Statehood. Settlement of the area continued slowly throughout the eighteenth century. In 1762 France ceded Louisiana to Spain. In order to encourage settlers, Spain offered free land and freedom from taxes to all who chose to live there. In 1783 British forces attacked Arkansas Post but were defeated by the Spanish and Quapaw. By 1799 Arkansas had nearly four hundred European settlers.

In 1800 Louisiana was returned to France. Three years later, the United States purchased this vast area, doubling the size of the young nation, for a payment of more than twenty-seven million dollars. At first a part of the huge Louisiana Territory, in 1812 Arkansas became part of the newly created Missouri Territory, then became a separate territory in 1819. In 1824 the western section of the area became part of the Indian Territory (Oklahoma), giving Arkansas its modern boundaries. By 1836 Arkansas had the sixty thousand residents necessary for statehood, primarily settlers from eastern states, and it was admitted as the twenty-fifth state.

The Civil War. The 1840's and 1850's brought large numbers of Irish and German immigrants to the area, along with those who arrived from the eastern United States. The mountains and plateaus of the northwest supported small farms, while the lowlands of the southeast developed large cotton plantations dependent on slaves. By 1860 the population of Arkansas reached 435,000. About one-quarter of the inhabitants were slaves.

Arkansas seceded from the Union on May 6, 1861, nearly a month after the Civil War broke out. The delay in joining the Confederacy may have been due to strong Union sympathies in the northwest part of the state. About six thousand residents of the state fought for the Union, while about fifty-eight thousand fought for the Confederacy. Several important Civil War battles were fought in northern Arkansas, near the border with Missouri. The Battle of Pea Ridge (March 7-8, 1862) led to heavy losses on both sides, as Union forces drove back an attack by the Confederates, ending the threat of a Confederate invasion of Missouri. In September of 1863, Union forces took control of Little Rock.

From the end of the war until the middle of the 1870's, a period known as Reconstruction, Arkansas and the other former Confederate states were occupied by federal troops and ruled by state governments dominated by the Republican Party. Arkansas was readmitted to the Union under Republican control in 1868. The Republican government, which attempted to win civil rights for freed slaves, was seen as an artificial structure imposed by the northern states. It was opposed, often violently, by many white Arkansans, leading to increased repression of African Americans after Reconstruction. After federal troops were withdrawn, the Democratic Party returned to power in 1874, completely dominating state politics for nearly a century.

After the War. Economic recovery after the devastation of the Civil War was difficult for Arkansans. The plantation system of the southeastern region of the state, which relied on slavery, was replaced with sharecropping. Under this system, tenants lived on and farmed a landowner's property, paying rent in the form of crops, usually cotton. The social and economic gap between the farmer and the landlord was often a large one.

An economic depression in the southern states in the late nineteenth century led to widespread poverty. The situation became even worse in 1885, when the state government defaulted on huge debts, including fourteen million dollars of interest payments. Race relations were also a severe problem, with the state government completely controlled by the Democratic Party, which excluded African Americans.

The Twentieth Century. Along with the rest of the country, Arkansas experienced a large increase in the number of European immigrants at the end of the nineteenth century. Although the pace of economic growth remained slow, the state began to develop new resources in the early years of the twentieth century. Rice, which would later become a major crop, was first planted in 1904. With the rise of the automobile and the increasing industrialization of the United States, the discovery of oil and natural gas deposits in 1921 was an important boost to the economy. The many rivers in Arkansas became an important resource, and modern dams were built beginning in the 1920's.

Arkansas, along with the rest of the United States, suffered a severe economic setback with the Great Depression of the 1930's. Adding to the problem, years of drought forced many farmers to abandon their lands. The Southern Farm Tenants Union, created by Arkansas sharecroppers at this time, had an important influence on national farm policies. It was not until the United States entered World War II in 1941 that the economy began to recover. The enormous defense industry created by the war effort, as well as the technological and economic growth that followed the war, led to major changes in Arkansas society.

The number of Arkansans living in rural areas decreased, and many small family farms were replaced by large agricultural enterprises. Little

Little Rock's Central High School, the scene of one of the nation's first major civil rights confrontations during the 1950's. (Tim Schick/Arkansas Department of Parks & Tourism)

Barge loaded with agricultural produce on the Arkansas River, a major tributary of the Mississippi. (A. C. Haralson/ Arkansas Department of Parks & Tourism)

Rock and other major cities experienced a rapid increase in population. Women entered the workplace in greater numbers. The most important social change in the middle of the twentieth century was the struggle to win civil rights for African Americans.

The attention of the world was focused on race relations in Arkansas in September of 1957. Three years earlier, the Supreme Court had declared public school segregation unconstitutional. To comply with the Court's decision, the school board of Little Rock created a plan to desegregate the city's schools. When nine African American students attempted to attend the city's Central High School, Governor Orval E. Faubus ordered the state militia to prevent them from entering. In response, President Dwight David Eisenhower sent federal troops to enforce the desegregation process.

Economic Growth. Economic development continued steadily throughout the second half of the twentieth century. In the 1960's, rice, soybeans, and poultry replaced cotton as the most important agricultural products. The McClellan-Kerr Arkansas River Navigation System, an ambitious project of building dams and locks, was completed after twenty-five years of work, in January of 1971. The project, the largest ever undertaken by the United States Army Corps of Engineers, made Little Rock an important river port and contributed greatly to the state's economy.

By the end of the twentieth century, important sources of income included fish farming, hydroelectric and nuclear power production, food processing, retail merchandising, computer software development, and financial services. The manufacturing sector of the economy produced clothing, furniture, machinery, electrical equipment, metal products, and electronic devices. With improvements in transportation, tourism became a particularly important source of revenue, with thousands of visitors traveling to attractions such as Hot Springs National Park and the Ozark Mountains each year. Despite this growth, Arkansas continued to have one of the lowest per-capita incomes in the United States.

Rose Secrest

Arkansas Time Line

June 18, 1541	Hernando de Soto crosses the Mississippi River and leads the first Europeans to the area.
July, 1673	Jacques Marquette and Louis Jolliet lead the first French expedition to the area.
Mar. 13, 1682	René-Robert Cavalier, sieur de La Salle, explores the area and claims the entire Mississippi valley for France, naming it Louisiana.
1686	Henri de Tonti establishes the first permanent European settlement at Arkansas Post.
1722	Bernard de la Harpe explores the Arkansas River and names Little Rock.
1762	Louisiana is ceded to Spain.
1783	British forces attack Arkansas Post.
1800	Louisiana is returned to France.
1803	United States purchases Louisiana.
1811-1812	Series of large earthquakes centered in New Madrid, Missouri, damage the area.
1812	Arkansas becomes part of the Missouri Territory.
1817	First post office is established.
Mar. 2, 1819	Arkansas Territory is created.
Nov. 20, 1819	First Arkansas newspaper, the *Arkansas Gazette*, is established.
1820	Border between Missouri and Arkansas is established as the line dividing future slave states and free states.
Oct. 25, 1821	Capital is moved from Arkansas Post to Little Rock.
1824	Western part of Arkansas becomes part of the Indian Territory.
1830	Congress marks boundary between Arkansas and Indian Territory.
June 15, 1836	Arkansas becomes the twenty-fifth state.
1858	First railroad is established.
1859	All free blacks are ordered out of the state by the end of the year.
1860	Population reaches 435,450, including 111,115 slaves.
May 6, 1861	Arkansas secedes from the Union.
Sept. 10, 1863	Union forces occupy Little Rock.
1864	State government dominated by the Republican Party is established.
1864	Unionists abolish slavery in Arkansas and adopt a new state constitution.
Aug., 1866	Laws passed prohibiting blacks from jury duty, militia service, and attendance of white schools.
Mar. 2, 1867	Reconstruction Act is passed in Congress, voiding the governments of Arkansas and nine other southern states.
Mar. 13, 1868	New constitution is adopted, freeing blacks and disfranchising former Confederate soldiers.
June 22, 1868	Arkansas is readmitted to the Union.
Nov., 1868	Martial law is declared in much of the state, as battles with the Ku Klux Klan become more frequent.
1872	University of Arkansas is established.

Oct. 13, 1874	New constitution restores franchise to all whites and gives full civil rights to blacks.
1885	State government defaults on millions of dollars of debt.
1891	Jim Crow laws go into effect, segregating trains and waiting stations.
1898	Whites-only primary elections are established.
1900	Population reaches 1.3 million.
1904	First rice crop is planted.
1906	Diamonds are discovered near Murfreesboro, leading to the only diamond-mining site in the United States.
1908	Ozark National Forest is established.
1921	Hot Springs National Park is established.
1921	Oil and natural gas are discovered.
1921	Commercial radio broadcasts begin.
1928	Law is passed prohibiting teaching of evolution theory in public schools, which would not be overturned until 1968, by the U.S. Supreme Court.
1931	Hattie W. Caraway is first woman elected to U.S. Senate.
1930's	Drought and economic depression lead to widespread poverty.
1930's	Southern Farm Tenants Union is created.
1940's	World War II defense industry leads to economic recovery.
1953	Commercial television broadcasts begin.
1957	Federal troops enter Little Rock after the state militia is called out to prevent school integration.
1960's	Rice, soybeans, and poultry replace cotton as the leading agricultural products.
1966	Winthrop Rockefeller is elected the first Republican governor since 1874.
1971	McClellan-Kerr Arkansas River Navigation System is completed.
1983	Arkansas requires teachers to pass basic skills tests, becoming the first state to do so.
1990	Population reaches 2.35 million.
Nov. 3, 1992	Bill Clinton becomes the first Arkansan elected president of the United States.
1993	M. Jocelyn Elders, former director of the state Department of Health, becomes the first African American Surgeon General of the United States.
1996	Severe tornadoes kill at least twelve people and do more than $300 million worth of property damage.
1998	Eleven-year-old and thirteen-year-old boys kill four fellow students and a teacher, wounding ten others, in a schoolyard shooting in Jonesboro, leading to a national debate on the issue of school violence.

Notes for Further Study

Published Sources. Countless books are devoted to all aspects of the state. For an overall view of the area's physical geography, the *Arkansas Atlas and Gazetteer* (1997) from the DeLorme Mapping Company is an excellent resource. The state government can be understood by reading *The Arkansas Constitution: A Reference Guide*

(1993) by Kay Collett Goss. The botany of the state is discussed in *Keys to the Flora of Arkansas* (1994) by Edwin B. Smith.

Among the many outstanding books devoted to the state's past are *Cultural Encounters in the Early South: Indians and Europeans in Arkansas* (1995) by Jeannie M. Whayne; *Colonial Arkansas, 1686-1804: A Social and Cultural History* (1991) by Morris S. Arnold; *Territorial Ambition: Land and Society in Arkansas, 1800-1840* (1993) by Charles S. Bolton; *Rebellion and Realignment: Arkansas's Road to Secession* (1987) by James M. Woods; *Rugged and Sublime: The Civil War in Arkansas* (1994), edited by Mark K. Christ; *War and Wartime Changes: The Transformation of Arkansas, 1940-1945* (1986) by Calvin C. Smith; and *Warriors Don't Cry: A Searing Memoir of the Battle to Integrate Little Rock's Central High* (1994) by Melba Pattillo Beals. More detailed resources can be found in *Arkansas History: An Annotated Bibliography* (1995), compiled by Michael B. Dougan, Tom W. Dillard, and Timothy G. Nutt.

Web Resources. A number of excellent Web sites devoted to Arkansas have been developed by government agencies, universities, and private organizations and individuals. A good place to start is The Unofficial Arkansas Page (http://ourworld.compuserve.com/homepages/mikenewman/indexark.htm), which includes maps, accounts of the state's history and government, biographies of famous Arkansans, and several links to other sites. Two sites that allow the user to search for informa-

tion from hundreds of Web sites are Arkansas Direct (http://www.arkansasdirect.com) and Arkansas Comcast (http://www.inarkansas.com). The state government provides information at Welcome to the State of Arkansas (http://www.state.ar.us), which includes detailed accounts of government agencies, tourism, business, local communities, and state laws. More specific sites include Arkansas—Vacation in the Natural State (http://www.arkansas.com) from the Arkansas Department of Parks and Tourism; ArkansasUSA (http://arkansasusa.com/buttonsindex.html), which provides detailed information on local communities; The Arkansas Economic Development Commission (http://www.1800arkansas.com) for information on business; and Arkansas Profiles (http://www.census.gov/datamap/www/05.htm) from the United States Census Bureau, which provides county statistics.

Arkansas history is presented in numerous Web sites. Good places to start include Arkansas History Questions and Answers (http://www.state.ar.us/ahc/q_and_a.htm) and A Brief History of Arkansas (http://www.sosweb.state.ar.us/brief.html). More specific information can be found in Web sites such as The Civil War in Arkansas (http://www.civilwarbuff.org), The Official Quapaw Website (http://www.geocities.com/Athens/Aegean/1388), and Persistence of the Spirit (http://www.aristotle.net/persistence), which concerns African Americans.

Counties

County	Sq. miles	1996 pop.	County	Sq. miles	1996 pop.
Arkansas	988.5	21,046	Cross	615.9	19,363
Ashley	921.4	24,543	Dallas	667.5	9,335
Baxter	554.4	36,382	Desha	765.0	15,513
Benton	843.3	125,956	Drew	828.2	17,863
Boone	591.2	31,906	Faulkner	647.4	73,909
Bradley	650.7	11,617	Franklin	609.6	16,453
Calhoun	628.3	5,714	Fulton	618.2	10,708
Carroll	633.8	22,492	Garland	678.1	82,038
Chicot	644.1	15,130	Grant	631.8	15,463
Clark	865.5	22,087	Greene	577.6	35,037
Clay	639.3	17,588	Hempstead	728.8	22,064
Cleburne	553.1	22,447	Hot Spring	615.0	28,242
Cleveland	597.8	8,337	Howard	587.5	13,882
Columbia	766.2	25,469	Independence	763.8	33,003
Conway	556.2	19,885	Izard	580.7	12,794
Craighead	710.8	76,155	Jackson	633.6	18,485
Crawford	595.5	49,074	Jefferson	884.8	83,007
Crittenden	610.5	49,604	Johnson	662.2	20,898

County	Sq. miles	1996 pop.	County	Sq. miles	1996 pop.
Lafayette	526.5	9,231	Pope	812.0	51,326
Lawrence	586.6	17,436	Prairie	646.0	9,273
Lee	601.7	12,802	Pulaski	771.0	352,305
Lincoln	561.2	14,309	Randolph	651.9	17,742
Little River	531.8	13,333	Saint Francis	633.9	28,348
Logan	709.9	21,188	Saline	724.8	74,555
Lonoke	765.5	47,583	Scott	893.9	10,775
Madison	837.0	13,094	Searcy	667.2	7,728
Marion	597.7	14,298	Sebastian	536.4	105,827
Miller	624.1	38,950	Sevier	564.0	14,754
Mississippi	898.3	50,606	Sharp	604.4	16,467
Monroe	606.7	10,381	Stone	606.6	10,877
Montgomery	781.0	8,448	Union	1,039.0	46,036
Nevada	620.0	10,067	Van Buren	711.6	15,325
Newton	823.0	7,966	Washington	950.2	134,984
Ouachita	732.5	28,374	White	1,034.1	61,954
Perry	551.0	9,312	Woodruff	586.6	9,203
Phillips	692.7	27,906	Yell	927.9	19,000
Pike	603.1	10,485			
Poinsett	757.8	24,720			
Polk	859.5	19,336			

Source: U.S. Census Bureau; National Association of Counties.

Cities

With 10,000 or more residents

Rank	City	Population	Rank	City	Population
1	Little Rock	175,303	17	El Dorado	21,848
2	Fort Smith	75,637	18	Sherwood	20,965
3	North Little Rock	59,184	19	Bentonville	19,691
4	Fayetteville	53,300	20	Van Buren	19,277
5	Pine Bluff	52,968	21	Blytheville	18,566
6	Jonesboro	52,250	22	Searcy	18,217
7	Springdale	40,287	23	Cabot	14,445
8	Conway	39,164	24	Camden	13,205
9	Hot Springs	37,961	25	Forrest City	13,064
10	Rogers	37,073	26	Harrison	11,594
11	Jacksonville	28,840	27	Magnolia	10,739
12	West Memphis	26,581	28	Siloam Springs	10,734
13	Russellville	25,340	29	Arkadelphia	10,407
14	Texarkana	23,693	30	Mountain Home	10,129
15	Benton	23,121			
16	Paragould	21,971			

Population figures are estimated for mid-1998.
Source: U.S. Bureau of the Census.

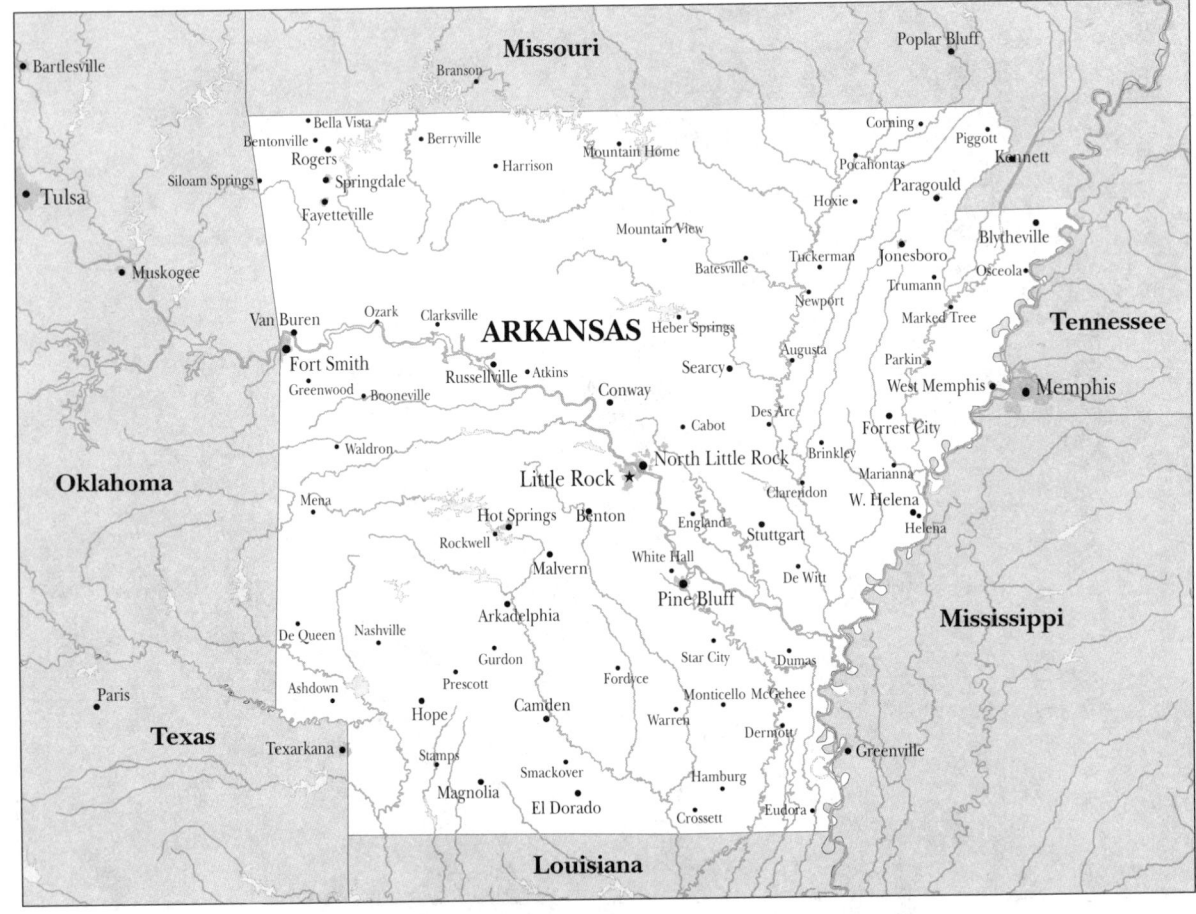

Index to Tables

NA = Reliable data are not available.

DEMOGRAPHICS

Resident state and national populations, 1970-1997

Population figures given in thousands

	State pop.	U.S. pop.	Share	Rank
1970	1,923	203,302	0.9%	32
1980	2,286	226,546	1.0%	33
1985	2,327	237,924	1.0%	33
1990	2,351	248,765	0.9%	33
1995	2,481	262,761	0.9%	33
1997	2,523	267,636	0.9%	33

Source: U.S. Bureau of the Census.

Resident population by age, 1997

Age group	Total population
Under 5 years	177,000
5 to 17 years	486,000
18 to 24 years	248,000
25 to 34 years	336,000
35 to 44 years	373,000
45 to 54 years	312,000
55 to 64 years	230,000
65 to 74 years	192,000
75 to 84 years	125,000
85 years and over	42,000
Portion of residents 65 and older	14.3%
National average	12.7%

Population figures are rounded to nearest thousand persons;
 figures include armed forces personnel stationed in state.
Source: U.S. Bureau of the Census.

Resident population by race, Hispanic origin, 1997

	State pop.	Share	U.S.
All residents	2,523,000	100.0%	100.0%
Hispanic white	40,000	1.6%	10.0%
non-Hispanic white	2,046,000	81.1%	72.7%
African American	406,000	16.1%	12.7%
Native American	13,000	0.5%	0.9%
Asian, Pacific Islander	18,000	0.7%	3.8%

Source: U.S. Bureau of the Census.

Projections of state population, 2000-2025

	Model A Uses interstate migration observed from 1975-1994	Model B Uses Bureau of Economic Analysis employment projections
Year	Population	Population
2000	2,631,000	2,623,000
2005	2,750,000	2,757,000
2010	2,840,000	2,887,000
2015	2,922,000	3,008,000
2020	2,997,000	3,109,000
2025	3,055,000	3,184,000

All population projections, including those for 2000, were calculated in 1997.

Source: U.S. Bureau of the Census, Population Paper Listings PPL-47.

VITAL STATISTICS

Average lifetime in years by race, 1989-1991

	State	U.S.	Rank
All residents	74.33	75.37	41
White residents	75.20	76.13	43
Black residents	68.93	69.16	23

Ranks are from longest-lived to least longest-lived. Ranks exclude Alaska, for which reliable data are not available. Rank for black residents is based on the 32 states for which reliable data are available.

Source: U.S. National Center for Health Statistics.

Infant mortality rates, 1980 and 1995

	State	U.S.
All residents		
1980	12.7	12.6
1995	8.8	7.6
White residents		
1980	10.3	11.0
1995	7.2	6.3
Black residents		
1980	20.0	21.4
1995	14.3	15.1

Figures represent deaths per 1,000 live births of resident infants under 1 year old, exclusive of fetal deaths; all-residents figures include other races not listed separately.

Source: U.S. National Center for Health Statistics.

Marriages and divorces

Marriages in 1996 36,200
Rate per 1,000 population, 1995 . . . . 14.7
U.S. rate, 1995 . . . . 8.9
Rank among all states 4

Divorces in 1996 15,200
Rate per 1,000 population, 1995 . . . . 6.5
U.S. rate, 1995 . . . . 4.4
Rank among all states 6

Rank is from highest to lowest in country.
Source: U.S. National Center for Health Statistics.

Death rates by leading causes, 1995
Deaths per 100,000 resident population

Cause	State	U.S.
Heart disease	339.8	280.7
Cancer	244.7	204.9
Cerebrovascular diseases	91.5	60.1
Accidents and adverse effects	48.8	35.5
Motor vehicle accidents	26.3	16.5
Chronic obstructive pulmonary diseases	45.0	39.2
Diabetes mellitus	22.4	22.6
HIV	6.8	NA
Suicide	14.5	11.9
Homicide	11.6	8.7
All causes	1,075.1	880.0
Rank in overall death rate among states		3

Figures exclude nonresidents who die in state. Causes of death follow International Classification of Diseases. Rank is from highest to lowest in country.

Source: U.S. National Center for Health Statistics.

ECONOMY

Gross state product, 1990-1996
In current dollars

	State product	Increase
1990	$37.9 billion	
1993	$46.5 billion	
1994	$50.4 billion	8.39%
1995	$53.4 billion	5.95%
1996	$56.4 billion	5.62%

Source: U.S. Bureau of Economic Analysis; *Survey of Current Business,* June, 1998.

Gross state product by industry, 1996
In billions

Farms, forestry, fisheries	$2.5
Construction	1.9
Manufacturing	13.2
Transportation, public utilities	5.9
Wholesale trade	3.3
Retail trade	5.6
Finance, insurance, real estate	5.5
Services	7.2
Government	6.0
State total	$51.5
Total U.S.	$6,923.8
State share	0.74%
Rank among states	33

Total figures include mining, not listed separately.
Source: U.S. Bureau of Economic Analysis; *Survey of Current Business,* June, 1998.

Personal income per capita, 1990 and 1997
In current dollars

	1990	1997
Per capita income	$14,042	$19,585
U.S. average	$19,188	$25,598
Rank among states	49	48

1997 data are preliminary.
Source: U.S. Bureau of Economic Analysis; *Survey of Current Business,* May, 1998.

Energy consumption, 1995
In trillions of British thermal units (BTU)

End-use sectors

Residential	187.1
Commercial	114.0
Industrial	433.1
Transportation	263.7

Sources of energy

Petroleum	308.8
Natural gas	276.6
Coal	237.4
Hydroelectric power	33.1
Nuclear electric power	124.2
Total state per capita consumption	401.6
Total U.S. per capita consumption	344.4
Rank among states	14
Total state energy consumption	997.9
Total U.S. energy consumption	90,547.4
State share of U.S. total	1.10%
Rank among states	32

Total figures include items not listed separately.
Source: U.S. Energy Information Administration; *State Energy Data Report.*

Nonfarm employment by sectors, 1997

Total	1,103,000
Construction	48,000
Manufacturing	253,000
Transportation, public utilities	66,000
Wholesale trade, retail trade	252,000
Finance, insurance, real estate	44,000
Services	254,000
Government	184,000

Figures are rounded to nearest thousand persons. Total includes mining, not listed separately.
Source: U.S. Bureau of Labor Statistics; *Employment and Earnings,* monthly.

Foreign exports, 1990-1997
In millions of dollars

Year	State	U.S.	State share
1990	920	394,045	0.23%
1996	2,003	624,767	0.32%
1997	2,305	688,896	0.33%

Source: U.S. Bureau of the Census; *U.S. Merchandise Trade,* series FT 900.

LAND USE

Federally owned land, 1996

	State	U.S.	State share
Total acres	33,599,000	2,271,343,000	1.48%
Federally owned	2,740,000	563,129,000	0.49%
Federal share	8.2%	24.8%	—

Areas are rounded to nearest thousand acres. Figures for
federally owned land do not include trust properties.
Source: U.S. General Services Administration; *Inventory Report
on Real Property Owned by the United States Throughout the
World,* annual.

Land use, 1992
In acres, rounded to nearest thousand

Total surface area	34,040,000
Federal land	3,207,000
Total nonfederal	29,803,000
Developed	1,322,000
Total rural	28,480,000
Cropland.	7,730,000
Pasture land	5,727,000
Range land.	159,000
Forest land	14,267,000
Minor cover/use.	598,000

Total surface area figures include water area not shown
separately.
Source: U.S. Dept. of Agriculture; Soil Conservation Service;
Iowa State University, Statistical Laboratory; *Summary
Report, 1992 National Resources Inventory.*

Farms and crop acreage, 1997

	State	U.S.	Share	Rank
Farms (thousands)	43	2,058	2.09%	20
Acres (millions)	15	968	1.55%	21
Acres per farm	348	471	—	20
Acres planted	8,345	334,139	2.50%	14
Acres harvested	8,206	319,894	2.57%	14
Farm value (mill.)	$2,527	$108,805	2.32%	16

Numbers of farms are rounded to nearest thousand.
Source: U.S. Dept. of Agriculture; National Agricultural
Statistics Service.

GOVERNMENT AND FINANCE

Units of local government, 1997

	State	Total U.S.	Rank
All local governments	1,516	87,453	20
Counties	75	3,043	18
Municipalities	491	19,372	17
Townships	0	16,629	—
School districts	311	13,726	17
Special districts	639	34,683	17

County ranks are based on the 48 states with county
governments; township ranks are based on the 20 states
with township governments; school district ranks are based
on the 46 states with such districts.
Source: U.S. Bureau of the Census; *1997 Census of Governments,
Government Organization,* Series GC97(1).

State government revenue, 1996

Total revenue	$8,653 mill.
General revenue	7,023 mill.
Per capita.	2,802
U.S. per capita average	2,910
Rank among states.	25
Intergovernmental revenue	
Total	$2,163 mill.
From federal government	2,156 mill.
From local government.	7 mill.
Charges and Miscellaneous	
Total	$1,152 mill.
Current charges	736 mill.
Misc. general revenue	415 mill.
Taxes	
Total	$3,709 mill.
General sales	1,376 mill.
Selective sales.	564 mill.
License taxes	216 mill.
Individual income	1,162 mill.
Corporate income	229 mill.
Other	162 mill.
Insurance trust revenue	1,630 mill.

Total revenue figures include items not listed separately.
Source: U.S. Bureau of the Census.

State government expenditures, 1996

General expenditures

Intergovernmental	$1,636 mill.
Direct expenditures	4,845 mill.
Total	6,481 mill.

Selected direct expenditures

Education	$2,509 mill.
Public welfare	1,583 mill.
Health, hospital	589 mill.
Highways	698 mill.
Police	52 mill.
Corrections	171 mill.
Natural resources	136 mill.
Parks and recreation	39 mill.
Government administration	206 mill.
Interest on debt	121 mill.

Other

State per capita expenditures	$2,586
U.S. per capita average	2,854
Rank among states	34
Total state expenditures	7,050 mill.
Total U.S. expenditures	859,959 mill.

Totals include items not listed separately.
Source: U.S. Bureau of the Census.

POLITICS

Governors since statehood

D = Democrat; R = Republican; O = other;
(r) resigned; (d) died in office; (i) removed from office

James S. Conway (D)	1836-1840
Archibald Yell (D)	(r) 1840-1844
Samuel Adams (D)	1844
Thomas S. Drew (D)	1844-1849
Richard C. Byrd (D)	1849
John S. Roane (D)	1849-1852
Elias N. Conway (D)	1852-1860
Henry M. Rector (D)	(r) 1860-1862
Thomas Fletcher (D)	1862
Harris Flanagin (D)	(i) 1862-1864
Isaac Murphy (O)	1864-1868
Powell Clayton (R)	(r) 1868-1871
Ozra A. Hadley (R)	1871-1873
Elisha Baxter (R)	1873-1874
Augustus H. Garland (D)	1874-1877
William R. Miller (D)	1877-1881
Thomas J. Churchill (D)	1881-1883
James H. Berry (D)	1883-1885

Simon P. Hughes (D)	1885-1889
James P. Eagle (D)	1889-1893
William M. Fishback (D)	1893-1895
James P. Clarke (D)	1895-1897
Daniel W. Jones (D)	1897-1901
Jefferson Davis (D)	1901-1907
John S. Little (D)	1907-1909
George W. Donaghey (D)	1909-1913
James T. Robinson (D)	(r) 1913
William K. Oldham (D)	1913
J. Marion Futrell (D)	1913
George W. Hays (D)	1913-1917
Charles H. Brough (D)	1917-1921
Thomas C. McRae (D)	1921-1925
Thomas J. Terral (D)	1925-1927
John E. Martineau (D)	(r) 1927-1928
Harvey Parnell (D)	1928-1933
J. Marion Futrell (D)	1933-1937
Carl E. Bailey (D)	1937-1941
Homer M. Adkins (D)	1941-1945
Benjamin T. Laney (D)	1945-1949
Sidney S. McMath (D)	1949-1953
Francis A. Cherry (D)	1953-1955
Orval E. Faubus (D)	1955-1967
Winthrop Rockefeller (R)	1967-1971
Dale L. Bumpers (D)	(r) 1971-1975
Robert C. Riley (D)	1975
David H. Pryor (D)	1975-1979
William J. Clinton (D)	1979-1992
Jim Guy Tucker (D)	(r) 1992-1996
Mike Huckabee (R)	1996-

Composition of state legislature, 1990-1998

	Democrats	Republicans
State House (100 seats)		
1990	90	9
1992	88	11
1994	88	12
1996	86	13
1998	75	25
State Senate (35 seats)		
1990	31	4
1992	30	5
1994	28	7
1996	28	6
1998	29	6

Figures for total seats may include independents and minor
party members.
Source: Council of State Governments; *State Elective Officials
and the Legislatures.*

Composition of congressional delegations, 1989-1999

	Dem	Rep	Total
House of Representatives			
101st Congress, 1989			
State delegates	3	1	4
Total U.S.	259	174	433
102d Congress, 1991			
State delegates	3	1	4
Total U.S.	267	167	434
103d Congress, 1993			
State delegates	2	2	4
Total U.S.	258	176	434
104th Congress, 1995			
State delegates	2	2	4
Total U.S.	197	236	433
105th Congress, 1997			
State delegates	2	2	4
Total U.S.	206	228	434
106th Congress, 1999			
State delegates	2	2	4
Total U.S.	211	222	433
Senate			
101st Congress, 1989			
State delegates	2	0	2
Total U.S.	55	45	100
102d Congress, 1991			
State delegates	2	0	2
Total U.S.	56	44	100
103d Congress, 1993			
State delegates	2	0	2
Total U.S.	57	43	100
104th Congress, 1995			
State delegates	1	1	2
Total U.S.	46	53	99
105th Congress, 1997			
State delegates	1	1	2
Total U.S.	45	55	100
106th Congress, 1999			
State delegates	1	1	2
Total U.S.	45	54	99

Figures are for starts of first sessions. Figure for U.S. Representatives for 101st Congress does not include Alabama and Indiana, which had vacancies. Figures for total U.S. Representatives for 102d, 103d, and 106th Congresses do not include Vermont, which had 1 Independent-Socialist. Figure for U.S. Representatives for 104th Congress does not include Vermont, which had 1 Independent-Socialist, and California, which had 1 vacancy. Figure for U.S. Representatives for 105th Congress does not include New York, which had 1 vacancy. Figure for U.S. Senators for 104th Congress does not include Oregon, which had 1 vacancy. Figure for U.S. Senators for 106th Congress does not include New Hampshire, which had 1 Independent.
Source: U.S. Congress; Congressional Directory, biennial.

Voter participation in presidential elections, 1992 and 1996

	1992	1996
State voting age pop.	1,774,000	1,860,000
Total U.S. voting age pop.	189,524,000	196,509,000
State share of U.S. total	0.9%	1.0%
Rank among states	33	33
Percent of state casting vote	53.6	58.0
Percent of U.S. total voting	55.1	49.0
Rank among states	33	7

Source: U.S. Bureau of the Census.

HEALTH AND MEDICAL CARE

Medicare, 1997

	Recipients	Payments
State	429,000	$1,906 mill.
Total U.S.	37,514,000	$206,064 mill.
State share	1.14%	0.92%
Rank among states	31	30

Recipient figures are rounded to nearest thousand persons. Ranks are from highest to lowest.
Source: U.S. Health Care Financing Administration.

Medicaid, 1996

	Recipients	Payments
State	363,000	$1,224 mill.
Total U.S.	35,028,000	$121,419 mill.
State share	1.04%	1.01%
Rank among states	29	28

Recipient figures are rounded to nearest thousand persons. Payment figures for fiscal year reflect federal and state contribution payments. Ranks are from highest to lowest.
Source: U.S. Health Care Financing Administration.

Health insurance coverage, 1996

	State	U.S.
Total persons covered	2,041,000	225,070,000
Total persons not covered	566,000	41,716,000
Part not covered	21.7%	15.6%
Rank among states	4	—
Children not covered	155,000	10,554,000
Part not covered	20.7%	14.8%
Rank among states	4	—

Ranks are from most to fewest uninsured. Population figures are rounded to nearest thousand persons.
Source: U.S. Bureau of the Census.

AIDS, syphilis, tuberculosis, and measles cases, 1997

Cases	U.S.	State	Share
AIDS	58,443	242	0.41%
Syphilis	8,550	173	2.02%
Tuberculosis	18,534	179	0.97%
Measles	148,000	NA	NA

Measles figures are rounded to nearest thousand cases.
Source: U.S. Centers for Disease Control and Prevention.

HOUSING

Homeownership rates, 1985-1997

	1985	1990	1997
State	66.6%	67.8%	66.7%
Total U.S.	63.9%	63.9%	65.7%
Rank among states	32	24	35

Source: U.S. Bureau of the Census.

Home sales, 1990 and 1997
In thousands of units

Existing home sales	1990	1997	Change
State sales	44.8	58.7	13.9
Total U.S. sales	3,560	4,730	1,170
State share of U.S. total	1.26%	1.24%	-0.02%
Rank among states	28	28	—

Source: National Association of Realtors; *Real Estate Outlook: Market Trends and Insights.*

EDUCATION

Public school enrollment, 1995

State K-8 enrollment	322,000
Total U.S. K-8 enrollment	32,341,000
State share of total U.S.	1.00%
State 9-12 enrollment	131,000
Total U.S. 9-12 enrollment	12,500,000
State share of U.S. total	1.05%
State public school enroll. rate	94.9%
Overall U.S. rate.	91.6%
Rank among states.	11

Enrollment figures (which include unclassified students) are rounded to nearest thousand pupils in fall term; kindergarten (K)-8 grade enrollment figures include some prekindergarten students. Enrollment rate is based on percentage of persons 5-17 years old. Rank is from highest to lowest.
Source: U.S. National Center for Education Statistics.

A duck hunter on an Arkansas river. (A. C. Haralson/ Arkansas Department of Parks & Tourism)

Public college finances, 1996

State FTE enrollment. 74,300
Total U.S. FTE enrollment 8,268,800
State share of total U.S. 0.90%
Rank among states. 33
State and local appropriations $334,800,000
Total U.S. state and local
    appropriations. . . . . $39,699 mill.
State share of total U.S. 0.84%
Rank among states. 35
State net tuition revenues. $162,300,000
Total U.S. net tuition $18,348,100,000
State share of total U.S. 0.88%
Rank among states. 34

FTE=Full-time equivalent; credit and noncredit enrollment
    including summer session in academic year ending in
    1996.
Enrollments are rounded to nearest thousand students. Net
    tuition revenues exclude appropriation to students
    attending in-state public institutions. Rankings are from
    highest shares to lowest.
Source: Research Associates of Washington.

Motor vehicle registrations and driver licenses, 1996
In thousands

Vehicle registrations	State	U.S.	Share	Rank
Autos, trucks, buses	1,633	206,365	0.79%	33
Autos only	853	128,439	0.66%	33
Motorcycles	16	3,832	0.42%	45
Driver licenses	1,752	179,539	0.98%	33

Figures do not include vehicles owned by military services.
Source: U.S. Federal Highway Administration; *Highway
    Statistics; Selected Highway Statistics and Charts.*

Domestic travel expenditures, 1995
Spending by U.S. residents on overnight trips and day
trips of at least 100 miles

Total expenditures in state . . . . $3,078 mill.
Total expenditures in U.S. . . . . $360,314 mill.
State share of total U.S. 0.85%
Rank among states. 33

Source: Travel Industry Association of America.

TRANSPORTATION AND TRAVEL

Highway mileage, 1996

Interstate 541
Other arterial. 6,885
Collector roads 21,057
Local roads 50,192
Urban roads 7,698
Rural roads 70,048
Total state 77,746
U.S. total 3,933,985
State share 2.0%
Rank among states. 26

Source: U.S. Federal Highway Administration.

CRIME AND LAW ENFORCEMENT

State and local police officers, 1996

Local police 3,244
State police 522
Sheriffs 1,410
Total 5,819
Officers per 10,000 residents 23
U.S. average 25
Rank among states. 21

Figures cover full-time sworn officers; totals include special
    police not shown separately.
Source: U.S. Bureau of Justice Statistics; *Census of State and
    Local Law Enforcement Agencies, 1996.*

Crime rates, 1996

Rates per 100,000 resident population

Violent crimes	State	U.S.
Total violent	524	634
Murder	8.7	7.4
Forcible rape	41.7	36.1
Robbery	114	202
Aggravated assault	360	388
Property crimes		
Total property	4,175	4,445
Burglary	953	943
Larceny/theft	2,909	2,976
Motor vehicle theft	313	526
Totals	4,699	5,079

Source: U.S. Federal Bureau of Investigation; *Crime in the United States,* annual.

State prison populations, 1980-1996

	State	U.S.	State share
1980	2,911	305,458	0.95%
1990	7,322	708,393	1.03%
1996	9,407	1,025,624	0.92%

Figures exclude prisoners in federal penitentiaries.
Source: U.S. Bureau of Justice Statistics.

California

Location: West Coast of continental United States

Area and rank: 155,973 square miles (403,970 square kilometers); 163,707 square miles (424,000 square kilometers) including water; third largest state in area

Coastline: 840 miles (1,352 kilometers)

Shoreline: 3,427 miles (5,514 kilometers)

Population and rank: 32,268,301 (1997); largest state in population

Capital: Sacramento

Largest city: Los Angeles (3,781,500 people at beginning of 1999)

Entered Union and rank: September 9, 1850; 31st state

Present constitution adopted: 1879

Counties: 58

State name: "California" is believed to have derived from a name in a Spanish romance written around 1500

State nickname: Golden State

Motto: *Eureka*! (Greek for "I have found it!")

State flag: Star above grizzly bear on white background above red stripe

Highest point: Mount Whitney — 14,494 feet (4,418 meters); highest point in continental United States

Lowest point: Death Valley — 282 feet (87 meters) below sea level; lowest point in United States

Highest recorded temperature: 134 degrees Fahrenheit (57 degrees Celsius) — Death Valley, 1913

Lowest recorded temperature: −45 degrees Fahrenheit (−43 degrees Celsius) — Boca, 1937

State song: "I Love You, California"

State tree: California redwoods

State flower: Golden poppy

State bird: California valley quail

State fish: Golden trout

State animal: California grizzly bear

National parks: Channel Islands, Kings Canyon, Lassen Volcanic, Redwood, Sequoia, Yosemite

Completed in 1937, the Golden Gate Bridge spans the mile-wide gap separating San Francisco Bay from the Pacific Ocean. (PhotoDisc)

California History

To a much greater extent than in other states, California is a naturally defined region with a distinct history of its own. Its differences begin with its natural geography. Bounded by the Pacific Ocean on the west and the Sierra Madre range along the east, California had limited contacts with the outside world until the mid-nineteenth century. Until then, little was known about its abundant natural resources beyond the fact it had an equable climate and fertile land.

An estimated 300,000 Native Americans inhabited the region before Europeans arrived. Though they were among the most numerous and prosperous Indian societies in North America, most of them lived outside the main currents of Native American history. Compared to many cultures outside California, their culture was simple. Metallurgy, pottery, intensive cultivation, horses, and draft animals were all unknown to them. With economies based mostly on fishing, hunting, and gathering, they nevertheless achieved comparatively high levels of prosperity and lived largely peaceful lives.

Early Exploration. European contact with California began in 1542, when the Spanish navigator Juan Rodríguez Cabrillo found San Diego Bay. English navigator Francis Drake followed thirty-seven years later, when he reached Northern California. Little came out of these early explorations. Busy colonizing Mexico, Spain paid little attention to the California region over the next two centuries. Permanent European interest in the region finally began in the late eighteenth century, when Spain authorized members of the Franciscan order to build a chain of mission stations up the California coast. Father Junipero Serra founded California's first mission at San Diego in 1769; twenty other mission stations followed over the next fifty-four years.

During those years California was nominally a Spanish colony, but the government exercised only light control, and the burden of imposing European culture on California's peoples was left to the Franciscans. The missionaries began systematic agricultural development and gathered Indian communities around their mission stations. Meanwhile, Russian traders established posts north of the mission chain without interference. After a half century of formal Spanish colonization, the non-Indian residents of California numbered only about 3,300—a small fraction of the number of Indians.

Mexican Rule. By this time, Spain was losing its hold on its New World empire and Mexico was in open revolt. When Mexico won its independence from Spain in 1821, California's Spanish governor peacefully recognized Mexican rule, and California became a Mexican province. Mexico then followed Spain's example by taking little active interest in the region until the early 1830's, when it began secularizing California's mission stations and distributing titles to large blocs of land among favored families. In 1837 the Mexican government granted California's administration a large measure of autonomy, continuing California's tradition of comparative isolation.

Secularization was a disaster to the Indian communities attached to the former mission stations. The departure of the Franciscans left the Indians at the mercy of private landlords, who had little interest in their welfare. Most of the Indians left the missions for their original homes, where harsh economic conditions and European diseases reduced their numbers greatly. By the turn of the twentieth century their numbers fell to their lowest level ever—about 15,000 people, about one-twentieth their precolonial number.

By the early 1840's, Americans hungry for land and new opportunities were moving west and settling in California. Conflicts soon arose between these new, non-Spanish-speaking residents and the established Spanish and Mexican settlers, known as *Californios*. Soon, the U.S. government took an interest in the region, which it feared might be occupied by Great Britain or Russia. In 1845 it instructed its consul in Monterey to promote local interest in annexation to the United States. The following year, disgruntled American settlers in northern California found an excuse for rebelling against the Mexican regime and proclaimed an independent republic in Sonoma—a short-lived rebellion known as the "Bear Flag Revolt," after the flag the rebels used.

For reasons largely unrelated to California, the United States declared war against Mexico in 1846. Placed under military rule by Mexico, California played a small role in the Mexican-American War.

The Mexican government surrendered California to the United States when John C. Frémont arrived with an occupation force in 1847. In the peace accord that followed, Mexico formally ceded California, along with most of what became the American Southwest, to the United States. California offi-

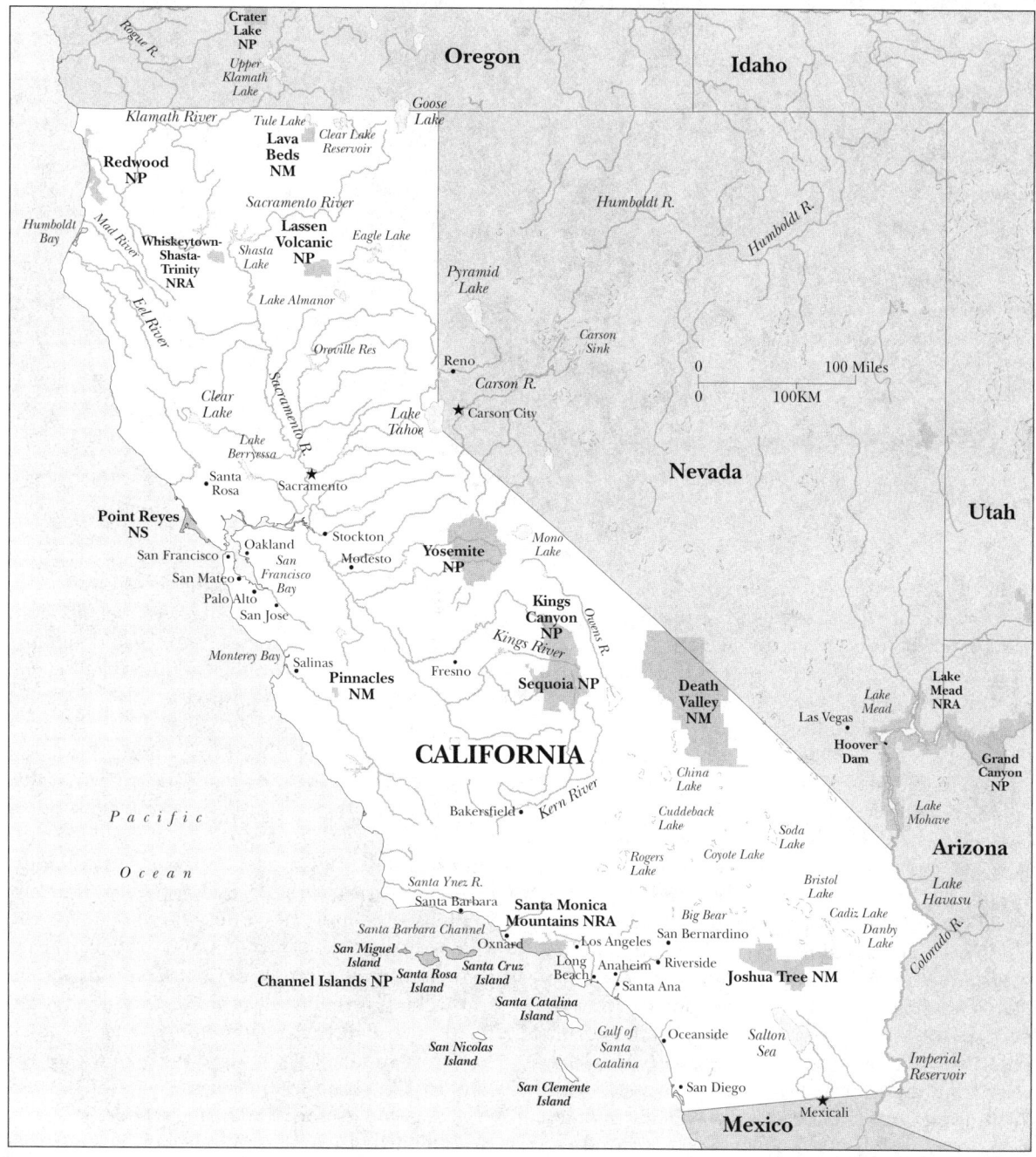

Now a historic state park, the town of Bodie is a vivid reminder of the state's nineteenth century mining boom. (PhotoDisc)

cially became an American territory in early 1848; however, its territorial status was short-lived. Two years later, before its territorial government was fully organized, California entered the Union as a state. Its rapid transition to statehood owed much to an unexpected and spectacular event that fundamentally changed the region's future: the discovery of gold near Sacramento.

The Gold Rush and Statehood. Scarcely a week before the treaty ending the Mexican-American War was signed, news of the discovery of gold in northern California became public, and one of the world's great gold rushes began. The effect the gold rush had on California would be difficult to overstate. Within a matter of only a few years, California was transformed from a sleepy backwater to perhaps the fastest-growing economy in the world. Hundreds of thousands of people poured into the state from the East and other parts of the world. Within ten years California's non-Indian population rose from less than 10,000 to several hundred

thousand. Meanwhile, San Francisco grew from little more than village to a booming metropolitan center offering virtually every service and amenity available in big eastern cities and controlling the commerce of the West Coast.

The multitudes who rushed to California dreamed of striking it rich from mineral wealth; however, the real fortunes made there grew mostly out of the many enterprises that arose to support the gold industry. Great profits were made in agriculture, retail trade, transportation, and countless other industries and services. For the first time, agriculture was undertaken on a large scale. As the gold rush made food production a critical priority, the agricultural potential of California's great Central Valley was finally recognized. Eventually, California's agricultural production would not only lead the nation but reach a level exceeded by only a handful of nations in the world.

The gold rush peaked during the early 1850's. By 1861, when the Civil War began, it was essentially over. Nevertheless, California's economy continued to expand. The war interrupted commerce with the eastern United States but actually helped the local economy. Once again isolated from the East, California had to diversity its production to make up for what it could not import. Pro-Unionists outnumbered Confederate sympathizers within California, but the state played no direct role in the war.

Communications. When California attained statehood in 1850, it was separated from the rest of the states by the Central Plains, Rocky Mountains, and arid Southwest. With people and goods arriving at increasing rates, cheaper and more rapid transportation became a paramount need. With overland transportation slow and expensive, many goods and people reaching the state came by ship—by way of Central America. In 1860 the Pony Express was begun to speed mail service between California and the East. It lasted little more than a year—but only because it was displaced by transcontinental telegraph service. Completion of the first transcontinental railroad in 1869 linked California's capital, Sacramento, with St. Joseph, Missouri. These new links with the East were major steps in ending California's isolation.

With the building of the railway and the end of the Civil War, California settled down to a period of steady growth and development. Settlers continued to pour in from the East, doubling the state's population every decade—a rate of growth that continued through the twentieth century. As the proportion of European Americans rose, their tolerance for other immigrants diminished and racially discriminatory laws were passed. Particular targets of white intolerance were the thousands of Chinese workers who had come to California to help build the railroads. Most of these people stayed working at low-paying jobs shunned by whites, who pressed the state government to legislate against Asians.

Agricultural production grew and diversified until California led the nation in production in the late 1940's. Mean-while, other industries arose to contribute to the state's growing economy. In 1895 oil was discovered in Southern California, just as the invention of motor-driven automobiles was creating new demand for petroleum products. Through the first four decades of the twentieth century, California led all states in oil production.

Most of California's early development occurred in the northern part of the state. During the twentieth century, the balance shifted to the south, where such new industries as petrochemicals, aeronautics, and entertainment attracted new immigrants from the East. By 1920 most of the state's residents lived in southern counties; however, its bicameral legislative system left the balance of political power in the north. With most of the water resources also in the north, supplying water to the largely arid south became a critical issue in state

Mission San Carlos Carmel, near Monterey, is one of the most famous Franciscan missions founded by Father Junipero Serra. (Library of Congress)

California's diverse terrain, which includes Sahara-like sand dunes in Death Valley, is one of the reasons it developed into the center of the film industry. (PhotoDisc)

politics. Correction of the political imbalance finally came during the early 1960's, after a U.S. Supreme Court decision forced reapportionment of the state legislature. By this time, California ranked as the most populous state in the nation.

Over the next three decades, a central issue in state politics was the changing composition of the population. Opposition to immigrants of all kinds is an issue with roots going back to the late nineteenth century. During the Great Depression of the 1930's, for example, the state tried, unsuccessfully to keep out swarms of poor farmers fleeing the drought-stricken Midwest. After World War II, Californians became alarmed by the rising influx of Mexicans seeking higher-paying jobs—particularly in agriculture. Immigration from Asia, Mexico, and Central America grew through the rest of the twentieth century, making California the most multicultural state in the Union.

R. Kent Rasmussen

California Time Line

1521	Spain conquers Mexico.
Sept. 28, 1542	Juan Rodríguez Cabrillo is the first European to sight California's coast.
1579	Sir Francis Drake lands in Northern California.
1602	Sebastían Vizcaíno sails along California coast.
1700's	Estimated Indian population is nearly 300,000 people.
1769-1823	Franciscans build twenty-one mission stations between San Diego and Sonoma.
1773	Spanish colonization begins.
1812	Russians establish trading posts in Northern California.
1820	Estimated *non*-Indian population is 3,270.
1821	Newly independent, Mexico makes California a province.
1833-1840	Mexico secularizes California missions and distributes lands among favored families.

1837	Mexico grants California government considerable autonomy.
1841	American settlers begin migrating to California from Missouri.
June 14, 1846	Americans raise "Bear Flag" republic revolt in Sonoma.
May, 1846	United States declares war on Mexico, which places California under military rule.
1847	California becomes U.S. territory when Mexico surrenders it to John C. Frémont's force.
1848	Signing of Treaty of Guadalupe Hildago ends Mexican-American War
Jan. 24, 1848	Discovery of gold near Sacramento launches gold rush, promoting rapid, long-term development.
1849	Convention votes against forming a territorial government, instead drafts bilingual state constitution, which voters ratify.
Sept. 9, 1850	California is admitted to the Union.
1854	Sacramento becomes permanent state capital.
1860-1861	Pony Express improves mail service with the East
Oct. 1861	Transcontinental telegraph reaches California.
1868	University of California is founded in Berkeley.
1869	Completion of transcontinental railroad ends California's isolation.
1872	State laws are codified for the first time.
May 7, 1879	Voters ratify new constitution.
1890	Yosemite becomes state's first national park.
1895	Oil is discovered in Southern California.
1900	Indian population drops to about 15,500 people.
Oct., 1906	Earthquake and fire level San Francisco.
1908	Film industry begins in Los Angeles.
1914	Opening of Panama Canal improves communications with the East Coast, lowering shipping and transportation costs.
1920	Southern California overtakes the north in population, but legislature refuses to reapportion.
Feb. 3, 1923	Mount Lassen erupts.
1930's	Great Depression sends many farmers from the Great Plains to California, which tries to keep them out.
1931	Master plan for distributing water throughout the state is created.
Nov., 1934	Voters endorse calling of new constitutional convention, but legislature never acts to organize it.
1937	Golden Gate Bridge opens in San Francisco Bay.
Nov., 1938	Culbert Olson is first Democrat elected governor.
1940	First freeway in United States opens in Pasadena.
Feb., 1942	Federal government orders internment of state's Japanese American population after World War II begins.
1942-1945	World War II spurs industrial and economic growth.
1945	State Water Resources Board is created to distribute state's limited water supplies.

(continued)

1947	State's agriculture ranks first among U.S. states.
1953	Governor Earl Warren becomes chief justice of the United States.
1959	California is first state to adopt master highway plan.
1960	State prepares master plan for higher education.
1964	California surpasses New York as most populous state.
Nov., 1964	Ronald Reagan is elected governor.
Aug., 1965	Nation's first modern racially motivated rioting erupts in Los Angeles's Watts district.
Nov., 1966	First elections after reapportionment are held.
Feb. 9, 1971	Massive earthquake devastates Los Angeles area.
June 6, 1978	Voters approve Proposition 13, mandating statewide reduction in property tax of 57 percent.
Nov., 1980	Ronald Reagan is elected president of the United States.
Oct. 17, 1989	Earthquake devastates San Francisco Bay region.
Oct. 20, 1991	Most destructive urban wildfire in U.S. history burns parts of Berkeley and Oakland.
Apr. 29, 1992	Acquittal of policemen charged with beating Rodney King touches off rioting in Los Angeles.
Jan. 17, 1994	Massive earthquake devastates Southern California.
Nov., 1998	Gray Davis is first democrat elected governor since 1978.

Notes for Further Study

Published Sources. As the largest state in the nation, California offers the most abundant resources for further study. Thousands of published books cover every imaginable aspect of the state's history, peoples, politics, economy, and natural resources. Especially abundant are travel guides. These not only provide practical guides to the state as a whole, its major cities, and its regions, but also are filled with statistics, historical facts, and other useful information. Vast amounts of diverse information can also be obtained from government agencies at all levels. A good starting point for general information on the state is James S. Fay, ed., *California Almanac* (7th ed. 1996). Warren A. Beck and Ynez D. Haase's *Historical Atlas of California* (1975) remains a standard source on historical geography. C. L. Keyworth, *California Indians* (1999), is a comprehensive guide to the history, cultures, and modern condition of the state's diverse Native American peoples. Also useful is Robert Fleming Heizer and M. A. Whipple's *The California Indians: A Source Book* (1983). For an updated version of a classic history text emphasizing forces that have made California unique, see Carey McWilliams and Lewis H. Lapham's *California: The Great Exception* (1999). A more modern overview can be found in *California: An Interpretive History* (7th ed. 1997), by James J. Rawls and Walton Bean. An authoritative analysis of how government works in the state can be found in Mona Field and Charles P. Sohner's *California Government and Politics Today* (8th ed. 1998)

Web Resources. The range of Web sites offering useful information on California is too broad even to summarize. However, many of the sites are so well connected by links and are so easy to find with Web search engines that the addresses of only a few will suffice to direct users to most of the rest. An excellent starting point is the official California Tourist Bureau site (http://gocalif.ca.gov/index2.html). In addition to its expected maps and travel information, it provides links to a variety of other sites, including the state government's history and culture site (http://www.ca.gov/s/history). This latter site rotates essays on aspects of state history and provides still more links to other historical sites, including those of other government agencies, counties, cities, and other places. Among the specialized sites to which it is linked is that of the Demographic Research Unit of the California Department of Finance (http://www.dof.ca.gov/html/Demograp/druhpar.htm), which offers large amounts of up-to-date statistics.

Another good starting point on the Web is the Guide to California Officials, Agencies and Laws (http://library.ca.gov/gov/official.html), which is linked to many useful basic sites. For example, the California State Association of Counties Web site (http://www.csac.counties.org/counties_close_up/county_web/index.html) offers profiles of every county, as well as links to individual Web sites for most of them. The county sites, in turn, provide additional information on local matters and government agencies. The Official California Legislative Information site (http://www.leginfo.ca.gov) provides full information on current legislative activity and pending legislation.

Counties

County	Sq. miles	1996 pop.
Alameda	737.5	1,328,139
Alpine	738.7	1,232
Amador	592.6	33,315
Butte	1,639.6	192,507
Calaveras	1,020.2	38,437
Colusa	1,150.8	18,223
Contra Costa	720.3	881,490
Del Norte	1,007.9	26,947
El Dorado	1,711.5	151,706
Fresno	5,963.2	751,272
Glenn	1,314.9	26,202
Humboldt	3,572.8	123,023
Imperial	4,175.1	142,651
Inyo	10,192.1	18,433
Kern	8,141.6	622,729
Kings	1,389.5	113,351
Lake	1,258.5	55,261
Lassen	4,557.5	31,431
Los Angeles	4,060.0	9,127,751
Madera	2,138.4	110,481
Marin	519.8	233,230
Mariposa	1,451.2	15,869
Mendocino	3,509.3	83,298
Merced	1,928.9	192,311
Modoc	3,944.4	9,693
Mono	3,044.5	10,497
Monterey	3,321.9	339,047
Napa	753.9	116,512
Nevada	957.7	89,016
Orange	789.7	2,636,888

County	Sq. miles	1996 pop.
Placer	1,404.4	213,227
Plumas	2,554.0	20,597
Riverside	7,208.2	1,417,425
Sacramento	965.7	1,117,275
San Benito	1,389.1	44,503
San Bernardino	20,062.2	1,598,358
San Diego	4,204.5	2,655,463
San Francisco	46.7	735,315
San Joaquin	1,399.3	533,392
San Luis Obispo	3,304.5	229,437
San Mateo	449.1	686,909
Santa Barbara	2,738.5	385,573
Santa Clara	1,291.2	1,599,604
Santa Cruz	445.7	237,821
Shasta	3,785.7	161,740
Sierra	953.4	3,409
Siskiyou	6,287.3	44,193
Solano	828.2	365,536
Sonoma	1,576.2	420,872
Stanislaus	1,494.6	415,786
Sutter	602.7	75,650
Tehama	2,951.0	54,108
Trinity	3,178.9	13,418
Tulare	4,824.3	349,922
Tuolumne	2,235.6	52,196
Ventura	1,845.9	714,733
Yolo	1,012.4	149,925
Yuba	630.5	60,905

Source: U.S. Census Bureau; National Association of Counties.

Cities
With more than 10,000 residents

Rank	City	Population
1	Los Angeles	3,781,500
2	San Diego	1,254,300
3	San Jose	909,100
4	San Francisco	790,500
5	Long Beach	452,900
6	Fresno	415,400
7	Oakland	399,900
8	Sacramento	396,200

Rank	City	Population
9	Santa Ana	315,000
10	Anaheim	306,300
11	Riverside	254,300
12	Stockton	243,700
13	Bakersfield	230,800
14	Fremont	203,600
15	Glendale	199,200
16	Huntington Beach	196,700

Rank	City	Population	Rank	City	Population
17	San Bernardino	185,000	70	Citrus Heights	88,300
18	Modesto	184,600	71	Westminster	86,200
19	Chula Vista	166,900	72	Whittier	85,300
20	Oxnard	158,300	73	Vista	84,400
21	Oceanside	157,900	74	Rialto	82,600
22	Garden Grove	156,500	75	Antioch	81,500
23	Santa Clarita	147,000	76	Lakewood	80,100
24	Ontario	145,900	77	Hawthorne	79,700
25	Torrance	145,800	78	Redding	78,700
26	Pomona	145,400	79	Carlsbad	77,600
27	Pasadena	142,500	80	Redwood City	76,600
28	Moreno Valley	139,100	81	Baldwin Park	76,300
29	Santa Rosa	138,700	82	Buena Park	75,900
30	Irvine	136,600	83	San Leandro	75,400
31	Sunnyvale	132,900	84	Mountain View	75,200
32	Salinas	131,100	85	Newport Beach	74,000
33	Lancaster	130,100	86	Livermore	73,600
34	Hayward	127,700	87	Alameda	73,100
35	Orange	127,600	88	Santa Maria	72,000
36	Fullerton	126,800	89	Roseville	71,600
37	Escondido	125,600	90	Napa	69,900
38	Rancho Cucamonga	121,800	91	Clovis	68,800
39	Palmdale	120,100	92	Lynwood	68,500
40	Inglewood	120,100	93	Upland	67,900
41	El Monte	118,600	94	Bellflower	67,600
42	Thousand Oaks	117,600	95	Redlands	66,900
43	Corona	117,300	96	Redondo Beach	66,800
44	Concord	114,500	97	Tustin	66,800
45	Vallejo	112,800	98	Monterey Park	66,600
46	Fontana	111,800	99	Chino	65,700
47	Simi Valley	108,900	100	Union City	65,400
48	Berkeley	108,900	101	Montebello	64,300
49	West Covina	106,500	102	Milpitas	64,300
50	Costa Mesa	105,600	103	Pleasanton	64,300
51	Burbank	105,300	104	Walnut Creek	63,900
52	Daly City	104,200	105	Pico Rivera	63,900
53	Norwalk	103,500	106	Huntington Park	62,900
54	Santa Clara	102,700	107	Merced	62,800
55	San Buenaventura	102,300	108	Victorville	62,800
56	Downey	101,100	109	Hesperia	62,100
57	Compton	96,800	110	Yorba Linda	61,800
58	Mission Viejo	96,300	111	Camarillo	61,500
59	El Cajon	95,500	112	Palo Alto	61,200
60	Visalia	94,800	113	Hemet	61,100
61	South Gate	94,400	114	South San Francisco	60,900
62	Santa Monica	94,200	115	Encinitas	60,400
63	San Mateo	94,100	116	Lake Forest	59,400
64	Richmond	93,800	117	Laguna Niguel	59,200
65	Fairfield	92,400	118	Gardena	58,800
66	Santa Barbara	91,900	119	La Mesa	58,700
67	Carson	91,900	120	Diamond Bar	58,300
68	Alhambra	91,600	121	Chino Hills	58,100
69	Vacaville	89,400	122	Cerritos	57,500

(continued)

Rank	City	Population
123	Santee	57,400
124	Lodi	56,900
125	Rosemead	56,700
126	Fountain Valley	56,400
127	Paramount	56,000
128	Davis	56,000
129	La Habra	55,800
130	Santa Cruz	55,700
131	Apple Valley	55,200
132	National City	55,000
133	San Rafael	54,400
134	Chico	54,100
135	Glendora	53,200
136	Arcadia	53,200
137	Pittsburg	53,000
138	San Marcos	52,100
139	Turlock	51,900
140	Petaluma	51,700
141	Tracy	50,300
142	San Clemente	49,250
143	Placentia	49,150
144	Temecula	48,850
145	La Mirada	48,800
146	Cypress	48,500
147	Poway	48,400
148	Folsom	48,250
149	Manteca	48,050
150	Novato	47,750
151	Cupertino	47,650
152	Covina	47,550
153	Colton	46,650
154	Azusa	45,700
155	Woodland	45,600
156	Bell Gardens	45,300
157	San Ramon	44,700
158	Indio	44,500
159	Rancho Palos Verdes	44,350
160	Palm Springs	42,900
161	Highland	42,850
162	San Luis Obispo	42,850
163	Newark	42,750
164	Lompoc	42,450
165	Culver City	42,250
166	La Puente	41,800
167	San Bruno	41,600
168	Murrieta	41,550
169	Tulare	41,350
170	San Gabriel	41,100
171	Pacifica	40,700
172	Monrovia	40,550
173	Hanford	40,300
174	Rohnert Park	40,050
175	Danville	39,900
176	Campbell	39,850
177	Gilroy	39,050
178	Yucaipa	38,850
179	West Hollywood	38,550
180	El Centro	37,950
181	Bell	37,700
182	Watsonville	37,500
183	Dana Point	37,350
184	Porterville	37,000
185	San Dimas	36,950
186	Cathedral City	36,750
187	Madera	36,650
188	Martinez	36,600
189	Brea	36,400
190	Palm Desert	36,300
191	Claremont	35,400
192	Manhattan Beach	35,350
193	Yuba City	35,050
194	Beverly Hills	34,550
195	Delano	34,450
196	Temple City	34,350
197	La Verne	34,000
198	Stanton	33,850
199	Monterey	33,100
200	Pleasant Hill	32,900
201	Walnut	32,850
202	Ceres	32,400
203	San Juan Capistrano	32,100
204	Morgan Hill	31,900
205	Rocklin	31,700
206	Perris	31,550
207	Menlo Park	31,550
208	Saratoga	31,250
209	Laguna Hills	30,750
210	Foster City	30,700
211	Lawndale	30,600
212	Montclair	30,550
213	West Sacramento	30,450
214	Los Gatos	30,250
215	Maywood	30,100
216	Seaside	30,000
217	Moorpark	29,600
218	Burlingame	29,300
219	Lake Elsinore	29,300
220	Imperial Beach	28,900
221	San Carlos	28,750
222	Dublin	28,700
223	Coronado	28,700
224	Benicia	28,700
225	Los Altos	28,500
226	Hollister	28,400
227	Eureka	27,750
228	Ridgecrest	27,500

Rank	City	Population
229	Seal Beach	27,200
230	Santa Paula	27,100
231	Suisun City	26,750
232	San Pablo	26,750
233	Paradise	26,250
234	Calexico	26,150
235	Belmont	26,100
236	South Pasadena	25,750
237	Lemon Grove	25,700
238	East Palo Alto	25,550
239	Norco	25,500
240	Atascadero	25,450
241	Cudahy	25,350
242	Banning	25,300
243	San Jacinto	25,250
244	Laguna Beach	24,950
245	San Fernando	24,450
246	Lafayette	24,250
247	El Cerrito	23,800
248	Soledad	23,200
249	Barstow	23,050
250	South Lake Tahoe	23,000
251	Duarte	22,650
252	Port Hueneme	22,600
253	El Paso de Robles	22,500
254	South El Monte	22,500
255	Atwater	22,250
256	Los Banos	22,200
257	Coachella	22,200
258	Agoura Hills	21,900
259	La Quinta	21,750
260	Brawley	21,650
261	Millbrae	21,600
262	Loma Linda	21,550
263	Blythe	20,950
264	Corcoran	20,900
265	La Canada Flintridge	20,850
266	Lomita	20,750
267	Reedley	20,550
268	Windsor	20,400
269	Wasco	20,350
270	Calabasas	20,100
271	Brentwood	20,050
272	Hermosa Beach	19,400
273	Hercules	19,250
274	Yucca Valley	18,950
275	Sanger	18,850
276	Pinole	18,600
277	Selma	18,450
278	Marina	18,350
279	Lemoore	18,300
280	Albany	17,750
281	Pacific Grove	17,450

Rank	City	Population
282	Orinda	17,350
283	Galt	17,200
284	Susanville	17,050
285	Artesia	17,000
286	Moraga	16,750
287	El Segundo	16,650
288	Arcata	16,500
289	La Palma	16,400
290	Santa Fe Springs	16,300
291	Arroyo Grande	16,000
292	Dinuba	15,400
293	Desert Hot Springs	15,400
294	Dixon	15,100
295	Hawaiian Gardens	15,050
296	Twentynine Palms	15,000
297	Ukiah	15,000
298	Carpinteria	14,950
299	Adelanto	14,900
300	Oakdale	14,700
301	Palos Verdes Estates	14,550
302	Riverbank	14,450
303	Solana Beach	14,150
304	Mill Valley	14,100
305	Chowchilla	14,050
306	San Marino	13,900
307	Grand Terrace	13,400
308	Commerce	13,250
309	Fillmore	13,200
310	Red Bluff	13,100
311	Malibu	12,950
312	Oroville	12,650
313	Grover Beach	12,650
314	San Anselmo	12,450
315	Truckee	12,450
316	Avenal	12,400
317	Marysville	12,150
318	Los Alamitos	12,050
319	Larkspur	11,950
320	Clearlake	11,900
321	Canyon Lake	11,850
322	Shafter	11,650
323	Hillsborough	11,600
324	Auburn	11,600
325	Piedmont	11,600
326	Sierra Madre	11,600
327	Arvin	11,400
328	Rancho Mirage	11,400
329	Half Moon Bay	11,200
330	Capitola	11,150
331	Clayton	11,100
332	Parlier	11,100
333	Beaumont	10,850
334	Scotts Valley	10,700

(continued)

Rank	City	Population
335	Livingston	10,550
336	King City	10,500
337	Coalinga	10,450
338	Greenfield	10,450
339	Patterson	10,400
340	Fortuna	10,250

Rank	City	Population
341	Ripon	10,000
342	Healdsburg	10,000

Population figures are estimated for January, 1999.

Source: Demographic Research Unit of California Department of Finance.

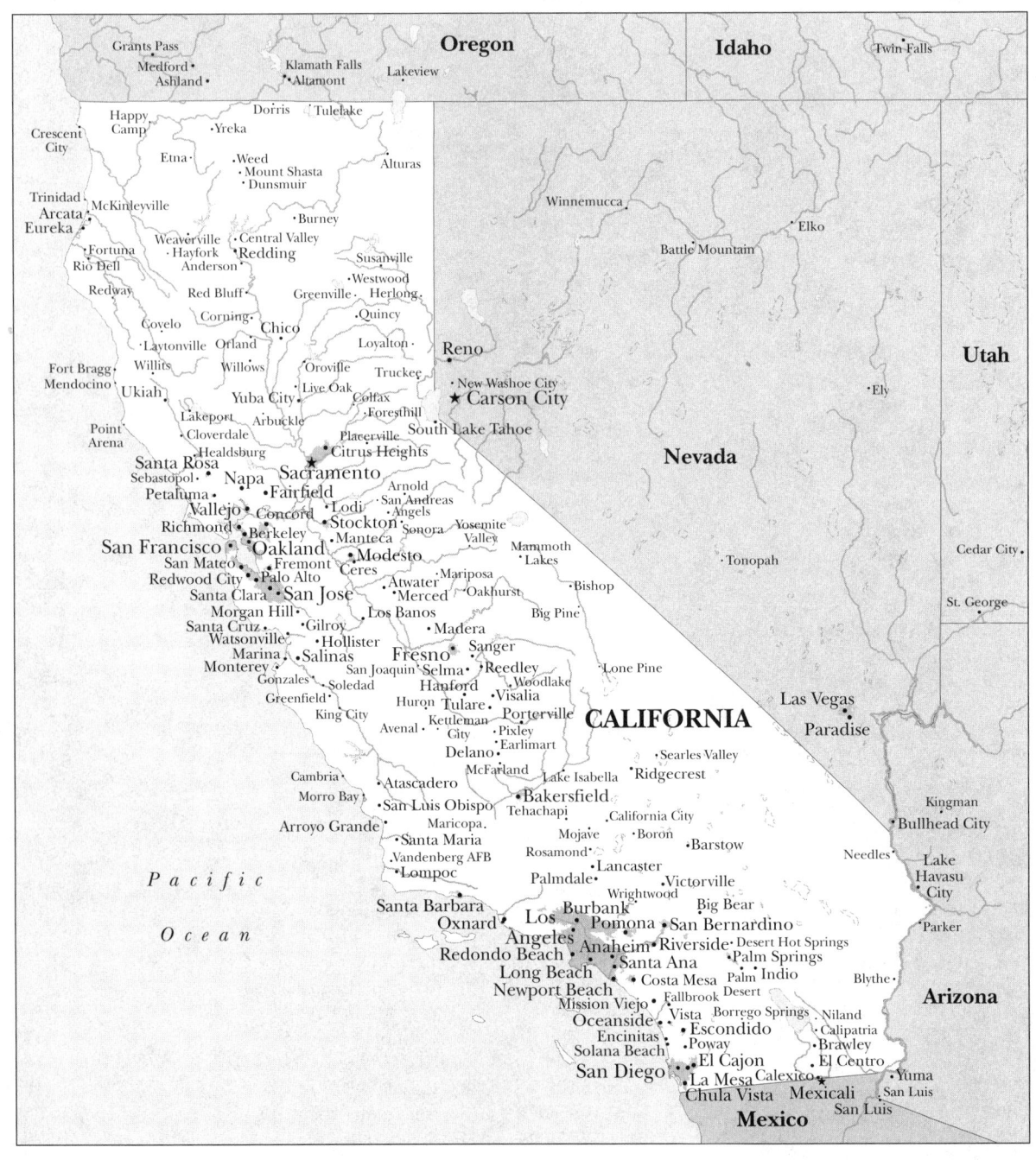

Index to Tables

NA = Reliable data are not available.

DEMOGRAPHICS

Resident state and national populations, 1970-1997

Population figures given in thousands

	State pop.	U.S. pop.	Share	Rank
1970	19,971	203,302	9.8%	1
1980	23,668	226,546	10.4%	1
1985	26,441	237,924	11.1%	1
1990	29,786	248,765	12.0%	1
1995	31,558	262,761	12.0%	1
1997	32,268	267,636	12.1%	1

Source: U.S. Bureau of the Census.

Resident population by age, 1997

Age group	Total population
Under 5 years	2,661,000
5 to 17 years	6,291,000
18 to 24 years	3,049,000
25 to 34 years	5,285,000
35 to 44 years	5,373,000
45 to 54 years	3,789,000
55 to 64 years	2,249,000
65 to 74 years	1,954,000
75 to 84 years	1,229,000
85 years and over	389,000
Portion of residents 65 and older	11.1%
National average	12.7%

Population figures are rounded to nearest thousand persons;
figures include armed forces personnel stationed in state.
Source: U.S. Bureau of the Census.

Resident population by race, Hispanic origin, 1997

	State pop.	Share	U.S.
All residents	32,268,000	100.0%	100.0%
Hispanic white	9,306,000	28.8%	10.0%
non-Hispanic white	16,482,000	51.1%	72.7%
African American	2,397,000	7.4%	12.7%
Native American	307,000	1.0%	0.9%
Asian, Pacific Islander	3,777,000	11.7%	3.8%

Source: U.S. Bureau of the Census.

Projections of state population, 2000-2025

	Model A Uses interstate migration observed from 1975-1994	Model B Uses Bureau of Economic Analysis employment projections
Year	Population	Population
2000	32,521,000	32,423,000
2005	34,441,000	33,511,000
2010	37,644,000	34,968,000
2015	41,373,000	36,838,000
2020	45,278,000	39,034,000
2025	49,285,000	41,480,000

All population projections, including those for 2000, were calculated in 1997.
Source: U.S. Bureau of the Census, Population Paper Listings PPL-47.

VITAL STATISTICS

Average lifetime in years by race, 1989-1991

	State	U.S.	Rank
All residents	75.86	75.37	23
White residents	75.92	76.13	33
Black residents	69.65	69.16	16

Ranks are from longest-lived to least longest-lived. Ranks exclude Alaska, for which reliable data are not available. Rank for black residents is based on the 32 states for which reliable data are available.
Source: U.S. National Center for Health Statistics.

Infant mortality rates, 1980 and 1995

	State	U.S.
All residents		
1980	11.1	12.6
1995	6.3	7.6
White residents		
1980	10.6	11.0
1995	5.8	6.3
Black residents		
1980	18.0	21.4
1995	14.4	15.1

Figures represent deaths per 1,000 live births of resident infants under 1 year old, exclusive of fetal deaths; all-residents figures include other races not listed separately.
Source: U.S. National Center for Health Statistics.

Aerial view of Hollywood's famous Capitol Records building, which was designed to resemble a record turntable. (PhotoDisc)

Marriages and divorces

Marriages in 1996 202,800
Rate per 1,000 population, 1995. . . . . 6.3
U.S. rate, 1995 . . . . 8.9
Rank among all states 48

Divorces in 1996 . . . . NA
Rate per 1,000 population, 1995. . . . . NA
U.S. rate, 1995 . . . . 4.4
Rank among all states . . . . NA

Rank is from highest to lowest in country.
Includes nonlicensed registered marriages
Source: U.S. National Center for Health Statistics.

Death rates by leading causes, 1995
Deaths per 100,000 resident population

Cause	State	U.S.
Heart disease	216.3	280.7
Cancer	162.8	204.9
Cerebrovascular diseases	51.4	60.1
Accidents and adverse effects	29.3	35.5
Motor vehicle accidents	14.1	16.5
Chronic obstructive pulmonary diseases	34.2	39.2
Diabetes mellitus	16.2	22.6
HIV	20.4	NA
Suicide	11.7	11.9
Homicide	11.6	8.7
All causes	709.8	880.0

Rank in overall death rate among states 46

Figures exclude nonresidents who die in state. Causes of
death follow International Classification of Diseases. Rank
is from highest to lowest in country.
Source: U.S. National Center for Health Statistics.

ECONOMY

Gross state product, 1990-1996
In current dollars

	State product	Increase
1990	$792.7 billion	
1993	$843.1 billion	
1994	$876.0 billion	3.90%
1995	$913.5 billion	4.28%
1996	$962.7 billion	5.39%

Source: U.S. Bureau of Economic Analysis; *Survey of Current
Business,* June, 1998.

Gross state product by industry, 1996
In billions

Farms, forestry, fisheries $18.1
Construction. 27.3
Manufacturing 138.7
Transportation, public utilities 62.8
Wholesale trade 62.9
Retail trade 83.0
Finance, insurance, real estate 189.7
Services 194.8
Government 99.6

State total $880.1
Total U.S. $6,923.8
State share 12.71%
Rank among states 1

Total figures include mining, not listed separately.
Source: U.S. Bureau of Economic Analysis; *Survey of Current
Business,* June, 1998.

Energy consumption, 1995
In trillions of British thermal units (BTU)

End-use sectors
Residential 1,310.3
Commercial 1,206.6
Industrial 2,237.7
Transportation 2,833.4

Sources of energy
Petroleum 3,293.9
Natural gas 1,955.9
Coal 61.0
Hydroelectric power 529.6
Nuclear electric power 322.4

Total state per capita consumption 240.0
Total U.S. per capita consumption 344.4
Rank among states. 47
Total state energy consumption 7,577.0
Total U.S. energy consumption 90,547.4
State share of U.S. total 8.37%
Rank among states 2

Total figures include items not listed separately.
Source: U.S. Energy Information Administration; *State Energy
Data Report.*

Personal income per capita, 1990 and 1997
In current dollars

	1990	1997
Per capita income	$21,393	$26,570
U.S. average	$19,188	$25,598
Rank among states	8	13

1997 data are preliminary.
Source: U.S. Bureau of Economic Analysis; *Survey of Current Business,* May, 1998.

Nonfarm employment by sectors, 1997

Total	13,167,000
Construction	554,000
Manufacturing	1,914,000
Transportation, public utilities	663,000
Wholesale trade, retail trade	3,057,000
Finance, insurance, real estate	756,000
Services	4,051,000
Government	2,144,000

Figures are rounded to nearest thousand persons. Total includes mining, not listed separately.
Source: U.S. Bureau of Labor Statistics; *Employment and Earnings,* monthly.

Foreign exports, 1990-1997
In millions of dollars

Year	State	U.S.	State share
1990	44,520	394,045	11.30%
1996	93,418	624,767	14.95%
1997	99,161	688,896	14.39%

Source: U.S. Bureau of the Census; *U.S. Merchandise Trade,* series FT 900.

LAND USE

Federally owned land, 1996

	State	U.S.	State share
Total acres	100,207,000	2,271,343,000	4.41%
Federally owned	44,757,000	563,129,000	7.95%
Federal share	44.7%	24.8%	—

Areas are rounded to nearest thousand acres. Figures for federally owned land do not include trust properties.
Source: U.S. General Services Administration; *Inventory Report on Real Property Owned by the United States Throughout the World,* annual.

Land use, 1992
In acres, rounded to nearest thousand

Total surface area	101,572,000
Federal land	46,792,000
Total nonfederal	52,892,000
Developed	5,001,000
Total rural	47,892,000
Cropland	10,052,000
Pasture land	1,161,000
Range land	17,140,000
Forest land	14,794,000
Minor cover/use	4,746,000

Total surface area figures include water area not shown separately.
Source: U.S. Dept. of Agriculture; Soil Conservation Service; Iowa State University, Statistical Laboratory; *Summary Report, 1992 National Resources Inventory.*

Farms and crop acreage, 1997

	State	U.S.	Share	Rank
Farms (thousands)	84	2,058	4.08%	6
Acres (millions)	30	968	3.10%	13
Acres per farm	357	471	—	19
Acres planted	5,172	334,139	1.55%	19
Acres harvested	4,678	319,894	1.46%	20
Farm value (mill.)	$15,554	$108,805	14.3%	1

Numbers of farms are rounded to nearest thousand.
Source: U.S. Dept. of Agriculture; National Agricultural Statistics Service.

GOVERNMENT AND FINANCE

Units of local government, 1997

	State	Total U.S.	Rank
All local governments	4,607	87,453	4
Counties	58	3,043	26
Municipalities	471	19,372	18
Townships	0	16,629	—
School districts	1,069	13,726	2
Special districts	3,010	34,683	2

County ranks are based on the 48 states with county governments; township ranks are based on the 20 states with township governments; school district ranks are based on the 46 states with such districts.
Source: U.S. Bureau of the Census; *1997 Census of Governments, Government Organization,* Series GC97(1).

State government revenue, 1996

Total revenue . . . . $123,342 mill.
General revenue . . . . 98,185 mill.
Per capita . . . . 3,082 mill.
U.S. per capita average 2,910
Rank among states. 21

Intergovernmental revenue
Total . . . . $29,087 mill.
From federal government . . . . 26,731 mill.
From local government . . . . 2,356 mill.

Charges and Miscellaneous
Total . . . . $11,351 mill.
Current charges . . . . 6,743 mill.
Misc. general revenue . . . . 4,609 mill.

Taxes
Total . . . . $57,747 mill.
General sales . . . . 18,980 mill.
Selective sales. . . . . 5,113 mill.
License taxes . . . . 3,035 mill.
Individual income. . . . . 20,760 mill.
Corporate income . . . . 5,831 mill.
Other . . . . 4,028 mill.
Insurance trust revenue . . . . 25,014 mill.

Total revenue figures include items not listed separately.
Source: U.S. Bureau of the Census.

State government expenditures, 1996

General expenditures
Intergovernmental. . . . . $48,759 mill.
Direct expenditures. . . . . 50,024 mill.
Total . . . . 98,783 mill.

Selected direct expenditures
Education . . . . $34,780 mill.
Public welfare . . . . 28,805 mill.
Health, hospital . . . . 8,344 mill.
Highways . . . . 4,522 mill.
Police . . . . 1,012 mill.
Corrections . . . . 3,843 mill.
Natural resources. . . . . 1,876 mill.
Parks and recreation . . . . 210 mill.
Government administration . . . . 3,095 mill.
Interest on debt . . . . 2,448 mill.

Other
State per capita expenditures $3,101
U.S. per capita average 2,854
Rank among states. 16
Total state expenditures. . . . . 113,361 mill.
Total U.S. expenditures . . . . 859,959 mill.

Totals include items not listed separately.
Source: U.S. Bureau of the Census.

Pacific Ocean coastline near Northern California's Big Sur. (PhotoDisc)

POLITICS

Governors since statehood

D = Democrat; R = Republican; O = other;
(r) resigned; (d) died in office; (i) removed from office

Peter H. Burnett (D) . . . . (r) 1849-1851
John McDougal (D) 1851-1852
John Bigler (D) 1852-1856
John Neely Johnson (O) 1856-1858
John B. Weller (D) 1858-1860
Milton S. Latham (D) . . . . (r) 1860-1860
John G. Downey (D) 1860-1862
Leland Stanford (R) 1862-1863
Frederick F. Low (O) 1863-1867
Henry H. Haight (D) 1867-1871
Newton Booth (R) . . . . (r) 1871-1875
Romualdo Pacheco (R) 1875-1875
William Irwin (D) 1875-1880
George C. Perkins (R) 1880-1883
George Stoneman (D) 1883-1887
Washington Bartlett (D) . . . . (d) 1887-1887
Robert W. Waterman (R) 1887-1891
Henry H. Markham (R) 1891-1895
James H. Budd (D) 1895-1899
Henry T. Gage (R) 1899-1903
George C. Pardee (R) 1903-1907
James N. Gillette (R) 1907-1911
Hiram W. Johnson (R) . . . . (r) 1911-1917
William D. Stephens (R) 1917-1923
Friend W. Richardson (R) 1923-1927
Clement C. Young (R) 1927-1931
James Rolph, Jr. (R) . . . . (d) 1931-1934
Frank F. Merriam (R) 1934-1939
Culbert L. Olson (D) 1939-1943
Earl Warren (R) . . . . (r) 1943-1953
Goodwin J. Knight (R) 1953-1959
Edmund G. ("Pat") Brown (D) 1959-1967
Ronald W. Reagan (R) 1967-1975
Edmund G. ("Jerry") Brown, Jr. (D) 1975-1983
George Deukmejian (R) 1983-1991
Pete Wilson (R) 1991-1999
Gray Davis (D) 1999-

Composition of state legislature, 1990-1998

	Democrats	Republicans
State Assembly (80 seats)		
1990	47	33
1992	47	33
1994	39	40
1996	43	37
1998	47	32
State Senate (40 seats)		
1990	25	13
1992	21	16
1994	21	17
1996	25	15
1998	25	15

Figures for total seats may include independents and minor party members.

Source: Council of State Governments; *State Elective Officials and the Legislatures.*

Composition of congressional delegations, 1989-1999

	Dem	Rep	Total
House of Representatives			
101st Congress, 1989			
State delegates	27	18	45
Total U.S.	259	174	433
102d Congress, 1991			
State delegates	26	19	45
Total U.S.	267	167	434
103d Congress, 1993			
State delegates	30	22	52
Total U.S.	258	176	434
104th Congress, 1995			
State delegates	29	23	52
Total U.S.	197	236	433
105th Congress, 1997			
State delegates	28	24	52
Total U.S.	206	228	434
106th Congress, 1999			
State delegates	28	24	52
Total U.S.	211	222	433
Senate			
101st Congress, 1989			
State delegates	1	1	2
Total U.S.	55	45	100
102d Congress, 1991			
State delegates	1	1	2
Total U.S.	56	44	100
103d Congress, 1993			
State delegates	2	0	2
Total U.S.	57	43	100

	Dem	Rep	Total
104th Congress, 1995			
State delegates	2	0	2
Total U.S.	46	53	99
105th Congress, 1997			
State delegates	2	0	2
Total U.S.	45	55	100
106th Congress, 1999			
State delegates	2	0	2
Total U.S.	45	54	99

Figures are for starts of first sessions. Figure for U.S. Representatives for 101st Congress does not include Alabama and Indiana, which had vacancies. Figures for total U.S. Representatives for 102d, 103d, and 106th Congresses do not include Vermont, which had 1 Independent-Socialist. Figure for U.S. Representatives for 104th Congress does not include Vermont, which had 1 Independent-Socialist, and California, which had 1 vacancy. Figure for U.S. Representatives for 105th Congress does not include New York, which had 1 vacancy. Figure for U.S. Senators for 104th Congress does not include Oregon, which had 1 vacancy. Figure for U.S. Senators for 106th Congress does not include New Hampshire, which had 1 Independent.
Source: U.S. Congress; *Congressional Directory*, biennial.

Voter participation in presidential elections, 1992 and 1996

	1992	1996
State voting age pop.	22,521,000	23,133,000
Total U.S. voting age pop.	189,524,000	196,509,000
State share of U.S. total	11.9%	11.8%
Rank among states	1	1
Percent of state casting vote	49.4	58.6
Percent of U.S. total voting	55.1	49.0
Rank among states	46	5

Source: U.S. Bureau of the Census.

HEALTH AND MEDICAL CARE

Medicare, 1997

	Recipients	Payments
State	3,727,000	$22,088 mill.
Total U.S.	37,514,000	$206,064 mill.
State share	9.93%	10.72%
Rank among states	1	1

Recipient figures are rounded to nearest thousand persons. Ranks are from highest to lowest.
Source: U.S. Health Care Financing Administration.

Medicaid, 1996

	Recipients	Payments
State	5,107,000	$11,124 mill.
Total U.S.	35,028,000	$121,419 mill.
State share	14.58%	9.16%
Rank among states	1	2

Recipient figures are rounded to nearest thousand persons. Payment figures for fiscal year reflect federal and state contribution payments. Ranks are from highest to lowest.
Source: U.S. Health Care Financing Administration.

Health insurance coverage, 1996

	State	U.S.
Total persons covered	25,853,000	225,070,000
Total persons not covered	6,514,000	41,716,000
Part not covered	20.1%	15.6%
Rank among states	6	—
Children not covered	1,631,000	10,554,000
Part not covered	17.8%	14.8%
Rank among states	13	—

Ranks are from most to fewest uninsured. Population figures are rounded to nearest thousand persons.
Source: U.S. Bureau of the Census.

AIDS, syphilis, tuberculosis, and measles cases, 1997

Cases	U.S.	State	Share
AIDS	58,443	7,029	12.03%
Syphilis	8,550	386	4.51%
Tuberculosis	18,534	3,527	19.03%
Measles	148,000	30,000	20.27%

Measles figures are rounded to nearest thousand cases.
Source: U.S. Centers for Disease Control and Prevention.

HOUSING

Homeownership rates, 1985-1997

	1985	1990	1997
State	54.2%	53.8%	55.7%
Total U.S.	63.9%	63.9%	65.7%
Rank among states	48	49	48

Source: U.S. Bureau of the Census.

Home sales, 1990 and 1997
In thousands of units

Existing home sales	1990	1997	Change
State sales	453.0	555.4	102.4
Total U.S. sales	3,560	4,730	1,170
State share of U.S. total	12.72%	11.74%	-0.98%
Rank among states	1	1	—

Source: National Association of Realtors; *Real Estate Outlook: Market Trends and Insights.*

EDUCATION

Public school enrollment, 1995

State K-8 enrollment	4,041,000
Total U.S. K-8 enrollment	32,341,000
State share of total U.S.	12.50%
State 9-12 enrollment	1,495,000
Total U.S. 9-12 enrollment	12,500,000
State share of U.S. total	11.96%
State public school enroll. rate	92.8%
Overall U.S. rate	91.6%
Rank among states	24

Enrollment figures (which include unclassified students) are rounded to nearest thousand pupils in fall term; kindergarten (K)-8 grade enrollment figures include some prekindergarten students. Enrollment rate is based on percentage of persons 5-17 years old. Rank is from highest to lowest.
Source: U.S. National Center for Education Statistics.

Public college finances, 1996

State FTE enrollment	1,263,100
Total U.S. FTE enrollment	8,268,800
State share of total U.S.	15.28%
Rank among states	1
State and local appropriations	$6,059,900,000
Total U.S. state and local appropriations	$39,699 mill.
State share of total U.S.	15.26%
Rank among states	1
State net tuition revenues	$1,362 mill.
Total U.S. net tuition	$18,348,100,000
State share of total U.S.	7.42%
Rank among states	1

FTE=Full-time equivalent; credit and noncredit enrollment including summer session in academic year ending in 1996.

Enrollments are rounded to nearest thousand students. Net tuition revenues exclude appropriation to students attending in-state public institutions. Rankings are from highest shares to lowest.
Source: Research Associates of Washington.

TRANSPORTATION AND TRAVEL

Highway mileage, 1996

Interstate	2,424
Other arterial	28,067
Collector roads	42,136
Local roads	107,904
Urban roads	83,109
Rural roads	87,397
Total state	170,506
U.S. total	3,933,985
State share	4.3%
Rank among states	2

Source: U.S. Federal Highway Administration.

Motor vehicle registrations and driver licenses, 1996
In thousands

Vehicle registrations	State	U.S.	Share	Rank
Autos, trucks, buses	25,214	206,365	12.22%	1
Autos only	15,223	128,439	11.85%	1
Motorcycles	513	3,832	13.39%	1
Driver licenses	20,249	179,539	11.28%	1

Figures do not include vehicles owned by military services.
Source: U.S. Federal Highway Administration; *Highway Statistics; Selected Highway Statistics and Charts.*

Domestic travel expenditures, 1995
Spending by U.S. residents on overnight trips and day trips of at least 100 miles

Total expenditures in state	$46,672 mill.
Total expenditures in U.S.	$360,314 mill.
State share of total U.S.	12.95%
Rank among states	1

Source: Travel Industry Association of America.

CRIME AND LAW ENFORCEMENT

State and local police officers, 1996

Local police.	35,939
State police.	6,219
Sheriffs	22,869
Total.	69,134
Officers per 10,000 residents	22
U.S. average	25
Rank among states.	28

Figures cover full-time sworn officers; totals include special police not shown separately.
Source: U.S. Bureau of Justice Statistics; *Census of State and Local Law Enforcement Agencies, 1996.*

Crime rates, 1996

Rates per 100,000 resident population

Violent crimes	*State*	*U.S.*
Total violent	863	634
Murder	9.1	7.4
Forcible rape	32.1	36.1
Robbery	296	202
Aggravated assault	526	388
Property crimes		
Total property	4,345	4,445
Burglary	979	943
Larceny/theft	2,605	2,976
Motor vehicle theft	761	526
Totals	5,208	5,079

Source: U.S. Federal Bureau of Investigation; *Crime in the United States,* annual.

State prison populations, 1980-1996

	State	*U.S.*	*State share*
1980	24,569	305,458	8.04%
1990	97,309	708,393	13.74%
1996	146,049	1,025,624	14.24%

Figures exclude prisoners in federal penitentiaries.
Source: U.S. Bureau of Justice Statistics.

Colorado

Location: Western continental United States

Area and rank: 103,730 square miles (268,660 square kilometers); 104,100 square miles (269,619 square kilometers) including water; eighth largest state in area

Population and rank: 3,892,644 (1997); twenty-fifth largest state in population

Capital: Denver

Largest city: Denver (499,055 people in 1998)

Became territory: February 28, 1861

Entered Union and rank: August 1, 1876; thirty-eighth state

Present constitution adopted: 1876

Counties: 63

State name: "Colorado" is derived from the Spanish for "ruddy" or "red"

State nickname: Centennial State

Motto: *Nil sine Numine* (Nothing Without Providence)

State flag: Blue and white stripes with red letter C and yellow disk in center

Highest point: Mount Elbert — 14,433 feet (4,399 meters)

Lowest point: Arkansas River — 3,350 feet (1,021 meters)

Highest recorded temperature: 118 degrees Fahrenheit (48 degrees Celsius) — Bennett, 1888

State capitol building in Denver. (Denver Metro Convention & Visitors Bureau)

Lowest recorded temperature: −61 degrees Fahrenheit (−52 degrees Celsius) — Maybell, 1985

State song: "Where the Columbines Grow"

State tree: Colorado blue spruce

State flower: Rocky Mountain columbine

State bird: Lark bunting

State animal: Rocky Mountain bighorn sheep

National parks: Mesa Verde, Rocky Mountain

Colorado History

The history of Colorado is marked by its geographical features, divided as it is by the Rocky Mountains, with rugged territory lying to the west and agriculturally productive plains to the east. Mining in the central and western parts of the state was influential in its early history, while agriculture, and its thirst for water in the parched eastern plains, was influential in later decades. Colorado's mountainous terrain has attracted generations of tourists, who flock to winter and summer recreational attractions.

Colorado History. The earliest inhabitants of the area were nomadic hunters, around 10,000 B.C.E. About the first century C.E., the southwestern area of the state was populated by a people known as the Basket Makers. By 800, the Cliff Dwellers had established their civilization in the state's mesa country. From 1000 the civilization of the Cliff Dwellers flourished, but around 1300, for unknown reasons, it died out.

Though their origins are unknown, many other Native American peoples populated today's Colorado when whites arrived. A number of Apache bands raided Colorado territory, but only one such band, the Jicarilla, lived permanently in Colorado and its environs, mainly in the southeastern portion. Bannock and Shoshone Indians roamed over the northwestern corner of the state. The Cheyenne, Arapaho, and Comanche tribes hunted and made war in eastern areas, as did the Kiowa and the Kiowa Apaches, who always accompanied them. The Navahos occasionally entered the state from New Mexico, but the Ute occupied the state's entire central and western portions. Most of the Pueblos inhabited the state's north, in Colorado's famous cliff ruins, sometimes intermarrying with the Utes.

Spanish Exploration. In the sixteenth century the Spanish became the area's first European explorers. Searching for rich cities of gold, Francisco Vásquez de Coronado arrived in 1541. During the next 250 years, a number of Spanish explorers traversed parts of what became Colorado, among them Juan de Ulibarri, who claimed the territory for the Spanish crown.

American Exploration and Settlement. In 1803 parts of Colorado were sold to the United States when the administration of Thomas Jefferson concluded the Louisiana Purchase with France. Thereafter, the territory was explored by a series of American expeditions: in 1806 by Zebulon Pike, for whom Pike's Peak is named; in 1820 by Stephen Long; from 1842 to 1853 by John C. Frémont; and in 1853 by the Gunnison-Beckwith expedition. In 1833 Bent's Fort, the first permanent American settlement in Colorado, was completed. The area was also inhabited by various nomadic Indian tribes, as well as by American "mountain men," who lived by trapping and fur trading. Among them were those who became the subjects of American folklore, such as Kit Carson and Jim Bridger.

From Territory to Statehood. In 1848 Mexico ceded part of Colorado to the United States with the Treaty of Guadalupe Hidalgo, which ended the Mexican-American War. Two years later, a portion of the western area of modern Colorado became part of Utah Territory. In 1854 some eastern areas were incorporated into Kansas and Nebraska Territories. In 1858 gold was found in Colorado, first at Cherry Creek, near Denver. The next year, a rich vein was discovered in Central City. These finds brought thousands of adventurers in search of a new life, who adopted the slogan "Pike's Peak or Bust." The miners ignored the claims of Indians to the land that had been deeded to them in past treaties. In place of Indian lands, newcomers attempted to set up a new, so-called Jefferson Territory, which Congress did not approve. After Kansas became a state in 1861, Colorado Territory was organized, with much the same boundaries as the subsequent state.

Colorado entered the Civil War on the Union side in 1861 and was the scene of significant fighting in the western phases of the war. Other notable events of these early years were wars between whites and American Indians, and a number of gold and silver strikes. By the late 1860's new mining methods brought both further prosperity and more immigration from the East. The increased population was a key factor in the territory's seeking statehood. After several failures, statehood was finally attained in 1876.

Economic and Social Development. The formation of modern Colorado was preceded by a society and economy dominated by decades of gold and silver mining followed by agricultural development. The same year statehood was achieved, the Leadville area began to surrender its millions of dollars of gold and silver ore. More than a decade later, Cripple Creek was the scene of another notable gold strike. This discovery was especially welcome, because the free coinage of silver sent silver mining into a tailspin that the Cripple Creek find helped to offset.

The last of the battles with Indian tribes came in 1879, when the Utes rebelled. In the last uprising by Native Americans in the American West, the Utes massacred Nathan Meeker, an Indian agent, and his workers in what would become the town of Meeker, in the White River Valley in northwestern Colorado. This massacre resulted in the Utes' forcible removal to eastern Utah. Some Indians, however, appear to have maintained their presence, though in modest numbers. For example, in 1845, the Jicarilla Apaches were said to number 800. According to the census of 1910, there were 694, and in 1937, the Report of the U.S. Indian Office said there were 714.

If Indian wars were at an end, other conflicts were not long in arriving. When a depression struck in 1893, serious labor problems erupted after the federal government canceled its agreement to purchase substantial amounts of silver. Silver miners were thrown out of work; strikes by miners,

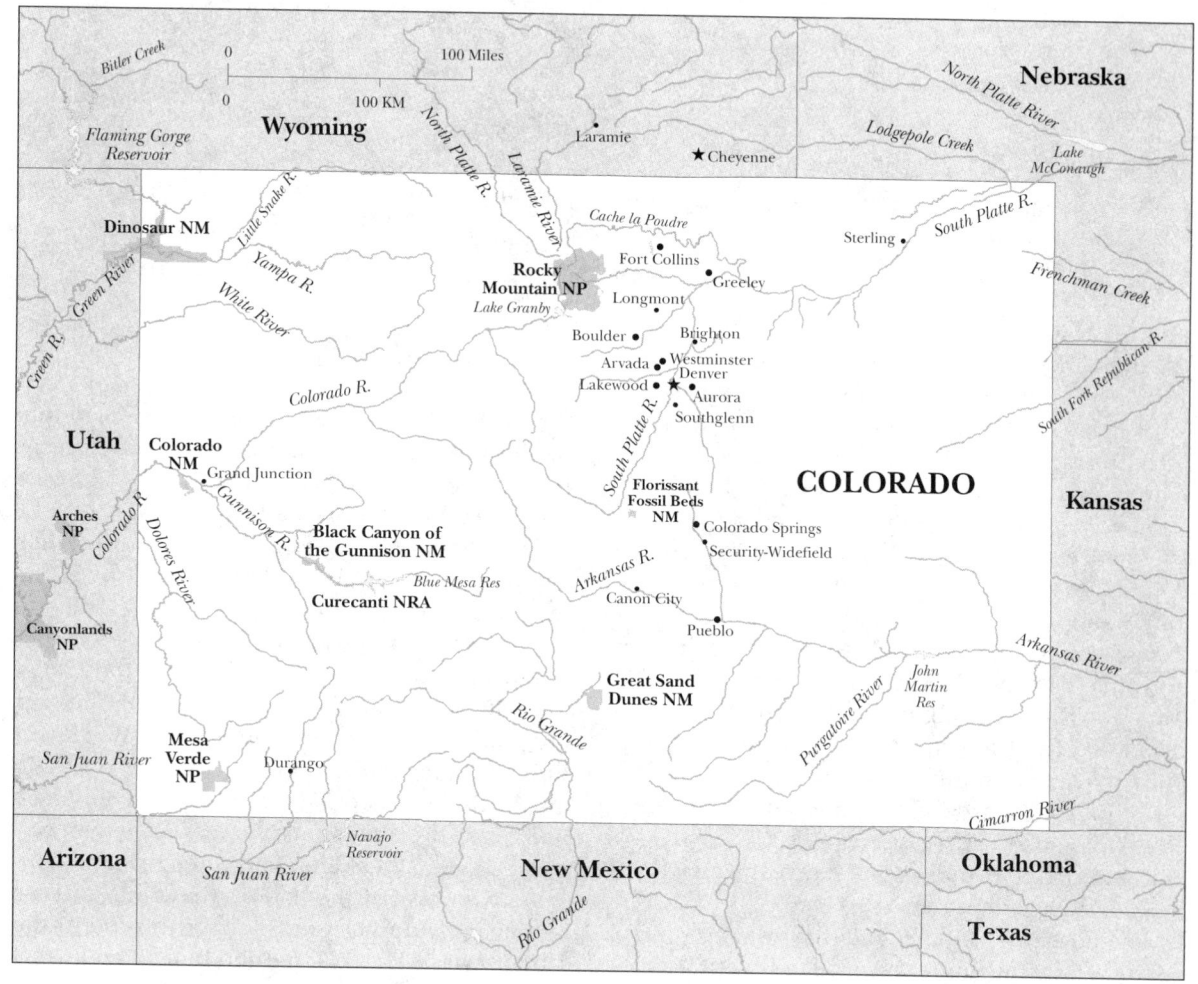

Last occupied during the thirteenth century, the Cliff Palace ruins in Mesa Verde National Park contain some of the oldest and best-preserved dwellings in North America. (PhotoDisc)

now employees of mining companies, not independent adventurers, occurred in silver mines in 1893-1894 and 1903-1904 and in coal mines in 1913-1914. These strikes were settled with military force, a graphic reminder that the days of the romantic West were over.

The Twentieth Century. The opening of the twentieth century saw the beginning of the natural conservation movement that attracted tourists. In 1906 Congress created Mesa Verde National Park to preserve the remains of ancient Indian culture, and nine years later Rocky Mountain National Park was established. During these years, the economy depended on agriculture, as Colorado became the most irrigated state in the Union. Canning and other industries grew along with agriculture. In 1899 Colorado's first sugar beet factory began operations at Grand Junction; seven years later the U.S. Mint opened in Denver.

The advent of another industry, however, augured well for the future, when oil production and refining became prominent sources of income. With the plentiful availability of oil throughout the nation came the advent of the automobile. America's love affair with the automobile, coupled with the unsurpassed beauty of western Colorado, gave rise to the state's considerable tourist industry, which developed rapidly after World War I. Colorado, moreover, has its own oil sources. Small amounts of oil had been discovered in the nineteenth century, when in 1862 the first oil well was drilled near Canon City. But in the next century more, and larger, fields were found. By the 1920's, the importance of oil surpassed that of all other minerals, though not until after World War II and the development of the Rangley oil field in 1946 in northwest Colorado did oil production approach its zenith. Oil production rose from 1.7 million barrels in 1940 to 23 million barrels in 1950.

Like the rest of the nation, Colorado suffered considerably during the Great Depression of the 1930's. World War II lifted the state from its doldrums, as its oil and minerals were in great demand. Military and other federal installations opened in several areas, especially around Denver, the state's capital.

Postwar Developments. Colorado's population, which had grown to 800,000 in 1910, grew swiftly after World War II. With population increase and demand for expansion of agriculture came the need for water. Irrigation had begun in the nineteenth century. Large irrigation projects existed from the 1860's, but after the war a series of irrigation projects were carried out. In 1947 the Alva B. Adams Tunnel, which carries water eastward through the Rocky Mountains, was completed. Two years later Cherry Creek Dam, near Denver, was finished. In 1959 the Colorado-Big Thompson Project, a series of dams, reservoirs, and tunnels, was completed, of which the Adams Tunnel is a part. More water-conservation projects were carried out between the 1950's and the 1980's, such as the Colorado River Storage Project, begun in 1956, and the Frying Pan-Arkansas project, begun in the early 1960's and completed in 1985.

Other significant postwar changes in the state's economy changed the complexion of its society. Manufacturing replaced agriculture in importance by the mid-1950's. Federal agencies sank important new roots in the state, opening the laboratory of the National Bureau of Standards in Boulder in 1954, the United States Air Force Academy in 1958, and the North American Air Defense Command in 1966, sunk some twelve hundred feet deep in Cheyenne Mountain.

By the 1990's Colorado had emerged as both a significant area of urban development below the eastern slopes of the Rocky Mountains and one of the nation's most popular recreation areas. The upscale mountain community of Vail, for example, serves as an icon of winter sports, and the state's national parks and other scenic wonders draw millions of vacationers each year. At the same time, the nation's academic life benefited from its universities, and several of its political figures reached national stature. If in its early decades, Colorado, seemingly connected more to the West, felt marginal to powerful eastern states, a century after its admittance to the Union the state became fully integrated into the nation's life. Signs of this integration include its thriving urban life, especially in its capital and environs; its significant defense installations; and its sports teams, such as those in professional baseball, basketball, and football.

Charles F. Bahmueller

Colorado Time Line

c. 1000 C.E.	Indian cliff dwellers live in southwestern part of state.
1500's	Spanish explorers searching for legendary golden cities travel through parts of the state.
1541	Spaniard Francisco Vásquez de Coronado probably crosses southeastern corner of the state.
1700	French explorers reach the Rocky Mountains.
1706	Juan de Uribarri, leader of a Spanish expedition to capture runaway Indian slaves, claims the area for Philip V of Spain.
c. 1776	Two Franciscan monks explore much of western and southwestern areas seeking a route to the California missions.
1779	Juan Bautista de Anza explores territory for Spain.
1803	Portions of Colorado become part of the United States through the Louisiana Purchase.
1806	Zebulon Pike explores Pike's Peak.
1820	Stephen Long explores western boundary of Colorado.

(continued)

1833	Bent's Old Fort is founded; first permanent American settlement of future state.
1842-1853	Sponsored by the federal government, John C. Frémont explores Colorado on five occasions.
1845	Portion of future state is acquired in connection with annexation of Texas.
1848	Entirety of Colorado is acquired in the Treaty of Guadalupe Hidalgo, which ended the Mexican-American War.
1854	Parts of Colorado are incorporated in the Kansas and Nebraska Territories.
1858	Gold is discovered at Cherry Creek, near Denver.
1859	Rich gold vein is discovered in Central City; Colorado Gold Rush attracts thousands of fortune hunters.
1858-1859	Agricultural irrigation begins.
1859	Production of gold begins; reaches peak in 1900.
1860's	Wars with Indians take place.
Feb. 28, 1861	Colorado Territory is organized; Cheyenne Indians give up most of their lands.
1861-1865	Entering on Union side, Colorado Territory is scene of Civil War fighting.
1867	Denver becomes permanent capital.
1867	Treaty of Medicine Lodge is signed; Cheyenne and Arapaho move to Indian Territory (Oklahoma).
1870	Denver Pacific Railroad is completed to Denver.
Aug. 1, 1876	Colorado enters the Union as the thirty-eighth state.
1876	Convention meeting in Denver adopts state constitution (March), which is ratified by voters (July).
1876	Gold mining in Leadville area is especially productive.
1877	University of Colorado at Boulder is founded.
1878	Adoption of Bland-Allison Act stimulates production of silver, causing silver boom.
1879	Ute Indians, originally given most of western Colorado, are relocated after massacre of Indian Agent Nathan Meeker and his colleagues.
1891	Gold production begins at Cripple Creek mine.
1890's	Following rapid growth, state experiences economic depression and severe labor strife.
Nov. 2, 1893	Women receive voting rights.
1906	U.S. Mint opens in Denver.
1906	Congress establishes Mesa Verde National Park.
Apr. 20, 1914	National Guardsmen burn a tent colony of striking Colorado Fuel and Iron Corporation miners, killing twenty; ten-day uprising follows, resulting in dispatch of federal troops.
1915	Rocky Mountain National Park is established.
1924	Ku Klux Klan members are elected to major state offices; Klan-endorsed politicians become governor and senator.
1927	Moffat Tunnel through the Rocky Mountains is completed.
1942	Relocation center for West Coast Japanese Americans is established near Granada.

Nineteenth century painter Frederic Remington's fanciful depiction of Coronado's march through Colorado in 1541. (Library of Congress)

1954	Air Force Academy is authorized by Congress, with temporary quarters at Lowry Air Force Base; permanent quarters at Colorado Springs open four years later.
1957	North American Air Defense Command (NORAD) is established in Colorado Springs.
1959	Series of dams for irrigation, known as Colorado-Big Thompson Project, is completed.
1961	National Center for Atmospheric Research is created at Boulder.
Apr. 25, 1967	Colorado is first to pass liberal abortion laws.
1990's	Economic boom turns state's electorate toward political right.
1998	Marked Republican plurality of 120,000 voters replaces previous slight Democratic Party advantage.

Notes for Further Study

Published Sources. A standard history of Colorado is *Colorado: A History of the Centennial State* (3d ed. 1994) by Carl Abbott et al. Informal volumes of colorful incidents and facets of the state's past are Abott Fay's *I Never Knew That About Colorado: A Quaint Volume of Forgotten Lore* (1997) and Muriel Marshall's *Where Rivers Meet: Lore from* the Colorado Frontier (1996). Maxine Benson's *1001 Colorado Place Names* (1995) discusses place names chosen for their historical, geographical, or geological significance. A good guide to the state is *Colorado* (4th ed. 1998) by Jon Klusmire and Paul Chesley. For the state's politics and government, readers should consult Roger A. Walton's *Colorado: A Practical Guide to Its Government and Politics* (6th rev. ed. 1991). A useful guide to the state's geography is *Colorado: A Geography* (1983), by Mel Griffiths and Lynell Rubright. Sally Crum's *People of the Red Earth: Native Americans of Colorado* (1998) uses archeological evidence in discussing Colorado's original inhabitants.

Web Resources. Those visiting the state or wishing to know more about it might begin with the state of Colorado home page (http://www.state.co.us). The site opens with a message from the governor and includes pages on points of current interest; road conditions; ski, weather, and air pollution conditions; and other topics. Those seeking more information on the state's history might consult a history site (http://coloradohistory.com/index.html).

For public affairs, one can turn to Citizen's Guide to Colorado, published by the Colorado governor's office (http://governor.state.co.us/citizens.html), which includes links both to state agencies and to nonstate resources, as well as to organizational phone listings. Another site providing links to a multitude of Colorado sites is (http://beherenow.com/colorado/links.html). This site provides links to others such as The Colorado Mall, which has information on the state's people, geography, history, recreation, and other subjects, and to Colorado Links, a source on "everything from real estate to sports."

Counties

County	Sq. miles	1996 pop.
Adams	1,192.0	309,928
Alamosa	722.8	14,300
Arapahoe	803.2	455,035
Archuleta	1,349.4	7,953
Baca	2,555.9	4,491
Bent	1,514.0	5,478
Boulder	742.5	258,234
Chaffee	1,013.5	14,672
Cheyenne	1,781.5	2,323
Clear Creek	395.5	8,448
Conejos	1,287.3	7,869
Costilla	1,227.0	3,567
Crowley	789.0	4,200
Custer	738.9	3,062
Delta	1,142.2	25,563
Denver	153.3	497,840
Dolores	1,067.0	1,677
Douglas	840.2	111,647
Eagle	1,688.0	30,525
El Paso	2,126.7	472,924
Elbert	1,850.9	16,209
Fremont	1,533.0	41,694
Garfield	2,947.5	36,499
Gilpin	149.9	3,725
Grand	1,849.8	9,536
Gunnison	3,239.2	12,148
Hinsdale	1,117.8	666
Huerfano	1,590.9	6,564
Jackson	1,613.3	1,521
Jefferson	772.2	492,528
Kiowa	1,771.1	1,646
Kit Carson	2,161.0	7,218
La Plata	1,692.1	39,453
Lake	376.9	6,212
Larimer	2,601.4	221,725
Las Animas	4,773.0	14,485
Lincoln	2,586.3	5,578
Logan	1,838.6	18,021
Mesa	3,327.9	108,371
Mineral	875.8	681
Moffat	4,742.5	12,086
Montezuma	2,036.9	21,999
Montrose	2,240.7	29,601
Morgan	1,285.5	24,788
Otero	1,262.9	20,901
Ouray	542.1	3,140
Park	2,200.8	11,602
Phillips	687.7	4,340
Pitkin	970.2	13,489
Prowers	1,640.5	13,689
Pueblo	2,388.8	131,217
Rio Blanco	3,221.2	6,348
Rio Grande	912.6	11,319
Routt	2,361.8	16,975
Saguache	3,168.7	5,784
San Juan	387.5	564
San Miguel	1,286.5	5,208
Sedgwick	548.3	2,651

County	Sq. miles	1996 pop.
Summit	608.2	17,896
Teller	557.1	18,717
Washington	2,521.2	4,673

County	Sq. miles	1996 pop.
Weld	3,992.8	152,189
Yuma	2,366.1	9,284

Source: U.S. Census Bureau; National Association of Counties.

Cities
With 10,000 or more residents

Rank	City	Population
1	Denver	499,055
2	Colorado Springs	344,987
3	Aurora	250,604
4	Lakewood	136,883
5	Fort Collins	108,905
6	Pueblo	107,301
7	Arvada	97,610
8	Westminster	95,691

Rank	City	Population
9	Boulder	90,543
10	Thornton	74,139
11	Greeley	70,434
12	Longmont	62,078
13	Loveland	47,116
14	Grand Junction	41,265
15	Littleton	41,059
16	Broomfield	34,391

(continued)

Rank	City	Population
17	Englewood	31,593
18	Northglenn	29,892
19	Wheat Ridge	29,870
20	Lafayette	20,487
21	Louisville	17,871
22	Commerce City	17,355
23	Brighton	16,841
24	Golden	15,259
25	Parker	15,248
26	Canon City	15,239

Rank	City	Population
27	Castle Rock	14,798
28	Greenwood Village	14,449
29	Fountain	13,900
30	Durango	13,854
31	Federal Heights	11,572
32	Montrose	11,451
33	Sterling	10,431
34	Fort Morgan	10,049

Population figures are estimated for mid-1998.

Source: U.S. Bureau of the Census.

Index to Tables

NA = Reliable data are not available.

DEMOGRAPHICS

Resident state and national populations, 1970-1997

Population figures given in thousands

	State pop.	U.S. pop.	Share	Rank
1970	2,210	203,302	1.1%	30
1980	2,890	226,546	1.3%	28
1985	3,209	237,924	1.4%	26
1990	3,294	248,765	1.3%	26
1995	3,742	262,761	1.4%	25
1997	3,893	267,636	1.5%	25

Source: U.S. Bureau of the Census.

Resident population by age, 1997

Age group	Total population
Under 5 years	274,000
5 to 17 years	742,000
18 to 24 years	363,000
25 to 34 years	547,000
35 to 44 years	701,000
45 to 54 years	553,000
55 to 64 years	321,000
65 to 74 years	220,000
75 to 84 years	130,000
85 years and over	44,000
Portion of residents 65 and older	10.1%
National average	12.7%

Population figures are rounded to nearest thousand persons;
figures include armed forces personnel stationed in state.
Source: U.S. Bureau of the Census.

Resident population by race, Hispanic origin, 1997

	State pop.	Share	U.S.
All residents	3,893,000	100.0%	100.0%
Hispanic white	522,000	13.4%	10.0%
non-Hispanic white	3,076,000	79.0%	72.7%
African American	168,000	4.3%	12.7%
Native American	36,000	0.9%	0.9%
Asian, Pacific Islander	90,000	2.3%	3.8%

Source: U.S. Bureau of the Census.

Projections of state population, 2000-2025

	Model A Uses interstate migration observed from 1975-1994	Model B Uses Bureau of Economic Analysis employment projections
Year	Population	Population
2000	4,168,000	4,154,000
2005	4,468,000	4,510,000
2010	4,658,000	4,837,000
2015	4,833,000	5,152,000
2020	5,012,000	5,454,000
2025	5,188,000	5,743,000

All population projections, including those for 2000, were calculated in 1997.
Source: U.S. Bureau of the Census, Population Paper Listings PPL-47.

VITAL STATISTICS

Average lifetime in years by race, 1989-1991

	State	U.S.	Rank
All residents	76.96	75.37	6
White residents	77.06	76.13	10
Black residents	72.41	69.16	2

Ranks are from longest-lived to least longest-lived. Ranks exclude Alaska, for which reliable data are not available. Rank for black residents is based on the 32 states for which reliable data are available.
Source: U.S. National Center for Health Statistics.

Infant mortality rates, 1980 and 1995

	State	U.S.
All residents		
1980	10.1	12.6
1995	6.5	7.6
White residents		
1980	9.8	11.0
1995	6.0	6.3
Black residents		
1980	19.1	21.4
1995	16.8	15.1

Figures represent deaths per 1,000 live births of resident infants under 1 year old, exclusive of fetal deaths; all-residents figures include other races not listed separately.
Source: U.S. National Center for Health Statistics.

Marriages and divorces

Marriages in 1996	34,500
Rate per 1,000 population, 1995	9.2
U.S. rate, 1995	8.9
Rank among all states	17
Divorces in 1996	NA
Rate per 1,000 population, 1995	NA
U.S. rate, 1995	4.4
Rank among all states	NA

Rank is from highest to lowest in country.
Source: U.S. National Center for Health Statistics.

Death rates by leading causes, 1995
Deaths per 100,000 resident population

Cause	State	U.S.
Heart disease	172.1	280.7
Cancer	145.9	204.9
Cerebrovascular diseases	42.7	60.1
Accidents and adverse effects	39.8	35.5
Motor vehicle accidents	18.6	16.5
Chronic obstructive pulmonary diseases	42.3	39.2
Diabetes mellitus	14.3	22.6
HIV	10.9	NA
Suicide	17.5	11.9
Homicide	5.7	8.7
All causes	667.6	880.0
Rank in overall death rate among states		47

Figures exclude nonresidents who die in state. Causes of death follow International Classification of Diseases. Rank is from highest to lowest in country.
Source: U.S. National Center for Health Statistics.

ECONOMY

Gross state product, 1990-1996
In current dollars

	State product	Increase
1990	$74.4 billion	
1993	$92.9 billion	
1994	$100.7 billion	8.40%
1995	$107.9 billion	7.15%
1996	$116.2 billion	7.69%

Source: U.S. Bureau of Economic Analysis; *Survey of Current Business,* June, 1998.

Gross state product by industry, 1996
In billions

Farms, forestry, fisheries	$1.8
Construction	5.4
Manufacturing.	14.4
Transportation, public utilities	12.1
Wholesale trade.	7.0
Retail trade	10.9
Finance, insurance, real estate	17.7
Services	22.1
Government	13.8
State total	$106.8
Total U.S.	$6,923.8
State share	1.54%
Rank among states.	23

Total figures include mining, not listed separately.
Source: U.S. Bureau of Economic Analysis; *Survey of Current Business,* June, 1998.

Personal income per capita, 1990 and 1997
In current dollars

	1990	1997
Per capita income	$19,322	$27,051
U.S. average	$19,188	$25,598
Rank among states	18	9

1997 data are preliminary.
Source: U.S. Bureau of Economic Analysis; *Survey of Current Business,* May, 1998.

Energy consumption, 1995
In trillions of British thermal units (BTU)

End-use sectors
Residential	242.0
Commercial	225.0
Industrial	282.8
Transportation	325.4

Sources of energy
Petroleum	390.5
Natural gas	288.7
Coal	337.3
Hydroelectric power.	22.9
Nuclear electric power	0
Total state per capita consumption	286.9
Total U.S. per capita consumption	344.4
Rank among states.	39
Total state energy consumption	1,075.2
Total U.S. energy consumption	90,547.4
State share of U.S. total	1.19%
Rank among states.	26

Total figures include items not listed separately.
Source: U.S. Energy Information Administration; *State Energy Data Report.*

Nonfarm employment by sectors, 1997

Total	1,977,000
Construction.	118,000
Manufacturing.	204,000
Transportation, public utilities	122,000
Wholesale trade, retail trade	481,000
Finance, insurance, real estate	127,000
Services	597,000
Government	315,000

Figures are rounded to nearest thousand persons. Total includes mining, not listed separately.
Source: U.S. Bureau of Labor Statistics; *Employment and Earnings,* monthly.

Foreign exports, 1990-1997
In millions of dollars

Year	State	U.S.	State share
1990	2,274	394,045	0.58%
1996	4,883	624,767	0.78%
1997	5,120	688,896	0.74%

Source: U.S. Bureau of the Census; *U.S. Merchandise Trade,* series FT 900.

LAND USE

Federally owned land, 1996

	State	U.S.	State share
Total acres	66,486,000	2,271,343,000	2.93%
Federally owned	24,129,000	563,129,000	4.28%
Federal share	36.3%	24.8%	—

Areas are rounded to nearest thousand acres. Figures for federally owned land do not include trust properties.
Source: U.S. General Services Administration; *Inventory Report on Real Property Owned by the United States Throughout the World*, annual.

Land use, 1992
In acres, rounded to nearest thousand

Total surface area	66,618,000
Federal land	23,923,000
Total nonfederal	42,240,000
Developed	1,694,000
Total rural	40,547,000
Cropland.	8,940,000
Pasture land	1,256,000
Range land	23,537,000
Forest land.	3,755,000
Minor cover/use.	3,059,000

Total surface area figures include water area not shown separately.
Source: U.S. Dept. of Agriculture; Soil Conservation Service; Iowa State University, Statistical Laboratory; *Summary Report, 1992 National Resources Inventory.*

Farms and crop acreage, 1997

	State	U.S.	Share	Rank
Farms (thousands)	25	2,058	1.21%	30
Acres (millions)	33	968	3.41%	11
Acres per farm	1,327	471	—	8
Acres planted	6,479	334,139	1.94%	17
Acres harvested	6,100	319,894	1.91%	17
Farm value (mill.)	$1,580	$108,805	1.45%	22

Numbers of farms are rounded to nearest thousand.
Source: U.S. Dept. of Agriculture; National Agricultural Statistics Service.

GOVERNMENT AND FINANCE

Units of local government, 1997

	State	Total U.S.	Rank
All local governments	1,869	87,453	16
Counties	63	3,043	24
Municipalities	269	19,372	29
Townships	0	16,629	—
School districts	180	13,726	25
Special districts	1,358	34,683	7

County ranks are based on the 48 states with county governments; township ranks are based on the 20 states with township governments; school district ranks are based on the 46 states with such districts.
Source: U.S. Bureau of the Census; *1997 Census of Governments, Government Organization*, Series GC97(1).

State government revenue, 1996

Total revenue	$11,866 mill.
General revenue	9,461 mill.
Per capita.	2,479
U.S. per capita average	2,910
Rank among states.	43
Intergovernmental revenue	
Total	$2,746 mill.
From federal government	2,726 mill.
From local government	20 mill.
Charges and Miscellaneous	
Total	$1,895 mill.
Current charges	1,071 mill.
Misc. general revenue	824 mill.
Taxes	
Total	$4,820 mill.
General sales	1,322 mill.
Selective sales.	716 mill.
License taxes	256 mill.
Individual income	2,274 mill.
Corporate income	206 mill.
Other.	47 mill.
Insurance trust revenue	2,405 mill.

Total revenue figures include items not listed separately.
Source: U.S. Bureau of the Census.

State government expenditures, 1996

General expenditures
Intergovernmental . . . . $2,850 mill.
Direct expenditures . . . . 6,052 mill.
Total. 8,902 mill.

Selected direct expenditures
Education . . . . $3,945 mill.
Public welfare. . . . . 2,081 mill.
Health, hospital . . . . 381 mill.
Highways . . . . 796 mill.
Police. 52 mill.
Corrections. . . . . 353 mill.
Natural resources. . . . . 158 mill.
Parks and recreation. . . . . 43 mill.
Government administration . . . . 294 mill.
Interest on debt . . . . 335 mill.

Other
State per capita expenditures $2,333
U.S. per capita average 2,854
Rank among states. 47
Total state expenditures . . . . 10,312 mill.
Total U.S. expenditures . . . . 859,959 mill.

Totals include items not listed separately.
Source: U.S. Bureau of the Census.

Jesse F. McDonald (R) 1905-1907
Henry A. Buchtel (R). 1907-1909
John F. Shafroth (D) 1909-1913
Elias M. Ammons (D). 1913-1915
George A. Carlson (R) 1915-1917
Julius C. Gunter (D) 1917-1919
Oliver H. Shoup (R) 1919-1923
William E. Sweet (D) 1923-1925
Clarence J. Morley (R) 1925-1927
William H. Adams (D) 1927-1933
Edwin C. Johnson (D) . . . . (r) 1933-1937
Ray H. Talbot (D). 1937
Teller Ammons (D). 1937-1939
Ralph L. Carr (R). 1939-1943
John C. Vivian (R) 1943-1947
William L. Knous (D). . . . . (r) 1947-1950
Walter W. Johnson (D) 1950-1951
Daniel I. J. Thornton (R). 1951-1955
Edwin C. Johnson (D) 1955-1957
Stephen L. R. McNichols (D) 1957-1963
John A. Love (R) . . . . (r) 1963-1973
John D. Vanderhoof (R) 1973-1975
Richard D. Lamm (D) 1975-1987
Roy Romer (D) 1987-1999
Bill Owens (R) 1999-

POLITICS

Governors since statehood
D = Democrat; R = Republican; O = other;
(r) resigned; (d) died in office; (i) removed from office

John L. Routt (R) 1876-1879
Frederick W. Pitkin (R). 1879-1883
James B. Grant (D) 1883-1885
Benjamin H. Eaton (R). 1885-1887
Alva Adams (D) 1887-1889
Job A. Cooper (R) 1889-1891
John L. Routt (R) 1891-1893
Davis H. Waite (D) 1893-1895
Albert W. McIntire (R) 1895-1897
Alva Adams (D) 1897-1899
Charles S. Thomas (O) 1899-1901
James B. Orman (O) 1901-1903
James H. Peabody (R) 1903-1905
Alva Adams (D) . . . . (r) 1905
James H. Peabody (R) 1905

Composition of state legislature, 1990-1998

	Democrats	Republicans
State House (65 seats)		
1990	27	38
1992	31	34
1994	24	41
1996	24	41
1998	25	40
State Senate (35 seats)		
1990	12	23
1992	16	19
1994	16	19
1996	15	20
1998	15	20

Figures for total seats may include independents and minor party members.
Source: Council of State Governments; *State Elective Officials and the Legislatures.*

Composition of congressional delegations, 1989-1999

	Dem	Rep	Total
House of Representatives			
101st Congress, 1989			
State delegates	3	3	6
Total U.S.	259	174	433
102d Congress, 1991			
State delegates	3	3	6
Total U.S.	267	167	434
103d Congress, 1993			
State delegates	2	4	6
Total U.S.	258	176	434
104th Congress, 1995			
State delegates	2	4	6
Total U.S.	197	236	433
105th Congress, 1997			
State delegates	2	4	6
Total U.S.	206	228	434
106th Congress, 1999			
State delegates	2	4	6
Total U.S.	211	222	433
Senate			
101st Congress, 1989			
State delegates	1	1	2
Total U.S.	55	45	100
102d Congress, 1991			
State delegates	1	1	2
Total U.S.	56	44	100
103d Congress, 1993			
State delegates	1	1	2
Total U.S.	57	43	100
104th Congress, 1995			
State delegates	0	2	2
Total U.S.	46	53	99
105th Congress, 1997			
State delegates	0	2	2
Total U.S.	45	55	100
106th Congress, 1999			
State delegates	0	2	2
Total U.S.	45	54	99

Figures are for starts of first sessions. Figure for U.S. Representatives for 101st Congress does not include Alabama and Indiana, which had vacancies. Figures for total U.S. Representatives for 102d, 103d, and 106th Congresses do not include Vermont, which had 1 Independent-Socialist. Figure for U.S. Representatives for 104th Congress does not include Vermont, which had 1 Independent-Socialist, and California, which had 1 vacancy. Figure for U.S. Representatives for 105th Congress does not include New York, which had 1 vacancy. Figure for U.S. Senators for 104th Congress does not include Oregon, which had 1 vacancy. Figure for U.S. Senators for 106th Congress does not include New Hampshire, which had 1 Independent.
Source: U.S. Congress; *Congressional Directory,* biennial.

Voter participation in presidential elections, 1992 and 1996

	1992	1996
State voting age pop.	2,579,000	2,843,000
Total U.S. voting age pop.	189,524,000	196,509,000
State share of U.S. total	1.4%	1.5%
Rank among states	25	25
Percent of state casting vote	60.8	55.3
Percent of U.S. total voting	55.1	49.0
Rank among states	20	16

Source: U.S. Bureau of the Census.

HEALTH AND MEDICAL CARE

Medicare, 1997

	Recipients	Payments
State	442,000	$2,216 mill.
Total U.S.	37,514,000	$206,064 mill.
State share	1.18%	1.08%
Rank among states	30	28

Recipient figures are rounded to nearest thousand persons. Ranks are from highest to lowest.
Source: U.S. Health Care Financing Administration.

Medicaid, 1996

	Recipients	Payments
State	271,000	$1,032 mill.
Total U.S.	35,028,000	$121,419 mill.
State share	0.77%	0.85%
Rank among states	34	31

Recipient figures are rounded to nearest thousand persons. Payment figures for fiscal year reflect federal and state contribution payments. Ranks are from highest to lowest.
Source: U.S. Health Care Financing Administration.

Health insurance coverage, 1996

	State	U.S.
Total persons covered	3,240,000	225,070,000
Total persons not covered	644,000	41,716,000
Part not covered	16.6%	15.6%
Rank among states	14	—
Children not covered	191,000	10,554,000
Part not covered	18.4%	14.8%
Rank among states	10	—

Ranks are from most to fewest uninsured. Population figures
are rounded to nearest thousand persons.
Source: U.S. Bureau of the Census.

AIDS, syphilis, tuberculosis, and measles cases, 1997

Cases	U.S.	State	Share
AIDS	58,443	380	0.65%
Syphilis	8,550	15	0.18%
Tuberculosis	18,534	93	0.50%
Measles	148,000	1,000	0.68%

Measles figures are rounded to nearest thousand cases.
Source: U.S. Centers for Disease Control and Prevention.

HOUSING

Homeownership rates, 1985-1997

	1985	1990	1997
State	63.6%	59.0%	64.1%
Total U.S.	63.9%	63.9%	65.7%
Rank among states	38	43	39

Source: U.S. Bureau of the Census.

Home sales, 1990 and 1997
In thousands of units

Existing home sales	1990	1997	Change
State sales	54.2	86.6	32.4
Total U.S. sales	3,560	4,730	1,170
State share of U.S. total	1.52%	1.83%	0.31%
Rank among states	25	20	—

Source: National Association of Realtors; *Real Estate Outlook: Market Trends and Insights.*

With nearly a half million residents, Denver is both Colorado's capital and its largest city. (PhotoDisc)

EDUCATION

Public school enrollment, 1995

State K-8 enrollment	479,000
Total U.S. K-8 enrollment	32,341,000
State share of total U.S.	1.48%
State 9-12 enrollment	177,000
Total U.S. 9-12 enrollment	12,500,000
State share of U.S. total	1.42%
State public school enroll. rate	92.5%
Overall U.S. rate	91.6%
Rank among states	25

Enrollment figures (which include unclassified students) are rounded to nearest thousand pupils in fall term; kindergarten (K)-8 grade enrollment figures include some prekindergarten students. Enrollment rate is based on percentage of persons 5-17 years old. Rank is from highest to lowest.

Source: U.S. National Center for Education Statistics.

Public college finances, 1996

State FTE enrollment	136,100
Total U.S. FTE enrollment	8,268,800
State share of total U.S.	1.65%
Rank among states	22
State and local appropriations	$482,300,000
Total U.S. state and local appropriations	$39,699 mill.
State share of total U.S.	1.21%
Rank among states	27
State net tuition revenues	$432,500,000
Total U.S. net tuition	$18,348,100,000
State share of total U.S.	2.36%
Rank among states	13

FTE=Full-time equivalent; credit and noncredit enrollment including summer session in academic year ending in 1996.

Enrollments are rounded to nearest thousand students. Net tuition revenues exclude appropriation to students attending in-state public institutions. Rankings are from highest shares to lowest.

Source: Research Associates of Washington.

TRANSPORTATION AND TRAVEL

Highway mileage, 1996

Interstate	954
Other arterial	8,337
Collector roads	17,885
Local roads	58,930
Urban roads	13,658
Rural roads	71,139
Total state	84,797
U.S. total	3,933,985
State share	2.2%
Rank among states	22

Source: U.S. Federal Highway Administration.

Motor vehicle registrations and driver licenses, 1996

In thousands

Vehicle registrations	State	U.S.	Share	Rank
Autos, trucks, buses	3,433	206,365	1.66%	21
Autos only	1,891	128,439	1.47%	22
Motorcycles	94	3,832	2.45%	14
Driver licenses	2,757	179,539	1.54%	21

Figures do not include vehicles owned by military services.

Source: U.S. Federal Highway Administration; *Highway Statistics; Selected Highway Statistics and Charts.*

Domestic travel expenditures, 1995

Spending by U.S. residents on overnight trips and day trips of at least 100 miles

Total expenditures in state	$6,707 mill.
Total expenditures in U.S.	$360,314 mill.
State share of total U.S.	1.86%
Rank among states	17

Source: Travel Industry Association of America.

CRIME AND LAW ENFORCEMENT

State and local police officers, 1996

Local police	5,451
State police	581
Sheriffs	3,324
Total	9,896
Officers per 10,000 residents	26
U.S. average	25
Rank among states	10

Figures cover full-time sworn officers; totals include special police not shown separately.
Source: U.S. Bureau of Justice Statistics; *Census of State and Local Law Enforcement Agencies, 1996.*

Crime rates, 1996

Rates per 100,000 resident population

Violent crimes	State	U.S.
Total violent	405	634
Murder	4.7	7.4
Forcible rape	46.2	36.1
Robbery	98	202
Aggravated assault	255	388
Property crimes		
Total property	4,714	4,445
Burglary	901	943
Larceny/theft	3,416	2,976
Motor vehicle theft	398	526
Totals	5,119	5,079

Source: U.S. Federal Bureau of Investigation; *Crime in the United States,* annual.

State prison populations, 1980-1996

	State	U.S.	State share
1980	2,629	305,458	0.86%
1990	7,671	708,393	1.08%
1996	12,438	1,025,624	1.21%

Figures exclude prisoners in federal penitentiaries.
Source: U.S. Bureau of Justice Statistics.

Connecticut

Location: New England (northeastern continental United States)

Area and rank: 4,845 square miles (12,550 square kilometers); 5,544 square miles (14,359 square kilometers) including water; forty-eighth largest state in area

Coastline: 0 miles (0 kilometers)

Shoreline: 618 miles (995 kilometers)

Population and rank: 3,269,858 (1997); twenty-eighth largest state in population

Capital: Hartford

Largest city: Bridgeport (137,425 people in 1998)

Entered Union and rank: January 9, 1788; fifth state

Present constitution adopted: December 30, 1965

Counties: 8

State name: "Connecticut" is derived from the Indian word "Quinnehtukqut," meaning "beside the long tidal river"

State nickname: Nutmeg State

Motto: *Qui transtulit sustinet* (He who transplanted still sustains)

State flag: Azure field with state coat of arms above banner with state motto

Hartford, Connecticut's capital and second-largest city, after Bridgeport. (Connecticut Office of Tourism/John Muldoon)

Highest point: Mount Frissell — 2,380 feet (725 meters)

Lowest point: Long Island Sound — sea level

Highest recorded temperature: 105 degrees Fahrenheit (41 degrees Celsius) — Waterbury, 1926

Lowest recorded temperature: −32 degrees Fahrenheit (−36 degrees Celsius) — Falls Village, 1943

State song: "Yankee Doodle"

State tree: White Oak

State flower: Mountain Laurel

State bird: American Robin

State animal: Sperm Whale

Connecticut History

Connecticut is the third smallest state in area in the Union, after Rhode Island and Delaware. It is also the fourth most densely populated state. Positioned at the southernmost part of New England, Connecticut is bordered by New York on the west, Rhode Island on the east, Massachusetts on the north, and Long Island Sound—an arm of the Atlantic Ocean—on the south. Like most New England states, Connecticut is shaped by its abundance of water. It has more than 1,000 lakes and 8,400 miles of rivers and streams. The three major rivers flowing through the state, the Connecticut, the Housatonic, and the Thames, provide ports, fishing, and power for industry.

The Connecticut River Valley has very fertile land; potatoes, corn, onions, lettuce, tobacco, and other crops are grown there. Forests cover 60 percent of the state, making Connecticut one of the most wooded states in the United States. Maple trees are used to supply sugar and syrup. Until the nineteenth century, salmon fishing was a highly profitable industry. After a dam was built on the Connecticut River, preventing salmon from reaching their spawning grounds, the salmon supply was depleted.

Early History. Connecticut was inhabited by American Indian tribes for thousands of years before the first Europeans came to North America. By the 1600's approximately twenty thousand Algonquian Indians lived in the region. The dominant tribe was the Pequot, a warrior group who conquered most of the Connecticut River Valley in the 1500's. Other tribes included the Narragansetts, Quinnipiacs, Mohegans, and Saukiogs, who hunted moose, deer, and bear and grew corn, beans, and squash.

Dutch explorer Adriaen Block sailed the Connecticut River in 1614, meeting friendly Podunk Indians. In 1633 Dutch settlers built the House of Good Hope trading post near modern Hartford, where they traded with the Native Americans. In the same year, English settlers founded Windsor. Violence erupted between the settlers and the Pequots in 1637 over land disputes. The Native Americans were defeated during the Pequot War,

with losses of six hundred people. Many remaining Native Americans left the state, and by 1990, Indians made up only 0.2 percent of the population.

Colonization. In 1638, 250 Puritans from the Massachusetts Bay Colony established the New Haven Colony. The government was based on the Fundamental Agreement, which stated that the Bible was the supreme law. The colony was not inclusive; only Puritans were allowed to vote or hold office.

The residents of Wethersfield, Windsor, and Hartford joined to form the Colony of Connecticut in 1639. This colony's government was based

Harkness Tower at Yale University, which was founded in New Haven in 1701. (Connecticut Office of Tourism/Bob Gregson)

on the teachings of Reverend Thomas Hooker, which were known as the Fundamental Orders. A Puritan preacher, Hooker believed that the right to vote should belong to all, regardless of their religion. The Fundamental Orders, which served as Connecticut's constitution for many years, were the first document in the New World to give the government its power from the "free consent of the people."

In 1643 Connecticut, New Haven, Massachussetts, and Plymouth colonies banded together, forming the Confederation of New England. The colonies stayed independent of each other but made a pact to act together in times of war. In 1662, the Connecticut colony received a royal charter, allowing it self-rule. The charter was revoked, however, twenty-three years later by King James. Edmund Andros, acting for the Duke of York, tried to claim the area west of the Connecticut River for the New York colony. The residents of Connecticut refused to turn over their charter, supposedly hiding it in an oak tree, and they were able to resume self-rule in 1689. Connecticut became a state, the fifth in the Union, in 1788.

The American Revolution. Connecticut played a major role in the American Revolution. It sent thirty thousand soldiers into action—more, in relation to its population, than any other colony. These men included more than three hundred black soldiers. General George Washington called Connecticut the "Provisions State" because it sent so many supplies and munitions to the soldiers. The colony's navy captured more than forty British ships.

Connecticut produced both villains and heroes. One of its residents, Benedict Arnold, became a spy for the British, led English troops in an attack at Fort Griswold, and burned down the city of New London. Connecticut's Nathan Hale was a spy for the Union and became famous for the last words he uttered before the British hanged him.

Slavery in Connecticut. In the mid-1700's about three to five thousand blacks lived in the colony, most of them slaves. A law was passed in 1774 prohibiting residents from bringing in new slaves, and the 1784 Connecticut Emancipation Law allowed children born to slaves to be freed at the age of twenty-five. After the Revolution, all slaves who fought were freed.

A well-publicized Connecticut court case in 1839 brought the issue of slavery to national attention. Africans carried in the Spanish slave ship *Amistad* mutinied and tried to force the crew to turn the ship back to Africa. The crew instead secretly headed for Long Island, and the rebels, led by Joseph Cinqué, stood trial in Hartford for murder and piracy. In 1840 the U.S. Supreme Court ruled that the Africans were born free and taken as slaves against their will, so they were returned home. Slavery was banished in Connecticut in 1848. Later, the antislavery state sent more than fifty-seven thousand men to fight in the Civil War on the Union side.

Industry. In its early days, Connecticut's economy depended on agriculture and fishing. Its economy grew during the early 1800's with the construction of cotton, wool, and paper mills. Samuel Colt invented the six-shooter, the first repeating pistol, and its factories boomed. A machine to remove seeds from cotton, the cotton gin, invented in 1793 by Eli Whitney, added to the growth of industry.

Connecticut was hit hard by the Great Depression of the 1930's, with 22 percent of the state's workers unemployed. However, its economy bounced back during World War II. Connecticut produced more war supplies per person than any other state. In the late 1940's, more than half of its adult population worked in factories. Most of the industry was centered in ten towns, especially New Haven, Bridgeport, and Danbury, and half of Connecticut residents lived in these factory towns.

After the 1950's, textile production and other factory work subsided, and service jobs grew. Most middle-class families left the cities, and poverty increased in urban areas. Urban renewal programs initiated in the 1950's-1970's could not counter the riots that took place in poor areas in 1967.

Economy. By the end of the twentieth century, Hartford was the insurance capital of the world, a position it had held since the late 1700's. Groton was the submarine capital of the world in the early part of the century, but massive layoffs in the defense industry in the 1990's forced the closure of many shipyards and factories. Connecticut's population fell by several thousand during this period.

The state's economy was revitalized by the Mashantucket Pequot Indian Foxwoods Casino,

The Connecticut River was historically the state's principal transportation route and the center of its richest agricultural region. (Connecticut Office of Tourism/John Muldoon)

which opened in 1993 as the largest casino in the Western Hemisphere. Paying the state one-quarter of its earnings, the casino pumps about $1 billion per year into Connecticut's economy. Nevertheless, the state imposed its first income tax in 1993, to the dismay of many.

Politics. Connecticut traditionally has been a Republican state. In 1974, however, Ella T. Grasso, a Democrat and the first Connecticut governor of Italian descent, became the first woman governor of a state elected in her own right. In 1981 Thirman Milner of Hartford became the first African American mayor of a New England city.

Crime rates fell in the 1990's, and efforts were being made to clean up Connecticut's deteriorating inner cities. The state government instituted a drug-policy reform in which drug addicts received methadone (a heroin substitute) treatments and thereby possibly avoided long-term imprisonment. Connecticut was the first state to place drug courts in every jurisdiction. About 75 percent of the defendants stay in the program, compared to about 25 percent in regular drug-treatment programs.

Lauren M. Mitchell

Connecticut Time Line

1600's	Connecticut area is inhabited by Native American Algonquians dominated by Pequots.
1614	Dutch explorer Adriaen Block sails up Connecticut River and claims region for Holland.
June 6, 1633	Dutch buy land from Pequot Indians and build trading post at modern Hartford.
1633	English settle Windsor.
1636	Thomas Hooker and followers settle at Hartford.
1637	Pequot War ends with defeat of Indians.
1638	New Haven is founded.
1639	Hartford, Wethersfield, and Windsor unite, forming Connecticut Colony.
Jan. 14, 1639	Fundamental Orders of Connecticut, the first written constitution, is adopted.
1647	Connecticut is first New England colony to hang a woman convicted of witchcraft.
1662	Connecticut Colony is officially chartered.
Jan. 5, 1665	New Haven becomes part of Connecticut Colony.
1701	Yale University is founded in New Haven.
1740	First tinware in New World is made in central Connecticut by Edward and William Pattison.
1779	New Haven is attacked, and Fairfield and Norwalk are burned during Revolutionary War.
1781	Benedict Arnold, a Connecticut traitor leading British troops, burns New London.
1784	First American law school is founded in New Litchfield.
1784	Connecticut Emancipation Law rules children born to slaves become free at age twenty-five.
Jan. 9, 1788	Connecticut becomes fifth state in Union.
1794	Eli Whitney of Connecticut invents cotton gin.
1798	Whitney establishes mass production at gun-making plant in Whitneyville.
1810	First silk mill in the Union is built in Mansfield.
1818	New state constitution is ratified.

(continued)

1833	Hartford and New Haven Railroad opens.
1835	Samuel Colt of Connecticut invents six-shooter pistol.
1841	Africans sold into slavery win freedom in Hartford trials after mutiny of *Amistad*.
1861-1865	Connecticut sends more than 57,000 men to fight in the Civil War for the Union.
1882	Knights of Columbus brotherhood is founded in New Haven.
1888	Great Blizzard of 1888 leaves hundreds dead.
1910	U.S. Coast Guard Academy moves to New London.
1917	U.S. naval submarine base opens at Groton.
1917-1918	During World War I, Connecticut is supply center; sends more than 60,000 men to fight.
1930's	Great Depression hits the industrial state hard; 150,000 are unemployed.
1941-1945	During World War II, Connecticut is supply center.
1943	Connecticut is first state to establish a civil rights commission.
Jan., 1954	First atomic-powered submarine, *Nautilus*, is launched at Groton.
1965	New state constitution is ratified.
1969	Race riots occur in black and Puerto Rican parts of Hartford.
1973	Waste agency opens, to combat widespread pollution.
1974	Connecticut's Ella Grasso is first woman to be elected a state governor without succeeding her husband.
1979	State bans construction of new nuclear plants.
1981	Thomas Milner of Hartford becomes first black mayor of a New England city.
1984	Ellen Ash Peters is first woman named to Connecticut supreme court.
1991	City of Bridgeport files for bankruptcy.
1991	First state income tax is established.
1996	*Sheff v. O'Neill* case, claiming racial segregation in schools, reaches state supreme court.

Notes for Further Study

Published Sources. Among the many books on Connecticut state history, a good place to start is *Connecticut* (1989) by William Hubbell and Roger Eddy. *Connecticut: An Explorer's Guide* (1999), by Barnett D. Laschever and Andi Marie Fusco, and *Connecticut: Driving through History* (1998), by Suzanne Staubach, are excellent travel books that give tourist information, as well as history lessons. Useful books on Native Americans in Connecticut include *Algonquians of the East Coast* (1996), published by Time-Life Books. It reveals the history, customs, and mythology of this important Connecticut tribe, with many photos. Alfred A. Cave's excellent *The Pequot War* (1997)

explains the Puritan belief that Native Americans were "agents of Satan" and were to be destroyed. *The Puritan Family: Religion and Domestic Relations in Seventeenth Century New England* (1990), by Edmund Sears Morgan, discusses the Puritan ideal of social virtue and the communities they established in New England.

Howard Jones's *Mutiny on the Amistad: The Saga of a Slave Revolt and Its Impact on American Abolition, Law and Diplomacy* (1988) is a full-scale treatment of the infamous case in which African slaves won their freedom. Another excellent study is *Black Mutiny: The Revolt on the Schooner Amistad* (1953) by William A. Owens and Michael E.

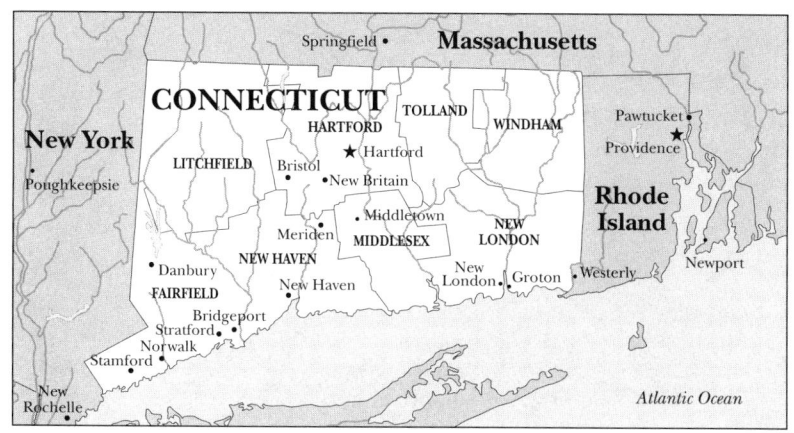

Counties

County	Sq. miles	1996 pop.
Fairfield	827,645	625.9
Hartford	851,783	735.5
Litchfield	174,092	920.0
Middlesex	143,196	369.3
New Haven	804,219	605.8
New London	254,957	666.1
Tolland	128,699	410.1
Windham	102,525	512.8

Source: U.S. Census Bureau; National Association of Counties.

Dyson, which provides one of the most detailed accounts of the Amistad mutiny. *Colt: The Making of an American Legend* (1996), by William Hosley, Constance Mc-Laughlin Green's *Eli Whitney and the Birth of American Technology* (1998), and *Eli Whitney, Great Inventor: Discovery Biography* (1991), by Jean Lee Latham and Louis F. Cary, are good biographies of these important Connecticut industrial leaders.

Web Resources. The best starting place on the World Wide Web is the official state of Connecticut site (http://www.state.ct.us), which covers government information, news, history, and tourist attractions. Other good tourist sites are the Connecticut Tourism Home Page (http://www.state.ct.us/tourism), Visit Connecticut (http://www.visitconnecticut. com), and Connecticut.com (http://www.connecticut.com), which also provides a list of the state's firsts.

For state and county data from the U.S. Census Bureau, see Connecticut Profiles (http://www.census.gov/datamap/www/09.html). Two good resources for state news, which are updated daily, are Connecticut Central (http://www.ctcentral.com), with news from the *New Haven Register* and *The Middletown Press,* and *The Hartford Courant* (http://www.courant.com), which also provides the history of the newspaper. For specific history, the Pequot Web site (http://ourworld .compuserve.com/homepages/cclemmons) has much data on the Pequot War in Connecticut. More information on Native Americans can be found at Nipmuc Indian Association of Connecticut (http://www.nativeweb.org/NativeTech/Nipmuc), with news of Nipmucs and links to other American Indian Web sites. The Fundamental Orders of 1639 site (http://www.constitution.org/bcp/fo_1639.htm) gives the history of the constitution and reprints it. The Amistad mutiny is discussed at The Amistad Case (http://www.nara.gov/education/teaching/amistad/home.html), which even provides legal documents.

Cities
With 10,000 or more residents

Rank	City	Population
1	Bridgeport	137,425
2	Hartford	131,523
3	New Haven	123,189
4	Stamford	110,689
5	Waterbury	105,346
6	Norwalk	78,064
7	New Britain	70,492
8	Danbury	65,829
9	Bristol	59,158
10	Meriden	56,667
11	West Haven	51,639

Rank	City	Population
12	Milford (remainder)	48,254
13	Middletown	43,640
14	Shelton	37,873
15	Norwich	34,931
16	Torrington	34,451
17	Naugatuck	30,231
18	New London	23,869
19	Ansonia	17,716
20	Derby	11,942

Population figures are estimated for mid-1998.
Source: U.S. Bureau of the Census.

Replica of the Amistad *slave ship at Mystic Harbor.* (PhotoDisc)

Index to Tables

NA = Reliable data are not available.

DEMOGRAPHICS

Resident state and national populations, 1970-1997
Population figures given in thousands

	State pop.	U.S. pop.	Share	Rank
1970	3,032	203,302	1.5%	24
1980	3,108	226,546	1.4%	25
1985	3,201	237,924	1.3%	27
1990	3,287	248,765	1.3%	27
1995	3,267	262,761	1.2%	28
1997	3,270	267,636	1.2%	28

Source: U.S. Bureau of the Census.

Resident population by age, 1997

Age group	Total population
Under 5 years	217,000
5 to 17 years	575,000
18 to 24 years	258,000
25 to 34 years	489,000
35 to 44 years	563,000
45 to 54 years	429,000
55 to 64 years	269,000
65 to 74 years	242,000
75 to 84 years	169,000
85 years and over	59,000
Portion of residents 65 and older	14.4%
National average	12.7%

Population figures are rounded to nearest thousand persons; figures include armed forces personnel stationed in state.
Source: U.S. Bureau of the Census.

Resident population by race, Hispanic origin, 1997

	State pop.	Share	U.S.
All residents	3,270,000	100.0%	100.0%
Hispanic white	229,000	7.0%	10.0%
non-Hispanic white	2,657,000	81.3%	72.7%
African American	300,000	9.2%	12.7%
Native American	8,000	0.2%	0.9%
Asian, Pacific Islander	76,000	2.3%	3.8%

Source: U.S. Bureau of the Census.

Projections of state population, 2000-2025

	Model A Uses interstate migration observed from 1975-1994	Model B Uses Bureau of Economic Analysis employment projections
Year	Population	Population
2000	3,284,000	3,286,000
2005	3,317,000	3,291,000
2010	3,400,000	3,303,000
2015	3,506,000	3,332,000
2020	3,621,000	3,376,000
2025	3,739,000	3,428,000

All population projections, including those for 2000, were calculated in 1997.
Source: U.S. Bureau of the Census, Population Paper Listings PPL-47.

VITAL STATISTICS

Average lifetime in years by race, 1989-1991

	State	U.S.	Rank
All residents	76.91	75.37	8
White residents	77.44	76.13	6
Black residents	70.84	69.16	7

Ranks are from longest-lived to least longest-lived. Ranks exclude Alaska, for which reliable data are not available. Rank for black residents is based on the 32 states for which reliable data are available.
Source: U.S. National Center for Health Statistics.

Infant mortality rates, 1980 and 1995

	State	U.S.
All residents		
1980	11.2	12.6
1995	7.2	7.6
White residents		
1980	10.2	11.0
1995	6.5	6.3
Black residents		
1980	19.1	21.4
1995	12.6	15.1

Figures represent deaths per 1,000 live births of resident infants under 1 year old, exclusive of fetal deaths; all-residents figures include other races not listed separately.
Source: U.S. National Center for Health Statistics.

Marriages and divorces

Marriages in 1996.	21,400
Rate per 1,000 population, 1995.	6.7
U.S. rate, 1995	8.9
Rank among all states	46
Divorces in 1996	10,500
Rate per 1,000 population, 1995.	2.9
U.S. rate, 1995	4.4
Rank among all states	45

Rank is from highest to lowest in country.
Source: U.S. National Center for Health Statistics.

Death rates by leading causes, 1995

Deaths per 100,000 resident population

Cause	State	U.S.
Heart disease	298.9	280.7
Cancer	215.6	204.9
Cerebrovascular diseases	57.2	60.1
Accidents and adverse effects	32.9	35.5
Motor vehicle accidents	10.7	16.5
Chronic obstructive pulmonary diseases	35.5	39.2
Diabetes mellitus	18.1	22.6
HIV	18.4	NA
Suicide	9.9	11.9
Homicide	-	8.7
All causes	899.5	880.0
Rank in overall death rate among states		27

Figures exclude nonresidents who die in state. Causes of death follow International Classification of Diseases. Rank is from highest to lowest in country.
Source: U.S. National Center for Health Statistics.

ECONOMY

Gross state product, 1990-1996
In current dollars

	State product	Increase
1990	$98.5 billion	
1993	$107.5 billion	
1994	$112.6 billion	4.74%
1995	$118.6 billion	5.33%
1996	$124.0 billion	4.55%

Source: U.S. Bureau of Economic Analysis; *Survey of Current Business,* June, 1998.

Gross state product by industry, 1996
In billions

Farms, forestry, fisheries	$0.8
Construction	3.5
Manufacturing	20.8
Transportation, public utilities	7.2
Wholesale trade	7.9
Retail trade	8.9
Finance, insurance, real estate	30.3
Services	23.6
Government	9.9
State total	$113.0
Total U.S.	$6,923.8
State share	1.63%
Rank among states	21

Total figures include mining, not listed separately.
Source: U.S. Bureau of Economic Analysis; *Survey of Current Business,* June, 1998.

Personal income per capita, 1990 and 1997
In current dollars

	1990	1997
Per capita income	$26,507	$36,263
U.S. average	$19,188	$25,598
Rank among states	1	1

1997 data are preliminary.
Source: U.S. Bureau of Economic Analysis; *Survey of Current Business,* May, 1998.

Energy consumption, 1995
In trillions of British thermal units (BTU)

End-use sectors

Residential	242.1
Commercial	180.1
Industrial	165.3
Transportation	204.5

Sources of energy

Petroleum	370.4
Natural gas	136.0
Coal	23.7
Hydroelectric power	14.0
Nuclear electric power	199.8
Total state per capita consumption	240.4
Total U.S. per capita consumption	344.4
Rank among states	46
Total state energy consumption	786.3
Total U.S. energy consumption	90,547.4
State share of U.S. total	0.87%
Rank among states	34

Total figures include items not listed separately.
Source: U.S. Energy Information Administration; *State Energy Data Report.*

Nonfarm employment by sectors, 1997

Total	1,616,000
Construction	57,000
Manufacturing	276,000
Transportation, public utilities	75,000
Wholesale trade, retail trade	354,000
Finance, insurance, real estate	131,000
Services	497,000
Government	226,000

Figures are rounded to nearest thousand persons. Total includes mining, not listed separately.
Source: U.S. Bureau of Labor Statistics; *Employment and Earnings,* monthly.

Foreign exports, 1990-1997
In millions of dollars

Year	State	U.S.	State share
1990	4,356	394,045	1.11%
1996	6,100	624,767	0.98%
1997	7,058	688,896	1.02%

Source: U.S. Bureau of the Census; *U.S. Merchandise Trade,* series FT 900.

LAND USE

Federally owned land, 1996

	State	U.S.	State share
Total acres	3,135,000	2,271,343,000	0.14%
Federally owned	7,000	563,129,000	0.00%
Federal share	0.2%	24.8%	—

Areas are rounded to nearest thousand acres. Figures for
federally owned land do not include trust properties.
Source: U.S. General Services Administration; *Inventory Report
on Real Property Owned by the United States Throughout the
World,* annual.

Land use, 1992
In acres, rounded to nearest thousand

Total surface area	3,212,000
Federal land.	15,000
Total nonfederal.	3,054,000
Developed	816,000
Total rural	2,238,000
Cropland.	229,000
Pasture land	110,000
Range land	0
Forest land.	1,760,000
Minor cover/use.	140,000

Total surface area figures include water area not shown
separately.
Source: U.S. Dept. of Agriculture; Soil Conservation Service;
Iowa State University, Statistical Laboratory; *Summary
Report, 1992 National Resources Inventory.*

Farms and crop acreage, 1997

	State	U.S.	Share	Rank
Farms (thousands)	4	2,058	0.19%	45
Acres (millions)	—	968	—	—
Acres per farm	97	471	—	47
Acres planted	112	334,139	0.03%	46
Acres harvested	109	319,894	0.03%	46
Farm value (mill.)	$76	$108,805	0.07%	47

State acreage total is less than 500,000 acres
Numbers of farms are rounded to nearest thousand.
Source: U.S. Dept. of Agriculture; National Agricultural
Statistics Service.

GOVERNMENT AND FINANCE

Units of local government, 1997

	State	Total U.S.	Rank
All local governments	583	87,453	41
Counties	0	3,043	—
Municipalities	30	19,372	45
Townships	149	16,629	19
School districts	17	13,726	43
Special districts	387	34,683	31

County ranks are based on the 48 states with county
governments; township ranks are based on the 20 states
with township governments; school district ranks are based
on the 46 states with such districts.
Township figures include "town" governments.
Source: U.S. Bureau of the Census; *1997 Census of Governments,
Government Organization,* Series GC97(1).

State government revenue, 1996

Total revenue	$14,349 mill.
General revenue	12,357 mill.
Per capita.	3,782
U.S. per capita average	2,910
Rank among states	6

Intergovernmental revenue

Total	$2,734 mill.
From federal government	2,729 mill.
From local government.	5 mill.

Charges and Miscellaneous

Total	$1,793 mill.
Current charges	845 mill.
Misc. general revenue	948 mill.

Taxes

Total	$7,830 mill.
General sales	2,445 mill.
Selective sales.	1,487 mill.
License taxes	331 mill.
Individual income	2,614 mill.
Corporate income	641 mill.
Other	311 mill.
Insurance trust revenue	1,972 mill.

Total revenue figures include items not listed separately.
Source: U.S. Bureau of the Census.

State government expenditures, 1996

General expenditures

Intergovernmental	$2,424 mill.
Direct expenditures	9,311 mill.
Total	11,736 mill.

Selected direct expenditures

Education	$2,888 mill.
Public welfare	2,815 mill.
Health, hospital	1,340 mill.
Highways	712 mill.
Police	105 mill.
Corrections	465 mill.
Natural resources	72 mill.
Parks and recreation	48 mill.
Government administration	536 mill.
Interest on debt	912 mill.

Other

State per capita expenditures	$3,592
U.S. per capita average	2,854
Rank among states	8
Total state expenditures	13,530 mill.
Total U.S. expenditures	859,959 mill.

Totals include items not listed separately.
Source: U.S. Bureau of the Census.

POLITICS

Governors since statehood

D = Democrat; R = Republican; O = other;
(r) resigned; (d) died in office; (i) removed from office

Jonathan Trumbull	1776-1784
Matthew Griswold	1784-1786
Samuel Huntington (O)	(d) 1786-1796
Oliver Wolcott (O)	(d) 1796-1797
Jonathan Trumbull, Jr. (O)	(d) 1797-1809
John Treadwell (O)	1809-1811
Robert Griswold (O)	(d) 1811-1812
John Cotton Smith (O)	1812-1817
Oliver Wolcott II (O)	1817-1827
Gideon Tomlinson (O)	1827-1831
John S. Peters (O)	1831-1833
Henry W. Edwards (D)	1833-1834
Samuel A. Foot (O)	1834-1835
Henry W. Edwards (D)	1835-1838
William W. Ellsworth (O)	1838-1842
Chauncey F. Cleveland (D)	1842-1844
Roger S. Baldwin (O)	1844-1846
Isaac Toucey (D)	1846-1847

Clark Bissell (O)	1847-1849
Joseph Trumbull (O)	1849-1850
Thomas H. Seymour (D)	(r) 1850-1853
Charles H. Pond (D)	1853-1854
Henry Dutton (O)	1854-1855
William T. Minor (O)	1855-1857
Alexander H. Holley (R)	1857-1858
William A. Buckingham (R)	1858-1866
Joseph R. Hawley (R)	1866-1867
James E. English (D)	1867-1869
Marshall Jewell (R)	1869-1870
James E. English (D)	1870-1871
Marshall Jewell (R)	1871-1873
Charles R. Ingersoll (R)	1873-1877
Richard D. Hubbard (D)	1877-1879
Charles B. Andrews (R)	1879-1881
Hobart B. Bigelow (R)	1881-1883
Thomas M. Waller (D)	1883-1885
Henry B. Harrison (R)	1885-1887
Phineas C. Lounsbury (R)	1887-1889
Morgan G. Bulkeley (R)	1889-1893
Luzon B. Morris (D)	1893-1895
Owen Vincent Coffin (R)	1895-1897
Lorrin A. Cooke (R)	1897-1899
George S. Lounsbury (R)	1899-1901
George P. McLean (R)	1901-1903
Abiram Chamberlain (R)	1903-1905
Harry Roberts (R)	1905-1907
Rollin S. Woodruff (R)	1907-1909
George L. Lilley (R)	(d) 1909
Frank B. Weeks (R)	1909-1911
Simeon E. Baldwin (D)	1911-1915
Marcus H. Holcomb (R)	1915-1921
Everett J. Lake (R)	1921-1923
Charles A. Templeton (R)	1923-1925
Hiram Bingham (R)	(r) 1925
John H. Trumbull (R)	1925-1931
Wilbur L. Cross (D)	1931-1939
Raymond E. Baldwin (R)	1939-1941
Robert A. Hurley (D)	1941-1943
Raymond E. Baldwin (R)	(r) 1943-1946
Wilbert Snow (D)	1946-1947
James L. McConaughty (R)	(d) 1947-1948
James C. Shannon (R)	1948-1949
Charles B. Bowles (D)	1949-1951
John D. Lodge (R)	1951-1955
Abraham Ribicoff (D)	(r) 1955-1961
John N. Dempsey (D)	1961-1971
Thomas J. Meskill (R)	1971-1975
Ella T. Grasso (D)	1975-1980
William A. O'Neill (D)	1981-1991
Lowell P. Weicker, Jr. (O)	1991-1995
John G. Rowland (R)	1995-1999

Composition of state legislature, 1990-1998

	Democrats	Republicans
State House (151 seats)		
1990	87	64
1992	85	64
1994	90	61
1996	97	54
1998	96	54
State Senate (36 seats)		
1990	20	16
1992	19	17
1994	17	19
1996	19	17
1998	19	17

Figures for total seats may include independents and minor
party members.
Source: Council of State Governments; *State Elective Officials
and the Legislatures.*

Composition of congressional delegations, 1989-1999

	Dem	Rep	Total
House of Representatives			
101st Congress, 1989			
State delegates	3	3	6
Total U.S.	259	174	433
102d Congress, 1991			
State delegates	3	3	6
Total U.S.	267	167	434
103d Congress, 1993			
State delegates	3	3	6
Total U.S.	258	176	434
104th Congress, 1995			
State delegates	4	2	6
Total U.S.	197	236	433
105th Congress, 1997			
State delegates	4	2	6
Total U.S.	206	228	434
106th Congress, 1999			
State delegates	4	2	6
Total U.S.	211	222	433

	Dem	Rep	Total
Senate			
101st Congress, 1989			
State delegates	2	0	2
Total U.S.	55	45	100
102d Congress, 1991			
State delegates	2	0	2
Total U.S.	56	44	100
103d Congress, 1993			
State delegates	2	0	2
Total U.S.	57	43	100
104th Congress, 1995			
State delegates	2	0	2
Total U.S.	46	53	99
105th Congress, 1997			
State delegates	2	0	2
Total U.S.	45	55	100
106th Congress, 1999			
State delegates	2	0	2
Total U.S.	45	54	99

Figures are for starts of first sessions. Figure for U.S. Representatives for 101st Congress does not include Alabama
and Indiana, which had vacancies. Figures for total U.S.
Representatives for 102d, 103d, and 106th Congresses do
not include Vermont, which had 1 Independent-Socialist.
Figure for U.S. Representatives for 104th Congress does
not include Vermont, which had 1 Independent-Socialist,
and California, which had 1 vacancy. Figure for U.S.
Representatives for 105th Congress does not include
New York, which had 1 vacancy. Figure for U.S. Senators
for 104th Congress does not include Oregon, which had
1 vacancy. Figure for U.S. Senators for 106th Congress does not include New Hampshire, which had
1 Independent.
Source: U.S. Congress; *Congressional Directory*, biennial.

Voter participation in presidential elections, 1992 and 1996

	1992	1996
State voting age pop.	2,508,000	2,468,000
Total U.S. voting age pop.	189,524,000	196,509,000
State share of U.S. total	1.3%	1.3%
Rank among states	27	27
Percent of state casting vote	64.4	52.0
Percent of U.S. total voting	55.1	49.0
Rank among states	10	22

Source: U.S. Bureau of the Census.

HEALTH AND MEDICAL CARE

Medicare, 1997

	Recipients	Payments
State	508,000	$3,082 mill.
Total U.S.	37,514,000	$206,064 mill.
State share	1.35%	1.50%
Rank among states	26	22

Recipient figures are rounded to nearest thousand persons.
Ranks are from highest to lowest.
Source: U.S. Health Care Financing Administration.

Medicaid, 1996

	Recipients	Payments
State	329,000	$2,030 mill.
Total U.S.	35,028,000	$121,419 mill.
State share	0.94%	1.67%
Rank among states	31	18

Recipient figures are rounded to nearest thousand persons.
Payment figures for fiscal year reflect federal and state
contribution payments. Ranks are from highest to lowest.
Source: U.S. Health Care Financing Administration.

Health insurance coverage, 1996

	State	U.S.
Total persons covered	2,985,000	225,070,000
Total persons not covered	368,000	41,716,000
Part not covered	11.0%	15.6%
Rank among states	40	—
Children not covered	108,000	10,554,000
Part not covered	11.6%	14.8%
Rank among states	25	—

Ranks are from most to fewest uninsured. Population figures
are rounded to nearest thousand persons.
Source: U.S. Bureau of the Census.

AIDS, syphilis, tuberculosis, and measles cases, 1997

Cases	U.S.	State	Share
AIDS	58,443	1,222	2.09%
Syphilis	8,550	62	0.73%
Tuberculosis	18,534	126	0.68%
Measles	148,000	1,000	0.68%

Measles figures are rounded to nearest thousand cases.
Source: U.S. Centers for Disease Control and Prevention.

HOUSING

Homeownership rates, 1985-1997

	1985	1990	1997
State	69.0%	67.9%	68.1%
Total U.S.	63.9%	63.9%	65.7%
Rank among states	19	23	26

Source: U.S. Bureau of the Census.

Home sales, 1990 and 1997
In thousands of units

Existing home sales	1990	1997	Change
State sales	34.3	55.0	20.7
Total U.S. sales	3,560	4,730	1,170
State share of U.S. total	0.96%	1.16%	0.20%
Rank among states	34	30	—

Source: National Association of Realtors; *Real Estate Outlook: Market Trends and Insights.*

EDUCATION

Public school enrollment, 1995

State K-8 enrollment	384,000
Total U.S. K-8 enrollment	32,341,000
State share of total U.S.	1.19%
State 9-12 enrollment	134,000
Total U.S. 9-12 enrollment	12,500,000
State share of U.S. total	1.07%
State public school enroll. rate	91.7%
Overall U.S. rate.	91.6%
Rank among states.	28

Enrollment figures (which include unclassified students) are
rounded to nearest thousand pupils in fall term; kindergarten (K)-8 grade enrollment figures include some prekindergarten students. Enrollment rate is based on percentage of persons 5-17 years old. Rank is from highest to lowest.
Source: U.S. National Center for Education Statistics.

Public college finances, 1996

State FTE enrollment. 57,000
Total U.S. FTE enrollment 8,268,800
State share of total U.S.. . . . . 0.69%
Rank among states. 37
State and local appropriations $428,700,000
Total U.S. state and local
    appropriations. . . . . $39,699 mill.
State share of total U.S.. . . . . 1.08%
Rank among states. 32
State net tuition revenues. $192,800,000
Total U.S. net tuition $18,348,100,000
State share of total U.S.. . . . . 1.05%
Rank among states. 32

FTE=Full-time equivalent; credit and noncredit enrollment
    including summer session in academic year ending in
    1996.
Enrollments are rounded to nearest thousand students. Net
    tuition revenues exclude appropriation to students
    attending in-state public institutions. Rankings are from
    highest shares to lowest.
Source: Research Associates of Washington.

Motor vehicle registrations and driver licenses, 1996
In thousands

Vehicle registrations	State	U.S.	Share	Rank
Autos, trucks, buses	2,609	206,365	1.26%	30
Autos only	1,930	128,439	1.50%	21
Motorcycles	48	3,832	1.25%	27
Driver licenses	2,344	179,539	1.31%	30

Figures do not include vehicles owned by military services.
Source: U.S. Federal Highway Administration; *Highway
    Statistics; Selected Highway Statistics and Charts.*

Domestic travel expenditures, 1995
Spending by U.S. residents on overnight trips and day
trips of at least 100 miles

Total expenditures in state . . . . $3,810 mill.
Total expenditures in U.S.. . . . . $360,314 mill.
State share of total U.S.. . . . . 1.06%
Rank among states. 30

Source: Travel Industry Association of America.

TRANSPORTATION AND TRAVEL

Highway mileage, 1996

Interstate 344
Other arterial. 3,045
Collector roads. 4,162
Local roads 14,239
Urban roads. 11,680
Rural roads 8,920
Total state 20,600
U.S. total 3,933,985
State share 0.5%
Rank among states. 44

Source: U.S. Federal Highway Administration.

CRIME AND LAW ENFORCEMENT

State and local police officers, 1996

Local police 6,411
State police 1,022
Sheriffs 886
Total 8,525
Officers per 10,000 residents 26
U.S. average 25
Rank among states. 10

Figures cover full-time sworn officers; totals include special
    police not shown separately.
Source: U.S. Bureau of Justice Statistics; *Census of State and
    Local Law Enforcement Agencies, 1996.*

Crime rates, 1996

Rates per 100,000 resident population

Violent crimes	State	U.S.
Total violent	412	634
Murder	4.8	7.4
Forcible rape	23.1	36.1
Robbery	170	202
Aggravated assault	215	388

Property crimes		
Total property	3,816	4,445
Burglary	842	943
Larceny/theft	2,484	2,976
Motor vehicle theft	489	526
Totals	4,228	5,079

Source: U.S. Federal Bureau of Investigation; *Crime in the United States*, annual.

State prison populations, 1980-1996

	State	U.S.	State share
1980	4,308	305,458	1.41%
1990	10,500	708,393	1.48%
1996	15,007	1,025,624	1.46%

Figures exclude prisoners in federal penitentiaries.
Source: U.S. Bureau of Justice Statistics.

Delaware

Location: East Coast of continental United States

Area and rank: 1,982 square miles (5,153 square kilometers); 2,489 square miles (6,447 square kilometers) including water; forty-ninth largest state in area

Coastline: 28 miles (45 kilometers)

Shoreline: 381 miles (613 kilometers)

Population and rank: 739,337 (1998); forty-fifth largest state in population

Capital: Dover

Governor Ross mansion in Dover. (Courtesy Delaware Tourism Office)

Largest city: Wilmington (71,678 people in 1998)

Entered Union and rank: December 7, 1787; first state

Present constitution adopted: 1897

Counties: 3

State name: "Delaware" was named after the Delaware River and Bay, which was named for Sir Thomas West, Baron De La Warr

DECEMBER 7, 1787

State nicknames: Diamond State; First State; Small Wonder

Motto: Liberty and independence

State flag: Blue field with yellow diamond with state coat of arms and date of entrance to Union

Highest point: Ebright Road — 442 feet (135 meters)

Lowest point: Atlantic Ocean — sea level

Highest recorded temperature: 110 degrees Fahrenheit (43 degrees Celsius) — Millsboro, 1930

Lowest recorded temperature: –17 degrees Fahrenheit (–27 degrees Celsius) — Millsboro, 1893

State song: "Our Delaware"

State tree: American holly

State flower: Peach blossom

State bird: Blue Hen chicken

State fish: Weakfish

Delaware History

Of the fifty states, only Rhode Island is smaller in land mass than Delaware, which stretches one hundred miles from north to south and varies in width from ten to thirty-five miles. Bounded on the north by Pennsylvania, on the south and west by Maryland, and on the east by the Atlantic Ocean and the Delaware River, whose east bank is in New Jersey, this small state, with a land mass of 1,982 square miles, has just three counties, New Castle in the north, Kent in the middle, and Sussex in the south. The state's mean elevation is about sixty feet.

Early History. As early as 1609, English explorer Henry Hudson sailed on what became known as the Delaware River and the Delaware Bay. By 1631, the Dutch had established the first European settlement in the area around present-day Lewes, in the southeastern part of the state. Long before European settlement began in the region, prehistoric Indians occupied the area. Archaeological excavations at Island Field, twenty miles south of Dover, Delaware's capital, unearthed Indian graves that were close to one thousand years old. The Native Americans in this area are thought to have been the Owascos, a tribe related to the Iroquois, who inhabited the Finger Lakes region in New York.

Later Indian inhabitants in northern Delaware included the Lenni-Lenape Indians, also called the Delaware. Near the ocean and on the Delaware Bay lived the Nanticoke and Assateague Indians. These Indians massacred the first Dutch settlers in the area near Lewes. When more permanent settlement occurred with the arrival of the Swedes, these Indians disappeared from the area.

Permanent Settlements in Delaware. By 1638 a permanent Swedish settlement was established at Fort Christina, which is close to Wilmington on the Delaware River in the state's north. Peter Minuit, who had been colonial governor of New Amsterdam (present-day New York), helped create this settlement for the New Sweden Company, partly sponsored by the Dutch. They soon withdrew their support, leaving a hearty band of Swedes to manage as well as they could on their own. Their governor, Johan Printz, was an able leader who almost single-handedly sustained the beleaguered community.

This settlement, which eventually extended from below Wilmington to Philadelphia, had about one thousand inhabitants. It was eventually overcome in 1655 by Dutch forces sent from New Amsterdam. In 1664, however, the British, rankling at the inroads the Dutch were making on English trade, assaulted New Amsterdam and captured it, then, after a considerable battle, took the Dutch fort at New Castle. The whole of New York and Delaware became part of the province of New York. Delaware remained so until 1682, when the Duke of York gave Delaware to William Penn, who owned Pennsylvania.

At first, Penn, whose colony needed more direct access to the ocean, tried to merge his two holdings, but the people in southern Delaware feared that their colony might in time be overwhelmed by Pennsylvania, many times its size. In 1704 Penn finally permitted the people of Delaware to form their own assembly and, although the area had the same governor as Pennsylvania, to make their own laws.

The Revolt Against England. Although sentiment about gaining independence from England was spreading, Delaware had many loyalists among its inhabitants. George Read, one of Delaware's three delegates to the Continental Congress in 1774, voted against the colonies' declaring independence from England. Had another delegate, Caesar Rodney, not ridden on horseback all night from Dover, Delaware, to Philadelphia to cast the deciding vote, Delaware might not have joined the twelve other colonies in supporting the Declaration of Independence.

In 1777 British forces making their way from the Chesapeake Bay to Philadelphia invaded Delaware. George Washington's army had dug in close to Wilmington, but the British troops cut into Pennsylvania south of Wilmington and finally met Washington's men at Brandywine. After the Battle of Brandywine, the British took Wilmington and controlled it until they gained complete control of the Delaware River in June, 1778.

After the Revolutionary War, Delaware, in 1787, became the first of the newly formed states to ratify the United States Constitution, thereby earning one of its nicknames, the First State. Because of its size, Delaware feared it would be viewed as politically inferior to larger states. During the Constitutional Convention in 1787, Delaware called for equal representation for all states. Finally, the Delaware delegation accepted a compromise whereby every state would have two senators but would have representation in the House of Representatives based on each state's population.

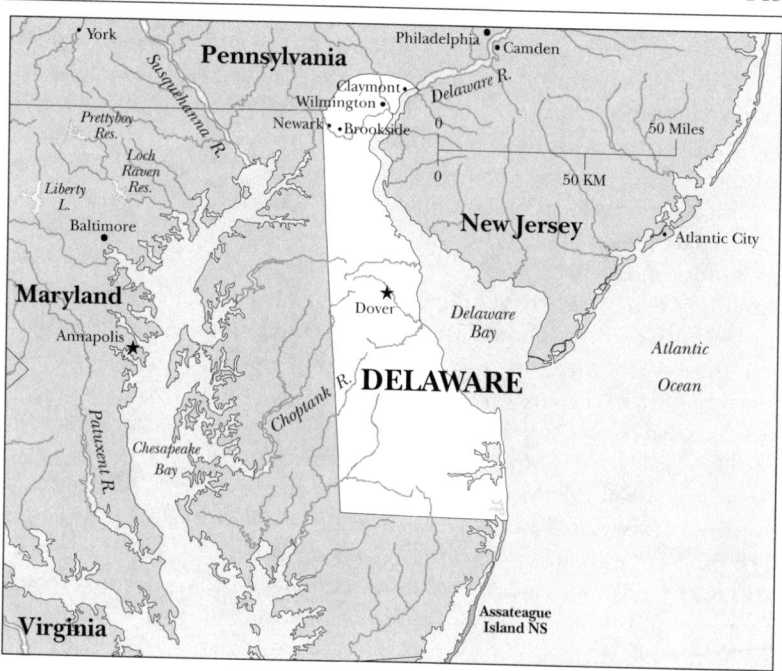

The War of 1812. Delaware, which was a Federalist state, opposed the War of 1812. Once the United States entered that war, however, Delaware gave its reluctant support. Residents of the state feared an invasion when the British took Washington, D.C., and, after burning the executive mansion, attacked Baltimore. Delaware was spared by the British, whose only assault on it was an abortive bombardment of Lewes in 1813.

The du Pont Company. In 1802 E. I. du Pont built a munitions factory on the Brandywine River. This marked the beginning of the highly influential enterprise E. I. du Pont de Nemours and Company, which grew into one of the most important chemical companies in the world. The presence of this company in Delaware eventually attracted other corporations to the region.

In time changing its name to the du Pont Company, having long since expanded from its original munitions manufacturing, it boasts a large nylon plant in Seaford, in the southwestern part of Delaware, and two major pigment factories in other parts of the state. Its home offices and laboratories are located in both Wilmington and Newark, Delaware. A large refinery in Delaware City drew many petrochemical companies to the state.

The Civil War. In 1790 Delaware had about nine thousand slaves, although the state was divided on the slavery issue and many abolitionists were active in helping African slaves escape from the South through Delaware. The state's first constitution, in 1776, made the further importation of slaves illegal. Because the state's tobacco industry was dependent upon slave labor, abolition bills introduced in the 1790's and again in 1847 were narrowly defeated. Nevertheless, by 1860, the slave population in the state had declined to about two thousand.

Although Delaware was staunchly opposed to secession, Abraham Lincoln won no electoral votes from the state in 1860 or in 1864. Delaware was more northern in its outlook and orientation than states in the Deep South. Some men from Delaware joined the Confederate forces, but most Delawareans fought on the Union side.

Despite its Union leanings, Delaware was occupied during the war by Union troops sent by President Lincoln to disarm some of the militia whose loyalty was suspect and to guard the polling places during elections. At war's end, many of the people in Delaware were so incensed by the federal government's punitive measures that the state became solidly Democrat, as did much of the Deep South.

Economy. Strategically situated on the Delaware River, Wilmington became a center of industrial activity in the state. In the city and its environs are textile mills, a steel foundry, automobile assembly operations, paper mills, and tanneries. Many large national corporations established their headquarters in Delaware, primarily in Wilmington, because of the state's favorable business climate.

Because of its location near the point where the Delaware River flows into the Atlantic Ocean, Wilmington has proved an ideal location for shipbuilders, who built iron-hulled ships during the nineteenth century. During World War II, the largest employer in the state was a shipbuilding company based in Wilmington that produced ships for the U.S. Navy and Merchant Marine.

The Dover Air Force Base helped Delaware's economy substantially. The national headquarters of the International Reading Association in Newark, whose outreach is enormous, serves ninety thousand members in ninety-nine countries and employs more than eighty people in its headquarters. In 1998 nearly one-third of the people who worked in Delaware worked in the service sector, whereas slightly more than 20 percent were engaged in construction and about 15 percent in

some aspect of manufacturing. The unemployment rate in that year was about 4 percent. The 1997 per-capita income was $29,022, up from $10,339 in 1980. The state had 2,667 federal employees in 1997 with average annual salaries of $40,159.

Despite its size, Delaware has a thriving agricultural industry that produces soybeans, lima beans, corn, potatoes, mushrooms, and various grains. It also produces considerable livestock, mainly chickens, hogs, and cattle. Its timber industry produced fifteen million board feet in 1998. Although it is not rich in minerals, Delaware produces magnesium, as well as sand, gravel, and gemstones.

Delaware's Population. A few of Delaware's Native American population, especially descendants of the Nanticoke and Moor Indians, remain in Kent and Sussex counties, although most of the native population was driven out or killed in combat with the Europeans who settled the state. In 1770, more than 20 percent of Delaware's population was African American; in 1998, 16.9 percent was black and less than 3 percent Hispanic.

Skyline of Wilmington, Delaware's largest city. (Courtesy Delaware Tourism Office)

Kent County farm country. (Courtesy Delaware Tourism Office)

During the mid-nineteenth century, many Germans and Irish came to Delaware. By the end of the century, southern and eastern Europeans began to arrive in large numbers, seeking work in the state's thriving industries. The first decades of the twentieth century saw the arrival of many Ukrainians and Greeks. As industry grew, many people arrived from other states to take advantage of Delaware's economic opportunities. In 1998 about 3 percent of the state's population was foreign-born.

Delaware, lying in the highly urbanized corridor that runs from Boston to Richmond, Virginia, experienced rapid population growth in the last third of the twentieth century. It population density of 340.8 people per square mile is among the greatest in the United States, and its population of three-quarters of a million should exceed the million mark well before 2010.

R. Baird Shuman

Delaware Time Line

1609   Henry Hudson explores the Delaware River and Delaware Bay for the Dutch East Indies.

1610   Samuel Argall of Virginia blown off course into a bay that he names for his governor, Lord De La Warr.

1631   Dutch found a settlement near present-day Lewes.

(continued)

1632	Native Americans destroy the Dutch settlement.
1638	Swedish settlement is established at Fort Christina.
1655	Dutch conquer the Swedish settlement and add it to the New Netherland settlement.
1664	New Netherland is taken by the British and renamed New York.
1682	Duke of York gives Delaware to William Penn.
1704	Delaware's General Assembly meets apart from Pennsylvania's legislature and makes its own laws.
1739	Wilmington receives its royal charter.
1743	University of Delaware opens in Newark.
1776	Delaware breaks from England, writes constitution for Delaware State.
1777	British capture Wilmington; Delaware General Assembly moves to Dover from New Castle.
Dec. 7, 1787	Delaware becomes the first state to ratify the United States Constitution.
1792	Delaware adopts second state constitution.
1802	E. I. du Pont opens powder mill on the Brandywine.
1813	British bombard Lewes in War of 1812.
1829	Chesapeake and Delaware Canal opens.
1829	Free public schools are mandated.
1831	Third state constitution is adopted.
1838	Philadelphia, Wilmington, and Baltimore Railroad is completed.
1861	Delaware refuses to join secession movement.
1897	New state constitution is adopted.
1912	Wilmington Society of the Fine Arts opens its museum, which grows into the Delaware Art Museum.
1917	Passage of state income and inheritance taxes.
1924	Completion of first highway running the length of Delaware.
1951	Delaware Memorial Bridge opens, linking Delaware and New Jersey.
1956	International Reading Association is established in Newark.
1966	Reorganized state government is established in New Castle County.
1968	Legislative reapportionment is completed.
1969	Henry Francis du Pont dies, leaving Winterthur, his 125-room residence, and most of its contents as a public museum in Wilmington.
1976	Rockwood Museum opens in New Castle; Willington Square with its six restored colonial homes relocated in a Wilmington park.
1981	Financial Center Development Act is enacted.
1987	Senator Joseph Biden withdraws presidential bid after being charged with plagiarism.
1988	Legislature passes law restricting hostile takeovers of businesses incorporated in-state.
1990	Laws passed enabling banks to sell and underwrite insurance.
1997	Seventeen hazardous waste sites placed on National Priority List.

Notes for Further Study

Published Sources. The best comprehensive history of Delaware is John A. Munroe's *History of Delaware* (3d ed. 1993). It relates how the state came into being and is especially effective in outlining clearly the chaotic situation that resulted in Delaware's once being a part of New York. Slavery existed but never really flourished in Delaware; Alice Dunbar-Nelson's essay, "Delaware: A Jewel of Inconsistencies," written in the 1920's and reproduced in *These "Colored" United States: African American Essays from the 1920's* (Tom Lutz and Susanne Ashton, eds., 1996) offers an interesting retrospective view of the situation by an African American who was affected by the ambivalent situation regarding people of color in the state. William H. Williams's *Slavery and Freedom in Delaware, 1639-1865* (1996) examines how slavery existed in a state that had few slave owners and many active abolitionists.

Jay F. Custer's *Delaware Prehistoric Archaeology: An Ecological Approach* (1984) reaches useful conclusions about the earliest history of the Delaware area based on archaelogical findings. His *Prehistoric Culture in the Delmarva Peninsula: An Archeological Study* (1989) also delves into some of the state's ancient history as revealed in artifacts and ancient burial grounds. David McCutchen offers cogent insights into early Indian cultures in *The Red Record: The Wallam Plum: The Oldest Native North American History* (1993). A reliable study of later Native Americans in Delaware is found in C. A. Weslager's *The Delaware Indians: A History* (1972) and in John Bierhorst's *Myth of the Lenape: Guide and Texts* (1995). The latter

presents the folk traditions of these Delaware Indians. In *New Sweden in America* (1995), edited by Carol E. Hoffecker and others, one will find six informative essays that touch on the early Swedish settlement of Delaware in the seventeenth century.

Web Resources. A reasonable starting point for finding out more about Delaware, and for locating other Web sites and their addresses, is the state's Web site (http://www.delaware.com/stateinfo.html). This Web site offers material about many aspects of state government, tourism, history, commerce, economy, and population. A Web site run by the state's department of tourism (http://www.state.de.us/tourism/intro.html) also provides comprehensive information about many of the state's attractions and facilities.

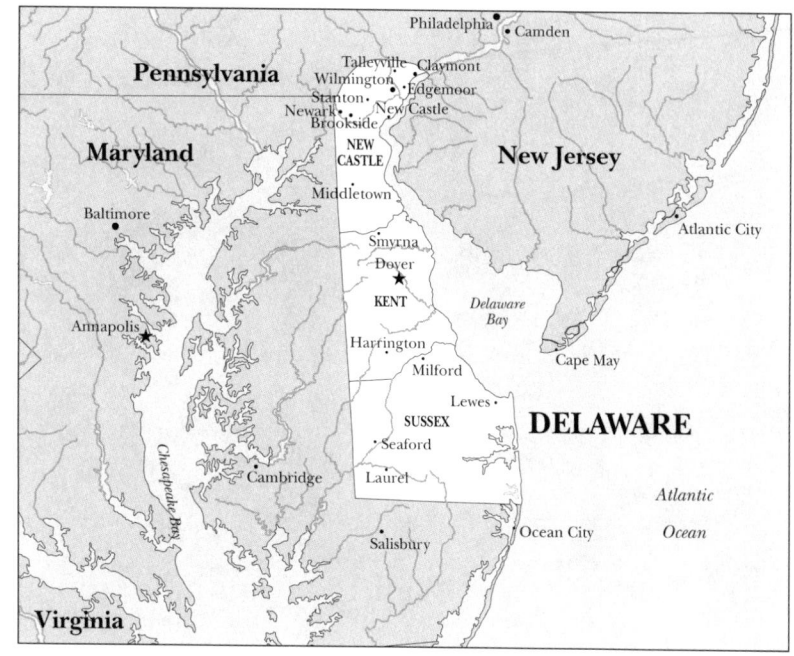

Counties

County	Sq. miles	1996 pop.
Kent	590.7	122,244
New Castle	426.3	471,417

County	Sq. miles	1996 pop.
Sussex	937.7	131,181

Source: U.S. Census Bureau; National Association of Counties.

The Delaware Art Museum's Web site (http://www .delart.mus.de.us) provides pertinent information about the museum and shows reproductions of some of its more notable holdings. The Winterthur Museum's Web site (http://www.winterthur.org) provides a useful bibliography of books about the Winterthur and its founder, Henry Francis du Pont. Rockwood Gardens is a popular attraction that features a Gothic house and well-attended gardens; its Web site (http://www.rockwood. org) provides information about hours, entrance fees, and the holdings of the museum. Information about Delaware libraries and research resources can be found on the Delaware Library Web site (http://www.ib.de.us) and on the University of Delaware Library's Web site (http://www .lib.udel.edu). More general information about the university is found on its Web site (http://www.udel.edu).

The best source for information about business and commerce is found on the Delaware Business Net Web site (http://www/ dvbiznet.com).

Cities

With 10,000 or more residents

Rank	City	Population
1	Wilmington	71,678
2	Dover	30,369

Rank	City	Population
3	Newark	28,000

Population figures are estimated for mid-1998.
Source: U.S. Bureau of the Census.

Index to Tables

NA = Reliable data are not available.

DEMOGRAPHICS

Resident state and national populations, 1970-1997

Population figures given in thousands

	State pop.	U.S. pop.	Share	Rank
1970	548	203,302	0.3%	46
1980	594	226,546	0.3%	47
1985	618	237,924	0.3%	47
1990	666	248,765	0.3%	46
1995	716	262,761	0.3%	46
1997	732	267,636	0.3%	46

Source: U.S. Bureau of the Census.

Resident population by age, 1997

Age group	Total population
Under 5 years	49,000
5 to 17 years	128,000
18 to 24 years	65,000
25 to 34 years	119,000
35 to 44 years	125,000
45 to 54 years	91,000
55 to 64 years	60,000
65 to 74 years	54,000
75 to 84 years	31,000
85 years and over	9,000
Portion of residents 65 and older	12.9%
National average	12.7%

Population figures are rounded to nearest thousand persons;
figures include armed forces personnel stationed in state.
Source: U.S. Bureau of the Census.

Resident population by race, Hispanic origin, 1997

	State pop.	Share	U.S.
All residents	732,000	100.0%	100.0%
Hispanic white	21,000	2.9%	10.0%
non-Hispanic white	554,000	75.7%	72.7%
African American	140,000	19.1%	12.7%
Native American	2,000	0.3%	0.9%
Asian, Pacific Islander	14,000	1.9%	3.8%

Source: U.S. Bureau of the Census.

Projections of state population, 2000-2025

	Model A Uses interstate migration observed from 1975-1994	Model B Uses Bureau of Economic Analysis employment projections
Year	Population	Population
2000	768,000	758,000
2005	800,000	793,000
2010	817,000	823,000
2015	832,000	851,000
2020	847,000	877,000
2025	861,000	899,000

All population projections, including those for 2000, were calculated in 1997.

Source: U.S. Bureau of the Census, Population Paper Listings PPL-47.

VITAL STATISTICS

Average lifetime in years by race, 1989-1991

	State	U.S.	Rank
All residents	74.76	75.37	37
White residents	75.76	76.13	36
Black residents	69.26	69.16	20

Ranks are from longest-lived to least longest-lived. Ranks exclude Alaska, for which reliable data are not available. Rank for black residents is based on the 32 states for which reliable data are available.

Source: U.S. National Center for Health Statistics.

Infant mortality rates, 1980 and 1995

	State	U.S.
All residents		
1980	13.9	12.6
1995	7.5	7.6
White residents		
1980	9.8	11.0
1995	6.0	6.3
Black residents		
1980	27.9	21.4
1995	13.1	15.1

Figures represent deaths per 1,000 live births of resident infants under 1 year old, exclusive of fetal deaths; all-residents figures include other races not listed separately.

Source: U.S. National Center for Health Statistics.

Marriages and divorces

Marriages in 1996	5,200
Rate per 1,000 population, 1995	7.5
U.S. rate, 1995	8.9
Rank among all states	37
Divorces in 1996	3,300
Rate per 1,000 population, 1995	5.1
U.S. rate, 1995	4.4
Rank among all states	15

Rank is from highest to lowest in country.

Source: U.S. National Center for Health Statistics.

Death rates by leading causes, 1995

Deaths per 100,000 resident population

Cause	State	U.S.
Heart disease	276.1	280.7
Cancer	227.3	204.9
Cerebrovascular diseases	47.8	60.1
Accidents and adverse effects	37.1	35.5
Motor vehicle accidents	17.6	16.5
Chronic obstructive pulmonary diseases	36.0	39.2
Diabetes mellitus	26.9	22.6
HIV	22.7	NA
Suicide	11.2	11.9
Homicide	5.9	8.7
All causes	875.9	880.0
Rank in overall death rate among states		32

Figures exclude nonresidents who die in state. Causes of death follow International Classification of Diseases. Rank is from highest to lowest in country.

Source: U.S. National Center for Health Statistics.

ECONOMY

Gross state product, 1990-1996
In current dollars

	State product	Increase
1990	$21.0 billion	
1993	$23.7 billion	
1994	$24.1 billion	1.69%
1995	$26.9 billion	11.62%
1996	$28.3 billion	5.20%

Source: U.S. Bureau of Economic Analysis; Survey of Current
Business, June, 1998.

Gross state product by industry, 1996
In billions

Farms, forestry, fisheries	$0.3
Construction	0.8
Manufacturing	5.6
Transportation, public utilities.	1.4
Wholesale trade.	1.1
Retail trade	1.6
Finance, insurance, real estate	13.0
Services	3.5
Government.	2.4
State total.	$28.9
Total U.S.	$6,923.8
State share.	0.42%
Rank among states.	41

Total figures include mining, not listed separately.
Source: U.S. Bureau of Economic Analysis; Survey of Current
Business, June, 1998.

Personal income per capita, 1990 and 1997
In current dollars

	1990	1997
Per capita income	$21,648	$29,022
U.S. average	$19,188	$25,598
Rank among states	6	5

1997 data are preliminary.
Source: U.S. Bureau of Economic Analysis; Survey of Current
Business, May, 1998.

Energy consumption, 1995
In trillions of British thermal units (BTU)

End-use sectors

Residential	54.3
Commercial	39.5
Industrial	109.3
Transportation.	60.9

Sources of energy

Petroleum	122.9
Natural gas.	62.7
Coal	52.4
Hydroelectric power	0
Nuclear electric power	0
Total state per capita consumption	368.1
Total U.S. per capita consumption	344.4
Rank among states.	21
Total state energy consumption.	264.0
Total U.S. energy consumption	90,547.4
State share of U.S. total.	0.29%
Rank among states.	46

Total figures include items not listed separately.
Source: U.S. Energy Information Administration; State Energy
Data Report.

Nonfarm employment by sectors, 1997

Total	388,000
Construction	22,000
Manufacturing	57,000
Transportation, public utilities.	16,000
Wholesale trade, retail trade	86,000
Finance, insurance, real estate	47,000
Services	107,000
Government.	53,000

Figures are rounded to nearest thousand persons. Total
includes mining, not listed separately.
Source: U.S. Bureau of Labor Statistics; Employment and
Earnings, monthly.

Foreign exports, 1990-1997
In millions of dollars

Year	State	U.S.	State share
1990	1,344	394,045	0.34%
1996	1,594	624,767	0.26%
1997	2,067	688,896	0.30%

Source: U.S. Bureau of the Census; U.S. Merchandise Trade,
series FT 900.

LAND USE

Federally owned land, 1996

	State	U.S.	State share
Total acres	1,266,000	2,271,343,000	0.06%
Federally owned	2,000	563,129,000	0.00%
Federal share	0.2%	24.8%	—

Areas are rounded to nearest thousand acres. Figures for federally owned land do not include trust properties.
Source: U.S. General Services Administration; *Inventory Report on Real Property Owned by the United States Throughout the World,* annual.

Land use, 1992
In acres, rounded to nearest thousand

Total surface area	1,309,000
Federal land.	33,000
Total nonfederal.	1,213,000
Developed	205,000
Total rural	1,008,000
Cropland.	499,000
Pasture land.	26,000
Range land	0
Forest land.	353,000
Minor cover/use.	130,000

Total surface area figures include water area not shown separately.
Source: U.S. Dept. of Agriculture; Soil Conservation Service; Iowa State University, Statistical Laboratory; *Summary Report, 1992 National Resources Inventory.*

Farms and crop acreage, 1997

	State	U.S.	Share	Rank
Farms (thousands)	2	2,058	0.10%	47
Acres (millions)	1	968	0.10%	45
Acres per farm	235	471	—	30
Acres planted	509	334,139	0.15%	41
Acres harvested	494	319,894	0.15%	41
Farm value (mill.)	$155	$108,805	0.14%	44

Numbers of farms are rounded to nearest thousand.
Source: U.S. Dept. of Agriculture; National Agricultural Statistics Service.

GOVERNMENT AND FINANCE

Units of local government, 1997

	State	Total U.S.	Rank
All local governments	336	87,453	46
Counties	3	3,043	47
Municipalities	57	19,372	42
Townships	0	16,629	—
School districts	19	13,726	41
Special districts	257	34,683	40

County ranks are based on the 48 states with county governments; township ranks are based on the 20 states with township governments; school district ranks are based on the 46 states with such districts.
Source: U.S. Bureau of the Census; *1997 Census of Governments, Government Organization,* Series GC97(1).

State government revenue, 1996

Total revenue	$3,619 mill.
General revenue	3,303 mill.
Per capita	4,565
U.S. per capita average	2,910
Rank among states	2

Intergovernmental revenue

Total	$662 mill.
From federal government	633 mill.
From local government	29 mill.

Charges and Miscellaneous

Total	$952 mill.
Current charges	466 mill.
Misc. general revenue	487 mill.

Taxes

Total	$1,688 mill.
General sales	NA
Selective sales	253 mill.
License taxes	533 mill.
Individual income	632 mill.
Corporate income	166 mill.
Other	105 mill.
Insurance trust revenue	309 mill.

Total revenue figures include items not listed separately.
Source: U.S. Bureau of the Census.

State government expenditures, 1996

General expenditures
Intergovernmental . . . . $511 mill.
Direct expenditures . . . . 2,414 mill.
Total. . . . . 2,926 mill.

Selected direct expenditures
Education . . . . $962 mill.
Public welfare. . . . . 463 mill.
Health, hospital . . . . 211 mill.
Highways . . . . 257 mill.
Police. . . . . 48 mill.
Corrections. . . . . 113 mill.
Natural resources . . . . 44 mill.
Parks and recreation. . . . . 43 mill.
Government administration . . . . 171 mill.
Interest on debt . . . . 270 mill.

Other
State per capita expenditures $4,044
U.S. per capita average 2,854
Rank among states 3
Total state expenditures . . . . 3,248 mill.
Total U.S. expenditures . . . . 859,959 mill.

Totals include items not listed separately.
Source: U.S. Bureau of the Census.

POLITICS

Governors since statehood
D = Democrat; R = Republican; O = other;
(r) resigned; (d) died in office; (i) removed from office

Governor	Term
John McKinly	1777
Thomas McKean	1777
George Read	1777-1778
Caesar Rodney	1778-1781
John Dickinson	(r) 1781-1782
John Cook	1782-1783
Nicholas Van Dyke	1783-1786
Thomas Collins	(d) 1786-1789
Jehu Davis	1789
Joshua Clayton (O)	1789-1796
Gunning Bedford (O)	(d) 1796-1797
Daniel Rogers (O)	1797-1799
Richard Bassett (O)	(r) 1799-1801
James Sykes (O)	1801-1802
David Hall (O)	1802-1805
Nathaniel Mitchell (O)	1805-1808
George Truitt (O)	1808-1811
Joseph Haslet (O)	1811-1814
Daniel Rodney (O)	1814-1817
John Clark (O)	1817-1820
Jacob Stout (O)	1820-1821
John Collins (O)	(d) 1821-1822
Caleb Rodney (O)	1822-1823
Joseph Haslet (O)	(d) 1823
Charles Thomas (O)	1823-1824
Samuel Paynter (O)	1824-1827
Charles Polk (O)	1827-1830
David Hazzard (D)	1830-1833
Caleb P. Bennett (D)	(d) 1833-1836
Charles Polk (O)	1836-1837
Cornelius P. Comegys (O)	1837-1841
William B. Cooper (O)	1841-1845
Thomas Stockton (O)	(d) 1845-1846
Joseph Maull (O)	(d) 1846
William Temple (O)	1846-1847
William Tharp (D)	1847-1851
William H. H. Ross (D)	1851-1855
Peter F. Causey (O)	1855-1859
William Burton (D)	1859-1863
William Cannon (O)	(d) 1863-1865
Gove Saulsbury (D)	1865-1871
James Ponder (D)	1871-1875
John P. Cochran (D)	1875-1879
John W. Hall (D)	1879-1883
Charles C. Stockley (D)	1883-1887
Benjamin T. Biggs (D)	1887-1891
Robert J. Reynolds (D)	1891-1895
Joshua H. Marvel (R)	(d) 1895
William T. Watson (D)	1895-1897
Ebe W. Tunnell (D)	1897-1901
John Hunn (R)	1901-1905
Preston Lea (R)	1905-1909
Simeon S. Pennewell (R)	1909-1913
Charles R. Miller (R)	1913-1917
John G. Townsend, Jr. (R)	1917-1921
William D. Denney (R)	1921-1925
Robert P. Robinson (R)	1925-1929
Clayton Douglass Buck (R)	1929-1937
Richard C. McMullen (D)	1937-1941
Walter W. Bacon (R)	1941-1949
Elbert N. Carvel (D)	1949-1953
James Caleb Boggs (R)	(r) 1953-1960
David P. Buckson (R)	1960-1961
Elbert N. Carvel (D)	1961-1965
Charles L. Terry, Jr. (D)	1965-1969
Russell W. Peterson (R)	1969-1973
Sherman W. Tribbitt (D)	1973-1977
Pierre Samuel du Pont IV (R)	1977-1985
Michael N. Castle (R)	1985-1993
Thomas R. Carper (D)	1993-

Governors were called state presidents before 1792.

Composition of state legislature, 1990-1998

	Democrats	Republicans
State House (41 seats)		
1990	17	24
1992	18	23
1994	14	27
1996	14	27
1998	15	26
State Senate (21 seats)		
1990	15	6
1992	15	6
1994	12	9
1996	13	8
1998	13	8

Figures for total seats may include independents and minor party members.

Source: Council of State Governments; *State Elective Officials and the Legislatures.*

Composition of congressional delegations, 1989-1999

	Dem	Rep	Total
House of Representatives			
101st Congress, 1989			
State delegates	1	0	1
Total U.S.	259	174	433
102d Congress, 1991			
State delegates	1	0	1
Total U.S.	267	167	434
103d Congress, 1993			
State delegates	0	1	1
Total U.S.	258	176	434
104th Congress, 1995			
State delegates	0	1	1
Total U.S.	197	236	433
105th Congress, 1997			
State delegates	0	1	1
Total U.S.	206	228	434
106th Congress, 1999			
State delegates	0	1	1
Total U.S.	211	222	433

	Dem	Rep	Total
Senate			
101st Congress, 1989			
State delegates	1	1	2
Total U.S.	55	45	100
102d Congress, 1991			
State delegates	1	1	2
Total U.S.	56	44	100
103d Congress, 1993			
State delegates	1	1	2
Total U.S.	57	43	100
104th Congress, 1995			
State delegates	1	1	2
Total U.S.	46	53	99
105th Congress, 1997			
State delegates	1	1	2
Total U.S.	45	55	100
106th Congress, 1999			
State delegates	1	1	2
Total U.S.	45	54	99

Figures are for starts of first sessions. Figure for U.S. Representatives for 101st Congress does not include Alabama and Indiana, which had vacancies. Figures for total U.S. Representatives for 102d, 103d, and 106th Congresses do not include Vermont, which had 1 Independent-Socialist. Figure for U.S. Representatives for 104th Congress does not include Vermont, which had 1 Independent-Socialist, and California, which had 1 vacancy. Figure for U.S. Representatives for 105th Congress does not include New York, which had 1 vacancy. Figure for U.S. Senators for 104th Congress does not include Oregon, which had 1 vacancy. Figure for U.S. Senators for 106th Congress does not include New Hampshire, which had 1 Independent.

Source: U.S. Congress; *Congressional Directory,* biennial.

Voter participation in presidential elections, 1992 and 1996

	1992	1996
State voting age pop.	521,000	547,000
Total U.S. voting age pop.	189,524,000	196,509,000
State share of U.S. total	0.3%	0.3%
Rank among states	45	45
Percent of state casting vote	55.6	56.4
Percent of U.S. total voting	55.1	49.0
Rank among states	29	13

Source: U.S. Bureau of the Census.

HEALTH AND MEDICAL CARE

Medicare, 1997

	Recipients	Payments
State	105,000	$471 mill.
Total U.S.	37,514,000	$206,064 mill.
State share	0.28%	0.23%
Rank among states	46	46

Recipient figures are rounded to nearest thousand persons.
Ranks are from highest to lowest.
Source: U.S. Health Care Financing Administration.

Medicaid, 1996

	Recipients	Payments
State	82,000	$308 mill.
Total U.S.	35,028,000	$121,419 mill.
State share	0.23%	0.25%
Rank among states	45	44

Recipient figures are rounded to nearest thousand persons.
Payment figures for fiscal year reflect federal and state
contribution payments. Ranks are from highest to lowest.
Source: U.S. Health Care Financing Administration.

Health insurance coverage, 1996

	State	U.S.
Total persons covered	636,000	225,070,000
Total persons not covered	98,000	41,716,000
Part not covered	13.4%	15.6%
Rank among states	26	—
Children not covered	24,000	10,554,000
Part not covered	12.9%	14.8%
Rank among states	21	—

Ranks are from most to fewest uninsured. Population figures
are rounded to nearest thousand persons.
Source: U.S. Bureau of the Census.

AIDS, syphilis, tuberculosis, and measles cases, 1997

Cases	U.S.	State	Share
AIDS	58,443	231	0.40%
Syphilis	8,550	22	0.26%
Tuberculosis	18,534	18	0.10%
Measles	148,000	NA	NA

Measles figures are rounded to nearest thousand cases.
Source: U.S. Centers for Disease Control and Prevention.

HOUSING

Homeownership rates, 1985-1997

	1985	1990	1997
State	70.3%	67.7%	69.2%
Total U.S.	63.9%	63.9%	65.7%
Rank among states	11	26	20

Source: U.S. Bureau of the Census.

Home sales, 1990 and 1997
In thousands of units

Existing home sales	1990	1997	Change
State sales	9.7	NA	NA
Total U.S. sales	3,560	4,730	1,170
State share of U.S. total	0.27%	NA	-0.27%
Rank among states	44	NA	—

Source: National Association of Realtors; *Real Estate Outlook: Market Trends and Insights.*

EDUCATION

Public school enrollment, 1995

State K-8 enrollment	77,000
Total U.S. K-8 enrollment	32,341,000
State share of total U.S..	0.24%
State 9-12 enrollment.	31,000
Total U.S. 9-12 enrollment	12,500,000
State share of U.S. total	0.25%
State public school enroll. rate.	86.6%
Overall U.S. rate.	91.6%
Rank among states.	48

Enrollment figures (which include unclassified students) are
rounded to nearest thousand pupils in fall term; kindergarten (K)-8 grade enrollment figures include some prekindergarten students. Enrollment rate is based on percentage of persons 5-17 years old. Rank is from highest to lowest.
Source: U.S. National Center for Education Statistics.

Public college finances, 1996

State FTE enrollment.	26,800
Total U.S. FTE enrollment	8,268,800
State share of total U.S..	0.32%
Rank among states.	45
State and local appropriations	$134 mill.
Total U.S. state and local appropriations.	$39,699 mill.
State share of total U.S..	0.34%
Rank among states.	44
State net tuition revenues.	$168,600,000
Total U.S. net tuition	$18,348,100,000
State share of total U.S..	0.92%
Rank among states.	33

FTE=Full-time equivalent; credit and noncredit enrollment including summer session in academic year ending in 1996.

Enrollments are rounded to nearest thousand students. Net tuition revenues exclude appropriation to students attending in-state public institutions. Rankings are from highest shares to lowest.

Source: Research Associates of Washington.

Chesapeake and Delaware Canal Bridge. (Courtesy Delaware Tourism Office)

TRANSPORTATION AND TRAVEL

Highway mileage, 1996

Interstate.	41
Other arterial.	626
Collector roads.	1,166
Local roads.	4,105
Urban roads	1,982
Rural roads	3,733
Total state.	5,715
U.S. total	3,933,985
State share	0.2%
Rank among states.	49

Source: U.S. Federal Highway Administration.

Motor vehicle registrations and driver licenses, 1996
In thousands

Vehicle registrations	State	U.S.	Share	Rank
Autos, trucks, buses	593	206,365	0.29%	47
Autos only	391	128,439	0.30%	45
Motorcycles	10	3,832	0.26%	50
Driver licenses	529	179,539	0.29%	47

Figures do not include vehicles owned by military services.
Source: U.S. Federal Highway Administration; *Highway Statistics; Selected Highway Statistics and Charts.*

Domestic travel expenditures, 1995
Spending by U.S. residents on overnight trips and day trips of at least 100 miles

Total expenditures in state	$886 mill.
Total expenditures in U.S..	$360,314 mill.
State share of total U.S..	0.25%
Rank among states.	49

Source: Travel Industry Association of America.

CRIME AND LAW ENFORCEMENT

State and local police officers, 1996

Local police	923
State police	540
Sheriffs	24
Total	1,660
Officers per 10,000 residents	23
U.S. average	25
Rank among states.	21

Figures cover full-time sworn officers; totals include special
   police not shown separately.
Source: U.S. Bureau of Justice Statistics; *Census of State and
   Local Law Enforcement Agencies, 1996.*

Crime rates, 1996

Rates per 100,000 resident population

Violent crimes	State	U.S.
Total violent	668	634
Murder	4.3	7.4
Forcible rape	62.6	36.1
Robbery	180	202
Aggravated assault	422	388
Property crimes		
Total property	4,227	4,445
Burglary	804	943
Larceny/theft	2,988	2,976
Motor vehicle theft	434	526
Totals	4,895	5,079

Source: U.S. Federal Bureau of Investigation; *Crime in the
   United States,* annual.

State prison populations, 1980-1996

	State	U.S.	State share
1980	1,474	305,458	0.48%
1990	3,471	708,393	0.49%
1996	5,110	1,025,624	0.50%

Figures exclude prisoners in federal penitentiaries.
Source: U.S. Bureau of Justice Statistics.

Florida

Location: Southeast coast of continental United States

Area and rank: 53,997 square miles (139,852 square kilometers); 65,758 square miles (170,313 square kilometers) including water; twenty-sixth largest state in area

Coastline: 1,350 miles (2,172 kilometers)

Shoreline: 8,426 miles (13,558 kilometers)

Population and rank: 14,653,945 (1997); fourth largest state in population

State capitol building in Tallahassee. (Visit Florida)

Capital: Tallahassee

Largest city: Jacksonville (consolidated city, coextensive with Duval County) (693,630 people in 1998)

Became territory: March 30, 1822

Entered Union and rank: March 3, 1845; twenty-seventh state

Present constitution adopted: 1969

Counties: 67

State name: "Florida" comes from the Spanish for "feast of flowers," which relates to Easter celebrations

State nickname: Sunshine State

Motto: In God we trust

State flag: White field with red cross of Saint Andrew and state seal in center

Highest point: Geological survey section 30, T6 north, R20 west — 345 feet (105 meters)

Lowest point: Atlantic Ocean — sea level

Highest recorded temperature: 109 degrees Fahrenheit (43 degrees Celsius) — Monticello, 1931

Lowest recorded temperature: −2 degrees Fahrenheit (−19 degrees Celsius) — Tallahassee, 1899

State song: "Suwannee River"

State flower: Orange blossom

State bird: Mockingbird

National parks: Biscayne, Dry Tortugas, Everglades

Florida History

Although Florida has a long and varied history, many of the most important developments in the state, especially in terms of economic, political, and demographic changes, took place after the 1950's. Because of its geographic location, which promotes the influence of West Indian and Caribbean cultures, and its pleasant, tropical climate, which has attracted large numbers of residents from both the Northern and Southern Hemispheres, Florida developed a unique and distinctive character.

Early History. Native Americans arrived in Florida sometime around 10,000 B.C.E. and slowly made their way south, not reaching the southern tip of the peninsula until about 1400 B.C.E. Archaeological evidence from northeastern Florida and southeastern Georgia indicates that inhabitants of these areas invented pottery in the period around 2000 B.C.E. This would place their development of pottery approximately eight hundred years before other North American cultures.

Because of the abundance of game and marine life, early Native Americans in the Florida area were primarily hunters and fishers, rather than farmers. Great respect was paid to the dead, who were interred in large burial mounds. By 1500 C.E. a sun worship cult, also centered around large earthen mounds, spread through the region. The tribes discovered agriculture and grew corn, beans, and squash, among other crops.

Along the northern Gulf coast lived the Panzacola, Chatot, and Apalachicola; further west were the Apalachee. The lower part of the peninsula, from Tampa Bay extending south, was inhabited by the warrior Calusa, for whom warfare seemed to be part of their religious practice. In the north, the dominant group was the Timucua, who were the first Native Americans to encounter Europeans. By far the most famous of Florida tribes, however, were the Seminoles, who entered the state in 1750. The word *seminole* means "runaway" in the Creek language, and the people themselves were Creek Indians who came from Alabama and Georgia. At first scattered in small groups, the Seminoles united against those who wanted to remove them from Florida, first the Spanish and English and later the Americans.

Exploration and Colonization. The first European contact with Florida began in 1513, when Juan Ponce de León landed on the coast, claimed the land for Spain, and bestowed its current name, either because it was Easter (*Pascua Florida*, in Spanish) or because of the many flowering plants he discovered (*florida* also means "flowery" in Spanish). After Ponce de León's death during a battle with Native Americans in 1521, several other Spanish explorers, including Hernando de Soto, sought to establish a permanent presence in Florida. It was not until 1566, however, that a Spanish colony was founded at St. Augustine, becoming the first permanent European settlement in what is now the United States.

As they did elsewhere with their New World colonies, the Spanish implemented both imperial rule and the Catholic religion. Settlements and missions were established throughout Florida, but these were destroyed in the early 1700's in raids by Native Americans and British settlers from South Carolina. In 1763, as part of the treaties which ended the French and Indian War, Spain ceded Florida to the British in exchange for Cuba. The British divided the colony into East and West Florida.

Immigration increased the English population of Florida, and during the American Revolution the residents remained loyal to that crown. However, in 1778, Spain, which had become an American ally, seized West Florida. In 1783, at the end of the Revolution, Spain regained all of Florida. While many English settlers left for British possessions in the West Indies, others remained behind, stubbornly defiant to the Spanish and fearful of possible takeover by French forces.

Steps to Statehood. During the War of 1812 the British used Pensacola as a naval base, prompting its capture by American forces under General Andrew Jackson. In 1819, Spain ceded Florida to the United States, and Jackson returned in 1822 as military governor of the new territory. The northwestern portion of the region, along the panhandle, became the site of numerous cotton plantations worked by slaves. Tallahassee was named the capital in 1823. In 1845 Florida was admitted to the Union.

Even before Florida officially became part of the United States, efforts had been under way to remove Native Americans from the territory. This ongoing conflict was concentrated on the Seminoles, who had formed a formidable presence against the threat from the Americans. From 1835 to 1842 the

United States waged the Seminole War against the tribe. The war was begun when Osceola, a young Seminole chief, publicly rejected a harsh treaty with the United States by plunging his dagger through the document. Outnumbered by the Americans, Osceola led the Seminoles into the Everglades and conducted guerrilla warfare. He was captured while under a flag of truce and imprisoned in Fort Moultrie at Charleston, South Carolina; he died there in 1838. Without his lead-

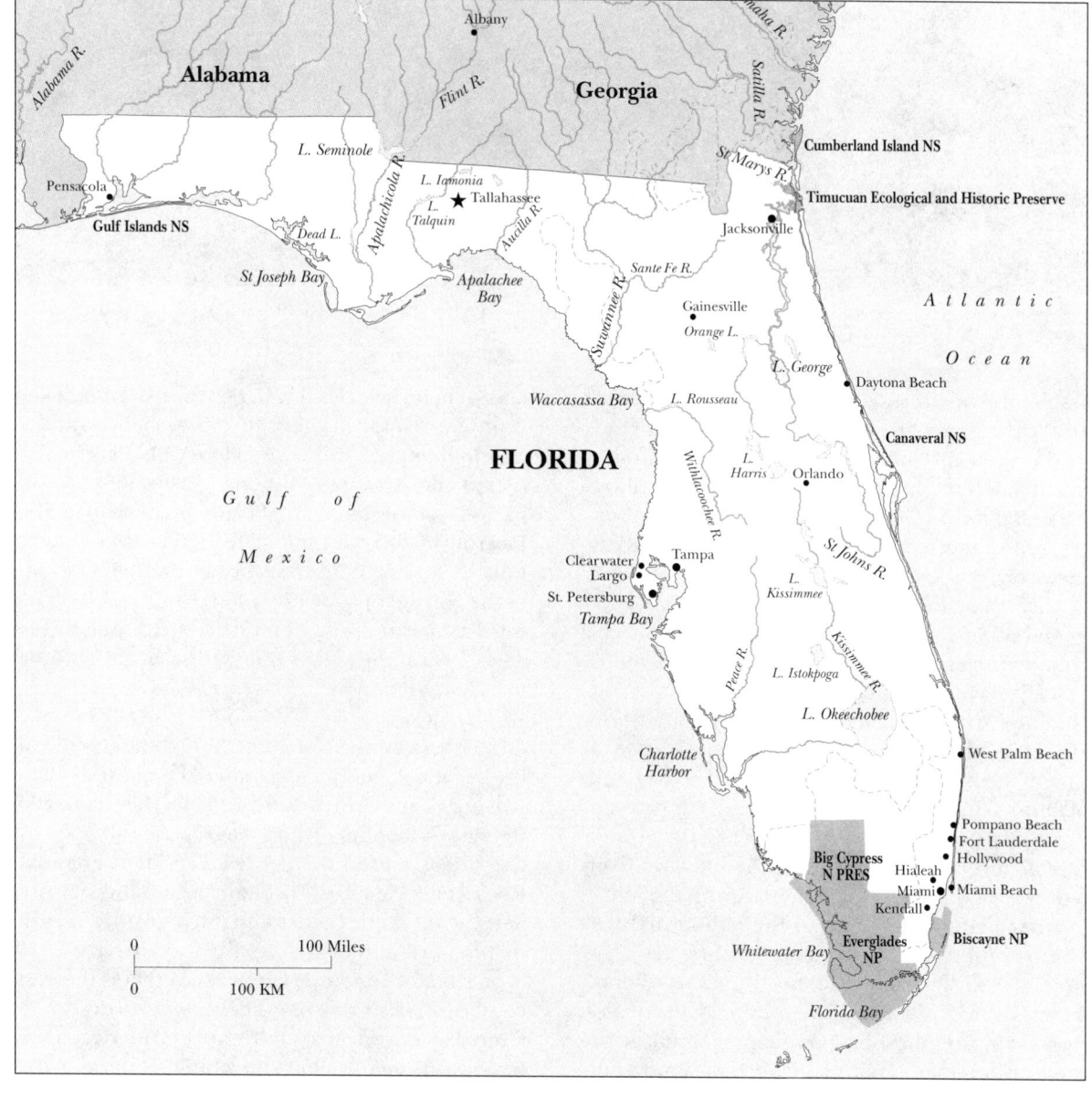

Hernando de Soto landing at Tampa Bay in 1539. (Library of Congress)

ership, the tide turned against the Seminoles, and after their final defeat they were removed to lands in the western United States. Only a handful remained behind, hidden in the swamps and wilderness of Florida. The number of Seminoles increased in the state during the twentieth century, however.

Civil War and Reconstruction. In 1861 Florida joined other southern states in seceding from the Union. During the Civil War, Union naval forces quickly captured strong points along the coast, including Fernandina, Pensacola, and St. Augustine. However, when Union troops attempted an invasion of the interior, they were defeated at the battle of Olustee in 1864. A second Union attempt to capture Tallahassee failed in March, 1865; the Florida capital and Austin, Texas, were the only two Confederate capitals never captured during the war.

After being readmitted to the Union in 1868, Florida entered Reconstruction and began a period of transformation of the state's economic base. Citrus fruits replaced cotton as the major cash crop, and phosphate mining for fertilizer became a dominant industry. Tourism, almost un-

known before the Civil War, began to become a key economic factor in the 1880's, especially with the development of railroads. Henry B. Plant completed the Kissimmee-Tampa cross-state railroad in 1884, and Henry M. Flagler inaugurated the Jacksonville-Miami Line in 1896. The two systems linked Florida and its produce to the rich markets of the Northeast and encouraged the growth of the tourism and retirement industries. Starting in the early 1900's, the state's population began to double approximately every twenty years.

The Florida real estate boom of the 1920's saw a dramatic increase in settlers, but by the middle of the decade the boom had ended. In addition, massive hurricanes in 1926 and 1928 further damaged the state's economy, which was severely affected by the Great Depression of 1929. President Franklin Roosevelt's New Deal brought relief and massive defense spending before and during World War II, helping bring the state into the modern age.

A Mixed Economy. Cape Canaveral on the east coast of Florida was one of the oldest sites to be named by Europeans on the North American continent. During the 1950's and 1960's it became the site of the nation's newest explorers, as the National Aeronautics and Space Administration (NASA) chose it for the site of the American space program. In 1958 it saw the launch of the first U.S. satellite, in 1961 and 1962 the first American manned space flight and orbital mission, and in 1969 the first lunar mission.

Modern Florida developed a mixed economy that depends upon traditional areas such as manufacturing and agriculture and also relies heavily on tourism. Companies that produce computer equipment and accessories have taken the lead in manufacturing. Citrus fruits, first introduced to Florida in the 1570's, are a strong staple, with Florida producing more than three-quarters of the total U.S. harvest of grapefruit and oranges. In addition, the state's pine forests are valuable sources of materials for pulp and paper, as well as turpentine and other products. The almost year-round growing season has made Florida a leader in truck-

farming agriculture, shipping tomatoes, vegetables, and other produce throughout the nation.

A Multicultural State. The Cuban Revolution of 1959, which brought Fidel Castro and the Communist Party to power, saw a massive emigration from that island, largely among the professional, upper, and middle classes. Conservative in politics and religion, Cubans brought with them a tradition of respect for learning and for the free enterprise system. Although their initial plans had been for an early return to their home, these immigrants established themselves in south Florida, especially in the Miami area, where they developed a strong economy and thriving culture. By the late 1970's, south Florida had become a multicultural, bilingual area.

These developments were not without difficulty. In 1986 Bob Martinez became the first Hispanic to be elected governor of Florida. Significantly, he won election as a Republican. However, many conservatives, disturbed at the increasing power of His-

Highway connecting the islands of the Florida Keys at the southern tip of the state. (PhotoDisc)

panic voters, pushed hard to win approval in 1988 of an amendment to the state constitution that made English the official language of state government. Adding to the situation were sometimes tense relations between the white, Hispanic, and African American populations; in the early 1980's these tensions caused riots to flare in the Miami area.

Tourism and Nature. Tourism, long a staple of the modern Florida economy, received a major boost in 1971 with the opening of Walt Disney World near Orlando. Disney's Epcot Center followed in 1982. Soon, Disney World became the single most popular tourist destination in the United States. Other attractions, including Sea World, Universal Studios theme park, and Busch Gardens, increased Florida's appeal as a tourist destination. Added to these are the state's natural attractions, such as the Everglades, the Florida Keys, and the unique John Pennekamp Coral Reef State Park near Key Largo, which is entirely underwater and features living coral formations. In 1990, a record-breaking 41 million visitors from around the world visited Florida.

Although much of Florida's appeal rested upon its environment, much of that environment had been devastated by natural forces or harmed by human intervention. In 1992 the state was struck by Hurricane Andrew, at that time the costliest natural disaster in U.S. history. The storm raged through south Florida, ruining entire communities and causing more than $20 billion in damages.

As the state entered the twenty-first century, it began to address a potentially fatal threat to its environment. Decades of systematic draining of wetlands, including the vast expanse of the Everglades, to accommodate expanding human population and development seriously endangered the environment and wildlife. Finally realizing the seriousness of the situation, the U.S. Army Corps of Engineers and other organizations abandoned long-standing projects such as the Cross Florida Barge Canal and began efforts to reverse years of neglect and active damage. These efforts became critical for a state more dependent than most on its natural environment for its prosperity and continued growth.

Michael Witkoski

Florida Time Line

Apr. 3, 1513	Juan Ponce de León discovers territory he calls Florida and claims for Spain.
May, 1539	Hernando de Soto lands near what is now Tampa Bay and begins exploration.
1564	French Huguenots establish settlement on St. Johns River.
1565	Spanish mariner Pedro Menéndez de Avilés founds St. Augustine, the oldest city in the Union, and kills French Huguenot colonists, establishing Spanish power.
1570's	Citrus trees are introduced into Florida.
1698	Spanish establish settlement at Pensacola.
1750	Seminoles migrate to Florida from Georgia.
1763	Spain trades Florida to Britain.
1783	Britain cedes Florida back to Spain.
1814	General Andrew Jackson seizes Pensacola in War of 1812.
1819	Spain sells East Florida to United States.
Mar. 30, 1822	Territory of Florida is established.
1835-1845	Seminole War rages as settlers try to push Native Americans from area.

Mar. 3, 1845	Florida enters the Union as the twenty-seventh state.
1853	University of Florida is founded at Gainesville.
Jan. 10, 1861	Florida is the third state to secede from the Union.
July 4, 1868	Florida is readmitted to the Union.
1884	Phosphate deposits are found on Peace River.
1884	Henry B. Plant completes cross-state railroad.
1886	Henry M. Flagler opens Jacksonville-Miami railroad.
1906	Draining operations begin in the Everglades.
1947	Everglades National Park is created.
1958	NASA begins administration of Cape Canaveral aerospace center.
1954	Sunshine Skyway across Tampa Bay opens.
1963	Cape Canaveral is renamed Cape Kennedy.
1968	New state constitution is adopted.
1969	All public schools, including colleges and universities, come under a unified system.
1971	Construction on Cross Florida Barge Canal halted for environmental reasons.
1971	Walt Disney World opens.
1973	Cape Kennedy is renamed Cape Canaveral.
1982	Epcot Center opens at Walt Disney World.
1985	Xavier Suarez becomes first Cuban American elected mayor of Miami.
1986	Republican Bob Martinez becomes first Hispanic elected governor.
1988	English is made the official language of state government through a constitutional amendment.
1990	41 million people visit Florida, a state record.
Aug. 24, 1992	Hurricane Andrew devastates south Florida.

Notes for Further Study

Published Sources. Charlton Tebeau's *A History of Florida* (1981) provides a good start to understanding the growth and development of the state, especially from statehood to Civil War and Reconstruction. *Florida: A Short History* (1993), by Michael Gannon, is another excellent introductory survey of the state and its development. David Nolan's *Fifty Feet in Paradise: The Booming of Florida* (1984) discusses Florida's checkered history in the modern era, as the state went through several periods of growth and recession.

Hernando de Soto and the Indians of Florida (1993), by Jerald T. Milanich and Charles Hudson, looks at the beginning of an often troubled relationship between Native Americans and later arriving European settlers. David Colburn's *The African American Heritage of Florida* (1995) is an important and interesting survey of African American contributions to the state during its history.

Web Resources. Practically every aspect of Florida history, culture, politics, economics, and leisure can be accessed through a Web site, and most of the general sites provide easy reference to specific areas. Both the All Florida Directory (http://www.allflorida.com) and Florida Web Centers (http://www.webguide.aol.com/local/north_america/united_florida) are excellent starting places. For official information about the state, including statistics and links to agencies and departments, the best site is Florida Access to Government (http://www.state.fl.us/fgsh_html/access.html).

For those who are interested in Florida history, there are a variety of sites that offer valuable information and links to other pages. History and Culture (http://www.dlis.dos.state.fl.us/fgils/history.htm) and Florida Facts and History (http://www.dhr.dos.state.fl.us./flafacts) have extensive links. A Short History of Florida (http://dhr.dos.state.fl.us/flafacts/shorthis.html) and The Florida Story (http://www.floridastory.com) provide both links and a generous helping of historical information. The Broward County Library site also provides extensive information and links for Florida history (http://www.shadow.net/~donnah/referral.html). For those who wish information about Florida's Native Americans, the Seminole Tribe of Florida has its own site (http://www.seminoletribe.com).

Counties

County	Sq. miles	1996 pop.	County	Sq. miles	1996 pop.
Alachua	874.3	196,525	Lake	953.1	186,631
Baker	585.2	20,556	Lee	803.6	380,001
Bay	763.7	144,637	Leon	666.8	215,593
Bradford	293.2	24,130	Levy	1,118.4	30,296
Brevard	1,018.5	453,998	Liberty	835.9	6,542
Broward	1,208.9	1,438,228	Madison	692.0	17,513
Calhoun	567.4	12,217	Manatee	741.2	232,285
Charlotte	693.7	130,426	Marion	1,579.0	230,068
Citrus	583.6	109,389	Martin	555.7	112,527
Clay	601.1	128,912	Monroe	997.3	80,730
Collier	2,025.5	188,187	Nassau	651.6	52,079
Columbia	797.2	49,291	Okaloosa	935.8	165,873
Dade	1,944.7	2,076,175	Okeechobee	774.3	30,894
DeSoto	637.3	25,253	Orange	907.6	758,980
Dixie	704.1	12,352	Osceola	1,322.0	135,812
Duval	773.9	721,139	Palm Beach	2,034.3	992,840
Escambia	663.6	277,634	Pasco	745.0	311,556
Flagler	485.0	42,142	Pinellas	280.2	868,887
Franklin	534.0	10,271	Polk	1,874.9	440,954
Gadsden	516.2	43,787	Putnam	722.2	69,704
Gilchrist	348.9	12,871	Saint Johns	609.0	106,503
Glades	773.5	7,851	Saint Lucie	572.5	174,728
Gulf	565.1	13,327	Santa Rosa	1,015.8	108,186
Hamilton	514.9	12,288	Sarasota	571.8	296,518
Hardee	637.4	20,130	Seminole	308.2	335,868
Hendry	1,152.7	29,821	Sumter	545.7	35,948
Hernando	478.3	121,266	Suwannee	687.7	30,901
Highlands	1,028.5	74,836	Taylor	1,041.9	18,173
Hillsborough	1,051.0	897,522	Union	240.3	12,451
Holmes	482.5	18,174	Volusia	1,105.9	414,322
Indian River	503.2	96,490	Wakulla	606.7	18,105
Jackson	915.8	44,728	Walton	1,057.7	35,255
Jefferson	597.8	13,260	Washington	579.9	19,212
Lafayette	542.8	6,237			

Source: U.S. Census Bureau; National Association of Counties.

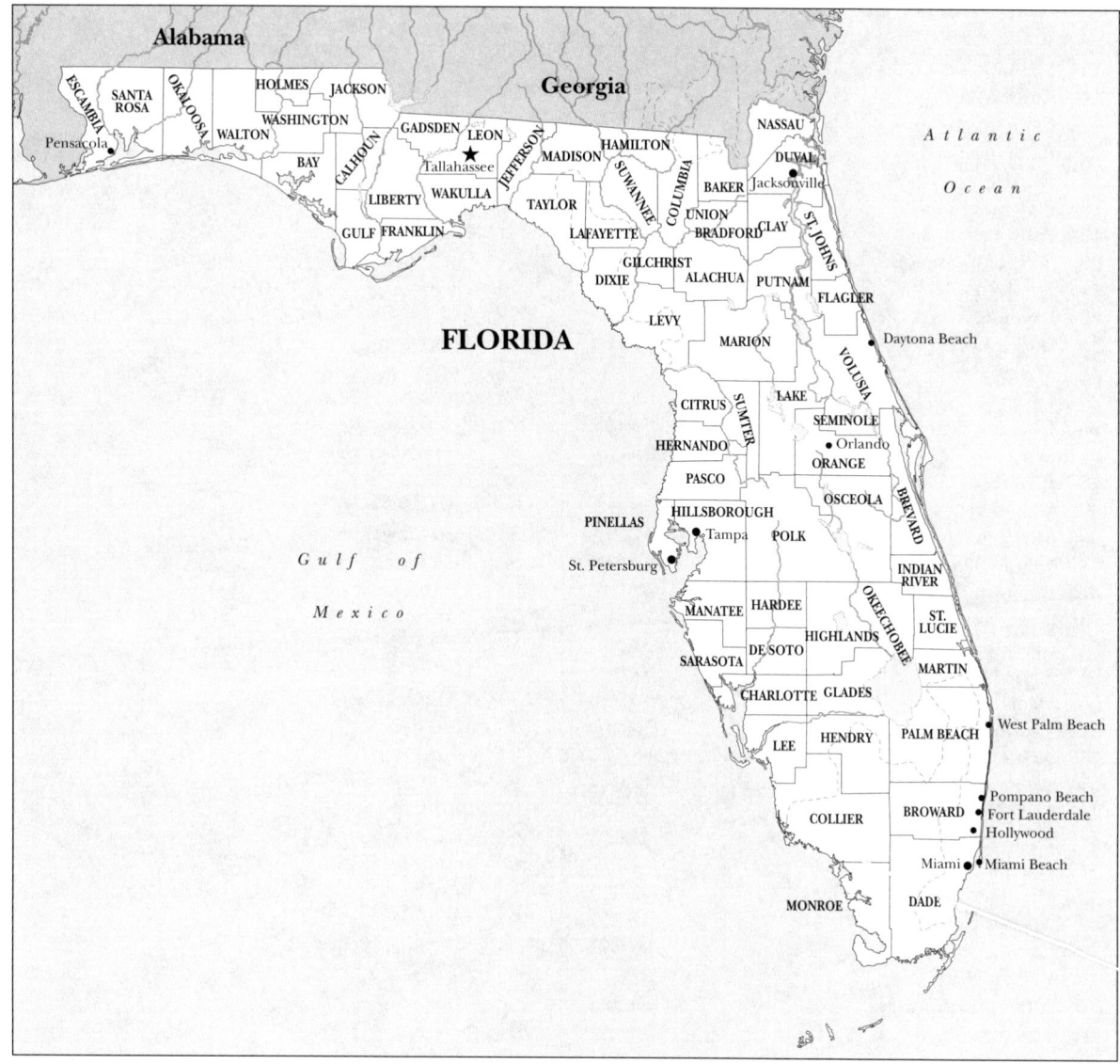

Cities

With 10,000 or more residents

Rank	City	Population
1	Jacksonville	693,630
2	Miami	368,624
3	Tampa	289,156
4	St. Petersburg	236,029
5	Hialeah	211,392
6	Orlando	181,175

Rank	City	Population
7	Fort Lauderdale	153,728
8	Tallahassee	136,628
9	Hollywood	130,026
10	Pembroke Pines	115,361
11	Coral Springs	111,744
12	Clearwater	101,474

(continued)

Rank	City	Population	Rank	City	Population
13	Miami Beach	97,053	66	Plant City	27,093
14	Gainesville	92,648	67	Greenacres	25,811
15	Cape Coral	91,180	68	Winter Haven	25,724
16	Plantation	81,424	69	Key West	25,701
17	Sunrise	80,338	70	Casselberry	24,768
18	Port St. Lucie	79,351	71	Winter Park	23,377
19	Palm Bay	77,486	72	Oviedo	22,162
20	West Palm Beach	76,308	73	Fort Walton Beach	21,501
21	Pompano Beach	75,982	74	Ocoee	21,089
22	Lakeland	74,204	75	Jacksonville Beach	20,643
23	BocaRaton	71,761	76	Apopka	19,657
24	Melbourne	69,057	77	Rockledge	19,416
25	Largo	66,264	78	Naples	19,404
26	Daytona Beach	65,136	79	Royal Palm Beach	19,170
27	Davie	62,061	80	Tarpon Springs	19,016
28	Pensacola	58,193	81	De Land	18,769
29	Deltona	58,168	82	Cocoa	18,508
30	Miramar	57,215	83	New Smyrna Beach	18,167
31	Delray Beach	53,618	84	Edgewater	17,757
32	Boynton Beach	53,607	85	Temple Terrace	17,713
33	Tamarac	52,929	86	Venice	17,686
34	Margate	51,268	87	Belle Glade	17,224
35	Sarasota	51,035	88	Hialeah Gardens	17,076
36	Deerfield Beach	50,921	89	Leesburg	16,911
37	Lauderhill	50,814	90	Vero Beach	16,387
38	North Miami	50,772	91	North Port	16,307
39	Bradenton	47,049	92	Safety Harbor	16,146
40	Ocala	47,035	93	Opa-locka	15,378
41	Fort Myers	45,697	94	St. Cloud	15,193
42	Pinellas Park	44,179	95	Dania	15,162
43	Port Orange	43,020	96	Eustis	15,137
44	Titusville	41,533	97	Bartow	15,025
45	Coral Gables	40,858	98	New Port Richey	15,024
46	Panama City	39,477	99	Sweetwater	14,370
47	Altamonte Springs	39,278	100	Longwood	14,004
48	Kissimmee	38,542	101	Sebastian	13,942
49	Coconut Creek	37,437	102	Miami Springs	13,416
50	Sanford	36,951	103	South Daytona	13,381
51	Fort Pierce	36,341	104	Punta Gorda	13,280
52	North Miami Beach	35,554	105	Atlantic Beach	12,960
53	Dunedin	34,990	106	Callaway	12,780
54	Palm Beach Gardens	34,880	107	Lady Lake	12,701
55	Ormond Beach	33,060	108	Haines City	12,684
56	Hallandale	31,260	109	Lynn Haven	12,604
57	Jupiter	30,970	110	St. Augustine	12,573
58	Riviera Beach	30,050	111	Crestview	12,556
59	North Lauderdale	29,453	112	Cocoa Beach	12,548
60	Cooper City	29,207	113	North Palm Beach	12,398
61	Lake Worth	29,116	114	Stuart	12,385
62	Homestead	29,072	115	Parkland	12,348
63	Winter Springs	28,606	116	Wilton Manors	12,147
64	Oakland Park	28,476	117	Niceville	11,973
65	Lauderdale Lakes	28,235	118	Winter Garden	11,871

Rank	City	Population
119	Gulfport	11,549
120	Holly Hill	11,529
121	De Bary	11,026
122	Destin	11,021
123	Palatka	10,891
124	Lake City	10,756
125	South Miami	10,710
126	Lighthouse Point	10,706

Rank	City	Population
127	Palmetto	10,605
128	Fernandina Beach	10,408
129	Oldsmar	10,287
130	Satellite Beach	10,128
131	Orange Park	10,105

Population figures are estimated for mid-1998.
Source: U.S. Bureau of the Census.

Index to Tables

NA = Reliable data are not available.

DEMOGRAPHICS

Resident state and national populations, 1970-1997

Population figures given in thousands

	State pop.	U.S. pop.	Share	Rank
1970	6,791	203,302	3.3%	9
1980	9,746	226,546	4.3%	7
1985	11,351	237,924	4.8%	6
1990	12,938	248,765	5.2%	4
1995	14,181	262,761	5.4%	4
1997	14,654	267,636	5.5%	4

Source: U.S. Bureau of the Census.

Resident population by age, 1997

Age group	Total population
Under 5 years	951,000
5 to 17 years	2,520,000
18 to 24 years	1,180,000
25 to 34 years	1,968,000
35 to 44 years	2,261,000
45 to 54 years	1,753,000
55 to 64 years	1,312,000
65 to 74 years	1,458,000
75 to 84 years	958,000
85 years and over	293,000
Portion of residents 65 and older	18.5%
National average	12.7%

Population figures are rounded to nearest thousand persons;
figures include armed forces personnel stationed in state.
Source: U.S. Bureau of the Census.

Resident population by race, Hispanic origin, 1997

	State pop.	Share	U.S.
All residents	14,654,000	100.0%	100.0%
Hispanic white	1,952,000	13.3%	10.0%
non-Hispanic white	10,141,000	69.2%	72.7%
African American	2,253,000	15.4%	12.7%
Native American	55,000	0.4%	0.9%
Asian, Pacific Islander	253,000	1.7%	3.8%

Source: U.S. Bureau of the Census.

Projections of state population, 2000-2025

	Model A Uses interstate migration observed from 1975-1994	Model B Uses Bureau of Economic Analysis employment projections
Year	Population	Population
2000	15,233,000	15,250,000
2005	16,279,000	16,273,000
2010	17,363,000	17,299,000
2015	18,497,000	18,318,000
2020	19,634,000	19,262,000
2025	20,710,000	20,066,000

All population projections, including those for 2000, were calculated in 1997.
Source: U.S. Bureau of the Census, Population Paper Listings PPL-47.

VITAL STATISTICS

Average lifetime in years by race, 1989-1991

	State	U.S.	Rank
All residents	75.84	75.37	24
White residents	76.82	76.13	15
Black residents	68.77	69.16	27

Ranks are from longest-lived to least longest-lived. Ranks exclude Alaska, for which reliable data are not available. Rank for black residents is based on the 32 states for which reliable data are available.
Source: U.S. National Center for Health Statistics.

Infant mortality rates, 1980 and 1995

	State	U.S.
All residents		
1980	14.6	12.6
1995	7.5	7.6
White residents		
1980	11.8	11.0
1995	6.0	6.3
Black residents		
1980	22.8	21.4
1995	13.0	15.1

Figures represent deaths per 1,000 live births of resident infants under 1 year old, exclusive of fetal deaths; all-residents figures include other races not listed separately.
Source: U.S. National Center for Health Statistics.

Marriages and divorces

Marriages in 1996	149,900
Rate per 1,000 population, 1995	10.2
U.S. rate, 1995	8.9
Rank among all states	12
Divorces in 1996	80,200
Rate per 1,000 population, 1995.	5.6
U.S. rate, 1995	4.4
Rank among all states	11

Rank is from highest to lowest in country.
Source: U.S. National Center for Health Statistics.

Death rates by leading causes, 1995
Deaths per 100,000 resident population

Cause	State	U.S.
Heart disease	351.6	280.7
Cancer	263.5	204.9
Cerebrovascular diseases	69.9	60.1
Accidents and adverse effects	38.1	35.5
Motor vehicle accidents	19.8	16.5
Chronic obstructive pulmonary diseases	52.9	39.2
Diabetes mellitus	26.0	22.6
HIV	30.8	NA
Suicide	15.3	11.9
Homicide	8.8	8.7
All causes	1,081.3	880.0
Rank in overall death rate among states		2

Figures exclude nonresidents who die in state. Causes of death follow International Classification of Diseases. Rank is from highest to lowest in country.
Source: U.S. National Center for Health Statistics.

ECONOMY

Gross state product, 1990-1996
In current dollars

	State product	Increase
1990	$255.2 billion	
1993	$300.7 billion	
1994	$321.7 billion	6.98%
1995	$339.0 billion	5.38%
1996	$360.5 billion	6.34%

Source: U.S. Bureau of Economic Analysis; *Survey of Current Business,* June, 1998.

Gross state product by industry, 1996
In billions

Farms, forestry, fisheries	$5.8
Construction	14.7
Manufacturing	28.8
Transportation, public utilities	30.4
Wholesale trade	25.2
Retail trade	39.2
Finance, insurance, real estate	67.8
Services	73.4
Government	40.1
State total	$326.1
Total U.S.	$6,923.8
State share	4.71%
Rank among states	5

Total figures include mining, not listed separately.
Source: U.S. Bureau of Economic Analysis; *Survey of Current Business,* June, 1998.

Personal income per capita, 1990 and 1997
In current dollars

	1990	1997
Per capita income	$19,185	$25,255
U.S. average	$19,188	$25,598
Rank among states	19	20

1997 data are preliminary.
Source: U.S. Bureau of Economic Analysis; *Survey of Current Business,* May, 1998.

Energy consumption, 1995
In trillions of British thermal units (BTU)

End-use sectors

Residential	973.0
Commercial	750.3
Industrial	570.0
Transportation	1,225.3

Sources of energy

Petroleum	1,620.2
Natural gas	532.6
Coal	653.0
Hydroelectric power	2.4
Nuclear electric power	306.3
Total state per capita consumption	248.1
Total U.S. per capita consumption	344.4
Rank among states	42
Total state energy consumption	3,518.6
Total U.S. energy consumption	90,547.4
State share of U.S. total	3.89%
Rank among states	8

Total figures include items not listed separately.
Source: U.S. Energy Information Administration; *State Energy Data Report.*

Nonfarm employment by sectors, 1997

Total	6,427,000
Construction	333,000
Manufacturing	491,000
Transportation, public utilities	327,000
Wholesale trade, retail trade	1,652,000
Finance, insurance, real estate	410,000
Services	2,265,000
Government	943,000

Figures are rounded to nearest thousand persons. Total includes mining, not listed separately.
Source: U.S. Bureau of Labor Statistics; *Employment and Earnings,* monthly.

Foreign exports, 1990-1997
In millions of dollars

Year	State	U.S.	State share
1990	11,634	394,045	2.95%
1996	20,744	624,767	3.32%
1997	23,234	688,896	3.37%

Source: U.S. Bureau of the Census; *U.S. Merchandise Trade,* series FT 900.

LAND USE

Federally owned land, 1996

	State	U.S.	State share
Total acres	34,721,000	2,271,343,000	1.53%
Federally owned	2,645,000	563,129,000	0.47%
Federal share	7.6%	24.8%	—

Areas are rounded to nearest thousand acres. Figures for federally owned land do not include trust properties.

Source: U.S. General Services Administration; *Inventory Report on Real Property Owned by the United States Throughout the World,* annual.

Land use, 1992

In acres, rounded to nearest thousand

Total surface area	37,545,000
Federal land	3,791,000
Total nonfederal	30,406,000
Developed	4,645,000
Total rural	25,761,000
Cropland	2,997,000
Pasture land	4,373,000
Range land	3,467,000
Forest land	12,378,000
Minor cover/use	2,545,000

Total surface area figures include water area not shown separately.

Source: U.S. Dept. of Agriculture; Soil Conservation Service; Iowa State University, Statistical Laboratory; *Summary Report, 1992 National Resources Inventory.*

Farms and crop acreage, 1997

	State	U.S.	Share	Rank
Farms (thousands)	40	2,058	1.94%	23
Acres (millions)	10	968	1.03%	30
Acres per farm	258	471	—	28
Acres planted	1,089	334,139	0.33%	37
Acres harvested	1,060	319,894	0.33%	37
Farm value (mill.)	$3,793	$108,805	3.49%	9

Numbers of farms are rounded to nearest thousand.

Source: U.S. Dept. of Agriculture; National Agricultural Statistics Service.

GOVERNMENT AND FINANCE

Units of local government, 1997

	State	Total U.S.	Rank
All local governments	1,081	87,453	28
Counties	66	3,043	21
Municipalities	394	19,372	21
Townships	0	16,629	—
School districts	95	13,726	34
Special districts	526	34,683	22

County ranks are based on the 48 states with county governments; township ranks are based on the 20 states with township governments; school district ranks are based on the 46 states with such districts.

Source: U.S. Bureau of the Census; *1997 Census of Governments, Government Organization,* Series GC97(1).

State government revenue, 1996

Total revenue	$41,680 mill.
General revenue	32,994 mill.
Per capita	2,288
U.S. per capita average	2,910
Rank among states	49
Intergovernmental revenue	
Total	$8,493 mill.
From federal government	8,171 mill.
From local government	322 mill.
Charges and Miscellaneous	
Total	$4,801 mill.
Current charges	1,818 mill.
Misc. general revenue	2,983 mill.
Taxes	
Total	$19,699 mill.
General sales	11,429 mill.
Selective sales	3,812 mill.
License taxes	1,315 mill.
Individual income	NA
Corporate income	1,008 mill.
Other	2,136 mill.
Insurance trust revenue	8,681 mill.

Total revenue figures include items not listed separately.

Source: U.S. Bureau of the Census.

State government expenditures, 1996

General expenditures

Intergovernmental . . . . $11,140 mill.
Direct expenditures. . . . . . . 22,479 mill.
Total . . . . 33,619 mill.

Selected direct expenditures

Education . . . . $10,872 mill.
Public welfare . . . . 7,318 mill.
Health, hospital . . . . 2,606 mill.
Highways . . . . 3,241 mill.
Police . . . . 295 mill.
Corrections. . . . . 1,647 mill.
Natural resources . . . . 1,241 mill.
Parks and recreation . . . . 125 mill.
Government administration. . . . 1,253 mill.
Interest on debt . . . . 1,112 mill.

Other

State per capita expenditures $2,332
U.S. per capita average 2,854
Rank among states 48
Total state expenditures . . . . . 36,454 mill.
Total U.S. expenditures . . . . . 859,959 mill.

Totals include items not listed separately.
Source: U.S. Bureau of the Census.

Launch of a space shuttle flight from Cape Canaveral. (Photo-Disc)

POLITICS

Governors since statehood

D = Democrat; R = Republican; O = other;
(r) resigned; (d) died in office; (i) removed from office

William D. Moseley (D) 1845-1849
Thomas Brown (O). 1849-1853
James E. Broome (D). 1853-1857
Madison S. Perry (D) 1857-1861
John Milton (D) . . . . (d) 1861-1865
Abram K. Allison (D) . . . . (i) 1865
William Marvin 1865
David S. Walker 1865-1868
Harrison Reed (R) 1868-1873

Ossian B. Hart (R) . . . . (d) 1873-1874
Marcellus L. Stearns (R) 1874-1877
George F. Drew (D). 1877-1881
William D. Bloxham (D) 1881-1885
Edward A. Perry (D) 1885-18489
Francis P. Fleming (D) 1889-1893
Henry L. Mitchell (D) 1893-1897
William D. Bloxham (D) 1897-1901
William S. Jennings (D) 1901-1905
Napoleon B. Broward (D) 1905-1909
Albert W. Gilchrist (D) 1909-1913
Park Trammell (D) 1913-1917
Sidney J. Catts (O) 1917-1921
Gary A. Hardee (D) 1921-1925
John W. Martin (D). 1925-1929
Doyle E. Carlton (D) 1929-1933

David Sholtz (D) 1933-1937
Frederick P. Cone (D) 1937-1941
Spessard L. Holland (D) 1941-1945
Millard F. Caldwell, Jr. (D) 1945-1949
Fuller Warren (D) 1949-1953
Daniel T. McCarty (D) . . . . (d) 1953
Charles E. Johns (D) 1953-1955
Thomas Leroy Collins (D) 1955-1961
Cecil Farris Bryant (D) 1961-1965
William Hayden Burns (D). 1965-1967
Claude R. Kirk, Jr. (R) 1967-1971
Reubin O. Askew (D) 1971-1979
Robert Graham (D) 1979-1987
Bob Martinez (R) 1987-1991
Lawton Chiles (D) 1991-1999
Jeb Bush (R) 1999-

Composition of state legislature, 1990-1998

	Democrats	Republicans
State House (120 seats)		
1990	74	46
1992	71	49
1994	63	57
1996	59	61
1998	46	73
State Senate (40 seats)		
1990	22	18
1992	20	20
1994	19	21
1996	17	23
1998	15	25

Figures for total seats may include independents and minor
party members.

Source: Council of State Governments; *State Elective Officials
and the Legislatures.*

Composition of congressional delegations, 1989-1999

	Dem	Rep	Total
House of Representatives			
101st Congress, 1989			
State delegates	10	9	19
Total U.S.	259	174	433
102d Congress, 1991			
State delegates	9	10	19
Total U.S.	267	167	434
103d Congress, 1993			
State delegates	10	13	23
Total U.S.	258	176	434
104th Congress, 1995			
State delegates	8	15	23
Total U.S.	197	236	433
105th Congress, 1997			
State delegates	8	15	23
Total U.S.	206	228	434
106th Congress, 1999			
State delegates	8	15	23
Total U.S.	211	222	433
Senate			
101st Congress, 1989			
State delegates	1	1	2
Total U.S.	55	45	100
102d Congress, 1991			
State delegates	1	1	2
Total U.S.	56	44	100
103d Congress, 1993			
State delegates	1	1	2
Total U.S.	57	43	100
104th Congress, 1995			
State delegates	1	1	2
Total U.S.	46	53	99
105th Congress, 1997			
State delegates	1	1	2
Total U.S.	45	55	100
106th Congress, 1999			
State delegates	1	1	2
Total U.S.	45	54	99

Figures are for starts of first sessions. Figure for U.S. Representatives for 101st Congress does not include Alabama
and Indiana, which had vacancies. Figures for total U.S.
Representatives for 102d, 103d, and 106th Congresses do
not include Vermont, which had 1 Independent-Socialist.
Figure for U.S. Representatives for 104th Congress does
not include Vermont, which had 1 Independent-Socialist,
and California, which had 1 vacancy. Figure for U.S.
Representatives for 105th Congress does not include
New York, which had 1 vacancy. Figure for U.S. Senators
for 104th Congress does not include Oregon, which had
1 vacancy. Figure for U.S. Senators for 106th Congress does
not include New Hampshire, which had 1 Independent.

Source: U.S. Congress; *Congressional Directory,* biennial.

Miami Beach. (PhotoDisc)

Voter participation in presidential elections, 1992 and 1996

	1992	1996
State voting age pop.	10,422,000	11,043,000
Total U.S. voting age pop.	189,524,000	196,509,000
State share of U.S. total	5.5%	5.6%
Rank among states	4	4
Percent of state casting vote	51.0	46.5
Percent of U.S. total voting	55.1	49.0
Rank among states	40	40

Source: U.S. Bureau of the Census.

HEALTH AND MEDICAL CARE

Medicare, 1997

	Recipients	Payments
State	2,703,000	$17,525 mill.
Total U.S.	37,514,000	$206,064 mill.
State share	7.21%	8.50%
Rank among states	2	2

Recipient figures are rounded to nearest thousand persons.
Ranks are from highest to lowest.
Source: U.S. Health Care Financing Administration.

Medicaid, 1996

	Recipients	Payments
State	1,638,000	$4,670 mill.
Total U.S.	35,028,000	$121,419 mill.
State share	4.68%	3.85%
Rank among states	4	6

Recipient figures are rounded to nearest thousand persons. Payment figures for fiscal year reflect federal and state contribution payments. Ranks are from highest to lowest.
Source: U.S. Health Care Financing Administration.

HOUSING

Homeownership rates, 1985-1997

	1985	1990	1997
State	67.2%	65.1%	66.9%
Total U.S.	63.9%	63.9%	65.7%
Rank among states	30	32	33

Source: U.S. Bureau of the Census.

Health insurance coverage, 1996

	State	U.S.
Total persons covered	11,654,000	225,070,000
Total persons not covered	2,722,000	41,716,000
Part not covered	18.9%	15.6%
Rank among states	7	—
Children not covered	615,000	10,554,000
Part not covered	18.4%	14.8%
Rank among states	10	—

Ranks are from most to fewest uninsured. Population figures are rounded to nearest thousand persons.
Source: U.S. Bureau of the Census.

Home sales, 1990 and 1997
In thousands of units

Existing home sales	1990	1997	Change
State sales	183.3	234.4	51.1
Total U.S. sales	3,560	4,730	1,170
State share of U.S. total	5.15%	4.96%	-0.19%
Rank among states	3	3	—

Source: National Association of Realtors; *Real Estate Outlook: Market Trends and Insights.*

EDUCATION

Public school enrollment, 1995

State K-8 enrollment	1,614,000
Total U.S. K-8 enrollment	32,341,000
State share of total U.S.	4.99%
State 9-12 enrollment	563,000
Total U.S. 9-12 enrollment	12,500,000
State share of U.S. total	4.50%
State public school enroll. rate	91.0%
Overall U.S. rate	91.6%
Rank among states	31

Enrollment figures (which include unclassified students) are rounded to nearest thousand pupils in fall term; kindergarten (K)-8 grade enrollment figures include some prekindergarten students. Enrollment rate is based on percentage of persons 5-17 years old. Rank is from highest to lowest.
Source: U.S. National Center for Education Statistics.

AIDS, syphilis, tuberculosis, and measles cases, 1997

Cases	U.S.	State	Share
AIDS	58,443	6,098	10.43%
Syphilis	8,550	296	3.46%
Tuberculosis	18,534	1,401	7.56%
Measles	148,000	9,000	6.08%

Measles figures are rounded to nearest thousand cases.
Source: U.S. Centers for Disease Control and Prevention.

Public college finances, 1996

State FTE enrollment	403,000
Total U.S. FTE enrollment	8,268,800
State share of total U.S.	4.87%
Rank among states	4
State and local appropriations	$1,660,500,000
Total U.S. state and local appropriations.	$39,699 mill.
State share of total U.S.	4.18%
Rank among states	5
State net tuition revenues.	$509,800,000
Total U.S. net tuition	$18,348,100,000
State share of total U.S.	2.78%
Rank among states	9

FTE=Full-time equivalent; credit and noncredit enrollment including summer session in academic year ending in 1996.

Enrollments are rounded to nearest thousand students. Net tuition revenues exclude appropriation to students attending in-state public institutions. Rankings are from highest shares to lowest.

Source: Research Associates of Washington.

Motor vehicle registrations and driver licenses, 1996
In thousands

Vehicle registrations	State	U.S.	Share	Rank
Autos, trucks, buses	10,889	206,365	5.28%	3
Autos only	7,192	128,439	5.60%	4
Motorcycles	198	3,832	5.17%	3
Driver licenses	11,400	179,539	6.35%	3

Figures do not include vehicles owned by military services.
Source: U.S. Federal Highway Administration; *Highway Statistics; Selected Highway Statistics and Charts.*

Domestic travel expenditures, 1995
Spending by U.S. residents on overnight trips and day trips of at least 100 miles

Total expenditures in state	$30,879 mill.
Total expenditures in U.S.	$360,314 mill.
State share of total U.S.	8.57%
Rank among states	2

Source: Travel Industry Association of America.

TRANSPORTATION AND TRAVEL

Highway mileage, 1996

Interstate	1,471
Other arterial	12,384
Collector roads	21,135
Local roads	85,338
Urban roads.	48,339
Rural roads	66,083
Total state	114,422
U.S. total	3,933,985
State share	2.9%
Rank among states.	10

Source: U.S. Federal Highway Administration.

CRIME AND LAW ENFORCEMENT

State and local police officers, 1996

Local police	19,652
State police	1,740
Sheriffs	14,124
Total	37,395
Officers per 10,000 residents	26
U.S. average	25
Rank among states.	10

Figures cover full-time sworn officers; totals include special police not shown separately.
Source: U.S. Bureau of Justice Statistics; *Census of State and Local Law Enforcement Agencies, 1996.*

Crime rates, 1996

Rates per 100,000 resident population

Violent crimes	State	U.S.
Total violent	1,051	634
Murder	7.5	7.4
Forcible rape	52.1	36.1
Robbery	289	202
Aggravated assault	702	388
Property crimes		
Total property	6,446	4,445
Burglary	1,521	943
Larceny/theft	4,205	2,976
Motor vehicle theft	721	526
Totals	7,497	5,079

Source: U.S. Federal Bureau of Investigation; *Crime in the United States*, annual.

State prison populations, 1980-1996

	State	U.S.	State share
1980	20,735	305,458	6.79%
1990	44,387	708,393	6.27%
1996	63,763	1,025,624	6.22%

Figures exclude prisoners in federal penitentiaries.
Source: U.S. Bureau of Justice Statistics.

Georgia

Location: Southeast coast of continental United States

Area and rank: 57,919 square miles (150,010 square kilometers); 59,441 square miles (153,952 square kilometers) including water; twenty-second largest state in area

Coastline: 100 miles (161 kilometers)

Shoreline: 2,344 miles (3,771 kilometers)

Population and rank: 7,486,242 (1997); tenth largest state in population

Atlanta, Georgia's capital and largest city. (PhotoDisc)

Capital: Atlanta

Largest city: Atlanta (403,819 people in 1998)

Entered Union and rank: January 2, 1788; fourth state

Present constitution adopted: 1977

Counties: 159

State name: Georgia takes its name from King George II of England

State nicknames: Peach State; Empire State of the South

Motto: Wisdom, justice, and moderation

State flag: One-third is blue field with state coat of arms; two-thirds are the Confederate flag — red field with blue and white cross of Saint Andrew and thirteen white stars

Highest point: Brasstown Bald — 4,784 feet (1,458 meters)

Lowest point: Atlantic Ocean — sea level

Highest recorded temperature: 113 degrees Fahrenheit (45 degrees Celsius) — Greenville, 1978

Lowest recorded temperature: −17 degrees Fahrenheit (−27 degrees Celsius) — CCC Camp F-16, 1940

State song: "Georgia on My Mind"

State tree: Live oak

State flower: Cherokee rose

State bird: Brown thrasher

Georgia History

The last of the original thirteen English colonies to be founded, and the largest state east of the Mississippi River, Georgia has twice led its region in being the forerunner of the "New South," first following the Civil War and then during the second half of the twentieth century. A state of immense geographical variation, changing in height from one mile to sea level, it transformed itself from a primarily agricultural state to one that embraced modern manufacturing and technology. Its capital, Atlanta, is one of the largest and fastest-growing cities in the South and a metropolis of truly international distinction.

Early History. In approximately 12,000 B.C.E. the first inhabitants lived along the rivers and coasts of what would become Georgia with a diet of fish and shellfish. They were followed first by nomadic hunters and then by more settled residents who developed agriculture. When Europeans arrived during the mid-1500's, the Native American Cherokee and Creek tribes were dominant in the eastern and coastal areas. Along the coast the Yamacraw, a group of the Creek, were well established. The Chickasaw and Choctaw inhabited the western portion of the territory.

A Native American chief named Guale was the first to make lasting contact with the Europeans, meeting the Spanish soldier Pedro Menéndez de Avilés in 1566. As a result, for a time the entire coastal region was called Guale. British, French, and Spanish competed to make the Native American tribes their allies, with hopes of using them to defend their own colonies and eliminate those of their competitors. After the Yamasee War (1715-1728) nearly destroyed the British colony of Carolina, the British were determined to settle a buffer colony between themselves and the Spanish in Florida. That colony would become Georgia.

Exploration and Settlement. Spain, with strongholds established throughout the Caribbean and in Florida, sent the first European explorers into the area of Georgia. In 1540 Hernando de Soto passed through Georgia on his lengthy and difficult expedition in search of the fabled Seven Cities of Gold, which were rumored to possess wealth in excess of anything yet found in the New World. French Huguenots under Jean Ribaut landed along the coast in 1562, the same year Ribaut sought to colonize the Port Royal region to the north, in what is now South Carolina. Both attempts were failures. In order to strengthen its position and defend its Florida possessions, Spain established a string of missions and forts running along the coast from northern Florida to the sea islands.

The English responded by thrusting south, forcing the Spanish back to St. Augustine. To create a barrier between the Spanish and the rapidly growing colonies to the north, King George II granted a charter for a colony in 1732. General James Edward Oglethorpe, who wished to open the colony for debtors to give them a fresh start on life, was placed in command of the venture. In 1733, with just over one hundred colonists, Oglethorpe arrived at the bluffs of the Savannah River and struck a deal with Yamacraw chief Tomochichi for land along the river. Oglethorpe laid out the city of Savannah with a gridlike pattern of squares, which would remain.

The Spanish threat was effectively ended in 1742 with Oglethorpe's victory at the battle of Bloody Marsh on Saint Simons Island. Georgia grew rapidly with an economy based on rice, indigo, and cotton. Slavery had been banned in the colony in 1735, but crops were grown best under the plantation system, and in 1749 the slave trade was legalized. The territory up the Savannah River was explored and settled; in 1753 the city of Augusta was founded. In 1754 Georgia became a royal colony.

Revolution and the New Nation. As the colonies moved toward independence, Georgia convened a Provincial Congress in 1775, and its Council of Safety sent delegates to the Continental Congress in Philadelphia. The year following the declaration of American independence, Georgia ratified its first state constitution. In 1778, as the British pursued a southern strategy to pacify the rebellion, their troops seized Savannah. American and French troops were repulsed in a bloody attempt to

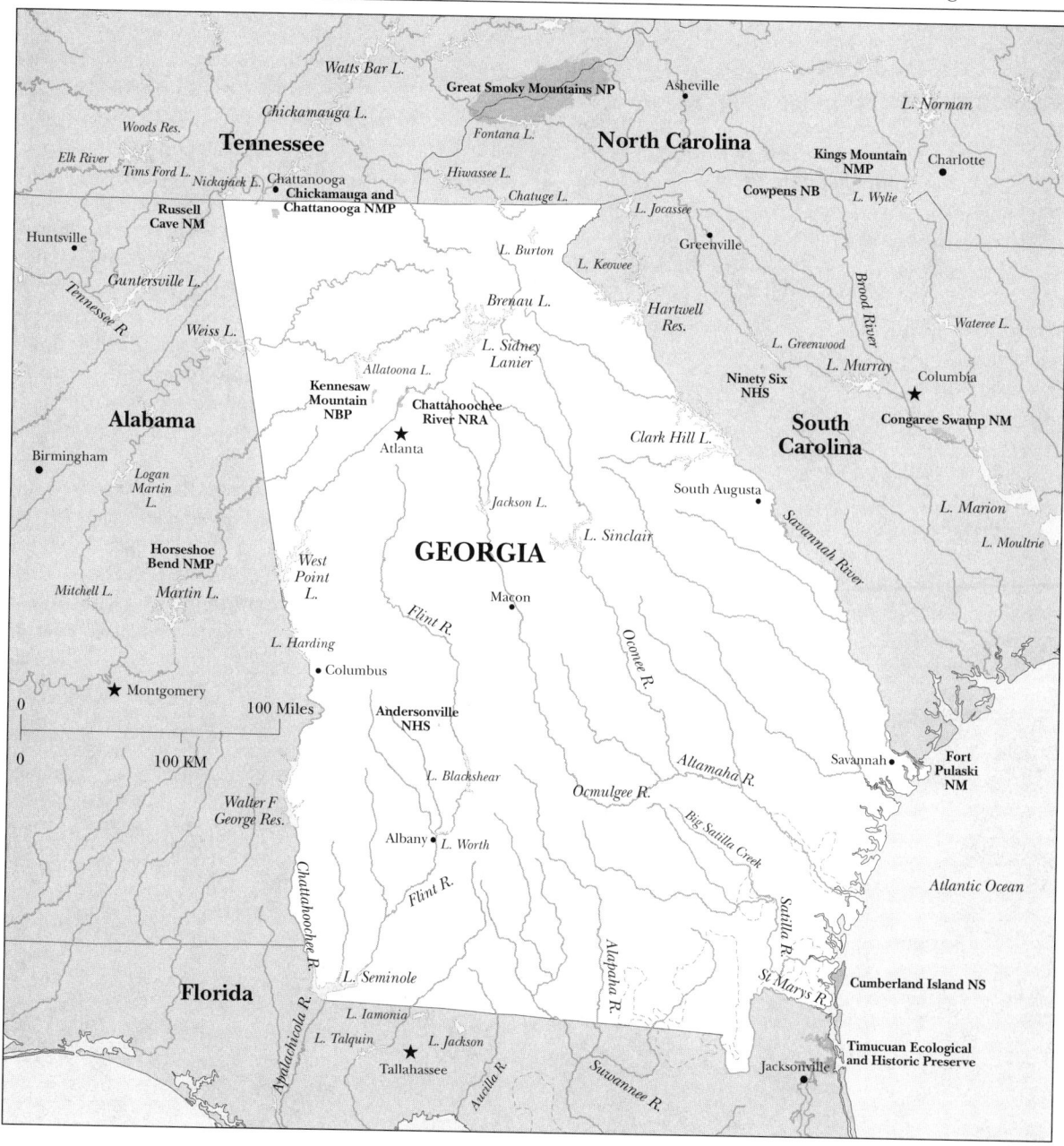

retake the city, which the British continued to hold until the end of the Revolution.

Georgia became the fourth state to ratify the Constitution, and it joined the Union in 1788, with Augusta, on the Savannah River, as its capital. Its western lands were rapidly developed, and this growth led to the Yazoo Fraud, during which members of the state legislature sold 50 million acres to phantom land companies (most of which were owned by the legislators themselves), which resold them to the public. In the end, the federal government had to pay more than $4 million to settle claims from the incident.

The western movement also prompted the removal of the Cherokee and Creek Indians from Georgia. The Creek sold their lands in 1827 and moved to Arkansas. Although the Cherokee had tried to fashion a compromise with the European settlers, the discovery of gold on their territory doomed those efforts. Georgia ordered the removal of the Native Americans in 1832, and six years later the tribe began its Trail of Tears to Indian Territory, now the state of Oklahoma.

One of the most important developments in American history occurred near Savannah in 1793, when Eli Whitney invented the cotton gin. This device automatically separated cotton seed from cotton fiber, a time-consuming task which before had been done only by hand. The cotton gin made possible the booming growth of cotton farming in the South, including Georgia, where the rich soil in central part of the state made the crop highly profitable.

Civil War and Reconstruction. In 1861 Georgia joined with seven other southern states and seceded from the Union. Later that year, in the temporary capital of Montgomery, Alabama, Alexander H. Stephens of Georgia was elected vice president of the Confederacy. While Georgia soldiers were fighting along the front lines in Tennessee and Virginia, Union forces bombarded and captured Fort Pulaski at the mouth of the Savannah River and clamped a tight blockade on the Georgia coastline. In 1863, after capturing Chattanooga, Tennessee, a Union army advancing into Georgia was surprised and overcome at the Battle of Chickamauga. The following year, the Federals returned under General William Tecumseh Sherman to strike at the strategic railroad center of Atlanta. After months of siege, Atlanta fell and was burned. Sherman then embarked on his March to the Sea, leaving a swath of destruction through Georgia sixty miles wide and capturing Savannah in December.

Following the war, Georgia, like the rest of the defeated South, entered a period of Reconstruction. It attempted to rejoin the Union in 1868 but was refused reentry in 1869 because it refused to ratify the Fifteenth Amendment, which prohibits denying voting rights because of race. When Geor-

This monumental relief carved on Stone Mountain, near Atlanta, honors (left to right) Confederate leaders Jefferson Davis, Robert E. Lee, and Thomas "Stonewall" Jackson. (PhotoDisc)

One of the great plantation houses of nineteenth century Savannah. (Georgia Department of Industry, Trade & Tourism)

gia complied with this amendment it was readmitted to the Union, in 1870.

During Reconstruction, Georgia began to rebuild its economy, repairing and expanding its railroad system, which had been largely destroyed during the Civil War, and diversifying its agricultural base to include corn, fruit—especially peaches—tobacco, and livestock. However, cotton, which had been a major crop before the Civil War, remained an essential part of the state's economy, and when a boll weevil infestation struck in the 1920's, it was a severe blow to Georgia's farmers and the entire state.

The state was making strides in other areas. In 1879 Henry Grady had become one of the owners of the Atlanta *Constitution*, the state's largest newspaper. As an unofficial spokesperson for Georgia, Grady prophesied the "New South," which would embrace progress, introduce industry and manufacturing, and move away from the wounds of the Civil War. Atlanta took as its symbol the phoe-

nix, since the city had literally risen anew from the ashes of destruction. It became the headquarters of large regional companies, an economic powerhouse in the Southeast, and a literal symbol of Grady's New South. Among the local success stories was the rise of Coca-Cola, invented by pharmacist John Styth Pemberton in 1886 and, after a few years, the most popular soft drink in the nation.

The Modern Age. During the 1940's and 1950's, manufacturing in Georgia passed agriculture, forestry, and fishing as the major source of income. Textile mills, in particular, became a major force in the state's economy. Georgia became one of the world's largest sources of kaolin and fullers earth, the first used in producing paper and dishware, the second used for cat litter. High-quality granite was also mined in the upper portion of the state. Meanwhile, the growth of banking and financial institutions continued to the point that Atlanta became known as the "Wall Street of the South," while busi-

Modern cotton-reaping machinery has replaced the labor-intensive hand-picking methods built on slave labor in the nineteenth century. (Georgia Department of Industry, Trade & Tourism)

nesses involved with modern technology also contributed to the growth of the state.

Georgia's passage through the civil rights era was aided by a tradition of moderation among its political leadership. From 1877 on, the state had only Democratic governors. Although Democrat Lester Maddox was elected governor in 1966 with an openly segregationist agenda, broad-minded Atlanta mayor Ivan Allen and progressive governors such as Ellis Arnall, Carl Sanders, and Jimmy Carter were more representative and helped bring the state through a potentially difficult period. Carter in 1976 was elected president of the United States. In 1972 Maynard Jackson was elected mayor of Atlanta, the first African American chosen to lead a large southern city. Also that year, Andrew Young became the first African American elected to Congress from Georgia since the end of Reconstruction. This period of Georgia's history is regarded as marking the birth of the second "New South," which combined economic development with racial progress.

Georgia's economy is strong, with its deep-water port of Savannah one of the most active on the East Coast. Atlanta's Hartsville International Airport is one of the largest and best equipped in the world. Natural resources contribute to the state's revenues.

Michael Witkoski

Georgia Time Line

1540	Spanish explorer Hernando de Soto marches through part of Georgia in his quest for gold.
1566	Spanish mariner Pedro Menéndez de Avilés builds a fort on Saint Catherine's Island.
June 9, 1732	George II grants charter giving imprisoned English debtors the right to settle in Georgia.
Feb. 12, 1733	General James Oglethorpe founds Savannah.

1735	Georgia bans importation of slaves.
1736	Methodist preachers John and Charles Wesley arrive at Savannah.
1742	Oglethorpe's troops defeat Spaniards at battle of Bloody Marsh on Saint Simons Island.
1749	Slave trade is legalized.
1754	Georgia becomes a royal province.
1775	Provincial Congress meets in Savannah.
Feb. 5, 1777	First state constitution is ratified in Savannah.
1778	British troops capture Savannah during the Revolution.
July 12, 1782	British abandon Savannah.
1785	University of Georgia is founded at Athens.
1786	Augusta is named state capital.
Jan. 2, 1788	Georgia enters the Union as the fourth state.
June 20, 1793	Eli Whitney invents the cotton gin near Savannah.
1795	Louisville is named state capital.
1804	Milledgeville is named state capital.
Feb. 12, 1825	Creek Indians cede all remaining lands east of Flint River to Georgia.
1828-1838	Conflicts with Cherokee over land claims lead to their removal from Georgia.
1836	Georgia Female College, now Wesleyan College, the first college chartered to grant degrees to women, opens in Macon.
1837	City of Terminus, later Atlanta, is founded.
Jan. 19, 1861	Georgia secedes from Union.
1861	Georgian Alexander H. Stephens is elected vice president of the Confederacy.
Sept. 20, 1863	Union army is defeated at Battle of Chickamauga.
1864	Union general William Tecumseh Sherman captures and burns Atlanta; Union army marches to the sea and captures Savannah.
1868	Federal troops leave state.
1868	Atlanta is named state capital.
July 15, 1870	Georgia is readmitted to Union.
1875	First commercial peach orchard in Georgia is established.
1886	Pharmacist John Styth Pemberton of Atlanta invents Coca-Cola.
1888	Georgia Institute of Technology opens in Atlanta.
1912	Girl Scouts of America is formed by Juliette Gordon Low of Savannah.
1921	Boll weevil infestation damages Georgia's cotton crop.
1960	Future governor Lester Maddox organizes Georgians Unwilling to Surrender (GUTS), which boycotts businesses that change their segregation policies.
1966	Race riots take place in Atlanta.
1972	Maynard Jackson becomes the first African American elected mayor of Atlanta.

(continued)

1972	Andrew Young is elected the first African American congressman from Georgia since Reconstruction.
1976	Former governor Jimmy Carter is elected president of United States.
1980	World's largest airport terminal opens in Atlanta.
1982	New state constitution is adopted.
1987	Gwinnett County in Atlanta is the fastest-growing county in the United States for the second year.
1991	Georgia holds the most executions in the country.
1992	Governor Zell Miller announces legislation to remove the Confederate battle symbol from the state flag.

Notes for Further Study

Published Sources. A good starting place for information on the state is *A History of Georgia* (2d ed. 1991), edited by Kenneth Coleman. This is a solid traditional history of the state, well-researched and documented, which explores a wide range of topics. Two good sources on Georgia residents are James C. Cobb's *Georgia Odyssey* (1997) and Lane Mills's *The People of Georgia: An Illustrated History* (1992), a popular history on individuals and groups, from the earliest times to the modern era, who shaped developments in the Peach State. *Civil War Savannah* (1997), by Derek Smith, explores one of the South's most important cities during the Civil War.

Web Resources. A very useful general link to a variety of Web sites about Georgia is the aptly named Links to Georgia Sites (http://www.icad.uga.edu/Publications/ gatrink.html). The state of Georgia has a Web site that provides a wealth of information and directs visitors to other locations (http://www.state.ga.us). A valuable source of information can be found at the site hosted by the Georgia Department of Industry, Trade and Tourism (http://www.georgia.org). For information specifically about Georgia's rich historical heritage, the Georgia History site (http://www.cviog.uga.edu/projects/gainfor/ gahist.htm) is an excellent starting place. It is well supplemented and amplified by a visit to the site of the Georgia Department of Archives and History (http:// www.sos.state.ga.us/archives). For those interested in Georgia's natural resources, an excellent site is Links to Georgia Geoscience Sites (http://www.dc.peachtree .edu/~pgore/georgia.htm).

Counties

County	Sq. miles	1996 pop.	County	Sq. miles	1996 pop.
Appling	508.8	16,333	Bartow	459.9	66,293
Atkinson	338.1	7,022	Ben Hill	251.8	17,322
Bacon	285.0	10,344	Berrien	452.5	15,784
Baker	343.2	3,686	Bibb	250.0	155,573
Baldwin	258.5	41,947	Bleckley	217.4	10,930
Banks	233.7	11,918	Brantley	444.4	13,048
Barrow	162.2	37,407	Brooks	493.7	15,820

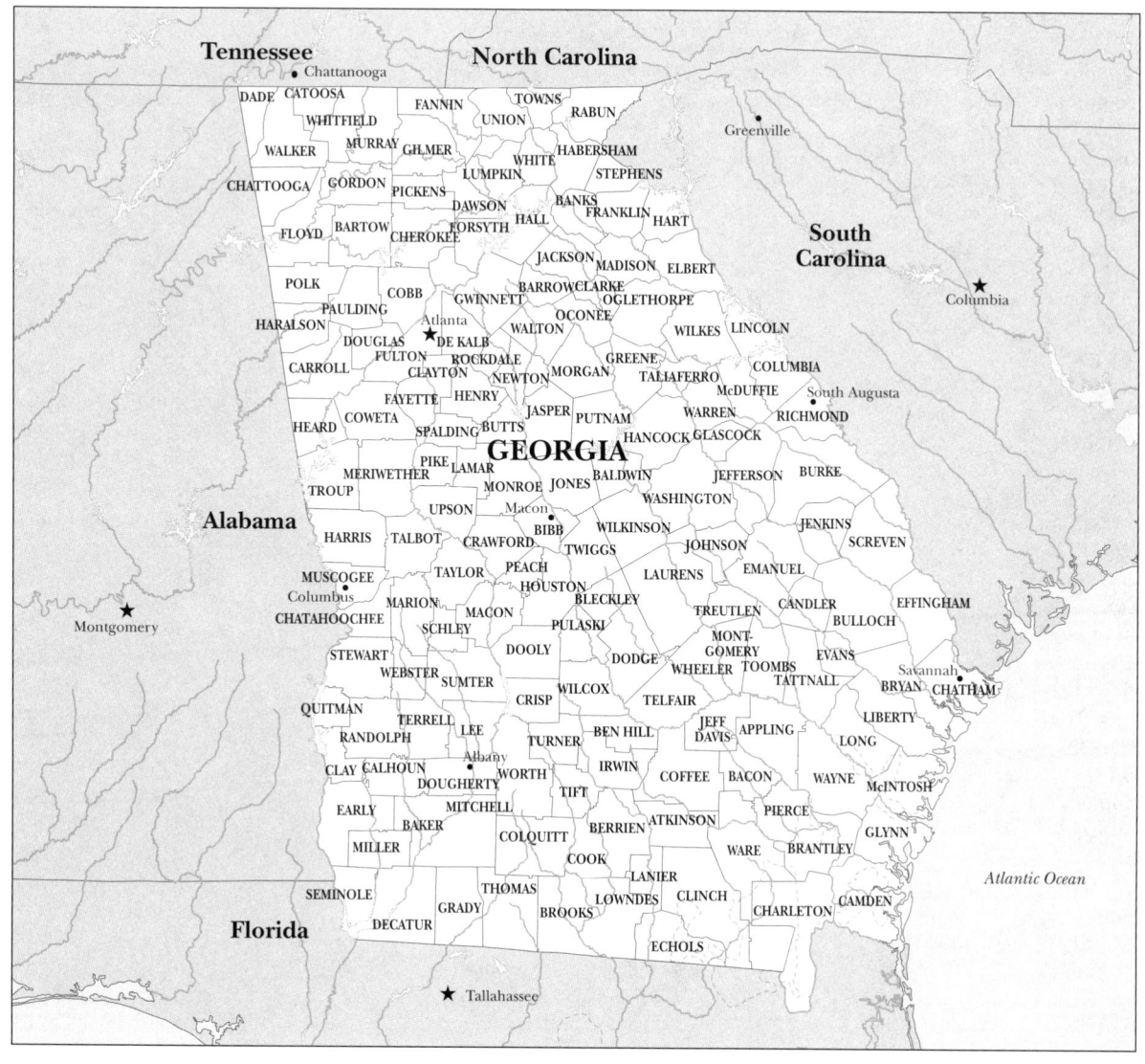

County	Sq. miles	1996 pop.	County	Sq. miles	1996 pop.
Bryan	441.8	22,286	Chatham	440.4	226,961
Bulloch	682.6	49,328	Chattahoochee	248.8	16,137
Burke	830.6	21,542	Chattooga	313.8	22,953
Butts	186.6	16,583	Cherokee	423.7	121,496
Calhoun	280.2	4,844	Clarke	120.8	90,602
Camden	629.9	42,798	Clay	195.2	3,360
Candler	247.0	8,676	Clayton	142.6	202,427
Carroll	499.3	79,307	Clinch	809.4	6,582
Catoosa	162.2	48,541	Cobb	340.2	538,832
Charlton	780.8	9,293	Coffee	599.1	33,188

(continued)

County	Sq. miles	1996 pop.	County	Sq. miles	1996 pop.
Colquitt	552.3	38,960	Lee	355.8	20,705
Columbia	290.0	86,173	Liberty	519.1	59,063
Cook	229.1	14,351	Lincoln	211.1	8,026
Coweta	443.1	76,295	Long	401.0	8,151
Crawford	325.1	10,514	Lowndes	504.3	83,982
Crisp	273.8	20,643	Lumpkin	284.5	17,286
Dade	173.9	14,486	McDuffie	259.8	21,474
Dawson	211.0	13,016	McIntosh	433.5	9,592
Decatur	596.8	26,529	Macon	403.3	13,141
DeKalb	268.3	589,796	Madison	284.4	24,192
Dodge	500.6	17,936	Marion	367.1	6,345
Dooly	393.0	10,416	Meriwether	503.4	22,944
Dougherty	329.7	96,581	Miller	283.1	6,144
Douglas	199.3	84,463	Mitchell	512.0	20,990
Early	511.3	12,149	Monroe	395.7	19,368
Echols	404.2	2,325	Montgomery	245.3	7,700
Effingham	479.5	33,363	Morgan	349.7	14,171
Elbert	368.8	19,286	Murray	344.4	30,777
Emanuel	686.0	21,030	Muscogee	216.3	183,394
Evans	185.0	9,519	Newton	276.4	52,709
Fannin	385.8	17,745	Oconee	185.8	22,410
Fayette	197.4	81,891	Oglethorpe	441.1	10,899
Floyd	513.3	84,422	Paulding	313.6	64,072
Forsyth	225.8	69,127	Peach	151.1	23,529
Franklin	263.3	18,184	Pickens	232.1	17,570
Fulton	528.7	718,336	Pierce	343.0	15,270
Gilmer	426.7	16,868	Pike	218.4	11,702
Glascock	144.2	2,429	Polk	311.2	35,370
Glynn	422.4	65,608	Pulaski	247.4	8,268
Gordon	355.2	39,369	Putnam	344.5	16,511
Grady	458.2	21,454	Quitman	151.6	2,463
Greene	388.4	13,010	Rabun	371.1	13,013
Gwinnett	432.9	478,001	Randolph	429.3	7,989
Habersham	278.2	30,794	Richmond	324.1	193,784
Hall	393.7	113,033	Rockdale	130.7	65,219
Hancock	473.3	9,023	Schley	167.6	3,763
Haralson	282.2	23,871	Screven	648.5	14,286
Harris	463.8	21,303	Seminole	238.1	9,252
Hart	232.2	21,005	Spalding	198.0	57,713
Heard	296.1	9,855	Stephens	179.3	25,246
Henry	322.7	90,969	Stewart	458.7	5,532
Houston	376.8	101,384	Sumter	485.3	30,668
Irwin	356.8	8,871	Talbot	393.2	6,865
Jackson	342.4	35,230	Taliaferro	195.4	1,861
Jasper	370.5	9,556	Tattnall	483.7	18,728
Jeff Davis	333.4	12,612	Taylor	377.5	8,189
Jefferson	527.7	17,860	Telfair	441.2	11,662
Jenkins	349.8	8,471	Terrell	335.5	11,092
Johnson	304.4	8,252	Thomas	548.4	41,908
Jones	393.8	22,330	Tift	265.1	36,850
Lamar	184.8	14,029	Toombs	366.7	25,463
Lanier	186.8	6,610	Towns	166.5	7,990
Laurens	812.6	43,342	Treutlen	200.7	5,903

County	Sq. miles	1996 pop.
Troup	413.9	58,568
Turner	286.1	9,003
Twiggs	360.4	9,873
Union	322.7	14,923
Upson	325.5	26,923
Walker	446.3	61,163
Walton	329.3	49,307
Ware	902.6	35,568
Warren	285.5	6,001
Washington	680.5	19,910

County	Sq. miles	1996 pop.
Wayne	644.7	24,636
Webster	209.6	2,242
Wheeler	297.7	4,933
White	241.6	16,140
Whitfield	290.0	80,296
Wilcox	380.4	7,320
Wilkes	471.4	10,583
Wilkinson	446.6	10,801
Worth	569.8	22,003

Source: U.S. Census Bureau; National Association of Counties.

Cities
With 10,000 or more residents

Rank	City	Population
1	Atlanta	403,819
2	Augusta-Richmond County (remainder)	187,689
3	Columbus (remainder)	182,219
4	Savannah	131,674
5	Macon	114,336
6	Athens-Clarke County(remainder)	89,361
7	Albany	77,545
8	Roswell	57,102
9	Marietta	51,362
10	Warner Robins	46,698
11	Valdosta	41,390
12	Smyrna	35,899
13	East Point	33,670
14	Peachtree City	31,086
15	Rome	30,899
16	Hinesville	26,435
17	La Grange	25,111
18	Alpharetta	24,831
19	Dalton	23,127
20	Statesboro	21,314
21	Griffin	21,052
22	Lawrenceville	20,008
23	College Park	19,990
24	Gainesville	19,900
25	Milledgeville	17,917
26	Duluth	17,722
27	Thomasville	17,451
28	Decatur	17,414

Rank	City	Population
29	Dublin	17,193
30	Forest Park	16,999
31	Americus	16,887
32	Carrollton	16,867
33	Douglasville	16,073
34	Snellville	15,703
35	Kennesaw	15,655
36	Moultrie	15,635
37	Waycross	15,466
38	Brunswick	15,163
39	Newnan	14,027
40	Tifton	13,867
41	St. Marys	13,823
42	Cartersville	13,470
43	Vidalia	11,726
44	Kingsland	11,584
45	Lilburn	11,239
46	Douglas	10,973
47	Bainbridge	10,941
48	Powder Springs	10,836
49	Cordele	10,599
50	Monroe	10,444
51	Union City	10,284
52	Riverdale	10,202
53	Buford	10,156
54	Covington	10,056

Population figures are estimated for mid-1998.
Source: U.S. Bureau of the Census.

Index to Tables

NA = Reliable data are not available.

DEMOGRAPHICS

Resident state and national populations, 1970-1997

Population figures given in thousands

	State pop.	U.S. pop.	Share	Rank
1970	4,588	203,302	2.3%	15
1980	5,463	226,546	2.4%	13
1985	5,963	237,924	2.5%	11
1990	6,478	248,765	2.6%	11
1995	7,192	262,761	2.7%	10
1997	7,486	267,636	2.8%	10

Source: U.S. Bureau of the Census.

Resident population by age, 1997

Age group	Total population
Under 5 years	558,000
5 to 17 years	1,430,000
18 to 24 years	738,000
25 to 34 years	1,220,000
35 to 44 years	1,274,000
45 to 54 years	955,000
55 to 64 years	573,000
65 to 74 years	416,000
75 to 84 years	245,000
85 years and over	77,000
Portion of residents 65 and older	9.9%
National average	12.7%

Population figures are rounded to nearest thousand persons;
figures include armed forces personnel stationed in state.
Source: U.S. Bureau of the Census.

Resident population by race, Hispanic origin, 1997

	State pop.	Share	U.S.
All residents	7,486,000	100.0%	100.0%
Hispanic white	181,000	2.4%	10.0%
non-Hispanic white	5,024,000	67.1%	72.7%
African American	2,126,000	28.4%	12.7%
Native American	17,000	0.2%	0.9%
Asian, Pacific Islander	137,000	1.8%	3.8%

Source: U.S. Bureau of the Census.

Projections of state population, 2000-2025

	Model A Uses interstate migration observed from 1975-1994	Model B Uses Bureau of Economic Analysis employment projections
Year	Population	Population
2000	7,875,000	7,893,000
2005	8,413,000	8,540,000
2010	8,824,000	9,167,000
2015	9,200,000	9,785,000
2020	9,552,000	10,386,000
2025	9,869,000	10,962,000

All population projections, including those for 2000, were calculated in 1997.
Source: U.S. Bureau of the Census, Population Paper Listings PPL-47.

VITAL STATISTICS

Average lifetime in years by race, 1989-1991

	State	U.S.	Rank
All residents	73.61	75.37	46
White residents	75.24	76.13	41
Black residents	68.79	69.16	26

Ranks are from longest-lived to least longest-lived. Ranks exclude Alaska, for which reliable data are not available. Rank for black residents is based on the 32 states for which reliable data are available.
Source: U.S. National Center for Health Statistics.

Infant mortality rates, 1980 and 1995

	State	U.S.
All residents		
1980	14.5	12.6
1995	9.4	7.6
White residents		
1980	10.8	11.0
1995	6.5	6.3
Black residents		
1980	21.0	21.4
1995	15.1	15.1

Figures represent deaths per 1,000 live births of resident infants under 1 year old, exclusive of fetal deaths; all-residents figures include other races not listed separately.
Source: U.S. National Center for Health Statistics.

Marriages and divorces

Marriages in 1996	60,100
Rate per 1,000 population, 1995	8.5
U.S. rate, 1995	8.9
Rank among all states	26
Divorces in 1996	35,900
Rate per 1,000 population, 1995	5.2
U.S. rate, 1995	4.4
Rank among all states	14

Rank is from highest to lowest in country.
Source: U.S. National Center for Health Statistics.

Death rates by leading causes, 1995
Deaths per 100,000 resident population

Cause	State	U.S.
Heart disease	242.4	280.7
Cancer	177.3	204.9
Cerebrovascular diseases	56.2	60.1
Accidents and adverse effects	41.1	35.5
Motor vehicle accidents	21.4	16.5
Chronic obstructive pulmonary diseases	34.2	39.2
Diabetes mellitus	16.7	22.6
HIV	22.0	NA
Suicide	11.5	11.9
Homicide	10.3	8.7
All causes	810.8	880.0
Rank in overall death rate among states		38

Figures exclude nonresidents who die in state. Causes of death follow International Classification of Diseases. Rank is from highest to lowest in country.
Source: U.S. National Center for Health Statistics.

ECONOMY

Gross state product, 1990-1996
In current dollars

	State product	Increase
1990	$140.5 billion	
1993	$170.9 billion	
1994	$186.0 billion	8.84%
1995	$200.8 billion	7.96%
1996	$216.0 billion	7.57%

Source: U.S. Bureau of Economic Analysis; *Survey of Current Business,* June, 1998.

Gross state product by industry, 1996
In billions

Farms, forestry, fisheries	$3.3
Construction	7.2
Manufacturing	37.9
Transportation, public utilities	22.7
Wholesale trade	18.1
Retail trade	18.8
Finance, insurance, real estate	29.9
Services	34.0
Government	24.4
State total	$197.1
Total U.S.	$6,923.8
State share	2.85%
Rank among states	10

Total figures include mining, not listed separately.
Source: U.S. Bureau of Economic Analysis; *Survey of Current Business,* June, 1998.

Personal income per capita, 1990 and 1997
In current dollars

	1990	1997
Per capita income	$17,407	$24,061
U.S. average	$19,188	$25,598
Rank among states	28	25

1997 data are preliminary.
Source: U.S. Bureau of Economic Analysis; *Survey of Current Business,* May, 1998.

Energy consumption, 1995
In trillions of British thermal units (BTU)

End-use sectors

Residential	530.1
Commercial	373.4
Industrial	807.2
Transportation	801.4

Sources of energy

Petroleum	963.6
Natural gas	380.0
Coal	728.5
Hydroelectric power	48.8
Nuclear electric power	326.8
Total state per capita consumption	348.5
Total U.S. per capita consumption	344.4
Rank among states	26
Total state energy consumption	2,512.1
Total U.S. energy consumption	90,547.4
State share of U.S. total	2.77%
Rank among states	12

Total figures include items not listed separately.
Source: U.S. Energy Information Administration; *State Energy Data Report.*

Nonfarm employment by sectors, 1997

Total	3,620,000
Construction	169,000
Manufacturing	589,000
Transportation, public utilities	230,000
Wholesale trade, retail trade	916,000
Finance, insurance, real estate	187,000
Services	944,000
Government	578,000

Figures are rounded to nearest thousand persons. Total includes mining, not listed separately.
Source: U.S. Bureau of Labor Statistics; *Employment and Earnings,* monthly.

Foreign exports, 1990-1997
In millions of dollars

Year	State	U.S.	State share
1990	5,763	394,045	1.46%
1996	10,982	624,767	1.76%
1997	12,949	688,896	1.88%

Source: U.S. Bureau of the Census; *U.S. Merchandise Trade,* series FT 900.

LAND USE

Federally owned land, 1996

	State	U.S.	State share
Total acres	37,295,000	2,271,343,000	1.64%
Federally owned	1,460,000	563,129,000	0.26%
Federal share	3.9%	24.8%	—

Areas are rounded to nearest thousand acres. Figures for federally owned land do not include trust properties.

Source: U.S. General Services Administration; *Inventory Report on Real Property Owned by the United States Throughout the World,* annual.

Land use, 1992
In acres, rounded to nearest thousand

Total surface area	37,702,000
Federal land	2,087,000
Total nonfederal	34,599,000
Developed	3,077,000
Total rural	31,523,000
Cropland.	5,173,000
Pasture land	3,075,000
Range land	0
Forest land	21,714,000
Minor cover/use.	1,560,000

Total surface area figures include water area not shown separately.

Source: U.S. Dept. of Agriculture; Soil Conservation Service; Iowa State University, Statistical Laboratory; *Summary Report, 1992 National Resources Inventory.*

Farms and crop acreage, 1997

	State	U.S.	Share	Rank
Farms (thousands)	43	2,058	2.09%	20
Acres (millions)	12	968	1.24%	26
Acres per farm	274	471	—	27
Acres planted	4,419	334,139	1.32%	24
Acres harvested	4,062	319,894	1.27%	26
Farm value (mill.)	$2,051	$108,805	1.89%	40

Numbers of farms are rounded to nearest thousand.

Source: U.S. Dept. of Agriculture; National Agricultural Statistics Service.

GOVERNMENT AND FINANCE

Units of local government, 1997

	State	Total U.S.	Rank
All local governments	1,344	87,453	24
Counties	156	3,043	2
Municipalities	535	19,372	13
Townships	0	16,629	—
School districts	180	13,726	24
Special districts	473	34,683	26

County ranks are based on the 48 states with county governments; township ranks are based on the 20 states with township governments; school district ranks are based on the 46 states with such districts.

Source: U.S. Bureau of the Census; *1997 Census of Governments, Government Organization,* Series GC97(1).

State government revenue, 1996

Total revenue	$22,409 mill.
General revenue	18,345 mill.
Per capita.	2,501
U.S. per capita average	2,910
Rank among states.	41

Intergovernmental revenue

Total	$5,420 mill.
From federal government	5,319 mill.
From local government	101 mill.

Charges and Miscellaneous

Total	$2,633 mill.
Current charges	1,425 mill.
Misc. general revenue	1,207 mill.

Taxes

Total	$10,292 mill.
General sales	3,824 mill.
Selective sales	962 mill.
License taxes	420 mill.
Individual income	4,244 mill.
Corporate income	719 mill.
Other	123 mill.
Insurance trust revenue	4,064 mill.

Total revenue figures include items not listed separately.

Source: U.S. Bureau of the Census.

State government expenditures, 1996

General expenditures
Intergovernmental	$5,285 mill.
Direct expenditures	13,304 mill.
Total	18,589 mill.

Selected direct expenditures
Education	$7,933 mill.
Public welfare	4,623 mill.
Health, hospital	1,289 mill.
Highways	1,228 mill.
Police	150 mill.
Corrections	817 mill.
Natural resources	355 mill.
Parks and recreation	184 mill.
Government administration	399 mill.
Interest on debt	345 mill.

Other
State per capita expenditures	$2,535
U.S. per capita average	2,854
Rank among states	38
Total state expenditures	20,013 mill.
Total U.S. expenditures	859,959 mill.

Totals include items not listed separately.
Source: U.S. Bureau of the Census.

POLITICS

Governors since statehood
D = Democrat; R = Republican; O = other;
(r) resigned; (d) died in office; (i) removed from office

John A. Treutlen	1777-1778
John Houstoun	1778-1779
George Walton	1779-1780
Richard Howley	1780-1781
Nathan Brownson	1781-1782
John Martin	1782-1783
Lyman Hall	1783-1784
John Houstoun	1784-1785
Samuel Elbert	1785-1786
Edward Telfair	1786-1787
George Mathews	1787-1788
George Handley	1788-1789
George Walton (O)	1789
Edward Telfair (O)	1789-1793
George Mathews (O)	1793-1796
Jared Irwin (O)	1796-1798
James Jackson (O)	(r) 1798-1801
David Emanuel (O)	1801
Josiah Tattnall (O)	(r) 1801-1802
John Milledge (O)	(r) 1802-1806
Jared Irwin (O)	1806-1809
David B. Mitchell (O)	1809-1813
William Rabun (O)	(d) 1813-1819
Matthew Talbot (O)	1819
John Clark (O)	1819-1823
George M. Troup (O)	1823-1827
John Forsyth (O)	1827-1829
George R. Gilmer (D)	1829-1831
Wilson Lumpkin (D)	1831-1835
William Schley (D)	1835-1837
George R. Gilmer (O)	1837-1839
Charles J. McDonald (D)	1839-1843
George W. Crawford (O)	1843-1847
George W. B. Towns (D)	1847-1851
Howell Cobb (D)	1851-1853
Herschel V. Johnson (D)	1853-1857
Joseph E. Brown (D)	(i) 1857-1865
James Johnson (D)	1865
Charles J. Jenkins (D)	(i) 1865-1868
Thomas H. Ruger	(i) 1868
Rufus B. Bullock (R)	(r) 1868-1871
Benjamin Conley (R)	1871-1872
James M. Smith (R)	1872-1877
Alfred M. Colquitt (D)	1877-1882
Alexander H. Stephens (D)	(d) 1882-1883
James S. Boynton (D)	1883
Henry D. McDaniel (D)	1883-1886
John B. Gordon (D)	1886-1890
William J. Northern (D)	1890-1894
William Y. Atkinson (D)	1894-1898
Allen D. Candler (D)	1898-1902
Joseph M. Terrell (D)	1902-1907
Michael Hoke Smith (D)	1907-1909
Joseph M. Brown (D)	1909-1911
Michael Hoke Smith (D)	(r) 1911
John M. Slaton (D)	1911-1912
Joseph M. Brown (D)	1912-1913
John M. Slaton (D)	1913-1915
Nathaniel E. Harris (D)	1915-1917
Hugh M. Dorsey (D)	1917-1921
Thomas W. Hardwick (D)	1921-1923
Clifford M. Walker (D)	1923-1927
Lamartine G. Hardman (D)	1927-1931
Richard B. Russell, Jr. (D)	1931-1933
Eugene Talmadge (D)	1933-1937
Eurith D. Rivers (D)	1937-1941
Eugene Talmadge (D)	1941-1943
Ellis G. Arnall (D)	1943-1947
Herman Talmadge (D)	(i) 1947
Ellis G. Arnall (D)	(r) 1947
Melvin E. Thompson (D)	1947-1948
Herman Talmadge (D)	1948-1955

(continued)

Samuel Marvin Griffin (D) 1955-1959
Samuel Ernest Vandiver, Jr. (D) 1959-1963
Carl E. Sanders (D) 1963-1967
Lester G. Maddox (D) 1967-1971
Jimmy (James E.) Carter (D) 1971-1975
George D. Busbee (D) 1975-1983
Joe Frank Harris (D) 1983-1991
Zell Miller (D) 1991-1999
Roy Barnes (D) 1999-

Composition of state legislature, 1990-1998

	Democrats	Republicans
State House (180 seats)		
1990	145	35
1992	128	51
1994	114	65
1996	106	74
1998	102	78
State Senate (56 seats)		
1990	45	11
1992	41	15
1994	35	20
1996	34	22
1998	33	22

Figures for total seats may include independents and minor
party members.
Source: Council of State Governments; *State Elective Officials
and the Legislatures.*

Composition of congressional delegations, 1989-1999

	Dem	Rep	Total
House of Representatives			
101st Congress, 1989			
State delegates	9	1	10
Total U.S.	259	174	433
102d Congress, 1991			
State delegates	9	1	10
Total U.S.	267	167	434
103d Congress, 1993			
State delegates	7	4	11
Total U.S.	258	176	434

	Dem	Rep	Total
104th Congress, 1995			
State delegates	3	8	11
Total U.S.	197	236	433
105th Congress, 1997			
State delegates	3	8	11
Total U.S.	206	228	434
106th Congress, 1999			
State delegates	3	8	11
Total U.S.	211	222	433
Senate			
101st Congress, 1989			
State delegates	2	0	2
Total U.S.	55	45	100
102d Congress, 1991			
State delegates	2	0	2
Total U.S.	56	44	100
103d Congress, 1993			
State delegates	1	1	2
Total U.S.	57	43	100
104th Congress, 1995			
State delegates	1	1	2
Total U.S.	46	53	99
105th Congress, 1997			
State delegates	1	1	2
Total U.S.	45	55	100
106th Congress, 1999			
State delegates	1	1	2
Total U.S.	45	54	99

Figures are for starts of first sessions. Figure for U.S. Representatives for 101st Congress does not include Alabama
and Indiana, which had vacancies. Figures for total U.S.
Representatives for 102d, 103d, and 106th Congresses do
not include Vermont, which had 1 Independent-Socialist.
Figure for U.S. Representatives for 104th Congress does
not include Vermont, which had 1 Independent-Socialist,
and California, which had 1 vacancy. Figure for U.S.
Representatives for 105th Congress does not include
New York, which had 1 vacancy. Figure for U.S. Senators
for 104th Congress does not include Oregon, which had
1 vacancy. Figure for U.S. Senators for 106th Congress does not include New Hampshire, which had
1 Independent.
Source: U.S. Congress; *Congressional Directory,* biennial.

Voter participation in presidential elections, 1992 and 1996

	1992	1996
State voting age pop.	5,006,000	5,396,000
Total U.S. voting age pop.	189,524,000	196,509,000
State share of U.S. total	2.6%	2.8%
Rank among states	11	11
Percent of state casting vote	46.4	51.2
Percent of U.S. total voting	55.1	49.0
Rank among states	48	23

Source: U.S. Bureau of the Census.

HEALTH AND MEDICAL CARE

Medicare, 1997

	Recipients	Payments
State	866,000	$4,725 mill.
Total U.S.	37,514,000	$206,064 mill.
State share	2.31%	2.29%
Rank among states	12	12

Recipient figures are rounded to nearest thousand persons. Ranks are from highest to lowest.
Source: U.S. Health Care Financing Administration.

Medicaid, 1996

	Recipients	Payments
State	1,185,000	$3,085 mill.
Total U.S.	35,028,000	$121,419 mill.
State share	3.38%	2.54%
Rank among states	8	12

Recipient figures are rounded to nearest thousand persons. Payment figures for fiscal year reflect federal and state contribution payments. Ranks are from highest to lowest.
Source: U.S. Health Care Financing Administration.

Health insurance coverage, 1996

	State	U.S.
Total persons covered	6,080,000	225,070,000
Total persons not covered	1,319,000	41,716,000
Part not covered	17.8%	15.6%
Rank among states	9	—

	State	U.S.
Children not covered	297,000	10,554,000
Part not covered	15.2%	14.8%
Rank among states	18	—

Ranks are from most to fewest uninsured. Population figures are rounded to nearest thousand persons.
Source: U.S. Bureau of the Census.

AIDS, syphilis, tuberculosis, and measles cases, 1997

Cases	U.S.	State	Share
AIDS	58,443	1,722	2.95%
Syphilis	8,550	515	6.02%
Tuberculosis	18,534	595	3.21%
Measles	148,000	1,000	0.68%

Measles figures are rounded to nearest thousand cases.
Source: U.S. Centers for Disease Control and Prevention.

HOUSING

Homeownership rates, 1985-1997

	1985	1990	1997
State	62.7%	64.3%	70.9%
Total U.S.	63.9%	63.9%	65.7%
Rank among states	39	38	14

Source: U.S. Bureau of the Census.

Home sales, 1990 and 1997
In thousands of units

Existing home sales	1990	1997	Change
State sales	73.2	NA	NA
Total U.S. sales	3,560	4,730	1,170
State share of U.S. total	2.06%	NA	-2.06%
Rank among states	18	NA	—

Source: National Association of Realtors; *Real Estate Outlook: Market Trends and Insights.*

EDUCATION

Public school enrollment, 1995

State K-8 enrollment 966,000
Total U.S. K-8 enrollment 32,341,000
State share of total U.S. 2.99%
State 9-12 enrollment 345,000
Total U.S. 9-12 enrollment 12,500,000
State share of U.S. total 2.76%
State public school enroll. rate 95.7%
Overall U.S. rate. 91.6%
Rank among states 7

Enrollment figures (which include unclassified students) are
   rounded to nearest thousand pupils in fall term;
   kindergarten (K)-8 grade figures include some
   prekindergarten students. Enrollment rate is based on
   percentage of persons 5-17 years old. Rank is from highest
   to lowest.
Source: U.S. National Center for Education Statistics.

Public college finances, 1996

State FTE enrollment 212,800
Total U.S. FTE enrollment 8,268,800
State share of total U.S. 2.57%
Rank among states. 11
State and local appropriations $1,186,600,000
Total U.S. state and local
   appropriations. . . . . $39,699 mill.
State share of total U.S. 2.99%
Rank among states. 10
State net tuition revenues. $369,200,000
Total U.S. net tuition $18,348,100,000
State share of total U.S. 2.01%
Rank among states. 17

FTE=Full-time equivalent; credit and noncredit enrollment
   including summer session in academic year ending in
   1996.
Enrollments are rounded to nearest thousand students. Net
   tuition revenues exclude appropriation to students
   attending in-state public institutions. Rankings are from
   highest shares to lowest.
Source: Research Associates of Washington.

TRANSPORTATION AND TRAVEL

Highway mileage, 1996

Interstate 1,241
Other arterial 13,226
Collector roads 25,222
Local roads 74,166

Urban roads. 26,655
Rural roads 85,091

Total state 111,746
U.S. total 3,933,985
State share 2.8%
Rank among states. 14

Source: U.S. Federal Highway Administration.

Motor vehicle registrations and driver licenses, 1996

In thousands

Vehicle registrations	State	U.S.	Share	Rank
Autos, trucks, buses	6,283	206,365	3.04%	9
Autos only	3,818	128,439	2.97%	10
Motorcycles	73	3,832	1.91%	18
Driver licenses	4,966	179,539	2.77%	9

Figures do not include vehicles owned by military services.
Source: U.S. Federal Highway Administration; *Highway
   Statistics; Selected Highway Statistics and Charts.*

Domestic travel expenditures, 1995

Spending by U.S. residents on overnight trips and day
trips of at least 100 miles

Total expenditures in state . . . . $10,457 mill.
Total expenditures in U.S. . . . . $360,314 mill.
State share of total U.S. 2.90%
Rank among states 9

Source: Travel Industry Association of America.

CRIME AND LAW ENFORCEMENT

State and local police officers, 1996

Local police	10,241
State police	878
Sheriffs	6,752
Total	19,115
Officers per 10,000 residents	26
U.S. average	25
Rank among states	10

Figures cover full-time sworn officers; totals include special police not shown separately.
Source: U.S. Bureau of Justice Statistics; *Census of State and Local Law Enforcement Agencies, 1996.*

Crime rates, 1996

Rates per 100,000 resident population

Violent crimes	State	U.S.
Total violent	639	634
Murder	8.6	7.4
Forcible rape	32.1	36.1
Robbery	205	202
Aggravated assault	393	388
Property crimes		
Total property	5,671	4,445
Burglary	1,115	943
Larceny/theft	3,928	2,976
Motor vehicle theft	629	526
Totals	6,310	5,079

Source: U.S. Federal Bureau of Investigation; *Crime in the United States,* annual.

State prison populations, 1980-1996

	State	U.S.	State share
1980	12,178	305,458	3.99%
1990	22,411	708,393	3.16%
1996	35,139	1,025,624	3.43%

Figures exclude prisoners in federal penitentiaries.
Source: U.S. Bureau of Justice Statistics.

Hawaii

Location: South Pacific Ocean, west of continental United States

Area and rank: 6,423 square miles (16,637 square kilometers); 10,932 square miles (28,314 square kilometers) including water; forty-seventh largest state in area

Coastline: 750 miles (1,207 kilometers)

Shoreline: 1,052 miles (1,693 kilometers)

Population and rank: 1,186,602 (1997); forty-first largest state in population

Capital: Honolulu

Honolulu, Hawaii's capital city, is home to a third of the state's residents, as well as a large tourist population.
(PhotoDisc)

Largest city: Honolulu (395,789 people in 1998)

Became territory: 1900

Entered Union and rank: August 21, 1959; fiftieth state

Present constitution adopted: 1950

Counties: 4 and Kalawao, a nonfunctioning county

State name: Hawaii appears to have taken its name from either Hawaii Loa, the islands' traditional discoverer, or the traditional home of the Polynesians, known as Hawaii or Hawaiki.

State nickname: Aloha State

Motto: *Ua Mau Ke Ea O Ka Aina I Ka Pono* (The life of the land is perpetuated in righteousness)

State flag: Eight stripes of red, white, and blue, with the Union Jack in the upper left corner

Highest point: Puu Wekiu — 13,796 feet (4,205 meters)

Lowest point: Pacific Ocean — sea level

Highest recorded temperature: 100 degrees Fahrenheit (38 degrees Celsius) — Pahala, 1931

Lowest recorded temperature: 14 degrees Fahrenheit (–10 degrees Celsius) — Haleukala, 1961

State song: "Hawaii Ponoi"

State tree: Kukui (Candlenut)

State flower: Hibiscus

State bird: Nene (Hawaiian goose)

National parks: Haleakala, Hawaii Volcanoes

Hawaii History

Hawaii is unique in many ways. It is the only one of the fifty United States that lies outside the northern hemisphere and is, with Alaska, one of two states that is not part of the contiguous forty-eight states that, until 1959, constituted the United States of America. It is the only state that is composed of a group of islands, running from the big island of Hawaii to the islet of Kure at Hawaii's northwest extreme. Ka Lae, or South Cape, on the big island, is the southernmost point in the United States.

Hawaii is also the most multiethnic state in the Union. Some 40 percent of Hawaiian marriages are interracial. In this state of idyllic islands with inviting beaches, one can ascend the big island's Mauna Loa volcano in winter and, at an altitude of almost fourteen thousand feet, go skiiing. Although 80 percent of its population lives in bustling, crowded cities, mainly Honolulu, Hawaiians are probably the most relaxed of all Americans.

Early History. As early as the middle of the eighth century, people sailed from the South Seas to Hawaii, presumably intent on colonizing some of its islands. Most of these people were southeast Asians who had made their arduous way to Tahiti and the Marquesa Islands. In time, sailing in large double-hulled canoes, they continued to Hawaii, carrying with them roots and seeds to plant, as well as animals, mostly pigs and chickens, to raise.

These seamen knew enough about sailing and about the currents of the Pacific Ocean, presumably, to make trips from Tahiti to Hawaii and safely back to Tahiti. Seemingly they did this regularly between 1100 and 1400. An influx of foreigners resumed, however, in the eighteenth century, this time from Europe as well as Asia. The native Hawaiian population, which exceeded 225,000 toward the end of that century, plummeted to about fifty thousand one hundred years later, as many natives fell victim to diseases that visitors brought to the islands.

Although Spanish seamen sailed from Manila in the Philippines to the west coast of Mexico in the seventeenth century, they seem to have passed north of the Hawaiian archipelago and were unaware of this chain of volcanic islands. Captain James Cook, in January, 1778, was probably the first European to find the Hawaiian islands, calling them the Sandwich Islands after the Earl of Sandwich, from whom he had financial support for his explorations. In February, 1779, Captain Cook was killed by natives on the big island of Hawaii in an argument over some thefts from his ship. In time, trade with white merchants began to flourish, Hawaii's chief export being sandalwood. As foreign merchants came to Hawaii to trade, the social structure of the islands began to change.

The Kingdom of Hawaii. In 1810, Kamehameha I, a warrior chief, founded the Kingdom of Hawaii after gaining the loyal support of Kauai's chieftain. Although a native Hawaiian gained political control, the islands had already been altered appreciably by the influx of people from the West who came there to do business. Upon the king's death in 1819, Kamehameha II, who welcomed traders from the West, was given the reins of power. Under his jurisdiction, the kapu system, based on the ancient laws and taboos that had long prevailed in the islands, began to give way to Western customs.

The following year, the first Christian missionaries arrived from New England. These Congregationalists were soon followed by Methodists from the United States, Roman Catholics from France, Anglicans from Britain, and Lutherans from Germany. Mormon missionaries arrived considerably later and had such great success in winning Hawaiians to Mormonism that they ultimately established a branch of Brigham Young University and a Mormon temple and information center on Oahu's northeast coast.

The pusillanimous Hawaiians, who were traditionally polytheistic, were easy to convert to Christianity, although they still preserved the myths of many of their deities, such as Pele and Maui. The arrival of the missionaries marked a wave of immigration to the islands and also heralded an era of interracial interchanges and interracial marriage, thereby minimizing many of the ethnic divisions that characterize some societies.

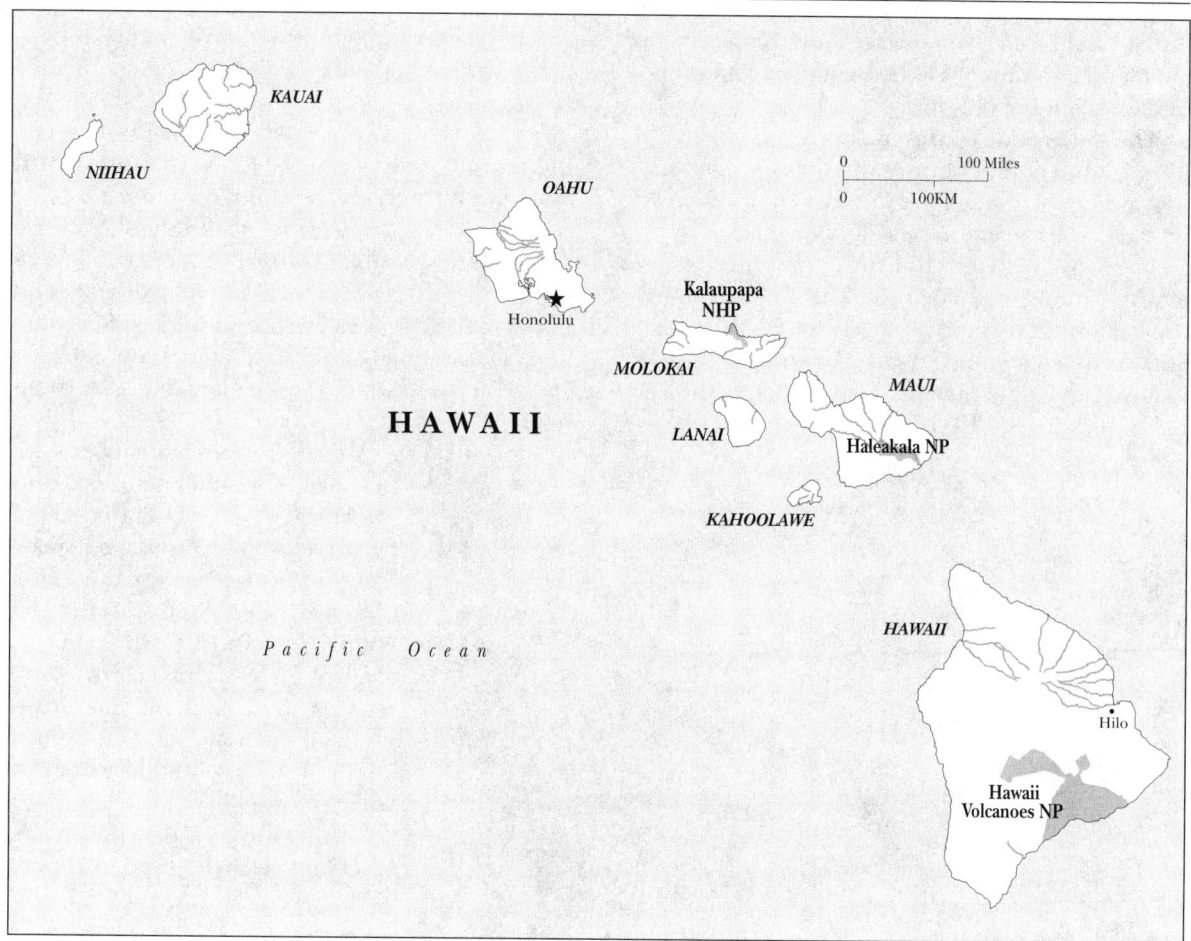

The next wave of immigration came in the 1850's, when large numbers of Chinese immigrants arrived, drawn to Hawaii by its climate, its strategic location, and its commercial possibilities. The Chinese, many of whom initially worked on the sugar and pineapple plantations, soon gravitated to urban centers, mostly to Honolulu, to establish businesses. Soon they had the highest family income of all the ethnic groups in the islands.

During the nineteenth century, significant numbers of immigrants arrived, first from Japan around 1860, then from Scandinavia, Spain, Madeira, the Azores, Puerto Rico, and Germany. The overwhelming influx was from Asia. About half of Hawaii's population is of Asian ancestry. Intermarriage reduced the number of full-blooded Hawaiians from about 225,000 at the end of the eigh-

teenth century to less than 10,000 at the end of the twentieth century.

Land Ownership. The king originally owned most of the state's land, held as crown lands. These properties, broken up in 1848, eventually reverted to the territorial government, which now owns about 40 percent of Hawaii's land. The federal government owns another 10 percent, and private land barons own all but about 3 percent of the remaining land. As a result, many people who own houses or other buildings in Hawaii built them on leased land. Long-term leases offer homeowners some protection, but when the leases come up for renewal, substantial increases are usually imposed.

The Bishop Estate is the largest private landowner in Hawaii, holding about 9 percent of all the land in the state. It uses the large income that these lands produce to fund the Kamehameha School, initially established to educate children of Hawaiian blood and thought to be the most affluent secondary school in the world.

The Annexation of Hawaii. By the middle of the nineteenth century, during the reign of Kamehameha III, the kingdom was increasingly influenced by American missionaries. Kamehameha III in 1843 ceded the islands to Britain, but within a few months, the United States had strongly protested this action, and, shortly thereafter, both Britain and France acknowledged Hawaii's independence. The kingdom was reformed under the Organic Acts of 1845-1847.

A statue of King Kamehameha I stands in front of Hawaii's judiciary building in Honolulu. (Hawaii Visitors & Convention Bureau/ Robert Coello)

The reigns of Kamehameha IV and Kamehameha V witnessed the growth of huge sugar plantations owned mostly by Americans. U.S. financial interests in Hawaii grew before the reign of Queen Liliuokalani, who ascended to the throne in 1891. She showed signs of becoming a more absolute ruler than her predecessors, so in 1893 she was deposed, and a republic, whose president was American Sanford B. Dole, was soon created. Dole and his legislature requested that the United States annex Hawaii, which, after some hesitation, it did in 1898. It officially became a United States territory in 1900.

Moving Toward Statehood. With the advent of military aircraft during World War I, Hawaii began to be viewed by military leaders as a first line of defense for the continental United States. With the bombing of Pearl Harbor on December 7, 1941, Americans soon realized how vulnerable Hawaii was to attack and how vital it was both as a line of defense and as a staging area for a Pacific war.

During the early days of the war, Nisei Japanese who lived in Hawaii were viewed with a combination of distrust and contempt. They were barred from service in the U.S. armed forces, although they were not incarcerated in camps, as their counterparts on the mainland West Coast had been. Eventually they were admitted to the armed forces and, as members of the 100th Infantry Battalion and the 442d Regimental Combat Team, performed heroically in some of the most desperate battles of the conflict, proving their loyalty.

Shortly after the war, mainland labor unions called plantation strikes in Hawaii that paralyzed shipping in 1946, 1948, and 1958. The five business cartels that controlled a great deal of the islands' economy were forced to make substantial concessions to plantation workers. Many Japanese Americans

Japan's surprise attack on the U.S. Naval Base at Pearl Harbor on December 7, 1941, brought the United States into World War II. (National Archives)

rose to political power and did a great deal to reform state government. As the territory attracted large numbers of new inhabitants and gained considerable affluence, agitation for statehood grew. In 1959 statehood was conferred.

The Growth of Tourism. Hawaii's economy during the nineteenth century and the first half of the twentieth came largely from the sale of sandalwood, sugar, and pineapples, although the federal and territorial governments increasingly provided jobs that bolstered the economy. In 1970 seventy thousand of the islands' population of less than one million were employed in state and federal jobs. By 1997 the federal government employed only 20,221 people in Hawaii at an average salary of $39,984.

Although the federal government spends a billion dollars a year in Hawaii, its expenditures are far exceeded by the revenues generated for the state through tourism, which in 1996 amounted to more than fourteen billion dollars. The Hawaiian Chamber of Commerce is among the most efficient and accommodating in the United States. The five islands that are most often visited, Oahu, Maui, Hawaii, Molokai, and Kauai, have excellent tourist facilities and offer breathtaking beaches and waves that attract surfers from around the world. Of the inhabited islands, only Lanai, owned by the Dole Corporation, discourages tourism.

Honolulu is Hawaii's most-visited city. Waikiki Beach, close to the main section of Honolulu, is lined with elegant hotels. Its beaches are filled with tourists and surfers throughout the year. Such natural attractions as the Haleakala Volcano on Maui, the Mauna Loa and Mauna Kea volcanos on Hawaii, Diamond Head on Oahu, and the Waimea Canyon on Kauai are popular among tourists.

R. Baird Shuman

Hawaii Time Line

750-800	First Polynesians begin to colonize the islands.
Jan. 18, 1778	James Cook discovers the Hawaiian archipelago and calls it the Sandwich Islands.
1810	Kamehameha I conquers the islands and establishes the Kingdom of Hawaii.
1819	Kamehameha I dies; Kamehameha II abolishes the kapu system.
1820	First Christian missionaries arrive from the United States.
1835	Ladd and Company establishes first sugar plantation on Kauai.
1840	Kamahameha III drafts first Hawaiian constitution.
1846	Redistribution of Hawaiian land begins, most going to the state.
1851	First Chinese laborers arrive to work on sugar plantations.
1868	First Japanese laborers arrive to work on Hawaiian plantations.
1886	Exportable pineapple strain, "Smooth Cayenne," introduced.
Jan. 17, 1893	Queen Liliuokalani deposed; republic is established by American business leaders.
July 4, 1894	New constitution introduced, establishing Republic of Hawaii; Sanford B. Dole is president.
Aug. 12, 1898	United States annexes Hawaii.
1900	Hawaii given territorial status by Organic Act; Sanford Dole named first territorial governor.
1901	First successful pineapple cannery is established.
1903	Territorial legislature asks Congress for statehood.
1907	University of Hawaii is established.
1916	Hawaii Volcanoes National Park and Haleakala National Park are established.
1927	First nonstop flight is made from American mainland.
1929	Regular air service is established among Hawaii's islands.
1935	Pan American Airlines launches first commercial flight across the Pacific with the China Clipper.
Dec. 7, 1941	Japanese attack Pearl Harbor.
1943	100th Infantry Battalion and 442d Regimental Combat Team admit Nisei Japanese.
1946	Plantation strikes launched by International Longshoremen's and Warehousemen's Union (ILWU).
1947	First statehood bill fails in U.S. Congress.
1949	Hawaiian waterfront is paralyzed for 178 days by ILWU strike.
1950	Constitutional Convention drafts constitution for state of Hawaii.
1955	Democrats take control of both legislative houses for the first time in Hawaii's history.
Aug. 20, 1959	Hawaii becomes fiftieth state.

May 23, 1960	Thirty-five-foot tidal wave kills fifty-seven, causes $50 million in damage.
1967	Mauna Kea Observatory opens.
1968	President Lyndon B. Johnson confers with South Vietnam's President Nguyen Van Thieu in Honolulu.
1972	First full Hawaiian medical school is approved.
1973	First Hawaiian school of law is established.
1985	Marijuana crop is estimated at $4 billion, ten times the worth of the sugar crop.
1986	Kilauea volcano erupts, destroying everything in its path.
1994	United States Navy negates 1941 agreement that gave it Kahoolawe Island as a gunnery site.

Notes for Further Study

Published Sources. One of the best brief accounts of Hawaii's ethnic situation is found in William Petersen's *Ethnicity Counts* (1997), which devotes ten pages to the multiethnicity of the islands. The book is excellent for its comparisons and contrasts with other venues. Wayne S. Wooden's *Return to Paradise: Continuity and Change in Hawaii* (1995) also touches on the islands' ethnicity, as does Mary Ann Lynch's *Hawaii: The Land, the People, the Cities* (1991), which is richly illustrated. E. C. Nordyke's *The Peopling of Hawaii*'s second edition (1989) offers specifics about the origins of the Hawaiian people and about the state's ethnicity. Nancy J. Morris and Love Dean compiled *Hawai'i* (1992), a fine source about the prehistory and languages of the islands. Bonnie Friedman, Paul Wood, and others offer eyewitness views of the islands in *Hawaii* (1998) and provide useful maps of the areas about which the many contributors write. A good supplement to this book is Suzi Forbes's *Hawaii: A Photographic Journey* (1991), whose photographs are superb and whose accompanying text by Forbes is readable and instructive. George Chaplin and Glenn D. Paige's *Hawaii 2000: Continuing Experiment in Anticipatory Democracy* (1973) looks ahead to the islands' future.

For young readers interested in knowing more about Hawaii, Dennis Brindell Fradin's *Hawaii* (1994), which is short and attractively illustrated, should prove enticing. Also of interest is Sylvia McNair's *America the Beautiful: Hawaii* (1990), which is well written and highly informative.

Web Resources. The most comprehensive Web site on Hawaii is that run by the state government (http://www.hawaii.gov), which has very extensive offerings. The Visitors' Department Web site (http://www.gohawaii.com) offers extensive, up-to-date information about every aspect of tourism in the state. The Web site of Honolulu's newspaper, *The Star-Bulletin* (http://www.starbulletin.com), is excellent for developments in the state generally and in Honolulu more particularly. It includes classified advertisements that can be useful. The *Islander Magazine* (http://www.islander-magazine.com) offers specific information about tourist attractions and coming events that might interest tourists.

The individual islands most visited by tourists have their own Web sites: for Maui (http://www.visitmaui.com), for Molokai (http://www.visitmoloki.com), for Hawaii (http://www.visithawaii.com) and (http://www.bigisland.com), for Kauai (http://www.kauaivisitorsbureau.org) and (http://www.kauai-hawaii.com), and for Oahu (http://www.oahuvacations.com). The Hawaii Guide (http://www.hawaiibigisland.com) is also useful for the island of Hawaii. The Hawaii Visitors Bureau maintains its own Web site (http://www.visit.hawaii.org). Those interested in Hawaii's volcanoes or in volcanology should consult the volcano Web sites (http://www.volcano-hawaii.com) and (http://www.nps.gov.havo) or the volcanologist Web site (http://www.volcanologist.com). Users interested in the cultural aspects of the islands will find valuable information on the Web site of the Honolulu Arts Academy (http://www.honoluluacademy.org) or the Hawaii Art Web site (http://www.hawaiiart.com). Those wishing to learn more about business in Hawaii should consult the Hawaii Business Web site (http://www.hawaiibusiness.com).

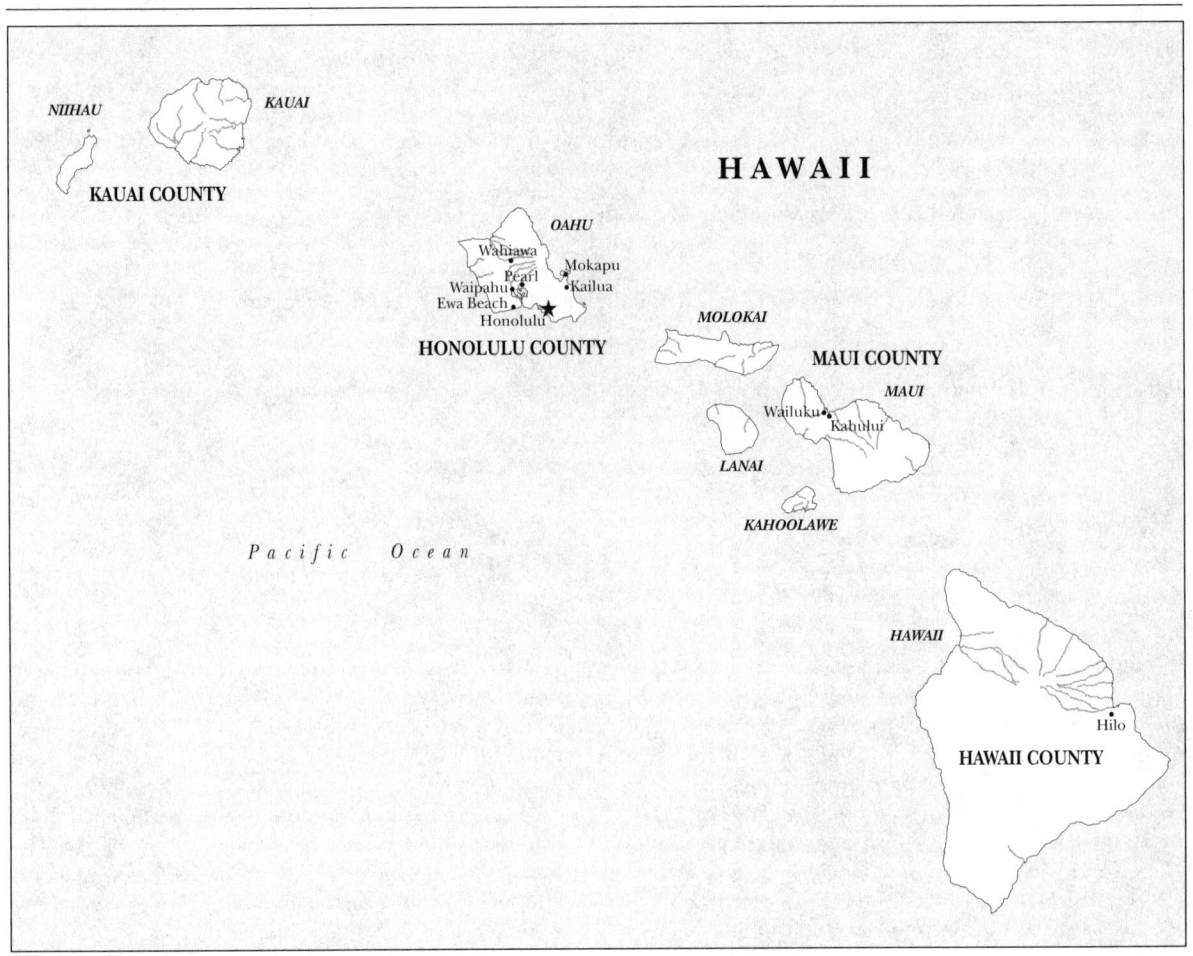

Counties

County	Sq. miles	1996 pop.
Hawaii	4,028.2	138,422
Honolulu	600.2	871,766
Kauai	622.5	56,435
Maui	1,159.3	117,013

Molokai's "Kalawao County" is administratively part of Maui County.
Source: U.S. Bureau of the Census; National Association of Counties.

Cities
With 10,000 or more residents

Rank	City	Population
1	Honolulu	395,789

Population figures are estimated for mid-1998.
Source: U.S. Bureau of the Census.

Mount Kilauea, on the island of Hawaii, has the world's largest crater among active volcanoes. (Hawaii Visitors & Convention Bureau/Warren Bolster)

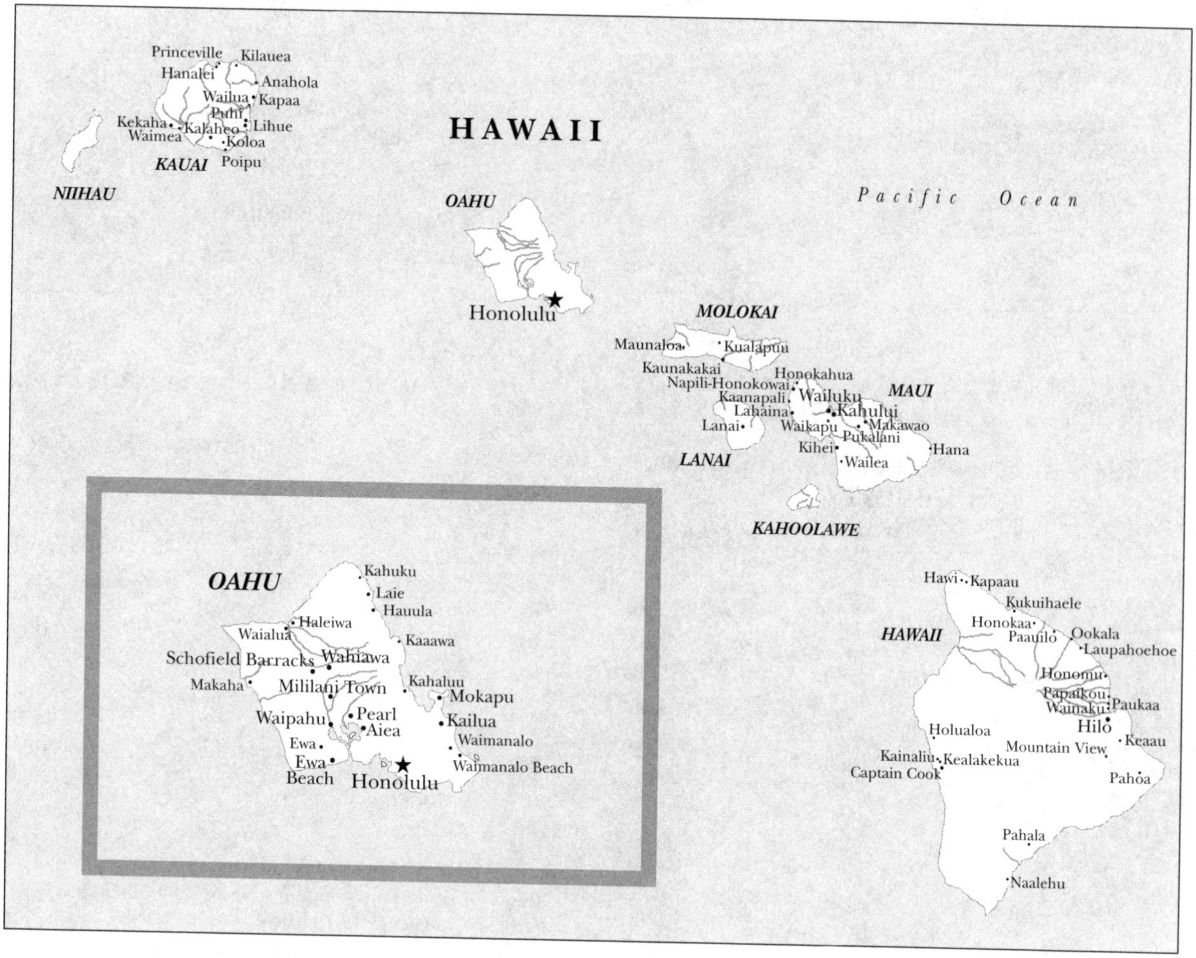

HAWAII

Pacific Ocean

Princeville Kilauea
Hanalei ·Anahola
Wailua ·Kapaa
Kekaha· Puhi·
Waimea·Kalaheo· Lihue
·Koloa
KAUAI Poipu

NIIHAU

OAHU

Honolulu ★

MOLOKAI
Maunaloa· ·Kualapuu
Kaunakakai ·Honokahua
Napili-Honokowai· ·Wailuku
Kaanapali· **MAUI**
Lahaina· ·Kahului
Lanai· Waikapu· ·Makawao
Kihei· ·Pukalani
·Wailea ·Hana

LANAI

KAHOOLAWE

Hawi· ·Kapaau
Kukuihaele
Honokaa
HAWAII Paauilo· ·Ookala
·Laupahoehoe
·Honomu
Papaikou·
Waiaku·Paukaa
Holualoa· Hilo·
Mountain View ·Keaau
Kainaliu·Kealakekua
Captain Cook· Pahoa·

Pahala·

Naalehu·

OAHU
·Kahuku
·Laie
·Hauula
·Haleiwa
Waialua· ·Kaaawa
Schofield Barracks· Wahiawa·
Makaha· Mililani Town· Kahaluu
·Mokapu
Waipahu· ·Pearl ·Kailua
·Aiea
Ewa· ·Waimanalo
Ewa ★ ·Waimanalo Beach
Beach Honolulu

Index to Tables

NA = Reliable data are not available.

DEMOGRAPHICS

Resident state and national populations, 1970-1997

Population figures given in thousands

	State pop.	U.S. pop.	Share	Rank
1970	770	203,302	0.4%	40
1980	965	226,546	0.4%	39
1985	1,040	237,924	0.4%	39
1990	1,108	248,765	0.4%	41
1995	1,179	262,761	0.4%	40
1997	1,187	267,636	0.4%	41

Source: U.S. Bureau of the Census.

Resident population by age, 1997

Age group	Total population
Under 5 years	88,000
5 to 17 years	214,000
18 to 24 years	117,000
25 to 34 years	161,000
35 to 44 years	199,000
45 to 54 years	156,000
55 to 64 years	95,000
65 to 74 years	90,000
75 to 84 years	52,000
85 years and over	15,000
Portion of residents 65 and older	13.2%
National average	12.7%

Population figures are rounded to nearest thousand persons;
figures include armed forces personnel stationed in state.
Source: U.S. Bureau of the Census.

Resident population by race, Hispanic origin, 1997

	State pop.	Share	U.S.
All residents	1,187,000	100.0%	100.0%
Hispanic white	49,000	4.1%	10.0%
non-Hispanic white	347,000	29.2%	72.7%
African American	35,000	2.9%	12.7%
Native American	7,000	0.6%	0.9%
Asian, Pacific Islander	749,000	63.1%	3.8%

Source: U.S. Bureau of the Census.

Projections of state population, 2000-2025

	Model A Uses interstate migration observed from 1975-1994	Model B Uses Bureau of Economic Analysis employment projections
Year	Population	Population
2000	1,257,000	1,238,000
2005	1,342,000	1,297,000
2010	1,440,000	1,367,000
2015	1,553,000	1,447,000
2020	1,677,000	1,537,000
2025	1,812,000	1,634,000

All population projections, including those for 2000, were
calculated in 1997.
Source: U.S. Bureau of the Census, Population Paper Listings
PPL-47.

VITAL STATISTICS

Average lifetime in years by race, 1989-1991

	State	U.S.	Rank
All residents	78.21	75.37	1
White residents	77.92	76.13	3
Black residents	NA	69.16	NA

Ranks are from longest-lived to least longest-lived. Ranks
exclude Alaska, for which reliable data are not available.
Rank for black residents is based on the 32 states for which
reliable data are available.
Source: U.S. National Center for Health Statistics.

Infant mortality rates, 1980 and 1995

	State	U.S.
All residents		
1980	10.3	12.6
1995	5.8	7.6
White residents		
1980	11.6	11.0
1995	NA	6.3
Black residents		
1980	11.8	21.4
1995	NA	15.1

Figures represent deaths per 1,000 live births of resident
infants under 1 year old, exclusive of fetal deaths; all-
residents figures include other races not listed separately.
Source: U.S. National Center for Health Statistics.

Marriages and divorces

Marriages in 1996. 19,500
Rate per 1,000 population, 1995 . . . . 15.8
U.S. rate, 1995 . . . . 8.9
Rank among all states. 2

Divorces in 1996 4,800
Rate per 1,000 population, 1995. . . . . 4.6
U.S. rate, 1995 . . . . 4.4
Rank among all states 24

Rank is from highest to lowest in country.
Source: U.S. National Center for Health Statistics.

Death rates by leading causes, 1995
Deaths per 100,000 resident population

Cause	State	U.S.
Heart disease	196.0	280.7
Cancer	156.4	204.9
Cerebrovascular diseases	51.5	60.1
Accidents and adverse effects	27.6	35.5
Motor vehicle accidents	12.0	16.5
Chronic obstructive pulmonary diseases	20.4	39.2
Diabetes mellitus	14.2	22.6
HIV	10.4	NA
Suicide	12.0	11.9
Homicide	4.9	8.7
All causes	643.1	880.0

Rank in overall death rate among states	48

Figures exclude nonresidents who die in state. Causes of
death follow International Classification of Diseases. Rank
is from highest to lowest in country.
Source: U.S. National Center for Health Statistics.

ECONOMY

Gross state product, 1990-1996
In current dollars

	State product	Increase
1990	$32.4 billion	
1993	$35.2 billion	
1994	$35.2 billion	0.00%
1995	$36.0 billion	2.27%
1996	$36.3 billion	0.83%

Source: U.S. Bureau of Economic Analysis; *Survey of Current Business,* June, 1998.

Gross state product by industry, 1996
In billions

Farms, forestry, fisheries	$0.4
Construction	1.5
Manufacturing	1.0
Transportation, public utilities.	3.5
Wholesale trade.	1.4
Retail trade	4.1
Finance, insurance, real estate	9.3
Services	7.0
Government.	7.0
State total.	$34.9
Total U.S.	$6,923.8
State share.	0.50%
Rank among states.	39

Total figures include mining, not listed separately.

Source: U.S. Bureau of Economic Analysis; *Survey of Current Business,* June, 1998.

Personal income per capita, 1990 and 1997
In current dollars

	1990	1997
Per capita income	$21,564	$26,034
U.S. average	$19,188	$25,598
Rank among states	7	16

1997 data are preliminary.

Source: U.S. Bureau of Economic Analysis; *Survey of Current Business,* May, 1998.

Energy consumption, 1995
In trillions of British thermal units (BTU)

End-use sectors

Residential	20.8
Commercial	24.4
Industrial.	73.7
Transportation	135.8

Sources of energy

Petroleum	234.8
Natural gas	2.9
Coal	2.6
Hydroelectric power	1.0
Nuclear electric power	0
Total state per capita consumption	216.1
Total U.S. per capita consumption	344.4
Rank among states.	49
Total state energy consumption	254.8
Total U.S. energy consumption	90,547.4
State share of U.S. total	0.28%
Rank among states.	47

Total figures include items not listed separately.

Source: U.S. Energy Information Administration; *State Energy Data Report.*

Nonfarm employment by sectors, 1997

Total	532,000
Construction	22,000
Manufacturing	17,000
Transportation, public utilities.	41,000
Wholesale trade, retail trade	135,000
Finance, insurance, real estate	36,000
Services	169,000
Government	112,000

Figures are rounded to nearest 1,000.

Source: U.S. Bureau of Labor Statistics; *Employment and Earnings,* monthly.

Foreign exports, 1990-1997
In millions of dollars

Year	State	U.S.	State share
1990	179	394,045	0.05%
1996	284	624,767	0.05%
1997	334	688,896	0.05%

Source: U.S. Bureau of the Census; *U.S. Merchandise Trade,* series FT 900.

LAND USE

Federally owned land, 1996

	State	U.S.	State share
Total acres	4,106,000	2,271,343,000	0.18%
Federally owned	350,000	563,129,000	0.06%
Federal share	8.5%	24.8%	—

Areas are rounded to nearest thousand acres. Figures for federally owned land do not include trust properties.
Source: U.S. General Services Administration; *Inventory Report on Real Property Owned by the United States Throughout the World*, annual.

Land use, 1992
In acres, rounded to nearest thousand

Total surface area	4,093,000
Federal land	432,000
Total nonfederal.	3,621,000
Developed	170,000
Total rural	3,451,000
Cropland.	274,000
Pasture land.	88,000
Range land.	925,000
Forest land.	1,483,000
Minor cover/use.	680,000

Total surface area figures include water area not shown separately.
Source: U.S. Dept. of Agriculture; Soil Conservation Service; Iowa State University, Statistical Laboratory; *Summary Report, 1992 National Resources Inventory.*

Farms and crop acreage, 1997

	State	U.S.	Share	Rank
Farms (thousands)	5	2,058	0.24%	44
Acres (millions)	2	968	0.21%	40
Acres per farm	346	471	—	21
Acres planted	35	334,139	0.01%	48
Acres harvested	35	319,894	0.01%	48
Farm value (mill.)	$303	$108,805	0.28%	19

Numbers of farms are rounded to nearest thousand.
Source: U.S. Dept. of Agriculture; National Agricultural Statistics Service.

GOVERNMENT AND FINANCE

Units of local government, 1997

	State	Total U.S.	Rank
All local governments	19	87,453	50
Counties	3	3,043	47
Municipalities	1	19,372	50
Townships	0	16,629	—
School districts	0	13,726	—
Special districts	15	34,683	49

County ranks are based on the 48 states with county governments; township ranks are based on the 20 states with township governments; school district ranks are based on the 46 states with such districts.
Source: U.S. Bureau of the Census; *1997 Census of Governments, Government Organization*, Series GC97(1).

State government revenue, 1996

Total revenue	$6,383 mill.
General revenue	5,379 mill.
Per capita.	4,547
U.S. per capita average	2,910
Rank among states	3

Intergovernmental revenue

Total	$1,228 mill.
From federal government	1,220 mill.
From local government.	8 mill.

Charges and Miscellaneous

Total	$1,072 mill.
Current charges	756 mill.
Misc. general revenue	316 mill.

Taxes

Total	$3,079 mill.
General sales	1,432 mill.
Selective sales.	473 mill.
License taxes.	85 mill.
Individual income.	1 mill.
Corporate income	66 mill.
Other.	24 mill.
Insurance trust revenue	1,004 mill.

Total revenue figures include items not listed separately.
Source: U.S. Bureau of the Census.

State government expenditures, 1996

General expenditures

Intergovernmental	$144 mill.
Direct expenditures	5,085 mill.
Total.	5,229 mill.

Selected direct expenditures

Education	$1,548 mill.
Public welfare.	915 mill.
Health, hospital	487 mill.
Highways	270 mill.
Police	9 mill.
Corrections	106 mill.
Natural resources	75 mill.
Parks and recreation	109 mill.
Government administration	224 mill.
Interest on debt	333 mill.

Other

State per capita expenditures	$4,420
U.S. per capita average	2,854
Rank among states	2
Total state expenditures	5,947 mill.
Total U.S. expenditures	859,959 mill.

Totals include items not listed separately.
Source: U.S. Bureau of the Census.

POLITICS

Governors since statehood

D = Democrat; R = Republican; O = other;
(r) resigned; (d) died in office; (i) removed from office

William F. Quinn (R)	1959-1962
John A. Burns (D)	1962-1974
George R. Ariyoshi (D)	1974-1986
John Waihee (D)	1986-1998
Benjamin J. Cayetano (D)	1998-

Composition of state legislature, 1990-1998

	Democrats	Republicans
State House (51 seats)		
1990	45	6
1992	47	4
1994	44	7
1996	39	12
1998	39	12

	Democrats	Republicans
State Senate (25 seats)		
1990	22	3
1992	22	3
1994	23	2
1996	23	2
1998	23	2

Figures for total seats may include independents and minor party members.
Source: Council of State Governments; *State Elective Officials and the Legislatures.*

Composition of congressional delegations, 1989-1999

	Dem	Rep	Total
House of Representatives			
101st Congress, 1989			
State delegates	1	1	2
Total U.S.	259	174	433
102d Congress, 1991			
State delegates	2	0	2
Total U.S.	267	167	434
103d Congress, 1993			
State delegates	2	0	2
Total U.S.	258	176	434
104th Congress, 1995			
State delegates	2	0	2
Total U.S.	197	236	433
105th Congress, 1997			
State delegates	2	0	2
Total U.S.	206	228	434
106th Congress, 1999			
State delegates	2	0	2
Total U.S.	211	222	433
Senate			
101st Congress, 1989			
State delegates	2	0	2
Total U.S.	55	45	100
102d Congress, 1991			
State delegates	2	0	2
Total U.S.	56	44	100
103d Congress, 1993			
State delegates	2	0	2
Total U.S.	57	43	100
104th Congress, 1995			
State delegates	2	0	2
Total U.S.	46	53	99

	Dem	Rep	Total
105th Congress, 1997			
State delegates	2	0	2
Total U.S.	45	55	100
106th Congress, 1999			
State delegates	2	0	2
Total U.S.	45	54	99

Figures are for starts of first sessions. Figure for U.S. Representatives for 101st Congress does not include Alabama and Indiana, which had vacancies. Figures for total U.S. Representatives for 102d, 103d, and 106th Congresses do not include Vermont, which had 1 Independent-Socialist. Figure for U.S. Representatives for 104th Congress does not include Vermont, which had 1 Independent-Socialist, and California, which had 1 vacancy. Figure for U.S. Representatives for 105th Congress does not include New York, which had 1 vacancy. Figure for U.S. Senators for 104th Congress does not include Oregon, which had 1 vacancy. Figure for U.S. Senators for 106th Congress does not include New Hampshire, which had 1 Independent.
Source: U.S. Congress; *Congressional Directory*, biennial.

Voter participation in presidential elections, 1992 and 1996

	1992	1996
State voting age pop.	866,000	882,000
Total U.S. voting age pop.	189,524,000	196,509,000
State share of U.S. total	0.5%	0.4%
Rank among states	40	40
Percent of state casting vote	43.1	49.0
Percent of U.S. total voting	55.1	49.0
Rank among states	50	29

Source: U.S. Bureau of the Census.

HEALTH AND MEDICAL CARE

Medicare, 1997

	Recipients	Payments
State	156,000	$655 mill.
Total U.S.	37,514,000	$206,064 mill.
State share	0.42%	0.32%
Rank among states	42	42

Recipient figures are rounded to nearest thousand persons. Ranks are from highest to lowest.
Source: U.S. Health Care Financing Administration.

Medicaid, 1996

	Recipients	Payments
State	41,000	$266 mill.
Total U.S.	35,028,000	$121,419 mill.
State share	0.12%	0.22%
Rank among states	50	48

Recipient figures are rounded to nearest thousand persons. Payment figures for fiscal year reflect federal and state contribution payments. Ranks are from highest to lowest.
Source: U.S. Health Care Financing Administration.

Health insurance coverage, 1996

	State	U.S.
Total persons covered	1,073,000	225,070,000
Total persons not covered	101,000	41,716,000
Part not covered	8.6%	15.6%
Rank among states	49	—
Children not covered	16,000	10,554,000
Part not covered	5.3%	14.8%
Rank among states	50	—

Ranks are from most to fewest uninsured. Population figures are rounded to nearest thousand persons.
Source: U.S. Bureau of the Census.

AIDS, syphilis, tuberculosis, and measles cases, 1997

Cases	U.S.	State	Share
AIDS	58,443	94	0.16%
Syphilis	8,550	1	0.01%
Tuberculosis	18,534	167	0.90%
Measles	148,000	6,000	4.05%

Measles figures are rounded to nearest thousand cases.
Source: U.S. Centers for Disease Control and Prevention.

HOUSING

Homeownership rates, 1985-1997

	1985	1990	1997
State	51.0%	55.5%	50.2%
Total U.S.	63.9%	63.9%	65.7%
Rank among states	49	48	50

Source: U.S. Bureau of the Census.

Home sales, 1990 and 1997

In thousands of units

Existing home sales	1990	1997	Change
State sales	19.2	11.1	-8.1
Total U.S. sales	3,560	4,730	1,170
State share of U.S. total	0.54%	0.23%	-0.31%
Rank among states	39	44	—

Source: National Association of Realtors; *Real Estate Outlook: Market Trends and Insights.*

EDUCATION

Public college finances, 1996

State FTE enrollment.	32,700
Total U.S. FTE enrollment	8,268,800
State share of total U.S.	0.40%
Rank among states.	40
State and local appropriations	$242,700,000
Total U.S. state and local appropriations.	$39,699 mill.
State share of total U.S.	0.61%
Rank among states.	37
State net tuition revenues	$33,400,000
Total U.S. net tuition	$18,348,100,000
State share of total U.S.	0.18%
Rank among states.	50

FTE=Full-time equivalent; credit and noncredit enrollment including summer session in academic year ending in 1996.

Enrollments are rounded to nearest thousand students. Net tuition revenues exclude appropriation to students attending in-state public institutions. Rankings are from highest shares to lowest.

Source: Research Associates of Washington.

Public school enrollment, 1995

State K-8 enrollment	136,000
Total U.S. K-8 enrollment	32,341,000
State share of total U.S.	0.42%
State 9-12 enrollment.	52,000
Total U.S. 9-12 enrollment	12,500,000
State share of U.S. total	0.42%
State public school enroll. rate	88.3%
Overall U.S. rate.	91.6%
Rank among states.	43

Enrollment figures (which include unclassified students) are rounded to nearest thousand pupils in fall term; kindergarten (K)-8 grade figures include some prekindergarten students. Enrollment rate is based on percentage of persons 5-17 years old. Rank is from highest to lowest.

Source: U.S. National Center for Education Statistics.

TRANSPORTATION AND TRAVEL

Highway mileage, 1996

Interstate.	43
Other arterial.	786
Collector roads.	1,128
Local roads.	2,524
Urban roads	1,851
Rural roads	2,291
Total state.	4,142
U.S. total.	3,933,985
State share	0.1%
Rank among states.	50

Source: U.S. Federal Highway Administration.

Motor vehicle registrations and driver licenses, 1996

In thousands

Vehicle registrations	State	U.S.	Share	Rank
Autos, trucks, buses	786	206,365	0.38%	43
Autos only	500	128,439	0.39%	42
Motorcycles	25	3,832	0.65%	37
Driver licenses	733	179,539	0.41%	43

Figures do not include vehicles owned by military services.
Source: U.S. Federal Highway Administration; *Highway Statistics; Selected Highway Statistics and Charts.*

View of Oahu's Diamond Head, with Magic Island in the foreground and Honolulu to the left. (Hawaii Visitors & Convention Bureau/Warren Bolster)

Domestic travel expenditures, 1995

Spending by U.S. residents on overnight trips and day trips of at least 100 miles

Total expenditures in state	$6,434 mill.
Total expenditures in U.S.	$360,314 mill.
State share of total U.S.	1.79%
Rank among states.	18

Source: Travel Industry Association of America.

CRIME AND LAW ENFORCEMENT

State and local police officers, 1996

Local police	2,746
State police	0
Sheriffs	0
Total	2,989
Officers per 10,000 residents	25
U.S. average	25
Rank among states.	14

Figures cover full-time sworn officers; totals include special police not shown separately.
Source: U.S. Bureau of Justice Statistics; *Census of State and Local Law Enforcement Agencies, 1996.*

Crime rates, 1996

Rates per 100,000 resident population

Violent crimes	*State*	*U.S.*
Total violent	281	634
Murder	3.4	7.4
Forcible rape	27.5	36.1
Robbery	136	202
Aggravated assault	114	388
Property crimes		
Total property	6,304	4,445
Burglary	1,080	943
Larceny/theft	4,620	2,976
Motor vehicle theft	605	526
Totals	6,585	5,079

Source: U.S. Federal Bureau of Investigation; *Crime in the United States,* annual.

State prison populations, 1980-1996

	State	*U.S.*	*State share*
1980	985	305,458	0.32%
1990	2,533	708,393	0.36%
1996	4,011	1,025,624	0.39%

Figures exclude prisoners in federal penitentiaries.
Source: U.S. Bureau of Justice Statistics.

Idaho

Location: Northwestern continental United States

Area and rank: 82,751 square miles (214,325 square kilometers); 83,574 square miles (216,457 square kilometers) including water; eleventh largest state in area

Population and rank: 1,210,232 (1997); fortieth largest state in population

Capital: Boise

Largest city: Boise (157,452 people in 1998)

Became territory: March 3, 1863

Entered Union and rank: July 3, 1890; forty-third state

Boise skyline, showing the capitol building. (Idaho Department of Commerce)

Present constitution adopted: 1890

Counties: 44, as well as a small part of Yellowstone National Park

State name: "Idaho" is an invented name whose meaning is unknown

State nicknames: Gem State; Spud State; Panhandle State

Motto: *Esto perpetua* (It is forever)

State flag: Blue field with state seal and red band with words "State of Idaho"

Highest point: Borah Peak — 12,662 feet (3,859 meters)

Lowest point: Snake River — 5,000 feet (1,524 meters)

Highest recorded temperature: 118 degrees Fahrenheit (48 degrees Celsius) — Orotino, 1934

Lowest recorded temperature: −60 degrees Fahrenheit (−51 degrees Celsius) — Island Park Dam, 1943

State song: "Here We Have Idaho"

State tree: White pine

State flower: Syringa

State bird: Mountain bluebird

State fish: Cutthroat trout

National park: Yellowstone

Idaho History

Idaho's history is marked by its frontier origins. The state was settled later than neighboring Washington and Oregon, as pioneers passed through in the 1840's without stopping to settle until valuable gold strikes brought miners in significant numbers. The rough character of Idaho's early days was reflected in the violence of its first decades as a state, which came to a close only around the time of the U.S. entrance into World War I.

This background is sometimes still apparent in extremist political groups, some of which are racist or anarchist.

Early History. Idaho was first inhabited by various American Indian tribes, such as the Nez Perce, Coeur d'Alene, Pend d'Oreille, Kutenai, Paiute Shoshone, and Bannock. The origins of the indigenous inhabitants extend back around fourteen thousand years. Other ancient cultures flourished from eight thousand years ago until about the seventeenth century. By the eighteenth century, Shoshone bands (fragments of tribes) had obtained horses from European contacts, but these contacts decimated them by spreading smallpox among the Indians.

No whites are known to have explored Idaho before Meriwether Lewis and William Clark led their famous expedition through Lemhi Pass in Idaho in 1805. Traveling through the Bitterroot Mountains, the explorers built canoes with the assistance of the Shoshone and Nez Perce and floated down the Clearwater and Snake Rivers to the Columbia. Four years later, Canadian explorer David Thompson built Kullyspell House, known as the first non-native house in the Pacific Northwest, near Pend Oreille Lake. Decades later, in the 1830's, Forts Hall and Boise, site of the future state's capital, were founded.

Presettlement Decades. Missionaries, a constant feature of the early days of the Pacific Northwest, soon made their appearance in Idaho, bringing Christianity and—in

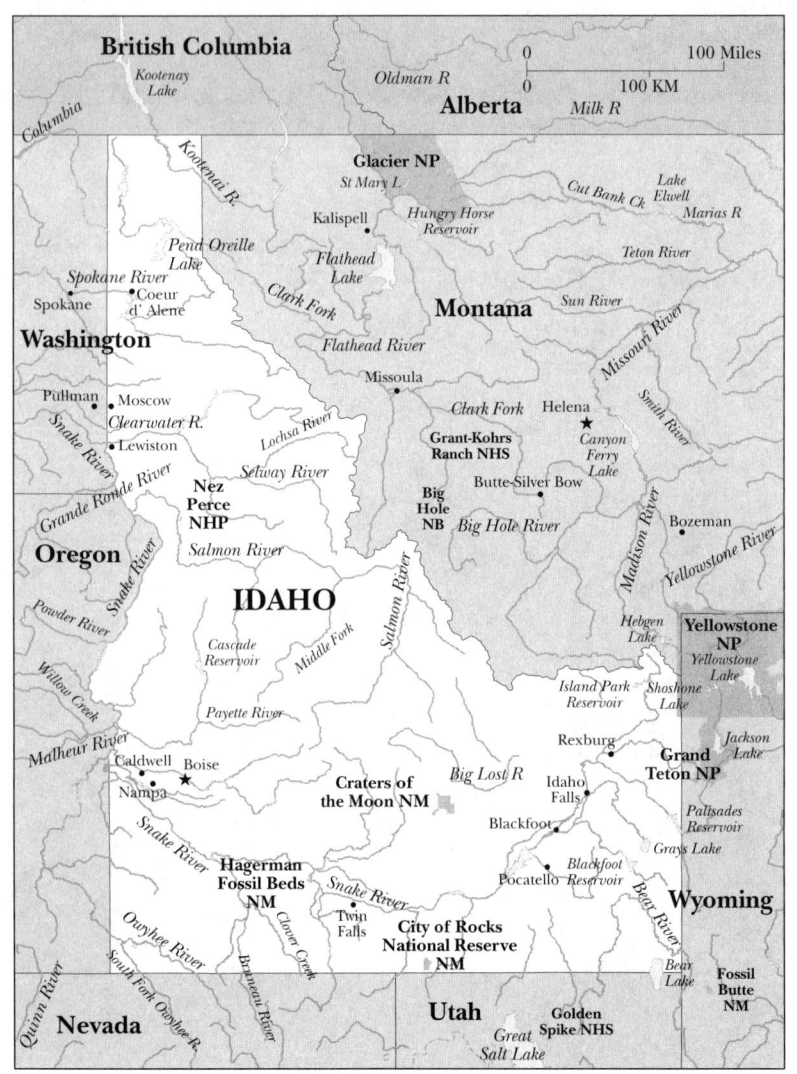

their eyes—civilization to the native tribes. Henry Spalding arrived in 1836 and established the state's first school. He also created its first irrigation system and planted its first potatoes, both of which were to play significant roles in Idaho's later economic development. The 1840's saw the arrival of the wagon trains headed west on the Oregon Trail. The steady stream of humanity became a flood in 1849, as twenty thousand forty-niners came through on their way to California's gold fields. Continuing heavy traffic led to the establishment of the U.S. military post Cantonment Loring near Fort Hall. There were still no settlers, however, even after French Canadians discovered gold on the Pend Oreille River in 1852, the year before a large piece of Oregon Territory broke off to form Washington Territory, of which Idaho was a part. The first permanent community had not even been founded when Oregon was admitted to the Union at the end of the decade. Mormon missionaries had established the Salmon River Mission (Fort Lemhi) in mid-decade, but it was not a success and was abandoned in 1858.

From Territory to State. Only in 1860, when much of the rest of the nation was gearing up for a bloody civil war, were roots for the first town put down, when Franklin, just over the Utah border, was founded by Mormons. The next several years, however, were to change Idaho's sparsely populated character, as major mining strikes were made in Pierce, Florence, Idaho City, and Silver City. Just two years after the first town was settled, the new community of Lewiston saw the region's first newspaper, the *Golden Age*. By 1863, the region east of Washington and Oregon was ready to take a giant step to statehood when it became a territory, with Lewiston as its capital.

This rapid invasion by European settlers was viewed with great alarm by the Native Americans. American Indian wars followed until the end of the 1870's, as Nez Perce, Bannock, and Sheepeater Indian wars followed in successive years. Thus, in 1877, after years of abuse by settlers, the Nez Perce resisted efforts to send them from Oregon to Lapwai Reservation in Idaho. In June, they crushed U.S. Army troops and settler volunteers at

Frederic Remington's depiction of Nez Perce Chief Joseph surrendering to U.S. cavalry troops in northern Montana in 1877 after leading five thousand troops on a five-month chase. (Library of Congress)

White Bird Canyon, in north-central Idaho. Forced to retreat after federal reinforcements arrived, the Nez Perce surrendered in Montana in October.

Other American Indians, in accordance with federal policy, were also settled on reservations provided by treaties. Conditions on reservations were in some cases so poor that rebellions took place. Thus, the Bannock Indians rebelled in 1878, when food on their reservation became inadequate and settlers objected to their foraging on cattle grazing land. However, they too were defeated by federal troops.

Economic Development and Statehood. In the meantime, other events were unfolding that foretold the new territory's social and economic future. The first wave of modern technology made its appearance in 1866, as the first telegraph service reached the territory. A harbinger of modern social conflict arrived the next year, when the Owyhee Miners' League, Idaho's first labor union, made its appearance. Early in the following decade the first U.S. assay office and Idaho's first prison were built. Soon after, railroad service came to Franklin, and the way was open for even greater emigration from the restless East. By the next century these immigrants included English, Chinese, Czech, Dutch, French, French Canadian, German, Mexican, and Scandinavian settlers.

From the 1880's on, technological developments and their economic consequences followed with stunning speed for a region that was so recently an untamed wilderness. In the early 1880's electric light was introduced, and telephone service followed in 1883. The following year, an enormous silver strike, eventually recognized as the nation's largest, was registered in the Coeur d'Alene mining district, and more settlers arrived. By the close of the decade, Idaho was ready to trade its position as territory for the status of state. In 1889 a constitutional convention convened on Independence Day to institute a new frame of government. The next year Idaho was admitted to the Union.

Government and Social Conflict. Government under the new state constitution, as in neighboring Washington, reflected the frontier distrust of power in the form of a powerful state governor. Accordingly, executive control was divided into a number of elective offices in which the secretary of state, state controller, state treasurer, attorney general, and superintendent of public instruction are separately elected rather than appointed by the governor. The governor is also denied the power of pardoning criminals. The state constitution underlines a commitment to liberal democracy. It opens with a declaration of the "inalienable rights of man" and a detailed enumeration of individual rights, the central idea of classical liberalism. Immediately following is the forthright statement that "All political power is inherent in the people," the key democratic idea of popular sovereignty. In keeping with a strong tradition of frontier democracy, voters have the right to the initiative, referendum, and recall.

While a framework for orderly government was in place, Idaho's rough-and-ready frontier origins could hardly disappear overnight. This became evident in the 1890's as serious violence broke out between union miners and mine owners. In 1892 the Coeur d'Alene mining area was the scene of dynamiting and shootings. More violence broke out when a new strike occurred in 1899. The strike was broken when the governor, Frank Steunenberg, called out federal troops.

Much bitterness remained, however. In 1905 former governor Steunenberg was murdered by a bomb. The perpetrator, a member of the Western Federation of Miners, an organization of the militant Marxist International Workers of the World (IWW), confessed but implicated three union officials. When a sensational trial was held in 1907, renowned defense attorney Clarence Darrow gained acquittals of two officials, and charges against the third were dropped. The prosecutor, William E. Borah, nevertheless won national fame and was elected six times to the U.S. Senate, where he became a stalwart foreign policy isolationist.

Two World Wars and Depression. Before World War I, the state's economy benefited from irrigation projects. A dam on the Snake River completed in 1906, for example, opened more than 100,000 acres of land for agriculture. The war created an agricultural boom when wartime food shortages brought demand for farm products. The end of the war, however, brought an economic downturn, whose effects were felt into the 1920's. Matters were worse in the Great Depression of the 1930's, when many banks collapsed. Federal spending helped to a degree through a highway construction program and employment in the Civilian Conservation Corps (CCC).

World War II brought renewed prosperity, as with the rest of the nation, with massive federal spending for war needs. Japanese who were relocated from western portions of Oregon and Washington went to work in agriculture, where conscription had made labor scarce. Wartime industry made a lasting change in the economy, since in the postwar period manufacturing begun by defense needs continued, resulting in increased urbanization. By 1960, half of the population lived in cities or towns.

Postwar Economy and Society. As in neighboring states, postwar economic growth was also stimulated by development of cheap hydroelectric power. A series of dams was built in the 1950's, and projects continued in the 1960's. In 1976 one of the dams collapsed, and several rural communities were inundated, causing loss of life and considerable damage. In the 1970's, the state's prosperity brought a rapid increase in population, which rose nearly one-third between 1970 and 1980.

By the 1990's, Idaho's economy was balanced between agriculture, mining, and nonagricultural industries. Various high-tech industries moved to the Boise area; food processing and wood products

Idaho's lowest altitude is found in the basin of the Snake River. (PhotoDisc)

remained important. A tourist industry that, led by development of winter sports in Sun Valley, had grown up beginning in the 1950's was also important. Politically, the state was divided between conservationists and their opponents, and outsiders frequently noted the activity of unsavory fringe political groups, such as anarchists and neo-Nazis. Observers noted that the wise and efficient use of the state's natural resources would principally determine its future prosperity.

Charles F. Bahmueller

Idaho Time Line

6000 B.C.E.-1700's	American Indian cultures flourish.
1810	Fort Henry, first American fur post west of Rocky Mountains, is established near St. Anthony.
1811	Party based at Astoria on the Pacific Coast explores portions of the future Oregon Trail in Idaho.
1819	Canadian Donald Mackenzie holds rendezvous with American Indians on the Boise River; attempts to establish post.
1820	Mackenzie negotiates peace treaty with the Shoshone on Little Lost River.
1821	Hudson's Bay Company and North West Company merge.
1822	Founding of Rocky Mountain Fur Company.

(continued)

1830	Captain B. L. E. Bonneville leads wagon train across South Pass to Green River.
1834	Forts Laramie, Boise, and Hall are established.
1843	First Oregon Trail wagons cross Idaho.
June 15, 1846	Treaty with Great Britain settles the Oregon boundary dispute; all land below the forty-ninth parallel is American.
Aug. 14, 1848	Oregon Territory is created, which includes Idaho.
1852	French Canadians discover gold on the Pend Oreille River.
1853	Idaho becomes part of Washington Territory.
1863	Major mining strikes take place near Pierce, Florence, Idaho City, and Silver City.
Mar. 3, 1863	Idaho Territory is established.
1864	Territorial legislature approves moving capital to Boise.
1867	Owyhee Miners' League, state's first labor union, is organized.
1874	First railroad service in Idaho begins at Franklin.
1877-1879	Nez Perce, Bannock, and Sheepeater Indians war with settlers.
1884	Silver is discovered in the Coeur d'Alene mining district.
Nov. 5, 1889	State constitution is ratified.
1889	Territorial legislature establishes University of Idaho.
July 3, 1890	Idaho becomes the forty-third state.
1904	Completion of Milner Dam brings irrigation to the south side of the Snake River.
1910	Forest fires consume one-sixth of north Idaho's forests.
1912	State Board of Education is established.
1914	Moses Alexander is elected the first Jewish governor in the United States.
1924	Craters of the Moon National Monument is established.
1926	First commercial airmail service in the U.S. begins in Boise.
1934	Idaho is nation's leading silver producer.
1936	Sun Valley winter sports resort is established by Union Pacific Railroad; world's first ski chair lift opens there.
1942	Almost ten thousand Japanese Americans are placed in an internment camp near Eden.
1949	National Reactor Testing Station (NRTS) is established.
1951	NRTS becomes site of the world's first use of nuclear fission to produce electricity.
1958	Idaho leads the nation in mining of silver, lead, and cobalt.
1966	Voters uphold 3 percent state sales tax.
1975	Port of Lewiston opens Idaho to oceangoing shipping.
June 5, 1976	Teton Dam collapses, killing eleven and forcing thousands to flee.
1978	Voters approve tax limitation placing severe restrictions on the use of the property tax.
1985	Idaho produces one-fourth of U.S. potatoes.

| 1986 | Voters adopt constitutional amendment prohibiting the payment of union dues as a necessity for employment. |
| 1992 | First woman appointed to Idaho Supreme Court. |

Notes for Further Study

Published Sources. For an introduction to the state, see Rick Ardinger and M. L. Peterson's *Celebrating Idaho: The Centennial in Words and Pictures* (1991). Books on Idaho's history include Leonard J. Arrington's *History of Idaho* (2 vols., 1994), Dorothy Dutton's *A Rendezvous with Idaho History* (1994), and, for younger readers, Virgil M. Young's *The Story of Idaho* (1990). One facet of ethnic history is described in *History of the Jews in Utah and Idaho, 1853-1950* (1973), by Juanita Brooks.

Good books on Idaho geography include Lalia Phipps Boone's *Idaho Place Names: A Geographical Dictionary* (1988) and Delorme Mapping's *Idaho Atlas and Gazetteer* (1992). American Indian history is surveyed in *Indians of Idaho* (1978) by Deward Walker. For information on the great Nez Perce leader Chief Joseph, readers should consult Clifford E. Trafzer's *Chief Joseph's Allies: The Palouse Indians and the Nez Perce* (1992). The Bannock Indians are studied in Brigham D. Mardsen's *The Bannock of Idaho* (1996). The state's government is discussed in *Paradox Politics: People and Power in Idaho* (1988) by Randy Strapilus. Idaho's constitution is examined in Dennis C. Colson's *Idaho's Constitution: The Tie That Binds* (1991). Jennifer Eastman Attebery's *Building Idaho: An Architectural History* (1991) treats the state's architecture. Those interested in archaeology of the state should see Mark Plew's *Introduction to the Archaeology of Southern Idaho* (1986). For the story of Idaho's most famous winter sports destination, Wendolyn Holland's *Sun Valley: An Extraordinary History* (1999) is an excellent resource.

Web Resources. For information on politics and government in Idaho, a good place to start is the state of Idaho home page (http://www2.state.id.us), which contains information on and links to state agencies and major offices as well as commerce, education, the environment, and many related topics. A federal government agency particularly significant in Idaho is the Bureau of Land Management (BLM), whose work is outlined on its home page (http://id.blm.gov/fed.html). The Idaho section of the American Local History Network (http://www.usgennet.org/~alhnidus) has a wealth of information and links to a wide variety of topics, such as local, ethnic, and cultural history; schools and education; genealogy, geography, government (including the Idaho Constitution), military records, and museums; and other topics. Other information on the state is found on the Libraries Linking Idaho (LiLI) home page (http://www.lili.org/idaho/index.html). The state historical society home page (http://www.state.id.us/ishi/SiteIndex.html) is useful for learning about the early days of Idaho. State geography information especially suitable to young people can be accessed at Kidport (http://kidport.com/UsaGeography/facts/Idaho.htm). Travelers may wish to consult The Virtual Tourist: Travel in Idaho (http://www.vtourist.com/North_America/USA/Idaho/travel).

For information on Native Americans, readers should view the home pages maintained by various tribes, for example the Nez Perce home page (http://www.uidaho.edu/nezperce/neemepoo.htm). The site for Bannock, Cayuse, and other Idaho Native Americans (http://emayzine.com/lectures/nwtribes.html), along with that for Coeur d'Alene tribal history (http://www.rootsweb.com/~idreserv/cdhist.html), is also informative.

Counties

County	Sq. miles	1996 pop.	County	Sq. miles	1996 pop.
Ada	1,055.0	260,057	Blaine	2,644.9	16,975
Adams	1,364.7	3,891	Boise	1,902.5	4,864
Bannock	1,113.2	73,608	Bonner	1,737.6	33,976
Bear Lake	971.4	6,534	Bonneville	1,868.6	79,670
Benewah	776.0	8,982	Boundary	1,268.8	9,823
Bingham	2,094.8	41,366	Butte	2,232.9	3,126

(continued)

County	Sq. miles	1996 pop.
Camas	1,075.0	860
Canyon	589.8	112,530
Caribou	1,766.1	7,398
Cassia	2,566.6	21,482
Clark	1,764.7	830
Clearwater	2,461.6	9,373
Custer	4,925.6	4,311
Elmore	3,077.8	23,894
Franklin	665.5	10,515
Fremont	1,866.8	11,594
Gem	562.6	14,129
Gooding	730.8	13,335
Idaho	8,485.2	14,924
Jefferson	1,095.1	18,903
Jerome	599.9	17,339
Kootenai	1,245.2	95,535
Latah	1,076.7	33,173
Lemhi	4,564.3	8,098
Lewis	479.1	4,002
Lincoln	1,205.6	3,777
Madison	471.6	23,458
Minidoka	759.7	20,756
Nez Perce	849.1	36,670
Oneida	1,200.4	3,871
Owyhee	7,678.4	10,012
Payette	407.5	19,957
Power	1,405.7	8,234
Shoshone	2,634.0	14,024
Teton	450.4	5,168
Twin Falls	1,925.1	60,403
Valley	3,678.2	7,988
Washington	1,456.4	9,836

Source: U.S. Census Bureau; National Association of Counties.

Cities
With 10,000 or more residents

Rank	City	Population
1	Boise	157,452
2	Pocatello	53,074
3	Idaho Falls	48,122
4	Nampa	41,951
5	Twin Falls	33,296
6	Coeur d'Alene	32,565
7	Lewiston	30,363
8	Meridian	25,377
9	Caldwell	22,340
10	Moscow	19,312
11	Post Falls	15,732
12	Rexburg	14,303
13	Blackfoot	10,453
14	Mountain Home	10,202

Population figures are estimated for mid-1998.
Source: U.S. Bureau of the Census.

Coeur d'Alene, the largest city in northern Idaho. (PhotoDisc)

Index to Tables

NA = Reliable data are not available.

DEMOGRAPHICS

Resident state and national populations, 1970-1997

Population figures given in thousands

	State pop.	U.S. pop.	Share	Rank
1970	713	203,302	0.4%	42
1980	944	226,546	0.4%	41
1985	994	237,924	0.4%	41
1990	1,007	248,765	0.4%	42
1995	1,165	262,761	0.4%	41
1997	1,210	267,636	0.5%	40

Source: U.S. Bureau of the Census.

Resident population by age, 1997

Age group	Total population
Under 5 years	92,000
5 to 17 years	260,000
18 to 24 years	135,000
25 to 34 years	151,000
35 to 44 years	187,000
45 to 54 years	150,000
55 to 64 years	99,000
65 to 74 years	72,000
75 to 84 years	49,000
85 years and over	16,000
Portion of residents 65 and older	11.3%
National average	12.7%

Population figures are rounded to nearest thousand persons;
figures include armed forces personnel stationed in state.
Source: U.S. Bureau of the Census.

Resident population by race, Hispanic origin, 1997

	State pop.	Share	U.S.
All residents	1,210,000	100.0%	100.0%
Hispanic white	80,000	6.6%	10.0%
non-Hispanic white	1,094,000	90.4%	72.7%
African American	7,000	0.6%	12.7%
Native American	16,000	1.3%	0.9%
Asian, Pacific Islander	13,000	1.1%	3.8%

Source: U.S. Bureau of the Census.

Projections of state population, 2000-2025

	Model A Uses interstate migration observed from 1975-1994	Model B Uses Bureau of Economic Analysis employment projections
Year	Population	Population
2000	1,347,000	1,332,000
2005	1,480,000	1,489,000
2010	1,557,000	1,637,000
2015	1,622,000	1,775,000
2020	1,683,000	1,900,000
2025	1,739,000	2,008,000

All population projections, including those for 2000, were calculated in 1997.

Source: U.S. Bureau of the Census, Population Paper Listings PPL-47.

VITAL STATISTICS

Average lifetime in years by race, 1989-1991

	State	U.S.	Rank
All residents	76.88	75.37	10
White residents	76.89	76.13	14
Black residents	NA	69.16	NA

Ranks are from longest-lived to least longest-lived. Ranks exclude Alaska, for which reliable data are not available. Rank for black residents is based on the 32 states for which reliable data are available.

Source: U.S. National Center for Health Statistics.

Infant mortality rates, 1980 and 1995

	State	U.S.
All residents		
1980	10.7	12.6
1995	6.1	7.6
White residents		
1980	10.7	11.0
1995	5.8	6.3
Black residents		
1980	NA	21.4
1995	NA	15.1

Figures represent deaths per 1,000 live births of resident infants under 1 year old, exclusive of fetal deaths; all-residents figures include other races not listed separately.

Source: U.S. National Center for Health Statistics.

Marriages and divorces

Marriages in 1996.	15,000
Rate per 1,000 population, 1995	13.3
U.S. rate, 1995	8.9
Rank among all states.	5
Divorces in 1996	7,000
Rate per 1,000 population, 1995.	5.8
U.S. rate, 1995	4.4
Rank among all states	10

Rank is from highest to lowest in country.

Source: U.S. National Center for Health Statistics.

Death rates by leading causes, 1995

Deaths per 100,000 resident population

Cause	State	U.S.
Heart disease	212.3	280.7
Cancer	172.4	204.9
Cerebrovascular diseases	54.8	60.1
Accidents and adverse effects	45.2	35.5
Motor vehicle accidents	22.7	16.5
Chronic obstructive pulmonary diseases	38.2	39.2
Diabetes mellitus	17.7	22.6
HIV	3.7	NA
Suicide	16.0	11.9
Homicide	4.0	8.7
All causes	732.1	880.0

Rank in overall death rate among states	45

Figures exclude nonresidents who die in state. Causes of death follow International Classification of Diseases. Rank is from highest to lowest in country.

Source: U.S. National Center for Health Statistics.

ECONOMY

Gross state product, 1990-1996
In current dollars

	State product	Increase
1990	$17.5 billion	
1993	$22.4 billion	
1994	$24.5 billion	9.38%
1995	$26.9 billion	9.80%
1996	$27.9 billion	3.72%

Source: U.S. Bureau of Economic Analysis; *Survey of Current Business,* June, 1998.

Gross state product by industry, 1996
In billions

Farms, forestry, fisheries	$1.5
Construction	1.4
Manufacturing	5.8
Transportation, public utilities.	2.4
Wholesale trade.	1.6
Retail trade	2.7
Finance, insurance, real estate.	3.0
Services	4.0
Government.	3.3
State total.	$25.9
Total U.S.	$6,923.8
State share.	0.37%
Rank among states.	43

Total figures include mining, not listed separately.
Source: U.S. Bureau of Economic Analysis; *Survey of Current Business,* June, 1998.

Personal income per capita, 1990 and 1997
In current dollars

	1990	1997
Per capita income	$15,368	$20,478
U.S. average	$19,188	$25,598
Rank among states	40	43

1997 data are preliminary.
Source: U.S. Bureau of Economic Analysis; *Survey of Current Business,* May, 1998.

Energy consumption, 1995
In trillions of British thermal units (BTU)

End-use sectors

Residential	85.6
Commercial	73.1
Industrial	184.8
Transportation	112.8

Sources of energy

Petroleum	146.0
Natural gas.	65.7
Coal	8.9
Hydroelectric power	113.6
Nuclear electric power	0
Total state per capita consumption	391.2
Total U.S. per capita consumption	344.4
Rank among states.	17
Total state energy consumption	456.2
Total U.S. energy consumption	90,547.4
State share of U.S. total.	0.50%
Rank among states.	41

Total figures include items not listed separately.
Source: U.S. Energy Information Administration; *State Energy Data Report.*

Nonfarm employment by sectors, 1997

Total	509,000
Construction	32,000
Manufacturing	74,000
Transportation, public utilities.	24,000
Wholesale trade, retail trade	129,000
Finance, insurance, real estate	25,000
Services	122,000
Government.	99,000

Figures are rounded to nearest thousand persons. Total includes mining, not listed separately.
Source: U.S. Bureau of Labor Statistics; *Employment and Earnings,* monthly.

Foreign exports, 1990-1997
In millions of dollars

Year	State	U.S.	State share
1990	898	394,045	0.23%
1996	1,571	624,767	0.25%
1997	1,664	688,896	0.24%

Source: U.S. Bureau of the Census; *U.S. Merchandise Trade,* series FT 900.

LAND USE

Federally owned land, 1996

	State	U.S.	State share
Total acres	52,933,000	2,271,343,000	2.33%
Federally owned	32,992,000	563,129,000	5.86%
Federal share	62.3%	24.8%	—

Areas are rounded to nearest thousand acres. Figures for federally owned land do not include trust properties.
Source: U.S. General Services Administration; *Inventory Report on Real Property Owned by the United States Throughout the World,* annual.

Land use, 1992
In acres, rounded to nearest thousand

Total surface area	53,481,000
Federal land	33,298,000
Total nonfederal	19,521,000
Developed	587,000
Total rural	18,934,000
Cropland.	5,600,000
Pasture land	1,243,000
Range land.	6,668,000
Forest land.	4,024,000
Minor cover/use.	1,399,000

Total surface area figures include water area not shown separately.
Source: U.S. Dept. of Agriculture; Soil Conservation Service; Iowa State University, Statistical Laboratory; *Summary Report, 1992 National Resources Inventory.*

Farms and crop acreage, 1997

	State	U.S.	Share	Rank
Farms (thousands)	22	2,058	1.07%	32
Acres (millions)	14	968	1.45%	24
Acres per farm	614	471	—	14
Acres planted	4,493	334,139	1.34%	23
Acres harvested	4,336	319,894	1.36%	23
Farm value (mill.)	$2,193	$108,805	2.02%	3

Numbers of farms are rounded to nearest thousand.
Source: U.S. Dept. of Agriculture; National Agricultural Statistics Service.

GOVERNMENT AND FINANCE

Units of local government, 1997

	State	Total U.S.	Rank
All local governments	1,147	87,453	25
Counties	44	3,043	32
Municipalities	200	19,372	35
Townships	0	16,629	—
School districts	114	13,726	31
Special districts	789	34,683	13

County ranks are based on the 48 states with county governments; township ranks are based on the 20 states with township governments; school district ranks are based on the 46 states with such districts.
Source: U.S. Bureau of the Census; *1997 Census of Governments, Government Organization,* Series GC97(1).

State government revenue, 1996

Total revenue	$4,384 mill.
General revenue	3,305 mill.
Per capita.	2,783
U.S. per capita average	2,910
Rank among states.	27

Intergovernmental revenue

Total	$850 mill.
From federal government	844 mill.
From local government.	7 mill.

Charges and Miscellaneous

Total	$597 mill.
Current charges	280 mill.
Misc. general revenue	318 mill.

Taxes

Total	$1,857 mill.
General sales	600 mill.
Selective sales.	252 mill.
License taxes	156 mill.
Individual income	655 mill.
Corporate income	153 mill.
Other.	41 mill.
Insurance trust revenue	1,032 mill.

Total revenue figures include items not listed separately.
Source: U.S. Bureau of the Census.

State government expenditures, 1996

General expenditures

Intergovernmental	$999 mill.
Direct expenditures	2,083 mill.
Total.	3,083 mill.

Selected direct expenditures

Education	$1,361 mill.
Public welfare.	528 mill.
Health, hospital	106 mill.
Highways	346 mill.
Police.	30 mill.
Corrections	98 mill.
Natural resources.	115 mill.
Parks and recreation.	20 mill.
Government administration	99 mill.
Interest on debt	93 mill.

Other

State per capita expenditures	$2,596
U.S. per capita average	2,854
Rank among states.	32
Total state expenditures	3,501 mill.
Total U.S. expenditures	859,959 mill.

Totals include items not listed separately.
Source: U.S. Bureau of the Census.

POLITICS

Governors since statehood

D = Democrat; R = Republican; O = other;
(r) resigned; (d) died in office; (i) removed from office

George L. Shoup (R)	(r) 1890
Norman B. Willey (R)	1890-1893
William J. McConnell (R)	1893-1897
Frank Steunenberg (D)	1897-1901
Frank W. Hunt (D)	1901-1903
John T. Morrison (R)	1903-1905
Frank R. Gooding (R)	1905-1909
James H. Brady (R)	1909-1911
James W. Hawley (D)	1911-1913
John M. Haines (R)	1913-1915
Moses Alexander (D)	1915-1919
David W. Davis (R)	1919-1923
Charles C. Moore (R).	1923-1927
H. Clarence Baldridge (R)	1927-1931
Charles Ben Ross (D)	1931-1937
Barzilla W. Clark (D)	1937-1939
Clarence A. Bottolfsen (R)	1939-1941
Chase A. Clark (D)	1941-1943
Clarence A. Bottolfsen (R)	1943-1945
Charles C. Gossett (D)	(r) 1945
Arnold Williams (D)	1945-1947
Charles A. Robins (R)	1947-1951
Leonard B. Jordan (R)	1951-1955
Robert E. Smylie (R)	1955-1967
Donald W. Samuelson (R)	1967-1971
Cecil D. Andrus (D)	(r) 1971-1977
John V. Evans (D).	1977-1987
Cecil D. Andrus (D)	1987-1995
Phillip E. Batt (R)	1995-1999
Dirk Kempthorne (R)	1999-

Composition of congressional delegations, 1989-1999

	Dem	Rep	Total
House of Representatives			
101st Congress, 1989			
State delegates	1	1	2
Total U.S.	259	174	433
102d Congress, 1991			
State delegates	2	0	2
Total U.S.	267	167	434
103d Congress, 1993			
State delegates	1	1	2
Total U.S.	258	176	434
104th Congress, 1995			
State delegates	0	2	2
Total U.S.	197	236	433
105th Congress, 1997			
State delegates	0	2	2
Total U.S.	206	228	434
106th Congress, 1999			
State delegates	0	2	2
Total U.S.	211	222	433
Senate			
101st Congress, 1989			
State delegates	0	2	2
Total U.S.	55	45	100
102d Congress, 1991			
State delegates	0	2	2
Total U.S.	56	44	100
103d Congress, 1993			
State delegates	0	2	2
Total U.S.	57	43	100

	Dem	Rep	Total
104th Congress, 1995			
State delegates	0	2	2
Total U.S.	46	53	99
105th Congress, 1997			
State delegates	0	2	2
Total U.S.	45	55	100
106th Congress, 1999			
State delegates	0	2	2
Total U.S.	45	54	99

Figures are for starts of first sessions. Figure for U.S. Representatives for 101st Congress does not include Alabama and Indiana, which had vacancies. Figures for total U.S. Representatives for 102d, 103d, and 106th Congresses do not include Vermont, which had 1 Independent-Socialist. Figure for U.S. Representatives for 104th Congress does not include Vermont, which had 1 Independent-Socialist, and California, which had 1 vacancy. Figure for U.S. Representatives for 105th Congress does not include New York, which had 1 vacancy. Figure for U.S. Senators for 104th Congress does not include Oregon, which had 1 vacancy. Figure for U.S. Senators for 106th Congress does not include New Hampshire, which had 1 Independent.

Source: U.S. Congress; *Congressional Directory,* biennial.

Composition of state legislature, 1990-1998

	Democrats	Republicans
State House (84 seats in 1990; 70 seats thereafter)		
1990	28	56
1992	20	50
1994	13	57
1996	11	59
1998	12	58
State Senate (42 seats in 1990; 35 seats thereafter)		
1990	21	21
1992	12	23
1994	8	27
1996	5	30
1998	4	31

Figures for total seats may include independents and minor party members.

Source: Council of State Governments; *State Elective Officials and the Legislatures.*

Voter participation in presidential elections, 1992 and 1996

	1992	1996
State voting age pop.	750,000	845,000
Total U.S. voting age pop.	189,524,000	196,509,000
State share of U.S. total	0.4%	0.4%
Rank among states	42	42
Percent of state casting vote	64.3	54.2
Percent of U.S. total voting	55.1	49.0
Rank among states	11	19

Source: U.S. Bureau of the Census.

HEALTH AND MEDICAL CARE

Medicare, 1997

	Recipients	Payments
State	155,000	$565 mill.
Total U.S.	37,514,000	$206,064 mill.
State share	0.41%	0.27%
Rank among states	43	43

Recipient figures are rounded to nearest thousand persons. Ranks are from highest to lowest.
Source: U.S. Health Care Financing Administration.

Medicaid, 1996

	Recipients	Payments
State	119,000	$405 mill.
Total U.S.	35,028,000	$121,419 mill.
State share	0.34%	0.33%
Rank among states	40	40

Recipient figures are rounded to nearest thousand persons. Payment figures for fiscal year reflect federal and state contribution payments. Ranks are from highest to lowest.
Source: U.S. Health Care Financing Administration.

Health insurance coverage, 1996

	State	U.S.
Total persons covered	990,000	225,070,000
Total persons not covered	196,000	41,716,000
Part not covered	16.5%	15.6%
Rank among states	15	—
Children not covered	44,000	10,554,000
Part not covered	13.2%	14.8%
Rank among states	20	—

Ranks are from most to fewest uninsured. Population figures are rounded to nearest thousand persons.
Source: U.S. Bureau of the Census.

AIDS, syphilis, tuberculosis, and measles cases, 1997

Cases	U.S.	State	Share
AIDS	58,443	52	0.09%
Syphilis	8,550	1	0.01%
Tuberculosis	18,534	17	0.09%
Measles	148,000	NA	NA

Measles figures are rounded to nearest thousand cases.
Source: U.S. Centers for Disease Control and Prevention.

HOUSING

Homeownership rates, 1985-1997

	1985	1990	1997
State	71.0%	69.4%	72.3%
Total U.S.	63.9%	63.9%	65.7%
Rank among states	7	11	12

Source: U.S. Bureau of the Census.

Home sales, 1990 and 1997
In thousands of units

Existing home sales	1990	1997	Change
State sales	18.1	20.7	2.6
Total U.S. sales	3,560	4,730	1,170
State share of U.S. total	0.51%	0.44%	-0.07%
Rank among states	40	38	—

Source: National Association of Realtors; *Real Estate Outlook: Market Trends and Insights.*

EDUCATION

Public school enrollment, 1995

State K-8 enrollment	170,000
Total U.S. K-8 enrollment	32,341,000
State share of total U.S.	0.53%
State 9-12 enrollment.	74,000
Total U.S. 9-12 enrollment	12,500,000
State share of U.S. total	0.59%
State public school enroll. rate	95.2%
Overall U.S. rate.	91.6%
Rank among states.	10

Enrollment figures (which include unclassified students) are rounded to nearest thousand pupils in fall term; kindergarten (K)-8 grade figures include some prekindergarten students. Enrollment rate is based on percentage of persons 5-17 years old. Rank is from highest to lowest.
Source: U.S. National Center for Education Statistics.

Public college finances, 1996

State FTE enrollment.	39,000
Total U.S. FTE enrollment	8,268,800
State share of total U.S.	0.47%
Rank among states.	38
State and local appropriations	$226,100,000
Total U.S. state and local appropriations.	$39,699 mill.
State share of total U.S.	0.57%
Rank among states.	38
State net tuition revenues	$49,000,000
Total U.S. net tuition	$18,348,100,000
State share of total U.S.	0.27%
Rank among states.	46

FTE=Full-time equivalent; credit and noncredit enrollment including summer session in academic year ending in 1996.
Enrollments are rounded to nearest thousand students. Net tuition revenues exclude appropriation to students attending in-state public institutions. Rankings are from highest shares to lowest.
Source: Research Associates of Washington.

TRANSPORTATION AND TRAVEL

Highway mileage, 1996

Interstate	611
Other arterial	3,678
Collector roads	10,059
Local roads	45,836
Urban roads	3,773
Rural roads	55,901
Total state	59,674
U.S. total	3,933,985
State share	1.5%
Rank among states	33

Source: U.S. Federal Highway Administration.

Motor vehicle registrations and driver licenses, 1996
In thousands

Vehicle registrations	State	U.S.	Share	Rank
Autos, trucks, buses	1,061	206,365	0.51%	40
Autos only	479	128,439	0.37%	43
Motorcycles	34	3,832	0.89%	33
Driver licenses	820	179,539	0.46%	40

Figures do not include vehicles owned by military services.
Source: U.S. Federal Highway Administration; *Highway Statistics; Selected Highway Statistics and Charts.*

Domestic travel expenditures, 1995
Spending by U.S. residents on overnight trips and day trips of at least 100 miles

Total expenditures in state	$1,650 mill.
Total expenditures in U.S.	$360,314 mill.
State share of total U.S.	0.46%
Rank among states	40

Source: Travel Industry Association of America.

CRIME AND LAW ENFORCEMENT

State and local police officers, 1996

Local police	1,142
State police	192
Sheriffs	1,053
Total	2,524
Officers per 10,000 residents	21
U.S. average	25
Rank among states	30

Figures cover full-time sworn officers; totals include special police not shown separately.
Source: U.S. Bureau of Justice Statistics; *Census of State and Local Law Enforcement Agencies, 1996.*

Crime rates, 1996
Rates per 100,000 resident population

Violent crimes	State	U.S.
Total violent	267	634
Murder	3.6	7.4
Forcible rape	26.3	36.1
Robbery	20	202
Aggravated assault	217	388
Property crimes		
Total property	3,745	4,445
Burglary	709	943
Larceny/theft	2,849	2,976
Motor vehicle theft	188	526
Totals	4,013	5,079

Source: U.S. Federal Bureau of Investigation; *Crime in the United States,* annual.

State prison populations, 1980-1996

	State	U.S.	State share
1980	817	305,458	0.27%
1990	1,961	708,393	0.28%
1996	3,832	1,025,624	0.37%

Figures exclude prisoners in federal penitentiaries.
Source: U.S. Bureau of Justice Statistics.

Illinois

Location: Midwestern continental United States

Area and rank: 55,593 square miles (143,987 square kilometers); 57,918 square miles (150,008 square kilometers) including water; twenty-fourth largest state in area

Population and rank: 11,895,849 (1997); sixth largest state in population

Capital: Springfield

Illinois's chief city, Chicago, is the third largest in the United States. (PhotoDisc)

Largest city: Chicago (2,802,079 people in 1998)

Became territory: February 3, 1809

Entered Union and rank: December 3, 1818; twenty-first state

Present constitution adopted: 1970

Counties: 102

ILLINOIS

State name: "Illinois" is an invented name with no known meaning

State nickname: Prairie State

Motto: State sovereignty, national union

State flag: White field with state seal and name "Illinois" in blue

Highest point: Charles Mound — 1,235 feet (376 meters)

Lowest point: Mississippi River — 279 feet (85 meters)

Highest recorded temperature: 117 degrees Fahrenheit (47 degrees Celsius) — East St. Louis, 1954

Lowest recorded temperature: −35 degrees Fahrenheit (−37 degrees Celsius) — Mount Carroll, 1930

State song: "Illinois"

State tree: White oak

State flower: Violet

State bird: Cardinal

State fish: Bluegill

State animal: White-tailed deer

Illinois History

Situated between the major waterways of the Mississippi River and Lake Michigan, and possessing unusually rich soil for agricultural purposes, Illinois has been an important area of human activity since the earliest days of habitation. The historical development of the region has been sharply divided among the urban northeast area, dominated by Chicago; the central area, a mixture of urban and rural cultures; and the rural southern area, which resembles its southern neighbors, Missouri and Kentucky, more than it does the rest of the state.

Early History. The earliest humans to inhabit the area were hunters and gatherers who roamed the southern part of the region ten thousand years ago. Over the next several thousand years, cultures developed that built permanent villages and depended primarily on the growing of corn. By the year 1300, the Mississippian culture, a highly developed society based on the raising of corn, squash, and beans, dominated central North America. This society, the largest Native American culture north of Mexico, built large, fortified cities and extensive earth-mound monuments. The largest of these monuments were found at Cahokia, the culture's religious center, located in southwestern Illinois.

By the time Europeans arrived in the New World, a large number of Native American peoples, belonging to the Algonquin language group, inhabited the region. Among these were the Kickapoo, Sauk, and Fox in the north; the Potawatomi, Ottawa, and Ojibwa near Lake Michigan; the Illinois, a confederation of five peoples, in the central prairies; and the Cahokia and Tamaroa in the south. These societies relied on agriculture and buffalo hunting for survival. By the end of the first third of the nineteenth century, all these peoples had sold, ceded, or been forced off their native lands and had settled in other areas.

Exploration and Settlement. The first Europeans to visit the Illinois area were led by the French explorers Louis Jolliet and Jacques Marquette in 1673 as they traveled south from Wisconsin along the Mississippi River as far as Arkansas. This expedition also explored the Illinois River on its return journey north. In 1680 the French explorers René-Robert Cavalier, sieur de La Salle, and Henri de Tonti founded Fort Crevecoeur near the modern city of Peoria, followed two years later by Fort Saint Louis near the modern city of Ottawa. After a century of French settlement, the area became British territory at the end of the French and Indian War.

British policy was unfavorable to the economic development of the area, and settlements often lacked any form of government. Combined with violent encounters with Native Americans living in the area, these factors tended to discourage settlers. By 1773, the number of Europeans in Illinois had declined to about one thousand. The population also included a few hundred slaves.

During the American Revolution, American forces under George Rogers Clark captured British settlements at Kaskaskia and Cahokia in May of 1778, winning the region for the newly created United States. American control of the area was confirmed by the Treaty of Paris, which ended the war in 1783. At first a part of the state of Virginia, the region became part of the new Northwest Territory in 1787; part of the new Indiana Territory in 1800; a separate territory, including parts of modern Wisconsin and Minnesota, in 1809; and a state, with its modern borders, in 1818.

Conflict with Native Americans. Battles between European settlers and Native Americans began long before statehood. In 1730 French forces defeated Fox forces in east central Illinois. In 1803 the Kaskaskia ceded their lands to the United States. In 1812 Potawatomi forces killed fifty-two Americans and destroyed Fort Dearborn, a military establishment on the site of modern Chicago. The Kickapoo left their native lands in 1819, followed by the Ojibwa, Ottawa, and Potawatomi in 1829. The Illinois sold their land in 1832.

One of the most violent encounters between settlers and American Indians was the Black Hawk War of 1832. Although some leaders of the Sauk and Fox had ceded their lands to the United States in 1804, others refused to leave. Black Hawk, a leader of these people, was driven into Iowa in 1831 but crossed back over the Mississippi River into Illinois the next year with about one thousand followers. Although at first Black Hawk was able to defeat the Illinois militia, lack of supplies forced him to retreat northward into Wisconsin, where most of his followers were killed. The destruction of Black Hawk's people, including women, children, and the elderly, was an important factor in the decision of nearly all Native Americans to leave the area by 1837.

Slavery and the Civil War. At the time of statehood, slaves in Illinois were given the status of indentured servants, due to the fear that permitting slavery would block admission to the Union. In 1824 voters rejected a proposal to hold a constitutional convention for the purpose of making slavery legal. Increasing numbers of settlers from free states in the 1830's and 1840's led to a new state constitution in 1848, which abolished slavery and made it illegal to bring slaves into Illinois.

During the Civil War, most residents of the state were loyal to the Union and to President Abraham Lincoln, who was himself from Illinois. An attempt was made to unite southern Illinois, which was less sympathetic to the Union cause, to the Confederacy, but it ended in failure. About 250,000 residents of Illinois fought for the Union, including Ulysses S. Grant, one of its most capable generals.

The Rise of Chicago. During the early nineteenth century, about two-thirds of the population of Illinois lived in the southern part of the state. Although Jean Baptist Point du Sable, known as the father of Chicago, founded a trading post at the site in 1779, it remained a small settlement for nearly half a century. The opening of the Erie Canal in 1825, linking the Hudson River to Lake Erie, made transportation from eastern states to northern Illinois much easier. In 1837 Chicago had a population of 4,200 and was incorporated as a city.

The opening of the Illinois and Michigan canal in 1848 linked Lake Michigan and the Illinois River, providing Chicago with a waterway to the Mississippi River. By 1852 two railroad lines linked Chicago to eastern states. By 1856 it was the nation's most important railroad center.

The second half of the nineteenth century saw rapid economic growth in Chicago, with the city becoming dominant in iron and steel production, lumber distribution, slaughtering and meat packing, and marketing of produce. The Great Chicago Fire, lasting for two days in October, 1871, killed more than two hundred people, left ninety thousand homeless, and destroyed $200 million worth of property. Despite this disaster, Chicago continued to experience rapid growth. From 1850 to 1880 the population of the city grew from about thirty thousand to more than half a million.

The Twentieth Century. Although Illinois harbored a number of German and Irish immigrants in the 1840's, it was not until the turn of the century that large numbers of immigrants from other nations, including Poland, Hungary, Italy, Norway, Sweden, Austria, and Russia, arrived in the state.

Chicago was the center of immigration, with more than three-fourths of its population in 1900 consisting of those born in other countries and their children.

The same period also saw a large increase in the number of African Americans in Illinois. From 1870 to 1910, the population of African Americans increased from 29,000 to more than 100,000. Prior to World War II, large numbers of European Jews immigrated to Illinois. In later years, increasing numbers of Asians and Latin Americans immigrated to the state.

The late nineteenth century and the early twentieth century brought Illinois a reputation for violence, particularly in Chicago, where the Haymarket Riot of 1886 resulted in numerous deaths in a confrontation between police and labor activists. Railroad worker strikes in Chicago in 1894 also led to violence. Elsewhere in the state, strikes by mine workers led to violence in 1898 and 1922. Race riots broke out in Springfield in 1908, in East St. Louis in 1917, and in Chicago in 1919. The 1920's saw an increase in violence against African Americans by the Ku Klux Klan. During the 1920's

Fanciful depiction of Chicago in 1779, showing Jean Baptist Point du Sable, believed to be the town's first settler. (Library of Congress)

Contemporary magazine illustration of the 1886 Haymarket Riot. (Library of Congress)

and 1930's, Chicago was a center of organized crime. Perhaps the most infamous event in the history of crime in Chicago occurred in 1929, when crime leader Al Capone had seven rivals killed in the Saint Valentine's Day Massacre.

Throughout the twentieth century, the Democratic and Republican parties struggled for control of Illinois. This fact, combined with the state's large number of electoral votes, made Illinois a key target of presidential election campaigns. In general, the city of Chicago has been strongly Democratic, the suburbs and farmlands of the north and central regions strongly Republican, and the southern region mixed.

After the economic recession of the 1970's, the electronic and computer technology industries in Illinois became an important part of the state's economy in the 1980's. Illinois also became a leader in nuclear power production in the 1990's, when it had thirteen operating nuclear power plants, more than any other state. These plants supplied more than half of the state's electricity.

Rose Secrest

Illinois Time Line

1673	Louis Jolliet and Jacques Marquette lead the first European expedition to the area.
1680	René-Robert Cavalier, sieur de La Salle, and Henri de Tonti found Fort Crevecoeur.
1682	La Salle and Tonti found Fort Saint Louis.

(continued)

1730	Fox forces are defeated in a battle with French settlers.
1763	End of the French and Indian War brings the area under British control.
1778	George Rogers Clark leads American forces to victory over British forces in Kaskaskia and Cahokia.
1779	Jean Baptist Point du Sable founds a trading post at Chicago.
1783	End of the American Revolution brings the area under American control.
1787	Illinois becomes part of the Northwest Territory.
1803	Kaskaskia cede their land to the United States.
1803	Fort Dearborn is established at Chicago.
1809	Illinois Territory is established.
1811-1812	Earthquakes centered near New Madrid, Missouri, cause extensive damage in southern Illinois.
1812	Potawatomi forces destroy Fort Dearborn.
1814	First newspaper, the *Illinois Herald*, is established.
1816	Fort Dearborn is rebuilt.
1816	First bank in Illinois is established.
Dec. 3, 1818	Illinois becomes the twenty-first state.
1818	Population is nearly thirty-five thousand.
1819	Kickapoo leave their native lands.
1820	Capital is moved from Kaskaskia to Vandalia.
1824	Voters defeat a plan for a constitutional convention which would legalize slavery in the state.
1825	Opening of the Erie Canal brings more settlers to Chicago.
1827	Rock Spring Seminary, the first college, is established.
1829	Ojibwa, Ottawa, and Potawatomi cede their lands to the United States.
1832	Black Hawk War leads to the defeat of the Sauk and Fox.
1837	Chicago is incorporated as a city.
1839	Capital is moved to Springfield.
1848	New state constitution abolishes slavery.
1850	Population reaches 850,000; Chicago is home to 30,000.
1852	Railroads connect Chicago with eastern cities.
1867	University of Illinois is established.
1871	Great Chicago Fire devastates the city.
1880	Population of Chicago reaches 500,000.
1883	Ten-story Home Insurance Building, the world's first skyscraper, is built in Chicago.
1886	Haymarket Riot, a confrontation between police and labor activists, breaks out in Chicago.
1894	Strike by railroad workers leads to violence in Chicago.
1898	Strike by mine workers leads to violence in Pana and Virden.
1900	Population reaches nearly five million.

1908	Race riot breaks out in Springfield.
1917	Race riot breaks out in East St. Louis.
1919	Race riot breaks out in Chicago.
1922	Strike by mine workers leads to violence in Williamson County.
1929	Seven Chicago crime leaders are murdered in the Saint Valentine's Day Massacre.
1942	First controlled nuclear chain reaction is achieved at the University of Chicago.
1950	Population reaches nearly nine million.
1957	First nuclear power plant in the United States is established.
1968	Violence breaks out between police and protesters during the Democratic National Convention in Chicago.
1990	Population reaches 11.5 million.
1992	Carol Moseley-Braun of Chicago becomes the first African American woman elected to the United States Senate.
1993	Worst floods in the state's history do $1.5 billion worth of damage in western and southern Illinois.
1994	Members of the Republican Party hold all statewide offices and control both chambers of the state assembly.
1997	Population reaches nearly 12 million, with 85 percent living in urban areas, including 65 percent in the Chicago metropolitan area.

Illinois's Lake Michigan shoreline. (PhotoDisc)

Notes for Further Study

Published Sources. A good place for the beginning student to start is Andrew Santella's *Illinois* (1998), a simple but clear account of the state's history, geography, ecology, people, economy, cities, and attractions. An extremely detailed discussion of the state's physical structure can be found in A. Doyne Horsley's *Illinois: A Geography* (1986), which includes extensive maps. The land and its inhabitants are described in *The Natural Resources of Illinois* (1987), compiled by R. Dan Neely and Carla G. Heister.

Of the many books dealing with Chicago, one of the best for the general reader is *Chicago Sketches: Urban Tales, Stories, and Legends from Chicago History* (1995) by June Skinner Sawyers, a collection of seventy-two colorful essays. A more serious book about the city is David Farber's *Chicago '68* (1988), a dramatic account of the riots that occurred during the Democratic National Convention in 1968. Two of the best books dealing with the early history of the state are *Frontier Illinois* (1998) by James E. Davis and *French Roots in the Illinois Country: The Mississippi Frontier in Colonial Times* (1998) by Carl J. Ekberg. For more detailed information, the University of Illinois publishes numerous volumes dealing with all aspects of the state's past. In 1987, the University of Illinois also reprinted a series of books from 1920 in the Centennial History of Illinois series, with useful information on the history of the state from 1673 to 1918.

Web Resources. Like most sources of information on the Internet, the Web sites devoted to Illinois are always changing. An excellent place to start is the state of Illinois site (http://www.state.il.us) from the state government. This site provides information on governmental agencies, tourism, cities and counties, and state facts. For local information, Illinois Counties (http://www.mclean.gov/county.html) provides data on all the state's counties. Tourist attractions in the state are discussed in the Illinois Travel Notes site (http://www.travelnotes.rog/NorthAmerica/illinois.htm). Regularly updated business news can be found at Illinois Economy (http://www.admin.uiuc.edu/NB/98.04/economytip.html) from the University of Illinois at Urbana-Champaign. The physical structure of the region is described in Geologic Information About Illinois (http://geology.er.usgs.gov/states/IL.html) from the United States Geologic Survey.

One of the many Web sites devoted to Illinois history, with discussions of Chicago, Abraham Lincoln, Native Americans, early settlers, and the history of transportation, is The Illinois History Resource Page (http://alexia.lis.uiuc.edu/~sorensen/hist.html). An excellent timeline can be found at Illinois Chronology (http://www.state.il.us/gov/bio/history.htm). Numerous history sites can be reached through links provided by Illinois History (http://squire.cmi.k12.il.us/Urbana/king/illinois_history.htm). A detailed history of Chicago is found at Chicago Timeline from 1673 (http://www.chipublib.org/04chicago/chihist.html).

Counties

County	Sq. miles	1996 pop.	County	Sq. miles	1996 pop.
Adams	856.7	67,816	Clinton	474.3	35,368
Alexander	236.4	10,228	Coles	508.3	51,186
Bond	380.2	17,069	Cook	945.7	5,096,540
Boone	281.4	37,389	Crawford	443.6	21,071
Brown	305.7	6,400	Cumberland	346.0	11,169
Bureau	868.6	35,739	De Kalb	634.2	82,703
Calhoun	253.8	5,011	DeWitt	397.6	16,795
Carroll	444.2	16,907	Douglas	416.9	19,799
Cass	376.0	13,284	DuPage	334.4	859,310
Champaign	997.2	167,392	Edgar	623.6	20,106
Christian	709.1	34,730	Edwards	222.4	7,129
Clark	501.5	17,571	Effingham	478.7	33,337
Clay	469.3	14,397	Fayette	716.5	21,362

County	Sq. miles	1996 pop.	County	Sq. miles	1996 pop.
Ford	485.9	14,164	Iroquois	1,116.5	31,625
Franklin	412.1	40,948	Jackson	588.1	61,154
Fulton	865.7	38,650	Jasper	494.4	10,635
Gallatin	323.7	6,753	Jefferson	571.1	39,090
Greene	543.1	15,733	Jersey	369.2	21,308
Grundy	420.1	35,712	Jo Daviess	601.2	21,783
Hamilton	435.2	8,622	Johnson	346.0	12,954
Hancock	794.7	21,205	Kane	520.7	370,361
Hardin	178.3	5,068	Kankakee	677.5	101,949
Henderson	378.8	8,526	Kendall	320.7	47,894
Henry	823.3	51,807	Knox	716.3	55,936

(continued)

County	Sq. miles	1996 pop.
Lake	447.8	582,983
LaSalle	1,135.0	109,462
Lawrence	372.0	15,865
Lee	725.4	35,959
Livingston	1,043.8	40,597
Logan	618.2	31,499
McDonough	589.3	34,152
McHenry	604.1	230,555
McLean	1,183.6	139,133
Macon	580.6	115,416
Macoupin	863.7	48,994
Madison	725.1	256,007
Marion	572.3	42,295
Marshall	386.1	12,789
Mason	539.0	16,820
Massac	239.1	15,336
Menard	314.3	12,359
Mercer	561.1	17,605
Monroe	388.3	25,358
Montgomery	703.8	31,059
Morgan	568.8	36,252
Moultrie	335.6	14,319
Ogle	758.9	50,107
Peoria	619.6	183,337
Perry	441.0	21,498
Piatt	440.0	16,357
Pike	830.3	17,251
Pope	370.9	4,735

County	Sq. miles	1996 pop.
Pulaski	200.8	7,348
Putnam	159.8	5,715
Randolph	578.4	34,240
Richland	360.2	16,747
Rock Island	426.8	148,640
Saint Clair	663.9	264,419
Saline	383.3	26,476
Sangamon	868.3	191,771
Schuyler	437.4	7,702
Scott	251.0	5,615
Shelby	758.6	22,660
Stark	287.9	6,402
Stephenson	564.3	49,167
Tazewell	648.9	128,366
Union	416.2	18,079
Vermilion	899.1	85,260
Wabash	223.5	12,681
Warren	542.6	18,901
Washington	562.7	15,204
Wayne	713.9	17,049
White	494.9	15,840
Whiteside	684.8	60,225
Will	837.3	427,818
Williamson	424.2	60,764
Winnebago	513.8	264,873
Woodford	528.0	34,798

Source: U.S. Census Bureau; National Association of Counties.

Cities

With 10,000 or more residents

Rank	City	Population
1	Chicago	2,802,079
2	Rockford	143,656
3	Aurora	124,736
4	Springfield	117,098
5	Naperville	117,091
6	Peoria	111,148
7	Joliet	92,285
8	Elgin	87,507
9	Decatur	79,972
10	Arlington Heights	76,522
11	Waukegan	75,999
12	Schaumburg	74,481
13	Evanston	71,928
14	Cicero	71,289

Rank	City	Population
15	Champaign	64,280
16	Bloomington	58,841
17	Skokie	58,628
18	Oak Lawn	57,730
19	Wheaton	55,308
20	Des Plaines	55,272
21	Bolingbrook	54,288
22	Mount Prospect	53,581
23	Downers Grove	51,716
24	Oak Park	50,646
25	Hoffman Estates	48,516
26	Orland Park	47,856
27	Tinley Park	45,825
28	Palatine	45,513

Rank	City	Population
29	Normal	44,221
30	Elmhurst	43,505
31	Berwyn	43,030
32	Lombard	42,215
33	Moline	41,919
34	Buffalo Grove	41,857

Rank	City	Population
35	Belleville	40,734
36	Quincy	39,918
37	Glenview	39,873
38	Rock Island	38,714
39	East St. Louis	37,390
40	Park Ridge	37,390

(continued)

Rank	City	Population	Rank	City	Population
41	Carol Stream	36,968	94	Blue Island	20,585
42	Calumet City	36,916	95	Charleston	20,437
43	De Kalb	36,094	96	Lake in the Hills	20,417
44	Hanover Park	36,027	97	Melrose Park	20,400
45	Streamwood	34,984	98	Evergreen Park	20,389
46	Urbana	34,872	99	East Moline	20,205
47	Elk Grove Village	34,693	100	Algonquin	20,093
48	Bartlett	34,511	101	Bloomingdale	19,995
49	Addison	34,074	102	Libertyville	19,976
50	Northbrook	33,107	103	Bellwood	19,932
51	Crystal Lake	33,078	104	Machesney Park	19,831
52	Galesburg	32,791	105	Homewood	19,536
53	North Chicago	32,175	106	McHenry	19,451
54	Pekin	31,958	107	O'Fallon	19,414
55	Danville	31,761	108	Alsip	19,378
56	Chicago Heights	31,635	109	Lake Forest	19,128
57	Alton	31,457	110	Romeoville	19,015
58	Highland Park	31,310	111	Deerfield	18,802
59	Granite City	31,078	112	Palos Hills	18,732
60	Wheeling	30,564	113	Belvidere	18,445
61	Glendale Heights	30,277	114	Vernon Hills	18,441
62	Niles	29,502	115	Geneva	18,382
63	Woodridge	29,382	116	Jacksonville	18,239
64	Harvey	28,756	117	Loves Park	18,183
65	Mundelein	28,518	118	Brookfield	18,155
66	Lansing	28,512	119	Mattoon	18,115
67	Burbank	27,807	120	Bensenville	18,105
68	Oak Forest	27,718	121	Ottawa	18,026
69	Carpentersville	27,271	122	Franklin Park	17,941
70	St. Charles	26,516	123	West Chicago	17,865
71	Kankakee	26,456	124	Macomb	17,778
72	Carbondale	26,454	125	Woodstock	17,734
73	Wilmette	26,219	126	Westchester	17,476
74	Glen Ellyn	25,956	127	Godfrey	17,340
75	Maywood	25,833	128	Lake Zurich	17,181
76	Freeport	25,806	129	Edwardsville	16,961
77	Gurnee	25,016	130	Mount Vernon	16,850
78	Park Forest	24,365	131	Hinsdale	16,589
79	Dolton	23,882	132	Country Club Hills	16,433
80	Darien	23,629	133	Cahokia	16,149
81	Roselle	23,627	134	Grayslake	15,853
82	Collinsville	23,308	135	Marion	15,810
83	Round Lake Beach	23,140	136	Bourbonnais	15,511
84	Rolling Meadows	22,844	137	Bridgeview	15,487
85	Westmont	22,654	138	Prospect Heights	15,398
86	Villa Park	22,635	139	Dixon	15,374
87	Zion	22,518	140	La Grange	15,002
88	Elmwood Park	22,461	141	Lincoln	14,966
89	Batavia	22,306	142	South Elgin	14,910
90	Morton Grove	22,180	143	Midlothian	14,865
91	East Peoria	22,117	144	New Lenox	14,830
92	South Holland	21,794	145	Fairview Heights	14,795
93	Lisle	20,820	146	Morton	14,742

Rank	City	Population
147	Sterling	14,623
148	Norridge	14,311
149	Forest Park	14,301
150	Centralia	14,229
151	Hickory Hills	14,113
152	Chicago Ridge	14,091
153	Cary	14,069
154	Rantoul	13,945
155	Hazel Crest	13,859
156	Canton	13,820
157	Streator	13,726
158	Warrenville	13,508
159	Wood Dale	13,402
160	Lockport	13,401
161	Riverdale	13,220
162	Markham	12,971
163	Crest Hill	12,821
164	Effingham	12,820
165	Mokena	12,715
166	Bradley	12,604
167	Matteson	12,490
168	Kewanee	12,481
169	La Grange Park	12,463
170	Western Springs	12,435
171	Palos Heights	12,164
172	Winnetka	11,853

Rank	City	Population
173	Northlake	11,847
174	Richton Park	11,720
175	Crestwood	11,658
176	Justice	11,528
177	Morris	11,477
178	Pontiac	11,440
179	Lincolnwood	11,277
180	Sycamore	11,237
181	Taylorville	11,236
182	Worth	11,152
183	River Forest	11,130
184	Herrin	11,107
185	WoodRiver	11,000
186	Sauk Village	10,973
187	Schiller Park	10,941
188	Washington	10,611
189	Lindenhurst	10,602
190	Lemont	10,544
191	Oswego	10,536
192	Burr Ridge	10,379
193	Beach Park	10,320
194	Frankfort	10,123
195	Glen Carbon	10,012

Population figures are estimated for mid-1998.
Source: U.S. Bureau of the Census.

Index to Tables

NA = Reliable data are not available.

DEMOGRAPHICS

Resident state and national populations, 1970-1997

Population figures given in thousands

	State pop.	U.S. pop.	Share	Rank
1970	11,110	203,302	5.5%	5
1980	11,427	226,546	5.0%	5
1985	11,400	237,924	4.8%	5
1990	11,431	248,765	4.6%	6
1995	11,795	262,761	4.5%	6
1997	11,896	267,636	4.4%	6

Source: U.S. Bureau of the Census.

Resident population by age, 1997

Age group	Total population
Under 5 years	904,000
5 to 17 years	2,271,000
18 to 24 years	1,095,000
25 to 34 years	1,764,000
35 to 44 years	1,950,000
45 to 54 years	1,469,000
55 to 64 years	963,000
65 to 74 years	788,000
75 to 84 years	517,000
85 years and over	177,000
Portion of residents 65 and older	12.5%
National average	12.7%

Population figures are rounded to nearest thousand persons;
figures include armed forces personnel stationed in state.
Source: U.S. Bureau of the Census.

Resident population by race, Hispanic origin, 1997

	State pop.	Share	U.S.
All residents	11,896,000	100.0%	100.0%
Hispanic white	1,107,000	9.3%	10.0%
non-Hispanic white	8,564,000	72.0%	72.7%
African American	1,815,000	15.3%	12.7%
Native American	27,000	0.2%	0.9%
Asian, Pacific Islander	383,000	3.2%	3.8%

Source: U.S. Bureau of the Census.

Projections of state population, 2000-2025

	Model A Uses interstate migration observed from 1975-1994	Model B Uses Bureau of Economic Analysis employment projections
Year	Population	Population
2000	12,051,000	12,069,000
2005	12,266,000	12,314,000
2010	12,515,000	12,601,000
2015	12,808,000	12,945,000
2020	13,121,000	13,323,000
2025	13,440,000	13,717,000

All population projections, including those for 2000, were calculated in 1997.

Source: U.S. Bureau of the Census, Population Paper Listings PPL-47.

VITAL STATISTICS

Average lifetime in years by race, 1989-1991

	State	U.S.	Rank
All residents	74.90	75.37	35
White residents	76.16	76.13	28
Black residents	67.46	69.16	32

Ranks are from longest-lived to least longest-lived. Ranks exclude Alaska, for which reliable data are not available. Rank for black residents is based on the 32 states for which reliable data are available.

Source: U.S. National Center for Health Statistics.

Infant mortality rates, 1980 and 1995

	State	U.S.
All residents		
1980	14.8	12.6
1995	9.4	7.6
White residents		
1980	11.7	11.0
1995	7.2	6.3
Black residents		
1980	26.3	21.4
1995	18.7	15.1

Figures represent deaths per 1,000 live births of resident infants under 1 year old, exclusive of fetal deaths; all-residents figures include other races not listed separately.

Source: U.S. National Center for Health Statistics.

Marriages and divorces

Marriages in 1996.	90,200
Rate per 1,000 population, 1995.	7.0
U.S. rate, 1995	8.9
Rank among all states	45
Divorces in 1996	40,400
Rate per 1,000 population, 1995.	3.3
U.S. rate, 1995	4.4
Rank among all states	40

Rank is from highest to lowest in country.

Source: U.S. National Center for Health Statistics.

Death rates by leading causes, 1995

Deaths per 100,000 resident population

Cause	State	U.S.
Heart disease	304.4	280.7
Cancer	212.2	204.9
Cerebrovascular diseases	63.3	60.1
Accidents and adverse effects	33.9	35.5
Motor vehicle accidents	14.7	16.5
Chronic obstructive pulmonary diseases	38.0	39.2
Diabetes mellitus	22.5	22.6
HIV	12.1	NA
Suicide	9.5	11.9
Homicide	11.0	8.7
All causes	916.9	880.0
Rank in overall death rate among states		22

Figures exclude nonresidents who die in state. Causes of death follow International Classification of Diseases. Rank is from highest to lowest in country.

Source: U.S. National Center for Health Statistics.

ECONOMY

Gross state product, 1990-1996
In current dollars

	State product	Increase
1990	$273.4 billion	
1993	$312.3 billion	
1994	$336.9 billion	7.88%
1995	$352.9 billion	4.75%
1996	$370.8 billion	5.07%

Source: U.S. Bureau of Economic Analysis; *Survey of Current Business,* June, 1998.

Gross state product by industry, 1996
In billions

Farms, forestry, fisheries	$4.4
Construction.	13.4
Manufacturing.	71.9
Transportation, public utilities	32.3
Wholesale trade	27.2
Retail trade	29.0
Finance, insurance, real estate	65.3
Services	67.2
Government	33.4
State total	$345.5
Total U.S.	$6,923.8
State share	4.99%
Rank among states	4

Total figures include mining, not listed separately.
Source: U.S. Bureau of Economic Analysis; *Survey of Current Business,* June, 1998.

Personal income per capita, 1990 and 1997
In current dollars

	1990	1997
Per capita income	$20,534	$28,202
U.S. average	$19,188	$25,598
Rank among states	11	7

1997 data are preliminary.
Source: U.S. Bureau of Economic Analysis; *Survey of Current Business,* May, 1998.

Energy consumption, 1995
In trillions of British thermal units (BTU)

End-use sectors

Residential	955.5
Commercial	703.3
Industrial	1,333.6
Transportation	811.9

Sources of energy

Petroleum	1,236.6
Natural gas	1,100.1
Coal	816.9
Hydroelectric power	1.3
Nuclear electric power	836.4
Total state per capita consumption	322.7
Total U.S. per capita consumption	344.4
Rank among states	34
Total state energy consumption	3,804.3
Total U.S. energy consumption	90,547.4
State share of U.S. total	4.20%
Rank among states	7

Total figures include items not listed separately.
Source: U.S. Energy Information Administration; *State Energy Data Report.*

Nonfarm employment by sectors, 1997

Total	5,773,000
Construction.	235,000
Manufacturing.	974,000
Transportation, public utilities	337,000
Wholesale trade, retail trade	1,324,000
Finance, insurance, real estate	399,000
Services	1,686,000
Government	806,000

Figures are rounded to nearest thousand persons. Total includes mining, not listed separately.
Source: U.S. Bureau of Labor Statistics; *Employment and Earnings,* monthly.

Foreign exports, 1990-1997
In millions of dollars

Year	State	U.S.	State share
1990	12,965	394,045	3.29%
1996	24,176	624,767	3.87%
1997	26,455	688,896	3.84%

Source: U.S. Bureau of the Census; *U.S. Merchandise Trade,* series FT 900.

LAND USE

Federally owned land, 1996

	State	U.S.	State share
Total acres	35,795,000	2,271,343,000	1.58%
Federally owned	405,000	563,129,000	0.07%
Federal share	1.1%	24.8%	—

Areas are rounded to nearest thousand acres. Figures for federally owned land do not include trust properties.
Source: U.S. General Services Administration; *Inventory Report on Real Property Owned by the United States Throughout the World,* annual.

Land use, 1992

In acres, rounded to nearest thousand

Total surface area	36,061,000
Federal land	521,000
Total nonfederal	34,766,000
Developed	3,094,000
Total rural	31,672,000
Cropland	24,100,000
Pasture land	2,764,000
Range land	0
Forest land	3,419,000
Minor cover/use	1,390,000

Total surface area figures include water area not shown separately.
Source: U.S. Dept. of Agriculture; Soil Conservation Service; Iowa State University, Statistical Laboratory; *Summary Report, 1992 National Resources Inventory.*

Farms and crop acreage, 1997

	State	U.S.	Share	Rank
Farms (thousands)	76	2,058	3.69%	9
Acres (millions)	28	968	2.89%	16
Acres per farm	368	471	—	18
Acres planted	23,740	334,139	7.10%	2
Acres harvested	23,534	319,894	7.36%	2
Farm value (mill.)	$7,366	$108,805	6.77%	8

Numbers of farms are rounded to nearest thousand.
Source: U.S. Dept. of Agriculture; National Agricultural Statistics Service.

GOVERNMENT AND FINANCE

Units of local government, 1997

	State	Total U.S.	Rank
All local governments	6,835	87,453	1
Counties	102	3,043	6
Municipalities	1,288	19,372	1
Townships	1,433	16,629	3
School districts	944	13,726	3
Special districts	3,068	34,683	1

County ranks are based on the 48 states with county governments; township ranks are based on the 20 states with township governments; school district ranks are based on the 46 states with such districts.
Source: U.S. Bureau of the Census; *1997 Census of Governments, Government Organization,* Series GC97(1).

State government revenue, 1996

Total revenue	$36,991 mill.
General revenue	30,306 mill.
Per capita	2,559
U.S. per capita average	2,910
Rank among states	38

Intergovernmental revenue	
Total	$8,394 mill.
From federal government	7,873 mill.
From local government	521 mill.

Charges and Miscellaneous	
Total	$4,635 mill.
Current charges	1,891 mill.
Misc. general revenue	2,744 mill.

Taxes	
Total	$17,277 mill.
General sales	5,057 mill.
Selective sales	3,428 mill.
License taxes	952 mill.
Individual income	5,781 mill.
Corporate income	1,621 mill.
Other	437 mill.
Insurance trust revenue	6,684 mill.

Total revenue figures include items not listed separately.
Source: U.S. Bureau of the Census.

State government expenditures, 1996

General expenditures

Intergovernmental	$8,549 mill.
Direct expenditures	21,543 mill.
Total	30,092 mill.

Selected direct expenditures

Education	$8,773 mill.
Public welfare	9,377 mill.
Health, hospital	2,310 mill.
Highways	2,435 mill.
Police	295 mill.
Corrections	873 mill.
Natural resources	266 mill.
Parks and recreation	203 mill.
Government administration	836 mill.
Interest on debt	1,493 mill.

Other

State per capita expenditures	$2,540
U.S. per capita average	2,854
Rank among states	37
Total state expenditures	34,111 mill.
Total U.S. expenditures	859,959 mill.

Totals include items not listed separately.
Source: U.S. Bureau of the Census.

Shelby L. Cullom (R)	(r) 1877-1883
John M. Hamilton (R)	1883-1885
Richard J. Oglesby (R)	1885-1889
Joseph W. Fifer (R)	1889-1893
John P. Altgeld (D)	1893-1897
John R. Tanner (R)	1897-1901
Richard Yates, Jr. (R)	1901-1905
Charles S. Deneen (R)	1905-1913
Edward F. Dunne (D)	1913-1917
Frank O. Lowden (R)	1917-1921
Lennington Small (R)	1921-1929
Louis L. Emmerson (R)	1929-1933
Henry Horner (D)	(d) 1933-1940
John H. Stelle (D)	1940-1941
Dwight H. Green (R)	1941-1949
Adlai E. Stevenson II (D)	1949-1953
William G. Stratton (R)	1953-1961
Otto Kerner, Jr. (D)	(r) 1961-1968
Samuel H. Shapiro (D)	1968-1969
Richard B. Ogilvie (R)	1969-1973
Daniel Walker (D)	1973-1977
James R. Thompson (R)	1977-1991
Jim Edgar (R)	1991-1999
George H. Ryan (R)	1999-

POLITICS

Governors since statehood

D = Democrat; R = Republican; O = other;
(r) resigned; (d) died in office; (i) removed from office

Shadrach Bond (O)	1818-1822
Edward Coles (O)	1822-1826
Ninian Edwards (O)	1826-1830
John Reynolds (O)	(r) 1830-1834
William L. D. Ewing (O)	1834
Joseph Duncan (O)	1834-1838
Thomas Carlin (D)	1838-1842
Thomas Ford (D)	1842-1846
Augustus C. French (D)	1846-1853
Joel A. Matteson (D)	1853-1857
William H. Bissell (R)	(d) 1857-1860
John Wood (R)	1860-1861
Richard Yates (R)	1861-1865
Richard J. Oglesby (R)	1865-1869
John M. Palmer (R)	1869-1873
Richard J. Oglesby (R)	(r) 1873
John L. Beveridge (R)	1873-1877

Composition of state legislature, 1990-1998

	Democrats	Republicans
State House (118 seats)		
1990	72	46
1992	67	51
1994	54	64
1996	60	58
1998	62	56
State Senate (59 seats)		
1990	31	28
1992	27	32
1994	26	33
1996	28	31
1998	27	32

Figures for total seats may include independents and minor
party members.
Source: Council of State Governments; *State Elective Officials
and the Legislatures.*

Composition of congressional delegations, 1989-1999

	Dem	Rep	Total
House of Representatives			
101st Congress, 1989			
State delegates	14	8	22
Total U.S.	259	174	433
102d Congress, 1991			
State delegates	15	7	22
Total U.S.	267	167	434
103d Congress, 1993			
State delegates	12	8	20
Total U.S.	258	176	434
104th Congress, 1995			
State delegates	10	10	20
Total U.S.	197	236	433
105th Congress, 1997			
State delegates	10	10	20
Total U.S.	206	228	434
106th Congress, 1999			
State delegates	10	10	20
Total U.S.	211	222	433
Senate			
101st Congress, 1989			
State delegates	2	0	2
Total U.S.	55	45	100
102d Congress, 1991			
State delegates	2	0	2
Total U.S.	56	44	100
103d Congress, 1993			
State delegates	2	0	2
Total U.S.	57	43	100
104th Congress, 1995			
State delegates	2	0	2
Total U.S.	46	53	99
105th Congress, 1997			
State delegates	2	0	2
Total U.S.	45	55	100
106th Congress, 1999			
State delegates	1	1	2
Total U.S.	45	54	99

Figures are for starts of first sessions. Figure for U.S. Representatives for 101st Congress does not include Alabama and Indiana, which had vacancies. Figures for total U.S. Representatives for 102d, 103d, and 106th Congresses do not include Vermont, which had 1 Independent-Socialist. Figure for U.S. Representatives for 104th Congress does not include Vermont, which had 1 Independent-Socialist, and California, which had 1 vacancy. Figure for U.S. Representatives for 105th Congress does not include New York, which had 1 vacancy. Figure for U.S. Senators for 104th Congress does not include Oregon, which had 1 vacancy. Figure for U.S. Senators for 106th Congress does not include New Hampshire, which had 1 Independent.

Source: U.S. Congress; *Congressional Directory,* biennial.

Voter participation in presidential elections, 1992 and 1996

	1992	1996
State voting age pop.	8,598,000	8,764,000
Total U.S. voting age pop.	189,524,000	196,509,000
State share of U.S. total	4.5%	4.5%
Rank among states	6	6
Percent of state casting vote	58.7	52.6
Percent of U.S. total voting	55.1	49.0
Rank among states	27	21

Source: U.S. Bureau of the Census.

HEALTH AND MEDICAL CARE

Medicare, 1997

	Recipients	Payments
State	1,620,000	$8,314 mill.
Total U.S.	37,514,000	$206,064 mill.
State share	4.32%	4.03%
Rank among states	7	7

Recipient figures are rounded to nearest thousand persons. Ranks are from highest to lowest.

Source: U.S. Health Care Financing Administration.

Medicaid, 1996

	Recipients	Payments
State	1,454,000	$5,365 mill.
Total U.S.	35,028,000	$121,419 mill.
State share	4.15%	4.42%
Rank among states	6	5

Recipient figures are rounded to nearest thousand persons. Payment figures for fiscal year reflect federal and state contribution payments. Ranks are from highest to lowest.

Source: U.S. Health Care Financing Administration.

Health insurance coverage, 1996

	State	U.S.
Total persons covered	10,511,000	225,070,000
Total persons not covered	1,337,000	41,716,000
Part not covered	11.3%	15.6%
Rank among states	38	—
Children not covered	322,000	10,554,000
Part not covered	9.8%	14.8%
Rank among states	34	—

Ranks are from most to fewest uninsured. Population figures
are rounded to nearest thousand persons.
Source: U.S. Bureau of the Census.

AIDS, syphilis, tuberculosis, and measles cases, 1997

Cases	U.S.	State	Share
AIDS	58,443	1,842	3.15%
Syphilis	8,550	435	5.09%
Tuberculosis	18,534	974	5.26%
Measles	148,000	8,000	5.41%

Measles figures are rounded to nearest thousand cases.
Source: U.S. Centers for Disease Control and Prevention.

HOUSING

Homeownership rates, 1985-1997

	1985	1990	1997
State	60.6%	63.0%	68.1%
Total U.S.	63.9%	63.9%	65.7%
Rank among states	44	40	26

Source: U.S. Bureau of the Census.

Home sales, 1990 and 1997
In thousands of units

Existing home sales	1990	1997	Change
State sales	160.9	199.7	38.8
Total U.S. sales	3,560	4,730	1,170
State share of U.S. total	4.52%	4.22%	-0.30%
Rank among states	5	6	—

Source: National Association of Realtors; *Real Estate Outlook:
Market Trends and Insights.*

EDUCATION

Public school enrollment, 1995

State K-8 enrollment	1,390,000
Total U.S. K-8 enrollment	32,341,000
State share of total U.S.	4.30%
State 9-12 enrollment	553,000
Total U.S. 9-12 enrollment	12,500,000
State share of U.S. total	4.42%
State public school enroll. rate	88.1%
Overall U.S. rate	91.6%
Rank among states	44

Enrollment figures (which include unclassified students) are
rounded to nearest thousand pupils in fall term;
kindergarten (K)-8 grade figures include some
prekindergarten students. Enrollment rate is based on
percentage of persons 5-17 years old. Rank is from highest
to lowest.
Source: U.S. National Center for Education Statistics.

Public college finances, 1996

State FTE enrollment	353,200
Total U.S. FTE enrollment	8,268,800
State share of total U.S.	4.27%
Rank among states	5
State and local appropriations	$1,844,900,000
Total U.S. state and local appropriations	$39,699 mill.
State share of total U.S.	4.65%
Rank among states	4
State net tuition revenues	$459,600,000
Total U.S. net tuition	$18,348,100,000
State share of total U.S.	2.51%
Rank among states	11

FTE=Full-time equivalent; credit and noncredit enrollment
including summer session in academic year ending in
1996.
Enrollments are rounded to nearest thousand students. Net
tuition revenues exclude appropriation to students
attending in-state public institutions. Rankings are from
highest shares to lowest.
Source: Research Associates of Washington.

TRANSPORTATION AND TRAVEL

Highway mileage, 1996

Interstate	2,163
Other arterial	13,956
Collector roads	25,239
Local roads	99,981
Urban roads	35,689
Rural roads	101,888
Total state	137,577
U.S. total	3,933,985
State share	3.5%
Rank among states	3

Source: U.S. Federal Highway Administration.

Motor vehicle registrations and driver licenses, 1996
In thousands

Vehicle registrations	State	U.S.	Share	Rank
Autos, trucks, buses	8,817	206,365	4.27%	6
Autos only	6,232	128,439	4.85%	6
Motorcycles	171	3,832	4.46%	5
Driver licenses	7,610	179,539	4.24%	6

Figures do not include vehicles owned by military services.
Source: U.S. Federal Highway Administration; *Highway Statistics; Selected Highway Statistics and Charts.*

Domestic travel expenditures, 1995
Spending by U.S. residents on overnight trips and day trips of at least 100 miles

Total expenditures in state	$15,852 mill.
Total expenditures in U.S.	$360,314 mill.
State share of total U.S.	4.40%
Rank among states	5

Source: Travel Industry Association of America.

CRIME AND LAW ENFORCEMENT

State and local police officers, 1996

Local police	26,151
State police	1,988
Sheriffs	8,426
Total	38,192
Officers per 10,000 residents	32
U.S. average	25
Rank among states	4

Figures cover full-time sworn officers; totals include special police not shown separately.
Source: U.S. Bureau of Justice Statistics; *Census of State and Local Law Enforcement Agencies, 1996.*

Crime rates, 1996
Rates per 100,000 resident population

Violent crimes	State	U.S.
Total violent	886	634
Murder	10.0	7.4
Forcible rape	34.2	36.1
Robbery	279	202
Aggravated assault	563	388
Property crimes		
Total property	4,430	4,445
Burglary	913	943
Larceny/theft	3,026	2,976
Motor vehicle theft	490	526
Totals	5,316	5,079

Crime counts are estimated due to incomplete data.
Source: U.S. Federal Bureau of Investigation; *Crime in the United States,* annual.

State prison populations, 1980-1996

	State	U.S.	State share
1980	11,899	305,458	3.90%
1990	27,516	708,393	3.88%
1996	38,852	1,025,624	3.79%

Figures exclude prisoners in federal penitentiaries.
Source: U.S. Bureau of Justice Statistics.

Indiana

Location: Midwestern continental United States

Area and rank: 35,870 square miles (92,904 square kilometers); 36,420 square miles (94,328 square kilometers) including water; thirty-eighth largest state in area

Population and rank: 5,864,108 (1997); fourteenth largest state in population

Capital: Indianapolis

Largest city: Indianapolis (741,304 people in 1998)

Became territory: May 7, 1800

Entered Union and rank: December 11, 1816; nineteenth state

Present constitution adopted: 1851

Counties: 92

State name: "Indiana" means "land of Indians"

State nickname: Hoosier State

Motto: The Crossroads of America

State flag: Blue field with gold torch

Highest point: Franklin Township — 1,257 feet (383 meters)

Lowest point: Ohio River — 320 feet (98 meters)

Highest recorded temperature: 116 degrees Fahrenheit (47 degrees Celsius) — Collegeville, 1936

Lowest recorded temperature: −35 degrees Fahrenheit (−37 degrees Celsius) — Greensburg, 1951

State song: "On the Banks of the Wabash, Far Away"

State tree: Tulip tree

State flower: Peony

State bird: Cardinal

State capitol building in Indianapolis. (Jim West)

Indiana History

Indiana's central position between earlier settled regions to the east and south and more recently settled regions to the north and west have made it an important area of commerce and transportation since the early years of the United States. Urban areas of the state, particularly in the northwest corner, which is located near the giant city of Chicago, have developed a multiethnic culture in sharp contrast to the white, western European, Protestant culture which dominates the rest of the state.

Early History. Several thousand years ago, early hunting, gathering, and crop-growing societies inhabited areas near the Ohio River. The oldest artifacts from this period have been discovered at Angel Mounds, a large archaeological site near Evansville. By the time Europeans arrived in the New World, the northern and central regions of the area were inhabited by the Miami Confederation, a group of Native Americans belonging to the Algonquin language group. The Miami, who depended largely on the growing of corn and the hunting of buffalo for survival, were organized into a confederation in order to protect their lands from the Iroquois, a large group of various Native American peoples living to the east. During the nineteenth century, the Miami ceded most of their land to the United States. Most of the Miami moved to Oklahoma, but some remained in Indiana.

French and British Settlement. During the seventeenth century, the Iroquois, who were generally hostile to the French, agreed to treaties which allowed the French to trade with the Miami. In 1679 the French explorer René-Robert Cavalier, sieur de La Salle, led an expedition into the northern part of the region by traveling south from Michigan down the Saint Joseph River. At about the same time, traders from the British colonies along the Atlantic coast began to settle in the region along the Wabash River and the Ohio River.

In order to protect their access to the Wabash River, which led to the vital waterway of the Mississippi River, the French built a series of forts in the area. The first was Fort Miami, built in 1704, followed by Fort Ouiatanon, built in 1719, and Fort Vincennes, built in 1732. The effort to win the region for France ended in failure in 1763, when the Treaty of Paris, which ended the French and Indian War, brought the area under British control. Although the British officially banned any further European settlement of the area, this prohibition was largely ignored. The area became part of the British province of Quebec in 1774.

American Settlement. In 1779, during the American Revolution, American forces led by George Rogers Clark brought the region under the control of the newly created United States in a surprise attack on British forces in Vincennes. The Peace of Paris, which ended the war in 1783, officially made the area part of the new nation. The first American settlement in the region was established in 1784 in Clarkville, across the Ohio River from Louisville, Kentucky.

The area was part of the Northwest Territory from 1787 to 1800, when the Indiana Territory, which included Michigan, Illinois, Wisconsin, and part of Minnesota, was created. The Michigan Territory was created in 1805, giving the region its modern northern border. In 1809 the Illinois Territory was created, giving the area its modern western border. Indiana became a state in 1816, with its first capital at Corydon.

Wars with Native Americans. Violent conflict with the Native Americans inhabiting the region began as soon as European settlers entered the area. The first phase of American Indian resistance ended in 1794 with the Battle of Fallen Timbers, near the border between Ohio and Indiana. About one thousand Americans led by Anthony Wayne defeated about two thousand Native Americans of the Northwest Indian Confederation, including members of the Miami, Potawatomi, Shawnee, Delaware, Ottawa, Ojibwa, and Iroquois, led by Shawnee chief Bluejacket. As a result of the battle, in 1795 Miami chief Little Turtle ceded much of his people's land to the United States in the Treaty of Fort Greenville.

The opening of this land to non-Indians led to a large increase in the number of settlers from Southern states. As a result, Indiana became culturally more Southern than other states in the area and was inhabited primarily by Protestants of English, Scottish, Irish, and German ancestry. This rapid increase in the rate of European settlement led to an increase in the number of violent encounters with Native Americans.

The second phase of Native American resistance ended on November 7, 1811, at the Battle of Tippecanoe, near the modern city of Lafayette. During the battle, American forces led by William Henry Harrison defeated Shawnee forces led by Tenskwatawa. Although the two sides suffered equal losses, the battle was generally considered a decisive American victory, and it helped Harrison, a war hero, become president in 1840. Between 1820 and 1840 most Native Americans left the state.

Indianapolis. Settlement in Indiana in the first half of the nineteenth century was centered in the southern part of the state. The economy was based primarily on agriculture and transportation of goods along the Ohio River and the Wabash River. Indianapolis, a planned city designed to resemble Washington, D.C., was founded in 1821 in the center of the state and became the state capital in 1825. With the rise of railroads in the middle of the nineteenth century and the increase in motor-vehicle traffic in the twentieth century, Indianapolis became one of the largest cities in the world not located on a major waterway. It also went on to be served by more major highways than any other city in the United States.

Education and Industry. The first college in Indiana was founded in Vincennes in 1801. The first major institute of higher education, Indiana University, was founded in Bloomington in 1820. This university went on to become one of the most respected in the United States, with a particularly

well-regarded university press. Indiana later became the home of other outstanding universities, with the founding of the University of Notre Dame, near South Bend, in 1842, and Purdue University, in West Lafayette, in 1869.

The Civil War, in which many Indianans fought for the Union, brought a rapid increase in the growth of industry in the state, particularly in the northern region. Natural resources that contributed to this growth included limestone, found in the southern part of the state, and coal, found in the southwest area. The southern half of the state was also the site of the world's largest natural gas field in 1880's, but this resource was depleted by 1898.

Steel production became one of the state's most important industries, particularly with the founding of Gary, located near Chicago, in 1906. At about the same time, automobile manufacturing began in South Bend and Indianapolis. Certain cities specialized in the manufacturing of particular products. Elkhart became known for producing musical instruments in 1875, while Fort Wayne produces a large part of the world's diamond tools. Overall, Indiana is one of the top ten manufacturing states in the nation. Manufacturing accounts for about 40 percent of the state's income. Environmental destruction to the state's unique sand dunes along Lake Michigan, an indirect result of industrial growth, was slowed by the creation of Indiana Dunes National Lakeshore in 1972.

The Twentieth Century. Although much of Indiana retains its character as an enclave of white, Anglo-Saxon, Protestant culture, the growth of the state's cities and the powerful influence of Chicago on the northwest region brought a mixture of ethnic groups to the area. World War I brought a steady flow of African Americans to the industrial centers of the state. By the late twentieth century, African Americans made up about 20 percent of the population of Indianapolis and about 70 percent of the population of Gary. Indianans of Polish ancestry constitute an important ethnic group in South Bend. Other ethnic groups in the state, particularly in northern cities, include Indianans whose ancestors arrived from Hungary, Belgium, and Italy. These groups give northern Indiana a higher percentage of Roman Catholics than the rest of the state, which is about two-thirds Protestant.

Politically, Indiana is generally conservative. The state spends less per capita on education, welfare, and health care than many other states. The amount of federal aid which the state receives per capita is one of the lowest in the nation. Change is slow to come to the state's political system, which still uses the state constitution of 1851. Although

In the Battle of Tippecanoe, fought near Lafayette, American troops under William Henry Harrison defeated Shawnee forces. Harrison was afterward dubbed "Tippecanoe" and went on to be elected president of the United States in 1840. (Library of Congress)

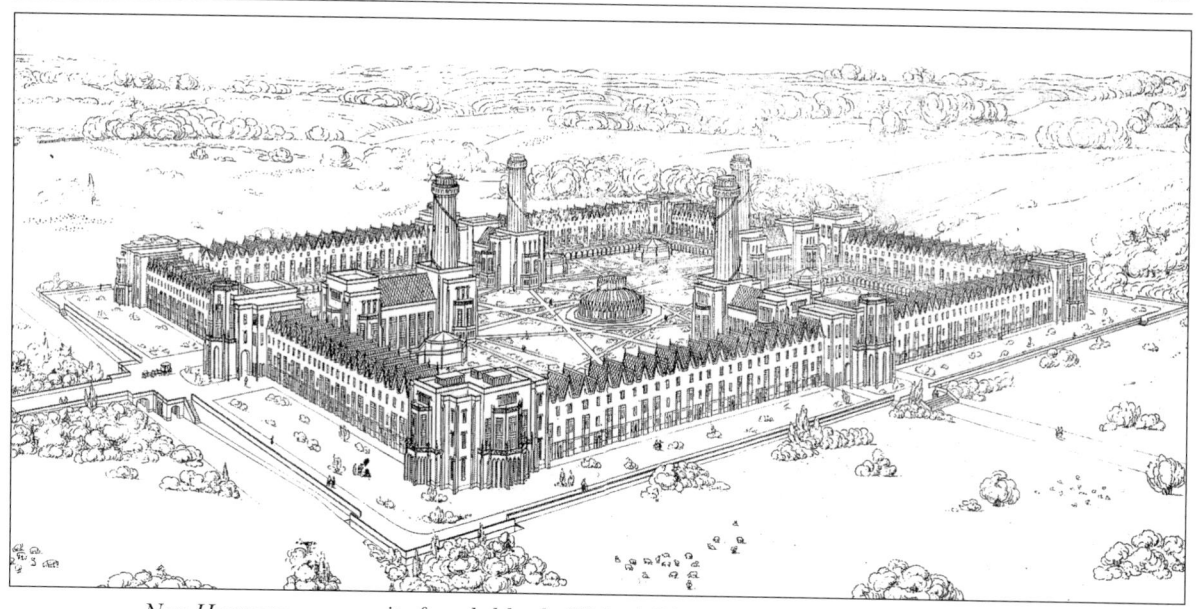

New Harmony community founded by the Wabash River in 1815. (Library of Congress)

this constitution requires changes to be made in legislative districts based on population changes, this rule was disregarded from 1923 to 1963, giving the rural areas more political power than their dwindling population should have allowed. Also, it was not until 1970 that voters approved a proposal to have the state legislature meet annually rather than every two years.

Despite this conservatism, the Republican party held only a slight advantage in the state after the Civil War. Indiana counties are about one-third Republican, one-third Democratic, and one-third variable. Almost as many liberals and Democrats have been elected from the state as conservatives and Republicans. Indiana state politics are sometimes surprisingly innovative, as when Indianapolis merged with Marion County in 1969 to form a unique type of city/county government.

Rose Secrest

Indiana Time Line

Dec. 5, 1679	René-Robert Cavalier, sieur de La Salle, leads a French expedition down the Saint Joseph River from Michigan into Indiana.
1686	Trading post is established at the future site of Fort Wayne.
1704	Fort Miami is founded.
1719	Fort Ouiatanon is founded.
1732	Fort Vincennes is founded.
1763	Defeat of the French in the French and Indian War brings the region under British control.
1774	Indiana becomes part of the British province of Quebec.
Feb. 25, 1779	American forces led by George Rogers Clark defeat British forces at Vincennes.

(continued)

1783	Defeat of the British in the American Revolution brings the region under American control.
1784	First American settlement in Indiana is founded at Clarkville.
1787	Indiana becomes part of the Northwest Territory.
1794	Battle of Fallen Timbers results in the defeat of a confederation of Native Americans.
1795	Miami people cede much of their land to the United States.
May 7, 1800	Indiana Territory is created.
1801	First college is founded at Vincennes.
1805	Michigan Territory is created from the northern part of the Indiana Territory.
1809	Illinois Territory is created from the western part of the Indiana Territory.
Nov. 7, 1811	Battle of Tippecanoe results in the defeat of the Shawnee.
1815	New Harmony, a utopian community, is founded on the Wabash River.
Dec. 11, 1816	Indiana becomes the nineteenth state.
1818	Bloomington is founded.
1820	Trading post is founded at the future site of South Bend.
1820	Indiana University is founded.
1821	Indianapolis is founded.
1825	Indianapolis becomes the state capital.
1832	Elkhart is founded.
1835	First railroad in the state, a horse-drawn single car, arrives in Shelbyville.
1840	William Henry Harrison, hero of the Battle of Tippecanoe, is elected president of the United States.
1842	University of Notre Dame is founded.
1851	State constitution is adopted.
1869	Purdue University is founded.
1880's	Indiana's "Gas Belt," the world's largest producing natural gas field, is developed.
1888	Indianapolis resident Benjamin Harrison, grandson of William Henry Harrison, is elected president.
1893	American Railway Union, the first industrial union in the United States, is founded in Terre Haute.
1894	Strike by the American Railway Union leads to violence and intervention by Federal troops.
1898	Indiana's natural gas supplies are depleted.
1906	Gary is founded.
May 30, 1911	First Indianapolis 500 automobile race is held.
1912	Indiana native Thomas R. Marshall is elected vice president.
1923-1963	State legislature disregards the state constitutional requirement that legislative districts be changed to reflect changes in population.
1969	Indianapolis merges with Marion County to form a single government.

1970	Voters approve a proposal to increase meetings of the state legislature from every two years to every year.
1970	Port of Indiana, an artificial harbor, is opened on Lake Michigan, linking the state to worldwide water traffic.
1972	University of Notre Dame begins accepting female students.
1972	Indiana Dunes National Lakeshore is created.
1975	Indiana and Michigan Electric Company begins generating nuclear power.
1988	Indiana native Dan Quayle is elected vice president.
Oct. 7, 1991	Rose-Hulman Institute of Terre Haute, an all-male school for 117 years, admits women.

Notes for Further Study

Published Sources. For those unfamiliar with basic facts about the history of Indiana, an excellent starting point is Howard Henry Peckham's *Indiana: A Bicentennial History* (1978), a clear, concise, colorful account of the state's past. For more advanced students, the Indiana Historical Bureau and the Indiana Historical Society, based in Indianapolis, have published several volumes in a series, which includes *Indiana to 1816: The Colonial Period* (1971), by John D. Barnhart and Dorothy L. Riker; *Indiana, 1816-1850: The Pioneer Era* (1998), by Donald F. Carmony; *Indiana in the Civil War Era, 1850-1880* (1965), by Emma Lou Thornburgh; *Indiana in Transition: The Emergence of an Industrial Commonwealth, 1880-1920* (1968), by Clifton J. Phillips; and *Indiana Through Transition and Change: A History of the Hoosier State and its People, 1920-1945* (1968), by James H. Madison.

A detailed and scholarly account of the early years of the state can be found in *Frontier Indiana* by Andrew R. L. Cayton (1996), one of many outstanding historical works published by Indiana University Press, located in Bloomington. The often overlooked story of African Americans in the state is found in a series of articles collected in *Indiana's African-American Heritage: Essays from Black History News and Notes* (1993), edited by Wilma L. Gibbs.

Web Resources. Several excellent Web sites, supplied by government agencies, private organizations, and individuals, are dedicated to the history of Indiana. A good place to start for the student new to the subject is the official Web site of the state government of Indiana. The section called "General Facts" (http://state.in.us/sic/HTML/general_facts.html) offers basic information on the state, a list of famous Indianans and the accomplishments for which they are noted, a discussion of the structure of the state government, and links to historical Web sites.

A unique, detailed, and interactive time line is found at (http://home.att.net/~Local_History/IN_Timeline.htm). This site is particularly helpful for information on the prehistory of the state, pre-Columbian Native American archaeology, French settlement, and early statehood. Purdue University has an extensive Web site dedicated to Indiana history (http://www.ipfw.edu/ipfwhist/indihist.htm) with an extensive collection of links to other historical sites. Two historical organizations in the state possess Web sites which are frequently updated. The Indiana Historical Bureau (http://www.state.lib.in.us/www/ihb/ihb.HTML) includes numerous historical documents and links to historical periodicals. The Indiana Historical Society (http://www2.ihs1830.org/ihs1830) includes links to publications, a collection of essays on subjects ranging from biographies of noted Indianans to a history of the state's constitution, and an interesting section entitled "Today in Indiana History."

Counties

County	Sq. miles	1996 pop.	County	Sq. miles	1996 pop.
Adams	339.4	32,686	Bartholomew	406.9	68,441
Allen	657.3	310,803	Benton	406.3	9,669

(continued)

County	Sq. miles	1996 pop.
Fulton	368.5	20,223
Gibson	488.9	32,058
Grant	414.0	73,469
Greene	542.1	32,942
Hamilton	398.0	147,719
Hancock	306.2	52,000
Harrison	485.3	33,349
Hendricks	408.4	89,343
Henry	393.0	49,135
Howard	293.1	84,126
Huntington	382.6	37,024
Jackson	509.3	40,467
Jasper	559.9	28,368
Jay	383.7	21,733
Jefferson	361.4	31,039
Jennings	377.3	26,747
Johnson	320.2	104,280
Knox	515.9	39,667
Kosciusko	537.5	69,932
La Porte	598.3	109,604
Lagrange	379.6	32,103
Lake	497.0	479,940
Lawrence	448.9	45,361
Madison	452.2	132,782
Marion	396.4	817,525
Marshall	444.3	45,173
Martin	336.2	10,581
Miami	375.8	32,686
Monroe	394.4	116,176
Montgomery	504.6	36,349
Morgan	406.5	63,244
Newton	401.9	14,611
Noble	411.1	41,449
Ohio	86.7	5,490
Orange	399.6	19,221
Owen	385.2	20,158
Parke	444.8	16,339
Perry	381.4	19,210
Pike	336.2	12,569
Porter	418.2	142,363
Posey	408.5	26,505
Pulaski	433.7	13,103
Putnam	480.3	33,451
Randolph	452.9	27,530
Ripley	446.4	26,932
Rush	408.3	18,285
Saint Joseph	457.3	257,740
Scott	190.4	22,652
Shelby	412.7	42,951
Spencer	398.7	20,540
Starke	309.3	23,399
Steuben	308.7	30,831
Sullivan	447.2	20,115

County	Sq. miles	1996 pop.
Blackford	165.1	14,134
Boone	422.7	42,453
Brown	312.3	15,485
Carroll	372.3	19,643
Cass	412.9	38,829
Clark	375.2	92,530
Clay	357.6	26,491
Clinton	405.1	32,876
Crawford	305.7	10,559
Daviess	430.7	28,760
Dearborn	305.2	45,236
Decatur	372.6	25,105
DeKalb	362.9	38,272
Delaware	393.3	118,600
Dubois	430.1	39,088
Elkhart	463.8	168,941
Fayette	215.0	26,237
Floyd	148.0	70,746
Fountain	395.7	18,207
Franklin	386.0	21,530

County	Sq. miles	1996 pop.
Switzerland	221.2	8,380
Tippecanoe	499.8	138,324
Tipton	260.4	16,453
Union	161.6	7,345
Vanderburgh	234.6	167,716
Vermillion	256.9	16,791
Vigo	403.3	106,389
Wabash	413.2	34,661

County	Sq. miles	1996 pop.
Warren	364.9	8,188
Warrick	384.1	50,070
Washington	514.5	26,689
Wayne	403.6	72,017
Wells	370.0	26,651
White	505.3	25,081
Whitley	335.5	29,863

Source: U.S. Census Bureau; National Association of Counties.

Cities

With 10,000 or more residents

Rank	City	Population
1	Indianapolis (remainder)	741,304
2	Fort Wayne	185,716
3	Evansville	122,779
4	Gary	108,469
5	South Bend	99,417
6	Hammond	78,212
7	Muncie	67,476
8	Bloomington	65,065
9	Anderson	58,528
10	Terre Haute	53,355
11	Mishawaka	45,310
12	Kokomo	45,149
13	Lafayette	44,583
14	Elkhart	43,673
15	Carmel	42,074
16	New Albany	38,265
17	Richmond	37,091
18	Lawrence	34,561
19	Greenwood	33,419
20	Portage	33,030
21	Michigan City	32,626
22	Columbus	32,250
23	East Chicago	30,885
24	Merrillville	30,571
25	Marion	28,812
26	West Lafayette	27,975
27	Jeffersonville	26,018
28	Noblesville	25,983
29	Valparaiso	25,931
30	Fishers	25,591
31	Goshen	25,262

Rank	City	Population
32	Hobart	24,841
33	Schererville	24,062
34	Highland	23,730
35	Munster	20,485
36	La Porte	20,226
37	Clarksville	19,688
38	Crown Point	19,403
39	Vincennes	18,875
40	Griffith	17,816
41	Plainfield	17,739
42	Franklin	17,259
43	Seymour	17,026
44	NewCastle	16,932
45	Shelbyville	16,562
46	Logansport	15,831
47	Huntington	15,469
48	Frankfort	15,291
49	Connersville	15,266
50	Bedford	14,619
51	Crawfordsville	14,108
52	Lake Station	13,903
53	Greenfield	13,869
54	Lebanon	13,840
55	New Haven	13,809
56	Dyer	13,485
57	Beech Grove	13,246
58	Madison	12,510
59	Speedway	12,213
60	Martinsville	12,096
61	Brownsburg	11,779
62	Peru	11,324

(continued)

Rank	City	Population
63	Jasper	11,174
64	Wabash	11,138
65	Auburn	11,015
66	Washington	10,949
67	Warsaw	10,797

Rank	City	Population
68	Greensburg	10,360
69	Chesterton	10,163
70	Plymouth	10,140

Population figures are estimated for mid-1998.
Source: U.S. Bureau of the Census.

Index to Tables

NA = Reliable data are not available.

DEMOGRAPHICS

Resident state and national populations, 1970-1997

Population figures given in thousands

	State pop.	U.S. pop.	Share	Rank
1970	5,195	203,302	2.6%	11
1980	5,490	226,546	2.4%	12
1985	5,459	237,924	2.3%	14
1990	5,544	248,765	2.2%	14
1995	5,788	262,761	2.2%	14
1997	5,864	267,636	2.2%	14

Source: U.S. Bureau of the Census.

Resident population by age, 1997

Age group	Total population
Under 5 years	407,000
5 to 17 years	1,090,000
18 to 24 years	569,000
25 to 34 years	859,000
35 to 44 years	961,000
45 to 54 years	748,000
55 to 64 years	496,000
65 to 74 years	399,000
75 to 84 years	251,000
85 years and over	84,000
Portion of residents 65 and older	12.5%
National average	12.7%

Population figures are rounded to nearest thousand persons;
figures include armed forces personnel stationed in state.
Source: U.S. Bureau of the Census.

Resident population by race, Hispanic origin, 1997

	State pop.	Share	U.S.
All residents	5,864,000	100.0%	100.0%
Hispanic white	125,000	2.1%	10.0%
non-Hispanic white	5,188,000	88.5%	72.7%
African American	484,000	8.3%	12.7%
Native American	14,000	0.2%	0.9%
Asian, Pacific Islander	53,000	0.9%	3.8%

Source: U.S. Bureau of the Census.

Projections of state population, 2000-2025

	Model A Uses interstate migration observed from 1975-1994	Model B Uses Bureau of Economic Analysis employment projections
Year	Population	Population
2000	6,045,000	6,060,000
2005	6,215,000	6,301,000
2010	6,318,000	6,532,000
2015	6,404,000	6,758,000
2020	6,481,000	6,969,000
2025	6,546,000	7,158,000

All population projections, including those for 2000, were calculated in 1997.
Source: U.S. Bureau of the Census, Population Paper Listings PPL-47.

VITAL STATISTICS

Average lifetime in years by race, 1989-1991

	State	U.S.	Rank
All residents	75.39	75.37	27
White residents	75.82	76.13	35
Black residents	69.80	69.16	12

Ranks are from longest-lived to least longest-lived. Ranks exclude Alaska, for which reliable data are not available. Rank for black residents is based on the 32 states for which reliable data are available.
Source: U.S. National Center for Health Statistics.

Infant mortality rates, 1980 and 1995

	State	U.S.
All residents		
1980	11.9	12.6
1995	8.4	7.6
White residents		
1980	10.5	11.0
1995	7.3	6.3
Black residents		
1980	23.4	21.4
1995	17.5	15.1

Figures represent deaths per 1,000 live births of resident infants under 1 year old, exclusive of fetal deaths; all-residents figures include other races not listed separately.
Source: U.S. National Center for Health Statistics.

Marriages and divorces

Marriages in 1996	49,200
Rate per 1,000 population, 1995	8.7
U.S. rate, 1995	8.9
Rank among all states	21
Divorces in 1996	NA
Rate per 1,000 population, 1995	NA
U.S. rate, 1995	4.4
Rank among all states	NA

Rank is from highest to lowest in country.
Source: U.S. National Center for Health Statistics.

Death rates by leading causes, 1995
Deaths per 100,000 resident population

Cause	State	U.S.
Heart disease	294.3	280.7
Cancer	216.3	204.9
Cerebrovascular diseases	68.9	60.1
Accidents and adverse effects	38.0	35.5
Motor vehicle accidents	17.1	16.5
Chronic obstructive pulmonary diseases	41.3	39.2
Diabetes mellitus	24.8	22.6
HIV	6.7	NA
Suicide	12.0	11.9
Homicide	7.8	8.7
All causes	918.2	880.0
Rank in overall death rate among states		21

Figures exclude nonresidents who die in state. Causes of death follow International Classification of Diseases. Rank is from highest to lowest in country.
Source: U.S. National Center for Health Statistics.

ECONOMY

Gross state product, 1990-1996
In current dollars

	State product	Increase
1990	$109.6 billion	
1993	$129.7 billion	
1994	$141.4 billion	9.02%
1995	$148.8 billion	5.23%
1996	$155.8 billion	4.70%

Source: U.S. Bureau of Economic Analysis; *Survey of Current Business,* June, 1998.

Gross state product by industry, 1996
In billions

Farms, forestry, fisheries	$2.4
Construction	6.2
Manufacturing	48.3
Transportation, public utilities	11.9
Wholesale trade	9.0
Retail trade	13.8
Finance, insurance, real estate	17.4
Services	20.7
Government	13.7
State total	$144.1
Total U.S.	$6,923.8
State share	2.08%
Rank among states	14

Total figures include mining, not listed separately.
Source: U.S. Bureau of Economic Analysis; *Survey of Current Business,* June, 1998.

Personal income per capita, 1990 and 1997
In current dollars

	1990	1997
Per capita income	$17,191	$23,604
U.S. average	$19,188	$25,598
Rank among states	31	29

1997 data are preliminary.
Source: U.S. Bureau of Economic Analysis; *Survey of Current Business,* May, 1998.

Energy consumption, 1995
In trillions of British thermal units (BTU)

End-use sectors

Residential	478.8
Commercial	295.0
Industrial	1,185.0
Transportation	633.4

Sources of energy

Petroleum	864.2
Natural gas	541.7
Coal	1,341.9
Hydroelectric power	4.8
Nuclear electric power	0
Total state per capita consumption	447.2
Total U.S. per capita consumption	344.4
Rank among states	9
Total state energy consumption	2,592.1
Total U.S. energy consumption	90,547.4
State share of U.S. total	2.86%
Rank among states	10

Total figures include items not listed separately.
Source: U.S. Energy Information Administration; *State Energy Data Report.*

Nonfarm employment by sectors, 1997

Total	2,860,000
Construction	141,000
Manufacturing	677,000
Transportation, public utilities	140,000
Wholesale trade, retail trade	682,000
Finance, insurance, real estate	139,000
Services	683,000
Government	391,000

Figures are rounded to nearest thousand persons. Total includes mining, not listed separately.
Source: U.S. Bureau of Labor Statistics; *Employment and Earnings,* monthly.

Foreign exports, 1990-1997
In millions of dollars

Year	State	U.S.	State share
1990	5,273	394,045	1.34%
1996	10,984	624,767	1.76%
1997	12,029	688,896	1.75%

Source: U.S. Bureau of the Census; *U.S. Merchandise Trade,* series FT 900.

LAND USE

Federally owned land, 1996

	State	U.S.	State share
Total acres	23,158,000	2,271,343,000	1.02%
Federally owned	394,000	563,129,000	0.07%
Federal share	1.7%	24.8%	—

Areas are rounded to nearest thousand acres. Figures for federally owned land do not include trust properties.
Source: U.S. General Services Administration; *Inventory Report on Real Property Owned by the United States Throughout the World,* annual.

Land use, 1992

In acres, rounded to nearest thousand

Total surface area	23,159,000
Federal land	487,000
Total nonfederal	22,287,000
Developed	2,095,000
Total rural	20,193,000
Cropland	13,513,000
Pasture land	1,866,000
Range land	0
Forest land	3,626,000
Minor cover/use	1,188,000

Total surface area figures include water area not shown separately.
Source: U.S. Dept. of Agriculture; Soil Conservation Service; Iowa State University, Statistical Laboratory; *Summary Report, 1992 National Resources Inventory.*

Farms and crop acreage, 1997

	State	U.S.	Share	Rank
Farms (thousands)	62	2,058	3.01%	13
Acres (millions)	16	968	1.65%	20
Acres per farm	256	471	—	29
Acres planted	12,964	334,139	3.88%	10
Acres harvested	12,786	319,894	4.00%	10
Farm value (mill.)	$4,031	$108,805	3.70%	2

Numbers of farms are rounded to nearest thousand.
Source: U.S. Dept. of Agriculture; National Agricultural Statistics Service.

GOVERNMENT AND FINANCE

Units of local government, 1997

	State	Total U.S.	Rank
All local governments	3,198	87,453	10
Counties	91	3,043	12
Municipalities	569	19,372	12
Townships	1,008	16,629	9
School districts	294	13,726	19
Special districts	1,236	34,683	8

County ranks are based on the 48 states with county governments; township ranks are based on the 20 states with township governments; school district ranks are based on the 46 states with such districts.
Source: U.S. Bureau of the Census; *1997 Census of Governments, Government Organization,* Series GC97(1).

State government revenue, 1996

Total revenue	$16,550 mill.
General revenue	15,065 mill.
Per capita	2,585
U.S. per capita average	2,910
Rank among states	37
Intergovernmental revenue	
Total	$3,750 mill.
From federal government	3,625 mill.
From local government	125 mill.
Charges and Miscellaneous	
Total	$2,878 mill.
Current charges	1,678 mill.
Misc. general revenue	1,200 mill.
Taxes	
Total	$8,437 mill.
General sales	2,868 mill.
Selective sales	894 mill.
License taxes	202 mill.
Individual income	3,478 mill.
Corporate income	894 mill.
Other	102 mill.
Insurance trust revenue	1,485 mill.

Total revenue figures include items not listed separately.
Source: U.S. Bureau of the Census.

State government expenditures, 1996

General expenditures
Intergovernmental	$5,091 mill.
Direct expenditures	9,331 mill.
Total	14,422 mill.

Selected direct expenditures
Education	$6,142 mill.
Public welfare	3,155 mill.
Health, hospital	608 mill.
Highways	1,532 mill.
Police	146 mill.
Corrections	378 mill.
Natural resources	160 mill.
Parks and recreation	43 mill.
Government administration	293 mill.
Interest on debt	271 mill.

Other
State per capita expenditures	$2,475
U.S. per capita average	2,854
Rank among states	41
Total state expenditures	15,368 mill.
Total U.S. expenditures	859,959 mill.

Totals include items not listed separately.
Source: U.S. Bureau of the Census.

POLITICS

Governors since statehood
D = Democrat; R = Republican; O = other;
(r) resigned; (d) died in office; (i) removed from office

Jonathan Jennings (O)	(r) 1816-1822
Ratliff Boon (O)	1822
William Hendricks (O)	(r) 1822-1825
James B. Ray (O)	1825-1831
Noah Noble (O)	1831-1837
David Wallace (O)	1837-1840
Samuel Rigger (O)	1840-1843
James Whitcomb (D)	(r) 1843-1848
Paris C. Dunning (D)	1848-1849
Joseph A. Wright (D)	1849-1857
Ashbel P. Willard (D)	(d) 1857-1860
Abram A. Hammond (D)	1860-1861
Henry S. Lane (R)	(r) 1861
Oliver H. P. T. Morton (R)	(r) 1861-1865
Conrad Baker (R)	1865-1873
Thomas A. Hendricks (D)	1873-1877
James D. Williams (D)	(d) 1877-1880
Isaac P. Gray (D)	1880-1881
Albert G. Porter (R)	1881-1885
Isaac P. Gray (D)	1885-1889
Alvin P. Hovey (R)	(d) 1889-1891
Ira J. Chase (R)	1891-1893
Claude Matthews (D)	1893-1897
James A. Mount (R)	1897-1901
Winfield T. Durbin (R)	1901-1905
James Franklin Hanly (R)	1905-1909
Thomas R. Marshall (D)	1909-1913
Samuel M. Ralston (D)	1913-1917
James P. Goodrich (R)	1917-1921
Warren T. McCray (R)	(i) 1921-1924
Emmett F. Branch (R)	1924-1925
Edward F. Jackson (R)	1925-1929
Harry G. Leslie (R)	1929-1933
Paul V. McNutt (D)	1933-1937
Maurice Clifford Townsend (D)	1937-1941
Henry F. Schricker (D)	1941-1945
Ralph F. Gates (R)	1945-1949
Henry F. Schricker (D)	1949-1953
George N. Craig (R)	1953-1957
Harold W. Handley (R)	1957-1961
Matthew E. Welsh (D)	1961-1965
Roger D. Branigan (D)	1965-1969
Edgar D. Whitcomb (R)	1969-1973
Otis R. Bowen (R)	1973-1981
Robert D. Orr (R)	1981-1989
Evan Bayh (D)	1989-1997
Frank O'Bannon (D)	1997-

Composition of state legislature, 1990-1998

	Democrats	Republicans
State House (100 seats)		
1990	52	48
1992	55	45
1994	44	56
1996	50	50
1998	53	47
State Senate (50 seats)		
1990	24	26
1992	22	28
1994	20	30
1996	19	31
1998	19	31

Figures for total seats may include independents and minor party members.
Source: Council of State Governments; *State Elective Officials and the Legislatures.*

Composition of congressional delegations, 1989-1999

	Dem	Rep	Total
House of Representatives			
101st Congress, 1989			
State delegates	6	3	9
Total U.S.	259	174	433
102d Congress, 1991			
State delegates	8	2	10
Total U.S.	267	167	434
103d Congress, 1993			
State delegates	7	3	10
Total U.S.	258	176	434
104th Congress, 1995			
State delegates	4	6	10
Total U.S.	197	236	433
105th Congress, 1997			
State delegates	4	6	10
Total U.S.	206	228	434
106th Congress, 1999			
State delegates	4	6	10
Total U.S.	211	222	433
Senate			
101st Congress, 1989			
State delegates	0	2	2
Total U.S.	55	45	100
102d Congress, 1991			
State delegates	0	2	2
Total U.S.	56	44	100
103d Congress, 1993			
State delegates	0	2	2
Total U.S.	57	43	100
104th Congress, 1995			
State delegates	0	2	2
Total U.S.	46	53	99
105th Congress, 1997			
State delegates	0	2	2
Total U.S.	45	55	100
106th Congress, 1999			
State delegates	1	1	2
Total U.S.	45	54	99

Figures are for starts of first sessions. Figure for U.S. Representatives for 101st Congress does not include Alabama and Indiana, which had vacancies. Figures for total U.S. Representatives for 102d, 103d, and 106th Congresses do not include Vermont, which had 1 Independent-Socialist. Figure for U.S. Representatives for 104th Congress does not include Vermont, which had 1 Independent-Socialist, and California, which had 1 vacancy. Figure for U.S. Representatives for 105th Congress does not include New York, which had 1 vacancy. Figure for U.S. Senators for 104th Congress does not include Oregon, which had 1 vacancy. Figure for U.S. Senators for 106th Congress does not include New Hampshire, which had 1 Independent.

Source: U.S. Congress; *Congressional Directory,* biennial.

Voter participation in presidential elections, 1992 and 1996

	1992	1996
State voting age pop.	4,209,000	4,369,000
Total U.S. voting age pop.	189,524,000	196,509,000
State share of U.S. total	2.2%	2.2%
Rank among states	14	14
Percent of state casting vote	54.8	54.3
Percent of U.S. total voting	55.1	49.0
Rank among states	30	18

Source: U.S. Bureau of the Census.

HEALTH AND MEDICAL CARE

Medicare, 1997

	Recipients	Payments
State	833,000	$4,080 mill.
Total U.S.	37,514,000	$206,064 mill.
State share	2.22%	1.98%
Rank among states	15	16

Recipient figures are rounded to nearest thousand persons. Ranks are from highest to lowest.
Source: U.S. Health Care Financing Administration.

Medicaid, 1996

	Recipients	Payments
State	594,000	$2,452 mill.
Total U.S.	35,028,000	$121,419 mill.
State share	1.70%	2.02%
Rank among states	19	15

Recipient figures are rounded to nearest thousand persons. Payment figures for fiscal year reflect federal and state contribution payments. Ranks are from highest to lowest.
Source: U.S. Health Care Financing Administration.

Health insurance coverage, 1996

	State	U.S.
Total persons covered	5,081,000	225,070,000
Total persons not covered	600,000	41,716,000
Part not covered	10.6%	15.6%
Rank among states	41	—
Children not covered	132,000	10,554,000
Part not covered	9.6%	14.8%
Rank among states	37	—

Ranks are from most to fewest uninsured. Population figures are rounded to nearest thousand persons.
Source: U.S. Bureau of the Census.

AIDS, syphilis, tuberculosis, and measles cases, 1997

Cases	U.S.	State	Share
AIDS	58,443	523	0.89%
Syphilis	8,550	151	1.77%
Tuberculosis	18,534	160	0.86%
Measles	148,000	NA	NA

Measles figures are rounded to nearest thousand cases.
Source: U.S. Centers for Disease Control and Prevention.

HOUSING

Homeownership rates, 1985-1997

	1985	1990	1997
State	67.6%	67.0%	74.1%
Total U.S.	63.9%	63.9%	65.7%
Rank among states	27	29	5

Source: U.S. Bureau of the Census.

Home sales, 1990 and 1997
In thousands of units

Existing home sales	1990	1997	Change
State sales	80.1	111.5	31.4
Total U.S. sales	3,560	4,730	1,170
State share of U.S. total	2.25%	2.36%	0.11%
Rank among states	16	15	—

Source: National Association of Realtors; *Real Estate Outlook: Market Trends and Insights.*

EDUCATION

Public school enrollment, 1995

State K-8 enrollment	684,000
Total U.S. K-8 enrollment	32,341,000
State share of total U.S.	2.12%
State 9-12 enrollment	293,000
Total U.S. 9-12 enrollment	12,500,000
State share of U.S. total	2.34%
State public school enroll. rate	90.6%
Overall U.S. rate	91.6%
Rank among states	33

Enrollment figures (which include unclassified students) are rounded to nearest thousand pupils in fall term; kindergarten (K)-8 grade figures include some prekindergarten students. Enrollment rate is based on percentage of persons 5-17 years old. Rank is from highest to lowest.
Source: U.S. National Center for Education Statistics.

Public college finances, 1996

State FTE enrollment	174,000
Total U.S. FTE enrollment	8,268,800
State share of total U.S.	2.10%
Rank among states	16
State and local appropriations	$802,200,000
Total U.S. state and local appropriations	$39,699 mill.
State share of total U.S.	2.02%
Rank among states	16
State net tuition revenues	$551,200,000
Total U.S. net tuition	$18,348,100,000
State share of total U.S.	3.00%
Rank among states	8

FTE=Full-time equivalent; credit and noncredit enrollment including summer session in academic year ending in 1996.

Enrollments are rounded to nearest thousand students. Net tuition revenues exclude appropriation to students attending in-state public institutions. Rankings are from highest shares to lowest.
Source: Research Associates of Washington.

TRANSPORTATION AND TRAVEL

Highway mileage, 1996

Interstate	1,172
Other arterial	8,037
Collector roads	24,803
Local roads	61,161
Urban roads	19,644
Rural roads	73,326
Total state	92,970
U.S. total	3,933,985
State share	2.4%
Rank among states	18

Source: U.S. Federal Highway Administration.

Motor vehicle registrations and driver licenses, 1996
In thousands

Vehicle registrations	*State*	*U.S.*	*Share*	*Rank*
Autos, trucks, buses	5,216	206,365	2.53%	13
Autos only	3,146	128,439	2.45%	14
Motorcycles	96	3,832	2.51%	13
Driver licenses	3,704	179,539	2.06%	13

Figures do not include vehicles owned by military services.
Source: U.S. Federal Highway Administration; *Highway Statistics; Selected Highway Statistics and Charts.*

Domestic travel expenditures, 1995
Spending by U.S. residents on overnight trips and day trips of at least 100 miles

Total expenditures in state	$4,634 mill.
Total expenditures in U.S.	$360,314 mill.
State share of total U.S.	1.29%
Rank among states	26

Source: Travel Industry Association of America.

Michael Andretti and Mario Andretti leading the field during the 1992 running of the Indianapolis 500. The nation's premier automobile racing event began at the Indianapolis Motor Speedway in 1911. (AP/Wide World Photos)

CRIME AND LAW ENFORCEMENT

State and local police officers, 1996

Local police	6,426
State police	1,207
Sheriffs	2,618
Total	10,931
Officers per 10,000 residents	19
U.S. average	25
Rank among states	39

Figures cover full-time sworn officers; totals include special police not shown separately.
Source: U.S. Bureau of Justice Statistics; *Census of State and Local Law Enforcement Agencies, 1996.*

Crime rates, 1996

Rates per 100,000 resident population

Violent crimes	State	U.S.
Total violent	537	634
Murder	7.2	7.4
Forcible rape	34.1	36.1
Robbery	124	202
Aggravated assault	372	388
Property crimes		
Total property	3,961	4,445
Burglary	784	943
Larceny/theft	2,753	2,976
Motor vehicle theft	425	526
Totals	4,498	5,079

Source: U.S. Federal Bureau of Investigation; *Crime in the United States*, annual.

State prison populations, 1980-1996

	State	U.S.	State share
1980	6,683	305,458	2.19%
1990	12,736	708,393	1.80%
1996	16,960	1,025,624	1.65%

Figures exclude prisoners in federal penitentiaries.
Source: U.S. Bureau of Justice Statistics.

Iowa

Location: Midwestern continental United States

Area and rank: 55,875 square miles (144,716 square kilometers); 56,276 square miles (145,755 square kilometers) including water; twenty-third largest state in area

Population and rank: 2,852,423 (1997); thirtieth largest state in population

Capital: Des Moines

Largest city: Des Moines (191,293 people in 1998)

Iowa's capital and largest city, Des Moines. (PhotoDisc)

Became territory:
June 12, 1838

Entered Union and rank: December 28, 1846; twenty-ninth state

Present constitution adopted: 1857

Counties: 99

State name: "Iowa" probably derives from an Indian word meaning either "this is the place" or "the beautiful land"

State nickname: Hawkeye State

Motto: Our liberties we prize and our rights we will maintain

State flag: Red, white, and blue stripes with the state seal and the name "Iowa"

Highest point: Geographical survey section 29, T100N, R41W — 1,670 feet (509 meters)

Lowest point: Mississippi River — 480 feet (146 meters)

Highest recorded temperature: 118 degrees Fahrenheit (48 degrees Celsius) — Keokuk, 1934

Lowest recorded temperature: –47 degrees Fahrenheit (–44 degrees Celsius) — Washta, 1912

State song: "Song of Iowa"

State flower: Wild rose

State bird: Eastern goldfinch

Iowa History

Defined by the Mississippi River on the east and the Missouri River on the west, Iowa is a rolling stretch of lush, green prairie with rich, black soil and ample rainfall for growing crops. The fertility of the earth and the lack of trees make for excellent farmland, and as a result, Iowa has been and remains a state focused on agriculture.

Early History. The Paleo-Indians, nomadic hunters and gatherers, lived in the Iowa region more than ten thousand years ago. They were followed by other nomadic Indians and the mound builders. The Ioway, who controlled most of Iowa in the seventeenth century, left their name to the state and to one of its rivers but gave up all claim to land in the state in 1838, settling in Kansas and Nebraska. About seventeen different tribes are believed to have lived in what became Iowa.

In 1673 Father Jacques Marquette and explorer-mapmaker Louis Jolliet entered the Mississippi River from the Wisconsin River and gazed on Iowa, the "land across the river." They went ashore on June 25, finding members of the Illini tribe, who probably actually lived on the east side of the Mississippi. In 1682 France claimed all the lands along the Mississippi River, and in 1803, in the Louisiana Purchase, the United States bought the land from France. The following year, Meriwether Lewis and William Clark traveled up the Missouri River searching for a waterway that would take them to the Pacific Ocean.

In 1812 Iowa became part of the Territory of Missouri. Eight years later, Missouri became a state, and in 1834, the Territory of Michigan was expanded to include Iowa. In 1838 the Territory of Iowa was created.

The Indians. The U.S. government pushed the Sauk and the Mesquaki (Fox) Indians out of western Illinois and into Iowa, where the Sioux already lived. In 1832 Chief Black Hawk, a respected Sauk leader, sought to reclaim his tribe's land on the Illinois side of the Mississippi River. For three months, in what is known as the Black Hawk War, the Illinois militia pursued Black Hawk, chasing him to the

Usher's Ferry Historic Village, a re-creation of a turn-of-the-twentieth-century Iowa farming town in Cedar Rapids. (Paul Rehn)

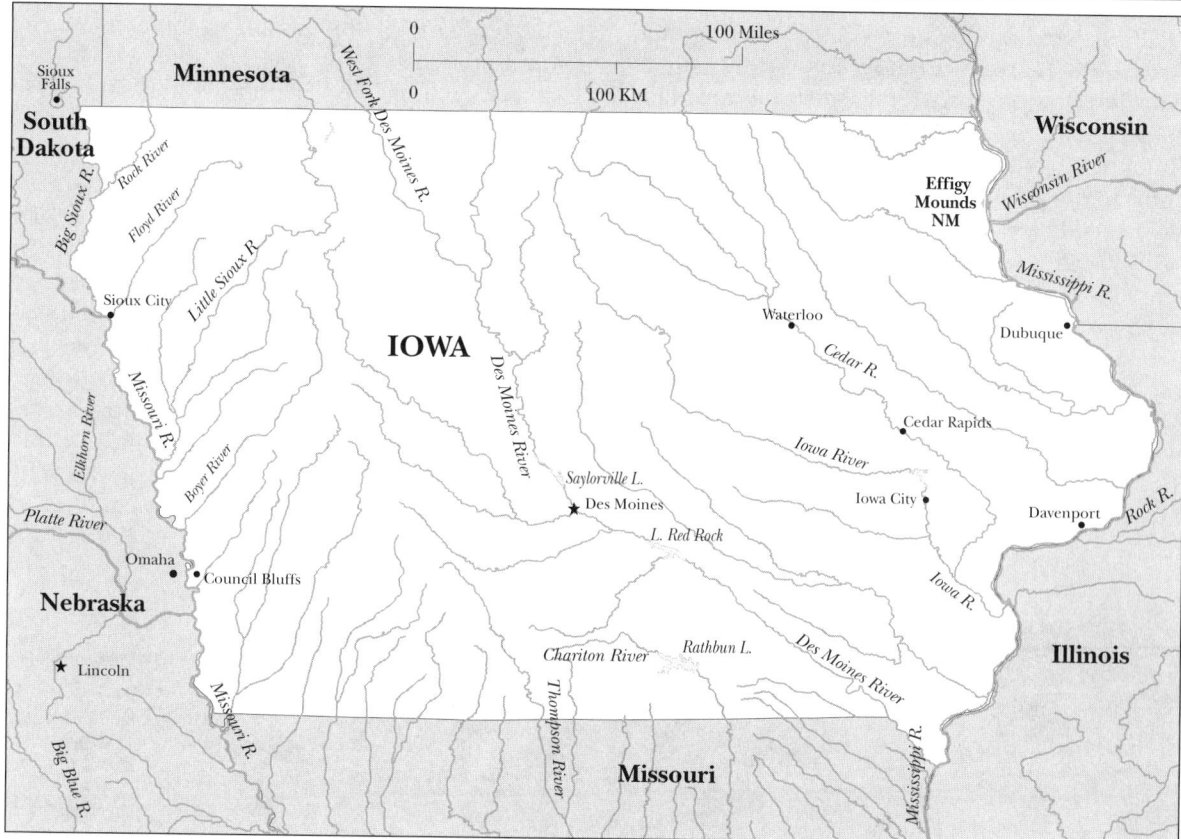

mouth of the Bad Axe River in Wisconsin, where he gave up. In a treaty signed on September 21, 1832, the Mesquaki and Sauk were required to relinquish a strip of land along the Mississippi River and vacate the land by June 1, 1833. Large numbers of white settlers began to move into Iowa, pushing the Indians farther west or into Missouri. In 1842 the Sauk and Mesquaki signed a treaty agreeing to leave Iowa by May, 1845. By 1851 the Sioux had also been forced to give up all land in Iowa. In 1856, a few Mesquaki negotiated with the governor of Iowa to buy back a portion of their former land in modern-day Tama County, eventually buying back about 3,200 acres.

White Settlement and Statehood. In 1838, 23,000 people settled on land in the newly established Territory of Iowa, buying the land for $1.25 an acre. The first settlers were primarily of northern European ancestry. Many were families who had lived in eastern states such as New York, Penn-

sylvania, or Ohio, and many were originally from Germany. The 1840 census showed Iowa to have a population of 43,000, exclusive of American Indians. By 1846 the population of Iowa had reached 96,088. Iowa became the twenty-ninth state of the Union in 1846.

Industry, Education, and Religion. In the early 1850's, railroad companies sprang up in Iowa. The Chicago, Iowa, and Nebraska line became the first railroad to cross the state, in 1867. Soon tracks crisscrossed Iowa, providing year-round transportation to markets and giving birth to new industries such as an oat-processing plant that would come to be known as Quaker Oats.

Early settlers soon established township elementary schools, but high schools were not common until after 1900. State officials created the University of Iowa in 1855 to provide traditional and professional education, Iowa State College of Science and Technology (later Iowa State University) in

1858 for agricultural and technical training, and Iowa State Teachers' College (later University of Northern Iowa) in 1876 for teacher training. Many religious groups, including Congregationalists, Roman Catholics, and Methodists, which had come to the state beginning in the 1830's, founded private colleges.

Although major religious denominations usually set up churches across the state, smaller religious groups tended to settle in specific areas. The Quakers settled in West Branch and Springdale, the Reorganized Church of the Latter-day Saints (a Mormon offshoot) in Lamoni, and the Mennonites in Johnson and Washington Counties. From 1855 to 1865, a group of German Pietists established the seven cities of Amana in Iowa County.

The residents of the Amana colonies practiced communal living for about eighty years. The Amana name lives on in refrigerators, air conditioners, and microwaves, although the colonies sold the business in 1937.

The Civil War. The biggest change the Civil War brought in Iowa was to create a one-party state. At the beginning of Iowa's statehood, the state was largely Democratic, although it contained some Whigs. However, many Iowans opposed slavery, and Iowa would later become an important station in the Underground Railroad. The identification of the Democratic Party with a proslavery stance, among other issues, caused many Iowans to turn to the new Republican Party. By the mid-1850's, the state was solidly Republican and would

Iowa's location on the Mississippi River has enhanced the value of its farm produce by providing access to relatively inexpensive bulk cargo carriage. (PhotoDisc)

Iowa field of corn—an agricultural product with which the state has almost become synonymous. (PhotoDisc)

stay that way through the first half of the twentieth century.

After the outbreak of the war, Iowans quickly responded to President Abraham Lincoln's call for troops. During the course of the war, the state sent 70,000 soldiers, of whom 13,001 died and 8,500 were seriously wounded. Iowans fought at Wilson's Creek to keep Missouri in the Union, accompanied Ulysses S. Grant to Vicksburg, and participated in Sherman's March to the Sea.

Immigration. The population of Iowa grew from 674,913 in 1860 to 1,194,020 in 1870. The state encouraged immigration from northern Europe and attracted many Germans, Swedes, Norwegians, Danes, and Hollanders, as well as people from the British Isles. Many of these immigrant groups created rural neighborhoods with distinct ethnic identities and churches. The coal mines in central and southern Iowa, which promised immediate employment and required few skills, drew people from Italy and Wales and large numbers of former slaves, who formed camps near the mines.

Farming and Economic Growth. By the 1870's, Iowa had become blanketed with small towns and family farms, connected by railroads. Farmers were raising cattle and hogs and, increasingly, corn instead of wheat. Scientific research led to the introduction in the early 1900's of soybeans, which eventually became second only to corn in terms of acreage and value. During World War I, farmers prospered, but after the war ended and farm subsidies were eliminated, farmers began to experience difficulties in paying off the money they had borrowed during boom times. A group of farmers formed the Farm Holiday Association, which attempted to withhold farm products from the market in order to force prices up, but the association's efforts had little impact.

Native Iowan Henry A. Wallace became secretary of agriculture under President Franklin D. Roosevelt in 1933. He believed that farmers would prosper if production was restricted and farmers were compensated for withholding land from production, and he incorporated these ideas into the Agricultural Adjustment Act of 1933, part of the New Deal. In 1926 Wallace and a partner founded what became Pioneer Seed Company, the first commercial company to produce hybrid seed corn, which led to increased yields and a more uniform plant that made mechanization of the harvest much easier. By 1944 nearly all corn planted in Iowa came from hybrid seed.

Farmers prospered when World War II and the Korean War boosted corn prices and again in the 1970's, when land prices rose, and many farmers borrowed money to expand their operations. In the 1980's, however, land prices crashed, and many farmers lost their farms, initiating a trend away from family farms and toward farming corporations. In 1985 the Iowa legislature introduced legislation designed to help troubled farmers deal with creditors and keep their farms. In the 1990's, the family farm was challenged on another front as large-scale hog-producing corporations moved into the state, driving down hog prices and forcing small hog producers out of business.

Although agriculture dominates Iowa's economy, the state has also supported business and manufacturing operations, some of which are farm-related. Major concerns include farm-implement producer John Deere, washing machine and appliance company Maytag, Winnebago motor homes, the Sheaffer pen company, and Iowa Beef Processors. In 1991 Iowa legalized riverboat gambling, creating a somewhat controversial source of revenue.

Middle America. Iowa is largely rural, an assemblage of small towns and family farms. In 1998 the state's population reached 2.8 million, and the population of its largest city, Des Moines, was 191,293. During the 1970's, 1980's, and to a lesser extent in the 1990's, the state became the focus of national attention early in each presidential election year during the Iowa caucuses. These early tests of presidential strength provided boosts to some candidates, including Jimmy Carter in 1976 and George Bush in 1980. Although the state is not a microcosm of the nation, its reputation as Middle America—a stable place where family values dominate—lends weight to its preferences. As more and more farm corporations are formed and the number of family farms decreases, the nature of Iowa, its character and makeup, which reflect this rural dominance, may undergo a transformation.

Rowena Wildin

Iowa Time Line

1673	French explorers Jacques Marquette and Louis Jolliet are the first Europeans to reach Iowa.
1788	French trader Julien Dubuque begins mining lead near modern-day Dubuque, with the permission of the Mesquaki Indians.
Dec. 30, 1803	United States purchases the Louisiana Territory, which includes Iowa, from France.
1804	Explorers Meriwether Lewis and William Clark cross Iowa on their journey to the Pacific Ocean.
Sept. 21, 1832	Sauk chief Black Hawk signs a treaty in which the Sauk and Mesquaki agree to vacate a strip of land near the Mississippi River by June, 1833.
June 12, 1838	Territory of Iowa is created.

1838	Land offices begin to sell Iowa land for $1.25 per acre.
Oct. 11, 1842	Sauk and Fox agree to leave Iowa within three years.
1846	Mormons begin crossing Iowa on their trek to Utah from Nauvoo, Illinois.
Dec. 28, 1846	Iowa becomes the twenty-ninth state of the Union.
1851	The Sioux, the last Indians with land in the state, agree to leave Iowa.
1855	University of Iowa is founded.
1855-1865	German immigrants form the Amana colonies, a communal society that lasts for eighty years.
1857	Group of Mesquaki purchase land in Tama County, part of their former homeland.
1857	Group of Sioux kill thirty-four settlers along the shores of Spirit Lake and capture four women, two of whom are later ransomed.
1857	State capital moves from Iowa City to Des Moines.
1858	Iowa State University is founded.
1858	"Cardiff Giant," a prehistoric man, is found to be a hoax.
1861-1865	Iowa sends seventy thousand soldiers to the Civil War; thirteen thousand die.
1867	First railroad, the Chicago, Iowa, and Nebraska, reaches the state's western edge.
1868	Iowa supreme court rules that segregated schools are unconstitutional in Iowa; blacks are given voting rights.
1876	University of Northern Iowa is founded.
1880	Five major and spur railroad lines, more than five thousand miles of track, cover Iowa.
1896	Free rural mail delivery begins.
1900-1918	Buxton, a town in Monroe county inhabited predominantly by African American coal miners, flourishes until its coal mines are depleted.
1906-1920	Bicycle shop owner Fred Duesenberg and attorney Edward R. Mason build cars, designed by Duesenberg, in Iowa.
1910	Iowa State Experiment Station tests soybeans as a potential crop.
1912	Walter Sheaffer, a jeweler in Fort Madison, develops an easily inked fountain pen.
1926	Henry A. Wallace creates Pioneer Seed Corn, devoted to producing hybrid seed corn.
Mar. 4, 1929	Herbert Hoover, from Iowa, becomes president of the United States.
1935	Rural Electrification Administration brings electricity to Iowa farms.
1950's	Forrest City furniture dealer John Hanon creates the Winnebago motor home.
1965	Des Moines students are suspended for wearing black armbands protesting the Vietnam War; four years later, the U.S. Supreme Court supports their right to protest.
1985	Country musician Willie Nelson holds Farm Aid benefit concert for farmers suffering from falling land values in Iowa.
1991	Iowa legalizes riverboat gambling.
Jan. 23, 2000	Caucuses held throughout Iowa launch the 2000 presidential campaigns in the United States.

Notes for Further Study

Published Sources. *Iowa: The Middle Land* (1996), by Dorothy Schwieder, presents a thorough history of Iowa from its earliest days to the mid-1990's. Allan Carpenter's *Between the Two Rivers: Iowa Year by Year, 1846-1996* (1997) examines the first 150 years of Iowa's statehood. Two older but still useful books on Iowa history are Joseph F. Wall's *Iowa, a Bicentennial History* (1978) and Leland L. Sage's *A History of Iowa* (1974). *Iowa History Reader* (1996), edited by Marvin Bergman, offers readings in Iowa history selected by the State Historical Society of Iowa. *Iowa's Ethnic Roots* (1993), edited by Ron E. Roberts, examines the ethnic history of Iowa, and Charles O. Musser's *Soldier Boy: The Civil War Letters of Charles O. Musser, 29th Iowa* (1995), edited by Barry Popchock, presents a look at the Civil War through the eyes of a soldier with the 29th Iowa Infantry Regiment.

Web Resources. A good place to start searching for information about Iowa on the Internet is through the state of Iowa's site (http://www.state.ia.us). It provides current Iowa news and weather; information on tourism, travel, and special events; and links to many other sites. Other excellent sources of information are the many sites furnished by the Iowa secretary of state (http:// www.sos.state.ia.us). These include the official register of Iowa (http://sos.state.ia.us/register/register.htm), which contains information on the various branches of Iowa government as well as a history and profile of Iowa. The Iowa general assembly's site (http://www.legis.state .ia.us) contains information about the assembly and legislation.

A site that the Cedar Rapids *Gazette* assembled for the state's 150th birthday celebration in 1996 (http:// www.gazetteonline.com/history) presents an interesting and informative look at various aspects of Iowa history, including the Civil War, settlements, agriculture, and religion. Another source is the Iowa Tourism Bureau's site (http://www.iowa.tourism), which offers a brief history of Iowa, interesting facts, and travel-related information, including events and attractions. The on-line version of *Iowan* magazine (http://www.iowan.com) provides articles about the state and allows a search of back issues. A compilation of sites on Iowa can be found at (http://www.iowanet.com). This site contains an index of organizations, attractions, events, companies, and resources throughout Iowa.

Counties

County	Sq. miles	1996 pop.	County	Sq. miles	1996 pop.
Adair	569.3	8,224	Cherokee	577.2	13,477
Adams	423.6	4,494	Chickasaw	504.7	13,493
Allamakee	639.6	14,002	Clarke	431.2	8,255
Appanoose	496.3	13,616	Clay	568.9	17,598
Audubon	443.2	6,894	Clayton	778.8	18,893
Benton	716.5	24,510	Clinton	695.0	50,471
Black Hawk	567.4	122,806	Crawford	714.4	16,503
Boone	571.5	25,875	Dallas	586.5	33,900
Bremer	437.9	23,280	Davis	503.3	8,447
Buchanan	571.3	21,175	Decatur	532.3	8,232
Buena Vista	574.8	19,862	Delaware	577.9	18,506
Butler	580.4	15,781	Des Moines	416.2	42,564
Calhoun	570.2	11,478	Dickinson	381.1	15,725
Carroll	569.3	21,536	Dubuque	608.2	88,201
Cass	564.3	14,930	Emmet	395.8	11,114
Cedar	579.6	17,809	Fayette	731.0	22,061
Cerro Gordo	568.4	46,584	Floyd	500.6	16,538

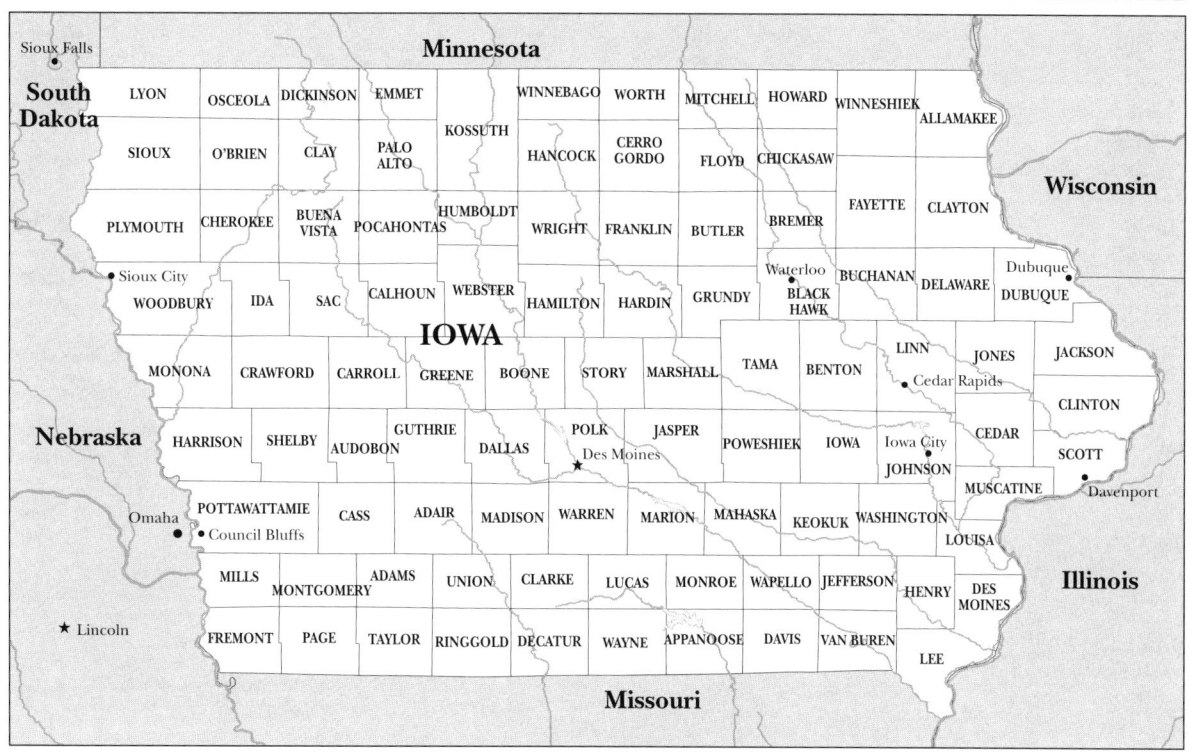

County	Sq. miles	1996 pop.	County	Sq. miles	1996 pop.
Franklin	582.5	11,017	Louisa	401.9	12,017
Fremont	511.3	7,918	Lucas	430.6	9,054
Greene	568.4	10,120	Lyon	587.6	11,962
Grundy	502.6	12,340	Madison	561.2	13,663
Guthrie	590.6	11,420	Mahaska	570.9	21,757
Hamilton	576.7	16,102	Marion	554.3	31,359
Hancock	571.1	12,152	Marshall	572.4	38,868
Hardin	569.3	18,682	Mills	436.6	14,054
Harrison	696.9	15,230	Mitchell	469.0	11,130
Henry	434.5	19,867	Monona	693.2	9,981
Howard	473.4	9,766	Monroe	433.4	8,113
Humboldt	434.4	10,431	Montgomery	423.9	11,908
Ida	431.7	8,109	Muscatine	438.7	41,158
Iowa	586.5	15,381	O'Brien	573.1	15,030
Jackson	636.1	20,057	Osceola	398.8	7,095
Jasper	730.0	35,470	Page	534.9	16,784
Jefferson	435.4	16,901	Palo Alto	563.9	10,136
Johnson	614.5	101,609	Plymouth	863.6	24,482
Jones	575.4	20,593	Pocahontas	577.7	9,001
Keokuk	579.2	11,594	Polk	569.5	354,150
Kossuth	973.1	18,021	Pottawattamie	954.3	84,939
Lee	517.4	38,879	Poweshiek	585.1	18,975
Linn	717.5	179,411	Ringgold	537.7	5,345

(continued)

County	Sq. miles	1996 pop.
Sac	575.8	11,986
Scott	457.9	157,353
Shelby	590.9	13,065
Sioux	767.9	31,191
Story	572.9	74,610
Tama	721.4	17,678
Taylor	534.0	7,186
Union	424.4	12,613
Van Buren	485.3	7,807
Wapello	431.8	35,766

County	Sq. miles	1996 pop.
Warren	571.7	39,386
Washington	568.8	20,706
Wayne	525.6	6,847
Webster	715.3	39,014
Winnebago	400.5	11,984
Winneshiek	689.7	20,963
Woodbury	872.7	102,580
Worth	400.0	7,865
Wright	580.8	14,327

Source: U.S. Census Bureau; National Association of Counties.

Cities
With 10,000 or more residents

Rank	City	Population
1	Des Moines	191,293
2	Cedar Rapids	114,563

Rank	City	Population
3	Davenport	96,842
4	Sioux City	82,697

Rank	City	Population	Rank	City	Population
5	Waterloo	63,703	21	Marion	23,777
6	Iowa City	60,897	22	Muscatine	22,932
7	Dubuque	56,467	23	Newton	15,371
8	Council Bluffs	56,312	24	Indianola	13,023
9	Ames	48,415	25	Boone	12,754
10	West Des Moines	42,333	26	Coralville	12,688
11	Cedar Falls	34,721	27	Keokuk	12,179
12	Bettendorf	31,737	28	Fort Madison	11,332
13	Mason City	28,718	29	Spencer	11,170
14	Urbandale	27,907	30	Clive	11,125
15	Clinton	27,626	31	Oskaloosa	10,673
16	Burlington	26,855	32	Carroll	10,331
17	Marshalltown	25,201	33	Fairfield	10,322
18	Ankeny	25,086			
19	Fort Dodge	24,738			
20	Ottumwa	23,854			

Population figures are estimated for mid-1998.

Source: U.S. Bureau of the Census.

Index to Tables

NA = Reliable data are not available.

DEMOGRAPHICS

Resident state and national populations, 1970-1997

Population figures given in thousands

	State pop.	U.S. pop.	Share	Rank
1970	2,825	203,302	1.4%	25
1980	2,914	226,546	1.3%	27
1985	2,830	237,924	1.2%	29
1990	2,777	248,765	1.1%	30
1995	2,841	262,761	1.1%	30
1997	2,852	267,636	1.1%	30

Source: U.S. Bureau of the Census.

Resident population by age, 1997

Age group	Total population
Under 5 years	184,000
5 to 17 years	542,000
18 to 24 years	270,000
25 to 34 years	376,000
35 to 44 years	445,000
45 to 54 years	357,000
55 to 64 years	251,000
65 to 74 years	214,000
75 to 84 years	154,000
85 years and over	61,000
Portion of residents 65 and older	15.0%
National average	12.7%

Population figures are rounded to nearest thousand persons;
figures include armed forces personnel stationed in state.
Source: U.S. Bureau of the Census.

Resident population by race, Hispanic origin, 1997

	State pop.	Share	U.S.
All residents	2,852,000	100.0%	100.0%
Hispanic white	48,000	1.7%	10.0%
non-Hispanic white	2,704,000	94.8%	72.7%
African American	56,000	2.0%	12.7%
Native American	9,000	0.3%	0.9%
Asian, Pacific Islander	36,000	1.3%	3.8%

Source: U.S. Bureau of the Census.

Projections of state population, 2000-2025

	Model A Uses interstate migration observed from 1975-1994	Model B Uses Bureau of Economic Analysis employment projections
Year	Population	Population
2000	2,900,000	2,891,000
2005	2,941,000	2,939,000
2010	2,968,000	2,992,000
2015	2,994,000	3,047,000
2020	3,019,000	3,095,000
2025	3,040,000	3,133,000

All population projections, including those for 2000, were calculated in 1997.

Source: U.S. Bureau of the Census, Population Paper Listings PPL-47.

VITAL STATISTICS

Average lifetime in years by race, 1989-1991

	State	U.S.	Rank
All residents	77.29	75.37	5
White residents	77.38	76.13	7
Black residents	NA	69.16	NA

Ranks are from longest-lived to least longest-lived. Ranks exclude Alaska, for which reliable data are not available. Rank for black residents is based on the 32 states for which reliable data are available.

Source: U.S. National Center for Health Statistics.

Infant mortality rates, 1980 and 1995

	State	U.S.
All residents		
1980	11.8	12.6
1995	8.2	7.6
White residents		
1980	11.5	11.0
1995	7.8	6.3
Black residents		
1980	27.2	21.4
1995	21.2	15.1

Figures represent deaths per 1,000 live births of resident infants under 1 year old, exclusive of fetal deaths; all-residents figures include other races not listed separately.

Source: U.S. National Center for Health Statistics.

Marriages and divorces

Marriages in 1996.	23,800
Rate per 1,000 population, 1995	7.8
U.S. rate, 1995	8.9
Rank among all states	34
Divorces in 1996	9,900
Rate per 1,000 population, 1995	3.7
U.S. rate, 1995	4.4
Rank among all states	35

Rank is from highest to lowest in country.

Source: U.S. National Center for Health Statistics.

Death rates by leading causes, 1995
Deaths per 100,000 resident population

Cause	State	U.S.
Heart disease	332.0	280.7
Cancer	219.1	204.9
Cerebrovascular diseases	77.5	60.1
Accidents and adverse effects	41.1	35.5
Motor vehicle accidents	19.2	16.5
Chronic obstructive pulmonary diseases	48.3	39.2
Diabetes mellitus	22.4	22.6
HIV	-	NA
Suicide	11.8	11.9
Homicide	-	8.7
All causes	986.0	880.0

Rank in overall death rate among states	9

Figures exclude nonresidents who die in state. Causes of death follow International Classification of Diseases. Rank is from highest to lowest in country.

Source: U.S. National Center for Health Statistics.

ECONOMY

Gross state product, 1990-1996
In current dollars

	State product	Increase
1990	$55.0 billion	
1993	$62.0 billion	
1994	$68.7 billion	10.81%
1995	$71.4 billion	3.93%
1996	$76.3 billion	6.86%

Source: U.S. Bureau of Economic Analysis; *Survey of Current Business*, June, 1998.

Gross state product by industry, 1996
In billions

Farms, forestry, fisheries	$4.9
Construction	2.7
Manufacturing	18.4
Transportation, public utilities	5.8
Wholesale trade	5.0
Retail trade	6.1
Finance, insurance, real estate	9.3
Services	10.1
Government	7.8
State total	$70.3
Total U.S.	$6,923.8
State share	1.02%
Rank among states	29

Total figures include mining, not listed separately.
Source: U.S. Bureau of Economic Analysis; *Survey of Current Business*, June, 1998.

Personal income per capita, 1990 and 1997
In current dollars

	1990	1997
Per capita income	$16,911	$23,102
U.S. average	$19,188	$25,598
Rank among states	33	32

1997 data are preliminary.
Source: U.S. Bureau of Economic Analysis; *Survey of Current Business*, May, 1998.

Energy consumption, 1995
In trillions of British thermal units (BTU)

End-use sectors

Residential	232.2
Commercial	150.9
Industrial	422.3
Transportation	262.0

Sources of energy

Petroleum	378.1
Natural gas	263.6
Coal	368.8
Hydroelectric power	10.3
Nuclear electric power	39.8
Total state per capita consumption	375.4
Total U.S. per capita consumption	344.4
Rank among states	20
Total state energy consumption	1,067.3
Total U.S. energy consumption	90,547.4
State share of U.S. total	1.18%
Rank among states	27

Total figures include items not listed separately.
Source: U.S. Energy Information Administration; *State Energy Data Report.*

Nonfarm employment by sectors, 1997

Total	1,405,000
Construction	60,000
Manufacturing	254,000
Transportation, public utilities	65,000
Wholesale trade, retail trade	345,000
Finance, insurance, real estate	79,000
Services	365,000
Government	234,000

Figures are rounded to nearest thousand persons. Total includes mining, not listed separately.
Source: U.S. Bureau of Labor Statistics; *Employment and Earnings*, monthly.

Foreign exports, 1990-1997
In millions of dollars

Year	State	U.S.	State share
1990	2,189	394,045	0.56%
1996	4,400	624,767	0.70%
1997	5,118	688,896	0.74%

Source: U.S. Bureau of the Census; *U.S. Merchandise Trade*, series FT 900.

LAND USE

Federally owned land, 1996

	State	U.S.	State share
Total acres	35,860,000	2,271,343,000	1.58%
Federally owned	30,000	563,129,000	0.01%
Federal share	0.1%	24.8%	—

Areas are rounded to nearest thousand acres. Figures for federally owned land do not include trust properties.

Source: U.S. General Services Administration; *Inventory Report on Real Property Owned by the United States Throughout the World*, annual.

Land use, 1992
In acres, rounded to nearest thousand

Total surface area	36,016,000
Federal land	184,000
Total nonfederal	35,363,000
Developed	1,779,000
Total rural	33,584,000
Cropland	24,988,000
Pasture land	3,712,000
Range land	0
Forest land	1,931,000
Minor cover/use	2,953,000

Total surface area figures include water area not shown separately.

Source: U.S. Dept. of Agriculture; Soil Conservation Service; Iowa State University, Statistical Laboratory; *Summary Report, 1992 National Resources Inventory.*

Farms and crop acreage, 1997

	State	U.S.	Share	Rank
Farms (thousands)	98	2,058	4.76%	3
Acres (millions)	33	968	3.41%	12
Acres per farm	339	471	—	23
Acres planted	24,711	334,139	7.40%	1
Acres harvested	24,513	319,894	7.66%	1
Farm value (mill.)	$7,830	$108,805	7.20%	7

Numbers of farms are rounded to nearest thousand.

Source: U.S. Dept. of Agriculture; National Agricultural Statistics Service.

GOVERNMENT AND FINANCE

Units of local government, 1997

	State	Total U.S.	Rank
All local governments	1,876	87,453	15
Counties	99	3,043	8
Municipalities	950	19,372	4
Townships	0	16,629	—
School districts	394	13,726	13
Special districts	433	34,683	27

County ranks are based on the 48 states with county governments; township ranks are based on the 20 states with township governments; school district ranks are based on the 46 states with such districts.

Source: U.S. Bureau of the Census; *1997 Census of Governments, Government Organization*, Series GC97(1).

State government revenue, 1996

Total revenue	$9,245 mill.
General revenue	8,133 mill.
Per capita	2,890
U.S. per capita average	2,910
Rank among states	24
Intergovernmental revenue	
Total	$2,139 mill.
From federal government	2,057 mill.
From local government	82 mill.
Charges and Miscellaneous	
Total	$1,554 mill.
Current charges	979 mill.
Misc. general revenue	574 mill.
Taxes	
Total	$4,441 mill.
General sales	1,456 mill.
Selective sales	691 mill.
License taxes	414 mill.
Individual income	1,588 mill.
Corporate income	203 mill.
Other	88 mill.
Insurance trust revenue	1,024 mill.

Total revenue figures include items not listed separately.

Source: U.S. Bureau of the Census.

State government expenditures, 1996

General expenditures

Intergovernmental	$2,672 mill.
Direct expenditures	5,511 mill.
Total.	8,183 mill.

Selected direct expenditures

Education	$3,263 mill.
Public welfare.	1,710 mill.
Health, hospital	698 mill.
Highways	1,046 mill.
Police.	61 mill.
Corrections	184 mill.
Natural resources.	204 mill.
Parks and recreation.	17 mill.
Government administration	300 mill.
Interest on debt	125 mill.

Other

State per capita expenditures	$2,873
U.S. per capita average	2,854
Rank among states.	24
Total state expenditures	8,853 mill.
Total U.S. expenditures	859,959 mill.

Totals include items not listed separately.
Source: U.S. Bureau of the Census.

Leslie M. Shaw (R)	1898-1902
Albert B. Cummins (R).	(r) 1902-1908
Warren Garst (R)	1908-1909
Beryl F. Carroll (R)	1909-1913
George W. Clarke (R)	1913-1917
William L. Harding (R)	1917-1921
Nathan E. Kendall (R)	1921-1925
John Hammill (R)	1925-1931
Daniel W. Turner (R).	1931-1933
Clyde L. Herring (D)	1933-1937
Nelson C. Kraschel (D).	1937-1939
George A. Wilson (R)	1939-1943
Bourke B. Hickenlooper (R).	1943-1945
Robert D. Blue (R)	1945-1949
William S. Beardsley (R)	(d) 1949-1954
Leo Elthon (R)	1954-1955
Leo A. Hoegh (R)	1955-1957
Herschel C. Loveless (D)	1957-1961
Norman A. Erbe (R)	1961-1963
Harold E. Hughes (D)	(r) 1963-1969
Robert D. Fulton (D)	1969
Robert D. Ray (R).	1969-1983
Terry E. Branstad (R)	1983-1999
Thomas Vilsack (D).	1999-

POLITICS

Governors since statehood

D = Democrat; R = Republican; O = other;
(r) resigned; (d) died in office; (i) removed from office

Ansel Briggs (D)	1846-1850
Stephen P. Hempstead (D).	1850-1854
James W. Grimes (R)	1854-1858
Ralph P. Lowe (R)	1858-1860
Samuel J. Kirkwood (R)	1860-1864
William H. Stone (O).	1864-1868
Samuel Merrill (R)	1868-1872
Cyrus C. Carpenter (R).	1872-1876
Samuel J. Kirkwood (R)	(r) 1876-1877
Joshua G. Newbold (R)	1877-1878
John H. Gear (R)	1878-1882
Buren R. Sherman (R)	1882-1886
William Larrabee (R).	1886-1890
Horace Boies (D)	1890-1894
Frank D. Jackson (R)	1894-1896
Francis M. Drake (R)	1896-1898

Composition of state legislature, 1990-1998

	Democrats	Republicans
State House (100 seats)		
1990	55	45
1992	49	51
1994	36	64
1996	46	54
1998	44	56
State Senate (50 seats)		
1990	29	21
1992	27	23
1994	27	23
1996	21	29
1998	20	30

Figures for total seats may include independents and minor
party members.
Source: Council of State Governments; *State Elective Officials
and the Legislatures.*

Composition of congressional delegations, 1989-1999

	Dem	Rep	Total
House of Representatives			
101st Congress, 1989			
State delegates	2	4	6
Total U.S.	259	174	433
102d Congress, 1991			
State delegates	2	4	6
Total U.S.	267	167	434
103d Congress, 1993			
State delegates	1	4	5
Total U.S.	258	176	434
104th Congress, 1995			
State delegates	1	4	5
Total U.S.	197	236	433
105th Congress, 1997			
State delegates	0	5	5
Total U.S.	206	228	434
106th Congress, 1999			
State delegates	1	4	5
Total U.S.	211	222	433
Senate			
101st Congress, 1989			
State delegates	1	1	2
Total U.S.	55	45	100
102d Congress, 1991			
State delegates	1	1	2
Total U.S.	56	44	100
103d Congress, 1993			
State delegates	1	1	2
Total U.S.	57	43	100
104th Congress, 1995			
State delegates	1	1	2
Total U.S.	46	53	99
105th Congress, 1997			
State delegates	1	1	2
Total U.S.	45	55	100
106th Congress, 1999			
State delegates	1	1	2
Total U.S.	45	54	99

Figures are for starts of first sessions. Figure for U.S. Representatives for 101st Congress does not include Alabama and Indiana, which had vacancies. Figures for total U.S. Representatives for 102d, 103d, and 106th Congresses do not include Vermont, which had 1 Independent-Socialist.

Figure for U.S. Representatives for 104th Congress does not include Vermont, which had 1 Independent-Socialist, and California, which had 1 vacancy. Figure for U.S. Representatives for 105th Congress does not include New York, which had 1 vacancy. Figure for U.S. Senators for 104th Congress does not include Oregon, which had 1 vacancy. Figure for U.S. Senators for 106th Congress does not include New Hampshire, which had 1 Independent.
Source: U.S. Congress; *Congressional Directory*, biennial.

Voter participation in presidential elections, 1992 and 1996

	1992	1996
State voting age pop.	2,073,000	2,138,000
Total U.S. voting age pop.	189,524,000	196,509,000
State share of U.S. total	1.1%	1.1%
Rank among states	30	30
Percent of state casting vote	65.3	48.9
Percent of U.S. total voting	55.1	49.0
Rank among states	9	30

Source: U.S. Bureau of the Census.

HEALTH AND MEDICAL CARE

Medicare, 1997

	Recipients	Payments
State	475,000	$1,738 mill.
Total U.S.	37,514,000	$206,064 mill.
State share	1.27%	0.84%
Rank among states	28	32

Recipient figures are rounded to nearest thousand persons. Ranks are from highest to lowest.
Source: U.S. Health Care Financing Administration.

Medicaid, 1996

	Recipients	Payments
State	308,000	$1,088 mill.
Total U.S.	35,028,000	$121,419 mill.
State share	0.88%	0.90%
Rank among states	33	30

Recipient figures are rounded to nearest thousand persons. Payment figures for fiscal year reflect federal and state contribution payments. Ranks are from highest to lowest.
Source: U.S. Health Care Financing Administration.

Health insurance coverage, 1996

	State	U.S.
Total persons covered	2,565,000	225,070,000
Total persons not covered	335,000	41,716,000
Part not covered	11.6%	15.6%
Rank among states	33	—
Children not covered	78,000	10,554,000
Part not covered	9.4%	14.8%
Rank among states	39	—

Ranks are from most to fewest uninsured. Population figures are rounded to nearest thousand persons.
Source: U.S. Bureau of the Census.

AIDS, syphilis, tuberculosis, and measles cases, 1997

Cases	U.S.	State	Share
AIDS	58,443	101	0.17%
Syphilis	8,550	7	0.08%
Tuberculosis	18,534	73	0.39%
Measles	148,000	NA	NA

Measles figures are rounded to nearest thousand cases.
Source: U.S. Centers for Disease Control and Prevention.

HOUSING

Homeownership rates, 1985-1997

	1985	1990	1997
State	69.9%	70.7%	72.7%
Total U.S.	63.9%	63.9%	65.7%
Rank among states	15	7	10

Source: U.S. Bureau of the Census.

Home sales, 1990 and 1997
In thousands of units

Existing home sales	1990	1997	Change
State sales	51.9	57.7	5.8
Total U.S. sales	3,560	4,730	1,170
State share of U.S. total	1.46%	1.22%	-0.24%
Rank among states	27	29	—

Source: National Association of Realtors; *Real Estate Outlook: Market Trends and Insights.*

EDUCATION

Public school enrollment, 1995

State K-8 enrollment	344,000
Total U.S. K-8 enrollment	32,341,000
State share of total U.S.	1.06%
State 9-12 enrollment	158,000
Total U.S. 9-12 enrollment	12,500,000
State share of U.S. total	1.26%
State public school enroll. rate	93.2%
Overall U.S. rate.	91.6%
Rank among states.	20

Enrollment figures (which include unclassified students) are rounded to nearest thousand pupils in fall term; kindergarten (K)-8 grade figures include some prekindergarten students. Enrollment rate is based on percentage of persons 5-17 years old. Rank is from highest to lowest.
Source: U.S. National Center for Education Statistics.

Public college finances, 1996

State FTE enrollment	100,400
Total U.S. FTE enrollment	8,268,800
State share of total U.S.	1.21%
Rank among states.	30
State and local appropriations	$555,500,000
Total U.S. state and local appropriations.	$39,699 mill.
State share of total U.S.	1.40%
Rank among states.	23
State net tuition revenues.	$284,700,000
Total U.S. net tuition	$18,348,100,000
State share of total U.S.	1.55%
Rank among states.	26

FTE=Full-time equivalent; credit and noncredit enrollment including summer session in academic year ending in 1996.
Enrollments are rounded to nearest thousand students. Net tuition revenues exclude appropriation to students attending in-state public institutions. Rankings are from highest shares to lowest.
Source: Research Associates of Washington.

TRANSPORTATION AND TRAVEL

Highway mileage, 1996

Interstate	781
Other arterial	9,429
Collector roads	32,419
Local roads	71,010
Urban roads	9,349
Rural roads	103,359
Total state	112,708
U.S. total	3,933,985
State share	2.9%
Rank among states	11

Source: U.S. Federal Highway Administration.

Motor vehicle registrations and driver licenses, 1996

In thousands

Vehicle registrations	State	U.S.	Share	Rank
Autos, trucks, buses	2,869	206,365	1.39%	26
Autos only	1,642	128,439	1.28%	28
Motorcycles	132	3,832	3.44%	10
Driver licenses	1,956	179,539	1.09%	26

Figures do not include vehicles owned by military services.
Source: U.S. Federal Highway Administration; *Highway Statistics; Selected Highway Statistics and Charts.*

Domestic travel expenditures, 1995

Spending by U.S. residents on overnight trips and day trips of at least 100 miles

Total expenditures in state	$3,172 mill.
Total expenditures in U.S.	$360,314 mill.
State share of total U.S.	0.88%
Rank among states	32

Source: Travel Industry Association of America.

CRIME AND LAW ENFORCEMENT

State and local police officers, 1996

Local police	3,037
State police	433
Sheriffs	1,343
Total	5,043
Officers per 10,000 residents	18
U.S. average	25
Rank among states	43

Figures cover full-time sworn officers; totals include special police not shown separately.
Source: U.S. Bureau of Justice Statistics; *Census of State and Local Law Enforcement Agencies, 1996.*

Crime rates, 1996

Rates per 100,000 resident population

Violent crimes	State	U.S.
Total violent	273	634
Murder	1.9	7.4
Forcible rape	19.7	36.1
Robbery	45	202
Aggravated assault	206	388

Property crimes		
Total property	3,376	4,445
Burglary	665	943
Larceny/theft	2,521	2,976
Motor vehicle theft	191	526
Totals	3,649	5,079

Source: U.S. Federal Bureau of Investigation; *Crime in the United States,* annual.

State prison populations, 1980-1996

	State	U.S.	State share
1980	2,481	305,458	0.81%
1990	3,967	708,393	0.56%
1996	6,342	1,025,624	0.62%

Figures exclude prisoners in federal penitentiaries.
Source: U.S. Bureau of Justice Statistics.

Kansas

Location: Midwestern continental United States

Area and rank: 81,823 square miles (211,922 square kilometers); 82,282 square miles (213,110 square kilometers) including water; thirteenth largest state in area

Population and rank: 2,594,840 (1997); thirty-second largest state in population

Capital: Topeka

Largest city: Wichita (329,211 people in 1998)

State capitol building in Topeka. (©James Blank/Weststock)

Became territory: May 30, 1854

Entered Union and rank: January 29, 1861; thirty-fourth state

Present constitution adopted: 1859

Counties: 105

State name: "Kansas" derives from a Sioux name for "people of the south wind"

State nicknames: Sunflower State; Jayhawk State

Motto: *Ad astra per aspera* (To the stars through difficulties)

State flag: Blue field with state seal, state flower, and name "Kansas"

Highest point: Mount Sunflower — 4,039 feet (1,231 meters)

Lowest point: Verdigris River — 679 feet (207 meters)

Highest recorded temperature: 121 degrees Fahrenheit (49 degrees Celsius) — near Alton, 1936

Lowest recorded temperature: −40 degrees Fahrenheit (−40 degrees Celsius) — Lebanon, 1905

State song: "Home on the Range"

State tree: Cottonwood

State flower: Sunflower

State bird: Western meadowlark

State animal: Buffalo

Kansas History

Within Kansas, slightly northwest of Lebanon, is the geographical center of the forty-eight contiguous states. The Spanish explorer Francisco Vásquez de Coronado first ventured into the area in 1541 seeking gold. Native Americans had occupied the region since prehistoric times, possibly as early as 14,000 B.C.E. The Pawnee, Osage, Wichita, and Kansa Indians lived there during the early Spanish exploration. They were mostly hunters and farmers living along the Kansas River.

Later members of some seminomadic tribes, mainly the Kiowa, Cheyenne, Arapaho, and Comanche Indians, also dwelled in the area. After 1830, however, the federal government forcibly moved many Native Americans from eastern tribes into the territory it had acquired through the Louisiana Purchase of 1803. Among the tribes whose members were relocated were the Cherokee, Miami, Potawatomi, Ottawa, Creek, Chickasaw, Choctaw, Delaware, and Shawnee. In all, about thirty tribes were assigned to Kansas for relocation.

French and American Settlement. The French moved into the area after the Spanish had been defeated by the Pawnee Indians in Nebraska. In the early 1700's, the French, attracted by the fur trade, built a trading post and military outpost, Fort Cavagnial, near present-day Leavenworth.

With the Louisiana Purchase, American exploration began. Meriwether Lewis and William Clark set out to explore the newly acquired area, which included all but a small part of southwestern Kansas bought in 1850 from Texas.

These explorers were followed in 1806 by Zebulon Pike, who made an east-west journey across the territory. As the eastern United States began to be developed, the federal government was under pressure to claim Native American lands for development. Relocating American Indians to the West provided the government with a convenient solution to a difficult problem. The Native Americans who were relocated are usually referred to as the emigrant tribes.

Between 1827 and 1853, Kansas was inhabited mostly by Indians. Some thirty-four thousand Indians from over thirty tribes and only fifteen hundred white inhabitants, mostly missionaries and the personnel that maintained the government forts constructed at Leavenworth, Fort Scott, and Fort Riley, lived there.

The Kansas-Nebraska Act of 1854. So great was the incursion of European settlers to the area after 1854, that the Native Americans who lived there, both original dwellers and the emigrant tribes, were removed from the state and settled elsewhere. In 1854 Kansas was created as a territory in the western part of what had previously been called the Missouri Territory. The early borders of the rectangular-shaped territory were much as they are today. Kansas is bounded by Missouri on the east and Colorado on the west. To the north, the boundary is Nebraska, and the southern border is Oklahoma. The only natural boundary is in the northeast, where the Missouri River constitutes part of the state line.

Soon after Kansas gained territorial status, the Kansas-Nebraska Act of 1854, which replaced the Missouri Compromise, opened the territory to settlement. Under the terms of this act, citizens of a territory decided whether it would be slave or free, whereas under the Missouri Compromise, an artificial balance between slave and free states was imposed.

Opinions were strongly divided about which choice Kansas should make. Its neighboring state, Missouri, had slaves. Nebraska opted to be free, but proslavery sentiment was strong in Kansas. When the issue came to a vote, hundreds of land-hungry people who had come to Kansas stuffed the ballot boxes.

Kansas was plunged into controversy between the pro- and antislavery forces. Abolitionists were recruited to come to Kansas from New England and make it a free state. Abolitionist John Brown led the Pottawatomie Massacre in May of 1856. In 1863 an angry proslavery mob, led by William Clarke Quantrill, attacked Lawrence, Kansas, killing around 150 of its citizens.

Moving Toward Statehood. With the pro- and antislavery forces fighting against each other, both

sides drew up constitutions, neither of them acceptable to the United States Congress. Finally, in 1859, the antislavery Wyandotte Constitution was approved. This cleared the way for Kansas to achieve statehood on January 29, 1861, just as many Southern states were seceding from the Union. Kansas was the thirty-fourth state admitted to the Union.

The Homestead Act of 1862. Following passage of the Homestead Act of 1862, Kansas grew rapidly. Under the terms of this act, upon the payment of a ten-dollar filing fee, heads of family or anyone over twenty-one years old could receive 160 acres of government land, which they would own if they lived on it for five years and improved the property. This opportunity was a magnet that drew thousands of easterners to Kansas.

The railroads that served the area received large land grants, chunks of which they sold to the early settlers. The Union Pacific Railroad began operating in Kansas in 1857, the Atchison and Topeka Railroad was chartered in 1859, and the Missouri,

Kansas, and Texas line soon followed. Eventually twelve railroads operated on more than six thousand miles of track in Kansas.

The Kansas Economy. Because of the nature of its founding, Kansas was originally a rural state concentrating heavily on agriculture. During the Civil War, it sided with the North, and many of its citizens joined the Union army. Shortly after the war, cow towns began to develop in Kansas. These were towns that had railway connections, notably Abilene, Dodge City, Ellsworth, and Wichita.

Texas at this time had no railroad service, so until the mid-1880's, when rail service became available, Texan cattle ranchers drove their herds across Oklahoma to the railroad towns of Kansas, from which they were shipped to other destinations.

Eastern Kansas was settled early, but soon other settlers moved into the central and western regions, as far as Great Bend near the Colorado border. A diverse population developed as Europeans from Russia, Germany, Bohemia, France, England, and Italy came to the state, which also had a sizable

African American population, being one of the free states that attracted freed slaves following the Civil War in what was called the "exodus movement."

Kansas, with a growing season of about 150 days in its northern reaches and more than 200 days in the southeast, is hospitable to agriculture. The rainfall ranges from sixteen inches annually in the west to more than forty inches in the east, although droughts have been a frequent problem, particularly in the early to mid-1930's, when the dust bowls of Kansas and Oklahoma put many farmers out of business.

The state constructed more than twenty large reservoirs to control flooding, provide drinking water, and afford irrigation to farmers. Also, early Russian immigrants into Kansas brought with them a drought-resistant strain of wheat, Turkey Red, which is grown extensively in the state.

Although Kansas was originally rural, it increasingly moved toward manufacturing, commerce, and service occupations, causing a population shift to urban areas. Of its more than six hundred incorporated cites, fifty have populations exceeding five thousand. More than two-thirds of the total 1990 population of about 2.5 million lived in urban areas.

Besides its agricultural and cattle industries, Kansas has a thriving aircraft industry centered in Wichita, where both private planes and commercial aircraft are produced by such companies as Boeing and Cessna. One of the nation's leading mental hospitals, the Menninger Neuropsychiatric Clinic, is located in Topeka. Kansas also has impressive oil reserves, as well as natural gas, coal, lead, salt, and zinc.

Kansas Conservatism. Kansas has traditionally been a conservative state, largely a Republican stronghold, although it has strong Populist leanings as well and has elected Populists as governors and representatives. It gave a moderate, Nancy Landon Kassebaum, three terms in the United States Senate.

In 1880 the state adopted prohibition and essentially remained a dry state. In 1899, Kansan Carry

The building of the transcontinental railroad accelerated the development of Kansas, while also hastening the annihilation of the once-great buffalo herds. (Library of Congress)

Silhouette figures of cattle drivers erected near Caldwell, at the Oklahoma border, recall the days when great herds moved between Abilene and Texas on the Chisholm Trail. (Kansas Department of Commerce & Housing, Travel and Tourism)

Nation single-handedly undertook the enforcement of Kansas's prohibition law by destroying saloons with her renowned axe.

Kansas Economy in the 1900's. The economy of Kansas had a significant resurgence during World War I, when the price of wheat escalated, bringing considerable money into the state's economy. The economy grew until the 1930's, when a drought that continued for several years devastated wheat farming.

The financial woes of the 1930's did not end until World War II again stimulated the economy and brought considerable industry into the state. The road building in the state during and after World War II resulted in one of the best road systems in the country. Kansas is served by 125 public and 250 private airports that provide excellent commercial air transport and encourage private ownership of airplanes.

R. Baird Shuman

Kansas Time Line

1541	Francisco Vásquez de Coronado explores central Kansas.
1723	Fort Orleans is built by French explorer Etienne de Bourgmont.

(continued)

1744	French establish trading post at Fort Cavagnial, near Leavenworth.
1803	Area that becomes Kansas becomes part of the United States through the Louisiana Purchase.
1804	Meriwether Lewis and William Clark explore Kansas on their way to the Pacific Coast.
1806	Captain Zebulon Pike crosses Kansas from east to west.
June 4, 1812	Territory of Missouri, which includes Kansas, is established.
Aug. 10, 1819	Stephen H. Long makes first steamboat expedition in Kansas.
1821	William Becknell establishes Santa Fe Trail.
1824	Founding of Presbyterian mission on Neosho River.
1827	Fort Leavenworth becomes the first permanent white settlement in Kansas.
1827	Daniel Boone establishes American Indian school in Jefferson County.
1830	United States government relocates Native Americans from the eastern states to Kansas.
1830	Shawnee Methodist Mission for Indians is established near Turner.
June 20, 1834	Kansas is declared Indian Country by Congress.
1839	Shawnee Methodist Mission moved to location near Shawnee.
1842	First of several expeditions by John C. Frémont passes through Kansas.
1842	Fort Scott is established.
1843	Great migration to Oregon begins.
1853	Fort Riley is established.
May 30, 1854	Kansas-Nebraska Act passed, giving Kansas territorial status.
July 2, 1855	First territorial legislature meeting at Pawnee and later at the Shawnee Mission legalizes slavery in Kansas.
1855	Free State antislavery party is established as conflict grows over slavery.
May 21, 1856	Lawrence Massacre results in 150 deaths when proslavery groups attack.
May 23-24, 1856	John Brown leads free-state massacre along Pottawatomie Creek.
1857	Union Pacific Railroad begins operating in Kansas.
1858	Congress rejects proslavery Lecompton Constitution.
Oct. 4, 1859	Antislavery Wyandotte Constitution is adopted.
1859	Atchison and Topeka Railroad chartered.
Apr., 1860	Pony Express crosses Kansas.
1860	First oil well drilled in Kansas near Paola.
Jan. 29, 1861	Kansas admitted to Union as thirty-fourth state.
1863	William Quantrill's Confederate troops attack Lawrence.
1864	University of Kansas opens at Lawrence.
1864	Confederate General Sterling Price leads his troops to Kansas.
1867	First Texas cattle run to Kansas.
1874	Mennonites from Russia introduce drought-resistant Turkey Red wheat to Kansas.

1878	Last Indian skirmish launched by Cheyenne Indians.
1880	Kansas imposes prohibition.
1899	Carry Nation begins her antisaloon raids.
1903	State capitol is completed.
1918	Economy bolstered by wheat sales during World War I.
1935	Dust storms devastate Kansas farm land.
1936	Alfred M. Landon is Republican candidate for president, losing with only 8 electoral votes.
1945	Growth of Kansas aircraft industry following World War II.
1948	Kanopolis Dam is completed on Smoky Hill River.
1949	Fall River Dam is completed.
1951	Cedar Bluff Dam on Smoky Hill River is completed.
1951	Kansas is devastated by floods.
1952	Kansan Dwight D. Eisenhower becomes thirty-fourth president of the United States.
1954	Eisenhower Museum opens in Abilene.
1954	U.S. Supreme Court rules against school board of Topeka in segregation case *Brown v. Board of Education of Topeka*.
1956	Kansas Turnpike is completed.
1965	Agricultural Hall of Fame and National Center opens near Kansas City.
1965	Fort Scott named a national historic monument.
1972	Terms of governor and other state officials increased from two to four years.
1976	Mid-American All-Indian Center opens in Wichita.
1988	Drought and wind erosion destroy more than 865,000 acres in Kansas.
1991	Largest remaining plot of Kansas prairie is plowed under.
Nov., 1991	Joan Finney is first woman elected governor of Kansas.

Notes for Further Study

Published Sources. *Natural Kansas* (1985), edited by Joseph T. Collins, provides interesting essays about biological, geological, geographical, and physical aspects of Kansas. Robert Richmond's *Kansas: A Land of Contrasts* (3d. ed. 1989) also presents varied information about the state, emphasizing that it is not entirely flat, soaring to an elevation of 4,039 feet at Mount Sunflower and having a mean elevation of 2,000 feet.

Robert S. Bader's *Prohibition in Kansas: A History* (1986) offers interesting information about this phase of the state's history and the state's role in the passage of the Eighteenth Amendment to the U.S. Constitution. Thomas Goodrich relates details of the Lawrence Massacre of 1863 in *Bloody Dawn: The Story of the Lawrence Massacre* (1991). Pamela Riney-Kehrbert's *Rooted in Dust: Surviving Drought and Depression in Southwestern Kansas* (1994) offers the best coverage of how widespread droughts in the early 1930's led to a rapid deterioration of the Kansas economy, followed by the Great Depression.

Numerous books on Kansas are directed primarily to juvenile readers. Allen Carpenter's *Kansas* (1979) remains a useful resource despite its datedness. Zachary Kent's later *Kansas* (1990) is an excellent brief account of the state. Both of these books can be supplemented by Dennis Fradin's *Kansas: In Words and Pictures* (1980). Dennis B. Fredeen's *Kansas* (1995) will appeal to juvenile readers, as will Patricia K. Kummer's *Kansas* (1999).

Web Resources. The state of Kansas maintains a Web site (http:/www.ink.org) that provides useful information about the state and its government. The state's department of tourism has a Web site (http:/www.kansas commerce.com) that includes information about tourist attractions, lodging, restaurants, and public transportation. The Web site of the University of Kansas (http:/www.ukans.edu) offers information about the various branches of the university and their attractions. Various libraries around the state have Web sites through which their catalogues can be accessed. Chief among these are the sites of the University of Kansas Medical School Library (http:/www.kumc.edu) and the libraries of Kansas City (http:/www.kcpl.lib.mo.us) and (http:/www.kcmlin .org), Manhattan (http:/www.manhattan.lib.ks.us), Hutchinson (http:/www.hplsck.org), Southeast Kansas (http:/www.sekls.lib.ks.us), Topeka (http:/www.tscpl .org), and Winfield (http:/www.wpl.org). Topeka has an active theater community, whose activities can be accessed through the Topeka Theater Web site (http:/ www.topekacivictheater.com).

Those interested in employment opportunities in Kansas should consult the Web site of the Department of Human Resources (http:/www.hr.state.ks.us) or the classified pages of the Kansas City *Star* (http:/www.kcstar .com). Employment opportunities within the University of Kansas Medical School are listed in the Web site of that school (http:/www.kumc.edu). News developments that affect Kansas are found on the Kanza Net Web site (http:/www.kansasnews.com).

Counties

County	Sq. miles	1996 pop.	County	Sq. miles	1996 pop.
Allen	503.1	14,645	Ellis	900.0	26,186
Anderson	583.0	8,054	Ellsworth	715.9	6,372
Atchison	432.4	16,234	Finney	1,300.2	35,545
Barber	1,134.2	5,484	Ford	1,098.6	29,309
Barton	894.0	28,097	Franklin	573.9	23,565
Bourbon	637.1	15,159	Geary	384.3	26,341
Brown	570.7	10,965	Gove	1,071.5	3,089
Butler	1,428.2	59,226	Graham	898.3	3,260
Chase	775.9	2,886	Grant	574.9	7,697
Chautauqua	641.7	4,379	Gray	868.9	5,527
Cherokee	587.2	22,505	Greeley	778.1	1,754
Cheyenne	1,019.9	3,220	Greenwood	1,139.8	8,090
Clark	974.7	2,382	Hamilton	996.5	2,296
Clay	643.9	9,319	Harper	801.5	6,524
Cloud	715.7	10,247	Harvey	539.4	31,302
Coffey	630.3	8,743	Haskell	577.4	3,922
Comanche	788.4	2,072	Hodgeman	860.0	2,231
Cowley	1,126.3	37,055	Jackson	656.9	11,978
Crawford	593.0	36,337	Jefferson	536.2	17,514
Decatur	893.6	3,521	Jewell	909.2	4,011
Dickinson	848.4	19,856	Johnson	476.8	408,341
Doniphan	392.2	7,766	Kearny	870.0	4,216
Douglas	457.0	89,899	Kingman	863.7	8,545
Edwards	622.1	3,471	Kiowa	722.4	3,571
Elk	647.9	3,393	Labette	648.9	22,869

County	Sq. miles	1996 pop.	County	Sq. miles	1996 pop.
Lane	717.3	2,211	Rice	726.6	10,044
Leavenworth	463.3	69,904	Riley	609.6	64,716
Lincoln	718.9	3,388	Rooks	888.4	5,849
Linn	598.8	8,974	Rush	718.2	3,537
Logan	1,073.1	3,113	Russell	884.7	7,658
Lyon	851.0	34,384	Saline	719.6	51,782
McPherson	899.8	27,548	Scott	717.6	5,029
Marion	943.2	12,898	Sedgwick	1,000.2	422,437
Marshall	902.6	11,286	Seward	639.6	20,002
Meade	978.5	4,436	Shawnee	549.9	164,938
Miami	576.8	25,933	Sheridan	896.4	2,760
Mitchell	699.9	7,096	Sherman	1,055.9	6,733
Montgomery	645.3	37,414	Smith	895.5	4,741
Morris	697.4	6,340	Stafford	792.1	5,129
Morton	730.0	3,315	Stanton	680.1	2,297
Nemaha	719.1	10,389	Stevens	727.6	5,347
Neosho	571.9	16,893	Sumner	1,181.9	26,901
Ness	1,074.8	3,663	Thomas	1,074.9	8,326
Norton	877.9	5,762	Trego	888.4	3,440
Osage	703.6	16,726	Wabaunsee	797.5	6,664
Osborne	892.6	4,606	Wallace	914.1	1,812
Ottawa	721.2	5,815	Washington	898.5	6,738
Pawnee	754.2	7,470	Wichita	718.6	2,725
Phillips	886.3	6,194	Wilson	573.9	10,353
Pottawatomie	844.3	17,908	Woodson	500.7	3,980
Pratt	735.0	9,746	Wyandotte	151.4	153,427
Rawlins	1,069.7	3,249			
Reno	1,254.5	62,901			
Republic	716.5	6,253			

Source: U.S. Census Bureau; National Association of Counties.

Cities
With 10,000 or more residents

Rank	City	Population
1	Wichita	329,211
2	Kansas City	141,297
3	Overland Park	139,685
4	Topeka	118,977
5	Olathe	85,035
6	Lawrence	74,244
7	Shawnee	45,250
8	Salina	44,022
9	Manhattan	41,318
10	Leavenworth	39,227
11	Hutchinson	39,016
12	Lenexa	38,826
13	Garden City	26,039
14	Leawood	25,886
15	Emporia	24,462
16	Prairie Village	23,365
17	Dodge City	22,456
18	Hays	18,866

Rank	City	Population
19	Pittsburg	18,508
20	Derby	18,327
21	Newton	18,070
22	Liberal	17,486
23	Junction City	16,970
24	Great Bend	14,461
25	McPherson	13,284
26	El Dorado	13,078
27	Arkansas City	12,300
28	Merriam	12,103
29	Coffeyville	12,031
30	Ottawa	11,963
31	Winfield	11,533
32	Parsons	11,163
33	Atchison	10,594

Population figures are estimated for mid-1998.
Source: U.S. Bureau of the Census.

Index to Tables

NA = Reliable data are not available.

DEMOGRAPHICS

Resident state and national populations, 1970-1997

Population figures given in thousands

	State pop.	U.S. pop.	Share	Rank
1970	2,249	203,302	1.1%	28
1980	2,364	226,546	1.0%	32
1985	2,427	237,924	1.0%	32
1990	2,478	248,765	1.0%	32
1995	2,570	262,761	1.0%	32
1997	2,595	267,636	1.0%	32

Source: U.S. Bureau of the Census.

Resident population by age, 1997

Age group	Total population
Under 5 years	179,000
5 to 17 years	509,000
18 to 24 years	252,000
25 to 34 years	356,000
35 to 44 years	423,000
45 to 54 years	317,000
55 to 64 years	207,000
65 to 74 years	179,000
75 to 84 years	124,000
85 years and over	49,000
Portion of residents 65 and older	13.5%
National average	12.7%

Population figures are rounded to nearest thousand persons;
figures include armed forces personnel stationed in state.
Source: U.S. Bureau of the Census.

Resident population by race, Hispanic origin, 1997

	State pop.	Share	U.S.
All residents	2,595,000	100.0%	100.0%
Hispanic white	120,000	4.6%	10.0%
non-Hispanic white	2,255,000	86.9%	72.7%
African American	153,000	5.9%	12.7%
Native American	23,000	0.9%	0.9%
Asian, Pacific Islander	44,000	1.7%	3.8%

Source: U.S. Bureau of the Census.

Projections of state population, 2000-2025

	Model A Uses interstate migration observed from 1975-1994	Model B Uses Bureau of Economic Analysis employment projections
Year	Population	Population
2000	2,668,000	2,675,000
2005	2,761,000	2,788,000
2010	2,849,000	2,908,000
2015	2,939,000	3,034,000
2020	3,026,000	3,158,000
2025	3,108,000	3,273,000

All population projections, including those for 2000, were calculated in 1997.
Source: U.S. Bureau of the Census, Population Paper Listings PPL-47.

VITAL STATISTICS

Average lifetime in years by race, 1989-1991

	State	U.S.	Rank
All residents	76.76	75.37	13
White residents	77.06	76.13	10
Black residents	71.22	69.16	4

Ranks are from longest-lived to least longest-lived. Ranks exclude Alaska, for which reliable data are not available. Rank for black residents is based on the 32 states for which reliable data are available.
Source: U.S. National Center for Health Statistics.

Infant mortality rates, 1980 and 1995

	State	U.S.
All residents		
1980	10.4	12.6
1995	7.0	7.6
White residents		
1980	9.5	11.0
1995	6.2	6.3
Black residents		
1980	20.6	21.4
1995	17.6	15.1

Figures represent deaths per 1,000 live births of resident infants under 1 year old, exclusive of fetal deaths; all-residents figures include other races not listed separately.
Source: U.S. National Center for Health Statistics.

Marriages and divorces

Marriages in 1996.	20,600
Rate per 1,000 population, 1995	8.6
U.S. rate, 1995	8.9
Rank among all states	24
Divorces in 1996	11,700
Rate per 1,000 population, 1995	4.2
U.S. rate, 1995	4.4
Rank among all states	29

Rank is from highest to lowest in country.
Source: U.S. National Center for Health Statistics.

Death rates by leading causes, 1995

Deaths per 100,000 resident population

Cause	State	U.S.
Heart disease	297.7	280.7
Cancer	205.9	204.9
Cerebrovascular diseases	70.6	60.1
Accidents and adverse effects	38.7	35.5
Motor vehicle accidents	17.6	16.5
Chronic obstructive pulmonary diseases	44.9	39.2
Diabetes mellitus	22.5	22.6
HIV	5.6	NA
Suicide	11.3	11.9
Homicide	6.3	8.7
All causes	933.0	880.0
Rank in overall death rate among states		16

Figures exclude nonresidents who die in state. Causes of death follow International Classification of Diseases. Rank is from highest to lowest in country.
Source: U.S. National Center for Health Statistics.

ECONOMY

Gross state product, 1990-1996
In current dollars

	State product	Increase
1990	$51.3 billion	
1993	$58.2 billion	
1994	$61.9 billion	6.36%
1995	$64.1 billion	3.55%
1996	$68.0 billion	6.08%

Source: U.S. Bureau of Economic Analysis; *Survey of Current Business,* June, 1998.

Gross state product by industry, 1996
In billions

Farms, forestry, fisheries	$2.6
Construction	2.5
Manufacturing	11.8
Transportation, public utilities	7.1
Wholesale trade	5.1
Retail trade	6.4
Finance, insurance, real estate	7.4
Services	9.9
Government	8.6
State total	$62.0
Total U.S.	$6,923.8
State share	0.90%
Rank among states	31

Total figures include mining, not listed separately.
Source: U.S. Bureau of Economic Analysis; *Survey of Current Business,* June, 1998.

Personal income per capita, 1990 and 1997
In current dollars

	1990	1997
Per capita income	$17,968	$24,379
U.S. average	$19,188	$25,598
Rank among states	22	24

1997 data are preliminary.
Source: U.S. Bureau of Economic Analysis; *Survey of Current Business,* May, 1998.

Energy consumption, 1995
In trillions of British thermal units (BTU)

End-use sectors

Residential	197.7
Commercial	171.7
Industrial	391.0
Transportation	280.2

Sources of energy

Petroleum	367.8
Natural gas	369.1
Coal	290.9
Hydroelectric power	0.1
Nuclear electric power	107.2
Total state per capita consumption	405.9
Total U.S. per capita consumption	344.4
Rank among states	13
Total state energy consumption	1,040.6
Total U.S. energy consumption	90,547.4
State share of U.S. total	1.15%
Rank among states	31

Total figures include items not listed separately.
Source: U.S. Energy Information Administration; *State Energy Data Report.*

Nonfarm employment by sectors, 1997

Total	1,268,000
Construction	59,000
Manufacturing	206,000
Transportation, public utilities	72,000
Wholesale trade, retail trade	310,000
Finance, insurance, real estate	61,000
Services	317,000
Government	236,000

Figures are rounded to nearest thousand persons. Total includes mining, not listed separately.
Source: U.S. Bureau of Labor Statistics; *Employment and Earnings,* monthly.

Foreign exports, 1990-1997
In millions of dollars

Year	State	U.S.	State share
1990	2,113	394,045	0.54%
1996	3,784	624,767	0.61%
1997	4,292	688,896	0.62%

Source: U.S. Bureau of the Census; *U.S. Merchandise Trade,* series FT 900.

LAND USE

Federally owned land, 1996

	State	U.S.	State share
Total acres	52,511,000	2,271,343,000	2.31%
Federally owned	350,000	563,129,000	0.06%
Federal share	0.7%	24.8%	—

Areas are rounded to nearest thousand acres. Figures for federally owned land do not include trust properties.
Source: U.S. General Services Administration; *Inventory Report on Real Property Owned by the United States Throughout the World,* annual.

Land use, 1992
In acres, rounded to nearest thousand

Total surface area	52,658,000
Federal land	606,000
Total nonfederal	51,488,000
Developed	1,997,000
Total rural	49,491,000
Cropland	26,565,000
Pasture land	2,306,000
Range land	15,723,000
Forest land	1,331,000
Minor cover/use	3,565,000

Total surface area figures include water area not shown separately.
Source: U.S. Dept. of Agriculture; Soil Conservation Service; Iowa State University, Statistical Laboratory; *Summary Report, 1992 National Resources Inventory.*

Farms and crop acreage, 1997

	State	U.S.	Share	Rank
Farms (thousands)	64	2,058	3.11%	12
Acres (millions)	48	968	4.96%	3
Acres per farm	747	471	—	12
Acres planted	23,497	334,139	7.03%	3
Acres harvested	22,850	319,894	7.14%	3
Farm value (mill.)	$4,411	$108,805	4.05%	21

Numbers of farms are rounded to nearest thousand.
Source: U.S. Dept. of Agriculture; National Agricultural Statistics Service.

GOVERNMENT AND FINANCE

Units of local government, 1997

	State	Total U.S.	Rank
All local governments	3,950	87,453	5
Counties	105	3,043	5
Municipalities	627	19,372	8
Townships	1,370	16,629	4
School districts	324	13,726	16
Special districts	1,524	34,683	5

County ranks are based on the 48 states with county governments; township ranks are based on the 20 states with township governments; school district ranks are based on the 46 states with such districts.
Source: U.S. Bureau of the Census; *1997 Census of Governments, Government Organization,* Series GC97(1).

State government revenue, 1996

Total revenue	$7,864 mill.
General revenue	6,892 mill.
Per capita	2,672
U.S. per capita average	2,910
Rank among states	34
Intergovernmental revenue	
Total	$1,694 mill.
From federal government	1,658 mill.
From local government	37 mill.
Charges and Miscellaneous	
Total	$1,219 mill.
Current charges	729 mill.
Misc. general revenue	490 mill.
Taxes	
Total	$3,979 mill.
General sales	1,401 mill.
Selective sales	530 mill.
License taxes	203 mill.
Individual income	1,377 mill.
Corporate income	255 mill.
Other	213 mill.
Insurance trust revenue	973 mill.

Total revenue figures include items not listed separately.
Source: U.S. Bureau of the Census.

State government expenditures, 1996

General expenditures

Intergovernmental	$2,263 mill.
Direct expenditures	4,417 mill.
Total	6,680 mill.

Selected direct expenditures

Education	$2,961 mill.
Public welfare	1,102 mill.
Health, hospital	565 mill.
Highways	996 mill.
Police	40 mill.
Corrections	195 mill.
Natural resources	159 mill.
Parks and recreation	5 mill.
Government administration	235 mill.
Interest on debt	72 mill.

Other

State per capita expenditures	$2,590
U.S. per capita average	2,854
Rank among states	33
Total state expenditures	7,276 mill.
Total U.S. expenditures	859,959 mill.

Totals include items not listed separately.
Source: U.S. Bureau of the Census.

George H. Hodges (D)	1913-1915
Arthur Capper (R)	1915-1919
Henry J. Allen (R)	1919-1923
Jonathan M. Davis (D)	1923-1925
Benjamin S. Paulen (R)	1925-1929
Clyde M. Reed (R)	1929-1931
Harry H. Woodring (D)	1931-1933
Alfred M. Landon (R)	1933-1937
Walter A. Huxman (D)	1937-1939
Payne H. Ratner (R)	1939-1943
Andrew F. Schoeppel (R)	1943-1947
Frank Carlson (R)	(r) 1947-1950
Frank L. Hagaman (R)	1950-1951
Edward F. Arn (R)	1951-1955
Fred L. Hall (R)	(r) 1955-1957
John B. McCuish (R)	1957
George Docking (D)	1957-1961
John A. Anderson, Jr. (R)	1961-1965
William H. Avery (R)	1965-1967
Robert B. Docking (D)	1967-1973
Robert F. Bennett (R)	1973-1979
John W. Carlin (D)	1979-1987
Mike Hayden (R)	1987-1991
Joan Finney (D)	1991-1995
Bill Graves (R)	1995-

POLITICS

Governors since statehood

D = Democrat; R = Republican; O = other;
(r) resigned; (d) died in office; (i) removed from office

Charles Robinson (R)	1861-1863
Thomas Carney (R)	1863-1865
Samuel J. Crawford (R)	(r) 1865-1868
Nehemiah Green (R)	1868-1869
James M. Harvey (R)	1869-1873
Thomas A. Osborn (R)	1873-1877
George T. Anthony (R)	1877-1879
John P. St. John (R)	1879-1883
George W. Glick (D)	1883-1885
John A. Martin (R)	1885-1889
Lyman U. Humphrey (R)	1889-1893
Lorenzo D. Lewelling (O)	1893-1895
Edmund N. Morrill (R)	1895-1897
John W. Leedy (D)	1897-1899
William E. Stanley (R)	1899-1903
Willis J. Bailey (R)	1903-1905
Edward W. Hoch (R)	1905-1909
Walter R. Stubbs (R)	1909-1913

Composition of state legislature, 1990-1998

	Democrats	Republicans
State House (125 seats)		
1990	63	62
1992	59	66
1994	45	80
1996	48	77
1998	48	77
State Senate (50 seats)		
1990	18	22
1992	13	27
1994	13	27
1996	13	27
1998	13	27

Figures for total seats may include independents and minor
party members.
Source: Council of State Governments; *State Elective Officials
and the Legislatures.*

Composition of congressional delegations, 1989-1999

	Dem	Rep	Total
House of Representatives			
101st Congress, 1989			
State delegates	2	3	5
Total U.S.	259	174	433
102d Congress, 1991			
State delegates	2	3	5
Total U.S.	267	167	434
103d Congress, 1993			
State delegates	2	2	4
Total U.S.	258	176	434
104th Congress, 1995			
State delegates	0	4	4
Total U.S.	197	236	433
105th Congress, 1997			
State delegates	0	4	4
Total U.S.	206	228	434
106th Congress, 1999			
State delegates	1	3	4
Total U.S.	211	222	433
Senate			
101st Congress, 1989			
State delegates	0	2	2
Total U.S.	55	45	100
102d Congress, 1991			
State delegates	0	2	2
Total U.S.	56	44	100
103d Congress, 1993			
State delegates	0	2	2
Total U.S.	57	43	100
104th Congress, 1995			
State delegates	0	2	2
Total U.S.	46	53	99
105th Congress, 1997			
State delegates	0	2	2
Total U.S.	45	55	100
106th Congress, 1999			
State delegates	0	2	2
Total U.S.	45	54	99

Figures are for starts of first sessions. Figure for U.S. Representatives for 101st Congress does not include Alabama and Indiana, which had vacancies. Figures for total U.S. Representatives for 102d, 103d, and 106th Congresses do not include Vermont, which had 1 Independent-Socialist. Figure for U.S. Representatives for 104th Congress does not include Vermont, which had 1 Independent-Socialist, and California, which had 1 vacancy. Figure for U.S. Representatives for 105th Congress does not include New York, which had 1 vacancy. Figure for U.S. Senators for 104th Congress does not include Oregon, which had 1 vacancy. Figure for U.S. Senators for 106th Congress does not include New Hampshire, which had 1 Independent.

Source: U.S. Congress; *Congressional Directory,* biennial.

Voter participation in presidential elections, 1992 and 1996

	1992	1996
State voting age pop.	1,840,000	1,898,000
Total U.S. voting age pop.	189,524,000	196,509,000
State share of U.S. total	1.0%	1.0%
Rank among states	32	32
Percent of state casting vote	62.9	49.2
Percent of U.S. total voting	55.1	49.0
Rank among states	16	28

Source: U.S. Bureau of the Census.

HEALTH AND MEDICAL CARE

Medicare, 1997

	Recipients	Payments
State	386,000	$1,691 mill.
Total U.S.	37,514,000	$206,064 mill.
State share	1.03%	0.82%
Rank among states	33	33

Recipient figures are rounded to nearest thousand persons. Ranks are from highest to lowest.

Source: U.S. Health Care Financing Administration.

Medicaid, 1996

	Recipients	Payments
State	251,000	$860 mill.
Total U.S.	35,028,000	$121,419 mill.
State share	0.72%	0.71%
Rank among states	35	34

Recipient figures are rounded to nearest thousand persons. Payment figures for fiscal year reflect federal and state contribution payments. Ranks are from highest to lowest.

Source: U.S. Health Care Financing Administration.

Health insurance coverage, 1996

	State	U.S.
Total persons covered	2,280,000	225,070,000
Total persons not covered	292,000	41,716,000
Part not covered	11.4%	15.6%
Rank among states	35	—
Children not covered	82,000	10,554,000
Part not covered	11.0%	14.8%
Rank among states	30	—

Ranks are from most to fewest uninsured. Population figures are rounded to nearest thousand persons.
Source: U.S. Bureau of the Census.

HOUSING

Homeownership rates, 1985-1997

	1985	1990	1997
State	68.3%	69.0%	66.5%
Total U.S.	63.9%	63.9%	65.7%
Rank among states	23	14	37

Source: U.S. Bureau of the Census.

AIDS, syphilis, tuberculosis, and measles cases, 1997

Cases	U.S.	State	Share
AIDS	58,443	159	0.27%
Syphilis	8,550	29	0.34%
Tuberculosis	18,534	78	0.42%
Measles	148,000	NA	NA

Measles figures are rounded to nearest thousand cases.
Source: U.S. Centers for Disease Control and Prevention.

Home sales, 1990 and 1997
In thousands of units

Existing home sales	1990	1997	Change
State sales	38.8	61.6	22.8
Total U.S. sales	3,560	4,730	1,170
State share of U.S. total	1.09%	1.30%	0.21%
Rank among states	32	26	—

Source: National Association of Realtors; *Real Estate Outlook: Market Trends and Insights.*

Arapaho and Comanche council at Medicine Lodge Creek in 1867, where their leaders signed a treaty with the U.S. government designed to end wars on southern plains. (Library of Congress)

EDUCATION

Public school enrollment, 1995

State K-8 enrollment	329,000
Total U.S. K-8 enrollment	32,341,000
State share of total U.S.	1.02%
State 9-12 enrollment	134,000
Total U.S. 9-12 enrollment	12,500,000
State share of U.S. total	1.07%
State public school enroll. rate	91.7%
Overall U.S. rate.	91.6%
Rank among states.	28

Enrollment figures (which include unclassified students) are rounded to nearest thousand pupils in fall term; kindergarten (K)-8 grade figures include some prekindergarten students. Enrollment rate is based on percentage of persons 5-17 years old. Rank is from highest to lowest.

Source: U.S. National Center for Education Statistics.

Public college finances, 1996

State FTE enrollment	105,800
Total U.S. FTE enrollment	8,268,800
State share of total U.S.	1.28%
Rank among states.	28
State and local appropriations	$496,900,000
Total U.S. state and local appropriations.	$39,699 mill.
State share of total U.S.	1.25%
Rank among states.	24
State net tuition revenues.	$214,700,000
Total U.S. net tuition	$18,348,100,000
State share of total U.S.	1.17%
Rank among states.	29

FTE=Full-time equivalent; credit and noncredit enrollment including summer session in academic year ending in 1996.

Enrollments are rounded to nearest thousand students. Net tuition revenues exclude appropriation to students attending in-state public institutions. Rankings are from highest shares to lowest.

Source: Research Associates of Washington.

TRANSPORTATION AND TRAVEL

Highway mileage, 1996

Interstate	872
Other arterial.	9,320
Collector roads	34,255
Local roads	89,948
Urban roads	9,757
Rural roads	123,629
Total state	133,386
U.S. total	3,933,985
State share	3.4%
Rank among states	4

Source: U.S. Federal Highway Administration.

Motor vehicle registrations and driver licenses, 1996

In thousands

Vehicle registrations	State	U.S.	Share	Rank
Autos, trucks, buses	2,110	206,365	1.02%	32
Autos only	1,151	128,439	0.90%	32
Motorcycles	49	3,832	1.28%	26
Driver licenses	1,788	179,539	1.00%	32

Figures do not include vehicles owned by military services.
Source: U.S. Federal Highway Administration; *Highway Statistics*; *Selected Highway Statistics and Charts.*

Domestic travel expenditures, 1995

Spending by U.S. residents on overnight trips and day trips of at least 100 miles

Total expenditures in state	$2,729 mill.
Total expenditures in U.S.	$360,314 mill.
State share of total U.S.	0.76%
Rank among states.	37

Source: Travel Industry Association of America.

CRIME AND LAW ENFORCEMENT

State and local police officers, 1996

Local police	3,616
State police	552
Sheriffs	1,683
Total	6,183
Officers per 10,000 residents	24
U.S. average	25
Rank among states	17

Figures cover full-time sworn officers; totals include special police not shown separately.

Source: U.S. Bureau of Justice Statistics; *Census of State and Local Law Enforcement Agencies, 1996.*

State prison populations, 1980-1996

	State	U.S.	State share
1980	2,494	305,458	0.82%
1990	5,775	708,393	0.82%
1996	7,756	1,025,624	0.76%

Figures exclude prisoners in federal penitentiaries.
Source: U.S. Bureau of Justice Statistics.

Crime rates, 1996

Rates per 100,000 resident population

Violent crimes	State	U.S.
Total violent	414	634
Murder	6.6	7.4
Forcible rape	42.6	36.1
Robbery	96	202
Aggravated assault	268	388
Property crimes		
Total property	4,268	4,445
Burglary	981	943
Larceny/theft	3,038	2,976
Motor vehicle theft	248	526
Totals	4,682	5,079

Crime counts are estimated due to incomplete data

Source: U.S. Federal Bureau of Investigation; *Crime in the United States,* annual.

Kentucky

Location: Eastern central continental United States

Area and rank: 39,732 square miles (102,907 square kilometers); 40,411 square miles (104,664 square kilometers) including water; thirty-sixth largest state in area

Population and rank: 3,908,124 (1997); twenty-fourth largest state in population

Louisville, Kentucky's largest city. (PhotoDisc)

Capital: Frankfort

Largest city: Louisville (255,045 people in 1998)

Entered Union and rank: June 1, 1792; fifteenth state

Present constitution adopted: 1891

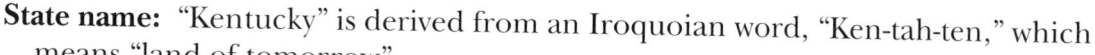

Counties: 120

State name: "Kentucky" is derived from an Iroquoian word, "Ken-tah-ten," which means "land of tomorrow"

State nickname: Bluegrass State

Motto: United we stand, divided we fall

State flag: Blue field with state seal, goldenrod sprigs below, and legend "Commonwealth of Kentucky" above

Highest point: Black Mountain — 4,139 feet (1,262 meters)

Lowest point: Mississippi River — 257 feet (78 meters)

Highest recorded temperature: 114 degrees Fahrenheit (46 degrees Celsius) — Greensburg, 1930

Lowest recorded temperature: −34 degrees Fahrenheit (−37 degrees Celsius) — Cynthiana, 1963

State song: "My Old Kentucky Home"

State tree: Tulip poplar

State flower: Goldenrod

State bird: Kentucky cardinal

National park: Mammoth Cave

Kentucky History

Kentucky, popularly known as the Bluegrass State, was the first state west of Appalachian Mountains populated by settlers from the original thirteen English colonies. From its earliest days it served as a gateway from east to west and as a border state between the North and South. For most of its history an agricultural and mining state, during the second half of the twentieth century Kentucky began a rapid transformation into a modern industrial economy.

Early History and Settlement. Evidence suggests that Native Americans first entered the area of modern Kentucky as long as fifteen thousand years ago and were primarily hunters and gatherers. Later, agriculture and trade were established leading to a period around 450 B.C.E. known as the Adena culture, when burial mounds were constructed in the northern Kentucky area. Around 1000 C.E. two distinct Native American cultures developed in the area, the Mississippian in the west and the Fort Ancient in the east; the two groups had many similarities, including the cultivation of beans and corn from the south and the use of agricultural implements including the hoe. The first European explorers found the Cherokee, Delaware, Iroquois, and Shawnee Indian tribes in the territory, although the central portion was not permanently settled by any of these groups. Instead, it seems to have been used as a common hunting ground by all of them. It may also have been reserved for a battlefield for their disputes.

During the mid-1700's English settlers from the colonies on the East Coast, in particular from Virginia, began to push over the mountains into the area known as Kentucky. The word itself is derived from an Indian word which most likely means "land of tomorrow." Among these English explorers and settlers was Dr. Thomas Walker, who charted the Cumberland Gap, the entryway to Kentucky, and was the first European to build a permanent shelter in the area.

Another and more famous traveler was Daniel Boone, who explored the area first in 1767 and again in 1769. In his second journey, Boone reached as far as the central plateau of the state, soon known as "bluegrass country" from its distinctive vegetation. Boone's initial attempt at settlement in 1773 was a failure, but the following year James Harrod and colonists from Pennsylvania established Harrodstown. Boone returned the year after, and Fort Boonesborough was established in 1775. In 1776 the state of Virginia formally claimed the entire territory, giving it the name of the County of Kentucky.

Revolution and Statehood. Native Americans were bewildered and angered by the various treaties they had made with the settlers. The Native Americans felt that these treaties had robbed them of the use of the lands which had been common to all for generations; ownership, in the European sense of the word, was an alien concept to the American Indians. As a result, many tribes throughout the area beyond the mountains allied themselves with the British during the American Revolution, and their attacks on Kentucky threatened the entire American settlement. In response, pioneer George Rogers Clark launched an offensive against the British and Native American strongholds north of the Ohio River. In a campaign that pitted small forces against one another in extremely difficult terrain in the middle of winter, Clark won a crucial victory when he forced the besieged British to surrender the frontier fort of Vincennes in 1779. However, Kentucky remained under threat from British and Native American attack until the Battle of Blue Licks in 1782, which has been called "the last battle of the Revolution."

Shortly after the Revolution ended in American independence, Kentuckians began agitating for their own independence, with the creation of a state separate from Virginia. During the 1780's, ten separate conventions were held, which gradually drafted the provisions that eventually established Kentucky as a state in its own right. On June 1, 1792, Kentucky was admitted to the Union as the fifteenth state, with Frankfort as its capital. It was the first state of the new United States established west of the Alleghenies.

During the years that followed, Kentucky encouraged one struggle, the War of 1812 against En-

gland, and sought to avoid a second, the American Civil War. Kentucky's most famous statesman of the years before the Civil War, Henry Clay, played a key role in both efforts. As a War Hawk congressman in the early 1800's, Clay advocated a conflict with Great Britain that he and others hoped could lead to the United States acquiring Canada. Later, as a U.S. Senator, Clay helped craft the Missouri Compromise of 1820 and the Compromise of 1850, which delayed, if they did not prevent, war between the states over slavery.

The Civil War and Early Modern Times. As a border state, Kentucky shared qualities of both the North and South. The majority of its residents were small farmers who owned few or no slaves, and they were inclined to neutrality in the Civil War. There were a number of slaveholders in the broad central portion of the state, and while their sympathies were with the South, they also sought to remain aloof from the struggle. The northern part of the state shared in the developing commerce of the Ohio Valley, and crops of tobacco and cotton were often shipped south down the Mississippi to New Orleans; thus all parts of the state feared that war would disrupt this commerce. Along the eastern, more mountainous portions of the state, where slaves were few, pro-Union sentiment was strongest. Perhaps the fact that most dramatically illustrated the state's precariously balanced position was the fact that both Abraham Lincoln, president of the Union, and Jefferson Davis, president of the Confederacy, were born in Kentucky within a year of one another.

As the controversy over slavery grew more intense and the nation drifted toward war, Kentucky hoped to find yet one more compromise to avert struggle. When the Civil War finally erupted in 1861, Kentucky declared its official neutrality and was promptly invaded by both the Confederacy and the Union, which seized strategic points in the state. Some seventy thousand Kentuckians served with the Union forces; approximately thirty thousand rallied to the Confederacy. After a powerful Confederate thrust north was turned back in the summer of 1862, Kentucky was kept firmly in Union hands for the duration of the war.

Following the Civil War, Kentucky continued to develop its agriculture, most notably the tobacco industry. In addition, the state expanded its reputation for outstanding horse breeding and racing; the first Kentucky Derby was held in Louisville in 1875. Whiskey, especially bourbon, had been produced in the state since the 1820's and became world famous for its quality. The expansion of the railroads into the eastern, more mountainous portions of the state opened new coal fields for exploitation, often through the destructive process of strip-mining, which left a barren wasteland behind. Life for coal miners and their families was hard and often dangerous.

The Great Depression, which began in 1929, coupled with years of drought and then flood, caused enormous damage to Kentucky's economy. By 1940 Kentucky ranked last in the nation for per capita income. President Franklin Roosevelt's New Deal and then the economic energy unleashed by World War II brought a measure of recovery to the state, including even parts of the Appalachian Mountains. However, poverty remained an endemic problem, especially in Appalachia, even through President Lyndon Johnson's Great Society programs of the mid-1960's.

The Modern Era. After World War II, northern Kentucky in particular experienced an economic boom, with growth in manufacturing companies, which supplied industries in fields such as chemicals, automotives, office supplies, electric appliances, and wood products. In addition, the state took the lead in fields such as health care, with Humana, a Kentucky-formed company and one of the largest health-care corporations in the United States, having established its headquarters in Louisville. State government actively sought to recruit industry, especially "light industry" which can fit into the Kentucky environment with minimal impact on natural resources. Such concerns are important, as horse breeding and tourism are major parts of Kentucky's overall economic picture and depend on precisely these natural resources for their continued viability.

President Abraham Lincoln is closely identified with Illinois, but he was born in Hardin County, Kentucky, where this memorial marks his birthplace. (PhotoDisc)

Kentucky also took its place in the developing automobile industry in the Southeast. Under Democratic governor Martha Layne Collins, the state recruited a $3.5 billion investment by Japanese automaker Toyota in Kentucky, which, by the early 1990's, was employing more than twenty thousand workers. The success of Toyota in Kentucky was one of the reasons that other international automobile makers chose to locate in the area, most notably BMW in South Carolina in 1993 and Mercedes-Benz in Alabama in 1994. In addition to the automobile manufacturing plants themselves, the companies also attracted large numbers of suppliers for the parts needed in the production of the finished vehicle.

Michael Witkoski

Thunder Gulch, ridden by Gary Stevens, winning the 121st running of the Kentucky Derby, the nation's most prestigious thoroughbred horse racing event, at Louisville's Churchill Downs, in May, 1995. (AP/Wide World Photos)

Kentucky Time Line

1671	Thomas Batts and Robert Fallam of Virginia reach Ohio Valley.
1682	René-Robert Cavalier, sieur de La Salle, claims Kentucky as part of Louisiana Territory for France.
1750	Dr. Thomas Walker discovers Cumberland Gap.
1751	Christopher Gist explores area along Ohio River.
1763	France cedes Louisiana Territory to Britain.
1769	Daniel Boone and John Finley explore Kentucky.
1774	James Harrod founds Harrodstown, later Harrodsburg.
1775	Daniel Boone blazes Wilderness Road and founds Boonesborough.
Dec. 6, 1776	Kentucky County is created by Virginia.
1778	Settlers break American Indian siege of Boonesborough.
1778	George Rogers Clark organizes expedition against British in Ohio valley.
Aug. 19, 1782	Last battle of American Revolution fought at Blue Licks, near Mount Olivet.
June 1, 1792	Kentucky ratifies Constitution to become fifteenth state.
1794	General "Mad Anthony" Wayne defeats Native Americans at Fallen Timbers, ending their attacks on settlers in Kentucky.
1796	Wilderness Road opens to wagons.

(continued)

1798	Legislature passes Kentucky Resolutions, opposing Alien and Sedition Acts.
1811	Henry Clay is elected to Congress.
1819	While drilling for salt, Martin Beatty finds petroleum in Cumberland River.
1830	Louisville and Portland Canal opens.
1849	Zachary Taylor, Kentucky native, is elected 12th president of United States.
1861	Kentucky declares itself neutral in Civil War, but is invaded by both Union and Confederate troops.
1862	Union forces win victory over Confederates at Perryville.
1865	University of Kentucky is founded at Lexington.
May 17, 1875	First Kentucky Derby is held at Churchill Downs near Louisville.
1891	New state constitution is adopted.
1926	Mammoth Cave National Park is established.
1937	Worst recorded flood of Ohio River occurs.
1937	United States builds gold depository at Fort Knox.
1944	Tennessee Valley Authority completes Kentucky Dam on Tennessee River.
1950	Atomic energy plant is built near Paducah.
1959	Cumberland Gap National Historical Park is dedicated.
1962	Federal government gives Kentucky control of certain nuclear energy materials, making it the first state granted this power.
1966	Kentucky passes a wide-ranging civil rights law, making it the first southern state to do so.
1966	Barkley Dam on Cumberland River is dedicated.
1982	Martha Layne Collins becomes first woman elected governor of Kentucky.
1985	Toyota automotive company announces construction of manufacturing plant near Georgetown, Kentucky.
1988	Voters approve state lottery.

Notes for Further Study

Published Sources. Two good books of introductory studies of Kentucky are M.Wharton's *Bluegrass Land and Life* (1992), which concentrates on the broad sweep of its historical development, economics, and popular culture, and Lowell H. Harrison and James C. Klotter's *A New History of Kentucky* (1997), a comprehensive survey of Kentucky from prehistoric to modern times, with a thorough review of developments in the twentieth century. In *Our Kentucky: A Study of the Bluegrass State* (1992), edited by James C. Klotter, a variety of authors and scholars examine the state's historical development and current status.

The state's agriculture is discussed in Thomas D. Clark's *Agrarian Kentucky* (1977). *Kentucky Government and Politics* (1984), edited by Joel Goldstein, examines the state's political system. Economic difficulty in Kentucky's Appalachians is explored in *Poverty, Politics, and Health Care: An Appalachian Experience* (1975), by Richard A. Couto. Interesting Kentucky facts can be found in Ernie Couch and Jill Couch's *Kentucky Trivia* (1992).

Web Resources. An excellent place to begin is the commonwealth of Kentucky homepage, the official site of the Kentucky state government (http://www.state .ky.us). This site is especially useful when supplemented with the home page of the Kentucky legislature (http:// www.lrc.state.ky.us/home.htm) and the Kentucky State Government Links (http:www.kentuckycoal.org/kygov .htm), both of which are connected with a wealth of official information, statistics, and data. The Kentucky State History Center (http://www.state.ky.us/agencies/khs/hcenter), which opened in 1999, also has a Web site worth visiting. Those interested in business conditions in the state should consult the Kentucky Chamber of Commerce site (http://www.kentuckychamber.com). For contemporary events, the Lexington Herald-Leader Online (http://www.kentuckyconnect.com/herald leader) has outstanding resources. As one of Kentucky's premiere newspapers, the *Herald-Leader* offers excellent insights into the state's economic, political, and cultural events.

The cultural and scenic sides of Kentucky can be found at a number of Web sites. One good entry is the Great Kentucky Getaway Guide (http://tour/tour.htm). This gives visitors a good overview of what the state has to offer both casual tourists and permanent residents. Kentucky has a wealth of folk art, especially in its Appalachian region, which can be studied through the Folk Art Center Web site (http://www.kyfolkart.org). For western Kentucky, and indeed the entire Ohio Valley, one of the most important natural wonders is Mammoth Cave, the Web site of which can be visited at Mammoth Cave Online (http://www.mammothcave.com).

Counties

County	Sq. miles	1996 pop.	County	Sq. miles	1996 pop.
Adair	406.9	16,460	Floyd	394.3	43,744
Allen	346.1	15,844	Franklin	210.5	46,410
Anderson	202.7	17,734	Fulton	209.0	7,794
Ballard	251.2	8,252	Gallatin	98.8	6,409
Barren	491.0	36,255	Garrard	231.2	13,251
Bath	279.4	10,143	Grant	259.9	19,269
Bell	360.8	30,193	Graves	555.7	35,601
Boone	246.3	72,926	Grayson	503.7	22,910
Bourbon	291.4	19,199	Green	288.7	10,582
Boyd	160.2	50,263	Greenup	346.2	37,183
Boyle	181.6	26,945	Hancock	188.8	8,750
Bracken	203.2	8,237	Hardin	628.0	89,404
Breathitt	495.2	15,640	Harlan	467.2	35,411
Breckinridge	572.4	16,901	Harrison	309.7	17,170
Bullitt	299.1	57,161	Hart	416.0	16,328
Butler	428.1	11,701	Henderson	440.2	44,444
Caldwell	347.0	13,290	Henry	289.3	14,581
Calloway	386.3	32,579	Hickman	244.5	5,306
Campbell	151.6	87,233	Hopkins	550.6	46,545
Carlisle	192.5	5,309	Jackson	346.3	12,832
Carroll	130.1	9,516	Jefferson	385.1	673,040
Carter	410.6	26,328	Jessamine	173.2	35,426
Casey	445.6	14,512	Johnson	261.6	24,147
Christian	721.4	65,445	Kenton	162.6	145,597
Clark	254.3	31,604	Knott	352.2	18,214
Clay	471.0	22,736	Knox	387.7	31,514
Clinton	197.5	9,269	Larue	263.4	12,760
Crittenden	362.2	9,400	Laurel	435.7	49,185
Cumberland	305.8	6,977	Lawrence	418.9	15,468
Daviess	462.4	90,818	Lee	209.9	7,906
Edmonson	302.6	11,076	Leslie	404.0	13,523
Elliott	234.0	6,584	Letcher	339.1	26,744
Estill	254.0	15,494	Lewis	484.5	13,516
Fayette	284.5	239,942	Lincoln	336.6	21,781
Fleming	351.1	13,161	Livingston	316.1	9,290

(continued)

County	Sq. miles	1996 pop.
Logan	555.7	25,902
Lyon	215.8	7,849
McCracken	251.1	64,940
McCreary	427.7	16,583
McLean	254.3	9,756
Madison	440.7	64,297
Magoffin	309.5	13,804
Marion	346.7	17,001
Marshall	304.9	29,683
Martin	230.7	12,658
Mason	241.1	16,891
Meade	308.5	27,522
Menifee	203.9	5,483
Mercer	250.9	20,412
Metcalfe	290.9	9,369
Monroe	330.8	11,314
Montgomery	198.6	20,492
Morgan	381.3	13,420
Muhlenberg	474.7	31,857
Nelson	422.7	34,332
Nicholas	196.6	6,942
Ohio	593.8	21,826
Oldham	189.2	42,287
Owen	352.2	9,905
Owsley	198.1	5,481
Pendleton	280.0	13,757
Perry	342.2	31,199
Pike	787.7	73,389
Powell	180.1	12,409
Pulaski	661.6	55,065
Robertson	100.1	2,209
Rockcastle	317.5	15,627
Rowan	280.8	21,768
Russell	253.5	16,401
Scott	285.2	28,565
Shelby	384.2	28,227
Simpson	236.2	16,084
Spencer	185.9	8,649
Taylor	269.8	22,712
Todd	376.4	11,225
Trigg	443.4	11,857
Trimble	148.9	7,246
Union	345.1	16,508
Warren	545.2	85,545
Washington	300.6	10,815
Wayne	459.4	18,703
Webster	334.7	13,524
Whitley	440.2	35,668
Wolfe	222.8	7,363
Woodford	190.7	22,040

Source: U.S. Census Bureau; National Association of Counties.

Cities
With 10,000 or more residents

Rank	City	Population
1	Louisville	255,045
2	Lexington-Fayette	241,749

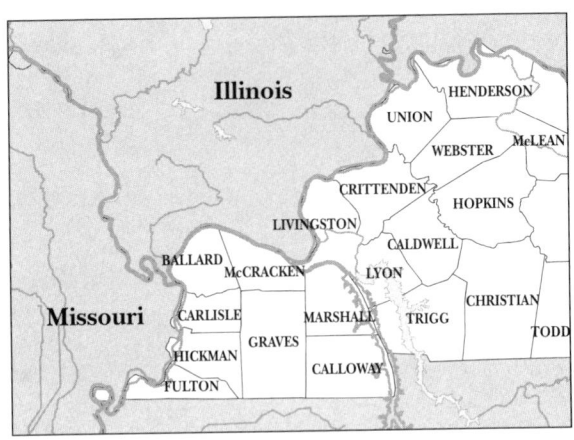

Rank	City	Population
3	Owensboro	54,041
4	Bowling Green	44,822
5	Covington	40,389
6	Hopkinsville	32,045
7	Richmond	27,644
8	Henderson	26,457
9	Frankfort	26,418
10	Paducah	25,883
11	Jeffersontown	25,678
12	Ashland	22,402
13	Elizabethtown	19,905
14	Florence	19,501
15	Radcliff	19,472
16	Madisonville	19,034
17	Nicholasville	17,099
18	Erlanger	16,900
19	Shively	16,608
20	St. Matthews	16,583
21	Danville	16,470
22	Newport	16,455
23	Winchester	15,937
24	Murray	15,905
25	Fort Thomas	14,929
26	Georgetown	14,365
27	Glasgow	14,062
28	Independence	13,745

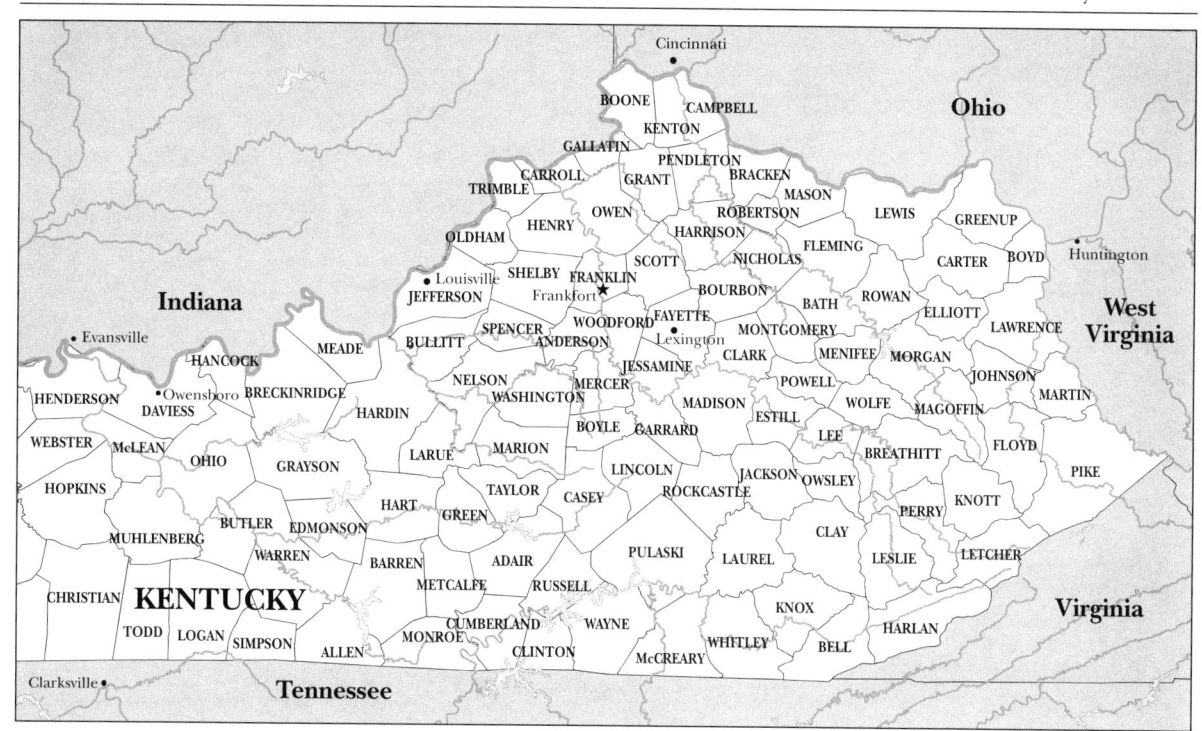

Rank	City	Population
29	Somerset	12,618
30	Campbellsville	10,776
31	Middlesborough	10,397
32	Mayfield	10,370

Rank	City	Population
33	Berea	10,341

Population figures are estimated for mid-1998.
Source: U.S. Bureau of the Census.

Index to Tables

NA = Reliable data are not available.

DEMOGRAPHICS

Resident state and national populations, 1970-1997

Population figures given in thousands

	State pop.	U.S. pop.	Share	Rank
1970	3,221	203,302	1.6%	23
1980	3,661	226,546	1.6%	23
1985	3,695	237,924	1.6%	23
1990	3,687	248,765	1.5%	23
1995	3,856	262,761	1.5%	24
1997	3,908	267,636	1.5%	24

Source: U.S. Bureau of the Census.

Resident population by age, 1997

Age group	Total population
Under 5 years	257,000
5 to 17 years	704,000
18 to 24 years	399,000
25 to 34 years	563,000
35 to 44 years	633,000
45 to 54 years	512,000
55 to 64 years	351,000
65 to 74 years	269,000
75 to 84 years	164,000
85 years and over	55,000
Portion of residents 65 and older	12.5%
National average	12.7%

Population figures are rounded to nearest thousand persons; figures include armed forces personnel stationed in state.
Source: U.S. Bureau of the Census.

Resident population by race, Hispanic origin, 1997

	State pop.	Share	U.S.
All residents	3,908,000	100.0%	100.0%
Hispanic white	26,000	0.7%	10.0%
non-Hispanic white	3,567,000	91.3%	72.7%
African American	283,000	7.2%	12.7%
Native American	6,000	0.2%	0.9%
Asian, Pacific Islander	26,000	0.7%	3.8%

Source: U.S. Bureau of the Census.

Projections of state population, 2000-2025

	Model A Uses interstate migration observed from 1975-1994	Model B Uses Bureau of Economic Analysis employment projections
Year	Population	Population
2000	3,995,000	3,990,000
2005	4,098,000	4,109,000
2010	4,170,000	4,220,000
2015	4,231,000	4,322,000
2020	4,281,000	4,411,000
2025	4,314,000	4,480,000

All population projections, including those for 2000, were calculated in 1997.

Source: U.S. Bureau of the Census, Population Paper Listings PPL-47.

VITAL STATISTICS

Average lifetime in years by race, 1989-1991

	State	U.S.	Rank
All residents	74.37	75.37	40
White residents	74.65	76.13	47
Black residents	70.16	69.16	9

Ranks are from longest-lived to least longest-lived. Ranks exclude Alaska, for which reliable data are not available. Rank for black residents is based on the 32 states for which reliable data are available.

Source: U.S. National Center for Health Statistics.

Infant mortality rates, 1980 and 1995

	State	U.S.
All residents		
1980	12.9	12.6
1995	7.6	7.6
White residents		
1980	12.0	11.0
1995	7.4	6.3
Black residents		
1980	22.0	21.4
1995	10.7	15.1

Figures represent deaths per 1,000 live births of resident infants under 1 year old, exclusive of fetal deaths; all-residents figures include other races not listed separately.
Source: U.S. National Center for Health Statistics.

Marriages and divorces

Marriages in 1996. 43,300
Rate per 1,000 population, 1995 . . . . 12.3
U.S. rate, 1995 . . . . 8.9
Rank among all states. 6

Divorces in 1996 21,200
Rate per 1,000 population, 1995. . . . . 5.9
U.S. rate, 1995 . . . . 4.4
Rank among all states. 9

Rank is from highest to lowest in country.
Source: U.S. National Center for Health Statistics.

Death rates by leading causes, 1995
Deaths per 100,000 resident population

Cause	State	U.S.
Heart disease	315.8	280.7
Cancer	229.2	204.9
Cerebrovascular diseases	63.9	60.1
Accidents and adverse effects	44.2	35.5
Motor vehicle accidents	22.0	16.5
Chronic obstructive pulmonary diseases	48.1	39.2
Diabetes mellitus	25.1	22.6
HIV	5.6	NA
Suicide	12.4	11.9
Homicide	6.5	8.7
All causes	963.7	880.0
Rank in overall death rate among states		12

Figures exclude nonresidents who die in state. Causes of death follow International Classification of Diseases. Rank is from highest to lowest in country.
Source: U.S. National Center for Health Statistics.

ECONOMY

Gross state product, 1990-1996
In current dollars

	State product	Increase
1990	$67.7 billion	
1993	$79.9 billion	
1994	$86.1 billion	7.76%
1995	$90.6 billion	5.23%
1996	$95.4 billion	5.30%

Source: U.S. Bureau of Economic Analysis; *Survey of Current Business*, June, 1998.

Gross state product by industry, 1996
In billions

Farms, forestry, fisheries	$2.1
Construction	3.2
Manufacturing	26.6
Transportation, public utilities	7.6
Wholesale trade	5.3
Retail trade	8.2
Finance, insurance, real estate	9.1
Services	12.4
Government	11.7
State total	$89.3
Total U.S.	$6,923.8
State share	1.29%
Rank among states	26

Total figures include mining, not listed separately.
Source: U.S. Bureau of Economic Analysis; *Survey of Current Business*, June, 1998.

Personal income per capita, 1990 and 1997
In current dollars

	1990	1997
Per capita income	$15,106	$20,657
U.S. average	$19,188	$25,598
Rank among states	43	41

1997 data are preliminary.
Source: U.S. Bureau of Economic Analysis; *Survey of Current Business*, May, 1998.

Energy consumption, 1995
In trillions of British thermal units (BTU)

End-use sectors

Residential	317.2
Commercial	196.0
Industrial	826.4
Transportation	430.8

Sources of energy

Petroleum	620.4
Natural gas	245.6
Coal	927.6
Hydroelectric power	35.3
Nuclear electric power	0
Total state per capita consumption	459.0
Total U.S. per capita consumption	344.4
Rank among states	6
Total state energy consumption	1,770.4
Total U.S. energy consumption	90,547.4
State share of U.S. total	1.96%
Rank among states	18

Total figures include items not listed separately.
Source: U.S. Energy Information Administration; *State Energy Data Report*.

Nonfarm employment by sectors, 1997

Total	1,714,000
Construction	82,000
Manufacturing	316,000
Transportation, public utilities	97,000
Wholesale trade, retail trade	410,000
Finance, insurance, real estate	69,000
Services	425,000
Government	291,000

Figures are rounded to nearest thousand persons. Total includes mining, not listed separately.
Source: U.S. Bureau of Labor Statistics; *Employment and Earnings*, monthly.

Foreign exports, 1990-1997
In millions of dollars

Year	State	U.S.	State share
1990	3,175	394,045	0.81%
1996	6,385	624,767	1.02%
1997	7,953	688,896	1.15%

Source: U.S. Bureau of the Census; *U.S. Merchandise Trade*, series FT 900.

LAND USE

Federally owned land, 1996

	State	U.S.	State share
Total acres	25,512,000	2,271,343,000	1.12%
Federally owned	1,083,000	563,129,000	0.19%
Federal share	4.2%	24.8%	—

Areas are rounded to nearest thousand acres. Figures for federally owned land do not include trust properties.

Source: U.S. General Services Administration; *Inventory Report on Real Property Owned by the United States Throughout the World,* annual.

Land use, 1992
In acres, rounded to nearest thousand

Total surface area	25,862,000
Federal land	1,201,000
Total nonfederal	23,985,000
Developed	1,653,000
Total rural	22,332,000
Cropland.	5,092,000
Pasture land	5,859,000
Range land	0
Forest land	10,312,000
Minor cover/use.	1,069,000

Total surface area figures include water area not shown separately.

Source: U.S. Dept. of Agriculture; Soil Conservation Service; Iowa State University, Statistical Laboratory; *Summary Report, 1992 National Resources Inventory.*

Farms and crop acreage, 1997

	State	U.S.	Share	Rank
Farms (thousands)	88	2,058	4.28%	4
Acres (millions)	14	968	1.45%	23
Acres per farm	158	471	—	43
Acres planted	5,852	334,139	1.75%	18
Acres harvested	5,648	319,894	1.77%	18
Farm value (mill.)	$1,953	$108,805	1.80%	24

Numbers of farms are rounded to nearest thousand.

Source: U.S. Dept. of Agriculture; National Agricultural Statistics Service.

GOVERNMENT AND FINANCE

Units of local government, 1997

	State	Total U.S.	Rank
All local governments	1,366	87,453	23
Counties	119	3,043	3
Municipalities	434	19,372	20
Townships	0	16,629	—
School districts	176	13,726	27
Special districts	637	34,683	18

County ranks are based on the 48 states with county governments; township ranks are based on the 20 states with township governments; school district ranks are based on the 46 states with such districts.

Source: U.S. Bureau of the Census; *1997 Census of Governments, Government Organization,* Series GC97(1).

State government revenue, 1996

Total revenue	$13,788 mill.
General revenue	11,571 mill.
Per capita.	2,981
U.S. per capita average	2,910
Rank among states.	22
Intergovernmental revenue	
Total	$3,152 mill.
From federal government	3,141 mill.
From local government	11 mill.
Charges and Miscellaneous	
Total	$1,929 mill.
Current charges	1,085 mill.
Misc. general revenue	844 mill.
Taxes	
Total	$6,489 mill.
General sales	1,784 mill.
Selective sales.	1,282 mill.
License taxes	381 mill.
Individual income	2,075 mill.
Corporate income	285 mill.
Other	683 mill.
Insurance trust revenue	2,218 mill.

Total revenue figures include items not listed separately.

Source: U.S. Bureau of the Census.

State government expenditures, 1996

General expenditures

Intergovernmental	$2,825 mill.
Direct expenditures	7,778 mill.
Total	10,603 mill.

Selected direct expenditures

Education	$4,263 mill.
Public welfare	2,770 mill.
Health, hospital	638 mill.
Highways	1,059 mill.
Police	115 mill.
Corrections	226 mill.
Natural resources	255 mill.
Parks and recreation	91 mill.
Government administration	429 mill.
Interest on debt	376 mill.

Other

State per capita expenditures	$2,731
U.S. per capita average	2,854
Rank among states	28
Total state expenditures	11,842 mill.
Total U.S. expenditures	859,959 mill.

Totals include items not listed separately.
Source: U.S. Bureau of the Census.

POLITICS

Governors since statehood

D = Democrat; R = Republican; O = other;
(r) resigned; (d) died in office; (i) removed from office

Isaac Shelby (O)	1792-1796
James Garrard (O)	1796-1804
Christopher Greenup (O)	1804-1808
Charles Scott (O)	1808-1812
Isaac Shelby (O)	1812-1816
George Madison (O)	(d) 1816
Gabriel Slaughter (O)	1816-1820
John Adair (O)	1820-1824
Joseph Desha (O)	1824-1828
Thomas Metcalfe (O)	1828-1832
John Breathitt (D)	(d) 1832-1834
James T. Morehead (O)	1834-1836
James Clark (O)	(d) 1836-1839
Charles A. Wickliffe (O)	1839-1840
Robert P. Letcher (O)	1840-1844
William Owsley (O)	1844-1848
John J. Crittenden (O)	(r) 1848-1850
John L. Helm (O)	1850-1851

Lazarus W. Powell (D)	1851-1855
Charles S. Morehead (O)	1855-1859
Beriah Magoffin (D)	(r) 1859-1862
James F. Robinson (O)	1862-1863
Thomas E. Bramlette (O)	1863-1867
John L. Helm (D)	(d) 1867
John W. Stevenson (D)	(r) 1867-1871
Preston H. Leslie (D)	1871-1875
James B. McCreary (D)	1875-1879
Luke P. Blackburn (D)	1879-1883
James Proctor Knott (D)	1883-1887
Simon B. Buckner (D)	1887-1891
John Young Brown (D)	1891-1895
William O. Bradley (R)	(r) 1895-1899
William S. Taylor (R)	(i) 1899-1900
William Goebel (D)	(d) 1900
John C. W. Beckham (D)	1900-1907
Augustus E. Willson (R)	1907-1911
James B. McCreary (D)	1911-1915
Augustus O. Stanley (D)	(r) 1915-1919
James D. Black (D)	1919
Edwin P. Morrow (R)	1919-1923
William J. Fields (D)	1923-1927
Flemon D. Sampson (R)	1927-1931
Ruby Laffoon (D)	1931-1935
Albert B. Chandler (D)	(r) 1935-1939
Keen Johnson (D)	1939-1943
Simeon S. Willis (R)	1943-1947
Earle C. Clements (D)	(r) 1947-1950
Lawrence W. Wetherby (D)	1950-1955
Albert B. Chandler (D)	1955-1959
Bert T. Combs (D)	1959-1963
Edward T. Breathitt (D)	1963-1967
Louis B. Nunn (R)	1967-1971
Wendell H. Ford (D)	(r) 1971-1974
Julian M. Carroll (D)	1974-1980
John Y. Brown, Jr. (D)	1980-1984
Martha Layne Collins (D)	1984-1987
Wallace G. Wilkinson (D)	1987-1991
Brereton C. Jones (D)	1991-1995
Paul E. Patton (D)	1995-1999

Composition of state legislature, 1990-1998

	Democrats	Republicans
State House (100 seats)		
1990	68	32
1992	71	29
1994	64	36
1996	64	36
1998	65	35

	Democrats	Republicans
State Senate (38 seats)		
1990	27	11
1992	25	13
1994	21	17
1996	20	18
1998	18	20

Figures for total seats may include independents and minor party members.

Source: Council of State Governments; *State Elective Officials and the Legislatures.*

Composition of congressional delegations, 1989-1999

	Dem	Rep	Total
House of Representatives			
101st Congress, 1989			
State delegates	4	3	7
Total U.S.	259	174	433
102d Congress, 1991			
State delegates	4	3	7
Total U.S.	267	167	434
103d Congress, 1993			
State delegates	4	2	6
Total U.S.	258	176	434
104th Congress, 1995			
State delegates	1	5	6
Total U.S.	197	236	433
105th Congress, 1997			
State delegates	1	5	6
Total U.S.	206	228	434
106th Congress, 1999			
State delegates	1	5	6
Total U.S.	211	222	433
Senate			
101st Congress, 1989			
State delegates	1	1	2
Total U.S.	55	45	100
102d Congress, 1991			
State delegates	1	1	2
Total U.S.	56	44	100
103d Congress, 1993			
State delegates	1	1	2
Total U.S.	57	43	100
104th Congress, 1995			
State delegates	1	1	2
Total U.S.	46	53	99

	Dem	Rep	Total
105th Congress, 1997			
State delegates	1	1	2
Total U.S.	45	55	100
106th Congress, 1999			
State delegates	0	2	2
Total U.S.	45	54	99

Figures are for starts of first sessions. Figure for U.S. Representatives for 101st Congress does not include Alabama and Indiana, which had vacancies. Figures for total U.S. Representatives for 102d, 103d, and 106th Congresses do not include Vermont, which had 1 Independent-Socialist. Figure for U.S. Representatives for 104th Congress does not include Vermont, which had 1 Independent-Socialist, and California, which had 1 vacancy. Figure for U.S. Representatives for 105th Congress does not include New York, which had 1 vacancy. Figure for U.S. Senators for 104th Congress does not include Oregon, which had 1 vacancy. Figure for U.S. Senators for 106th Congress does not include New Hampshire, which had 1 Independent.

Source: U.S. Congress; *Congressional Directory*, biennial.

Voter participation in presidential elections, 1992 and 1996

	1992	1996
State voting age pop.	2,798,000	2,924,000
Total U.S. voting age pop.	189,524,000	196,509,000
State share of U.S. total	1.5%	1.5%
Rank among states	24	24
Percent of state casting vote	53.4	54.5
Percent of U.S. total voting	55.1	49.0
Rank among states	35	17

Source: U.S. Bureau of the Census.

HEALTH AND MEDICAL CARE

Medicare, 1997

	Recipients	Payments
State	601,000	$2,889 mill.
Total U.S.	37,514,000	$206,064 mill.
State share	1.60%	1.40%
Rank among states	23	24

Recipient figures are rounded to nearest thousand persons.
Ranks are from highest to lowest.

Source: U.S. Health Care Financing Administration.

Medicaid, 1996

	Recipients	Payments
State	641,000	$1,931 mill.
Total U.S.	35,028,000	$121,419 mill.
State share	1.83%	1.59%
Rank among states	15	20

Recipient figures are rounded to nearest thousand persons.
Payment figures for fiscal year reflect federal and state
contribution payments. Ranks are from highest to lowest.
Source: U.S. Health Care Financing Administration.

Health insurance coverage, 1996

	State	U.S.
Total persons covered	3,295,000	225,070,000
Total persons not covered	601,000	41,716,000
Part not covered	15.4%	15.6%
Rank among states	18	—
Children not covered	177,000	10,554,000
Part not covered	17.4%	14.8%
Rank among states	15	—

Ranks are from most to fewest uninsured. Population figures
are rounded to nearest thousand persons.
Source: U.S. Bureau of the Census.

AIDS, syphilis, tuberculosis, and measles cases, 1997

Cases	U.S.	State	Share
AIDS	58,443	361	0.62%
Syphilis	8,550	135	1.58%
Tuberculosis	18,534	199	1.07%
Measles	148,000	NA	NA

Measles figures are rounded to nearest thousand cases.
Source: U.S. Centers for Disease Control and Prevention.

HOUSING

Homeownership rates, 1985-1997

	1985	1990	1997
State	68.5%	65.8%	75.0%
Total U.S.	63.9%	63.9%	65.7%
Rank among states	22	31	2

Source: U.S. Bureau of the Census.

Home sales, 1990 and 1997
In thousands of units

Existing home sales	1990	1997	Change
State sales	66.4	81.1	14.7
Total U.S. sales	3,560	4,730	1,170
State share of U.S. total	1.87%	1.71%	−0.15%
Rank among states	20	23	—

Source: National Association of Realtors; *Real Estate Outlook: Market Trends and Insights.*

EDUCATION

Public school enrollment, 1995

State K-8 enrollment	468,000
Total U.S. K-8 enrollment	32,341,000
State share of total U.S.	1.45%
State 9-12 enrollment	192,000
Total U.S. 9-12 enrollment	12,500,000
State share of U.S. total	1.54%
State public school enroll. rate	93.0%
Overall U.S. rate.	91.6%
Rank among states.	22

Enrollment figures (which include unclassified students) are
rounded to nearest thousand pupils in fall term;
kindergarten (K)-8 grade figures include some
prekindergarten students. Enrollment rate is based on
percentage of persons 5-17 years old. Rank is from highest
to lowest.
Source: U.S. National Center for Education Statistics.

Public college finances, 1996

State FTE enrollment	115,800
Total U.S. FTE enrollment	8,268,800
State share of total U.S.	1.40%
Rank among states.	26
State and local appropriations	$440,700,000
Total U.S. state and local appropriations.	$39,699 mill.
State share of total U.S.	1.11%
Rank among states.	30
State net tuition revenues.	$254,700,000
Total U.S. net tuition	$18,348,100,000
State share of total U.S.	1.39%
Rank among states.	28

FTE=Full-time equivalent; credit and noncredit enrollment
including summer session in academic year ending in
1996.
Enrollments are rounded to nearest thousand students. Net

tuition revenues exclude appropriation to students attending in-state public institutions. Rankings are from highest shares to lowest.

Source: Research Associates of Washington.

TRANSPORTATION AND TRAVEL

Highway mileage, 1996

Interstate	762
Other arterial	5,526
Collector roads	18,753
Local roads	49,263
Urban roads	10,283
Rural roads	62,875
Total state	73,158
U.S. total	3,933,985
State share	1.9%
Rank among states	28

Source: U.S. Federal Highway Administration.

Motor vehicle registrations and driver licenses, 1996
In thousands

Vehicle registrations	State	U.S.	Share	Rank
Autos, trucks, buses	2,696	206,365	1.31%	29
Autos only	1,585	128,439	1.23%	29
Motorcycles	37	3,832	0.97%	30
Driver licenses	2,567	179,539	1.43%	29

Figures do not include vehicles owned by military services.
Source: U.S. Federal Highway Administration; *Highway Statistics; Selected Highway Statistics and Charts.*

Domestic travel expenditures, 1995
Spending by U.S. residents on overnight trips and day trips of at least 100 miles

Total expenditures in state	$4,034 mill.
Total expenditures in U.S.	$360,314 mill.
State share of total U.S.	1.12%
Rank among states	29

Source: Travel Industry Association of America.

CRIME AND LAW ENFORCEMENT

State and local police officers, 1996

Local police	4,089
State police	984
Sheriffs	1,113
Total	6,466
Officers per 10,000 residents	17
U.S. average	25
Rank among states	46

Figures cover full-time sworn officers; totals include special police not shown separately.
Source: U.S. Bureau of Justice Statistics; *Census of State and Local Law Enforcement Agencies, 1996.*

Crime rates, 1996
Rates per 100,000 resident population

Violent crimes	State	U.S.
Total violent	321	634
Murder	5.9	7.4
Forcible rape	31.7	36.1
Robbery	94	202
Aggravated assault	189	388
Property crimes		
Total property	2,846	4,445
Burglary	688	943
Larceny/theft	1,896	2,976
Motor vehicle theft	261	526
Totals	3,166	5,079

Crime counts are estimated due to incomplete data
Source: U.S. Federal Bureau of Investigation; *Crime in the United States,* annual.

State prison populations, 1980-1996

	State	U.S.	State share
1980	3,588	305,458	1.17%
1990	9,023	708,393	1.27%
1996	12,910	1,025,624	1.26%

Figures exclude prisoners in federal penitentiaries.
Source: U.S. Bureau of Justice Statistics.

Louisiana

Location: Southern continental United States

Area and rank: 43,566 square miles (112,836 square kilometers); 51,843 square miles (134,273 square kilometers) including water; thirty-third largest state in area

Coastline: 397 miles (639 kilometers)

Shoreline: 7,721 miles (12,423 kilometers)

Population and rank: 4,351,769 (1997); twenty-second largest state in population

State capitol building in Baton Rouge. (Louisiana Office of Tourism)

Capital: Baton Rouge

Largest city: New Orleans (465,538 people in 1998)

Became territory: March 26, 1804

Entered Union and rank: April 30, 1812; eighteenth state

Present constitution adopted: 1974

Parishes (counties): 64

State name: Louisiana takes its name from France's King Louis XIV

State nicknames: Pelican State; Sportsman's Paradise; Creole State; Sugar State

Motto: Union, justice, and confidence

State flag: Blue field with state seal design and the state motto on a banner below

Highest point: Driskill Mountain — 535 feet (163 meters)

Lowest point: New Orleans — −8 feet (−2 meters)

Highest recorded temperature: 114 degrees Fahrenheit (46 degrees Celsius) — Plain Dealing, 1936

Lowest recorded temperature: −16 degrees Fahrenheit (−27 degrees Celsius) — Minden, 1899

State songs: "Give Me Louisiana"; "You Are My Sunshine"

State tree: Bald cypress

State flower: Magnolia

State bird: Pelican

Louisiana History

Much of Louisiana lies in the Mississippi Alluvial Plain, flat lands that stretch from each side of the Mississippi River. As the river moves south to the Gulf of Mexico, the elevation of the land becomes progressively lower, and most of it is damp and swampy. Far western and northwestern Louisiana is part of the West Gulf Coastal Plain. In the northern area of this region, the land is hilly, and it becomes prairie further south. On the eastern side, near Mississippi, lies the East Gulf Coastal Plain, which is similar to the territory in the west. These three regions correspond roughly to the historical and cultural divisions of Louisiana. The swampy south central and southwestern areas have corresponded to French Roman Catholic Louisiana. The western region and the eastern region have been home to mostly Protestant, English-speaking people.

Early History. During prehistoric times, Louisiana was populated by people who lived in highly organized farming societies. These societies are often known as the Mound Builders, after the great ceremonial earth mounds they constructed. The Mound Builders may be divided into the people of the Hopewell culture, who flourished from about the first century until about 800 C.E., and the people of the Mississippian culture, who were present from about 800 C.E. until about 1500.

When the Europeans arrived, Louisiana was inhabited by Native Americans of three language groups. Those of the Caddoan language group lived in the northwestern area. Those who spoke Muskogean languages lived in east central Louisiana near the Mississippi River. Speakers of the Tunican languages generally lived near the coast of the Gulf of Mexico. Louisiana's Native American population declined as a result of warfare, diseases introduced by the Europeans, and intermarriages with Americans of European and African descent. Some, such as the majority of the Choctaw nation, were forced westward into Indian Territory in modern Oklahoma by the U.S. government in the 1830's. Contemporary Louisiana is home to communities of the Chitimacha, Houma, Tunica-Biloxi, Coushatta, and Choctaw.

European Exploration and Colonization. The Spanish and the French were the first Europeans to explore the territory of the lower Mississippi River. In 1542 a Spanish expedition led by Hernando de Soto crossed through Louisiana. At the end of the 1600's, the French explorer René-Robert Cavalier, sieur de La Salle, journeyed down the Mississippi River to its mouth and claimed all of the land drained by the Mississippi in the name of France. La Salle named this huge expanse of territory Louisiana, in honor of King Louis XIV of France.

In 1718 the French explorer Jean Baptiste Le Moyne, sieur de Bienville, founded a settlement at a strategic location near the mouth of the Mississippi on the shores of the lake that the French had named Lake Pontchartrain. Bienville named his settlement *Nouvelle-Orléans* (New Orleans) in honor of the regent of France, the Duke of Orleans. In 1722 New Orleans would become the capital of Louisiana.

The Acadians, or Cajuns, one of Louisiana's best-known population groups, arrived in the region between 1763 and 1788. These were French-speaking people from the former French colony of Acadia in Canada expelled by British troops in the French and Indian Wars (1754-1763). The Acadians settled in the swampy areas of southwestern Louisiana and on the Mississippi just north of New Orleans. Isolation enabled them to keep the French language. Although the use of French largely disappeared in other parts of Louisiana after World War I, it would continue to be spoken in the Acadian region.

The British conquest of Canada also greatly reduced the strategic value of Louisiana for France. In order to entice the Spanish into entering the war against Britain, France transferred ownership of Louisiana to Spain in 1762. The following year, France and Spain lost the war. The Louisiana territories east of the Mississippi River became the property of Britain, and Spain was allowed to keep the lands west of the Mississippi, including New Orleans. Many of the French Louisianians had been born in America—Creoles—but they retained a devotion to France. The French Creoles revolted

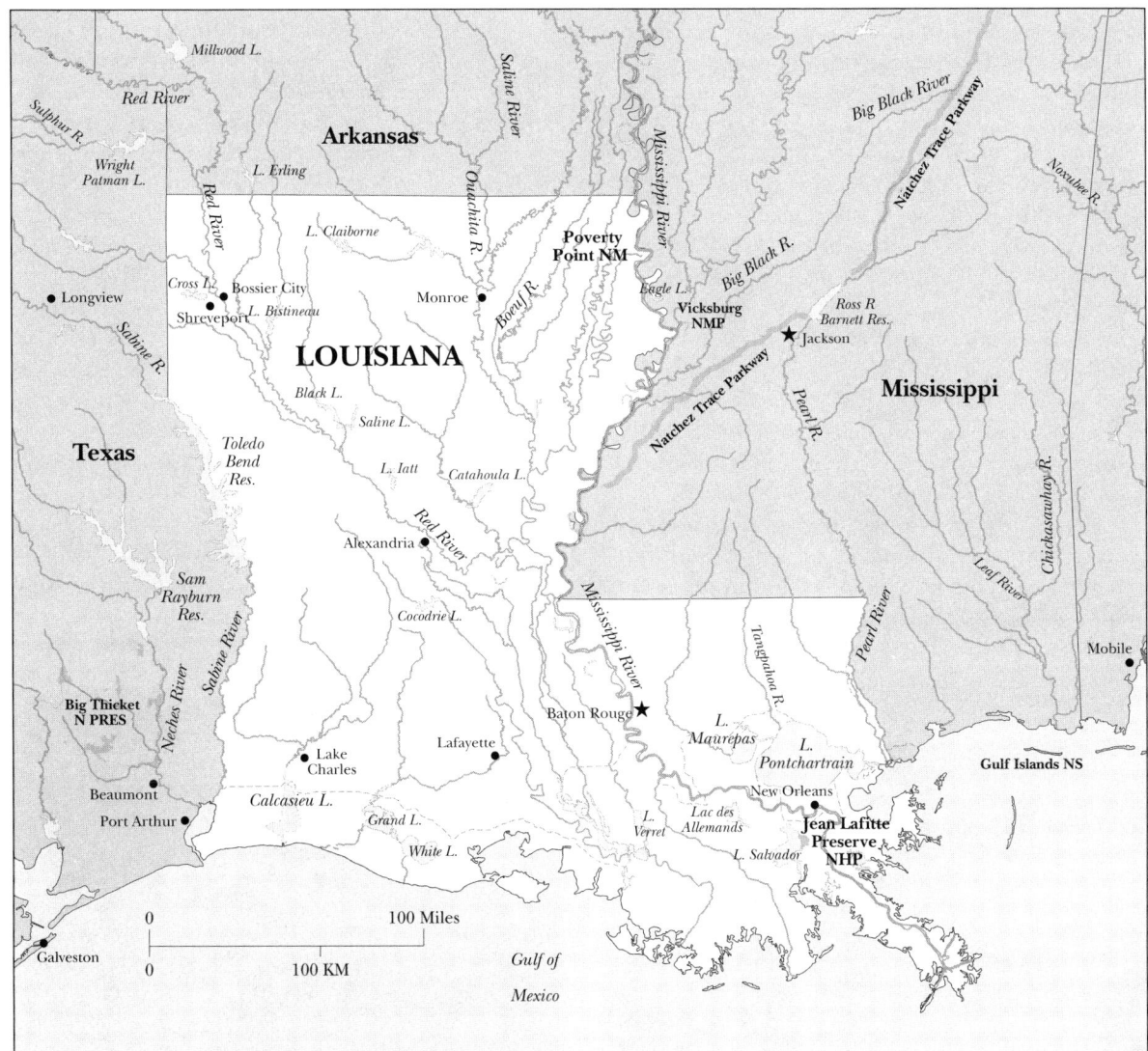

against Spanish rule, but Spanish troops quickly put down the rebellion. Spain, under the influence of French ruler Napoleon Bonaparte, returned the Louisiana territories to France in 1800. Bonaparte then sold the colony to the United States in 1803 in order to fund his own wars.

The American Period. The year after the United States purchased the huge Louisiana Territory, which extended the length of the Mississippi River, the United States split the region into the Territory of Louisiana and the Territory of Orleans. The Territory of Orleans became modern Louisiana. In 1810 American settlers in Spanish West Florida de-

clared their independence from Spain and asked to join the United States. The American governor of Louisiana, William C. C. Claiborne, incorporated West Florida, as far as the Pearl River, into Orleans Territory. In 1812 the Territory of Orleans entered the United States as the state of Louisiana.

English-speaking settlers from other areas of the United States moved into Louisiana in large numbers. Most white Louisianians, both French-speaking and English-speaking, were small farmers. The most prosperous crops, though, were cotton and sugarcane. Both of these were plantation crops, which required intensive labor. As a result, slavery became a prominent part of the economic and social life of the state, especially in the southwestern bayou country, where the sugarcane flourished. Slave markets also became important to the economy of New Orleans.

One of the unique racial characteristics of Louisiana was the existence of a large group of free people of mixed race, known as the *gens de couleur libres*, or free people of color. Free people of color were sometimes quite prosperous and even owned slaves. According to historian John Hope Franklin, 3,000 of the 10,689 free people of color in New Orleans were slaveowners.

Civil War and Reconstruction. By the 1850's, the southern states, which were dependent on agriculture and slavery, were losing control of the U.S. Congress and presidency to the industrialized North. Many southerners believed that the southern way of life, including the institution of slavery, could only be preserved by seceding from the United States. In 1861, after the election of U.S. president Abraham Lincoln, southern states began declaring their independence. Louisiana withdrew from the union on April 12, 1861. One year later, though, the U.S. Navy captured New Orleans and soon afterward captured Baton Rouge.

Louisiana still had a large number of people of mixed race after the Civil War, and many of them were well educated. They made up the core of Louisiana's black political leadership during Reconstruction (1866-1877), when about one-third of the state's governmental leaders were black. In 1872 Louisiana's P. B. S. Pinchback became the first black governor in the United States.

After the withdrawal of Union troops, whites in the state reacted violently against Reconstruction. Taking control of the government, whites systematically excluded African Americans from many areas of public life. Legal segregation and the prevention of voting and political organization by African

New Orleans's famous French Quarter recalls Louisiana's early history as a French colony. (PhotoDisc)

The crowding of carnival masks in a store window foretokens the coming of New Orleans's annual Mardi Gras, a festival with roots going back to 1838. (PhotoDisc)

Americans continued until the 1960's, when Louisiana became a focal point of the Civil Rights movement.

The Legacy of Huey Long. Louisiana continued to be a rural and agricultural state after the Civil War. During the 1920's, prices of agricultural goods, especially cotton, dropped. The charismatic politician Huey P. Long rose to power by championing the interests of workers and small farmers. One of Long's chief targets was Standard Oil Company, which had begun operating in Louisiana after the discovery of oil and gas deposits in the early twentieth century. Brilliant and ruthless, Long became governor in 1928. In 1930 he was elected U.S. senator, but he waited until 1932 to take his seat in the Senate, placing a hand-picked successor in the governor's position.

By the time Long was assassinated in 1935, he had almost total control over the Louisiana govern-

ment. He helped to improve the lives of many Louisianians, but he also raised the level of corruption in state government. The Long political machine continued to operate under Huey's brother Earl Long through the 1950's, and the good and bad legacies of Huey Long would long remain with Louisiana politics.

Social and Economic Change. Although historically Louisiana has been a rural and agricultural state, the period after World War II saw substantial movement to cities. By 1990, 68 percent of Louisiana's people lived in urban areas. Sugarcane and rice farming continued to be economically important, but these agricultural activities became heavily mechanized and use only a small amount of human labor, mostly at planting and harvest times. Oil mining became increasingly important in the late twentieth century, and among the states Louisiana is second only to Texas in oil production.

Baton Rouge, the state capital and chief port. (Louisiana Office of Tourism/S. C. Spencer)

Louisiana has one of the largest African American populations in the United States. About one out of every three Louisianians was African American in 1997. Despite the state's history of slavery and racial segregation, black Louisianians have made substantial progress toward political equality. During the 1990's, the state legislature was 16 percent black, and by 1992 there were two black Louisianians in the U.S. House of Representatives. One of these representatives, Cleo Fields, made it into the run-offs for governor in 1996. Despite these advances, incomes and living conditions of African Americans in Louisiana lagged far behind those of whites. It also appeared that racism was still prevalent. David Duke, a former leader of the Ku Klux Klan, won a majority of white votes in the 1991 election for governor. Duke was defeated only because black voters turned out in record numbers.

Carl L. Bankston III

Louisiana Time Line

1500's	Mound Builder cultures flourish along the Mississippi River and in other areas of eastern North America.
1541-1542	Hernando de Soto discovers the Mississippi River.
Apr. 9, 1682	Robert Cavalier, sieur de La Salle, claims all the territory drained by the Mississippi River for Louis XIV of France, for whom Louisiana is named.

1718	New Orleans is founded.
1723	France moves capital of the Louisiana colonies from Biloxi to New Orleans.
1763	Treaty of Paris transfers Louisiana to Spain.
1764	First Acadian families begin arriving in Louisiana.
Dec. 30, 1803	United States purchases the Louisiana Territory from France for fifteen million dollars.
Mar. 26, 1804	Louisiana is divided into the Territory of Orleans (modern Louisiana) and the District of Louisiana at 33 degrees latitude.
1810	American settlers in Spanish West Florida rebel against Spain; after a brief period of independence, West Florida becomes part of the Territory of Orleans.
Apr. 30, 1812	Territory of Orleans enters the United States as the state of Louisiana.
Jan. 8, 1815	U.S. general Andrew Jackson wins the Battle of New Orleans against the invading British.
1838	New Orleans holds its first Mardi Gras parade.
1849	State capital is moved from New Orleans to Baton Rouge.
1861	Louisiana votes to secede from the Union.
Apr. 25, 1862	U.S. Navy captures New Orleans.
1868	Louisiana ratifies a new state constitution, granting blacks social and civil rights, and is readmitted to the United States.
Nov., 1872	After the impeachment of Governor Henry C. Warmoth for corruption, Lieutenant Governor P. B. S. Pinchback becomes the first black governor in the United States.
1877	Reconstruction in Louisiana ends with the election of Democratic governor Francis T. Nicholls.
May 12, 1898	Louisiana adopts a new set of voting qualifications that take the vote away from almost all black Louisianians and many poor whites.
1901	First oil in Louisiana is discovered near the town of Jennings.
1915	New Orleans-style music becomes popularly known as "jazz."
1928	Huey P. Long is elected governor of Louisiana.
Sept. 8, 1935	Dr. Carl D. Weiss assassinates Long in Baton Rouge.
1947	Kerr-McGee Corporation drills the first deep-water, off-shore oil well off the Louisiana coast, with operations based in Morgan City.
1958	State legislature votes to close desegregated schools.
1963	In the midst of controversy over integration, Tulane University in New Orleans accepts its first black students.
1975	Super Dome in New Orleans is completed.
1977	Ernest N. (Dutch) Morial is elected the first black mayor of New Orleans.
1979	David Treen becomes the first Republican governor of Louisiana since Reconstruction.
1983	Edwin W. Edwards becomes the first Louisiana governor to be elected to three terms.
1988	Louisiana has the country's highest high school dropout rate.
1991	Edwards wins a historic fourth term in a run-off against former Ku Klux Klansman David Duke.

Notes for Further Study

Published Sources. Author Carl A. Brasseaux is one of the most prolific and respected authorities on Louisiana history, especially on the history of Acadian Louisiana. Brasseaux's *Acadian to Cajun: Transformation of a People, 1803-1877* (1992) is particularly recommended for its accurate, well-documented view of changing life in southwestern Louisiana. *Creoles of Color in the Bayou Country* (1996), also by Brasseaux, gives a fascinating account of Louisiana's free people of color. The *Historical Atlas of Louisiana* (1995) gives the places and facts of Louisiana history. For a short general overview of Louisiana history, readers should consult *A Guide to the History of Louisiana* (1982), edited by Light Townsend Cummins and Glen Jeansonne.

One of the best books on Louisiana's complicated political history is T. Harry Williams's biography *Huey Long* (1969). *Socks on a Rooster: Louisiana's Earl K. Long* (1967), by Richard B. McCaughan, is an engaging look at Huey's eccentric brother, Earl, who was committed to a mental institution while serving as governor, escaped, and retook control of the state government. For later political history, two books by Louisiana political commentator John Maginnis are highly recommended. *The Last Hayride* (1984) looks at the controversial political career of three-term governor Edwin W. Edwards. In *Cross to Bear* (1992), Maginnis looks at the 1991 Louisiana gubernatorial campaign, in which Edwards, who was accused of massive corruption and frequently indicted by federal authorities, ran against David Duke, former Grand Wizard of the Ku Klux Klan and alleged neo-Nazi.

New Orleans is the subject of many books and articles. *Classic New Orleans* (1993), with text by William R. Mitchell and photographs by James R. Lockhart, is a beautifully illustrated guide to the architecture and neighborhoods of the city.

Web Resources. A good starting place for obtaining information about Louisiana is Info Louisiana (http://www.state.la.us), which offers access to Louisiana state government sites. By clicking on "Learn about Louisiana," the internet user can find sites on the state's people, culture, history, archaeology, architecture, music, maps and geography, demographics and census information, and other topics. Those interested in the Civil War history of Louisiana should look at the Louisiana Civil War Map of Battles (http://californiacentralcoast.com/commun/map/civil/statepic/la.html), which provides a map of the battles fought in Louisiana and histories of each one.

Louisiana is known for its unique culture, especially for its music. One of the most interesting cultural sites on the Web is the Louisiana Author's Index (http://indigo.lib.lsu.edu/la/la.html), provided by the library of Louisiana State University. This is an alphabetical index of Louisiana writers that provides bibliographies and short biographical sketches. Those interested in learning about Louisiana music will want to visit the Web sites of the Louisiana Blues Hall of Fame (http://commerce.usunwired.net/blues) and the Rootsworld site (http://www.rootsworld.com). LouisianaRadio.com (http://www.louisianaradio.com) is devoted entirely to the music of Louisiana. Louisiana.com (http://www.lousiana.com) offers updated news on entertainment and tourist attractions in the state.

Counties

County	Sq. miles	1996 pop.
Acadia	655.3	57,590
Allen	764.6	23,892
Ascension	291.6	67,958
Assumption	338.7	22,681
Avoyelles	832.5	40,433
Beauregard	1,160.2	31,771
Bienville	810.7	16,676
Bossier	838.5	91,811
Caddo	882.1	245,095

County	Sq. miles	1996 pop.
Calcasieu	1,071.2	178,881
Caldwell	529.5	10,189
Cameron	1,313.0	8,733
Catahoula	703.7	11,155
Claiborne	754.7	17,185
Concordia	696.4	20,854
DeSoto	877.3	23,428
East Baton Rouge	455.7	395,914
East Carroll	421.5	9,154

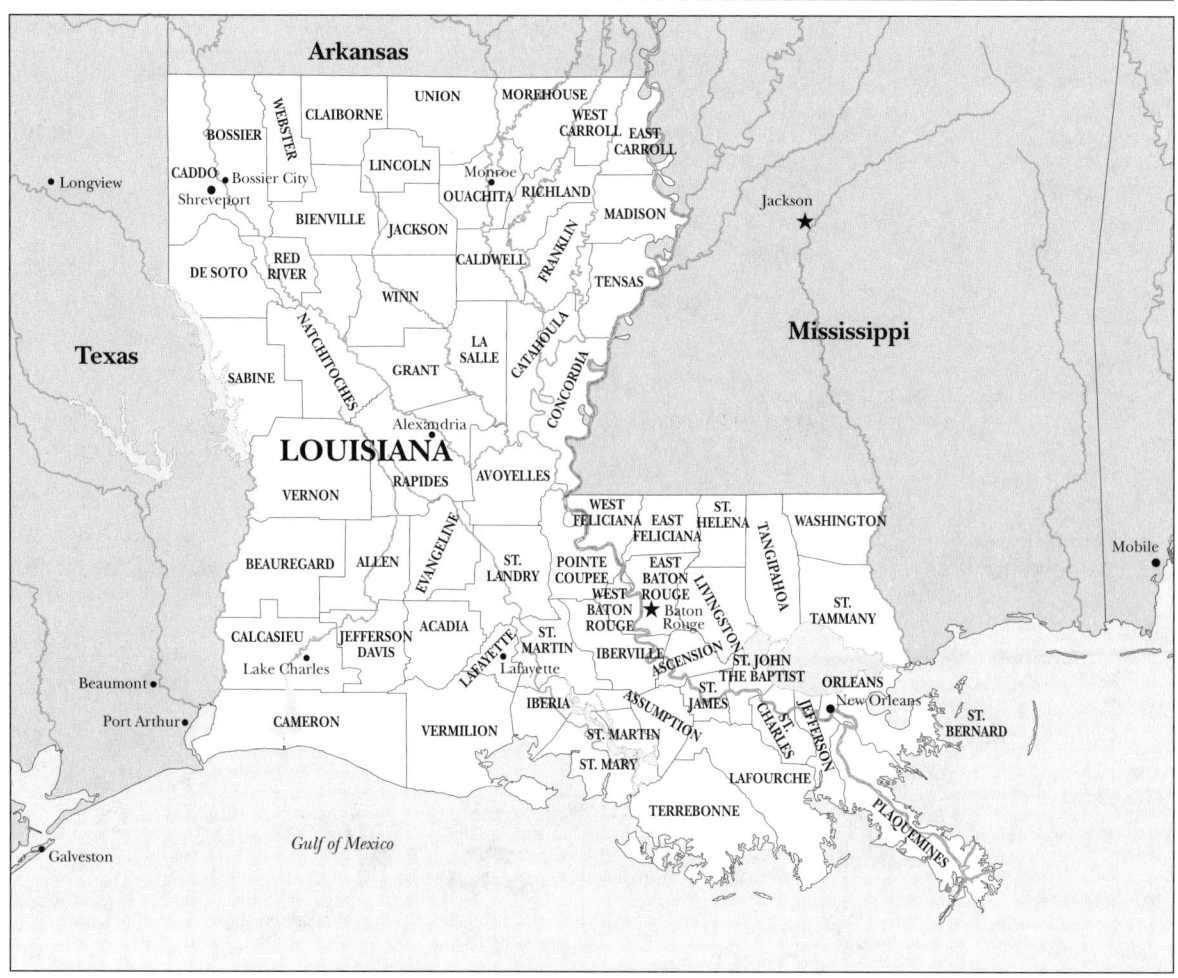

County	Sq. miles	1996 pop.	County	Sq. miles	1996 pop.
East Feliciana	453.4	20,833	Orleans	180.6	476,625
Evangeline	664.3	34,281	Ouachita	611.0	147,302
Franklin	623.4	22,078	Plaquemines	844.6	25,848
Grant	645.1	18,591	Pointe Coupee	557.4	23,200
Iberia	575.2	71,685	Rapides	1,322.7	126,290
Iberville	618.7	30,929	Red River	388.6	9,746
Jackson	570.0	15,492	Richland	558.5	20,892
Jefferson Davis	652.4	31,753	Sabine	865.3	23,741
Jefferson	305.9	455,043	Saint Bernard	465.2	66,641
Lafayette	269.9	181,851	Saint Charles	283.7	47,031
Lafourche	1,084.8	87,772	Saint Helena	408.4	9,748
LaSalle	623.9	13,840	Saint James	246.1	20,959
Lincoln	471.4	42,302	Saint John the Baptist	218.9	42,260
Livingston	648.1	82,900	Saint Landry	928.7	82,955
Madison	624.1	12,997	Saint Martin	739.9	46,239
Morehouse	794.3	31,969	Saint Mary	612.9	57,425
Natchitoches	1,256.4	38,173	Saint Tammany	854.4	178,483

(continued)

County	Sq. miles	1996 pop.
Tangipahoa	790.3	94,273
Tensas	602.5	6,883
Terrebonne	1,255.1	102,097
Union	877.7	21,607
Vermilion	1,173.9	51,299
Vernon	1,328.5	54,546
Washington	669.6	43,315

County	Sq. miles	1996 pop.
Webster	595.9	42,690
West Baton Rouge	191.2	20,616
West Carroll	359.4	12,191
West Feliciana	406.0	12,964
Winn	950.6	16,824

Louisiana's counties are called parishes.
Source: U.S. Census Bureau; National Association of Counties.

Cities
With 10,000 or more residents

Rank	City	Population
1	New Orleans	465,538
2	Baton Rouge	211,551

Rank	City	Population
3	Shreveport	188,319
4	Lafayette	113,615

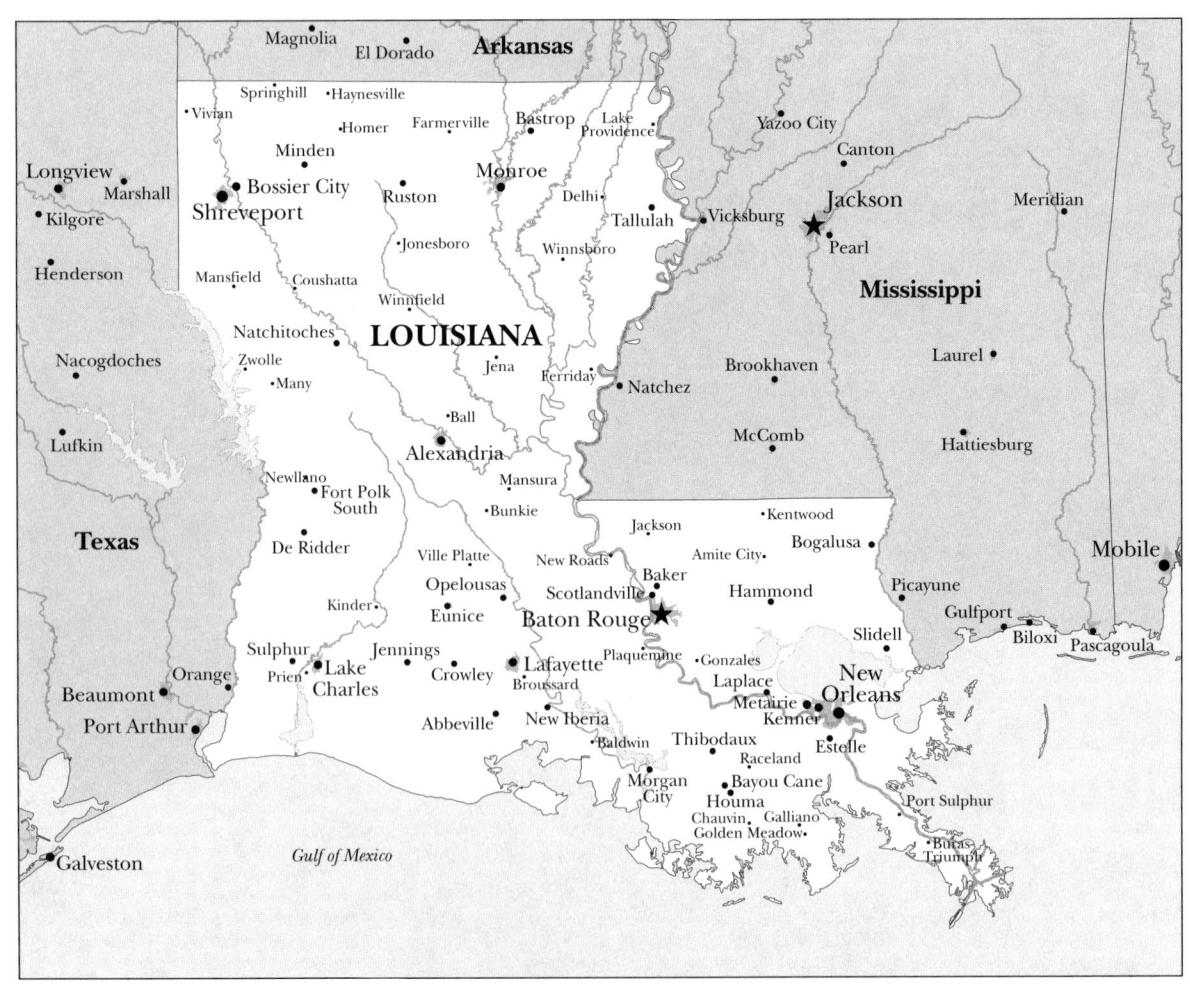

Rank	City	Population	Rank	City	Population
5	Kenner	71,641	21	West Monroe	13,901
6	Lake Charles	70,766	22	Morgan City	13,671
7	Bossier City	56,637	23	Crowley	13,554
8	Monroe	53,612	24	Bastrop	13,516
9	Alexandria	45,800	25	Bogalusa	13,444
10	New Iberia	32,664	26	Minden	13,309
11	Houma	29,964	27	Baker	13,009
12	Slidell	26,123	28	Abbeville	11,402
13	Sulphur	21,065	29	Jennings	11,314
14	Ruston	19,615	30	De Ridder	11,152
15	Opelousas	18,984	31	Eunice	11,112
16	Natchitoches	16,713	32	Westwego	11,004
17	Hammond	16,617	33	Zachary	10,353
18	Gretna	16,569			
19	Thibodaux	14,175			
20	Pineville	14,030			

Population figures are estimated for mid-1998.
Source: U.S. Bureau of the Census.

Index to Tables

NA = Reliable data are not available.

DEMOGRAPHICS

Resident state and national populations, 1970-1997

Population figures given in thousands

	State pop.	U.S. pop.	Share	Rank
1970	3,645	203,302	1.8%	20
1980	4,206	226,546	1.9%	19
1985	4,408	237,924	1.9%	19
1990	4,222	248,765	1.7%	21
1995	4,329	262,761	1.6%	21
1997	4,352	267,636	1.6%	22

Source: U.S. Bureau of the Census.

Resident population by age, 1997

Age group	Total population
Under 5 years	314,000
5 to 17 years	877,000
18 to 24 years	468,000
25 to 34 years	608,000
35 to 44 years	686,000
45 to 54 years	538,000
55 to 64 years	365,000
65 to 74 years	280,000
75 to 84 years	164,000
85 years and over	53,000
Portion of residents 65 and older	11.4%
National average	12.7%

Population figures are rounded to nearest thousand persons;
figures include armed forces personnel stationed in state.
Source: U.S. Bureau of the Census.

Resident population by race, Hispanic origin, 1997

	State pop.	Share	U.S.
All residents	4,352,000	100.0%	100.0%
Hispanic white	97,000	2.2%	10.0%
non-Hispanic white	2,785,000	64.0%	72.7%
African American	1,396,000	32.1%	12.7%
Native American	19,000	0.4%	0.9%
Asian, Pacific Islander	53,000	1.2%	3.8%

Source: U.S. Bureau of the Census.

Projections of state population, 2000-2025

	Model A Uses interstate migration observed from 1975-1994	Model B Uses Bureau of Economic Analysis employment projections
Year	Population	Population
2000	4,425,000	4,445,000
2005	4,535,000	4,558,000
2010	4,683,000	4,687,000
2015	4,840,000	4,828,000
2020	4,991,000	4,972,000
2025	5,133,000	5,111,000

All population projections, including those for 2000, were calculated in 1997.
Source: U.S. Bureau of the Census, Population Paper Listings PPL-47.

VITAL STATISTICS

Average lifetime in years by race, 1989-1991

	State	U.S.	Rank
All residents	73.05	75.37	48
White residents	74.87	76.13	45
Black residents	68.62	69.16	28

Ranks are from longest-lived to least longest-lived. Ranks exclude Alaska, for which reliable data are not available. Rank for black residents is based on the 32 states for which reliable data are available.
Source: U.S. National Center for Health Statistics.

Infant mortality rates, 1980 and 1995

	State	U.S.
All residents		
1980	14.3	12.6
1995	9.8	7.6
White residents		
1980	10.5	11.0
1995	6.2	6.3
Black residents		
1980	20.6	21.4
1995	15.3	15.1

Figures represent deaths per 1,000 live births of resident infants under 1 year old, exclusive of fetal deaths; all-residents figures include other races not listed separately.
Source: U.S. National Center for Health Statistics.

Marriages and divorces

Marriages in 1996.	38,900
Rate per 1,000 population, 1995.	9.4
U.S. rate, 1995	8.9
Rank among all states	16
Divorces in 1996	NA
Rate per 1,000 population, 1995.	NA
U.S. rate, 1995	4.4
Rank among all states	NA

Rank is from highest to lowest in country.
Source: U.S. National Center for Health Statistics.

Death rates by leading causes, 1995

Deaths per 100,000 resident population

Cause	State	U.S.
Heart disease	279.4	280.7
Cancer	214.3	204.9
Cerebrovascular diseases	58.6	60.1
Accidents and adverse effects	42.4	35.5
Motor vehicle accidents	21.0	16.5
Chronic obstructive pulmonary diseases	32.7	39.2
Diabetes mellitus	34.4	22.6
HIV	16.8	NA
Suicide	12.5	11.9
Homicide	17.6	8.7
All causes	914.4	880.0
Rank in overall death rate among states		23

Figures exclude nonresidents who die in state. Causes of death follow International Classification of Diseases. Rank is from highest to lowest in country.
Source: U.S. National Center for Health Statistics.

ECONOMY

Gross state product, 1990-1996
In current dollars

	State product	Increase
1990	$91.1 billion	
1993	$94.7 billion	
1994	$103.9 billion	9.71%
1995	$112.9 billion	8.66%
1996	$121.1 billion	7.26%

Source: U.S. Bureau of Economic Analysis; *Survey of Current Business,* June, 1998.

Gross state product by industry, 1996
In billions

Farms, forestry, fisheries	$1.3
Construction	4.4
Manufacturing	21.9
Transportation, public utilities	10.2
Wholesale trade	6.2
Retail trade	9.2
Finance, insurance, real estate	13.4
Services	16.5
Government	11.8
State total	$109.6
Total U.S.	$6,923.8
State share	1.58%
Rank among states	22

Total figures include mining, not listed separately.
Source: U.S. Bureau of Economic Analysis; *Survey of Current Business,* June, 1998.

Personal income per capita, 1990 and 1997
In current dollars

	1990	1997
Per capita income	$14,790	$20,680
U.S. average	$19,188	$25,598
Rank among states	45	40

1997 data are preliminary.
Source: U.S. Bureau of Economic Analysis; *Survey of Current Business,* May, 1998.

Energy consumption, 1995
In trillions of British thermal units (BTU)

End-use sectors

Residential	319.3
Commercial	216.1
Industrial	2,520.0
Transportation	758.2

Sources of energy

Petroleum	1,476.5
Natural gas	1,778.0
Coal	217.5
Hydroelectric power	9.9
Nuclear electric power	167.2
Total state per capita consumption	879.1
Total U.S. per capita consumption	344.4
Rank among states	2
Total state energy consumption	3,813.6
Total U.S. energy consumption	90,547.4
State share of U.S. total	4.21%
Rank among states	6

Total figures include items not listed separately.
Source: U.S. Energy Information Administration; *State Energy Data Report.*

Nonfarm employment by sectors, 1997

Total	1,847,000
Construction	116,000
Manufacturing	190,000
Transportation, public utilities	110,000
Wholesale trade, retail trade	430,000
Finance, insurance, real estate	86,000
Services	498,000
Government	364,000

Figures are rounded to nearest thousand persons. Total includes mining, not listed separately.
Source: U.S. Bureau of Labor Statistics; *Employment and Earnings,* monthly.

Foreign exports, 1990-1997
In millions of dollars

Year	State	U.S.	State share
1990	14,199	394,045	3.60%
1996	21,667	624,767	3.47%
1997	18,732	688,896	2.72%

Source: U.S. Bureau of the Census; *U.S. Merchandise Trade,* series FT 900.

LAND USE

Federally owned land, 1996

	State	U.S.	State share
Total acres	28,868,000	2,271,343,000	1.27%
Federally owned	745,000	563,129,000	0.13%
Federal share	2.6%	24.8%	—

Areas are rounded to nearest thousand acres. Figures for
  federally owned land do not include trust properties.
Source: U.S. General Services Administration; *Inventory Report
  on Real Property Owned by the United States Throughout the
  World,* annual.

Land use, 1992
In acres, rounded to nearest thousand

Total surface area	30,561,000
Federal land	1,264,000
Total nonfederal	26,373,000
Developed	1,764,000
Total rural	24,609,000
Cropland.	5,972,000
Pasture land	2,269,000
Range land.	227,000
Forest land	12,961,000
Minor cover/use.	3,181,000

Total surface area figures include water area not shown
  separately.
Source: U.S. Dept. of Agriculture; Soil Conservation Service;
  Iowa State University, Statistical Laboratory; *Summary
  Report, 1992 National Resources Inventory.*

Farms and crop acreage, 1997

	State	U.S.	Share	Rank
Farms (thousands)	27	2,058	1.31%	29
Acres (millions)	9	968	0.93%	35
Acres per farm	321	471	—	24
Acres planted	4,040	334,139	1.21%	27
Acres harvested	3,963	319,894	1.24%	27
Farm value (mill.)	$1,490	$108,805	1.37%	43

Numbers of farms are rounded to nearest thousand.
Source: U.S. Dept. of Agriculture; National Agricultural
  Statistics Service.

GOVERNMENT AND FINANCE

Units of local government, 1997

	State	Total U.S.	Rank
All local governments	467	87,453	44
Counties	60	3,043	25
Municipalities	302	19,372	26
Townships	0	16,629	—
School districts	66	13,726	37
Special districts	39	34,683	48

County ranks are based on the 48 states with county
  governments; township ranks are based on the 20 states
  with township governments; school district ranks are based
  on the 46 states with such districts.
Source: U.S. Bureau of the Census; *1997 Census of Governments,
  Government Organization,* Series GC97(1).

State government revenue, 1996

Total revenue	$14,296 mill.
General revenue	11,833 mill.
Per capita.	2,726
U.S. per capita average	2,910
Rank among states.	33
Intergovernmental revenue	
Total	$4,111 mill.
From federal government	4,084 mill.
From local government	26 mill.
Charges and Miscellaneous	
Total	$2,816 mill.
Current charges	1,621 mill.
Misc. general revenue	1,195 mill.
Taxes	
Total	$4,906 mill.
General sales	1,622 mill.
Selective sales.	937 mill.
License taxes	418 mill.
Individual income	1,160 mill.
Corporate income	328 mill.
Other	441 mill.
Insurance trust revenue	2,463 mill.

Total revenue figures include items not listed separately.
Source: U.S. Bureau of the Census.

State government expenditures, 1996

General expenditures

Intergovernmental	$3,026 mill.
Direct expenditures	9,565 mill.
Total	12,591 mill.

Selected direct expenditures

Education	$4,348 mill.
Public welfare	2,976 mill.
Health, hospital	1,494 mill.
Highways	858 mill.
Police	166 mill.
Corrections	384 mill.
Natural resources	319 mill.
Parks and recreation	132 mill.
Government administration	319 mill.
Interest on debt	745 mill.

Other

State per capita expenditures	$2,901
U.S. per capita average	2,854
Rank among states	21
Total state expenditures	14,030 mill.
Total U.S. expenditures	859,959 mill.

Totals include items not listed separately.
Source: U.S. Bureau of the Census.

POLITICS

Governors since statehood

D = Democrat; R = Republican; O = other;
(r) resigned; (d) died in office; (i) removed from office

William C. C. Claiborne		1812-1816
Jacques P. Villere		1816-1820
Thomas B. Robertson	(r)	1820-1824
Henry S. Thibodaux		1824
Henry Johnson		1824-1828
Pierre A. C. B. Derbigny	(d)	1828-1829
Armand Beauvais		1829-1830
Jacques Dupre		1830-1831
Andre B. Roman (O)		1831-1835
Edward D. White (O)		1835-1839
Andre B. Roman (O)		1839-1843
Alexandre Mouton (D)		1843-1846
Isaac Johnson (D)		1846-1850
Joseph M. Walker (D)		1850-1853
Paul O. Herbert (D)		1853
Robert C. Wickliffe (D)		1853-1860
Thomas O. Moore (D)		1860-1864
Henry W. Allen	(i)	1864

George Michael D. Hahn	(r)	1864-1865
J. Madison Wells (D)	(i)	1865-1867
Benjamin F. Flanders (D)	(i)	1867-1868
Joshua Baker (D)	(i)	1868
Henry C. Warmoth (R)	(r)	1868-1872
Pinckney B. S. Pinchback (R)		1872-1873
William P. Kellogg (R)		1873-1877
Francis R. T. Nicholls (D)		1877-1880
Louis A. Wiltz (D)	(d)	1880-1881
Samuel D. McEnery (D)		1881-1888
Francis R. T. Nicholls (D)		1888-1892
Murphy J. Foster (D)		1892-1900
William W. Heard (D)		1900-1904
Newton C. Blanchard (D)		1904-1908
Jared Y. Sanders (D)		1908-1912
Luther E. Hall (D)		1912-1916
Ruffin G. Pleasant (D)		1916-1920
John M. Parker (D)		1920-1924
Henry L. Fuqua (D)	(d)	1924-1926
Oramel H. Simpson (D)		1926-1928
Huey P. Long (D)	(r)	1928-1932
Alvin O. King (D)		1932
Oscar K. Allen (D)	(d)	1932-1936
James A. Noe (D)		1936
Richard W. Leche (D)	(r)	1936-1939
Earl K. Long (D)		1939-1940
Sam Houston Jones (D)		1940-1944
James H. (Jimmie) Davis (D)		1944-1948
Earl K. Long (D)		1948-1952
Robert F. Kennon (D)		1952-1956
Earl K. Long (D)		1956-1960
James H. (Jimmie) Davis (D)		1960-1964
John J. McKeithen (D)		1964-1972
Edwin W. Edwards (D)		1972-1988
Charles E. Roemer III (D)		1988-1992
Edwin W. Edwards (D)		1992-1996
Murphy J. (Mike) Foster (R)		1996-

Composition of congressional delegations, 1989-1999

	Dem	Rep	Total
House of Representatives			
101st Congress, 1989			
State delegates	4	4	8
Total U.S.	259	174	433
102d Congress, 1991			
State delegates	4	4	8
Total U.S.	267	167	434

	Dem	Rep	Total
103d Congress, 1993			
State delegates	4	3	7
Total U.S.	258	176	434
104th Congress, 1995			
State delegates	2	5	7
Total U.S.	197	236	433
105th Congress, 1997			
State delegates	2	5	7
Total U.S.	206	228	434
106th Congress, 1999			
State delegates	2	5	7
Total U.S.	211	222	433
Senate			
101st Congress, 1989			
State delegates	2	0	2
Total U.S.	55	45	100
102d Congress, 1991			
State delegates	2	0	2
Total U.S.	56	44	100
103d Congress, 1993			
State delegates	2	0	2
Total U.S.	57	43	100
104th Congress, 1995			
State delegates	2	0	2
Total U.S.	46	53	99
105th Congress, 1997			
State delegates	2	0	2
Total U.S.	45	55	100
106th Congress, 1999			
State delegates	2	0	2
Total U.S.	45	54	99

Figures are for starts of first sessions. Figure for U.S. Representatives for 101st Congress does not include Alabama and Indiana, which had vacancies. Figures for total U.S. Representatives for 102d, 103d, and 106th Congresses do not include Vermont, which had 1 Independent-Socialist. Figure for U.S. Representatives for 104th Congress does not include Vermont, which had 1 Independent-Socialist, and California, which had 1 vacancy. Figure for U.S. Representatives for 105th Congress does not include New York, which had 1 vacancy. Figure for U.S. Senators for 104th Congress does not include Oregon, which had 1 vacancy. Figure for U.S. Senators for 106th Congress does not include New Hampshire, which had 1 Independent.
Source: U.S. Congress; *Congressional Directory*, biennial.

Composition of state legislature, 1990-1998

	Democrats	Republicans
State House (105 seats)		
1990	89	16
1992	88	16
1994	86	17
1996	76	28
1998	74	28
State Senate (39 seats)		
1990	34	5
1992	33	6
1994	33	6
1996	25	14
1998	25	14

Figures for total seats may include independents and minor party members.
Source: Council of State Governments; *State Elective Officials and the Legislatures*.

Voter participation in presidential elections, 1992 and 1996

	1992	1996
State voting age pop.	3,045,000	3,137,000
Total U.S. voting age pop.	189,524,000	196,509,000
State share of U.S. total	1.6%	1.6%
Rank among states	22	22
Percent of state casting vote	58.8	57.4
Percent of U.S. total voting	55.1	49.0
Rank among states	26	9

Source: U.S. Bureau of the Census.

HEALTH AND MEDICAL CARE

Medicare, 1997

	Recipients	Payments
State	591,000	$4,286 mill.
Total U.S.	37,514,000	$206,064 mill.
State share	1.58%	2.08%
Rank among states	24	15

Recipient figures are rounded to nearest thousand persons. Ranks are from highest to lowest.
Source: U.S. Health Care Financing Administration.

Medicaid, 1996

	Recipients	Payments
State	778,000	$2,453 mill.
Total U.S.	35,028,000	$121,419 mill.
State share	2.22%	2.02%
Rank among states	12	14

Recipient figures are rounded to nearest thousand persons. Payment figures for fiscal year reflect federal and state contribution payments. Ranks are from highest to lowest.
Source: U.S. Health Care Financing Administration.

Health insurance coverage, 1996

	State	U.S.
Total persons covered	3,378,000	225,070,000
Total persons not covered	890,000	41,716,000
Part not covered	20.9%	15.6%
Rank among states	5	—
Children not covered	260,000	10,554,000
Part not covered	22.4%	14.8%
Rank among states	3	—

Ranks are from most to fewest uninsured. Population figures are rounded to nearest thousand persons.
Source: U.S. Bureau of the Census.

AIDS, syphilis, tuberculosis, and measles cases, 1997

Cases	U.S.	State	Share
AIDS	58,443	1,094	1.87%
Syphilis	8,550	364	4.26%
Tuberculosis	18,534	345	1.86%
Measles	148,000	NA	NA

Measles figures are rounded to nearest thousand cases.
Source: U.S. Centers for Disease Control and Prevention.

HOUSING

Homeownership rates, 1985-1997

	1985	1990	1997
State	70.2%	67.8%	66.4%
Total U.S.	63.9%	63.9%	65.7%
Rank among states	12	24	38

Source: U.S. Bureau of the Census.

Home sales, 1990 and 1997
In thousands of units

Existing home sales	1990	1997	Change
State sales	41.6	52.9	11.3
Total U.S. sales	3,560	4,730	1,170
State share of U.S. total	1.17%	1.12%	-0.05%
Rank among states	31	31	—

Source: National Association of Realtors; *Real Estate Outlook: Market Trends and Insights.*

EDUCATION

Public school enrollment, 1995

State K-8 enrollment	580,000
Total U.S. K-8 enrollment	32,341,000
State share of total U.S..	1.79%
State 9-12 enrollment	217,000
Total U.S. 9-12 enrollment	12,500,000
State share of U.S. total	1.74%
State public school enroll. rate	88.5%
Overall U.S. rate.	91.6%
Rank among states.	41

Enrollment figures (which include unclassified students) are rounded to nearest thousand pupils in fall term; kindergarten (K)-8 grade figures include some prekindergarten students. Enrollment rate is based on percentage of persons 5-17 years old. Rank is from highest to lowest.
Source: U.S. National Center for Education Statistics.

Public college finances, 1996

State FTE enrollment	136,200
Total U.S. FTE enrollment	8,268,800
State share of total U.S..	1.65%
Rank among states.	21
State and local appropriations	$433,400,000
Total U.S. state and local appropriations.	$39,699 mill.
State share of total U.S..	1.09%
Rank among states.	31
State net tuition revenues	$325 mill.
Total U.S. net tuition	$18,348,100,000
State share of total U.S..	1.77%
Rank among states.	22

FTE=Full-time equivalent; credit and noncredit enrollment including summer session in academic year ending in 1996.
Enrollments are rounded to nearest thousand students. Net

tuition revenues exclude appropriation to students attending in-state public institutions. Rankings are from highest shares to lowest.

Source: Research Associates of Washington.

TRANSPORTATION AND TRAVEL

Highway mileage, 1996

Interstate	893
Other arterial	5,332
Collector roads	13,844
Local roads	41,905
Urban roads	13,965
Rural roads	46,702
Total state	60,667
U.S. total	3,933,985
State share	1.5%
Rank among states	32

Source: U.S. Federal Highway Administration.

Motor vehicle registrations and driver licenses, 1996
In thousands

Vehicle registrations	State	U.S.	Share	Rank
Autos, trucks, buses	3,318	206,365	1.61%	23
Autos only	1,871	128,439	1.46%	23
Motorcycles	37	3,832	0.97%	30
Driver licenses	2,624	179,539	1.46%	23

Figures do not include vehicles owned by military services.
Source: U.S. Federal Highway Administration; *Highway Statistics; Selected Highway Statistics and Charts.*

Domestic travel expenditures, 1995
Spending by U.S. residents on overnight trips and day trips of at least 100 miles

Total expenditures in state	$6,059 mill.
Total expenditures in U.S.	$360,314 mill.
State share of total U.S.	1.68%
Rank among states	21

Source: Travel Industry Association of America.

CRIME AND LAW ENFORCEMENT

State and local police officers, 1996

Local police	5,733
State police	873
Sheriffs	8,720
Total	16,125
Officers per 10,000 residents	37
U.S. average	25
Rank among states	2

Figures cover full-time sworn officers; totals include special police not shown separately.
Source: U.S. Bureau of Justice Statistics; *Census of State and Local Law Enforcement Agencies, 1996.*

Crime rates, 1996
Rates per 100,000 resident population

Violent crimes	State	U.S.
Total violent	929	634
Murder	17.5	7.4
Forcible rape	41.5	36.1
Robbery	277	202
Aggravated assault	594	388
Property crimes		
Total property	5,910	4,445
Burglary	1,296	943
Larceny/theft	3,982	2,976
Motor vehicle theft	632	526
Totals	6,839	5,079

Source: U.S. Federal Bureau of Investigation; *Crime in the United States,* annual.

State prison populations, 1980-1996

	State	U.S.	State share
1980	8,889	305,458	2.91%
1990	18,599	708,393	2.63%
1996	26,779	1,025,624	2.61%

Figures exclude prisoners in federal penitentiaries.
Source: U.S. Bureau of Justice Statistics.

Maine

Location: New England (northeastern continental United States)

Area and rank: 30,865 square miles (79,939 square kilometers); 35,387 square miles (91,652 square kilometers) including water; thirty-ninth largest state in area

Coastline: 228 miles (367 kilometers)

Shoreline: 3,478 miles (5,596 kilometers)

Population and rank: 1,242,051 (1997); thirty-ninth largest state in population

Capital: Augusta

Largest city: Portland (62,786 people in 1998)

State capitol building in Augusta. (Maine Office of Tourism)

Entered Union and rank:
March 15, 1820; twenty-third state

Present constitution adopted: 1820

Counties: 16

State name: "Maine" was first used to distinguish the region's mainland from its offshore islands; the name was also considered a compliment to English king Charles I's consort, Henrietta Maria, of France's Mayne province

State nickname: Pine Tree State

Motto: *Dirigo* (I lead)

State flag: Blue field with the state coat of arms

Highest point: Mount Katahdin — 5,267 feet (1,605 meters)

Lowest point: Atlantic Ocean — sea level

Highest recorded temperature: 105 degrees Fahrenheit (41 degrees Celsius) — North Bridgton, 1911

Lowest recorded temperature: −48 degrees Fahrenheit (−44 degrees Celsius) — Van Buren, 1925

State song: "State of Maine Song"

State tree: White pine tree

State flower: White pine cone and tassel

State bird: Chickadee

State fish: Landlocked salmon

State animal: Moose

National park: Acadia

Maine History

Maine, the largest of the six New England states, is filled with natural wonder and beauty. It has more than 5,000 lakes and ponds, woodlands cover almost 90 percent of the state, and 2,500 miles of its Atlantic coastline twist from New Hampshire to Canada. The harsh, brutal winters have always made living there difficult, and the state remains relatively sparsely populated.

As far as it is known, the first Native Americans to settle in the area were members of the Abenaki (people of the dawnland) tribe. They, and the tribes that followed them, were hunters and gatherers, living on fish, deer, moose, beavers, and bears. Like many Native Americans of New England, they lived in wigwams and were generally peaceful—until European settlers began to come.

Early Exploration and Settlement. Viking leader Leif Eriksson and other Norse sailors most likely explored part of Maine during their travels in 1000. John Cabot, sent by King Henry VII of England, claimed Maine as territory for England around 1497. In 1524 explorer Giovanni da Verrazano claimed Maine for France. In 1605 British captain George Weymouth landed in Maine, kidnapped five Abenaki men, and took them back to England. Upon meeting the American Indians and hearing stories of the land, King James I agreed to sponsor a settlement there, sending Sir Ferdinando Gorges and Sir John Popham to lead the expedition. In 1607 the British explorers reached the coast where the Kennebec River meets the ocean. There they began the Popham colony, where they built the *Virginia*—the first English ship built in North America. Success was short-lived, however, as a typically bitter Maine winter, combined with attacks from the Abenakis, drove the entire colony back to England in 1608.

Soon, however, both English and French explorers returned and claimed different parts of the state for their kings. The English fought with the Native Americans often. Englishman John Winter founded one of Maine's first shipyards around 1637, and Maine was on its way to becoming a major shipbuilding center. The ships built in Maine supplied fish, fur, lumber, and masts to England's navy. The empty ships returning brought more settlers, and as settlers moved inland, farming gained importance. As in most of New England, native corn was Maine's primary crop. Primarily because of the harsh winters, Maine did not grow as quickly as the other New England colonies. The small population and weak government motivated the colonists there to merge with Massachusetts in 1658, and they remained part of it for nearly 150 years.

Two Wars. In 1754 tension over the colonies between France, which ruled Canada, and England broke into the French and Indian War. Thousands of Maine settlers fought against the French. The French and Indians were eventually defeated, and many of the warring tribes fled to Canada. The victory was costly, however, and it left Great Britain deeply in debt. When the war ended in 1763, Maine was doing well. The colony had 25,000 settlers and nearly fifty towns. Each year, Maine shipped millions of pounds of fish and lumber to cities in Europe. Like the other colonies, Maine started resenting Britain's meddling. Britain, trying to relieve its war debt, continually raised the taxes of the colonists.

In 1774 a group of men from York, Maine, burned English tea to protest the high taxes in what would be called the York Tea Party. In 1775 the Revolutionary War began in Massachusetts. On June 12 of that year, the first sea battle of the war occurred off Maine, when colonists from Machias rowed out and attacked an English ship. Soon after that the English retaliated, and the city of Falmouth (later Portland) was bombarded and burned. By the time the Union won the war, about 1,000 colonists from Maine had given their lives.

After the war, the Massachusetts government sold Maine land to new settlers for less than a dollar an acre. Maine's population increased significantly, and by 1785 Maine started lobbying for statehood. The new and growing country had other problems, however. In 1812 the United States again went to war with Great Britain. Britain, at that time at war with France, would attack and capture American ships and conscript Americans into service. Maine's growing dominance as a ship-

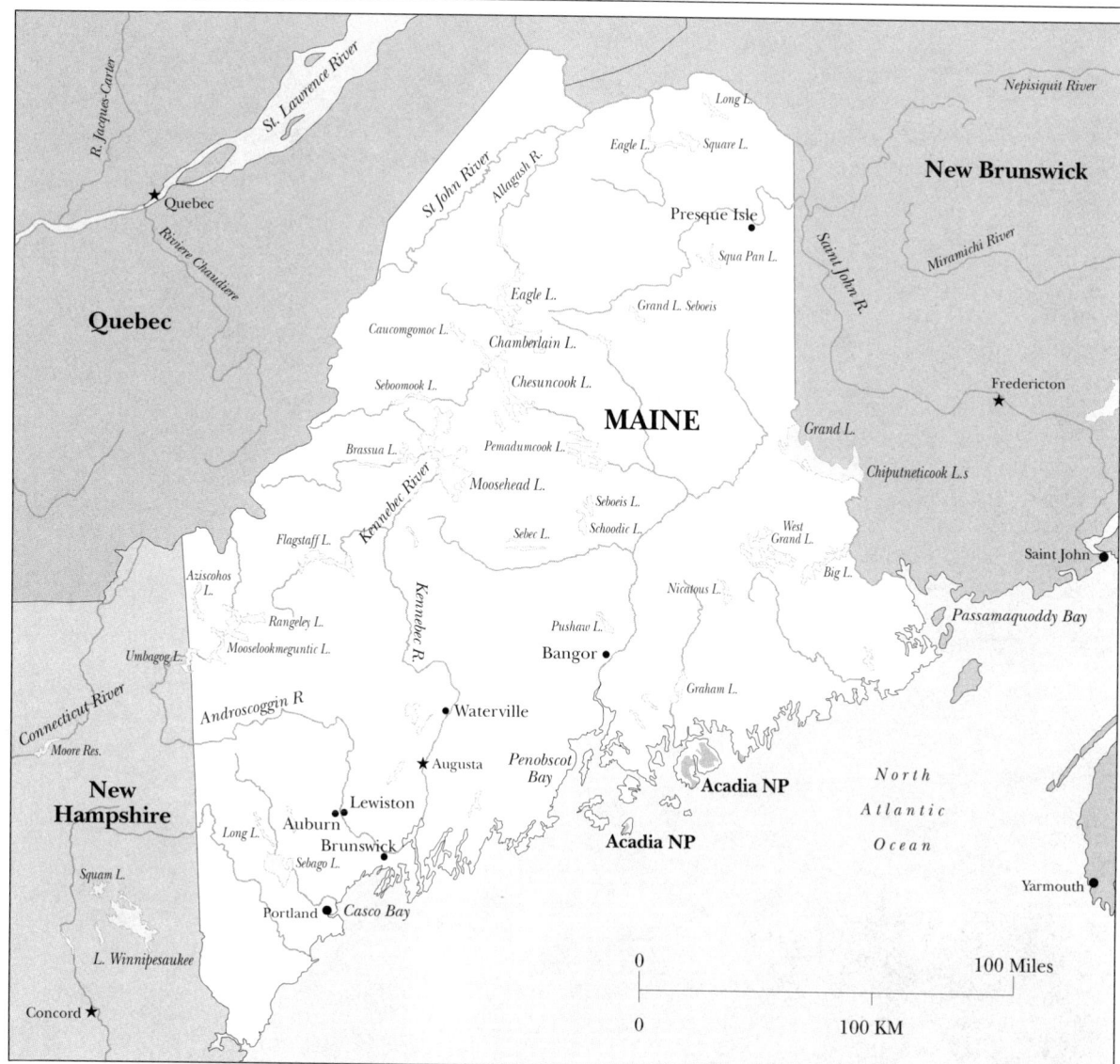

builder played a major role in the American success, and after the war, it pushed even harder for statehood.

Statehood. In 1820, in an effort to diffuse the hotly contested issue of slavery in America, it was proposed that Missouri be admitted as a slave state if Maine were admitted as a free state, thus keeping a balance of eleven proslavery states and eleven antislavery states. Known as the Missouri Compromise, this agreement is credited with postponing civil war. Maine then separated from Massachusetts and became the twenty-third state, and the last New England state accepted into the Union. Portland served as the state capital until 1832, when the more centrally located Augusta became the capital. By then, potatoes were replacing corn as the most profitable crop, and lumbering became the state's largest industry. The city of Bath became the leading shipbuilding city in the country.

Maine was admitted to the Union as a free state, as it had a history of supporting people of African descent: When Bowdoin College opened in Brunswick in 1802, it was the first U.S. college to admit black students. John Russwurm, the college's first black graduate, cofounded *Freedom's Journal*, the country's first black-run newspaper in 1827.

Antislavery Maine governor Hannibal Hamlin became President Abraham Lincoln's vice president in 1861. The Civil War erupted that year, and many Mainers heeded the call to arms. In the election of 1864, Lincoln was in political trouble, and he quietly allowed moderate southern Democrat Andrew Johnson to replace Hamlin as his vice president to ensure his reelection. By the time the Civil War ended in 1865, about 7,500 Maine soldiers had been killed fighting.

Industrial Revolution. In the 1850's the Industrial Revolution began to influence American cities, and Maine came to operate textile and leather factories. Like the rest of New England, Maine was successful at building factories, and thousands of French Canadians crossed the border to find jobs. Many Irish escaped the horrible potato famine that began in the 1840's and came to Maine. In 1894 the Arrostock Railroad was completed, and trains be-

gan to move the wealth of Maine potatoes to the markets of other American cities. During this time Maine became one of the country's great potato-growing areas.

Economic Decline. In the 1900's tourists discovered Maine: its mystique, unspoiled beauty, and lack of crowded cities. The upsurge in tourists helped Maine's economy, as the state's other industries began to falter. The development of iron steamships damaged Maine's wooden-ship building industry, and the traditional activities of lumbering, fishing, and farming did not provide enough jobs for everyone.

There was a small break in economic decline when World War I began in 1914. Many Mainers did not wait for the United States to enter the war and joined Canada's armed forces to fight the Germans. The United States entered the war in 1917, and 35,000 Mainers joined the U.S. forces. Maine's shipbuilding industry sprang back to life, and farmers and fisherman saw a significant increase in

With a population of less than twenty thousand people, Maine's capital city, Augusta, is only the seventh largest city in the state. (PhotoDisc)

Although Maine ranks only thirty-ninth in area among the states, it has nearly 3,500 miles of shoreline and is famous for its numerous lighthouses. (PhotoDisc)

price for their harvests. After the war ended, however, times were difficult in Maine. When the country entered World War II in 1941, Maine again sprang back to life. In the 1950's and 1960's, Air Force bases were built, which employed many locals, but unemployment remained higher in Maine than in the rest of the nation.

Modern Maine. In 1954 Edmund Muskie became the first modern Democrat elected governor in the traditionally Republican state. In 1957 he was the first Maine Democrat elected to the Senate. The popular senator went on to run unsuccessfully for the vice presidency in 1968 and for the presidential nomination of the Democratic Party in 1972.

In 1972 Maine's Native Americans filed a lawsuit against the United States, claiming their lands had been wrongly seized and showing a 1794 treaty as proof. In 1980 the federal government paid the tribes $81.5 million for their land. It was the largest such settlement ever awarded to Native Americans.

In the 1980's the state's economy became strong again, particularly in the largest city, Portland, although industry declined to the point that service industries represented 70 percent of the state's economy. Maine lobster is often referred to as the best in the country, and the state produces 22 million pounds of it each year. Maine also produces 98 percent of the nation's blueberries.

The state is relatively underpopulated, with only about one million residents. In the northern part of the state, there are few developed cities. In the 1990's less than 1 percent of the population was Native American, and most Mainers are descendants of emigrants from Great Britain, France, and Canada.

Kevin M. Mitchell

Maine Time Line

1400	Abenaki tribe inhabits Maine area.
1497	John Cabot claims Maine for England.
1524	Explorer Giovanni da Verrazano claims Maine for France.
1605	Captain George Weymouth kidnaps five Native Americans and takes them to England.
1607	Gorge Popham establishes a settlement near Kennebec River; the first English ship, the *Virginia*, is built.
1620's	Smallpox wipes out many Abenaki.
1628	Plymouth Pilgrims establish several fur-trading posts in Maine territory.
1634	First sawmill in Maine begins operation.
1637	First shipyard in Maine opens.
1640's	French establish missions and begin converting Indians.
1649	Government grants all Christians the right to form churches.
1652	Maine becomes a part of the Massachusetts Bay Colony.
1690's	French and Indians from Canada pillage Maine until only four English settlements remain inhabited.
1774	Patriots burn English tea to protest high taxes in York Tea Party.
May 12, 1775	Maine patriots capture English ship in first naval battle of the American Revolution.
1778	Continental Congress divides Massachusetts into three districts, including one province called Maine.
1785	Maine's first newspaper, the *Falmouth Gazette*, is published.
1791	First lighthouse on the Atlantic Coast begins operation in Portland.
1801	First free public library opens in Castine.
1802	Bowdoin College opens in Brunswick.
1819	Maine state representatives vote to separate from Massachusetts and adopt a state constitution.
Mar. 15, 1820	Maine gains statehood under terms of Missouri Compromise, becoming the twenty-third state of the Union.
1832	State capital is moved to Augusta.
1834	Maine's Antislavery Society is formed in Augusta.
1850's	Most remaining Native Americans live on reservations.
1851	Antidrinking legislation passes making Maine the first dry state.
1855	State militia fires on civilians as they descend upon Portland's City Hall, looking for liquor; one man is killed.
1861	Maine Republican Hannibal Hamlin is elected vice-president of the United States.
1894	Arrostock Railroad is completed; trains move potatoes to the markets of other American cities.

1912	Leon Bean founds clothing mail-order business L. L. Bean in Freeport.
1950	Margaret Chase Smith, becomes the first woman elected to both houses of the U.S. Congress.
1957	Governor Edmund S. Muskie is first Maine Democrat elected to the U.S. Senate.
1979	Maine's three Indian reservations have a total population of 1,247.
1981	Tourism continues to lead all industries; more than $500 million is spent by out-of-state visitors in Maine.
1999	Children's Rights Council names Maine the best state in which to raise children.

Founded in Freeport in 1912, L. L. Bean is one of the nation's largest mail-order clothing businesses in the country.
(Maine Office of Tourism)

Notes for Further Study

Published Sources. Those looking for short, historical and social overviews of Maine will find material in *Maine* (1990) by LeeAnne Engfer and *Maine: From Sea to Shining Sea* (1994) by Dennis B. Fradin. More information, particularly about Maine's beginnings, can be found in the book *Maine History! Surprising Secrets About Our State's Founding Mothers, Fathers and Kids!* (1996) by Carole Marsh. *Maine: A Narrative History* by Neil Rolde offers a more in-depth view of the state. *Maine: Heads of Families at*

the First Census of the U. S. Taken in 1790 (1987), edited by Robert Danbury, offers insight to Maine's early settlers and the first families of the state.

The French and Indian War (1997), by Christopher Collier and James Lincoln Collier, covers the many battles that took place on Maine's soil, as well as the hundred years between initial colonization and the American Revolution. *The Maine Reader: The Down East Experience, 1614 to the Present* (1997) edited by Charles Shain and

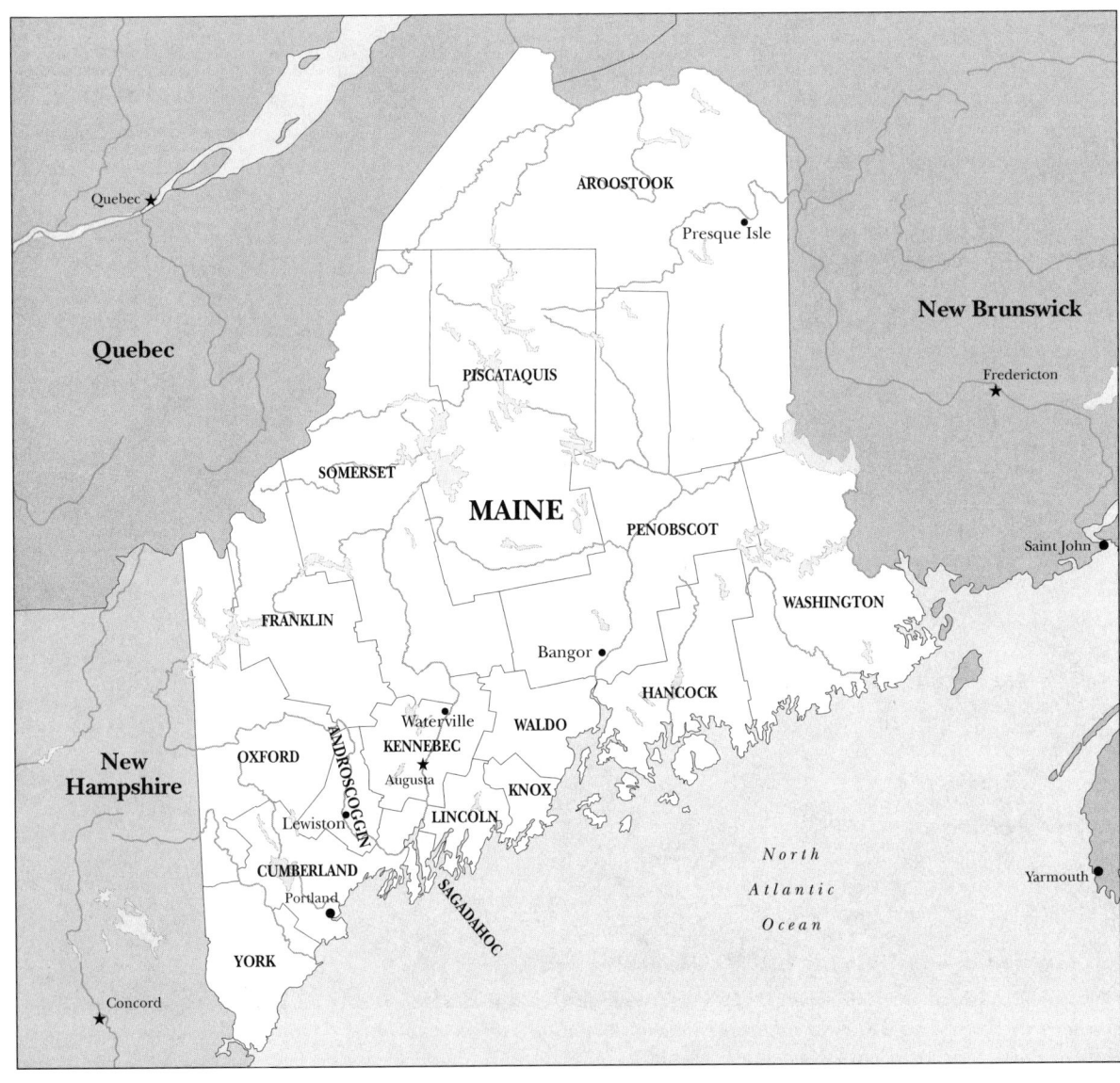

Samuella Shain, offers a sweeping history of the state through literature. Covering everything from ferry boats to the islands, in addition to coastal architecture, is *The Coast of Maine Book: A Complete Guide* (1999) by Rick Ackermann and Kathryn Buxton. *The Maine Handbook* (1998) by Kathy Brandes provides information on all Maine's natural beauty destinations. *The Maine Woods* (1988), the last book by New England's Henry David Thoreau, chronicles the famous American writer's exploration of Maine's backwoods. *Maine Trivia* (1998) compiled by John N. Cole, is a fun, insightful, small volume of the facts, figures, and firsts of the Pine Tree State.

Web Resources. There are many Maine sites on the World Wide Web, and those listed here often give links to others. A good starting point is the Center for Maine History (http://www.mainhistory.com). The Center comprises the Maine Historical Society Research Library, the Maine History Gallery, and the historic Wadsworth-Longfellow House. The Maine home page (http://www.maine.com) is a collection of information and other Web sites on such topics as arts, history, finance, and politics. Information on Margaret Chase Smith and the organization she inspired can be found at Margaret Chase Smith Quality Website (http://www.maine-quality.org). The state's largest newspaper, the *Press Herald* (http://www.portland.com), offers updated news on state happenings. The Portland Harbor Museum (http://www.portlandharbormuseum.com) is a fascinating maritime museum with information on the city's port and working lighthouse.

Counties

County	Sq. miles	1996 pop.
Androscoggin	470.3	101,754
Aroostook	6,671.9	78,113
Cumberland	835.6	251,087
Franklin	1,698.0	29,200
Hancock	1,589.1	49,500
Kennebec	867.5	116,214
Knox	365.6	37,487
Lincoln	455.6	31,303
Oxford	2,078.2	53,797
Penobscot	3,396.0	144,989
Piscataquis	3,966.5	18,329
Sagadahoc	254.0	35,508
Somerset	3,926.8	52,507
Waldo	729.8	35,822
Washington	2,568.6	36,224
York	991.0	171,482

Source: U.S. Census Bureau; National Association of Counties.

Cities
With 10,000 or more residents

Rank	City	Population
1	Portland	62,786
2	Lewiston	36,186
3	Bangor	30,508
4	South Portland	22,810
5	Auburn	22,617
6	Biddeford	20,851
7	Augusta	19,978
8	Westbrook	16,679
9	Waterville	16,263
10	Saco	16,068

Population figures are estimated for mid-1998.
Source: U.S. Bureau of the Census.

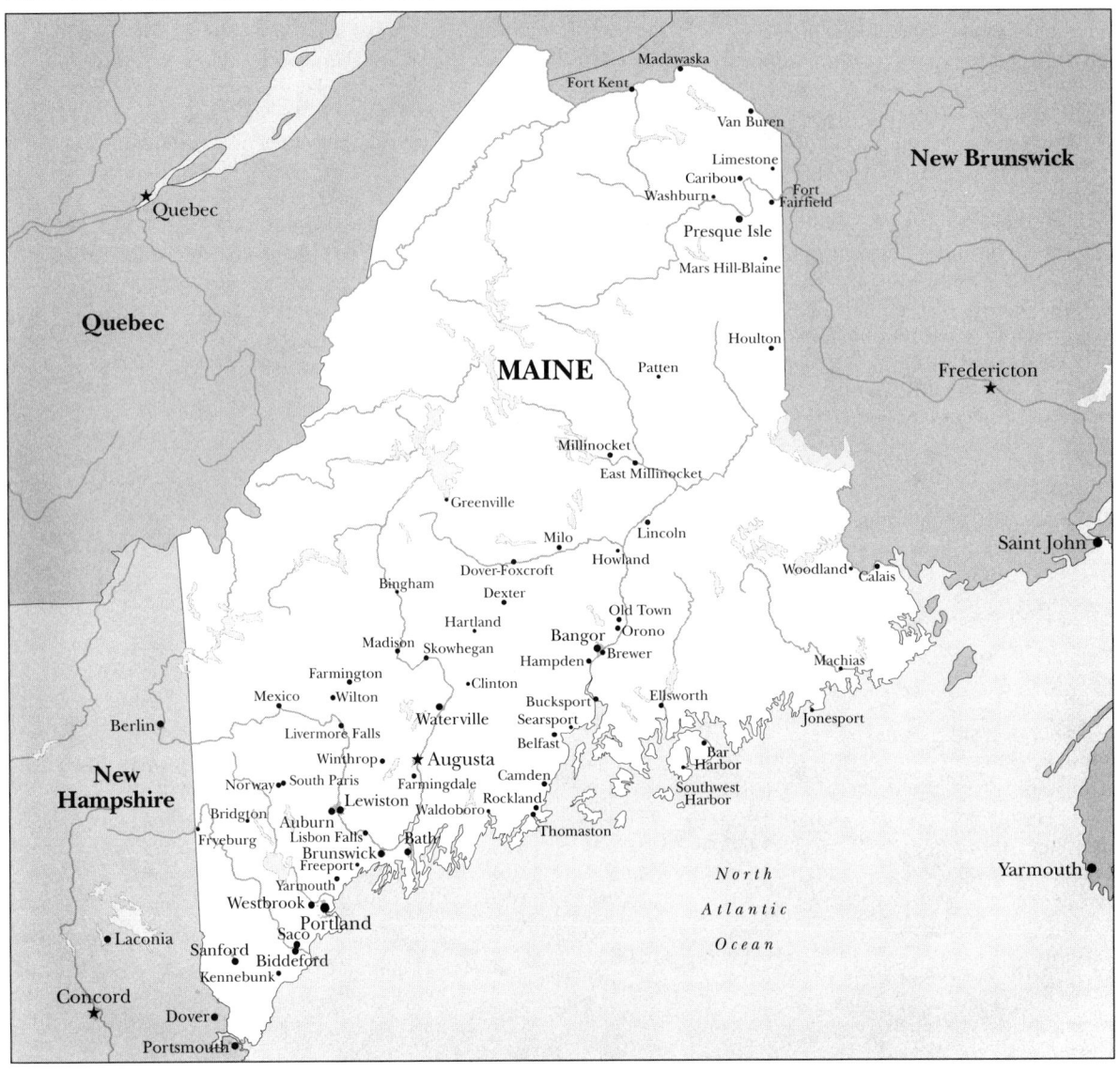

Madawaska

Fort Kent

Van Buren

Quebec

Limestone

Caribou

Washburn

Fort Fairfield

New Brunswick

Presque Isle

Quebec

Mars Hill-Blaine

Houlton

MAINE

Patten

Fredericton

Millinocket

East Millinocket

Greenville

Lincoln

Milo

Howland

Dover-Foxcroft

Bingham

Dexter

Woodland

Calais

Saint John

Hartland

Old Town

Orono

Madison

Skowhegan

Bangor

Brewer

Machias

Farmington

Hampden

Wilton

Clinton

Mexico

Waterville

Buckport

Searsport

Ellsworth

Jonesport

Berlin

Livermore Falls

Belfast

Winthrop

Augusta

Camden

Bar Harbor

New Hampshire

Norway

South Paris

Farmingdale

Rockland

Southwest Harbor

Bridgton

Lewiston

Waldoboro

Fryeburg

Auburn

Lisbon Falls

Freeport

Bath

Thomaston

North

Atlantic

Ocean

Yarmouth

Yarmouth

Westbrook

Laconia

Saco

Portland

Sanford

Biddeford

Kennebunk

Concord

Dover

Portsmouth

Index to Tables

NA = Reliable data are not available.

DEMOGRAPHICS

Resident state and national populations, 1970-1997

Population figures given in thousands

	State pop.	U.S. pop.	Share	Rank
1970	994	203,302	0.5%	38
1980	1,125	226,546	0.5%	38
1985	1,163	237,924	0.5%	38
1990	1,228	248,765	0.5%	38
1995	1,234	262,761	0.5%	39
1997	1,242	267,636	0.5%	39

Source: U.S. Bureau of the Census.

Resident population by age, 1997

Age group	Total population
Under 5 years	69,000
5 to 17 years	228,000
18 to 24 years	110,000
25 to 34 years	172,000
35 to 44 years	216,000
45 to 54 years	169,000
55 to 64 years	104,000
65 to 74 years	93,000
75 to 84 years	59,000
85 years and over	21,000
Portion of residents 65 and older	13.9%
National average	12.7%

Population figures are rounded to nearest thousand persons;
figures include armed forces personnel stationed in state.
Source: U.S. Bureau of the Census.

Resident population by race, Hispanic origin, 1997

	State pop.	Share	U.S.
All residents	1,242,000	100.0%	100.0%
Hispanic white	8,000	0.6%	10.0%
non-Hispanic white	1,214,000	97.7%	72.7%
African American	6,000	0.5%	12.7%
Native American	6,000	0.5%	0.9%
Asian, Pacific Islander	9,000	0.7%	3.8%

Source: U.S. Bureau of the Census.

Projections of state population, 2000-2025

	Model A Uses interstate migration observed from 1975-1994	Model B Uses Bureau of Economic Analysis employment projections
Year	Population	Population
2000	1,259,000	1,250,000
2005	1,285,000	1,259,000
2010	1,323,000	1,268,000
2015	1,362,000	1,276,000
2020	1,396,000	1,282,000
2025	1,423,000	1,282,000

All population projections, including those for 2000, were calculated in 1997.
Source: U.S. Bureau of the Census, Population Paper Listings PPL-47.

VITAL STATISTICS

Average lifetime in years by race, 1989-1991

	State	U.S.	Rank
All residents	76.35	75.37	19
White residents	76.35	76.13	23
Black residents	NA	69.16	NA

Ranks are from longest-lived to least longest-lived. Ranks exclude Alaska, for which reliable data are not available. Rank for black residents is based on the 32 states for which reliable data are available.
Source: U.S. National Center for Health Statistics.

Infant mortality rates, 1980 and 1995

	State	U.S.
All residents		
1980	9.2	12.6
1995	6.5	7.6
White residents		
1980	9.4	11.0
1995	6.3	6.3
Black residents		
1980	NA	21.4
1995	NA	15.1

Figures represent deaths per 1,000 live births of resident infants under 1 year old, exclusive of fetal deaths; all-residents figures include other races not listed separately.
Source: U.S. National Center for Health Statistics.

Marriages and divorces

Marriages in 1996	NA
Rate per 1,000 population, 1995	8.7
U.S. rate, 1995	8.9
Rank among all states	21
Divorces in 1996	NA
Rate per 1,000 population, 1995	4.4
U.S. rate, 1995	4.4
Rank among all states	26

Rank is from highest to lowest in country.
Source: U.S. National Center for Health Statistics.

Death rates by leading causes, 1995
Deaths per 100,000 resident population

Cause	State	U.S.
Heart disease	293.9	280.7
Cancer	242.9	204.9
Cerebrovascular diseases	59.9	60.1
Accidents and adverse effects	32.1	35.5
Motor vehicle accidents	14.7	16.5
Chronic obstructive pulmonary diseases	54.3	39.2
Diabetes mellitus	25.4	22.6
HIV	6.1	NA
Suicide	13.0	11.9
Homicide	-	8.7
All causes	946.8	880.0
Rank in overall death rate among states		15

Figures exclude nonresidents who die in state. Causes of death follow International Classification of Diseases. Rank is from highest to lowest in country.
Source: U.S. National Center for Health Statistics.

ECONOMY

Gross state product, 1990-1996
In current dollars

	State product	Increase
1990	$23.2 billion	
1993	$25.1 billion	
1994	$26.2 billion	4.38%
1995	$27.7 billion	5.73%
1996	$28.9 billion	4.33%

Source: U.S. Bureau of Economic Analysis; *Survey of Current Business,* June, 1998.

Gross state product by industry, 1996
In billions

Farms, forestry, fisheries	$0.5
Construction	1.1
Manufacturing	4.9
Transportation, public utilities.	2.0
Wholesale trade.	1.6
Retail trade	3.1
Finance, insurance, real estate	4.6
Services	4.7
Government.	3.5
State total.	$26.0
Total U.S.	$6,923.8
State share	0.38%
Rank among states.	42

Total figures include mining, not listed separately.

Source: U.S. Bureau of Economic Analysis; *Survey of Current Business,* June, 1998.

Personal income per capita, 1990 and 1997
In current dollars

	1990	1997
Per capita income	$17,190	$22,078
U.S. average	$19,188	$25,598
Rank among states	32	36

1997 data are preliminary.

Source: U.S. Bureau of Economic Analysis; *Survey of Current Business,* May, 1998.

Energy consumption, 1995
In trillions of British thermal units (BTU)

End-use sectors

Residential	97.9
Commercial	50.7
Industrial	278.3
Transportation	103.4

Sources of energy

Petroleum	243.0
Natural gas	5.5
Coal	7.1
Hydroelectric power.	66.4
Nuclear electric power	2.1
Total state per capita consumption	414.4
Total U.S. per capita consumption	344.4
Rank among states.	12
Total state energy consumption	513.3
Total U.S. energy consumption	90,547.4
State share of U.S. total	0.57%
Rank among states.	40

Total figures include items not listed separately.

Source: U.S. Energy Information Administration; *State Energy Data Report.*

Nonfarm employment by sectors, 1997

Total	554,000
Construction	24,000
Manufacturing	88,000
Transportation, public utilities.	23,000
Wholesale trade, retail trade	140,000
Finance, insurance, real estate	28,000
Services	158,000
Government.	93,000

Figures are rounded to nearest thousand persons. Total includes mining, not listed separately.

Source: U.S. Bureau of Labor Statistics; *Employment and Earnings,* monthly.

Foreign exports, 1990-1997
In millions of dollars

Year	State	U.S.	State share
1990	870	394,045	0.22%
1996	1,380	624,767	0.22%
1997	1,723	688,896	0.25%

Source: U.S. Bureau of the Census; *U.S. Merchandise Trade,* series FT 900.

LAND USE

Federally owned land, 1996

	State	U.S.	State share
Total acres	19,848,000	2,271,343,000	0.87%
Federally owned	193,000	563,129,000	0.03%
Federal share	1.0%	24.8%	—

Areas are rounded to nearest thousand acres. Figures for federally owned land do not include trust properties.
Source: U.S. General Services Administration; *Inventory Report on Real Property Owned by the United States Throughout the World,* annual.

Land use, 1992
In acres, rounded to nearest thousand

Total surface area	21,290,000
Federal land	164,000
Total nonfederal	19,517,000
Developed	697,000
Total rural	18,820,000
Cropland.	448,000
Pasture land	111,000
Range land	0
Forest land	17,557,000
Minor cover/use.	705,000

Total surface area figures include water area not shown separately.
Source: U.S. Dept. of Agriculture; Soil Conservation Service; Iowa State University, Statistical Laboratory; *Summary Report, 1992 National Resources Inventory.*

Farms and crop acreage, 1997

	State	U.S.	Share	Rank
Farms (thousands)	7	2,058	0.34%	41
Acres (millions)	1	968	0.10%	42
Acres per farm	184	471	—	39
Acres planted	296	334,139	0.09%	44
Acres harvested	287	319,894	0.09%	44
Farm value (mill.)	$170	$108,805	0.16%	36

Numbers of farms are rounded to nearest thousand.
Source: U.S. Dept. of Agriculture; National Agricultural Statistics Service.

GOVERNMENT AND FINANCE

Units of local government, 1997

	State	Total U.S.	Rank
All local governments	832	87,453	34
Counties	16	3,043	40
Municipalities	22	19,372	46
Townships	467	16,629	12
School districts	98	13,726	32
Special districts	229	34,683	42

County ranks are based on the 48 states with county governments; township ranks are based on the 20 states with township governments; school district ranks are based on the 46 states with such districts.
Township figures include "town" governments.
Source: U.S. Bureau of the Census; *1997 Census of Governments, Government Organization,* Series GC97(1).

State government revenue, 1996

Total revenue	$4,267 mill.
General revenue	3,836 mill.
Per capita.	3,097
U.S. per capita average	2,910
Rank among states.	20
Intergovernmental revenue	
Total	$1,245 mill.
From federal government	1,242 mill.
From local government.	3 mill.
Charges and Miscellaneous	
Total	$694 mill.
Current charges	287 mill.
Misc. general revenue	407 mill.
Taxes	
Total	$1,897 mill.
General sales	658 mill.
Selective sales	278 mill.
License taxes	114 mill.
Individual income	709 mill.
Corporate income	71 mill.
Other.	66 mill.
Insurance trust revenue	361 mill.

Total revenue figures include items not listed separately.
Source: U.S. Bureau of the Census.

State government expenditures, 1996

General expenditures

Intergovernmental	$743 mill.
Direct expenditures	2,992 mill.
Total	3,735 mill.

Selected direct expenditures

Education	$1,080 mill.
Public welfare	1,256 mill.
Health, hospital	235 mill.
Highways	362 mill.
Police	34 mill.
Corrections	64 mill.
Natural resources	106 mill.
Parks and recreation	8 mill.
Government administration	120 mill.
Interest on debt	170 mill.

Other

State per capita expenditures	$3,016
U.S. per capita average	2,854
Rank among states	18
Total state expenditures	4,240 mill.
Total U.S. expenditures	859,959 mill.

Totals include items not listed separately.
Source: U.S. Bureau of the Census.

POLITICS

Governors since statehood

D = Democrat; R = Republican; O = other;
(r) resigned; (d) died in office; (i) removed from office

William King (O)	(r) 1820-1821
William D. Williamson (O)	(r) 1821
Benjamin Ames (O)	1821-1822
Albion K. Parris (O)	1822-1827
Enoch Lincoln (O)	(d) 1827-1829
Nathan Cutler (O)	1829-1830
Joshua Hall (O)	1830
Jonathan G. Hunton (O)	1830-1831
Samuel E. Smith (O)	1831-1834
Robert P. Dunlap (D)	1834-1838
Edward Kent (O)	1838-1839
John Fairfield (D)	1839-1841
Edward Kent (O)	1841-1842
John Fairfield (D)	(r) 1842-1843
Edward Kavanagh (D)	1843-1844
Hugh J. Anderson (D)	1844-1847
John W. Dana (D)	1847-1850
John Hubbard (D)	1850-1853
William G. Crosby (O)	1853-1855
Anson P. Morrill (R)	1855-1856
Samuel Wells (D)	1856-1857
Hannibal Hamlin (R)	1857
Joseph H. Williams (R)	1857-1858
Lot M. Morrill (R)	1858-1861
Israel Washburn, Jr. (R)	1861-1863
Abner Coburn (R)	1863-1864
Samuel Cony (R)	1864-1867
Joshua L. Chamberlain (R)	1867-1871
Sidney Perham (R)	1871-1874
Nelson Dingley, Jr. (R)	1874-1876
Sheldon Connor (R)	1876-1879
Alonzo Garcelon (D)	1879-1880
Daniel F. Davis (R)	1880-1881
Harris M. Plaisted (O)	1881-1883
Frederick Robie (R)	1883-1887
Joseph R. Bodwell (R)	(d) 1887
Sebastian S. Marble (R)	1887-1889
Edwin C. Burleigh (R)	1889-1893
Henry B. Cleaves (R)	1893-1897
Llewellyn Powers (R)	1897-1901
John F. Hill (R)	1901-1905
William T. Cobb (R)	1905-1909
Bert M. Fernald (R)	1909-1911
Frederick W. Plaisted (D)	1911-1913
William T. Haines (R)	1913-1915
Oakley C. Curtis (D)	1915-1917
Carl E. Milliken (R)	1917-1921
Frederic H. Parkhurst (R)	(d) 1921
Percival P. Baxter (R)	1921-1925
Ralph O. Brewster (R)	1925-1929
William T. Gardiner (R)	1929-1933
Louis J. Brann (R)	1933-1937
Lewis O. Barrows (D)	1937-1941
Sumner Sewall (R)	1941-1945
Horace A. Hildreth (R)	1945-1949
Frederick G. Payne (R)	(r) 1949-1952
Burton M. Cross (R)	1952-1955
Edmund S. Muskie (D)	(r) 1955-1959
Robert N. Haskell (R)	1959
Clinton A. Clauson (D)	(d) 1959
John H. Reed (R)	1959-1967
Kenneth M. Curtis (D)	1967-1975
James B. Longley (O)	1975-1979
Joseph E. Brennan (D)	1979-1987
John R. McKernan, Jr. (R)	1987-1995
Angus S. King, Jr. (O)	1995-

Composition of state legislature, 1990-1998

	Democrats	Republicans
State House (151 seats)		
1990	97	54
1992	93	58
1994	77	74
1996	81	69
1998	79	71
State Senate (35 seats)		
1990	21	14
1992	20	15
1994	16	18
1996	19	15
1998	20	14

Figures for total seats may include independents and minor party members.
Source: Council of State Governments; *State Elective Officials and the Legislatures.*

Composition of congressional delegations, 1989-1999

	Dem	Rep	Total
House of Representatives			
101st Congress, 1989			
State delegates	1	1	2
Total U.S.	259	174	433
102d Congress, 1991			
State delegates	1	1	2
Total U.S.	267	167	434
103d Congress, 1993			
State delegates	1	1	2
Total U.S.	258	176	434
104th Congress, 1995			
State delegates	2	0	2
Total U.S.	197	236	433
105th Congress, 1997			
State delegates	2	0	2
Total U.S.	206	228	434
106th Congress, 1999			
State delegates	2	0	2
Total U.S.	211	222	433
Senate			
101st Congress, 1989			
State delegates	1	1	2
Total U.S.	55	45	100

	Dem	Rep	Total
102d Congress, 1991			
State delegates	1	1	2
Total U.S.	56	44	100
103d Congress, 1993			
State delegates	1	1	2
Total U.S.	57	43	100
104th Congress, 1995			
State delegates	0	2	2
Total U.S.	46	53	99
105th Congress, 1997			
State delegates	0	2	2
Total U.S.	45	55	100
106th Congress, 1999			
State delegates	0	2	2
Total U.S.	45	54	99

Figures are for starts of first sessions. Figure for U.S. Representatives for 101st Congress does not include Alabama and Indiana, which had vacancies. Figures for total U.S. Representatives for 102d, 103d, and 106th Congresses do not include Vermont, which had 1 Independent-Socialist. Figure for U.S. Representatives for 104th Congress does not include Vermont, which had 1 Independent-Socialist, and California, which had 1 vacancy. Figure for U.S. Representatives for 105th Congress does not include New York, which had 1 vacancy. Figure for U.S. Senators for 104th Congress does not include Oregon, which had 1 vacancy. Figure for U.S. Senators for 106th Congress does not include New Hampshire, which had 1 Independent.
Source: U.S. Congress; *Congressional Directory,* biennial.

Voter participation in presidential elections, 1992 and 1996

	1992	1996
State voting age pop.	932,000	939,000
Total U.S. voting age pop.	189,524,000	196,509,000
State share of U.S. total	0.5%	0.5%
Rank among states	39	39
Percent of state casting vote	72.9	58.1
Percent of U.S. total voting	55.1	49.0
Rank among states	1	6

Source: U.S. Bureau of the Census.

HEALTH AND MEDICAL CARE

Medicare, 1997

	Recipients	Payments
State	208,000	$879 mill.
Total U.S.	37,514,000	$206,064 mill.
State share	0.55%	0.43%
Rank among states	38	39

Recipient figures are rounded to nearest thousand persons.
  Ranks are from highest to lowest.
Source: U.S. Health Care Financing Administration.

Medicaid, 1996

	Recipients	Payments
State	167,000	$723 mill.
Total U.S.	35,028,000	$121,419 mill.
State share	0.48%	0.60%
Rank among states	37	35

Recipient figures are rounded to nearest thousand persons.
  Payment figures for fiscal year reflect federal and state
  contribution payments. Ranks are from highest to lowest.
Source: U.S. Health Care Financing Administration.

Health insurance coverage, 1996

	State	U.S.
Total persons covered	1,058,000	225,070,000
Total persons not covered	146,000	41,716,000
Part not covered	12.1%	15.6%
Rank among states	31	—
Children not covered	33,000	10,554,000
Part not covered	12.9%	14.8%
Rank among states	21	—

Ranks are from most to fewest uninsured. Population figures
  are rounded to nearest thousand persons.
Source: U.S. Bureau of the Census.

AIDS, syphilis, tuberculosis, and measles cases, 1997

Cases	U.S.	State	Share
AIDS	58,443	51	0.09%
Syphilis	8,550	2	0.02%
Tuberculosis	18,534	21	0.11%
Measles	148,000	1,000	0.68%

Measles figures are rounded to nearest thousand cases.
Source: U.S. Centers for Disease Control and Prevention.

HOUSING

Homeownership rates, 1985-1997

	1985	1990	1997
State	73.7%	74.2%	74.9%
Total U.S.	63.9%	63.9%	65.7%
Rank among states	2	1	3

Source: U.S. Bureau of the Census.

Home sales, 1990 and 1997

In thousands of units

Existing home sales	1990	1997	Change
State sales	NA	14.7	NA
Total U.S. sales	3,560	4,730	1,170
State share of U.S. total	NA	0.31%	0.31%
Rank among states	NA	41	—

Source: National Association of Realtors; *Real Estate Outlook:*
  Market Trends and Insights.

EDUCATION

Public school enrollment, 1995

State K-8 enrollment	156,000
Total U.S. K-8 enrollment	32,341,000
State share of total U.S.	0.48%
State 9-12 enrollment	58,000
Total U.S. 9-12 enrollment	12,500,000
State share of U.S. total	0.46%
State public school enroll. rate	93.5%
Overall U.S. rate	91.6%
Rank among states	17

Enrollment figures (which include unclassified students) are rounded to nearest thousand pupils in fall term; kindergarten (K)-8 grade figures include some prekindergarten students. Enrollment rate is based on percentage of persons 5-17 years old. Rank is from highest to lowest.
Source: U.S. National Center for Education Statistics.

Public college finances, 1996

State FTE enrollment	26,900
Total U.S. FTE enrollment	8,268,800
State share of total U.S.	0.33%
Rank among states	44
State and local appropriations	$161,700,000
Total U.S. state and local appropriations	$39,699 mill.
State share of total U.S.	0.41%
Rank among states	41
State net tuition revenues	$92,900,000
Total U.S. net tuition	$18,348,100,000
State share of total U.S.	0.51%
Rank among states	42

FTE=Full-time equivalent; credit and noncredit enrollment including summer session in academic year ending in 1996.
Enrollments are rounded to nearest thousand students. Net tuition revenues exclude appropriation to students attending in-state public institutions. Rankings are from highest shares to lowest.
Source: Research Associates of Washington.

TRANSPORTATION AND TRAVEL

Highway mileage, 1996

Interstate	368
Other arterial	2,327
Collector roads	6,397
Local roads	13,969
Urban roads	2,615
Rural roads	19,962
Total state	22,577
U.S. total	3,933,985
State share	0.6%
Rank among states	43

Source: U.S. Federal Highway Administration.

Motor vehicle registrations and driver licenses, 1996

In thousands

Vehicle registrations	State	U.S.	Share	Rank
Autos, trucks, buses	959	206,365	0.46%	42
Autos only	573	128,439	0.45%	40
Motorcycles	27	3,832	0.70%	36
Driver licenses	874	179,539	0.49%	42

Figures do not include vehicles owned by military services.
Source: U.S. Federal Highway Administration; *Highway Statistics; Selected Highway Statistics and Charts.*

Domestic travel expenditures, 1995

Spending by U.S. residents on overnight trips and day trips of at least 100 miles

Total expenditures in state	$1,600 mill.
Total expenditures in U.S.	$360,314 mill.
State share of total U.S.	0.44%
Rank among states	41

Source: Travel Industry Association of America.

CRIME AND LAW ENFORCEMENT

State and local police officers, 1996

Local police 1,426
State police 337
Sheriffs 321
Total 2,318
Officers per 10,000 residents 19
U.S. average 25
Rank among states. 39

Figures cover full-time sworn officers; totals include special
    police not shown separately.
Source: U.S. Bureau of Justice Statistics; *Census of State and
    Local Law Enforcement Agencies, 1996.*

Crime rates, 1996
Rates per 100,000 resident population

Violent crimes	State	U.S.
Total violent	125	634
Murder	2.0	7.4
Forcible rape	20.9	36.1
Robbery	24	202
Aggravated assault	79	388
Property crimes		
Total property	3,269	4,445
Burglary	748	943
Larceny/theft	2,378	2,976
Motor vehicle theft	143	526
Totals	3,394	5,079

Source: U.S. Federal Bureau of Investigation; *Crime in the
    United States*, annual.

State prison populations, 1980-1996

	State	U.S.	State share
1980	814	305,458	0.27%
1990	1,523	708,393	0.21%
1996	1,426	1,025,624	0.14%

Figures exclude prisoners in federal penitentiaries.
Source: U.S. Bureau of Justice Statistics.

Maryland

Location: East Coast of continental United States

Area and rank: 9,775 square miles (25,316 square kilometers); 12,407 square miles (32,134 square kilometers) including water; forty-second largest state in area

Coastline: 31 miles (50 kilometers)

Shoreline: 3,190 miles (5,133 kilometers)

Population and rank: 5,094,289 (1997); nineteenth largest state in population

Capital: Annapolis

Few states have cities as dominant as Baltimore, whose population exceeds that of Maryland's next fifty largest cities combined. (PhotoDisc)

Largest city: Baltimore (645,593 people in 1998)

Entered Union and rank: April 28, 1788; seventh state

Present constitution adopted: 1867

Counties: 23, as well as 1 independent city

State name: Maryland was named to honor Henrietta Maria, the queen of Charles I of England

State nicknames: Free State; Old Line State

Motto: *Fatti maschii, parole femine* (Manly deeds, womanly words)

State flag: Two quarters bear the arms of the Calvert family in gold and black; two quarters show the arms of the Crossland family in red and white

Highest point: Backbone Mountain — 3,360 feet (1,024 meters)

Lowest point: Atlantic Ocean — sea level

Highest recorded temperature: 109 degrees Fahrenheit (43 degrees Celsius) — Cumberland and Frederick, 1936

Lowest recorded temperature: −40 degrees Fahrenheit (−40 degrees Celsius) — Oakland, 1912

State song: "Maryland! My Maryland!"

State tree: White oak

State flower: Black-eyed susan

State bird: Baltimore oriole

State fish: Rockfish

Maryland History

In many ways, Maryland is a microcosm of much of the United States, combining elements from the north, south, east, and west. Physically located in the middle of the English colonies, it was the center state of the new nation and thus the logical site for a capital, which is located in the District of Columbia. After the Revolution, Maryland led efforts to develop the nation westward; it remained in the Union during the Civil War but sent soldiers to both the North and the South during that conflict. After World War II, the state managed to preserve its historic traditions and environmental legacy while advancing into the future.

Early History and Settlement. It is uncertain when Native Americans first entered the area now known as Maryland, but tribes of the Iroquoian and Algonquian peoples were certainly present several hundred years prior to European arrival. The major Iroquoian tribe was the Susquehannock, sometimes known as Conestoga, who came south from the Pennsylvania area. The Algonquians included the Choptank, Portobago, and Wicomico, names which still survive on the map of Maryland. The major Algonquian tribes were the Piscataway on the western shore (the mainland) of the Chesapeake Bay, and the Nanticoke on the eastern shore (the peninsula between the Chesapeake Bay and

Antietam, the site of the single bloodiest battle fought during the Civil War. (PhotoDisc)

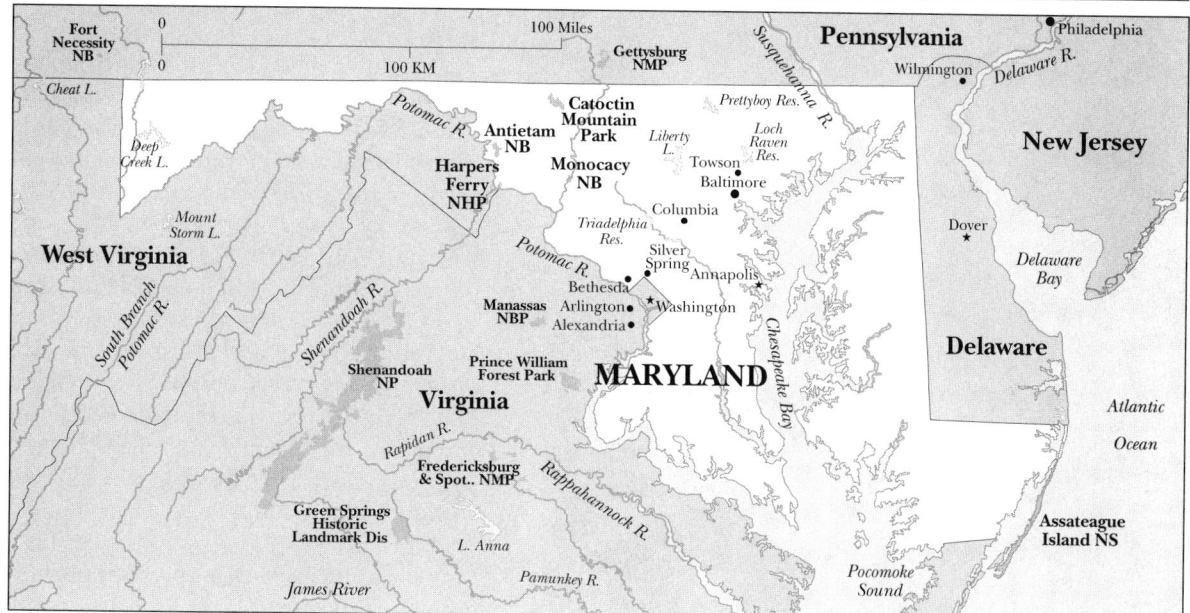

the Atlantic coast). Both Iroquoian and Algonquian Indians lived and farmed in permanent settlements.

The Algonquian tribes welcomed the English settlers, but the Susquehannock proved hostile, although their attacks were aimed as much against Native American allies of the English as against the English themselves. In any event, the colonists successfully defended themselves and in 1652 concluded a peace with the Susquehannock, which included the American Indians' departure from Maryland. Between the 1690's and the mid-1700's, first the Piscataway and then the other Native Americans also moved away from the area.

The Spanish were the first Europeans to explore the area, but the English were the first permanent settlers. English colonists from Virginia under councilman William Claiborne established a trading post on Kent Island in Chesapeake Bay in 1631. The following year, King Charles I granted George Calvert, Baron Baltimore, land north of the Potomac River, which included Maryland. It was on this land that Calvert's son Cecil, known as Lord Baltimore, established a colony in 1634. Led by Leonard Calvert, half brother of Cecil, the colonists included many Roman Catholics, among them two priests. At this time Roman Catholics were forbidden by British law from voting or

holding office. In part, Maryland was founded with the tacit understanding that it would be a refuge for English Catholics. In fact, the name of the colony, while officially honoring Queen Henrietta Maria of England, was often interpreted as referring to the Virgin Mary. In 1649 the colony adopted an "Act Concerning Religion," the first act of religious toleration in the colonies. Soon afterward, a group of Puritans arrived from Virginia.

In the meantime, Maryland settlers under Leonard Calvert disputed Virginia's claims to Kent Island. In 1654 Virginian Claiborne led the Puritans in a revolt that exiled Calvert, an action recognized by the English Commonwealth that had overthrown and executed Charles I. However, in 1658 Calvert and proprietary government were restored to Maryland. In 1692 Maryland became a royal colony, and the Church of England was declared established, or official, church. In 1718 Roman Catholics were denied the right to vote.

By far the most important influence on Maryland's history has been the Chesapeake Bay, the largest inlet on the East Coast. The bay is nearly two hundred miles long from north to south and as wide as twenty-five miles and is important for commercial fishing, oystering, and crabbing. At the head of the bay is Baltimore, one of the major

Cadets lining up at the U.S. Naval Academy, which opened at Maryland's state capital, Annapolis, in 1845. (Middleton Evans/Courtesy Maryland Office of Tourism)

In 1791 Maryland and Virginia ceded land to the United States to create the District of Columbia as the site of the new national capital. Construction of the White House began in 1793 and of the Capitol in 1794. In 1800 Congress moved to the new capital city from Philadelphia. During the War of 1812, British forces seized Washington and burned the White House but were unable to force their way past Fort McHenry to capture Baltimore. It was while watching this bombardment from Baltimore harbor that Francis Scott Key composed the poem "The Star Spangled Banner," which later became the national anthem of the United States.

In its key central position, Maryland took a leading role in the growth of the new nation, especially in its westward advancement. The Cumberland Road, also known as the National Pike, was a prime avenue for settlers heading into the interior of the continent; by 1818 it reached the Ohio River. Maryland was also active in the construction of canals, essential for transport of cargo during that period. Two vital waterways, the Chesapeake and Delaware and the Chesapeake and Ohio, connected the bay to those two rivers. The state also took the forefront in exploiting the new technology of the steam railroad, with the Baltimore and Ohio (B&O) starting operations in 1830 as the first American railroad to carry both passengers and freight.

Civil War. Slavery was legal in Maryland, and when the Civil War came there was considerable sentiment in the state for it to join others in the South in seceding from the Union. However, in 1861 the Maryland legislature rejected a bill of secession; still, many of the state's residents left to fight with the Confederate army, and many others were sympathizers. During the first months of the war mobs attacked Union troops as they marched through Baltimore. However, these disturbances were suppressed, and soon a ring of Union forts was erected to protect Washington, D.C., from Confederate attack.

There were a number of battles fought in Maryland during the Civil War, the largest being that of Antietam, fought in 1862. Antietam was the single

American ports since its founding in 1729 and Maryland's largest city.

Revolution and Growth. Marylanders joined with other colonists in their distaste for the high taxes imposed by Britain, and in 1774 a group of patriots boarded the *Peggy Stewart* in Annapolis Harbor and destroyed more than two thousand pounds of its cargo of tea. During the Revolution, when the British threatened the capital of Philadelphia, the Continental Congress moved to Baltimore, then to Annapolis. Maryland troops were among the best in the Continental Army, and their straight ranks and orderly battle lines earned Maryland the nickname "The Old Line State" from General George Washington.

bloodiest day of battle of the war, with more than twenty-three thousand casualties. It was a narrow Union victory, but enough for President Abraham Lincoln to feel justified in announcing the Emancipation Proclamation, which freed the slaves in the Confederacy and transformed the nature of the war to a crusade for liberty. During the summer of 1863, Confederate general Robert E. Lee's Army of Northern Virginia passed through the state on its way to the Battle of Gettysburg. In 1864 Confederate forces under General Jubal Early threatened Washington but were driven back at the last moment by Federal reinforcements.

Post-Civil War Progress. Agriculture had been dominant in Maryland prior to the Civil War, with the major crop of tobacco being shipped through the port of Baltimore. However, after the war the state's economy shifted toward manufacturing. Baltimore remained a key shipbuilding and weaponry production center; in the twentieth century the city would make rockets and missiles for the U.S. military. Both shipbuilding and weapons manufacture were spurred by government purchases during the two world wars.

Education in the state received an infusion of resources during the second half of the nineteenth century, especially with donations from philanthropists such as Johns Hopkins, who provided the financial backing to create the prestigious university that bears his name. Later, in the 1960's, federal funds were allocated for the National Institutes of Health at Bethesda and the Goddard Space Flight Center.

Toward the Future. As the twentieth century advanced, Maryland's agriculture remained important, with the chief crops being tobacco, corn, hay, and soybeans. Manufacturing continued to expand, primarily in ship building, transportation equipment, and modern technology such as electronics. Fishing in the renewed Chesapeake Bay

A Maryland horse farm. (Middleton Evans/Courtesy Maryland Office of Tourism)

provided much of the seafood sold nationally. However, it was commerce which led Maryland's revitalization, especially in its largest city.

Throughout most of Maryland's history, trade and commerce focused on Baltimore, which underwent a striking revival starting in the 1950's. Under Kurt Schmoke, the first African American elected mayor of the city, Baltimore completed an ambitious reconstruction of its inner harbor, with its centerpiece being the USS *Constellation*, the first warship commissioned by the U.S. Navy, in 1797. In 1992 the Baltimore Orioles opened their new stadium, Camden Yards, widely hailed as one of the most well designed and attractive of modern baseball parks.

Perhaps Maryland's most visible success is its reclaiming of Chesapeake Bay and its adoption of a policy of smart growth to combat urban sprawl. After decades of environmental neglect, including drainage of agriculture chemicals, unregulated dumping of waste, and overfishing, the Bay was seriously endangered. Governor Marvin Mandel established a Chesapeake Bay Interagency Planning Committee, and a widespread Save the Bay organization was created—two parts of a comprehensive effort that linked grassroots activists, government, and the private sector in addressing the problem. Spurred by the growing success of this effort, an association of environmental and citizen groups known as the Thousand Friends of Maryland began to campaign for strategic planning and "smart growth" to control urban sprawl, save Maryland's traditional farmlands, and preserve its small towns and their unique character. Supported by Governor Parris Glendening, who made smart growth an issue in his reelection campaign, the Maryland smart growth program became a national trendsetter for the twenty-first century.

Michael Witkoski

Maryland Time Line

1608	English Captain John Smith charts Chesapeake Bay region.
1631	Councilman William Claiborne establishes trading post on Kent Island as outpost of Virginia.
June 20, 1632	English King Charles I grants Cecil Calvert, Lord Baltimore, province of Maryland.
1634	Governor Leonard Calvert and settlers found St. Mary's City.
1635	St. Mary's City settlers fight Claiborne's colonists.
Apr. 21, 1649	Maryland enacts "Act Concerning Religion," the first act of religious toleration in colonies.
1652	Peace treaty is made with Susquehannock Indians.
1654	English Commonwealth ends Maryland's proprietary government.
1658	Proprietary government is restored by English Parliament.
1692	Maryland becomes a royal colony; Church of England made state church.
1694	Capital is moved to Annapolis.
1718	Roman Catholics lose the right to vote.
Oct. 19, 1774	Patriots burn cargo of tea aboard *Peggy Stewart* in Annapolis Harbor.
1776	Maryland Provincial Convention votes for independence; adopts state constitution.
1776	Continental Congress, fearing capture by British, flees Philadelphia to Baltimore.
Jan. 14, 1784	Continental Congress meets at Annapolis to sign Treaty of Paris.

Apr. 28, 1788	Maryland ratifies U.S. Constitution, becoming seventh state.
1791	Maryland cedes land to District of Columbia.
1796	Baltimore City is incorporated.
1809	First Roman Catholic parochial school in Union opens in Baltimore.
1812	University of Maryland is founded at Baltimore.
1814	British are defeated in attack on Fort McHenry outside Baltimore; Francis Scott Key writes "The Star-Spangled Banner."
1818	Cumberland Road (National Pike) reaches Ohio River.
1824-1829	Chesapeake and Delaware Canal is constructed.
1827	Baltimore and Ohio Railroad is chartered.
1830	Locomotive *Tom Thumb* races on Baltimore and Ohio Railroad line, the first U.S. railroad to carry both passengers and freight.
1828-1850	Chesapeake and Ohio Canal is constructed.
May 24, 1844	First telegraph line in United States links Baltimore with Washington, D.C.
1845	U.S. Naval Academy opens at Annapolis.
1849	Edgar Allan Poe dies in Baltimore.
Apr. 19, 1861	Baltimore mob attacks Union troops passing through state; sixteen are killed.
Sept. 16-17, 1862	Union wins a bloody victory over Confederate army at Antietam.
1864	State adopts new constitution abolishing slavery.
1867	State adopts revised constitution.
1876	The Johns Hopkins University opens in Baltimore.
1904	Great Baltimore Fire destroys downtown.
1920	Governor Albert Ritchie refuses to enforce national prohibition law.
1942	President Franklin D. Roosevelt establishes Shangri-La (now Camp David) as presidential retreat in Catoctin Mountains of Maryland.
1950	Friendship International Airport opens.
July, 1954	Chesapeake Bay Bridge is completed near Annapolis.
Sept., 1954	Baltimore desegregates public schools.
1957	Baltimore Harbor Tunnel opens.
1970	Perren Mitchell is elected to Congress, the first African American to represent Maryland.
1972	Maryland adopts state lottery.
1973	Parallel bridge of Chesapeake Bay Bridge is completed.
1980	Baltimore opens Harborplace, centerpiece of the renewed city.
1983	Chesapeake Bay Agreement to improve water quality and living resources of the bay is enacted.
1987	Updated and revised Chesapeake Bay Agreement to restore and protect the bay is enacted.

(continued)

1987	Kurt Schmoke becomes first African American mayor of Baltimore.
1992	Baltimore Orioles open Camden Yards baseball stadium.
1992	Maryland is first state to require public high school students to perform community service to graduate.
1994	Maryland adopts Smart Growth initiative to control urban sprawl.

Notes for Further Study

Published Sources. Maryland's history may best be studied in Robert J. Brugger's *Maryland: A Middle Temperament* (1989), a traditional but solid history that examines the state's unique character and contributions from colonial times to the modern era. *Maryland Lost and Found: People and Places from Chesapeake to Appalachia* (1986), by Eugene Meyer, is a genial approach to the cultures, communities, and diversity found between Maryland's coast and mountains. Two excellent guides to the state are *Maryland: A New Guide to the Old Line State* (1999), by Earl Arnett with Robert J. Brugger and Edward C. Papenfuse, and *The Chesapeake Bay Book: A Complete Guide* (3d ed. 1997), by Alison Blade and Tom Dove. Robert B. Harmon's *Government and Politics in Maryland* (1990) offers some excellent information and insights into Maryland's economic, cultural, and historical trends.

Web Resources. A good starting point for information on the state is Maryland Government—The Mary-

land Electronic Capital (http://www.mec.state.md.us), which has links to the various state agencies and departments and their wealth of resources. Of particular interest is the Maryland State Archives site (http://www.mdarchives.state.md.us), which has much material on Maryland's history and development from its settlement. A good supplement to these two sites is that of the Maryland Historical Society (http://www.mdhs.org). Two generalized sites are Maryland Manual Online (http://www.mdsa.net/msa/mdmanual/html/mmtoc.html) and Maryland Online (http://www.maryland-online.com), both of which contain information about contemporary Maryland. More specialized are the sites devoted to Maryland's Eastern Shore (http://www.esrl.lib.md.us/maryland/index.html) and to Women in Maryland (http://www.lib.umd.edu/UMCP/RATE/womenbib.html).

Counties

County	Sq. miles	1996 pop.	County	Sq. miles	1996 pop.
Allegany	425.3	73,037	Charles	461.1	113,557
Anne Arundel	416.0	465,582	Dorchester	557.6	29,988
Baltimore	598.6	717,859	Frederick	662.9	179,327
Calvert	215.2	66,779	Garrett	648.1	29,445
Caroline	320.2	29,189	Harford	440.4	209,121
Carroll	449.2	143,648	Howard	252.2	224,483
Cecil	348.2	79,475	Kent	279.4	18,889

County	Sq. miles	1996 pop.
Montgomery	494.6	816,999
Prince George's	486.4	773,810
Queen Anne's	372.2	38,024
Saint Mary's	361.3	82,655
Somerset	327.2	24,266
Talbot	269.2	32,381

County	Sq. miles	1996 pop.
Washington	458.2	127,278
Wicomico	377.2	79,253
Worcester	473.2	41,158

The city of Baltimore is independent of all counties.
Source: U.S. Census Bureau; National Association of Counties.

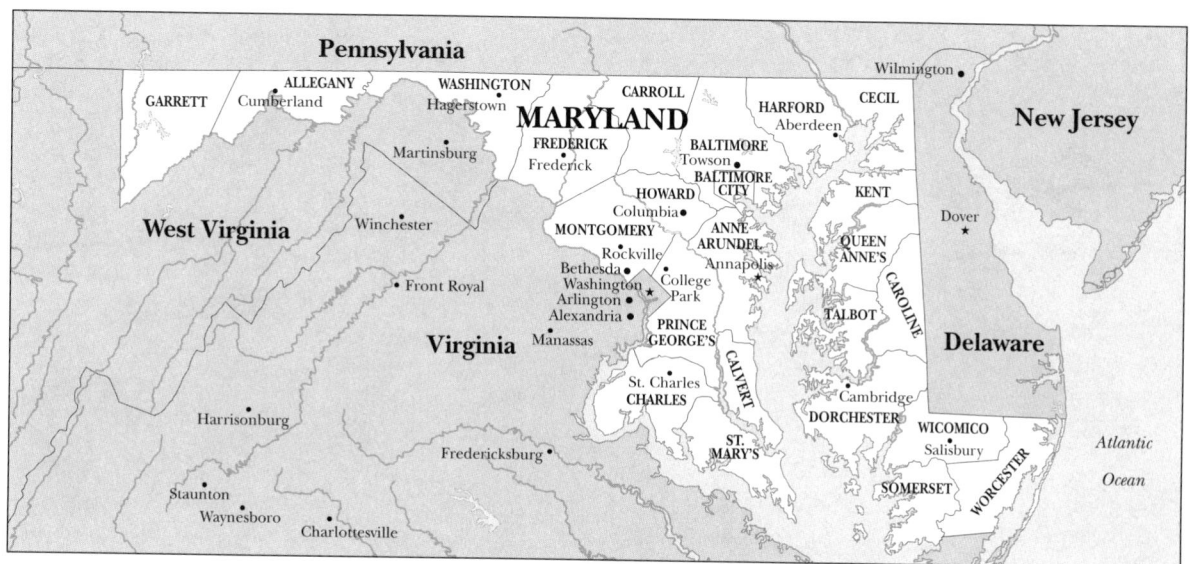

Cities

With 10,000 or more residents

Rank	City	Population
1	Baltimore	645,593
2	Frederick	47,468
3	Gaithersburg	46,980
4	Rockville	46,788
5	Bowie	40,704
6	Hagerstown	34,105

Rank	City	Population
7	Annapolis	33,585
8	College Park	25,855
9	Greenbelt	22,076
10	Cumberland	21,521
11	Salisbury	20,884
12	Laurel	18,825

(continued)

Rank	City	Population
13	Takoma Park	18,238
14	Westminster	15,776
15	Hyattsville	14,812
16	Aberdeen	13,278
17	New Carrollton	12,978
18	Elkton	10,870

Rank	City	Population
19	Cambridge	10,734
20	Easton	10,713
21	Havre de Grace	10,482

Population figures are estimated for mid-1998.
Source: U.S. Bureau of the Census.

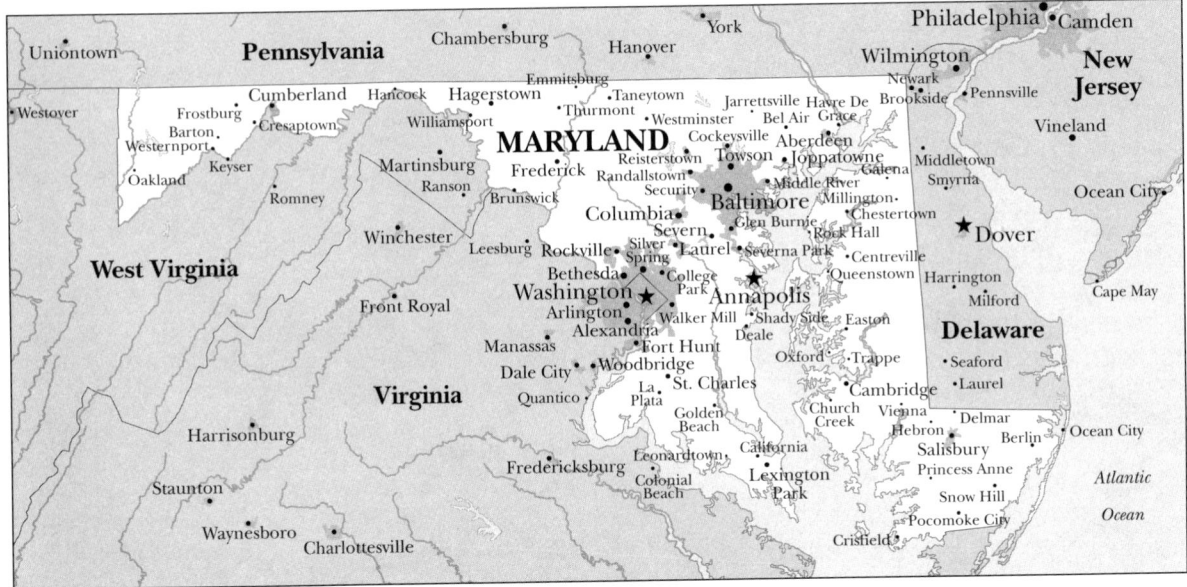

Index to Tables

NA = Reliable data are not available.

DEMOGRAPHICS

Resident state and national populations, 1970-1997

Population figures given in thousands

	State pop.	U.S. pop.	Share	Rank
1970	3,924	203,302	1.9%	18
1980	4,217	226,546	1.9%	18
1985	4,413	237,924	1.9%	18
1990	4,781	248,765	1.9%	19
1995	5,027	262,761	1.9%	19
1997	5,094	267,636	1.9%	19

Source: U.S. Bureau of the Census.

Resident population by age, 1997

Age group	Total population
Under 5 years	347,000
5 to 17 years	922,000
18 to 24 years	429,000
25 to 34 years	819,000
35 to 44 years	917,000
45 to 54 years	675,000
55 to 64 years	402,000
65 to 74 years	325,000
75 to 84 years	198,000
85 years and over	61,000
Portion of residents 65 and older	11.5%
National average	12.7%

Population figures are rounded to nearest thousand persons;
figures include armed forces personnel stationed in state.
Source: U.S. Bureau of the Census.

Resident population by race, Hispanic origin, 1997

	State pop.	Share	U.S.
All residents	5,094,000	100.0%	100.0%
Hispanic white	150,000	2.9%	10.0%
non-Hispanic white	3,337,000	65.5%	72.7%
African American	1,397,000	27.4%	12.7%
Native American	15,000	0.3%	0.9%
Asian, Pacific Islander	195,000	3.8%	3.8%

Source: U.S. Bureau of the Census.

Projections of state population, 2000-2025

	Model A Uses interstate migration observed from 1975-1994	Model B Uses Bureau of Economic Analysis employment projections
Year	Population	Population
2000	5,275,000	5,261,000
2005	5,467,000	5,426,000
2010	5,657,000	5,577,000
2015	5,862,000	5,736,000
2020	6,071,000	5,904,000
2025	6,274,000	6,072,000

All population projections, including those for 2000, were calculated in 1997.
Source: U.S. Bureau of the Census, Population Paper Listings PPL-47.

VITAL STATISTICS

Average lifetime in years by race, 1989-1991

	State	U.S.	Rank
All residents	74.79	75.37	36
White residents	76.30	76.13	26
Black residents	69.69	69.16	15

Ranks are from longest-lived to least longest-lived. Ranks exclude Alaska, for which reliable data are not available. Rank for black residents is based on the 32 states for which reliable data are available.
Source: U.S. National Center for Health Statistics.

Infant mortality rates, 1980 and 1995

	State	U.S.
All residents		
1980	14.0	12.6
1995	8.9	7.6
White residents		
1980	11.6	11.0
1995	6.0	6.3
Black residents		
1980	20.4	21.4
1995	15.3	15.1

Figures represent deaths per 1,000 live births of resident infants under 1 year old, exclusive of fetal deaths; all-residents figures include other races not listed separately.
Source: U.S. National Center for Health Statistics.

Marriages and divorces

Marriages in 1996	41,800
Rate per 1,000 population, 1995	8.5
U.S. rate, 1995	8.9
Rank among all states	26
Divorces in 1996	16,300
Rate per 1,000 population, 1995	3.0
U.S. rate, 1995	4.4
Rank among all states	44

Rank is from highest to lowest in country.
Source: U.S. National Center for Health Statistics.

Death rates by leading causes, 1995
Deaths per 100,000 resident population

Cause	State	U.S.
Heart disease	236.4	280.7
Cancer	201.9	204.9
Cerebrovascular diseases	52.5	60.1
Accidents and adverse effects	27.6	35.5
Motor vehicle accidents	13.5	16.5
Chronic obstructive pulmonary diseases	31.6	39.2
Diabetes mellitus	27.0	22.6
HIV	25.6	NA
Suicide	10.1	11.9
Homicide	12.7	8.7
All causes	829.8	880.0
Rank in overall death rate among states		35

Figures exclude nonresidents who die in state. Causes of death follow International Classification of Diseases. Rank is from highest to lowest in country.
Source: U.S. National Center for Health Statistics.

ECONOMY

Gross state product, 1990-1996
In current dollars

	State product	Increase
1990	$113.7 billion	
1993	$124.6 billion	
1994	$132.9 billion	6.66%
1995	$137.4 billion	3.39%
1996	$143.2 billion	4.22%

Source: U.S. Bureau of Economic Analysis; *Survey of Current Business,* June, 1998.

Gross state product by industry, 1996
In billions

Farms, forestry, fisheries	$1.2
Construction	6.2
Manufacturing	12.0
Transportation, public utilities	10.6
Wholesale trade	8.6
Retail trade	12.2
Finance, insurance, real estate	26.5
Services	29.1
Government	23.6
State total	$130.2
Total U.S.	$6,923.8
State share	1.88%
Rank among states	17

Total figures include mining, not listed separately.
Source: U.S. Bureau of Economic Analysis; *Survey of Current Business,* June, 1998.

Personal income per capita, 1990 and 1997
In current dollars

	1990	1997
Per capita income	$22,517	$28,969
U.S. average	$19,188	$25,598
Rank among states	5	6

1997 data are preliminary.
Source: U.S. Bureau of Economic Analysis; *Survey of Current Business,* May, 1998.

Energy consumption, 1995
In trillions of British thermal units (BTU)

End-use sectors

Residential	365.3
Commercial	323.3
Industrial	270.3
Transportation	353.0

Sources of energy

Petroleum	496.1
Natural gas	199.1
Coal	289.6
Hydroelectric power	14.9
Nuclear electric power	137.9
Total state per capita consumption	260.4
Total U.S. per capita consumption	344.4
Rank among states	40
Total state energy consumption	1,311.9
Total U.S. energy consumption	90,547.4
State share of U.S. total	1.45%
Rank among states	25

Total figures include items not listed separately.
Source: U.S. Energy Information Administration; *State Energy Data Report.*

Nonfarm employment by sectors, 1997

Total	2,257,000
Construction	138,000
Manufacturing	176,000
Transportation, public utilities	106,000
Wholesale trade, retail trade	536,000
Finance, insurance, real estate	131,000
Services	752,000
Government	417,000

Figures are rounded to nearest thousand persons. Total includes mining, not listed separately.
Source: U.S. Bureau of Labor Statistics; *Employment and Earnings,* monthly.

Foreign exports, 1990-1997
In millions of dollars

Year	State	U.S.	State share
1990	2,592	394,045	0.66%
1996	5,019	624,767	0.80%
1997	5,214	688,896	0.76%

Source: U.S. Bureau of the Census; *U.S. Merchandise Trade,* series FT 900.

LAND USE

Federally owned land, 1996

	State	U.S.	State share
Total acres	6,319,000	2,271,343,000	0.28%
Federally owned	157,000	563,129,000	0.03%
Federal share	2.5%	24.8%	—

Areas are rounded to nearest thousand acres. Figures for federally owned land do not include trust properties.
Source: U.S. General Services Administration; *Inventory Report on Real Property Owned by the United States Throughout the World,* annual.

Land use, 1992
In acres, rounded to nearest thousand

Total surface area	6,695,000
Federal land	167,000
Total nonfederal.	6,034,000
Developed	1,095,000
Total rural	4,939,000
Cropland.	1,673,000
Pasture land	545,000
Range land	0
Forest land.	2,364,000
Minor cover/use.	356,000

Total surface area figures include water area not shown separately.
Source: U.S. Dept. of Agriculture; Soil Conservation Service; Iowa State University, Statistical Laboratory; *Summary Report, 1992 National Resources Inventory.*

Farms and crop acreage, 1997

	State	U.S.	Share	Rank
Farms (thousands)	13	2,058	0.63%	36
Acres (millions)	2	968	0.21%	41
Acres per farm	162	471	—	42
Acres planted	1,556	334,139	0.47%	34
Acres harvested	1,500	319,894	0.47%	34
Farm value (mill.)	$420	$108,805	0.39%	41

Numbers of farms are rounded to nearest thousand.
Source: U.S. Dept. of Agriculture; National Agricultural Statistics Service.

GOVERNMENT AND FINANCE

Units of local government, 1997

	State	Total U.S.	Rank
All local governments	420	87,453	45
Counties	23	3,043	37
Municipalities	156	19,372	36
Townships	0	16,629	—
School districts	0	13,726	—
Special districts	241	34,683	41

County ranks are based on the 48 states with county governments; township ranks are based on the 20 states with township governments; school district ranks are based on the 46 states with such districts.
Source: U.S. Bureau of the Census; *1997 Census of Governments, Government Organization,* Series GC97(1).

State government revenue, 1996

Total revenue	$16,041 mill.
General revenue	14,011 mill.
Per capita.	2,769
U.S. per capita average	2,910
Rank among states.	28
Intergovernmental revenue	
Total	$3,240 mill.
From federal government	3,126 mill.
From local government	114 mill.
Charges and Miscellaneous	
Total	$2,605 mill.
Current charges	1,318 mill.
Misc. general revenue	1,286 mill.
Taxes	
Total	$8,167 mill.
General sales	2 mill.,000
Selective sales.	1,555 mill.
License taxes	358 mill.
Individual income	3,485 mill.
Corporate income	331 mill.
Other	439 mill.
Insurance trust revenue	1,941 mill.

Total revenue figures include items not listed separately.
Source: U.S. Bureau of the Census.

State government expenditures, 1996

General expenditures

Intergovernmental	$3,238 mill.
Direct expenditures	10,117 mill.
Total	13,355 mill.

Selected direct expenditures

Education	$4,050 mill.
Public welfare	2,923 mill.
Health, hospital	1,072 mill.
Highways	1,220 mill.
Police	274 mill.
Corrections	743 mill.
Natural resources	303 mill.
Parks and recreation	68 mill.
Government administration	621 mill.
Interest on debt	594 mill.

Other

State per capita expenditures	$2,639
U.S. per capita average	2,854
Rank among states	30
Total state expenditures	15,554 mill.
Total U.S. expenditures	859,959 mill.

Totals include items not listed separately.
Source: U.S. Bureau of the Census.

POLITICS

Governors since statehood

D = Democrat; R = Republican; O = other;
(r) resigned; (d) died in office; (i) removed from office

Thomas Johnson	1777-1779
Thomas Sim Lee	1779-1782
William Paca	1782-1785
William Smallwood	1785-1788
John Eager Howard (O)	1788-1791
George Plater (O)	(d) 1791-1792
James Brice (O)	1792
Thomas Sim Lee (O)	1792-1794
John Hoskins Stone (O)	1794-1797
John Henry (O)	1797-1798
Benjamin Ogle (O)	1798-1801
John Francis Mercer (O)	1801-1803
Robert Bowie (O)	1803-1806
Robert Wright (O)	(r) 1806-1809
James Butcher (O)	1809
Edward Lloyd (O)	1809-1811
Robert Bowie (O)	1811-1812
Levin Winder (O)	1812-1816
Charles Carnan Ridgley (O)	1816-1819
Charles Goldsborough (O)	1819
Samuel Sprigg (O)	1819-1822
Samuel Stevens, Jr. (O)	1822-1826
Joseph Kent (O)	1826-1829
Daniel Martin (O)	1829-1830
Thomas King Carroll (O)	1830-1831
Daniel Martin (O)	(d) 1831
George Howard (O)	1831-1833
James Thomas (O)	1833-1836
Thomas Ward Veazey (O)	1836-1839
William Grason (D)	1839-1842
Francis Thomas (D)	1842-1845
Thomas George Pratt (O)	1845-1848
Philip Francis Thomas (D)	1848-1851
Enoch Louis Lowe (D)	1851-1854
Thomas Watkins Ligon (D)	1854-1858
Thomas Holliday Hicks (O)	1858-1862
Augustus W. Bradford (O)	1862-1866
Thomas Swann (O)	1866-1869
Oden Bowie (D)	1869-1872
William Pinkney Whyte (D)	(r) 1872-1874
James Black Groome (D)	1874-1876
John Lee Carroll (D)	1876-1880
William Thomas Hamilton (D)	1880-1884
Robert Milligan McLane (D)	(r) 1884-1885
Henry Lloyd (D)	1885-1888
Elihu Emory Jackson (D)	1888-1892
Frank Brown (D)	1892-1896
Lloyd Lowndes (R)	1896-1900
John W. Smith (D)	1900-1904
Edwin Warfield (D)	1904-1908
Austin L. Crothers (D)	1908-1912
Phillips L. Goldsborough (R)	1912-1916
Emerson C. Harrington (D)	1916-1920
Albert C. Ritchie (D)	1920-1935
Harry W. Nice (R)	1935-1939
Herbert R. O'Conor (D)	1939-1947
William P. Lane, Jr. (D)	1947-1951
Theodore R. McKeldin (R)	1951-1959
J. Millard Tawes (D)	1959-1967
Spiro T. Agnew (R)	(r) 1967-1969
Marvin Mandel (D)	(i) 1969-1977
Blair Lee III (D)	1977-1979
Harry R. Hughes (D)	1979-1987
William Donald Schaefer (D)	1987-1991
Parris N. Glendening (D)	1995-

Composition of state legislature, 1990-1998

	Democrats	Republicans
State House (141 seats)		
1990	116	25
1992	116	25
1994	100	41
1996	100	41
1998	106	35
State Senate (47 seats)		
1990	38	9
1992	38	9
1994	32	15
1996	32	15
1998	32	15

Figures for total seats may include independents and minor
party members.
Source: Council of State Governments; *State Elective Officials
and the Legislatures.*

Composition of congressional delegations, 1989-1999

	Dem	Rep	Total
House of Representatives			
101st Congress, 1989			
State delegates	6	2	8
Total U.S.	259	174	433
102d Congress, 1991			
State delegates	5	3	8
Total U.S.	267	167	434
103d Congress, 1993			
State delegates	4	4	8
Total U.S.	258	176	434
104th Congress, 1995			
State delegates	4	4	8
Total U.S.	197	236	433
105th Congress, 1997			
State delegates	4	4	8
Total U.S.	206	228	434
106th Congress, 1999			
State delegates	4	4	8
Total U.S.	211	222	433

	Dem	Rep	Total
Senate			
101st Congress, 1989			
State delegates	2	0	2
Total U.S.	55	45	100
102d Congress, 1991			
State delegates	2	0	2
Total U.S.	56	44	100
103d Congress, 1993			
State delegates	2	0	2
Total U.S.	57	43	100
104th Congress, 1995			
State delegates	2	0	2
Total U.S.	46	53	99
105th Congress, 1997			
State delegates	2	0	2
Total U.S.	45	55	100
106th Congress, 1999			
State delegates	2	0	2
Total U.S.	45	54	99

Figures are for starts of first sessions. Figure for U.S. Representatives for 101st Congress does not include Alabama
and Indiana, which had vacancies. Figures for total U.S.
Representatives for 102d, 103d, and 106th Congresses do
not include Vermont, which had 1 Independent-Socialist.
Figure for U.S. Representatives for 104th Congress does
not include Vermont, which had 1 Independent-Socialist,
and California, which had 1 vacancy. Figure for U.S. Representatives for 105th Congress does not include New York,
which had 1 vacancy. Figure for U.S. Senators for 104th
Congress does not include Oregon, which had 1 vacancy.
Figure for U.S. Senators for 106th Congress does not
include New Hampshire, which had 1 Independent.
Source: U.S. Congress; *Congressional Directory,* biennial.

Voter participation in presidential elections, 1992 and 1996

	1992	1996
State voting age pop.	3,705,000	3,811,000
Total U.S. voting age pop.	189,524,000	196,509,000
State share of U.S. total	2.0%	1.9%
Rank among states	19	19
Percent of state casting vote	53.6	64.3
Percent of U.S. total voting	55.1	49.0
Rank among states	33	2

Source: U.S. Bureau of the Census.

HEALTH AND MEDICAL CARE

Medicare, 1997

	Recipients	Payments
State	618,000	$3,438 mill.
Total U.S.	37,514,000	$206,064 mill.
State share	1.65%	1.67%
Rank among states	22	19

Recipient figures are rounded to nearest thousand persons.
  Ranks are from highest to lowest.
Source: U.S. Health Care Financing Administration.

Medicaid, 1996

	Recipients	Payments
State	399,000	$2,047 mill.
Total U.S.	35,028,000	$121,419 mill.
State share	1.14%	1.69%
Rank among states	27	17

Recipient figures are rounded to nearest thousand persons.
  Payment figures for fiscal year reflect federal and state
  contribution payments. Ranks are from highest to lowest.
Source: U.S. Health Care Financing Administration.

Health insurance coverage, 1996

	State	U.S.
Total persons covered	4,507,000	225,070,000
Total persons not covered	581,000	41,716,000
Part not covered	11.4%	15.6%
Rank among states	35	—
Children not covered	107,000	10,554,000
Part not covered	8.1%	14.8%
Rank among states	43	—

Ranks are from most to fewest uninsured. Population figures
  are rounded to nearest thousand persons.
Source: U.S. Bureau of the Census.

AIDS, syphilis, tuberculosis, and measles cases, 1997

Cases	U.S.	State	Share
AIDS	58,443	1,875	3.21%
Syphilis	8,550	891	10.42%
Tuberculosis	18,534	340	1.83%
Measles	148,000	2,000	1.35%

Measles figures are rounded to nearest thousand cases.
Source: U.S. Centers for Disease Control and Prevention.

HOUSING

Homeownership rates, 1985-1997

	1985	1990	1997
State	65.6%	64.9%	70.5%
Total U.S.	63.9%	63.9%	65.7%
Rank among states	34	35	15

Source: U.S. Bureau of the Census.

Home sales, 1990 and 1997

In thousands of units

Existing home sales	1990	1997	Change
State sales	67.1	66.4	-0.7
Total U.S. sales	3,560	4,730	1,170
State share of U.S. total	1.88%	1.40%	-0.48%
Rank among states	19	24	—

Source: National Association of Realtors; *Real Estate Outlook:*
  Market Trends and Insights.

EDUCATION

Public school enrollment, 1995

State K-8 enrollment 590,000
Total U.S. K-8 enrollment 32,341,000
State share of total U.S. 1.82%
State 9-12 enrollment 215,000
Total U.S. 9-12 enrollment 12,500,000
State share of U.S. total 1.72%
State public school enroll. rate 89.0%
Overall U.S. rate. 91.6%
Rank among states. 37

Enrollment figures (which include unclassified students) are rounded to nearest thousand pupils in fall term; kindergarten (K)-8 grade figures include some prekindergarten students. Enrollment rate is based on percentage of persons 5-17 years old. Rank is from highest to lowest.
Source: U.S. National Center for Education Statistics.

Public college finances, 1996

State FTE enrollment 155,100
Total U.S. FTE enrollment 8,268,800
State share of total U.S. 1.88%
Rank among states. 19
State and local appropriations $716,800,000
Total U.S. state and local
　appropriations. . . . . $39,699 mill.
State share of total U.S. 1.81%
Rank among states. 19
State net tuition revenues. $432,200,000
Total U.S. net tuition $18,348,100,000
State share of total U.S. 2.36%
Rank among states. 14

FTE=Full-time equivalent; credit and noncredit enrollment including summer session in academic year ending in 1996.
Enrollments are rounded to nearest thousand students. Net tuition revenues exclude appropriation to students attending in-state public institutions. Rankings are from highest shares to lowest.
Source: Research Associates of Washington.

TRANSPORTATION AND TRAVEL

Highway mileage, 1996

Interstate 482
Other arterial. 3,780
Collector roads 6,292
Local roads 20,431
Urban roads. 13,899
Rural roads 15,781
Total state 29,680
U.S. total 3,933,985
State share 0.8%
Rank among states. 42

Source: U.S. Federal Highway Administration.

Motor vehicle registrations and driver licenses, 1996

In thousands

Vehicle registrations	State	U.S.	Share	Rank
Autos, trucks, buses	3,635	206,365	1.76%	20
Autos only	2,557	128,439	1.99%	18
Motorcycles	38	3,832	0.99%	29
Driver licenses	3,377	179,539	1.88%	20

Figures do not include vehicles owned by military services.
Source: U.S. Federal Highway Administration; *Highway Statistics; Selected Highway Statistics and Charts.*

Domestic travel expenditures, 1995

Spending by U.S. residents on overnight trips and day trips of at least 100 miles

Total expenditures in state . . . . $5,667 mill.
Total expenditures in U.S. . . . . $360,314 mill.
State share of total U.S. 1.57%
Rank among states. 22

Source: Travel Industry Association of America.

CRIME AND LAW ENFORCEMENT

State and local police officers, 1996

Local police 8,923
State police 1,625
Sheriffs 1,438
Total 13,828
Officers per 10,000 residents 27
U.S. average 25
Rank among states 8

Figures cover full-time sworn officers; totals include special
   police not shown separately.
Source: U.S. Bureau of Justice Statistics; *Census of State and
   Local Law Enforcement Agencies, 1996.*

Crime rates, 1996

Rates per 100,000 resident population

Violent crimes	State	U.S.
Total violent	931	634
Murder	11.6	7.4
Forcible rape	37.6	36.1
Robbery	393	202
Aggravated assault	489	388
Property crimes		
Total property	5,131	4,445
Burglary	992	943
Larceny/theft	3,427	2,976
Motor vehicle theft	711	526
Totals	6,062	5,079

Source: U.S. Federal Bureau of Investigation; *Crime in the
   United States,* annual.

State prison populations, 1980-1996

	State	U.S.	State share
1980	7,731	305,458	2.53%
1990	17,848	708,393	2.52%
1996	22,050	1,025,624	2.15%

Figures exclude prisoners in federal penitentiaries.
Source: U.S. Bureau of Justice Statistics.

Massachusetts

Location: New England (northeastern continental United States)

Area and rank: 7,838 square miles (20,300 square kilometers); 10,555 square miles (27,337 square kilometers) including water; forty-fifth largest state in area

Coastline: 192 miles (309 kilometers)

Shoreline: 1,519 miles (2,444 kilometers)

Population and rank: 6,117,520 (1997); thirteenth largest state in population

A view from the Charles River of Massachusetts's capital and largest city, Boston. (PhotoDisc)

Capital: Boston

Largest city: Boston (555,447 people in 1998)

Entered Union and rank: February 6, 1788; sixth state

Present constitution adopted: 1780 (oldest U.S. state constitution in effect today)

Counties: 14

State name: "Massachusetts" is derived from two Indian words meaning "great mountain place"

State nicknames: Bay State; Old Colony State

Motto: *Ense petit placidam sub libertate quietem* (By the sword we seek peace, but peace only under liberty)

State flag: White field with state coat of arms in blue and yellow

Highest point: Mount Greylock — 3,487 feet (1,063 meters)

Lowest point: Atlantic Ocean — sea level

Highest recorded temperature: 107 degrees Fahrenheit (42 degrees Celsius) — New Bedford and Chester, 1975

Lowest recorded temperature: −34 degrees Fahrenheit (−37 degrees Celsius) — Birch Hill Dam, 1957

State song: "All Hail to Massachusetts"

State tree: American elm

State flower: Mayflower

State bird: Chickadee

Massachusetts History

Massachusetts was one of the original thirteen colonies, and its capital, Boston, is considered the cradle of the American Revolution. The state was home to some of the United States' greatest leaders. Its reputation for excellent education is due to its many great universities and colleges, including the world-famous Harvard and Massachusetts Institute of Technology (MIT). Geographically, the state forms a narrow rectangle. Relatively small, it is forty-fifth in area among the states, yet thirteenth in state population.

Native American History. The Algonquians were a large family of tribes, related by language and customs, who lived throughout the northeastern United States. Several of these tribes made their homes in the fertile farming and hunting grounds of the area. The Nauset lived on Cape Cod, while the Wampanoag, the Massachusetts (for whom the state is named), and the Patuxet fished and hunted along the coast. Women played a central role in Algonquian society. They owned the tribe's land, which they cleared and farmed communally. When a young man married, he left home to become a member of his bride's family.

Early Exploration and the Pilgrims. In 1602 English navigator Bartholomew Gosnold visited Massachusetts Bay and named it Cape Cod. Two years later explorer Samuel de Champlain explored the coast, followed by Captain John Smith in 1614.

In September of 1620, an English merchant ship called the *Mayflower* set sail from the port of Southampton with 102 passengers bound for the

The landing of the pilgrims at Plymouth Rock in 1620 is traditionally considered the beginning of British North America. (Library of Congress)

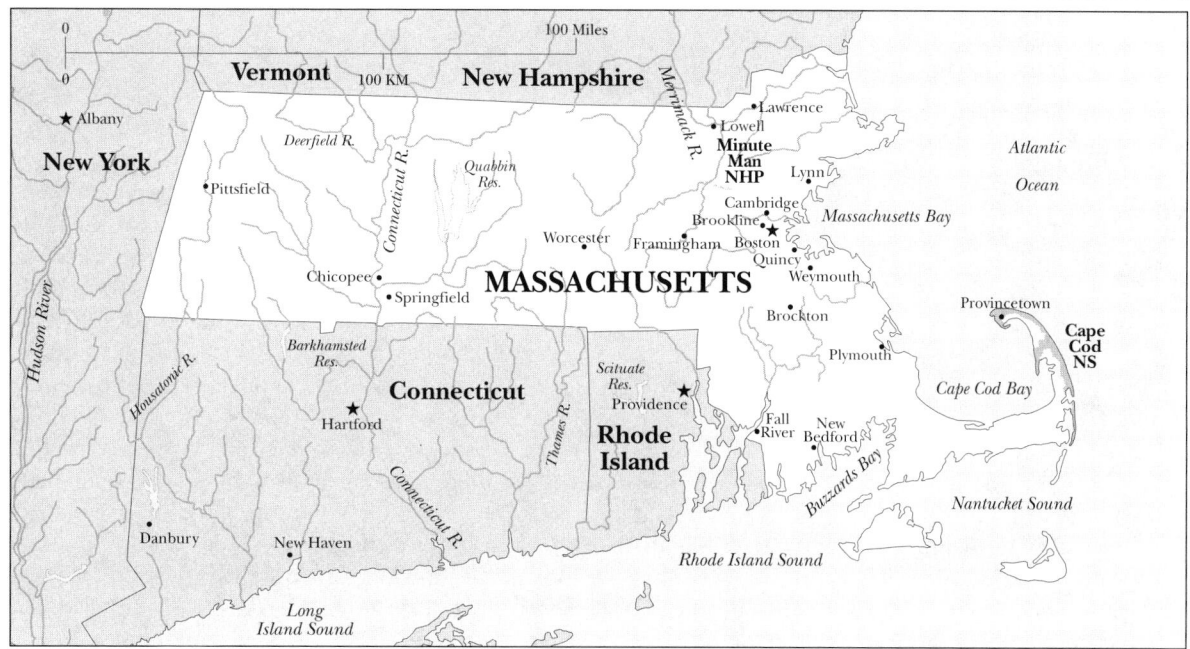

Americas. Of these passengers, 41 were Separatists, members of a renegade congregation that had broken away from the Church of England. These people considered themselves religious pilgrims. Before the pilgrims and the others left England, the group leaders wrote and signed a document that became the foundation of American democracy, the Mayflower Compact. It decreed a representative government.

Despite legend, the ship did not land at Plymouth Rock, but rather at the tip of Cape Cod, the site of modern Provincetown. After a little exploring, Plymouth proved a better place to found a village. After the harsh winter of 1621, however, half the settlers were dead. Spring came, and the pilgrims met a Patuxet Indian named Squanto. Years earlier he had been captured by slave traders and sold in Spain. After escaping to England and becoming fluent in English, he made his way back to his homeland, only to find his tribe wiped out by disease. Squanto taught the pilgrims how to farm and served as an interpreter, making treaties with other tribes. After the first harvest in October, 1621, for three days the pilgrims hosted about ninety Native Americans in a feast. It became the first Thanksgiving, a tradition that would long be celebrated in the United States.

The colony began to prosper, and every year brought more colonists seeking religious freedom. In 1630 John Winthrop, with a charter for "The Governor and Company of the Massachusetts Bay in New England," landed at Salem with more than one thousand colonists. Winthrop and his followers did not want to separate from the church, but they believed it needed to be purified from within and thus were called Puritans. The Puritans felt the law must be strictly obeyed if the community were to be strong. A set of wooden stocks stood in the center of many towns, and wrongdoers were put there for crimes as small as swearing.

The Witch Trials. Ironically, while Winthrop and his followers left England to seek religious freedom, they had little tolerance of others' religious philosophies. In the 1660's Puritan authorities hanged several Quakers as heretics. By 1692 this intolerance, mixed with superstition, turned into one of the New World's most shameful chapters, the Salem witch trials. Tituba, a West Indian slave woman, told locals tales of African magic. When some of the girls began to have fainting spells, they accused Tituba of casting spells over them. When Salem reverend Samuel Parris demanded to know who else had been practicing the evil arts, the girls started falsely accusing neighbors of witchery, and soon everyone was accusing everyone else. Nineteen men and women were burned as witches, and nearly 150 more were awaiting trail when authorities in Boston stopped the proceedings. Although the Puritans initiated an atmosphere of intolerance and fear in their society, they must also be remembered for their dedication to hard work and their respect for education; they founded Harvard, the first institution of higher learning in North America.

The American Revolution. By the mid-1700's Massachusetts was the center of shipbuilding and commerce in the British colonies. The people there were successful, well educated, and accustomed to managing their own affairs. The French and Indian War was won by the British, but at a great cost. To raise more money, Great Britain heavily taxed the colonies. The colonists were particularly upset about this because they were being taxed with no representation in Parliament: "No taxation without representation!" was the frequent cry of colonial protesters. The merchants of

Boston led a boycott of British goods, and Britain responded by stationing troops in the city. One night in March of 1770, mounting tension exploded in a skirmish that became known as the Boston Massacre. Five were killed, the first being a young black man named Crispus Attucks.

On December 16, 1773, a group of Boston men crept aboard three British ships and dumped the tea cargoes into the harbor to protest the high taxes, in what became known as the Boston Tea Party. In April of 1775, the British, intent on quelling the patriots by force, planned to send armed men to Lexington, Concord, and then Boston. Paul Revere, among others, was able to warn the Minutemen, Massachusetts fighters. While the British were able to take Lexington and then Concord in small battles, the patriots were able to defend Boston for a while. Eventually, however, the city succumbed to British force. The Revolutionary War had begun.

The next year, General George Washington took Boston back, chasing the British out of Massa-

One of the most famous incidents that led to the Revolutionary War was the dumping of British tea cargoes into Boston harbor in 1773—an event later celebrated as the "Boston Tea Party." (Library of Congress)

chusetts forever. The Treaty of Paris of 1783 granted independence to the colonies. No other colony had contributed more men or money to the war for independence than Massachusetts.

War and Immigration. The United States went to war with Britain again in 1812 for interfering with American trade, pirating U.S. ships, and forcing Americans to fight the British war with France. Boston, the largest American city of the time, suffered greatly. Boston developed industries to maintain the economy.

In the 1840's, the potato famine in Ireland sent more than one million Irish men and women to the United States, and hundreds of thousands settled in Massachusetts. They found work in the factories of Boston, Lawrence, Lowell, and Worcester. Many residents saw the flood of Irish Catholics as a threat to their Anglo-Protestant society. Discrimination against the Irish was prevalent, and it was not uncommon to see a Help Wanted sign include a No Irish Need Apply slogan. However, any labor was needed eventually as the state became a leader in the American Industrial Revolution. New mills producing textile, paper, boots, and shoes sprang up all over the state.

The Late 1800's. The Civil War began in 1861, and Massachusetts was the first state to respond, with a regiment of fifteen hundred soldiers. Throughout the war, the state supplied guns, uniforms, and boots to the Union army. When the war was over, the Irish, many of whom served in the war, began climbing the social ladder. They founded businesses, saved money, and bought their own homes. Still, they were discriminated against, and they looked to politics as a way to fight back. In 1880 Hugh O'Brien became Boston's first Irish mayor. In 1892 Patrick Joseph "P. J." Kennedy, son of an East Boston barrel maker, was elected to the state senate. Yet discrimination against Irish, as well as all immigrants, continued.

In the 1880's and 1890's, fresh waves of immigrants poured in. In 1896, U.S. Senator Henry Cabot Lodge, a descendant of Boston's most elite families, sponsored a bill to restrict immigration. He claimed scientific evidence to prove that southern and eastern Europeans were racially inferior and prone to crime. It was vetoed by the U.S. president but signed into law in 1924.

Economic Hard Times. By 1900 Massachusetts was an industrial state. Yet the large mills in the state would not always run smoothly. In 1912 more than twenty-two thousand textile workers staged a strike in Lawrence. There would be other labor problems, and men and women began to organize into unions to fight for better working conditions and higher wages.

After World War I, Massachusetts slipped into recession. When the country fell into the Depression of the 1930's, Massachusetts was hit hard. By 1931 only 44 percent of the state's workers were employed full-time. When World War II began in 1941, Massachusetts factories and shipyards rebounded. The state achieved almost full employment, and thousands of African Americans migrated from southern states to work in the war plants. After the war, the factories fell on hard times yet again. However, another industry, education, led by MIT and Harvard, proved to entice many great minds—and federal grants—to the state. Boston, meanwhile, emerged as a center for banking, insurance, and medicine.

The Kennedy Dynasty. The son of P. J. Kennedy, Joseph Kennedy graduated from Harvard in 1912 and entered the world of banking. At twenty-five, he became the youngest bank president in the nation. He rose in stature and was eventually named ambassador to England. His political career was ruined, however, when he supported appeasement of German leader Adolf Hitler. Three of his nine children would fulfill his ambitions by going into politics.

In 1960 his son and Massachusetts senator John F. Kennedy became the first Irish Catholic president of the United States. He would not be allowed to finish out his term, however, and the nation grieved when the young president was assassinated in Dallas in 1963. His brother, Robert, was also killed when running for president in 1968. Joseph Kennedy's youngest son, Edward "Ted" Kennedy, served in the U.S. Senate for many years, serving as the patriarch of the ill-fated family. Several of the next generation of Kennedys served in politics as well.

Great politicians and diversity continued to be a strength of the state. Michael S. Dukakis was the first Greek American to be elected governor, in 1972. He later won the Democratic nomination for U.S. president in 1988 but lost to George Bush.

Kevin M. Mitchell

Massachusetts Time Line

1620	*Mayflower* lands and its passengers begin settlement at Plymouth.
1621	Patuxet Indian named Squanto befriends the pilgrims and teaches them farming.
Oct., 1621	First Thanksgiving takes place.
1634	Boston Commons is established, making it the first city park in the nation.
1636	Harvard, America's first institution of higher learning, is founded.
1692	Salem witch trials begin, resulting in nineteen people being burned as witches.
Mar. 5, 1770	Five are killed, the first being Crispus Attucks, in Boston Massacre.
Dec. 16, 1773	Patriots sneak aboard a British cargo ship and dump tea into the harbor to protest the high taxes during the Boston Tea Party.
1775	First battle of the Revolutionary war occurs at Lexington; Paul Revere makes "midnight ride" to warn patriots.
1783	Treaty of Paris is signed, ending the Revolutionary War and granting the thirteen colonies independence.
1783	Massachusetts abolishes slavery.
1786	Pelham farmer Daniel Shay leads an armed uprising protesting high taxes from Boston in Shay's Rebellion.
Feb. 6, 1788	Massachusetts, led by Samuel Adams and John Hancock, ratifies Constitution, becoming the sixth state.
1792	John Adams of Massachusetts becomes second president of the United States.
1815	Newburyport businessman Francis Cabot Lowell, inspired by England and Scotland's textile mills, opens the state's first mill at Waltham.
Mar. 4, 1824	John Quincy Adams, son of the second president, becomes the fifth president of the United States.
1829	Journalist William Lloyd Garrison begins publishing his antislavery newspaper, the *Liberator*, in Boston.
1832	Perkins Institute, the first school for the blind in the Union, is founded.
1881	Boston Symphony is founded.
1897	First Boston Marathon is held.
1908	P. J. Kennedy is elected to the state senate.
1912	More than twenty-two thousand textile workers stage a massive strike in Lawrence.
1919	Republican governor Calvin Coolidge sends in state police to restore order in the Boston Police strike.
1924	Newly installed U.S. president Coolidge signs into law Massachusetts senator Henry Cabot Lodge's bill limiting immigration.
1937	Joseph Kennedy is named ambassador to England, the first Irish American to represent the country in England's court.
1956	Foster Furcolo becomes first Italian American governor of Massachusetts.
1960	Senator John F. Kennedy becomes thirty-fifth president of the United States; assassinated in 1963.

Founded in Cambridge in 1636, Harvard University is not only one of the nation's oldest universities, it is also one of its most prestigious. It is pictured here as it appeared in 1725. (Library of Congress)

1966	Republican Edward Brooke is first black man elected U.S. Senator in nearly a century.
1974	Federal judge orders Boston to start busing students in order to integrate its public schools, sparking years of turmoil.
July, 1999	John F. Kennedy, Jr., son of the slain president, is killed in a plane crash near Martha's Vineyard.

Notes for Further Study

Published Sources. Those interested in learning about Massachusetts history will find a wealth of materials on all aspects of the state's early years. For short, informational histories readers should consult *Massachusetts* (1998), by Sylvia McNair, and *Massachusetts: From Sea to Shining Sea* (1994), by Dennis B. Fradin. *Massachusetts Bay Company and Its Predecessors* (1974), by Frances Rose-

Troup, offers an in-depth overview of the earliest European settlers and their trials and tribulations. Marcia Sewall's *The Pilgrims of Plymouth* (1996) chronicles in text and illustrations the day-to-day life of the early pilgrims of the Plymouth Colony. *Pilgrims and Puritans: 1620-1676* (1994), by Christopher Collier and James Lincoln Collier, recounts the religious, political, and social history of the Massachusetts Bay Colony and its influence on modern life.

The Salem Witch Trials (1991), by Earle Rice, covers the social, legal, and political realities surrounding the trials. For a personal view of the American Revolution and such key events as the Tea Party and the Boston Massacre, a Boston shoemaker's account is available in *The Shoemaker and the Tea Party: Memory and the American Revolution* (1999), edited by Alfred F. Young. *Civil War Boston: Home Front and Battlefield* (1999), by Thomas H. O'Connor, examines the dramatic ways the Civil War affected Bostonians on the home front and discusses how residents contributed to the Union cause, focusing on businessmen, Irish Catholic immigrants, African Americans, and women. *The Boston Irish: A Political History* (1996), also by Thomas H. O'Connor, discusses how Irish political dominance in Boston grew out of generations of bitter and unyielding conflict between Yankees and Irish Catholic immigrants. There are a great deal of books available on the Kennedys, including *The Sins of the Father: Joseph P. Kennedy and the Dynasty He Founded* (1996) by Ronald Kessler.

Web Resources. There are many Massachusetts sites on the World Wide Web, and those listed here often give links to others. A good starting point is the Massachusetts home page (http://www.massachusetts.com), which lists a variety of sites, including links to all colleges and universities. A thorough overview of historical Massachusetts, as well as a Boston African American database, can be found at Masshist (http://www.masthist.org). Massachusetts's early history can be accessed at the History site (http://www.ftp.std.com/NE/mahistory.com), Mayflower and Early Families site (http://www.mayflowerfamilies.html), and the Wampanoag site (http://www.dickshovel.com/wampa.html). Salem Witchcraft hysteria (http://www.nationalgeographic.com/features/97/salem) is an intriguing account of the trials by a National Geographic historian. The Kennedy Presidential Library and Museum, located in Boston, has a site (http:// www.cs.umb.edu/jfklibrary) that is useful not only for learning more about the Kennedy political dynasty but also for keeping up with statewide travel information. The Massachusetts State Historical Board has an informative site (http://www.magnet.state.ma.us).

Now a picturesque resort region, Cape Cod is the actual site of the first pilgrim landing in 1620. (PhotoDisc)

Counties

County	Sq. miles	1996 pop.
Barnstable	395.8	201,970
Berkshire	931.4	134,788
Bristol	556.0	513,899
Dukes	103.8	13,259
Essex	498.1	670,080
Franklin	702.1	70,092
Hampden	618.5	456,310
Hampshire	529.0	146,568

County	Sq. miles	1996 pop.
Middlesex	823.5	1,398,468
Nantucket	47.8	7,267
Norfolk	399.6	637,388
Plymouth	660.6	456,820
Suffolk	58.5	645,068
Worcester	1,513.2	709,705

Source: U.S. Census Bureau; National Association of Counties.

Cities

With 10,000 or more residents

Rank	City	Population
1	Boston	555,447
2	Worcester	166,535
3	Springfield	148,144

Rank	City	Population
4	Lowell	101,075
5	New Bedford	96,353
6	Cambridge	93,352

(continued)

Rank	City	Population
7	Brockton	93,173
8	Fall River	90,654
9	Quincy	85,752
10	Lynn	81,075
11	Newton	80,345
12	Somerville	74,100
13	Lawrence	69,420
14	Waltham	58,540
15	Medford	55,981
16	Haverhill	55,321
17	Chicopee	54,049
18	Malden	52,644
19	Taunton	52,553
20	Peabody	49,204
21	Pittsfield	45,513
22	Barnstable	45,187
23	Methuen	41,988
24	Revere	41,663
25	Holyoke	40,964
26	Leominster	40,208

Rank	City	Population
27	Fitchburg	40,011
28	Attleboro	39,557
29	Beverly	39,037
30	Salem	38,351
31	Westfield	37,570
32	Woburn	37,070
33	Everett	34,922
34	Marlborough	33,278
35	Watertown	32,435
36	Gloucester	29,657
37	Northampton	28,680
38	Franklin	28,353
39	Chelsea	27,426
40	Melrose	27,376
41	Agawam	26,738
42	Gardner	20,261
43	Newburyport	16,808
44	North Adams	15,496

Population figures are estimated for mid-1998.
Source: U.S. Bureau of the Census.

Index to Tables

NA = Reliable data are not available.

DEMOGRAPHICS

Resident state and national populations, 1970-1997

Population figures given in thousands

	State pop.	U.S. pop.	Share	Rank
1970	5,689	203,302	2.8%	10
1980	5,737	226,546	2.5%	11
1985	5,881	237,924	2.5%	12
1990	6,016	248,765	2.4%	13
1995	6,061	262,761	2.3%	13
1997	6,118	267,636	2.3%	13

Source: U.S. Bureau of the Census.

Resident population by age, 1997

Age group	Total population
Under 5 years	399,000
5 to 17 years	1,052,000
18 to 24 years	500,000
25 to 34 years	1,014,000
35 to 44 years	1,028,000
45 to 54 years	782,000
55 to 64 years	479,000
65 to 74 years	446,000
75 to 84 years	307,000
85 years and over	109,000
Portion of residents 65 and older	14.1%
National average	12.7%

Population figures are rounded to nearest thousand persons;
figures include armed forces personnel stationed in state.
Source: U.S. Bureau of the Census.

Resident population by race, Hispanic origin, 1997

	State pop.	Share	U.S.
All residents	6,118,000	100.0%	100.0%
Hispanic white	284,000	4.6%	10.0%
non-Hispanic white	5,226,000	85.4%	72.7%
African American	384,000	6.3%	12.7%
Native American	14,000	0.2%	0.9%
Asian, Pacific Islander	210,000	3.4%	3.8%

Source: U.S. Bureau of the Census.

Projections of state population, 2000-2025

	Model A Uses interstate migration observed from 1975-1994	Model B Uses Bureau of Economic Analysis employment projections
Year	Population	Population
2000	6,199,000	6,224,000
2005	6,310,000	6,361,000
2010	6,431,000	6,498,000
2015	6,574,000	6,653,000
2020	6,734,000	6,824,000
2025	6,902,000	7,001,000

All population projections, including those for 2000, were calculated in 1997.
Source: U.S. Bureau of the Census, Population Paper Listings PPL-47.

VITAL STATISTICS

Average lifetime in years by race, 1989-1991

	State	U.S.	Rank
All residents	76.72	75.37	14
White residents	76.90	76.13	13
Black residents	72.45	69.16	1

Ranks are from longest-lived to least longest-lived. Ranks exclude Alaska, for which reliable data are not available. Rank for black residents is based on the 32 states for which reliable data are available.
Source: U.S. National Center for Health Statistics.

Infant mortality rates, 1980 and 1995

	State	U.S.
All residents		
1980	10.5	12.6
1995	5.2	7.6
White residents		
1980	10.1	11.0
1995	4.7	6.3
Black residents		
1980	16.8	21.4
1995	9.0	15.1

Figures represent deaths per 1,000 live births of resident infants under 1 year old, exclusive of fetal deaths; all-residents figures include other races not listed separately.
Source: U.S. National Center for Health Statistics.

Marriages and divorces

Marriages in 1996.	40,600
Rate per 1,000 population, 1995.	7.2
U.S. rate, 1995	8.9
Rank among all states.	41
Divorces in 1996	12,400
Rate per 1,000 population, 1995.	2.2
U.S. rate, 1995	4.4
Rank among all states.	46

Rank is from highest to lowest in country.
Source: U.S. National Center for Health Statistics.

Death rates by leading causes, 1995
Deaths per 100,000 resident population

Cause	State	U.S.
Heart disease	275.8	280.7
Cancer	231.9	204.9
Cerebrovascular diseases	57.0	60.1
Accidents and adverse effects	20.1	35.5
Motor vehicle accidents	8.0	16.5
Chronic obstructive pulmonary diseases	38.8	39.2
Diabetes mellitus	21.8	22.6
HIV	15.5	NA
Suicide	8.1	11.9
Homicide	3.7	8.7
All causes	913.4	880.0
Rank in overall death rate among states		24

Figures exclude nonresidents who die in state. Causes of death follow International Classification of Diseases. Rank is from highest to lowest in country.
Source: U.S. National Center for Health Statistics.

ECONOMY

Gross state product, 1990-1996
In current dollars

	State product	Increase
1990	$158.9 billion	
1993	$174.0 billion	
1994	$186.0 billion	6.90%
1995	$195.9 billion	5.32%
1996	$208.6 billion	6.48%

Source: U.S. Bureau of Economic Analysis; *Survey of Current Business,* June, 1998.

Gross state product by industry, 1996
In billions

Farms, forestry, fisheries	$1.1
Construction	5.7
Manufacturing	33.5
Transportation, public utilities	12.4
Wholesale trade	14.2
Retail trade	15.9
Finance, insurance, real estate	43.9
Services	47.2
Government	17.3
State total	$191.0
Total U.S.	$6,923.8
State share	2.76%
Rank among states	11

Total figures include mining, not listed separately.

Source: U.S. Bureau of Economic Analysis; *Survey of Current Business,* June, 1998.

Personal income per capita, 1990 and 1997
In current dollars

	1990	1997
Per capita income	$23,249	$31,524
U.S. average	$19,188	$25,598
Rank among states	3	3

1997 data are preliminary.

Source: U.S. Bureau of Economic Analysis; *Survey of Current Business,* May, 1998.

Energy consumption, 1995
In trillions of British thermal units (BTU)

End-use sectors

Residential	418.9
Commercial	356.4
Industrial	318.7
Transportation	405.5

Sources of energy

Petroleum	682.7
Natural gas	371.7
Coal	104.4
Hydroelectric power	11.0
Nuclear electric power	47.8
Total state per capita consumption	246.1
Total U.S. per capita consumption	344.4
Rank among states	44
Total state energy consumption	1,493.8
Total U.S. energy consumption	90,547.4
State share of U.S. total	1.65%
Rank among states	22

Total figures include items not listed separately.

Source: U.S. Energy Information Administration; *State Energy Data Report.*

Nonfarm employment by sectors, 1997

Total	3,119,000
Construction	100,000
Manufacturing	448,000
Transportation, public utilities	134,000
Wholesale trade, retail trade	711,000
Finance, insurance, real estate	213,000
Services	1,107,000
Government	405,000

Figures are rounded to nearest thousand persons. Total includes mining, not listed separately.

Source: U.S. Bureau of Labor Statistics; *Employment and Earnings,* monthly.

Foreign exports, 1990-1997
In millions of dollars

Year	State	U.S.	State share
1990	9,501	394,045	2.41%
1996	14,524	624,767	2.32%
1997	16,526	688,896	2.40%

Source: U.S. Bureau of the Census; *U.S. Merchandise Trade,* series FT 900.

LAND USE

Federally owned land, 1996

	State	U.S.	State share
Total acres	5,035,000	2,271,343,000	0.22%
Federally owned	52,000	563,129,000	0.01%
Federal share	1.0%	24.8%	—

Areas are rounded to nearest thousand acres. Figures for federally owned land do not include trust properties.
Source: U.S. General Services Administration; *Inventory Report on Real Property Owned by the United States Throughout the World,* annual.

Land use, 1992
In acres, rounded to nearest thousand

Total surface area	5,302,000
Federal land.	89,000
Total nonfederal.	4,839,000
Developed	1,309,000
Total rural	3,530,000
Cropland.	272,000
Pasture land	170,000
Range land	0
Forest land.	2,778,000
Minor cover/use.	310,000

Total surface area figures include water area not shown separately.
Source: U.S. Dept. of Agriculture; Soil Conservation Service; Iowa State University, Statistical Laboratory; *Summary Report, 1992 National Resources Inventory.*

Farms and crop acreage, 1997

	State	U.S.	Share	Rank
Farms (thousands)	6	2,058	0.29%	42
Acres (millions)	1	968	0.10%	43
Acres per farm	92	471	—	48
Acres planted	133	334,139	0.04%	45
Acres harvested	128	319,894	0.04%	45
Farm value (mill.)	$220	$108,805	0.20%	17

Numbers of farms are rounded to nearest thousand.
Source: U.S. Dept. of Agriculture; National Agricultural Statistics Service.

GOVERNMENT AND FINANCE

Units of local government, 1997

	State	Total U.S.	Rank
All local governments	861	87,453	33
Counties	12	3,043	44
Municipalities	44	19,372	44
Townships	307	16,629	15
School districts	85	13,726	36
Special districts	413	34,683	28

County ranks are based on the 48 states with county governments; township ranks are based on the 20 states with township governments; school district ranks are based on the 46 states with such districts.
Township figures include "town" governments.
Source: U.S. Bureau of the Census; *1997 Census of Governments, Government Organization,* Series GC97(1).

State government revenue, 1996

Total revenue	$25,197 mill.
General revenue	22,845 mill.
Per capita.	3,754
U.S. per capita average	2,910
Rank among states	7
Intergovernmental revenue	
Total	$5,827 mill.
From federal government	5,354 mill.
From local government	474 mill.
Charges and Miscellaneous	
Total	$4,562 mill.
Current charges	1,814 mill.
Misc. general revenue	2,748 mill.
Taxes	
Total	$12,455 mill.
General sales	2,610 mill.
Selective sales.	1,278 mill.
License taxes	398 mill.
Individual income	6,707 mill.
Corporate income	1,228 mill.
Other	235 mill.
Insurance trust revenue	2,283 mill.

Total revenue figures include items not listed separately.
Source: U.S. Bureau of the Census.

State government expenditures, 1996

General expenditures

Intergovernmental	$5,160 mill.
Direct expenditures	17,630 mill.
Total	22,790 mill.

Selected direct expenditures

Education	$4,492 mill.
Public welfare	5,999 mill.
Health, hospital	2,182 mill.
Highways	1,803 mill.
Police	287 mill.
Corrections	729 mill.
Natural resources	228 mill.
Parks and recreation	97 mill.
Government administration	901 mill.
Interest on debt	1,708 mill.

Other

State per capita expenditures	$3,745
U.S. per capita average	2,854
Rank among states	6
Total state expenditures	24,950 mill.
Total U.S. expenditures	859,959 mill.

Totals include items not listed separately.
Source: U.S. Bureau of the Census.

POLITICS

Governors since statehood

D = Democrat; R = Republican; O = other;
(r) resigned; (d) died in office; (i) removed from office

John Hancock	(r)	1780-1785
Thomas Cushing		1785
James Bowdoin		1785-1787
John Hancock	(d)	1787-1793
Samuel Adams (O)		1793-1797
Increase Sumner (O)	(d)	1797-1799
Moses Gill (O)	(d)	1799-1800
Thomas Dawes (O)		1800
Caleb Strong (O)		1800-1807
James Sullivan (O)	(d)	1807-1808
Levi Lincoln (O)		1808-1809
Christopher Gore (O)		1809-1810
Elbridge Gerry (O)		1810-1812
Caleb Strong (O)		1812-1816
John Brooks (O)		1816-1823
William Eustis (O)	(d)	1823-1825
Marcus Morton (O)		1825
Levi Lincoln, Jr. (O)		1825-1834
John Davis (O)	(r)	1834-1835
Samuel T. Armstrong (O)		1835-1836
Edward Everett (O)		1836-1840
Marcus Morton (D)		1840-1841
John Davis (O)		1841-1843
Marcus Morton (D)		1843-1844
George N. Briggs (O)		1844-1851
George S. Boutwell (D)		1851-1853
John H. Clifford (O)		1853-1854
Emory Washburn (O)		1854-1855
Henry J. Gardner (O)		1855-1858
Nathaniel P. Banks (R)		1858-1861
John A. Andrew (R)		1861-1866
Alexander H. Bullock (R)		1866-1869
William Claflin (R)		1869-1872
William B. Washburn (R)	(r)	1872-1874
William Talbot (R)		1874-1875
William Gaston (D)		1875-1876
Alexander H. Rice (R)		1876-1879
Thomas Talbot (R)		1879-1880
John D. Long (R)		1880-1883
Benjamin F. Butler (D)		1883-1884
George D. Robinson (R)		1884-1887
Oliver Ames (R)		1887-1890
John Q. A. Brackett (R)		1890-1891
William E. Russell (D)		1891-1894
Frederic T. Greenhalge (R)	(d)	1894-1896
Roger Wolcott (R)		1896-1900
Winthrop Murray Crane (R)		1900-1903
John L. Bates (R)		1903-1905
William L. Douglas (D)		1905-1906
Curtis Guild, Jr. (R)		1906-1909
Eben S. Draper (R)		1909-1911
Eugene N. Foss (D)		1911-1914
David T. Walsh (D)		1914-1916
Samuel W. McCall (R)		1916-1919
Calvin Coolidge (R)		1919-1921
Channing H. Cox (R)		1921-1925
Alvan T. Fuller (R)		1925-1929
Frank G. Allen (R)		1929-1931
Joseph B. Ely (D)		1931-1935
James M. Curley (D)		1935-1937
Charles F. Hurley (D)		1937-1939
Leverett Saltonstall (R)		1939-1945
Maurice J. Tobin (D)		1945-1947
Robert F. Bradford (R)		1947-1949
Paul A. Dever (D)		1949-1953
Christian A. Herter (R)		1953-1957
Foster Furcolo (D)		1957-1961
John A. Volpe (R)		1961-1963
Endicott Peabody (D)		1963-1965
John A. Volpe (R)	(r)	1965-1969
Francis W. Sargent (R)		1969-1975
Michael S. Dukakis (D)		1975-1979
Edward J. King (D)		1979-1983
Michael S. Dukakis (D)		1983-1991

(continued)

William Weld (R) . . . . (r) 1991-1997
Argeo Paul Cellucci (R) 1997-

Composition of state legislature, 1990-1998

	Democrats	Republicans
State House (160 seats)		
1990	118	37
1992	123	34
1994	125	34
1996	134	25
1998	130	27
State Senate (40 seats)		
1990	25	15
1992	31	9
1994	30	10
1996	34	6
1998	33	7

Figures for total seats may include independents and minor
party members.
Source: Council of State Governments; *State Elective Officials
and the Legislatures.*

Composition of congressional delegations, 1989-1999

	Dem	Rep	Total
House of Representatives			
101st Congress, 1989			
State delegates	10	1	11
Total U.S.	259	174	433
102d Congress, 1991			
State delegates	10	1	11
Total U.S.	267	167	434
103d Congress, 1993			
State delegates	8	2	10
Total U.S.	258	176	434
104th Congress, 1995			
State delegates	10	0	10
Total U.S.	197	236	433
105th Congress, 1997			
State delegates	10	0	10
Total U.S.	206	228	434
106th Congress, 1999			
State delegates	10	0	10
Total U.S.	211	222	433

	Dem	Rep	Total
Senate			
101st Congress, 1989			
State delegates	2	0	2
Total U.S.	55	45	100
102d Congress, 1991			
State delegates	2	0	2
Total U.S.	56	44	100
103d Congress, 1993			
State delegates	2	0	2
Total U.S.	57	43	100
104th Congress, 1995			
State delegates	2	0	2
Total U.S.	46	53	99
105th Congress, 1997			
State delegates	2	0	2
Total U.S.	45	55	100
106th Congress, 1999			
State delegates	2	0	2
Total U.S.	45	54	99

Figures are for starts of first sessions. Figure for U.S. Representatives for 101st Congress does not include Alabama
and Indiana, which had vacancies. Figures for total U.S.
Representatives for 102d, 103d, and 106th Congresses do
not include Vermont, which had 1 Independent-Socialist.
Figure for U.S. Representatives for 104th Congress does
not include Vermont, which had 1 Independent-Socialist,
and California, which had 1 vacancy. Figure for U.S. Representatives for 105th Congress does not include New York,
which had 1 vacancy. Figure for U.S. Senators for 104th
Congress does not include Oregon, which had 1 vacancy.
Figure for U.S. Senators for 106th Congress does not
include New Hampshire, which had 1 Independent.
Source: U.S. Congress; *Congressional Directory,* biennial.

Voter participation in presidential elections, 1992 and 1996

	1992	1996
State voting age pop.	4,616,000	4,623,000
Total U.S. voting age pop.	189,524,000	196,509,000
State share of U.S. total	2.4%	2.4%
Rank among states	13	13
Percent of state casting vote	60.1	57.7
Percent of U.S. total voting	55.1	49.0
Rank among states	22	8

Source: U.S. Bureau of the Census.

HEALTH AND MEDICAL CARE

Medicare, 1997

	Recipients	Payments
State	945,000	$6,455 mill.
Total U.S.	37,514,000	$206,064 mill.
State share	2.52%	3.13%
Rank among states	11	10

Recipient figures are rounded to nearest thousand persons.
  Ranks are from highest to lowest.
Source: U.S. Health Care Financing Administration.

Medicaid, 1996

	Recipients	Payments
State	715,000	$3,777 mill.
Total U.S.	35,028,000	$121,419 mill.
State share	2.04%	3.11%
Rank among states	13	8

Recipient figures are rounded to nearest thousand persons.
  Payment figures for fiscal year reflect federal and state
  contribution payments. Ranks are from highest to lowest.
Source: U.S. Health Care Financing Administration.

Health insurance coverage, 1996

	State	U.S.
Total persons covered	5,392,000	225,070,000
Total persons not covered	766,000	41,716,000
Part not covered	12.4%	15.6%
Rank among states	30	—
Children not covered	143,000	10,554,000
Part not covered	9.2%	14.8%
Rank among states	40	—

Ranks are from most to fewest uninsured. Population figures
  are rounded to nearest thousand persons.
Source: U.S. Bureau of the Census.

AIDS, syphilis, tuberculosis, and measles cases, 1997

Cases	U.S.	State	Share
AIDS	58,443	863	1.48%
Syphilis	8,550	78	0.91%
Tuberculosis	18,534	254	1.37%
Measles	148,000	16,000	10.81%

Measles figures are rounded to nearest thousand cases.
Source: U.S. Centers for Disease Control and Prevention.

HOUSING

Homeownership rates, 1985-1997

	1985	1990	1997
State	60.5%	58.6%	62.3%
Total U.S.	63.9%	63.9%	65.7%
Rank among states	46	44	43

Source: U.S. Bureau of the Census.

Home sales, 1990 and 1997
In thousands of units

Existing home sales	1990	1997	Change
State sales	44.0	94.3	50.3
Total U.S. sales	3,560	4,730	1,170
State share of U.S. total	1.24%	1.99%	0.76%
Rank among states	29	18	—

Source: National Association of Realtors; *Real Estate Outlook:
  Market Trends and Insights.*

EDUCATION

Public school enrollment, 1995

State K-8 enrollment	675,000
Total U.S. K-8 enrollment	32,341,000
State share of total U.S.	2.09%
State 9-12 enrollment	240,000
Total U.S. 9-12 enrollment	12,500,000
State share of U.S. total	1.92%
State public school enroll. rate	90.2%
Overall U.S. rate.	91.6%
Rank among states.	34

Enrollment figures (which include unclassified students) are
  rounded to nearest thousand pupils in fall term;
  kindergarten (K)-8 grade figures include some
  prekindergarten students. Enrollment rate is based on
  percentage of persons 5-17 years old. Rank is from highest
  to lowest.
Source: U.S. National Center for Education Statistics.

Public college finances, 1996

State FTE enrollment	116,700
Total U.S. FTE enrollment	8,268,800
State share of total U.S.	1.41%
Rank among states.	25
State and local appropriations	$593,500,000
Total U.S. state and local appropriations.	$39,699 mill.
State share of total U.S.	1.50%
Rank among states.	22
State net tuition revenues.	$311,300,000
Total U.S. net tuition	$18,348,100,000
State share of total U.S.	1.70%
Rank among states.	24

FTE=Full-time equivalent; credit and noncredit enrollment
  including summer session in academic year ending in
  1996.
Enrollments are rounded to nearest thousand students. Net
  tuition revenues exclude appropriation to students
  attending in-state public institutions. Rankings are from
  highest shares to lowest.
Source: Research Associates of Washington.

TRANSPORTATION AND TRAVEL

Highway mileage, 1996

Interstate	565
Other arterial.	5,843
Collector roads	8,023
Local roads	22,828
Urban roads.	22,675
Rural roads	12,050
Total state	34,725
U.S. total	3,933,985
State share	0.9%
Rank among states.	40

Source: U.S. Federal Highway Administration.

Motor vehicle registrations and driver licenses, 1996

In thousands

Vehicle registrations	State	U.S.	Share	Rank
Autos, trucks, buses	4,702	206,365	2.28%	15
Autos only	3,528	128,439	2.75%	12
Motorcycles	91	3,832	2.37%	15
Driver licenses	4,355	179,539	2.43%	15

Figures do not include vehicles owned by military services.
Source: U.S. Federal Highway Administration; *Highway
  Statistics; Selected Highway Statistics and Charts.*

Domestic travel expenditures, 1995

Spending by U.S. residents on overnight trips and day
trips of at least 100 miles

Total expenditures in state	$8,031 mill.
Total expenditures in U.S.	$360,314 mill.
State share of total U.S.	2.23%
Rank among states.	14

Source: Travel Industry Association of America.

CRIME AND LAW ENFORCEMENT

State and local police officers, 1996

Local police	13,068
State police	2,565
Sheriffs	1,540
Total	17,935
Officers per 10,000 residents	29
U.S. average	25
Rank among states	5

Figures cover full-time sworn officers; totals include special
  police not shown separately.
Source: U.S. Bureau of Justice Statistics; *Census of State and
  Local Law Enforcement Agencies, 1996.*

Crime rates, 1996
Rates per 100,000 resident population

Violent crimes	State	U.S.
Total violent	642	634
Murder	2.6	7.4
Forcible rape	29.0	36.1
Robbery	128	202
Aggravated assault	483	388

Property crimes	State	U.S.
Total property	3,195	4,445
Burglary	704	943
Larceny/theft	1,963	2,976
Motor vehicle theft	528	526
Totals	3,837	5,079

Source: U.S. Federal Bureau of Investigation; *Crime in the
  United States,* annual.

State prison populations, 1980-1996

	State	U.S.	State share
1980	3,185	305,458	1.04%
1990	8,345	708,393	1.18%
1996	11,796	1,025,624	1.15%

Figures exclude prisoners in federal penitentiaries.
Source: U.S. Bureau of Justice Statistics.

Michigan

Location: Upper Midwestern continental United States

Area and rank: 58,110 square miles (150,504 square kilometers); 96,810 square miles (250,738 square kilometers) including water; twenty-first largest state in area

Population and rank: 9,773,892 (1997); eighth largest state in population

Capital: Lansing

Largest city: Detroit (970,196 people in 1998)

State capitol building in Lansing. (Travel Michigan)

Became territory:
January 11, 1805

Entered Union and rank:
January 26, 1837;
twenty-sixth state

**Present constitution
adopted:** April 1, 1963
(effective January 1,
1964)

Counties: 83

State name: "Michigan"
comes from the Indian
word "Michigana,"
meaning "great or
large lake"

State nickname: Wolverine State

Motto: *Si quaeris peninsulam amoenam circumspice* (If you seek a pleasant peninsula, look around you)

State flag: Blue field with state coat of arms

Highest point: Mount Arvon — 1,979 feet (603 meters)

Lowest point: Lake Erie — 571 feet (174 meters)

Highest recorded temperature: 112 degrees Fahrenheit (44 degrees Celsius) — Mio, 1936

Lowest recorded temperature: −51 degrees Fahrenheit (−46 degrees Celsius) — Vanderbilt, 1934

State tree: White pine

State flower: Apple blossom

State bird: Robin

State fish: Trout; Brook trout

National park: Isle Royale

Michigan History

Michigan's abundant natural resources and access to major waterways, including four of the five Great Lakes, have made it an important area of human activity for more than ten thousand years. The unique geographic situation of Michigan, with the state divided into two separate land masses, has had a profound influence on its history. The southern land mass, known as the Lower Peninsula, developed into a heavily populated area of agriculture, forestry, and industry. The northern land mass, known as the Upper Peninsula, remained sparsely populated but provided important mineral resources.

Early History. The first inhabitants of the region hunted and fished about eleven thousand years ago. They also made tools from copper found in the Upper Peninsula. This is the earliest known use of metal in the New World. About three thousand years ago, agriculture began to develop in the southwestern part of the Lower Peninsula.

By the time Europeans arrived in North America, Michigan was primarily inhabited by Native Americans belonging to the Algonquian language group. These peoples included the Ottawa, the Ojibwa, the Miami, and the Potawatomi, mostly living in the northern regions. In the south lived the Huron, a Native American tribe belonging to the Iroquois language group. During the middle of the seventeenth century, conflict with other Iroquois peoples to the east drove the Huron and the Ottawa westward. At about the same time, the development of the French fur trade led many Native Americans in northern Michigan to move south.

Exploration and Settlement. The first European known to have visited the area was Étienne Brulé, who reached the Upper Peninsula from Canada in 1622. Another French explorer, Jean Nicolet, traveled through the narrow strait that separates the two peninsulas in 1634 during a journey from Canada to Wisconsin. The earliest permanent European settlements, located in the Upper Peninsula, were founded by the French missionary Jacques Marquette at Sault Sainte Marie in 1668 and St. Ignace in 1671. During the late seventeenth and early eighteenth centuries, several French mission-ary, fur trading, and military posts were established on both peninsulas. In 1701 Detroit was founded by Antoine Laumet de La Mothe, sieur de Cadillac. It soon became the most important French settlement in the Great Lakes region.

During the French and Indian War, a struggle between France and England for control of North America, Detroit was surrendered to the British in 1760. After the war, control of the region went to Great Britain. Fearful that the British would bring many more settlers to the area, many Native Americans united under the Ottawa leader Pontiac. After capturing several British forts in the area, Pontiac's forces laid siege to Detroit for nearly six months in 1763. Pontiac was forced to abandon the siege in October, and the British remained in control.

Steps to Statehood. Although the end of the American Revolution officially brought the area under American control, the British did not leave Detroit and other military posts until 1796. Michigan was part of the Northwest Territory from 1787 to 1800, when it became part of the newly created Indiana Territory. The Michigan Territory was created in 1805. In the same year, a fire destroyed several buildings in Detroit.

After being rebuilt, Detroit was an important military objective in the War of 1812, a conflict between the United States and England. Detroit was captured by the British in August of 1812 but recaptured in September of 1813. Control of the Great Lakes region was restored to the United States the same month, when American naval forces commanded by Oliver Hazard Perry defeated the British in the Battle of Lake Erie.

Michigan began growing quickly after the war. Settlement was encouraged by the beginning of steamship transportation on Lake Erie from Buffalo to Detroit. The completion of the Erie Canal in 1825, linking the Hudson River to Lake Erie, also led to rapid population growth. From 1820 to 1840, the number of settlers, mostly from eastern states, increased from less than 9,000 to more than 200,000. During this time, many Native Americans gave up their lands or were forced to leave. However, some remained on reservations that still exist.

Michigan reached the population of sixty thousand required for statehood as early as 1833. Before statehood could be approved by Congress, however, a border dispute arose between Michigan and Ohio. Ohio claimed lands in the southeastern part of the Michigan Territory. In the Toledo War of 1835, Michigan militia prevented Ohio officials from occupying the area. Michigan eventually gave up the disputed region in return for a large increase in the size of its lands in the Upper Peninsula. It became the twenty-sixth state in 1837.

Economic Development. Despite an economic depression in the late 1830's, Michigan experienced rapid growth in the two decades after statehood. Many of the new residents were immigrants from Germany, Ireland, and the Netherlands. The vast majority of settlers were drawn to Michigan by the rich, productive soil found in the southern part of the Lower Peninsula. In the 1850's, about 85 percent of the population was involved in agriculture.

The pine forests of the northern part of the Lower Peninsula and the mineral resources of the Upper Peninsula were also important parts of the state's economy. Iron, copper, and salt deposits began to be mined in the 1840's. Immigrants from Finland and Cornwall, a region of southwestern England, were involved in the development of the mining industry. An important stimulus to economic growth in the Upper Peninsula was the completion in 1855 of a series of locks at Sault Sainte Marie which allowed ships to travel from Lake Huron to Lake Superior. The growing importance of the northern regions of the state was a factor in the decision to move the capital from Detroit to Lansing in 1847.

The Republican Party and the Civil War. The Democratic Party dominated Michigan politics from before statehood until the national crisis over slavery in the 1850's. In 1854 antislavery members of the Democratic Party joined with members of the Whig Party and the Free-Soil Party to form the

Republican Party in Jackson. The new party would dominate Michigan politics for the next eight decades.

During the Civil War about ninety thousand residents of Michigan fought for the Union, and around fourteen thousand were killed. Among the forces representing Michigan was a regiment of African Americans drawn from several states.

The Rise of Industry. The late nineteenth century saw the beginnings of modern manufacturing in Michigan. Grand Rapids became a center of furniture making. Kalamazoo dominated the paper industry. The Dow Chemical Company and the Upjohn Company made the chemical and pharmaceutical industries an important part of the state's economy. Perhaps the most distinctive industry to arise in Michigan at this time was the manufacture of breakfast cereal. This industry, which grew out

Michigan Ford Motor Company Model T factory at Highland Park, where assembly-line production began in 1913. (Library of Congress)

Renaissance Center in Michigan's largest city, Detroit. (Travel Michigan)

of health resorts in the state that developed these products as part of a vegetarian diet, is centered in the city of Battle Creek.

By far the most important industry in Michigan during the twentieth century was automobile manufacturing. The industry began in 1901, when Ransom Eli Olds began marketing the Oldsmobile, the first successful American automobile. Inspired by this success, other automobile manufacturing companies soon appeared in the state. Henry Ford organized the Ford Motor Company in 1903 and began manufacturing the highly successful Model T in 1908. The same year, William C. Durant created the General Motors Corporation. Walter P. Chrysler founded the Chrysler Corporation in 1925. These and many other companies made the cities of Detroit, Flint, Pontiac, and Lansing dominant in the automobile industry.

The Twentieth Century. During the late nineteenth and early twentieth centuries, large numbers of immigrants from Ireland, Italy, Poland, and other European nations entered the state. At about the same time, African Americans from southern states began to arrive in large numbers. From 1900 to the late twentieth century, the number of African Americans in the state rose from less than sixteen thousand to well over one million. In the last few decades of the century, immigrants also arrived from Latin America, Asia, and the Middle East.

The Great Depression of the 1930's devastated the automobile industry. By 1932 half the industrial workers in Michigan were unemployed. This crisis ended the dominance of the Republican Party in the state. It also made organized labor an important force in Michigan. The entire automobile industry was unionized by the United Automobile Workers by 1941.

World War II revitalized industry in the state as automobile manufacturers turned to making military vehicles. Prosperity continued from the end of the war until the nationwide recession of the 1980's, which brought much higher unemployment to Michigan than to most other states. During the late 1980's and 1990's, the state made efforts to lessen its economic dependence on the automobile industry, particularly by developing technological industries and tourism.

Rose Secrest

Michigan Time Line

1622	French explorer Étienne Brulé reaches the Upper Peninsula.
1634	Jean Nicolet journeys between the Upper and Lower Peninsulas.
1668	Father Jacques Marquette founds Sault Sainte Marie.
1671	Marquette founds St. Ignace.
July 24, 1701	Antoine Laumet de La Mothe, sieur de Cadillac, founds Detroit.
Nov. 29, 1760	Detroit surrenders to the British during the French and Indian War.
1763	End of the war brings the area under British control.
1763	Native American forces under Pontiac unsuccessfully lay siege to Detroit.
1783	End of the American Revolution brings the area under American control.
1787	Michigan becomes part of the Northwest Territory.
July 11, 1796	British leave Detroit.
1800	Michigan becomes part of the Indiana Territory.
Jan. 11, 1805	Michigan Territory is created with Detroit as the capital.
1805	Fire devastates Detroit.
1806	First post office in the state is established in Detroit.
Aug. 16, 1812	Detroit surrenders to the British during the War of 1812.
1813	Detroit is recaptured by the United States; Michigan returns to American control after the defeat of the British in the Battle of Lake Erie.
1818	Steamship travel begins between Buffalo and Detroit.
1820	Number of settlers reaches nearly nine thousand.
1825	Opening of the Erie Canal allows water transportation from New York City to Detroit.
1833	Population reaches sixty thousand.
1835	Toledo War, a border dispute between Michigan and Ohio, breaks out.
1836	First railroad is completed, linking Toledo and Adrian.
Jan. 26, 1837	Michigan is admitted to the Union as the twenty-sixth state.
1837	University of Michigan is founded at Ann Arbor.
1840	Population reaches more than 200,000.
May 18, 1846	Michigan is first state to abolish the death penalty.
1847	Capital is moved to Lansing.

1854	Republican Party is founded in Jackson.
1855	Locks are completed at Sault Sainte Marie, linking Lake Huron and Lake Superior.
1901	Ransom Eli Olds begins selling the Oldsmobile.
1903	Henry Ford founds the Ford Motor Company.
1908	Ford begins manufacturing the Model T; William C. Durant founds the General Motors Corporation.
1914	Auto industry is responsible for 37 percent of state's manufacturing.
1920	For the first time, a majority of Michigan residents live in cities.
1925	Walter P. Chrysler founds the Chrysler Corporation.
1926	Commercial air travel from Detroit begins.
1932	Half of the state's industrial workers are unemployed due to the Great Depression.
1941	United Automobile Workers unionizes the entire automobile industry.
June 20-21, 1943	Race riot breaks out in Detroit, leaving thirty-four dead.
1957	Mackinac Bridge connects the Upper and Lower Peninsulas.
1963	New state constitution is the first in the nation to create a Department of Civil Rights.
July 21-23, 1967	Race riot occurs in Detroit, leaving forty-three dead.
1973	Coleman Young is elected the first African American mayor of Detroit.
Aug. 9, 1974	Michigan resident Gerald R. Ford becomes president of United States.
1982	Due to a nationwide recession, unemployment reaches 17.3 percent.
1988	Less than one-quarter of all wage earners work in factories, a decline of 30 percent in ten years.
1998	Population reaches 9.8 million.
1998	Chrysler Corporation merges with German automaker Daimler-Benz to form Daimler-Chrysler.

Notes for Further Study

Published Sources. For students new to the subject, several books intended for a general audience provide a basic introduction to the state. *Michigan* (1998), by Martin Hintz, is a good place to start, with a clear, simple account of the state's geography, plant, and animal life, history, economy, culture, and people. Similar information about Michigan and its neighboring states is found in *Eastern Great Lakes: Indiana, Michigan, Ohio* (1995) by Thomas G. Aylesworth. General information, with an emphasis on tourist attractions, is also found in Tina Lassen's *Michigan Handbook* (1999). An enjoyable way to learn about the state is *Michigan Trivia* (1995) by Ernie and Jill Couch. The importance of industry in the state is the subject of Burton W. Folsom's *Empire Builders: How Michigan Entrepreneurs Helped Make America Great* (1998).

Of the many volumes concerning the state's past, *A Historical Album of Michigan* (1996) by Charles Wills is a good introduction. A more scholarly account is found in *Michigan: A History of the Wolverine State* (1995) by Willis F. Dunbar and George S. May. The early history of the state's major city is the topic of Annick Hivert-Carthew's *Cadillac and the Dawn of Detroit* (1995). The important role of race relations in the city is the subject of Thomas J. Sugrue's *The Origins of the Urban Crisis: Race and Inequality in Postwar Detroit* (1996); the same subject is discussed in *Someone Else's House: America's Unfinished Struggle for Integration* (1998) by Tamar Jacoby, which compares the situation in Detroit to that in New York City and Atlanta.

Web Resources. An enormous variety of Internet resources exists with information about Michigan. A good place to begin exploring the many Web sites available is Welcome to Michigan! The Great Lakes State (http://

Shelter Bay on Lake Superior. Almost surrounded by Great Lakes, Michigan has thousands of miles of shoreline. (Travel Michigan)

munities. The structure of the state government is discussed in detail in Michigan Government Home Page (http://www.state.mi.us). The importance of farming to the state is studied at Michigan Department of Agriculture (http://www.mda.state.mi.us).

Statistical information is available in great detail from the U.S. Census Bureau at Michigan Profiles (http://www.census.gov/cgi-bin/datamap/state?26). A scholarly view of the tourism industry is provided by Michigan State University at Tourism Center (http://www.tourism.msu.edu/tourism.html). A less formal discussion of the same subject is found at The Michigan Travel Companion (http://yesmichigan.com/pcconnections/travelmichigan/home.htm). Of the many sites devoted to the state's history, one of the best is Michigan Historical Center (http://www.sos.state.mi.us/history/history2.html), which provides

www.inetmi.com/mi/index.htm), a general site with a large number of links to other sites. A similar Web site, more oriented to consumers, can be found at Michigan-Online (http://www.michigan-online.com), which supplies information on business, education, and local com-

information on state archives and museums, as well as biographies of famous residents. A similar Web site is provided by the Historical Society of Michigan at Michigan History Links (http://leslie.k12.mi.us/MI/~mwhfame/mhist.htm#4).

Counties

County	Sq. miles	1996 pop.	County	Sq. miles	1996 pop.
Alcona	674.5	10,799	Crawford	558.2	13,671
Alger	917.9	9,971	Delta	1,170.2	39,047
Allegan	827.5	99,019	Dickinson	766.4	27,285
Alpena	574.2	30,746	Eaton	576.5	99,562
Antrim	476.9	20,595	Emmet	468.0	27,870
Arenac	366.9	16,268	Genesee	639.7	436,128
Baraga	904.2	8,472	Gladwin	506.8	24,615
Barry	556.2	53,145	Gogebic	1,101.9	17,704
Bay	444.3	110,824	Grand Traverse	465.1	72,072
Benzie	321.3	14,037	Gratiot	570.2	39,978
Berrien	571.0	161,434	Hillsdale	598.9	45,887
Branch	507.4	42,991	Houghton	1,011.7	36,230
Calhoun	708.9	140,112	Huron	836.6	35,281
Cass	492.2	50,050	Ingham	559.2	285,737
Charlevoix	416.9	23,503	Ionia	573.2	60,378
Cheboygan	715.6	22,993	Iosco	549.1	24,761
Chippewa	1,561.1	37,289	Iron	1,166.5	13,121
Clare	566.9	28,618	Isabella	574.3	57,118
Clinton	571.5	62,239	Jackson	706.6	154,563

County	Sq. miles	1996 pop.	County	Sq. miles	1996 pop.
Kalamazoo	561.9	229,008	Mason	495.2	27,725
Kalkaska	561.0	15,325	Mecosta	555.8	38,460
Kent	856.2	536,103	Menominee	1,043.7	24,551
Keweenaw	541.2	2,010	Midland	521.2	80,669
Lake	567.6	9,874	Missaukee	566.8	13,607
Lapeer	654.3	85,479	Monroe	551.1	140,488
Leelanau	348.5	18,430	Montcalm	708.1	58,969
Lenawee	750.6	97,133	Montmorency	547.6	9,868
Livingston	568.4	137,616	Muskegon	509.2	164,913
Luce	903.1	6,180	Newaygo	842.4	44,285
Mackinac	1,021.6	11,096	Oakland	872.7	1,162,098
Macomb	480.4	734,625	Oceana	540.5	24,379
Manistee	543.9	22,902	Ogemaw	564.4	20,790
Marquette	1,821.3	62,017	Ontonagon	1,311.6	8,405

(continued)

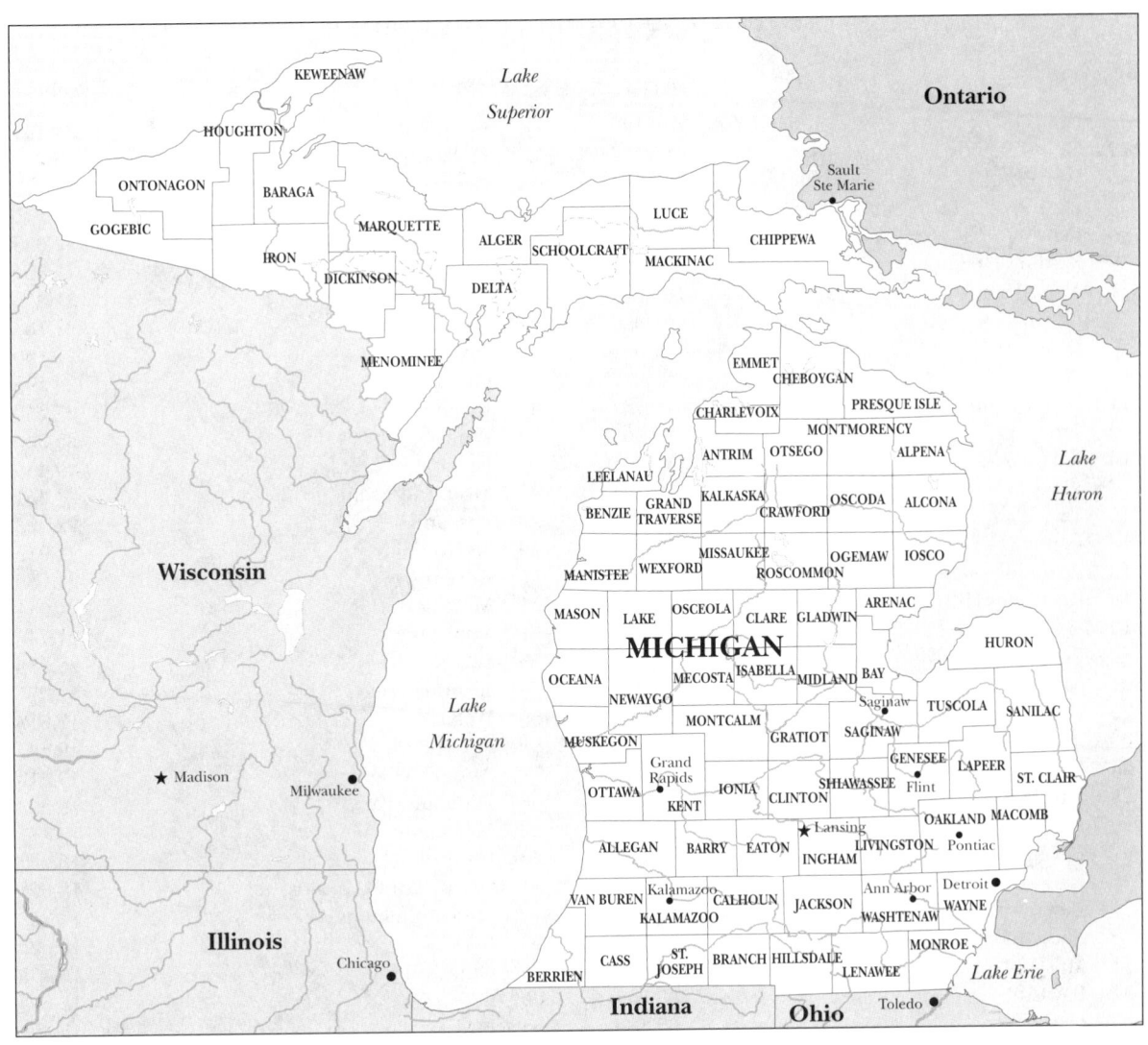

County	Sq. miles	1996 pop.
Osceola	566.1	22,047
Oscoda	565.0	8,775
Otsego	514.6	21,343
Ottawa	565.7	215,064
Presque Isle	660.1	14,407
Roscommon	521.4	22,847
Saginaw	809.0	211,808
Saint Clair	724.5	155,636
Saint Joseph	503.7	60,977
Sanilac	963.9	42,440

County	Sq. miles	1996 pop.
Schoolcraft	1,178.2	8,653
Shiawassee	538.8	72,333
Tuscola	812.6	57,837
Van Buren	611.0	75,308
Washtenaw	710.1	295,149
Wayne	614.1	2,039,819
Wexford	565.5	28,789

Source: U.S. Census Bureau; National Association of Counties.

Cities
With 10,000 or more residents

Rank	City	Population
1	Detroit	970,196
2	Grand Rapids	185,437
3	Warren	142,455
4	Flint	131,668
5	Lansing	127,825
6	Sterling Heights	124,339
7	Ann Arbor	109,967
8	Livonia	101,358
9	Dearborn	91,691
10	Westland	86,227
11	Farmington Hills	79,784
12	Troy	79,303
13	Kalamazoo	76,241
14	Southfield	75,104
15	Taylor	72,551
16	Pontiac	68,916
17	Wyoming	68,671
18	Rochester Hills	67,413
19	St. Clair Shores	66,056
20	Royal Oak	64,290
21	Saginaw	63,464
22	Dearborn Heights	59,805
23	Battle Creek	53,496
24	Roseville	51,390
25	East Lansing	46,509
26	Novi	44,760
27	Portage	43,707
28	Kentwood	42,316
29	Lincoln Park	42,283
30	Midland	39,956
31	Muskegon	39,017
32	Bay City	35,485
33	Jackson	35,183

Rank	City	Population
34	Eastpointe	34,145
35	Holland	33,249
36	Garden City	32,750
37	Southgate	32,375
38	Port Huron	32,256
39	Wyandotte	31,884
40	Madison Heights	31,854
41	Allen Park	31,764
42	Inkster	31,160
43	Oak Park	29,595
44	Burton	27,230
45	Romulus	25,326
46	Ferndale	24,458
47	Mount Pleasant	23,351
48	Ypsilanti	22,923
49	Norton Shores	22,919
50	Adrian	22,086
51	Monroe	21,981
52	Trenton	21,708
53	Wayne	20,880
54	Birmingham	19,991
55	Walker	19,813
56	Hazel Park	19,683
57	Auburn Hills	19,310
58	Highland Park	19,293
59	Marquette	19,147
60	Hamtramck	18,041
61	Grosse Pointe Woods	18,021
62	Mount Clemens	17,723
63	Berkley	16,620
64	Grandville	16,483
65	Owosso	15,617
66	Fraser	15,490

Rank	City	Population
67	Sault Ste. Marie	15,385
68	Traverse City	15,158
69	Harper Woods	15,094
70	Riverview	14,797
71	Woodhaven	13,736
72	Clawson	13,648
73	Escanaba	13,280
74	Grosse Pointe Park	13,037
75	Muskegon Heights	12,395
76	Grand Haven	11,982
77	Ecorse	11,913
78	Niles	11,899
79	Benton Harbor	11,885
80	Alpena	11,581

Rank	City	Population
81	Melvindale	11,251
82	Wixom	10,981
83	Ionia	10,848
84	River Rouge	10,835
85	Big Rapids	10,610
86	Cadillac	10,439
87	Grosse Pointe Farms	10,372
88	East Grand Rapids	10,318
89	Sturgis	10,297
90	Beverly Hills	10,289
91	Fenton	10,072

Population figures are estimated for mid-1998.

Source: U.S. Bureau of the Census.

Index to Tables

NA = Reliable data are not available.

DEMOGRAPHICS

Resident state and national populations, 1970-1997

Population figures given in thousands

	State pop.	U.S. pop.	Share	Rank
1970	8,882	203,302	4.4%	7
1980	9,262	226,546	4.1%	8
1985	9,076	237,924	3.8%	8
1990	9,295	248,765	3.7%	8
1995	9,655	262,761	3.7%	8
1997	9,774	267,636	3.7%	8

Source: U.S. Bureau of the Census.

Resident population by age, 1997

Age group	Total population
Under 5 years	653,000
5 to 17 years	1,852,000
18 to 24 years	922,000
25 to 34 years	1,434,000
35 to 44 years	1,641,000
45 to 54 years	1,261,000
55 to 64 years	797,000
65 to 74 years	664,000
75 to 84 years	417,000
85 years and over	132,000
Portion of residents 65 and older	12.4%
National average	12.7%

Population figures are rounded to nearest thousand persons;
figures include armed forces personnel stationed in state.
Source: U.S. Bureau of the Census.

Resident population by race, Hispanic origin, 1997

	State pop.	Share	U.S.
All residents	9,774,000	100.0%	100.0%
Hispanic white	225,000	2.3%	10.0%
non-Hispanic white	7,946,000	81.3%	72.7%
African American	1,392,000	14.2%	12.7%
Native American	60,000	0.6%	0.9%
Asian, Pacific Islander	151,000	1.5%	3.8%

Source: U.S. Bureau of the Census.

Projections of state population, 2000-2025

	Model A Uses interstate migration observed from 1975-1994	Model B Uses Bureau of Economic Analysis employment projections
Year	Population	Population
2000	9,679,000	9,711,000
2005	9,763,000	9,835,000
2010	9,836,000	9,966,000
2015	9,917,000	10,115,000
2020	10,002,000	10,272,000
2025	10,078,000	10,423,000

All population projections, including those for 2000, were calculated in 1997.
Source: U.S. Bureau of the Census, Population Paper Listings PPL-47.

VITAL STATISTICS

Average lifetime in years by race, 1989-1991

	State	U.S.	Rank
All residents	75.04	75.37	34
White residents	76.18	76.13	27
Black residents	68.49	69.16	29

Ranks are from longest-lived to least longest-lived. Ranks exclude Alaska, for which reliable data are not available. Rank for black residents is based on the 32 states for which reliable data are available.
Source: U.S. National Center for Health Statistics.

Infant mortality rates, 1980 and 1995

	State	U.S.
All residents		
1980	12.8	12.6
1995	8.3	7.6
White residents		
1980	10.6	11.0
1995	6.2	6.3
Black residents		
1980	24.2	21.4
1995	17.3	15.1

Figures represent deaths per 1,000 live births of resident infants under 1 year old, exclusive of fetal deaths; all-residents figures include other races not listed separately.
Source: U.S. National Center for Health Statistics.

Marriages and divorces

Marriages in 1996. 69,100
Rate per 1,000 population, 1995. . . . . 7.4
U.S. rate, 1995 . . . . 8.9
Rank among all states 39

Divorces in 1996 38,700
Rate per 1,000 population, 1995. . . . . 4.2
U.S. rate, 1995 . . . . 4.4
Rank among all states 29

Rank is from highest to lowest in country.
Source: U.S. National Center for Health Statistics.

Death rates by leading causes, 1995
Deaths per 100,000 resident population

Cause	State	U.S.
Heart disease	294.8	280.7
Cancer	203.5	204.9
Cerebrovascular diseases	61.4	60.1
Accidents and adverse effects	33.2	35.5
Motor vehicle accidents	17.0	16.5
Chronic obstructive pulmonary diseases	37.5	39.2
Diabetes mellitus	23.4	22.6
HIV	8.4	NA
Suicide	10.3	11.9
Homicide	9.9	8.7
All causes	876.1	880.0
Rank in overall death rate among states		31

Figures exclude nonresidents who die in state. Causes of death follow International Classification of Diseases. Rank is from highest to lowest in country.
Source: U.S. National Center for Health Statistics.

ECONOMY

Gross state product, 1990-1996
In current dollars

	State product	Increase
1990	$188.0 billion	
1993	$217.3 billion	
1994	$240.6 billion	10.72%
1995	$251.8 billion	4.66%
1996	$263.3 billion	4.57%

Source: U.S. Bureau of Economic Analysis; Survey of Current Business, June, 1998.

Gross state product by industry, 1996
In billions

Farms, forestry, fisheries	$2.2
Construction	8.7
Manufacturing.	68.6
Transportation, public utilities	16.5
Wholesale trade	18.0
Retail trade	22.7
Finance, insurance, real estate	36.0
Services	42.5
Government	24.6
State total.	241.0
Total U.S.	$6,923.8
State share	3.48%
Rank among states	9

Total figures include mining, not listed separately.

Source: U.S. Bureau of Economic Analysis; Survey of Current Business, June, 1998.

Personal income per capita, 1990 and 1997
In current dollars

	1990	1997
Per capita income	$18,730	$25,560
U.S. average	$19,188	$25,598
Rank among states	20	18

1997 data are preliminary.

Source: U.S. Bureau of Economic Analysis; Survey of Current Business, May, 1998.

Energy consumption, 1995
In trillions of British thermal units (BTU)

End-use sectors

Residential	770.9
Commercial	561.0
Industrial	1,073.9
Transportation	771.9

Sources of energy

Petroleum	991.0
Natural gas	987.4
Coal	775.8
Hydroelectric power	47.8
Nuclear electric power	260.6
Total state per capita consumption	331.0
Total U.S. per capita consumption	344.4
Rank among states	30
Total state energy consumption	3,157.0
Total U.S. energy consumption	90,547.4
State share of U.S. total	3.49%
Rank among states	9

Total figures include items not listed separately.

Source: U.S. Energy Information Administration; State Energy Data Report.

Nonfarm employment by sectors, 1997

Total	4,446,000
Construction	180,000
Manufacturing	967,000
Transportation, public utilities	173,000
Wholesale trade, retail trade	1,044,000
Finance, insurance, real estate	206,000
Services	1,219,000
Government	649,000

Figures are rounded to nearest thousand persons. Total includes mining, not listed separately.

Source: U.S. Bureau of Labor Statistics; Employment and Earnings, monthly.

Foreign exports, 1990-1997
In millions of dollars

Year	State	U.S.	State share
1990	18,474	394,045	4.69%
1996	27,553	624,767	4.41%
1997	32,254	688,896	4.68%

Source: U.S. Bureau of the Census; U.S. Merchandise Trade, series FT 900.

LAND USE

Federally owned land, 1996

	State	U.S.	State share
Total acres	36,492,000	2,271,343,000	1.61%
Federally owned	3,980,000	563,129,000	0.71%
Federal share	10.9%	24.8%	—

Areas are rounded to nearest thousand acres. Figures for federally owned land do not include trust properties.

Source: U.S. General Services Administration; *Inventory Report on Real Property Owned by the United States Throughout the World*, annual.

Land use, 1992

In acres, rounded to nearest thousand

Total surface area	37,457,000
Federal land	3,166,000
Total nonfederal	33,040,000
Developed	3,686,000
Total rural	29,354,000
Cropland	8,985,000
Pasture land	2,353,000
Range land	0
Forest land	15,608,000
Minor cover/use	2,408,000

Total surface area figures include water area not shown separately.

Source: U.S. Dept. of Agriculture; Soil Conservation Service; Iowa State University, Statistical Laboratory; *Summary Report, 1992 National Resources Inventory.*

Farms and crop acreage, 1997

	State	U.S.	Share	Rank
Farms (thousands)	51	2,058	2.48%	16
Acres (millions)	10	968	1.03%	29
Acres per farm	206	471	—	37
Acres planted	7,032	334,139	2.10%	16
Acres harvested	6,893	319,894	2.15%	16
Farm value (mill.)	$2,433	$108,805	2.24%	4

Numbers of farms are rounded to nearest thousand.

Source: U.S. Dept. of Agriculture; National Agricultural Statistics Service.

GOVERNMENT AND FINANCE

Units of local government, 1997

	State	Total U.S.	Rank
All local governments	2,775	87,453	13
Counties	83	3,043	15
Municipalities	534	19,372	15
Townships	1,242	16,629	8
School districts	584	13,726	7
Special districts	332	34,683	34

County ranks are based on the 48 states with county governments; township ranks are based on the 20 states with township governments; school district ranks are based on the 46 states with such districts.

Source: U.S. Bureau of the Census; *1997 Census of Governments, Government Organization*, Series GC97(1).

State government revenue, 1996

Total revenue	$38,047 mill.
General revenue	32,129 mill.
Per capita	3,302
U.S. per capita average	2,910
Rank among states	14
Intergovernmental revenue	
Total	$7,760 mill.
From federal government	7,313 mill.
From local government	447 mill.
Charges and Miscellaneous	
Total	$5,240 mill.
Current charges	3,200 mill.
Misc. general revenue	2,040 mill.
Taxes	
Total	$19,129 mill.
General sales	6,587 mill.
Selective sales	1,738 mill.
License taxes	982 mill.
Individual income	5,868 mill.
Corporate income	2,190 mill.
Other	1,764 mill.
Insurance trust revenue	5,443 mill.

Total revenue figures include items not listed separately.

Source: U.S. Bureau of the Census.

State government expenditures, 1996

General expenditures

Intergovernmental	$13,299 mill.
Direct expenditures	18,345 mill.
Total	31,644 mill.

Selected direct expenditures

Education	$13,812 mill.
Public welfare	6,440 mill.
Health, hospital	3,406 mill.
Highways	1,936 mill.
Police	229 mill.
Corrections	1,241 mill.
Natural resources	401 mill.
Parks and recreation	59 mill.
Government administration	684 mill.
Interest on debt	696 mill.

Other

State per capita expenditures	$3,252
U.S. per capita average	2,854
Rank among states	13
Total state expenditures	35,080 mill.
Total U.S. expenditures	859,959 mill.

Totals include items not listed separately.
Source: U.S. Bureau of the Census.

Josiah W. Begole (O)	1883-1885
Russell A. Alger (R)	1885-1887
Cyrus G. Luce (R)	1887-1891
Edwin B. Winans (D)	1891-1893
John T. Rich (R)	1893-1897
Hazen S. Pingree (R)	1897-1901
Aaron T. Bliss (R)	1901-1905
Fred M. Warner (R)	1905-1911
Chase M. Osborn (R)	1911-1913
Woodbridge N. Ferris (D)	1913-1917
Albert E. Sleeper (R)	1917-1921
Alexander J. Groesbeck (R)	1921-1927
Fred W. Green (R)	1927-1931
Wilbur M. Brucker (R)	1931-1933
William A. Comstock (D)	1933-1935
Frank D. Fitzgerald (R)	1935-1937
Frank Murphy (D)	1937-1939
Frank D. Fitzgerald (R)	(d) 1939
Luren D. Dickinson (R)	1939-1941
Murray D. Van Wagoner (D)	1941-1943
Harry F. Kelly (R)	1943-1947
Kim Sigler (R)	1947-1949
Gerhard Mennon Williams (D)	1949-1961
John B. Swainson (D)	1961-1963
George W. Romney (R)	(r) 1963-1969
William G. Milliken (R)	1969-1983
James J. Blanchard (D)	1983-1991
John Engler (R)	1991-

POLITICS

Governors since statehood

D = Democrat; R = Republican; O = other;
(r) resigned; (d) died in office; (i) removed from office

Stevens T. Mason (D)	1835-1840
William Woodbridge (O)	(r) 1840-1841
James Wright Gordon (O)	1841-1842
John S. Barry (D)	1842-1846
Alpheus Felch (D)	(r) 1846-1847
William L. Greely (D)	1847-1848
Epaphroditus Ransom (D)	1848-1850
John S. Barry (D)	1850-1852
Robert McClelland (D)	(r) 1852-1853
Andrew Parsons (D)	1853-1855
Kinsley S. Bingham (R)	1855-1859
Moses Wisner (R)	1859-1861
Austin Blair (R)	1861-1865
Henry H. Crapo (R)	1865-1869
Henry P. Baldwin (R)	1869-1873
John J. Bagley (R)	1873-1877
Charles M. Crosswell (R)	1877-1881
David H. Jerome (R)	1881-1883

Composition of state legislature, 1990-1998

	Democrats	Republicans
State House (110 seats)		
1990	61	49
1992	55	55
1994	53	56
1996	58	52
1998	52	58
State Senate (38 seats)		
1990	18	20
1992	16	22
1994	16	22
1996	16	22
1998	15	23

Figures for total seats may include independents and minor
party members.
Source: Council of State Governments; *State Elective Officials
and the Legislatures.*

Composition of congressional delegations, 1989-1999

	Dem	Rep	Total
House of Representatives			
101st Congress, 1989			
State delegates	11	7	18
Total U.S.	259	174	433
102d Congress, 1991			
State delegates	11	7	18
Total U.S.	267	167	434
103d Congress, 1993			
State delegates	10	6	16
Total U.S.	258	176	434
104th Congress, 1995			
State delegates	10	6	16
Total U.S.	197	236	433
105th Congress, 1997			
State delegates	10	6	16
Total U.S.	206	228	434
106th Congress, 1999			
State delegates	10	6	16
Total U.S.	211	222	433
Senate			
101st Congress, 1989			
State delegates	2	0	2
Total U.S.	55	45	100
102d Congress, 1991			
State delegates	2	0	2
Total U.S.	56	44	100
103d Congress, 1993			
State delegates	2	0	2
Total U.S.	57	43	100
104th Congress, 1995			
State delegates	1	1	2
Total U.S.	46	53	99
105th Congress, 1997			
State delegates	1	1	2
Total U.S.	45	55	100
106th Congress, 1999			
State delegates	1	1	2
Total U.S.	45	54	99

Figures are for starts of first sessions. Figure for U.S. Representatives for 101st Congress does not include Alabama and Indiana, which had vacancies. Figures for total U.S. Representatives for 102d, 103d, and 106th Congresses do not include Vermont, which had 1 Independent-Socialist. Figure for U.S. Representatives for 104th Congress does not include Vermont, which had 1 Independent-Socialist, and California, which had 1 vacancy. Figure for U.S. Representatives for 105th Congress does not include New York, which had 1 vacancy. Figure for U.S. Senators for 104th Congress does not include Oregon, which had 1 vacancy. Figure for U.S. Senators for 106th Congress does not include New Hampshire, which had 1 Independent.
Source: U.S. Congress; *Congressional Directory,* biennial.

Voter participation in presidential elections, 1992 and 1996

	1992	1996
State voting age pop.	6,947,000	7,067,000
Total U.S. voting age pop.	189,524,000	196,509,000
State share of U.S. total	3.7%	3.6%
Rank among states	8	8
Percent of state casting vote	61.5	54.2
Percent of U.S. total voting	55.1	49.0
Rank among states	18	19

Source: U.S. Bureau of the Census.

HEALTH AND MEDICAL CARE

Medicare, 1997

	Recipients	Payments
State	1,368,000	$7,401 mill.
Total U.S.	37,514,000	$206,064 mill.
State share	3.65%	3.59%
Rank among states	8	8

Recipient figures are rounded to nearest thousand persons. Ranks are from highest to lowest.
Source: U.S. Health Care Financing Administration.

Medicaid, 1996

	Recipients	Payments
State	1,172,000	$3,359 mill.
Total U.S.	35,028,000	$121,419 mill.
State share	3.35%	2.77%
Rank among states	9	11

Recipient figures are rounded to nearest thousand persons. Payment figures for fiscal year reflect federal and state contribution payments. Ranks are from highest to lowest.
Source: U.S. Health Care Financing Administration.

Health insurance coverage, 1996

	State	U.S.
Total persons covered	8,739,000	225,070,000
Total persons not covered	857,000	41,716,000
Part not covered	8.9%	15.6%
Rank among states	48	—
Children not covered	189,000	10,554,000
Part not covered	7.3%	14.8%
Rank among states	45	—

Ranks are from most to fewest uninsured. Population figures are rounded to nearest thousand persons.
Source: U.S. Bureau of the Census.

AIDS, syphilis, tuberculosis, and measles cases, 1997

Cases	U.S.	State	Share
AIDS	58,443	882	1.51%
Syphilis	8,550	153	1.79%
Tuberculosis	18,534	161	0.87%
Measles	148,000	8,000	5.41%

Measles figures are rounded to nearest thousand cases.
Source: U.S. Centers for Disease Control and Prevention.

HOUSING

Homeownership rates, 1985-1997

	1985	1990	1997
State	70.7%	72.3%	73.3%
Total U.S.	63.9%	63.9%	65.7%
Rank among states	8	4	8

Source: U.S. Bureau of the Census.

Home sales, 1990 and 1997
In thousands of units

Existing home sales	1990	1997	Change
State sales	145.0	180.3	35.3
Total U.S. sales	3,560	4,730	1,170
State share of U.S. total	4.07%	3.81%	-0.26%
Rank among states	7	8	—

Source: National Association of Realtors; *Real Estate Outlook: Market Trends and Insights.*

EDUCATION

Public school enrollment, 1995

State K-8 enrollment	1,192,000
Total U.S. K-8 enrollment	32,341,000
State share of total U.S.	3.69%
State 9-12 enrollment	450,000
Total U.S. 9-12 enrollment	12,500,000
State share of U.S. total	3.60%
State public school enroll. rate	88.9%
Overall U.S. rate	91.6%
Rank among states	38

Enrollment figures (which include unclassified students) are rounded to nearest thousand pupils in fall term; kindergarten (K)-8 grade figures include some prekindergarten students. Enrollment rate is based on percentage of persons 5-17 years old. Rank is from highest to lowest.
Source: U.S. National Center for Education Statistics.

Public college finances, 1996

State FTE enrollment	316,400
Total U.S. FTE enrollment	8,268,800
State share of total U.S.	3.83%
Rank among states	7
State and local appropriations	$1,633,500,000
Total U.S. state and local appropriations	$39,699 mill.
State share of total U.S.	4.11%
Rank among states	6
State net tuition revenues	$1,232 mill.
Total U.S. net tuition	$18,348,100,000
State share of total U.S.	6.72%
Rank among states	3

FTE=Full-time equivalent; credit and noncredit enrollment including summer session in academic year ending in 1996.
Enrollments are rounded to nearest thousand students. Net tuition revenues exclude appropriation to students attending in-state public institutions. Rankings are from highest shares to lowest.
Source: Research Associates of Washington.

TRANSPORTATION AND TRAVEL

Highway mileage, 1996

Interstate	1,239
Other arterial	12,409
Collector roads	28,343
Local roads	78,151
Urban roads.	28,142
Rural roads	89,478
Total state	117,620
U.S. total	3,933,985
State share	3.0%
Rank among states	8

Source: U.S. Federal Highway Administration.

Motor vehicle registrations and driver licenses, 1996
In thousands

Vehicle registrations	State	U.S.	Share	Rank
Autos, trucks, buses	8,010	206,365	3.88%	8
Autos only	5,045	128,439	3.93%	8
Motorcycles	149	3,832	3.89%	7
Driver licenses	6,717	179,539	3.74%	8

Figures do not include vehicles owned by military services.
Source: U.S. Federal Highway Administration; *Highway Statistics; Selected Highway Statistics and Charts.*

Domestic travel expenditures, 1995
Spending by U.S. residents on overnight trips and day trips of at least 100 miles

Total expenditures in state	$8,396 mill.
Total expenditures in U.S.	$360,314 mill.
State share of total U.S.	2.33%
Rank among states.	13

Source: Travel Industry Association of America.

CRIME AND LAW ENFORCEMENT

State and local police officers, 1996

Local police	13,288
State police	2,164
Sheriffs	4,435
Total	20,568
Officers per 10,000 residents	21
U.S. average	25
Rank among states.	30

Figures cover full-time sworn officers; totals include special police not shown separately.
Source: U.S. Bureau of Justice Statistics; *Census of State and Local Law Enforcement Agencies, 1996.*

Crime rates, 1996
Rates per 100,000 resident population

Violent crimes	State	U.S.
Total violent	635	634
Murder	7.5	7.4
Forcible rape	57.0	36.1
Robbery	176	202
Aggravated assault	395	388
Property crimes		
Total property	4,482	4,445
Burglary	895	943
Larceny/theft	2,886	2,976
Motor vehicle theft	701	526
Totals	5,118	5,079

Source: U.S. Federal Bureau of Investigation; *Crime in the United States,* annual.

State prison populations, 1980-1996

	State	U.S.	State share
1980	15,124	305,458	4.95%
1990	34,267	708,393	4.84%
1996	42,349	1,025,624	4.13%

Figures exclude prisoners in federal penitentiaries.
Source: U.S. Bureau of Justice Statistics.

Minnesota

Location: Upper Midwestern continental United States

Area and rank: 79,617 square miles (206,207 square kilometers); 86,943 square miles (225,182 square kilometers) including water; fourteenth largest state in area

Population and rank: 4,685,549 (1997); twentieth largest state in population

Capital: St. Paul

Largest city: Minneapolis (351,731 people in 1998)

Became territory: March 3, 1849

State capitol building at St. Paul. (©James Blank/Weststock)

Entered Union and rank: May 11, 1858; thirty-second state

Present constitution adopted: 1858

Counties: 87

State name: "Minnesota" is derived from a Dakota Indian word that means "sky-tinted water"

State nicknames: North Star State; Gopher State; Land of 10,000 Lakes

Motto: *L'Etoile du Nord* (The North Star)

State flag: Blue field with 1858 scene from state seal and border of state flower blossoms, name "Minnesota," and nineteen stars

Highest point: Eagle Mountain — 2,301 feet (701 meters)

Lowest point: Lake Superior — 602 feet (183 meters)

Highest recorded temperature: 114 degrees Fahrenheit (46 degrees Celsius) — Moorhead, 1936

Lowest recorded temperature: −59 degrees Fahrenheit (−51 degrees Celsius) — Pokegama Dam, 1903

State song: "Hail Minnesota"

State tree: Red (or Norway) pine

State flower: Showy lady slipper

State bird: Common loon (also known as Great Northern Diver)

State fish: Walleye

National park: Voyageurs

Minnesota History

Reaching farther north than any other state except Alaska, Minnesota was settled more slowly than other states in the center of the United States, which were more accessible to heavily populated eastern states. Despite its isolation, the fertile soils of the south and west, the pine forests of the northeast, and the hardwood forests between these regions eventually attracted settlers. The state's access to Lake Superior, numerous rivers, and countless lakes also brought economic growth to the area. Much of Minnesota remains rural, in sharp contrast to the Twin Cities of Minneapolis and St. Paul near the eastern edge of the state.

Early History. The earliest people to inhabit the area, known as the Paleo-Indian Culture, hunted bison and other large animals more than ten thousand years ago. About seven thousand years ago, the people of the Eastern Archaic Culture hunted small and large animals and made tools from copper. The Woodland Culture, starting about three thousand years ago, introduced the use of pottery and burial mounds. Starting about one thousand years ago, the Mississippian Culture built large, permanent villages located in fertile river valleys and raised corn, beans, and squash.

Both the Woodland Culture and Mississippian Culture lifestyles lasted until Europeans arrived about three hundred years ago. Until the middle of the nineteenth century, Minnesota was primarily inhabited by the Ojibwa in the north and east and the Dakota in the south and west. Conflicts between these peoples led to the Ojibwa forcing the Dakota to move further southwest in the middle of the eighteenth century.

Exploration and Settlement. The first European explorers to reach the area were the French fur traders Pierre Esprit Radisson and Médard Chouart des Groseilliers, who traveled from Canada through Wisconsin and into eastern Minnesota in 1658. In September of 1679, Daniel Greysolon, sieur du Lhut, met with Native Americans near Mille Lacs Lake near the center of the region. As a result of this meeting, peaceful relations were established among the French, the Ojibwa,

and the Dakota. Du Lhut also claimed the area for King Louis XIV of France.

In January of 1680, the French missionary Louis Hennepin began a journey north along the Mississippi River into eastern Minnesota. In April, Hennepin was captured by the Dakota. During his captivity, Hennepin named a waterfall on the Mississippi River the Falls of St. Anthony, near the future site of the Twin Cities. Hennepin was rescued by Du Lhut in July.

In 1682 the French explorer René-Robert Cavalier, sieur de La Salle, claimed the entire valley of the Mississippi River for France. He named this vast area, including western Minnesota, Louisiana. Meanwhile, French fur traders had established the first permanent European settlement in the region in the far north, at Grand Portage. Grand Portage soon became the center of the prosperous fur trade. Among the many noted French explorers who established settlements in the area were Nicolas Perrot, who founded Fort Antoine in 1686, and Pierre Gaultier de Varennes, sieur de La Vérendrye, who founded Fort Saint Charles in 1731.

The British and Americans. The wealth generated by the fur trade was part of the struggle for control of North America between France and England that led to the French and Indian War (1754-1763). The British took control of Minnesota east of the Mississippi River after the war. Western Minnesota, with the rest of Louisiana, had been ceded to Spain in 1762 but was returned to France in 1800.

Spain did little to settle the area, but England quickly established the North West Company at Grand Portage to take advantage of the lucrative fur trade. At the end of the American Revolution (1775-1783), eastern Minnesota officially became part of the United States. The North West Company did not leave Grand Portage until 1803, when it moved to Canada. It was replaced by the American Fur Company, established in 1808.

Eastern Minnesota became part of the newly created Northwest Territory in 1787. It became

part of several different territories as the vast Northwest Territory was reorganized in the early nineteenth century. Between 1800 and 1858, it was part of Indiana Territory, Illinois Territory, Michigan Territory, Wisconsin Territory, and Minnesota Territory.

Meanwhile, the United States purchased Louisiana, including western Minnesota, from France in 1803. From 1834 to 1849, eastern Minnesota was part of Michigan Territory, Wisconsin Territory, the Iowa Territory, again Wisconsin Territory, and Minnesota Territory.

Becoming a State. During this time, Minnesota remained a sparsely populated area isolated from the rest of the United States. In 1805, a military expedition led by Zebulon Pike failed to locate the source of the Mississippi but did manage to secure lands along a river from the Dakota Indians. In 1818 a treaty with England added a large area of land to northern Minnesota. In 1819 Fort Saint An-

Minnesota's largest city, Minneapolis, is separated from the state capital, St. Paul, by the Mississippi River. (PhotoDisc)

thony was established as the first permanent American settlement in the area. The site was renamed Fort Snelling in 1825 and went on to become the most important settlement in the area until the middle of the century.

The fur trade began to decline in 1837, with the first in a series of treaties with the Dakota and Ojibwa Indians that ceded large amounts of land to the United States. This encouraged settlers to enter the region and eventually made the lumber industry and agriculture more important than the fur trade.

The Minnesota Territory had about four thousand settlers in 1849, mostly near Fort Snelling. Most of these early settlers were from New England, although many had entered Minnesota from Canada. Within one year, the population jumped to more than six thousand. As the lumber industry grew more important, the population grew even more quickly. By 1857 the number of Minnesota residents, mostly from eastern states, reached more than 150,000.

The majority of new residents settled in the southeast part of the territory, near Fort Snelling. In the same area, St. Paul was founded in 1838 and became the territory capital in 1849. The nearby city of Minneapolis was founded in 1855. Minnesota became the thirty-second state, with much of its western lands removed and added to the Nebraska Territory, in 1858.

Wars and Industry. Minnesota was the first state to send volunteers to fight for the Union during the Civil War. More than twenty thousand residents of the state served in the war. Meanwhile, Minnesota faced its own violent conflict. In 1862 a rebellion by the Dakotas, confined to reservations within the state, eventually led to more than five hundred deaths within a few weeks. The defeated Dakotas were forced into reservations in western territories. The Ojibwas remained on reservations created for them in the north of the state.

After the Civil War, growth continued at a rapid pace. Germans, Swedes, and Norwegians arrived in large numbers. Other important sources of new

immigrants were Finland, Poland, Bohemia, Ireland, France, Canada, the Netherlands, Belgium, Iceland, Denmark, Wales, and Switzerland. During the 1880's, the period of the state's fastest growth, most settlers were homesteaders in western Minnesota or worked in the lumber industry. Flour milling was also a major industry in the Twin Cities, both of which tripled in population during this decade. Mining of iron ore began in 1884 and soon became a major source of income.

The Twentieth Century. Immigration during the early twentieth century was mostly to the Twin Cities and included Finns, Italians, Slovakians, Croatians, Serbs, Greeks, Jews, Ukrainians, Russians, and Hispanics. African Americans from southern states moved to the Twin Cities also. In later years, Asians also immigrated.

Throughout the twentieth century Minnesota tended to be politically independent. It supported traditionally a wide variety of small political parties that influence the policies of the major parties. The modern Democratic Party in Minnesota incorporates many of the ideas of the Farmer-Labor Party, while the modern Republican Party in the state is influenced by independents.

Loss of natural resources led to changes in the state's economy during the twentieth century. Much of the most valuable lumber was cut by 1920, forcing the industry to turn to other trees. At about the same time, flour milling was moved from Minneapolis to Buffalo. The best iron ore was depleted by the late 1950's. New techniques for using lower-grade iron ore led to a revitalization of the industry in the 1960's, but low-cost imports led to another decline in the 1980's. Despite a decline in agriculture after World War II, agriculture was still the state's largest industry.

The early 1980's brought a drop in crop prices, bringing hardship to farmers throughout the state. However, the nationwide recession of the late 1980's had only a minimal effect on Minnesota. In the 1990's, the state's economy turned to industries such as printing, health care, scientific instruments, chemicals, and recreational equipment.

Rose Secrest

Mass execution of participants in the Minnesota Dakota Sioux uprising of 1862. (Library of Congress)

Minnesota Time Line

1658	Pierre Esprit Radisson and Médard Chouart des Groseilliers are the first Europeans to explore the region.
1679	Daniel Greysolon, sieur Du Lhut, meets with Native Americans and claims the area for France.
1680	Father Louis Hennepin explores the area, is captured by the Dakota, and is rescued by Du Lhut.
1682	René-Robert Cavalier, sieur de La Salle, claims the entire valley of the Mississippi River for France, naming it Louisiana.
1686	Nicolas Perrot founds Fort Antoine.
1731	Pierre Gaultier de Varennes, sieur de La Vérendrye, founds Fort Saint Charles.
1762	Louisiana is ceded to Spain.
1763	End of the French and Indian War brings eastern Minnesota under British control.
1783	End of the American Revolution brings eastern Minnesota under American control.
1787	Eastern Minnesota becomes part of the Northwest Territory.
1800	Louisiana is returned to France.
1800	Eastern Minnesota becomes part of Indiana Territory.
1803	United States purchases Louisiana Territory from France.
1805	Explorer Zebulon Pike leads a military expedition to the region.
1808	American Fur Company is established.
1809	Eastern Minnesota becomes part of Illinois Territory.
1818	Eastern Minnesota becomes part of Michigan Territory.
1818	Part of Canada is ceded to the United States by England and is incorporated into Minnesota.
1819	Fort Saint Anthony (later Fort Snelling) is established.
1834	Western Minnesota becomes part of Michigan Territory
1836	Minnesota becomes part of Wisconsin Territory.
1837	Treaties with Native Americans open new lands for settlers.
1838	St. Paul is founded.
1838	Western Minnesota becomes part of Iowa Territory.
1846	Western Minnesota is returned to Wisconsin Territory.
Mar. 3, 1849	Minnesota Territory is created, with St. Paul as the capital.
1849	Population is about four thousand.
1850	Population is more than six thousand.
1851	University of Minnesota is established.
1855	Minneapolis is founded.
1857	Population reaches 150,000.
May 11, 1858	Minnesota is admitted to the Union as the thirty-second state.

1862	Rebellion by the Dakota Indians leads to five hundred deaths.
1862	First railroad, linking the Twin Cities, is built.
1867	Railroads link the Twin Cities to Chicago.
1880	Minneapolis surpasses St. Paul in population.
1880's	Minnesota experiences its period of fastest growth.
1884	Mining of iron ore begins.
1890's	Immigration shifts from rural areas to the Twin Cities.
1920's	Flour milling and lumber industries decline in importance.
1950's	High-grade iron ore is depleted.
1959	Great Lakes are opened to oceangoing vessels.
1960's	Methods are developed to use low-grade iron ore.
1970's	Asian immigrants begin to arrive in Minnesota.
1980's	Crop prices decline, leading to economic hardship.
1980's	Low-cost foreign iron ore leads to a decline in the iron business.
1990	Population reaches nearly 4.4 million; more than half live in the Minneapolis-St. Paul metropolitan area.
1998	Population reaches 4.7 million.
1998	In a campaign that draws national attention, former professional wrestler Jesse Ventura is elected governor, the first Reform Party member to win a statewide office.

Notes for Further Study

Published Sources. Of the many books that offer general information about the state, one of the most enjoyable for beginning students may be *Minnesota Trivia* (1990) by Laurel Winter. Minnesota's scenic beauty has led to the publications of many books about the land and the living things that reside there. Two of the best are *Minnesota's Natural Heritage: An Ecological Perspective* (1995), edited by John R. Tester and Mary Keinstead, and *Natural Wonders of Minnesota: Parks, Preserves, and Wild Places* (1997) by Martin Hintz. An interesting look at new ways of influencing political decisions, using the issue of school choice in Minnesota as an example, can be found in *Transforming Public Policy: Dynamics of Policy Entrepreneurship and Innovation* (1996) by Nancy C. Roberts and Paula J. King. Of the many volumes providing information about the Twin Cities, one of the clearest is Rick Nelson's *City-Smart Guidebook: Minneapolis-St. Paul* (1999).

For students of the state's history, an excellent starting place is *A Historical Album of Minnesota* (1993) by Jeffrey D. Carlson. A more scholarly account is found in *Minnesota: A History* (1998) by William E. Lass. An interesting account of Native Americans in the state is offered in Samuel W. Pond's *The Dakota or Sioux in Minnesota as They Were in 1834* (1986). A colorful account of the early days of fur trading can be found in *The Grand Portage Story* (1992) by Carolyn Gilman. The modern history of the state is discussed in detail in *Minnesota in a Century of Change: The State and Its People Since 1900* (1989), edited by Clifford E. Clark.

Web Resources. A wide variety of Web sites dealing with all aspects of Minnesota can be found on the Internet. Many of these are associated with the state government, which maintains a large number of informative sites. For the beginning student, two good places to visit for general information about the state are All About Minnesota (http://www.state.mn.us/aam) and Minnesota Information (http://www.wms.luminet.net/CurricSites/Minnesota/Minnesota_Information.html).

An extremely broad range of information is available at the state government's main Web site, North Star: Minnesota Government Information and Sources (http://www.state.mn.us/mainmenu.html). Statistical information from the U.S. Census Bureau can be found at Minnesota (http://www.census.gov/cgi-bin/data map/state?27).

Detailed information on economic activity in the state is available at Minnesota's Economy (http://www.dted.state.mn.us/mnecon/mnecon.html) A popular guide to tourism is offered at Explore Minnesota (http://www.exploreminnesota.com). An unusual Web site, dealing with public policy issues such as crime and the enviroment, can be found at Minnesota Planning (http://www.mnplan.state.mn.us). Of the many Web sites devoted to the state's past, a good starting place is Minnesota Historical Society (http://www.mnhs.org), which offers information about the state's historical museums, archives, and libraries.

Counties

County	Sq. miles	1996 pop.	County	Sq. miles	1996 pop.
Aitkin	1,819.4	13,715	Koochiching	3,102.4	15,858
Anoka	424.0	282,139	Lac qui Parle	764.9	8,228
Becker	1,310.5	29,161	Lake	2,099.4	10,707
Beltrami	2,505.4	38,274	Lake of the Woods	1,296.7	4,598
Benton	408.3	33,336	Le Sueur	448.5	24,715
Big Stone	497.0	5,839	Lincoln	537.1	6,687
Blue Earth	752.4	54,199	Lyon	714.2	24,791
Brown	610.9	27,262	McLeod	491.9	33,636
Carlton	860.4	30,426	Mahnomen	556.2	5,144
Carver	357.1	61,415	Marshall	1,772.3	10,563
Cass	2,017.7	25,329	Martin	709.4	22,462
Chippewa	582.8	13,132	Meeker	608.6	21,463
Chisago	417.7	38,123	Mille Lacs	574.5	20,312
Clay	1,045.3	51,848	Morrison	1,124.5	30,528
Clearwater	994.8	8,254	Mower	711.5	37,151
Cook	1,450.7	4,688	Murray	704.5	9,609
Cottonwood	640.0	12,321	Nicollet	452.3	29,846
Crow Wing	996.7	50,634	Nobles	715.5	20,060
Dakota	569.7	326,016	Norman	876.3	7,753
Dodge	439.5	16,855	Olmsted	653.0	113,182
Douglas	634.3	30,459	Otter Tail	1,979.8	53,889
Faribault	713.7	16,405	Pennington	616.6	13,564
Fillmore	861.3	20,860	Pine	1,411.2	23,331
Freeborn	707.7	31,972	Pipestone	465.9	10,124
Goodhue	758.6	42,366	Polk	1,970.5	32,433
Grant	546.5	6,154	Pope	670.2	11,051
Hennepin	556.6	1,058,746	Ramsey	155.8	484,484
Houston	558.4	19,226	Red Lake	432.4	4,342
Hubbard	922.6	16,406	Redwood	879.9	16,878
Isanti	439.1	29,017	Renville	983.0	17,075
Itasca	2,665.3	43,392	Rice	497.6	52,888
Jackson	701.9	11,718	Rock	482.6	9,948
Kanabec	525.0	13,838	Roseau	1,662.6	16,215
Kandiyohi	796.2	41,324	Saint Louis	6,225.7	196,414
Kittson	1,097.1	5,419	Scott	356.8	72,813

County	Sq. miles	1996 pop.	County	Sq. miles	1996 pop.
Sherburne	436.6	55,401	Waseca	423.3	17,998
Sibley	588.7	14,652	Washington	391.7	185,074
Stearns	1,344.6	126,990	Watonwan	434.5	11,600
Steele	429.6	31,567	Wilkin	751.5	7,381
Stevens	562.1	10,197	Winona	626.3	48,411
Swift	743.6	10,857	Wright	660.8	80,757
Todd	942.1	24,128	Yellow Medicine	758.0	11,559
Traverse	574.1	4,298			
Wabasha	525.0	20,752	*Source:* U.S. Census Bureau; National Association of Counties.		
Wadena	535.5	13,126			

Cities
With 10,000 or more residents

Rank	City	Population
1	Minneapolis	351,731
2	St. Paul	257,284
3	Bloomington	86,186
4	Duluth	81,228
5	Rochester	78,173
6	Coon Rapids	63,674
7	Brooklyn Park	63,115
8	Plymouth	61,509
9	Eagan	60,042
10	Burnsville	59,334
11	Minnetonka	50,952
12	St. Cloud	50,745

Rank	City	Population
13	Eden Prairie	50,279
14	Maple Grove	46,932
15	Edina	45,894
16	Apple Valley	45,428
17	Blaine	44,960
18	St. Louis Park	42,387
19	Woodbury	40,431
20	Lakeville	39,166
21	Maplewood	34,970
22	Roseville	34,465
23	Richfield	34,040
24	Moorhead	33,082
25	Cottage Grove	31,250
26	Mankato	30,780
27	Inver Grove Heights	29,292
28	Fridley	27,974
29	Brooklyn Center	27,851
30	Oakdale	26,663
31	Shoreview	26,157
32	White Bear Lake	25,999
33	Winona	24,187
34	Andover	23,918
35	Crystal	23,040
36	New Brighton	22,845
37	Austin	21,482
38	New Hope	21,204
39	Champlin	21,116
40	Owatonna	20,599
41	Golden Valley	20,349
42	South St. Paul	19,827
43	West St. Paul	19,228
44	Willmar	18,805
45	Faribault	18,645
46	Columbia Heights	18,285
47	Ramsey	18,226

Rank	City	Population
48	Chanhassen	18,185
49	Anoka	17,996
50	Albert Lea	17,593
51	Hastings	17,454
52	Hibbing	17,383
53	Savage	17,151
54	Shakopee	16,553
55	Hopkins	16,279
56	Northfield	16,174
57	Elk River	16,129
58	Red Wing	15,843
59	Stillwater	15,801
60	Chaska	15,348
61	Prior Lake	14,864
62	Lino Lakes	14,469
63	Robbinsdale	13,993
64	Fergus Falls	13,706
65	New Ulm	13,491
66	Vadnais Heights	13,366
67	Brainerd	13,323
68	Rosemount	13,249
69	Mounds View	12,874
70	Bemidji	12,591
71	North St. Paul	12,570
72	Hutchinson	12,521
73	Marshall	12,117
74	Ham Lake	11,793
75	North Mankato	11,595
76	Mendota Heights	11,529
77	Cloquet	10,868
78	Fairmont	10,862
79	East Bethel	10,302
80	Farmington	10,166

Population figures are estimated for mid-1998.
Source: U.S. Bureau of the Census.

Index to Tables

NA = Reliable data are not available.

DEMOGRAPHICS

Resident state and national populations, 1970-1997

Population figures given in thousands

	State pop.	U.S. pop.	Share	Rank
1970	3,806	203,302	1.9%	19
1980	4,076	226,546	1.8%	21
1985	4,184	237,924	1.8%	21
1990	4,376	248,765	1.8%	20
1995	4,607	262,761	1.8%	20
1997	4,686	267,636	1.8%	20

Source: U.S. Bureau of the Census.

Resident population by age, 1997

Age group	Total population
Under 5 years	316,000
5 to 17 years	935,000
18 to 24 years	427,000
25 to 34 years	671,000
35 to 44 years	805,000
45 to 54 years	587,000
55 to 64 years	367,000
65 to 74 years	294,000
75 to 84 years	205,000
85 years and over	79,000
Portion of residents 65 and older	12.3%
National average	12.7%

Population figures are rounded to nearest thousand persons;
figures include armed forces personnel stationed in state.
Source: U.S. Bureau of the Census.

Resident population by race, Hispanic origin, 1997

	State pop.	Share	U.S.
All residents	4,686,000	100.0%	100.0%
Hispanic white	70,000	1.5%	10.0%
non-Hispanic white	4,307,000	91.9%	72.7%
African American	133,000	2.8%	12.7%
Native American	57,000	1.2%	0.9%
Asian, Pacific Islander	118,000	2.5%	3.8%

Source: U.S. Bureau of the Census.

Projections of state population, 2000-2025

	Model A Uses interstate migration observed from 1975-1994	Model B Uses Bureau of Economic Analysis employment projections
Year	Population	Population
2000	4,830,000	4,822,000
2005	5,005,000	5,014,000
2010	5,147,000	5,212,000
2015	5,283,000	5,414,000
2020	5,406,000	5,606,000
2025	5,510,000	5,778,000

All population projections, including those for 2000, were calculated in 1997.

Source: U.S. Bureau of the Census, Population Paper Listings PPL-47.

VITAL STATISTICS

Average lifetime in years by race, 1989-1991

	State	U.S.	Rank
All residents	77.76	75.37	2
White residents	77.97	76.13	2
Black residents	NA	69.16	NA

Ranks are from longest-lived to least longest-lived. Ranks exclude Alaska, for which reliable data are not available. Rank for black residents is based on the 32 states for which reliable data are available.

Source: U.S. National Center for Health Statistics.

Infant mortality rates, 1980 and 1995

	State	U.S.
All residents		
1980	10.0	12.6
1995	6.7	7.6
White residents		
1980	9.6	11.0
1995	6.0	6.3
Black residents		
1980	20.0	21.4
1995	17.6	15.1

Figures represent deaths per 1,000 live births of resident infants under 1 year old, exclusive of fetal deaths; all-residents figures include other races not listed separately.
Source: U.S. National Center for Health Statistics.

Marriages and divorces

Marriages in 1996. 33,200
Rate per 1,000 population, 1995. . . . . 7.1
U.S. rate, 1995 . . . . 8.9
Rank among all states 43

Divorces in 1996 15,200
Rate per 1,000 population, 1995. . . . . 3.4
U.S. rate, 1995 . . . . 4.4
Rank among all states 37

Rank is from highest to lowest in country.
Source: U.S. National Center for Health Statistics.

Death rates by leading causes, 1995
Deaths per 100,000 resident population

Cause	State	U.S.
Heart disease	225.2	280.7
Cancer	188.6	204.9
Cerebrovascular diseases	67.8	60.1
Accidents and adverse effects	36.1	35.5
Motor vehicle accidents	14.4	16.5
Chronic obstructive pulmonary diseases	36.3	39.2
Diabetes mellitus	18.7	22.6
HIV	5.6	NA
Suicide	11.3	11.9
Homicide	-	8.7
All causes	813.7	880.0

Rank in overall death rate among states	37

Figures exclude nonresidents who die in state. Causes of death follow International Classification of Diseases. Rank is from highest to lowest in country.
Source: U.S. National Center for Health Statistics.

ECONOMY

Gross state product, 1990-1996
In current dollars

	State product	Increase
1990	$99.5 billion	
1993	$114.6 billion	
1994	$124.6 billion	8.73%
1995	$131.4 billion	5.46%
1996	$141.6 billion	7.76%

Source: U.S. Bureau of Economic Analysis; *Survey of Current Business,* June, 1998.

Gross state product by industry, 1996
In billions

Farms, forestry, fisheries	$3.6
Construction	5.3
Manufacturing	26.7
Transportation, public utilities	10.3
Wholesale trade	11.2
Retail trade	11.9
Finance, insurance, real estate	21.2
Services	24.0
Government	13.8
State total	$128.7
Total U.S.	$6,923.8
State share	1.86%
Rank among states	18

Total figures include mining, not listed separately.

Source: U.S. Bureau of Economic Analysis; *Survey of Current Business,* June, 1998.

Personal income per capita, 1990 and 1997
In current dollars

	1990	1997
Per capita income	$19,378	$26,797
U.S. average	$19,188	$25,598
Rank among states	17	10

1997 data are preliminary.

Source: U.S. Bureau of Economic Analysis; *Survey of Current Business,* May, 1998.

Energy consumption, 1995
In trillions of British thermal units (BTU)

End-use sectors

Residential	358.4
Commercial	214.2
Industrial	623.6
Transportation	440.1

Sources of energy

Petroleum	615.8
Natural gas	357.7
Coal	337.2
Hydroelectric power	46.0
Nuclear electric power	141.1
Total state per capita consumption	351.5
Total U.S. per capita consumption	344.4
Rank among states	24
Total state energy consumption	1,622.1
Total U.S. energy consumption	90,547.4
State share of U.S. total	1.79%
Rank among states	21

Total figures include items not listed separately.

Source: U.S. Energy Information Administration; *State Energy Data Report.*

Nonfarm employment by sectors, 1997

Total	2,485,000
Construction	94,000
Manufacturing	434,000
Transportation, public utilities	124,000
Wholesale trade, retail trade	600,000
Finance, insurance, real estate	146,000
Services	700,000
Government	380,000

Figures are rounded to nearest thousand persons. Total includes mining, not listed separately.

Source: U.S. Bureau of Labor Statistics; *Employment and Earnings,* monthly.

Foreign exports, 1990-1997
In millions of dollars

Year	State	U.S.	State share
1990	5,091	394,045	1.29%
1996	8,992	624,767	1.44%
1997	9,447	688,896	1.37%

Source: U.S. Bureau of the Census; *U.S. Merchandise Trade,* series FT 900.

LAND USE

Federally owned land, 1996

	State	U.S.	State share
Total acres	51,206,000	2,271,343,000	2.25%
Federally owned	4,069,000	563,129,000	0.72%
Federal share	7.9%	24.8%	—

Areas are rounded to nearest thousand acres. Figures for federally owned land do not include trust properties.

Source: U.S. General Services Administration; *Inventory Report on Real Property Owned by the United States Throughout the World,* annual.

Land use, 1992

In acres, rounded to nearest thousand

Total surface area	54,017,000
Federal land	3,383,000
Total nonfederal	47,092,000
Developed	2,418,000
Total rural	44,674,000
Cropland	21,356,000
Pasture land	3,282,000
Range land	0
Forest land	13,815,000
Minor cover/use	6,222,000

Total surface area figures include water area not shown separately.

Source: U.S. Dept. of Agriculture; Soil Conservation Service; Iowa State University, Statistical Laboratory; *Summary Report, 1992 National Resources Inventory.*

Farms and crop acreage, 1997

	State	U.S.	Share	Rank
Farms (thousands)	87	2,058	4.23%	5
Acres (millions)	30	968	3.10%	14
Acres per farm	343	471	—	22
Acres planted	20,510	334,139	6.14%	6
Acres harvested	20,079	319,894	6.28%	5
Farm value (mill.)	$5,403	$108,805	4.97%	23

Numbers of farms are rounded to nearest thousand.

Source: U.S. Dept. of Agriculture; National Agricultural Statistics Service.

GOVERNMENT AND FINANCE

Units of local government, 1997

	State	Total U.S.	Rank
All local governments	3,501	87,453	7
Counties	87	3,043	14
Municipalities	854	19,372	7
Townships	1,794	16,629	1
School districts	360	13,726	15
Special districts	406	34,683	29

County ranks are based on the 48 states with county governments; township ranks are based on the 20 states with township governments; school district ranks are based on the 46 states with such districts.

Township figures include "town" governments.

Source: U.S. Bureau of the Census; *1997 Census of Governments, Government Organization,* Series GC97(1).

State government revenue, 1996

Total revenue	$20,525 mill.
General revenue	16,192 mill.
Per capita	3,483
U.S. per capita average	2,910
Rank among states	9
Intergovernmental revenue	
Total	$3,620 mill.
From federal government	3,461 mill.
From local government	159 mill.
Charges and Miscellaneous	
Total	$2,330 mill.
Current charges	1,325 mill.
Misc. general revenue	1,005 mill.
Taxes	
Total	$10,243 mill.
General sales	2,900 mill.
Selective sales	1,592 mill.
License taxes	769 mill.
Individual income	4,136 mill.
Corporate income	703 mill.
Other	142 mill.
Insurance trust revenue	4,333 mill.

Total revenue figures include items not listed separately.

Source: U.S. Bureau of the Census.

State government expenditures, 1996

General expenditures

Intergovernmental	$6,068 mill.
Direct expenditures	9,681 mill.
Total	15,749 mill.

Selected direct expenditures

Education	$5,783 mill.
Public welfare	4,129 mill.
Health, hospital	1,117 mill.
Highways	1,214 mill.
Police	89 mill.
Corrections	302 mill.
Natural resources	329 mill.
Parks and recreation	88 mill.
Government administration	461 mill.
Interest on debt	288 mill.

Other

State per capita expenditures	$3,388
U.S. per capita average	2,854
Rank among states	10
Total state expenditures	17,325 mill.
Total U.S. expenditures	859,959 mill.

Totals include items not listed separately.
Source: U.S. Bureau of the Census.

Samuel R. Van Sant (R)	1901-1905
John A. Johnson (D)	(d) 1905-1909
Adolph O. Eberhart (R)	1909-1915
Winfield S. Hammond (D)	(d) 1915
Joseph A. A. Burnquist (R)	1915-1921
Jacob A. O. Preus (R)	1921-1925
Theodore Christianson (R)	1925-1931
Floyd B. Olson (O)	(d) 1931-1936
Hjalmar Petersen (O)	1936-1937
Elmer A. Benson (O)	1937-1939
Harold E. Stassen (R)	(r) 1939-1943
Edward J. Thye (R)	1943-1947
Luther W. Youngdahl (R)	(r) 1947-1951
Clyde Elmer Anderson (R)	1951-1955
Orville L. Freeman (O)	1955-1961
Elmer L. Anderson (R)	1961-1963
Karl F. Rolvaag (O)	1963-1967
Harold P. LeVander (R)	1967-1971
Wendell R. Anderson (O)	(r) 1971-1976
Rudy Perpich (O)	1976-1979
Albert H. Quie (R)	1979-1983
Rudolph Perpich (O)	1983-1991
Arne Carlson (R)	1991-1999
Jesse Ventura (O)	1999-

POLITICS

Governors since statehood

D = Democrat; R = Republican; O = other;
(r) resigned; (d) died in office; (i) removed from office

Henry H. Sibley (D)	1858-1860
Alexander Ramsey (R)	(r) 1860-1863
Henry A. Swift (R)	1863-1864
Stephen Miller (R)	1864-1868
William R. Marshall (R)	1868-1870
Horace Austin (R)	1870-1874
Cushman K. Davis (R)	1874-1876
John S. Pillsbury (R)	1876-1882
Lucius F. Hubbard (R)	1882-1887
Andrew R. McGill (R)	1887-1889
William R. Merriam (R)	1889-1893
Knute Nelson (R)	(r) 1893-1895
David M. Clough (R)	1895-1899
John Lind (D)	1899-1901

Composition of state legislature, 1990-1998

	Democrats	*Republicans*
State House (134 seats)		
1990	78	56
1992	85	49
1994	71	63
1996	70	64
1998	62	70
State Senate (67 seats)		
1990	46	21
1992	45	22
1994	43	21
1996	42	24
1998	40	26

Figures for total seats may include independents and minor
party members.
Source: Council of State Governments; *State Elective Officials
and the Legislatures.*

Composition of congressional delegations, 1989-1999

	Dem	Rep	Total
House of Representatives			
101st Congress, 1989			
State delegates	5	3	8
Total U.S.	259	174	433
102d Congress, 1991			
State delegates	6	2	8
Total U.S.	267	167	434
103d Congress, 1993			
State delegates	6	2	8
Total U.S.	258	176	434
104th Congress, 1995			
State delegates	6	2	8
Total U.S.	197	236	433
105th Congress, 1997			
State delegates	6	2	8
Total U.S.	206	228	434
106th Congress, 1999			
State delegates	6	2	8
Total U.S.	211	222	433
Senate			
101st Congress, 1989			
State delegates	0	2	2
Total U.S.	55	45	100
102d Congress, 1991			
State delegates	1	1	2
Total U.S.	56	44	100
103d Congress, 1993			
State delegates	1	1	2
Total U.S.	57	43	100
104th Congress, 1995			
State delegates	1	1	2
Total U.S.	46	53	99
105th Congress, 1997			
State delegates	1	1	2
Total U.S.	45	55	100
106th Congress, 1999			
State delegates	1	1	2
Total U.S.	45	54	99

Figures are for starts of first sessions. Figure for U.S. Representatives for 101st Congress does not include Alabama and Indiana, which had vacancies. Figures for total U.S. Representatives for 102d, 103d, and 106th Congresses do not include Vermont, which had 1 Independent-Socialist. Figure for U.S. Representatives for 104th Congress does not include Vermont, which had 1 Independent-Socialist, and California, which had 1 vacancy. Figure for U.S. Representatives for 105th Congress does not include New York, which had 1 vacancy. Figure for U.S. Senators for 104th Congress does not include Oregon, which had 1 vacancy. Figure for U.S. Senators for 106th Congress does not include New Hampshire, which had 1 Independent.

Source: U.S. Congress; *Congressional Directory*, biennial.

Voter participation in presidential elections, 1992 and 1996

	1992	1996
State voting age pop.	3,272,000	3,412,000
Total U.S. voting age pop.	189,524,000	196,509,000
State share of U.S. total	1.7%	1.7%
Rank among states	20	20
Percent of state casting vote	71.8	56.3
Percent of U.S. total voting	55.1	49.0
Rank among states	2	14

Source: U.S. Bureau of the Census.

HEALTH AND MEDICAL CARE

Medicare, 1997

	Recipients	Payments
State	639,000	$2,733 mill.
Total U.S.	37,514,000	$206,064 mill.
State share	1.70%	1.33%
Rank among states	20	25

Recipient figures are rounded to nearest thousand persons. Ranks are from highest to lowest.

Source: U.S. Health Care Financing Administration.

Medicaid, 1996

	Recipients	Payments
State	455,000	$2,430 mill.
Total U.S.	35,028,000	$121,419 mill.
State share	1.30%	2.00%
Rank among states	24	16

Recipient figures are rounded to nearest thousand persons. Payment figures for fiscal year reflect federal and state contribution payments. Ranks are from highest to lowest.

Source: U.S. Health Care Financing Administration.

Health insurance coverage, 1996

	State	U.S.
Total persons covered	4,229,000	225,070,000
Total persons not covered	480,000	41,716,000
Part not covered	10.2%	15.6%
Rank among states	42	—
Children not covered	114,000	10,554,000
Part not covered	8.4%	14.8%
Rank among states	42	—

Ranks are from most to fewest uninsured. Population figures are rounded to nearest thousand persons.
Source: U.S. Bureau of the Census.

AIDS, syphilis, tuberculosis, and measles cases, 1997

Cases	U.S.	State	Share
AIDS	58,443	214	0.37%
Syphilis	8,550	16	0.19%
Tuberculosis	18,534	318	1.72%
Measles	148,000	2,000	1.35%

Measles figures are rounded to nearest thousand cases.
Source: U.S. Centers for Disease Control and Prevention.

HOUSING

Homeownership rates, 1985-1997

	1985	1990	1997
State	70.0%	68.0%	75.4%
Total U.S.	63.9%	63.9%	65.7%
Rank among states	13	22	1

Source: U.S. Bureau of the Census.

Home sales, 1990 and 1997
In thousands of units

Existing home sales	1990	1997	Change
State sales	64.8	88.0	23.2
Total U.S. sales	3,560	4,730	1,170
State share of U.S. total	1.82%	1.86%	0.04%
Rank among states	21	19	—

Source: National Association of Realtors; *Real Estate Outlook: Market Trends and Insights.*

EDUCATION

Public school enrollment, 1995

State K-8 enrollment	586,000
Total U.S. K-8 enrollment	32,341,000
State share of total U.S.	1.81%
State 9-12 enrollment	249,000
Total U.S. 9-12 enrollment	12,500,000
State share of U.S. total	1.99%
State public school enroll. rate	90.8%
Overall U.S. rate.	91.6%
Rank among states.	32

Enrollment figures (which include unclassified students) are rounded to nearest thousand pupils in fall term; kindergarten (K)-8 grade figures include some prekindergarten students. Enrollment rate is based on percentage of persons 5-17 years old. Rank is from highest to lowest.
Source: U.S. National Center for Education Statistics.

Public college finances, 1996

State FTE enrollment	161,000
Total U.S. FTE enrollment	8,268,800
State share of total U.S.	1.95%
Rank among states.	18
State and local appropriations	$862,400,000
Total U.S. state and local appropriations.	$39,699 mill.
State share of total U.S.	2.17%
Rank among states.	14
State net tuition revenues.	$361,300,000
Total U.S. net tuition	$18,348,100,000
State share of total U.S.	1.97%
Rank among states.	18

FTE=Full-time equivalent; credit and noncredit enrollment including summer session in academic year ending in 1996.
Enrollments are rounded to nearest thousand students. Net tuition revenues exclude appropriation to students attending in-state public institutions. Rankings are from highest shares to lowest.
Source: Research Associates of Washington.

TRANSPORTATION AND TRAVEL

Highway mileage, 1996

Interstate	913
Other arterial	12,737
Collector roads	31,029
Local roads	87,462
Urban roads.	15,381
Rural roads	115,232
Total state	130,613
U.S. total	3,933,985
State share	3.3%
Rank among states	5

Source: U.S. Federal Highway Administration.

Motor vehicle registrations and driver licenses, 1996
In thousands

Vehicle registrations	State	U.S.	Share	Rank
Autos, trucks, buses	3,861	206,365	1.87%	19
Autos only	2,263	128,439	1.76%	20
Motorcycles	116	3,832	3.03%	11
Driver licenses	2,830	179,539	1.58%	19

Figures do not include vehicles owned by military services.
Source: U.S. Federal Highway Administration; *Highway Statistics; Selected Highway Statistics and Charts.*

Domestic travel expenditures, 1995
Spending by U.S. residents on overnight trips and day trips of at least 100 miles

Total expenditures in state	$4,931 mill.
Total expenditures in U.S.	$360,314 mill.
State share of total U.S.	1.37%
Rank among states.	24

Source: Travel Industry Association of America.

CRIME AND LAW ENFORCEMENT

State and local police officers, 1996

Local police	5,006
State police	484
Sheriffs	2,139
Total	7,994
Officers per 10,000 residents	17
U.S. average	25
Rank among states.	46

Figures cover full-time sworn officers; totals include special police not shown separately.
Source: U.S. Bureau of Justice Statistics; *Census of State and Local Law Enforcement Agencies, 1996.*

Crime rates, 1996
Rates per 100,000 resident population

Violent crimes	State	U.S.
Total violent	339	634
Murder	3.6	7.4
Forcible rape	50.0	36.1
Robbery	116	202
Aggravated assault	170	388
Property crimes		
Total property	4,124	4,445
Burglary	763	943
Larceny/theft	2,977	2,976
Motor vehicle theft	385	526
Totals	4,463	5,079

Source: U.S. Federal Bureau of Investigation; *Crime in the United States,* annual.

State prison populations, 1980-1996

	State	U.S.	State share
1980	2,001	305,458	0.66%
1990	3,176	708,393	0.45%
1996	5,158	1,025,624	0.50%

Figures exclude prisoners in federal penitentiaries.
Source: U.S. Bureau of Justice Statistics.

Mississippi

Location: Southeastern continental United States

Area and rank: 46,914 square miles (121,506 square kilometers); 48,434 square miles (125,444 square kilometers) including water; thirty-first largest state in area

Coastline: 44 miles (71 kilometers)

Shoreline: 359 miles (578 kilometers)

Population and rank: 2,730,501 (1997); thirty-first largest state in population

Capital: Jackson

Largest city: Jackson (188,419 people in 1998)

Became territory: April 7, 1798

Entered Union and rank: December 10, 1817; twentieth state

Present constitution adopted: 1890

Counties: 82

State capitol building in Jackson. (Mississippi Division of Tourism Development)

State name: Mississippi takes its name from an Indian expression for "father of waters"

State nickname: Magnolia State

Motto: *Virtute et armis* (By valor and arms)

State flag: Top left contains red field with Confederate flag; remainder contains red, white, and blue stripes

Highest point: Woodall Mountain — 806 feet (246 meters)

Lowest point: Gulf of Mexico — sea level

Highest recorded temperature: 115 degrees Fahrenheit (46 degrees Celsius) — Holly Springs, 1930

Lowest recorded temperature: −19 degrees Fahrenheit (−28 degrees Celsius) — Corinth, 1966

State song: "Go, Mississippi"

State tree: Magnolia

State flower: Flower of the magnolia or evergreen magnolia

State bird: Mockingbird

State fish: Largemouth or black bass

Mississippi History

Mississippi's climate has greatly influenced its history. Located in the Deep South of the United States, just above the Gulf of Mexico, Mississippi has long, humid summers and generally short, mild winters. Consequently the growing season throughout the state is more than two hundred days long. In the far South, the growing season can be as long as 280 days. This long growing period, combined with abundant rain, has made agriculture a prominent economic activity. Outside of the hilly region in the north, the soils are finely textured, composed of clays, sands, and other components.

In the nineteenth century, when cotton became a major export crop for the United States, climate and soil tended to make the state heavily dependent on production of cotton. The prominence of cotton, a plantation crop requiring heavy investment of labor, contributed to the development of slavery as a major feature of life before the Civil War. Slavery gave Mississippi a large African American population, and the legacy of slavery produced racial inequality and troubled race relations. Continuing reliance on agriculture also tended to make Mississippi one of the least industrialized and poorest states in the United States throughout the twentieth century.

Early History. During prehistoric times, the area of Mississippi was populated by people who lived in highly organized farming societies. These societies are known as the Mound Builders, after the great ceremonial earth mounds they constructed. The Mound Builders may be divided into the people of the Hopewell culture, who flourished from about the first century until about 800 C.E., and the people of the Mississippian culture, who lived from about 800 C.E. until about 1500. When the earliest French settlers arrived in what is now the southwestern part of Mississippi, the Natchez Indians were still building mounds, which were used for burials and as sites for public buildings.

By the time of European settlement in this area of North America, there were three major Native American nations in the Mississippi region, as well as a host of small Native American groups. The na-

tion of the Choctaw was the largest of the three. The Choctaw controlled most of central and southern Mississippi. In southwestern Mississippi, the Natchez nation was dominant. In the northern part of what is now the state of Mississippi, the Chickasaw were the largest and most powerful group.

The Choctaw were an agricultural people who lived in thatched-roof cabins made of mud and bark. The Chickasaw were closely related to the Choctaw, and both groups spoke languages of the Muskogean family, but they were traditional enemies before European settlement. The Natchez were the largest and most unified group in the area. However, war broke out between the Natchez and French settlers in the early 1700's. The French joined with the Choctaw to destroy the Natchez in 1729. Some Natchez were sold into slavery, and others were absorbed into other tribes. The Choctaw and Chickasaw continued to live in the Mississippi region, adopting many of the ways of European society. By 1842 though, the U.S. government, under pressure from land-hungry white settlers, forced most of the Native Americans of the Southeast to relocate in Indian Territory in Oklahoma.

European Exploration and Colonization. The Spanish and the French were the first Europeans to explore the territory of the lower Mississippi River. From 1539 to 1543, the Spaniard Hernando de Soto led an expedition that is believed to have crossed the northern part of the modern state of Mississippi. At the end of the 1600's, the French explorer René-Robert Cavalier, sieur de La Salle, journeyed down the Mississippi River to its mouth and claimed all of the land drained by the Mississippi in the name of France. La Salle named this huge expanse of territory Louisiana, in honor of King Louis XIV of France.

After the French and Indian War between France and Great Britain, from 1754 to 1763, France ceded all of the French land east of the Mississippi River to Great Britain. Although the British attempted to reserve the land of northern Mississippi for Native Americans and forbade white set-

tlement in that region, white Americans were drawn to the region for its rich soil. In 1783 the Spanish, who had acquired the Louisiana territories from France, took southern Mississippi from the British. In 1798 Spain recognized the northern part of modern Mississippi as territory of the new United States. That same year, the U.S. Congress organized this region as the Mississippi Territory.

American colonists in West Florida, the areas of modern Louisiana and southern Mississippi still under Spanish rule, revolted against Spain in 1810. West Florida became independent briefly, then it was annexed to the United States. In 1817 Mississippi was admitted to the United States as the twentieth state.

Cotton and the Civil War. In 1800 there were only 7,600 settlers in Mississippi. By 1820 this number had grown to 75,448. Ten years later, the U.S. Census put the state's population at 136,621. The 1860 census showed a population of 791,305. Much of this rapid growth was due to the immigration of farmers who were looking for land to grow cotton. Cotton was Mississippi's most important crop, and, by the eve of the Civil War, Mississippi pro-

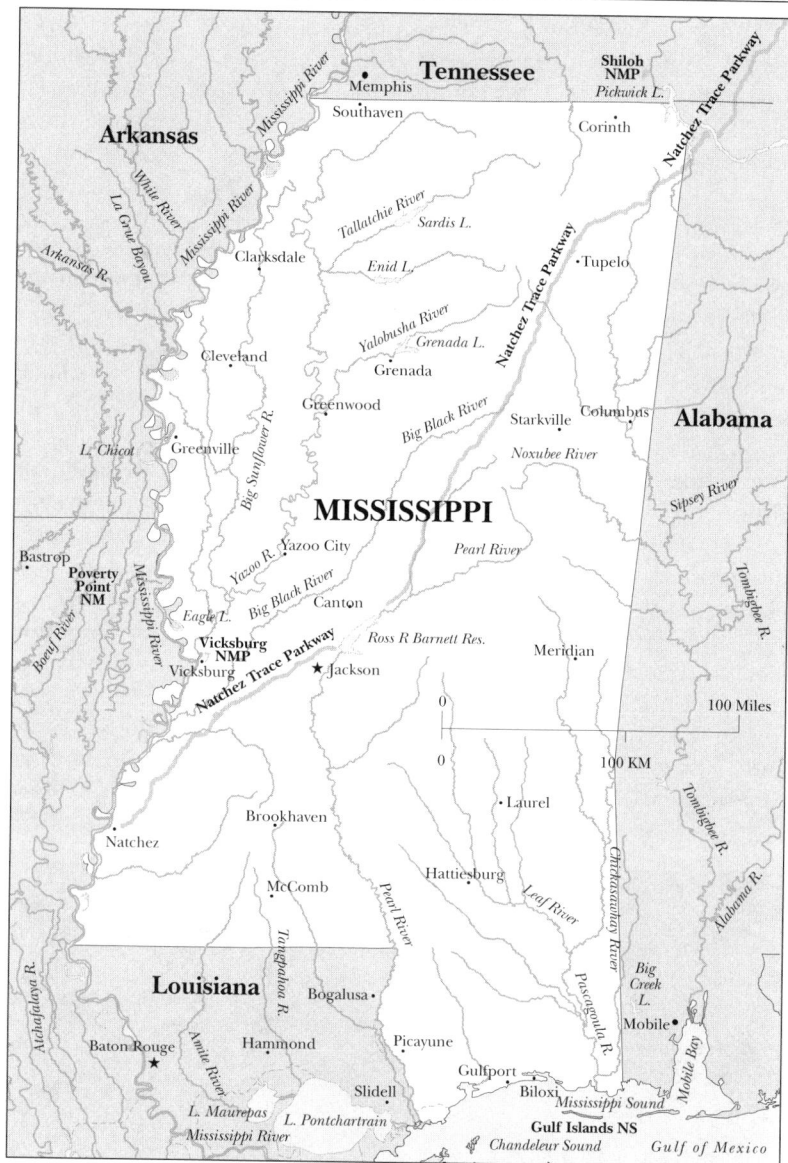

duced more cotton than any other state. Although only a small minority of the whites in the state were large plantation owners, owners of the big plantations held most of the economic and political power. Reliance on slave labor meant that the state had a huge slave population, with slaves of African descent outnumbering whites. Because there were so many people held in bondage, Mississippi's slave laws were among the harshest in the South.

By the 1850's the southern states, which were dependent on agriculture and slavery, were losing control over the U.S. Congress and presidency to the industrialized North. Many southerners believed that the southern way of life, including the institution of slavery, could only be preserved by seceding from the United States. In 1861, after the election of U.S. president Abraham Lincoln, southern states began declaring their independence. Mississippi was the second state to secede, and Mississippi planter and former U.S. senator Jefferson Davis became president of the Confederate States of America.

About eighty thousand Mississippians fought for the Confederacy, and almost one-third of them died in the Civil War. Many counties in Mississippi also saw an internal civil war, as small farmers who opposed secession organized themselves to fight against the Confederacy. Fighting ravaged the state, and the forces of U.S. general William T. Sherman were especially destructive in their efforts to defeat the rebellious southerners.

The Legacy of War and Slavery. Mississippi's history of slavery and civil war led to continuing problems of racial inequality. During Reconstruction, the period following the Civil War when northern troops occupied the defeated lands of the Confederacy, the state's freed slaves entered political life, although few had sufficient education or experience to hold more than minor offices. By 1875, though, the whites of Mississippi began to retake power. They instituted segregation and, by the early twentieth century, excluded African Americans from public life by laws and terrorism. In some of the counties of the Mississippi Delta, the region where the Mississippi and Yazoo Rivers join together, 80 to 90 percent of the people were African American. Most of them worked as sharecroppers, farmers working the land for a share of the crop, on land owned by whites.

As a consequence of this legacy of slavery, Mississippi became a central battleground of the Civil Rights movement. In 1964 black and white college students working with civil rights organizations traveled to the state for Freedom Summer, to provide educational opportunities to local African Americans and to encourage minority voter registration. After the passage of the Civil Rights Act of 1964 and the Voting Rights Act of 1965, segregation became illegal in the United States, and black Mississippians began to enter public life. By the 1990's, the Mississippi legislature had the highest percentage of blacks of any state legislature in the nation. Nevertheless, racial prejudice and poverty in Mississippi's black population continued to be problems.

Economy and Population After the War. Mississippi continued to have an economy based on agriculture well into the twentieth century. However, declining prices for cotton and other agricultural goods contributed to making it the poorest state in the nation by many measures. In 1936 Governor Hugh L. White began an effort to bring industry

Modern Mississippi riverboat recalls the great age of nineteenth century steamboating on the Mississippi River. (PhotoDisc)

James Meredith's admission to the University of Mississippi in 1962 marked a turning point in the Civil Rights movement. (Library of Congress)

into the state with his Balance Agriculture with Industry (BAWI) program. World War II helped industrialization, especially in the shipbuilding industry along the Gulf Coast. The period following World War II saw rapid industrialization. By 1990 less than 3 percent of Mississippi's labor force were employed in agriculture, while almost 23 percent were employed in factories. The state's largest areas of employment in the late twentieth century were lumber and wood products, furniture, food products, and the manufacture of clothing.

With the disappearance of agricultural jobs, many black Mississippians left the state. The state's African American population declined from 60 percent of all Mississippians in 1900 to 36 percent in 1990. Most small towns and villages grew smaller or even disappeared after World War II. Most of the state's population growth in this period took place in the urban areas of Jackson, Biloxi-Gulfport, and Pascagoula-Moss Point. By 1990 nearly half of all the people in the state lived in cities.

Carl L. Bankston III

Mississippi Time Line

1500's	Mound Builder cultures flourish along the Mississippi River and in other areas of eastern North America.
1540	Spanish explorer Hernando de Soto's expedition enters the northern part of modern Mississippi.

(continued)

1682	René-Robert Cavalier, sieur de La Salle, travels down the Mississippi to its mouth and claims all lands along the river in the name of France.
1699	French found Biloxi, the first permanent European settlement in Mississippi.
1729	French and the Choctaw together destroy the Natchez nation.
1763	Great Britain takes control of the Mississippi region after the French and Indian Wars.
Apr. 7, 1798	Spain recognizes northern Mississippi as part of the United States; U.S. Congress organizes the Mississippi Territory.
1816	Chickasaw sign a treaty ceding their lands to the United States.
Dec. 10, 1817	Mississippi is admitted to the United States as the twentieth state.
1822	Capital of Mississippi is moved from Columbia to Jackson.
1830	Choctaw sign a treaty ceding their lands in Mississippi to the United States.
1844	University of Mississippi is chartered by the state legislature.
Jan. 9, 1861	Mississippi is the second state to secede from the Union, joining the Confederacy.
Apr. 12, 1861	Civil War begins when Confederate forces attack Fort Sumter, South Carolina.
Feb. 22, 1862	Former U.S. senator Jefferson Davis of Mississippi is made Confederate president.
July 4, 1863	Vicksburg, Mississippi, falls to Union forces.
Feb. 23, 1870	Mississippi is readmitted to the Union.
1875	Democratic Party takes control of the Mississippi legislature from the Republicans, essentially ending Reconstruction in Mississippi.
1890	Mississippi legislature adopts a constitution that formally establishes racial segregation in the state and effectively takes the vote away from most black citizens.
1908	Mississippi state legislature prohibits the sale and consumption of alcohol.
1926	Public schools are forbidden to teach evolution.
Apr. 21, 1927	Mississippi River floods and devastates many areas of Mississippi.
1936	Governor Hugh L. White begins attempting to industrialize Mississippi with the Balance Agriculture with Industry (BAWI) program.
Apr. 5, 1955	Governor Hugh White signs a bill providing fines and a jail sentence for white students who attend schools with blacks.
Sept. 28, 1962	U.S. Court of Appeals orders Mississippi governor Ross R. Barnett to stop interfering with desegregation at the University of Mississippi.
Oct. 1, 1962	James Meredith is admitted to the University of Mississippi after riots that result in two deaths.
June 12, 1963	Medgar N. Evers, a Mississippi official of the National Association for the Advancement of Colored People, is shot to death.
June, 1964	Three young civil rights workers are murdered in Mississippi.
1969	Charles Evers, brother of Medgar Evers, becomes mayor of Fayette, making him the first black mayor in Mississippi.
1973	U.S. Supreme Court rules unconstitutional a Mississippi law enabling the state to purchase textbooks and distribute them free to segregated private schools.
1978	Mississippi elects its first Republican senator since Reconstruction.

County	Sq. miles	1996 pop.
Newton	578.1	21,455
Noxubee	694.9	12,414
Oktibbeha	457.8	39,303
Panola	684.3	32,615
Pearl River	811.5	44,359
Perry	647.2	11,874
Pike	408.9	38,093
Pontotoc	497.4	24,518
Prentiss	415.0	24,011
Quitman	404.9	9,888
Rankin	774.6	102,414
Scott	609.1	25,194
Sharkey	427.7	6,814
Simpson	588.8	25,221
Smith	635.9	15,069
Stone	445.4	12,670
Sunflower	693.8	36,266
Tallahatchie	644.0	15,033
Tate	404.5	22,842
Tippah	457.9	20,751
Tishomingo	424.2	18,430
Tunica	454.8	8,043
Union	415.5	23,117
Walthall	403.8	14,414
Warren	586.7	49,047
Washington	724.0	66,115
Wayne	810.4	20,003
Webster	422.8	10,437
Wilkinson	676.8	9,294
Winston	607.0	19,442
Yalobusha	467.2	12,212
Yazoo	919.6	25,295

Source: U.S. Census Bureau; National Association of Counties.

Cities

With 10,000 or more residents

Rank	City	Population		Rank	City	Population
1	Jackson	188,419		4	Biloxi	47,316
2	Gulfport	64,762		5	Greenville	42,042
3	Hattiesburg	48,806		6	Meridian	40,255

(continued)

Rank	City	Population
7	Tupelo	35,589
8	Vicksburg	27,221
9	Pascagoula	27,163
10	Southaven	23,434
11	Pearl	23,287
12	Columbus	22,297
13	Clinton	22,067
14	Clarksdale	20,461
15	Starkville	20,184
16	Laurel	18,299
17	Natchez	18,277
18	Greenwood	18,218
19	Moss Point	18,095
20	Long Beach	16,776
21	Ridgeland	16,545
22	Ocean Springs	16,519
23	Cleveland	14,834
24	Brandon	14,612
25	Horn Lake	13,885
26	Madison	12,618
27	Canton	12,221
28	Corinth	12,204
29	Oxford	12,096
30	Olive Branch	12,063
31	Picayune	12,058
32	Yazoo City	11,941
33	McComb	11,746
34	Indianola	11,514
35	Grenada	11,161
36	Gautier	11,139
37	Brookhaven	10,649

Population figures are estimated for mid-1998.

Source: U.S. Bureau of the Census.

Index to Tables

NA = Reliable data are not available.

DEMOGRAPHICS

Resident state and national populations, 1970-1997
Population figures given in thousands

	State pop.	U.S. pop.	Share	Rank
1970	2,217	203,302	1.1%	29
1980	2,521	226,546	1.1%	31
1985	2,588	237,924	1.1%	31
1990	2,575	248,765	1.0%	31
1995	2,691	262,761	1.0%	31
1997	2,731	267,636	1.0%	31

Source: U.S. Bureau of the Census.

Resident population by age, 1997

Age group	Total population
Under 5 years	202,000
5 to 17 years	551,000
18 to 24 years	298,000
25 to 34 years	385,000
35 to 44 years	412,000
45 to 54 years	322,000
55 to 64 years	228,000
65 to 74 years	183,000
75 to 84 years	110,000
85 years and over	39,000
Portion of residents 65 and older	12.2%
National average	12.7%

Population figures are rounded to nearest thousand persons; figures include armed forces personnel stationed in state.
Source: U.S. Bureau of the Census.

Resident population by race, Hispanic origin, 1997

	State pop.	Share	U.S.
All residents	2,731,000	100.0%	100.0%
Hispanic white	17,000	0.6%	10.0%
non-Hispanic white	1,691,000	61.9%	72.7%
African American	993,000	36.4%	12.7%
Native American	10,000	0.4%	0.9%
Asian, Pacific Islander	18,000	0.7%	3.8%

Source: U.S. Bureau of the Census.

Projections of state population, 2000-2025

	Model A	Model B
	Uses interstate migration observed from 1975-1994	Uses Bureau of Economic Analysis employment projections
Year	Population	Population
2000	2,816,000	2,826,000
2005	2,908,000	2,949,000
2010	2,974,000	3,072,000
2015	3,035,000	3,195,000
2020	3,093,000	3,310,000
2025	3,142,000	3,413,000

All population projections, including those for 2000, were calculated in 1997.
Source: U.S. Bureau of the Census, Population Paper Listings PPL-47.

VITAL STATISTICS

Average lifetime in years by race, 1989-1991

	State	U.S.	Rank
All residents	73.03	75.37	49
White residents	74.78	76.13	46
Black residents	69.41	69.16	17

Ranks are from longest-lived to least longest-lived. Ranks exclude Alaska, for which reliable data are not available. Rank for black residents is based on the 32 states for which reliable data are available.
Source: U.S. National Center for Health Statistics.

Infant mortality rates, 1980 and 1995

	State	U.S.
All residents		
1980	17.0	12.6
1995	10.5	7.6
White residents		
1980	11.1	11.0
1995	7.0	6.3
Black residents		
1980	23.7	21.4
1995	14.7	15.1

Figures represent deaths per 1,000 live births of resident infants under 1 year old, exclusive of fetal deaths; all-residents figures include other races not listed separately.
Source: U.S. National Center for Health Statistics.

Marriages and divorces

Marriages in 1996. 21,300
Rate per 1,000 population, 1995. . . . . 8.0
U.S. rate, 1995 . . . . 8.9
Rank among all states 33

Divorces in 1996 15,700
Rate per 1,000 population, 1995. . . . . 4.8
U.S. rate, 1995 . . . . 4.4
Rank among all states 20

Rank is from highest to lowest in country.
Source: U.S. National Center for Health Statistics.

Death rates by leading causes, 1995
Deaths per 100,000 resident population

Cause	State	U.S.
Heart disease	356.0	280.7
Cancer	213.1	204.9
Cerebrovascular diseases	69.3	60.1
Accidents and adverse effects	59.6	35.5
Motor vehicle accidents	33.5	16.5
Chronic obstructive pulmonary diseases	37.9	39.2
Diabetes mellitus	18.1	22.6
HIV	9.5	NA
Suicide	11.8	11.9
Homicide	15.9	8.7
All causes	1,002.0	880.0
Rank in overall death rate among states		7

Figures exclude nonresidents who die in state. Causes of death follow International Classification of Diseases. Rank is from highest to lowest in country.
Source: U.S. National Center for Health Statistics.

ECONOMY

Gross state product, 1990-1996
In current dollars

	State product	Increase
1990	$38.7 billion	
1993	$46.6 billion	
1994	$50.8 billion	9.01%
1995	$53.6 billion	5.51%
1996	$56.4 billion	5.22%

Source: U.S. Bureau of Economic Analysis; *Survey of Current Business,* June, 1998.

Gross state product by industry, 1996
In billions

Farms, forestry, fisheries	$1.5
Construction	1.9
Manufacturing	12.8
Transportation, public utilities	5.7
Wholesale trade	3.0
Retail trade	5.5
Finance, insurance, real estate	5.4
Services	7.8
Government	7.6
State total	$51.7
Total U.S.	$6,923.8
State share	0.75%
Rank among states	32

Total figures include mining, not listed separately.
Source: U.S. Bureau of Economic Analysis; *Survey of Current Business,* June, 1998.

Personal income per capita, 1990 and 1997
In current dollars

	1990	1997
Per capita income	$12,719	$18,272
U.S. average	$19,188	$25,598
Rank among states	50	50

1997 data are preliminary.
Source: U.S. Bureau of Economic Analysis; *Survey of Current Business,* May, 1998.

Energy consumption, 1995
In trillions of British thermal units (BTU)

End-use sectors

Residential	192.0
Commercial	109.7
Industrial	418.2
Transportation	338.9

Sources of energy

Petroleum	399.6
Natural gas	295.6
Coal	103.8
Hydroelectric power	0
Nuclear electric power	85.4
Total state per capita consumption	392.7
Total U.S. per capita consumption	344.4
Rank among states	16
Total state energy consumption	1,058.8
Total U.S. energy consumption	90,547.4
State share of U.S. total	1.17%
Rank among states	29

Total figures include items not listed separately.
Source: U.S. Energy Information Administration; *State Energy Data Report.*

Nonfarm employment by sectors, 1997

Total	1,106,000
Construction	51,000
Manufacturing	241,000
Transportation, public utilities	53,000
Wholesale trade, retail trade	237,000
Finance, insurance, real estate	41,000
Services	258,000
Government	219,000

Figures are rounded to nearest thousand persons. Total includes mining, not listed separately.
Source: U.S. Bureau of Labor Statistics; *Employment and Earnings,* monthly.

Foreign exports, 1990-1997
In millions of dollars

Year	State	U.S.	State share
1990	1,605	394,045	0.41%
1996	2,623	624,767	0.42%
1997	2,290	688,896	0.33%

Source: U.S. Bureau of the Census; *U.S. Merchandise Trade,* series FT 900.

LAND USE

Federally owned land, 1996

	State	U.S.	State share
Total acres	30,223,000	2,271,343,000	1.33%
Federally owned	1,276,000	563,129,000	0.23%
Federal share	4.2%	24.8%	—

Areas are rounded to nearest thousand acres. Figures for federally owned land do not include trust properties.
Source: U.S. General Services Administration; *Inventory Report on Real Property Owned by the United States Throughout the World*, annual.

Land use, 1992
In acres, rounded to nearest thousand

Total surface area	30,521,000
Federal land	1,726,000
Total nonfederal	27,992,000
Developed	1,337,000
Total rural	26,655,000
Cropland.	5,726,000
Pasture land	4,047,000
Range land	0
Forest land	15,765,000
Minor cover/use.	1,117,000

Total surface area figures include water area not shown separately.
Source: U.S. Dept. of Agriculture; Soil Conservation Service; Iowa State University, Statistical Laboratory; *Summary Report, 1992 National Resources Inventory.*

Farms and crop acreage, 1997

	State	U.S.	Share	Rank
Farms (thousands)	43	2,058	2.09%	20
Acres (millions)	13	968	1.34%	25
Acres per farm	291	471	—	26
Acres planted	4,770	334,139	1.43%	22
Acres harvested	4,696	319,894	1.47%	19
Farm value (mill.)	$1,498	$108,805	1.38%	12

Numbers of farms are rounded to nearest thousand.
Source: U.S. Dept. of Agriculture; National Agricultural Statistics Service.

GOVERNMENT AND FINANCE

Units of local government, 1997

	State	Total U.S.	Rank
All local governments	936	87,453	31
Counties	82	3,043	16
Municipalities	295	19,372	27
Townships	0	16,629	—
School districts	164	13,726	29
Special districts	395	34,683	30

County ranks are based on the 48 states with county governments; township ranks are based on the 20 states with township governments; school district ranks are based on the 46 states with such districts.
Source: U.S. Bureau of the Census; *1997 Census of Governments, Government Organization*, Series GC97(1).

State government revenue, 1996

Total revenue	$8,865 mill.
General revenue	7,461 mill.
Per capita.	2,752
U.S. per capita average	2,910
Rank among states.	30

Intergovernmental revenue	
Total	$2,696 mill.
From federal government	2,608 mill.
From local government	88 mill.

Charges and Miscellaneous	
Total	$904 mill.
Current charges	675 mill.
Misc. general revenue	229 mill.

Taxes	
Total	$3,861 mill.
General sales	1,832 mill.
Selective sales.	770 mill.
License taxes	247 mill.
Individual income	742 mill.
Corporate income	202 mill.
Other.	67 mill.
Insurance trust revenue	1,269 mill.

Total revenue figures include items not listed separately.
Source: U.S. Bureau of the Census.

State government expenditures, 1996

General expenditures

Intergovernmental	$2,506 mill.
Direct expenditures	4,931 mill.
Total	7,437 mill.

Selected direct expenditures

Education	$2,724 mill.
Public welfare	1,658 mill.
Health, hospital	623 mill.
Highways	718 mill.
Police	52 mill.
Corrections	230 mill.
Natural resources	168 mill.
Parks and recreation	108 mill.
Government administration	133 mill.
Interest on debt	136 mill.

Other

State per capita expenditures	$2,744
U.S. per capita average	2,854
Rank among states	27
Total state expenditures	8,217 mill.
Total U.S. expenditures	859,959 mill.

Totals include items not listed separately.
Source: U.S. Bureau of the Census.

POLITICS

Governors since statehood

D = Democrat; R = Republican; O = other;
(r) resigned; (d) died in office; (i) removed from office

David Holmes (O)		1817-1820
George Poindexter (O)		1820-1822
Walter Leake (O)	(d)	1822-1825
Gerard C. Brandon (O)		1825-1826
David Holmes (O)	(r)	1826
Gerard C. Brandon (O)		1826-1832
Abram M. Scott (O)	(d)	1832-1833
Charles Lynch (O)		1833
Hiram G. Runnells (O)		1833-1835
John A. Quitman (O)		1835-1836
Charles Lynch (O)		1836-1838
Alexander G. McNutt (D)		1838-1842
Tilghman M. Tucker (D)		1842-1844
Albert G. Brown (D)		1844-1848
Joseph M. Matthews (D)		1848-1850
John A. Quitman (D)	(r)	1850-1851
John I. Guion (D)		1851
James Whitfield (D)		1851-1852
Henry S. Foote (D)	(r)	1852-1854
John J. Pettus (D)		1854
John J. McRae (D)		1854-1857
William McWillie (D)		1857-1859
John J. Pettus (D)		1859-1863
Charles Clark (D)	(i)	1863-1865
William L. Sharkey (D)	(i)	1865
Benjamin G. Humphreys (D)	(i)	1865-1868
Adelbert Ames (R)		1868-1870
James L. Alcorn (R)	(r)	1870-1871
Ridgely C. Powers (R)		1871-1874
Adelbert Ames (R)	(r)	1874-1876
John M. Stone (D)		1876-1882
Robert Lowry, Jr. (D)		1882-1890
John M. Stone (D)		1890-1896
Anselm J. McLaurin (D)		1896-1900
Andrew H. Longbird (D)		1900-1904
James K. Vardman (D)		1904-1908
Edmund F. Noel (D)		1908-1912
Earl L. Brewer (D)		1912-1916
Theodore G. Bilbo (D)		1916-1920
Lee M. Russell (D)		1920-1924
Henry L. Whitfield (D)	(d)	1924-1927
Dennis Murphree (D)		1927-1928
Theodore G. Bilbo (D)		1928-1932
Martin S. Conner (D)		1932-1936
Hugh L. White (D)		1936-1940
Paul B. Johnson (D)	(d)	1940-1943
Dennis Murphree (D)		1943-1944
Thomas L. Bailey (D)	(d)	1944-1946
Fielding L. Wright (D)		1946-1952
Hugh L. White (D)		1952-1956
James F. Coleman (D)		1956-1960
Ross R. Barnett (D)		1960-1964
Paul B. Johnson, Jr. (D)		1964-1968
John Bell Williams (D)		1968-1972
William L. Waller (D)		1972-1976
Cliff Finch (D)		1976-1980
William Winter (D)		1980-1984
Bill Allain (D)		1984-1988
Ray Mabus (D)		1988-1992
Kirk Fordice (R)		1992-2000
David R. Musgrove (D)		2000-

Composition of state legislature, 1990-1998

	Democrats	Republicans
State House (121 seats)		
1990	98	23
1992	91	29
1994	89	31
1996	86	33
1998	83	37
State Senate (52 seats)		
1990	43	9
1992	37	15
1994	36	14
1996	34	18
1998	34	18

Figures for total seats may include independents and minor party members.

Source: Council of State Governments; *State Elective Officials and the Legislatures.*

Composition of congressional delegations, 1989-1999

	Dem	Rep	Total
House of Representatives			
101st Congress, 1989			
State delegates	4	1	5
Total U.S.	259	174	433
102d Congress, 1991			
State delegates	5	0	5
Total U.S.	267	167	434
103d Congress, 1993			
State delegates	5	0	5
Total U.S.	258	176	434
104th Congress, 1995			
State delegates	2	3	5
Total U.S.	197	236	433
105th Congress, 1997			
State delegates	2	3	5
Total U.S.	206	228	434
106th Congress, 1999			
State delegates	3	2	5
Total U.S.	211	222	433

	Dem	Rep	Total
Senate			
101st Congress, 1989			
State delegates	0	2	2
Total U.S.	55	45	100
102d Congress, 1991			
State delegates	0	2	2
Total U.S.	56	44	100
103d Congress, 1993			
State delegates	0	2	2
Total U.S.	57	43	100
104th Congress, 1995			
State delegates	0	2	2
Total U.S.	46	53	99
105th Congress, 1997			
State delegates	0	2	2
Total U.S.	45	55	100
106th Congress, 1999			
State delegates	0	2	2
Total U.S.	45	54	99

Figures are for starts of first sessions. Figure for U.S. Representatives for 101st Congress does not include Alabama and Indiana, which had vacancies. Figures for total U.S. Representatives for 102d, 103d, and 106th Congresses do not include Vermont, which had 1 Independent-Socialist. Figure for U.S. Representatives for 104th Congress does not include Vermont, which had 1 Independent-Socialist, and California, which had 1 vacancy. Figure for U.S. Representatives for 105th Congress does not include New York, which had 1 vacancy. Figure for U.S. Senators for 104th Congress does not include Oregon, which had 1 vacancy. Figure for U.S. Senators for 106th Congress does not include New Hampshire, which had 1 Independent.

Source: U.S. Congress; *Congressional Directory*, biennial.

Voter participation in presidential elections, 1992 and 1996

	1992	1996
State voting age pop.	1,873,000	1,961,000
Total U.S. voting age pop.	189,524,000	196,509,000
State share of U.S. total	1.0%	1.0%
Rank among states	31	31
Percent of state casting vote	52.4	61.1
Percent of U.S. total voting	55.1	49.0
Rank among states	38	4

Source: U.S. Bureau of the Census.

HEALTH AND MEDICAL CARE

Medicare, 1997

	Recipients	Payments
State	406,000	$2,214 mill.
Total U.S.	37,514,000	$206,064 mill.
State share	1.08%	1.07%
Rank among states	32	29

Recipient figures are rounded to nearest thousand persons.
Ranks are from highest to lowest.
Source: U.S. Health Care Financing Administration.

Medicaid, 1996

	Recipients	Payments
State	510,000	$1,342 mill.
Total U.S.	35,028,000	$121,419 mill.
State share	1.46%	1.11%
Rank among states	22	26

Recipient figures are rounded to nearest thousand persons.
Payment figures for fiscal year reflect federal and state
contribution payments. Ranks are from highest to lowest.
Source: U.S. Health Care Financing Administration.

Health insurance coverage, 1996

	State	U.S.
Total persons covered	2,279,000	225,070,000
Total persons not covered	518,000	41,716,000
Part not covered	18.5%	15.6%
Rank among states	8	—
Children not covered	154,000	10,554,000
Part not covered	18.4%	14.8%
Rank among states	10	—

Ranks are from most to fewest uninsured. Population figures
are rounded to nearest thousand persons.
Source: U.S. Bureau of the Census.

AIDS, syphilis, tuberculosis, and measles cases, 1997

Cases	U.S.	State	Share
AIDS	58,443	347	0.59%
Syphilis	8,550	390	4.56%
Tuberculosis	18,534	236	1.27%
Measles	148,000	NA	NA

Measles figures are rounded to nearest thousand cases.
Source: U.S. Centers for Disease Control and Prevention.

HOUSING

Homeownership rates, 1985-1997

	1985	1990	1997
State	69.6%	69.4%	73.7%
Total U.S.	63.9%	63.9%	65.7%
Rank among states	16	11	7

Source: U.S. Bureau of the Census.

Home sales, 1990 and 1997
In thousands of units

Existing home sales	1990	1997	Change
State sales	34.7	47.7	13
Total U.S. sales	3,560	4,730	1,170
State share of U.S. total	0.97%	1.01%	0.03%
Rank among states	33	32	—

Source: National Association of Realtors; *Real Estate Outlook:
Market Trends and Insights.*

EDUCATION

Public school enrollment, 1995

State K-8 enrollment	366,000
Total U.S. K-8 enrollment	32,341,000
State share of total U.S.	1.13%
State 9-12 enrollment	140,000
Total U.S. 9-12 enrollment	12,500,000
State share of U.S. total	1.12%
State public school enroll. rate	91.8%
Overall U.S. rate	91.6%
Rank among states	27

Enrollment figures (which include unclassified students) are rounded to nearest thousand pupils in fall term; kindergarten (K)-8 grade figures include some prekindergarten students. Enrollment rate is based on percentage of persons 5-17 years old. Rank is from highest to lowest.

Source: U.S. National Center for Education Statistics.

Public college finances, 1996

State FTE enrollment	101,600
Total U.S. FTE enrollment	8,268,800
State share of total U.S.	1.23%
Rank among states	29
State and local appropriations	$458,700,000
Total U.S. state and local appropriations	$39,699 mill.
State share of total U.S.	1.16%
Rank among states	28
State net tuition revenues	$208,500,000
Total U.S. net tuition	$18,348,100,000
State share of total U.S.	1.14%
Rank among states	31

FTE=Full-time equivalent; credit and noncredit enrollment including summer session in academic year ending in 1996.

Enrollments are rounded to nearest thousand students. Net tuition revenues exclude appropriation to students attending in-state public institutions. Rankings are from highest shares to lowest.

Source: Research Associates of Washington.

TRANSPORTATION AND TRAVEL

Highway mileage, 1996

Interstate	685
Other arterial	7,093
Collector roads	16,517
Local roads	49,887
Urban roads	7,921
Rural roads	65,281
Total state	73,202
U.S. total	3,933,985
State share	1.9%
Rank among states	27

Source: U.S. Federal Highway Administration.

Motor vehicle registrations and driver licenses, 1996

In thousands

Vehicle registrations	State	U.S.	Share	Rank
Autos, trucks, buses	2,182	206,365	1.06%	31
Autos only	1,257	128,439	0.98%	31
Motorcycles	30	3,832	0.78%	35
Driver licenses	1,700	179,539	0.95%	31

Figures do not include vehicles owned by military services.

Source: U.S. Federal Highway Administration; *Highway Statistics; Selected Highway Statistics and Charts.*

Domestic travel expenditures, 1995

Spending by U.S. residents on overnight trips and day trips of at least 100 miles

Total expenditures in state	$3,185 mill.
Total expenditures in U.S.	$360,314 mill.
State share of total U.S.	0.88%
Rank among states	31

Source: Travel Industry Association of America.

CRIME AND LAW ENFORCEMENT

State and local police officers, 1996

Local police	3,326
State police	535
Sheriffs	1,474
Total	5,813
Officers per 10,000 residents	21
U.S. average	25
Rank among states	30

Figures cover full-time sworn officers; totals include special
police not shown separately.
Source: U.S. Bureau of Justice Statistics; *Census of State and
Local Law Enforcement Agencies, 1996.*

Crime rates, 1996
Rates per 100,000 resident population

Violent crimes	State	U.S.
Total violent	488	634
Murder	11.1	7.4
Forcible rape	36.1	36.1
Robbery	134	202
Aggravated assault	307	388
Property crimes		
Total property	4,035	4,445
Burglary	1,132	943
Larceny/theft	2,552	2,976
Motor vehicle theft	351	526
Totals	4,523	5,079

Source: U.S. Federal Bureau of Investigation; *Crime in the
United States*, annual.

State prison populations, 1980-1996

	State	U.S.	State share
1980	3,902	305,458	1.28%
1990	8,375	708,393	1.18%
1996	13,859	1,025,624	1.35%

Figures exclude prisoners in federal penitentiaries.
Source: U.S. Bureau of Justice Statistics.

Missouri

Location: Midwestern continental United States

Area and rank: 68,898 square miles (178,446 square kilometers); 69,709 square miles (180,546 square kilometers) including water; eighteenth largest state in area

Population and rank: 5,402,058 (1997); sixteenth largest state in population

Capital: Jefferson City

Largest city: Kansas City (441,574 people in 1998)

Became territory: June 4, 1812

Entered Union and rank: August 10, 1821; twenty-fourth state

Present constitution adopted: 1945

Counties: 114, as well as 1 independent city

State capitol building in Jefferson City. (Missouri Division of Tourism)

State name: Missouri takes its name from the Missouri Indians, whose name means "town of the large canoes"

State nickname: Show-Me State

Motto: *Salus populi suprema lex esto* (The welfare of the people shall be the supreme law)

State flag: Red, white, and blue stripes with state coat of arms surrounded by twenty-four stars

Highest point: Taum Sauk Mountain — 1,772 feet (540 meters)

Lowest point: St. Francis River — 230 feet (70 meters)

Highest recorded temperature: 118 degrees Fahrenheit (48 degrees Celsius) — Warsaw and Union, 1954

Lowest recorded temperature: −40 degrees Fahrenheit (−40 degrees Celsius) — Warsaw, 1905

State song: "Missouri Waltz"

State tree: Flowering dogwood

State flower: Hawthorn

State bird: Bluebird

State fish: Paddlefish; channel catfish

State animal: Mule

Missouri History

Missouri lies almost in the center of the forty-eight contiguous states. It is the southernmost midwestern state. Its eastern boundary is the Mississippi River, its western boundary the Missouri River. It is bordered by eight states: west of Missouri are Nebraska, Kansas, and Oklahoma. To its east are Illinois and Kentucky. Iowa borders it on the north, and Arkansas and Tennessee are on the south. Missouri is about 300 miles from east to west and about 280 miles from north to south.

The earliest settlers in the area probably lived there more than twelve thousand years ago. By the seventeenth century, the Missouri and Osage Indian tribes were there. The first Europeans in the region were Jacques Marquette, a French missionary, and Louis Jolliet, a fur trader, known to be there in 1673. In 1683 René-Robert Cavalier, sieur de La Salle, claimed a vast expanse of land, including present-day Missouri, for France, calling it Louisiana after King Louis XIV.

Early Settlements. The first permanent French settlement in Missouri was Sainte Genevieve, on the Mississippi River south of present-day St. Louis, established in 1735. In 1764, Pierre Laclède and René Auguste Chouteau founded St. Louis, also on the Mississippi River.

In 1762 Spain claimed France's Louisiana territory and futilely attempted to coerce Spaniards to move there. When the United States became independent in 1776, Spain invited Americans east of the Mississippi to move into Missouri. Substantial numbers of farmers and miners accepted. By 1799 groups of settlers inhabited the area.

In 1800 France reclaimed the Louisiana territory, which, through the Louisiana Purchase, it sold to the United States for fifteen million dollars in 1803. The Missouri Territory, which included Kansas, had a population of about twenty thousand by 1812. Most settled on land that had been the property of Native Americans, who sought to reclaim it. Various treaties were signed between the indigenous people and the new arrivals, but by 1825, almost no American Indians remained in Missouri.

The Missouri Compromise. Black slaves came to Missouri as early as 1720, owned by French miners searching for gold and other minerals. These slaves were involved in building Missouri's first cities. Soon southern farmers and plantation owners relocated in Missouri, bringing their slaves with them.

Missouri applied to join the United States in 1818, coming in as a slave state. This would have made for one extra slave state in the country, and the federal government could not sanction an imbalance between slave and free states. The solution was the Missouri Compromise of 1821, which assured that the number of slave states and free states would remain equal. Maine was to be admitted as a free state, thereby permitting Missouri statehood as a slave state. In 1821 Missouri became the twenty-fourth state.

Early Economy. Missouri's land became fertile when advancing glaciers deposited rich topsoil upon it thousands of years ago. The state also has excellent river transportation in the the east and the west. Steamboats carried their cargos to points along the rivers that eventually became thriving ports. Trails running west from Missouri led into the Rocky Mountains, where independent fur traders lived.

Soon there were permanent settlements and thriving towns along the river banks and trade routes. In 1822 the Santa Fe Trail was opened between Independence, in western Missouri, and Santa Fe, New Mexico, then a possession of Mexico. The beginning of the two-thousand-mile-long Oregon Trail was in Independence. When the Gold Rush to California began in 1848, thousands of prospectors passed through Missouri.

The potato famine in Ireland in the mid-1840's resulted in an influx of Irish into Missouri, where they worked on railroad construction or as day laborers. Missouri was growing so fast that extra hands were welcome. By the late 1840's, a wave of Germans seeking a better life came to the area around St. Louis.

Slavery. Slavery was a contentious matter in Missouri. By 1860, nearly 115,000 slaves were held in servitude in Missouri, many of them working

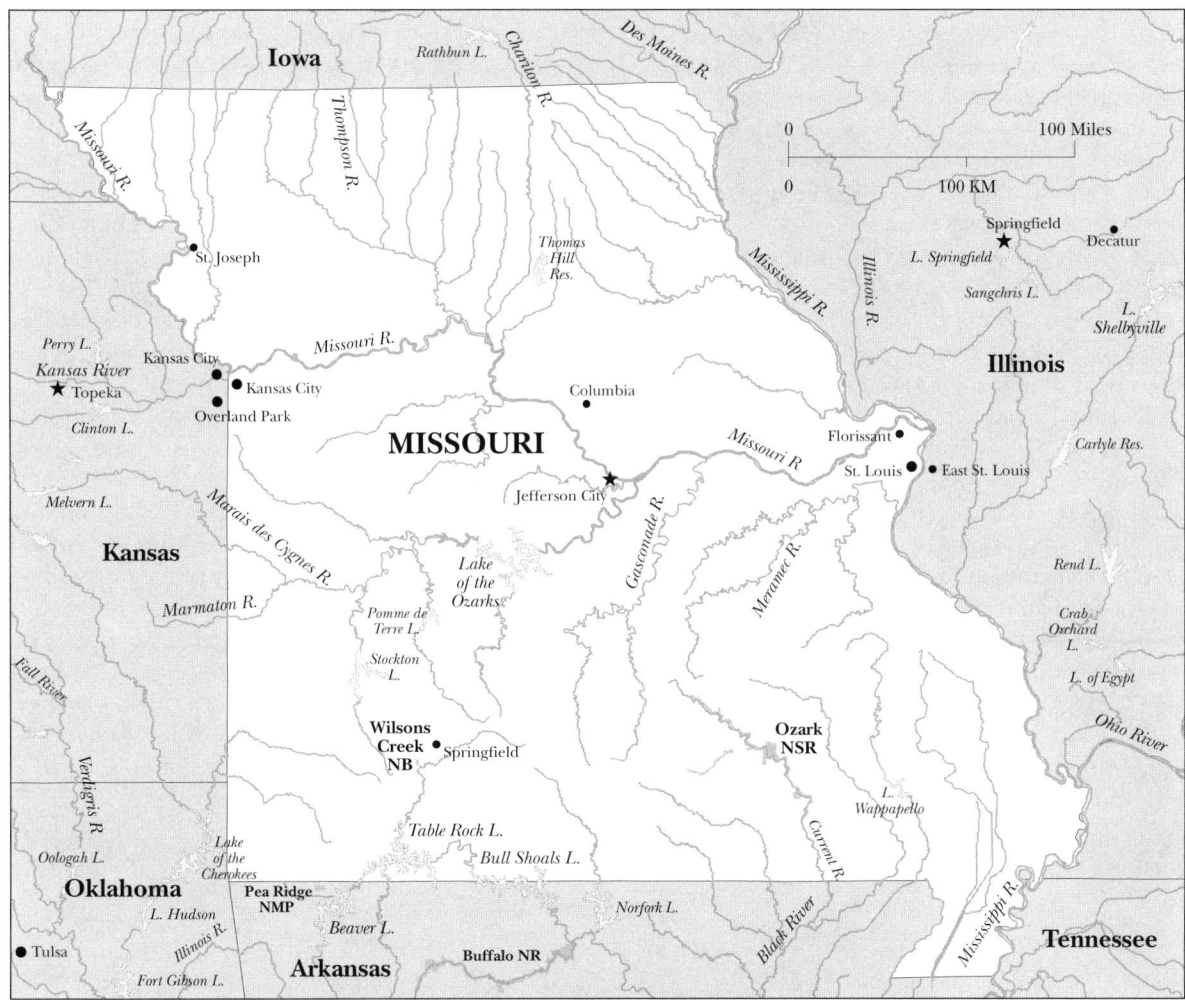

on farms in the western part of the state. Some 3,600 free African Americans also lived in the state prior to the Civil War, most of them settling around St. Louis.

Dred Scott and his wife, Harriet, were slaves in Missouri. In 1846 the Scotts sued for their freedom, claming that they were humans, not chattel. Their case reached the U.S. Supreme Court in 1857. The Court ultimately ruled that the Scotts were property owned by the master who had bought them. As such, they had no rights as citizens. This decision enraged northern abolitionists and was one of the crucial factors that led to the Civil War, which started in 1861.

Missouri and the Confederacy. In 1861 the southern slave states formed the Confederacy, a separate nation with its own government. As a border state, Missouri, despite pressure from many of its slave owners, voted to remain in the Union, although nearly thirty-five thousand Missourians joined the Confederate armed forces.

Months before the war ended, Missouri freed all of its slaves, many of whom remained in the state. At the end of the twentieth century, Missouri had an African American population of nearly 11 percent. During the Civil War, more than a thousand battles were fought in Missouri, which sent more than 150,000 of its men to fight. About 115,000 thousand of these fought in the Union forces.

Urban Growth. Missouri's strategic location and access to waterways and major trails resulted in the establishment of towns and cities along trade routes and encouraged urban development. The two cities that emerged as preeminent were St. Louis in the east and Kansas City on the western border with Kansas. Both cities became railroad centers, and Kansas City was known for its stockyards, first established in 1870, which still contribute substantially to its economy.

St. Louis became a major manufacturing center. In 1904 the city held a World's Fair that attracted people from around the world. In the same year, St. Louis also became the first U.S. city chosen as the site of the Olympic Games.

By 1990, 75 percent of Missouri's residents lived in urban areas. Chief among these, besides Kansas City and St. Louis, were Springfield, Joplin, St. Joseph, and Colombia, the site of the University of Missouri's main campus, established in 1841.

Other Factors in the Economy. Agriculture is a major contributor to Missouri's economy. Soybeans are the state's most lucrative crop, but Missouri farms produce sorghum, wheat, and hay as well. Cattle, hogs, and turkeys are also raised.

Its agricultural production nothwithstanding, manufacturing became the largest and most important factor in Missouri's economy. Among the major industries located in the state are General Motors and Ford, whose plants produce automobiles and trucks, McDonnell-Douglas, which makes commercial and private airplanes, and the Hallmark Card Company.

Tourism and commerce are also major factors in the economy. Tourists bring more than five billion dollars per year into the state, coming there to sightsee, gamble in the riverboat casinos, and attend the many shows in Branson, where nearly thirty well-known singers own theaters.

Missouri's Attractions. Besides the riverboat casinos and Branson's theaters, tourists are drawn to the state to view such attractions as the Gateway Arch in St. Louis, designed by Eero Saarinen and opened in 1965, which commemorates St. Louis as the jumping-off point for many pioneers heading into the western frontier.

Tourists also flock into New Madrid, a town on the Mississippi River that in 1811 and 1812 was rocked by three of the worst earthquakes ever recorded in North America. The New Madrid Museum provides detailed information about these

Modern depiction of a wagon train leaving Missouri to go west on the Oregon Trail in 1830. (Library of Congress)

earthquakes, which were so destructive they were felt as far away as Washington, D.C., and changed the course of the Mississippi River.

The Ozark Mountains and Lake of the Ozarks in southern Missouri offer excellent recreational facilities. This area attracts both tourists and retirees in large numbers. Tourists also flock into Florida and Hannibal in the north to visit the birthplace of Mark Twain and the town in which he grew up and used as the setting for some of his most popular stories.

R. Baird Shuman

Missouri Time Line

1673	Jacques Marquette, a missionary, and Louis Jolliet, a fur trader, sail the Mississippi, exploring Missouri and Tennessee.
1682	René-Robert Cavalier, sieur de La Salle, claims the Mississippi River Valley for France, naming it Louisiana.
1720	Philip Renault, searching for silver, brings black slaves to Missouri.
1724	Fort Orleans is built to protect French settlers from Spanish.
1750	Founding of Sainte Genevieve, the first permanent French settlement.
1763	Treaty of Paris cedes all of Canada and land west of the Mississippi River to Britain.
1764	René Auguste Chouteau and Pierre Laclède found St. Louis.
1799	Spanish encourage Americans to settle in Missouri.
1800	Spain returns western Louisiana territory to France.
1803	France sells area to the United States in Louisiana Purchase.
1804	Meriwether Lewis and William Clark leave St. Louis on their cross-country exploration.
1811	First of three earthquakes rocks New Madrid area.
1815	Indians in Missouri sign peace treaty with the United States.
1818	Missouri applies for statehood as a slave state.
1819	Steamship *Independence* sails the Missouri River, proving its navigability.
1820	Henry Clay brings the Missouri Compromise before Congress, which approves it.
Aug. 10, 1821	Missouri admitted to Union as twenty-fourth state.
1834	*St. Louis Herald*, first daily paper in the state, published in St. Louis.
1836	Missouri gains six northern counties from American Indians in Platte Purchase.
1839	University of Missouri chartered.
1841	University of Missouri opens in Columbia.
1847	St. Louis linked to eastern United States by telegraph.
1849	Major fire devastates much of the center of St. Louis.
1853	State opens first public high school in St. Louis.

(continued)

1857	U.S. Supreme Court renders Dred Scott decision, denying him freedom.
Apr. 3, 1860	First railroad across Missouri links St. Joseph and Hannibal.
1859	First railroad across Missouri links St. Joseph and Hannibal.

1857   U.S. Supreme Court renders Dred Scott decision, denying him freedom.

1859   First railroad across Missouri links St. Joseph and Hannibal.

Apr. 3, 1860   First Pony Express service begins in St. Joseph.

Mar. 6, 1861   Missouri votes against seceding from Union.

1865   Civil War ends, new Missouri constitution bans slavery.

1866   Lincoln Institute is founded for recently freed slaves.

1867   First women admitted to University of Missouri.

1869   First bridge across Missouri River opens at Kansas City.

1875   New constitution restores voting rights to Confederate sympathizers.

1880   First newspaper in Missouri for African Americans, the *Advocate*, is established.

1904   St. Louis hosts Olympic Games and World's Fair.

1908   University of Missouri launches first journalism school in the United States.

1921   Missouri's first radio station, WEW, begins broadcasting at St. Louis University.

1931   Bagnell Dam on Osage River opens and forms Lake of the Ozarks.

1945   Harry S Truman of Independence becomes thirty-third president of the United States.

1952   Drought ravages Missouri.

1955   Tornados kill 115 people in Missouri and Kansas.

1957   Harry S Truman Library opens in Independence.

1959   Tornadoes kill 22 and injure 5,350 in St. Louis.

1965   Gateway Arch opens in St. Louis.

1973   Floods devastate Missouri, causing $100 million in damage.

1982   Dioxin contamination closes Times Beach, threatens fifty other localities.

1986   State, suffering economic recession, institutes lottery.

1988   Court orders desegregation of Kansas City public schools.

1990   Governor signs educational bill allowing parental choice in public schools their children will attend.

1991   Kansas City elects its first black mayor, Emanuel Cleaver.

1993   St. Louis elects its first black mayor, Freeman Bosley, Jr.

1993   Floods cause five billion dollars damage in eastern Missouri.

Notes for Further Study

Published Sources. P. C. Nagel's *Missouri: A History* (1988) is useful and readable. It should be read in conjunction with M. D. Rafferty's *Missouri: A Geography* (1982), which gives graphic descriptions of the state's topography. Michael J. O'Brien delves into Missouri's distant past in *Paradigms of the Past: The Story of Missouri Archeology* (1996). W. E. Foley views the development of Missouri from a wilderness to a state in *The Genesis of Missouri: From Wilderness to Statehood* (1989), while Walter D. Kamphoefner considers the nineteenth century German immigration into the state in *The Westphalians: From Germany to Missouri* (1987). More specialized is John E.

Farley's *Earthquake Fears, Predictions, and Preparations in Mid-America* (1998), which offers a detailed account of the New Madrid earthquakes and explains the underlying geological structure that makes Missouri earthquake prone. Also somewhat specialized but of exceeding importance is Paul Finkelman's *Dred Scott v. Sandford: A Brief History with Documents* (1997). It offers an explanation of the case that helped to start the Civil War.

David Thelen's *Paths of Resistance: Tradition and Dignity in Industrializing Missouri* (1996) offers information about the industrialization of the state and the obstacles that the shift from agriculture to industry involved. *Dino, Godzilla, and the Pigs: My Life on Our Missouri Hog Farm* (1993) by Mary Elizabeth Fricke is a beguiling memoir that chronicles the author's growing up on a Missouri farm. It is interesting when read along with R. Douglas Hurt's *Agriculture and Slavery in Missouri's Little Dixie* (1992), focusing on the matter of what slavery meant to Missouri's agricultural economy. Joan Gilbert in *The Trail of Tears Across Missouri* (1996) deals with the dispossession of the Cherokee Indians from North Carolina and Tennessee, who were forced to go west to Missouri and Oklahoma. Cornelia Fleischer Mutel writes with feeling about the natural history of Missouri, Iowa, and Nebraska in *Fragile Giants: A Natural History of the Loess Hills* (1989).

Among the best accounts of the state aimed at juvenile readers are Patricia K. Kummer's *Missouri* (1998), Dennis B. and Judith Bloom Fradin's *Missouri* (1994), Rita C. La-Doux's *Missouri* (1991), and William R. Sanford's *America the Beautiful: Missouri* (1990), which will appeal to teenage readers.

Web Resources. The state of Missouri Web sites (http://www.state.mo.us) and (http://www.ecodev.state.mo.us) offer comprehensive information about Missouri and its economy. They also lead users to other pertinent Web sites. The state's tourist bureau provides a site (http://www.missouritourism.org) offering voluminous information about tourism in Missouri and will direct viewers to lodgings, restaurants, and tourist attractions, including the twenty-two caves in the state open to tourists. People interested in Branson and its offerings should consult some of its fourteen Web sites, among them (http://www.branson.com), (http://www

St. Louis's Gateway Arch, which opened in 1965, was built to symbolize the city's history as the gateway through which the West was settled. (PhotoDisc)

.branson-nights.com), (http://www.bransoninfo.com), and (http://www.bransonnow.com). Lake of the Ozarks Web sites include (http://www.lakeozarks.com) and (http:// www.lake-ozarks.com).

Web sites that detail cultural attractions are those of the St. Louis Art Museum (http://www.slam.org), the Kansas City Museum (http://www.kcmuseum.com), the St. Louis Concerts (http://www.stl-music.com), and the Kansas City Opera (http://www.kc-opera.org). The Harry S Truman site (http://www.nps.gov/hstr) provides information about Truman, his home, and the Truman Library. Information about higher education in the state is best obtained from the Web site of the university system (http://www.system.missouri.edu) or of its Rolla (http://www.unr.edu) or Kansas City (http://www.umkc.edu) campuses.

Counties

County	Sq. miles	1996 pop.
Adair	567.7	24,501
Andrew	435.2	15,270
Atchison	544.7	7,291
Audrain	693.4	23,385
Barry	779.1	32,325
Barton	594.3	11,829
Bates	848.5	15,608
Benton	705.6	16,050
Bollinger	620.8	11,361
Boone	685.4	125,676
Buchanan	409.8	82,066
Butler	697.6	40,217
Caldwell	429.4	8,589

County	Sq. miles	1996 pop.
Callaway	839.1	36,036
Camden	655.2	32,552
Cape Girardeau	578.7	65,719
Carroll	694.6	10,273
Carter	507.6	6,187
Cass	699.1	75,665
Cedar	476.0	13,012
Chariton	755.9	8,818
Christian	563.2	44,871
Clark	507.3	7,499
Clay	396.5	170,447
Clinton	418.8	18,115
Cole	391.6	68,185

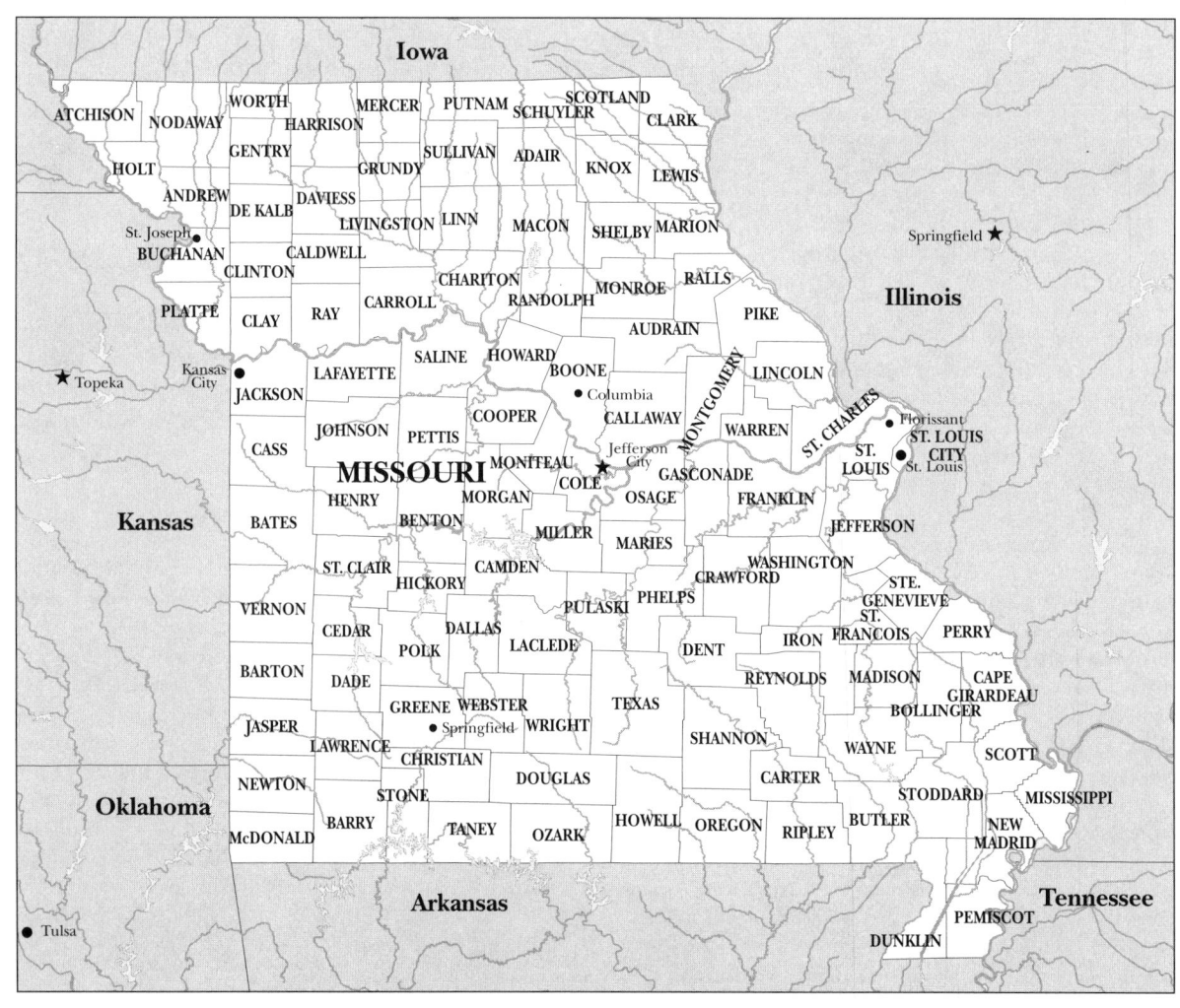

Kansas City, Missouri's largest city. (PhotoDisc)

County	Sq. miles	1996 pop.	County	Sq. miles	1996 pop.
Cooper	565.1	15,947	Jasper	639.8	97,965
Crawford	742.6	21,754	Jefferson	656.8	188,863
Dade	490.4	7,919	Johnson	830.6	46,491
Dallas	541.6	14,728	Knox	505.7	4,309
Daviess	567.0	7,814	Laclede	765.9	29,804
DeKalb	424.2	11,037	Lafayette	629.4	32,259
Dent	753.6	14,054	Lawrence	613.1	32,396
Douglas	814.6	12,235	Lewis	505.1	10,121
Dunklin	545.6	32,991	Lincoln	630.5	34,119
Franklin	922.1	89,485	Linn	620.4	14,007
Gasconade	519.5	14,615	Livingston	534.6	14,306
Gentry	491.6	6,887	McDonald	539.5	19,030
Greene	675.0	223,873	Macon	803.8	15,159
Grundy	435.9	10,238	Madison	496.8	11,379
Harrison	725.2	8,317	Maries	527.8	8,208
Henry	702.5	21,051	Marion	438.1	27,841
Hickory	398.7	8,493	Mercer	454.5	4,004
Holt	461.9	5,658	Miller	592.3	22,321
Howard	465.8	9,708	Mississippi	413.2	13,629
Howell	927.8	34,972	Moniteau	416.5	13,047
Iron	551.4	10,931	Monroe	646.0	8,872
Jackson	604.8	646,341	Montgomery	538.7	11,825

(continued)

County	Sq. miles	1996 pop.
Morgan	597.5	17,592
New Madrid	678.1	20,611
Newton	626.5	47,751
Nodaway	876.7	21,030
Oregon	791.5	10,095
Osage	606.1	12,396
Ozark	746.8	9,629
Pemiscot	493.1	21,666
Perry	474.7	17,433
Pettis	685.0	36,767
Phelps	672.9	37,848
Pike	672.9	16,169
Platte	420.4	67,251
Polk	637.2	25,148
Pulaski	547.1	34,334
Putnam	518.0	5,049
Ralls	471.0	8,905
Randolph	482.4	23,793
Ray	569.5	22,660
Reynolds	811.3	6,699
Ripley	629.5	13,626
Saint Charles	561.4	255,066
Saint Clair	676.7	9,100

County	Sq. miles	1996 pop.
Saint Francois	449.5	53,843
Saint Genevieve	502.4	16,853
Saint Louis	507.8	1,003,807
Saline	755.6	22,922
Schuyler	307.9	4,376
Scotland	438.5	4,800
Scott	421.0	40,241
Shannon	1,003.9	7,976
Shelby	500.9	6,845
Stoddard	827.2	29,625
Stone	463.3	25,875
Sullivan	651.0	6,648
Taney	632.4	33,271
Texas	1,178.6	22,385
Vernon	834.0	19,285
Warren	431.7	22,873
Washington	759.8	22,315
Wayne	761.1	12,842
Webster	593.4	27,601
Worth	266.5	2,335
Wright	682.3	19,241

The city of St. Louis is independent of all counties.
Source: U.S. Census Bureau; National Association of Counties.

Cities
With 10,000 or more residents

Rank	City	Population
1	Kansas City	441,574
2	St. Louis	339,316
3	Springfield	142,898
4	Independence	116,832
5	Columbia	78,915
6	St. Joseph	69,622
7	Lee's Summit	66,623
8	St. Charles	58,166
9	St. Peters	50,297
10	Florissant	47,069
11	Chesterfield	46,033
12	Joplin	44,612
13	Blue Springs	44,433
14	University City	36,858
15	Cape Girardeau	35,596
16	O'Fallon	35,019
17	Jefferson City	34,911

Rank	City	Population
18	Raytown	28,372
19	Gladstone	28,043
20	Kirkwood	26,804
21	Ballwin	25,909
22	Liberty	25,592
23	Grandview	23,703
24	Maryland Heights	23,470
25	Belton	21,778
26	Webster Groves	21,332
27	Arnold	21,052
28	Ferguson	20,490
29	Sedalia	20,447
30	Wildwood	18,123
31	Sikeston	17,792
32	Hannibal	17,728
33	Warrensburg	17,429
34	Poplar Bluff	17,029

Rank	City	Population
35	Kirksville	16,979
36	Overland	16,386
37	Bridgeton	16,243
38	Rolla	16,027
39	Jennings	14,694
40	Hazelwood	14,391
41	Farmington	13,849
42	St. Ann	13,507
43	Clayton	13,289
44	Washington	12,282
45	Crestwood	12,274
46	Marshall	12,163
47	Moberly	12,037
48	Creve Coeur	11,880

Rank	City	Population
49	Lebanon	11,704
51	Excelsior Springs	11,424
52	Carthage	11,360
53	Fulton	11,330
54	Jackson	11,258
55	Mexico	11,250
56	West Plains	11,135
57	Town and Country	10,909
58	Kennett	10,621
59	Berkeley	10,432
60	Bellefontaine	10,041
61	Maryville	10,012

Population figures are estimated for mid-1998.
Source: U.S. Bureau of the Census.

Index to Tables

NA = Reliable data are not available.

DEMOGRAPHICS

Resident state and national populations, 1970-1997

Population figures given in thousands

	State pop.	U.S. pop.	Share	Rank
1970	4,678	203,302	2.3%	13
1980	4,917	226,546	2.2%	15
1985	5,000	237,924	2.1%	15
1990	5,117	248,765	2.1%	15
1995	5,325	262,761	2.0%	16
1997	5,402	267,636	2.0%	16

Source: U.S. Bureau of the Census.

Resident population by age, 1997

Age group	Total population
Under 5 years	367,000
5 to 17 years	1,040,000
18 to 24 years	498,000
25 to 34 years	756,000
35 to 44 years	873,000
45 to 54 years	667,000
55 to 64 years	462,000
65 to 74 years	392,000
75 to 84 years	254,000
85 years and over	95,000
Portion of residents 65 and older	13.7%
National average	12.7%

Population figures are rounded to nearest thousand persons;
figures include armed forces personnel stationed in state.
Source: U.S. Bureau of the Census.

Resident population by race, Hispanic origin, 1997

	State pop.	Share	U.S.
All residents	5,402,000	100.0%	100.0%
Hispanic white	73,000	1.4%	10.0%
non-Hispanic white	4,645,000	86.0%	72.7%
African American	607,000	11.2%	12.7%
Native American	21,000	0.4%	0.9%
Asian, Pacific Islander	58,000	1.1%	3.8%

Source: U.S. Bureau of the Census.

Projections of state population, 2000-2025

	Model A Uses interstate migration observed from 1975-1994	Model B Uses Bureau of Economic Analysis employment projections
Year	Population	Population
2000	5,540,000	5,547,000
2005	5,718,000	5,750,000
2010	5,864,000	5,953,000
2015	6,005,000	6,153,000
2020	6,137,000	6,336,000
2025	6,250,000	6,492,000

All population projections, including those for 2000, were calculated in 1997.
Source: U.S. Bureau of the Census, Population Paper Listings PPL-47.

VITAL STATISTICS

Average lifetime in years by race, 1989-1991

	State	U.S.	Rank
All residents	75.25	75.37	30
White residents	76.02	76.13	31
Black residents	68.81	69.16	25

Ranks are from longest-lived to least longest-lived. Ranks exclude Alaska, for which reliable data are not available. Rank for black residents is based on the 32 states for which reliable data are available.
Source: U.S. National Center for Health Statistics.

Infant mortality rates, 1980 and 1995

	State	U.S.
All residents		
1980	12.4	12.6
1995	7.4	7.6
White residents		
1980	11.1	11.0
1995	6.4	6.3
Black residents		
1980	20.7	21.4
1995	13.8	15.1

Figures represent deaths per 1,000 live births of resident infants under 1 year old, exclusive of fetal deaths; all-residents figures include other races not listed separately.
Source: U.S. National Center for Health Statistics.

Marriages and divorces

Marriages in 1996.	46,100
Rate per 1,000 population, 1995.	8.4
U.S. rate, 1995	8.9
Rank among all states	28
Divorces in 1996	26,300
Rate per 1,000 population, 1995.	5.0
U.S. rate, 1995	4.4
Rank among all states	18

Rank is from highest to lowest in country.
Source: U.S. National Center for Health Statistics.

Death rates by leading causes, 1995

Deaths per 100,000 resident population

Cause	State	U.S.
Heart disease	345.3	280.7
Cancer	230.7	204.9
Cerebrovascular diseases	72.9	60.1
Accidents and adverse effects	43.5	35.5
Motor vehicle accidents	20.6	16.5
Chronic obstructive pulmonary diseases	46.1	39.2
Diabetes mellitus	23.4	22.6
HIV	8.8	NA
Suicide	13.5	11.9
Homicide	8.9	8.7
All causes	1,021.9	880.0
Rank in overall death rate among states		5

Figures exclude nonresidents who die in state. Causes of death follow International Classification of Diseases. Rank is from highest to lowest in country.
Source: U.S. National Center for Health Statistics.

ECONOMY

Gross state product, 1990-1996
In current dollars

	State product	Increase
1990	$104.1 billion	
1993	$118.3 billion	
1994	$129.1 billion	9.13%
1995	$137.5 billion	6.51%
1996	$145.1 billion	5.53%

Source: U.S. Bureau of Economic Analysis; *Survey of Current Business,* June, 1998.

Gross state product by industry, 1996
In billions

Farms, forestry, fisheries	$2.3
Construction	5.8
Manufacturing	29.6
Transportation, public utilities	14.1
Wholesale trade	10.2
Retail trade	12.8
Finance, insurance, real estate	18.8
Services	24.1
Government	14.7
State total	$132.8
Total U.S.	$6,923.8
State share	1.92%
Rank among states	16

Total figures include mining, not listed separately.
Source: U.S. Bureau of Economic Analysis; *Survey of Current Business,* June, 1998.

Personal income per capita, 1990 and 1997
In current dollars

	1990	1997
Per capita income	$17,672	$24,001
U.S. average	$19,188	$25,598
Rank among states	25	26

1997 data are preliminary.
Source: U.S. Bureau of Economic Analysis; *Survey of Current Business,* May, 1998.

Energy consumption, 1995
In trillions of British thermal units (BTU)

End-use sectors

Residential	432.6
Commercial	317.3
Industrial	363.5
Transportation	549.3

Sources of energy

Petroleum	700.1
Natural gas	281.0
Coal	591.4
Hydroelectric power	19.1
Nuclear electric power	87.8
Total state per capita consumption	312.6
Total U.S. per capita consumption	344.4
Rank among states	37
Total state energy consumption	1,662.8
Total U.S. energy consumption	90,547.4
State share of U.S. total	1.84%
Rank among states	20

Total figures include items not listed separately.
Source: U.S. Energy Information Administration; *State Energy Data Report.*

Nonfarm employment by sectors, 1997

Total	2,636,000
Construction	122,000
Manufacturing	419,000
Transportation, public utilities	164,000
Wholesale trade, retail trade	623,000
Finance, insurance, real estate	154,000
Services	736,000
Government	413,000

Figures are rounded to nearest thousand persons. Total includes mining, not listed separately.
Source: U.S. Bureau of Labor Statistics; *Employment and Earnings,* monthly.

Foreign exports, 1990-1997
In millions of dollars

Year	State	U.S.	State share
1990	3,130	394,045	0.79%
1996	5,404	624,767	0.86%
1997	6,724	688,896	0.98%

Source: U.S. Bureau of the Census; *U.S. Merchandise Trade,* series FT 900.

LAND USE

Federally owned land, 1996

	State	U.S.	State share
Total acres	44,248,000	2,271,343,000	1.95%
Federally owned	1,658,000	563,129,000	0.29%
Federal share	3.7%	24.8%	—

Areas are rounded to nearest thousand acres. Figures for
federally owned land do not include trust properties.
Source: U.S. General Services Administration; *Inventory Report
on Real Property Owned by the United States Throughout the
World,* annual.

Land use, 1992
In acres, rounded to nearest thousand

Total surface area	44,606,000
Federal land	2,017,000
Total nonfederal	41,710,000
Developed	2,336,000
Total rural	39,374,000
Cropland	13,347,000
Pasture land	11,911,000
Range land.	126,000
Forest land	11,656,000
Minor cover/use.	2,332,000

Total surface area figures include water area not shown
separately.
Source: U.S. Dept. of Agriculture; Soil Conservation Service;
Iowa State University, Statistical Laboratory; *Summary
Report, 1992 National Resources Inventory.*

Farms and crop acreage, 1997

	State	U.S.	Share	Rank
Farms (thousands)	102	2,058	4.96%	2
Acres (millions)	30	968	3.10%	15
Acres per farm	293	471	—	25
Acres planted	13,424	334,139	4.02%	9
Acres harvested	13,267	319,894	4.15%	9
Farm value (mill.)	$3,075	$108,805	2.83%	27

Numbers of farms are rounded to nearest thousand.
Source: U.S. Dept. of Agriculture; National Agricultural
Statistics Service.

GOVERNMENT AND FINANCE

Units of local government, 1997

	State	Total U.S.	Rank
All local governments	3,416	87,453	8
Counties	114	3,043	4
Municipalities	944	19,372	5
Townships	324	16,629	14
School districts	537	13,726	10
Special districts	1,497	34,683	6

County ranks are based on the 48 states with county
governments; township ranks are based on the 20 states
with township governments; school district ranks are based
on the 46 states with such districts.
Source: U.S. Bureau of the Census; *1997 Census of Governments,
Government Organization,* Series GC97(1).

State government revenue, 1996

Total revenue	$17,051 mill.
General revenue	13,022 mill.
Per capita.	2,428
U.S. per capita average	2,910
Rank among states.	46
Intergovernmental revenue	
Total	$3,711 mill.
From federal government	3,690 mill.
From local government	20 mill.
Charges and Miscellaneous	
Total	$2,101 mill.
Current charges	1,103 mill.
Misc. general revenue	998 mill.
Taxes	
Total	$7,210 mill.
General sales	2,465 mill.
Selective sales.	986 mill.
License taxes	516 mill.
Individual income	2,741 mill.
Corporate income	426 mill.
Other.	76 mill.
Insurance trust revenue	4,029 mill.

Total revenue figures include items not listed separately.
Source: U.S. Bureau of the Census.

State government expenditures, 1996

General expenditures
Intergovernmental	$3,434 mill.
Direct expenditures	8,317 mill.
Total	11,751 mill.

Selected direct expenditures
Education	$4,387 mill.
Public welfare.	2,898 mill.
Health, hospital	1,032 mill.
Highways	1,152 mill.
Police	130 mill.
Corrections.	312 mill.
Natural resources.	231 mill.
Parks and recreation.	28 mill.
Government administration	375 mill.
Interest on debt	307 mill.

Other
State per capita expenditures	$2,191
U.S. per capita average	2,854
Rank among states.	49
Total state expenditures	12,841 mill.
Total U.S. expenditures	859,959 mill.

Totals include items not listed separately.
Source: U.S. Bureau of the Census.

POLITICS

Governors since statehood
D = Democrat; R = Republican; O = other;
(r) resigned; (d) died in office; (i) removed from office

Alexander McNair (O)	1820-1824
Frederick Bates (O)	(d) 1824-1825
Abraham J. Williams (O)	1825-1826
John Miller (O)	1826-1832
Daniel Dunkin (D)	(r) 1832-1836
Lillburn W. Boggs (D)	1836-1840
Thomas Reynolds (D)	(d) 1840-1844
Meredith M. Marmaduke (D)	1844
John C. Edwards (D)	1844-1848
Austin A. King (D)	1848-1853
Sterling Price (D).	1853-1857
Truston Polk (D)	1857
Hancock L. Jackson (D)	1857
Robert M. Stewart (D)	1857-1861
Claiborne F. Jackson (D)	(i) 1861
Hamilton R. Gamble (O)	(d) 1861-1864
Willard P. Hall (O)	1864-1865
Thomas C. Fletcher (R)	1865-1869
Joseph W. McClurg (R).	1869-1871

Benjamin Gratz Brown (R).	1871-1873
Silas Woodson (D)	1873-1875
Charles H. Hardin (D)	1875-1877
John S. Phelps (D)	1877-1881
Thomas T. Crittenden (D)	1881-1885
John S. Marmaduke (D)	(d) 1885-1887
Albert P. Morehouse (D)	1887-1889
David R. Francis (D)	1889-1893
William J. Stone (D)	1893-1897
Lon V. Stephens (D)	1897-1901
Alexander M. Dockery (D).	1901-1905
Joseph W. Polk (D)	1905-1909
Herbert S. Hadley (R)	1909-1913
Elliott W. Major (D)	1913-1917
Frederick D. Gardner (D)	1917-1921
Arthur M. Hyde (R)	1921-1925
Samuel A. Baker (R)	1925-1929
Henry S. Caulfield (R)	1929-1933
Guy B. Park (D).	1933-1937
Lloyd C. Stark (D)	1937-1941
Forrest C. Donnell (R)	1941-1945
Phillip M. Donnelly (D)	1945-1949
Forest Smith (D)	1949-1953
Phillip M. Donnelly (D)	1953-1957
James T. Blair, Jr. (D)	1957-1961
John M. Dalton (D).	1961-1965
Warren E. Hearnes (D).	1965-1973
Christopher S. Bond (R)	1973-1977
Joseph P. Teasdale (D)	1977-1981
Christopher S. Bond (R)	1981-1985
John D. Ashcroft (R)	1985-1993
Mel Carnahan (D)	1993-

Composition of state legislature, 1990-1998

	Democrats	Republicans
State House (163 seats)		
1990	99	64
1992	98	65
1994	87	76
1996	88	75
1998	85	76
State Senate (34 seats)		
1990	23	11
1992	20	14
1994	19	15
1996	19	15
1998	18	16

Figures for total seats may include independents and minor
party members.
Source: Council of State Governments; *State Elective Officials
and the Legislatures.*

Composition of congressional delegations, 1989-1999

	Dem	Rep	Total
House of Representatives			
101st Congress, 1989			
State delegates	5	4	9
Total U.S.	259	174	433
102d Congress, 1991			
State delegates	6	3	9
Total U.S.	267	167	434
103d Congress, 1993			
State delegates	6	3	9
Total U.S.	258	176	434
104th Congress, 1995			
State delegates	5	4	9
Total U.S.	197	236	433
105th Congress, 1997			
State delegates	5	4	9
Total U.S.	206	228	434
106th Congress, 1999			
State delegates	5	4	9
Total U.S.	211	222	433
Senate			
101st Congress, 1989			
State delegates	0	2	2
Total U.S.	55	45	100
102d Congress, 1991			
State delegates	0	2	2
Total U.S.	56	44	100
103d Congress, 1993			
State delegates	0	2	2
Total U.S.	57	43	100
104th Congress, 1995			
State delegates	0	2	2
Total U.S.	46	53	99
105th Congress, 1997			
State delegates	0	2	2
Total U.S.	45	55	100
106th Congress, 1999			
State delegates	0	2	2
Total U.S.	45	54	99

Figures are for starts of first sessions. Figure for U.S. Representatives for 101st Congress does not include Alabama and Indiana, which had vacancies. Figures for total U.S. Representatives for 102d, 103d, and 106th Congresses do not include Vermont, which had 1 Independent-Socialist. Figure for U.S. Representatives for 104th Congress does not include Vermont, which had 1 Independent-Socialist, and California, which had 1 vacancy. Figure for U.S. Representatives for 105th Congress does not include New York, which had 1 vacancy. Figure for U.S. Senators for 104th Congress does not include Oregon, which had 1 vacancy. Figure for U.S. Senators for 106th Congress does not include New Hampshire, which had 1 Independent.
Source: U.S. Congress; *Congressional Directory*, biennial.

Voter participation in presidential elections, 1992 and 1996

	1992	1996
State voting age pop.	3,851,000	3,980,000
Total U.S. voting age pop.	189,524,000	196,509,000
State share of U.S. total	2.0%	2.0%
Rank among states	17	17
Percent of state casting vote	62.1	56.1
Percent of U.S. total voting	55.1	49.0
Rank among states	17	15

Source: U.S. Bureau of the Census.

HEALTH AND MEDICAL CARE

Medicare, 1997

	Recipients	Payments
State	843,000	$4,579 mill.
Total U.S.	37,514,000	$206,064 mill.
State share	2.25%	2.22%
Rank among states	14	14

Recipient figures are rounded to nearest thousand persons. Ranks are from highest to lowest.
Source: U.S. Health Care Financing Administration.

Medicaid, 1996

	Recipients	Payments
State	636,000	$2,018 mill.
Total U.S.	35,028,000	$121,419 mill.
State share	1.82%	1.66%
Rank among states	16	19

Recipient figures are rounded to nearest thousand persons. Payment figures for fiscal year reflect federal and state contribution payments. Ranks are from highest to lowest.
Source: U.S. Health Care Financing Administration.

Health insurance coverage, 1996

	State	U.S.
Total persons covered	4,591,000	225,070,000
Total persons not covered	700,000	41,716,000
Part not covered	13.2%	15.6%
Rank among states	27	—
Children not covered	168,000	10,554,000
Part not covered	11.7%	14.8%
Rank among states	24	—

Ranks are from most to fewest uninsured. Population figures
are rounded to nearest thousand persons.
Source: U.S. Bureau of the Census.

AIDS, syphilis, tuberculosis, and measles cases, 1997

Cases	U.S.	State	Share
AIDS	58,443	577	0.99%
Syphilis	8,550	114	1.33%
Tuberculosis	18,534	248	1.34%
Measles	148,000	1,000	0.68%

Measles figures are rounded to nearest thousand cases.
Source: U.S. Centers for Disease Control and Prevention.

HOUSING

Homeownership rates, 1985-1997

	1985	1990	1997
State	69.2%	64.0%	70.5%
Total U.S.	63.9%	63.9%	65.7%
Rank among states	18	39	15

Source: U.S. Bureau of the Census.

Home sales, 1990 and 1997
In thousands of units

Existing home sales	1990	1997	Change
State sales	84.1	115.9	31.8
Total U.S. sales	3,560	4,730	1,170
State share of U.S. total	2.36%	2.45%	0.09%
Rank among states	15	14	—

Source: National Association of Realtors; *Real Estate Outlook: Market Trends and Insights.*

EDUCATION

Public school enrollment, 1995

State K-8 enrollment	636,000
Total U.S. K-8 enrollment	32,341,000
State share of total U.S.	1.97%
State 9-12 enrollment	254,000
Total U.S. 9-12 enrollment	12,500,000
State share of U.S. total	2.03%
State public school enroll. rate	87.9%
Overall U.S. rate	91.6%
Rank among states	46

Enrollment figures (which include unclassified students) are
rounded to nearest thousand pupils in fall term;
kindergarten (K)-8 grade figures include some
prekindergarten students. Enrollment rate is based on
percentage of persons 5-17 years old. Rank is from highest
to lowest.
Source: U.S. National Center for Education Statistics.

Public college finances, 1996

State FTE enrollment	129,400
Total U.S. FTE enrollment	8,268,800
State share of total U.S.	1.56%
Rank among states	23
State and local appropriations	$689,500,000
Total U.S. state and local appropriations	$39,699 mill.
State share of total U.S.	1.74%
Rank among states	20
State net tuition revenues	$457,400,000
Total U.S. net tuition	$18,348,100,000
State share of total U.S.	2.49%
Rank among states	12

FTE=Full-time equivalent; credit and noncredit enrollment
including summer session in academic year ending in
1996.
Enrollments are rounded to nearest thousand students. Net
tuition revenues exclude appropriation to students
attending in-state public institutions. Rankings are from
highest shares to lowest.
Source: Research Associates of Washington.

TRANSPORTATION AND TRAVEL

Highway mileage, 1996

Interstate	1,178
Other arterial	9,582
Collector roads	26,673
Local roads	86,921
Urban roads	16,415
Rural roads	106,333
Total state	122,748
U.S. total	3,933,985
State share	3.1%
Rank among states	6

Source: U.S. Federal Highway Administration.

Motor vehicle registrations and driver licenses, 1996
In thousands

Vehicle registrations	State	U.S.	Share	Rank
Autos, trucks, buses	4,350	206,365	2.11%	17
Autos only	2,568	128,439	2.00%	17
Motorcycles	54	3,832	1.41%	24
Driver licenses	3,749	179,539	2.09%	17

Figures do not include vehicles owned by military services.
Source: U.S. Federal Highway Administration; *Highway Statistics; Selected Highway Statistics and Charts.*

Domestic travel expenditures, 1995
Spending by U.S. residents on overnight trips and day trips of at least 100 miles

Total expenditures in state	$6,989 mill.
Total expenditures in U.S.	$360,314 mill.
State share of total U.S.	1.94%
Rank among states	16

Source: Travel Industry Association of America.

CRIME AND LAW ENFORCEMENT

State and local police officers, 1996

Local police	8,836
State police	996
Sheriffs	2,421
Total	12,998
Officers per 10,000 residents	24
U.S. average	25
Rank among states	17

Figures cover full-time sworn officers; totals include special police not shown separately.
Source: U.S. Bureau of Justice Statistics; *Census of State and Local Law Enforcement Agencies, 1996.*

Crime rates, 1996
Rates per 100,000 resident population

Violent crimes	State	U.S.
Total violent	591	634
Murder	8.1	7.4
Forcible rape	29.2	36.1
Robbery	171	202
Aggravated assault	383	388
Property crimes		
Total property	4,493	4,445
Burglary	894	943
Larceny/theft	3,151	2,976
Motor vehicle theft	448	526
Totals	5,084	5,079

Source: U.S. Federal Bureau of Investigation; *Crime in the United States,* annual.

State prison populations, 1980-1996

	State	U.S.	State share
1980	5,726	305,458	1.87%
1990	14,943	708,393	2.11%
1996	22,003	1,025,624	2.15%

Figures exclude prisoners in federal penitentiaries.
Source: U.S. Bureau of Justice Statistics.

Montana

Location: Northwestern continental United States

Area and rank: 145,556 square miles (376,991 square kilometers); 147,046 square miles (380,849 square kilometers) including water; fourth largest state in area

Population and rank: 878,810 (1997); forty-fourth largest state in population

Capital: Helena

Largest city: Billings (91,750 people in 1998)

State capitol building in Helena. (Travel Montana/Donnie Sexton)

Became territory:
May 26, 1864

**Entered Union and
rank:** November 8,
1889; forty-first state

**Present constitution
adopted:** 1972

Counties: 56, as well as
a small part of
Yellowstone National
Park

State name: "Montana"
is a Latinized form for a Spanish word meaning "mountainous."

State nickname: Treasure State

Motto: *Oro y plata* (Gold and silver)

State flag: Dark blue field with the state seal emblem and name "Montana" above

Highest point: Granite Peak — 12, 799 feet (3,900 meters)

Lowest point: Kootenai River — 1,800 feet (549 meters)

Highest recorded temperature: 117 degrees Fahrenheit (47 degrees Celsius) —
Medicine Lake, 1937

Lowest recorded temperature: –70 degrees Fahrenheit (–57 degrees Celsius) —
Rogers Pass, 1954

State song: "Montana"

State tree: Ponderosa pine

State flower: Bitterroot

State bird: Western meadowlark

National parks: Glacier, Yellowstone

Montana History

Montana, one of the six Rocky Mountain states, lies directly south of the Canadian provinces of Saskatchewan and Alberta. To its east are North and South Dakota. Wyoming lies south of it, and Idaho borders it to the south and west. It is 570 miles from east to west. From Canada in the north to Wyoming in the south is 315 miles.

With an area exceeding 147,000 square miles, it ranks fourth in size among the fifty states. With a population density of 5.5 people per square mile, Montana ranks forty-fourth among the states in population. Montana lost population between 1980 and 1990 but experienced a slight population upsurge during the 1990's.

The Rocky Mountains dominate the western two-fifths of the state. The eastern three-fifths consist mostly of rolling hills and plains. The climate is dry and, in winter, extremely cold. Summers are hot. The rich soil of the plains, the hot summers, and the long summer days in this latitude are ideal for agriculture.

Early History. When French Canadian explorers first visited the area, it had already been inhabited by humans for more than nine thousand years. Evidence exists of cultures that date to 8000 B.C.E. Among the native tribes in the area were the Arapaho, Assiniboine, Blackfoot, Cheyenne, Crow, Kalispel, Kutenai, and Salish Indians.

In prehistoric times, dinosaurs roamed Montana. A nest of duck-billed dinosaur fossils was discovered there in 1978. In 1988 the most complete skeleton of a tyrannosaur ever unearthed was discovered. The earliest human inhabitants hunted bison and other indigenous animals with spears.

Early Exploration. The earliest known explorers to reach Montana were François and Louis Joseph de La Vérendrye, French Canadian brothers who arrived in 1743. Montana became part of the United States in 1803 through the Louisiana Purchase.

Explorers Meriwether Lewis and William Clark, guided by a young American Indian woman, Sacagawea, crossed the territory in 1805 en route to America's northwest coast. They returned in 1806 on their trip east. A Spanish trader, Manuel Lisa, established the Missouri Fur Company and went on a trading expedition up the Yellowstone River. In 1807 he established Montana's first trading post, Fort Manuel.

The following year Canadian David Thompson established a trading post on the Kootenai River and, in 1809, founded Salish House near Thompson Falls. By 1829, both the Hudson Bay Company and the American Fur Company traded in this area.

Montana's rivers and low mountain passes encouraged transportation. The second longest river in the United States, the 2,315-mile-long Missouri, begins in Montana. Other rivers—the Jefferson, the Madison, the Gallatin, and the Yellowstone—criss-cross the state.

By 1850 fur traders had overhunted and exploited Montana to the extent that most of the fur-bearing animals had been killed. Whole herds of bison, fox, and deer were wiped out by voracious traders.

The Discovery of Gold. When gold was discovered in California in 1848, thousands of easterners rushed across the country seeking instant wealth. Meanwhile, residents of Montana searched for gold in their area. In 1862 John White discovered small gold deposits at Grasshopper Creek. By 1863 more than five hundred miners had come there.

Soon a gold strike was made nearby. A settlement, Virginia City, which by 1865 had ten thousand inhabitants, sprang into being. Gold was discovered at Last Chance Gulch, where its discovery spawned another city, Helena. Meanwhile, rich veins of copper and silver were found around Butte in the Rocky Mountains.

Lawlessness soon became a considerable problem. Gangsters robbed stagecoaches of the gold and silver they transported. During 1863 one gang killed more than one hundred people. In the following year, vigilantes captured and hanged more than twenty such criminals, thereby reducing crime substantially.

Miners flocked into the area as well as merchants, who arrived with their families to open

stores and to establish an infrastructure. Cattle ranchers came to eastern Montana. In 1863 schools were opened in Bannack and Nevada City.

The Road to Statehood. Congress created the Montana Territory in 1864. In 1875 Helena became its capital. American Indian uprisings raged. In 1876 the Sioux and Cheyenne Indians killed Lieutenant Colonel George Armstrong Custer in the Battle of the Little Bighorn, but in 1877, Chief Joseph of the Nez Perce tribe surrendered, ending the American Indian wars that plagued the territory. By 1880, Montana's Native American population was deployed to seven American Indian reservations within the territory.

In 1880 the Utah and Northern Railroad laid tracks across Montana, enabling Montanans to ship produce and cattle to eastern markets. Montana's first bid for statehood in 1866 was premature because the state had a very small population, little access to eastern markets, and continuing problems with American Indian wars. Because the expansion of the railroad into the state resulted in the population quadrupling within a decade, a constitutional convention was called in 1884, and statehood was again requested but refused for political reasons.

In 1889 President Grover Cleveland signed an enabling bill guaranteeing that if North Dakota, South Dakota, Washington, and Montana submitted acceptable constitutions, statehood would be granted. Montana held a constitutional convention in July of that year, offered a constitution to its electorate, and was granted statehood in November, 1889, becoming the forty-first state. In 1894 Montana voters chose Helena as the capital.

Copper Mining in Montana. Although early prospectors found gold and silver around Butte, it was copper that brought the greatest wealth to Montana. Marcus Daly, seeking silver in the area, discovered one of the richest copper deposits in the world and in 1881 opened his copper mine in Anaconda. William Clark soon opened a copper operation nearby in Butte.

The copper found here was so abundant that Butte Hill was nicknamed "the Richest Hill on Earth." The copper industry attracted immigrants, mostly from Great Britain, to work in the mines. Daly established the Anaconda Copper Company, and in 1926 Clark's Butte holdings were sold to that corporation.

Montana Politics and Education. The two powerful copper barons who emerged from the Butte-

Anaconda area, Marcus Daly and William Clark, were business and political rivals. They engaged in a heated campaign to have their own towns declared capital of the state, with Clark prevailing. Each owned the newspaper in his respective town.

Clark was elected to the U.S. Senate in 1891 but resigned when a scandal, perpetrated by reports accusing him of bribery in Daly's newspaper, the *Anaconda Standard*, cast doubt upon Clark's integrity. He was, nevertheless, elected to the Senate when he ran again in 1900.

Montana was the first state to elect a woman to Congress. Jeanette Rankin was elected in 1917 and served for two years. She served again from 1941 to 1943. Rankin was the only member of Congress to vote against the United States' entry into World War I in 1917 and into World War II in 1941.

Montana's first constitution, ratified in 1889, was replaced when a constitutional convention called in 1972 produced a new constitution, narrowly ratified by the electorate and put into effect in 1973. This constitution combined more than one hundred state agencies into fifteen departments, whose heads report to the governor. In 1974 the constitution was amended to change the annual sixty-day legislative session to a ninety-day session to meet in odd-numbered years.

Montana prides itself on valuing education. Its 1990 literacy rate of 92 percent is 5 percent above the national average. Seventy-five percent of Montanans are high school graduates, whereas the national average is 67 percent.

Industrial Expansion. Natural gas was discovered in Glendive, near Montana's eastern border, in 1913. This was an important discovery because where there is natural gas, there is usually oil. It was not until 1950, however, that vast oil deposits were discovered on the Montana-North Dakota border. Oil revenues spurred the state's faltering economy. The strip mining of bituminous coal in the eastern part of the state also helped to advance Montana's economy, changing the nature of the plains con-

Decision Point, at the confluence of the Marias and Missouri Rivers—a key site in Meriwether Lewis and William Clark's exploration of the Louisiana Purchase territory. (Travel Montana/Victor Bjornberg)

siderably. Nevertheless, the Montana plains are among the most prolific producers of wheat in the United States.

In 1955 the Anaconda Aluminum Company began operation in Columbia Falls in northwestern Montana. In 1983, however, the once-powerful Anaconda Copper Company, having mined out the area around Butte, suspended operations.

Natural Disasters. Between 1917 and 1920, Montana suffered greatly from droughts that caused many farmers and cattle ranchers in eastern Montana to fail. In 1929 another drought began that again devastated eastern Montana and lasted for several years, during which the economic contractions of the Great Depression also affected that state's economy. During 1935 Helena was struck by more than one hundred earthquakes. Although no lives were lost, property damage was severe.

With federal aid, Montana strove to avert the devastation earlier droughts had inflicted upon the state. Although Flathead Lake, which covers two hundred square miles, is the largest freshwater lake west of the Mississippi River, it proved insufficient to provide irrigation during droughts. In 1934 Montana began a dam-building project that, in 1940, culminated in the creation of the four-hundred-square-mile Fort Peck Lake and several other artificial

The battlefield on which the Sioux annihilated the cavalry force commanded by George Armstrong Custer has been consecrated as a national monument. (PhotoDisc)

lakes that provide irrigation and hydroelectric power for Montana's farms and cattle ranches.

R. Baird Shuman

Montana Time Line

c. 8000 B.C.E.	People first settle Montana.
1743	French Canadians François and Louis Joseph de La Vérendrye explore the area.
1803	United States gains most of Montana through the Louisiana Purchase.
1805	Explorers Meriwether Lewis and William Clark are guided through Montana by American Indian Sacagawea.
1807	Spanish trader Manuel Lisa establishes Montana's first fur-trading post.
1846	Fort Benton is built.

(continued)

1862	John White discovers gold at Grasshopper Creek.
1863	Virginia City is established near Grasshopper Creek gold strike.
May 26, 1864	Montana Territory is created.
1875	Helena becomes capital of the territory.
June 25, 1876	Battle of the Little Bighorn takes place between Sioux and U.S. Army; Lieutenant Colonel George Armstrong Custer is killed.
Oct. 5, 1877	Chief Joseph of the Nez Perce surrenders, ending the American Indian wars.
1880	Most of Montana's Native Americans are placed on reservations.
Nov. 8, 1889	Montana becomes the forty-first state.
1893	Four public institutions of higher learning open in Montana.
1910	Congress establishes Glacier National Park.
1917	Jeannette Rankin becomes the first female member of Congress.
1917-1918	More than forty thousand Montanans serve in World War I.
1917-1920	Severe droughts devastate Montana farms and ranches.
1934	Work begins on Fort Peck Dam.
1935	Helena is hit by more than one hundred earthquakes.
1940	Jeannette Rankin is elected to a second term in Congress.
1941-1945	Some fifty-seven thousand Montanans serve in World War II.
1950	Large oil strike is made in eastern Montana.
1955	Anaconda Aluminum Company begins operation.
1959	Huge earthquake creates Quake Lake on Madison River.
1972	New state constitution is adopted.
1983	Anaconda Copper Company closes its Butte mining operations.
1984	Forest fires ravage state.
1996	Native Americans sue state over voting precinct districting.
1997	Montana farmers seek right to kill buffalo outside Yellowstone Park to control brucelosis.
1998	Montana farmers block border point to protest low Canadian produce prices.
1999	Montana replaces "reasonable and prudent" speed limit with one of 75 miles per hour on most highways.

Notes for Further Study

Published Sources. The most comprehensive study of Montana is *Montana: A History of Two Centuries* (rev. ed. 1991) by Michael P. Malone, Richard B. Roeder, and William L. Lang. This richly illustrated book presents the history of the state, considering its cultural, educational, and economic development. Janice Cohn in *The Christ-mas Menorahs: How a Town Fought Hate* (1995) explains how citizens of Billings, Montana, defended a Jewish family that fell victim to hate crimes. R. E. Mather in *Vigilante Victims: Montana's Hanging Spree* (1991) discusses the vigilantes who broke the Montana crime wave of the 1860's. Laura Ross focuses on America's dealings with

Montana's Native Americans in *Inventing the Savage: The Social Construction of Native American Criminality* (1998).

Richard Allan Fox, Jr., discusses the Battle of the Little Bighorn and George Custer's defeat in *Archeology, History, and Custer's Last Battle: The Little Big Horn Reexamined* (1993), updating *Archeological Insights into the Custer Battle: The Assessment of the 1984 Field Season* (1987) by Douglas D. Scott and Richard A. Fox, Jr. Duane A. Smith's *Rocky Mountain West: Colorado, Wyoming, and Montana* (1991) emphasizes the western part of the state, in which most of its mining occurs. Adolescent readers will find Ann Heinrichs's *Montana* (1991), in the America the Beautiful series, clear, well written, and detailed. Younger readers will appreciate *Montana* (1993) by Judith Bloom Fradin and Dennis Brindell Fradin in the From Sea to Shining Sea series.

Web Resources. The best Internet source for information about the government of Montana is its home page (http://www.mt.gov). For tourist information consult the Web sites of the tourist service (http://www.travel.mt .gov), Montana Tours (http://www .mhct.com), Big Sky (http://www.big sky.net), Glacier National Park (http://www.glacierparkinc.com), and Yellowstone National Park (http://www.nps.gov/yell). Information about hunting and fishing can be found at the Fish, Wildlife, and Parks Web site (http://www.swp.state.mt .us), the Montana Bowhunters site

Located on Montana's border with Canada, Glacier National Park was established by the U.S. Congress in 1910. (PhotoDisc)

(http://www.mtba.org), and the Living Country site (http://www.livingcountry.com). Montana's business and commerce is discussed at the Montana Business Web site (http://www.mbs.umt.edu). Information about real estate is available on the Montana Realtors Web site (http://www.mtmar.com) or on such regional Web sites as those of the Great Falls Realtors (http://www.gtfar .com) and Glacier Real Estate (http://www.glacierreal estate.com).

For information about legal matters, the Montana Bar Association's Web site (http://www.montanabar.org) is useful. The Montana Education Association maintains a Web site (http://www.mea-mt.org), as does the Montana

Medical Association (http://www.montanamed.com). The University of Montana's Web site (http://www .umt.edu) provides information about the school's resources. Other institutions of higher learning offer Web sites, including Carroll College (http://www.carroll .edu), Dawson Community College (http://www.daw son.cc.us), Dull Knife College (http://www.dkmc.cc.mt .us), Little Big Horn College (http://www.lbhc.cc.mt .us), Montana State University (http://www.montana .edu), Montana Tech (http://www.mtech.edu), Rocky Mountain College (http://www.rocky.edu), Salish Kootenai College (http://www.skc.edu), and West Montana College (http://www.wmc.edu).

Job opportunities in Montana are listed on the Montana Jobs Web site (http://www.jsd.dli.mt.gov). Various communities and counties also maintain Web sites, some of which have information about job opportunities, among them Bozeman (http://www.bozeman.org), Butte (http://www.butte-montana.com), Gallatin County (http://www.galico.org), Great Falls (http://www.city-of-great-falls.com), Lewistown (http://www.lewistown.net), Missoula (http://www.missoula.bigsky.net), Nez Perce (http://www.nps.gov/nepe), and Whitefish (http://www.whitefishmt.com).

Counties

County	Sq. miles	1996 pop.	County	Sq. miles	1996 pop.
Beaverhead	5,542.6	9,144	Glacier	2,994.7	12,675
Big Horn	4,994.9	12,308	Golden Valley	1,175.3	984
Blaine	4,226.2	7,114	Granite	1,727.5	2,585
Broadwater	1,191.5	4,012	Hill	2,896.4	17,730
Carbon	2,048.1	9,248	Jefferson	1,656.7	9,668
Carter	3,339.7	1,489	Judith Basin	1,869.9	2,278
Cascade	2,698.0	81,087	Lake	1,493.8	24,921
Chouteau	3,973.4	5,361	Lewis and Clark	3,461.0	53,345
Custer	3,783.3	12,285	Liberty	1,429.8	2,311
Daniels	1,426.1	2,136	Lincoln	3,612.8	18,833
Dawson	2,373.3	9,085	McCone	2,642.6	2,055
Deer Lodge	736.9	10,093	Madison	3,586.6	6,773
Fallon	1,620.4	2,992	Meagher	2,391.9	1,798
Fergus	4,339.3	12,697	Mineral	1,219.9	3,719
Flathead	5,098.6	71,253	Missoula	2,598.2	88,523
Gallatin	2,506.9	60,565	Musselshell	1,867.2	4,675
Garfield	4,668.2	1,410	Park	2,656.2	16,143

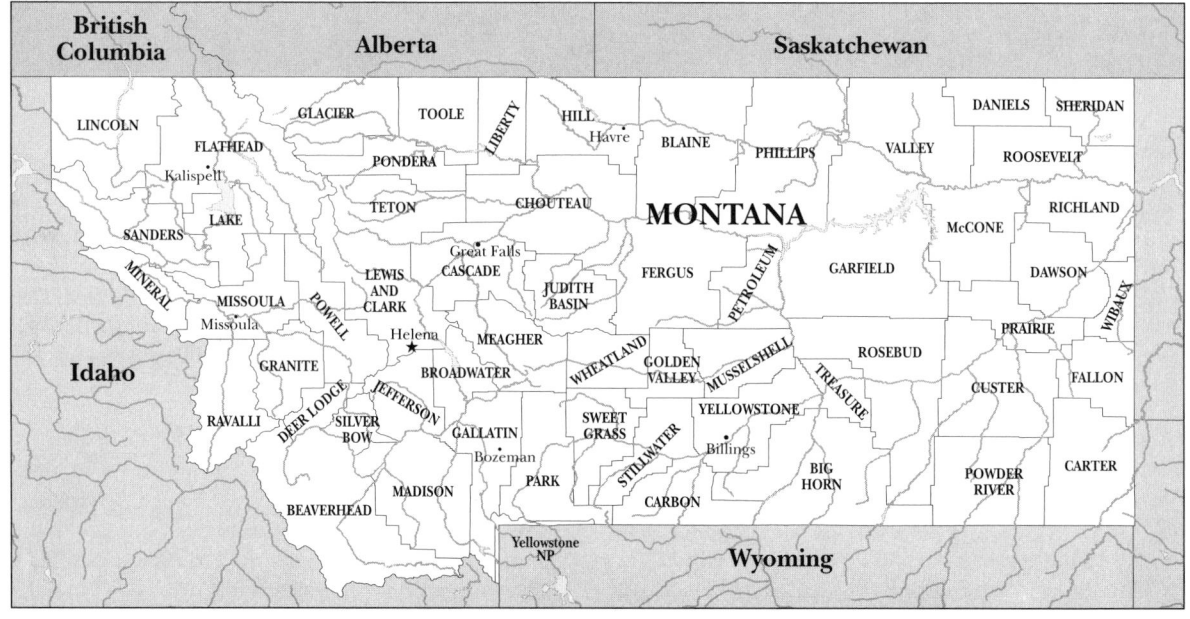

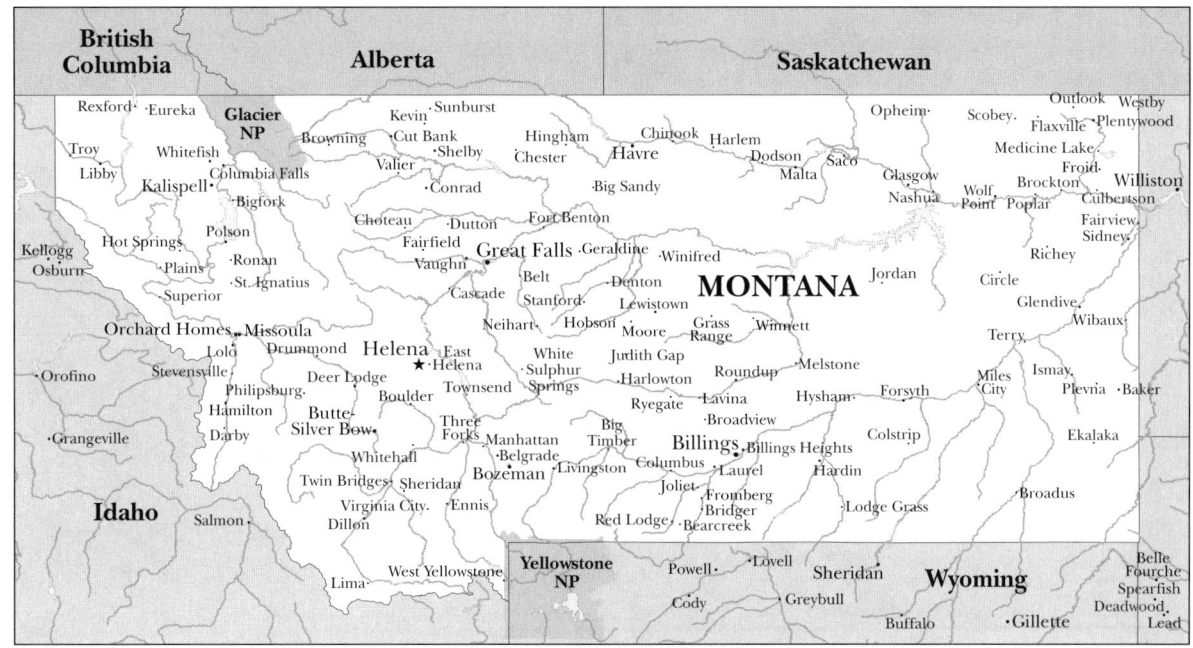

County	Sq. miles	1996 pop.
Petroleum	1,653.9	533
Phillips	5,139.9	5,025
Pondera	1,624.7	6,344
Powder River	3,297.3	1,930
Powell	2,326.0	7,115
Prairie	1,736.6	1,392
Ravalli	2,394.3	33,586
Richland	2,084.2	10,313
Roosevelt	2,355.7	11,065
Rosebud	5,012.4	10,457
Sanders	2,762.3	10,140
Sheridan	1,676.7	4,363

County	Sq. miles	1996 pop.
Silver Bow	718.3	34,634
Stillwater	1,794.7	7,653
Sweet Grass	1,855.2	3,437
Teton	2,272.6	6,371
Toole	1,910.9	4,918
Treasure	978.9	866
Valley	4,920.9	8,363
Wheatland	1,423.2	2,420
Wibaux	889.3	1,146
Yellowstone	2,635.2	125,966

Source: U.S. Census Bureau; National Association of Counties.

Cities
With 10,000 or more residents

Rank	City	Population
1	Billings	91,750
2	Great Falls	56,395
3	Missoula	52,239
4	Butte-Silver Bow (remainder)	33,994
5	Bozeman	29,936

Rank	City	Population
6	Helena	28,306
7	Kalispell	16,089
8	Havre	10,015

Population figures are estimated for mid-1998.
Source: U.S. Bureau of the Census.

Index to Tables

NA = Reliable data are not available.

DEMOGRAPHICS

Resident state and national populations, 1970-1997

Population figures given in thousands

	State pop.	U.S. pop.	Share	Rank
1970	694	203,302	0.3%	43
1980	787	226,546	0.3%	44
1985	822	237,924	0.3%	44
1990	799	248,765	0.3%	44
1995	869	262,761	0.3%	44
1997	879	267,636	0.3%	44

Source: U.S. Bureau of the Census.

Resident population by age, 1997

Age group	Total population
Under 5 years	54,000
5 to 17 years	175,000
18 to 24 years	87,000
25 to 34 years	98,000
35 to 44 years	144,000
45 to 54 years	123,000
55 to 64 years	82,000
65 to 74 years	61,000
75 to 84 years	41,000
85 years and over	14,000
Portion of residents 65 and older	13.2%
National average	12.7%

Population figures are rounded to nearest thousand persons;
figures include armed forces personnel stationed in state.
Source: U.S. Bureau of the Census.

Resident population by race, Hispanic origin, 1997

	State pop.	Share	U.S.
All residents	879,000	100.0%	100.0%
Hispanic white	13,000	1.5%	10.0%
non-Hispanic white	803,000	91.4%	72.7%
African American	3,000	0.3%	12.7%
Native American	55,000	6.3%	0.9%
Asian, Pacific Islander	5,000	0.6%	3.8%

Source: U.S. Bureau of the Census.

Projections of state population, 2000-2025

	Model A Uses interstate migration observed from 1975-1994	Model B Uses Bureau of Economic Analysis employment projections
Year	Population	Population
2000	950,000	937,000
2005	1,006,000	998,000
2010	1,040,000	1,056,000
2015	1,069,000	1,108,000
2020	1,097,000	1,152,000
2025	1,121,000	1,187,000

All population projections, including those for 2000, were calculated in 1997.
Source: U.S. Bureau of the Census, Population Paper Listings PPL-47.

VITAL STATISTICS

Average lifetime in years by race, 1989-1991

	State	U.S.	Rank
All residents	76.23	75.37	20
White residents	76.72	76.13	17
Black residents	NA	69.16	NA

Ranks are from longest-lived to least longest-lived. Ranks exclude Alaska, for which reliable data are not available. Rank for black residents is based on the 32 states for which reliable data are available.
Source: U.S. National Center for Health Statistics.

Infant mortality rates, 1980 and 1995

	State	U.S.
All residents		
1980	12.4	12.6
1995	7.0	7.6
White residents		
1980	11.8	11.0
1995	7.0	6.3
Black residents		
1980	NA	21.4
1995	NA	15.1

Figures represent deaths per 1,000 live births of resident infants under 1 year old, exclusive of fetal deaths; all-residents figures include other races not listed separately.
Source: U.S. National Center for Health Statistics.

Marriages and divorces

Marriages in 1996 6,600
Rate per 1,000 population, 1995 . . . . 7.6
U.S. rate, 1995 . . . . 8.9
Rank among all states 36

Divorces in 1996 4,300
Rate per 1,000 population, 1995 . . . . 4.8
U.S. rate, 1995 . . . . 4.4
Rank among all states 20

Rank is from highest to lowest in country.
Source: U.S. National Center for Health Statistics.

Death rates by leading causes, 1995
Deaths per 100,000 resident population

Cause	State	U.S.
Heart disease	230.3	280.7
Cancer	203.4	204.9
Cerebrovascular diseases	68.3	60.1
Accidents and adverse effects	43.7	35.5
Motor vehicle accidents	22.4	16.5
Chronic obstructive pulmonary diseases	55.2	39.2
Diabetes mellitus	24.1	22.6
HIV	-	NA
Suicide	23.1	11.9
Homicide	5.4	8.7
All causes	876.6	880.0
Rank in overall death rate among states		30

Figures exclude nonresidents who die in state. Causes of death follow International Classification of Diseases. Rank is from highest to lowest in country.
Source: U.S. National Center for Health Statistics.

ECONOMY

Gross state product, 1990-1996
In current dollars

	State product	Increase
1990	$13.3 billion	
1993	$16.1 billion	
1994	$16.9 billion	4.97%
1995	$17.7 billion	4.73%
1996	$18.5 billion	4.52%

Source: U.S. Bureau of Economic Analysis; *Survey of Current Business,* June, 1998.

Gross state product by industry, 1996
In billions

Farms, forestry, fisheries	$0.8
Construction	0.8
Manufacturing	1.3
Transportation, public utilities	2.3
Wholesale trade	1.1
Retail trade	1.8
Finance, insurance, real estate	2.2
Services	3.1
Government	2.7
State total	$16.9
Total U.S.	$6,923.8
State share	0.24%
Rank among states	47

Total figures include mining, not listed separately.
Source: U.S. Bureau of Economic Analysis; *Survey of Current Business,* June, 1998.

Personal income per capita, 1990 and 1997
In current dollars

	1990	1997
Per capita income	$15,067	$20,046
U.S. average	$19,188	$25,598
Rank among states	44	46

1997 data are preliminary.
Source: U.S. Bureau of Economic Analysis; *Survey of Current Business,* May, 1998.

Energy consumption, 1995
In trillions of British thermal units (BTU)

End-use sectors

Residential	63.8
Commercial	51.0
Industrial	162.5
Transportation	101.7

Sources of energy

Petroleum	159.6
Natural gas	59.6
Coal	171.2
Hydroelectric power	111.0
Nuclear electric power	0
Total state per capita consumption	435.4
Total U.S. per capita consumption	344.4
Rank among states	10
Total state energy consumption	378.9
Total U.S. energy consumption	90,547.4
State share of U.S. total	0.42%
Rank among states	43

Total figures include items not listed separately.
Source: U.S. Energy Information Administration; *State Energy Data Report.*

Nonfarm employment by sectors, 1997

Total	366,000
Construction	18,000
Manufacturing	24,000
Transportation, public utilities	21,000
Wholesale trade, retail trade	99,000
Finance, insurance, real estate	16,000
Services	105,000
Government	77,000

Figures are rounded to nearest thousand persons. Total includes mining, not listed separately.
Source: U.S. Bureau of Labor Statistics; *Employment and Earnings,* monthly.

Foreign exports, 1990-1997
In millions of dollars

Year	State	U.S.	State share
1990	229	394,045	0.06%
1996	440	624,767	0.07%
1997	530	688,896	0.08%

Source: U.S. Bureau of the Census; *U.S. Merchandise Trade,* series FT 900.

LAND USE

Federally owned land, 1996

	State	U.S.	State share
Total acres	93,271,000	2,271,343,000	4.11%
Federally owned	25,485,000	563,129,000	4.53%
Federal share	27.3%	24.8%	—

Areas are rounded to nearest thousand acres. Figures for federally owned land do not include trust properties.
Source: U.S. General Services Administration; *Inventory Report on Real Property Owned by the United States Throughout the World,* annual.

Land use, 1992
In acres, rounded to nearest thousand

Total surface area	94,109,000
Federal land	27,122,000
Total nonfederal	65,656,000
Developed	1,096,000
Total rural	64,561,000
Cropland	15,035,000
Pasture land	3,370,000
Range land	36,835,000
Forest land	5,156,000
Minor cover/use	4,165,000

Total surface area figures include water area not shown separately.
Source: U.S. Dept. of Agriculture; Soil Conservation Service; Iowa State University, Statistical Laboratory; *Summary Report, 1992 National Resources Inventory.*

Farms and crop acreage, 1997

	State	U.S.	Share	Rank
Farms (thousands)	24	2,058	1.17%	31
Acres (millions)	60	968	6.20%	2
Acres per farm	2,483	471	—	5
Acres planted	10,423	334,139	3.12%	13
Acres harvested	9,939	319,894	3.11%	12
Farm value (mill.)	$1,415	$108,805	1.30%	6

Numbers of farms are rounded to nearest thousand.
Source: U.S. Dept. of Agriculture; National Agricultural Statistics Service.

GOVERNMENT AND FINANCE

Units of local government, 1997

	State	Total U.S.	Rank
All local governments	1,144	87,453	26
Counties	54	3,043	29
Municipalities	128	19,372	38
Townships	0	16,629	—
School districts	362	13,726	14
Special districts	600	34,683	19

County ranks are based on the 48 states with county governments; township ranks are based on the 20 states with township governments; school district ranks are based on the 46 states with such districts.
Source: U.S. Bureau of the Census; *1997 Census of Governments, Government Organization,* Series GC97(1).

State government revenue, 1996

Total revenue	$3,476 mill.
General revenue	2,831 mill.
Per capita	3,229
U.S. per capita average	2,910
Rank among states	15
Intergovernmental revenue	
Total	$991 mill.
From federal government	977 mill.
From local government	15 mill.
Charges and Miscellaneous	
Total	$583 mill.
Current charges	250 mill.
Misc. general revenue	334 mill.
Taxes	
Total	$1,256 mill.
General sales	NA
Selective sales	269 mill.
License taxes	148 mill.
Individual income	383 mill.
Corporate income	76 mill.
Other	380 mill.
Insurance trust revenue	606 mill.

Total revenue figures include items not listed separately.
Source: U.S. Bureau of the Census.

State government expenditures, 1996

General expenditures
Intergovernmental . . . . $699 mill.
Direct expenditures . . . . 2,030 mill.
Total. . . . . 2,729 mill.

Selected direct expenditures
Education . . . . $1,014 mill.
Public welfare. . . . . 510 mill.
Health, hospital . . . . 168 mill.
Highways . . . . 340 mill.
Police. . . . . 30 mill.
Corrections . . . . 66 mill.
Natural resources. . . . . 110 mill.
Parks and recreation . . . . 6 mill.
Government administration . . . . 122 mill.
Interest on debt . . . . 136 mill.

Other
State per capita expenditures $3,113
U.S. per capita average 2,854
Rank among states. 15
Total state expenditures . . . . 3,136 mill.
Total U.S. expenditures . . . . 859,959 mill.

Totals include items not listed separately.
Source: U.S. Bureau of the Census.

POLITICS

Governors since statehood
D = Democrat; R = Republican; O = other;
(r) resigned; (d) died in office; (i) removed from office

Joseph K. Toole (D) 1889-1893
John E. Rickards (R) 1893-1897
Robert B. Smith (O) 1897-1901
Joseph K. Toole (D) . . . . (r) 1901-1908
Edwin L. Norris (D) 1908-1913
Samuel V. Stewart (D) 1913-1921
Joseph M. Dixon (R) 1921-1925
John E. Erickson (D) . . . . (r) 1925-1933
Frank H. Cooney (D) . . . . (d) 1933-1935
William Elmer Hoyt (D) 1935-1937
Roy E. Ayers (D) 1937-1941
Samuel C. Ford (R). 1941-1949
John W. Bonner (D) 1949-1953
John Hugo Aronson (R) 1953-1961
Donald G. Nutter (R) . . . . (d) 1961-1962
Tim M. Babcock (R) 1962-1969
Forrest H. Anderson (D) 1969-1973
Thomas L. Judge (D) 1973-1981

Ted Schwinden (D) 1981-1989
Stan Stephens (R) 1989-1993
Marc Racicot (R) 1993-

Composition of state legislature, 1990-1998

	Democrats	Republicans
State House (100 seats)		
1990	61	39
1992	47	53
1994	33	67
1996	35	65
1998	41	59
State Senate (50 seats)		
1990	29	21
1992	30	20
1994	19	31
1996	16	34
1998	18	32

Figures for total seats may include independents and minor
party members.
Source: Council of State Governments; *State Elective Officials
and the Legislatures.*

Composition of congressional delegations, 1989-1999

	Dem	Rep	Total
House of Representatives			
101st Congress, 1989			
State delegates	1	1	2
Total U.S.	259	174	433
102d Congress, 1991			
State delegates	1	1	2
Total U.S.	267	167	434
103d Congress, 1993			
State delegates	1	0	1
Total U.S.	258	176	434
104th Congress, 1995			
State delegates	0	1	1
Total U.S.	197	236	433
105th Congress, 1997			
State delegates	0	1	1
Total U.S.	206	228	434
106th Congress, 1999			
State delegates	0	1	1
Total U.S.	211	222	433

	Dem	Rep	Total
Senate			
101st Congress, 1989			
State delegates	1	1	2
Total U.S.	55	45	100
102d Congress, 1991			
State delegates	1	1	2
Total U.S.	56	44	100
103d Congress, 1993			
State delegates	1	1	2
Total U.S.	57	43	100
104th Congress, 1995			
State delegates	1	1	2
Total U.S.	46	53	99
105th Congress, 1997			
State delegates	1	1	2
Total U.S.	45	55	100
106th Congress, 1999			
State delegates	1	1	2
Total U.S.	45	54	99

Figures are for starts of first sessions. Figure for U.S. Representatives for 101st Congress does not include Alabama and Indiana, which had vacancies. Figures for total U.S. Representatives for 102d, 103d, and 106th Congresses do not include Vermont, which had 1 Independent-Socialist. Figure for U.S. Representatives for 104th Congress does not include Vermont, which had 1 Independent-Socialist, and California, which had 1 vacancy. Figure for U.S. Representatives for 105th Congress does not include New York, which had 1 vacancy. Figure for U.S. Senators for 104th Congress does not include Oregon, which had 1 vacancy. Figure for U.S. Senators for 106th Congress does not include New Hampshire, which had 1 Independent.
Source: U.S. Congress; *Congressional Directory*, biennial.

Voter participation in presidential elections, 1992 and 1996

	1992	1996
State voting age pop.	600,000	647,000
Total U.S. voting age pop.	189,524,000	196,509,000
State share of U.S. total	0.3%	0.3%
Rank among states	44	44
Percent of state casting vote	68.4	56.6
Percent of U.S. total voting	55.1	49.0
Rank among states	4	11

Source: U.S. Bureau of the Census.

HEALTH AND MEDICAL CARE

Medicare, 1997

	Recipients	Payments
State	133,000	$496 mill.
Total U.S.	37,514,000	$206,064 mill.
State share	0.35%	0.24%
Rank among states	44	44

Recipient figures are rounded to nearest thousand persons. Ranks are from highest to lowest.
Source: U.S. Health Care Financing Administration.

Medicaid, 1996

	Recipients	Payments
State	101,000	$352 mill.
Total U.S.	35,028,000	$121,419 mill.
State share	0.29%	0.29%
Rank among states	43	42

Recipient figures are rounded to nearest thousand persons. Payment figures for fiscal year reflect federal and state contribution payments. Ranks are from highest to lowest.
Source: U.S. Health Care Financing Administration.

Health insurance coverage, 1996

	State	U.S.
Total persons covered	788,000	225,070,000
Total persons not covered	124,000	41,716,000
Part not covered	13.6%	15.6%
Rank among states	22	—
Children not covered	29,000	10,554,000
Part not covered	11.1%	14.8%
Rank among states	28	—

Ranks are from most to fewest uninsured. Population figures are rounded to nearest thousand persons.
Source: U.S. Bureau of the Census.

AIDS, syphilis, tuberculosis, and measles cases, 1997

Cases	U.S.	State	Share
AIDS	58,443	41	0.07%
Syphilis	8,550	NA	NA
Tuberculosis	18,534	17	0.09%
Measles	148,000	NA	NA

Measles figures are rounded to nearest thousand cases.
Source: U.S. Centers for Disease Control and Prevention.

HOUSING

Homeownership rates, 1985-1997

	1985	1990	1997
State	66.5%	69.1%	67.5%
Total U.S.	63.9%	63.9%	65.7%
Rank among states	33	13	31

Source: U.S. Bureau of the Census.

Home sales, 1990 and 1997
In thousands of units

Existing home sales	1990	1997	Change
State sales	12.7	14.9	2.2
Total U.S. sales	3,560	4,730	1,170
State share of U.S. total	0.36%	0.32%	-0.04%
Rank among states	41	40	—

Source: National Association of Realtors; *Real Estate Outlook: Market Trends and Insights.*

EDUCATION

Public school enrollment, 1995

State K-8 enrollment	116,000
Total U.S. K-8 enrollment	32,341,000
State share of total U.S.	0.36%
State 9-12 enrollment.	49,000
Total U.S. 9-12 enrollment	12,500,000
State share of U.S. total	0.39%
State public school enroll. rate	93.6%
Overall U.S. rate.	91.6%
Rank among states.	16

Enrollment figures (which include unclassified students) are rounded to nearest thousand pupils in fall term; kindergarten (K)-8 grade figures include some prekindergarten students. Enrollment rate is based on percentage of persons 5-17 years old. Rank is from highest to lowest.
Source: U.S. National Center for Education Statistics.

Public college finances, 1996

State FTE enrollment.	32,400
Total U.S. FTE enrollment	8,268,800
State share of total U.S.	0.39%
Rank among states.	41

State and local appropriations	$113,700,000
Total U.S. state and local appropriations.	$39,699 mill.
State share of total U.S..	0.29%
Rank among states.	47
State net tuition revenues	$76,900,000
Total U.S. net tuition	$18,348,100,000
State share of total U.S..	0.42%
Rank among states.	43

FTE=Full-time equivalent; credit and noncredit enrollment including summer session in academic year ending in 1996.
Enrollments are rounded to nearest thousand students. Net tuition revenues exclude appropriation to students attending in-state public institutions. Rankings are from highest shares to lowest.
Source: Research Associates of Washington.

TRANSPORTATION AND TRAVEL

Highway mileage, 1996

Interstate	1,190
Other arterial.	6,002
Collector roads	16,703
Local roads	46,207
Urban roads	2,420
Rural roads	67,389
Total state	69,809
U.S. total	3,933,985
State share	1.8%
Rank among states.	29

Source: U.S. Federal Highway Administration.

Motor vehicle registrations and driver licenses, 1996
In thousands

Vehicle registrations	State	U.S.	Share	Rank
Autos, trucks, buses	973	206,365	0.47%	41
Autos only	431	128,439	0.34%	44
Motorcycles	21	3,832	0.55%	41
Driver licenses	574	179,539	0.32%	41

Figures do not include vehicles owned by military services.
Source: U.S. Federal Highway Administration; *Highway Statistics; Selected Highway Statistics and Charts.*

Domestic travel expenditures, 1995

Spending by U.S. residents on overnight trips and day trips of at least 100 miles

Total expenditures in state . . . . $1,546 mill.
Total expenditures in U.S. . . . . $360,314 mill.
State share of total U.S. 0.43%
Rank among states. 42

Source: Travel Industry Association of America.

CRIME AND LAW ENFORCEMENT

State and local police officers, 1996

Local police 690
State police 212
Sheriffs 616
Total 1,682
Officers per 10,000 residents 19
U.S. average 25
Rank among states. 39

Figures cover full-time sworn officers; totals include special
police not shown separately.
Source: U.S. Bureau of Justice Statistics; *Census of State and
Local Law Enforcement Agencies, 1996.*

Crime rates, 1996

Rates per 100,000 resident population

Violent crimes	State	U.S.
Total violent	161	634
Murder	3.9	7.4
Forcible rape	27.1	36.1
Robbery	30	202
Aggravated assault	100	388
Property crimes		
Total property	4,333	4,445
Burglary	558	943
Larceny/theft	3,519	2,976
Motor vehicle theft	256	526
Totals	4,494	5,079

Crime counts are estimated due to incomplete data.
Source: U.S. Federal Bureau of Investigation; *Crime in the
United States,* annual.

State prison populations, 1980-1996

	State	U.S.	State share
1980	739	305,458	0.24%
1990	1,425	708,393	0.20%
1996	2,293	1,025,624	0.22%

Figures exclude prisoners in federal penitentiaries.
Source: U.S. Bureau of Justice Statistics.

Nebraska

Location: Midwestern continental United States

Area and rank: 76,644 square miles (198,508 square kilometers); 77,358 square miles (200,357 square kilometers) including water; fifteenth largest state in area

Population and rank: 1,656,870 (1997); thirty-eighth largest state in population

Capital: Lincoln

Largest city: Omaha (371,291 people in 1998)

Became territory: May 30, 1854

Entered Union and rank: March 1, 1867; thirty-seventh state

Present constitution adopted: October 12, 1875 (extensively amended 1919-1920)

Counties: 93

State name: "Nebraska" is derived from an Oto Indian word meaning "flat water"

State nicknames: Cornhusker State; Beef State

Motto: Equality before the law

State flag: Blue field with state seal in gold and silver

Highest point: Johnson Township — 5,424 feet (1,653 meters)

Lowest point: Missouri River — 840 feet (256 meters)

Highest recorded temperature: 118 degrees Fahrenheit (48 degrees Celsius) — Minden, 1936

Lowest recorded temperature: –47 degrees Fahrenheit (–44 degrees Celsius) — Camp Clarke, 1899

State song: "Beautiful Nebraska"

State tree: Cottonwood

State flower: Goldenrod

State bird: Western meadowlark

State capitol building in Lincoln. (P. Michael Whye/Department of Economic Development, Nebraska Division of Travel and Tourism)

Nebraska History

Nebraska's eastern and northeastern borders are defined by the Missouri River, across which lie Iowa to the east and South Dakota to the north. It is 462 miles across Nebraska to its extreme western border at the Wyoming state line. West and south of the state is Colorado. From the northern border at the South Dakota line to the southern border at the Kansas line is 210 miles. With a land mass of 77,358 square miles, Nebraska ranks sixteenth in size of the states, although, with 1,656,870 residents in 1997, it ranked thirty-eighth in population. In 1990, it had a population density of about twenty people per square mile.

Nebraska is considered one of the midwestern states, although it is at the western extreme of the Midwest. Its climate is semi-arid, with hot, dry summers and very cold winters. Because glaciers pushed topsoil into the area as they advanced south more than two million years ago, the soil, called till, is fertile. However, droughts sometimes lead to dust storms that blow away some of the richest topsoil from thousands of acres.

Early History. Human habitation of the Nebraska area is estimated to have begun more than ten thousand years ago. Ancestors of the bison roamed the plains, supplying settlers with food and fur, from which they fashioned clothing and shelters in the form of tepees. They used animal bones to make buttons and such instruments as knives.

The largest mammoth skeleton ever recovered

Contemporary illustration of Crazy Horse's Sioux riding from Camp Sheridan to surrender in 1877. (Library of Congress)

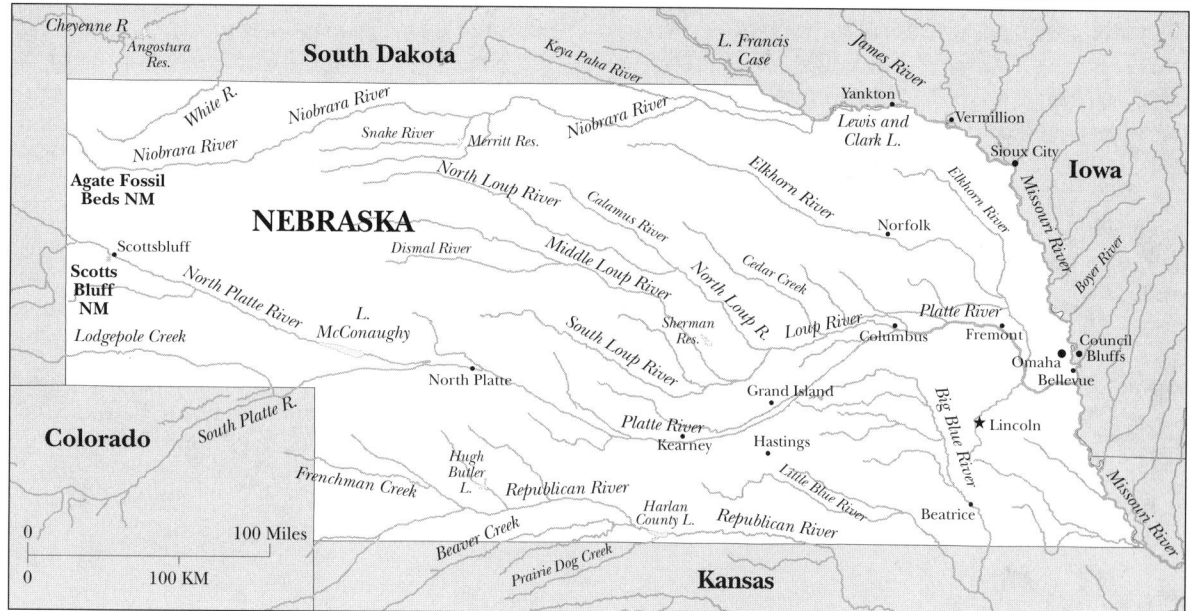

was found near North Platte. This animal, resembling an elephant, was nearly fourteen feet tall. When the Ice Age arrived more than two million years ago, many of these animals disappeared and eventually became extinct. At the end of the Ice Age, however, some animals, including bison and mammoths, survived, and the ancient people who lived in the area hunted them with spears. These people also farmed and made pottery.

By the 1500's, Native Americans, notably the Omaha, Oto, Pawnee, and Ponca, occupied the area, living in villages and raising crops of beans, corn, and squash. The Arapaho, Cheyenne, Comanche, and Sioux were more hunters than farmers. Living in tepees, they roved the plains hunting for animals, mostly bison. The largest Native American group at this time was the Pawnee.

Early European Exploration. Even before Europeans reached what is now Nebraska, Spanish explorers who had traveled to Texas, Oklahoma, Kansas, and Missouri had claimed for Spain all of the land they had visited and a great deal of land north and west of it that they had not seen. By 1541 both Francisco Vásquez de Coronado and Hernando de Soto had laid claim to much of this land for Spain.

In 1682 René-Robert Cavalier, sieur de La Salle, had claimed much of the same land for France,

naming the whole vast area between the Mississippi River and the Rocky Mountains Louisiana, in honor of King Louis XIV of France. It was not until 1803 that the United States, through the Louisiana Purchase, bought all of this land from France for fifteen million dollars.

Meanwhile, in 1714 Etienne Veniard de Bourgmont, a French explorer, made his way into the Missouri River Valley of Nebraska. Spanish forces were known to have been in the state in 1720, when they clashed with some of the natives, who soundly defeated them. Almost two decades later, in 1739, brothers Paul and Pierre Mallet crossed Nebraska, following the course of the Platte River.

The area was so sparsely populated that its development was slow. It was not until 1823 that the first white settlement was established at Bellevue on the Missouri River in the eastern part of the region. The United States Army had built Fort Atkinson on the Missouri's west bank four years earlier.

The Oregon Trail passed through Nebraska, so a steady stream of people who set out during the 1840's to seek their fortunes in the West passed through the area. These early travelers, however, had to keep moving because the government had designated Nebraska as an Indian territory and, at that time, would not permit further white settlement there.

The Homestead Act. By 1854 the federal government, in enacting the Kansas-Nebraska Act, made Kansas and Nebraska territories. Nebraska was now opened to anyone, mostly Europeans, who wished to settle there. In the same year, Omaha was founded.

The Homestead Act of 1862 gave families or any male over age twenty-one 160 acres of land that would become theirs after five years if they settled on it and improved it. This bonanza attracted so many people that by 1867 Nebraska had sufficient population numbers to justify statehood. With many of its residents still living on the prairie in sod houses, Nebraska became the thirty-seventh state in 1867. Lincoln became its capital. In 1871 the University of Nebraska was founded at Lincoln.

The Early Homesteaders. Life was not easy for most of the homesteaders who were given land in Nebraska. The winters were long and harsh. Driving winds howled outside as residents huddled in drafty homes, many of which had been fashioned from squares of sod cut from the prairie. Wood for stoves was scarce.

During the long winters, hungry animals, particularly wolves, roved the prairie looking for food and putting the settlers, especially small children, at risk. Until the late 1870's, there was the added threat of attacks by hostile American Indians, which subsided somewhat after the Sioux chief Crazy Horse surrendered at Fort Robinson, where he was murdered in 1877. These were difficult times for people living on the prairie.

Nebraska's largest city, Omaha. (PhotoDisc)

Water Problems. The eastern part of Nebraska always received more precipitation than the west, but droughts were common throughout the state, ruining agriculture. Permanent damage was done to the land as dust storms blew valuable topsoil away. A particularly devastating blizzard in 1888 resulted in the deaths of more than two hundred people in Nebraska. Floods in springtime plagued the areas along the Missouri and Platte Rivers.

It was not until late in the nineteenth century that Nebraska farmers began to irrigate their fields with water obtained from great reservoirs that had been constructed along the Platte. In 1895, largely at the instigation of the Populist Party that had been established three years earlier, the state set up a Board of Irrigation. In 1902 the U.S. government passed the Reclamation Act, which provided money for the development of irrigation projects.

Modern Nebraska faces significant water problems: On their way to Nebraska the state's rivers are siphoned by other states, depriving Nebraska of much-needed water. So great has been the problem that Nebraska has had to tap its aquifer, the subterranean water in porous rocks and gravel, that is not renewable. The use of pesticides and other agricultural chemicals has polluted much of Nebraska's water, including its aquifer.

Monument to the famous shelter for boys founded at Omaha in 1917. (Department of Economic Development, Nebraska Division of Travel and Tourism)

The Nebraska Economy. Nebraska is known for having had the lowest unemployment rate of any state in the United States for many years. During World War I, Nebraska farms supplied much of the food that the armed forces required, and 48,000 Nebraskans went off to serve their country in the war. Wheat and corn production was strong, as was the production of sorghum and soy beans. The state was prosperous until the late 1920's, when two coincident factors ruined the economy.

The stock market crash late in 1929 changed the economic picture all over the United States. Banks and businesses failed. People lost their life savings and their homes. Factories closed and armies of people were unemployed nationwide. Despite this economic chaos, farmers, who were usually self-sufficient, might have been expected to survive economically.

During the early 1930's, however, severe droughts plagued the Midwest, reducing farm production to all-time lows. Nebraska, like many other midwestern states, found itself hit hard by the Great Depression. In 1934 Nebraskans voted to establish a one-house legislature to speed up legislation and to cut costs. This unicameral system persisted.

More than sixty thousand desperate Nebraskans were forced by the economic meltdown to leave the state and find work elsewhere. By the end of the 1930's, Nebraska's weather had improved measurably, so farming again became profitable. War industries came into the state during World War II, bringing factory jobs. As rainfall increased substantially during the 1940's, farmers were again producing record crops.

The Move Away from Farms. After World War II, Nebraska's farms were bigger, but there were fewer of them. Many independent farmers sold their land and moved into cities and towns. Large agricultural corporations moved into the state, swallowing up small farms and turning agriculture into a much more specialized and scientific pursuit than it had once been. Omaha became a center for food processing. In 1953 the first frozen dinners in America were produced there.

By 1960 Nebraska had more city dwellers than rural inhabitants. By 1994 Omaha and Lincoln had only about a 2 percent unemployment rate. In the 1990's about half of Nebraska's work force of 800,000 were employed in sales or service occupations. Some 200,000 people were employed in sales and telemarketing, centered in Omaha. Another 200,000 worked as doctors, nurses, lawyers, bankers, insurance agents, automotive repair people, and other service personnel. The local, state, and federal governments offered employment to another 150,000. The state had one public school teacher for every fourteen students enrolled, which is much higher than the national average.

Despite the move to urban areas, Nebraska still has more than fifty thousand farms; farms and ranches occupy 90 percent of the state's land. In the western part of Nebraska, which is not suited to farming, the great grasslands provide excellent grazing for cattle, which are produced there in large numbers.

R. Baird Shuman

Nebraska Time Line

1541	Francisco Vásquez de Coronado claims America's Southwest, including present-day Nebraska, for Spain.
1682	René-Robert Cavalier, sieur de La Salle, claims all lands that drain into the Mississippi River, including modern Nebraska, for France.
1714	Etienne Veniard sails up the Missouri River to the Platte.
Aug. 13, 1720	Pawnee Indians defeat Spanish forces led by Pedro de Villasur.
1739	Paul and Pierre Mallet sail on the Missouri and Platte Rivers.
Apr. 30, 1803	United States buys the area that includes present-day Nebraska from France for fifteen million dollars in the Louisiana Purchase.
1806	Zebulon Pike visits south central Nebraska on his journey west.

1809	Manuel Lisa builds first trading posts along the Missouri River.
1813	Robert Stuart pioneers the Oregon Trail across Nebraska.
1819	Fort Atkinson is built.
1823	Bellevue, the first permanent non-Indian settlement in the area, is established as a trading post on the west bank of the Missouri River.
1843	Early travelers along the Oregon Trail pass through Nebraska, now designated an Indian territory.
May 30, 1854	Kansas-Nebraska Act establishes Kansas and Nebraska as territories.
1862	Congress passes the Homestead Act, increasing settlement in Nebraska and other parts of the Midwest.
1865	Union Pacific Railroad lays tracks west from Omaha.
Mar. 1, 1867	Nebraska becomes the thirty-seventh state.
1872	Nebraska initiates the nation's first Arbor Day to encourage the planting of trees on the prairie.
1877	Sioux Chief Crazy Horse surrenders at Fort Robinson.
1888	Huge blizzard kills more than two hundred Nebraskans.
1892	Populist Party is formed.
1895	Nebraska establishes Board of Irrigation.
1896	Nebraskan William Jennings Bryan runs unsuccessfully for president of the United States.
1902	Congress passes the Reclamation Act, providing money for irrigation.
1917	Near Omaha, Father Edward Flanagan begins shelter for boys that becomes Boys Town.
1917	United States enters World War I; 48,000 Nebraskans serve in armed forces.
1919	Law prohibits teaching of any subject in any foreign language; U.S. Supreme Court strikes it down in 1923.
1934	Nebraskans vote to have a unicameral state legislature, the only one in America.
1935	Severe dust storms turns state into "Great American Desert."
1939	Oil is discovered in southeastern Nebraska.
1941	United States enters World War II; 140,000 Nebraskans serve in armed forces.
1944	United States Congress approves Missouri River Basin Project.
1952	Missouri River floods devastate eastern Nebraska.
1953	First frozen dinner processed in Omaha.
1960	Census reveals more Nebraskans live in cities than in rural areas.
1967	Nebraska Department of Economic development is established to attract new industry into the state.
1974	Nebraska-born Gerald R. Ford becomes thirty-eighth president of the United States.
1982	Constitutional amendment passed prohibiting further corporate farming.
1986	Both the Republican and Democratic candidates for governor are women; Republican Kay Orr wins.

(continued)

1992	Omaha is telemarketing capital of the world.
1993	President Bill Clinton declares parts of Nebraska disaster areas after devastating Missouri River floods.
1994	Nebraska has record harvest of corn and soybeans.

Notes for Further Study

Published Sources. The most complete history of Nebraska is James C. Olson and Ronald C. Naugle's *History of Nebraska* (3d ed. 1997), which covers the history of the state from prehistoric times to the date of publication, offering valuable illustrations, maps, and statistical tables. It is especially strong in its presentation of the growth of the Populist movement in Nebraska. A less formal offering is Donald R. Hickey's *Nebraska Moments: Glimpses of Nebraska's Past* (1992). It provides insightful vignettes that help readers understand Nebraska's people, especially the homesteaders.

For information about Nebraska's Native Americans, one should turn to Mildred Mott Wedel's *The Wichita Indians, 1541-1750: Ethnohistorical Essays* (1988), which reproduces many essays relating to the state and its development. The dislocation of Nebraska's Indians is revealed in heart-rending terms in David J. Wishart's *An Unspeakable Sadness: The Dispossession of the Nebraska Indians* (1994). Donald Worster, in *Under Western Stars: A Nature and History of the American West* (1992), writes with feeling about its nature, prairies, and grasslands. *Dunwoody Pond: Reflections on the High Plains Wetlands and the Cultivation of Naturalists* (1994) by John Janovy, Jr., offers a well-considered ecological presentation that is nicely supplemented by Robert Hanna's *A Nebraska Portfolio* (1992), the pictures in which provide a sensitive visual record of the state. Juvenile readers should turn to *Nebraska* (1996), written by the publisher's geography department; to Dennis Brindell Fradin's *Nebraska* (1995); or to Kathleen Thompson's *Nebraska* (1996).

Web Resources. The Nebraska state government's Web site (http://www.state.ne.us) and its travel and tourism Web sites (http://www.travel.org/nebraska.html), (http://www.ded.state.ne.us/tourism.html) provide essential information about the state and its attractions. These sites also refer users to additional relevant sites, including the Western Nebraska Web site (http://www.westnebraska.com). The Nebraska City Web site (http://www.city.net/countries.united_states/nebraska) offers considerable information and statistics about Nebraska.

The Missouri River Web site (http://www.nps.gov/mnrr), frequently updated, gives information about the river, including flood warnings and information about irrigation projects. Omaha and Lincoln both have Web sites, (http://www.omaha.org and http://www.lincoln.org), that focus on their respective cities. The library systems of Omaha (http://www.omaha.lib.ne.us) and Lincoln (http://www.lcl.lib.ne.us) are both online. The Boys Town Web site (http://www.boystown.org) offers details about that establishment as well as pictures. The state's Department of Development has a Web site (http://www.ded.state.ne.us) that contains information about the state's economy, commerce, and trade. Related supplemental information is available on the Department of Labor's Web site (http://www.dol.state.ne.us).

Counties

County	Sq. miles	1996 pop.	County	Sq. miles	1996 pop.
Adams	563.4	29,698	Arthur	715.4	428
Antelope	857.1	7,453	Banner	746.3	859

South Dakota

DAWES
SIOUX
SHERIDAN
BOX BUTTE
SCOTTS BLUFF
MORRILL
BANNER
GARDEN
KIMBALL
CHEYENNE
DEUEL
KEITH
PERKINS
CHASE
HAYES
DUNDY
HITCHCOCK
RED WILLOW

CHERRY

NEBRASKA

GRANT HOOKER THOMAS BLAINE LOUP
ARTHUR McPHERSON LOGAN
CUSTER
North Platte
LINCOLN
FRONTIER
GOSPER
FURNAS HARLAN

KEYA PAHA BOYD
KNOX CEDAR DIXON
BROWN ROCK HOLT
DAKOTA
PIERCE WAYNE THURSTON
ANTELOPE
WHEELER STANTON
GARFIELD MADISON CUMING BURT
BOONE
GREELEY
VALLEY PLATTE COLFAX DODGE WASHINGTON
NANCE
SHERMAN HOWARD MERRICK POLK BUTLER DOUGLAS
SAUNDERS SARPY Omaha
DAWSON BUFFALO HALL HAMILTON YORK SEWARD Lincoln CASS
LANCASTER OTOE
PHELPS KEARNEY ADAMS CLAY FILLMORE SALINE JOHNSON NEMAHA
FRANKLIN NUCKOLLS JEFFERSON GAGE
WEBSTER THAYER PAWNEE RICHARDSON

Iowa

Colorado

Kansas

County	Sq. miles	1996 pop.	County	Sq. miles	1996 pop.
Blaine	710.8	651	Garden	1,704.6	2,242
Boone	686.7	6,536	Garfield	570.1	2,081
Box Butte	1,075.4	12,984	Gosper	458.2	2,256
Boyd	540.1	2,746	Grant	776.3	749
Brown	1,221.4	3,637	Greeley	569.9	2,969
Buffalo	968.1	40,037	Hall	546.4	51,485
Burt	492.8	7,944	Hamilton	543.7	9,245
Butler	583.6	8,623	Harlan	552.8	3,755
Cass	559.3	23,478	Hayes	713.1	1,136
Cedar	740.3	9,936	Hitchcock	710.1	3,401
Chase	894.5	4,265	Holt	2,412.8	12,163
Cherry	5,960.7	6,433	Hooker	721.2	707
Cheyenne	1,196.4	9,690	Howard	569.5	6,444
Clay	573.1	7,209	Jefferson	573.1	8,454
Colfax	413.2	10,388	Johnson	376.2	4,604
Cuming	572.0	10,126	Kearney	516.1	6,648
Custer	2,575.8	12,228	Keith	1,061.3	8,643
Dakota	264.0	18,528	Keya Paha	773.3	1,002
Dawes	1,396.3	9,086	Kimball	951.8	4,056
Dawson	1,012.9	23,126	Knox	1,108.2	9,387
Deuel	439.9	2,068	Lancaster	838.9	231,765
Dixon	476.4	6,337	Lincoln	2,564.2	33,619
Dodge	534.5	35,022	Logan	570.7	894
Douglas	331.0	438,835	Loup	569.7	698
Dundy	919.9	2,387	McPherson	859.0	565
Fillmore	576.5	6,871	Madison	572.6	34,702
Franklin	575.9	3,868	Merrick	484.6	8,149
Frontier	974.6	3,220	Morrill	1,423.9	5,376
Furnas	718.1	5,556	Nance	441.3	4,293
Gage	855.3	22,903	Nemaha	409.3	7,878

(continued)

County	Sq. miles	1996 pop.
Nuckolls	575.3	5,376
Otoe	615.9	14,515
Pawnee	431.7	3,261
Perkins	883.2	3,250
Phelps	540.0	9,995
Pierce	574.0	7,945
Platte	678.1	30,755
Polk	439.1	5,581
Red Willow	716.7	11,448
Richardson	553.5	9,689
Rock	1,008.5	1,807
Saline	575.4	12,988
Sarpy	240.7	116,271
Saunders	754.1	19,135
Scotts Bluff	739.3	36,679

County	Sq. miles	1996 pop.
Seward	574.8	16,194
Sheridan	2,441.2	6,645
Sherman	565.9	3,574
Sioux	2,066.7	1,509
Stanton	429.9	6,195
Thayer	574.6	6,418
Thomas	712.9	824
Thurston	393.8	7,274
Valley	568.1	4,850
Washington	390.5	18,175
Wayne	443.5	9,517
Webster	574.9	4,037
Wheeler	575.2	957
York	575.7	14,707

Source: U.S. Census Bureau; National Association of Counties.

Cities
With 10,000 or more residents

Rank	City	Population
1	Omaha	371,291
2	Lincoln	213,088

Rank	City	Population
3	Bellevue	44,047
4	Grand Island	41,392

Rank	City	Population	Rank	City	Population
5	Kearney	27,968	12	Scottsbluff	14,294
6	Fremont	24,429	13	Beatrice	12,376
7	Norfolk	23,476	14	La Vista	11,864
8	North Platte	23,307	15	South Sioux City	11,415
9	Hastings	21,356			
10	Columbus	20,898			
11	Papillion	20,603			

Population figures are estimated for mid-1998.
Source: U.S. Bureau of the Census.

Index to Tables

NA = Reliable data are not available.

DEMOGRAPHICS

Resident state and national populations, 1970-1997

Population figures given in thousands

	State pop.	U.S. pop.	Share	Rank
1970	1,485	203,302	0.7%	35
1980	1,570	226,546	0.7%	35
1985	1,585	237,924	0.7%	36
1990	1,578	248,765	0.6%	36
1995	1,636	262,761	0.6%	37
1997	1,657	267,636	0.6%	38

Source: U.S. Bureau of the Census.

Resident population by age, 1997

Age group	Total population
Under 5 years	114,000
5 to 17 years	330,000
18 to 24 years	164,000
25 to 34 years	218,000
35 to 44 years	264,000
45 to 54 years	203,000
55 to 64 years	135,000
65 to 74 years	116,000
75 to 84 years	79,000
85 years and over	33,000
Portion of residents 65 and older	13.7%
National average	12.7%

Population figures are rounded to nearest thousand persons;
figures include armed forces personnel stationed in state.
Source: U.S. Bureau of the Census.

Resident population by race, Hispanic origin, 1997

	State pop.	Share	U.S.
All residents	1,657,000	100.0%	100.0%
Hispanic white	62,000	3.7%	10.0%
non-Hispanic white	1,493,000	90.1%	72.7%
African American	66,000	4.0%	12.7%
Native American	15,000	0.9%	0.9%
Asian, Pacific Islander	21,000	1.3%	3.8%

Source: U.S. Bureau of the Census.

Projections of state population, 2000-2025

	Model A Uses interstate migration observed from 1975-1994	Model B Uses Bureau of Economic Analysis employment projections
Year	Population	Population
2000	1,705,000	1,700,000
2005	1,761,000	1,766,000
2010	1,806,000	1,837,000
2015	1,850,000	1,912,000
2020	1,892,000	1,984,000
2025	1,930,000	2,050,000

All population projections, including those for 2000, were calculated in 1997.
Source: U.S. Bureau of the Census, Population Paper Listings PPL-47.

VITAL STATISTICS

Average lifetime in years by race, 1989-1991

	State	U.S.	Rank
All residents	76.92	75.37	7
White residents	77.21	76.13	8
Black residents	NA	69.16	NA

Ranks are from longest-lived to least longest-lived. Ranks exclude Alaska, for which reliable data are not available. Rank for black residents is based on the 32 states for which reliable data are available.
Source: U.S. National Center for Health Statistics.

Infant mortality rates, 1980 and 1995

	State	U.S.
All residents		
1980	11.5	12.6
1995	7.4	7.6
White residents		
1980	10.7	11.0
1995	7.3	6.3
Black residents		
1980	25.2	21.4
1995	NA	15.1

Figures represent deaths per 1,000 live births of resident infants under 1 year old, exclusive of fetal deaths; all-residents figures include other races not listed separately.
Source: U.S. National Center for Health Statistics.

Marriages and divorces

Marriages in 1996.	12,800
Rate per 1,000 population, 1995.	7.4
U.S. rate, 1995	8.9
Rank among all states	39
Divorces in 1996	6,100
Rate per 1,000 population, 1995.	3.8
U.S. rate, 1995	4.4
Rank among all states	34

Rank is from highest to lowest in country.
Source: U.S. National Center for Health Statistics.

Death rates by leading causes, 1995
Deaths per 100,000 resident population

Cause	State	U.S.
Heart disease	312.0	280.7
Cancer	206.2	204.9
Cerebrovascular diseases	71.2	60.1
Accidents and adverse effects	35.2	35.5
Motor vehicle accidents	15.5	16.5
Chronic obstructive pulmonary diseases	44.6	39.2
Diabetes mellitus	17.5	22.6
HIV	-	NA
Suicide	11.4	11.9
Homicide	-	8.7
All causes	932.6	880.0
Rank in overall death rate among states		17

Figures exclude nonresidents who die in state. Causes of death follow International Classification of Diseases. Rank is from highest to lowest in country.
Source: U.S. National Center for Health Statistics.

ECONOMY

Gross state product, 1990-1996
In current dollars

	State product	Increase
1990	$33.2 billion	
1993	$38.4 billion	
1994	$42.1 billion	9.64%
1995	$43.7 billion	3.80%
1996	$47.2 billion	8.01%

Source: U.S. Bureau of Economic Analysis; Survey of Current Business, June, 1998.

Gross state product by industry, 1996
In billions

Farms, forestry, fisheries	$3.7
Construction	1.8
Manufacturing	6.6
Transportation, public utilities.	4.9
Wholesale trade.	3.3
Retail trade	3.8
Finance, insurance, real estate	5.9
Services	7.0
Government.	6.0
State total	$43.2
Total U.S.	$6,923.8
State share	0.62%
Rank among states	36

Total figures include mining, not listed separately.
Source: U.S. Bureau of Economic Analysis; Survey of Current Business, June, 1998.

Personal income per capita, 1990 and 1997
In current dollars

	1990	1997
Per capita income	$17,562	$23,803
U.S. average	$19,188	$25,598
Rank among states	26	27

1997 data are preliminary.
Source: U.S. Bureau of Economic Analysis; Survey of Current Business, May, 1998.

Energy consumption, 1995
In trillions of British thermal units (BTU)

End-use sectors

Residential	133.0
Commercial	120.1
Industrial	159.6
Transportation	167.6

Sources of energy

Petroleum	218.5
Natural gas	133.7
Coal	179.5
Hydroelectric power.	14.7
Nuclear electric power	79.8
Total state per capita consumption	354.0
Total U.S. per capita consumption	344.4
Rank among states.	23
Total state energy consumption	580.3
Total U.S. energy consumption	90,547.4
State share of U.S. total	0.64%
Rank among states.	37

Total figures include items not listed separately.
Source: U.S. Energy Information Administration; State Energy Data Report.

Nonfarm employment by sectors, 1997

Total	856,000
Construction	39,000
Manufacturing.	116,000
Transportation, public utilities.	53,000
Wholesale trade, retail trade	210,000
Finance, insurance, real estate	55,000
Services	229,000
Government	153,000

Figures are rounded to nearest thousand persons. Total includes mining, not listed separately.
Source: U.S. Bureau of Labor Statistics; Employment and Earnings, monthly.

Foreign exports, 1990-1997
In millions of dollars

Year	State	U.S.	State share
1990	693	394,045	0.18%
1996	1,907	624,767	0.31%
1997	1,971	688,896	0.29%

Source: U.S. Bureau of the Census; U.S. Merchandise Trade, series FT 900.

LAND USE

Federally owned land, 1996

	State	U.S.	State share
Total acres	49,032,000	2,271,343,000	2.16%
Federally owned	515,000	563,129,000	0.09%
Federal share	1.1%	24.8%	—

Areas are rounded to nearest thousand acres. Figures for federally owned land do not include trust properties.

Source: U.S. General Services Administration; *Inventory Report on Real Property Owned by the United States Throughout the World*, annual.

Land use, 1992
In acres, rounded to nearest thousand

Total surface area	49,507,000
Federal land	739,000
Total nonfederal	48,137,000
Developed	1,252,000
Total rural	46,885,000
Cropland	19,239,000
Pasture land	2,066,000
Range land	22,669,000
Forest land	777,000
Minor cover/use	2,135,000

Total surface area figures include water area not shown separately.

Source: U.S. Dept. of Agriculture; Soil Conservation Service; Iowa State University, Statistical Laboratory; *Summary Report, 1992 National Resources Inventory*.

Farms and crop acreage, 1997

	State	U.S.	Share	Rank
Farms (thousands)	55	2,058	2.67%	15
Acres (millions)	47	968	4.86%	4
Acres per farm	855	471	—	10
Acres planted	19,121	334,139	5.72%	7
Acres harvested	18,696	319,894	5.84%	7
Farm value (mill.)	$4,873	$108,805	4.48%	42

Numbers of farms are rounded to nearest thousand.

Source: U.S. Dept. of Agriculture; National Agricultural Statistics Service.

GOVERNMENT AND FINANCE

Units of local government, 1997

	State	Total U.S.	Rank
All local governments	2,894	87,453	12
Counties	93	3,043	10
Municipalities	535	19,372	13
Townships	455	16,629	13
School districts	681	13,726	5
Special districts	1,130	34,683	10

County ranks are based on the 48 states with county governments; township ranks are based on the 20 states with township governments; school district ranks are based on the 46 states with such districts.

Source: U.S. Bureau of the Census; *1997 Census of Governments, Government Organization*, Series GC97(1).

State government revenue, 1996

Total revenue	$4,999 mill.
General revenue	4,536 mill.
Per capita	2,751
U.S. per capita average	2,910
Rank among states	31
Intergovernmental revenue	
Total	$1,190 mill.
From federal government	1,164 mill.
From local government	26 mill.
Charges and Miscellaneous	
Total	$977 mill.
Current charges	640 mill.
Misc. general revenue	337 mill.
Taxes	
Total	$2,369 mill.
General sales	815 mill.
Selective sales	410 mill.
License taxes	158 mill.
Individual income	840 mill.
Corporate income	127 mill.
Other	20 mill.
Insurance trust revenue	463 mill.

Total revenue figures include items not listed separately.

Source: U.S. Bureau of the Census.

State government expenditures, 1996

General expenditures
Intergovernmental	$1,176 mill.
Direct expenditures	3,144 mill.
Total	4,320 mill.

Selected direct expenditures
Education	$1,514 mill.
Public welfare	976 mill.
Health, hospital	503 mill.
Highways	574 mill.
Police	43 mill.
Corrections	94 mill.
Natural resources	130 mill.
Parks and recreation	21 mill.
Government administration	119 mill.
Interest on debt	85 mill.

Other
State per capita expenditures	$2,620
U.S. per capita average	2,854
Rank among states	31
Total state expenditures	4,490 mill.
Total U.S. expenditures	859,959 mill.

Totals include items not listed separately.
Source: U.S. Bureau of the Census.

POLITICS

Governors since statehood
D = Democrat; R = Republican; O = other;
(r) resigned; (d) died in office; (i) removed from office

David Butler (R)	(i) 1867-1871
William H. James (R)	1871-1873
Robert W. Furnas (R)	1873-1875
Silas Garber (R)	1875-1879
Albinus Nance (R)	1879-1883
James W. Dawes (R)	1883-1887
John M. Thayer (R)	1887-1891
James E. Boyd (D)	(i) 1891
John M. Thayer (R)	(i) 1891-1892
James E. Boyd (D)	1892-1893
Lorenzo Crounse (R)	1893-1895
Silas A. Holcomb (O)	1895-1899
William A. Poynter (O)	1899-1901
Charles H. Dietrich (R)	(r) 1901
Ezra P. Savage (R)	1901-1903
John H. Mickey (R)	1903-1907
George L. Sheldon (R)	1907-1909
Ashton C. Shallenberger (D)	1909-1911
Chester H. Aldrich (R)	1911-1913
John H. Morehead (D)	1913-1917
Keith Neville (D)	1917-1919
Samuel R. McKelvie (R)	1919-1923
Charles W. Bryan (D)	1923-1925
Adam McMullen (R)	1925-1929
Arthur J. Weaver (R)	1929-1931
Charles W. Bryan (D)	1931-1935
Robert L. Cochran (D)	1935-1941
Dwight P. Griswold (R)	1941-1947
Frederick Val Peterson (R)	1947-1953
Robert B. Crosby (R)	1953-1955
Victor E. Anderson (R)	1955-1959
Ralph G. Brooks (D)	(d) 1959-1960
Dwight W. Burney (R)	1960-1961
Frank B. Morrison (D)	1961-1967
Norbert T. Tiemann (R)	1967-1971
John James Exon (D)	1971-1979
Charles Thone (R)	1979-1983
Robert Kerrey (D)	1983-1987
Kay A. Orr (R)	1987-1991
Ben Nelson (D)	1991-1999
Mike Johanns (R)	1999-

Composition of state legislature, 1990-1998

Nebraska has a unicameral legislature of 49 members who are elected without party affiliations.

Source: Council of State Governments; *State Elective Officials and the Legislatures.*

Composition of congressional delegations, 1989-1999

	Dem	Rep	Total
House of Representatives			
101st Congress, 1989			
State delegates	1	2	3
Total U.S.	259	174	433
102d Congress, 1991			
State delegates	1	2	3
Total U.S.	267	167	434
103d Congress, 1993			
State delegates	1	2	3
Total U.S.	258	176	434
104th Congress, 1995			
State delegates	0	3	3
Total U.S.	197	236	433
105th Congress, 1997			
State delegates	0	3	3
Total U.S.	206	228	434

	Dem	Rep	Total
106th Congress, 1999			
State delegates	0	3	3
Total U.S.	211	222	433

Senate			
101st Congress, 1989			
State delegates	2	0	2
Total U.S.	55	45	100
102d Congress, 1991			
State delegates	2	0	2
Total U.S.	56	44	100
103d Congress, 1993			
State delegates	2	0	2
Total U.S.	57	43	100
104th Congress, 1995			
State delegates	1	1	2
Total U.S.	46	53	99
105th Congress, 1997			
State delegates	1	1	2
Total U.S.	45	55	100
106th Congress, 1999			
State delegates	1	1	2
Total U.S.	45	54	99

Figures are for starts of first sessions. Figure for U.S. Representatives for 101st Congress does not include Alabama and Indiana, which had vacancies. Figures for total U.S. Representatives for 102d, 103d, and 106th Congresses do not include Vermont, which had 1 Independent-Socialist. Figure for U.S. Representatives for 104th Congress does not include Vermont, which had 1 Independent-Socialist, and California, which had 1 vacancy. Figure for U.S. Representatives for 105th Congress does not include New York, which had 1 vacancy. Figure for U.S. Senators for 104th Congress does not include Oregon, which had 1 vacancy. Figure for U.S. Senators for 106th Congress does not include New Hampshire, which had 1 Independent.
Source: U.S. Congress; *Congressional Directory,* biennial.

Voter participation in presidential elections, 1992 and 1996

	1992	1996
State voting age pop.	1,164,000	1,208,000
Total U.S. voting age pop.	189,524,000	196,509,000
State share of U.S. total	0.6%	0.6%
Rank among states	37	37
Percent of state casting vote	63.4	45.9
Percent of U.S. total voting	55.1	49.0
Rank among states	15	42

Source: U.S. Bureau of the Census.

HEALTH AND MEDICAL CARE

Medicare, 1997

	Recipients	Payments
State	251,000	$1,030 mill.
Total U.S.	37,514,000	$206,064 mill.
State share	0.67%	0.50%
Rank among states	35	36

Recipient figures are rounded to nearest thousand persons. Ranks are from highest to lowest.
Source: U.S. Health Care Financing Administration.

Medicaid, 1996

	Recipients	Payments
State	191,000	$678 mill.
Total U.S.	35,028,000	$121,419 mill.
State share	0.55%	0.56%
Rank among states	36	37

Recipient figures are rounded to nearest thousand persons. Payment figures for fiscal year reflect federal and state contribution payments. Ranks are from highest to lowest.
Source: U.S. Health Care Financing Administration.

Health insurance coverage, 1996

	State	U.S.
Total persons covered	1,483,000	225,070,000
Total persons not covered	190,000	41,716,000
Part not covered	11.4%	15.6%
Rank among states	35	—
Children not covered	46,000	10,554,000
Part not covered	9.8%	14.8%
Rank among states	34	—

Ranks are from most to fewest uninsured. Population figures are rounded to nearest thousand persons.
Source: U.S. Bureau of the Census.

AIDS, syphilis, tuberculosis, and measles cases, 1997

Cases	U.S.	State	Share
AIDS	58,443	91	0.16%
Syphilis	8,550	5	0.06%
Tuberculosis	18,534	22	0.12%
Measles	148,000	NA	NA

Measles figures are rounded to nearest thousand cases.
Source: U.S. Centers for Disease Control and Prevention.

HOUSING

Homeownership rates, 1985-1997

	1985	1990	1997
State	68.5%	67.3%	66.7%
Total U.S.	63.9%	63.9%	65.7%
Rank among states	21	27	35

Source: U.S. Bureau of the Census.

Home sales, 1990 and 1997
In thousands of units

Existing home sales	1990	1997	Change
State sales	19.3	23.4	4.1
Total U.S. sales	3,560	4,730	1,170
State share of U.S. total	0.54%	0.49%	-0.05%
Rank among states	38	37	—

Source: National Association of Realtors; *Real Estate Outlook: Market Trends and Insights.*

EDUCATION

Public school enrollment, 1995

State K-8 enrollment	203,000
Total U.S. K-8 enrollment	32,341,000
State share of total U.S.	0.63%
State 9-12 enrollment.	87,000
Total U.S. 9-12 enrollment	12,500,000
State share of U.S. total	0.70%
State public school enroll. rate	88.6%
Overall U.S. rate.	91.6%
Rank among states. 39

Enrollment figures (which include unclassified students) are rounded to nearest thousand pupils in fall term; kindergarten (K)-8 grade figures include some prekindergarten students. Enrollment rate is based on percentage of persons 5-17 years old. Rank is from highest to lowest.
Source: U.S. National Center for Education Statistics.

Public college finances, 1996

State FTE enrollment.	67,500
Total U.S. FTE enrollment	8,268,800
State share of total U.S.	0.82%
Rank among states.	35

State and local appropriations	$308 mill.
Total U.S. state and local appropriations.	$39,699 mill.
State share of total U.S.	0.78%
Rank among states.	36
State net tuition revenues	$120,500,000
Total U.S. net tuition	$18,348,100,000
State share of total U.S.	0.66%
Rank among states.	39

FTE=Full-time equivalent; credit and noncredit enrollment including summer session in academic year ending in 1996.
Enrollments are rounded to nearest thousand students. Net tuition revenues exclude appropriation to students attending in-state public institutions. Rankings are from highest shares to lowest.
Source: Research Associates of Washington.

TRANSPORTATION AND TRAVEL

Highway mileage, 1996

Interstate	480
Other arterial.	7,901
Collector roads	21,183
Local roads	63,651
Urban roads	5,121
Rural roads	87,684
Total state	92,805
U.S. total	3,933,985
State share	2.4%
Rank among states.	19

Source: U.S. Federal Highway Administration.

Motor vehicle registrations and driver licenses, 1996
In thousands

Vehicle registrations	State	U.S.	Share	Rank
Autos, trucks, buses	1,479	206,365	0.72%	35
Autos only	797	128,439	0.62%	35
Motorcycles	18	3,832	0.47%	42
Driver licenses	1,160	179,539	0.65%	35

Figures do not include vehicles owned by military services.
Source: U.S. Federal Highway Administration; *Highway Statistics; Selected Highway Statistics and Charts.*

Domestic travel expenditures, 1995

Spending by U.S. residents on overnight trips and day trips of at least 100 miles

Total expenditures in state . . . . $2,058 mill.
Total expenditures in U.S. . . . . $360,314 mill.
State share of total U.S. 0.57%
Rank among states. 38

Source: Travel Industry Association of America.

CRIME AND LAW ENFORCEMENT

State and local police officers, 1996

Local police 1,929
State police 464
Sheriffs 794
Total 3,297
Officers per 10,000 residents 20
U.S. average 25
Rank among states. 36

Figures cover full-time sworn officers; totals include special police not shown separately.
Source: U.S. Bureau of Justice Statistics; *Census of State and Local Law Enforcement Agencies, 1996.*

Crime rates, 1996

Rates per 100,000 resident population

Violent crimes	State	U.S.
Total violent	435	634
Murder	2.9	7.4
Forcible rape	27.1	36.1
Robbery	64	202
Aggravated assault	341	388

Property crimes		
Total property	4,002	4,445
Burglary	615	943
Larceny/theft	3,046	2,976
Motor vehicle theft	342	526
Totals	4,437	5,079

Source: U.S. Federal Bureau of Investigation; *Crime in the United States,* annual.

State prison populations, 1980-1996

	State	U.S.	State share
1980	1,446	305,458	0.47%
1990	2,403	708,393	0.34%
1996	3,287	1,025,624	0.32%

Figures exclude prisoners in federal penitentiaries.
Source: U.S. Bureau of Justice Statistics.

Nevada

Location: Western continental United States

Area and rank: 109,806 square miles (284,397 square kilometers); 110,567 square miles (286,369 square kilometers) including water; seventh largest state in area

Population and rank: 1,676,809 (1997); thirty-seventh largest state in population

Capital: Carson City

Largest city: Las Vegas (404,288 people in 1998)

State capitol building in Carson City. (Nevada Commission on Tourism)

Became territory: March 2, 1861

Entered Union and rank: October 31, 1864; thirty-sixth state

Present constitution adopted: 1864

Counties: 16, as well as 1 independent city

State name: "Nevada" is the Spanish word for "snowcapped"

State nicknames: Sagebrush State; Silver State; Battle Born State

Motto: All for Our Country

State flag: Cobalt field with silver star and the name "Nevada" above sagebrush in the upper left, with legend "Battle Born" on a scroll above

Highest point: Boundary Peak — 13,140 feet (4,005 meters)

Lowest point: Colorado River — 479 feet (146 meters)

Highest recorded temperature: 122 degrees Fahrenheit (50 degrees Celsius) — Overton, 1954

Lowest recorded temperature: –50 degrees Fahrenheit (–46 degrees Celsius) — San Jacinto, 1937

State song: "Home Means Nevada"

State trees: Single-leaf pinon; Bristlecone pine

State flower: Sagebrush

State bird: Mountain bluebird

State fish: Lahontan cutthroat trout

State animal: Desert bighorn sheep

National park: Great Basin

Nevada History

Nevada is mostly arid, its desert terrain broken up by a series of mountain ranges. Part of the Great Basin region, it lies between Utah to the east and California to the west. Nevada's geography has deeply influenced nearly every principal aspect of its economy and society. Nevada's history would hardly have been the same without its laws, all influenced by geography, governing gambling, personal and corporate taxation, and marriage and divorce—even prostitution, which, unique among American states, it permits in sparsely populated counties.

The role of the state's geography is most apparent in that, unlike its neighbors, especially California, Nevada has few natural hospitable areas for human settlement. The proximity of populous, wealthy California, however, provides an abundant source of tourism. This fact gave legalized gambling in Nevada an irresistible appeal. Gambling revenues, in turn, allow the state to dispense with state income tax, which now helps to persuade large numbers of retirees, many of them Californians, to settle in the state, especially in the Las Vegas area.

Nevada has had incredible wealth beneath its surface, though virtually all of its mining bonanzas have turned to busts, at least temporarily. Even with the precious metals and other minerals in the state, Nevada's population did not exceed one million until the 1980's; at the end of the twentieth century its population still totaled fewer than two million.

Early History. Human society in Nevada extends as much as ten thousand years into the past. Before the arrival of white settlers, American Indian peoples, including the Shoshone, Northern Paiute, and Washoe tribes, inhabited the region. In the eighteenth century, Spanish explorers were the first Europeans to visit the area. Spanish interest in the territory waned, however, after the report of Father Francisco Silvestre Vélez de Escalante, who accompanied an expedition, commented negatively on the area's steep, dry character.

By the early nineteenth century, Canadian and American explorers had arrived. Some were seeking animal furs, and others, such as John C. Frémont in the 1840's, led scientific expeditions. Frémont's systematic research of the area and reports on his findings provided the federal government with its first systematic account of the region and stimulated interest in the West among easterners. However, the harsh terrain was inhospitable to settlers, and those who passed through Nevada's deserts and mountains were usually on their way to kinder environs. One of the immigrant parties that crossed Nevada was the Donner party, which in 1846-1847 became snowbound while attempting to cross the Sierra Nevada Mountains west of Reno, and resorted to cannibalism to survive.

There appear to have been fewer conflicts between settlers and American Indians than in neighboring territories. The settler population was sparse and grouped in only a few locations, so that contacts with American Indians were fewer. That did not mean there was no conflict, however. For example, in 1855, when Mormons arrived in Las Vegas (Spanish for "the meadows") to convert Paiute Indians and supply travelers on their way to Salt Lake City from the Pacific, they found themselves attacked by American Indian raiding parties. Three years later, they abandoned their adobe fort.

In the 1870's, in accordance with federal American Indian policy, reservations were established, the largest of which were the Pyramid Lake Reservation north of Reno, and the Walker River Reservation southeast of Reno. These and a number of other smaller reservations, numbering fewer than a dozen, are scattered around the state.

From Territory to State. The United States acquired the land of modern Nevada, along with other territory, in 1848, after the signing of the Treaty of Guadalupe Hidalgo ended the Mexican-American War. In 1850, when New Mexico and Utah were established as territories, Nevada's land was incorporated into the new Utah Territory, administered from Salt Lake City by the Mormon regime.

Those seeking their fortunes in the gold fields of California undertook the first great trek through Nevada in 1849-1850. Their numbers led to the first white settlement in present Nevada, when Mormons from Salt Lake City established Mormon Station (later called Genoa), southeast of Carson City. The establishment was obliged to close in 1857, when Mormon leader Brigham Young recalled them, fearful of an attack by U.S. Army troops during a dispute with the federal government. Young had proposed a new state to be formed called "Deseret" but was turned down in Washington. Non-Mormons who flocked to the area two years later, who generally opposed living under Mormon rule, tried to set up a provisional territorial government, but Washington also refused to recognize this arrangement.

Miners began pouring into Nevada in 1859, when a rich silver lode was discovered, according to one story, by siblings Ethan and Hosea Grosh near Virginia City but credited to Henry Tompkins Comstock, who assumed the brothers' claims after they mysteriously died. This strike, which resulted in the extraction of some $400 million in silver, brought thousands of adventurers into Comstock and the surrounding area. Nearby Virginia City became the site's de facto capital, scene of fabulous luxury as well as lawless behavior, as fantastic fortunes were extracted from the ground. Among the invaders from California was the young Samuel Clemens, better known later as Mark Twain, who had become a reporter for Virginia City's *Territorial Enterprise*. Twain chronicled the raucous life of the era in his book *Roughing It* (1872). By the 1870's, however, wasteful mining methods and the demonetization of silver by the U.S. government, which lowered its price, combined to diminish the silver rush, and by 1898, Comstock was all but abandoned.

Although settlers were unsuccessful in their first attempt at establishing a territory, events were moving in their favor. Lawlessness needed to be curbed, but, perhaps more important, the Civil War looming early in 1861 inclined Washington to ensure the loyalty of the West. Accordingly, Nevada became a territory in 1861. The next step to statehood was the writing of a constitution. After voters rejected a first constitution in 1863, a second version—this time without objectionable mining taxes—was accepted the following year. Although the territory was unqualified for statehood because its population was too small (6,857 in 1860), Presi-

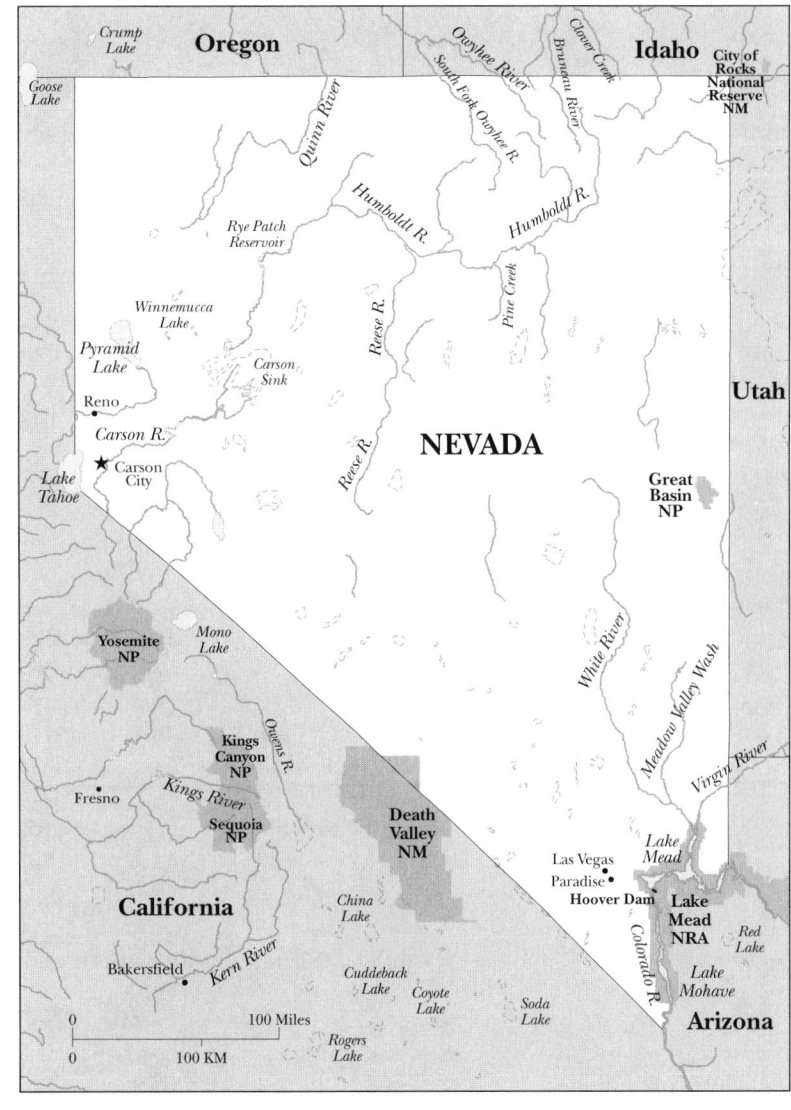

One of the most prosperous cities of the Far West during Nevada's nineteenth century silver boom, Virginia City is now little more than a curiosity for tourists. (Nevada Commission on Tourism)

dent Abraham Lincoln needed votes in the Senate to pass constitutional amendments and was anxious to add more. Accordingly, the entire text of the new constitution was sent to Washington for approval in the longest telegram up to then ever sent, at the astronomical cost of $3,416.77. The territory was made a state in 1864.

The formal institutions of government followed the lead of other states in splitting executive powers into a number of elective offices. This policy had the effect of keeping power out of the hands of a single chief executive, and it reflected traditional American, especially Western, distrust of executives, whether kings or presidents. The legislature is bicameral. Five justices sit on the Supreme Court of Nevada, all elected to six-year staggered terms. Nine district courts, with thirty-five district judges serving six-year terms, and a series of municipal courts, complete the judicial system.

Economy and Society. Life in the new state improved by the arrival in 1868 of a transcontinental railroad, a more satisfactory communications link than the Pony Express. In the 1870's the economy went sour when the nation turned to the gold standard and silver was no longer used in coins. Cattle and sheep ranching now assumed prominence in

the state's economy. Mining in the state revived after 1900 with new gold, silver, and copper discoveries. Moreover, the mining boom stimulated railroad building. In 1905 the Union Pacific Railroad constructed tracks from Salt Lake City to Los Angeles through Las Vegas. Prosperity had its dark side, too, as early in the century violent strikes took place, pitting workers against mining companies.

Mining boomed again when the nation entered World War I in 1917, but after the war demand fell off and declined in the 1920's. When the Depression came in 1930, to stimulate the economy the state legalized gambling, which had been outlawed since 1909. To attract more visitors, it also relaxed marriage and divorce laws, in time making a "Nevada divorce" a household term. Mining revived once more in the late 1930's and 1940's, as federal spending for war materiel increased.

Postwar Developments. After World War II society and the economy in Nevada changed dramatically. Contrary to some expectations, the demand for minerals remained high in the postwar years. Next, big-time gambling was inaugurated with the opening in Las Vegas of the Flamingo Hotel, built and financed by organized crime. By the mid-1950's dozens of large casinos had opened in Las Vegas and Reno, drawing gamblers and vacationers from throughout the nation with headline entertainment and inexpensive food and accommodations.

Last, the federal government dramatically increased spending in the state, opening an Air Force base north of Las Vegas and a bombing range, including a site for testing atomic weapons. In addition, irrigation projects brought water to make the desert bloom. By the 1980's a controversy had broken out between the state and the federal government, which owns nearly 80 percent of the state's domain, over use of federal land for storing atomic waste. In the 1990's the state lost key court decisions over the matter, and the federal government began creating storage facilities for nuclear waste.

Recreational Mecca. In the 1960's, the threat of organized crime to the state's gaming industry led Nevada to change its laws, allowing public companies to open casinos in the state. The advent of well-financed commercial gaming in the state was to revolutionize the industry. Gamblers, some of them very rich, began to arrive from all over the world. By the 1980's and 1990's casinos had adopted a policy of attracting families, and the tourist industry expanded significantly. Reno and neighboring Lake Tahoe prospered, and Las Vegas became an international center of postmodern architecture. Its cavernous casino-hotels, some de-signed with a touch of whimsy, often made thematic reference to lost civilizations such as ancient Egypt and Rome, or to contemporary cities such as New York and Paris.

The state also attracts increasing numbers of retirees. Las Vegas in particular, with its mild winter climate and proximity to Southern California, became a mecca for retirees. Other factors attracting retirees and others was housing made inexpensive by an inexhaustible supply of cheap land stretching endlessly into the desert, and the absence of a state income tax, made unnecessary by gambling revenues.

Charles F. Bahmueller

Nevada Time Line

1775   Spanish missionary Francisco Garces is the first white person to enter Nevada.

1826   Explorer and fur trader Jedediah Smith leads a party across southern Nevada and recrosses the
            region while returning east the following year.

(continued)

Completion of Hoover Dam in 1936 harnessed the Colorado River waters, which are vital to the Southwest, and created Nevada's Lake Mead. (Nevada Commission on Tourism)

c. 1830	Fur trader Peter S. Ogden discovers Humboldt River in northeastern Nevada.
1843-1846	Explorer John C. Frémont with scout Kit Carson leads three exploratory expeditions through Nevada.
1848	Nevada and other lands are acquired from Mexico by the United States through the Treaty of Guadalupe Hidalgo.
1849	Thousands of speculators cross northern Nevada on their way to the California gold fields near Sacramento.
1849	Mormon Station (later Genoa), Nevada's first non-American Indian settlement, is established in the Carson Valley to supply the forty-niners.
1850	Utah Territory, including most of modern Nevada, is established.
1855	First Mormon settlement is established in Las Vegas.
1859	Silver strike is made at Comstock, near Virginia City.
1860	Population of Nevada is 6,700, nearly all around the Carson City and Virginia City areas.
March 2, 1861	Nevada Territory is formed, with capital at Carson City.
1862	Voters reject first Nevada constitution.
Oct. 31, 1864	Nevada enters the Union as the thirty-sixth state.
1868	Transcontinental railroad crosses Nevada; is completed in Utah the following year.
1869	Legislature legalizes gambling.
1874	University of Nevada is founded at Elko.
1877-1881	Drop in the price of silver leaves many unemployed.
1880	Population reaches 62,266.
1881-1890	Depopulation occurs due to unemployment.
1900	Population falls to 42,335.
1900	Silver deposits found at Tonopah, gold at Goldfield, and copper at Ely revive state's mining industry.
1907	Construction begun on Newlands irrigation project to irrigate Fallon area, east of Reno.
1909	Gambling is made illegal.
1911	City of Las Vegas is incorporated.
1917-1918	U.S. entrance into World War I gives rise to short-lived mining boom.
1931	Gambling is legalized; residency required for divorce is reduced to six weeks.
1936	Boulder (later Hoover) Dam is completed.
1939-1945	World War II creates great demand for Nevada minerals.
1942-1945	Federal government establishes military installations in Nevada, stimulating economy and population growth.
1941	First casino-hotels open in Las Vegas.
1946	Flamingo Hotel on Las Vegas Strip is opened by mobster "Bugsy" Siegel; first state gambling taxes levied.
1950	Population is 160,083.

1951	U.S. Atomic Energy Commission inaugurates above-ground atomic testing in southern Nevada.
1963	U.S. Supreme Court settles long-standing dispute over water among Nevada and neighboring states.
1969	Corporate Gaming Act allows publicly traded companies to open casinos.
1971	Robert B. Griffith Water Project is completed.
1975	Nevada gaming revenues top $1 billion mark.
1980	Legislature acts to counter pollution of Lake Tahoe.
1990	State population is 1,206,152.
1990	Excaliber Hotel, with 4,032 rooms, opens as the world's largest hotel, beginning decade-long hotel-casino building boom.
1994	Visitors top 40 million, including 28.2 million to Las Vegas.
1998	State population estimated at 1,746,898.
1999	Metropolitan Las Vegas is one of the fastest growing urban areas in America, adding from four thousand to six thousand people monthly.

Notes for Further Study

Published Sources. For an overview of Nevada history, see Robert Laxalt's *Nevada: A Bicentennial History* (1991). The story of the Comstock silver bonanza is chronicled in Grant H. Smith and Joseph V. Tingley's *The History of the Comstock Lode* (1998). Another resource on Nevada's mining history is *Nevada's Twentieth-Century Mining Boom: Tonopah, Goldfield, Ely* (1966), by Russell R. Elliott. For information about the Donner Party tragedy, *The Donner Party Chronicles: A Day-by-Day Account of a Doomed Wagon Train, 1846-1847* (1997), by Frank Mullen and Will Bagley, is a good reference.

For an example of the state's ethnic history, students should begin with Malvin Miranda's *A History of Hispanics in Southern Nevada* (1997). An excellent resource on Native American history in the state is *The Washoe, Paiute, and Shoshone Indians of Nevada* (1961), by E. Haglund. In the Nevada Studies in History and Political Science series, see, for example, James W. Hulse, *Forty Years in the Wilderness: Impressions of Nevada, 1940-1980* (1986), and *East of Eden, West of Zion: Essays on Ne-* *vada* (1989), edited by Wilbur S. Shepperson. For place names, see Helen S. Carlson's *Nevada Place Names: A Geographical Dictionary* (1985) and Peter Browning's *Place Names of the Sierra Nevada: From Abbot to Zumwalt* (1986).

Web Resources. Web resources on Nevada begin with the state's home page (http://www.state.nv.us). The state legislature maintains its own home page (http://

Nevada's legalization of gambling during the Great Depression made possible the post-World War II transformation of Las Vegas into one of the world's leading casino and entertainment centers. (PhotoDisc)

www.leg.state.nv.us), where information on pending or existing legislation may be found. A number of Web sites exist for localities, such as an index that includes Nevada (http://wwwpiperinfo.com/state/slnv.html), which has links to sites of cities, counties, statewide offices, and similar organizations. The Library of Congress site (http://lcweb.loc.gov/global/state/nv-gov.html) is also a good reference. A variety of history links may be found in the Encyclopaedia Nevadaca (http://www.nevadaweb.com/nevadaca/historylinks.html).

Individual cities maintain sites that give a range of information relevant to tourists or to residents. The Nevada Index (http://www.nevadaindex.com/3ref2.htm) includes a detailed set of links to politics, public interest groups, and similar sites, some of which are specific to Nevada, such as the National Organization for Women of Southern Nevada and Law Officers from Nevada. The City of Las Vegas home page (http://www.ci/las-vegas.nv.us) is also helpful. Nevada universities' Web sites include, for example, those of the University of Nevada at Las Vegas (http://www.unlv.edu) and its counterpart at Reno (http://www.unr.edu). For resources on Native Americans, see the site on Nevada tribes (http://www.unr.edu/nnap/NT/nt_main.htm) or American Indian Tribes (http://www.members.tripod.com/~MGO/1Indian.html). Geographic information on the state can be found at the Nevada Geographic Information Society (http://www.ngis.org). For water shortages and other issues, see the site maintained by the U.S. Geological Survey (http://water.usgs/gov/wid/html/nv.html).

Counties

County	Sq. miles	1996 pop.
Churchill	4,929.3	21,792
Clark	7,910.7	1,048,717
Douglas	709.9	35,745
Elko	17,181.6	43,567
Esmeralda	3,588.7	1,180
Eureka	4,176.0	1,577
Humboldt	9,648.3	16,453
Lander	5,493.5	6,815
Lincoln	10,634.7	3,903
Lyon	1,993.8	27,357
Mineral	3,756.6	6,064
Nye	18,147.2	26,062
Pershing	6,009.1	4,708
Storey	263.5	2,917
Washoe	6,342.5	298,787
White Pine	8,876.6	10,282

Carson City is independent of all counties.

Source: U.S. Bureau of the Census; National Association of Counties.

Cities

With 10,000 or more residents

Rank	City	Population
1	Las Vegas	404,288
2	Reno	163,334
3	Henderson	152,717
4	North Las Vegas	94,218
5	Sparks	62,432
6	Carson City	49,301
7	Elko	19,204
8	Boulder City	14,166
9	Mesquite	10,125

Population figures are estimated for mid-1998.

Source: U.S. Bureau of the Census.

Index to Tables

NA = Reliable data are not available.

DEMOGRAPHICS

Resident state and national populations, 1970-1997

Population figures given in thousands

	State pop.	U.S. pop.	Share	Rank
1970	489	203,302	0.2%	47
1980	800	226,546	0.4%	43
1985	951	237,924	0.4%	43
1990	1,202	248,765	0.5%	39
1995	1,530	262,761	0.6%	38
1997	1,677	267,636	0.6%	37

Source: U.S. Bureau of the Census.

Resident population by age, 1997

Age group	Total population
Under 5 years	130,000
5 to 17 years	313,000
18 to 24 years	141,000
25 to 34 years	254,000
35 to 44 years	279,000
45 to 54 years	219,000
55 to 64 years	149,000
65 to 74 years	119,000
75 to 84 years	60,000
85 years and over	14,000
Portion of residents 65 and older	11.5%
National average	12.7%

Population figures are rounded to nearest thousand persons;
figures include armed forces personnel stationed in state.
Source: U.S. Bureau of the Census.

Resident population by race, Hispanic origin, 1997

	State pop.	Share	U.S.
All residents	1,677,000	100.0%	100.0%
Hispanic white	231,000	13.8%	10.0%
non-Hispanic white	1,218,000	72.6%	72.7%
African American	125,000	7.5%	12.7%
Native American	30,000	1.8%	0.9%
Asian, Pacific Islander	74,000	4.4%	3.8%

Source: U.S. Bureau of the Census.

Projections of state population, 2000-2025

	Model A Uses interstate migration observed from 1975-1994	Model B Uses Bureau of Economic Analysis employment projections
Year	Population	Population
2000	1,871,000	1,863,000
2005	2,070,000	2,130,000
2010	2,131,000	2,355,000
2015	2,179,000	2,547,000
2020	2,241,000	2,712,000
2025	2,312,000	2,854,000

All population projections, including those for 2000, were calculated in 1997.
Source: U.S. Bureau of the Census, Population Paper Listings PPL-47.

VITAL STATISTICS

Average lifetime in years by race, 1989-1991

	State	U.S.	Rank
All residents	74.18	75.37	44
White residents	74.44	76.13	48
Black residents	NA	69.16	NA

Ranks are from longest-lived to least longest-lived. Ranks exclude Alaska, for which reliable data are not available. Rank for black residents is based on the 32 states for which reliable data are available.
Source: U.S. National Center for Health Statistics.

Infant mortality rates, 1980 and 1995

	State	U.S.
All residents		
1980	10.7	12.6
1995	5.7	7.6
White residents		
1980	10.0	11.0
1995	5.5	6.3
Black residents		
1980	20.6	21.4
1995	NA	15.1

Figures represent deaths per 1,000 live births of resident infants under 1 year old, exclusive of fetal deaths; all-residents figures include other races not listed separately.
Source: U.S. National Center for Health Statistics.

Marriages and divorces

Marriages in 1996	141,200
Rate per 1,000 population, 1995	88.1
U.S. rate, 1995	8.9
Rank among all states.	1
Divorces in 1996	15,900
Rate per 1,000 population, 1995.	8.1
U.S. rate, 1995	4.4
Rank among all states.	1

Rank is from highest to lowest in country.
Source: U.S. National Center for Health Statistics.

Death rates by leading causes, 1995

Deaths per 100,000 resident population

Cause	State	U.S.
Heart disease	246.9	280.7
Cancer	194.5	204.9
Cerebrovascular diseases	46.4	60.1
Accidents and adverse effects	36.0	35.5
Motor vehicle accidents	19.9	16.5
Chronic obstructive pulmonary diseases	52.0	39.2
Diabetes mellitus	15.4	22.6
HIV	13.2	NA
Suicide	25.8	11.9
Homicide	11.2	8.7
All causes	818.6	880.0
Rank in overall death rate among states		36

Figures exclude nonresidents who die in state. Causes of death follow International Classification of Diseases. Rank is from highest to lowest in country.
Source: U.S. National Center for Health Statistics.

ECONOMY

Gross state product, 1990-1996
In current dollars

	State product	Increase
1990	$31.3 billion	
1993	$39.5 billion	
1994	$44.5 billion	12.66%
1995	$48.7 billion	9.44%
1996	$53.7 billion	10.27%

Source: U.S. Bureau of Economic Analysis; *Survey of Current Business,* June, 1998.

Gross state product by industry, 1996
In billions

Farms, forestry, fisheries	$0.4
Construction	3.9
Manufacturing	2.5
Transportation, public utilities.	3.9
Wholesale trade.	2.4
Retail trade	4.9
Finance, insurance, real estate	8.6
Services	15.1
Government.	4.8
State total.	$48.3
Total U.S.	$6,923.8
State share.	0.70%
Rank among states.	34

Total figures include mining, not listed separately.
Source: U.S. Bureau of Economic Analysis; *Survey of Current Business,* June, 1998.

Personal income per capita, 1990 and 1997
In current dollars

	1990	1997
Per capita income	$20,241	$26,791
U.S. average	$19,188	$25,598
Rank among states	12	11

1997 data are preliminary.
Source: U.S. Bureau of Economic Analysis; *Survey of Current Business,* May, 1998.

Energy consumption, 1995
In trillions of British thermal units (BTU)

End-use sectors

Residential.	97.4
Commercial	81.3
Industrial	196.1
Transportation	162.5

Sources of energy

Petroleum	202.6
Natural gas	114.7
Coal.	162.7
Hydroelectric power.	20.3
Nuclear electric power	0
Total state per capita consumption	350.3
Total U.S. per capita consumption	344.4
Rank among states.	25
Total state energy consumption.	537.2
Total U.S. energy consumption	90,547.4
State share of U.S. total.	0.59%
Rank among states.	39

Total figures include items not listed separately.
Source: U.S. Energy Information Administration; *State Energy Data Report.*

Nonfarm employment by sectors, 1997

Total	890,000
Construction	82,000
Manufacturing	41,000
Transportation, public utilities.	45,000
Wholesale trade, retail trade	179,000
Finance, insurance, real estate	40,000
Services	382,000
Government	106,000

Figures are rounded to nearest thousand persons. Total includes mining, not listed separately.
Source: U.S. Bureau of Labor Statistics; *Employment and Earnings,* monthly.

Foreign exports, 1990-1997
In millions of dollars

Year	State	U.S.	State share
1990	394	394,045	0.10%
1996	1,268	624,767	0.20%
1997	1,075	688,896	0.16%

Source: U.S. Bureau of the Census; *U.S. Merchandise Trade,* series FT 900.

LAND USE

Federally owned land, 1996

	State	U.S.	State share
Total acres	70,264,000	2,271,343,000	3.09%
Federally owned	56,082,000	563,129,000	9.96%
Federal share	79.8%	24.8%	—

Areas are rounded to nearest thousand acres. Figures for federally owned land do not include trust properties.

Source: U.S. General Services Administration; *Inventory Report on Real Property Owned by the United States Throughout the World,* annual.

Land use, 1992

In acres, rounded to nearest thousand

Total surface area	70,759,000
Federal land	60,290,000
Total nonfederal	10,025,000
Developed	394,000
Total rural	9,631,000
Cropland.	762,000
Pasture land	297,000
Range land.	7,854,000
Forest land.	353,000
Minor cover/use.	364,000

Total surface area figures include water area not shown separately.

Source: U.S. Dept. of Agriculture; Soil Conservation Service; Iowa State University, Statistical Laboratory; *Summary Report, 1992 National Resources Inventory.*

Farms and crop acreage, 1997

	State	U.S.	Share	Rank
Farms (thousands)	3	2,058	0.15%	46
Acres (millions)	9	968	0.93%	34
Acres per farm	3,520	471	—	3
Acres planted	520	334,139	0.16%	40
Acres harvested	517	319,894	0.16%	40
Farm value (mill.)	$187	$108,805	0.17%	48

Numbers of farms are rounded to nearest thousand.

Source: U.S. Dept. of Agriculture; National Agricultural Statistics Service.

GOVERNMENT AND FINANCE

Units of local government, 1997

	State	Total U.S.	Rank
All local governments	205	87,453	47
Counties	16	3,043	40
Municipalities	19	19,372	47
Townships	0	16,629	—
School districts	17	13,726	42
Special districts	153	34,683	45

County ranks are based on the 48 states with county governments; township ranks are based on the 20 states with township governments; school district ranks are based on the 46 states with such districts.

Source: U.S. Bureau of the Census; *1997 Census of Governments, Government Organization,* Series GC97(1).

State government revenue, 1996

Total revenue	$5,997 mill.
General revenue	4,146 mill.
Per capita.	2,590
U.S. per capita average	2,910
Rank among states.	36

Intergovernmental revenue

Total	$804 mill.
From federal government	764 mill.
From local government	40 mill.

Charges and Miscellaneous

Total	$452 mill.
Current charges	254 mill.
Misc. general revenue	199 mill.

Taxes

Total	$2,889 mill.
General sales	1,572 mill.
Selective sales.	863 mill.
License taxes	313 mill.
Individual income	NA
Corporate income	NA
Other	141 mill.
Insurance trust revenue	1,806 mill.

Total revenue figures include items not listed separately.

Source: U.S. Bureau of the Census.

State government expenditures, 1996

General expenditures

Intergovernmental	$1,624 mill.
Direct expenditures	2,400 mill.
Total.	4,024 mill.

Selected direct expenditures

Education	$1,539 mill.
Public welfare.	653 mill.
Health, hospital	140 mill.
Highways	400 mill.
Police.	39 mill.
Corrections	151 mill.
Natural resources	57 mill.
Parks and recreation.	14 mill.
Government administration	163 mill.
Interest on debt	129 mill.

Other

State per capita expenditures	$2,514
U.S. per capita average	2,854
Rank among states.	40
Total state expenditures	4,831 mill.
Total U.S. expenditures	859,959 mill.

Totals include items not listed separately.
Source: U.S. Bureau of the Census.

POLITICS

Governors since statehood

D = Democrat; R = Republican; O = other;
(r) resigned; (d) died in office; (i) removed from office

Henry G. Blasdel (R)		1864-1871
Lewis R. Bradley (D)		1871-1879
John H. Kinkead (R)		1879-1883
Jewett W. Adams (D)		1883-1887
Charles C. Stevenson (R).	(r)	1887-1890
Frank Bell (R).		1890-1891
Roswell K. Colcord (R)		1891-1895
John E. Jones (O)	(d)	1895-1896
Reinhold Sadler (O)		1896-1903
John Sparks (D)	(d)	1903-1908
Denver S. Dickerson (D)		1908-1911
Tasker L. Oddie (R)		1911-1915
Emmet D. Boyle (D)		1915-1923
James G. Scrugham (D)		1923-1927

Frederick B. Balzer (R)	(d)	1927-1934
Morley I. Griswold (R)		1934-1935
Richard Kirman (D)		1935-1939
Edward P. Carville (D)	(r)	1939-1945
Vail M. Pittman (D).		1945-1951
Charles H. Russell (R)		1951-1959
Grant Sawyer (R)		1959-1967
Paul D. Laxalt (R)		1967-1971
Mike O'Callaghan (D)		1971-1979
Robert F. List (R)		1979-1983
Richard H. Bryan (D)		1983-1991
Robert Miller (D).		1991-1999
Kenny C. Guinn (R)		1999-

Composition of state legislature, 1990-1998

	Democrats	*Republicans*
State Assembly (42 seats)		
1990	22	19
1992	27	12
1994	21	21
1996	25	17
1998	28	14
State Senate (21 seats)		
1990	10	10
1992	10	11
1994	8	13
1996	9	12
1998	9	12

Figures for total seats may include independents and minor
party members.
Source: Council of State Governments; *State Elective Officials
and the Legislatures.*

Composition of congressional delegations, 1989-1999

	Dem	*Rep*	*Total*
House of Representatives			
101st Congress, 1989			
State delegates	1	1	2
Total U.S.	259	174	433
102d Congress, 1991			
State delegates	1	1	2
Total U.S.	267	167	434

	Dem	Rep	Total
103d Congress, 1993			
State delegates	1	1	2
Total U.S.	258	176	434
104th Congress, 1995			
State delegates	0	2	2
Total U.S.	197	236	433
105th Congress, 1997			
State delegates	0	2	2
Total U.S.	206	228	434
106th Congress, 1999			
State delegates	1	1	2
Total U.S.	211	222	433
Senate			
101st Congress, 1989			
State delegates	2	0	2
Total U.S.	55	45	100
102d Congress, 1991			
State delegates	2	0	2
Total U.S.	56	44	100
103d Congress, 1993			
State delegates	2	0	2
Total U.S.	57	43	100
104th Congress, 1995			
State delegates	2	0	2
Total U.S.	46	53	99
105th Congress, 1997			
State delegates	2	0	2
Total U.S.	45	55	100
106th Congress, 1999			
State delegates	2	0	2
Total U.S.	45	54	99

Figures are for starts of first sessions. Figure for U.S. Representatives for 101st Congress does not include Alabama and Indiana, which had vacancies. Figures for total U.S. Representatives for 102d, 103d, and 106th Congresses do not include Vermont, which had 1 Independent-Socialist. Figure for U.S. Representatives for 104th Congress does not include Vermont, which had 1 Independent-Socialist, and California, which had 1 vacancy. Figure for U.S. Representatives for 105th Congress does not include New York, which had 1 vacancy. Figure for U.S. Senators for 104th Congress does not include Oregon, which had 1 vacancy. Figure for U.S. Senators for 106th Congress does not include New Hampshire, which had 1 Independent.

Source: U.S. Congress; *Congressional Directory,* biennial.

Voter participation in presidential elections, 1992 and 1996

	1992	1996
State voting age pop.	1,011,000	1,180,000
Total U.S. voting age pop.	189,524,000	196,509,000
State share of U.S. total	0.5%	0.6%
Rank among states	38	38
Percent of state casting vote	50.1	46.0
Percent of U.S. total voting	55.1	49.0
Rank among states	44	41

Source: U.S. Bureau of the Census.

HEALTH AND MEDICAL CARE

Medicare, 1997

	Recipients	Payments
State	212,000	$1,123 mill.
Total U.S.	37,514,000	$206,064 mill.
State share	0.57%	0.54%
Rank among states	37	35

Recipient figures are rounded to nearest thousand persons. Ranks are from highest to lowest.
Source: U.S. Health Care Financing Administration.

Medicaid, 1996

	Recipients	Payments
State	109,000	$365 mill.
Total U.S.	35,028,000	$121,419 mill.
State share	0.31%	0.30%
Rank among states	41	41

Recipient figures are rounded to nearest thousand persons. Payment figures for fiscal year reflect federal and state contribution payments. Ranks are from highest to lowest.
Source: U.S. Health Care Financing Administration.

Health insurance coverage, 1996

	State	U.S.
Total persons covered	1,381,000	225,070,000
Total persons not covered	255,000	41,716,000
Part not covered	15.6%	15.6%
Rank among states	17	—
Children not covered	78,000	10,554,000
Part not covered	19.0%	14.8%
Rank among states	7	—

Ranks are from most to fewest uninsured. Population figures
 are rounded to nearest thousand persons.
Source: U.S. Bureau of the Census.

AIDS, syphilis, tuberculosis, and measles cases, 1997

Cases	U.S.	State	Share
AIDS	58,443	592	1.01%
Syphilis	8,550	10	0.12%
Tuberculosis	18,534	46	0.25%
Measles	148,000	2,000	1.35%

Measles figures are rounded to nearest thousand cases.
Source: U.S. Centers for Disease Control and Prevention.

HOUSING

Homeownership rates, 1985-1997

	1985	1990	1997
State	57.0%	55.8%	61.2%
Total U.S.	63.9%	63.9%	65.7%
Rank among states	47	47	45

Source: U.S. Bureau of the Census.

Home sales, 1990 and 1997
In thousands of units

Existing home sales	1990	1997	Change
State sales	26.2	29.7	3.5
Total U.S. sales	3,560	4,730	1,170
State share of U.S. total	0.74%	0.63%	-0.11%
Rank among states	35	35	—

Source: National Association of Realtors; *Real Estate Outlook:*
 Market Trends and Insights.

EDUCATION

Public school enrollment, 1995

State K-8 enrollment	196,000
Total U.S. K-8 enrollment	32,341,000
State share of total U.S.	0.61%
State 9-12 enrollment.	69,000
Total U.S. 9-12 enrollment	12,500,000
State share of U.S. total	0.55%
State public school enroll. rate	95.7%
Overall U.S. rate.	91.6%
Rank among states	7

Enrollment figures (which include unclassified students) are
 rounded to nearest thousand pupils in fall term;
 kindergarten (K)-8 grade figures include some
 prekindergarten students. Enrollment rate is based on
 percentage of persons 5-17 years old. Rank is from highest
 to lowest.
Source: U.S. National Center for Education Statistics.

Public college finances, 1996

State FTE enrollment.	36,800
Total U.S. FTE enrollment	8,268,800
State share of total U.S.	0.45%
Rank among states.	39
State and local appropriations	$199,900,000
Total U.S. state and local appropriations.	$39,699 mill.
State share of total U.S.	0.50%
Rank among states.	39
State net tuition revenues	$41,700,000
Total U.S. net tuition	$18,348,100,000
State share of total U.S.	0.23%
Rank among states.	47

FTE=Full-time equivalent; credit and noncredit enrollment
 including summer session in academic year ending in
 1996.
Enrollments are rounded to nearest thousand students. Net
 tuition revenues exclude appropriation to students
 attending in-state public institutions. Rankings are from
 highest shares to lowest.
Source: Research Associates of Washington.

TRANSPORTATION AND TRAVEL

Highway mileage, 1996

Interstate	563
Other arterial	2,990
Collector roads	6,105
Local roads	36,283
Urban roads	5,298
Rural roads	39,741
Total state	45,039
U.S. total	3,933,985
State share	1.1%
Rank among states	36

Source: U.S. Federal Highway Administration.

Motor vehicle registrations and driver licenses, 1996

In thousands

Vehicle registrations	State	U.S.	Share	Rank
Autos, trucks, buses	1,096	206,365	0.53%	39
Autos only	610	128,439	0.47%	39
Motorcycles	22	3,832	0.57%	40
Driver licenses	1,117	179,539	0.62%	39

Figures do not include vehicles owned by military services.
Source: U.S. Federal Highway Administration; *Highway Statistics; Selected Highway Statistics and Charts.*

Domestic travel expenditures, 1995

Spending by U.S. residents on overnight trips and day trips of at least 100 miles

Total expenditures in state	$15,006 mill.
Total expenditures in U.S.	$360,314 mill.
State share of total U.S.	4.16%
Rank among states	6

Source: Travel Industry Association of America.

CRIME AND LAW ENFORCEMENT

State and local police officers, 1996

Local police	2,565
State police	375
Sheriffs	935
Total	4,363
Officers per 10,000 residents	27
U.S. average	25
Rank among states	8

Figures cover full-time sworn officers; totals include special police not shown separately.
Source: U.S. Bureau of Justice Statistics; *Census of State and Local Law Enforcement Agencies, 1996.*

Crime rates, 1996

Rates per 100,000 resident population

Violent crimes	State	U.S.
Total violent	811	634
Murder	13.7	7.4
Forcible rape	53.4	36.1
Robbery	308	202
Aggravated assault	437	388
Property crimes		
Total property	5,181	4,445
Burglary	1,220	943
Larceny/theft	3,262	2,976
Motor vehicle theft	698	526
Totals	5,992	5,079

Source: U.S. Federal Bureau of Investigation; *Crime in the United States*, annual.

State prison populations, 1980-1996

	State	U.S.	State share
1980	1,839	305,458	0.60%
1990	5,322	708,393	0.75%
1996	8,439	1,025,624	0.82%

Figures exclude prisoners in federal penitentiaries.
Source: U.S. Bureau of Justice Statistics.

New Hampshire

Location: New England (northeastern continental United States)

Area and rank: 8,969 square miles (23,231 square kilometers); 9,351 square miles (24,219 square kilometers) including water; forty-fourth largest state in area

Coastline: 13 miles (21 kilometers)

Shoreline: 131 miles (211 kilometers)

Population and rank: 1,172,709 (1997); forty-second largest state in population

A characteristic New Hampshire scene, with the spire of a Protestant church rising above a small town. (PhotoDisc)

Capital: Concord

Largest city: Manchester (102,524 people in 1998)

Entered Union and rank: June 21, 1788; ninth state

Present constitution adopted: 1784

Counties: 10

State name: New Hampshire was named after England's Hampshire county

State nickname: Granite State

Motto: Live free or die

State flag: Blue field with state seal bordered with laurel leaves and stars

Highest point: Mount Washington — 6,288 feet (1,917 meters)

Lowest point: Atlantic Ocean — sea level

Highest recorded temperature: 106 degrees Fahrenheit (41 degrees Celsius) — Nashua, 1911

Lowest recorded temperature: −46 degrees Fahrenheit (−43 degrees Celsius) — Pittsburg, 1925

State songs: "Old New Hampshire"; "New Hampshire, My New Hampshire"

State tree: White birch

State flower: Purple lilac

State bird: Purple finch

State fish: Striped bass (saltwater); Brook trout (freshwater)

State animal: White-tailed deer

New Hampshire History

Part of New England, New Hampshire is one of the original thirteen states. When the glaciers that once covered the North American continent retreated in the area now known as New Hampshire, they left behind a hard, gray granite rock called gneiss, which is why New Hampshire is called the Granite State. The state is relatively small: Its longest distance is 180 miles from north to south, and it is ranked forty-fourth in land area among states. Bounded by Canada in the north, its other borders are the New England states of Massachusetts, Maine, and Vermont. New Hampshire has a small coastline, stretching only eighteen miles, with Portsmouth serving as the state's only harbor. Because of the state's relatively small amount of arable land, farms produce mostly dairy and poultry products. The impressive water power available made New Hampshire attractive to industrialists in the early 1900s, and manufacturing is still an important segment of the state's economy. A fiercely independent people whose state motto is "Live free or die," this traditionally conservative state is one of the few without a state income tax.

Before 1800 New Hampshire was home to the Ossipee, Nashua, Pennacook, Piscataqua, Sqamscot, and Winnipeaukee Indians. These people, known collectively as the western Abenaki, belonged to the eastern branch of the Algonquian family, a large group of tribes related by similar languages and customs. They lived in wigwams and were primarily hunters and gathers, living off the area's fertile fishing waters and hunting grounds. The encroaching European settlements drove most of the early settlers off the land by the late 1700's. Native Americans comprised 0.2 percent of the population in 1997.

Early Exploration. Viking Leif Eriksson and other Norse sailors most likely explored some of New Hampshire during their travels in 1000. Explorer Martin Pring was at the mouth of the Piscataqua in 1603. In 1605, British captain George Weymouth landed in Maine, kidnapped five Abenaki men, and took them back to England. Upon meeting the tribesmen, King James I agreed to sponsor a settlement there. In 1620 he formed the Council for New England which gave out land grants, the first going to Captain John Mason, "the founder of New Hampshire." The following year, David Thomson started the first known English settlement in New Hampshire, now known as Rye. He headed a company that organized fishing and trading.

Religious Conflict. In 1636 Reverend John Wheelwright was banished from Massachusetts for his religious beliefs. Wheelwright was an Antinomian who believed that Christians do not need to observe moral laws if they are saved by God. Ironically, the Puritans, who had fled England because they were persecuted for their religious beliefs, had little tolerance of other religious philosophies.

Wheelwright turned down an offer from Roger Williams to come to Rhode Island because he wanted to establish a new colony. He went by boat as far as the site of present-day Portsmouth, New Hampshire. It was there that he and a settler named John explored further west and established the village of Exeter and the Laconia Company, a joint-stock company.

In the same year, Massachusetts encouraged Puritans to settle nearby Hampton. Tension quickly erupted between the Antinomians and the Puritans. Both New Hampshire and Massachusetts granted townships within New Hampshire territory. It took the Revolutionary War against Great Britain to unite the two factions in a greater cause.

The Wentworth Family. The Wentworths were New Hampshire's most influential family throughout much of the 1700's. In 1717 the king of England appointed John Wentworth, a wealthy, self-made merchant, lieutenant governor of New Hampshire. At the time a single royal governor administered both Massachusetts and New Hampshire.

When John Wentworth died in 1730, his son Benning worked to separate from Massachusetts. In 1740, the king's council established a boundary and the following year appointed Benning Wentworth as the first independent governor of the province. Like his father, he was a loyal representative of the Crown. His devotion to England was unpopular with most citizens, who found the King's taxes unjust, and he resigned from office in 1766. His nephew, John Wentworth, was the new royal appointee. He too tried to keep New Hampshire on the side of Britain, and in 1774, he dissolved the assembly for speaking of revolution. The colonists took matters into their own hands, and in June of 1775, Governor Wentworth was forced from office, ending 160 years of colonial rule in New Hampshire.

Revolution. In what some historians consider the first revolutionary act against Britain, four hundred New Hampshire men stormed the British fort at New Castle and carried off arms and ammunition in 1774. The following year the Revolutionary War began, and New Hampshire was represented in every important battle. Portsmouth's shipbuilding industry naturally grew significantly as naval vessels were needed to aid the war.

About four thousand of the state's men fought in the war. Another three thousand served the cause by privateering: These men sailed the coast capturing British supply ships and seized their cargoes for the

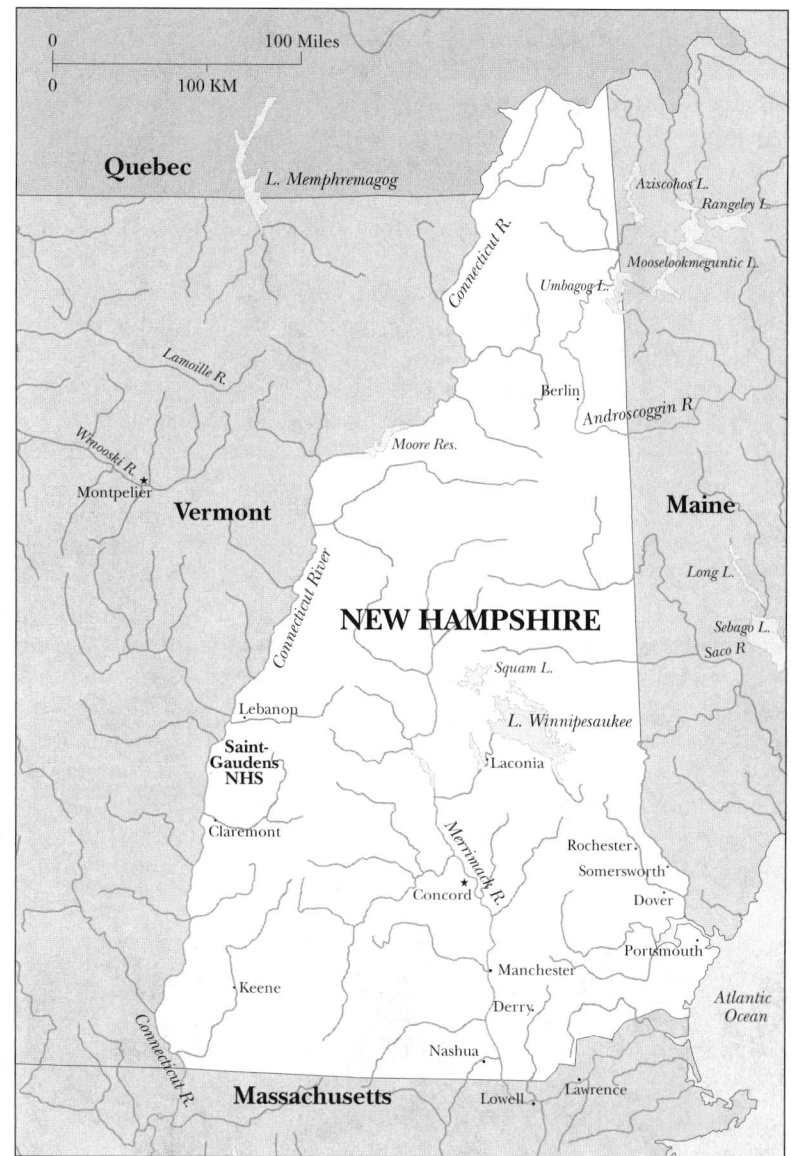

American army. Those at home did not have to suffer invasion—New Hampshire was the only one of the original thirteen states British armies never attacked.

The New State. New Hampshire was the first state to adopt its own constitution, in 1776, and also the first of the original thirteen states to call a convention to write a better one. In 1784 the permanent state constitution was adopted.

In 1808 the state's seat of government moved to Concord. Like most of the country's population,

New Hampshire's at this time was mainly made up of farmers. When the Industrial Revolution came to New England in the 1830's, it caused an upsurge in economic activity downriver from Concord in Manchester, which soon became the economic center of the state.

The first commercial buildings to appear were sawmills, which processed lumber, and gristmills, which ground grain. The rivers in the Merrimack Valley provided great power, and soon the area developed into one of the world's leading textile centers. The mill workers labored long hours, usually under dangerous conditions. The workers had no bargaining power to speak of, as in the 1840's the mill owners had an influx of cheap labor: Ireland's potato famine had driven many of that country's poorest to the shores of America, many ending up in New Hampshire. Wages remained low and working conditions harsh.

The Civil War. One of the country's most gifted orators and famous politicians, Daniel Webster, was born in Salisbury, New Hampshire, in 1782. After graduating from Dartmouth College, he served as New Hampshire's state representative from 1813 to 1817. He eventually moved to Massachusetts, however, representing that state in both houses of Congress.

In 1852 New Hampshire lawyer and former state representative Franklin Pierce came out of retirement to become the Democratic nominee for president. He was elected and became at that time the youngest president ever to serve. His inexperience led to several botched political moves, and in 1854 he backed the Kansas-Nebraska Act, which repealed the Missouri Compromise. Many historians believe that this act reignited the slavery issue on a national level and pushed the country quickly toward the Civil War, which began in 1860.

During the Civil War, New Hampshire was fortunate again in that no battles were fought on its soil. Yet the citizens were staunch defenders of the Union, and nearly half the state's male population at the time, thirty-nine thousand men, fought in the war.

The Twentieth Century. When the new century began, more people in New Hampshire made their living from manufacturing than from agriculture. Labor unions began forming in the factories, and a labor reform bill passed in 1907 that limited the workweek for women and children to fifty-eight hours.

The United States entered World War I in 1917, and New Hampshire citizens fought again in large numbers. The Portsmouth Naval Shipyard built warships, including submarines. After the war, the 1920's brought the beginning of years of decline for New England textile milling, and the state began an economic slump that would worsen through the Depression and only start to get better at the beginning of World War II.

Frank Knox, publisher of Manchester's *Union Leader,* was appointed secretary of the Navy. Production of U.S. submarines rapidly went into high gear at the Portsmouth Naval Shipyard—at one point during the war turning out two a week. About twenty thousand men and women worked in the yard.

The Primary State. In 1913, New Hampshire state legislators moved the date of their election year primary and began a long tradition of being the first primary of every political season. After World War II, presidential primaries became more important, as they were seen as a testing ground for potential candidates. The eyes of the nation focus on New Hampshire during this time every four years. Other states, jealous of the attention, have tried to move their primaries up, and New Hampshire has responded by passing a law dictating that their primary will be held the Tuesday before any other state's.

One of New Hampshire's many covered bridges. (PhotoDisc)

Beginning in 1952 no president was elected without first winning the New Hampshire primary—until 1992, when U.S. senator Paul Tsongas won the primary but later lost the nomination to Bill Clinton.

Kevin M. Mitchell

The Mount Washington Cog Railway. (State of New Hampshire Office of Travel and Tourism)

New Hampshire Time Line

1500's	Western Abenaki Indians inhabit New Hampshire.
1603	England's Martin Pring explores mouth of the Piscataqua River.
1605	French explorer Samuel de Champlain enters Piscataqua Bay.
1623	First English settlements are founded at Dover and at Little Harbor (later Rye).
1629	England's Captain John Mason receives a grant of land in the area and names it New Hampshire after England's Hampshire.
1634	Dover becomes site of the first church built in New Hampshire.
1641	Because of religious disagreements among Anglicans, Puritans, and Quakers, communities are unable to decide on a government and thus become part of Massachusetts.
1647	New Hampshire colonists pass an education act requiring towns to provide public education.
1679	New Hampshire becomes a royal province, separate from Massachusetts.
1693	New school law requires each town to provide a schoolmaster.
1756	*New Hampshire Gazette*, the state's first paper, is published.
1763	French and Indian War ends; most Native Americans are driven into Canada, and the French are driven out completely.
1768	Dartmouth College opens in Hanover.
1774	Colonists raid England's Fort William and Mary in Portsmouth, taking ammunition and gunpowder.
1776	New Hampshire becomes first colony to declare independence from Great Britain and becomes first state to adopt a constitution.

(continued)

1784	Revised state constitution is adopted.
1785	Two-party political system begins.
June 21, 1788	New Hampshire becomes ninth state.
1804	State's first cotton factory begins operation.
1819	Amoskeag Mills, in Manchester, introduces the power loom for weaving cloth.
1838	State's first railroad begins operation.
1847	First ten-hour-day law for factory workers is enacted.
1853	New Hampshire politician Franklin Pierce becomes fourteenth president of the United States.
1865	Fifth New Hampshire Regiment ends Civil War service with more casualties than any other regiment in the Union.
1871	School attendance is made compulsory.
1877	Law requiring that state's governor, senators, and representatives be Protestants is repealed.
1891	New Hampshire's Library Commission provides free public libraries with state aid.
1909	New Hampshire adopts direct primary law.
1922	State's first radio station begins operation.
1961	New Hampshire-born Alan B. Shepard, Jr., becomes first American to travel in space.
1963	John W. King becomes first Democrat to be elected governor in forty years.
1972	State ratifies Equal Rights Amendment.
1977	Two thousand demonstrators march on construction site of nuclear plant at Seabrook.
1980-1990	Median household income jumps 27.4 percent, the greatest increase in the nation.
1986	Concord teacher Christa McAuliffe is among crew members killed when the space shuttle *Challenger* explodes.
1999	New Hampshire senator Bob Smith leaves the Republican Party, which he says has become too liberal, to pursue an independent presidential bid.

Notes for Further Study

Published Sources. Those looking for short historical and social overviews will find material in *New Hampshire: From Sea to Shining Sea* (1994) by Dennis B. Fradin and *America the Beautiful: New Hampshire* (1992) by Sylvia McNair. Deeper analysis is found in *New Hampshire: Cross-currents in Its Development* (1996) by Nancy Coffeey Heffernan and Ann P. Stecker. The book covers the state's industry, from the prosperous ship-building trade to high-tech industry, and tells about its colorful political figures and New Hampshire's primary. *The New Hampshire Primary and the American Electoral Process* (1997) studies the peculiar role and history of the New Hampshire primary in American presidential elections. The work reviews the primary's history and analyzes the media's

treatment of New Hampshire results, including the role played by local media.

New Hampshire: Disaster and Catastrophes (1990), by Carole Marsh, provides coverage of the floods, fires, and other disasters the state's residents have had to endure. *New Hampshire: An Explorer's Guide* (1999), by Christina Tree and Christine Hamm, covers the state's recreation and natural world. Books on the American Industrial Revolution and the textile industry, revealing life in nineteenth century New England, include *The Growth of Manufacturing in Early Nineteenth Century New England* (1975), by Robert Brooke Zevin, and *The Lowell Offering: Writings by New England Mill Women, 1840-1845* (1997), edited by Benita Eisler. Based on a magazine produced at the time, it comprises personal essays of the first women to work in American mills.

Web Resources. There are many New Hampshire sites on the World Wide Web, and those listed here often give links to others. The best starting point is the state's official Web site, sponsored by the state's largest newspaper, the *Union Leader* (http://www.newhampshire.com). A brief history of New Hampshire (http://www.state.nh .us/nhinfo/ history) offers details emphasizing the state's beginnings. Specific town histories are also available on-line (http://www .state.nh.us nhinfo/guide). Information and biographical information on New Hampshire's Alan Shepard, Jr. and Christa McAuliffe may be found at the NASA Web site (http://www .nasa.hq.gov). The New Hampshire Primary site (http://www.newhamp shireprimary.com) provides updates to the beginning of the nation's presidential race.

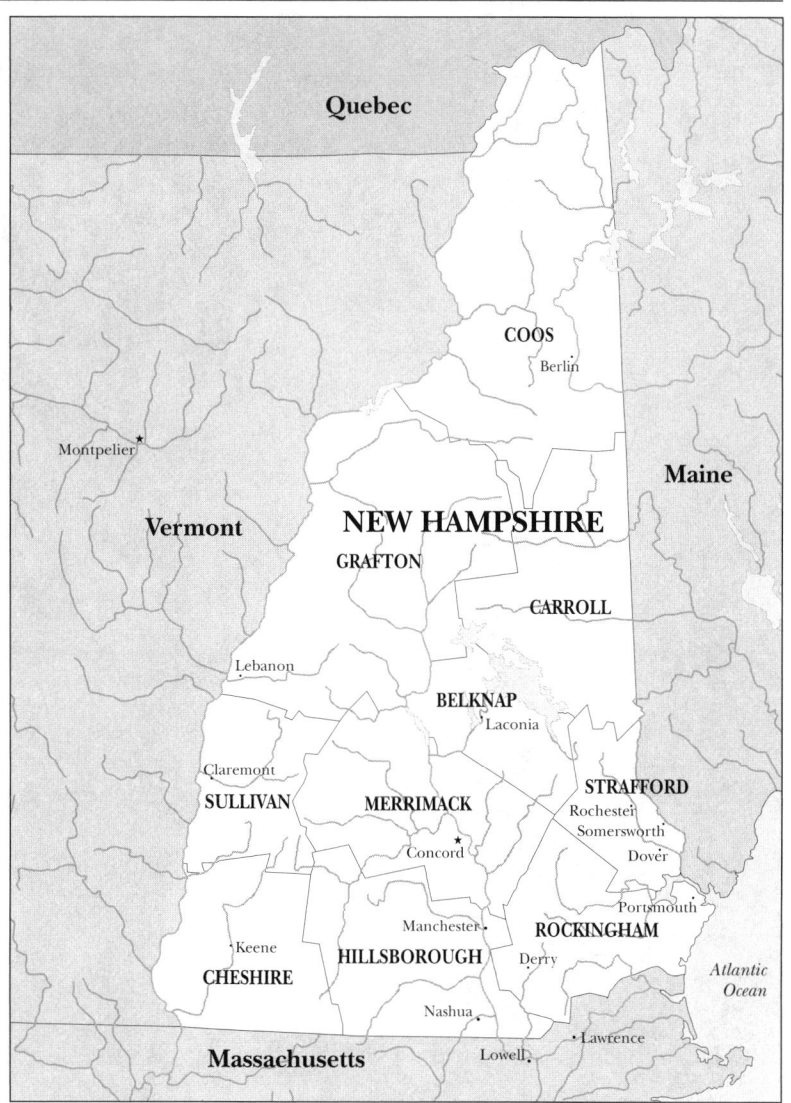

Counties

County	Sq. miles	1996 pop.
Belknap	401.3	51,466
Carroll	933.9	38,240
Cheshire	707.5	71,531
Coos	1,800.6	33,531
Grafton	1,713.5	78,329
Hillsborough	876.5	354,196

County	Sq. miles	1996 pop.
Merrimack	934.5	125,085
Rockingham	695.2	262,893
Strafford	368.8	107,344
Sullivan	537.4	39,866

Source: U.S. Bureau of the Census; National Association of Counties.

Cities
With 10,000 or more residents

Rank	City	Population
1	Manchester	102,524
2	Nashua	82,169
3	Concord	37,444
4	Rochester	27,869
5	Dover	25,953
6	Portsmouth	25,388
7	Keene	22,313
8	Laconia	16,435
9	Claremont	13,868
10	Lebanon	12,461
11	Somersworth	11,525
12	Berlin	10,120

Population figures are estimated for mid-1998.
Source: U.S. Bureau of the Census.

Index to Tables

NA = Reliable data are not available.

DEMOGRAPHICS

Resident state and national populations, 1970-1997

Population figures given in thousands

	State pop.	U.S. pop.	Share	Rank
1970	738	203,302	0.4%	41
1980	921	226,546	0.4%	42
1985	997	237,924	0.4%	40
1990	1,109	248,765	0.4%	40
1995	1,146	262,761	0.4%	42
1997	1,173	267,636	0.4%	42

Source: U.S. Bureau of the Census.

Resident population by age, 1997

Age group	Total population
Under 5 years	74,000
5 to 17 years	222,000
18 to 24 years	94,000
25 to 34 years	186,000
35 to 44 years	219,000
45 to 54 years	152,000
55 to 64 years	85,000
65 to 74 years	76,000
75 to 84 years	49,000
85 years and over	17,000
Portion of residents 65 and older	12.1%
National average	12.7%

Population figures are rounded to nearest thousand persons; figures include armed forces personnel stationed in state.
Source: U.S. Bureau of the Census.

Resident population by race, Hispanic origin, 1997

	State pop.	Share	U.S.
All residents	1,173,000	100.0%	100.0%
Hispanic white	15,000	1.3%	10.0%
non-Hispanic white	1,133,000	96.6%	72.7%
African American	8,000	0.7%	12.7%
Native American	2,000	0.2%	0.9%
Asian, Pacific Islander	13,000	1.1%	3.8%

Source: U.S. Bureau of the Census.

Projections of state population, 2000-2025

	Model A Uses interstate migration observed from 1975-1994	Model B Uses Bureau of Economic Analysis employment projections
Year	Population	Population
2000	1,224,000	1,217,000
2005	1,281,000	1,267,000
2010	1,329,000	1,307,000
2015	1,372,000	1,344,000
2020	1,410,000	1,377,000
2025	1,439,000	1,402,000

All population projections, including those for 2000, were calculated in 1997.
Source: U.S. Bureau of the Census, Population Paper Listings PPL-47.

VITAL STATISTICS

Average lifetime in years by race, 1989-1991

	State	U.S.	Rank
All residents	76.72	75.37	14
White residents	76.68	76.13	18
Black residents	NA	69.16	NA

Ranks are from longest-lived to least longest-lived. Ranks exclude Alaska, for which reliable data are not available. Rank for black residents is based on the 32 states for which reliable data are available.
Source: U.S. National Center for Health Statistics.

Infant mortality rates, 1980 and 1995

	State	U.S.
All residents		
1980	9.9	12.6
1995	5.5	7.6
White residents		
1980	9.9	11.0
1995	5.5	6.3
Black residents		
1980	22.5	21.4
1995	NA	15.1

Figures represent deaths per 1,000 live births of resident infants under 1 year old, exclusive of fetal deaths; all-residents figures include other races not listed separately.
Source: U.S. National Center for Health Statistics.

Marriages and divorces

Marriages in 1996	9,700
Rate per 1,000 population, 1995	8.4
U.S. rate, 1995	8.9
Rank among all states	28
Divorces in 1996	5,000
Rate per 1,000 population, 1995	4.2
U.S. rate, 1995	4.4
Rank among all states	29

Rank is from highest to lowest in country.
Source: U.S. National Center for Health Statistics.

Death rates by leading causes, 1995

Deaths per 100,000 resident population

Cause	State	U.S.
Heart disease	256.9	280.7
Cancer	205.2	204.9
Cerebrovascular diseases	55.2	60.1
Accidents and adverse effects	25.0	35.5
Motor vehicle accidents	11.8	16.5
Chronic obstructive pulmonary diseases	41.5	39.2
Diabetes mellitus	22.6	22.6
HIV	4.1	NA
Suicide	11.9	11.9
Homicide	-	8.7
All causes	803.6	880.0

Rank in overall death rate among states	39

Figures exclude nonresidents who die in state. Causes of death follow International Classification of Diseases. Rank is from highest to lowest in country.
Source: U.S. National Center for Health Statistics.

ECONOMY

Gross state product, 1990-1996
In current dollars

	State product	Increase
1990	$23.7 billion	
1993	$27.2 billion	
1994	$29.3 billion	7.72%
1995	$31.8 billion	8.53%
1996	$34.1 billion	7.23%

Source: U.S. Bureau of Economic Analysis; *Survey of Current Business,* June, 1998.

Gross state product by industry, 1996
In billions

Farms, forestry, fisheries	$0.2
Construction	1.0
Manufacturing	8.1
Transportation, public utilities	2.5
Wholesale trade	2.0
Retail trade	3.0
Finance, insurance, real estate	6.5
Services	5.8
Government	2.8
State total	$31.7
Total U.S.	$6,923.8
State share	0.46%
Rank among states	40

Total figures include mining, not listed separately.
Source: U.S. Bureau of Economic Analysis; *Survey of Current Business,* June, 1998.

Personal income per capita, 1990 and 1997
In current dollars

	1990	1997
Per capita income	$20,767	$28,047
U.S. average	$19,188	$25,598
Rank among states	10	8

1997 data are preliminary.
Source: U.S. Bureau of Economic Analysis; *Survey of Current Business,* May, 1998.

Energy consumption, 1995
In trillions of British thermal units (BTU)

End-use sectors

Residential	79.7
Commercial	52.5
Industrial	76.3
Transportation	81.7

Sources of energy

Petroleum	151.0
Natural gas	20.1
Coal	35.5
Hydroelectric power	24.7
Nuclear electric power	89.3
Total state per capita consumption	247.8
Total U.S. per capita consumption	344.4
Rank among states	43
Total state energy consumption	284.5
Total U.S. energy consumption	90,547.4
State share of U.S. total	0.31%
Rank among states	45

Total figures include items not listed separately.
Source: U.S. Energy Information Administration; *State Energy Data Report.*

Nonfarm employment by sectors, 1997

Total	568,000
Construction	21,000
Manufacturing	107,000
Transportation, public utilities	19,000
Wholesale trade, retail trade	148,000
Finance, insurance, real estate	29,000
Services	165,000
Government	78,000

Figures are rounded to nearest thousand persons. Total includes mining, not listed separately.
Source: U.S. Bureau of Labor Statistics; *Employment and Earnings,* monthly.

Foreign exports, 1990-1997
In millions of dollars

Year	State	U.S.	State share
1990	973	394,045	0.25%
1996	1,481	624,767	0.24%
1997	1,597	688,896	0.23%

Source: U.S. Bureau of the Census; *U.S. Merchandise Trade,* series FT 900.

LAND USE

Federally owned land, 1996

	State	U.S.	State share
Total acres	5,769,000	2,271,343,000	0.25%
Federally owned	734,000	563,129,000	0.13%
Federal share	12.7%	24.8%	—

Areas are rounded to nearest thousand acres. Figures for federally owned land do not include trust properties.
Source: U.S. General Services Administration; *Inventory Report on Real Property Owned by the United States Throughout the World,* annual.

Land use, 1992
In acres, rounded to nearest thousand

Total surface area	5,938,000
Federal land	747,000
Total nonfederal.	4,952,000
Developed	563,000
Total rural	4,389,000
Cropland.	142,000
Pasture land.	98,000
Range land	0
Forest land	3,932,000
Minor cover/use.	217,000

Total surface area figures include water area not shown separately.
Source: U.S. Dept. of Agriculture; Soil Conservation Service; Iowa State University, Statistical Laboratory; *Summary Report, 1992 National Resources Inventory.*

Farms and crop acreage, 1997

	State	U.S.	Share	Rank
Farms (thousands)	2	2,058	0.10%	47
Acres (millions)	—	968	—	—
Acres per farm	179	471	—	41
Acres planted	70	334,139	0.02%	47
Acres harvested	69	319,894	0.02%	47
Farm value (mill.)	$27	$108,805	0.02%	38

State acreage total is less than 500,000 acres.
Numbers of farms are rounded to nearest thousand.
Source: U.S. Dept. of Agriculture; National Agricultural Statistics Service.

GOVERNMENT AND FINANCE

Units of local government, 1997

	State	Total U.S.	Rank
All local governments	575	87,453	42
Counties	10	3,043	46
Municipalities	13	19,372	48
Townships	221	16,629	18
School districts	166	13,726	28
Special districts	165	34,683	43

County ranks are based on the 48 states with county governments; township ranks are based on the 20 states with township governments; school district ranks are based on the 46 states with such districts.
Township figures include "town" governments.
Source: U.S. Bureau of the Census; *1997 Census of Governments, Government Organization,* Series GC97(1).

State government revenue, 1996

Total revenue	$3,561 mill.
General revenue	2,706 mill.
Per capita.	2,333
U.S. per capita average	2,910
Rank among states.	48

Intergovernmental revenue	
Total	$1,011 mill.
From federal government	862 mill.
From local government	149 mill.

Charges and Miscellaneous	
Total	$858 mill.
Current charges	372 mill.
Misc. general revenue	486 mill.

Taxes	
Total	$837 mill.
General sales	NA
Selective sales	429 mill.
License taxes	108 mill.
Individual income	52 mill.
Corporate income	180 mill.
Other.	69 mill.
Insurance trust revenue	632 mill.

Total revenue figures include items not listed separately.
Source: U.S. Bureau of the Census.

State government expenditures, 1996

General expenditures

Intergovernmental	$392 mill.
Direct expenditures	2,449 mill.
Total	2,841 mill.

Selected direct expenditures

Education	$579 mill.
Public welfare	988 mill.
Health, hospital	146 mill.
Highways	224 mill.
Police	27 mill.
Corrections	62 mill.
Natural resources	35 mill.
Parks and recreation	13 mill.
Government administration	130 mill.
Interest on debt	376 mill.

Other

State per capita expenditures	$2,449
U.S. per capita average	2,854
Rank among states	42
Total state expenditures	3,240 mill.
Total U.S. expenditures	859,959 mill.

Totals include items not listed separately.
Source: U.S. Bureau of the Census.

POLITICS

Governors since statehood
D = Democrat; R = Republican; O = other;
(r) resigned; (d) died in office; (i) removed from office

Meshech Weare	1776-1785
John Langdon	1785-1786
John Sullivan	1786-1788
John Langdon	(r) 1788-1789
John Pickering	1789
John Sullivan	1789-1790
Josiah Bartlett	1790-1794
John T. Gilman (O)	1794-1805
John Langdon (O)	1805-1809
Jeremiah Smith (O)	1809-1810
John Langdon (O)	1810-1812
William Plumer (O)	1812-1813
John T. Gilman (O)	1813-1816
William Plumer (O)	1816-1819
Samuel Bell (O)	1819-1823
Levi Woodbury (O)	1823-1824
David L. Morril (O)	1824-1827
Benjamin Pierce (O)	1827-1828
John Bell (O)	1828-1829
Benjamin Pierce (O)	1829-1830
Matthew Harvey (O)	(r) 1830-1831
Joseph M. Harper (O)	1831
Samuel Dinsmoor (O)	1831-1834
William Badger (D)	1834-1836
Isaac Hill (D)	1836-1839
John Page (D)	1839-1842
Henry Hubbard (D)	1842-1844
John H. Steele (D)	1844-1846
Anthony Colby (O)	1846-1847
Jared W. Williams (D)	1847-1849
Samuel Dinsmoor, Jr. (D)	1849-1852
Noah Martin (D)	1852-1854
Nathaniel B. Baker (D)	1854-1855
Ralph Metcalf (O)	1855-1857
William Haile (R)	1857-1859
Ichabod Goodwin (R)	1859-1861
Nathaniel S. Berry (R)	1861-1863
Joseph A. Gilmore (R)	1863-1865
Frederick Smith (R)	1865-1867
Walter Harriman (R)	1867-1869
Onslow Stearns (R)	1869-1871
James A. Weston (D)	1871-1872
Ezekiel A. Straw (R)	1872-1874
James A. Weston (D)	1874-1875
Person C. Cheney (R)	1875-1877
Benjamin F. Prescott (R)	1877-1879
Nathaniel Head (R)	1879-1881
Charles H. Bell (R)	1881-1883
Samuel W. Hale (R)	1883-1885
Moody Currier (R)	1885-1887
Charles H. Sawyer (R)	1887-1889
David H. Goodell (R)	1889-1891
Hiram A. Tuttle (R)	1891-1893
John B. Smith (R)	1893-1895
Charles A. Busiel (R)	1895-1897
George A. Ramsdell (R)	1897-1899
Frank W. Rollins (R)	1899-1901
Chester B. Jordan (R)	1901-1903
Nahum J. Bachelder (R)	1903-1905
John McLane (R)	1905-1907
Charles M. Floyd (R)	1907-1909
Henry B. Quimby (R)	1909-1911
Robert P. Bass (R)	1911-1913
Samuel D. Felker (D)	1913-1915
Rolland H. Spaulding (R)	1915-1917
Henry W. Keyes (R)	1917-1919
John H. Bartlett (R)	1919-1921
Albert O. Brown (R)	1921-1923
Fred H. Brown (D)	1923-1925
John G. Winant (R)	1925-1927
Huntley N. Spaulding (R)	1927-1929
Charles W. Tobey (R)	1929-1931

(continued)

John G. Winant (R)	1931-1935
Henry Styles Bridges (R)	1935-1937
Francis P. Murphy (R)	1937-1941
Robert O. Blood (R)	1941-1945
Charles M. Dale (R)	1945-1949
Sherman Adams (R)	1949-1953
Hugh Gregg (R)	1953-1955
Lane Dwinell (R)	1955-1959
Wesley Powell (R)	1959-1963
John W. King (D)	1963-1969
Walter R. Peterson, Jr. (R)	1969-1973
Meldrim Thomson, Jr. (R)	1973-1979
Hugh J. Gallen (D)	1979-1982
Vesta Roy (R)	1982-1983
John H. Sununu (R)	1983-1989
Judd Gregg (R)	1989-1993
Steve Merrill (R)	1993-1997
Jeanne Shaheen (D)	1997-

Governors were called state presidents before 1792.

Composition of state legislature, 1990-1998

	Democrats	Republicans
State House (398 seats)		
1990	125	268
1992	136	258
1994	112	286
1996	143	255
1998	154	244
State Senate (24 seats)		
1990	11	13
1992	11	13
1994	6	18
1996	9	15
1998	13	11

Figures for total seats may include independents and minor party members.

Source: Council of State Governments; *State Elective Officials and the Legislatures.*

Composition of congressional delegations, 1989-1999

	Dem	Rep	Total
House of Representatives			
101st Congress, 1989			
State delegates	0	2	2
Total U.S.	259	174	433

	Dem	Rep	Total
102d Congress, 1991			
State delegates	1	1	2
Total U.S.	267	167	434
103d Congress, 1993			
State delegates	1	1	2
Total U.S.	258	176	434
104th Congress, 1995			
State delegates	0	2	2
Total U.S.	197	236	433
105th Congress, 1997			
State delegates	0	2	2
Total U.S.	206	228	434
106th Congress, 1999			
State delegates	0	2	2
Total U.S.	211	222	433
Senate			
101st Congress, 1989			
State delegates	0	2	2
Total U.S.	55	45	100
102d Congress, 1991			
State delegates	0	2	2
Total U.S.	56	44	100
103d Congress, 1993			
State delegates	0	2	2
Total U.S.	57	43	100
104th Congress, 1995			
State delegates	0	2	2
Total U.S.	46	53	99
105th Congress, 1997			
State delegates	0	2	2
Total U.S.	45	55	100
106th Congress, 1999			
State delegates	0	1	2
Total U.S.	45	54	99

Figures are for starts of first sessions. Figure for U.S. Representatives for 101st Congress does not include Alabama and Indiana, which had vacancies. Figures for total U.S. Representatives for 102d, 103d, and 106th Congresses do not include Vermont, which had 1 Independent-Socialist. Figure for U.S. Representatives for 104th Congress does not include Vermont, which had 1 Independent-Socialist, and California, which had 1 vacancy. Figure for U.S. Representatives for 105th Congress does not include New York, which had 1 vacancy. Figure for U.S. Senators for 104th Congress does not include Oregon, which had 1 vacancy. Figure for U.S. Senators for 106th Congress does not include New Hampshire, which had 1 Independent.

Source: U.S. Congress; *Congressional Directory,* biennial.

Voter participation in presidential elections, 1992 and 1996

	1992	1996
State voting age pop.	838,000	860,000
Total U.S. voting age pop.	189,524,000	196,509,000
State share of U.S. total	0.4%	0.4%
Rank among states	41	41
Percent of state casting vote	64.2	49.5
Percent of U.S. total voting	55.1	49.0
Rank among states	12	27

Source: U.S. Bureau of the Census.

HEALTH AND MEDICAL CARE

Medicare, 1997

	Recipients	Payments
State	162,000	$714 mill.
Total U.S.	37,514,000	$206,064 mill.
State share	0.43%	0.35%
Rank among states	41	41

Recipient figures are rounded to nearest thousand persons. Ranks are from highest to lowest.
Source: U.S. Health Care Financing Administration.

Medicaid, 1996

	Recipients	Payments
State	100,000	$547 mill.
Total U.S.	35,028,000	$121,419 mill.
State share	0.29%	0.45%
Rank among states	44	38

Recipient figures are rounded to nearest thousand persons. Payment figures for fiscal year reflect federal and state contribution payments. Ranks are from highest to lowest.
Source: U.S. Health Care Financing Administration.

Health insurance coverage, 1996

	State	U.S.
Total persons covered	1,033,000	225,070,000
Total persons not covered	109,000	41,716,000
Part not covered	9.5%	15.6%
Rank among states	45	—
Children not covered	27,000	10,554,000
Part not covered	9.6%	14.8%
Rank among states	37	—

Ranks are from most to fewest uninsured. Population figures are rounded to nearest thousand persons.
Source: U.S. Bureau of the Census.

AIDS, syphilis, tuberculosis, and measles cases, 1997

Cases	U.S.	State	Share
AIDS	58,443	55	0.09%
Syphilis	8,550	NA	NA
Tuberculosis	18,534	17	0.09%
Measles	148,000	1,000	0.68%

Measles figures are rounded to nearest thousand cases.
Source: U.S. Centers for Disease Control and Prevention.

HOUSING

Homeownership rates, 1985-1997

	1985	1990	1997
State	65.5%	65.0%	66.8%
Total U.S.	63.9%	63.9%	65.7%
Rank among states	35	33	34

Source: U.S. Bureau of the Census.

Home sales, 1990 and 1997
In thousands of units

Existing home sales	1990	1997	Change
State sales	7.9	NA	NA
Total U.S. sales	3,560	4,730	1,170
State share of U.S. total	0.22%	NA	NA
Rank among states	45	NA	—

Source: National Association of Realtors; *Real Estate Outlook: Market Trends and Insights.*

EDUCATION

Public school enrollment, 1995

State K-8 enrollment 142,000
Total U.S. K-8 enrollment 32,341,000
State share of total U.S. 0.44%
State 9-12 enrollment. 52,000
Total U.S. 9-12 enrollment 12,500,000
State share of U.S. total 0.42%
State public school enroll. rate 89.6%
Overall U.S. rate. 91.6%
Rank among states. 36

Enrollment figures (which include unclassified students) are
    rounded to nearest thousand pupils in fall term;
    kindergarten (K)-8 grade figures include some
    prekindergarten students. Enrollment rate is based on
    percentage of persons 5-17 years old. Rank is from highest
    to lowest.
Source: U.S. National Center for Education Statistics.

Public college finances, 1996

State FTE enrollment. 27,900
Total U.S. FTE enrollment 8,268,800
State share of total U.S. 0.34%
Rank among states. 43
State and local appropriations $78,800,000
Total U.S. state and local
    appropriations. . . . . $39,699 mill.
State share of total U.S. 0.20%
Rank among states. 49
State net tuition revenues . . . . $160 mill.
Total U.S. net tuition $18,348,100,000
State share of total U.S. 0.87%
Rank among states. 36

FTE=Full-time equivalent; credit and noncredit enrollment
    including summer session in academic year ending in
    1996.
Enrollments are rounded to nearest thousand students. Net
    tuition revenues exclude appropriation to students
    attending in-state public institutions. Rankings are from
    highest shares to lowest.
Source: Research Associates of Washington.

TRANSPORTATION AND TRAVEL

Highway mileage, 1996

Interstate 224
Other arterial. 1,582
Collector roads 2,998
Local roads 10,586
Urban roads 2,916
Rural roads 12,190
Total state 15,106
U.S. total 3,933,985
State share 0.4%
Rank among states. 45

Source: U.S. Federal Highway Administration.

Motor vehicle registrations and driver licenses, 1996
In thousands

Vehicle registrations	State	U.S.	Share	Rank
Autos, trucks, buses	1,112	206,365	0.54%	38
Autos only	733	128,439	0.57%	38
Motorcycles	52	3,832	1.36%	25
Driver licenses	915	179,539	0.51%	38

Figures do not include vehicles owned by military services.
Source: U.S. Federal Highway Administration; *Highway*
    Statistics; Selected Highway Statistics and Charts.

Domestic travel expenditures, 1995
Spending by U.S. residents on overnight trips and day
trips of at least 100 miles

Total expenditures in state . . . . $1,676 mill.
Total expenditures in U.S. . . . . $360,314 mill.
State share of total U.S. 0.47%
Rank among states. 39

Source: Travel Industry Association of America.

CRIME AND LAW ENFORCEMENT

State and local police officers, 1996

Local police	1,862
State police	245
Sheriffs	129
Total	2,305
Officers per 10,000 residents	20
U.S. average	25
Rank among states.	36

Figures cover full-time sworn officers; totals include special police not shown separately.
Source: U.S. Bureau of Justice Statistics; *Census of State and Local Law Enforcement Agencies, 1996.*

Crime rates, 1996
Rates per 100,000 resident population

Violent crimes	State	U.S.
Total violent	118	634
Murder	1.7	7.4
Forcible rape	34.8	36.1
Robbery	27	202
Aggravated assault	54	388
Property crimes		
Total property	2,705	4,445
Burglary	436	943
Larceny/theft	2,118	2,976
Motor vehicle theft	152	526
Totals	2,824	5,079

Source: U.S. Federal Bureau of Investigation; *Crime in the United States,* annual.

State prison populations, 1980-1996

	State	U.S.	State share
1980	326	305,458	0.11%
1990	1,342	708,393	0.19%
1996	2,062	1,025,624	0.20%

Figures exclude prisoners in federal penitentiaries.
Source: U.S. Bureau of Justice Statistics.

New Jersey

Location: East Coast of continental United States

Area and rank: 7,419 square miles (19,215 square kilometers); 8,722 square miles (22,590 square kilometers) including water; forty-sixth largest state in area

Coastline: 130 miles (209 kilometers)

Shoreline: 1,792 miles (2,883 kilometers)

Population and rank: 8,052,849 (1997); ninth largest state in population

Capital: Trenton

Boardwalk at Atlantic City, New Jersey's premier resort community. (PhotoDisc)

Largest city: Newark (267,823 people in 1998)

Entered Union and rank: December 18, 1787; third state

Present constitution adopted: 1947

Counties: 21

State name: New Jersey was named after the Channel Isle of Jersey

State nickname: Garden State

Motto: Liberty and prosperity

State flag: Buff field with state coat of arms

Highest point: High Point — 1,803 feet (550 meters)

Lowest point: Atlantic Ocean — sea level

Highest recorded temperature: 110 degrees Fahrenheit (43 degrees Celsius) — Runyon, 1936

Lowest recorded temperature: −34 degrees Fahrenheit (−37 degrees Celsius) — River Vale, 1904

State tree: Red oak

State flower: Purple violet

State bird: Eastern goldfinch

State fish: Brook trout

State animal: Horse

New Jersey History

Situated on a relatively narrow strip of land between the Atlantic Ocean and the Delaware River, New Jersey has been one of the most densely populated areas of the nation since the early years of the United States. Bordering the large cities of New York City to the northeast and Philadelphia to the southwest, New Jersey was heavily urbanized and industrialized at an early date but still retains scenic seacoasts and wilderness areas.

The New Jersey site where George Washington crossed the Delaware River during the Revolutionary War has been made into a state park. (Courtesy of New Jersey Commerce & Economic Growth Commission/Scott Barrow)

Early History. About six thousand years ago, the Delaware, a Native American people also known as the Lenni Lenape, arrived in the region between the Hudson River and the Delaware River. The Delaware practiced agriculture, hunted, fished in the rivers, and gathered shellfish from the Atlantic Ocean. Not long after European colonists established settlements in the area, the Delaware, reduced greatly in numbers by newly introduced European diseases, sold their native lands and moved westward. By the middle of the nineteenth century, the Delaware were removed to Oklahoma, where many of their descendants reside today.

The first European to reach New Jersey was the Italian navigator Giovanni da Verrazano. Working for the French, Verrazano explored the Atlantic coast from North Carolina to Canada in 1524. During this voyage, Verrazano entered what is now Newark Bay. In 1609, the English navigator Henry Hudson, working for the Dutch, explored what is now Sandy Hook Bay.

Colonization. Despite this early exploration, settlement of the area began slowly. Although Dutch trading posts were founded on the Hudson River as early as 1618, and Swedish trading posts on the Delaware River by 1638, the first permanent European settlement was not founded until 1660. This settlement, known as Bergen, was founded by the Dutch at the present site of Jersey City. The Dutch, who had taken control of the Swedish trading posts in 1655, retained ownership of the colony until 1664, when an English fleet sailed into New York Harbor and took control of the Dutch colonies of New York and New Jersey without a fight.

King Charles II of England granted all the lands between the Connecticut River and the Delaware River, including New York and New Jersey, to his brother, the Duke of York and Albany. The duke (later King James II) in turn granted the region between the Hudson River and the Delaware River to John Berkeley and George Carteret, two friends and allies of the king. This area was divided into East Jersey and West Jersey in 1676, when Berkeley sold his share of the land to a group of Quakers. The Quakers took possession of West Jersey, while Carteret retained control of East Jersey.

East Jersey was mostly settled by Puritans from Long Island and New England. The Quakers purchased East Jersey in 1682. In 1702 English Queen Anne united the two colonies under royal rule and placed them under the administration of the governor of New York. In 1738, New Jersey separated from New York, with Lewis Morris serving as its first governor.

Revolution. Located between the two important colonial cities of New York and Philadelphia, New Jersey soon became an important area of transportation, with more roads than any other colony. During the American Revolution (1775-1783), New Jersey's strategic position between these two vital cities led to more than one hundred battles in the area.

The British, who had captured New York City in late 1776, drove American troops commanded by General George Washington out of New York and New Jersey into Pennsylvania. Early on the morning of December 26, 1776, Washington crossed the Delaware River into New Jersey and captured Trenton. Although Trenton was recaptured by the British on January 2, 1777, Washington won another victory at Princeton the next day. These early successes, although not decisive, prevented the American war effort from failing during the early years of the Revolution. A later American victory on June 28, 1778, when Washing-

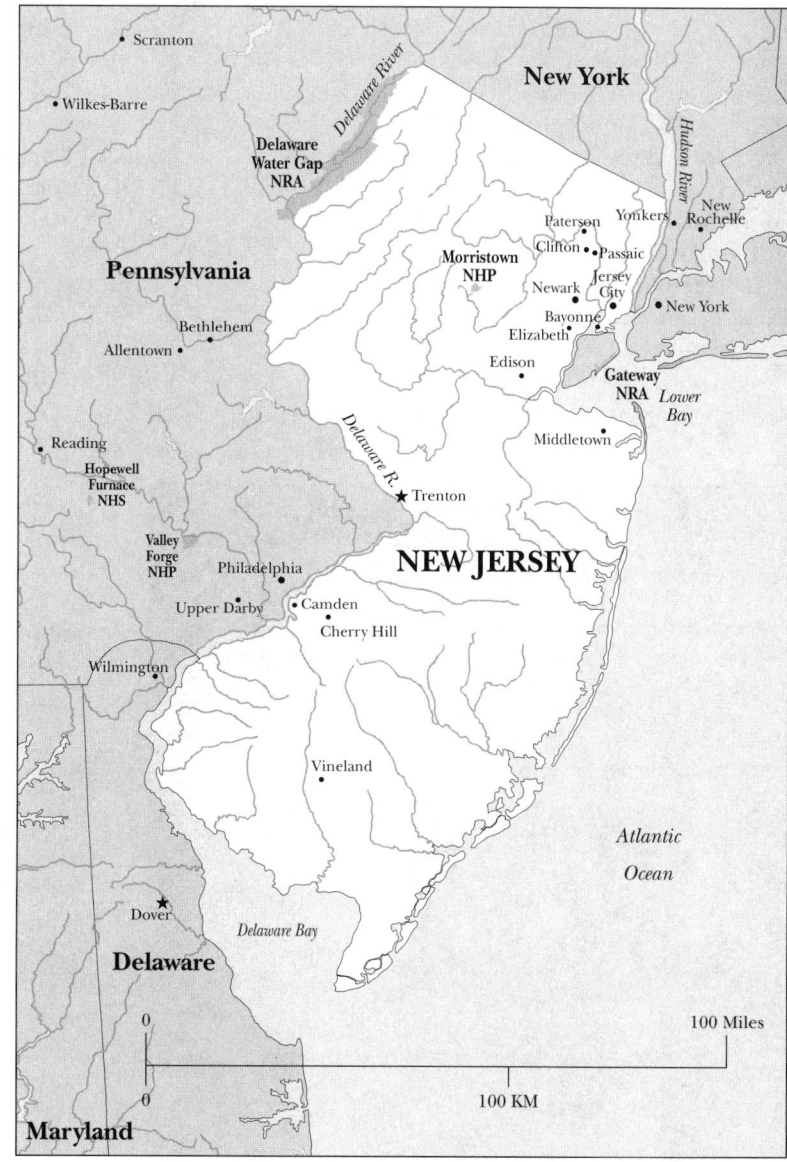

ton attacked British forces withdrawing from Philadelphia at Monmouth Court House, helped maintain a stalemate in the northern states, allowing the Revolution to continue until more critical victories in the southern states led to the end of the war.

After the war, Princeton served as the capital of the United States for brief periods in 1783 and 1784. New Jersey played a key role during the convention in Philadelphia in 1787 that created the U.S. Constitution. The New Jersey Plan, which advocated equal representation for each state, was combined with the Virginia Plan, which advocated representation based on population, to create the Senate and the House of Representatives. New Jersey ratified the Constitution on December 18, 1787, officially becoming the third state. It was the first state to ratify the first ten amendments to the Constitution, known as the Bill of Rights, on November 20, 1789.

Industry and Transportation. Although first noted in colonial days as a highly productive area for agriculture, hence the nickname of the "Garden State," New Jersey became one of the first states to develop an industrial economy. The pro-

The Statue of Liberty stands on an island claimed by both New Jersey and New York states. (Courtesy of New Jersey Commerce & Economic Growth Commission)

cess began during the American Revolution, when New Jersey supplied much of the iron needed for cannons and ammunition. In 1791 Alexander Hamilton founded the nation's first industrial town at Paterson, located at the Great Falls of the Passaic River, which supplied water power.

Much of the industrial growth during the early nineteenth century was due to improvements in transportation. During the 1830's, a series of canals linked the Hudson River and the Delaware River, allowing easier transport of goods between New York City and Philadelphia. During the same period, railroads began to appear in the state. An early industry that developed in New Jersey due to the transportation revolution was the dyeing and weaving of cloth. The textile industry would remain important to the state's economy.

The Civil War and Immigration. Its central position between Northern states and Southern states, combined with economic ties to Southern states, made New Jersey one of the most divided states during the Civil War (1861-1865). The Democratic Party in the state included many Peace Democrats, who advocated an end to the war through negotiation with the Confederacy. The Republican Party demanded complete victory over the Confederacy. This early struggle was reflected in later years, when the two parties continued to share almost equal power in the state. Although the military draft was strongly opposed in 1863, New Jersey supplied large numbers of troops and manufactured goods for the Union. After the war, many politicians opposed granting civil rights to African Americans, who were not allowed to vote in New Jersey until 1870.

Meanwhile, the first of many waves of immigration to the state brought many Germans and Irish to New Jersey in the 1840's. Most immigrants during the late nineteenth century arrived from southern and eastern Europe, particularly Italy, Russia, Poland, and Hungary. The increase in population, particularly in urban areas, combined with an increased demand for manufactured goods, continued the industrialization of the state. One of the largest factories in New Jersey was founded by Isaac M. Singer, who opened a sewing machine plant in Elizabeth in 1871. Other thriving industries at this time included oil refining along the Hudson River and pottery manufacturing in Trenton. Newark became one of the most prominent industrial cities in the state, with a variety of manufacturers, as well as an important insurance industry.

The Age of Wilson. New Jersey rose to prominence in national politics in the early years of the twentieth century. Woodrow Wilson, president of Princeton University since 1902, was elected governor in 1910. The success of his progressive policies led to his election as president of the United States in 1912. During his first term in office, Wilson was active in promoting legislation that reformed national economic policies. Reelected in 1916, Wilson helped to establish the League of Nations after World War I, winning him the Nobel Peace Prize in 1920.

In sharp contrast to Wilson's idealism, local politics in New Jersey were often highly corrupt. The most notorious of the state's political bosses was Frank Hague, who ruled Jersey City from 1917 to 1947. Hague was famous for his boast that "I am the law." Although reforms diminished the power of political bosses, New Jersey continued to have a reputation for political corruption and organized crime.

The Twentieth Century. World War I made New Jersey a center of shipbuilding and munitions manufacturing. The war also prevented German chemicals and pharmaceuticals from reaching the United States, and New Jersey became a leader in these developing industries domestically. Chemical production continued to be the most important industry in the state. After the Great Depression of the 1930's, New Jersey's economy recovered during World War II, when aircraft manufacturing became a major industry in the state, along

Harvesting cranberries, a major New Jersey crop. (Courtesy of New Jersey Commerce & Economic Growth Commission)

with a revival in the making of ships and armaments.

World War II also brought many African Americans to New Jersey. The 1950's and 1960's saw large numbers of Puerto Ricans enter the state. After Fidel Castro established a Communist government in Cuba in 1959, many Cubans immigrated to New Jersey. Later decades saw an increase in the number of immigrants from Asia and the Middle East.

After a recession in the 1970's and early 1980's, New Jersey's economy shifted from manufacturing to service industries. Unemployment dropped from 10 percent in the middle of the 1970's to 4 percent in 1988. Despite a strong economy in the 1990's, New Jersey faced the problems of crime, poverty, and pollution, which were inevitable for any heavily urbanized state.

Rose Secrest

New Jersey Time Line

1524	Explorer Giovanni da Verrazano, sailing for the French, reaches Newark Bay.
1609	English navigator Henry Hudson, working for the Dutch, reaches Sandy Hook Bay.
1618	Dutch trading posts are established on the Hudson River.
1638	Swedish trading posts are established on the Delaware River.
1655	Dutch take control of the Swedish trading posts.
1660	Dutch establish the first permanent European settlement in New Jersey at Bergen, at the modern site of Jersey City.
1664	English take control of New Jersey.
1676	New Jersey is divided into East Jersey and West Jersey, with Quakers purchasing West Jersey.
1682	Quakers purchase East Jersey.
1702	East Jersey and West Jersey are united under the control of English Queen Anne, who places them under the same administration as New York.
1738	Lewis Morris becomes the first governor of New Jersey after its administration is separated from that of New York.
1746	Princeton University is founded.
1758	American Indians sell all New Jersey lands to the state; first Indian reservation in the Union is established in Burlington County.
1766	Queens College, later known as Rutgers University, is founded.
Dec. 26, 1776	American forces led by General George Washington capture Trenton during the Revolution.
Jan. 3, 1777	British recapture Trenton but are defeated by Washington at Princeton.
1778	Washington defeats British at Monmouth Court House.
1783-1784	Princeton serves briefly twice as the national capital.
Dec. 18, 1787	New Jersey ratifies the U.S. Constitution, becoming the third state.
Nov. 20, 1789	New Jersey becomes the first state to ratify the Bill of Rights.
1791	Alexander Hamilton establishes the nation's first industrial town at Paterson.
1830's	Canals and railroads improve transportation in the state.
1840's	German and Irish immigrants arrive.

1850	Population reaches 500,000.
1863	Opposition to the military draft in the Civil War breaks out.
1870	African Americans are allowed to vote.
1870	First boardwalk is erected in Atlantic City.
1873	Isaac M. Singer establishes a sewing machine factory in Elizabeth.
1876	Thomas Edison establishes a research laboratory in Menlo Park.
1880	Population reaches 1,000,000.
1890's	Immigrants arrive from southern and eastern Europe.
1910	Woodrow Wilson is elected governor.
Nov. 5, 1912	Wilson is elected president of the United States; is reelected in 1916.
1917	Political boss Frank Hague takes control of Jersey City.
1921	New York and New Jersey form the Port of New York Authority, operating transportation facilities near New York City in both states.
1940's	Large numbers of African Americans migrate to New Jersey.
1946	State takes control of Rutgers University, establishing the State University of New Jersey.
1947	New state constitution is adopted.
1950's-1960's	Many Puerto Ricans and Cubans enter the state.
July, 1967	Four days of rioting take place in slums; twenty-three die.
1968	Amphitheater for drama, music, and dance opens at the Garden State Arts Center.
1970's	Economic recession leads to unemployment rate of 10 percent.
1976	Gambling is legalized in Atlantic City.
1978	Pinelands National Reserve, the nation's first national reserve, is established.
1988	Economic recovery reduces the unemployment rate to 4 percent.
1991	State prohibits ocean dumping after beaches become contaminated with medical waste.
1999	Severe drought leads to mandatory water rationing.

Notes for Further Study

Published Sources. Of the many books dealing with New Jersey, one of the best for students new to the subject is *New Jersey* (1998) by R. Conrad Stein, which discusses the state's geography, plant and animal life, history, economy, and people in a clear and concise manner. The ecology of one of the most unusual wilderness areas in the state is presented in detail in *Pine Barrens: Ecosystem and Landscape* (1998) edited by Richard T. T. Forman. A useful account of the foundations of the state government is provided by *The New Jersey Constitution: A Reference Guide* (1997) by Robert F. Williams. More details on the state government can be found in *New Jersey Poli-* *tics and Government: Suburban Politics Come of Age* (1998) by Barbara G. and Stephen A. Salmore.

An excellent description of the many different ethnic groups in the state is provided by *Keys to Successful Immigration: Implications of the New Jersey Experience* (1997) by Thomas J. Espenshade. A book that supplies a dramatic account of the serious problem of race relations in New Jersey is *Our Town: Race, Housing, and the Soul of Suburbia* (1995) by David L. Kirp, John P. Dwyer, and Larry A. Rosenthal.

An unusual guidebook with a great deal of information on lesser-known attractions in the state is provided by *Discover the Hidden New Jersey* (1995) by Russell Roberts. A lively history of New Jersey's most famous tourist attraction is found in Vicki Gold Levi's *Atlantic City: 125 Years of Ocean Madness* (1994).

Web Resources. A good starting point for exploring Internet resources dedicated to New Jersey is the state's official Web site, The State of New Jersey (http://www.state.nj.us), which supplies general information as well as a guide to the state government. Other general Web sites include New Jersey Online (http://www.nj.com), IN Jersey (http://www.injersey.com), and New Jersey Internet (http://www.nji.com). A guide to tourism in the state is supplied by New Jersey Travel and Tourism (http://www.state.nj.us/travel/index.html). A detailed account of transportation in New Jersey, vital to the state's economy, is found at Welcome to NJ Transit's Web site (http://www.njtransit.state.nj.us). Detailed weather information is provided by Rutgers University at the Office of the NJ State Climatologist site (http://www.climate.rutgers.edu/stateclim).

Of the many Web sites dedicated to New Jersey history, one of the best for a clear introduction to the subject is found at New Jersey History (http://www.state.nj.us/hangout/history.html). More detailed information is supplied by Rutgers University at Electronic New Jersey (http://www.scc01.rutgers.edu/njh). Links to archives, museums, and other historical resources are provided by New Jersey Historical Commission (http://www.state.nj.us/state/history/hisidx.html). An excellent account of the vital role New Jersey played in the American Revolution is provided by New Jersey in the Revolution (http://www.people/csnet.net/dpst/welcome.html). The life story of one of New Jersey's most renowned citizens is found at Woodrow Wilson Biography (http://gi.grolier.com/presidents/ea/bios/28pwils.html).

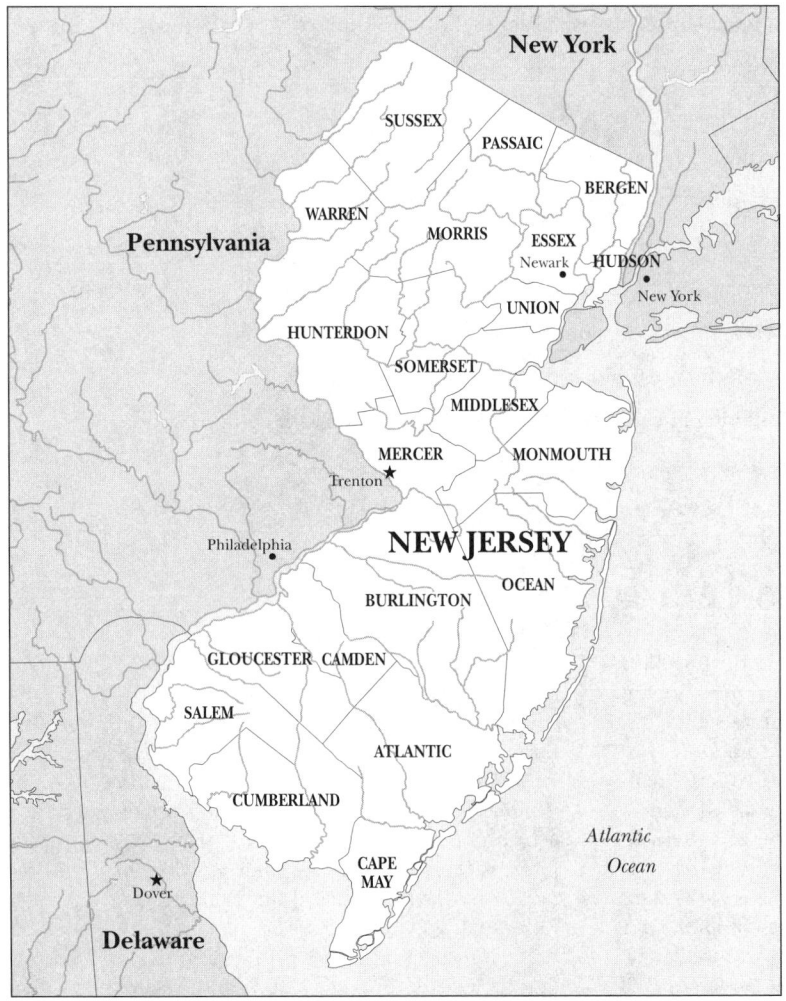

Counties

County	Sq. miles	1996 pop.
Atlantic	561.2	235,447
Bergen	234.2	846,498
Burlington	804.8	410,931
Camden	222.3	506,420
Cape May	255.2	98,252
Cumberland	489.3	135,943
Essex	126.3	755,089
Gloucester	324.9	244,203
Hudson	46.7	550,789
Hunterdon	430.1	118,737
Mercer	226.0	330,226
Middlesex	310.6	702,458
Monmouth	471.9	591,182
Morris	469.1	449,218
Ocean	636.3	474,102
Passaic	185.0	464,833
Salem	337.8	67,540
Somerset	304.7	269,902
Sussex	521.2	141,308
Union	103.3	497,281
Warren	357.9	97,574

Source: U.S. Bureau of the Census;
    National Association of Counties.

Cities
With 10,000 or more residents

Rank	City	Population	Rank	City	Population
1	Newark	267,823	49	Asbury Park	17,057
2	Jersey City	232,429	50	Morristown	16,629
3	Paterson	148,212	51	Pleasantville	16,619
4	Elizabeth	110,661	52	New Milford	16,425
5	Trenton	84,494	53	Hopatcong	16,241
6	Camden	83,546	54	Madison	15,828
7	Clifton	76,180	55	Tinton Falls	15,795
8	East Orange	69,598	56	Ocean City	15,760
9	Bayonne	61,051	57	Phillipsburg	15,533
10	Passaic	60,817	58	Dover	15,462
11	Union City	57,621	59	Palisades Park	15,060
12	Vineland	55,484	60	Collingswood	14,582
13	Plainfield	46,414	61	Ramsey	14,480
14	Perth Amboy	42,481	62	North Arlington	14,128
15	New Brunswick	41,768	63	Eatontown	14,077
16	Atlantic City	38,063	64	South River	14,045
17	Sayreville	38,042	65	Secaucus	13,975
18	West New York	38,020	66	Tenafly	13,595
19	Hackensack	37,813	67	Ringwood	13,504
20	Linden	37,204	68	Harrison	13,383
21	Kearny	35,441	69	Highland Park	13,266
22	Fort Lee	33,989	70	Middlesex	13,217
23	Hoboken	33,354	71	Metuchen	13,038
24	Fair Lawn	31,091	72	Roselle Park	12,771
25	Westfield	29,297	73	Ridgefield Park	12,603
26	Long Branch	28,905	74	Oakland	12,478
27	Garfield	27,262	75	Hammonton	12,447
28	Millville	26,359	76	Bellmawr	12,243
29	Paramus	26,103	77	Gloucester City	12,121
30	Rahway	25,336	78	New Providence	11,885
31	Englewood	25,321	79	Princeton	11,814
32	Bergenfield	24,827	80	Somerville	11,777
33	Ridgewood	24,577	81	Hasbrouck Heights	11,704
34	Lodi	22,917	82	West Paterson	11,704
35	Cliffside Park	21,141	83	Brigantine	11,599
36	South Plainfield	20,903	84	Lincoln Park	11,270
37	Roselle	20,297	85	Fairview	11,252
38	Summit	19,706	86	Pompton Lakes	11,180
39	Point Pleasant	19,349	87	Haddonfield	11,170
40	Carteret	19,094	88	Keansburg	11,166
41	North Plainfield	19,067	89	Somers Point	11,159
42	Hawthorne	18,304	90	Glen Rock	11,149
43	Elmwood Park	18,299	91	Wallington	11,099
44	Rutherford	18,116	92	Totowa	10,930
45	Bridgeton	18,096	93	Manville	10,899
46	Lindenwold	18,093	94	River Edge	10,862
47	Dumont	17,631	95	Red Bank	10,858
48	Glassboro	17,588	96	Ventnor City	10,857

(continued)

Rank	City	Population
97	Freehold	10,850
98	Westwood	10,779
99	Franklin Lakes	10,575
100	Wanaque	10,520
101	Woodbury	10,520
102	Pine Hill	10,468
103	Ridgefield	10,183
104	Little Ferry	10,176
105	Hillsdale	10,142
106	Beachwood	10,130
107	Waldwick	10,097

Population figures are estimated for mid-1998.

Source: U.S. Bureau of the Census.

Index to Tables

NA = Reliable data are not available.

DEMOGRAPHICS

Resident state and national populations, 1970-1997

Population figures given in thousands

	State pop.	U.S. pop.	Share	Rank
1970	7,171	203,302	3.5%	8
1980	7,365	226,546	3.3%	9
1985	7,566	237,924	3.2%	9
1990	7,748	248,765	3.1%	9
1995	7,956	262,761	3.0%	9
1997	8,053	267,636	3.0%	9

Source: U.S. Bureau of the Census.

Resident population by age, 1997

Age group	Total population
Under 5 years	557,000
5 to 17 years	1,430,000
18 to 24 years	667,000
25 to 34 years	1,170,000
35 to 44 years	1,385,000
45 to 54 years	1,055,000
55 to 64 years	683,000
65 to 74 years	596,000
75 to 84 years	386,000
85 years and over	124,000
Portion of residents 65 and older	13.7%
National average	12.7%

Population figures are rounded to nearest thousand persons;
figures include armed forces personnel stationed in state.
Source: U.S. Bureau of the Census.

Resident population by race, Hispanic origin, 1997

	State pop.	Share	U.S.
All residents	8,053,000	100.0%	100.0%
Hispanic white	826,000	10.3%	10.0%
non-Hispanic white	5,611,000	69.7%	72.7%
African American	1,170,000	14.5%	12.7%
Native American	21,000	0.3%	0.9%
Asian, Pacific Islander	424,000	5.3%	3.8%

Source: U.S. Bureau of the Census.

Projections of state population, 2000-2025

	Model A Uses interstate migration observed from 1975-1994	Model B Uses Bureau of Economic Analysis employment projections
Year	Population	Population
2000	8,178,000	8,185,000
2005	8,392,000	8,387,000
2010	8,638,000	8,594,000
2015	8,924,000	8,832,000
2020	9,238,000	9,096,000
2025	9,558,000	9,369,000

All population projections, including those for 2000, were calculated in 1997.
Source: U.S. Bureau of the Census, Population Paper Listings PPL-47.

VITAL STATISTICS

Average lifetime in years by race, 1989-1991

	State	U.S.	Rank
All residents	75.42	75.37	26
White residents	76.46	76.13	21
Black residents	68.47	69.16	30

Ranks are from longest-lived to least longest-lived. Ranks exclude Alaska, for which reliable data are not available. Rank for black residents is based on the 32 states for which reliable data are available.
Source: U.S. National Center for Health Statistics.

Infant mortality rates, 1980 and 1995

	State	U.S.
All residents		
1980	12.5	12.6
1995	6.6	7.6
White residents		
1980	10.3	11.0
1995	5.3	6.3
Black residents		
1980	21.9	21.4
1995	13.3	15.1

Figures represent deaths per 1,000 live births of resident infants under 1 year old, exclusive of fetal deaths; all-residents figures include other races not listed separately.
Source: U.S. National Center for Health Statistics.

Marriages and divorces

Marriages in 1996	51,700
Rate per 1,000 population, 1995	6.7
U.S. rate, 1995	8.9
Rank among all states	46
Divorces in 1996	25,000
Rate per 1,000 population, 1995	3.1
U.S. rate, 1995	4.4
Rank among all states	42

Rank is from highest to lowest in country.
Source: U.S. National Center for Health Statistics.

Death rates by leading causes, 1995
Deaths per 100,000 resident population

Cause	State	U.S.
Heart disease	303.3	280.7
Cancer	231.9	204.9
Cerebrovascular diseases	53.4	60.1
Accidents and adverse effects	29.1	35.5
Motor vehicle accidents	10.6	16.5
Chronic obstructive pulmonary diseases	34.5	39.2
Diabetes mellitus	30.1	22.6
HIV	30.7	NA
Suicide	7.3	11.9
Homicide	5.4	8.7
All causes	932.5	880.0
Rank in overall death rate among states		18

Figures exclude nonresidents who die in state. Causes of death follow International Classification of Diseases. Rank is from highest to lowest in country.
Source: U.S. National Center for Health Statistics.

ECONOMY

Gross state product, 1990-1996
In current dollars

	State product	Increase
1990	$214.1 billion	
1993	$243.9 billion	
1994	$255.8 billion	4.88%
1995	$266.1 billion	4.03%
1996	$276.4 billion	3.87%

Source: U.S. Bureau of Economic Analysis; *Survey of Current Business,* June, 1998.

Gross state product by industry, 1996
In billions

Farms, forestry, fisheries	$1.4
Construction	8.4
Manufacturing	36.8
Transportation, public utilities	25.6
Wholesale trade	24.0
Retail trade	19.6
Finance, insurance, real estate	55.8
Services	52.8
Government	26.6
State total	$251.1
Total U.S.	$6,923.8
State share	3.63%
Rank among states	8

Total figures include mining, not listed separately.
Source: U.S. Bureau of Economic Analysis; *Survey of Current Business,* June, 1998.

Personal income per capita, 1990 and 1997
In current dollars

	1990	1997
Per capita income	$24,930	$32,654
U.S. average	$19,188	$25,598
Rank among states	2	2

1997 data are preliminary.
Source: U.S. Bureau of Economic Analysis; *Survey of Current Business,* May, 1998.

Energy consumption, 1995
In trillions of British thermal units (BTU)

End-use sectors

Residential	529.5
Commercial	493.5
Industrial	655.4
Transportation	864.5

Sources of energy

Petroleum	1,238.4
Natural gas	610.9
Coal	55.1
Hydroelectric power	-0.9
Nuclear electric power	179.1
Total state per capita consumption	319.9
Total U.S. per capita consumption	344.4
Rank among states	36
Total state energy consumption	2,542.9
Total U.S. energy consumption	90,547.4
State share of U.S. total	2.81%
Rank among states	11

Total figures include items not listed separately.
A negative number occurs when more electricity is expended than is created
Source: U.S. Energy Information Administration; *State Energy Data Report.*

Nonfarm employment by sectors, 1997

Total	3,725,000
Construction	131,000
Manufacturing	482,000
Transportation, public utilities	257,000
Wholesale trade, retail trade	872,000
Finance, insurance, real estate	239,000
Services	1,172,000
Government	569,000

Figures are rounded to nearest thousand persons. Total includes mining, not listed separately.
Source: U.S. Bureau of Labor Statistics; *Employment and Earnings,* monthly.

Foreign exports, 1990-1997
In millions of dollars

Year	State	U.S.	State share
1990	7,633	394,045	1.94%
1996	13,119	624,767	2.10%
1997	15,167	688,896	2.20%

Source: U.S. Bureau of the Census; *U.S. Merchandise Trade,* series FT 900.

LAND USE

Federally owned land, 1996

	State	U.S.	State share
Total acres	4,813,000	2,271,343,000	1.32%
Federally owned	102,000	563,129,000	0.06%
Federal share	2.1%	24.8%	—

Areas are rounded to nearest thousand acres. Figures for federally owned land do not include trust properties.
Source: U.S. General Services Administration; *Inventory Report on Real Property Owned by the United States Throughout the World*, annual.

Land use, 1992
In acres, rounded to nearest thousand

Total surface area	4,984,000
Federal land	159,000
Total nonfederal.	4,549,000
Developed	1,588,000
Total rural	2,961,000
Cropland.	650,000
Pasture land	159,000
Range land	0
Forest land.	1,766,000
Minor cover/use.	386,000

Total surface area figures include water area not shown separately.
Source: U.S. Dept. of Agriculture; Soil Conservation Service; Iowa State University, Statistical Laboratory; *Summary Report, 1992 National Resources Inventory.*

Farms and crop acreage, 1997

	State	U.S.	Share	Rank
Farms (thousands)	9	2,058	0.44%	38
Acres (millions)	1	968	0.10%	46
Acres per farm	88	471	—	50
Acres planted	435	334,139	0.13%	42
Acres harvested	413	319,894	0.13%	42
Farm value (mill.)	$330	$108,805	0.30%	35

Numbers of farms are rounded to nearest thousand.
Source: U.S. Dept. of Agriculture; National Agricultural Statistics Service.

GOVERNMENT AND FINANCE

Units of local government, 1997

	State	Total U.S.	Rank
All local governments	1,421	87,453	22
Counties	21	3,043	39
Municipalities	324	19,372	24
Townships	243	16,629	16
School districts	552	13,726	9
Special districts	281	34,683	39

County ranks are based on the 48 states with county governments; township ranks are based on the 20 states with township governments; school district ranks are based on the 46 states with such districts.
Source: U.S. Bureau of the Census; *1997 Census of Governments, Government Organization*, Series GC97(1).

State government revenue, 1996

Total revenue	$35,857 mill.
General revenue	26,615 mill.
Per capita.	3,326
U.S. per capita average	2,910
Rank among states.	12
Intergovernmental revenue	
Total	$6,663 mill.
From federal government	6,424 mill.
From local government	240 mill.
Charges and Miscellaneous	
Total	$5,567 mill.
Current charges	2,529 mill.
Misc. general revenue	3,038 mill.
Taxes	
Total	$14,385 mill.
General sales	4,318 mill.
Selective sales.	3,045 mill.
License taxes	753 mill.
Individual income	4,734 mill.
Corporate income	1,155 mill.
Other	379 mill.
Insurance trust revenue	8,796 mill.

Total revenue figures include items not listed separately.
Source: U.S. Bureau of the Census.

State government expenditures, 1996

General expenditures

Intergovernmental	$7,771 mill.
Direct expenditures	18,264 mill.
Total	26,035 mill.

Selected direct expenditures

Education	$7,750 mill.
Public welfare	6,744 mill.
Health, hospital	1,588 mill.
Highways	1,812 mill.
Police	259 mill.
Corrections	875 mill.
Natural resources	163 mill.
Parks and recreation	382 mill.
Government administration	907 mill.
Interest on debt	1,329 mill.

Other

State per capita expenditures	$3,254
U.S. per capita average	2,854
Rank among states	12
Total state expenditures	32,315 mill.
Total U.S. expenditures	859,959 mill.

Totals include items not listed separately.
Source: U.S. Bureau of the Census.

POLITICS

Governors since statehood

D = Democrat; R = Republican; O = other;
(r) resigned; (d) died in office; (i) removed from office

William Livingston	(d) 1776-1790
Elisha Lawrence	1790
William Paterson (O)	(r) 1790-1793
Thomas Henderson (O)	1793
Richard Howell (O)	1793-1801
Joseph Bloomfield (O)	1801-1802
John Lambert (O)	1802-1803
Joseph Bloomfield (O)	(r) 1803-1812
Charles Clark (O)	1812
Aaron Ogden (O)	1812-1813
William S. Pennington (O)	(r) 1813-1815
William Kennedy (O)	1815
Mahlon Dickerson (O)	(r) 1815-1817
Isaac H. Williamson (O)	1817-1829
Peter D. Vroom (O)	1829-1832
Samuel L. Southard (O)	(r) 1832-1833
Elias P. Seeley (O)	1833
Peter D. Vroom (O)	1833-1836
Philemon Dickerson (D)	1836-1837
William Pennington (O)	1837-1843
Daniel Haines (D)	1843-1845
Charles C. Stratton (O)	1845-1848
Daniel Haines (D)	1848-1851
George F. Fort (D)	1851-1854
Rodman M. Price (D)	1854-1857
William A. Newell (R)	1857-1860
Charles S. Olden (R)	1860-1863
Joel Parker (D)	1863-1866
Marcus L. Ward (R)	1866-1869
Theodore F. Randolph (D)	1869-1872
Joel Parker (D)	1872-1875
Joseph D. Bedle (D)	1875-1878
George B. McClellan (D)	1878-1881
George C. Ludlow (D)	1881-1884
Leon Abbett (D)	1884-1887
Robert S. Green (D)	1887-1890
Leon Abbett (D)	1890-1893
George T. Werts (D)	1893-1896
John W. Griggs (R)	(r) 1896-1898
Foster M. Voorhees (R)	(r) 1898
David O. Watkins (R)	1898-1899
Foster M. Voorhees (R)	1899-1902
Franklin Murphy (R)	1902-1905
Edward C. Stokes (R)	1905-1908
John F. Fort (R)	1908-1911
Woodrow Wilson (D)	(r) 1911-1913
James F. Fielder (D)	(r) 1913
Leon R. Taylor (D)	1913-1914
James F. Fielder (D)	1914-1917
Walter E. Edge (R)	(r) 1917-1919
William N. Runyon (R)	1919-1920
Clarence E. Case (R)	1920
Edward I. Edwards (D)	1920-1923
George S. Silzer (D)	1923-1926
Arthur Harry Moore (D)	1926-1929
Morgan F. Larson (R)	1929-1932
Arthur Henry Moore (D)	(r) 1932-1935
Clifford R. Powell (D)	1935
Horace G. Prall (R)	1935
Harold G. Hoffman (R)	1935-1938
Arthur Henry Moore (D)	1938-1941
Charles Edison (D)	1941-1944
Walter E. Edge (R)	1944-1947
Alfred E. Driscoll (R)	1947-1954
Robert B. Meyner (D)	1954-1962
Richard J. Hughes (D)	1962-1970
William T. Cahill (D)	1970-1974
Brendan T. Byrne (D)	1974-1982
Thomas H. Kean (R)	1982-1990
James Florio (D)	1990-1994
Christine Todd Whitman (R)	1994-

Composition of state legislature, 1990-1998

	Democrats	Republicans
State Assembly (80 seats)		
1990	22	58
1992	27	53
1994	28	52
1996	30	50
1998	32	48
State Senate (40 seats)		
1990	13	27
1992	16	24
1994	16	24
1996	16	24
1998	16	24

Figures for total seats may include independents and minor party members.

Source: Council of State Governments; *State Elective Officials and the Legislatures.*

Composition of congressional delegations, 1989-1999

	Dem	Rep	Total
House of Representatives			
101st Congress, 1989			
State delegates	8	6	14
Total U.S.	259	174	433
102d Congress, 1991			
State delegates	8	6	14
Total U.S.	267	167	434
103d Congress, 1993			
State delegates	7	6	13
Total U.S.	258	176	434
104th Congress, 1995			
State delegates	6	7	13
Total U.S.	197	236	433
105th Congress, 1997			
State delegates	6	7	13
Total U.S.	206	228	434
106th Congress, 1999			
State delegates	7	6	13
Total U.S.	211	222	433

	Dem	Rep	Total
Senate			
101st Congress, 1989			
State delegates	2	0	2
Total U.S.	55	45	100
102d Congress, 1991			
State delegates	2	0	2
Total U.S.	56	44	100
103d Congress, 1993			
State delegates	2	0	2
Total U.S.	57	43	100
104th Congress, 1995			
State delegates	2	0	2
Total U.S.	46	53	99
105th Congress, 1997			
State delegates	2	0	2
Total U.S.	45	55	100
106th Congress, 1999			
State delegates	2	0	2
Total U.S.	45	54	99

Figures are for starts of first sessions. Figure for U.S. Representatives for 101st Congress does not include Alabama and Indiana, which had vacancies. Figures for total U.S. Representatives for 102d, 103d, and 106th Congresses do not include Vermont, which had 1 Independent-Socialist. Figure for U.S. Representatives for 104th Congress does not include Vermont, which had 1 Independent-Socialist, and California, which had 1 vacancy. Figure for U.S. Representatives for 105th Congress does not include New York, which had 1 vacancy. Figure for U.S. Senators for 104th Congress does not include Oregon, which had 1 vacancy. Figure for U.S. Senators for 106th Congress does not include New Hampshire, which had 1 Independent.

Source: U.S. Congress; *Congressional Directory*, biennial.

Voter participation in presidential elections, 1992 and 1996

	1992	1996
State voting age pop.	5,964,000	6,005,000
Total U.S. voting age pop.	189,524,000	196,509,000
State share of U.S. total	3.2%	3.1%
Rank among states	9	9
Percent of state casting vote	56.1	46.7
Percent of U.S. total voting	55.1	49.0
Rank among states	28	39

Source: U.S. Bureau of the Census.

HEALTH AND MEDICAL CARE

Medicare, 1997

	Recipients	Payments
State	1,181,000	$6,573 mill.
Total U.S.	37,514,000	$206,064 mill.
State share	3.15%	3.19%
Rank among states	9	9

Recipient figures are rounded to nearest thousand persons.
  Ranks are from highest to lowest.
Source: U.S. Health Care Financing Administration.

Medicaid, 1996

	Recipients	Payments
State	714,000	$3,726 mill.
Total U.S.	35,028,000	$121,419 mill.
State share	2.04%	3.07%
Rank among states	14	9

Recipient figures are rounded to nearest thousand persons.
  Payment figures for fiscal year reflect federal and state
  contribution payments. Ranks are from highest to lowest.
Source: U.S. Health Care Financing Administration.

Health insurance coverage, 1996

	State	U.S.
Total persons covered	6,546,000	225,070,000
Total persons not covered	1,317,000	41,716,000
Part not covered	16.7%	15.6%
Rank among states	13	—
Children not covered	349,000	10,554,000
Part not covered	18.6%	14.8%
Rank among states	9	—

Ranks are from most to fewest uninsured. Population figures
  are rounded to nearest thousand persons.
Source: U.S. Bureau of the Census.

AIDS, syphilis, tuberculosis, and measles cases, 1997

Cases	U.S.	State	Share
AIDS	58,443	3,226	5.52%
Syphilis	8,550	151	1.77%
Tuberculosis	18,534	728	3.93%
Measles	148,000	3,000	2.03%

Measles figures are rounded to nearest thousand cases.
Source: U.S. Centers for Disease Control and Prevention.

HOUSING

Homeownership rates, 1985-1997

	1985	1990	1997
State	62.3%	65.0%	63.1%
Total U.S.	63.9%	63.9%	65.7%
Rank among states	40	33	40

Source: U.S. Bureau of the Census.

Home sales, 1990 and 1997
In thousands of units

Existing home sales	1990	1997	Change
State sales	114.8	157.3	42.5
Total U.S. sales	3,560	4,730	1,170
State share of U.S. total	3.22%	3.33%	0.10%
Rank among states	10	10	—

Source: National Association of Realtors; *Real Estate Outlook:*
  Market Trends and Insights.

EDUCATION

Public school enrollment, 1995

State K-8 enrollment	880,000
Total U.S. K-8 enrollment	32,341,000
State share of total U.S.	2.72%
State 9-12 enrollment	317,000
Total U.S. 9-12 enrollment	12,500,000
State share of U.S. total	2.54%
State public school enroll. rate	86.5%
Overall U.S. rate.	91.6%
Rank among states.	49

Enrollment figures (which include unclassified students) are
  rounded to nearest thousand pupils in fall term;
  kindergarten (K)-8 grade figures include some
  prekindergarten students. Enrollment rate is based on
  percentage of persons 5-17 years old. Rank is from highest
  to lowest.
Source: U.S. National Center for Education Statistics.

Public college finances, 1996

State FTE enrollment 185,600
Total U.S. FTE enrollment 8,268,800
State share of total U.S. 2.24%
Rank among states. 13
State and local
    appropriations $1,119,700,000
Total U.S. state and local
    appropriations. . . . . $39,699 mill.
State share of total U.S. 2.82%
Rank among states. 11
State net tuition revenues. $495,300,000
Total U.S. net tuition $18,348,100,000
State share of total U.S. 2.70%
Rank among states. 10

Estimated by source.
FTE=Full-time equivalent; credit and noncredit enrollment
    including summer session in academic year ending in
    1996.
Enrollments are rounded to nearest thousand students. Net
    tuition revenues exclude appropriation to students
    attending in-state public institutions. Rankings are from
    highest shares to lowest.
Source: Research Associates of Washington.

Motor vehicle registrations and driver licenses, 1996

In thousands

Vehicle registrations	State	U.S.	Share	Rank
Autos, trucks, buses	5,822	206,365	2.82%	10
Autos only	4,348	128,439	3.39%	9
Motorcycles	91	3,832	2.37%	15
Driver licenses	5,486	179,539	3.06%	10

Figures do not include vehicles owned by military services.
Source: U.S. Federal Highway Administration; *Highway*
    Statistics; Selected Highway Statistics and Charts.

Domestic travel expenditures, 1995

Spending by U.S. residents on overnight trips and day
trips of at least 100 miles

Total expenditures in state . . . . $11,708 mill.
Total expenditures in U.S. . . . . $360,314 mill.
State share of total U.S. 3.25%
Rank among states 7

Source: Travel Industry Association of America.

TRANSPORTATION AND TRAVEL

CRIME AND LAW ENFORCEMENT

Highway mileage, 1996

Interstate 422
Other arterial. 5,724
Collector roads. 6,752
Local roads 25,191

Urban roads. 24,241
Rural roads 11,683

Total state 35,924
U.S. total 3,933,985
State share 0.9%
Rank among states. 38

Source: U.S. Federal Highway Administration.

State and local police officers, 1996

Local police 19,891
State police 2,702
Sheriffs 3,145
Total 28,058
Officers per 10,000 residents 35
U.S. average 25
Rank among states 3

Figures cover full-time sworn officers; totals include special
    police not shown separately.
Source: U.S. Bureau of Justice Statistics; *Census of State and*
    Local Law Enforcement Agencies, 1996.

Crime rates, 1996

Rates per 100,000 resident population

Violent crimes	State	U.S.
Total violent	532	634
Murder	4.2	7.4
Forcible rape	24.7	36.1
Robbery	236	202
Aggravated assault	267	388
Property crimes		
Total property	3,801	4,445
Burglary	792	943
Larceny/theft	2,428	2,976
Motor vehicle theft	581	526
Totals	4,333	5,079

Source: U.S. Federal Bureau of Investigation; *Crime in the United States*, annual.

State prison populations, 1980-1996

	State	U.S.	State share
1980	5,884	305,458	1.93%
1990	21,128	708,393	2.98%
1996	27,490	1,025,624	2.68%

Figures exclude prisoners in federal penitentiaries.
Source: U.S. Bureau of Justice Statistics.

New Mexico

Location: Southwestern continental United States

Area and rank: 121,365 square miles (314,334 square kilometers); 121,598 square miles (314,939 square kilometers) including water; fifth largest state in area

Population and rank: 1,729,751 (1997); thirty-sixth largest state in population

Capital: Santa Fe

Largest city: Albuquerque (419,311 people in 1998)

Nearly a quarter of New Mexico's residents live in Albuquerque, which has more people than the state's next ten largest cities combined. (PhotoDisc)

Became territory:
September 9, 1850

Entered Union and rank:
January 6, 1912; forty-
seventh state

**Present constitution
adopted:** 1911

Counties: 33

State name: New Mexico
is named after
neighboring Mexico

State nicknames: Land
of Enchantment;
Sunshine State

Motto: *Crescit eundo* (It grows as it goes)

State flag: Yellow field with red circle with four rays emanating from it

Highest point: Wheeler Peak — 13,161 feet (4,011 meters)

Lowest point: Red Bluff Reservoir — 2,842 feet (866 meters)

Highest recorded temperature: 116 degrees Fahrenheit (47 degrees Celsius) —
Orogrande, 1936

Lowest recorded temperature: −50 degrees Fahrenheit (−46 degrees Celsius) —
Gavilan, 1951

State songs: "O Fair New Mexico"; "Asi Es Nuevo Méjico"

State tree: Pinon

State flower: Yucca

State bird: Roadrunner

State fish: Cutthroat trout

State animal: Black bear

National park: Carlsbad Caverns

New Mexico History

New Mexico's arid climate and southwestern geographical position have deeply influenced its history. Known as the "Land of Enchantment," the state's high altitudes, clear air, and colorful mountains and deserts attract artists and tourists alike. Its lack of water, however, makes large-scale settlement difficult, and its proximity to Mexico has long been a factor in making its culture a Spanish-American hybrid. Added to these ingredients, the state's large American Indian population and late—1912—entry to statehood give New Mexico a unique flavor.

Early History. American Indians have lived in New Mexico for perhaps twenty-five thousand years. Evidence shows that they hunted in northeastern New Mexico about ten thousand years ago. Later, the Mogollons settled near the modern Arizona border, eventually building villages. The Anasazis, another ancient people, lived in "Four Corners," where Colorado, Arizona, New Mexico, and Utah meet, and created one of the most developed civilizations of the time. The Pueblo Indians are descendants of the Anasazis. In about 1500 B.C.E. the Navaho and Apache Indians arrived; Ute and Comanche tribes arrived shortly afterward.

Exploration. The Spanish conquistador Hernán Cortés invaded Mexico in 1519. Nine years later, another Spaniard, explorer Alvar Núñez Cabeza de Vaca, became shipwrecked off the Texas coast. When he finally made it to Mexico City in 1536, his reports of large wealthy cities sparked in-

With hundreds of fine Pueblo ruins such as this, New Mexico has one of the richest collections of major archaeological sites in North America. (PhotoDisc)

terest in further exploration. In 1538 Franciscan friar Marcos de Niza set out exploring and within a year returned with tales of golden cities larger than Mexico City.

Spanish authorities chose Franciso de Coronado, then twenty-nine, to explore the region. He set out in 1540 with more than 1,600 men but in two years had found no opulent cities. His travels did increase Spain's geographical knowledge of the region, however, and profoundly influenced the future.

After later expeditions, the Spanish finally decided in 1598 to found a colony in the region, with the capital at San Juan de las Caballeros, near the Chama River. In 1609 the capital was moved to Santa Fe ("holy faith"). The Spanish treated the American Indians harshly. Missionaries made inroads into their traditional culture, while secular rulers set up a system of forced labor tantamount to slavery. A revolt in 1680 left hundreds of Spaniards dead; the remainder fled. Twelve years later the Spanish reconquered the region, and for the next 125 years, the two sides lived in relative peace.

In 1821, however, Mexico gained its independence from Spain. Traders and trappers had been making uninvited forays into the New Mexico area, but now, with the suspicious Spanish gone, they were welcome. Also in 1821 American trader William Becknell established the Santa Fe Trail, over which millions of dollars in goods would travel until the trail was replaced by transcontinental railroads. New Mexico's Indians and the Mexicans themselves rebelled against the government in 1837 but the rebellion was crushed. In 1841 Texas, which had become an independent republic, invaded the region, but this venture also failed.

Matters changed again, this time decisively, after the United States and Mexico went to war in 1846.

Troops led by General Stephen W. Kearney occupied New Mexico with little difficulty. After American victory in 1848, New Mexico, along with a huge swathe of territory that included much of California, Colorado, Utah, Nevada, and Arizona, came under American rule. The stage was set for the future state to emerge.

Becoming a Territory. It took sixty-four years for New Mexico to join the American Union as a separate and equal state. Much conflict and agonizing over statehood lay ahead. First, in 1850, New Mexico, which then included Arizona, was organized into a territory. In 1853 the Gadsden Purchase added new land on the southern border. Yet statehood was little more than a dream. The region had too few inhabitants—about sixty thousand in 1850—to become part of the Union. And, while in time thousands of Americans came to live there, the territory's Mexican character drew hostility from certain forces in Congress. The fact that most inhabitants were Roman Catholic added to the distrust of the suspicious East.

Moreover, New Mexico, along with Arizona and other western regions, was a violent place, plagued with serious American Indian problems and often equally serious Anglo-American problems, in the form of range wars and general lawlessness. From the 1850's to the 1880's, when the last dangerous American Indian menace succumbed to peace and outlaws such as Billy the Kid were laid to rest, New Mexico was truly the Wild West.

Civil War. The territory experienced the Civil War in 1862, when an army of Texas Confederates commanded by General Henry J. Sibley invaded from the east. Sibley defeated a Union force at Valverde, more than one hundred miles south of Albuquerque on the east side of the Rio Grande, and advanced north toward Santa Fe and Albuquerque. His army was then to head north to Colorado and its gold regions around Pike's Peak and Denver. They never made it, however, because when they reached Glorietta Pass and Apache Canyon, near Santa Fe, Union soldiers turned them back in a battle sometimes called "the Gettysburg of the West."

Conflict. In 1863 Congress organized the territories of Arizona and Colorado, in the process reducing the size of New Mexico. After the Civil War ended in 1865, cattle ranchers, sheepherders, and others flocked to the state in search of prosperity or adventure. Affairs were hardly fit for the pursuit of wealth, however, since conflicts broke out repeatedly among settlers. Some of the worst of the hostilities came in the late 1870's in a county southeast of Albuquerque. The Lincoln County War saw cattlemen and others battling for political control. In this "war" Billy the Kid, a teenage bandit who survived only until age twenty-one, murdered twenty-one men before being shot by Sheriff Pat Garrett. To end the bloodshed, in 1878 the territorial governor pardoned the fighters. Over the next decade other territorial governors helped establish order.

Establishing peace between settlers and American Indians, however, was another matter. Apache chief Victorio led many murderous raids against his enemies until his death in 1880. Control was passed to Geronimo, last of the warring Apache warrior chiefs. Geronimo surrendered repeatedly, only to escape and regroup his army. In September, 1886, he finally surrendered after receiving per-

Contemporary illustration of a wagon train entering Santa Fe on the newly established Santa Fe Trail during the 1830's. (Museum of New Mexico)

New Mexico's dry, clear air and open spaces have made it an ideal site for the large array of radio telescopes. (New Mexico Department of Tourism)

sonal assurances of safety from President Grover Cleveland. Geronimo lived on to convert to Christianity and participate in President Theodore Roosevelt's inauguration in 1905.

New Mexico Economy. With peace established, economic progress could proceed. Without American Indian depredations, cattle ranching prospered. Mineral wealth had been discovered and would continue to be discovered well into the next century. Between 1880 and 1890 the population swelled by more than one-third, to just more than 160,000. By 1910, though New Mexico was still not a state, the population had more than doubled again, to 325,000.

As in much of the West, the advent of the transcontinental railroad changed life in New Mexico. When the first train entered in 1878, products such as cattle could be easily and cheaply transported east. The territory experienced a boom in cattle and mining products. New Mexico's economy, however, was handicapped by a lack of water; annual rainfall is less than ten inches. Sheriff Pat Garrett inaugurated far-reaching irrigation projects.

Statehood. New Mexicans desired statehood, but by 1901 this goal had not been accomplished, despite many attempts. Congress feared allowing a seemingly foreign territory to gain precious votes in the Senate. The territory appeared too Mexican for full membership. The Spanish-American War (1898) allowed the territory to demonstrate its loyalty. Lieutenant Colonel Theodore Roosevelt recruited many of his Rough Riders in New Mexico, and they proved their trustworthiness. Finally, in 1910 Congress passed a statehood bill, and two years later New Mexico entered the Union.

The state constitution, adopted in 1911, is considered conservative in comparison to other western states, since it omits the initiative, referendum, and recall, which allot extra powers to the electorate. Instead, all legislative power lies in the bicameral legislature. Along with a governor, a lieutenant governor, and five other executive officers, officials are elected to four-year terms. They may hold office no more than two successive terms. Members of the upper house serve four-year terms; lower-house members serve two-year terms. Provisions guaranteeing voting rights and education for Spanish-speaking people can be changed only by three-fourths of the legislature and three-fourths of the electorate.

Two World Wars. The state was soon called upon again for military service, and its soldiers fought in World Wars I and II. The postwar period proved problematic, however, as a long drought wreaked havoc with the state's economy. Livestock prices sank, ranchers went bankrupt, and banks collapsed. Providentially, however, new mineral wealth was discovered, and new businesses appeared. When Carlsbad Caverns became a national park in 1930, a focal point for tourism was born. Water projects begun in the 1920's eventually brought significant acreage under cultivation. While there was limited capacity for these supplies to be increased, New Deal projects during the Depression continued making inroads into this chronic problem.

Like neighboring states, New Mexico's economy gained considerably during World War II, when federal spending increased dramatically. A secret project begun at Los Alamos turned out to be development of the world's first atomic bombs. The first atomic explosion lighted up the New Mexico desert at Trinity, near Alamogordo, in 1945.

Postindustrial Society. New Mexico's postwar economy grew on the strength of federal spending, especially for defense. Key areas were research on the military, peacetime uses of nuclear power, and experiments with rockets. This effort was assisted when uranium was discovered in the state in 1950. In the 1960's, coal production rose markedly; the state's power supply is generated primarily by burning coal.

The economy and society of New Mexico dramatically changed with its passage from an industrial to a postindustrial and high-tech economy, with service industries far outweighing manufacturing, construction, agriculture, and mining in both income produced (70 percent) and number of employees (81 percent). In the 1990's the state ranked among the nation's leaders in nuclear and space research.

Charles F. Bahmueller

New Mexico Time Line

300 C.E.-1400 C.E.	Mogollon and Anasazi Indian cultures flourish.
1200-1500	Pueblo Indians establish villages along the Rio Grande and its tributaries.
1538	Franciscan friar Marcos de Niza leads expedition to find fabled cities of Cibola.
1540-1542	Francisco de Coronado explores the Southwest.
1598	Juan de Onate establishes the first capital, San Juan de los Caballeros.
1599	Battle at Aroma occurs between Native Americans and Spaniards.
1600	San Gabriel, the second capital, is founded.
1601	Mass desertion of San Gabriel by colonists takes place; new recruits from Spain and Mexico are sent.
1609	Santa Fe is made the capital.
1626	Spanish Inquisition is established in New Mexico.
1680	During Pueblo Indian Revolt, Spanish survivors flee to El Paso del Norte.
1706	Albuquerque is founded.
1743	French trappers reach Santa Fe and begin trade with Spanish.
1807	Zebulon Pike leads first American expedition to New Mexico.
1821	Mexico declares independence from Spain.

Sept., 1821	Santa Fe Trail is opened to trade.
1828	First major gold discovery in West made south of Santa Fe.
1841	Texan soldiers invade New Mexico but are stopped by Mexican troops.
1846	Mexican-American War begins; Stephen Kearny declares New Mexico annexed to U.S.
1848	Treaty of Guadalupe Hidalgo ends Mexican-American War.
Sept. 9, 1850	New Mexico Territory is created.
Dec. 30, 1853	Gadsden Purchase from Mexico adds land to southern New Mexico.
1861	Confederacy invades New Mexico during Civil War.
1862	Battles of Apache Canyon and Glorieta Pass end intrusion of Confederate troops.
1863	Navajos and Apaches are relocated to Bosque Redondo in the Long Walk from Arizona; they return five years later.
1863	Creation of Arizona Territory halves New Mexico's area.
1878	Lincoln County War erupts in southeast.
July 14, 1881	Outlaw Billy the Kid is shot by Sheriff Pat Garrett in Fort Sumner.
1886	Geronimo makes final surrender; American Indian hostilities cease in the Southwest.
1906	Joint statehood is approved by New Mexico but rejected by Arizona.
1910	New Mexico Constitution is drafted; it is adopted the following year.
Jan. 6, 1912	New Mexico is admitted to the Union as forty-seventh state.
Mar. 9, 1916	Mexican bandit Pancho Villa raids Columbus, killing eighteen.
1923	Oil is discovered on Navajo Reservation.
July 16, 1945	First atomic bomb is detonated near Alamogordo after development at Los Alamos.
1947	Rumors of unidentified flying object crash between Roswell and Corona; believers claim U.S. government covers up the incident.
1948	Native Americans gain right to vote in state elections.
1950	Uranium is discovered near Grants.
1969	Voters reject proposed new state constitution.
1970	U.S. Senate votes to return forty-eight thousand acres to Taos Indians.
mid-1970's	San Juan-Chama Project brings water to north-central area.
1977	First U.S. fusion reaction using electron beams is conducted in Albuquerque.
1988	Severe drought damages 1.4 million acres of the state.

Notes for Further Study

Published Sources. Those interested in New Mexican government should consult Paul L. Hain, et al., *New Mexico Government* (1994) and Maurilo E. Virgil, et al., *New Mexico Government and Politics* (1990). Of numerous historical resources, a good general history is Susan A. Roberts and Calvin A. Roberts's *A History of New Mexico* (1997); Marc Simmons's *New Mexico: An Interpretive History* (1988) is also helpful. A sample of the state's ethnic history is found in *A History of the Jews in New Mexico* (1992) by Henry J. Tobias.

The Lincoln County War is treated in Maurice Garland Fulton et al., *History of the Lincoln County War* (1997). New Mexico's Spanish past is discussed in Marc Simmons's *Coronado's Land: Essays on Daily Life in Colonial New Mexico* (1996). Civil War history in the state is amplified in Steve Cottrell's *Civil War in Texas and New Mexico Territory* (1998). For information on the state's Native American peoples, readers should consult Edmund J. Ladd's *The Zuni* (1999); *Indian Tribes of the Americas* (1999), edited by Fred L. Israel; and *Native Resistance and the Pax Colonial in New Spain* (1998), edited by Susan Schroeder. A good resource on natural history is *The Smithsonian Guide to Natural America: The Southwest, Arizona and New Mexico* (1995), by Jake Page and George H. H. Huey (photographer). Julie Kirgo's *New Mexico: Portrait of the Land and the People* (1990) presents a geographer's perspective.

Web Resources. The New Mexico state government home page (http://www.state.nm.us) contains a great deal of information on varied topics. Other information, including links to the offices of elected officials, is found at (http://alpha.mhpcc.edu/mhpcc/WW1011.html). A state legislator site (http://www.hcor/nmgov.html)

and a site for legislative links (http://www.aci.nm.org/legislat/legis.html) offer information about New Mexico law. Questions about legal resources are dealt with at Rominger (http://romingerlegal.com/state/new mexico.htm) and at Findlaw (http://www.findlaw.org/11stategov/nm/state.html).

New Mexico's geography is surveyed at Geography (http://geography.mioningco.com/library/maps/blusnm .htm). For an account of the state's history with main emphasis on the era prior to statehood, see the Cuarto Centennial History of New Mexico (http://nmgs .org/artcuarto.htm), written by a state historian. Examples of the municipal history of Las Cruces (http://www.lascruces-culture.org/families/html) are informative. The sites for the history of the state's northeast (http://www.nenewmexico.com/history) and for the Santa Fe Trail (http://www.cccok.org/trail.htm) give background and links to other sites. Examples of sites dealing with the state's American Indian population include Pueblo Indians of New Mexico (http://www .bhsedu.wmc/lzc/Puebloindians.html) and Historical Native American Photographs of the Southwest (http://www.sw scout.com/photos.html).

Counties

County	Sq. miles	1996 pop.
Bernalillo	1,166.2	526,614
Catron	6,928.3	2,657
Chaves	6,071.4	62,564
Cibola	4,539.6	25,473
Colfax	3,756.9	13,867
Curry	1,406.1	47,753
DeBaca	2,325.1	2,358
Dona Ana	3,807.4	163,849
Eddy	4,182.2	53,358
Grant	3,966.2	30,700
Guadalupe	3,030.6	4,195
Harding	2,125.5	946
Hidalgo	3,445.9	6,328
Lea	4,393.3	56,634
Lincoln	4,831.4	15,362
Los Alamos	109.4	18,212
Luna	2,965.3	23,089
McKinley	5,449.1	67,754
Mora	1,931.2	4,798
Otero	6,626.9	55,881
Quay	2,875.1	10,291
Rio Arriba	5,858.1	37,580
Roosevelt	2,448.7	18,700
San Juan	5,514.4	102,508

County	Sq. miles	1996 pop.	County	Sq. miles	1996 pop.
San Miguel	4,717.4	28,703	Torrance	3,345.1	13,584
Sandoval	3,709.7	83,264	Union	3,830.2	4,067
Santa Fe	1,909.4	119,011	Valencia	1,067.6	60,214
Sierra	4,180.5	10,953			
Socorro	6,647.1	16,155			
Taos	2,203.3	25,985			

Source: U.S. Bureau of the Census; National Association of Counties.

Cities

With 10,000 or more residents

Rank	City	Population
1	Albuquerque	419,311
2	Las Cruces	76,102
3	Santa Fe	67,879
4	Rio Rancho	50,041
5	Roswell	47,624
6	Farmington	39,028
7	Clovis	32,394
8	Alamogordo	28,312
9	Hobbs	27,156
10	Carlsbad	26,315
11	Gallup	20,120
12	Las Vegas	16,487
13	Deming	14,517
14	Silver City	12,064
15	Artesia	10,973
16	Portales	10,857

Population figures are estimated for mid-1998.

Source: U.S. Bureau of the Census.

Index to Tables

NA = Reliable data are not available.

DEMOGRAPHICS

Resident state and national populations, 1970-1997

Population figures given in thousands

	State pop.	U.S. pop.	Share	Rank
1970	1,017	203,302	0.5%	37
1980	1,303	226,546	0.6%	37
1985	1,438	237,924	0.6%	37
1990	1,515	248,765	0.6%	37
1995	1,686	262,761	0.6%	36
1997	1,730	267,636	0.6%	36

Source: U.S. Bureau of the Census.

Resident population by age, 1997

Age group	Total population
Under 5 years	134,000
5 to 17 years	365,000
18 to 24 years	174,000
25 to 34 years	225,000
35 to 44 years	281,000
45 to 54 years	216,000
55 to 64 years	142,000
65 to 74 years	110,000
75 to 84 years	63,000
85 years and over	20,000
Portion of residents 65 and older	11.2%
National average	12.7%

Population figures are rounded to nearest thousand persons;
figures include armed forces personnel stationed in state.
Source: U.S. Bureau of the Census.

Resident population by race, Hispanic origin, 1997

	State pop.	Share	U.S.
All residents	1,730,000	100.0%	100.0%
Hispanic white	663,000	38.3%	10.0%
non-Hispanic white	840,000	48.6%	72.7%
African American	44,000	2.5%	12.7%
Native American	158,000	9.1%	0.9%
Asian, Pacific Islander	24,000	1.4%	3.8%

Source: U.S. Bureau of the Census.

Projections of state population, 2000-2025

	Model A Uses interstate migration observed from 1975-1994	Model B Uses Bureau of Economic Analysis employment projections
Year	Population	Population
2000	1,860,000	1,858,000
2005	2,016,000	2,035,000
2010	2,155,000	2,223,000
2015	2,300,000	2,425,000
2020	2,454,000	2,636,000
2025	2,612,000	2,850,000

All population projections, including those for 2000, were calculated in 1997.
Source: U.S. Bureau of the Census, Population Paper Listings PPL-47.

VITAL STATISTICS

Average lifetime in years by race, 1989-1991

	State	U.S.	Rank
All residents	75.74	75.37	25
White residents	76.08	76.13	30
Black residents	NA	69.16	NA

Ranks are from longest-lived to least longest-lived. Ranks exclude Alaska, for which reliable data are not available. Rank for black residents is based on the 32 states for which reliable data are available.
Source: U.S. National Center for Health Statistics.

Infant mortality rates, 1980 and 1995

	State	U.S.
All residents		
1980	11.5	12.6
1995	6.2	7.6
White residents		
1980	11.3	11.0
1995	6.1	6.3
Black residents		
1980	23.1	21.4
1995	NA	15.1

Figures represent deaths per 1,000 live births of resident infants under 1 year old, exclusive of fetal deaths; all-residents figures include other races not listed separately.
Source: U.S. National Center for Health Statistics.

Marriages and divorces

Marriages in 1996.	16,000
Rate per 1,000 population, 1995.	9.0
U.S. rate, 1995	8.9
Rank among all states	19
Divorces in 1996	10,900
Rate per 1,000 population, 1995.	6.7
U.S. rate, 1995	4.4
Rank among all states.	2

Rank is from highest to lowest in country.
Source: U.S. National Center for Health Statistics.

Death rates by leading causes, 1995
Deaths per 100,000 resident population

Cause	State	U.S.
Heart disease	196.1	280.7
Cancer	159.5	204.9
Cerebrovascular diseases	42.7	60.1
Accidents and adverse effects	54.6	35.5
Motor vehicle accidents	26.7	16.5
Chronic obstructive pulmonary diseases	41.5	39.2
Diabetes mellitus	26.1	22.6
HIV	9.1	NA
Suicide	17.6	11.9
Homicide	10.1	8.7
All causes	744.3	880.0
Rank in overall death rate among states		43

Figures exclude nonresidents who die in state. Causes of death follow International Classification of Diseases. Rank is from highest to lowest in country.
Source: U.S. National Center for Health Statistics.

ECONOMY

Gross state product, 1990-1996
In current dollars

	State product	Increase
1990	$26.7 billion	
1993	$36.3 billion	
1994	$40.9 billion	12.67%
1995	$40.8 billion	−0.24%
1996	$42.7 billion	4.66%

Source: U.S. Bureau of Economic Analysis; *Survey of Current Business,* June, 1998.

Gross state product by industry, 1996
In billions

Farms, forestry, fisheries	$0.7
Construction	1.7
Manufacturing	8.2
Transportation, public utilities.	3.2
Wholesale trade.	1.7
Retail trade	3.7
Finance, insurance, real estate	5.1
Services	6.6
Government.	6.8
State total.	$40.4
Total U.S.	$6,923.8
State share	0.58%
Rank among states.	37

Total figures include mining, not listed separately.
Source: U.S. Bureau of Economic Analysis; *Survey of Current Business,* June, 1998.

Personal income per capita, 1990 and 1997
In current dollars

	1990	1997
Per capita income	$14,502	$19,587
U.S. average	$19,188	$25,598
Rank among states	46	47

1997 data are preliminary.
Source: U.S. Bureau of Economic Analysis; *Survey of Current Business,* May, 1998.

Energy consumption, 1995
In trillions of British thermal units (BTU)

End-use sectors

Residential	80.0
Commercial	96.2
Industrial	202.4
Transportation	196.3

Sources of energy

Petroleum	208.2
Natural gas	219.4
Coal	275.3
Hydroelectric power	2.7
Nuclear electric power	0
Total state per capita consumption	340.3
Total U.S. per capita consumption	344.4
Rank among states.	28
Total state energy consumption	575.0
Total U.S. energy consumption	90,547.4
State share of U.S. total	0.64%
Rank among states.	38

Total figures include items not listed separately.
Source: U.S. Energy Information Administration; *State Energy Data Report.*

Nonfarm employment by sectors, 1997

Total	707,000
Construction	43,000
Manufacturing	46,000
Transportation, public utilities.	32,000
Wholesale trade, retail trade	168,000
Finance, insurance, real estate	31,000
Services	195,000
Government	177,000

Figures are rounded to nearest thousand persons. Total includes mining, not listed separately.
Source: U.S. Bureau of Labor Statistics; *Employment and Earnings,* monthly.

Foreign exports, 1990-1997
In millions of dollars

Year	State	U.S.	State share
1990	249	394,045	0.06%
1996	931	624,767	0.15%
1997	1,776	688,896	0.26%

Source: U.S. Bureau of the Census; *U.S. Merchandise Trade,* series FT 900.

LAND USE

Federally owned land, 1996

	State	U.S.	State share
Total acres	77,766,000	2,271,343,000	3.42%
Federally owned	26,217,000	563,129,000	4.66%
Federal share	33.7%	24.8%	—

Areas are rounded to nearest thousand acres. Figures for federally owned land do not include trust properties.

Source: U.S. General Services Administration; *Inventory Report on Real Property Owned by the United States Throughout the World,* annual.

Land use, 1992
In acres, rounded to nearest thousand

Total surface area	77,819,000
Federal land	27,394,000
Total nonfederal	50,196,000
Developed	866,000
Total rural	49,330,000
Cropland.	1,892,000
Pasture land	212,000
Range land	39,792,000
Forest land.	4,600,000
Minor cover/use.	2,835,000

Total surface area figures include water area not shown separately.

Source: U.S. Dept. of Agriculture; Soil Conservation Service; Iowa State University, Statistical Laboratory; *Summary Report, 1992 National Resources Inventory.*

Farms and crop acreage, 1997

	State	U.S.	Share	Rank
Farms (thousands)	14	2,058	0.68%	35
Acres (millions)	44	968	4.55%	5
Acres per farm	3,222	471	—	4
Acres planted	1,290	334,139	0.39%	35
Acres harvested	1,137	319,894	0.36%	35
Farm value (mill.)	$505	$108,805	0.46%	31

Numbers of farms are rounded to nearest thousand.

Source: U.S. Dept. of Agriculture; National Agricultural Statistics Service.

GOVERNMENT AND FINANCE

Units of local government, 1997

	State	Total U.S.	Rank
All local governments	881	87,453	32
Counties	33	3,043	35
Municipalities	99	19,372	39
Townships	0	16,629	—
School districts	96	13,726	33
Special districts	653	34,683	16

County ranks are based on the 48 states with county governments; township ranks are based on the 20 states with township governments; school district ranks are based on the 46 states with such districts.

Source: U.S. Bureau of the Census; *1997 Census of Governments, Government Organization,* Series GC97(1).

State government revenue, 1996

Total revenue	$8,129 mill.
General revenue	6,318 mill.
Per capita.	3,692
U.S. per capita average	2,910
Rank among states	8

Intergovernmental revenue

Total	$1,794 mill.
From federal government	1,749 mill.
From local government	45 mill.

Charges and Miscellaneous

Total	$1,464 mill.
Current charges	599 mill.
Misc. general revenue	865

Taxes

Total	$3,061 mill.
General sales	1,284 mill.
Selective sales.	452 mill.
License taxes	165 mill.
Individual income	643 mill.
Corporate income	163 mill.
Other	354 mill.
Insurance trust revenue	1,811 mill.

Total revenue figures include items not listed separately.
Source: U.S. Bureau of the Census.

State government expenditures, 1996

General expenditures

Intergovernmental	$2,055 mill.
Direct expenditures	4,166 mill.
Total.	6,222 mill.

Selected direct expenditures

Education	$2,457 mill.
Public welfare.	1,118 mill.
Health, hospital	577 mill.
Highways	651 mill.
Police.	56 mill.
Corrections.	175 mill.
Natural resources	89 mill.
Parks and recreation.	31 mill.
Government administration	211 mill.
Interest on debt	110 mill.

Other

State per capita expenditures	$3,636
U.S. per capita average	2,854
Rank among states	7
Total state expenditures	6,740 mill.
Total U.S. expenditures	859,959 mill.

Totals include items not listed separately.
Source: U.S. Bureau of the Census.

POLITICS

Governors since statehood

D = Democrat; R = Republican; O = other;
(r) resigned; (d) died in office; (i) removed from office

William C. McDonald (D)	1912-1917
Ezequiel Cabeza DeBaca (D)	(d) 1917
Washington E. Lindsay (R).	1917-1919
Octaviano A. Larrazolo (R)	1919-1921
Merritt C. Mechem (R).	1921-1923
James F. Hinkle (D).	1923-1925
Arthur T. Hannett (D)	1925-1927
Richard C. Dillon (R).	1927-1931
Arthur Seligman (D).	(d) 1931-1933
Andrew W. Hockenbull (D)	1933-1935
Clyde Tingley (D).	1935-1939
John E. Miles (D).	1939-1943
John J. Dempsey (D)	1943-1947
Thomas L. Mabry (D)	1947-1951
Edwin L. Mechem (R)	1951-1955

John F. Sims, Jr. (D).	1955-1957
Edwin L. Mechem (R)	1957-1959
John Burroughs (D)	1959-1961
Edwin L. Mechem (R)	(r) 1961-1962
Thomas F. Bolack (R)	1962-1963
Jack M. Campbell (D)	1963-1967
David F. Cargo (R)	1967-1971
Bruce King (D)	1971-1975
Raymond S. (Jerry) Apodaca (D)	1975-1979
Bruce King (D)	1979-1983
Toney Anaya (D)	1983-1987
Garrey E. Carruthers (R).	1987-1991
Bruce King (D)	1991-1995
Gary E. Johnson (R)	1995-

Composition of state legislature, 1990-1998

	Democrats	Republicans
State House (70 seats)		
1990	49	21
1992	53	17
1994	46	24
1996	42	28
1998	40	30
State Senate (42 seats)		
1990	26	16
1992	27	15
1994	27	15
1996	25	17
1998	25	17

Figures for total seats may include independents and minor
party members.
Source: Council of State Governments; *State Elective Officials
and the Legislatures.*

Composition of congressional delegations, 1989-1999

	Dem	Rep	Total
House of Representatives			
101st Congress, 1989			
State delegates	1	2	3
Total U.S.	259	174	433
102d Congress, 1991			
State delegates	1	2	3
Total U.S.	267	167	434

	Dem	Rep	Total
103d Congress, 1993			
State delegates	1	2	3
Total U.S.	258	176	434
104th Congress, 1995			
State delegates	0	3	3
Total U.S.	197	236	433
105th Congress, 1997			
State delegates	1	2	3
Total U.S.	206	228	434
106th Congress, 1999			
State delegates	1	2	3
Total U.S.	211	222	433
Senate			
101st Congress, 1989			
State delegates	1	1	2
Total U.S.	55	45	100
102d Congress, 1991			
State delegates	1	1	2
Total U.S.	56	44	100
103d Congress, 1993			
State delegates	1	1	2
Total U.S.	57	43	100
104th Congress, 1995			
State delegates	1	1	2
Total U.S.	46	53	99
105th Congress, 1997			
State delegates	1	1	2
Total U.S.	45	55	100
106th Congress, 1999			
State delegates	1	1	2
Total U.S.	45	54	99

Figures are for starts of first sessions. Figure for U.S. Representatives for 101st Congress does not include Alabama and Indiana, which had vacancies. Figures for total U.S. Representatives for 102d, 103d, and 106th Congresses do not include Vermont, which had 1 Independent-Socialist. Figure for U.S. Representatives for 104th Congress does not include Vermont, which had 1 Independent-Socialist, and California, which had 1 vacancy. Figure for U.S. Representatives for 105th Congress does not include New York, which had 1 vacancy. Figure for U.S. Senators for 104th Congress does not include Oregon, which had 1 vacancy. Figure for U.S. Senators for 106th Congress does not include New Hampshire, which had 1 Independent.
Source: U.S. Congress; *Congressional Directory,* biennial.

Voter participation in presidential elections, 1992 and 1996

	1992	1996
State voting age pop.	1,121,000	1,210,000
Total U.S. voting age pop.	189,524,000	196,509,000
State share of U.S. total	0.6%	0.6%
Rank among states	36	36
Percent of state casting vote	50.8	42.7
Percent of U.S. total voting	55.1	49.0
Rank among states	41	47

Source: U.S. Bureau of the Census.

HEALTH AND MEDICAL CARE

Medicare, 1997

	Recipients	Payments
State	221,000	$873 mill.
Total U.S.	37,514,000	$206,064 mill.
State share	0.59%	0.42%
Rank among states	36	40

Recipient figures are rounded to nearest thousand persons. Ranks are from highest to lowest.
Source: U.S. Health Care Financing Administration.

Medicaid, 1996

	Recipients	Payments
State	318,000	$878 mill.
Total U.S.	35,028,000	$121,419 mill.
State share	0.91%	0.72%
Rank among states	32	33

Recipient figures are rounded to nearest thousand persons. Payment figures for fiscal year reflect federal and state contribution payments. Ranks are from highest to lowest.
Source: U.S. Health Care Financing Administration.

Health insurance coverage, 1996

	State	U.S.
Total persons covered	1,435,000	225,070,000
Total persons not covered	412,000	41,716,000
Part not covered	22.3%	15.6%
Rank among states	3	—
Children not covered	108,000	10,554,000
Part not covered	17.5%	14.8%
Rank among states	14	—

Ranks are from most to fewest uninsured. Population figures are rounded to nearest thousand persons.
Source: U.S. Bureau of the Census.

AIDS, syphilis, tuberculosis, and measles cases, 1997

Cases	U.S.	State	Share
AIDS	58,443	169	0.29%
Syphilis	8,550	9	0.11%
Tuberculosis	18,534	60	0.32%
Measles	148,000	NA	NA

Measles figures are rounded to nearest thousand cases.
Source: U.S. Centers for Disease Control and Prevention.

HOUSING

Homeownership rates, 1985-1997

	1985	1990	1997
State	68.2%	68.6%	69.6%
Total U.S.	63.9%	63.9%	65.7%
Rank among states	24	18	19

Source: U.S. Bureau of the Census.

Home sales, 1990 and 1997
In thousands of units

Existing home sales	1990	1997	Change
State sales	23.6	25.5	1.9
Total U.S. sales	3,560	4,730	1,170
State share of U.S. total	0.66%	0.54%	-0.12%
Rank among states	36	36	—

Source: National Association of Realtors; *Real Estate Outlook: Market Trends and Insights.*

EDUCATION

Public school enrollment, 1995

State K-8 enrollment	229,000
Total U.S. K-8 enrollment	32,341,000
State share of total U.S.	0.71%
State 9-12 enrollment	100,000
Total U.S. 9-12 enrollment	12,500,000
State share of U.S. total	0.80%
State public school enroll. rate	91.7%
Overall U.S. rate	91.6%
Rank among states	28

Enrollment figures (which include unclassified students) are rounded to nearest thousand pupils in fall term; kindergarten (K)-8 grade figures include some prekindergarten students. Enrollment rate is based on percentage of persons 5-17 years old. Rank is from highest to lowest.
Source: U.S. National Center for Education Statistics.

Public college finances, 1996

State FTE enrollment	70,900
Total U.S. FTE enrollment	8,268,800
State share of total U.S.	0.86%
Rank among states	34
State and local appropriations	$441,900,000
Total U.S. state and local appropriations	$39,699 mill.
State share of total U.S.	1.11%
Rank among states	29
State net tuition revenues	$98,900,000
Total U.S. net tuition	$18,348,100,000
State share of total U.S.	0.54%
Rank among states	41

FTE=Full-time equivalent; credit and noncredit enrollment including summer session in academic year ending in 1996.
Enrollments are rounded to nearest thousand students. Net tuition revenues exclude appropriation to students attending in-state public institutions. Rankings are from highest shares to lowest.
Source: Research Associates of Washington.

TRANSPORTATION AND TRAVEL

Highway mileage, 1996

Interstate	1,000
Other arterial	4,516
Collector roads	7,157
Local roads	47,236
Urban roads	6,133
Rural roads	53,322
Total state	59,455
U.S. total	3,933,985
State share	1.5%
Rank among states	34

Source: U.S. Federal Highway Administration.

Motor vehicle registrations and driver licenses, 1996
In thousands

Vehicle registrations	State	U.S.	Share	Rank
Autos, trucks, buses	1,545	206,365	0.75%	34
Autos only	759	128,439	0.59%	37
Motorcycles	31	3,832	0.81%	34
Driver licenses	1,179	179,539	0.66%	34

Figures do not include vehicles owned by military services.
Source: U.S. Federal Highway Administration; *Highway Statistics; Selected Highway Statistics and Charts.*

Domestic travel expenditures, 1995
Spending by U.S. residents on overnight trips and day trips of at least 100 miles

Total expenditures in state	$2,931 mill.
Total expenditures in U.S.	$360,314 mill.
State share of total U.S.	0.81%
Rank among states	36

Source: Travel Industry Association of America.

CRIME AND LAW ENFORCEMENT

State and local police officers, 1996

Local police	2,462
State police	435
Sheriffs	889
Total	4,134
Officers per 10,000 residents	24
U.S. average	25
Rank among states	17

Figures cover full-time sworn officers; totals include special police not shown separately.
Source: U.S. Bureau of Justice Statistics; *Census of State and Local Law Enforcement Agencies, 1996.*

Crime rates, 1996
Rates per 100,000 resident population

Violent crimes	State	U.S.
Total violent	841	634
Murder	11.5	7.4
Forcible rape	63.5	36.1
Robbery	162	202
Aggravated assault	603	388
Property crimes		
Total property	5,762	4,445
Burglary	1,377	943
Larceny/theft	3,803	2,976
Motor vehicle theft	582	526
Totals	6,602	5,079

Source: U.S. Federal Bureau of Investigation; *Crime in the United States,* annual.

State prison populations, 1980-1996

	State	U.S.	State share
1980	1,279	305,458	0.42%
1990	3,187	708,393	0.45%
1996	4,724	1,025,624	0.46%

Figures exclude prisoners in federal penitentiaries.
Source: U.S. Bureau of Justice Statistics.

New York

Location: Northeastern continental United States

Area and rank: 47,224 square miles (122,310 square kilometers); 54,475 square miles (141,090 square kilometers) including water; thirtieth largest state in area

Coastline: 127 miles (204 kilometers)

Shoreline: 1,850 miles (2,977 kilometers)

Population and rank: 18,137,226 (1997); third largest state in population

State capitol building in Albany. (© NYS Department of Economic Development)

Capital: Albany

Largest city: New York (7,420,166 people in 1998)

Entered Union and rank: July 26, 1788; eleventh state

Present constitution adopted: 1777 (last revised 1938)

Counties: 62

State name: New York takes its name from the Duke of York

State nickname: Empire State

Motto: *Excelsior* (Ever upward)

State flag: Blue field with state coat of arms

Highest point: Mount Marcy — 5,344 feet (1,629 meters)

Lowest point: Atlantic Ocean — sea level

Highest recorded temperature: 108 degrees Fahrenheit (42 degrees Celsius) — Troy, 1926

Lowest recorded temperature: –52 degrees Fahrenheit (–47 degrees Celsius) — Old Forge, 1979

State song: "I Love New York"

State tree: Sugar maple

State flower: Rose

State bird: Bluebird

State fish: Brook trout

State animal: Beaver

New York History

Dominated by the nation's most heavily populated city, New York has been an area of economic and political importance since the earliest years of the United States. Its position between the Atlantic Ocean and the Great Lakes made it a major area of population movement to the west, and New York City attracts immigrants from around the world.

Early History. The first humans to reside in the area arrived about ten thousand years ago and hunted bison and other large game. Thousands of years later, the culture known as the Mound Builders grew crops in southwestern New York. By the time Europeans arrived in the New World, the Atlantic coast was inhabited by the Mohegans and the Munsees, members of the Algonquian language group. Farther inland resided the Onondaga, the Oneida, the Seneca, the Cayuga, and the Mohawk tribes, members of the Iroquois language group. In 1570, these five peoples united into the Iroquois League, a powerful confederation that dominated the area for two centuries.

Exploration and Colonization. The first European to visit the area was the Italian navigator Giovanni da Verrazano. Working for the French, Verrazano explored the Atlantic coast from North Carolina to Canada, including New York Harbor, in 1524. The French explorer Samuel de Champlain journeyed from Canada to northern New York and reached Lake Champlain in 1609. The same year, the English navigator Henry Hudson, working for the Dutch, sailed up the Hudson River about as far as the modern site of Albany.

Despite this early exploration, settlement of New York began slowly. The Dutch established Fort Orange, later known as Albany, in 1624 as the first

Late nineteenth century illustration of Dutch leader Peter Minuit buying Manhattan from Indians in 1626. (Library of Congress)

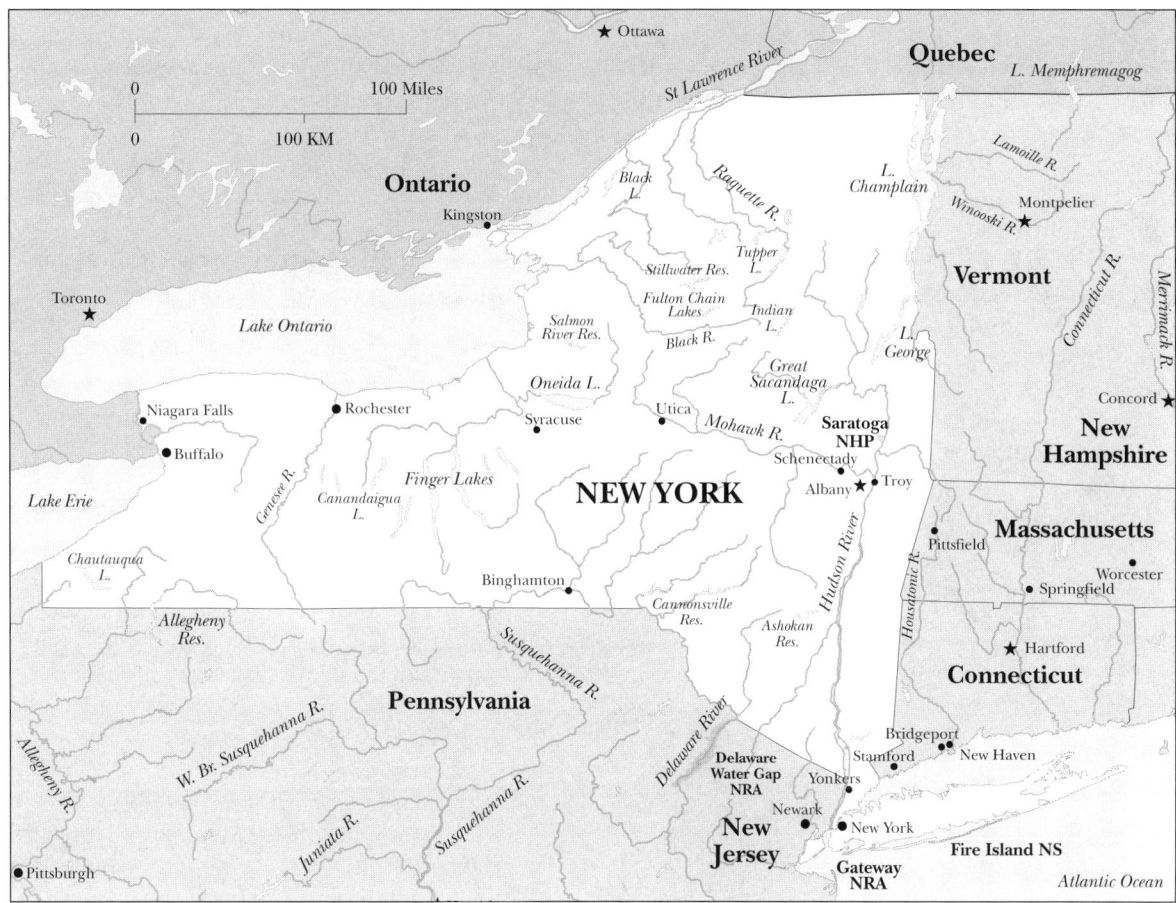

permanent European settlement in the area. The next year they established New Amsterdam, later known as New York City, on Manhattan Island. By 1650, the Dutch colony had about one thousand residents. In 1664 an English fleet sailed into New York Harbor and captured the colony without a fight. At this time the area had about eight thousand colonists, including Dutch, English, French, Germans, Finns, Swedes, Jews, and African slaves.

The colony was given by English King Charles II to his brother, the Duke of York and Albany, later King James II. After approving a charter adopted by the colonists in 1683, James II revoked it when he became king in 1685. Instead, he united New York and the colonies of New England to the north under a single administration. Strong resistance to the unification of the colonies led to a rebellion in 1689, after a political crisis in England forced James II to abdicate. Jacob Leisler, the leader of the rebellion, controlled New York until 1691, when the new king, William II, sent in a new royal governor, who had Leisler hanged for treason.

The next several decades brought conflict between the French and the English in the area. The French made a number of raids from Canada into central and northern New York, limiting settlement beyond Albany. An important factor in England's ability to retain control of the colony was an alliance with the Iroquois League. The struggle for control of North America led to the French and Indian War (1754-1763), which ended with the English in firm control of New York. The war also weakened the power of the Iroquois League, which ceded much of its land to the colonists.

Revolution and Population Growth. The British victory in the war encouraged settlement of the area. By the start of the American Revolution (1775-1783), New York had a population of 163,000.

About one-third of the battles of the Revolution took place in New York. American forces under Ethan Allen captured Fort Ticonderoga, in the northeastern part of the colony, in 1775. The British captured New York City in 1776 and recaptured Fort Ticonderoga in 1777. One of the most important events in the war took place in New York on October 17, 1777, when British general John Burgoyne surrendered his army at Saratoga, between Fort Ticonderoga and Albany. This American victory, often considered the turning point in the Revolution, helped bring France into the war against the British.

New York adopted its first state constitution on April 20, 1777, with Kingston, located between Albany and New York City, as the first state capital. After the war, New York City served as the capital of the United States from 1785 to 1790. It became the most populous city in the nation in 1790. New York officially became the eleventh state of the Union in 1788, when it ratified the U.S. Constitution. The state capital was moved to Albany nine years later.

Migration to the state from New England made New York the second most heavily populated state in 1800 and the most heavily populated state in 1810. The opening of the Erie Canal between the Hudson River and Lake Erie in 1825, linking New York to new territories in the west, contributed to the state's rapid growth.

The Civil War and Tammany Hall. New York abolished slavery in 1827 and was a center of the antislavery movement. Although the state was firmly on the side of the Union during the Civil War (1861-1865), violent draft riots in New York City in 1863 led to two thousand deaths, including those of many African Americans. Despite this crisis, the war was generally good for the state's growing economy.

Meanwhile, New York City became a stronghold of political corruption with the rise of Tammany Hall. This group had been founded in 1789 to represent the interests of the middle class against the policies of the Federalist Party. It later evolved into an organization that dominated the Democratic Party in New York City, giving it control of the city government. Tammany Hall reached its greatest power in the middle of the nineteenth century, when William "Boss" Tweed took control in 1857. Tweed stole millions of dollars from the city treasury. Tammany Hall lost much of its power when Tweed was arrested in 1872, but it continued to have an influence on city politics well into the twentieth century.

Economic Growth and Immigration. New York's position as one of the most economically important states in the nation began soon after statehood. Dairy farming, long the most important agricultural activity in the state, was established before the American Revolution. Poultry and egg production, as well as fruit and vegetable farming, began at an early date and would remain important parts of the state's economy.

New York City's Empire State Building nearing completion in 1930. (Library of Congress)

With more than seven million residents, New York City is by far the biggest city in the United States. (PhotoDisc)

Investment and finance, which began with the founding of the New York Stock Exchange in 1817, would remain centered in New York City's Wall Street. The textile industry began in the 1820's. International trade was also established at an early date, with New York handling half of the nation's imported goods as early as 1831.

The first railroad in the state was completed in 1831. The growth of the New York Central Railroad Company throughout the nineteenth century was a major factor in the rise of industry in the state. After the Civil War, during the so-called Gilded Age, rapid economic growth created many millionaires and led to the founding of nationally important companies such as Westinghouse, General Electric, and Eastman Kodak.

Meanwhile, the first of many waves of immigration brought large numbers of Germans and Irish to New York in the 1840's. During the late nine-teenth century, new residents from around the world arrived, particularly from eastern and southern Europe. New York's Ellis Island was the center of immigration in the United States from 1892 to 1943.

Large numbers of African Americans began to arrive in New York during World War I, followed by an even larger number during and after World War II. New York's African American population rose from less than 5 percent in the early 1940's to more than 20 percent by the end of the century. During the 1950's and 1960's, large numbers of Puerto Ricans arrived in the state. Later decades brought an increase in immigration from Asia and the Middle East.

The Twentieth Century. New York, long dominant in national politics, began a new era with the election of Franklin Delano Roosevelt as governor in 1928. Roosevelt's policy of increased govern-

New York City's Manhattan is the most densely populated residential area in the nation, but its crowding is relieved by Central Park, which stretches from 59th Street to 110th Street and from Fifth Avenue to Eighth Avenue. (Corbis)

ment spending on social services, particularly after the stock market crash of 1929 and the Great Depression, continued when he served as president of the United States from 1933 to 1945. This trend continued in New York City after World War II, leading to a financial crisis in 1975, when federal funds in the amount of $4.5 billion were needed to protect the city from bankruptcy.

In 1970 California surpassed New York in population. Between 1970 and 1980, New York was one of the few states to decrease in population. Despite a decline in manufacturing during the same de-

cade, the rise of service industries led to economic growth in the late 1970's and 1980's. This growth came to a sudden halt in late 1987, when a stock market crash led to a recession. In addition to economic problems, New York City faced an increase in racial violence in the late 1980's and early 1990's. Although New York City managed to improve its image as a center of crime and poverty in the late 1990's, it still faced numerous challenges in the twenty-first century.

Rose Secrest

New York Time Line

Apr. 17, 1524   Italian navigator Giovanni da Verrazano enters New York Harbor.

1570   Five Native American peoples unite into the Iroquois League.

1609	French explorer Samuel de Champlain reaches Lake Champlain; English navigator Henry Hudson, working for the Dutch, explores the Hudson River.
1624	Dutch establish Fort Orange, later known as Albany.
1625	Dutch establish New Amsterdam, later known as New York City, on Manhattan Island.
1650	Dutch colony has about one thousand residents.
Sept. 9, 1664	English fleet captures the colony, which now has about eight thousand residents.
1683	General assembly of colonists adopts a charter, which King James II revokes two years later.
1686	James II dissolves the assembly and unites New York and New England under a single administration.
1689	James II abdicates, leading to a rebellion against the administration, led by Jacob Leisler.
1754	King's College, later known as Columbia University, is established in New York City.
1763	Loss of the French and Indian War ends French attempts to win control of the area.
1776	British forces capture New York City during the American Revolution.
Apr. 20, 1777	New York adopts its first state constitution, with the state capital located at Kingston.
Oct. 17, 1777	British general John Burgoyne surrenders his army at Saratoga.
1784	University of the State of New York is founded.
1785	New York City becomes the capital of the United States.
July 26, 1788	New York ratifies the U.S. Constitution, becoming the eleventh state.
1789	Tammany Hall is created.
1790	New York City is the most populous city in the nation.
1790	National capital is moved to the newly created Washington, D.C.
1791	First public school is established.
1797	State capital is moved to Albany.
1800	New York is the second most populous state.
1810	New York is the most populous state.
1817	New York Stock Exchange is established.
1825	Erie Canal opens.
July 4, 1827	New York abolishes slavery.
1831	New York handles half the nation's imports.
1831	First railroad in the state is completed.
July 19, 1848	First women's rights convention in the nation is held at Seneca Falls.
1857	William Tweed takes control of Tammany Hall.
July 13-16, 1863	Antidraft riots in New York City lead to two thousand deaths.
1872	Tweed is arrested for stealing millions of dollars in state funds.
1892	Ellis Island begins serving as the center of immigration for the United States.

(continued)

1918	New York State Barge Canal System, the nation's largest inland waterway, is completed.
1928	Franklin Delano Roosevelt is elected governor.
1929	Stock market crashes, leading to the Great Depression.
1933	Roosevelt takes office as president of the United States.
Nov. 8, 1966	State lottery legalized.
1970	California surpasses New York in population.
1975	$4.5 billion in federal funds save New York City from bankruptcy.
1987	Stock market crashes, leading to a recession.
1989	One-quarter of lakes and ponds in Adirondacks polluted by acid rain.
Feb. 26, 1993	World Trade Center is bombed by terrorists, killing six.
1999	First Lady Hillary Rodham Clinton announces her candidacy for U.S. senator from New York, becoming the first presidential wife to run for the Senate.

Notes for Further Study

Published Sources. A good basic source of information on the state is *New York* (1999) by Ann Heinrichs, which discusses New York's geography, plants, animals, history, economy, and people. A broad discussion of the many issues facing New York in the future, including education, the environment, and the economy, can be found in *New York State in the Twenty-first Century* (1999), edited by Thomas A. Hirschl and Tim B. Heaton.

By far the largest number of books available deal with New York City. Two excellent histories of the city are *American Metropolis: A History of New York City* (1998) by George J. Lankevich, and *Gotham: A History of New York City to 1898* (1999) by Edwin G. Burrows and Mike Wallace. An updated version of a classic work dealing with the many different ethnic groups in the city is found in *Beyond the Melting Pot: The Negroes, Puerto Ricans, Jews, Italians, and Irish of New York City* (1990) by Nathan Glazer. A detailed account of the attempt in the 1990's to transform the city's most famous area from a place of crime and poverty to a tourist attraction is provided by Alexander J. Reichl in *Reconstructing Times Square: Politics and Culture in Urban Development* (1999).

Web Resources. As might be expected for a state with the largest city in the United States, an enormous variety of Web sites exist relating to New York. A good place to start is with the state government's official Web site, Welcome to New York State (http://www.state.ny.us), which provides information about government services as well as a discussion of important issues such as crime, education, the economy, the environment, health care, and welfare. A large number of relevant Web sites can be reached through The New York State Links Page (http://www.historyoftheworld.com/usa/nyork.htm). A similar site, with information for each county, is found at New York GenWeb Project (http://www.rootsweb.com/~nygenweb). Tourist attractions in the state are the subject of I Love New York (http://www.iloveny.state.ny.us).

Statistical information for the state can be found at New York Profiles (http://www.census.gov/datamap/www.36.htm), provided by the U.S. Census Bureau. A concise guide to the state's government is found at New York's Government (http://www.sara.nysed.gov/virtual/gov-one-page.html). A similar site with an emphasis on law is New York State Law and Government Information Resources (http://web.cuny.edu/library/libwebsites/NYGovInfo.html). Of the many Web sites dealing with the state's history, one of the best for the student new to the subject is New York History (http://www.encyclopedia.com/articles/09209.html). For more details, New York State Archives and Records Administration (http://unix6.nysed.gov) is a good resource. Among the countless Web sites dealing with New York City, New York City Information (http://www.nycballet.com.NYCsites.html) has numerous links. Sites dealing with two of the city's most famous institutions are The New York Stock Exchange (http://www.nyse.com) and The New York Times on the Web (http://nytimes.com).

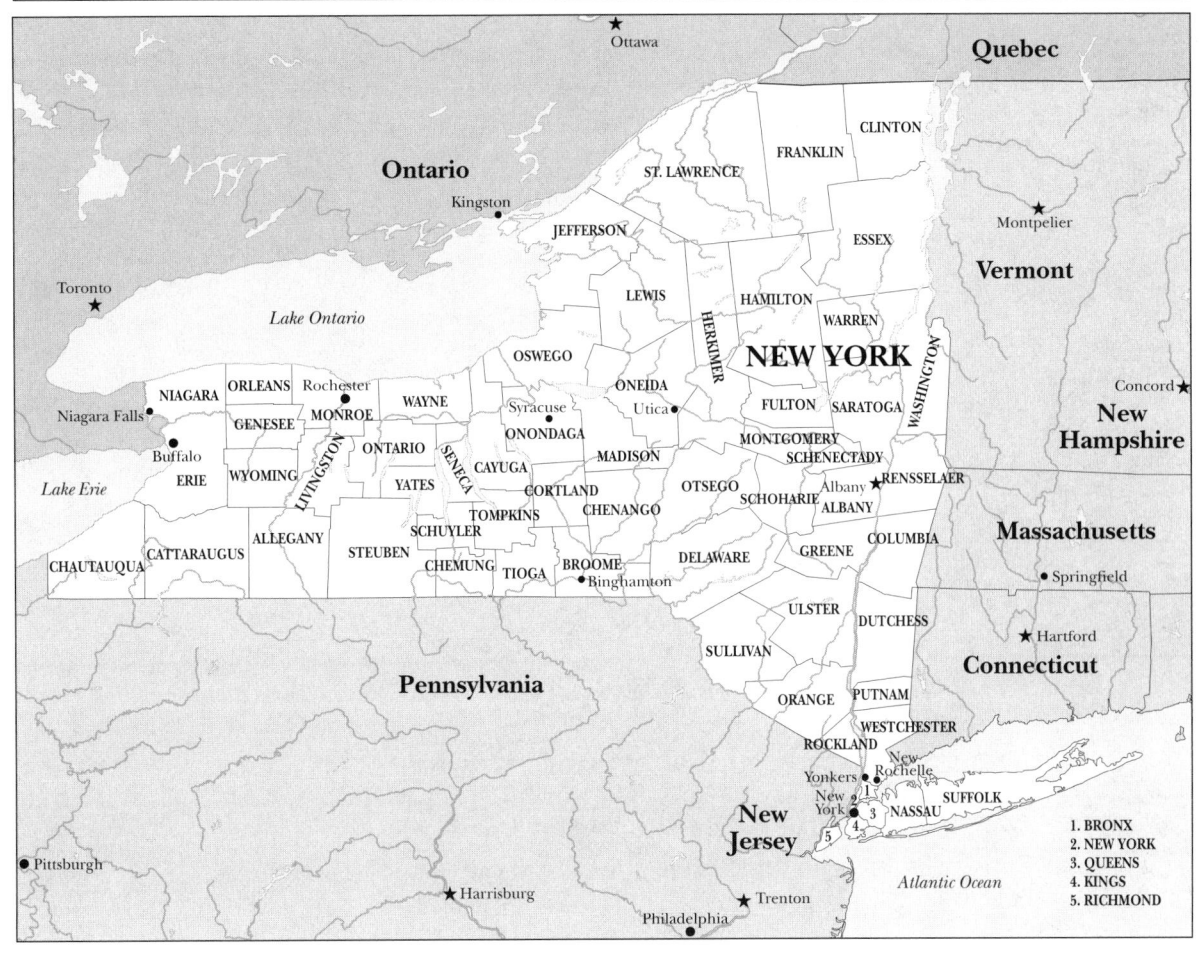

Counties

County	Sq. miles	1996 pop.	County	Sq. miles	1996 pop.
Albany	523.8	296,087	Franklin	1,631.6	49,335
Allegany	1,030.3	51,282	Fulton	496.2	53,965
Bronx	42.0	1,203,789	Genesee	494.1	61,206
Broome	706.9	201,533	Greene	647.9	47,291
Cattaraugus	1,309.9	85,680	Hamilton	1,720.7	5,232
Cayuga	693.3	82,062	Herkimer	1,411.8	65,968
Chautauqua	1,062.1	140,800	Jefferson	1,272.3	113,844
Chemung	408.2	93,282	Kings	26,796	70.5
Chenango	894.4	52,121	Lewis	1,275.6	27,799
Clinton	1,039.4	80,537	Livingston	632.2	65,898
Columbia	635.8	63,613	Madison	655.9	71,508
Cortland	499.7	48,573	Monroe	659.3	721,996
Delaware	1,446.4	47,287	Montgomery	404.8	51,894
Dutchess	801.7	262,675	Nassau	286.8	1,303,389
Erie	1,044.7	954,021	New York	28.4	7,533,774
Essex	1,797.0	37,789	Niagara	523.0	221,219

(continued)

County	Sq. miles	1996 pop.
Oneida	1,212.8	236,437
Onondaga	780.3	466,675
Ontario	644.4	99,634
Orange	816.4	324,422
Orleans	391.4	44,979
Oswego	953.3	125,446
Otsego	1,002.9	61,470
Putnam	231.5	90,983
Queens	109.4	1,951,598
Rensselaer	654.0	155,098
Richmond	58.6	378,977
Rockland	174.2	278,136
Saint Lawrence	2,685.7	114,759
Saratoga	811.9	194,837
Schenectady	206.1	147,599
Schoharie	621.8	33,012

County	Sq. miles	1996 pop.
Schuyler	328.7	19,108
Seneca	324.9	32,530
Steuben	1,392.7	99,201
Suffolk	911.2	1,356,896
Sullivan	969.8	70,346
Tioga	518.7	52,520
Tompkins	476.1	96,152
Ulster	1,126.6	167,082
Warren	869.7	61,490
Washington	835.5	60,777
Wayne	604.2	94,324
Westchester	432.9	893,412
Wyoming	593.0	44,357
Yates	338.2	24,300

Source: U.S. Bureau of the Census; National Association of Counties.

Cities

With 10,000 or more residents

Rank	City	Population
1	New York	7,420,166
2	Buffalo	300,717
3	Rochester	216,887
4	Yonkers	190,153
5	Syracuse	152,215
6	Albany	94,305
7	New Rochelle	67,225
8	Mount Vernon	66,824
9	Schenectady	61,698
10	Utica	59,334
11	Niagara Falls	56,768
12	Troy	51,320
13	White Plains	49,944
14	Binghamton	46,760
15	Hempstead	46,698
16	Freeport	39,963
17	Rome	39,792
18	Long Beach	34,244
19	Valley Stream	33,891
20	North Tonawanda	32,947
21	Jamestown	32,166
22	Elmira	31,367
23	Auburn	29,145
24	Ithaca	28,172
25	Watertown	27,759
26	Poughkeepsie	27,669

Rank	City	Population
27	Lindenhurst	26,433
28	Newburgh	26,114
29	Saratoga Springs	25,140
30	Glen Cove	24,935
31	Port Chester	24,777
32	Rockville Centre	24,639
33	Harrison	24,027
34	Middletown	23,953
35	Ossining	23,010
36	Lockport	22,650
37	Spring Valley	22,105
38	Kingston	21,860
39	Garden City	21,616
40	Peekskill	21,111
41	Lynbrook	19,341
42	Lackawanna	19,220
43	Amsterdam	19,176
44	Mineola	18,942
45	Plattsburgh	18,678
46	Cortland	18,409
47	Massapequa Park	18,108
48	Oswego	18,054
49	Scarsdale	17,802
50	Mamaroneck	17,394
51	Depew	16,675
52	Cohoes	16,333

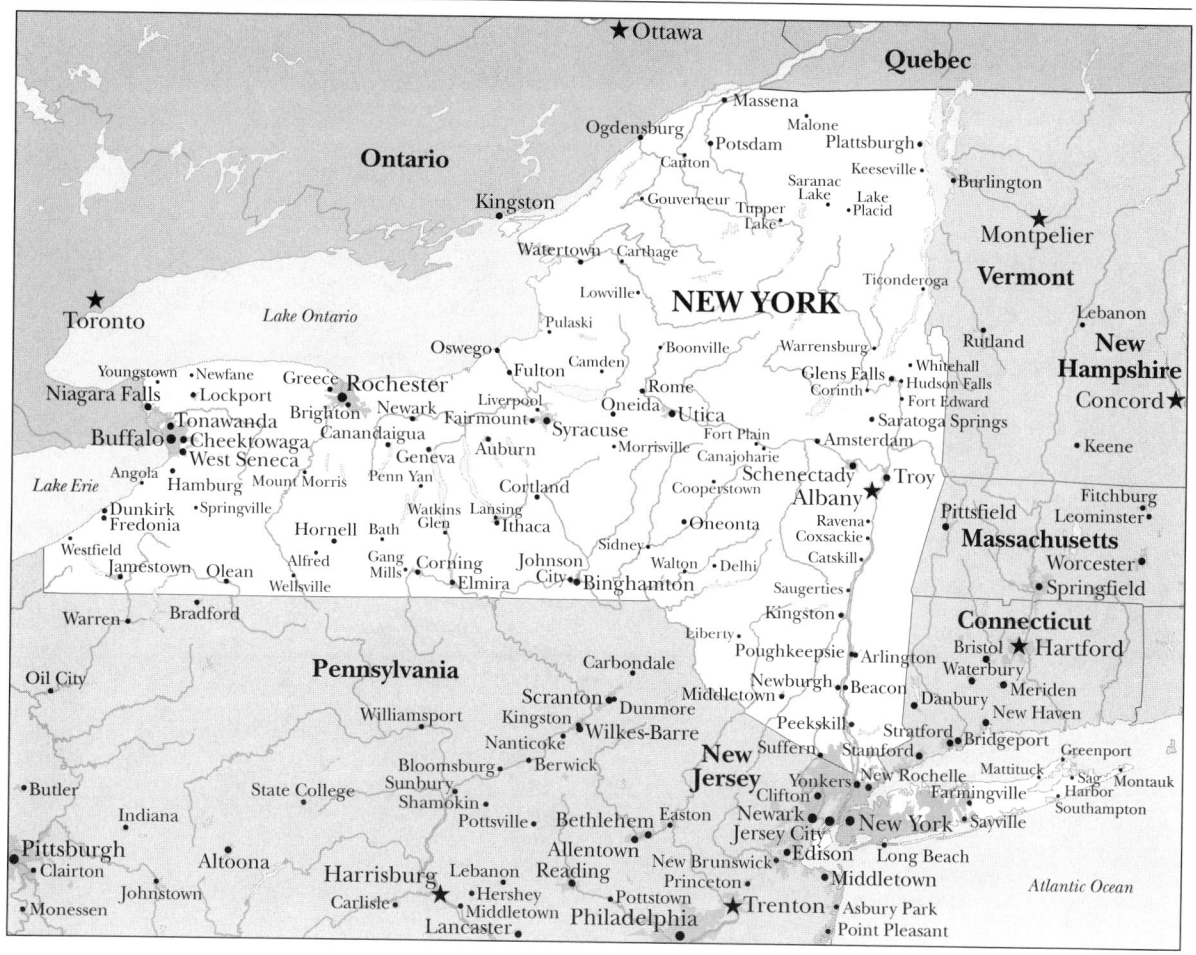

Rank	City	Population
53	Olean	16,170
54	Kenmore	15,911
55	Tonawanda	15,901
56	Floral Park	15,849
57	Batavia	15,784
58	Gloversville	15,488
59	Rye	15,326
60	Johnson City	14,962
61	Glens Falls	14,497
62	Geneva	13,720
63	Beacon	13,215
64	Westbury	13,189
65	Oneonta	12,965
66	Dunkirk	12,952
67	Ogdensburg	12,759
68	Fulton	12,195
69	Babylon	12,001

Rank	City	Population
70	Endicott	12,001
71	Massena	11,257
72	Tarrytown	11,228
73	Lancaster	11,087
74	Corning	11,080
75	Suffern	11,059
76	Patchogue	11,014
77	Oneida	10,854
78	Canandaigua	10,658
79	Watervliet	10,342
80	East Rockaway	10,155
81	West Haverstraw	10,091
82	Dobbs Ferry	10,070
83	Fredonia	10,016

Population figures are estimated for mid-1998.
Source: U.S. Bureau of the Census.

Index to Tables

NA = Reliable data are not available.

DEMOGRAPHICS

Resident state and national populations, 1970-1997

Population figures given in thousands

	State pop.	U.S. pop.	Share	Rank
1970	18,241	203,302	9.0%	2
1980	17,558	226,546	7.8%	2
1985	17,792	237,924	7.5%	2
1990	17,991	248,765	7.2%	2
1995	18,146	262,761	6.9%	3
1997	18,137	267,636	6.8%	3

Source: U.S. Bureau of the Census.

Resident population by age, 1997

Age group	Total population
Under 5 years	1,314,000
5 to 17 years	3,246,000
18 to 24 years	1,579,000
25 to 34 years	2,767,000
35 to 44 years	2,948,000
45 to 54 years	2,312,000
55 to 64 years	1,543,000
65 to 74 years	1,313,000
75 to 84 years	825,000
85 years and over	290,000
Portion of residents 65 and older	13.4%
National average	6.8%

Population figures are rounded to nearest thousand persons;
figures include armed forces personnel stationed in state.
Source: U.S. Bureau of the Census.

Resident population by race, Hispanic origin, 1997

	State pop.	Share	U.S.
All residents	18,137,000	100.0%	100.0%
Hispanic white	1,943,000	10.7%	10.0%
non-Hispanic white	11,958,000	65.9%	72.7%
African American	3,208,000	17.7%	12.7%
Native American	74,000	0.4%	0.9%
Asian, Pacific Islander	953,000	5.3%	3.8%

Source: U.S. Bureau of the Census.

Projections of state population, 2000-2025

	Model A Uses interstate migration observed from 1975-1994	Model B Uses Bureau of Economic Analysis employment projections
Year	Population	Population
2000	18,146,000	18,174,000
2005	18,250,000	18,227,000
2010	18,530,000	18,363,000
2015	18,916,000	18,616,000
2020	19,359,000	18,969,000
2025	19,830,000	19,396,000

All population projections, including those for 2000, were calculated in 1997.

Source: U.S. Bureau of the Census, Population Paper Listings PPL-47.

VITAL STATISTICS

Average lifetime in years by race, 1989-1991

	State	U.S.	Rank
All residents	74.68	75.37	38
White residents	75.61	76.13	38
Black residents	69.33	69.16	19

Ranks are from longest-lived to least longest-lived. Ranks exclude Alaska, for which reliable data are not available. Rank for black residents is based on the 32 states for which reliable data are available.

Source: U.S. National Center for Health Statistics.

Infant mortality rates, 1980 and 1995

	State	U.S.
All residents		
1980	12.5	12.6
1995	7.7	7.6
White residents		
1980	10.8	11.0
1995	6.2	6.3
Black residents		
1980	20.0	21.4
1995	13.9	15.1

Figures represent deaths per 1,000 live births of resident infants under 1 year old, exclusive of fetal deaths; all-residents figures include other races not listed separately.
Source: U.S. National Center for Health Statistics.

Marriages and divorces

Marriages in 1996	152,300
Rate per 1,000 population, 1995	8.1
U.S. rate, 1995	8.9
Rank among all states	31
Divorces in 1996	60,800
Rate per 1,000 population, 1995	3.1
U.S. rate, 1995	4.4
Rank among all states	42

Rank is from highest to lowest in country.
Source: U.S. National Center for Health Statistics.

Death rates by leading causes, 1995
Deaths per 100,000 resident population

Cause	State	U.S.
Heart disease	350.2	280.7
Cancer	213.3	204.9
Cerebrovascular diseases	44.8	60.1
Accidents and adverse effects	27.5	35.5
Motor vehicle accidents	9.9	16.5
Chronic obstructive pulmonary diseases	33.8	39.2
Diabetes mellitus	19.4	22.6
HIV	44.1	NA
Suicide	7.6	11.9
Homicide	8.7	8.7
All causes	928.4	880.0
Rank in overall death rate among states		20

Figures exclude nonresidents who die in state. Causes of death follow International Classification of Diseases. Rank is from highest to lowest in country.
Source: U.S. National Center for Health Statistics.

ECONOMY

Gross state product, 1990-1996
In current dollars

	State product	Increase
1990	$498.3 billion	
1993	$541.1 billion	
1994	$565.2 billion	4.45%
1995	$587.7 billion	3.98%
1996	$613.3 billion	4.36%

Source: U.S. Bureau of Economic Analysis; Survey of Current Business, June, 1998.

Gross state product by industry, 1996
In billions

Farms, forestry, fisheries	$2.5
Construction	15.2
Manufacturing	71.7
Transportation, public utilities	46.3
Wholesale trade	36.0
Retail trade	40.8
Finance, insurance, real estate	167.2
Services	122.6
Government	60.9
State total	$563.3
Total U.S.	$6,923.8
State share	8.14%
Rank among states	2

Total figures include mining, not listed separately.
Source: U.S. Bureau of Economic Analysis; Survey of Current Business, June, 1998.

Personal income per capita, 1990 and 1997
In current dollars

	1990	1997
Per capita income	$23,147	$30,752
U.S. average	$19,188	$25,598
Rank among states	4	4

1997 data are preliminary.
Source: U.S. Bureau of Economic Analysis; Survey of Current Business, May, 1998.

Energy consumption, 1995
In trillions of British thermal units (BTU)

End-use sectors

Residential	1,053.1
Commercial	1,088.1
Industrial	883.8
Transportation	916.4

Sources of energy

Petroleum	1,491.1
Natural gas	1,172.4
Coal	287.1
Hydroelectric power	319.3
Nuclear electric power	280.7
Total state per capita consumption	215.1
Total U.S. per capita consumption	344.4
Rank among states	50
Total state energy consumption	3,913.4
Total U.S. energy consumption	90,547.4
State share of U.S. total	4.32%
Rank among states	4

Total figures include items not listed separately.
Source: U.S. Energy Information Administration; State Energy Data Report.

Nonfarm employment by sectors, 1997

Total	8,027,000
Construction	264,000
Manufacturing	921,000
Transportation, public utilities	408,000
Wholesale trade, retail trade	1,640,000
Finance, insurance, real estate	720,000
Services	2,696,000
Government	1,374,000

Figures are rounded to nearest thousand persons. Total includes mining, not listed separately.
Source: U.S. Bureau of Labor Statistics; Employment and Earnings, monthly.

Foreign exports, 1990-1997
In millions of dollars

Year	State	U.S.	State share
1990	22,072	394,045	5.60%
1996	34,230	624,767	5.48%
1997	37,979	688,896	5.51%

Source: U.S. Bureau of the Census; U.S. Merchandise Trade, series FT 900.

LAND USE

Federally owned land, 1996

	State	U.S.	State share
Total acres	30,681,000	2,271,343,000	1.35%
Federally owned	197,000	563,129,000	0.03%
Federal share	0.6%	24.8%	—

Areas are rounded to nearest thousand acres. Figures for federally owned land do not include trust properties.

Source: U.S. General Services Administration; *Inventory Report on Real Property Owned by the United States Throughout the World,* annual.

Land use, 1992
In acres, rounded to nearest thousand

Total surface area	31,429,000
Federal land	231,000
Total nonfederal	29,788,000
Developed	3,005,000
Total rural	26,783,000
Cropland.	5,616,000
Pasture land	3,001,000
Range land	0
Forest land	17,178,000
Minor cover/use.	987,000

Total surface area figures include water area not shown separately.

Source: U.S. Dept. of Agriculture; Soil Conservation Service; Iowa State University, Statistical Laboratory; *Summary Report, 1992 National Resources Inventory.*

Farms and crop acreage, 1997

	State	U.S.	Share	Rank
Farms (thousands)	36	2,058	1.75%	25
Acres (millions)	8	968	0.83%	36
Acres per farm	214	471	—	34
Acres planted	3,070	334,139	0.92%	28
Acres harvested	3,017	319,894	0.94%	28
Farm value (mill.)	$1,070	$108,805	0.98%	15

Numbers of farms are rounded to nearest thousand.

Source: U.S. Dept. of Agriculture; National Agricultural Statistics Service.

GOVERNMENT AND FINANCE

Units of local government, 1997

	State	Total U.S.	Rank
All local governments	3,413	87,453	9
Counties	57	3,043	26
Municipalities	615	19,372	9
Townships	929	16,629	11
School districts	686	13,726	4
Special districts	1,126	34,683	11

County ranks are based on the 48 states with county governments; township ranks are based on the 20 states with township governments; school district ranks are based on the 46 states with such districts.

Township figures include "town" governments.

Source: U.S. Bureau of the Census; *1997 Census of Governments, Government Organization,* Series GC97(1).

State government revenue, 1996

Total revenue	$94,277 mill.
General revenue	71,219 mill.
Per capita.	3,927
U.S. per capita average	2,910
Rank among states	5

Intergovernmental revenue

Total	$27,668 mill.
From federal government	22,373 mill.
From local government	5,296 mill.

Charges and Miscellaneous

Total	$9,401 mill.
Current charges	3,941 mill.
Misc. general revenue	5,460 mill.

Taxes

Total	$34,150 mill.
General sales	6,963 mill.
Selective sales.	4,950 mill.
License taxes	974 mill.
Individual income.	17,399 mill.
Corporate income	2,730 mill.
Other	1,134 mill.
Insurance trust revenue	20,902 mill.

Total revenue figures include items not listed separately.

Source: U.S. Bureau of the Census.

State government expenditures, 1996

General expenditures

Intergovernmental.	$25,417 mill.
Direct expenditures.	43,449 mill.
Total	68,866 mill.

Selected direct expenditures

Education	$17,326 mill.
Public welfare	26,146 mill.
Health, hospital	6,433 mill.
Highways	2,841 mill.
Police	353 mill.
Corrections	2,377 mill.
Natural resources.	326 mill.
Parks and recreation	291 mill.
Government administration	2,750 mill.
Interest on debt	3,354 mill.

Other

State per capita expenditures	$3,798
U.S. per capita average	2,854
Rank among states	4
Total state expenditures	82,420 mill.
Total U.S. expenditures	859,959 mill.

Totals include items not listed separately.
Source: U.S. Bureau of the Census.

POLITICS

Governors since statehood

D = Democrat; R = Republican; O = other;
(r) resigned; (d) died in office; (i) removed from office

George Clinton	1777-1795
John Jay	1795-1801
George Clinton (O)	1801-1804
Morgan Lewis (O)	1804-1807
Daniel D. Tompkins (O)	1807-1817
John Tayler (O).	1817
DeWitt Clinton (O).	1817-1822
Joseph C. Yates (O).	1823-1824
DeWitt Clinton (O).	1825-1828
Nathaniel Pitcher (O)	1828
Martin Van Buren (D)	1829
Enos T. Throop (D)	1829-1832
William L. Marcy (D).	1833-1838
William H. Seward (O).	1839-1842
William C. Bouck (D)	1843-1844
Silas Wright (D).	1845-1846
John Young (O).	1847-1848
Hamilton Fish (O)	1849-1850
Washington Hunt (O)	1851-1852
Horatio Seymour (D)	1853-1854
Myron H. Clark (O)	1855-1856
John A. King (R)	1857-1858
Edwin D. Morgan (R)	1859-1862
Horatio Seymour (D)	1863-1864
Reuben E. Fenton (R)	1865-1868
John T. Hoffman (D)	1869-1872
John Adams Dix (R)	1873-1874
Samuel J. Tilden (D)	1875-1876
Lucius Robinson (D)	1877-1879
Alonzo B. Cornell (R)	1880-1882
Grover Cleveland (D)	1883-1885
David B. Hill (D)	1885-1891
Roswell P. Flower (D)	1892-1894
Levi P. Morton (R)	1895-1896
Frank S. Black (R)	1897-1898
Theodore Roosevelt (R)	1899-1900
Benjamin B. Odell, Jr. (R)	1901-1904
Frank W. Higgins (R).	1905-1906
Charles Evans Hughes (R)	1907-1910
Horace White (R).	1910
John Alden Dix (D).	1911-1912
William Sulzer (D)	1913
Martin Glynn (D).	1913-1914
Charles S. Whitman (R)	1915-1918
Alfred E. Smith (D).	1919-1920
Nathan L. Miller (R)	1921-1922
Alfred E. Smith (D).	1923-1928
Franklin D. Roosevelt (D)	1929-1932
Herbert H. Lehman (D)	1933-1942
Charles Poletti (D)	1942
Thomas E. Dewey (R)	1943-1954
Averell Harriman (D)	1955-1958
Nelson Rockefeller (R).	1959-1973
Malcolm Wilson (R)	1973-1974
Hugh J. Carey (D)	1975-1982
Mario M. Cuomo (D).	1983-1994
George E. Pataki (R)	1995-

Composition of state legislature, 1990-1998

	Democrats	Republicans
State Assembly (150 seats)		
1990	95	55
1992	100	50
1994	94	56
1996	96	54
1998	98	52

	Democrats	Republicans
State Senate (61 seats)		
1990	26	35
1992	26	35
1994	25	36
1996	26	35
1998	24	36

Figures for total seats may include independents and minor party members.

Source: Council of State Governments; *State Elective Officials and the Legislatures.*

Composition of congressional delegations, 1989-1999

	Dem	Rep	Total
House of Representatives			
101st Congress, 1989			
State delegates	21	13	34
Total U.S.	259	174	433
102d Congress, 1991			
State delegates	21	13	34
Total U.S.	267	167	434
103d Congress, 1993			
State delegates	18	13	31
Total U.S.	258	176	434
104th Congress, 1995			
State delegates	18	13	31
Total U.S.	197	236	433
105th Congress, 1997			
State delegates	18	12	30
Total U.S.	206	228	434
106th Congress, 1999			
State delegates	19	12	31
Total U.S.	211	222	433
Senate			
101st Congress, 1989			
State delegates	1	1	2
Total U.S.	55	45	100
102d Congress, 1991			
State delegates	1	1	2
Total U.S.	56	44	100
103d Congress, 1993			
State delegates	1	1	2
Total U.S.	57	43	100

	Dem	Rep	Total
104th Congress, 1995			
State delegates	1	1	2
Total U.S.	46	53	99
105th Congress, 1997			
State delegates	1	1	2
Total U.S.	45	55	100
106th Congress, 1999			
State delegates	2	0	2
Total U.S.	45	54	99

Figures are for starts of first sessions. Figure for U.S. Representatives for 101st Congress does not include Alabama and Indiana, which had vacancies. Figures for total U.S. Representatives for 102d, 103d, and 106th Congresses do not include Vermont, which had 1 Independent-Socialist. Figure for U.S. Representatives for 104th Congress does not include Vermont, which had 1 Independent-Socialist, and California, which had 1 vacancy. Figure for U.S. Representatives for 105th Congress does not include New York, which had 1 vacancy. Figure for U.S. Senators for 104th Congress does not include Oregon, which had 1 vacancy. Figure for U.S. Senators for 106th Congress does not include New Hampshire, which had 1 Independent.

Source: U.S. Congress; *Congressional Directory*, biennial.

Voter participation in presidential elections, 1992 and 1996

	1992	1996
State voting age pop.	13,705,000	13,579,000
Total U.S. voting age pop.	189,524,000	196,509,000
State share of U.S. total	7.2%	6.9%
Rank among states	3	3
Percent of state casting vote	50.5	47.5
Percent of U.S. total voting	55.1	49.0
Rank among states	42	33

Source: U.S. Bureau of the Census.

HEALTH AND MEDICAL CARE

Medicare, 1997

	Recipients	Payments
State	2,657,000	$16,451 mill.
Total U.S.	37,514,000	$206,064 mill.
State share	7.08%	7.98%
Rank among states	3	3

Recipient figures are rounded to nearest thousand persons. Ranks are from highest to lowest.

Source: U.S. Health Care Financing Administration.

Medicaid, 1996

	Recipients	Payments
State	3,281,000	$22,347 mill.
Total U.S.	35,028,000	$121,419 mill.
State share	9.37%	18.40%
Rank among states	2	1

Recipient figures are rounded to nearest thousand persons. Payment figures for fiscal year reflect federal and state contribution payments. Ranks are from highest to lowest.
Source: U.S. Health Care Financing Administration.

Health insurance coverage, 1996

	State	U.S.
Total persons covered	15,265,000	225,070,000
Total persons not covered	3,132,000	41,716,000
Part not covered	17.0%	15.6%
Rank among states	11	—
Children not covered	735,000	10,554,000
Part not covered	15.1%	14.8%
Rank among states	19	—

Ranks are from most to fewest uninsured. Population figures are rounded to nearest thousand persons.
Source: U.S. Bureau of the Census.

AIDS, syphilis, tuberculosis, and measles cases, 1997

Cases	U.S.	State	Share
AIDS	58,443	13,189	22.57%
Syphilis	8,550	138	1.61%
Tuberculosis	18,534	2,271	12.25%
Measles	148,000	16,000	10.81%

Measles figures are rounded to nearest thousand cases.
Source: U.S. Centers for Disease Control and Prevention.

HOUSING

Homeownership rates, 1985-1997

	1985	1990	1997
State	50.3%	53.3%	52.6%
Total U.S.	63.9%	63.9%	65.7%
Rank among states	50	50	49

Source: U.S. Bureau of the Census.

Home sales, 1990 and 1997
In thousands of units

Existing home sales	1990	1997	Change
State sales	125.5	171.0	45.5
Total U.S. sales	3,560	4,730	1,170
State share of U.S. total	3.53%	3.62%	0.09%
Rank among states	9	9	—

Source: National Association of Realtors; *Real Estate Outlook: Market Trends and Insights.*

EDUCATION

Public school enrollment, 1995

State K-8 enrollment	1,980,000
Total U.S. K-8 enrollment	32,341,000
State share of total U.S.	6.12%
State 9-12 enrollment	833,000
Total U.S. 9-12 enrollment	12,500,000
State share of U.S. total	6.66%
State public school enroll. rate	88.6%
Overall U.S. rate.	91.6%
Rank among states.	39

Enrollment figures (which include unclassified students) are rounded to nearest thousand pupils in fall term; kindergarten (K)-8 grade figures include some prekindergarten students. Enrollment rate is based on percentage of persons 5-17 years old. Rank is from highest to lowest.
Source: U.S. National Center for Education Statistics.

Public college finances, 1996

State FTE enrollment	439,300
Total U.S. FTE enrollment	8,268,800
State share of total U.S.	5.31%
Rank among states	3
State and local appropriations	$2,226,700,000
Total U.S. state and local appropriations.	$39,699 mill.
State share of total U.S.	5.61%
Rank among states	3
State net tuition revenues	$1,080,900,000
Total U.S. net tuition	$18,348,100,000
State share of total U.S.	5.89%
Rank among states	5

FTE=Full-time equivalent; credit and noncredit enrollment including summer session in academic year ending in 1996.
Enrollments are rounded to nearest thousand students. Net tuition revenues exclude appropriation to students attending in-state public institutions. Rankings are from highest shares to lowest.
Source: Research Associates of Washington.

TRANSPORTATION AND TRAVEL

Highway mileage, 1996

Interstate	1,499
Other arterial	14,453
Collector roads	24,543
Local roads	75,878
Urban roads	40,646
Rural roads	71,701
Total state	112,347
U.S. total	3,933,985
State share	2.9%
Rank among states	13

Source: U.S. Federal Highway Administration.

Motor vehicle registrations and driver licenses, 1996
In thousands

Vehicle registrations	State	U.S.	Share	Rank
Autos, trucks, buses	10,636	206,365	5.15%	4
Autos only	7,915	128,439	6.16%	2
Motorcycles	135	3,832	3.52%	9
Driver licenses	10,484	179,539	5.84%	4

Figures do not include vehicles owned by military services.
Source: U.S. Federal Highway Administration; *Highway Statistics; Selected Highway Statistics and Charts.*

Domestic travel expenditures, 1995
Spending by U.S. residents on overnight trips and day trips of at least 100 miles

Total expenditures in state	$21,647 mill.
Total expenditures in U.S.	$360,314 mill.
State share of total U.S.	6.01%
Rank among states	4

Source: Travel Industry Association of America.

CRIME AND LAW ENFORCEMENT

State and local police officers, 1996

Local police	54,657
State police	3,972
Sheriffs	5,852
Total	71,221
Officers per 10,000 residents	39
U.S. average	25
Rank among states	1

Figures cover full-time sworn officers; totals include special police not shown separately.
Source: U.S. Bureau of Justice Statistics; *Census of State and Local Law Enforcement Agencies, 1996.*

Crime rates, 1996
Rates per 100,000 resident population

Violent crimes	State	U.S.
Total violent	727	634
Murder	7.4	7.4
Forcible rape	23.0	36.1
Robbery	340	202
Aggravated assault	357	388
Property crimes		
Total property	3,405	4,445
Burglary	714	943
Larceny/theft	2,197	2,976
Motor vehicle theft	494	526
Totals	4,132	5,079

Source: U.S. Federal Bureau of Investigation; *Crime in the United States,* annual.

State prison populations, 1980-1996

	State	U.S.	State share
1980	21,815	305,458	7.14%
1990	54,895	708,393	7.75%
1996	69,709	1,025,624	6.80%

Figures exclude prisoners in federal penitentiaries.
Source: U.S. Bureau of Justice Statistics.

North Carolina

Location: East Coast of continental United States

Area and rank: 48,718 square miles (126,180 square kilometers); 53,821 square miles (139,396 square kilometers) including water; twenty-ninth largest state in area

Coastline: 301 miles (484 kilometers)

Shoreline: 3,375 miles (5,430 kilometers)

Population and rank: 7,428,194 (1997); eleventh largest state in population

Capital: Raleigh

State capitol building in Raleigh. (Courtesy of the North Carolina Division of Tourism, Film & Sports Development)

Largest city: Charlotte (504,637 people in 1998)

Entered Union and rank: November 21, 1789; twelfth state

Present constitution adopted: 1971

Counties: 100

State name: North Carolina was named after Charles II of England

State nickname: Tar Heel State

Motto: *Esse quam videri* (To be rather than to seem)

State flag: One-third is blue with a white star surrounded by letters N and C, with gold scrolls above and below reading "May 20th, 1775" and "April 12th, 1776"; other two thirds are red and white

Highest point: Mount Mitchell — 6,684 feet (2,037 meters)

Lowest point: Atlantic Ocean — sea level

Highest recorded temperature: 110 degrees Fahrenheit (43 degrees Celsius) — Fayetteville, 1983

Lowest recorded temperature: −34 degrees Fahrenheit (−37 degrees Celsius) — Mount Mitchell, 1985

State song: "The Old North State"

State tree: Pine

State flower: Dogwood

State bird: Cardinal

National park: Great Smoky Mountains

North Carolina History

Although sometimes historically overshadowed by its neighbors, Virginia and South Carolina, North Carolina has contributed much to the development of the United States. A relatively narrow state, it stretches from the Great Smoky Mountains, a part of the Appalachian system, through the Piedmont Plateau to the coastal plain, which terminates at the long, narrow islands known as the Outer Banks, where Europeans first attempted to settle the land in the late 1500's.

Native Americans and Early Europeans. Sometime around 8000 B.C.E., Native Americans began settling what is now North Carolina. By the period 500 B.C.E., what is known as the Woodland culture had developed throughout much of the area, with cultivation of corn, beans, and squash and the hunting of game. By the time Europeans arrived there were around thirty tribes in the area, belonging to three basic linguistic groups: the Algonquian, Iroquoian, and Siouan. The five most powerful and important tribes were the Hatteras (also known as Croatoan), Chowanoe, Tuscarora, Catawba, and Cherokee. The relationship between these Native Americans and the Europeans, especially the English, would have a major impact on the development of North Carolina.

Giovanni da Verrazano, an Italian explorer in the service of France, was the first European to chart the Carolina coast. He was followed by the Spanish in 1526 with an unsuccessful attempt at settlement and in 1540 with Spanish explorer Hernando de Soto's travel through the state. The first serious attempts at European settlement came through England's Sir Walter Raleigh, who had been granted land by Queen Elizabeth. In 1585 and 1586 the first two expeditions sponsored, but not led, by Raleigh were unsuccessful. However, in 1587 a third group established itself on Roanoke Island on the Outer Banks. A few weeks after the colony was founded, Eleanor Dare gave birth to a daughter named Virginia, the first English child born in the New World. John White, father of Eleanor Dare and the colony's governor, sailed to England for supplies. Hostile Spanish fleets prevented his return until 1590, when he found the colony deserted and the word "Croatoan" carved into a tree. Although this may have signaled the community's move to Croatoan Island, south of Cape Hatteras, the mystery of the so-called Lost Colony has never been solved.

English Settlement and Revolution. In 1663 King Charles II of England granted a charter to

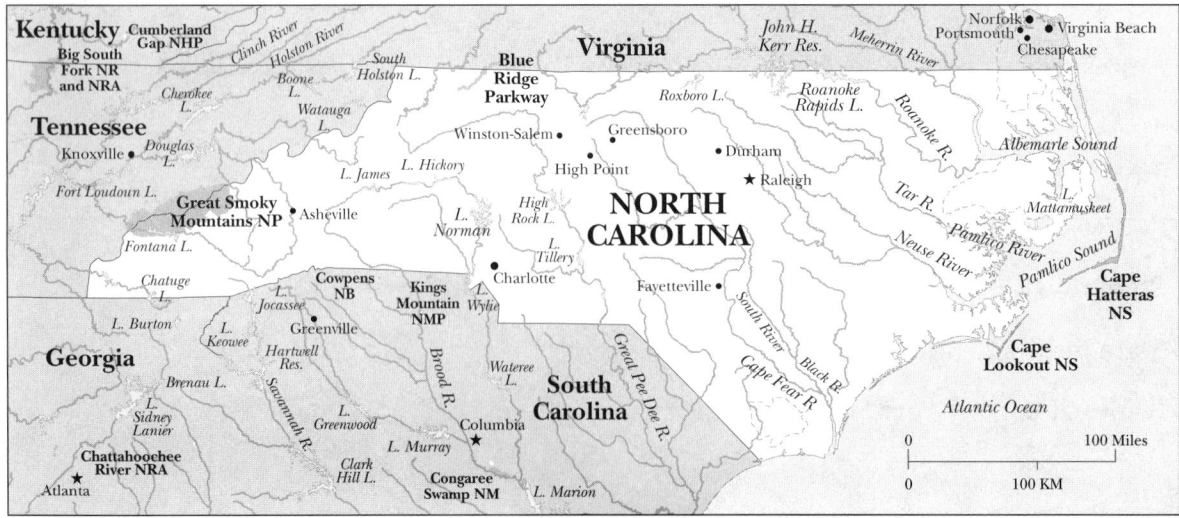

Orville and Wilbur Wright making the first successful powered flight at Kittyhawk in December, 1903. (Library of Congress)

eight Lord Proprietors for a colony to be called Carolina, after himself. A northern county, known as Albemarle, became the foundation of North Carolina. Settlers came from England and Virginia. Initial growth was slow, marked by frequent disputes, sometimes breaking into open rebellion, between settlers and representatives of the Proprietors. The colony faced numerous dangers, including the ravages of pirates, such as Edward Teach or Blackbeard, and the colony was hard-pressed during the Tuscarora War with that tribe, which raged from 1711 through 1713. However, it overcame these difficulties, and in 1712 North and South Carolina were officially recognized as two separate and distinct colonies. In 1729 North Carolina became a royal colony.

After an initially slow start, North Carolina's population grew steadily, and its economy prospered from the production of naval staples such as turpentine and tar. It was during this period that "Tarheel" became a popular nickname for the state and its residents, because of the abundance of that

material. As high British taxes and unfair treatment pushed the colonies toward rebellion, North Carolina joined the movement for independence and took a dramatic step in advance of other American colonies: In 1775 citizens of Mecklenburg County adopted a set of "resolves," which declared North Carolina independent of Great Britain. In Halifax in April, 1776, a provincial congress again voted in favor of independence.

Revolution and Statehood. The only two battles during the Revolution in North Carolina were those of Moore's Creek Bridge in 1776 and Guilford Courthouse in 1781. However, there was a vicious partisan struggle during the Revolution between loyalists and rebels, as well as uprisings by Cherokee Indians in the mountain areas throughout the conflict.

North Carolina initially rejected the proposed U.S. Constitution from fear of a strong central government but ratified it in 1789, after the Bill of Rights was proposed. Until the mid-1830's, it lagged behind the rest of the new nation in economic development, educational initiatives, and overall prosperity. During this time, North Carolina was sometimes scornfully referred to as the "Rip Van Winkle State" because of its stagnation. However, state leaders pushed through important changes, writing a new state constitution and making the state capital Raleigh, near the center of the state. Railroads, canals, public schools, and other civic improvements led to economic development and population growth.

Civil War. When the Civil War was brewing, North Carolina resisted joining other Southern states in seceding from the Union. There was strong antislavery and pro-Union sentiment in North Carolina, especially in the western portion of the state, and efforts were made to find a peaceful solution to the conflict. It was not until 1861, when Confederate forces fired on Fort Sumter and President Abraham Lincoln issued a call for troops to put down the rebellion that North Carolina left the Union.

Despite coming late to the conflict, North Carolina sent more troops to the Confederate army than any other Southern state, and more than one-quarter of its soldiers were killed. During the war, Union forces quickly captured the Outer Banks and much of the coastline; only the port of Wilmington remained open for Confederate blockade runners until the spring of 1865. The last major battle of the war was fought at Bentonville on March 19-21, 1865, between the forces of Union General William T. Sherman and Confederate Joseph E. Johnston. Johnston's defeat and surrender to Sherman shortly after Confederate general Robert E. Lee's effectively ended the Civil War.

Reconstruction. The Reconstruction period in North Carolina was one of intense struggle between defenders of the old order against newly freed African Americans and whites who had not been slave owners before the war. Under a new constitution, North Carolina was readmitted to the Union in 1868, and a series of reforms was enacted,

North Carolina's largest city, Charlotte, has a population double that of its nearest rival, Raleigh. (Courtesy of the North Carolina Division of Tourism, Film & Sports Development)

Tobacco, the crop on which North Carolina's agricultural economy is built. (Courtesy of the North Carolina Division of Tourism, Film & Sports Development)

of benefit to both whites and blacks. However, conservative forces regained power in the state legislature in 1870, and in 1876, when federal troops left and Reconstruction ended, blacks and poor whites found themselves again under the domination of landlords and the rich.

Antebellum North Carolina's economy had relied primarily upon agriculture, with the state split between larger farms and plantations dependent upon slave labor in the east and smaller farms in the west. Following the Civil War, small farms leased out to sharecroppers became a dominant pattern, with tobacco and cotton the primary cash crops. Textile mills, many of them using the water power abundant in the state's piedmont area, were established. Tobacco became a major crop, and North Carolina a major manufacturer of tobacco products. In 1890 James B. Duke founded the

American Tobacco Company, and his rival, Richard Joshua Reynolds, made his company, R. J. Reynolds, one of the nation's leading industries. Meanwhile, the abundant forests and water power of western North Carolina and the wood-working technology it powered caused furniture making to become a growth industry that remained important throughout the twentieth century. Technology of another kind was literally launched on December 17, 1903, when Wilbur and Orville Wright made the first powered flight of an aircraft at Kitty Hawk on the windswept Outer Banks.

Modern North Carolina. North Carolina, like so much of the South, was hard hit by the Great Depression, but Franklin Roosevelt's New Deal and the economic mobilization brought about by World War II began massive changes in the state. By offering tax breaks and other incentives,

North Carolina was highly successful in recruiting new business, including high-technology firms. Research Triangle Park, located in the Raleigh-Durham-Chapel Hill area, became the site of research and development efforts by many national and international companies, often in conjunction with North Carolina's colleges and universities. During the 1980's, North Carolina became a major player in the financial world as regional and national banks located their headquarters in the state.

Under Governor Terry Sanford, from 1961 to 1965, North Carolina developed a progressive attitude toward education and the arts. Many community and technical colleges were established to provide training and education for workers in high-technology industries, and the nation's first state-supported school for the performing arts was launched in Winston-Salem. During this time North Carolina's institutions of higher education, such as the University of North Carolina at Chapel Hill, Duke University, and Wake Forest, became recognized as among the finest in the United States.

However, economic development and academic achievement were not always matched evenly to social progress. The nation's first sit-in to protest racial segregation occurred in Greensboro in 1960 and provoked reactions from the Ku Klux Klan and other white supremacist groups, including the murder of five protesters at an anti-Klan rally in 1979. At the same time, the Republican Party grew in strength in North Carolina, at times by appealing to the "white backlash" vote. In 1972 Jesse Helms became the first Republican elected to the U.S. Senate from North Carolina in the twentieth century.

The state was also battered by natural disasters in the 1980's and 1990's. In March, 1984, a series of tornadoes in the state's eastern counties killed forty-four people. Only six months later, Hurricane Diana caused more than $65 million in damage. In 1989 Hurricane Hugo, one of the strongest storms ever to come ashore in the United States, caused millions of dollars of damage in Charlotte, hundreds of miles inland. In 1996 two hurricanes, Bertha in July and Fran in September, left massive destruction behind them, and twenty-one people died in Fran's fury. With potential prosperity and growth on one hand, and unresolved racial tensions on the other, North Carolina is ever more mindful of its motto, *Esse quam videri*—To be rather than to seem.

Michael Witkoski

North Carolina Time Line

1524	Giovanni da Verrazano commands French expedition along coast of North Carolina.
1540	Hernando de Soto leads Spanish exploration through North Carolina mountains.
1584	Queen Elizabeth grants Sir Walter Raleigh right to found colony; English explore Roanoke Island.
Aug., 1585	Raleigh establishes first English colony in America on Roanoke Island.
1586	English abandon Roanoke colony.
1587	English found second colony on Roanoke Island.
Aug. 18, 1587	Virginia Dare is born, first English child born in North America.
1590	Governor John White returns from England to find colony deserted under mysterious circumstances.
1629	King Charles I of England grants territory to Sir Robert Heath, who names it "Carolina" after the king.

1663	King Charles II of England grants region to eight Lord Proprietors.
1705	First school opens in Pasquotank County.
1706	Bath is incorporated as first town.
1710	New Bern is founded.
Sept., 1711	Tuscarora War begins with massacre of settlers by Native Americans.
1712	Carolina is divided into two colonies, North and South Carolina.
1713	Tuscarora War ends with defeat of Native Americans.
1729	North Carolina becomes a royal province.
1768	Backcountry farmers known as "Regulators" oppose British rule and threaten to rebel.
May 17, 1771	Regulators are defeated by colonial militia in battle of Alamance Creek.
Aug. 25, 1774	Provincial congress is organized at New Bern.
May 20, 1775	Mecklenburg Resolves are adopted, effectively declaring North Carolina independent.
Feb. 27, 1776	Rebels defeat loyalists at Moore's Creek Bridge.
Apr. 12, 1776	Halifax Resolves instruct North Carolina delegates to Continental Congress to vote for independence.
Dec. 18, 1776	First state constitution is adopted.
1780	British General Charles Cornwallis occupies Charlotte.
Mar. 15, 1781	Cornwallis wins Battle of Guilford Courthouse but is forced to retreat.
Nov. 21, 1789	North Carolina enters the Union as the twelfth state to ratify the Constitution.
1789	University of North Carolina is chartered.
1792	Raleigh is made the capital.
1795	University of North Carolina becomes first state university to open, at Chapel Hill.
Early 1800's	First gold rush in United States takes place in North Carolina piedmont.
1813	First cotton mill in North Carolina opens.
1830's	Cherokees are forcibly removed to western territories along "Trail of Tears."
1835	Changes in state constitution give more representation to western part of state and disenfranchise free blacks.
1840	State's first railroad opens.
May 20, 1861	North Carolina secedes from Union as Civil War begins.
1865	Confederate general Joseph E. Johnston surrenders to General William T. Sherman.
1865	Washington Duke begins packaging tobacco near Durham.
June 25, 1868	North Carolina is readmitted to Union.
1890	James B. Duke founds American Tobacco Company.
Dec. 17, 1903	Wright brothers make first successful powered flight near Kitty Hawk.
1920	Tobacco becomes the state's major crop.
1924	Duke University is founded.
1936	Intracoastal Waterway is completed.

(continued)

1944	Fontana Dam, the largest in the Tennessee Valley Authority system, is completed.
1958	Research Triangle Park is established.
Feb. 1, 1960	First sit-in to protest segregation takes place in Greensboro.
1965	Nation's first state-supported school for the performing arts opens in Winston-Salem.
1966	Cape Lookout National Seashore is established.
1972	Jesse Helms becomes first Republican in the twentieth century elected to U.S. Senate from North Carolina.
1972	James E. Holshouser, Jr., becomes first Republican in the twentieth century elected governor of North Carolina.
1976	Section of historic New River designated a "scenic river" to prevent construction of a dam.
1979	Ku Klux Klan members murder five protesters at anti-Klan rally in Greensboro.
1980's	Charlotte becomes one of the largest banking centers in the United States.
1984	Severe tornadoes strike eastern counties, killing forty-four; Hurricane Diana strikes, causing millions in damages.
1988	Drought disaster declared worst since heat wave of the 1930's.
1989	Hurricane Hugo cripples Charlotte.
1996	Hurricanes Bertha and Fran strike state, causing billions in damage and twenty-one deaths.
1999	Cape Hatteras Lighthouse is moved to protect it from erosion; Hurricane Floyd devastates eastern part of the state.

Notes for Further Study

Published Sources. The beginning student should consult *North Carolina: A History* (1988), by William S. Powell, which begins in prehistoric times and includes original documents. Powell's *North Carolina Through Four Centuries* (1990) is the definitive history of the state from European colonization to the twentieth century, and offers excellent discussions of all aspects of the state's development, including the colonial and Civil War periods. *Discovering North Carolina: A Tar Heel Reader* (1991), edited by Jack Claiborne and William Price, contains a sampling of North Carolina scenes and personalities, presented by North Carolina writers.

Jack Fleer's *North Carolina Government and Politics* (1994) is a serious study of the changing nature of North Carolina government from colonial times to the present and how the political landscape has shifted during that period. Paul Luebke's *Tar Heel Politics* (1990) is another study of the politics of North Carolina from the colonial days with its "east versus west" rivalry to the rise of the Republican Party.

Web Resources. Many Web sites provide information on North Carolina, and a good place to start is the North Carolina Page (http://www.ipass.net/~kestep/nclink .htm), especially when supplemented by the North Carolina site (http://www.plcmc.lib.nc.us/online/links/knc .htm) and the North Carolina Encyclopedia (http:// www.statelibrary.dcr.state.nc.us/nc/cover.htm). For students who want more specific information and links relating to North Carolina history and culture there are the North Carolina Museum of History site (http:// www.nchistory.dcr.state.nc.us/museums), the North Carolina links from the American History site (http:// www.mcdougall:ttell.com/amhist/nc/nclinks.htm), the North Carolina Humanities Council (http://www.nc humanities.org), and the North Carolina Department of Cultural Resources (http://www.web.dcr.state.nc.us).

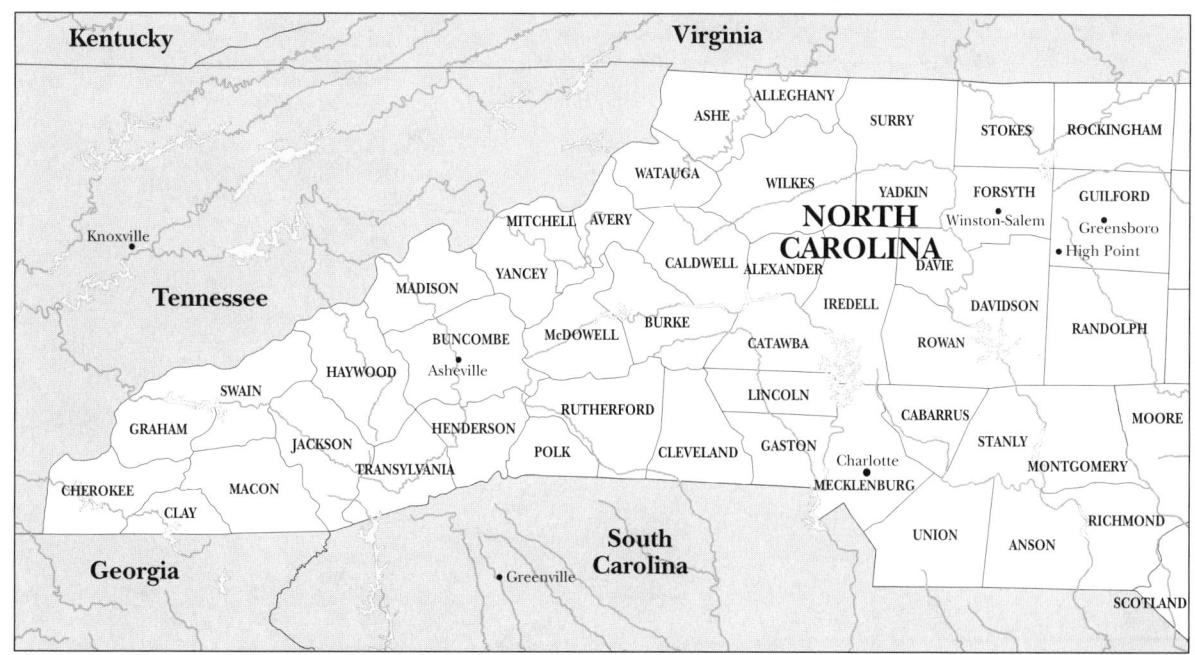

(continued)

Counties

County	Sq. miles	1996 pop.	County	Sq. miles	1996 pop.
Alamance	430.7	116,514	Columbus	936.8	51,975
Alexander	260.3	30,192	Craven	695.6	86,352
Alleghany	234.7	9,849	Cumberland	653.1	284,800
Anson	531.6	24,302	Currituck	261.7	16,766
Ashe	426.2	23,792	Dare	381.7	26,803
Avery	247.0	15,626	Davidson	552.2	137,395
Beaufort	827.6	44,027	Davie	265.2	30,243
Bertie	699.2	20,722	Duplin	817.8	42,802
Bladen	875.0	30,330	Durham	290.6	197,352
Brunswick	854.9	63,225	Edgecombe	505.1	56,166
Buncombe	656.3	191,800	Forsyth	409.7	284,207
Burke	506.7	80,986	Franklin	491.6	42,872
Cabarrus	364.4	113,165	Gaston	356.5	182,623
Caldwell	471.7	74,683	Gates	340.6	9,911
Camden	240.7	6,523	Graham	292.1	7,616
Carteret	531.4	58,773	Granville	531.2	41,622
Caswell	425.7	21,585	Greene	265.4	17,660
Catawba	400.0	129,104	Guilford	650.1	379,201
Chatham	683.1	43,870	Halifax	725.4	57,183
Cherokee	455.2	21,934	Harnett	595.0	79,052
Chowan	172.6	14,099	Haywood	553.9	50,387
Clay	214.7	8,132	Henderson	373.8	77,940
Cleveland	464.3	91,381	Hertford	353.7	22,447

(continued)

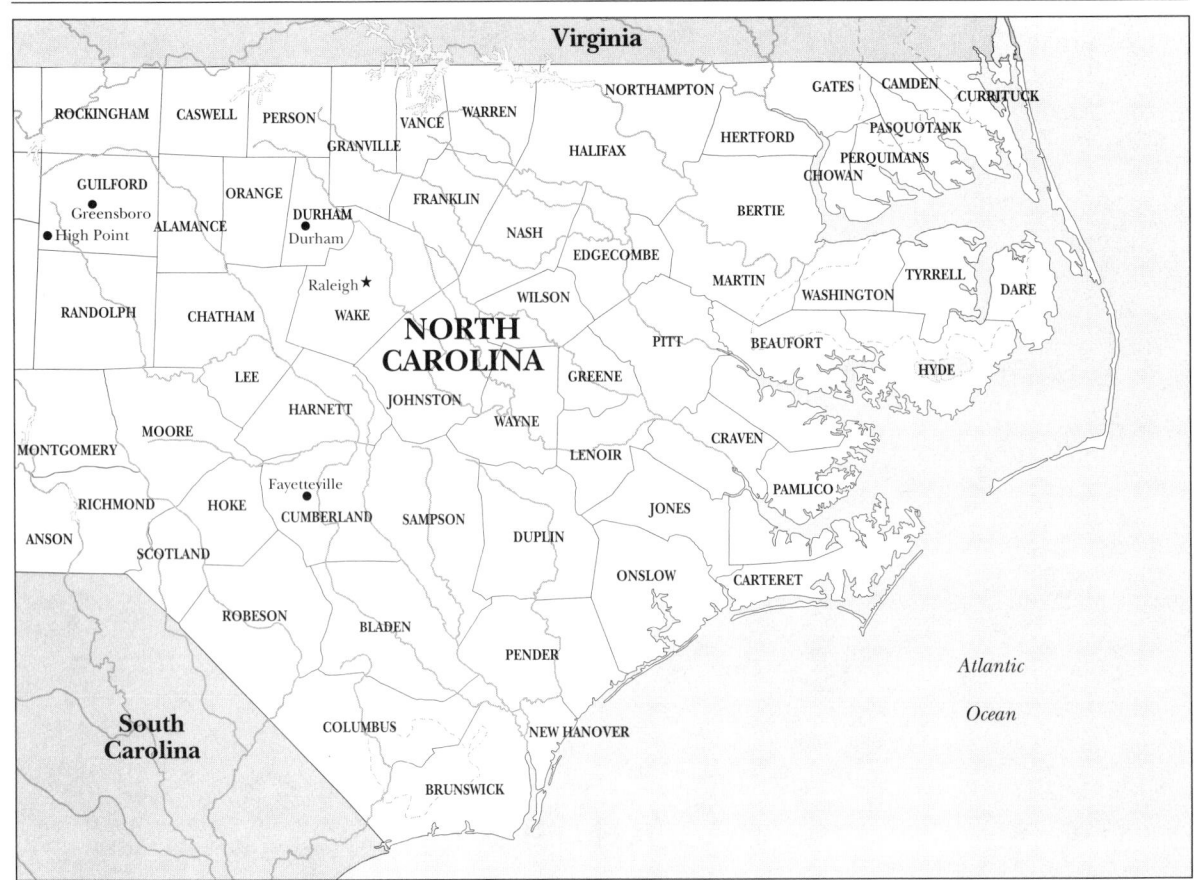

County	Sq. miles	1996 pop.	County	Sq. miles	1996 pop.
Hoke	391.2	28,471	Onslow	766.9	144,533
Hyde	612.8	5,413	Orange	399.8	108,795
Iredell	574.4	106,383	Pamlico	336.9	12,188
Jackson	490.6	29,668	Pasquotank	226.9	34,036
Johnston	792.0	98,289	Pender	870.7	36,601
Jones	473.3	9,501	Perquimans	247.2	10,913
Lee	257.3	47,483	Person	392.3	32,793
Lenoir	399.9	59,355	Pitt	651.6	119,064
Lincoln	298.8	56,235	Polk	237.8	16,226
McDowell	441.7	38,057	Randolph	787.5	117,455
Macon	516.5	27,114	Richmond	474.0	45,665
Madison	449.4	18,242	Robeson	948.9	113,169
Martin	462.6	26,438	Rockingham	566.5	89,575
Mecklenburg	527.4	597,589	Rowan	5 11.4	121,785
Mitchell	221.5	14,719	Rutherford	564.2	59,723
Montgomery	491.1	24,144	Sampson	945.5	50,675
Moore	698.8	68,483	Scotland	319.2	35,404
Nash	540.3	87,991	Stanly	395.1	54,850
New Hanover	198.9	143,513	Stokes	451.9	42,062
Northampton	536.1	21,180	Surry	536.6	65,848

County	Sq. miles	1996 pop.
Swain	528.1	12,008
Transylvania	378.4	27,499
Tyrrell	389.9	3,820
Union	637.4	102,372
Vance	253.5	41,312
Wake	833.9	534,075
Warren	428.7	18,039
Washington	347.8	13,956
Watauga	312.5	40,357

County	Sq. miles	1996 pop.
Wayne	552.6	111,581
Wilkes	757.2	61,884
Wilson	371.1	67,809
Yadkin	335.6	34,161
Yancey	312.4	16,380

Source: U.S. Bureau of the Census; National Association of Counties.

Cities

With 10,000 or more residents

Rank	City	Population
1	Charlotte	504,637
2	Raleigh	259,423
3	Greensboro	197,910
4	Winston-Salem	164,316
5	Durham	153,513
6	Cary	82,071
7	Fayetteville	77,295
8	High Point	76,117
9	Jacksonville	68,380
10	Wilmington	68,062
11	Asheville	63,031
12	Greenville	57,005

Rank	City	Population
13	Gastonia	56,977
14	Rocky Mount	56,901
15	Chapel Hill	42,865
16	Goldsboro	40,909
17	Burlington	40,531
18	Wilson	40,192
19	Kannapolis	36,975
20	Concord	34,617
21	Hickory	31,523
22	Salisbury	25,100
23	Kinston	24,470
24	Monroe	23,792

(continued)

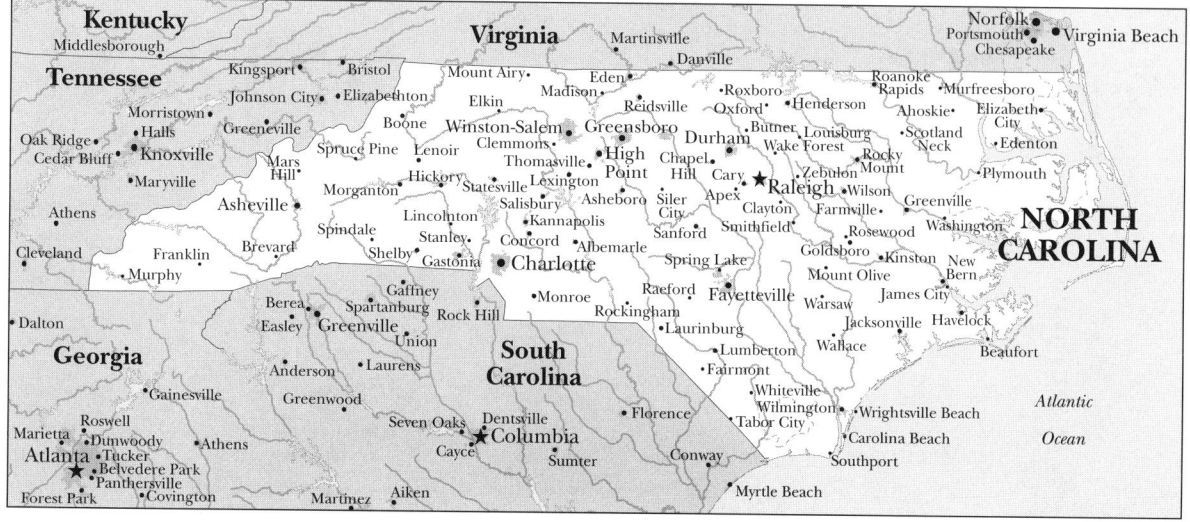

Rank	City	Population
25	Sanford	21,784
26	New Bern	21,770
27	Havelock	20,274
28	Statesville	20,121
29	Lumberton	19,076
30	Thomasville	18,070
31	Asheboro	17,551
32	Garner	17,511
33	Matthews	17,119
34	Mint Hill	17,000
35	Elizabeth City	16,704
36	Lenoir	16,434
37	Lexington	16,150
38	Laurinburg	15,998
39	Albemarle	15,612
40	Shelby	15,568
41	Roanoke Rapids	15,521

Rank	City	Population
42	Henderson	14,934
43	Morganton	14,892
44	Carrboro	14,733
45	Eden	14,661
46	Apex	14,528
47	Reidsville	13,840
48	Boone	13,600
49	Newton	12,026
50	Graham	11,806
51	Mooresville	11,621
52	Kernersville	11,580
53	Smithfield	10,839
54	Southern Pines	10,412
55	Wake Forest	10,156
56	Tarboro	10,082

Population figures are estimated for mid-1998.
Source: U.S. Bureau of the Census.

Index to Tables

NA = Reliable data are not available.

DEMOGRAPHICS

Resident state and national populations, 1970-1997

Population figures given in thousands

	State pop.	U.S. pop.	Share	Rank
1970	5,084	203,302	2.5%	12
1980	5,882	226,546	2.6%	10
1985	6,254	237,924	2.6%	10
1990	6,632	248,765	2.7%	10
1995	7,187	262,761	2.7%	11
1997	7,425	267,636	2.8%	11

Source: U.S. Bureau of the Census.

Resident population by age, 1997

Age group	Total population
Under 5 years	519,000
5 to 17 years	1,355,000
18 to 24 years	696,000
25 to 34 years	1,147,000
35 to 44 years	1,201,000
45 to 54 years	946,000
55 to 64 years	635,000
65 to 74 years	524,000
75 to 84 years	309,000
85 years and over	94,000
Portion of residents 65 and older	12.5%
National average	12.7%

Population figures are rounded to nearest thousand persons;
figures include armed forces personnel stationed in state.
Source: U.S. Bureau of the Census.

Resident population by race, Hispanic origin, 1997

	State pop.	Share	U.S.
All residents	7,425,000	100.0%	100.0%
Hispanic white	129,000	1.7%	10.0%
non-Hispanic white	5,466,000	73.6%	72.7%
African American	1,643,000	22.1%	12.7%
Native American	95,000	1.3%	0.9%
Asian, Pacific Islander	92,000	1.2%	3.8%

Source: U.S. Bureau of the Census.

Projections of state population, 2000-2025

	Model A Uses interstate migration observed from 1975-1994	Model B Uses Bureau of Economic Analysis employment projections
Year	Population	Population
2000	7,777,000	7,789,000
2005	8,227,000	8,312,000
2010	8,552,000	8,780,000
2015	8,840,000	9,206,000
2020	9,111,000	9,588,000
2025	9,349,000	9,916,000

All population projections, including those for 2000, were calculated in 1997.
Source: U.S. Bureau of the Census, Population Paper Listings PPL-47.

VITAL STATISTICS

Average lifetime in years by race, 1989-1991

	State	U.S.	Rank
All residents	74.48	75.37	39
White residents	75.89	76.13	34
Black residents	69.38	69.16	18

Ranks are from longest-lived to least longest-lived. Ranks exclude Alaska, for which reliable data are not available. Rank for black residents is based on the 32 states for which reliable data are available.
Source: U.S. National Center for Health Statistics.

Infant mortality rates, 1980 and 1995

	State	U.S.
All residents		
1980	14.5	12.6
1995	9.2	7.6
White residents		
1980	12.1	11.0
1995	6.7	6.3
Black residents		
1980	20.0	21.4
1995	15.9	15.1

Figures represent deaths per 1,000 live births of resident infants under 1 year old, exclusive of fetal deaths; all-residents figures include other races not listed separately.
Source: U.S. National Center for Health Statistics.

Marriages and divorces

Marriages in 1996.	61,900
Rate per 1,000 population, 1995.	8.6
U.S. rate, 1995	8.9
Rank among all states	24
Divorces in 1996	35,900
Rate per 1,000 population, 1995.	5.1
U.S. rate, 1995	4.4
Rank among all states	15

Rank is from highest to lowest in country.
Source: U.S. National Center for Health Statistics.

Death rates by leading causes, 1995

Deaths per 100,000 resident population

Cause	State	U.S.
Heart disease	269.5	280.7
Cancer	206.8	204.9
Cerebrovascular diseases	72.3	60.1
Accidents and adverse effects	41.0	35.5
Motor vehicle accidents	20.7	16.5
Chronic obstructive pulmonary diseases	39.7	39.2
Diabetes mellitus	24.3	22.6
HIV	14.1	NA
Suicide	12.6	11.9
Homicide	9.6	8.7
All causes	902.2	880.0
Rank in overall death rate among states		26

Figures exclude nonresidents who die in state. Causes of death follow International Classification of Diseases. Rank is from highest to lowest in country.
Source: U.S. National Center for Health Statistics.

ECONOMY

Gross state product, 1990-1996
In current dollars

	State product	Increase
1990	$142.5 billion	
1993	$168.6 billion	
1994	$182.3 billion	8.13%
1995	$192.2 billion	5.43%
1996	$204.2 billion	6.24%

Source: U.S. Bureau of Economic Analysis; Survey of Current Business, June, 1998.

Gross state product by industry, 1996
In billions

Farms, forestry, fisheries	$4.1
Construction	7.4
Manufacturing	56.8
Transportation, public utilities	15.2
Wholesale trade	12.5
Retail trade	17.7
Finance, insurance, real estate	25.2
Services	27.4
Government	24.1
State total	$190.9
Total U.S.	$6,923.8
State share	2.76%
Rank among states	12

Total figures include mining, not listed separately.
Source: U.S. Bureau of Economic Analysis; Survey of Current Business, June, 1998.

Personal income per capita, 1990 and 1997
In current dollars

	1990	1997
Per capita income	$16,674	$23,345
U.S. average	$19,188	$25,598
Rank among states	34	31

1997 data are preliminary.
Source: U.S. Bureau of Economic Analysis; Survey of Current Business, May, 1998.

Energy consumption, 1995
In trillions of British thermal units (BTU)

End-use sectors

Residential	544.8
Commercial	388.7
Industrial	784.5
Transportation	610.1

Sources of energy

Petroleum	845.8
Natural gas	209.4
Coal	601.1
Hydroelectric power	59.8
Nuclear electric power	382.7
Total state per capita consumption	323.2
Total U.S. per capita consumption	344.4
Rank among states	32
Total state energy consumption	2,328.1
Total U.S. energy consumption	90,547.4
State share of U.S. total	2.57%
Rank among states	13

Total figures include items not listed separately.
Source: U.S. Energy Information Administration; State Energy Data Report.

Nonfarm employment by sectors, 1997

Total	3,667,000
Construction	204,000
Manufacturing	835,000
Transportation, public utilities	170,000
Wholesale trade, retail trade	838,000
Finance, insurance, real estate	166,000
Services	871,000
Government	579,000

Figures are rounded to nearest thousand persons. Total includes mining, not listed separately.
Source: U.S. Bureau of Labor Statistics; Employment and Earnings, monthly.

Foreign exports, 1990-1997
In millions of dollars

Year	State	U.S.	State share
1990	8,010	394,045	2.03%
1996	15,734	624,767	2.52%
1997	16,402	688,896	2.38%

Source: U.S. Bureau of the Census; U.S. Merchandise Trade, series FT 900.

LAND USE

Federally owned land, 1996

	State	U.S.	State share
Total acres	31,403,000	2,271,343,000	1.38%
Federally owned	2,028,000	563,129,000	0.36%
Federal share	6.5%	24.8%	—

Areas are rounded to nearest thousand acres. Figures for federally owned land do not include trust properties.
Source: U.S. General Services Administration; *Inventory Report on Real Property Owned by the United States Throughout the World*, annual.

Land use, 1992
In acres, rounded to nearest thousand

Total surface area	33,708,000
Federal land	2,448,000
Total nonfederal	28,476,000
Developed	3,542,000
Total rural	24,933,000
Cropland.	5,960,000
Pasture land	2,019,000
Range land	0
Forest land	15,979,000
Minor cover/use.	975,000

Total surface area figures include water area not shown separately.
Source: U.S. Dept. of Agriculture; Soil Conservation Service; Iowa State University, Statistical Laboratory; *Summary Report, 1992 National Resources Inventory.*

Farms and crop acreage, 1997

	State	U.S.	Share	Rank
Farms (thousands)	57	2,058	2.77%	14
Acres (millions)	9	968	0.93%	33
Acres per farm	158	471	—	44
Acres planted	4,916	334,139	1.47%	21
Acres harvested	4,671	319,894	1.46%	22
Farm value (mill.)	$2,575	$108,805	2.37%	14

Numbers of farms are rounded to nearest thousand.
Source: U.S. Dept. of Agriculture; National Agricultural Statistics Service.

GOVERNMENT AND FINANCE

Units of local government, 1997

	State	Total U.S.	Rank
All local governments	952	87,453	29
Counties	100	3,043	7
Municipalities	527	19,372	16
Townships	0	16,629	—
School districts	0	13,726	—
Special districts	325	34,683	35

County ranks are based on the 48 states with county governments; township ranks are based on the 20 states with township governments; school district ranks are based on the 46 states with such districts.
Source: U.S. Bureau of the Census; *1997 Census of Governments, Government Organization*, Series GC97(1).

State government revenue, 1996

Total revenue	$23,387 mill.
General revenue	20,047 mill.
Per capita.	2,743
U.S. per capita average	2,910
Rank among states.	32
Intergovernmental revenue	
Total	$5,758 mill.
From federal government	5,300 mill.
From local government	458 mill.
Charges and Miscellaneous	
Total	$2,407 mill.
Current charges	1,525 mill.
Misc. general revenue	882 mill.
Taxes	
Total	$11,882 mill.
General sales	2,971 mill.
Selective sales.	2,173 mill.
License taxes	733 mill.
Individual income	4,929 mill.
Corporate income	939 mill.
Other	137 mill.
Insurance trust revenue	3,340 mill.

Total revenue figures include items not listed separately.
Source: U.S. Bureau of the Census.

State government expenditures, 1996

General expenditures
Intergovernmental . . . . $6,653 mill.
Direct expenditures. . . . . 12,757 mill.
Total . . . . 19,410 mill.

Selected direct expenditures
Education . . . . $8,051 mill.
Public welfare. . . . . 4,419 mill.
Health, hospital . . . . 1,577 mill.
Highways . . . . 1,733 mill.
Police . . . . 195 mill.
Corrections . . . . 873 mill.
Natural resources. . . . . 403 mill.
Parks and recreation. . . . . 87 mill.
Government administration . . . . 582 mill.
Interest on debt . . . . 251 mill.

Other
State per capita expenditures $2,656
U.S. per capita average 2,854
Rank among states. 29
Total state expenditures . . . . 21,221 mill.
Total U.S. expenditures . . . . 859,959 mill.

Totals include items not listed separately.
Source: U.S. Bureau of the Census.

POLITICS

Governors since statehood
D = Democrat; R = Republican; O = other;
(r) resigned; (d) died in office; (i) removed from office

Richard Caswell. 1777-1780
Abner Nash 1780-1781
Thomas Burke 1781
Alexander Martin. 1781-1782
Thomas Burke 1782
Alexander Martin. 1782-1785
Richard Caswell. 1785-1787
Samuel Johnston 1787-1789
Alexander Martin (O) 1789-1792
Richard D. Spaight (O). 1792-1795
Samuel Ashe (O) 1795-1798
William R. Davie (O) 1798-1799
Benjamin Williams (O). 1799-1802
James Turner (O). 1802-1805
Nathaniel Alexander (O) 1805-1807
Benjamin Williams (O). 1807-1808
David Stone (O) 1808-1810
Benjamin Smith (O) 1810-1811
William Hawkins (O). 1811-1814

William Miller (O) 1814-1817
John Branch (O) 1817-1820
Jesse Franklin (O) 1820-1821
Gabriel Holmes (O) 1821-1824
Hutchins G. Burton (O) 1824-1827
James Iredell, Jr. (O) 1827-1828
John Owen (D) 1828-1830
Montfort Stokes (D) 1830-1832
David L. Swain (D) 1832-1835
Richard D. Spaight, Jr. (D) 1835-1836
Edward B. Dudley (O) 1836-1841
John M. Morehead (O). 1841-1845
William A. Graham (O) 1845-1849
Charles Manly (O) 1849-1851
David S. Reid (D) . . . . (r) 1851-1854
Warren Winslow (D) 1854-1855
Thomas Bragg (D) 1855-1859
John W. Ellis (D) . . . . (d) 1859-1861
Henry T. Clark (D) 1861-1862
Zebulon B. Vance (D). . . . . (i) 1862-1865
William W. Holden 1865
Jonathan Worth (D) 1865-1868
William W. Holden (R) . . . . (i) 1868-1870
Tod R. Caldwell (R) . . . . (d) 1870-1874
Curtis H. Brogden (R) 1874-1877
Zebulon B. Vance (D) . . . . (r) 1877-1879
Thomas J. Jarvis (D) 1879-1885
Alfred M. Scales (D) 1885-1889
Daniel G. Fowle (D) . . . . (d) 1889-1891
Thomas M. Holt (D) 1891-1893
Elias Carr (D) 1893-1897
Daniel L. Russell (D) 1897-1901
Charles B. Aycock (D) 1901-1905
Robert B. Glenn (D) 1905-1909
William W. Kitchen (D) 1909-1913
Locke Craig (D) 1913-1917
Thomas W. Bickett (D) 1917-1921
Cameron Morrison (D) 1921-1925
Angus W. McLean (D) 1925-1929
Oliver Max Gardner (D) 1929-1933
John C. B. Ehringhouse (D) 1933-1937
Clyde R. Hoey (D) 1937-1941
Joseph Melville Broughton (D) 1941-1945
Robert Gregg Cherry (D) 1945-1949
William Kerr Scott (D) 1949-1953
William B. Umstead (D) . . . . (d) 1953-1954
Luther H. Hodges (D) 1954-1961
Terry Sanford (D) 1961-1965
Daniel K. Moore (D) 1965-1969
Robert W. Scott (D) 1969-1973
James E. Holshouser, Jr. (R) 1973-1977
James Baxter Hunt, Jr. (R) 1977-1985
James G. Martin (R) 1985-1993
James Baxter Hunt, Jr. (R) 1993-

Composition of state legislature, 1990-1998

	Democrats	Republicans
State House (120 seats)		
1990	81	39
1992	78	42
1994	52	68
1996	59	61
1998	66	54
State Senate (50 seats)		
1990	36	14
1992	39	11
1994	26	24
1996	30	20
1998	35	15

Figures for total seats may include independents and minor party members.

Source: Council of State Governments; *State Elective Officials and the Legislatures.*

Composition of congressional delegations, 1989-1999

	Dem	Rep	Total
House of Representatives			
101st Congress, 1989			
State delegates	8	3	11
Total U.S.	259	174	433
102d Congress, 1991			
State delegates	7	4	11
Total U.S.	267	167	434
103d Congress, 1993			
State delegates	8	4	12
Total U.S.	258	176	434
104th Congress, 1995			
State delegates	6	6	12
Total U.S.	197	236	433
105th Congress, 1997			
State delegates	6	6	12
Total U.S.	206	228	434
106th Congress, 1999			
State delegates	5	7	12
Total U.S.	211	222	433

	Dem	Rep	Total
Senate			
101st Congress, 1989			
State delegates	1	1	2
Total U.S.	55	45	100
102d Congress, 1991			
State delegates	1	1	2
Total U.S.	56	44	100
103d Congress, 1993			
State delegates	0	2	2
Total U.S.	57	43	100
104th Congress, 1995			
State delegates	0	2	2
Total U.S.	46	53	99
105th Congress, 1997			
State delegates	0	2	2
Total U.S.	45	55	100
106th Congress, 1999			
State delegates	1	1	2
Total U.S.	45	54	99

Figures are for starts of first sessions. Figure for U.S. Representatives for 101st Congress does not include Alabama and Indiana, which had vacancies. Figures for total U.S. Representatives for 102d, 103d, and 106th Congresses do not include Vermont, which had 1 Independent-Socialist. Figure for U.S. Representatives for 104th Congress does not include Vermont, which had 1 Independent-Socialist, and California, which had 1 vacancy. Figure for U.S. Representatives for 105th Congress does not include New York, which had 1 vacancy. Figure for U.S. Senators for 104th Congress does not include Oregon, which had 1 vacancy. Figure for U.S. Senators for 106th Congress does not include New Hampshire, which had 1 Independent.

Source: U.S. Congress; *Congressional Directory,* biennial.

Voter participation in presidential elections, 1992 and 1996

	1992	1996
State voting age pop.	5,190,000	5,499,000
Total U.S. voting age pop.	189,524,000	196,509,000
State share of U.S. total	2.7%	2.8%
Rank among states	10	10
Percent of state casting vote	50.3	45.0
Percent of U.S. total voting	55.1	49.0
Rank among states	43	46

Source: U.S. Bureau of the Census.

HEALTH AND MEDICAL CARE

Medicare, 1997

	Recipients	Payments
State	1,071,000	$5,079 mill.
Total U.S.	37,514,000	$206,064 mill.
State share	2.85%	2.46%
Rank among states	10	11

Recipient figures are rounded to nearest thousand persons.
   Ranks are from highest to lowest.
Source: U.S. Health Care Financing Administration.

Medicaid, 1996

	Recipients	Payments
State	1,130,000	$3,678 mill.
Total U.S.	35,028,000	$121,419 mill.
State share	3.23%	3.03%
Rank among states	11	10

Recipient figures are rounded to nearest thousand persons.
   Payment figures for fiscal year reflect federal and state
   contribution payments. Ranks are from highest to lowest.
Source: U.S. Health Care Financing Administration.

Health insurance coverage, 1996

	State	U.S.
Total persons covered	6,103,000	225,070,000
Total persons not covered	1,160,000	41,716,000
Part not covered	16.0%	15.6%
Rank among states	16	—
Children not covered	310,000	10,554,000
Part not covered	17.2%	14.8%
Rank among states	16	—

Ranks are from most to fewest uninsured. Population figures
   are rounded to nearest thousand persons.
Source: U.S. Bureau of the Census.

AIDS, syphilis, tuberculosis, and measles cases, 1997

Cases	U.S.	State	Share
AIDS	58,443	850	1.45%
Syphilis	8,550	721	8.43%
Tuberculosis	18,534	462	2.49%
Measles	148,000	2,000	1.35%

Measles figures are rounded to nearest thousand cases.
Source: U.S. Centers for Disease Control and Prevention.

HOUSING

Homeownership rates, 1985-1997

	1985	1990	1997
State	68.0%	69.0%	70.2%
Total U.S.	63.9%	63.9%	65.7%
Rank among states	25	14	17

Source: U.S. Bureau of the Census.

Home sales, 1990 and 1997
In thousands of units

Existing home sales	1990	1997	Change
State sales	135.9	228.0	92.1
Total U.S. sales	3,560	4,730	1,170
State share of U.S. total	3.82%	4.82%	1.00%
Rank among states	8	5	—

Source: National Association of Realtors; *Real Estate Outlook:*
   Market Trends and Insights.

EDUCATION

Public school enrollment, 1995

State K-8 enrollment	871,000
Total U.S. K-8 enrollment	32,341,000
State share of total U.S.	2.69%
State 9-12 enrollment	312,000
Total U.S. 9-12 enrollment	12,500,000
State share of U.S. total	2.50%
State public school enroll. rate	92.0%
Overall U.S. rate	91.6%
Rank among states	26

Enrollment figures (which include unclassified students) are rounded to nearest thousand pupils in fall term; kindergarten (K)-8 grade figures include some prekindergarten students. Enrollment rate is based on percentage of persons 5-17 years old. Rank is from highest to lowest.

Source: U.S. National Center for Education Statistics.

Public college finances, 1996

State FTE enrollment	238,900
Total U.S. FTE enrollment	8,268,800
State share of total U.S.	2.89%
Rank among states	9
State and local appropriations	$1,403,500,000
Total U.S. state and local appropriations	$39,699 mill.
State share of total U.S.	3.54%
Rank among states	9
State net tuition revenues	$355,200,000
Total U.S. net tuition	$18,348,100,000
State share of total U.S.	1.94%
Rank among states	19

FTE=Full-time equivalent; credit and noncredit enrollment including summer session in academic year ending in 1996.

Enrollments are rounded to nearest thousand students. Net tuition revenues exclude appropriation to students attending in-state public institutions. Rankings are from highest shares to lowest.

Source: Research Associates of Washington.

TRANSPORTATION AND TRAVEL

Highway mileage, 1996

Interstate	981
Other arterial	9,162
Collector roads	19,456
Local roads	69,578
Urban roads	22,432
Rural roads	75,077
Total state	97,509
U.S. total	3,933,985
State share	2.5%
Rank among states	16

Source: U.S. Federal Highway Administration.

Motor vehicle registrations and driver licenses, 1996

In thousands

Vehicle registrations	State	U.S.	Share	Rank
Autos, trucks, buses	5,759	206,365	2.79%	11
Autos only	3,474	128,439	2.70%	13
Motorcycles	67	3,832	1.75%	20
Driver licenses	5,187	179,539	2.89%	11

Figures do not include vehicles owned by military services.

Source: U.S. Federal Highway Administration; *Highway Statistics; Selected Highway Statistics and Charts.*

Domestic travel expenditures, 1995

Spending by U.S. residents on overnight trips and day trips of at least 100 miles

Total expenditures in state	$9,056 mill.
Total expenditures in U.S.	$360,314 mill.
State share of total U.S.	2.51%
Rank among states	12

Source: Travel Industry Association of America.

CRIME AND LAW ENFORCEMENT

State and local police officers, 1996

Local police	9,505
State police	1,380
Sheriffs	5,264
Total	16,953
Officers per 10,000 residents	23
U.S. average	25
Rank among states	21

Figures cover full-time sworn officers; totals include special police not shown separately.

Source: U.S. Bureau of Justice Statistics; *Census of State and Local Law Enforcement Agencies, 1996.*

Crime rates, 1996

Rates per 100,000 resident population

Violent crimes	State	U.S.
Total violent	588	634
Murder	8.5	7.4
Forcible rape	31.3	36.1
Robbery	164	202
Aggravated assault	385	388
Property crimes		
Total property	4,938	4,445
Burglary	1,346	943
Larceny/theft	3,257	2,976
Motor vehicle theft	336	526
Totals	5,526	5,079

Source: U.S. Federal Bureau of Investigation; *Crime in the United States,* annual.

State prison populations, 1980-1996

	State	U.S.	State share
1980	15,513	305,458	5.08%
1990	18,411	708,393	2.60%
1996	30,647	1,025,624	2.99%

Figures exclude prisoners in federal penitentiaries.
Source: U.S. Bureau of Justice Statistics.

North Dakota

Location: North-central continental United States

Area and rank: 68,994 square miles (178,695 square kilometers); 70,704 square miles (183,123 square kilometers) including water; seventeenth largest state in area

Population and rank: 640,883 (1997); forty-seventh largest state in population

Capital: Bismarck

Largest city: Fargo (86,718 people in 1998)

Became territory: March 2, 1861

State capitol building in Bismarck. (North Dakota Tourism Department)

Entered Union and rank: November 2, 1889; thirty-ninth state

Present constitution adopted: 1889

Counties: 53

State name: "Dakota" is a Sioux word meaning "allies"

State nicknames: Sioux State; Flickertail State; Peace Garden State

Motto: Liberty and union, now and forever: one and inseparable

State flag: Blue field with eagle holding olive branch, arrows, and scroll reading *E Pluribus Unum*, bearing shield of the Stars and Stripes on its breast; double arch of thirteen stars with a sunburst above, scroll with name "North Dakota" below

Highest point: White Butte — 3,506 feet (1,069 meters)

Lowest point: Red River — 750 feet (229 meters)

Highest recorded temperature: 121 degrees Fahrenheit (49 degrees Celsius) — Steele, 1936

Lowest recorded temperature: −60 degrees Fahrenheit (−51 degrees Celsius) — Parshall, 1936

State song: "North Dakota Hymn"

State tree: American elm

State flower: Wild prairie rose

State bird: Western meadowlark

State fish: Northern pike

National park: Theodore Roosevelt

North Dakota History

With a 1997 population of about 641,000, North Dakota ranked forty-eighth among the fifty states in population. Its total area of 71,000 square miles makes it the seventeenth largest state in land mass. Its population density of 9.3 people per square mile is among America's lowest.

Bordered on the north by the Canadian provinces of Saskatchewan and Manitoba, on the east by Minnesota, on the south by South Dakota, and on the west by Montana, North Dakota runs 360 miles from east to west and 210 miles from north to south.

Early History. North Dakota had human inhabitants more than ten thousand years ago. Millions of years earlier, dinosaurs and mastodons roamed the area. During the Ice Age, the Dakotas were covered by glaciers, which melted around 10,000 B.C.E., leaving a huge lake in what is now the Red River Valley in eastern North Dakota. Topsoil trapped in the glacier was deposited in the lake as the ice melted. When the lake evaporated, that topsoil created fertile fields.

Prehistoric settlers lived beside the Red and Missouri Rivers. The Mandan Indians, around 1300 C.E., were the earliest of the Native American settlers, followed some three hundred years later by the Hidatsa and Arikara, all groups that created settlements and engaged in farming, growing mostly squash, sunflowers, corn, and beans. They hunted indigenous animals, particularly bison, for their meat and fur.

This blockhouse at Fort Lincoln is a vestige of the late nineteenth century wars with Native Americans. (North Dakota Tourism Department)

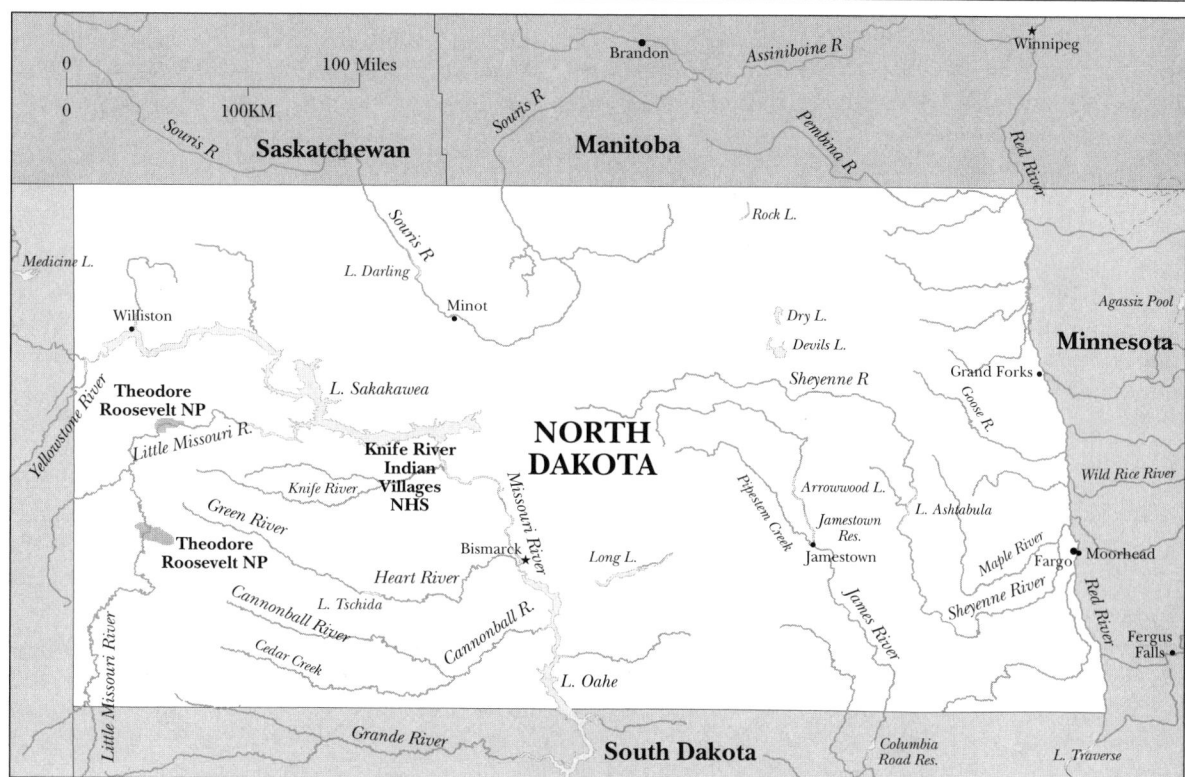

The more migratory Sioux and Chippewa entered the area in pursuit of the bison. Other tribes, notably the Assiniboine, Cheyenne, Cree, and Crow, lived in North Dakota for short periods. The first Europeans in the area were Pierre Gaultier de Varennes, sieur de La Vérendrye, his sons, and a nephew, who visited Mandan villages in 1738.

The Fur Trade. Relations between North Dakota's Native Americans and visiting Europeans were amicable initially. The American Indians had an abundance of furs, and the European traders had ready markets for these furs. By the 1780's, a thriving fur trade flourished in the region, largely stimulated by the Hudson Bay Company, headquartered in Manitoba. In 1801 Alexander Henry established a fur-trading post at Pembina, the first European settlement in the area.

In 1713 the French gave England the northern part of North Dakota, which bordered Canada. In 1812 a group of Canadians started a town at the Pembina trading post, building a school and some permanent buildings. In 1818, however, the United States, through a treaty with Great Britain, was given Britain's section of North Dakota, establishing the territory's northern border. Canadians living there returned to Canada.

Early Growth. Few people other than American Indians came to North Dakota in its early days, although Congress established the Dakota Territory in 1861. By 1870, the territory had 2,405 inhabitants. By 1880, however, the population had ballooned to about 37,000.

Three major factors brought about this increase. The Homestead Act of 1862, designed to encourage settlement of the sparsely inhabited territory west of the Mississippi, permitted people to stake claims to the 160 acres allotted to each homesteader, to improve the land and live on it for five years, and then to receive a clear title to that land. Although homesteading became more prevalent in the 1870's, there was no immediate rush of homesteaders to the Dakotas.

Homesteading was difficult. In a land bereft of forests, timber was scarce, forcing early settlers to build sod houses made by cutting square chunks of sod from the prairie for roofs and walls. Sod houses extended below ground; these small houses offered adequate shelter and were warm in winter but were quite unlike the dwellings to which homesteaders were accustomed.

The establishment of towns in the area also spurred population growth. Fargo and Grand Forks were established in 1871, and the following year Bismarck was founded in the middle of the state. In 1873 Bismarck began publishing its own newspaper, the Bismarck *Tribune.* Concurrent with the establishment of towns was the spread of railroads, first from Minnesota to Fargo in 1872 and, in 1873, to Bismarck. Railroad service enabled farmers and cattle ranchers to send their products to eastern markets.

By 1875 farmers in the Red River Valley of eastern North Dakota were producing huge amounts of wheat on their fertile soil. North Dakota is second only to Kansas in the amount of wheat it produces, and it ranks first in its production of sunflower seed and barley. Long, hot summer days and abundant topsoil make the eastern half of the state agriculturally productive.

In 1878 large-scale cattle ranching began in the western Dakota Territory, whose stubby grasses proved perfect for grazing. Growing railroad service made it easy to transport cattle to markets in Chicago, St. Louis, and Kansas City.

American Indian Relations. Although North Dakota's Native Americans generally had amicable relations with the early European traders, relations became strained when the federal government reneged on treaties it had entered into with Native Americans. In 1875, when the government permitted white settlement on American Indian lands in abrogation of the 1868 Fort Laramie Treaty, major Indian uprisings occurred.

The following year, in neighboring Montana, the Sioux killed many Americans, including Lieutenant Colonel George Armstrong Custer in the Battle of the Little Bighorn. In 1877, the federal government confiscated Sioux lands in the Dakotas. Within a year, most of the Native American population was deployed to reservations.

Achieving Statehood. The Dakotas were growing and moving irrevocably toward statehood, although

Remnants of the immense herds of buffalo that once roamed the Great Plains graze near a modern North Dakota power plant. (North Dakota Tourism Department)

Congress resisted admitting the entire territory as a single state. Between 1880 and 1900, North Dakota's population increased tenfold to about 320,000. In 1883 the territorial capital was moved from Yankton in the southeast to Bismarck.

In 1889 the Enabling Act passed by Congress divided the Dakota Territory into two separate states and guaranteed statehood as soon as each territory submitted acceptable constitutions. North Dakota drew up a constitution that the electorate approved, and late in 1889 President Benjamin Harrison signed papers admitting North Dakota as the thirty-ninth state and South Dakota as the fortieth.

North Dakota is one of the nation's leading producers of wheat and other grain crops. (North Dakota Tourism Department)

The Early Twentieth Century. Between 1900 and 1915, inequities existed for North Dakota's farmers and cattle ranchers. Their labors were enriching the state's banks, flour mills, and railroads, but life was difficult for those providing the basic labor. In 1915, discouraged by these inequities, thirty thousand farmers joined the Nonpartisan League, which helped to elect Lynn Frazier, a reform candidate, governor.

Frazier helped establish the Bank of North Dakota in Bismarck in 1919. This state-operated bank offered farmers and cattle ranchers low-interest loans. In 1922 the state opened the North Dakota Mill and Elevator, in which wheat farmers could store their crops until they could sell them at favorable prices. Farmers' taxes were lowered, and an increased percentage of state revenues was earmarked for rural schools, which extended educational opportunities to farm children.

During World Wars I and II, North Dakota provided produce to feed members of the armed forces. Although North Dakota opposed entry into both of these wars, the citizens served valiantly in the armed forces.

During the 1920's, agriculture boomed in North Dakota. Sugar beets and red potatoes became profitable crops. The upsurge in agriculture caused the population to more than double between 1900 and 1930.

No state was more severely damaged by the Great Depression than North Dakota. During most of the 1930's, widespread droughts and dust storms that blew away precious topsoil plagued the state. By 1936 half the state's citizens required public assistance. A third of North Dakota's farmers lost their farms. Nearly forty thousand people had left the state by 1940.

In 1937, realizing the need for water conservation, North Dakota established the Water Conservation Commission. All its fifty-three counties embarked upon water-conservation projects. It was not until 1960, however, that the Garrison Dam was completed, creating Lake Sakakawea, which provides irrigation and whose dam generates hydroelectric power.

Recovery. During the 1950's, many farmers moved to cities, entering new walks of life. The state's first television station opened in Minot in 1953. Interstate Highway 94 crossed the state in 1956. Air transportation became more accessible, and North Dakota, which had suffered from isolation, was now linked more closely to mainstream America.

Oil was discovered in Tioga in 1951, but not until 1978 did an enormous oil boom begin around Williston. In the same general area is substantial mining of lignite, which is burned to fuel electrical generating plants.

North Dakota again experienced an upsurge in population near the end of the twentieth century. People are drawn to it from more populous states by its fine schools, which boast the lowest dropout rate in the nation, its clean air and water, and its low crime rate.

R. Baird Shuman

North Dakota Time Line

c. 9000 B.C.E.	Early human habitation of the North Dakota area begins.
c. 550-400 B.C.E.	Woodlands people live in southeastern North Dakota.
c. 100 B.C.E.	Inhabitants build burial mounds.
c. 1200 C.E.	Jamestown mounds are abandoned.
c. 1610	Explorer Henry Hudson claims northeastern Dakota for England.
1682	René-Robert Cavalier, sieur de La Salle, claims area as part of France's Louisiana Territory.
Dec. 3, 1738	Pierre Gaultier de Varennes, sieur de La Vérendrye, visits American Indian villages along Missouri River.
1762	Louisiana Territory ceded by France to Spain.
1801	Alexander Henry establishes fur-trading post at Pembina, spawning the first white settlement in North Dakota.
Dec. 20, 1803	United States gains major portion of North Dakota through the Louisiana Purchase.
1804-1805	Meriwether Lewis and William Clark spend winter in North Dakota en route to the Pacific Northwest.
1812	Canadians attempt to establish town at Pembina.
1818	Treaty with Great Britain establishes northern border of North Dakota.
1829	Fort Union Trading Post is founded on the Upper Missouri River.
1842	Road opens between eastern North Dakota and St. Paul, Minnesota.
1857	Fort Abercrombie is established on the Red River.
1861	Congress establishes the Dakota Territory.
1863	North Dakota opens for homesteading.
1867	Sioux Indians accept treaty to cede lands to the federal government.
1868	Standing Rock Indian Reservation is established.
1870's	Homesteaders flock to North Dakota, spawning a land boom.
1872	Railway service from Minnesota to Fargo begins.
July 11, 1873	Bismarck *Tribune* begins publication.
1875	American Indian uprisings occur, caused by federal government's violation of the Fort Laramie Treaty.
1880	Population grows from 2,405 in 1870 to 36,909.
1882	Turtle Mountain Indian Reservation is established.
1883	Territorial capital is moved from Yankton to Bismarck.

1883	University of North Dakota is established at Grand Forks.
Nov. 2, 1889	North Dakota becomes thirty-ninth state.
1890	North Dakota State University opens at Fargo.
1897	State's first public library opens in Grafton.
1915	Nonpartisan League is established to aid farmers.
1919	Bank of North Dakota begins operation in Bismarck.
1920	Electorate adds recall provision to state constitution.
1921	Lynn J. Frazier is first state governor in U.S. history to be recalled.
1930's	Prolonged drought and the Great Depression devastate North Dakota.
1937	North Dakota Water Conservation Commission is established.
1944	Congress passes Pick-Sloan Plan to build dams on Missouri River.
Apr. 4, 1951	Oil is discovered in northwestern North Dakota.
1960	Garrison Dam is completed.
1979	Oil boom occurs in western North Dakota.
1980	Beulah's coal gasification plant is built, the first in the United States.
1988	Devastating drought bankrupts many farmers and cattle ranchers.
1989	Legislature passes bill legalizing home schooling.
1997	Severe floods devastate Red River Valley.
1998	Per capita income rises 7.8 percent in one year.

Notes for Further Study

Published Sources. John C. Hudson's *Plains Country Towns* (1985) contains well-presented information about small-town North Dakota. For a sensitive rendering of North Dakota's educational development consult Esther Burnett Horne and Sally McBeth's *Essie's Story: The Life and Legacy of a Shoshone Teacher* (1998), in which Horne relates her early experiences as a teacher in North Dakota. Her material on off-reservation boarding schools is valuable, particularly if read in conjunction with Brenda J. Child's *Boarding School Seasons: American Indian Families, 1900-1940* (1998). Carrie Young's *Nothing to Do But Stay: My Pioneer Mother* (1991) is extremely interesting anecdotally. *Rachel Calof's Story: Jewish Homesteader on the Northern Plains* (1995) tells how a member of a religious and ethnic minority was treated in early North Dakota, offering an interesting sociological treatment in a book written many years ago but later translated and edited by Jacob Calof and Molly Shaw.

Kathleen Norris's *Dakota: A Spiritual Geography* (1993) offers insights into the varied cultures of the area.

Catherine McNicol Stock's *Main Street in Crisis: The Great Depression and the Old Middle Class on the Northern Plains* (1992) provides the best socioeconomic analysis of the plains states during the 1930's.

Web Resources. The Web site of North Dakota's state government (http://www.state.nd.us) provides information about the state's history, economy, industry, population, and political organization. Information about tourism is available on several Web sites, including those of the state tourist office (http://www.glness.com/tourism), Breezy Point Resort (http://breezypoint.com), Dahkota Lodge (http://www.dahkotalodge.com), Detroit Lakes (http://www.detroitlakes.com), Dickinson Visitors' Bureau (http://www.diskinsonvb.com), Red River Net (http://www.rrnet.com), Red River (http://www.rmh.com), and Roosevelt National Park (http://www.nps.gov/thro). Individual North Dakota towns and counties with Web sites include Elgin (http://www.elginnd.com), Fargo (http://www.fedc.com), Grand Forks (http://www.grandforks.com), and Red River (http://

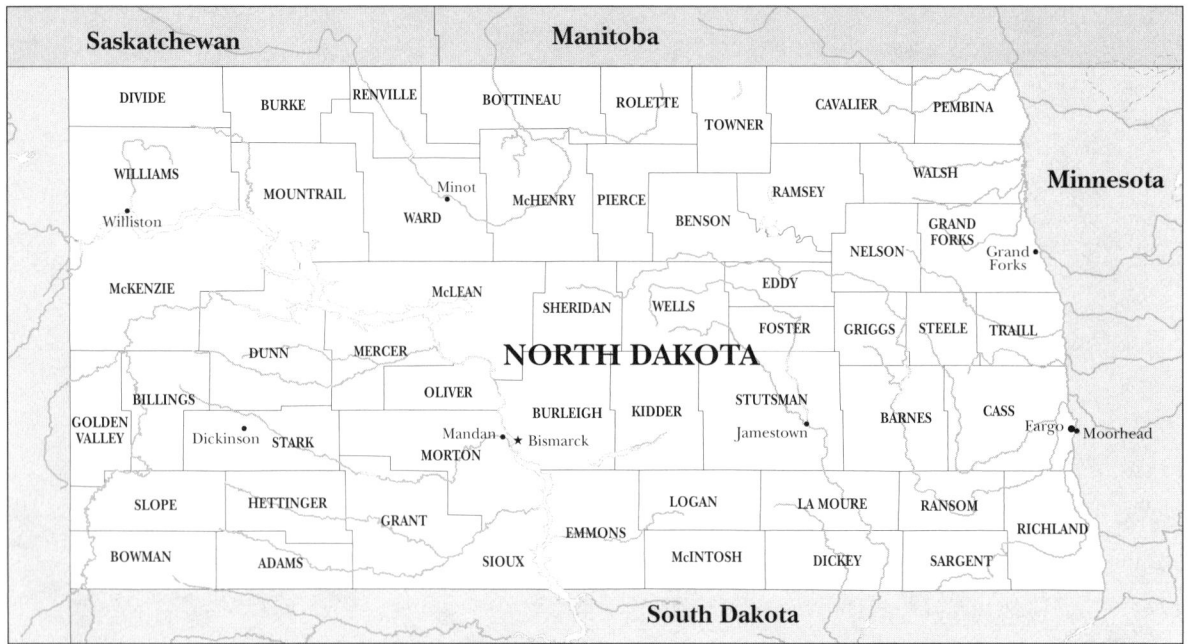

www.rrnh.com). Each offers information about the economy, governance, and attractions of its area.

The North Dakota Art Museum Web site (http://www.ndmoa.com) is well illustrated and informative. Institutions of higher learning within the state have serviceable Web sites, among them Bismarck State College (http://www.bsc.nodak.edu), the North Dakota University System (http://www.nodak.edu), and the University of North Dakota (http://www.und.edu). The State Uni-

versity Library's Web site (http://www.lib.ndsu.nodak.edu) provides access to its resources. Fargo's Economic Development Web site (http://www.fedc.com) provides information about business and commerce in the Fargo area. Agricultural information is available through the Web sites of the North Dakota Corn Growers (http://www.ndcorn.com) and the North Dakota Wheat Association (http://www.ndwheat.com).

Counties

County	Sq. miles	1996 pop.	County	Sq. miles	1996 pop.
Adams	988.0	2,841	Foster	635.3	3,866
Barnes	1,491.8	12,114	Golden Valley	1,002.0	1,932
Benson	1,388.6	6,905	Grand Forks	1,437.9	71,450
Billings	1,151.5	1,129	Grant	1,659.6	3,114
Bottineau	1,668.7	7,538	Griggs	708.5	2,984
Bowman	1,162.1	3,303	Hettinger	1,132.3	2,982
Burke	1,103.6	2,469	Kidder	1,351.6	2,997
Burleigh	1,633.2	65,681	LaMoure	1,147.2	4,970
Cass	1,765.7	113,343	Logan	992.7	2,443
Cavalier	1,489.1	5,270	McHenry	1,874.2	6,161
Dickey	1,131.1	5,676	McIntosh	975.3	3,642
Divide	1,259.4	2,523	McKenzie	2,742.2	5,851
Dunn	2,010.0	3,751	McLean	2,110.4	9,897
Eddy	632.1	2,876	Mercer	1,045.4	9,548
Emmons	1,510.0	4,443	Morton	1,926.4	24,422

County	Sq. miles	1996 pop.
Mountrail	1,824.0	6,753
Nelson	981.7	3,905
Oliver	723.6	2,234
Pembina	1,118.8	8,741
Pierce	1,017.9	4,718
Ramsey	1,186.2	12,455
Ransom	862.8	5,794
Renville	874.8	2,843
Richland	1,436.9	18,162
Rolette	902.5	14,029
Sargent	858.8	4,441
Sheridan	971.8	1,859
Sioux	1,094.2	4,095

County	Sq. miles	1996 pop.
Slope	1,218.0	827
Stark	1,338.3	22,694
Steele	712.4	2,277
Stutsman	2,221.5	21,338
Towner	1,025.4	3,209
Traill	861.9	8,706
Walsh	1,282.0	12,799
Ward	2,013.0	59,734
Wells	1,271.4	5,271
Williams	2,070.6	20,534

Source: U.S. Bureau of the Census; National Association of Counties.

Cities
With 10,000 or more residents

Rank	City	Population
1	Fargo	86,718
2	Bismarck	54,040
3	Grand Forks	47,327
4	Minot	35,286
5	Dickinson	16,221
6	Mandan	15,860

Rank	City	Population
7	Jamestown	14,713
8	West Fargo	14,091
9	Williston	12,446

Population figures are estimated for mid-1998.
Source: U.S. Bureau of the Census.

Index to Tables

NA = Reliable data are not available.

DEMOGRAPHICS

Resident state and national populations, 1970-1997

Population figures given in thousands

	State pop.	U.S. pop.	Share	Rank
1970	618	203,302	0.3%	45
1980	653	226,546	0.3%	46
1985	677	237,924	0.3%	46
1990	639	248,765	0.3%	47
1995	641	262,761	0.2%	47
1997	641	267,636	0.2%	47

Source: U.S. Bureau of the Census.

Resident population by age, 1997

Age group	Total population
Under 5 years	41,000
5 to 17 years	125,000
18 to 24 years	67,000
25 to 34 years	85,000
35 to 44 years	101,000
45 to 54 years	77,000
55 to 64 years	54,000
65 to 74 years	45,000
75 to 84 years	33,000
85 years and over	14,000
Portion of residents 65 and older	14.4%
National average	12.7%

Population figures are rounded to nearest thousand persons;
figures include armed forces personnel stationed in state.
Source: U.S. Bureau of the Census.

Resident population by race, Hispanic origin, 1997

	State pop.	Share	U.S.
All residents	641,000	100.0%	100.0%
Hispanic white	6,000	0.9%	10.0%
non-Hispanic white	596,000	93.0%	72.7%
African American	4,000	0.6%	12.7%
Native American	30,000	4.7%	0.9%
Asian, Pacific Islander	5,000	0.8%	3.8%

Source: U.S. Bureau of the Census.

Projections of state population, 2000-2025

	Model A Uses interstate migration observed from 1975-1994	Model B Uses Bureau of Economic Analysis employment projections
Year	Population	Population
2000	662,000	657,000
2005	677,000	677,000
2010	690,000	701,000
2015	704,000	727,000
2020	717,000	754,000
2025	729,000	778,000

All population projections, including those for 2000, were calculated in 1997.

Source: U.S. Bureau of the Census, Population Paper Listings PPL-47.

VITAL STATISTICS

Average lifetime in years by race, 1989-1991

	State	U.S.	Rank
All residents	77.62	75.37	4
White residents	77.99	76.13	1
Black residents	NA	69.16	NA

Ranks are from longest-lived to least longest-lived. Ranks exclude Alaska, for which reliable data are not available. Rank for black residents is based on the 32 states for which reliable data are available.

Source: U.S. National Center for Health Statistics.

Infant mortality rates, 1980 and 1995

	State	U.S.
All residents		
1980	12.1	12.6
1995	7.2	7.6
White residents		
1980	11.7	11.0
1995	6.7	6.3
Black residents		
1980	27.5	21.4
1995	NA	15.1

Figures represent deaths per 1,000 live births of resident infants under 1 year old, exclusive of fetal deaths; all-residents figures include other races not listed separately.

Source: U.S. National Center for Health Statistics.

Marriages and divorces

Marriages in 1996	5,000
Rate per 1,000 population, 1995.	7.2
U.S. rate, 1995	8.9
Rank among all states	41
Divorces in 1996	2,200
Rate per 1,000 population, 1995.	3.4
U.S. rate, 1995	4.4
Rank among all states	37

Rank is from highest to lowest in country.

Source: U.S. National Center for Health Statistics.

Death rates by leading causes, 1995

Deaths per 100,000 resident population

Cause	State	U.S.
Heart disease	304.3	280.7
Cancer	214.4	204.9
Cerebrovascular diseases	77.3	60.1
Accidents and adverse effects	32.7	35.5
Motor vehicle accidents	13.1	16.5
Chronic obstructive pulmonary diseases	37.9	39.2
Diabetes mellitus	24.3	22.6
HIV	-	NA
Suicide	14.7	11.9
Homicide	-	8.7
All causes	931.6	880.0

Rank in overall death rate among states	19

Figures exclude nonresidents who die in state. Causes of death follow International Classification of Diseases. Rank is from highest to lowest in country.

Source: U.S. National Center for Health Statistics.

ECONOMY

Gross state product, 1990-1996
In current dollars

	State product	Increase
1990	$11.4 billion	
1993	$12.7 billion	
1994	$13.7 billion	7.87%
1995	$14.5 billion	5.84%
1996	$15.7 billion	8.28%

Source: U.S. Bureau of Economic Analysis; Survey of Current Business, June, 1998.

Gross state product by industry, 1996
In billions

Farms, forestry, fisheries	$1.4
Construction	0.7
Manufacturing	1.2
Transportation, public utilities.	1.7
Wholesale trade.	1.3
Retail trade	1.4
Finance, insurance, real estate	1.7
Services	2.4
Government.	2.1
State total.	$14.3
Total U.S.	$6,923.8
State share	0.21%
Rank among states.	49

Total figures include mining, not listed separately.
Source: U.S. Bureau of Economic Analysis; Survey of Current Business, June, 1998.

Personal income per capita, 1990 and 1997
In current dollars

	1990	1997
Per capita income	$15,281	$20,271
U.S. average	$19,188	$25,598
Rank among states	41	45

1997 data are preliminary.
Source: U.S. Bureau of Economic Analysis; Survey of Current Business, May, 1998.

Energy consumption, 1995
In trillions of British thermal units (BTU)

End-use sectors

Residential.	57.0
Commercial	43.6
Industrial.	175.9
Transportation.	74.6

Sources of energy

Petroleum	118.0
Natural gas.	47.6
Coal.	399.8
Hydroelectric power.	28.5
Nuclear electric power	0
Total state per capita consumption	545.8
Total U.S. per capita consumption	344.4
Rank among states	5
Total state energy consumption.	350.1
Total U.S. energy consumption	90,547.4
State share of U.S. total.	0.39%
Rank among states.	44

Total figures include items not listed separately.
Source: U.S. Energy Information Administration; State Energy Data Report.

Nonfarm employment by sectors, 1997

Total	313,000
Construction	15,000
Manufacturing	23,000
Transportation, public utilities.	18,000
Wholesale trade, retail trade	81,000
Finance, insurance, real estate	15,000
Services	87,000
Government.	71,000

Figures are rounded to nearest thousand persons. Total includes mining, not listed separately.
Source: U.S. Bureau of Labor Statistics; Employment and Earnings, monthly.

Foreign exports, 1990-1997
In millions of dollars

Year	State	U.S.	State share
1990	360	394,045	0.09%
1996	707	624,767	0.11%
1997	778	688,896	0.11%

Source: U.S. Bureau of the Census; U.S. Merchandise Trade, series FT 900.

LAND USE

Federally owned land, 1996

	State	U.S.	State share
Total acres	44,452,000	2,271,343,000	1.96%
Federally owned	1,413,000	563,129,000	0.25%
Federal share	3.2%	24.8%	—

Areas are rounded to nearest thousand acres. Figures for federally owned land do not include trust properties.

Source: U.S. General Services Administration; *Inventory Report on Real Property Owned by the United States Throughout the World,* annual.

Land use, 1992
In acres, rounded to nearest thousand

Total surface area	45,250,000
Federal land	1,951,000
Total nonfederal	42,187,000
Developed	1,344,000
Total rural	40,843,000
Cropland	24,743,000
Pasture land	1,168,000
Range land	10,325,000
Forest land	426,000
Minor cover/use	4,181,000

Total surface area figures include water area not shown separately.

Source: U.S. Dept. of Agriculture; Soil Conservation Service; Iowa State University, Statistical Laboratory; *Summary Report, 1992 National Resources Inventory.*

Farms and crop acreage, 1997

	State	U.S.	Share	Rank
Farms (thousands)	31	2,058	1.51%	28
Acres (millions)	40	968	4.13%	7
Acres per farm	1,318	471	—	9
Acres planted	22,271	334,139	6.67%	5
Acres harvested	21,091	319,894	6.59%	4
Farm value (mill.)	$2,593	$108,805	2.38%	10

Numbers of farms are rounded to nearest thousand.

Source: U.S. Dept. of Agriculture; National Agricultural Statistics Service.

GOVERNMENT AND FINANCE

Units of local government, 1997

	State	Total U.S.	Rank
All local governments	2,758	87,453	14
Counties	53	3,043	30
Municipalities	363	19,372	22
Townships	1,341	16,629	5
School districts	237	13,726	22
Special districts	764	34,683	14

County ranks are based on the 48 states with county governments; township ranks are based on the 20 states with township governments; school district ranks are based on the 46 states with such districts.

Source: U.S. Bureau of the Census; *1997 Census of Governments, Government Organization,* Series GC97(1).

State government revenue, 1996

Total revenue	$2,569 mill.
General revenue	2,144 mill.
Per capita	3,337
U.S. per capita average	2,910
Rank among states	11

Intergovernmental revenue	
Total	$660 mill.
From federal government	631 mill.
From local government	29 mill.

Charges and Miscellaneous	
Total	$499 mill.
Current charges	361 mill.
Misc. general revenue	138 mill.

Taxes	
Total	$985 mill.
General sales	282 mill.
Selective sales	278 mill.
License taxes	78 mill.
Individual income	152 mill.
Corporate income	74 mill.
Other	122 mill.
Insurance trust revenue	424 mill.

Total revenue figures include items not listed separately.

Source: U.S. Bureau of the Census.

State government expenditures, 1996

General expenditures

Intergovernmental	$411 mill.
Direct expenditures	1,449 mill.
Total	1,860 mill.

Selected direct expenditures

Education	$705 mill.
Public welfare	361 mill.
Health, hospital	84 mill.
Highways	209 mill.
Police	6 mill.
Corrections	17 mill.
Natural resources	77 mill.
Parks and recreation	7 mill.
Government administration	59 mill.
Interest on debt	55 mill.

Other

State per capita expenditures	$2,895
U.S. per capita average	2,854
Rank among states	22
Total state expenditures	2,064 mill.
Total U.S. expenditures	859,959 mill.

Totals include items not listed separately.
Source: U.S. Bureau of the Census.

POLITICS

Governors since statehood

D = Democrat; R = Republican; O = other;
(r) resigned; (d) died in office; (i) removed from office

John Miller (R)	1889-1891
Andrew H. Burke (R)	1891-1893
Eli C. D. Shortridge (O)	1893-1895
Roger Allin (R)	1895-1897
Frank A. Briggs (R)	1897-1898
Joseph N. Devine (R)	1898-1899
Frederick B. Fancher (R)	1899-1901
Frank White (R)	1901-1905
Elmore Y. Sarles (R)	1905-1907
John Burke (D)	1907-1913
Louis B. Hanna (R)	1913-1917
Lynn J. Frazier (R)	(i) 1917-1921
Ragnvald A. Nestos (R)	1921-1925
Arthur C. Sorlie (R)	(d) 1925-1928
Walter J. Maddock (R)	1928-1929
George F. Shafer (R)	1929-1933
William Langer (R)	(i) 1933-1934
Ole H. Olson (R)	1934-1935
Thomas Moodie (D)	(i) 1935
Walter H. Welford (R)	1935-1937
William Langer (O)	1937-1939
John Moses (D)	1939-1945
Fred G. Aandahl (R)	1945-1951
Norman Brunsdale (R)	1951-1957
John E. Davis (R)	1957-1961
William L. Guy (D)	1961-1973
Arthur A. Link (D)	1973-1981
Allen I. Olson (R)	1981-1985
George A. Sinner (D)	1985-1993
Edward T. Schafer (R)	1993-

Composition of state legislature, 1990-1998

	Democrats	Republicans
State House (106 seats in 1990; 98 seats thereafter)		
1990	48	58
1992	33	65
1994	23	75
1996	26	72
1998	34	64
State Senate (49 seats)		
1990	27	26
1992	25	24
1994	20	29
1996	19	30
1998	18	31

Figures for total seats may include independents and minor
party members.
Source: Council of State Governments; *State Elective Officials
and the Legislatures.*

Composition of congressional delegations, 1989-1999

	Dem	Rep	Total
House of Representatives			
101st Congress, 1989			
State delegates	1	0	1
Total U.S.	259	174	433
102d Congress, 1991			
State delegates	1	0	1
Total U.S.	267	167	434

	Dem	Rep	Total
103d Congress, 1993			
State delegates	1	0	1
Total U.S.	258	176	434
104th Congress, 1995			
State delegates	1	0	1
Total U.S.	197	236	433
105th Congress, 1997			
State delegates	1	0	1
Total U.S.	206	228	434
106th Congress, 1999			
State delegates	1	0	1
Total U.S.	211	222	433

Senate

	Dem	Rep	Total
101st Congress, 1989			
State delegates	2	0	2
Total U.S.	55	45	100
102d Congress, 1991			
State delegates	2	0	2
Total U.S.	56	44	100
103d Congress, 1993			
State delegates	2	0	2
Total U.S.	57	43	100
104th Congress, 1995			
State delegates	2	0	2
Total U.S.	46	53	99
105th Congress, 1997			
State delegates	2	0	2
Total U.S.	45	55	100
106th Congress, 1999			
State delegates	2	0	2
Total U.S.	45	54	99

Figures are for starts of first sessions. Figure for U.S. Representatives for 101st Congress does not include Alabama and Indiana, which had vacancies. Figures for total U.S. Representatives for 102d, 103d, and 106th Congresses do not include Vermont, which had 1 Independent-Socialist. Figure for U.S. Representatives for 104th Congress does not include Vermont, which had 1 Independent-Socialist, and California, which had 1 vacancy. Figure for U.S. Representatives for 105th Congress does not include New York, which had 1 vacancy. Figure for U.S. Senators for 104th Congress does not include Oregon, which had 1 vacancy. Figure for U.S. Senators for 106th Congress does not include New Hampshire, which had 1 Independent.
Source: U.S. Congress; *Congressional Directory,* biennial.

Voter participation in presidential elections, 1992 and 1996

	1992	1996
State voting age pop.	462,000	473,000
Total U.S. voting age pop.	189,524,000	196,509,000
State share of U.S. total	0.2%	0.2%
Rank among states	47	47
Percent of state casting vote	66.7	45.8
Percent of U.S. total voting	55.1	49.0
Rank among states	6	43

Source: U.S. Bureau of the Census.

HEALTH AND MEDICAL CARE

Medicare, 1997

	Recipients	Payments
State	103,000	$468 mill.
Total U.S.	37,514,000	$206,064 mill.
State share	0.27%	0.23%
Rank among states	47	47

Recipient figures are rounded to nearest thousand persons. Ranks are from highest to lowest.
Source: U.S. Health Care Financing Administration.

Medicaid, 1996

	Recipients	Payments
State	61,000	$298 mill.
Total U.S.	35,028,000	$121,419 mill.
State share	0.17%	0.25%
Rank among states	48	46

Recipient figures are rounded to nearest thousand persons. Payment figures for fiscal year reflect federal and state contribution payments. Ranks are from highest to lowest.
Source: U.S. Health Care Financing Administration.

Health insurance coverage, 1996

	State	U.S.
Total persons covered	568,000	225,070,000
Total persons not covered	62,000	41,716,000
Part not covered	9.8%	15.6%
Rank among states	44	—
Children not covered	16,000	10,554,000
Part not covered	9.7%	14.8%
Rank among states	36	—

Ranks are from most to fewest uninsured. Population figures are rounded to nearest thousand persons.
Source: U.S. Bureau of the Census.

AIDS, syphilis, tuberculosis, and measles cases, 1997

Cases	U.S.	State	Share
AIDS	58,443	13	0.02%
Syphilis	8,550	NA	NA
Tuberculosis	18,534	12	0.06%
Measles	148,000	NA	NA

Measles figures are rounded to nearest thousand cases.
Source: U.S. Centers for Disease Control and Prevention.

HOUSING

Homeownership rates, 1985-1997

	1985	1990	1997
State	69.9%	67.2%	68.1%
Total U.S.	63.9%	63.9%	65.7%
Rank among states	14	28	26

Source: U.S. Bureau of the Census.

Home sales, 1990 and 1997
In thousands of units

Existing home sales	1990	1997	Change
State sales	10.4	11.9	1.5
Total U.S. sales	3,560	4,730	1,170
State share of U.S. total	0.29%	0.25%	-0.04%
Rank among states	43	43	—

Source: National Association of Realtors; *Real Estate Outlook: Market Trends and Insights.*

EDUCATION

Public school enrollment, 1995

State K-8 enrollment	82,000
Total U.S. K-8 enrollment	32,341,000
State share of total U.S.	0.25%
State 9-12 enrollment	37,000
Total U.S. 9-12 enrollment	12,500,000
State share of U.S. total	0.30%
State public school enroll. rate	93.2%
Overall U.S. rate	91.6%
Rank among states	20

Enrollment figures (which include unclassified students) are rounded to nearest thousand pupils in fall term; kindergarten (K)-8 grade figures include some prekindergarten students. Enrollment rate is based on percentage of persons 5-17 years old. Rank is from highest to lowest.
Source: U.S. National Center for Education Statistics.

Public college finances, 1996

State FTE enrollment	30,700
Total U.S. FTE enrollment	8,268,800
State share of total U.S.	0.37%
Rank among states	42
State and local appropriations	$122,700,000
Total U.S. state and local appropriations	$39,699 mill.
State share of total U.S.	0.31%
Rank among states	46
State net tuition revenues	$65 mill.
Total U.S. net tuition	$18,348,100,000
State share of total U.S.	0.35%
Rank among states	44

FTE=Full-time equivalent; credit and noncredit enrollment including summer session in academic year ending in 1996.
Enrollments are rounded to nearest thousand students. Net tuition revenues exclude appropriation to students attending in-state public institutions. Rankings are from highest shares to lowest.
Source: Research Associates of Washington.

TRANSPORTATION AND TRAVEL

Highway mileage, 1996

Interstate	571
Other arterial	5,872
Collector roads	11,621
Local roads	68,965
Urban roads	1,823
Rural roads	84,985
Total state	86,808
U.S. total	3,933,985
State share	2.2%
Rank among states	20

Source: U.S. Federal Highway Administration.

Motor vehicle registrations and driver licenses, 1996
In thousands

Vehicle registrations	State	U.S.	Share	Rank
Autos, trucks, buses	679	206,365	0.33%	46
Autos only	334	128,439	0.26%	47
Motorcycles	16	3,832	0.42%	45
Driver licenses	449	179,539	0.25%	46

Figures do not include vehicles owned by military services.
Source: U.S. Federal Highway Administration; *Highway Statistics; Selected Highway Statistics and Charts.*

Domestic travel expenditures, 1995
Spending by U.S. residents on overnight trips and day trips of at least 100 miles

Total expenditures in state	$897 mill.
Total expenditures in U.S.	$360,314 mill.
State share of total U.S.	0.25%
Rank among states	48

Source: Travel Industry Association of America.

CRIME AND LAW ENFORCEMENT

State and local police officers, 1996

Local police	561
State police	120
Sheriffs	364
Total	1,141
Officers per 10,000 residents	18
U.S. average	25
Rank among states	43

Figures cover full-time sworn officers; totals include special police not shown separately.
Source: U.S. Bureau of Justice Statistics; *Census of State and Local Law Enforcement Agencies, 1996.*

Crime rates, 1996
Rates per 100,000 resident population

Violent crimes	State	U.S.
Total violent	84	634
Murder	2.2	7.4
Forcible rape	24.1	36.1
Robbery	11	202
Aggravated assault	47	388
Property crimes		
Total property	2,585	4,445
Burglary	309	943
Larceny/theft	2,086	2,976
Motor vehicle theft	190	526
Totals	2,669	5,079

Source: U.S. Federal Bureau of Investigation; *Crime in the United States,* annual.

State prison populations, 1980-1996

	State	U.S.	State share
1980	253	305,458	0.08%
1990	483	708,393	0.07%
1996	722	1,025,624	0.07%

Figures exclude prisoners in federal penitentiaries.
Source: U.S. Bureau of Justice Statistics.

Ohio

Location: Midwestern continental United States

Area and rank: 40,953 square miles (106,067 square kilometers); 44,828 square miles (116,105 square kilometers) including water; thirty-fifth largest state in area

Population and rank: 11,186,331 (1997); seventh largest state in population

Capital: Columbus

Largest city: Columbus (670,234 people in 1998)

Though perhaps less famous than Cleveland and Cincinnati, Columbus is Ohio's largest city, as well as its capital. (PhotoDisc)

Entered Union and rank: March 1, 1803; seventeenth state

Present constitution adopted: 1912

Counties: 88

State name: "Ohio" derives from an Iroquoian word for "great river"

State nickname: Buckeye State

Motto: With God, all things are possible

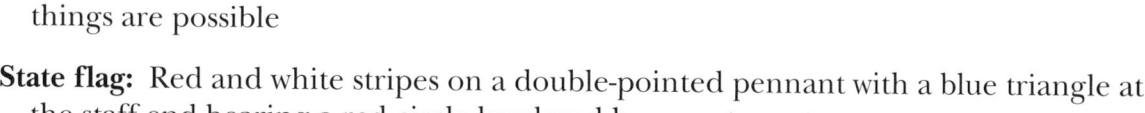

State flag: Red and white stripes on a double-pointed pennant with a blue triangle at the staff end bearing a red circle bordered by seventeen stars

Highest point: Campbell Hill — 1,549 feet (472 meters)

Lowest point: Ohio River — 455 feet (139 meters)

Highest recorded temperature: 113 degrees Fahrenheit (45 degrees Celsius) — near Gallipolis, 1934

Lowest recorded temperature: −39 degrees Fahrenheit (−39 degrees Celsius) — Milligan, 1899

State song: "Beautiful Ohio"

State tree: Buckeye

State flower: Scarlet carnation

State bird: Cardinal

Ohio History

Located between previously settled eastern states and newer territories in the Midwest, Ohio was one of the first states to be established after the creation of the United States. Ease of transportation, supplied by Lake Erie along the northern border and the Ohio River along the southern border, quickly made Ohio one of the most populous states in the Union. Ohio's rich soils and abundant natural resources have made it one of the most important areas of agricultural and industrial activity in the nation.

Early History. About eleven thousand years ago, the earliest humans to reside in the area used stone tools to hunt bison as well as extinct species such as mammoths and mastodons. About 2,500 years ago, the people of the Adena culture, located in southern Ohio, built mounds, lived in villages, made pottery, and subsisted by hunting, fishing, and gathering wild plant foods. About five hundred years later, the people of the Hopewell culture, living in the same area, established agriculture with the growing of corn. They also produced the most advanced metal artifacts, mostly made from copper, found in North America until the Europeans arrived. About fifteen hundred years ago, the Hopewell culture began to decline. By the time Europeans first arrived in the region in the late seventeenth century, Ohio was mostly uninhabited.

In the early eighteenth century, however, before Europeans were established in the area, Native Americans returned to Ohio. The Wyandot, originally residing in Ontario, were driven south into northern Ohio by the devastation caused by newly introduced European diseases and by their enemies, the Iroquois League, a powerful confederation of eastern Native Americans. The Delaware, originally residing along the Atlantic coast, were driven west into northern Ohio by the Iroquois League and European settlers. The Miami, originally residing in eastern Wisconsin, expanded south and east into many areas, including southern Ohio. The Shawnee, who had originally resided along the Ohio River, were driven out by the Iroquois League but returned to southern Ohio in 1725.

Exploration and Settlement. The first European known to have visited the area was the French explorer René-Robert Cavalier, sieur de La Salle, who journeyed southwest from Canada along the Saint Lawrence River, past Lake Ontario and Lake Erie, and into Ohio in 1670. During the first half of the eighteenth century, French traders from Canada and British traders from eastern colonies provided manufactured goods to the Native Americans in the area in exchange for deer and beaver skins. The lucrative fur trade led both sides to attempt to win control of the area. In 1749 the French sent an expedition led by Celeron de Bienville from Canada into Ohio, in order to make trade agreements with the inhabitants. The next year, the British sent a similar expedition, led by Christopher Gist, from Virginia to Ohio.

The conflict between France and England for control of North America led to the French and Indian War, which ended with the British in control of the area. During the American Revolution, American forces led by George Rogers Clark seized British outposts in Ohio. Clark also destroyed villages of the Shawnee, who were allied with the British. The war ended with the United States in control of the region. It became part of the newly created Northwest Territory in 1787.

The first permanent settlement in Ohio was founded in 1788 at Marietta by veterans of the Revolutionary War. The next year, settlers from New Jersey led by John Cleves Symes established a settlement at the future site of Cincinnati. These and other early settlements, located along the Ohio River, caused conflicts with the Native Americans inhabiting the region. On August 20, 1794, American forces led by Anthony Wayne defeated an alliance of Native Americans under Shawnee leader Bluejacket at the Battle of Fallen Timbers. The next year Wayne negotiated a treaty that resulted in Native Americans ceding much of their land in Ohio to the United States.

Statehood. Settlements continued to be located almost entirely in the southern part of Ohio until 1796, when settlers from Connecticut arrived in northeast Ohio. By 1802 Ohio had the sixty thou-

sand white adult male residents required for statehood, and it became the seventeenth state the next year. The capital was located at Chillicothe until 1810, when it was briefly moved to Zanesville. After returning to Chillicothe in 1812, the capital was moved to the newly founded city of Columbus in 1816.

During the early years of statehood, Shawnee leader Tecumseh organized an alliance of Native Americans who attempted to win back control of the region from the United States. During the War of 1812 Tecumseh was allied with the British against the Americans. Tecumseh and British general Henry A. Proctor led an invasion of Ohio in 1812 but were driven back into Canada the next year.

After the war, the population of Ohio grew rapidly. In addition to settlers from eastern and southern states, emigrants from England, Ireland, and Germany arrived in large numbers after 1830. Advances in transportation contributed to this growth. Steamboats appeared on the Ohio River as early as 1811. The opening of the Erie Canal in 1825, linking the Hudson River with Lake Erie, improved transportation to Ohio and the territories beyond it. From 1825 to 1841, a series of canals linked the Ohio River and Lake Erie. The first railroad in the state was established in 1832. Between 1825 and 1838, the federal government extended the National Road across Ohio, linking the state to Pennsylvania and Maryland. By 1850, Ohio was the third most populous state in the Union.

At this time, agriculture was the most important part of the state's economy. In 1850 Ohio had a larger agricultural output than any other state. Coal was discovered in Ohio in 1808 and was later of great importance to the iron and steel industry. Other important mineral resources developed at this time include limestone, sandstone, clay, shale, and rock salt.

The Civil War. During the Civil War, Ohio was divided in loyalty. The strongest support for the Union was found in northern Ohio. Southern Ohio, bordering on Kentucky and Virginia, was more sympathetic to the Confederacy. Ohio supplied 320,000 volunteers for the Union. Three of the Union's most important generals, Ulysses S. Grant, William T. Sherman, and Philip H. Sheridan, were from Ohio.

Ohio was an important center of the Peace Democrats, known to their opponents as Copperheads. The Peace Democrats advocated an end to the war through negotiation with the Confederacy. Clement L. Vallandigham, a leader of the Peace Democrats, was nominated for governor of Ohio in 1863 but was defeated by Union supporter John Brough. The same year, Confederate soldiers led by John Hunt Morgan raided southern Ohio, reaching farther north than any other Confederate forces.

Industry and Immigration. The demand for manufactured goods during the war led to the growth of industry in Ohio, particularly in the northern part of the state. Iron ore from states to the northwest was transported via the Great Lakes

Ohio is rich in Native American archaeological sites, such as this pyramid-shaped mound at Miamisburg. (Ohio Division of Travel and Tourism)

The riverboat under Cincinnati's modern skyline recalls the city's origins as a steamboat port on the Ohio River. (Ohio Division of Travel and Tourism)

to the steelmaking cities of Toledo, Cleveland, and Youngstown. During the 1870's, Akron became a center of the rubber industry. Oil and natural gas were discovered in 1860. The Standard Oil Company, founded in Cleveland in 1870, soon controlled almost all oil production in the United States.

Immigrants from Italy, Poland, Hungary, and Russia arrived in large numbers after 1880. The ethnic origins of the new residents of Cleveland were particularly diverse, with immigrants arriving from Austria, the Netherlands, Portugal, Greece, China, Japan, Turkey, and Mexico. A large number of African Americans moved into the state at this time also, increasing the black population from about twenty-five thousand in 1850 to more than sixty-three thousand in 1870.

The Twentieth Century. Ohio was dominant in national politics around the turn of the century. Of the twelve U.S. presidents who held office from 1869 to 1923, seven were born in Ohio. Ohio was also the birthplace of Victoria Woodhull, who in 1872 became the first woman to run for president.

The state's economy expanded during World War I. The increase in automobile manufacturing after the war strengthened Ohio's oil, rubber, and glass industries. The Great Depression of the 1930's led to widespread unemployment, and the economy did not recover until World War II. Although economic conditions were generally favorable until the late 1970's, Ohio faced serious problems, including pollution in Lake Erie, race riots in Cleveland, poverty in the cities, and a decline in the quality of education.

A recession in the late 1970's and 1980's led to Ohio having 14 percent unemployment in 1982. During the 1980's and 1990's, Ohio shifted much of its economy away from manufacturing to the service and technology sectors. The state also took steps to encourage new businesses, provide vocational training, and protect the environment.

Rose Secrest

Put-in-Bay on Lake Erie, near the site of Commodore Perry's naval victory over a British fleet during the War of 1812. (Ohio Division of Travel and Tourism)

Ohio Time Line

1670	French explorer René-Robert Cavalier, sieur de La Salle, reaches Ohio.
1725	Shawnee, previously driven out by the Iroquois League, return to southern Ohio.
1749	French explorer Celeron de Bienville leads a trade expedition to Ohio.
1750	British explorer Christopher Gist leads a trade expedition to Ohio.
1763	End of the French and Indian War brings the area under British control.
1783	End of the American Revolution brings the area under American control.
1787	Ohio becomes part of the newly created Northwest Territory.
Apr. 7, 1788	First permanent settlement in Ohio is founded at Marietta.
1789	Settlement is founded at the future site of Cincinnati.
Aug. 20, 1794	United States defeats an alliance of Native Americans at the Battle of Fallen Timbers.
Aug. 3, 1795	Treaty of Greenville results in Native Americans ceding most of their lands in Ohio to the United States.
1796	First permanent American settlement in northern Ohio is founded.

1800	*Chillicothe Gazette*, Ohio's oldest newspaper, is founded.
Mar. 1, 1803	Ohio is admitted to the Union as the seventeenth state; its capital is Chillicothe.
1804	Ohio University is founded in Athens.
1808	Coal is discovered in Ohio.
1810	State capital is moved to Zanesville.
1811	Steamboat travel begins on the Ohio River.
1812	Capital is moved back to Chillicothe.
1812-1813	Allied British and Native American forces invade Ohio.
1816	State capital is moved to Columbus.
1825	Erie Canal, linking the Hudson River to Lake Erie, is opened, increasing water traffic to Ohio.
1825-1838	National Road is extended through Ohio, increasing land traffic into the state.
1832	First railroad in Ohio is established.
1850	With two million residents, Ohio becomes the third most populous state in the Union; ranks first among the states in agricultural production.
1860	Oil and natural gas production begins in Ohio.
July, 1863	Confederate forces under John Hunt Morgan raid Ohio.
1870	Standard Oil Company is founded in Cleveland.
1872	Ohio native Victoria Woodhull becomes the first woman to run for U.S. president.
1912	Ohio adopts its fourth constitution.
1934	State sales tax is enacted.
1959	Completion of the Saint Lawrence Seaway, linking the Great Lakes to the Atlantic Ocean, allows ocean vessels to reach Ohio.
1968	Carl B. Stokes of Cleveland becomes the first African American mayor of a major city.
May 4, 1970	Four students are killed at Kent State University in a confrontation with the National Guard during a protest against the Vietnam War.
1980	Unemployment reaches 14 percent.
1998	Population reaches more than eleven million.
1999	Federal judge stops the state of Ohio from providing taxed-funded tuition vouchers to students attending religious schools.

Notes for Further Study

Published Sources. An excellent resource for the student new to the subject of Ohio is *Eastern Great Lakes: Indiana, Michigan, Ohio* (1995) by Thomas G. Aylesworth, which provides basic information on the state and compares it to other states in the region. A similar work, with an emphasis on the culture and society of Ohio, is George W. Knepper's *Ohio and Its People* (1997). The physical geography of the state is presented in a popular style in *Natural Wonders of Ohio: Exploring Wild and Scenic Places* (1998) by Gordon and Janet Groene. A more scholarly discussion of the same subject is found in *A Geography of Ohio* (1996), edited by Leonard Peacefull. An enjoyable way to learn about many different locations in the state is Larry L. Miller's *Ohio Place Names* (1996).

Of the many different books that discuss Ohio's history, one of the most dramatic is Allan W. Eckert's *That Dark and Bloody River: Chronicles of the Ohio River Valley* (1995). An outstanding discussion of the early history of the state is found in *The Ohio Frontier: Crucible of the Old Northwest, 1720-1830* (1996) by R. Douglas Hurt. The role that Ohio played in the Civil War is included in *Rebel Raider: The Life of General John Hunt Morgan* (1986) by James A. Ramage. An excellent review of racial tensions in Ohio is found in Joseph Watras's *Politics, Race, and Schools: Racial Integration, 1954-1994* (1997), which uses the city of Dayton as an example. The state's largest city is the topic of *Cleveland: A Concise History, 1796-1990* (1997) by Carol Poh Miller.

Web Resources. As one of the most heavily populated states in the Union, Ohio provides an enormous variety of Web sites with information on the state. A good place to start is State of Ohio Government Information and Services (http://www.state.oh.us), the official site for the state government. Besides the information on government services usually provided by similar Web sites, this site also provides links to a large number of sites with general information about the state. For a concise but clear and accurate overview of Ohio, Ohio (http://www.infoplease.com/ipa/a0108258.htm) is an excellent summary of basic facts. Numerous links are also found at Ohio.com (http://www.ohio.com), provided by the *Akron Beacon Journal*. This site emphasizes news events and Ohio businesses. A similar site, which even provides a message board and chat room for discussion of Ohio topics, is found at Virtual Ohio (http://www.virtual ohio.com).

Statistical information on the state is provided by the U.S. Census Bureau at Ohio Profiles (http://www.census .gov/datamap/www/39.htm). A guide to attractions and events within Ohio can be found at Ohio Tourism (http://www.ohiotourism.com). The flora and fauna of the state are discussed in detail at Ohio Biological Survey (http://www-obs.biosci.ohio-state.edu/obshme.htm), an ambitious project involving ninety-one colleges, universities, museums, and other organizations. The complete text of the state's constitution, with all amendments, can be found at Anderson's Ohio Constitution (http://204.89.181.223/oconst.htm).

Counties

County	Sq. miles	1996 pop.	County	Sq. miles	1996 pop.
Adams	584.0	28,093	Franklin	540.0	1,013,724
Allen	404.5	108,440	Fulton	406.8	41,180
Ashland	424.4	51,372	Gallia	468.8	32,820
Ashtabula	702.7	102,207	Geauga	404.1	86,054
Athens	506.8	61,162	Greene	414.9	139,936
Auglaize	401.3	47,059	Guernsey	522.0	40,509
Belmont	537.3	70,022	Hamilton	407.4	857,616
Brown	491.8	39,358	Hancock	531.4	68,562
Butler	467.3	323,579	Hardin	470.3	31,629
Carroll	394.7	28,522	Harrison	403.6	16,001
Champaign	428.6	37,910	Henry	416.5	29,901
Clark	400.0	147,472	Highland	553.3	39,388
Clermont	452.1	169,670	Hocking	422.8	28,413
Clinton	410.9	38,645	Holmes	423.0	36,786
Columbiana	532.5	111,406	Huron	493.1	59,563
Coshocton	564.1	36,131	Jackson	420.3	32,352
Crawford	402.3	47,290	Jefferson	409.6	77,037
Cuyahoga	458.3	1,401,552	Knox	527.2	51,702
Darke	599.9	54,259	Lake	228.2	223,301
Defiance	411.2	40,059	Lawrence	455.4	64,258
Delaware	442.5	83,245	Licking	686.5	137,584
Erie	254.5	78,913	Logan	458.5	45,606
Fairfield	505.7	119,182	Lorain	492.6	281,231
Fayette	406.6	28,395	Lucas	340.4	452,691

County	Sq. miles	1996 pop.	County	Sq. miles	1996 pop.
Madison	465.2	41,184	Pickaway	502.2	52,727
Mahoning	415.3	260,107	Pike	441.5	27,156
Marion	403.9	65,323	Portage	492.4	149,571
Medina	421.6	138,943	Preble	424.8	42,633
Meigs	429.5	23,938	Putnam	483.9	35,199
Mercer	463.3	40,890	Richland	497.0	128,151
Miami	407.0	96,941	Ross	688.5	74,407
Monroe	455.6	15,268	Sandusky	409.2	62,732
Montgomery	461.7	566,312	Scioto	612.3	80,905
Morgan	417.7	14,599	Seneca	550.6	60,368
Morrow	405.5	30,481	Shelby	409.3	46,837
Muskingum	664.6	84,349	Stark	576.2	374,406
Noble	399.0	12,134	Summit	412.8	530,571
Ottawa	255.1	40,535	Trumbull	615.8	227,069
Paulding	416.3	20,344	Tuscarawas	567.6	87,803
Perry	410.0	33,834	Union	436.7	37,396

(continued)

County	Sq. miles	1996 pop.
Van Wert	410.1	30,426
Vinton	414.1	12,068
Warren	399.9	134,791
Washington	635.2	63,827
Wayne	555.4	108,556

County	Sq. miles	1996 pop.
Williams	421.8	37,950
Wood	617.4	117,546
Wyandot	405.6	22,718

Source: U.S. Bureau of the Census; National Association of Counties.

Cities

With 10,000 or more residents

Rank	City	Population
1	Columbus	670,234
2	Cleveland	495,817
3	Cincinnati	336,400
4	Toledo	312,174
5	Akron	215,712
6	Dayton	167,475
7	Youngstown	84,650
8	Parma	83,347
9	Canton	79,259
10	Lorain	68,857
11	Springfield	65,568
12	Hamilton	61,808
13	Kettering	57,205
14	Elyria	56,278
15	Lakewood	55,682
16	Cleveland Heights	53,533
17	Euclid	50,644
18	Cuyahoga Falls	49,913
19	Mansfield	49,802
20	Mentor	49,227
21	Middletown	48,590
22	Newark	48,245
23	Warren	46,866
24	Lima	42,382
25	Fairfield	41,765
26	Strongsville	41,304
27	Beavercreek	40,014
28	Lancaster	37,701
29	Findlay	37,132
30	Huber Heights	36,997
31	North Olmsted	33,546
32	Westerville	33,437
33	Brunswick	32,634
34	Marion	32,281
35	Upper Arlington	31,699
36	Gahanna	31,579
37	Fairborn	31,390
38	Stow	31,357
39	Massillon	30,894
40	East Cleveland	29,937
41	Westlake	29,740
42	Reynoldsburg	29,473
43	Garfield Heights	29,160
44	Sandusky	28,223
45	Bowling Green	28,200
46	Shaker Heights	28,116
47	Trotwood	27,964
48	Barberton	27,097
49	Kent	26,833
50	Zanesville	26,831
51	Dublin	25,506
52	Maple Heights	25,302
53	North Royalton	25,016
54	Xenia	24,994
55	Wooster	23,609
56	North Ridgeville	23,411
57	Centerville	23,035
58	Medina	22,928
59	Alliance	22,448
60	South Euclid	22,355
61	Chillicothe	22,275
62	Portsmouth	22,213
63	Brook Park	22,084
64	Green	21,975
65	Athens	21,706
66	Troy	21,672
67	Ashland	21,521
68	Willoughby	21,494
69	Ashtabula	21,472
70	Norwood	21,450
71	Hudson Village	21,226
72	Eastlake	20,976

Rank	City	Population
73	Parma Heights	20,624
74	Niles	20,593
75	Steubenville	20,224
76	Solon	20,017
77	Hilliard	19,934
78	Piqua	19,810
79	Rocky River	19,506
80	Forest Park	19,442
81	Whitehall	19,237
82	Sidney	19,197
83	Oregon	19,136
84	Delaware	18,962

Rank	City	Population
85	Grove City	18,938
86	Mason	18,850
87	Oxford	18,789
88	Mayfield Heights	18,519
89	Berea	18,380
90	Miamisburg	18,304
91	Tiffin	18,007
92	Sylvania	17,664
93	Wadsworth	17,567
94	AvonLake	17,171
95	Fremont	17,010
96	Fairview Park	16,897

(continued)

Rank	City	Population
97	New Philadelphia	16,615
98	Defiance	16,458
99	Tallmadge	16,054
100	Painesville	15,896
101	Bay Village	15,859
102	Norwalk	15,694
103	North Canton	15,601
104	Twinsburg	15,179
105	Lyndhurst	15,109
106	Mount Vernon	14,973
107	Maumee	14,955
108	Middleburg Heights	14,877
109	Marietta	14,857
110	Warrensville Heights	14,822
111	Willowick	14,448
112	Perrysburg	14,411
113	Fostoria	14,379
114	Broadview Heights	14,187
115	Worthington	14,103
116	Vandalia	14,021
117	Wickliffe	13,953
118	Sharonville	13,870
119	Lebanon	13,802
120	Bedford	13,800
121	West Carrollton City	13,709
122	University Heights	13,409
123	Washington	13,283
124	Bucyrus	13,192
125	East Liverpool	13,151
126	Greenville	13,099
127	Bellefontaine	13,037
128	Marysville	13,010
129	Conneaut	12,836
130	Ironton	12,724
131	Brecksville	12,623

Rank	City	Population
132	Blue Ash	12,374
133	Struthers	12,342
134	Seven Hills	12,276
135	Bexley	12,216
136	Coshocton	12,183
137	Indian Springs	12,112
138	Circleville	12,107
139	Norton	12,077
140	Streetsboro	11,996
141	Ravenna	11,961
142	Salem	11,894
143	Englewood	11,870
144	Wilmington	11,866
145	Dover	11,844
146	Cambridge	11,791
147	Loveland	11,780
148	Franklin	11,664
149	Aurora	11,530
150	Reading	11,488
151	Bedford Heights	11,471
152	Brooklyn	11,462
153	Galion	11,396
154	Amherst	11,364
155	Vermilion	11,344
156	Urbana	11,142
157	Beachwood	10,955
158	Girard	10,872
159	Avon	10,615
160	Celina	10,615
161	Van Wert	10,608
162	Springboro	10,520
163	North College Hill	10,363
164	Springdale	10,081

Population figures are estimated for mid-1998.
Source: U.S. Bureau of the Census.

Index to Tables

NA = Reliable data are not available.

DEMOGRAPHICS

Resident state and national populations, 1970-1997

Population figures given in thousands

	State pop.	U.S. pop.	Share	Rank
1970	10,657	203,302	5.2%	6
1980	10,798	226,546	4.8%	6
1985	10,735	237,924	4.5%	7
1990	10,847	248,765	4.4%	7
1995	11,133	262,761	4.2%	7
1997	11,186	267,636	4.2%	7

Source: U.S. Bureau of the Census.

Resident population by age, 1997

Age group	Total population
Under 5 years	749,000
5 to 17 years	2,090,000
18 to 24 years	1,045,000
25 to 34 years	1,602,000
35 to 44 years	1,831,000
45 to 54 years	1,423,000
55 to 64 years	952,000
65 to 74 years	817,000
75 to 84 years	513,000
85 years and over	165,000
Portion of residents 65 and older	13.4%
National average	12.7%

Population figures are rounded to nearest thousand persons;
figures include armed forces personnel stationed in state.
Source: U.S. Bureau of the Census.

Resident population by race, Hispanic origin, 1997

	State pop.	Share	U.S.
All residents	11,186,000	100.0%	100.0%
Hispanic white	153,000	1.4%	10.0%
non-Hispanic white	9,610,000	85.9%	72.7%
African American	1,278,000	11.4%	12.7%
Native American	22,000	0.2%	0.9%
Asian, Pacific Islander	123,000	1.1%	3.8%

Source: U.S. Bureau of the Census.

Projections of state population, 2000-2025

	Model A Uses interstate migration observed from 1975-1994	Model B Uses Bureau of Economic Analysis employment projections
Year	Population	Population
2000	11,319,000	11,352,000
2005	11,428,000	11,534,000
2010	11,505,000	11,726,000
2015	11,588,000	11,937,000
2020	11,671,000	12,148,000
2025	11,744,000	12,343,000

All population projections, including those for 2000, were calculated in 1997.
Source: U.S. Bureau of the Census, Population Paper Listings PPL-47.

VITAL STATISTICS

Average lifetime in years by race, 1989-1991

	State	U.S.	Rank
All residents	75.32	75.37	29
White residents	75.93	76.13	32
Black residents	70.15	69.16	10

Ranks are from longest-lived to least longest-lived. Ranks exclude Alaska, for which reliable data are not available. Rank for black residents is based on the 32 states for which reliable data are available.
Source: U.S. National Center for Health Statistics.

Infant mortality rates, 1980 and 1995

	State	U.S.
All residents		
1980	12.8	12.6
1995	8.7	7.6
White residents		
1980	11.2	11.0
1995	7.3	6.3
Black residents		
1980	23.0	21.4
1995	17.5	15.1

Figures represent deaths per 1,000 live births of resident infants under 1 year old, exclusive of fetal deaths; all-residents figures include other races not listed separately.
Source: U.S. National Center for Health Statistics.

Marriages and divorces

Marriages in 1996.	82,800
Rate per 1,000 population, 1995.	8.1
U.S. rate, 1995	8.9
Rank among all states	31
Divorces in 1996	44,600
Rate per 1,000 population, 1995.	4.4
U.S. rate, 1995	4.4
Rank among all states	26

Rank is from highest to lowest in country.
Source: U.S. National Center for Health Statistics.

Death rates by leading causes, 1995
Deaths per 100,000 resident population

Cause	State	U.S.
Heart disease	317.4	280.7
Cancer	226.1	204.9
Cerebrovascular diseases	60.0	60.1
Accidents and adverse effects	29.1	35.5
Motor vehicle accidents	12.4	16.5
Chronic obstructive pulmonary diseases	44.2	39.2
Diabetes mellitus	30.0	22.6
HIV	7.9	NA
Suicide	9.7	11.9
Homicide	-	8.7
All causes	950.1	880.0
Rank in overall death rate among states		13

Figures exclude nonresidents who die in state. Causes of death follow International Classification of Diseases. Rank is from highest to lowest in country.
Source: U.S. National Center for Health Statistics.

ECONOMY

Gross state product, 1990-1996
In current dollars

	State product	Increase
1990	$227.1 billion	
1993	$256.6 billion	
1994	$276.7 billion	7.83%
1995	$292.1 billion	5.57%
1996	$304.4 billion	4.21%

Source: U.S. Bureau of Economic Analysis; Survey of Current Business, June, 1998.

Gross state product by industry, 1996
In billions

Farms, forestry, fisheries	$2.9
Construction	10.1
Manufacturing	80.7
Transportation, public utilities	22.3
Wholesale trade	20.6
Retail trade	27.2
Finance, insurance, real estate	40.3
Services	46.9
Government	28.6
State total	$280.7
Total U.S.	$6,923.8
State share	4.05%
Rank among states	7

Total figures include mining, not listed separately.
Source: U.S. Bureau of Economic Analysis; Survey of Current Business, June, 1998.

Personal income per capita, 1990 and 1997
In current dollars

	1990	1997
Per capita income	$18,147	$24,661
U.S. average	$19,188	$25,598
Rank among states	21	21

1997 data are preliminary.
Source: U.S. Bureau of Economic Analysis; Survey of Current Business, May, 1998.

Energy consumption, 1995
In trillions of British thermal units (BTU)

End-use sectors

Residential	904.5
Commercial	626.9
Industrial	1,639.3
Transportation	867.3

Sources of energy

Petroleum	1,190.0
Natural gas	930.1
Coal	1,379.8
Hydroelectric power	2.4
Nuclear electric power	178.7
Total state per capita consumption	362.7
Total U.S. per capita consumption	344.4
Rank among states	22
Total state energy consumption	4,038.0
Total U.S. energy consumption	90,547.4
State share of U.S. total	4.46%
Rank among states	3

Total figures include items not listed separately.
Source: U.S. Energy Information Administration; State Energy Data Report.

Nonfarm employment by sectors, 1997

Total	5,386,000
Construction	224,000
Manufacturing	1,090,000
Transportation, public utilities	233,000
Wholesale trade, retail trade	1,311,000
Finance, insurance, real estate	287,000
Services	1,469,000
Government	760,000

Figures are rounded to nearest thousand persons. Total includes mining, not listed separately.
Source: U.S. Bureau of Labor Statistics; Employment and Earnings, monthly.

Foreign exports, 1990-1997
In millions of dollars

Year	State	U.S.	State share
1990	13,378	394,045	3.40%
1996	22,677	624,767	3.63%
1997	24,903	688,896	3.61%

Source: U.S. Bureau of the Census; U.S. Merchandise Trade, series FT 900.

LAND USE

Federally owned land, 1996

	State	U.S.	State share
Total acres	26,222,000	2,271,343,000	1.15%
Federally owned	280,000	563,129,000	0.05%
Federal share	1.1%	24.8%	—

Areas are rounded to nearest thousand acres. Figures for federally owned land do not include trust properties.
Source: U.S. General Services Administration; *Inventory Report on Real Property Owned by the United States Throughout the World*, annual.

Land use, 1992
In acres, rounded to nearest thousand

Total surface area	26,451,000
Federal land	375,000
Total nonfederal	25,654,000
Developed	3,558,000
Total rural	22,096,000
Cropland	11,929,000
Pasture land	2,269,000
Range land	0
Forest land	6,624,000
Minor cover/use	1,275,000

Total surface area figures include water area not shown separately.
Source: U.S. Dept. of Agriculture; Soil Conservation Service; Iowa State University, Statistical Laboratory; *Summary Report, 1992 National Resources Inventory.*

Farms and crop acreage, 1997
In millions of acres

	State	U.S.	Share	Rank
Farms (thousands)	73	2,058	3.55%	10
Acres (millions)	15	968	1.55%	22
Acres per farm	207	471	—	36
Acres planted	10,726	334,139	3.21%	12
Acres harvested	10,528	319,894	3.29%	11
Farm value (mill.)	$3,460	$108,805	3.18%	28

Numbers of farms are rounded to nearest thousand.
Source: U.S. Dept. of Agriculture; National Agricultural Statistics Service.

GOVERNMENT AND FINANCE

Units of local government, 1997

	State	Total U.S.	Rank
All local governments	3,597	87,453	6
Counties	88	3,043	13
Municipalities	941	19,372	6
Townships	1,310	16,629	6
School districts	666	13,726	6
Special districts	592	34,683	20

County ranks are based on the 48 states with county governments; township ranks are based on the 20 states with township governments; school district ranks are based on the 46 states with such districts.
Source: U.S. Bureau of the Census; *1997 Census of Governments, Government Organization,* Series GC97(1).

State government revenue, 1996

Total revenue	$43,823 mill.
General revenue	29,467 mill.
Per capita	2,640
U.S. per capita average	2,910
Rank among states	35
Intergovernmental revenue	
Total	$8,726 mill.
From federal government	8,485 mill.
From local government	241 mill.
Charges and Miscellaneous	
Total	$5,091 mill.
Current charges	2,882 mill.
Misc. general revenue	2,209 mill.
Taxes	
Total	$15,649 mill.
General sales	4,991 mill.
Selective sales	2,613 mill.
License taxes	1,219 mill.
Individual income	5,903 mill.
Corporate income	807 mill.
Other	116 mill.
Insurance trust revenue	13,983 mill.

Total revenue figures include items not listed separately.
Source: U.S. Bureau of the Census.

State government expenditures, 1996

General expenditures
Intergovernmental.	$10,054 mill.
Direct expenditures.	18,439 mill.
Total	28,492 mill.

Selected direct expenditures
Education	$10,315 mill.
Public welfare.	7,392 mill.
Health, hospital	2,268 mill.
Highways	2,203 mill.
Police	192 mill.
Corrections	1,144 mill.
Natural resources.	284 mill.
Parks and recreation.	80 mill.
Government administration	898 mill.
Interest on debt	822 mill.

Other
State per capita expenditures	$2,552
U.S. per capita average	2,854
Rank among states.	36
Total state expenditures	35,517 mill.
Total U.S. expenditures	859,959 mill.

Totals include items not listed separately.
Source: U.S. Bureau of the Census.

POLITICS

Governors since statehood
D = Democrat; R = Republican; O = other;
(r) resigned; (d) died in office; (i) removed from office

Edward Tiffin (O)	(r) 1803-1807
Thomas Kirker (O)	1807-1808
Samuel Huntington (O)	1808-1810
Return J. Meigs, Jr. (O)	(r) 1810-1814
Othniel Looker (O)	1814
Thomas Worthington (O)	1814-1818
Ethen A. Brown (O)	(r) 1818-1822
Allen Trimble (O)	1822
Jeremiah Morrow (O)	1822-1826
Allen Trimble (O)	1826-1830
Duncan McArthur (O)	1830-1832
Robert Lucas (D)	1832-1836
Joseph Vance (O)	1836-1838
Wilson Shannon (D)	1838-1840
Thomas Corwin (O)	1840-1842
Wilson Shannon (D)	(r) 1842-1844
Thomas W. Bartley (D)	1844
William Bebb (O)	1844-1846
Seabury Ford (O)	1846-1849
Reuben Wood (O)	(r) 1849-1850
William Medill (D)	1850-1856
Salmon P. Chase (R)	1856-1860
William Dennison (R)	1860-1862
David Tod (O)	1862-1864
John Brough (O)	(d) 1864-1865
Charles Anderson (O)	1865-1866
Jacob D. Cox (O)	1866-1868
Rutherford B. Hayes (R)	1868-1872
Edward F. Noyes (R)	1872-1874
William Allen (D)	1874-1876
Rutherford B. Hayes (R)	(r) 1876-1877
Thomas L. Young (R)	1877-1878
Richard M. Bishop (D)	1878-1880
Charles Foster (R)	1880-1884
George Hoadly (D)	1884-1886
Joseph B. Foraker (R)	1886-1890
James E. Campbell (D)	1890-1892
William McKinley (R)	1892-1896
Asa S. Bushnell (R)	1896-1900
George E. Nash (R)	1900-1904
Myron T. Merrick (R)	1904-1906
John M. Pattison (D)	(d) 1906
Andrew L. Harris (R)	1906-1909
Judson Harmon (D)	1909-1913
James M. Cox (D)	1913-1915
Frank B. Willis (R)	1915-1917
James M. Cox (D)	1917-1921
Harry L. Davis (R)	1921-1923
Alvin Victor Donahey (D)	1923-1929
Myers T. Cooper (R)	1929-1931
George White (D)	1931-1935
Martin L. Davey (D)	1935-1939
John W. Bricker (R)	1939-1945
Frank J. Lausche (D)	1945-1947
Thomas J. Herbert (R)	1947-1949
Frank J. Lausche (D)	(r) 1949-1957
John W. Brown (R)	1957
Crone William O'Neill (R)	1957-1959
Michael V. Disalle (D)	1959-1963
James A. Rhodes (R)	1963-1971
John J. Gilligan (D)	1971-1975
James A. Rhodes (R)	1975-1983
Richard F. Celeste (D)	1983-1991
George Voinovich (R)	1991-1999
Bob Taft (R)	1999-

Composition of state legislature, 1990-1998

	Democrats	Republicans
State House (99 seats)		
1990	61	38
1992	53	46
1994	43	56
1996	39	60
1998	39	58
State Senate (33 seats)		
1990	12	21
1992	13	20
1994	13	20
1996	12	21
1998	12	21

Figures for total seats may include independents and minor party members.

Source: Council of State Governments; *State Elective Officials and the Legislatures.*

Composition of congressional delegations, 1989-1999

	Dem	Rep	Total
House of Representatives			
101st Congress, 1989			
State delegates	11	10	21
Total U.S.	259	174	433
102d Congress, 1991			
State delegates	11	10	21
Total U.S.	267	167	434
103d Congress, 1993			
State delegates	10	9	20
Total U.S.	258	176	434
104th Congress, 1995			
State delegates	8	11	19
Total U.S.	197	236	433
105th Congress, 1997			
State delegates	8	11	19
Total U.S.	206	228	434
106th Congress, 1999			
State delegates	8	11	19
Total U.S.	211	222	433

	Dem	Rep	Total
Senate			
101st Congress, 1989			
State delegates	2	0	2
Total U.S.	55	45	100
102d Congress, 1991			
State delegates	2	0	2
Total U.S.	56	44	100
103d Congress, 1993			
State delegates	2	0	2
Total U.S.	57	43	100
104th Congress, 1995			
State delegates	1	1	2
Total U.S.	46	53	99
105th Congress, 1997			
State delegates	1	1	2
Total U.S.	45	55	100
106th Congress, 1999			
State delegates	0	2	2
Total U.S.	45	54	99

Figures are for starts of first sessions. Figure for U.S. Representatives for 101st Congress does not include Alabama and Indiana, which had vacancies. Figures for total U.S. Representatives for 102d, 103d, and 106th Congresses do not include Vermont, which had 1 Independent-Socialist. Figure for U.S. Representatives for 104th Congress does not include Vermont, which had 1 Independent-Socialist, and California, which had 1 vacancy. Figure for U.S. Representatives for 105th Congress does not include New York, which had 1 vacancy. Figure for U.S. Senators for 104th Congress does not include Oregon, which had 1 vacancy. Figure for U.S. Senators for 106th Congress does not include New Hampshire, which had 1 Independent.

Source: U.S. Congress; *Congressional Directory,* biennial.

Voter participation in presidential elections, 1992 and 1996

	1992	1996
State voting age pop.	8,207,000	8,358,000
Total U.S. voting age pop.	189,524,000	196,509,000
State share of U.S. total	4.3%	4.3%
Rank among states	7	7
Percent of state casting vote	60.2	41.5
Percent of U.S. total voting	55.1	49.0
Rank among states	21	49

Source: U.S. Bureau of the Census.

HEALTH AND MEDICAL CARE

Medicare, 1997

	Recipients	Payments
State	1,679,000	$8,556 mill.
Total U.S.	37,514,000	$206,064 mill.
State share	4.48%	4.15%
Rank among states	6	6

Recipient figures are rounded to nearest thousand persons. Ranks are from highest to lowest.
Source: U.S. Health Care Financing Administration.

Medicaid, 1996

	Recipients	Payments
State	1,478,000	$5,512 mill.
Total U.S.	35,028,000	$121,419 mill.
State share	4.22%	4.54%
Rank among states	5	4

Recipient figures are rounded to nearest thousand persons. Payment figures for fiscal year reflect federal and state contribution payments. Ranks are from highest to lowest.
Source: U.S. Health Care Financing Administration.

Health insurance coverage, 1996

	State	U.S.
Total persons covered	9,974,000	225,070,000
Total persons not covered	1,292,000	41,716,000
Part not covered	11.5%	15.6%
Rank among states	34	—
Children not covered	305,000	10,554,000
Part not covered	10.1%	14.8%
Rank among states	33	—

Ranks are from most to fewest uninsured. Population figures are rounded to nearest thousand persons.
Source: U.S. Bureau of the Census.

AIDS, syphilis, tuberculosis, and measles cases, 1997

Cases	U.S.	State	Share
AIDS	58,443	848	1.45%
Syphilis	8,550	218	2.55%
Tuberculosis	18,534	286	1.54%
Measles	148,000	NA	NA

Measles figures are rounded to nearest thousand cases.
Source: U.S. Centers for Disease Control and Prevention.

HOUSING

Homeownership rates, 1985-1997

	1985	1990	1997
State	67.9%	68.7%	69.0%
Total U.S.	63.9%	63.9%	65.7%
Rank among states	26	17	22

Source: U.S. Bureau of the Census.

Home sales, 1990 and 1997
In thousands of units

Existing home sales	1990	1997	Change
State sales	151.6	187.3	35.7
Total U.S. sales	3,560	4,730	1,170
State share of U.S. total	4.26%	3.96%	-0.30%
Rank among states	6	7	—

Source: National Association of Realtors; *Real Estate Outlook: Market Trends and Insights.*

EDUCATION

Public school enrollment, 1995

State K-8 enrollment 1,297,000
Total U.S. K-8 enrollment 32,341,000
State share of total U.S.. . . . . 4.01%
State 9-12 enrollment 539,000
Total U.S. 9-12 enrollment 12,500,000
State share of U.S. total 4.31%
State public school enroll. rate 88.4%
Overall U.S. rate. 91.6%
Rank among states. 42

Enrollment figures (which include unclassified students) are
rounded to nearest thousand pupils in fall term;
kindergarten (K)-8 grade figures include some
prekindergarten students. Enrollment rate is based on
percentage of persons 5-17 years old. Rank is from highest
to lowest.
Source: U.S. National Center for Education Statistics.

Public college finances, 1996

State FTE enrollment 338,400
Total U.S. FTE enrollment 8,268,800
State share of total U.S.. . . . . 4.09%
Rank among states 6
State and local appropriations $1,414,500,000
Total U.S. state and local
    appropriations. . . . . $39,699 mill.
State share of total U.S.. . . . . 3.56%
Rank among states 7
State net tuition revenues. $1,069,100,000
Total U.S. net tuition $18,348,100,000
State share of total U.S.. . . . . 5.83%
Rank among states 6

FTE=Full-time equivalent; credit and noncredit enrollment
including summer session in academic year ending in
1996.
Enrollments are rounded to nearest thousand students. Net
tuition revenues exclude appropriation to students
attending in-state public institutions. Rankings are from
highest shares to lowest.
Source: Research Associates of Washington.

TRANSPORTATION AND TRAVEL

Highway mileage, 1996

Interstate 1,573
Other arterial 11,015
Collector roads 25,739
Local roads 79,872

Urban roads. 33,191
Rural roads 81,451

Total state 114,642
U.S. total 3,933,985
State share 2.9%
Rank among states 9

Source: U.S. Federal Highway Administration.

Motor vehicle registrations and driver licenses, 1996

In thousands

Vehicle registrations	State	U.S.	Share	Rank
Autos, trucks, buses	9,770	206,365	4.73%	5
Autos only	6,570	128,439	5.12%	5
Motorcycles	219	3,832	5.72%	2
Driver licenses	7,853	179,539	4.37%	5

Figures do not include vehicles owned by military services.
Source: U.S. Federal Highway Administration; *Highway
Statistics; Selected Highway Statistics and Charts.*

Domestic travel expenditures, 1995

Spending by U.S. residents on overnight trips and day
trips of at least 100 miles

Total expenditures in state . . . . $9,641 mill.
Total expenditures in U.S. . . . . $360,314 mill.
State share of total U.S.. . . . . 2.68%
Rank among states. 11

Source: Travel Industry Association of America.

CRIME AND LAW ENFORCEMENT

State and local police officers, 1996

Local police	15,932
State police	1,391
Sheriffs	5,179
Total	23,811
Officers per 10,000 residents	21
U.S. average	25
Rank among states	30

Figures cover full-time sworn officers; totals include special
  police not shown separately.
Source: U.S. Bureau of Justice Statistics; *Census of State and
  Local Law Enforcement Agencies, 1996.*

Crime rates, 1996

Rates per 100,000 resident population

Violent crimes	State	U.S.
Total violent	429	634
Murder	4.8	7.4
Forcible rape	41.3	36.1
Robbery	164	202
Aggravated assault	218	388
Property crimes		
Total property	4,027	4,445
Burglary	835	943
Larceny/theft	2,784	2,976
Motor vehicle theft	408	526
Totals	4,456	5,079

Source: U.S. Federal Bureau of Investigation; *Crime in the
  United States,* annual.

State prison populations, 1980-1996

	State	U.S.	State share
1980	13,489	305,458	4.42%
1990	31,822	708,393	4.49%
1996	46,174	1,025,624	4.50%

Figures exclude prisoners in federal penitentiaries.
Source: U.S. Bureau of Justice Statistics.

Oklahoma

Location: Midwestern continental United States

Area and rank: 68,679 square miles (177,877 square kilometers); 69,903 square miles (181,049 square kilometers) including water; nineteenth largest state in area

Population and rank: 3,317,091 (1997); twenty-seventh largest state in population

Capital: Oklahoma City

Largest city: Oklahoma City (472,221 people in 1998)

Became territory: May 2, 1890

Entered Union and rank: November 16, 1907; forty-sixth state

Present constitution adopted: 1907

Counties: 77

State name: "Oklahoma" derives from two Choctaw Indian words meaning "red people"

State nickname: Sooner State

Motto: *Labor omnia vincit* (Labor conquers all things)

State flag: Blue field with American Indian shield bearing six red crosses, seven eagle feathers, a peace pipe, and an olive branch, with the name "Oklahoma" below

Highest point: Black Mesa — 4,973 feet (1,516 meters)

Lowest point: Little River — 289 feet (88 meters)

Highest recorded temperature: 120 degrees Fahrenheit (49 degrees Celsius) — Tishomingo, 1943

Lowest recorded temperature: −27 degrees Fahrenheit (−33 degrees Celsius) — Watts, 1930

State song: "Oklahoma"

State tree: Redbud

State flower: Mistletoe

State bird: Scissor-tailed flycatcher

State fish: White or sand bass

State animal: Bison

State capitol building in Oklahoma City. (Oklahoma Tourism/Fred W. Marvel)

Oklahoma History

Oklahoma is almost square except for its northwestern extreme, called the Panhandle, a strip about 40 miles wide and 120 miles long that reaches to Colorado, which, with Kansas, forms the state's northern border. To the west lie New Mexico and Texas, which also forms its southern boundary. On the east are Missouri and Arkansas. Although some geographers consider Oklahoma a southwestern state, along with New Mexico, Arizona, and Nevada, others call it a south central state.

Early History. The first humans probably settled in the Oklahoma region more than twenty thousand years ago, living in caves, where their drawings have been discovered on cave walls near Kenton. These early dwellers lived on roots and berries as well as the meat they obtained from the animals they hunted.

When Spanish explorer Francisco Vásquez de Coronado first came to the area in 1541, he found a place in which few people lived, although a few Native American tribes, notably the Plains Indians, eked out an existence there. Chief among these were the Apache, Comanche, and Kiowa, although the area also had some village-dwelling Indians, notably the Caddo, Pawnee, and Wichita, who had inhabited the area prior to 1500. These Native American groups were joined between 1815 and 1840 by the Cherokee, Chickasaw, Choctaw, Creek, and Seminole Indians, known as the Five Civilized Tribes. The federal government had driven them from their homes and forcibly relocated them in large enclaves in Oklahoma and other nearby areas, called Indian Territory.

The Earliest Explorers. It has been speculated that Vikings from Greenland reached Oklahoma

This 1942 painting, titled Trail of Tears, *by Robert Lindneux is a romanticized depiction of the forced removal of Cherokee from Georgia to what later became Oklahoma during the 1830's. Most Cherokee actually made the arduous journey on foot.* (Woolaroc Museum, Bartlesville, Oklahoma)

as early as 1012. The evidence for this, however, a huge stone found at Heavener in eastern Oklahoma with the date carved into it in the kind of runic letters used by the Vikings, has not been authenticated. It is known that Spanish explorers crossed the Oklahoma Panhandle in 1541, coming from Mexico in search of gold. In the same year, Hernando de Soto, also seeking gold, came into the area from the east, traveling along the Arkansas River. All explorers claimed the area for Spain.

In 1682 René-Robert Cavalier, sieur de La Salle, explored the Mississippi River, claiming for France all the lands drained by the Mississippi and naming it Louisiana in honor of his king, Louis XIV. The vast area he claimed included most of present-day Oklahoma. The early explorers traded trinkets with the native dwellers for furs.

The Louisiana Territory changed hands several times. In 1762 Spain took it from France. In 1800 Spain returned it to France, and in 1803 the United States, in the Louisiana Purchase, bought it from France for fifteen million dollars. It must be remembered that at the time of the Louisiana Purchase, fewer than five hundred Europeans lived in the entire area called Louisiana, which included parts of Texas, Oklahoma, Arkansas, Kansas, and Missouri.

The first non-Indian settlement in Oklahoma, near present-day Salina, was established in 1823 by Auguste Pierre Chouteau, whose trading post served the area's fur traders. In 1830 the U.S. Congress passed the Indian Removal Act, under which the government was permitted to relocate Indians from the East Coast of the United States. Between 1830 and 1842, around 75,000 Native Americans were deployed to the area, many dying en route. Those who survived lived much as white people in the east did, creating villages, building schools and churches, farming, and raising cattle and poultry. Some became so affluent that they owned slaves.

The government promised the relocated Indians that the land they were given in the eastern and southern parts of the area, known as the Indian Territory, would always be theirs. The various tribes set up their own governments and functioned as separate nations.

The Civil War. Because the Indian Territory had not achieved statehood, it could not secede from the Union during the Civil War. Many of the Native Americans who dwelled there owned slaves, and about six thousand of the Indians fought for the Confederacy during the war, although some joined the Union forces. Most of these people held a grudge against the federal government for having taken them from their native lands and relocated them. This caused many who were not slave owners to side with the South.

After the war, in 1866, representatives of the Indian Territory were forced to sign the Reconstruction Treaty. The government retaliated against the Native Americans for their support of the Confederacy by taking back much of their land and by forcing them to permit railroads to cross their property.

Land Disputes. In the 1870's, Texan cattle men drove their herds to Kansas railroad towns from which livestock could be shipped to market, crossing Oklahoma. Irritated, Kansans tried to pressure the government into opening more land in the area to white settlement. The Missouri-Kansas-Texas Railroad crossed eastern Oklahoma by 1872 and brought many people into the region.

Many white farmers rented the land they tilled from the Native Americans. In time the federal government bought five thousand square miles of the Indian Territory and, in 1889, opened it to settlers on a first come, first served basis. Each family could claim 160 acres merely by placing themselves upon

Oklahoma City, the state's capital and largest city. (Oklahoma Tourism/Fred W. Marvel)

it. About fifty thousand land-hungry people arrived. At noon, the great Land Run of 1889 began, marking an important phase in Oklahoma's development. A tent city in Guthrie housed fifteen thousand people temporarily. On that single day, the settlements of Kingfisher, Norman, Oklahoma City, and Stillwater were started.

After development started there, the U.S. Congress established the Oklahoma Territory, which lay west of the Indian Territory. The two areas were called the Twin Territories. The federal purchase of more Indian land was followed by more land runs, so that by the early 1900's, the area had a substantial white population. The Native Americans wanted to establish their own state, but their desires were overlooked. In 1907 the Twin Territories were admitted to the Union as the state of Oklahoma, the forty-sixth of the United States, with Guthrie as its capital. Three years later, the capital was moved to Oklahoma City.

The Discovery of Oil. In 1901 Oklahoma began its journey toward affluence. Oil was discovered near Tulsa. An oil rush began, with many petroleum companies establishing offices in Tulsa. As oil was discovered in other parts of the state, many boomtowns grew, and the entire state experienced an economic upsurge.

The decade following World War I was a time of considerable prosperity for the state. Oil fueled the economy, but agriculture was also important. The state's prosperity, based on these two enterprises, was not to last, however.

Dust Bowls and the Great Depression. The economic chaos following the collapse of the stock market in 1929 affected the entire United States. Oklahoma, however, suffered more than most other states because, combined with a national economic downturn that devastated the oil industry, a continued drought resulted in huge dust storms and reduced agriculture production to below the subsistence level.

The Great Depression was so devastating to Oklahoma that more than sixty thousand of its citizens, labeled "Okies," left the state, many of them heading for the West Coast, particularly California.

World War II and After. World War II brought renewed prosperity to Oklahoma. The weather improved to the point that agriculture again contributed significantly to the economy. War industries

Port of Muskogee on the Arkansas River, which links Oklahoma to the Mississippi River and the world's oceans. (Oklahoma Tourism/Fred W. Marvel)

came into the state, notably aeronautical and munitions factories. The state's oil wells produced much-needed petroleum products for the war effort. Some two hundred thousand Oklahomans served in the nation's armed forces.

Shortly after the war, in 1947, the McClellan-Kerr Arkansas River Navigation Project was begun. When it was completed in 1970, the Arkansas River had been made navigable by widening and deepening. The system of dams and locks on the river made it navigable by large ships. Muskogee and Tulsa became important port cities once the waterway was opened.

Other dams were built on rivers throughout Oklahoma as a means of flood control and irrigation. The lakes these dams formed offer visitors extensive recreational facilities and attracted many tourists. The hydroelectric power the dams generate stimulated industrial growth.

This industrial growth, mainly in companies that make airplanes, rockets, automobile parts, and computers, brought an influx of new people into the state, which, from 1970 to 1980, attracted 466,000 new residents. During the 1970's, three groups of Oklahoma Indians—the Cherokee, the Choctaw, and the Chickasaw—regained ninety-six

miles of the Arkansas River, increasing their prosperity.

In 1971 the voters of Oklahoma City elected Patience Latting mayor, making her the first female mayor of a major metropolis. Three years later, the state selected thirty-three-year-old David Boren as governor, making him the youngest governor in the United States.

The Federal Building Bombing. The 1990's were marked by tragedy in Oklahoma. In a horrible act of domestic terrorism, on April 19, 1995, Timothy McVeigh loaded a rental truck with explosives, parked it outside the Alfred P. Murrah Federal Building in Oklahoma City, retreated a safe distance, and detonated the explosives.

The Murrah Building collapsed, killing 168 people and seriously injuring scores of others, among them many young children in a day-care center housed in the building. The city and state were devastated by this crime and erected a memorial on the site of the demolished building. Timothy McVeigh, granted a change of venue for his court case, was tried in Denver, Colorado. He was convicted of first-degree murder, for which he received the death sentence.

R. Baird Shuman

Oklahoma Time Line

1541	Spanish explorer Francisco Vásquez de Coronado crosses the Oklahoma Panhandle.
1541	Spanish explorer Hernando de Soto travels to eastern Oklahoma.
1682	René-Robert Cavalier, sieur de La Salle, claims the Louisiana Territory, which includes much of Oklahoma, for France.
1762	France cedes Louisiana, including Oklahoma, to Spain.
1800	Spain returns Louisiana to France.
1803	United States buys the area from France for fifteen million dollars in the Louisiana Purchase.
1823	Auguste Pierre Chouteau establishes a trading post and the first permanent non-Indian settlement near present-day Salina.
1830	U.S. Congress passes the Indian Removal Act, through which Native American tribes are brought to Oklahoma between 1830 and 1842.
1834	U.S. government creates the Indian Territory in eastern Oklahoma.
1844	Relocated Cherokees publish Oklahoma's first newspaper, the *Cherokee Advocate*.
1861	Six thousand Oklahomans support the Confederacy during the Civil War.
1865	Oklahoma's black slaves are freed at the conclusion of the Civil War.
1866	Government retaliates against Indians for their support of the Confederacy by taking back some of their land.
1872	Missouri-Kansas-Texas Railroad crosses eastern Oklahoma.
1880	Pressure exerted for the government to open more land for white settlement.
Apr. 22, 1889	Great Land Run brings more than 50,000 people to the area to compete for the newly available land.
1890	Congress creates the Oklahoma Territory, calling it and the Indian Territory the Twin Territories; U.S. government buys more Indian land for redistribution to white settlers.
1892	University of Oklahoma opens at Norman.
Sept. 16, 1893	Great Land Run draws 100,000 participants.
1901	Oil is discovered near Tulsa.
1905	Indians try to create their own separate state, Sequoyah.
Nov. 16, 1907	Twin Territories admitted to the Union as Oklahoma, the forty-sixth state, with Guthrie as its capital.
1910	Oklahoma City named state capital.
1917	Ninety thousand Oklahomans join armed forces in World War I.
1930's	Oklahoma's agriculture devastated by extended drought; thousands leave the state.
1941	United States enters World War II; defense industries bring renewed prosperity to Oklahoma.
1953	Toll road, the Turner Turnpike, is completed between Tulsa and Oklahoma City.
1970	McClellan-Kerr Arkansas River Navigation System is completed.
1971	Patience Latting is elected mayor of Oklahoma City, the first woman mayor of a city of more than 200,000.
1974	David Boren, age thirty-three, is elected governor, becoming the youngest governor in the United States.

1980	Oklahoma suffers devastating drought.
Sept.-Oct., 1986	Severe floods lead to great property damage.
1991	University of Oklahoma law professor Anita F. Hill accuses U.S. Supreme Court nominee Clarence Thomas of sexual harassment.
April 19, 1995	Timothy McVeigh bombs the Alfred P. Murrah Federal Building in Oklahoma City, killing 168.
June 3, 1997	Timothy McVeigh convicted of eleven counts of murder and on June 13 is sentenced to death.

Notes for Further Study

Published Sources. Arrel M. Gibson's *Oklahoma: A History of Five Centuries* (2d ed. 1989) provides an encompassing history of the state through its various stages of development. *Oklahoma: The Story of Its Past and Present* (rev. ed. 1985) by Edwin C. McReynolds, et al., covers the essentials of the state's development accurately and thoroughly. Although quite specialized, Bradford Koplowitz's *Guide to the Historical Records of Oklahoma* (1998) is an indispensable guide for those wishing to undertake research on the state.

Rennard Strickland's *The Indians in Oklahoma* (1980) reviews the convoluted history of the various Native American tribes in Oklahoma with special and valuable emphasis on the Five Civilized Tribes, who were relocated in the state. W. Dale Mason focuses on some of the problems of Native Americans in Oklahoma and their solutions in *Interest Group Federalism: Indian Gaming and the Status of Indian Tribes in the American Political System* (1992). In *Professors, Presidents, and Politicians: Civil Rights and the University of Oklahoma, 1890-1968* (1981), George Lynn Cross considers the broad question of human rights in Oklahoma.

Written specifically for juvenile readers are Dennis B. and Judith Bloom Fradin's *From Sea to Shining Sea: Oklahoma* (1995), which is nicely illustrated and well written, and Ann Heinrichs's *America the Beautiful: Oklahoma* (1989), which will appeal to teenage readers.

Web Resources. The state of Oklahoma's Web site (http://www.state.ok.us) and the Oklahoma Department of Tourism's Web site (http://www.otrd.state.ok.us) both provide extensive information about the state and its attractions. Information about the state's American Indian population is available on the Caddo Indian Tribe's Web site (http://www.caddonation.com) and the Chickasaw Nation Net Web site (http://www.chicka saw.com). The Heartland Internet Web site (http://www.heartserv.com) also provides useful historical information and statistics. The state's Department of Commerce Web site (http://www.odoc.state.ok.us) offers information about Oklahoma's economy and state commerce. The Department of Agriculture also has a site (http://www.state.ok.us) that is connected with the state's major Web site; agricultural statistics are available there. Additional economic information is available on the Oklahoma Small Business Web site (http://www.osbdc.org).

Among the individual municipal Web sites, the most useful are Oklahoma City's (http://www.okccvb.org) and (http://www.okconline.com), Norman's (http://www.ci .norman.ok.us), Shawnee's (http://www.shawneenet .com), Stillwater's (http://www.ci.stillwater.ok.us), and Lawton's (http://www.lawtonok.com). Tulsa's Chamber of Commerce also maintains a Web site (http:// www .tulsachamber.com) that provides varied information about that city.

Counties

County	Sq. miles	1996 pop.	County	Sq. miles	1996 pop.
Adair	575.7	19,914	Canadian	899.9	83,342
Alfalfa	866.7	6,155	Carter	823.9	44,280
Atoka	978.4	13,250	Cherokee	751.1	37,879
Beaver	1,814.5	6,013	Choctaw	774.0	15,250
Beckham	901.9	18,552	Cimarron	1,835.1	3,087
Blaine	928.6	10,748	Cleveland	536.2	194,687
Bryan	908.9	33,920	Coal	518.2	6,162
Caddo	1,278.4	30,663	Comanche	1,069.4	111,171

(continued)

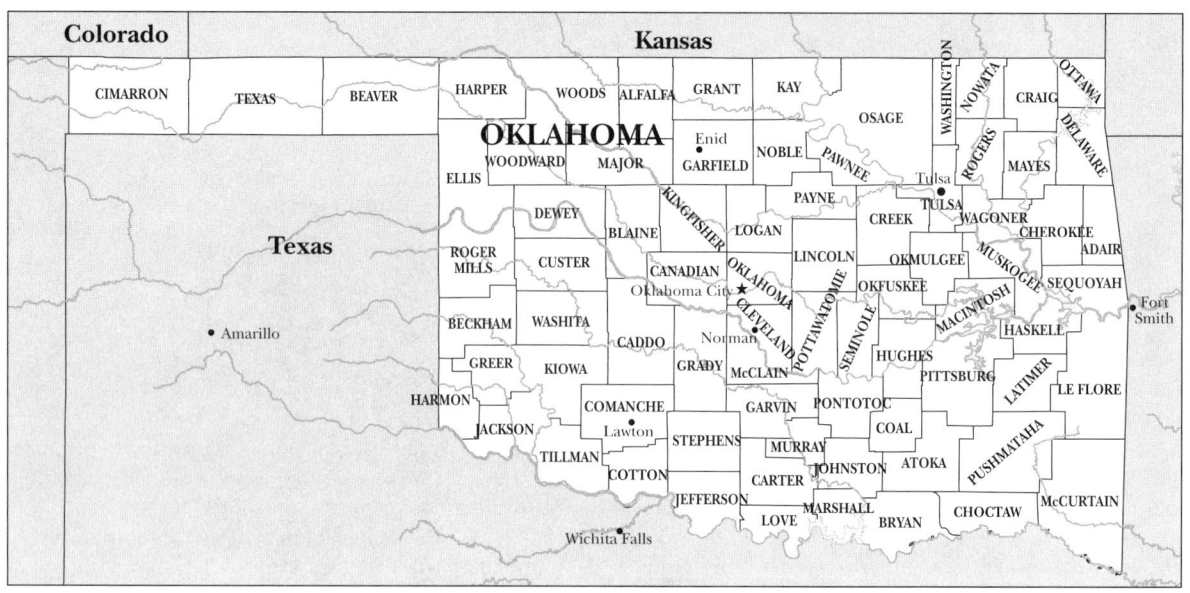

County	Sq. miles	1996 pop.
Cotton	636.7	6,879
Craig	761.1	14,440
Creek	955.6	65,469
Custer	986.6	25,937
Delaware	740.7	33,141
Dewey	1,000.2	5,112
Ellis	1,229.2	4,185
Garfield	1,058.5	57,312
Garvin	809.2	26,733
Grady	1,101.0	44,896
Grant	1,000.6	5,546
Greer	639.4	6,750
Harmon	537.9	3,592
Harper	1,039.1	3,781
Haskell	577.1	11,283
Hughes	806.8	13,077
Jackson	802.8	29,990
Jefferson	758.9	6,724
Johnston	644.6	10,458
Kay	918.8	47,285
Kingfisher	903.1	13,471
Kiowa	1,014.7	10,859
Latimer	722.2	10,235
Le Flore	1,586.0	46,037
Lincoln	958.6	30,945
Logan	744.6	30,940
Love	515.4	8,637
McClain	569.7	25,475
McCurtain	1,852.4	34,754
McIntosh	620.0	18,556
Major	956.8	7,758
Marshall	371.1	11,869

County	Sq. miles	1996 pop.
Mayes	656.2	36,565
Murray	418.3	12,400
Muskogee	813.9	69,298
Noble	732.0	11,239
Nowata	565.0	9,846
Okfuskee	624.8	11,358
Oklahoma	709.2	630,531
Okmulgee	697.0	37,821
Osage	2,251.0	42,503
Ottawa	471.4	30,310
Pawnee	569.5	16,043
Payne	686.4	64,219
Pittsburg	1,306.0	43,101
Pontotoc	719.7	34,822
Pottawatomie	787.9	61,682
Pushmataha	1,397.4	11,586
Roger Mills	1,141.9	3,721
Rogers	675.0	63,536
Seminole	632.5	24,960
Sequoyah	673.9	36,581
Stephens	877.2	43,336
Texas	2,037.3	17,322
Tillman	872.4	9,634
Tulsa	570.3	531,596
Wagoner	563.1	53,389
Washington	416.9	47,423
Washita	1,003.5	11,698
Woods	1,286.6	8,516
Woodward	1,242.4	18,667

Source: U.S. Bureau of the Census; National Association of Counties.

Cities
With 10,000 or more residents

Rank	City	Population
1	Oklahoma City	472,221
2	Tulsa	381,393
3	Norman	93,019
4	Lawton	81,107
5	Broken Arrow	72,564
6	Edmond	64,962
7	Midwest City	54,037
8	Moore	45,318
9	Enid	45,234
10	Stillwater	38,765
11	Muskogee	38,386
12	Bartlesville	33,672
13	Shawnee	27,008
14	Ponca City	25,943
15	Del City	23,817
16	Ardmore	23,436
17	Yukon	22,897
18	Duncan	21,816
19	Altus	21,552
20	Bethany	20,269

Rank	City	Population
21	Claremore	20,085
22	Sapulpa	19,844
23	Sand Springs	17,255
24	McAlester	17,074
25	Chickasha	16,180
26	El Reno	15,786
27	Ada	15,313
28	Owasso	15,032
29	Okmulgee	13,981
30	Durant	13,187
31	Miami	12,760
32	Bixby	12,694
33	Mustang	12,409
34	Tahlequah	12,336
35	Woodward	12,034
36	Elk City	11,062
37	The Village	10,289
38	Guthrie	10,281

Population figures are estimated for mid-1998.
Source: U.S. Bureau of the Census.

Index to Tables

NA = Reliable data are not available.

DEMOGRAPHICS

Resident state and national populations, 1970-1997

Population figures given in thousands

	State pop.	U.S. pop.	Share	Rank
1970	2,559	203,302	1.3%	27
1980	3,025	226,546	1.3%	26
1985	3,271	237,924	1.4%	25
1990	3,146	248,765	1.3%	28
1995	3,271	262,761	1.2%	27
1997	3,317	267,636	1.2%	27

Source: U.S. Bureau of the Census.

Resident population by age, 1997

Age group	Total population
Under 5 years	226,000
5 to 17 years	652,000
18 to 24 years	332,000
25 to 34 years	437,000
35 to 44 years	510,000
45 to 54 years	416,000
55 to 64 years	300,000
65 to 74 years	240,000
75 to 84 years	150,000
85 years and over	55,000
Portion of residents 65 and older	13.4%
National average	12.7%

Population figures are rounded to nearest thousand persons;
figures include armed forces personnel stationed in state.
Source: U.S. Bureau of the Census.

Resident population by race, Hispanic origin, 1997

	State pop.	Share	U.S.
All residents	3,317,000	100.0%	100.0%
Hispanic white	102,000	3.1%	10.0%
non-Hispanic white	2,655,000	80.0%	72.7%
African American	257,000	7.7%	12.7%
Native American	260,000	7.8%	0.9%
Asian, Pacific Islander	43,000	1.3%	3.8%

Source: U.S. Bureau of the Census.

Projections of state population, 2000-2025

	Model A Uses interstate migration observed from 1975-1994	Model B Uses Bureau of Economic Analysis employment projections
Year	Population	Population
2000	3,373,000	3,370,000
2005	3,491,000	3,471,000
2010	3,639,000	3,578,000
2015	3,789,000	3,684,000
2020	3,930,000	3,784,000
2025	4,057,000	3,871,000

All population projections, including those for 2000, were calculated in 1997.
Source: U.S. Bureau of the Census, Population Paper Listings PPL-47.

VITAL STATISTICS

Average lifetime in years by race, 1989-1991

	State	U.S.	Rank
All residents	75.10	75.37	33
White residents	75.21	76.13	42
Black residents	70.85	69.16	6

Ranks are from longest-lived to least longest-lived. Ranks exclude Alaska, for which reliable data are not available. Rank for black residents is based on the 32 states for which reliable data are available.
Source: U.S. National Center for Health Statistics.

Infant mortality rates, 1980 and 1995

	State	U.S.
All residents		
1980	12.7	12.6
1995	8.3	7.6
White residents		
1980	12.1	11.0
1995	8.0	6.3
Black residents		
1980	21.8	21.4
1995	15.1	15.1

Figures represent deaths per 1,000 live births of resident infants under 1 year old, exclusive of fetal deaths; all-residents figures include other races not listed separately.
Source: U.S. National Center for Health Statistics.

Marriages and divorces

Marriages in 1996	26,700
Rate per 1,000 population, 1995	8.7
U.S. rate, 1995	8.9
Rank among all states	21
Divorces in 1996	19,300
Rate per 1,000 population, 1995	6.7
U.S. rate, 1995	4.4
Rank among all states	2

Rank is from highest to lowest in country.
Source: U.S. National Center for Health Statistics.

Death rates by leading causes, 1995
Deaths per 100,000 resident population

Cause	State	U.S.
Heart disease	340.4	280.7
Cancer	217.9	204.9
Cerebrovascular diseases	72.5	60.1
Accidents and adverse effects	44.9	35.5
Motor vehicle accidents	22.1	16.5
Chronic obstructive pulmonary diseases	48.1	39.2
Diabetes mellitus	19.5	22.6
HIV	7.1	NA
Suicide	15.3	11.9
Homicide	13.5	8.7
All causes	1,002.3	880.0
Rank in overall death rate among states		6

Figures exclude nonresidents who die in state. Causes of death follow International Classification of Diseases. Rank is from highest to lowest in country.
Source: U.S. National Center for Health Statistics.

ECONOMY

Gross state product, 1990-1996
In current dollars

	State product	Increase
1990	$56.9 billion	
1993	$64.0 billion	
1994	$66.0 billion	3.13%
1995	$68.6 billion	3.94%
1996	$72.8 billion	6.12%

Source: U.S. Bureau of Economic Analysis; Survey of Current Business, June, 1998.

Gross state product by industry, 1996
In billions

Farms, forestry, fisheries	$1.3
Construction	2.0
Manufacturing.	12.7
Transportation, public utilities.	6.9
Wholesale trade.	4.2
Retail trade	7.1
Finance, insurance, real estate	7.7
Services	11.0
Government	10.6
State total	$66.7
Total U.S.	$6,923.8
State share	0.96%
Rank among states.	30

Total figures include mining, not listed separately.
Source: U.S. Bureau of Economic Analysis; Survey of Current Business, June, 1998.

Personal income per capita, 1990 and 1997
In current dollars

	1990	1997
Per capita income	$15,633	$20,556
U.S. average	$19,188	$25,598
Rank among states	37	42

1997 data are preliminary.
Source: U.S. Bureau of Economic Analysis; Survey of Current Business, May, 1998.

Energy consumption, 1995
In trillions of British thermal units (BTU)

End-use sectors	
Residential	253.3
Commercial	183.6
Industrial	556.3
Transportation	366.3

Sources of energy	
Petroleum	446.2
Natural gas	579.5
Coal	343.5
Hydroelectric power.	28.0
Nuclear electric power	0

Total state per capita consumption	415.2
Total U.S. per capita consumption	344.4
Rank among states.	11
Total state energy consumption	1,359.6
Total U.S. energy consumption	90,547.4
State share of U.S. total	1.50%
Rank among states.	24

Total figures include items not listed separately.
Source: U.S. Energy Information Administration; State Energy Data Report.

Nonfarm employment by sectors, 1997

Total	1,387,000
Construction	51,000
Manufacturing.	180,000
Transportation, public utilities.	79,000
Wholesale trade, retail trade	324,000
Finance, insurance, real estate	69,000
Services	378,000
Government	275,000

Figures are rounded to nearest thousand persons. Total includes mining, not listed separately.
Source: U.S. Bureau of Labor Statistics; Employment and Earnings, monthly.

Foreign exports, 1990-1997
In millions of dollars

Year	State	U.S.	State share
1990	1,646	394,045	0.42%
1996	2,365	624,767	0.38%
1997	2,728	688,896	0.40%

Source: U.S. Bureau of the Census; U.S. Merchandise Trade, series FT 900.

LAND USE

Federally owned land, 1996

	State	U.S.	State share
Total acres	44,088,000	2,271,343,000	1.94%
Federally owned	678,000	563,129,000	0.12%
Federal share	1.5%	24.8%	—

Areas are rounded to nearest thousand acres. Figures for federally owned land do not include trust properties.

Source: U.S. General Services Administration; *Inventory Report on Real Property Owned by the United States Throughout the World,* annual.

Land use, 1992
In acres, rounded to nearest thousand

Total surface area	44,772,000
Federal land	1,202,000
Total nonfederal	42,395,000
Developed	1,875,000
Total rural	40,520,000
Cropland	10,081,000
Pasture land	7,720,000
Range land	14,061,000
Forest land	6,988,000
Minor cover/use	1,672,000

Total surface area figures include water area not shown separately.

Source: U.S. Dept. of Agriculture; Soil Conservation Service; Iowa State University, Statistical Laboratory; *Summary Report, 1992 National Resources Inventory.*

Farms and crop acreage, 1997

	State	U.S.	Share	Rank
Farms (thousands)	73	2,058	3.55%	10
Acres (millions)	34	968	3.51%	10
Acres per farm	466	471	—	16
Acres planted	10,935	334,139	3.27%	11
Acres harvested	9,295	319,894	2.91%	13
Farm value (mill.)	$1,310	$108,805	1.20%	26

Numbers of farms are rounded to nearest thousand.

Source: U.S. Dept. of Agriculture; National Agricultural Statistics Service.

GOVERNMENT AND FINANCE

Units of local government, 1997

	State	Total U.S.	Rank
All local governments	1,799	87,453	19
Counties	77	3,043	17
Municipalities	592	19,372	10
Townships	0	16,629	—
School districts	578	13,726	8
Special districts	552	34,683	21

County ranks are based on the 48 states with county governments; township ranks are based on the 20 states with township governments; school district ranks are based on the 46 states with such districts.

Source: U.S. Bureau of the Census; *1997 Census of Governments, Government Organization,* Series GC97(1).

State government revenue, 1996

Total revenue . . . . $10,609 mill.
General revenue . . . . 8,156 mill.
Per capita 2,475
U.S. per capita average 2,910
Rank among states 44

Intergovernmental revenue
Total . . . . $2,197 mill.
From federal government . . . . 2,119 mill.
From local government . . . . 78 mill.

Charges and Miscellaneous
Total . . . . $1,341 mill.
Current charges . . . . 934 mill.
Misc. general revenue . . . . 407 mill.

Taxes
Total . . . . $4,618 mill.
General sales . . . . 1,210 mill.
Selective sales . . . . 660 mill.
License taxes . . . . 658 mill.
Individual income . . . . 1,512 mill.
Corporate income . . . . 164 mill.
Other . . . . 413 mill.
Insurance trust revenue . . . . 2,207 mill.

Total revenue figures include items not listed separately.

Source: U.S. Bureau of the Census.

State government expenditures, 1996

General expenditures

Intergovernmental	$2,537 mill.
Direct expenditures	5,375 mill.
Total.	7,912 mill.

Selected direct expenditures

Education	$3,476 mill.
Public welfare.	1,658 mill.
Health, hospital	593 mill.
Highways	832 mill.
Police.	51 mill.
Corrections.	296 mill.
Natural resources.	133 mill.
Parks and recreation.	50 mill.
Government administration	326 mill.
Interest on debt	159 mill.

Other

State per capita expenditures	$2,401
U.S. per capita average	2,854
Rank among states.	46
Total state expenditures	9,265 mill.
Total U.S. expenditures	859,959 mill.

Totals include items not listed separately.
Source: U.S. Bureau of the Census.

POLITICS

Governors since statehood

D = Democrat; R = Republican; O = other;
(r) resigned; (d) died in office; (i) removed from office

Charles N. Haskell (D)	1907-1911
Lee Cruce (D)	1911-1915
Robert L. Williams (D)	1915-1919
James B. A. Robertson (D)	1919-1923
John C. Walton (D)	(i) 1923
Martin E. Trapp (D)	1923-1927
Henry S. Johnston (D)	(i) 1927-1929
William J. Holloway (D)	1929-1931
William H. Murray (D)	1931-1935
Ernest W. Marland (D)	1935-1939
Leon C. Phillips (D)	1939-1943
Robert S. Kerr (D)	1943-1947
Roy J. Turner (D).	1947-1951
Johnston Murray (D).	1951-1955
Raymond D. Gary (D)	1955-1959
James Howard Edmondson (D)	(r) 1959-1963
George P. Nigh (D).	1963
Henry L. Bellmon (R)	1963-1967
Dewey F. Bartlett (R)	1967-1971
David Hall (D)	1971-1975
David L. Boren (D)	1975-1979
George P. Nigh (D)	1979-1987
Henry Bellmon (R)	1987-1991
David Walters (D)	1991-1995
Frank Keating (R)	1995-

Composition of state legislature, 1990-1998

	Democrats	Republicans
State House (101 seats)		
1990	68	33
1992	70	31
1994	65	36
1996	65	36
1998	61	40
State Senate (48 seats)		
1990	37	11
1992	37	11
1994	35	13
1996	33	15
1998	33	15

Figures for total seats may include independents and minor
party members.
Source: Council of State Governments; *State Elective Officials
and the Legislatures.*

Composition of congressional delegations, 1989-1999

	Dem	Rep	Total
House of Representatives			
101st Congress, 1989			
State delegates	4	2	6
Total U.S.	259	174	433
102d Congress, 1991			
State delegates	4	2	6
Total U.S.	267	167	434
103d Congress, 1993			
State delegates	4	2	6
Total U.S.	258	176	434
104th Congress, 1995			
State delegates	0	6	6
Total U.S.	197	236	433
105th Congress, 1997			
State delegates	0	5	5
Total U.S.	206	228	434

	Dem	Rep	Total
106th Congress, 1999			
State delegates	0	6	6
Total U.S.	211	222	433

Senate			
101st Congress, 1989			
State delegates	1	1	2
Total U.S.	55	45	100
102d Congress, 1991			
State delegates	1	1	2
Total U.S.	56	44	100
103d Congress, 1993			
State delegates	1	1	2
Total U.S.	57	43	100
104th Congress, 1995			
State delegates	0	2	2
Total U.S.	46	53	99
105th Congress, 1997			
State delegates	0	2	2
Total U.S.	45	55	100
106th Congress, 1999			
State delegates	0	2	2
Total U.S.	45	54	99

Figures are for starts of first sessions. Figure for U.S. Representatives for 101st Congress does not include Alabama and Indiana, which had vacancies. Figures for total U.S. Representatives for 102d, 103d, and 106th Congresses do not include Vermont, which had 1 Independent-Socialist. Figure for U.S. Representatives for 104th Congress does not include Vermont, which had 1 Independent-Socialist, and California, which had 1 vacancy. Figure for U.S. Representatives for 105th Congress does not include New York, which had 1 vacancy. Figure for U.S. Senators for 104th Congress does not include Oregon, which had 1 vacancy. Figure for U.S. Senators for 106th Congress does not include New Hampshire, which had 1 Independent.
Source: U.S. Congress; *Congressional Directory*, biennial.

Voter participation in presidential elections, 1992 and 1996

	1992	1996
State voting age pop.	2,352,000	2,419,000
Total U.S. voting age pop.	189,524,000	196,509,000
State share of U.S. total	1.2%	1.2%
Rank among states	28	28
Percent of state casting vote	59.1	42.6
Percent of U.S. total voting	55.1	49.0
Rank among states	24	48

Source: U.S. Bureau of the Census.

HEALTH AND MEDICAL CARE

Medicare, 1997

	Recipients	Payments
State	495,000	$2,677 mill.
Total U.S.	37,514,000	$206,064 mill.
State share	1.32%	1.30%
Rank among states	27	26

Recipient figures are rounded to nearest thousand persons. Ranks are from highest to lowest.
Source: U.S. Health Care Financing Administration.

Medicaid, 1996

	Recipients	Payments
State	358,000	$1,021 mill.
Total U.S.	35,028,000	$121,419 mill.
State share	1.02%	0.84%
Rank among states	30	32

Recipient figures are rounded to nearest thousand persons. Payment figures for fiscal year reflect federal and state contribution payments. Ranks are from highest to lowest.
Source: U.S. Health Care Financing Administration.

Health insurance coverage, 1996

	State	U.S.
Total persons covered	2,784,000	225,070,000
Total persons not covered	570,000	41,716,000
Part not covered	17.0%	15.6%
Rank among states	11	—
Children not covered	195,000	10,554,000
Part not covered	20.6%	14.8%
Rank among states	6	—

Ranks are from most to fewest uninsured. Population figures are rounded to nearest thousand persons.
Source: U.S. Bureau of the Census.

AIDS, syphilis, tuberculosis, and measles cases, 1997

Cases	U.S.	State	Share
AIDS	58,443	283	0.48%
Syphilis	8,550	117	1.37%
Tuberculosis	18,534	194	1.05%
Measles	148,000	1,000	0.68%

Measles figures are rounded to nearest thousand cases.
Source: U.S. Centers for Disease Control and Prevention.

HOUSING

Homeownership rates, 1985-1997

	1985	1990	1997
State	70.5%	70.3%	68.5%
Total U.S.	63.9%	63.9%	65.7%
Rank among states	9	8	23

Source: U.S. Bureau of the Census.

Home sales, 1990 and 1997
In thousands of units

Existing home sales	1990	1997	Change
State sales	53.4	64.2	10.8
Total U.S. sales	3,560	4,730	1,170
State share of U.S. total	1.50%	1.36%	-0.14%
Rank among states	26	25	—

Source: National Association of Realtors; *Real Estate Outlook: Market Trends and Insights.*

EDUCATION

Public school enrollment, 1995

State K-8 enrollment	446,000
Total U.S. K-8 enrollment	32,341,000
State share of total U.S.	1.38%
State 9-12 enrollment	171,000
Total U.S. 9-12 enrollment	12,500,000
State share of U.S. total	1.37%
State public school enroll. rate	95.5%
Overall U.S. rate	91.6%
Rank among states	9

Enrollment figures (which include unclassified students) are rounded to nearest thousand pupils in fall term; kindergarten (K)-8 grade figures include some prekindergarten students. Enrollment rate is based on percentage of persons 5-17 years old. Rank is from highest to lowest.
Source: U.S. National Center for Education Statistics.

Public college finances, 1996

State FTE enrollment	111,400
Total U.S. FTE enrollment	8,268,800
State share of total U.S.	1.35%
Rank among states	27
State and local appropriations	$493,300,000
Total U.S. state and local appropriations	$39,699 mill.
State share of total U.S.	1.24%
Rank among states	25
State net tuition revenues	$213,300,000
Total U.S. net tuition	$18,348,100,000
State share of total U.S.	1.16%
Rank among states	30

FTE=Full-time equivalent; credit and noncredit enrollment including summer session in academic year ending in 1996.
Enrollments are rounded to nearest thousand students. Net tuition revenues exclude appropriation to students attending in-state public institutions. Rankings are from highest shares to lowest.
Source: Research Associates of Washington.

TRANSPORTATION AND TRAVEL

Highway mileage, 1996

Interstate	930
Other arterial	7,973
Collector roads	26,372
Local roads	78,371
Urban roads	13,034
Rural roads	99,630
Total state	112,664
U.S. total	3,933,985
State share	2.9%
Rank among states	12

Source: U.S. Federal Highway Administration.

Motor vehicle registrations and driver licenses, 1996
In thousands

Vehicle registrations	State	U.S.	Share	Rank
Autos, trucks, buses	3,082	206,365	1.49%	24
Autos only	1,675	128,439	1.30%	27
Motorcycles	59	3,832	1.54%	22
Driver licenses	2,396	179,539	1.33%	24

Figures do not include vehicles owned by military services.
Source: U.S. Federal Highway Administration; *Highway Statistics; Selected Highway Statistics and Charts.*

Domestic travel expenditures, 1995
Spending by U.S. residents on overnight trips and day trips of at least 100 miles

Total expenditures in state	$3,015 mill.
Total expenditures in U.S.	$360,314 mill.
State share of total U.S.	0.84%
Rank among states.	35

Source: Travel Industry Association of America.

CRIME AND LAW ENFORCEMENT

State and local police officers, 1996

Local police	4,951
State police	756
Sheriffs	1,014
Total	7,232
Officers per 10,000 residents	22
U.S. average	25
Rank among states.	28

Figures cover full-time sworn officers; totals include special police not shown separately.
Source: U.S. Bureau of Justice Statistics; *Census of State and Local Law Enforcement Agencies, 1996.*

Crime rates, 1996
Rates per 100,000 resident population

Violent crimes	State	U.S.
Total violent	597	634
Murder	6.8	7.4
Forcible rape	46.8	36.1
Robbery	107	202
Aggravated assault	437	388
Property crimes		
Total property	5,056	4,445
Burglary	1,256	943
Larceny/theft	3,317	2,976
Motor vehicle theft	483	526
Totals	5,653	5,079

Source: U.S. Federal Bureau of Investigation; *Crime in the United States*, annual.

State prison populations, 1980-1996

	State	U.S.	State share
1980	4,796	305,458	1.57%
1990	12,285	708,393	1.73%
1996	19,593	1,025,624	1.91%

Figures exclude prisoners in federal penitentiaries.
Source: U.S. Bureau of Justice Statistics.

Oregon

Location: Northwest coast of continental United States

Area and rank: 96,003 square miles (248,647 square kilometers); 98,386 square miles (254,820 square kilometers) including water; tenth largest state in area

Coastline: 296 miles (476 kilometers)

Shoreline: 1,410 miles (2,269 kilometers)

Population and rank: 3,243,487 (1997); twenty-ninth largest state in population

Capital: Salem

Largest city: Portland (503,891 people in 1998)

Became territory: August 14, 1848

Mall of the state capitol in Salem. (Oregon Tourism Commission)

Entered Union and rank: February 14, 1859; thirty-third state

Present constitution adopted: 1859

Counties: 36

State name: The derivation of "Oregon" is uncertain; the name was first used by Jonathan Carver in 1778 and taken from the writings of Major Robert Rogers, an English army officer.

State nickname: Beaver State

Motto: *Alis volat Propriis* (She flies with her own wings)

State flag: Navy blue field with, on one side, coat of arms and legends "State of Oregon" and "1859" below; gold beaver on other side

Highest point: Mount Hood — 11,239 feet (3,426 meters)

Lowest point: Pacific Ocean — sea level

Highest recorded temperature: 119 degrees Fahrenheit (48 degrees Celsius) — Pendleton, 1898

Lowest recorded temperature: –54 degrees Fahrenheit (–48 degrees Celsius) — Seneca, 1933

State song: "Oregon, My Oregon"

State tree: Douglas fir

State flower: Oregon grape

State bird: Western meadowlark

State fish: Chinook salmon

State animal: Beaver

National park: Crater Lake

Oregon History

Oregon's special character, like that of every state, was shaped by its geography and geographical position in the nation, combined with the formative events of its history. Oregon's character marries the independent spirit of the frontier West inherited from the nineteenth century with modern, urban America, the result of the economic development of the World War II era and the years of steady growth that followed. The cool, wet western portion of the state coexists with a semiarid eastern segment in whose economy irrigation has played a major role. Oregon's society and politics exhibit a unique blend of liberalism and conservatism, making it a fascinating laboratory of democracy.

Early History. Before the arrival of white settlers, the region of Oregon was inhabited by numerous Native Americans. These included the Clackma, the Multnomah, the Tillamook, and the Kalapuya in the northwest. Also present were the Bannock, Cayuse, Nez Perce, Paiute, and Umatilla, who lived east of the Cascade Mountains. Near today's California border were the Klamath and the Rogue peoples.

Exploration. Oregon was explored by a succession of European nations before Americans arrived. In the sixteenth century, Spanish adventurers first explored the region. Two centuries later English and more Spaniards searched for the Northwest Passage linking eastern North America to the Pacific, eliminating a voyage around South America. In 1774 Juan Pérez sailed the coast, and the following year Bruno Heceta was the first European to find the Columbia River.

Oregon's largest city, Portland, has access to the Pacific Ocean on the Columbia River. (PhotoDisc)

In 1778 the famed English navigator Captain James Cook, also searching for the Northwest Passage and the twenty-thousand-pound finders' reward, sailed up the coast to Yaqina Bay. In 1788 the first American ships arrived, including those of John Kendrick and Robert Gray. In 1792 Gray became the first white man to sail up the Columbia River, which he named after his ship. Soon afterward, William Brougham, a lieutenant of British Captain George Vancouver, who was exploring the region, sailed into the Columbia and continued well inland. At this time, too, Russian traders were pushing south from posts in Alaska, and British fur traders were exploring the West, since Oregon furs were seen as a promising component of the growing trade with China.

American Exploration and Settlement. Spain abandoned exploration of the area after 1795, leaving it to the British and Americans. In 1805, Meriwether Lewis and William Clark, leading the expedition sent by President Thomas Jefferson to explore the territory of the Louisiana Purchase, arrived at Fort Clatsop, where the Columbia River meets the Pacific Ocean.

A more permanent American presence first appeared in the form of fur trappers and traders, and only later in the form of agricultural settlers. The first American fur company was established in the region by John Jacob Astor, who brought his Pacific Fur Company to Oregon, basing it in Astoria in 1811. Two years later, during the War of 1812, he sold it to the North West Company, which in turn sold it to Hudson's Bay Company in 1821. By then, however, Great Britain and the United States had signed a treaty establishing joint occupation of the region by both countries.

Joint occupation brought both British and American influence. By the 1820's, Britain's Hudson's Bay Company was a dominant force in the region, guided by Dr. John McLoughlin at Fort Vancouver, on the Columbia River. Americans were also arriving: Mountain men such as Jedediah S. Smith rivaled the trappers of Hudson's Bay Company in the southeast of the region. In 1829 Hall J.

Kelley founded the American Society for the Settlement of Oregon Territory. One of his followers, Nathaniel J. Wyeth, attempted to establish a permanent post on the Columbia River.

Missionaries added their numbers to the fur trappers and traders, especially after Marcus Whitman arrived in the region in 1836. The missionaries awakened American interest in the region. Two years after Whitman, the first Roman Catholic missionaries, François N. Blanchet and Modeste Demers, arrived, and others followed.

The 1840's saw the advent of the "Great Migration" of Americans moving steadily westward in covered wagons across the Great Plains. In 1842 and 1843 enormous wagon trains braved American Indian attacks and hardship to cross the prairies and mountain chains of the Oregon Trail. Friction soon arose between Americans and British. It had not been so long, after all, since Britain had attempted to undo the results of the American Revolution in the War of 1812. American leaders such as Jesse Applegate advocated establishment of an American government in the area. Thus, in 1843 about one hundred settlers, missionaries, and retired fur traders met at Champoeg and created an Oregon provisional government, modeled on American lines, despite objections by the British-oriented among them.

Conflict with Native Americans and Statehood. The national spirit of the young American republic was now sufficiently stirred to demand removal of British authority in its entirely from the area. The 1844 election slogan "Fifty-four Forty or Fight" expressed American demands for ousting the British

Crater Lake, a natural lake in an extinct volcanic crater in southern Oregon, is one of North America's scenic wonders. (PhotoDisc)

Columbia River gorge, which separates Oregon from Washington to the north. (PhotoDisc)

up to that latitude. Fighting proved unnecessary, however, since in 1846 the two nations agreed on borders dividing the Oregon Country.

The next year, the slaughter by American Indians of Marcus Whitman and thirteen others near present-day Walla Walla, Washington, brought demands for protection. The massacre led to the Cayuse War of 1847-1848 and the execution in 1850 of five Indians found guilty of its perpetration. Demands for protection from Indians also led to the establishment of Oregon Territory. The territory embraced far more than the present state but was reduced in 1853 with the creation of a separate Washington Territory. Finally, in 1859 Oregon became the nation's thirty-third state.

The discovery of gold in Oregon's southwest led to fighting with the Rogue Indians, who resisted abuse at the hands of miners. Conflict with Indians often arose on account of settlers' abuse or Native American resistance to their forcible removal to reservations, as occurred with the Medoc tribe in the early 1870's.

Economic Development. The period from 1850 to 1880 was marked by Indians wars. Nevertheless, Oregon's economy was developing. The California gold rush brought thousands of people to nearby Oregon. Discovery of gold in Oregon had a similar effect.

In 1867-1868 a bumper wheat crop made it possible to ship grain to England, beginning a large wheat export industry in the state. The most important stimulus came later in the century, however, with the arrival of the transcontinental railroad. Under the direction of Henry Villard, the North Pacific Railroad was completed in the

1880's, bringing with it new trade and the onset of manufacturing. The lumber industry was already important to the state's economy, much of the timber being shipped overseas. Australian newspapers of the period invariably carried advertisements for Oregon lumber. With the arrival of the transcontinental railroad from the east, however, wood could be shipped throughout the United States, and for a time timber dominated the state's economy. The railroad was also extended to California, facilitating transport of Oregon goods to the growing state to the south.

Political Developments. After 1900, with the state's growing prosperity, Oregon's politics tended to conservatism. This conservatism, however, has long been punctuated with a pronounced streak of reformism and a taste for grass roots democracy. The latter is illustrated by a series of measures enacted early in the century, designed to ensure the influence of popular will over government. In 1902 the initiative and referendum were adopted. The former gave the right of citizens to propose laws to be voted upon in general elections. The referendum secured the electorate's right to reject certain laws passed by the state legislature. In 1904 direct primary elections were instituted. These empowered the electorate at the expense of political party organizations, since candidates for office at general elections were to be chosen directly by the electorate at "primary" elections. In 1908 the state adopted the "recall" election, whereby office holders can be voted from office in special elections. Finally, in 1912, woman suffrage was adopted, after a long and difficult struggle led by Abigail Jane Scott Duniway.

Depression and War. Oregon's twentieth century economic and social life saw continued emigration from the East. Electric power and irrigation projects propelled agriculture and manufacturing to the fore. The Great Depression of the 1930's dramatically increased the role of the federal government in economic affairs. Federal law allowed the lumber industry to set production quotas and prices. Farmers were paid to lower crop production. The federal government also completed the Bonneville Dam on the Columbia River in 1937, bringing important economic benefits as well as flood control to the region.

After the economic hardships of the 1930's, World War II saw a tremendous lift to the state's manufacturing industries. The war brought the state an aluminum industry and revitalized Portland's shipbuilding industry. The city also became an important port for shipping war material to U.S. forces and the Soviet Union. Thousands of workers migrated from the East to work in wartime industries, and many stayed after the war. The federal government built and operated an entire city called Vanport in the Portland-Vancouver, Washington, area to house the huge influx of wartime workers. The city was not well situated, however, and was washed away in the great Columbia River floods of 1948.

Postwar Developments. Growing prosperity punctuated by a thriving tourist industry marked the postwar era. Visitors flocked to see the state's scenic wonders, including Crater Lake National Park. Cheap hydroelectric power became more plentiful from a series of federally funded dams, such as The Dalles and McNary on the Columbia River. By 1956 natural gas became available, adding to the energy supply. Mechanization and diversification of products aided the state's farms and agricultural industries. In the 1960's, forest products also became more diversified, as new uses were found for previously discarded refuse.

The postwar state's population also became predominantly urban. In 1880 only 15 percent lived in towns. In 1910, the figure was 44 percent, but by 1993, 62 percent of the population lived in incorporated cities and towns. These demographic changes were reflected in the state's politics. The state's early history was marked by domination of the Republican Party. With the urbanization of the 1950's and 1960's and the influx of migrants from other parts of the country, the pattern was reversed and a majority of voters were Democrats. From the 1970's to the end of the 1990's reformist politics was prominent. Oregonians, however, showed themselves independent minded, repeatedly electing Independent Wayne Morse, an outspoken critic of the Vietnam War, to the U.S. Senate. Indicative of this spirit was Oregon's passage of the nation's first "bottle law," requiring deposits on disposable bottles and cans. The state's century-long tradition of conservation continued, and in 1998, the nation's first "right to die" law, which passed as an initiative in 1994, went into effect.

Charles F. Bahmueller

Oregon Time Line

1542	Spanish explorers sail near Oregon coast.
1579	English explorer Sir Francis Drake may have landed on Oregon coast.
1774	Spanish explorer Juan Pérez, seeking Northwest Passage, arrives in Oregon; other Spaniards follow.
Mar. 7, 1778	Captain James Cook explores Oregon coast.
1788	First American ships arrive off Oregon coast.
May 11, 1792	Captain Robert Gray sails into the Columbia River.
1795	George Vancouver, a British officer, explores much of the region.
1805-1806	Expedition of Meriwether Lewis and William Clark reaches mouth of Columbia via land, establishing strong American claim to the land.
Apr. 12, 1811	John Jacob Astor establishes fur trading post at Astoria, the first white settlement in Oregon.
1811	Great Britain-United States treaty allows citizens of both countries to trade and live in the region.
1824-1825	Russia cedes claims south of fifty-four degrees, forty minutes.
1829	Hall J. Kelley founds American Society for the Settlement of Oregon Territory.
1834	Methodist missionaries establish first American settlement in Willamette Valley.
1843	Nine hundred settlers arrive in Oregon; they create provisional government to prevent British occupation.
May 2, 1843	Willamette Valley settlers organize provisional government based on the laws of Iowa.
1843	Acts passed to prohibit slavery and to exclude blacks and mulattoes from Oregon.
1846	Forty-ninth parallel is established as principal border between British and American territories in the Pacific Northwest.
1847	Massacre by Cayuse Indians of fourteen American settlers leads to war.
Aug. 14, 1848	Oregon Territory created.
1847	Congress passes Oregon Donation Land Law; ensuing increase in settler migration sparks Indian-white hostilities.
1850-1855	Indian agents sign more than twenty treaties with Oregon Indians, but none are ratified in the Senate.
1850's	Discovery of gold leads to conflict with American Indians.
1856	Rogue River Indian War begins with Indian resistance to abuse by miners, ends with removal of Indians to distant reservations.
Feb. 14, 1859	Oregon becomes thirty-third state.
1860's	Cattle become significant part of state's economy.
1861-1862	Gold strikes worth tens of millions of dollars achieved; state economy vitalized.
1870's	Indian wars break out; Modoc Indians, dissatisfied with forced removal and mistreatment on Klamath Reserve, are defeated and sent permanently to Oklahoma.
1877	Nez Perce War; defeated tribal members sent to Oklahoma; most eventually return to the Northwest.

(continued)

1890	Population reaches 300,000, rising from about 52,000 in 1860.
1902	Crater Lake National Park is established.
1912	Woman suffrage is adopted.
1937	Completion of Bonneville Dam.
1940	Population exceeds one million.
1942-1945	World War II raises prosperity of state; Portland is major transshipment point for war material.
May 30, 1948	City of Vanport is swept away in massive flood.
1950's	McNary and The Dalles Dams make available cheap, plentiful electric power.
1950's	Oregon industry prospers; marked increase in urbanization.
1960's	Oregon's timber industry transformed by new uses for forestry products and large replantation projects.
1964	Heavy floods ravage western part of the state.
1973	Establishment of Land Conservation and Development Commission.
1982	Completion of second powerhouse at Bonneville Dam more than doubles its electric power production.
1994	Passage of nation's first assisted suicide law.
1998	Assisted suicide law becomes effective.

Notes for Further Study

Published Sources. A detailed discussion of state and local government in Oregon is Richard Sanders's *Government in Oregon* (1991). Place names are examined in *Oregon Geographic Names* (1992), a work originating in 1928, comprising more than 5,400 entries. *The Oregon Atlas and Gazetteer* (1998), published by the Delorme Mapping Company, is one of a series of imaginative atlases and encompasses information about the state's parks, forests, wilderness areas, campgrounds, cycling routes, hiking, fishing, and the like.

Comprehensive histories are Gordon B. Dobbs's *Oregon: A Bicentennial History* (1977) and Herman Leonard's *History of the Oregon Territory from Its First Discovery up to the Present Time* (1980). The story of the state's first American settlers is told in *Blazing a Wagon Trail to Oregon: A Weekly Chronicle of the Great Migration of 1843* (1993), by Lloyd W. Coffman. For a history of Oregon's indigenous peoples, see Jeff Zucker, et al., *Oregon Indians* (1983) and Bert Webber's *Indians Along the Oregon Trail: The Tribes of Nebraska, Wyoming, Idaho, Oregon, and Washington Identified* (1992). The relationship between the state's history and its geography is treated in *Making Oregon: A Study in Histor-*

ical Geography (1981) by Samuel Dicken. Finally, for Oregon's wildlife, see Blair A. Csuti, et al., eds., *Atlas of Oregon's Wildlife: Distribution, Habitat, and Natural History* (1997).

Web Resources. A starting place on the Web for those seeking information on the state's politics and government is the Active Access site dealing with state and local government (http://activeaccess.com/links/oregon.html; see also http://www.lawresearch.com/csor.htm). This site contains links to each branch of state government, and includes individual agencies, government documents, and general information. It also has links to county and city government, as well as to Oregon law sites. An engagingly written account of the state's history is Oregon History Narrative (http://www.teleport.com/~garski/oregon_history2.htm). Numerous links to information about historical topics are at Oregon Historical Links (http://www.usgennet.org/~alhnorus/links history.html). A number of sites are dedicated to Oregon's Native Americans. A good one is an account of Eastern Oregon Indians (http://www.halcyon.com/rdpayne/jdfbnm-lee.html). An informative site on the state's coastal regions, including an events calendar, maps, whale watching, lodging, and other intelligence, is Oregon Coast (http://www.oregoncoast.com). Those researching higher education in the state might start with the Oregon State University system's home page (http:///www.uoregon.edu). Those wishing to examine the state's controversial Death with Dignity program can access it at http://www.dwd.org. The Oregon Directory (http://www.touroregon.com) serves both Oregonians and tourists, with business listings and tourist information.

Counties

County	Sq. miles	1996 pop.	County	Sq. miles	1996 pop.
Baker	3,068.3	16,410	Douglas	5,036.8	101,076
Benton	676.5	75,926	Gilliam	1,204.1	1,948
Clackamas	1,868.3	324,043	Grant	4,528.8	7,973
Clatsop	827.3	35,132	Harney	10,134.9	7,075
Columbia	656.8	42,969	Hood River	522.4	19,338
Coos	1,600.5	63,036	Jackson	2,785.4	168,609
Crook	2,979.5	16,615	Jefferson	1,780.9	16,360
Curry	1,627.4	21,038	Josephine	1,639.5	72,182
Deschutes	3,018.3	98,524	Klamath	5,944.6	62,502

(continued)

County	Sq. miles	1996 pop.
Lake	8,136.3	7,303
Lane	4,554.2	306,862
Lincoln	979.7	45,041
Linn	2,291.4	102,217
Malheur	9,887.7	28,425
Marion	1,185.0	260,919
Morrow	2,032.8	9,229
Multnomah	435.3	624,903
Polk	741.1	58,501
Sherman	823.3	1,825

County	Sq. miles	1996 pop.
Tillamook	1,102.2	24,098
Umatilla	3,215.3	64,547
Union	2,036.7	25,012
Wallowa	3,145.4	7,495
Wasco	2,381.2	23,093
Washington	723.8	383,603
Wheeler	1,715.0	1,658
Yamhill	715.6	78,248

Source: U.S. Bureau of the Census; National Association of Counties.

Cities
With 10,000 or more residents

Rank	City	Population
1	Portland	503,891
2	Eugene	128,240
3	Salem	126,702

Rank	City	Population
4	Gresham	85,021
5	Beaverton	62,111
6	Hillsboro	61,111

Rank	City	Population
7	Medford	57,156
8	Springfield	50,682
9	Corvallis	50,202
10	Albany	38,832
11	Tigard	36,920
12	Lake Oswego	34,704
13	Bend	34,321
14	Keizer	28,967
15	McMinnville	24,086
16	Grants Pass	21,366
17	West Linn	21,202
18	Oregon City	20,940
19	Tualatin	19,978
20	Milwaukie	19,895
21	Roseburg	19,289
22	Klamath Falls	18,538
23	Ashland	18,095
24	Newberg	16,962
25	Pendleton	16,060

Rank	City	Population
26	Coos Bay	15,259
27	Forest Grove	15,200
28	Woodburn	14,981
29	Troutdale	13,576
30	Wilsonville	13,124
31	Lebanon	12,471
32	Dallas	12,331
33	Canby	12,084
34	La Grande	12,060
35	Gladstone	11,762
36	Redmond	11,728
37	Hermiston	11,514
38	City of the Dalles	11,211
39	Ontario	10,848
40	Central Point	10,583

Population figures are estimated for mid-1998.
Source: U.S. Bureau of the Census.

Index to Tables

NA = Reliable data are not available.

DEMOGRAPHICS

Resident state and national populations, 1970-1997

Population figures given in thousands

	State pop.	U.S. pop.	Share	Rank
1970	2,092	203,302	1.0%	31
1980	2,633	226,546	1.2%	30
1985	2,673	237,924	1.1%	30
1990	2,842	248,765	1.1%	29
1995	3,143	262,761	1.2%	29
1997	3,243	267,636	1.2%	29

Source: U.S. Bureau of the Census.

Resident population by age, 1997

Age group	Total population
Under 5 years	213,000
5 to 17 years	598,000
18 to 24 years	296,000
25 to 34 years	434,000
35 to 44 years	542,000
45 to 54 years	457,000
55 to 64 years	274,000
65 to 74 years	224,000
75 to 84 years	155,000
85 years and over	51,000
Portion of residents 65 and older	13.3%
National average	12.7%

Population figures are rounded to nearest thousand persons;
figures include armed forces personnel stationed in state.
Source: U.S. Bureau of the Census.

Resident population by race, Hispanic origin, 1997

	State pop.	Share	U.S.
All residents	3,243,000	100.0%	100.0%
Hispanic white	174,000	5.4%	10.0%
non-Hispanic white	2,866,000	88.4%	72.7%
African American	58,000	1.8%	12.7%
Native American	44,000	1.4%	0.9%
Asian, Pacific Islander	101,000	3.1%	3.8%

Source: U.S. Bureau of the Census.

Projections of state population, 2000-2025

	Model A Uses interstate migration observed from 1975-1994	Model B Uses Bureau of Economic Analysis employment projections
Year	Population	Population
2000	3,397,000	3,397,000
2005	3,613,000	3,625,000
2010	3,803,000	3,837,000
2015	3,992,000	4,036,000
2020	4,177,000	4,213,000
2025	4,349,000	4,361,000

All population projections, including those for 2000, were calculated in 1997.
Source: U.S. Bureau of the Census, Population Paper Listings PPL-47.

VITAL STATISTICS

Average lifetime in years by race, 1989-1991

	State	U.S.	Rank
All residents	76.44	75.37	18
White residents	76.51	76.13	19
Black residents	NA	69.16	NA

Ranks are from longest-lived to least longest-lived. Ranks exclude Alaska, for which reliable data are not available. Rank for black residents is based on the 32 states for which reliable data are available.
Source: U.S. National Center for Health Statistics.

Infant mortality rates, 1980 and 1995

	State	U.S.
All residents		
1980	12.2	12.6
1995	6.1	7.6
White residents		
1980	12.2	11.0
1995	5.9	6.3
Black residents		
1980	15.9	21.4
1995	NA	15.1

Figures represent deaths per 1,000 live births of resident infants under 1 year old, exclusive of fetal deaths; all-residents figures include other races not listed separately.
Source: U.S. National Center for Health Statistics.

Marriages and divorces

Marriages in 1996	25,600
Rate per 1,000 population, 1995	8.2
U.S. rate, 1995	8.9
Rank among all states	30
Divorces in 1996	15,000
Rate per 1,000 population, 1995	4.8
U.S. rate, 1995	4.4
Rank among all states	20

Rank is from highest to lowest in country.
Source: U.S. National Center for Health Statistics.

Death rates by leading causes, 1995
Deaths per 100,000 resident population

Cause	State	U.S.
Heart disease	240.1	280.7
Cancer	214.7	204.9
Cerebrovascular diseases	77.7	60.1
Accidents and adverse effects	43.5	35.5
Motor vehicle accidents	18.9	16.5
Chronic obstructive pulmonary diseases	45.4	39.2
Diabetes mellitus	21.7	22.6
HIV	9.2	NA
Suicide	15.8	11.9
Homicide	4.7	8.7
All causes	898.4	880.0
Rank in overall death rate among states		28

Figures exclude nonresidents who die in state. Causes of death follow International Classification of Diseases. Rank is from highest to lowest in country.
Source: U.S. National Center for Health Statistics.

ECONOMY

Gross state product, 1990-1996
In current dollars

	State product	Increase
1990	$57.0 billion	
1993	$68.9 billion	
1994	$74.7 billion	8.42%
1995	$80.8 billion	8.17%
1996	$87.0 billion	7.67%

Source: U.S. Bureau of Economic Analysis; Survey of Current Business, June, 1998.

Gross state product by industry, 1996
In billions

Farms, forestry, fisheries	$2.3
Construction	4.1
Manufacturing	17.4
Transportation, public utilities	6.3
Wholesale trade	6.6
Retail trade	7.4
Finance, insurance, real estate	12.1
Services	13.9
Government	9.3
State total	$79.4
Total U.S.	$6,923.8
State share	1.15%
Rank among states	28

Total figures include mining, not listed separately.
Source: U.S. Bureau of Economic Analysis; Survey of Current Business, June, 1998.

Personal income per capita, 1990 and 1997
In current dollars

	1990	1997
Per capita income	$17,452	$24,393
U.S. average	$19,188	$25,598
Rank among states	27	23

1997 data are preliminary.
Source: U.S. Bureau of Economic Analysis; Survey of Current Business, May, 1998.

Energy consumption, 1995
In trillions of British thermal units (BTU)

End-use sectors

Residential	220.1
Commercial	171.8
Industrial	365.0
Transportation	297.3

Sources of energy

Petroleum	361.2
Natural gas	151.7
Coal	20.2
Hydroelectric power	431.1
Nuclear electric power	0
Total state per capita consumption	332.9
Total U.S. per capita consumption	344.4
Rank among states	29
Total state energy consumption	1,048.2
Total U.S. energy consumption	90,547.4
State share of U.S. total	1.16%
Rank among states	30

Total figures include items not listed separately.
Source: U.S. Energy Information Administration; State Energy Data Report.

Nonfarm employment by sectors, 1997

Total	1,525,000
Construction	82,000
Manufacturing	244,000
Transportation, public utilities	74,000
Wholesale trade, retail trade	378,000
Finance, insurance, real estate	95,000
Services	401,000
Government	250,000

Figures are rounded to nearest thousand persons. Total includes mining, not listed separately.
Source: U.S. Bureau of Labor Statistics; Employment and Earnings, monthly.

Foreign exports, 1990-1997
In millions of dollars

Year	State	U.S.	State share
1990	4,065	394,045	1.03%
1996	8,948	624,767	1.43%
1997	9,151	688,896	1.33%

Source: U.S. Bureau of the Census; U.S. Merchandise Trade, series FT 900.

LAND USE

Federally owned land, 1996

	State	U.S.	State share
Total acres	61,599,000	2,271,343,000	2.71%
Federally owned	31,809,000	563,129,000	5.65%
Federal share	51.6%	24.8%	—

Areas are rounded to nearest thousand acres. Figures for federally owned land do not include trust properties.
Source: U.S. General Services Administration; *Inventory Report on Real Property Owned by the United States Throughout the World*, annual.

Land use, 1992
In acres, rounded to nearest thousand

Total surface area	62,127,000
Federal land	32,291,000
Total nonfederal	29,155,000
Developed	1,125,000
Total rural	28,030,000
Cropland.	3,776,000
Pasture land	1,900,000
Range land.	9,375,000
Forest land	11,839,000
Minor cover/use.	1,142,000

Total surface area figures include water area not shown separately.
Source: U.S. Dept. of Agriculture; Soil Conservation Service; Iowa State University, Statistical Laboratory; *Summary Report, 1992 National Resources Inventory.*

Farms and crop acreage, 1997

	State	U.S.	Share	Rank
Farms (thousands)	38	2,058	1.85%	24
Acres (millions)	18	968	1.86%	17
Acres per farm	467	471	—	15
Acres planted	2,390	334,139	0.72%	30
Acres harvested	2,293	319,894	0.72%	30
Farm value (mill.)	$1,423	$108,805	1.31%	25

Numbers of farms are rounded to nearest thousand.
Source: U.S. Dept. of Agriculture; National Agricultural Statistics Service.

GOVERNMENT AND FINANCE

Units of local government, 1997

	State	Total U.S.	Rank
All local governments	1,493	87,453	21
Counties	36	3,043	34
Municipalities	240	19,372	31
Townships	0	16,629	—
School districts	258	13,726	21
Special districts	959	34,683	12

County ranks are based on the 48 states with county governments; township ranks are based on the 20 states with township governments; school district ranks are based on the 46 states with such districts.
Source: U.S. Bureau of the Census; *1997 Census of Governments, Government Organization*, Series GC97(1).

State government revenue, 1996

Total revenue	$15,432 mill.
General revenue	9,958 mill.
Per capita.	3,115
U.S. per capita average	2,910
Rank among states.	19
Intergovernmental revenue	
Total	$3,334 mill.
From federal government	3,267 mill.
From local government	67 mill.
Charges and Miscellaneous	
Total	$2,208 mill.
Current charges	1,141 mill.
Misc. general revenue	1,067 mill.
Taxes	
Total	$4,416 mill.
General sales	NA
Selective sales.	591 mill.
License taxes	581 mill.
Individual income	2,823 mill.
Corporate income	300 mill.
Other	120 mill.
Insurance trust revenue	5,290 mill.

Total revenue figures include items not listed separately.
Source: U.S. Bureau of the Census.

State government expenditures, 1996

General expenditures
Intergovernmental . . . . $3,110 mill.
Direct expenditures . . . . 6,523 mill.
Total. . . . . 9,633 mill.

Selected direct expenditures
Education . . . . $3,473 mill.
Public welfare. . . . . 2,116 mill.
Health, hospital . . . . 809 mill.
Highways . . . . 933 mill.
Police . . . . 120 mill.
Corrections. . . . . 291 mill.
Natural resources. . . . . 239 mill.
Parks and recreation. . . . . 32 mill.
Government administration . . . . 613 mill.
Interest on debt . . . . 343 mill.

Other
State per capita expenditures $3,014
U.S. per capita average 2,854
Rank among states. 19
Total state expenditures . . . . 11,858 mill.
Total U.S. expenditures . . . . 859,959 mill.

Totals include items not listed separately.
Source: U.S. Bureau of the Census.

POLITICS

Governors since statehood

D = Democrat; R = Republican; O = other;
(r) resigned; (d) died in office; (i) removed from office

John Whiteaker (D) 1859-1862
Addison C. Gibbs (O) 1862-1866
George L. Woods (R) 1866-1870
LaFayette Grover (D) . . . . (r) 1870-1877
Stephen F. Chadwick (D). 1877-1878
William W. Thayer (D) 1878-1882
Zenas F. Moody (R). 1882-1887
Sylvester Pennoyer (D) 1887-1895
William P. Lord (R). 1895-1899
Theodore T. Geer (R) 1899-1903
George E. Chamberlain (R) . . . . (r) 1903-1909

Frank W. Benson (R) . . . . (r) 1909-1910
Jay Bowerman (R) 1910-1911
Oswald West (D) 1911-1915
James Withycombe (R). . . . . (d) 1915-1919
Benjamin W. Olcott (R) 1919-1923
Walter M. Pierce (D) 1923-1927
Isaac L. Patterson (R) . . . . (d) 1927-1929
Albin W. Norblad (R). 1929-1931
Julius L. Meier (O) 1931-1935
Charles H. Martin (D) 1935-1939
Charles A. Sprague (R) 1939-1943
Earl W. Snell (R) . . . . (d) 1943-1947
John H. Hall (R) 1947-1949
Douglas McKay (R) . . . . (r) 1949-1952
Paul L. Patterson (R). . . . . (d) 1952-1956
Elmo Smith (R). 1956-1957
Robert D. Holmes (D) 1957-1959
Mark O. Hatfield (R) 1959-1967
Tom L. McCall (R) 1967-1975
Robert W. Straub (D). 1975-1979
Victor Atiyeh (R) 1979-1987
Neil Goldschmidt (D) 1987-1991
Barbara Roberts (D) 1991-1995
John A. Kitzhaber (D) 1995-

Composition of state legislature, 1990-1998

	Democrats	Republicans
State House (60 seats)		
1990	28	32
1992	28	32
1994	26	34
1996	29	31
1998	25	34
State Senate (30 seats)		
1990	20	10
1992	16	14
1994	11	19
1996	10	20
1998	13	17

Figures for total seats may include independents and minor
party members.
Source: Council of State Governments; *State Elective Officials
and the Legislatures.*

Composition of congressional delegations, 1989-1999

	Dem	Rep	Total
House of Representatives			
101st Congress, 1989			
State delegates	3	2	5
Total U.S.	259	174	433
102d Congress, 1991			
State delegates	4	1	5
Total U.S.	267	167	434
103d Congress, 1993			
State delegates	4	1	5
Total U.S.	258	176	434
104th Congress, 1995			
State delegates	4	1	5
Total U.S.	197	236	433
105th Congress, 1997			
State delegates	4	1	5
Total U.S.	206	228	434
106th Congress, 1999			
State delegates	4	1	5
Total U.S.	211	222	433
Senate			
101st Congress, 1989			
State delegates	0	2	2
Total U.S.	55	45	100
102d Congress, 1991			
State delegates	0	2	2
Total U.S.	56	44	100
103d Congress, 1993			
State delegates	0	2	2
Total U.S.	57	43	100
104th Congress, 1995			
State delegates	1	1	2
Total U.S.	46	53	99
105th Congress, 1997			
State delegates	1	1	2
Total U.S.	45	55	100
106th Congress, 1999			
State delegates	1	1	2
Total U.S.	45	54	99

Figures are for starts of first sessions. Figure for U.S. Representatives for 101st Congress does not include Alabama and Indiana, which had vacancies. Figures for total U.S. Representatives for 102d, 103d, and 106th Congresses do not include Vermont, which had 1 Independent-Socialist. Figure for U.S. Representatives for 104th Congress does not include Vermont, which had 1 Independent-Socialist, and California, which had 1 vacancy. Figure for U.S. Representatives for 105th Congress does not include New York, which had 1 vacancy. Figure for U.S. Senators for 104th Congress does not include Oregon, which had 1 vacancy. Figure for U.S. Senators for 106th Congress does not include New Hampshire, which had 1 Independent.

Source: U.S. Congress; *Congressional Directory,* biennial.

Voter participation in presidential elections, 1992 and 1996

	1992	1996
State voting age pop.	2,220,000	2,396,000
Total U.S. voting age pop.	189,524,000	196,509,000
State share of U.S. total	1.2%	1.2%
Rank among states	29	29
Percent of state casting vote	65.9	48.0
Percent of U.S. total voting	55.1	49.0
Rank among states	8	31

Source: U.S. Bureau of the Census.

HEALTH AND MEDICAL CARE

Medicare, 1997

	Recipients	Payments
State	475,000	$1,887 mill.
Total U.S.	37,514,000	$206,064 mill.
State share	1.27%	0.92%
Rank among states	29	31

Recipient figures are rounded to nearest thousand persons. Ranks are from highest to lowest.

Source: U.S. Health Care Financing Administration.

Medicaid, 1996

	Recipients	Payments
State	450,000	$1,313 mill.
Total U.S.	35,028,000	$121,419 mill.
State share	1.28%	1.08%
Rank among states	25	27

Recipient figures are rounded to nearest thousand persons. Payment figures for fiscal year reflect federal and state contribution payments. Ranks are from highest to lowest.

Source: U.S. Health Care Financing Administration.

Health insurance coverage, 1996

	State	U.S.
Total persons covered	2,743,000	225,070,000
Total persons not covered	496,000	41,716,000
Part not covered	15.3%	15.6%
Rank among states	19	—
Children not covered	138,000	10,554,000
Part not covered	17.0%	14.8%
Rank among states	17	—

Ranks are from most to fewest uninsured. Population figures
are rounded to nearest thousand persons.
Source: U.S. Bureau of the Census.

AIDS, syphilis, tuberculosis, and measles cases, 1997

Cases	U.S.	State	Share
AIDS	58,443	305	0.52%
Syphilis	8,550	10	0.12%
Tuberculosis	18,534	157	0.85%
Measles	148,000	NA	NA

Measles figures are rounded to nearest thousand cases.
Source: U.S. Centers for Disease Control and Prevention.

HOUSING

Homeownership rates, 1985-1997

	1985	1990	1997
State	61.5%	64.4%	61.0%
Total U.S.	63.9%	63.9%	65.7%
Rank among states	41	37	46

Source: U.S. Bureau of the Census.

Home sales, 1990 and 1997

In thousands of units

Existing home sales	1990	1997	Change
State sales	56.6	60.1	3.5
Total U.S. sales	3,560	4,730	1,170
State share of U.S. total	1.59%	1.27%	-0.32%
Rank among states	24	27	—

Source: National Association of Realtors; *Real Estate Outlook:
Market Trends and Insights.*

EDUCATION

Public school enrollment, 1995

State K-8 enrollment 376,000
Total U.S. K-8 enrollment 32,341,000
State share of total U.S. 1.16%
State 9-12 enrollment 152,000
Total U.S. 9-12 enrollment 12,500,000
State share of U.S. total 1.22%
State public school enroll. rate 90.1%
Overall U.S. rate. 91.6%
Rank among states. 35

Enrollment figures (which include unclassified students) are
rounded to nearest thousand pupils in fall term;
kindergarten (K)-8 grade figures include some
prekindergarten students. Enrollment rate is based on
percentage of persons 5-17 years old. Rank is from highest
to lowest.
Source: U.S. National Center for Education Statistics.

Public college finances, 1996

State FTE enrollment. 93,500
Total U.S. FTE enrollment 8,268,800
State share of total U.S. 1.13%
Rank among states. 31
State and local appropriations $388,700,000
Total U.S. state and local
   appropriations. . . . . $39,699 mill.
State share of total U.S. 0.98%
Rank among states. 33
State net tuition revenues. $267,700,000
Total U.S. net tuition $18,348,100,000
State share of total U.S. 1.46%
Rank among states. 27

FTE=Full-time equivalent; credit and noncredit enrollment
including summer session in academic year ending in
1996.
Enrollments are rounded to nearest thousand students. Net
tuition revenues exclude appropriation to students
attending in-state public institutions. Rankings are from
highest shares to lowest.
Source: Research Associates of Washington.

TRANSPORTATION AND TRAVEL

Highway mileage, 1996

Interstate	728
Other arterial	6,539
Collector roads	18,970
Local roads	58,139
Urban roads	10,151
Rural roads	73,039
Total state	83,190
U.S. total	3,933,985
State share	2.1%
Rank among states	24

Source: U.S. Federal Highway Administration.

Motor vehicle registrations and driver licenses, 1996
In thousands

Vehicle registrations	State	U.S.	Share	Rank
Autos, trucks, buses	2,851	206,365	1.38%	27
Autos only	1,503	128,439	1.17%	30
Motorcycles	60	3,832	1.57%	21
Driver licenses	2,613	179,539	1.46%	27

Figures do not include vehicles owned by military services.
Source: U.S. Federal Highway Administration; *Highway Statistics; Selected Highway Statistics and Charts.*

Domestic travel expenditures, 1995
Spending by U.S. residents on overnight trips and day trips of at least 100 miles

Total expenditures in state	$4,263 mill.
Total expenditures in U.S.	$360,314 mill.
State share of total U.S.	1.18%
Rank among states	27

Source: Travel Industry Association of America.

CRIME AND LAW ENFORCEMENT

State and local police officers, 1996

Local police	3,245
State police	824
Sheriffs	1,921
Total	6,064
Officers per 10,000 residents	19
U.S. average	25
Rank among states	39

Figures cover full-time sworn officers; totals include special police not shown separately.
Source: U.S. Bureau of Justice Statistics; *Census of State and Local Law Enforcement Agencies, 1996.*

Crime rates, 1996
Rates per 100,000 resident population

Violent crimes	State	U.S.
Total violent	463	634
Murder	4.0	7.4
Forcible rape	39.7	36.1
Robbery	122	202
Aggravated assault	297	388
Property crimes		
Total property	5,534	4,445
Burglary	988	943
Larceny/theft	4,014	2,976
Motor vehicle theft	531	526
Totals	5,997	5,079

Source: U.S. Federal Bureau of Investigation; *Crime in the United States,* annual.

State prison populations, 1980-1996

	State	U.S.	State share
1980	3,177	305,458	1.04%
1990	6,492	708,393	0.92%
1996	8,661	1,025,624	0.84%

Figures exclude prisoners in federal penitentiaries.
Source: U.S. Bureau of Justice Statistics.

Pennsylvania

Location: Northeastern continental United States

Area and rank: 44,820 square miles (116,083 square kilometers); 46,058 square miles (119,290 square kilometers) including water; thirty-second largest state in area

Coastline: 0 miles (0 kilometers)

Shoreline: 89 miles (143 kilometers)

Population and rank: 12,019,661 (1997); fifth largest state in population

Capital: Harrisburg

With a population of nearly 1.5 million people, Philadelphia is more than four times larger than Pennsylvania's next largest city, Pittsburgh. (PhotoDisc)

Largest city: Philadelphia (1,436,287 people in 1998)

Entered Union and rank: December 12, 1787; second state

Present constitution adopted: 1968

Counties: 67

State name: Meaning "Penn's Woodland," Pennsylvania was named for Admiral Sir William Penn, the father of William Penn, who founded the state's first English colony

State nickname: Keystone State

Motto: Virtue, liberty, and independence

State flag: Blue field with state coat of arms

Highest point: Mount Davis — 3,213 feet (979 meters)

Lowest point: Delaware River — sea level

Highest recorded temperature: 111 degrees Fahrenheit (44 degrees Celsius) — Phoenixville, 1936

Lowest recorded temperature: −42 degrees Fahrenheit (−41 degrees Celsius) — Smethport, 1904

State song: "Pennsylvania"

State tree: Hemlock

State flower: Mountain laurel

State bird: Ruffed grouse

Pennsylvania History

Even though Pennsylvania is located in the northeastern part of the United States and is called a mid-Atlantic state, it is not on the Atlantic Ocean, as are Delaware, New Jersey, and New York. It has access to the Atlantic Ocean's important shipping routes from the Delaware River, which marks Pennsylvania's eastern boundary. New York is east and north of it, New Jersey east, and Delaware east and south. Maryland borders it to the south, and West Virginia lies both south and west of it. Its western boundary is eastern Ohio.

Located in the middle the original thirteen colonies, Pennsylvania is known as the Keystone State. The state is quite mountainous, with the Appalachian Mountains running through much of it. In the east are the Pocono Mountains and to the south the Blue Ridge. These mountains have more than two hundred lakes, the largest of which is Lake Wallenpaupack in northeastern Pennsylvania, between Milford and Scranton.

Early History. Humans lived in Pennsylvania as much as twelve thousand years ago, probably drawn there by its network of rivers. Besides the Delaware, Susquehanna, Schuylkill, and Lackawanna Rivers in the east, the Monongahela, Ohio, Juniata, and Allegheny Rivers run through the western part of the state. The northwestern section of Pennsylvania borders on Lake Erie, one of the five Great Lakes. These waterways afforded the earliest settlers mobility, food, and water.

Among the people who originally inhabited the area were Algonquian, Delaware, Erie, Lenape,

On November 19, 1863, President Abraham Lincoln (circled) spoke at Pennsylvania's Gettysburg battlefield, where more than fifty thousand Union and Confederate soldiers had died four months earlier. (Corbis)

Monongahela, and Susquehannock Indians. The state's Native American population in the 1990's of about fourteen thousand were mostly descendants of the Algonquians.

The first Europeans in the area were Dutch explorers Cornelius Mey, who sailed into the Delaware River in 1614, and Cornelius Hendrickson, who, in 1616, sailed up the Delaware to its junction with the Schuylkill, near modern Philadelphia. By 1638, Swedish immigrants had built the first European settlement, New Sweden, establishing Fort New Gothenburg on Tinicum Island south of present-day Philadelphia. The Dutch captured New Sweden in 1655. In 1664 the British took it from the Dutch. Shortly thereafter, in 1681, King Charles II of England granted William Penn's father the area which today is Pennsylvania. The following year, William Penn founded the Pennsylvania colony and the city of Philadelphia, after making peace with the American Indians who lived in the region.

The Importance of Philadelphia. Pennsylvania lay midway between the New England colonies and those in the south. When official business was to be transacted, Philadelphia, a well-developed colonial city, was the logical meeting place. Benjamin

Franklin had settled there in 1723 and established a library in 1731. The State House, later renamed Independence Hall, provided a good venue for delegates from the other colonies. Its famed bell, later known as the Liberty Bell, was placed in its tower in 1753.

England was engaged in war against France during the period immediately before the Revolutionary War. To finance the war, the English raised the colonies' taxes. The outcry against taxation without representation became strident. Beginning in 1774, the leaders of the thirteen original colonies met in Philadelphia. In 1775, they named George Washington to head the Continental Army, and on July 4, 1776, they approved the Declaration of Independence, which was read publicly four days later.

In effect, this declaration began England's war against the colonies. Although they were clearly the underdogs in this conflict, the colonists ultimately prevailed. England surrendered in 1781 and signed a peace treaty in 1783. A Constitutional Convention was called and met in Philadelphia in 1787, out of which the United States Constitution, ratified on December 12, 1787, evolved. Pennsylvania became the second of the United States. Philadelphia, because of its central location, was the capital of the country from 1790 to 1800.

Pennsylvania's Growth. From 1732, although England laid claim to the whole of Pennsylvania, the French were building forts in the western part of Penn's land grant. Conflicts over the ownership of western Pennsylvania resulted in a war between England and France, and it was the financing of this war that led indirectly to the Revolutionary War.

By 1763 England controlled all of Pennsylvania. In 1759 the English raised Fort Pitt beside the Monongahela River, where modern Pittsburgh stands. This area, because of its geographical isolation, was slower to develop than the eastern region of Penn's grant, but its rivers and Lake Erie provided it with the potential to grow quickly.

The Pennsylvania colony was quite progressive. It had a circulating library as early as 1731 and a volunteer fire department by 1736. The first hospital in the colonies opened in Philadelphia in 1751. With the discovery of bituminous coal near Pittsburgh in 1759 and anthracite coal in the Wyoming Valley in 1762, ready sources of power became available. This, combined with navigable waterways throughout the state, led to rapid development. The state decreed in 1780 that no black born in Pennsylvania would be a slave. It remained a free state throughout its existence.

By 1812 steamboats transported people and goods down the Ohio River. Canals and roads were being built. In 1829 the state's first commercial railroad was functioning. The state became a trading center. In 1859 the first commercially successful oil well in the United States was drilled at Titusville in western Pennsylvania.

With plentiful oil, coal, and iron ore available in the western part of the state, it was clear that steel manufacturing would become a major enterprise in and around Pittsburgh, where the first steel mill was established in 1873. Later the Bethlehem Steel Company was established in the eastern part of the state.

The Civil War. A free state since its inception, Pennsylvania was a staunch supporter of the Union during the Civil War. Many towns in the state had, since the early 1800's, been significant waystations

As modern as this Amish farm near Lancaster appears, it lacks such modern advances as electricity. (©Commonwealth Media Services)

The Fallingwater house in Fayette County, designed by Frank Lloyd Wright, is one of North America's most famous examples of residential architectural design. (© Commonwealth Media Services/Terry Way)

along the Underground Railroad, an informal complex of safe havens for slaves escaping from the South and heading to either New England or Canada. Safe houses throughout Pennsylvania offered shelter and food to runaway slaves.

Following President Abraham Lincoln's call for volunteers to fight in the war, Pennsylvanians, in two weeks, created twenty-five regiments to fight against the Confederate forces. A total of more than 340,000 men from Pennsylvania served in the Union forces between 1861 and 1865.

General Robert E. Lee's army invaded Pennsylvania in 1863. As Lee made his incursions into the state, the Army of the Potomac stood between his army and Washington, D.C., in an attempt to protect the nation's capital. On July 1, 1863, the two armies met outside Gettysburg in the southern part of the state and, for three days, engaged in the bloodiest battle of the Civil War, leaving more than fifty thousand dead or wounded soldiers on the

battlefield. This battle was the turning point in the war, although before the war ended, Confederate forces attacked Chambersburg in July, 1864.

Pennsylvania's People. Most Pennsylvanians are descendants of early settlers from Europe. More than 70 percent of all Pennsylvanians live in cities, chief among them Philadelphia, Pittsburgh, Allentown, Bethlehem, Scranton, Lancaster, Williamsport, Erie, and Harrisburg, the state's capital since 1812. Nearly four million Pennsylvanians live on farms or in small towns, however, giving the state the largest rural population in the nation.

The earliest European settlers were from Germany, France, the Netherlands, Scandinavia, and Britain. Immigrants from Ireland arrived in the 1840's. In the 1880's, people began arriving in large numbers from central and eastern Europe, notably Czechoslovakia, Poland, and Russia.

Unique among Pennsylvanians are the Pennsylvania Dutch, German immigrants who live mostly in Lancaster County. These Amish farmers lead simple lives, eschewing electricity, telephones, and automobiles.

About 9 percent of Pennsylvanians are of African American descent. Some lived there as free men before the Civil War, but many flooded into Pennsylvania after the war and again during World Wars I and II, when the defense industries offered them ready work.

The Pennsylvania Economy. About four million Pennsylvanians work in such service industries as banking, insurance, and retail. John Wanamaker established the first American department store in Philadelphia in 1876, mostly to serve visitors to the United States Bicentennial Exposition, which was held in Philadelphia's Fairmount Park.

Manufacturing industries, mainly of steel, food products, and chemicals, employ almost one million people. Another hundred thousand work on farms. Mining, which was once a major industry, now, because of mechanization, employs around twenty thousand miners. Philadelphia, Pittsburgh, and Erie are thriving ports that employ many people, and Hershey has the world's largest chocolate factory. Tourism, which brings in ten billion dollars annually, also contributes significantly to the state's economy.

Dairy products are the leading farm product. The state's leading agricultural crop is mushrooms. Pennsylvania also has a large timber industry that produces wood for building.

R. Baird Shuman

Pennsylvania Time Line

1614	Dutch explorer Cornelius Mey sails up the Delaware River.
1615	French explorer Etienne Brule sails the Susquehanna River from its source to its mouth.
1616	Dutch explorer Cornelius Hendrickson sails up the Delaware to the Schuylkill.
1638	Swedish settlers found New Sweden on the Delaware River.
1655	Dutch forces from New Netherlands (New York) take possession of New Sweden.
1664	British forces overwhelm Dutch, driving them from Pennsylvania.
Mar. 4, 1681	King Charles II of England gives 45,000 square miles of Pennsylvania to Admiral William Penn.
1682	William Penn, Jr., founds the colony of Pennsylvania.
Mar. 19, 1683	First Pennsylvania Assembly meets in Philadelphia and enacts Penn's Charter of Liberties, an early constitution.
1723	Benjamin Franklin, age seventeen, arrives in Philadelphia.
1731	First colonial circulating library is opened by Benjamin Franklin.
1732	Benjamin Franklin publishes first issue of *Poor Richard's Almanac*.
1751	Benjamin Rush establishes the first colonial hospital in Philadelphia.
1753	Liberty Bell placed in State House tower.
1754	General George Washington builds Fort Necessity near Uniontown.
1759	British build Fort Pitt at Pittsburgh.
1759	Bituminous coal found in western Pennsylvania.
1762	Anthracite coal found in the Wyoming Valley of northeastern Pennsylvania.

1767	Mason-Dixon line sets boundary between Pennsylvania and Maryland, essentially the boundary between north and south.
1768	Pennsylvania Assembly renounces British imposition of taxation without representation.
Sept. 5, 1774	First Continental Congress meets in Philadelphia.
1775	Second Continental Congress meets in Philadelphia, names George Washington commander of the Continental Army.
July 4, 1776	Declaration of Independence is adopted.
1776	Washington defeats the British at Trenton, across the Delaware River.
1777	British occupy Philadelphia, defeat Continental Army at Germantown.
1777	Washington's Continental Army winters at Valley Forge.
1778	British leave Philadelphia, intimidated by Washington's regenerated army.
1780	Pennsylvania declares that no black born in state shall be a slave.
Dec. 12, 1787	Pennsylvania ratifies Constitution during Constitutional Convention and joins Union as second state.
1792	U.S. Mint is established in Philadelphia.
1792	Purchase of the Erie Triangle completes Pennsylvania's boundaries.
1800	U.S. capital moved from Philadelphia to Washington, D.C.
1812	Harrisburg becomes state capital.
1829	First commercial railway in state begins operation.
1857	Pennsylvanian James Buchanan becomes fifteenth president of the United States.
Aug. 2, 1859	First commercially successful oil well in United States drilled at Titusville.
July 1-3, 1863	Battle of Gettysburg marks turning point in Civil War.
1873	Andrew Carnegie opens first steel mill in Pittsburgh.
May 31, 1889	Johnstown flood kills 2,200 people.
Jan. 1, 1901	Philadelphia holds first annual Mummers' Parade.
1920	First public radio broadcast in the United States is made by KDKA in Pittsburgh.
1951	Pennsylvania Turnpike, running from Philadelphia to the Ohio border, is completed.
1957	First nuclear power plant in the United States opens at Shippingport.
1967	Long, violent steelworkers strike disrupts state's economy.
1968	Pennsylvania adopts new state constitution.
June, 1972	Hurricane Agnes devastates eastern Pennsylvania.
Mar. 28, 1979	Dangerous nuclear power plant accident occurs at Three Mile Island, near Harrisburg.
1984	W. Wilson Goode is elected Philadelphia's first black mayor.
1988	Collapse of oil storage tank south of Pittsburgh spills a million gallons of diesel oil into the Monongahela and Ohio Rivers.
Nov. 18, 1989	Pennsylvania is first state to pass law restricting abortion.
1998	Democrats and Republicans in Pennsylvania's legislature pass bill to make it difficult for third-party candidates to get on ballot; Governor Tom Ridge vetoes the bill.

Notes for Further Study

Published Sources. A solid overall history of Pennsylvania is Dennis B. Downey and Francis J. Bremer's *A Guide to the History of Pennsylvania* (1993). Also informative are P. S. Klein and Ari Hoogenboom's *A History of Pennsylvania* (1980) and T. C. Cochran's *Pennsylvania: A Bicentennial History* (1978). Richard Ammon's *Growing up Amish* (1989) presents an inside view of the Pennsylvania Dutch in Lancaster County. Charles L. Blockson's *The Underground Railroad in Pennsylvania* (1981) provides a fascinating account of how Pennsylvanians helped slaves escape from the South. Two extremely provocative books, Gary B. Nash's *Freedom by Degrees: Emancipation in Pennsylvania and Its Aftermath* (1991) and Edward Raymond Turner's *The Negro in Pennsylvania: Slavery, Servitude, Freedom, 1639-1861* (1969), focus on the slavery question, emancipation, and Pennsylvania's role in dealing with runaway slaves.

James T. Lemon's *The Best Poor Man's Country: A Geographical Study of Early Southeastern Pennsylvania* (1972) and R. Eugene Harper's *The Transformation of Western Pennsylvania, 1770-1800* (1991) present contrasting views of the settlement of the two major portions of Pennsylvania, the east, dominated by Philadelphia, and the west, dominated by Pittsburgh. John Brodnar's *Steelton: Immigration and Industrialization* (1990) discusses the growth of the steel industry in western Pennsylvania and the people who came to that part of the state to work. Gerald G. Eggert's *Harrisburg Industrializes: The Coming of Factories to an American Community* (1993) shows how the state's capital, in need of industrial development, achieved its ends.

Directed toward juvenile readers are Capston Press's *Pennsylvania* (1996), compiled by the publisher's geography department, and Deborah Kent's *America the Beautiful: Pennsylvania* (1988), which should appeal to teenage readers.

Web Resources. The state of Pennsylvania Web site (http://www.state.pa.us) and the Tourism site (http://www.state.pa.us/visit) are the best starting places for information about the state. The Pennsylvania Press site (http://www.pa.press.net) is also useful, as is the Pennsylvania Today Web site (http://www.pa-today.com). All of these sources are regularly updated. The Philadelphia Zoo, one of the best in the country, has a Web site (http://www.phillyzoo.org) that offers information about the zoo, including pictures of the facility and its animals. The Philadelphia Orchestra maintains a Web site (http://www.philorch.org) as does the Philadelphia Opera (http://www.operaphilly.com). Art offerings are presented on the Philadelphia Art World site (http://www.phillyart.com) and on the Arts Festival (http://www.arts-festival.com) and Arts Net (http://www.artsnet.org) sites. The University of the Arts Web site (http://www.uarts.edu) is also easily accessible and highly informative.

Information about tourist attractions in Gettysburg, including comprehensive data about the famed Civil War battleground, is available on two Gettysburg Web sites (http://www.gettysburgguide.com), (http://www.gettysburg.com). The best overall Web sites for individual cities or areas are Pittsburgh's (http://www.pghguide.com), Philadelphia's (http://www.philanet.com), Bethlehem's (http://www.bethtour.org), Lancaster County's (http://www.co.lancaster.pa.us), and York County's (http://www.yorkpa.com).

Counties

County	Sq. miles	1996 pop.	County	Sq. miles	1996 pop.
Adams	520.1	84,921	Butler	788.6	167,732
Allegheny	730.2	1,296,037	Cambria	688.1	158,500
Armstrong	654.0	73,872	Cameron	397.2	5,745
Beaver	435.3	187,009	Carbon	382.6	58,783
Bedford	1,014.6	49,322	Centre	1,107.6	131,489
Berks	859.2	352,353	Chester	756.0	410,744
Blair	525.8	131,450	Clarion	602.5	42,205
Bradford	1,150.7	62,352	Clearfield	1,147.4	79,640
Bucks	607.6	578,715	Clinton	890.9	37,130

County	Sq. miles	1996 pop.	County	Sq. miles	1996 pop.
Columbia	485.6	64,079	Monroe	607.3	119,581
Crawford	1,012.9	89,175	Montgomery	483.1	708,782
Cumberland	550.2	207,042	Montour	130.8	18,044
Dauphin	525.3	246,807	Northampton	373.9	257,719
Delaware	184.2	547,592	Northumberland	459.9	95,897
Elk	828.7	35,141	Perry	553.6	43,727
Erie	802.0	280,570	Philadelphia	135.1	1,478,002
Fayette	790.1	145,628	Pike	547.1	38,139
Forest	428.1	4,942	Potter	1,081.2	17,103
Franklin	772.0	127,035	Schuylkill	778.6	152,630
Fulton	437.6	14,435	Snyder	331.2	38,034
Greene	575.9	42,054	Somerset	1,074.8	80,517
Huntingdon	875.4	44,977	Sullivan	450.0	6,145
Indiana	829.5	90,073	Susquehanna	823.0	42,002
Jefferson	655.5	46,624	Tioga	1,133.8	41,510
Juniata	391.6	21,793	Union	316.8	40,826
Lackawanna	458.8	213,323	Venango	675.1	58,820
Lancaster	949.1	450,834	Warren	883.5	44,624
Lawrence	360.5	95,780	Washington	857.1	206,708
Lebanon	361.8	117,179	Wayne	729.4	44,718
Lehigh	346.7	297,802	Westmoreland	1,022.6	376,297
Luzerne	891.0	321,309	Wyoming	397.2	29,362
Lycoming	1,234.9	119,083	York	904.6	368,332
McKean	981.6	48,156			
Mercer	671.9	122,155	*Source:* U.S. Bureau of the Census; National Association of		
Mifflin	410.7	47,006	Counties.		

Cities

With 10,000 or more residents

Rank	City	Population	Rank	City	Population
1	Philadelphia	1,436,287	22	Easton	25,361
2	Pittsburgh	340,520	23	Lebanon	23,442
3	Erie	102,640	24	McKeesport	23,089
4	Allentown	100,757	25	Hazleton	22,542
5	Reading	74,762	26	West Mifflin	22,111
6	Scranton	74,683	27	Pottstown	21,465
7	Bethlehem	69,383	28	Baldwin	20,512
8	Lancaster	52,951	29	Municipality of Murrysville	19,143
9	Harrisburg	49,502	30	Wilkinsburg	19,128
10	Altoona	49,226	31	West Chester	17,988
11	Wilkes-Barre	42,828	32	Carlisle	17,720
12	Chester	40,221	33	Chambersburg	17,295
13	York	39,978	34	Sharon	16,373
14	State College	39,550	35	Hermitage	16,274
15	Bethel Park	32,869	36	Lansdale	15,936
16	Williamsport	29,891	37	Greensburg	15,531
17	Norristown	29,763	38	Pottsville	15,374
18	Municipality of Monroeville	27,964	39	Phoenixville	15,207
19	Plum	26,469	40	Butler	14,871
20	New Castle	26,178	41	New Kensington	14,805
21	Johnstown	25,390	42	Washington	14,805

Rank	City	Population
43	Indiana	14,399
44	Hanover	14,269
45	Dunmore	14,253
46	Meadville	14,004
47	St. Marys	13,842
48	Whitehall	13,728
49	Kingston	13,146
50	Ephrata	13,000
51	Bloomsburg	12,495
52	Aliquippa	12,448
53	Lower Burrell	12,211
54	Munhall	12,019
55	Yeadon	11,452
56	Emmaus	11,409
57	Uniontown	11,197
58	Oil City	11,185

Rank	City	Population
59	Lansdowne	11,151
60	Nanticoke	11,122
61	Franklin Park	11,070
62	Coatesville	10,687
63	Darby	10,658
64	Elizabethtown	10,619
65	Sunbury	10,483
66	Columbia	10,465
67	Jeannette	10,449
68	Berwick	10,389
69	Bristol	10,142
70	Beaver Falls	10,104
71	East Stroudsburg	10,056

Population figures are estimated for mid-1998.
Source: U.S. Bureau of the Census.

Index to Tables

NA = Reliable data are not available.

DEMOGRAPHICS

Resident state and national populations, 1970-1997

Population figures given in thousands

	State pop.	U.S. pop.	Share	Rank
1970	11,801	203,302	5.8%	3
1980	11,864	226,546	5.2%	4
1985	11,771	237,924	5.0%	4
1990	11,883	248,765	4.8%	5
1995	12,046	262,761	4.6%	5
1997	12,020	267,636	4.5%	5

Source: U.S. Bureau of the Census.

Resident population by age, 1997

Age group	Total population
Under 5 years	738,000
5 to 17 years	2,126,000
18 to 24 years	1,023,000
25 to 34 years	1,670,000
35 to 44 years	1,963,000
45 to 54 years	1,546,000
55 to 64 years	1,049,000
65 to 74 years	1,015,000
75 to 84 years	676,000
85 years and over	213,000
Portion of residents 65 and older	15.8%
National average	12.7%

Population figures are rounded to nearest thousand persons;
figures include armed forces personnel stationed in state.
Source: U.S. Bureau of the Census.

Resident population by race, Hispanic origin, 1997

	State pop.	Share	U.S.
All residents	12,020,000	100.0%	100.0%
Hispanic white	254,000	2.1%	10.0%
non-Hispanic white	10,394,000	86.5%	72.7%
African American	1,164,000	9.7%	12.7%
Native American	17,000	0.1%	0.9%
Asian, Pacific Islander	191,000	1.6%	3.8%

Source: U.S. Bureau of the Census.

Projections of state population, 2000-2025

	Model A Uses interstate migration observed from 1975-1994	Model B Uses Bureau of Economic Analysis employment projections
Year	Population	Population
2000	12,202,000	12,220,000
2005	12,281,000	12,329,000
2010	12,352,000	12,443,000
2015	12,449,000	12,580,000
2020	12,567,000	12,727,000
2025	12,683,000	12,854,000

All population projections, including those for 2000, were
calculated in 1997.
Source: U.S. Bureau of the Census, Population Paper Listings
PPL-47.

VITAL STATISTICS

Average lifetime in years by race, 1989-1991

	State	U.S.	Rank
All residents	75.38	75.37	28
White residents	76.15	76.13	29
Black residents	68.27	69.16	31

Ranks are from longest-lived to least longest-lived. Ranks
exclude Alaska, for which reliable data are not available.
Rank for black residents is based on the 32 states for which
reliable data are available.
Source: U.S. National Center for Health Statistics.

Infant mortality rates, 1980 and 1995

	State	U.S.
All residents		
1980	13.2	12.6
1995	7.8	7.6
White residents		
1980	11.9	11.0
1995	6.2	6.3
Black residents		
1980	23.1	21.4
1995	17.6	15.1

Figures represent deaths per 1,000 live births of resident
infants under 1 year old, exclusive of fetal deaths; all-
residents figures include other races not listed separately.
Source: U.S. National Center for Health Statistics.

Marriages and divorces

Marriages in 1996.	70,200
Rate per 1,000 population, 1995.	6.3
U.S. rate, 1995	8.9
Rank among all states	48
Divorces in 1996	38,300
Rate per 1,000 population, 1995.	3.3
U.S. rate, 1995	4.4
Rank among all states	40

Rank is from highest to lowest in country.
Source: U.S. National Center for Health Statistics.

Death rates by leading causes, 1995
Deaths per 100,000 resident population

Cause	State	U.S.
Heart disease	359.7	280.7
Cancer	250.7	204.9
Cerebrovascular diseases	68.6	60.1
Accidents and adverse effects	35.3	35.5
Motor vehicle accidents	13.1	16.5
Chronic obstructive pulmonary diseases	43.9	39.2
Diabetes mellitus	28.2	22.6
HIV	11.5	NA
Suicide	12.1	11.9
Homicide	6.5	8.7
All causes	1,059.2	880.0
Rank in overall death rate among states		4

Figures exclude nonresidents who die in state. Causes of
death follow International Classification of Diseases. Rank
is from highest to lowest in country.
Source: U.S. National Center for Health Statistics.

ECONOMY

Gross state product, 1990-1996
In current dollars

	State product	Increase
1990	$245.8 billion	
1993	$283.1 billion	
1994	$296.8 billion	4.84%
1995	$313.3 billion	5.56%
1996	$328.5 billion	4.85%

Source: U.S. Bureau of Economic Analysis; Survey of Current Business, June, 1998.

Gross state product by industry, 1996
In billions

Farms, forestry, fisheries	$2.9
Construction	10.8
Manufacturing	66.7
Transportation, public utilities	27.5
Wholesale trade	18.4
Retail trade	27.5
Finance, insurance, real estate	51.8
Services	60.5
Government	31.0
State total	$298.7
Total U.S.	$6,923.8
State share	4.31%
Rank among states	6

Total figures include mining, not listed separately.
Source: U.S. Bureau of Economic Analysis; Survey of Current Business, June, 1998.

Personal income per capita, 1990 and 1997
In current dollars

	1990	1997
Per capita income	$19,410	$26,058
U.S. average	$19,188	$25,598
Rank among states	16	15

1997 data are preliminary.
Source: U.S. Bureau of Economic Analysis; Survey of Current Business, May, 1998.

Energy consumption, 1995
In trillions of British thermal units (BTU)

End-use sectors

Residential	901.6
Commercial	585.7
Industrial	1,484.5
Transportation	913.9

Sources of energy

Petroleum	1,330.5
Natural gas	746.7
Coal	1,386.5
Hydroelectric power	8.2
Nuclear electric power	708.3
Total state per capita consumption	322.2
Total U.S. per capita consumption	344.4
Rank among states	35
Total state energy consumption	3,885.7
Total U.S. energy consumption	90,547.4
State share of U.S. total	4.29%
Rank among states	5

Total figures include items not listed separately.
Source: U.S. Energy Information Administration; State Energy Data Report.

Nonfarm employment by sectors, 1997

Total	5,398,000
Construction	214,000
Manufacturing	936,000
Transportation, public utilities	278,000
Wholesale trade, retail trade	1,217,000
Finance, insurance, real estate	313,000
Services	1,707,000
Government	713,000

Figures are rounded to nearest thousand persons. Total includes mining, not listed separately.
Source: U.S. Bureau of Labor Statistics; Employment and Earnings, monthly.

Foreign exports, 1990-1997
In millions of dollars

Year	State	U.S.	State share
1990	8,491	394,045	2.15%
1996	14,364	624,767	2.30%
1997	16,069	688,896	2.33%

Source: U.S. Bureau of the Census; U.S. Merchandise Trade, series FT 900.

LAND USE

Federally owned land, 1996

	State	U.S.	State share
Total acres	28,804,000	2,271,343,000	1.27%
Federally owned	623,000	563,129,000	0.11%
Federal share	2.2%	24.8%	—

Areas are rounded to nearest thousand acres. Figures for federally owned land do not include trust properties.

Source: U.S. General Services Administration; *Inventory Report on Real Property Owned by the United States Throughout the World*, annual.

Land use, 1992

In acres, rounded to nearest thousand

Total surface area	28,997,000
Federal land	682,000
Total nonfederal	28,997,000
Developed	682,000
Total rural	27,813,000
Cropland.	3,432,000
Pasture land	24,381,000
Range land.	5,596,000
Forest land.	2,326,000
Minor cover/use	1,143 15,3160

Total surface area figures include water area not shown separately.

Source: U.S. Dept. of Agriculture; Soil Conservation Service; Iowa State University, Statistical Laboratory; *Summary Report, 1992 National Resources Inventory*.

Farms and crop acreage, 1997

	State	U.S.	Share	Rank
Farms (thousands)	50	2,058	2.43%	17
Acres (millions)	8	968	0.83%	37
Acres per farm	154	471	—	45
Acres planted	4,313	334,139	1.29%	26
Acres harvested	4,202	319,894	1.31%	25
Farm value (mill.)	$1,481	$108,805	1.36%	49

Numbers of farms are rounded to nearest thousand.

Source: U.S. Dept. of Agriculture; National Agricultural Statistics Service.

GOVERNMENT AND FINANCE

Units of local government, 1997

	State	Total U.S.	Rank
All local governments	5,070	87,453	2
Counties	66	3,043	21
Municipalities	1,023	19,372	3
Townships	1,546	16,629	2
School districts	516	13,726	11
Special districts	1,919	34,683	4

County ranks are based on the 48 states with county governments; township ranks are based on the 20 states with township governments; school district ranks are based on the 46 states with such districts.

Source: U.S. Bureau of the Census; *1997 Census of Governments, Government Organization*, Series GC97(1).

State government revenue, 1996

Total revenue	$42,796 mill.
General revenue	33,512 mill.
Per capita.	2,783
U.S. per capita average	2,910
Rank among states.	26

Intergovernmental revenue	
Total	$9,151 mill.
From federal government	9,063 mill.
From local government	88 mill.

Charges and Miscellaneous	
Total	$6,066 mill.
Current charges	3,512 mill.
Misc. general revenue	2,554 mill.

Taxes	
Total	$18,295 mill.
General sales	5,701 mill.
Selective sales.	3,056 mill.
License taxes	1,809 mill.
Individual income	5,214 mill.
Corporate income	1,504 mill.
Other	1,010 mill.
Insurance trust revenue	8,592 mill.

Total revenue figures include items not listed separately.

Source: U.S. Bureau of the Census.

State government expenditures, 1996

General expenditures

Intergovernmental	$9,676 mill.
Direct expenditures	23,460 mill.
Total	33,136 mill.

Selected direct expenditures

Education	$10,526 mill.
Public welfare	9,835 mill.
Health, hospital	3,005 mill.
Highways	2,427 mill.
Police	625 mill.
Corrections	1,077 mill.
Natural resources	432 mill.
Parks and recreation	113 mill.
Government administration	1,028 mill.
Interest on debt	1,088 mill.

Other

State per capita expenditures	$2,752
U.S. per capita average	2,854
Rank among states	26
Total state expenditures	38,699 mill.
Total U.S. expenditures	859,959 mill.

Totals include items not listed separately.
Source: U.S. Bureau of the Census.

POLITICS

Governors since statehood

D = Democrat; R = Republican; O = other;
(r) resigned; (d) died in office; (i) removed from office

Thomas Wharton, Jr.	(d) 1777-1778
George Bryan	1778
Joseph Reed	1778-1781
William Moore	1781-1782
John Dickinson	1782-1785
Benjamin Franklin	1785-1788
Thomas Mifflin	1788-1799
Thomas McKean (O)	1799-1808
Simon Snyder (O)	1808-1817
William Findlay (O)	1817-1820
Joseph Hiester (O)	1820-1823
John A. Schulze (O)	1823-1829
George Wolf (O)	1829-1835
Joseph Ritner (D)	1835-1839
David R. Porter (D)	1839-1845
Francis R. Shunk (D)	(r) 1845-1848
William F. Johnston (O)	1848-1852
William Bigler (D)	1852-1855
James Pollock (O)	1855-1858
William F. Packer (D)	1858-1861

Andrew G. Curtin (R)	1861-1867
John W. Geary (R)	1867-1873
John F. Hartranft (R)	1873-1879
Henry M. Hoyt (R)	1879-1883
Robert E. Pattison (D)	1883-1887
James A. Beaver (R)	1887-1891
Robert E. Pattison (D)	1891-1895
Daniel W. Hastings (R)	1895-1899
William A. Stone (R)	1899-1903
Samuel W. Pennypacker (R)	1903-1907
Edwin S. Stuart (R)	1907-1911
John K. Tener (R)	1911-1915
Martin G. Brumbaugh (R)	1915-1919
William C. Sproul (R)	1919-1923
Gifford Pinchot (R)	1923-1927
John S. Fisher (R)	1927-1931
Gifford Pinchot (R)	1931-1935
George H. Earle III (D)	1935-1939
Arthur H. James (R)	1939-1943
Edward Martin (R)	(r) 1943-1947
John C. Bell (R)	1947
James H. Duff (R)	1947-1951
John S. Fine (R)	1951-1955
George M. Leader (D)	1955-1959
David L. Lawrence (D)	1959-1963
William W. Scranton (R)	1963-1967
Raymond P. Shafer (R)	1967-1971
Milton J. Shapp (D)	1971-1979
Richard L. Thornburgh (R)	1979-1987
Robert P. Casey (D)	1987-1995
Tom Ridge (R)	1995-

Governors were called state council presidents before 1790.

Composition of state legislature, 1990-1998

	Democrats	Republicans
State House (203 seats)		
1990	107	94
1992	105	98
1994	101	102
1996	99	104
1998	100	103
State Senate (50 seats)		
1990	24	26
1992	24	25
1994	21	29
1996	20	30
1998	20	30

Figures for total seats may include independents and minor
party members.
Source: Council of State Governments; *State Elective Officials
and the Legislatures.*

Composition of congressional delegations, 1989-1999

	Dem	Rep	Total
House of Representatives			
101st Congress, 1989			
State delegates	12	11	23
Total U.S.	259	174	433
102d Congress, 1991			
State delegates	11	12	23
Total U.S.	267	167	434
103d Congress, 1993			
State delegates	11	10	21
Total U.S.	258	176	434
104th Congress, 1995			
State delegates	11	10	21
Total U.S.	197	236	433
105th Congress, 1997			
State delegates	12	10	21
Total U.S.	206	228	434
106th Congress, 1999			
State delegates	11	10	21
Total U.S.	211	222	433
Senate			
101st Congress, 1989			
State delegates	0	2	2
Total U.S.	55	45	100
102d Congress, 1991			
State delegates	0	2	2
Total U.S.	56	44	100
103d Congress, 1993			
State delegates	1	1	2
Total U.S.	57	43	100
104th Congress, 1995			
State delegates	0	2	2
Total U.S.	46	53	99
105th Congress, 1997			
State delegates	0	2	2
Total U.S.	45	55	100
106th Congress, 1999			
State delegates	0	2	2
Total U.S.	45	54	99

Figures are for starts of first sessions. Figure for U.S. Representatives for 101st Congress does not include Alabama and Indiana, which had vacancies. Figures for total U.S. Representatives for 102d, 103d, and 106th Congresses do not include Vermont, which had 1 Independent-Socialist. Figure for U.S. Representatives for 104th Congress does not include Vermont, which had 1 Independent-Socialist, and California, which had 1 vacancy. Figure for U.S. Representatives for 105th Congress does not include New York, which had 1 vacancy. Figure for U.S. Senators for 104th Congress does not include Oregon, which had 1 vacancy. Figure for U.S. Senators for 106th Congress does not include New Hampshire, which had 1 Independent.

Source: U.S. Congress; *Congressional Directory,* biennial.

Voter participation in presidential elections, 1992 and 1996

	1992	1996
State voting age pop.	9,161,000	9,196,000
Total U.S. voting age pop.	189,524,000	196,509,000
State share of U.S. total	4.8%	4.7%
Rank among states	5	5
Percent of state casting vote	54.1	47.1
Percent of U.S. total voting	55.1	49.0
Rank among states	32	37

Source: U.S. Bureau of the Census.

HEALTH AND MEDICAL CARE

Medicare, 1997

	Recipients	Payments
State	2,079,000	$12,445 mill.
Total U.S.	37,514,000	$206,064 mill.
State share	5.54%	6.04%
Rank among states	5	5

Recipient figures are rounded to nearest thousand persons. Ranks are from highest to lowest.

Source: U.S. Health Care Financing Administration.

Medicaid, 1996

	Recipients	Payments
State	1,168,000	$4,663 mill.
Total U.S.	35,028,000	$121,419 mill.
State share	3.33%	3.84%
Rank among states	10	7

Recipient figures are rounded to nearest thousand persons. Payment figures for fiscal year reflect federal and state contribution payments. Ranks are from highest to lowest.

Source: U.S. Health Care Financing Administration.

Health insurance coverage, 1996

	State	U.S.
Total persons covered	10,763,000	225,070,000
Total persons not covered	1,133,000	41,716,000
Part not covered	9.5%	15.6%
Rank among states	45	—
Children not covered	214,000	10,554,000
Part not covered	7.3%	14.8%
Rank among states	45	—

Ranks are from most to fewest uninsured. Population figures
are rounded to nearest thousand persons.
Source: U.S. Bureau of the Census.

AIDS, syphilis, tuberculosis, and measles cases, 1997

Cases	U.S.	State	Share
AIDS	58,443	1,912	3.27%
Syphilis	8,550	123	1.44%
Tuberculosis	18,534	459	2.48%
Measles	148,000	8,000	5.41%

Measles figures are rounded to nearest thousand cases.
Source: U.S. Centers for Disease Control and Prevention.

EDUCATION

Public school enrollment, 1995

State K-8 enrollment	1,257,000
Total U.S. K-8 enrollment	32,341,000
State share of total U.S.	3.89%
State 9-12 enrollment	531,000
Total U.S. 9-12 enrollment	12,500,000
State share of U.S. total	4.25%
State public school enroll. rate	84.6%
Overall U.S. rate	91.6%
Rank among states	50

Enrollment figures (which include unclassified students) are
rounded to nearest thousand pupils in fall term;
kindergarten (K)-8 grade figures include some
prekindergarten students. Enrollment rate is based on
percentage of persons 5-17 years old. Rank is from highest
to lowest.
Source: U.S. National Center for Education Statistics.

HOUSING

Homeownership rates, 1985-1997

	1985	1990	1997
State	71.6%	73.8%	73.3%
Total U.S.	63.9%	63.9%	65.7%
Rank among states	5	2	8

Source: U.S. Bureau of the Census.

Home sales, 1990 and 1997
In thousands of units

Existing home sales	1990	1997	Change
State sales	182.7	233.3	50.6
Total U.S. sales	3,560	4,730	1,170
State share of U.S. total	5.13%	4.93%	-0.20%
Rank among states	4	4	—

Source: National Association of Realtors; *Real Estate Outlook:
Market Trends and Insights.*

Public college finances, 1996

State FTE enrollment	279,900
Total U.S. FTE enrollment	8,268,800
State share of total U.S.	3.39%
Rank among states	8
State and local appropriations	$1,410,800,000
Total U.S. state and local appropriations	$39,699 mill.
State share of total U.S.	3.55%
Rank among states	8
State net tuition revenues	$1,237,600,000
Total U.S. net tuition	$18,348,100,000
State share of total U.S.	6.75%
Rank among states	2

FTE=Full-time equivalent; credit and noncredit enrollment
including summer session in academic year ending in
1996.
Enrollments are rounded to nearest thousand students. Net
tuition revenues exclude appropriation to students
attending in-state public institutions. Rankings are from
highest shares to lowest.
Source: Research Associates of Washington.

TRANSPORTATION AND TRAVEL

Highway mileage, 1996

Interstate	1,750
Other arterial	13,621
Collector roads	23,526
Local roads	83,809
Urban roads	33,202
Rural roads	85,750
Total state	118,952
U.S. total	3,933,985
State share	3.0%
Rank among states	7

Source: U.S. Federal Highway Administration.

Motor vehicle registrations and driver licenses, 1996
In thousands

Vehicle registrations	State	U.S.	Share	Rank
Autos, trucks, buses	8,640	206,365	4.19%	7
Autos only	5,893	128,439	4.59%	7
Motorcycles	178	3,832	4.65%	4
Driver licenses	8,221	179,539	4.58%	7

Figures do not include vehicles owned by military services.
Source: U.S. Federal Highway Administration; *Highway Statistics; Selected Highway Statistics and Charts.*

Domestic travel expenditures, 1995
Spending by U.S. residents on overnight trips and day trips of at least 100 miles

Total expenditures in state	$11,186 mill.
Total expenditures in U.S.	$360,314 mill.
State share of total U.S.	3.10%
Rank among states	8

Source: Travel Industry Association of America.

CRIME AND LAW ENFORCEMENT

State and local police officers, 1996

Local police	17,655
State police	4,114
Sheriffs	1,239
Total	24,873
Officers per 10,000 residents	21
U.S. average	25
Rank among states	30

Figures cover full-time sworn officers; totals include special police not shown separately.
Source: U.S. Bureau of Justice Statistics; *Census of State and Local Law Enforcement Agencies, 1996.*

Crime rates, 1996
Rates per 100,000 resident population

Violent crimes	State	U.S.
Total violent	433	634
Murder	5.7	7.4
Forcible rape	25.3	36.1
Robbery	201	202
Aggravated assault	200	388
Property crimes		
Total property	2,960	4,445
Burglary	551	943
Larceny/theft	1,997	2,976
Motor vehicle theft	412	526
Totals	3,393	5,079

Source: U.S. Federal Bureau of Investigation; *Crime in the United States,* annual.

State prison populations, 1980-1996

	State	U.S.	State share
1980	8,171	305,458	2.67%
1990	22,290	708,393	3.15%
1996	34,537	1,025,624	3.37%

Figures exclude prisoners in federal penitentiaries.
Source: U.S. Bureau of Justice Statistics.

Rhode Island

Location: New England (northeastern continental United States)

Area and rank: 1,045 square miles (2,706 square kilometers); 1,545 square miles (4,002 square kilometers) including water; fiftieth largest state in area

Coastline: 40 miles (64 kilometers)

Shoreline: 384 miles (618 kilometers)

Population and rank: 987,429 (1997); forty-third largest state in population

Capital: Providence

Rhode Island's State House in Providence. (Frederick E. D'Andrea)

Largest city: Providence (150,890 people in 1998)

Entered Union and rank: May 29, 1790; thirteenth state

Present constitution adopted: 1843

Counties: 5

State name: Rhode Island may have taken its name from the Greek island of Rhodes or it may come from the Dutch *roodt eylandt* (red island)

State nickname: Ocean State

Motto: Hope

State flag: White field with state coat of arms

Highest point: Jerimoth Hill — 812 feet (247 meters)

Lowest point: Atlantic Ocean — sea level

Highest recorded temperature: 104 degrees Fahrenheit (40 degrees Celsius) — Providence, 1975

Lowest recorded temperature: −23 degrees Fahrenheit (−31 degrees Celsius) — Kingston, 1942

State song: "Rhode Island"

State tree: Red maple

State flower: Violet (unofficial)

State bird: Rhode Island Red

Rhode Island History

Though the smallest state in the Union in area, Rhode Island has the longest name: Rhode Island and Providence Plantations. Rhode Island, though it is only 48 miles long and 37 miles wide, has 384 miles of coastline, which earned for it the nickname the Ocean State. The state is practically divided by Narragansett Bay, which extends twenty-eight miles into the interior. As a result, no town in Rhode Island is more than twenty-five miles from water. The state's geography played a major role in its development, with fishing, boatbuilding, and international trade being its early major industries. The numerous and swift rivers running through the state also shaped industry, being harnessed for power to the nation's first mills. Due to its small size, Rhode Island has always been intimately linked to its neighbors, Connecticut on the west and Massachusetts on the east and north.

Native American Presence. Archaeological evidence shows that Rhode Island has been inhabited for at least eight thousand years. During the 1600's, the area of Rhode Island, Connecticut, and Massachusetts was inhabited by about thirty thousand American Indians of the Algonquian family, roughly split into five tribes: Narragansetts, Wampanoags, Niantics, Nipmucs, and Pequots. They farmed the land for corn, squash, beans, and tobacco.

The first European settlers of the state in the 1630's lived peaceably among the Native Americans; Indians even gave portions of their land to the English. Eventually, however, discord between the groups arose, when whites began taking Ameri-

Providence, Rhode Island's capital and largest city, viewed through Prospect Park. (Rhode Island Tourism Division)

can Indian land. In the 1637 Pequot War, Pequots unsuccessfully tried to drive out the colonists who had taken over their land. The continued disintegration of ties led to King Philip's War in 1675. The Wampanoags, their leader King Philip, and their violent behavior provoked Connecticut and Massachusetts to declare war against them. The Rhode Island Narragansetts joined with the Wampanoags eventually, but the Native Americans were defeated, with thousands of Indians and more than six hundred whites killed and most of the city of Providence burned. After the war, Indians were shipped to the South or to the West Indies as slaves. Most eventually left the state, and by the year 2000, Native Americans made up less than ½ percent of Rhode Island's population.

Discovery and Colonization. Rhode Island may have been visited by Norwegian Vikings as early as 1000 C.E. In 1524 the Italian explorer Giovanni da Verrazano, sailing for France, found Narragansett Bay. He may have named the state, comparing it to the Greek island of Rhodes. The state's name is also often attributed to Dutch trader Adriaen Block, who visited the region in 1614 and called it *roodt eylandt* (red island).

Rhode Island was first settled by Europeans in 1636, when the city of Providence was founded by religious dissenter Roger Williams. Williams was about to be exiled from the Massachusetts Bay Colony to England due to his unpopular views that religion and state should be separate. He escaped, and his Native American friends, the Narragansetts, gave him land that he named Providence. He declared the region "a shelter for persons distressed of conscience."

In 1638 Anne Hutchinson was banished from the Massachusetts Bay Colony for preaching against the established church. She settled in Portsmouth, at the north end of Aquidneck Island. A year later William Coddington broke from Hutchinson's group and founded Newport. After the future Warwick was founded by Samuel Gorton in 1643, the four towns received a charter from England to become one colony, with freedom of religion guaranteed to all. Soon all those seeking asylum from persecution—Quakers, Jews, Congregationalists, Baptists—made their homes there, and the region became known for its tolerance. Because of its open-mindedness, the colony was considered by outsiders a haven for misfits and thus was scorned.

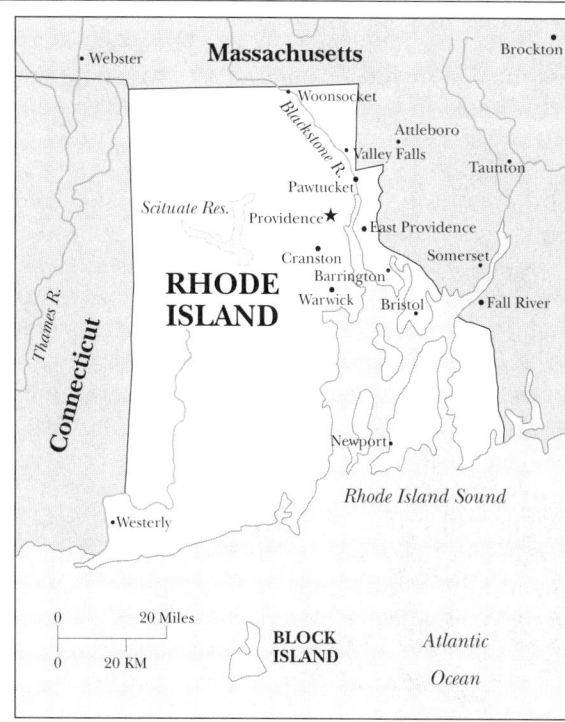

Although the first antislavery law in the Union was signed in Rhode Island in 1652, Rhode Island, especially Newport and Bristol, was a hub of the so-called "triangle trade" in the 1700's. Rum, which Rhode Islanders manufactured, was traded in Africa for slaves, who were traded in the West Indies for molasses, which was used in New England to make more rum. Slavery was abolished in 1784, and the triangle trade ended by 1800.

Steps to Revolution. By 1750 the main industries in Rhode Island were fishing, rum manufacture, and the rum trade. After Great Britain imposed taxes on trade, Rhode Islanders became smugglers to maintain their livelihoods. In 1764 they fired on a British ship, one of the first acts of aggression and rebellion against England. In 1772 the British ship *Gaspee* was burned by Providence residents, in an act thought to be the first of the Revolution.

Always progressive, Rhode Island's general assembly voted to end allegiance to Britain on May 4, 1776—two months before the rest of the colonies. Rhode Island played an active part in the fighting; the Battle of Rhode Island took place in Newport in 1778. A company of freed slaves, known as the

Black Regiment, fought with the colonists, becoming the first such regiment to fight in America. After winning independence, Rhode Island was the last of the original thirteen colonies to ratify the Constitution, in 1790, refusing to sign until the Bill of Rights was added. Desiring a balance of power, until 1854 Rhode Island had five capital cities: Providence, Newport, East Greenwich, Bristol, and South Kingstown. From 1854 to 1900, Providence and Newport shared capital status, and in 1900 Providence became the sole capital.

Industry. The American Industrial Revolution began in Pawtucket, Rhode Island, in 1790. Harnessing the power of the mighty Blackstone River, resident Samuel Slater built the first water-powered cotton mill in the Union. Later, in 1827, Slater erected the first steam-powered cotton mill. Rhode Island thrived during the 1800's due to the prosperity of its mills. Though the state's land was arable, by 1860 about 50 percent of Rhode Islanders worked in industrial jobs, while only 10 percent were farmers.

Production remained steady during the Civil War, and after the war the state's industry shifted from production of textiles to that of metals and jewelry. By the second half of the twentieth century an estimated 85 percent of U.S. costume jewelry was produced in Providence, though many factories faced difficulties when low-cost imports from Asia threatened to bankrupt them. Rhode Island is also home to Hasbro, the second-largest toy manufacturer in the world. The three largest employers in the state are industry, tourism, and health care.

Political Makeup. Rhode Island expanded its trend of tolerance into the political arena. In 1842 Thomas Dorr founded the People's Party to try to give all citizens the right to vote. After illegitimately claiming governorship during what is known as Dorr's Rebellion, he was suppressed. However, because of his work, all adult males were given the right to vote, regardless of color. Rhode Island was the only state before the Civil War in which blacks and whites voted as equals.

The Cliffwalk-Breakers mansion reflects the wealthy and aristocratic lifestyle for which Newport has traditionally been known. (Rhode Island Tourism Division)

From 1930 through the mid-1980's, the world's premier yachting race, the America's Cup, was held off the coast of Newport. (Rhode Island Tourism Division)

Until the 1900's, the majority of Rhode Island voters were Republicans. Democrats came into power, however, when diverse immigrants began arriving in the early part of the century. Democrats dominated politics beginning in 1935, never losing control of the General Assembly throughout the century.

During the 1980's, Rhode Island became known as a hotbed of political corruption. After 1986, two mayors in the state were convicted on corruption charges, two chief justices of the state supreme court resigned in disgrace, and a superior court judge was arrested for taking bribes. Possible reasons for the state's scandals include the longtime dominance of one political party, the small size of the state, and the fact that Rhode Island is considered the New England headquarters of the Mafia. Residents hoping for a turn for the better elected Patrick Kennedy to the U.S. House of Representatives in 1988. Although Kennedy was just a twenty-one-year-old attending Provi-

dence College, he proved himself worthy of reelection twice.

Ethnic and Religious Heritage. Italian Americans make up a large percentage of the Rhode Island population, second only to Irish Americans. Irish and Italian immigrants helped make Roman Catholicism the prevalent religion in the state. Rhode Island is about 70 percent Catholic, making it the state with the highest percentage of Roman Catholics.

Revitalization of Providence. Though at the turn of the twentieth century Providence was one of the nation's richest and most thriving cities, after 1925 residents began fleeing to suburban and rural areas. Mayor Vincent "Buddy" Cianci, Jr., was mostly responsible for bringing the city back to life beginning in the 1970's. In the 1990's the two downtown rivers that had been covered by pavement were uncovered, and bridges, walkways, and an amphitheater highlighted the center of the city, replacing unused train tracks and freight yards.

Providence became a haven for artists and attracted multitudes with the building of new hotels, a convention center, a giant mall, and an outdoor ice rink. The city experienced a 40 percent drop in crime in the early 1990's, providing more reason for residents to return to the once-empty downtown area.

Lauren M. Mitchell

Rhode Island Time Line

1500's	Algonquian Indians are dominant society throughout New England area.
1524	Italian navigator Giovanni da Verrazano, sailing for France, explores Narragansett Bay.
1614	Dutch explorer Adriaen Block lands at Block Island.
1636	Roger Williams founds Providence.
1638	Anne Hutchinson settles Portsmouth.
1639	Williams and Ezekiel Holliman found the first Baptist church in the New World, in Providence.
1639	William Coddington settles Newport.
1643	Samuel Gorton founds Shawomet (later Warwick).
1644	Williams is granted a charter for Rhode Island.
1652	Union's first antislavery law is passed, in Rhode Island.
July 8, 1663	King Charles II grants Rhode Island a charter guaranteeing religious freedom and self-governance.
1675	King Philip's War begins as Massachusetts and Connecticut fight American Indians, eventually bringing Rhode Island into the war.
1732	First Rhode Island newspaper, *Rhode Island Gazette*, is published.
1763	Rhode Island College is established (becomes Brown University in 1804).
1763	Touro Synagogue, the first Jewish house of worship in the colonies, is built in Newport.
June 9, 1772	Colonists burn the British ship *Gaspee* to protest trade restrictions.
1774	Rhode Island outlaws the importation of slaves.
May 4, 1776	Rhode Island is first colony to declare independence from Great Britain.
Aug. 29, 1778	British seize Newport during Battle of Rhode Island.
1778	Black Regiment, the nation's first battalion of freed slaves, begins fighting in the Revolution.
1784	Colony abolishes slavery.
May 29, 1790	Rhode Island ratifies U.S. Constitution, becoming the thirteenth state in the Union.
1790	Samuel Slater builds the first water-powered cotton mill in the Union, in Pawtucket.
1835	Train line connects Boston and Providence.
1827	Samuel Slater builds first steam-powered cotton mill.
1828	Providence Arcade, the first enclosed shopping mall in the Union, is opened.
1842	Dorr's Rebellion results in voting rights for all adult males in the state.
1854	The five capitals—Providence, Newport, East Greenwich, Bristol, and South Kingston—are reduced to two: Providence and Newport.

1861	More than 24,000 Rhode Islanders serve on Union side in Civil War.
1880	Nearly half the population of the state is of Irish ancestry.
1882	Public schooling is made mandatory.
1883	U.S. Navy opens station at Newport.
1890's	Italian Americans become the state's second-largest ethnic group.
1900	Providence becomes the sole capital of the state.
1910	Roman Catholicism becomes the major religion in the state.
1917-1918	Almost 28,000 Rhode Islanders serve in World War I.
1920	Rhode Island refuses to ratify national prohibition amendment.
1935	Democrats take control of state's General Assembly, which they will retain throughout twentieth century.
1938	Severe hurricane costs 317 deaths and more than $100 million in damage.
1946	Rhode Island legislates equal pay rates for women and men.
1969	Newport Bridge is completed across Narragansett Bay.
1971	First state income tax is enacted.
1983	After general depression, state's economy improves.
1990	Prominent banker steals $13 million from bank, causing forty-five banks and credit unions to close temporarily.
1991	Sewage pollution in Narragansett Bay declines 13 percent from 1990.

Notes for Further Study

Published Sources. Those interested in learning about Rhode Island's history will find a wealth of materials on all aspects of the state's early years. For information on the founding of the colony, Edwin S. Gaustad's *Liberty of Conscience: Roger Williams in America* (1991) is excellent. *Flintlock and Tomahawk: New England in King Philip's War* (1992), by Douglas Edward Leach, describes the conflict of the Native Americans and white settlers. *Inventing New England's Slave Paradise: Master/Slave Relations in Eighteenth-Century Narragansett, Rhode Island* (1998), by Robert K. Fitts, is one of the few books that examines slavery in the state. Rhode Island's role in the Revolution is discussed in *The Documentary History of the Destruction of the Gaspee* (1990), by William R. Staples. Barbara Tucker analyzes the American Industrial Revolution in *Samuel Slater and the Origins of the American Textile Industry, 1790-1860* (1984). Carole Marsh's *Rhode Island Bandits, Bushwackers, Outlaws, Crooks, Devils, Ghosts, Desperadoes, and Other Assorted and Sundry Characters!* (1994) describes the colorful characters who have inhabited the state throughout its history, and her *Rhode Island Classic*

Christmas Trivia: Stories, Recipes, Trivia, Legends, Lore, and More! (1994) offers interesting bits of Rhode Island information. A good book for visitors to the state is *The Smithsonian Guides to Historic America: Southern New England* (1998), by Henry Wiencek.

Web Resources. There are many Rhode Island sites on the World Wide Web, and those listed here often give links to others. A good starting point is the Rhode Island Home Page (http://www.state.ri.us), which gives information on state government, history, and visitor information. A Hotlist on Rhode Island (http://www.usoe .k12.ut.us/curr/internet/listrhodeisla.html) has links on state government, history, recreation, and other useful information. R.I. History (http://www.sec.state.ri.us/ submenus/rihstlnk.htm) provides government information and history, including the texts of the state constitution and Royal Charter. The state of Rhode Island Parks and Recreation site (http://www.riparks.com) offers details about the state's many nature areas, history, maps, and park events. The Narragansett Bay site (http://inlet.geol.sc.edu/NAR/home.html) gives information on locations and trails available to nature lovers.

Good sites for information about Newport include Newport Notables (http://www.redwood1747.org/notables/nntitle.htm#h), which offers biographies of prominent Newport citizens from the colony's earliest years. The Touro Synagogue site (http://www.nps.gov/tosy) gives history and information about the country's oldest standing synagogue. Newport's International Tennis Hall of Fame's site (http://www.tennisfame.org) preserves the historical location. The Web site of the *Providence Journal*, the state's main newspaper (http://www.projo.com), offers daily news on events in and around the state. Brown University (http://www.brown.edu) and University of Rhode Island (http://www.uri.edu) maintain updated sites about the respective schools.

Counties

County	Sq. miles	1996 pop.
Bristol	24.7	48,859
Kent	170.1	161,135
Newport	104.1	87,194
Providence	413.3	596,270
Washington	332.9	110,006

Source: U.S. Bureau of the Census; National Association of Counties.

Cities
With 10,000 or more residents

Rank	City	Population
1	Providence	150,890
2	Warwick	84,094
3	Cranston	74,521
4	Pawtucket	68,169
5	East Providence	47,882
6	Woonsocket	41,034
7	Newport	24,279
8	Central Falls	16,364

Population figures are estimated for mid-1998.
Source: U.S. Bureau of the Census.

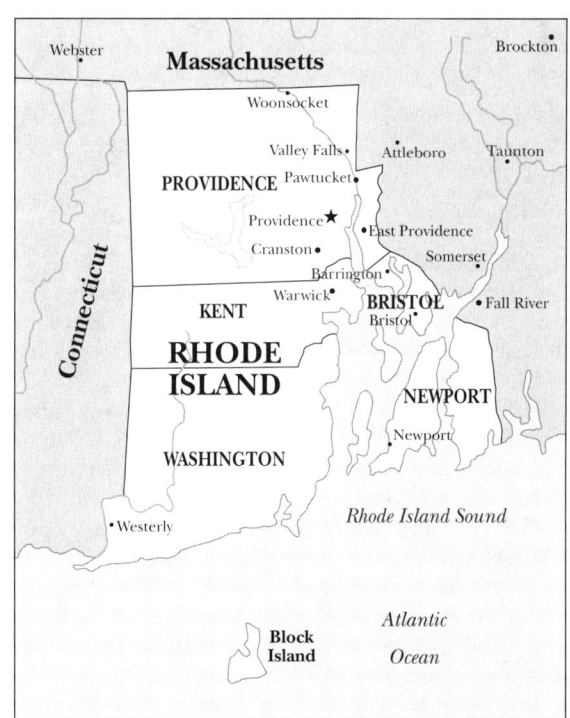

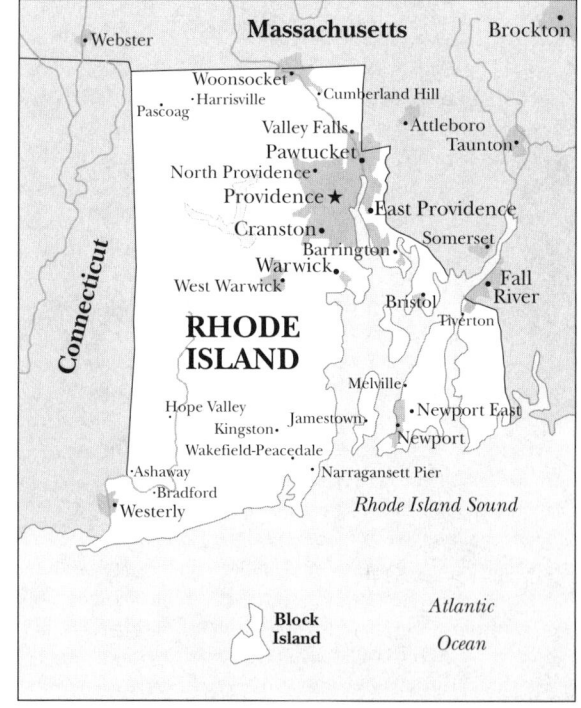

Index to Tables

NA = Reliable data are not available.

DEMOGRAPHICS

Resident state and national populations, 1970-1997

Population figures given in thousands

	State pop.	U.S. pop.	Share	Rank
1970	950	203,302	0.5%	39
1980	947	226,546	0.4%	40
1985	969	237,924	0.4%	42
1990	1,003	248,765	0.4%	43
1995	990	262,761	0.4%	43
1997	987	267,636	0.4%	43

Source: U.S. Bureau of the Census.

Resident population by age, 1997

Age group	Total population
Under 5 years	62,000
5 to 17 years	171,000
18 to 24 years	83,000
25 to 34 years	157,000
35 to 44 years	163,000
45 to 54 years	120,000
55 to 64 years	75,000
65 to 74 years	80,000
75 to 84 years	56,000
85 years and over	20,000
Portion of residents 65 and older	15.8%
National average	12.7%

Population figures are rounded to nearest thousand persons;
figures include armed forces personnel stationed in state.
Source: U.S. Bureau of the Census.

Resident population by race, Hispanic origin, 1997

	State pop.	Share	U.S.
All residents	987,000	100.0%	100.0%
Hispanic white	49,000	5.0%	10.0%
non-Hispanic white	864,000	87.5%	72.7%
African American	47,000	4.8%	12.7%
Native American	5,000	0.5%	0.9%
Asian, Pacific Islander	22,000	2.2%	3.8%

Source: U.S. Bureau of the Census.

Projections of state population, 2000-2025

	Model A Uses interstate migration observed from 1975-1994	Model B Uses Bureau of Economic Analysis employment projections
Year	Population	Population
2000	998,000	989,000
2005	1,012,000	986,000
2010	1,038,000	986,000
2015	1,070,000	989,000
2020	1,105,000	998,000
2025	1,141,000	1,007,000

All population projections, including those for 2000, were calculated in 1997.
Source: U.S. Bureau of the Census, Population Paper Listings PPL-47.

VITAL STATISTICS

Average lifetime in years by race, 1989-1991

	State	U.S.	Rank
All residents	76.54	75.37	16
White residents	76.80	76.13	16
Black residents	NA	69.16	NA

Ranks are from longest-lived to least longest-lived. Ranks exclude Alaska, for which reliable data are not available. Rank for black residents is based on the 32 states for which reliable data are available.
Source: U.S. National Center for Health Statistics.

Infant mortality rates, 1980 and 1995

	State	U.S.
All residents		
1980	11.0	12.6
1995	7.2	7.6
White residents		
1980	10.9	11.0
1995	7.0	6.3
Black residents		
1980	NA	21.4
1995	NA	15.1

Figures represent deaths per 1,000 live births of resident infants under 1 year old, exclusive of fetal deaths; all-residents figures include other races not listed separately.
Source: U.S. National Center for Health Statistics.

Marriages and divorces

Marriages in 1996	7,800
Rate per 1,000 population, 1995.	7.5
U.S. rate, 1995	8.9
Rank among all states	37
Divorces in 1996	3,200
Rate per 1,000 population, 1995.	3.7
U.S. rate, 1995	4.4
Rank among all states	35

Rank is from highest to lowest in country.
Source: U.S. National Center for Health Statistics.

Death rates by leading causes, 1995
Deaths per 100,000 resident population

Cause	State	U.S.
Heart disease	334.1	280.7
Cancer	250.4	204.9
Cerebrovascular diseases	64.8	60.1
Accidents and adverse effects	21.9	35.5
Motor vehicle accidents	8.1	16.5
Chronic obstructive pulmonary diseases	42.0	39.2
Diabetes mellitus	24.7	22.6
HIV	10.0	NA
Suicide	9.0	11.9
Homicide	-	8.7
All causes	975.7	880.0
Rank in overall death rate among states		11

Figures exclude nonresidents who die in state. Causes of death follow International Classification of Diseases. Rank is from highest to lowest in country.
Source: U.S. National Center for Health Statistics.

ECONOMY

Gross state product, 1990-1996
In current dollars

	State product	Increase
1990	$21.5 billion	
1993	$23.3 billion	
1994	$23.9 billion	2.58%
1995	$25.0 billion	4.60%
1996	$25.6 billion	2.40%

Source: U.S. Bureau of Economic Analysis; *Survey of Current Business,* June, 1998.

Gross state product by industry, 1996
In billions

Farms, forestry, fisheries	$0.2
Construction	0.8
Manufacturing	4.3
Transportation, public utilities.	1.7
Wholesale trade.	1.4
Retail trade	2.2
Finance, insurance, real estate.	5.0
Services	5.1
Government.	2.8
State total.	$23.3
Total U.S.	$6,923.8
State share.	0.34%
Rank among states.	44

Total figures include mining, not listed separately.

Source: U.S. Bureau of Economic Analysis; *Survey of Current Business,* June, 1998.

Personal income per capita, 1990 and 1997
In current dollars

	1990	1997
Per capita income	$19,729	$25,760
U.S. average	$19,188	$25,598
Rank among states	14	17

1997 data are preliminary.

Source: U.S. Bureau of Economic Analysis; *Survey of Current Business,* May, 1998.

Energy consumption, 1995
In trillions of British thermal units (BTU)

End-use sectors

Residential.	68.4
Commercial	49.5
Industrial.	64.3
Transportation.	58.6

Sources of energy

Petroleum	98.7
Natural gas.	72.0
Coal	0.1
Hydroelectric power.	10.5
Nuclear electric power	0
Total state per capita consumption	237.0
Total U.S. per capita consumption	344.4
Rank among states.	48
Total state energy consumption.	235.1
Total U.S. energy consumption	90,547.4
State share of U.S. total.	0.26%
Rank among states.	49

Total figures include items not listed separately.

Source: U.S. Energy Information Administration; *State Energy Data Report.*

Nonfarm employment by sectors, 1997

Total	449,000
Construction	15,000
Manufacturing	80,000
Transportation, public utilities.	15,000
Wholesale trade, retail trade	98,000
Finance, insurance, real estate.	27,000
Services	151,000
Government.	64,000

Figures are rounded to nearest thousand persons. Total includes mining, not listed separately.

Source: U.S. Bureau of Labor Statistics; *Employment and Earnings,* monthly.

Foreign exports, 1990-1997
In millions of dollars

Year	State	U.S.	State share
1990	595	394,045	0.15%
1996	919	624,767	0.15%
1997	1,088	688,896	0.16%

Source: U.S. Bureau of the Census; *U.S. Merchandise Trade,* series FT 900.

LAND USE

Federally owned land, 1996

	State	U.S.	State share
Total acres	677,000	2,271,343,000	0.03%
Federally owned	3,000	563,129,000	0.00%
Federal share	0.5%	24.8%	—

Areas are rounded to nearest thousand acres. Figures for federally owned land do not include trust properties.

Source: U.S. General Services Administration; *Inventory Report on Real Property Owned by the United States Throughout the World*, annual.

Land use, 1992
In acres, rounded to nearest thousand

Total surface area	776,000
Federal land	4,000
Total nonfederal.	661,000
Developed	190,000
Total rural	472,000
Cropland	25,000
Pasture land.	24,000
Range land	0
Forest land	393,000
Minor cover/use	30,000

Total surface area figures include water area not shown separately.

Source: U.S. Dept. of Agriculture; Soil Conservation Service; Iowa State University, Statistical Laboratory; *Summary Report, 1992 National Resources Inventory.*

Farms and crop acreage, 1997

	State	U.S.	Share	Rank
Farms (thousands)	1	2,058	0.05%	49
Acres (millions)	—	968	—	—
Acres per farm	90	471	—	49
Acres planted	10	334,139	0.00%	49
Acres harvested	10	319,894	0.00%	49
Farm value (mill.)	$7	$108,805	0.01%	33

State acreage total is less than 500,000 acres.

Numbers of farms are rounded to nearest thousand.

Source: U.S. Dept. of Agriculture; National Agricultural Statistics Service.

GOVERNMENT AND FINANCE

Units of local government, 1997

	State	Total U.S.	Rank
All local governments	119	87,453	49
Counties	0	3,043	—
Municipalities	8	19,372	49
Townships	31	16,629	20
School districts	4	13,726	45
Special districts	76	34,683	47

County ranks are based on the 48 states with county governments; township ranks are based on the 20 states with township governments; school district ranks are based on the 46 states with such districts.

Township figures include "town" governments.

Source: U.S. Bureau of the Census; *1997 Census of Governments, Government Organization*, Series GC97(1).

State government revenue, 1996

Total revenue	$4,271 mill.
General revenue	3,346 mill.
Per capita	3,385
U.S. per capita average	2,910
Rank among states	10
Intergovernmental revenue	
Total	$1,110 mill.
From federal government	1,053 mill.
From local government	57 mill.
Charges and Miscellaneous	
Total	$686 mill.
Current charges	253 mill.
Misc. general revenue	433 mill.
Taxes	
Total	$1,549 mill.
General sales	465 mill.
Selective sales	313 mill.
License taxes	80 mill.
Individual income	581 mill.
Corporate income	87 mill.
Other	23 mill.
Insurance trust revenue	917 mill.

Total revenue figures include items not listed separately.

Source: U.S. Bureau of the Census.

State government expenditures, 1996

General expenditures

Intergovernmental	$505 mill.
Direct expenditures	2,895 mill.
Total	3,400 mill.

Selected direct expenditures

Education	$886 mill.
Public welfare	882 mill.
Health, hospital	332 mill.
Highways	210 mill.
Police	30 mill.
Corrections	116 mill.
Natural resources	28 mill.
Parks and recreation	30 mill.
Government administration	181 mill.
Interest on debt	295 mill.

Other

State per capita expenditures	$3,441
U.S. per capita average	2,854
Rank among states	9
Total state expenditures	4,061 mill.
Total U.S. expenditures	859,959 mill.

Totals include items not listed separately.
Source: U.S. Bureau of the Census.

POLITICS

Governors since statehood

D = Democrat; R = Republican; O = other;
(r) resigned; (d) died in office; (i) removed from office

Nicholas Cooke	1776-1778
William Greene	1778-1786
John Collins	1786-1790
Arthur Fenner (O)	(d) 1790-1805
Henry Smith (O)	1805-1806
Isaac Wilbour (O)	1806-1807
James Fenner (O)	1807-1811
William Jones (O)	1811-1817
Nehemiah Knight (O)	1817-1821
Edward Wilcox (O)	1821
William C. Gibbs (O)	1821-1824
James Fenner (O)	1824-1831
Lemuel H. Arnold (D)	1831-1833
John B. Francis (D)	1833-1838
William Sprague (O)	1838-1839
Samuel W. King (O)	1839-1843
James Fenner (O)	1843-1845
Charles Jackson (O)	1845-1846
Byron Diman (O)	1846-1847
Elisha Harris (O)	1847-1849
Henry B. Anthony (O)	1849-1851
Philip Allen (D)	(r) 1851-1853
Francis M. Dimond (D)	1853-1854
William W. Hoppin (O)	1854-1857
Elisha Dyer II (R)	1857-1859
Thomas G. Turner (R)	1859-1860
William Sprague II (O)	(r) 1860-1863
William C. Cozzens (O)	1863
James Y. Smith (O)	1863-1866
Ambrose E. Burnside (R)	1866-1869
Seth Padelford (R)	1869-1873
Henry Howard (R)	1873-1875
Henry Lippitt (R)	1875-1877
Charles C. Van Zandt (R)	1877-1880
Alfred H. Littlefield (R)	1880-1883
Augustus O. Bourne (R)	1883-1885
George P. Wetmore (R)	1885-1887
John W. Davis (D)	1887-1888
Royal C. Taft (R)	1888-1889
Herbert W. Ladd (R)	1889-1890
John W. Davis (D)	1890-1891
Herbert W. Ladd (R)	1891-1892
Daniel Russell Brown (R)	1892-1895
Charles W. Lippitt (R)	1895-1897
Elisha Dyer III (R)	1897-1900
William Gregory (R)	(d) 1900-1901
Charles D. Kimball (R)	1901-1903
Lucius F. C. Garvin (D)	1903-1905
George H. Utter (R)	1905-1907
James H. Higgins (D)	1907-1909
Aram J. Pothier (R)	1909-1915
Robert Livingston Beeckman (R)	1915-1921
Emery J. San Souci (R)	1921-1923
William S. Flynn (D)	1923-1925
Aram J. Pothier (R)	(d) 1925-1928
Norman S. Case (R)	1928-1933
Theodore F. Green (D)	1933-1937
Robert E. Quinn (D)	1937-1939
William H. Vanderbilt (R)	1939-1941
James Howard McGrath (D)	(r) 1941-1945
John O. Pastore (D)	(r) 1945-1950
John S. McKiernan (D)	1950-1951
Dennis J. Roberts (D)	1951-1959
Christopher Del Sesto (R)	1959-1961
John A. Notte, Jr. (D)	1961-1963
John H. Chafee (R)	1963-1969
Frank R. Licht (D)	1969-1973
Philip W. Noel (D)	1973-1977
J. Joseph Garrahy (D)	1977-1985
Edward D. DiPrete (R)	1985-1991
Bruce Sundlun (D)	1991-1995
Lincoln Almond (R)	1995-

Composition of state legislature, 1990-1998

	Democrats	Republicans
State House (100 seats)		
1990	89	11
1992	85	15
1994	84	16
1996	84	16
1998	86	13
State Senate (50 seats)		
1990	45	5
1992	39	11
1994	40	10
1996	41	9
1998	42	8

Figures for total seats may include independents and minor party members.
Source: Council of State Governments; *State Elective Officials and the Legislatures.*

Composition of congressional delegations, 1989-1999

	Dem	Rep	Total
House of Representatives			
101st Congress, 1989			
State delegates	0	2	2
Total U.S.	259	174	433
102d Congress, 1991			
State delegates	1	1	2
Total U.S.	267	167	434
103d Congress, 1993			
State delegates	1	1	2
Total U.S.	258	176	434
104th Congress, 1995			
State delegates	2	0	2
Total U.S.	197	236	433
105th Congress, 1997			
State delegates	2	0	2
Total U.S.	206	228	434
106th Congress, 1999			
State delegates	2	0	2
Total U.S.	211	222	433

	Dem	Rep	Total
Senate			
101st Congress, 1989			
State delegates	1	1	2
Total U.S.	55	45	100
102d Congress, 1991			
State delegates	1	1	2
Total U.S.	56	44	100
103d Congress, 1993			
State delegates	1	1	2
Total U.S.	57	43	100
104th Congress, 1995			
State delegates	1	1	2
Total U.S.	46	53	99
105th Congress, 1997			
State delegates	1	1	2
Total U.S.	45	55	100
106th Congress, 1999			
State delegates	1	1	2
Total U.S.	45	54	99

Figures are for starts of first sessions. Figure for U.S. Representatives for 101st Congress does not include Alabama and Indiana, which had vacancies. Figures for total U.S. Representatives for 102d, 103d, and 106th Congresses do not include Vermont, which had 1 Independent-Socialist. Figure for U.S. Representatives for 104th Congress does not include Vermont, which had 1 Independent-Socialist, and California, which had 1 vacancy. Figure for U.S. Representatives for 105th Congress does not include New York, which had 1 vacancy. Figure for U.S. Senators for 104th Congress does not include Oregon, which had 1 vacancy. Figure for U.S. Senators for 106th Congress does not include New Hampshire, which had 1 Independent.
Source: U.S. Congress; *Congressional Directory*, biennial.

Voter participation in presidential elections, 1992 and 1996

	1992	1996
State voting age pop.	768,000	750,000
Total U.S. voting age pop.	189,524,000	196,509,000
State share of U.S. total	0.4%	0.4%
Rank among states	43	43
Percent of state casting vote	59.0	47.5
Percent of U.S. total voting	55.1	49.0
Rank among states	25	33

Source: U.S. Bureau of the Census.

HEALTH AND MEDICAL CARE

Medicare, 1997

	Recipients	Payments
State	169,000	$989 mill.
Total U.S.	37,514,000	$206,064 mill.
State share	0.45%	0.48%
Rank among states	40	37

Recipient figures are rounded to nearest thousand persons.
  Ranks are from highest to lowest.
Source: U.S. Health Care Financing Administration.

Medicaid, 1996

	Recipients	Payments
State	130,000	$684 mill.
Total U.S.	35,028,000	$121,419 mill.
State share	0.37%	0.56%
Rank among states	39	36

Recipient figures are rounded to nearest thousand persons.
  Payment figures for fiscal year reflect federal and state
  contribution payments. Ranks are from highest to lowest.
Source: U.S. Health Care Financing Administration.

Health insurance coverage, 1996

	State	U.S.
Total persons covered	847,000	225,070,000
Total persons not covered	93,000	41,716,000
Part not covered	9.9%	15.6%
Rank among states	43	—
Children not covered	13,000	10,554,000
Part not covered	6.3%	14.8%
Rank among states	47	—

Ranks are from most to fewest uninsured. Population figures
  are rounded to nearest thousand persons.
Source: U.S. Bureau of the Census.

AIDS, syphilis, tuberculosis, and measles cases, 1997

Cases	U.S.	State	Share
AIDS	58,443	152	0.26%
Syphilis	8,550	2	0.02%
Tuberculosis	18,534	39	0.21%
Measles	148,000	NA	NA

Measles figures are rounded to nearest thousand cases.
Source: U.S. Centers for Disease Control and Prevention.

HOUSING

Homeownership rates, 1985-1997

	1985	1990	1997
State	61.4%	58.5%	58.7%
Total U.S.	63.9%	63.9%	65.7%
Rank among states	42	45	47

Source: U.S. Bureau of the Census.

Home sales, 1990 and 1997
In thousands of units

Existing home sales	1990	1997	Change
State sales	7.8	14.3	6.5
Total U.S. sales	3,560	4,730	1,170
State share of U.S. total	0.22%	0.30%	0.08%
Rank among states	46	42	—

Source: National Association of Realtors; *Real Estate Outlook: Market Trends and Insights.*

EDUCATION

Public school enrollment, 1995

State K-8 enrollment	110,000
Total U.S. K-8 enrollment	32,341,000
State share of total U.S.	0.34%
State 9-12 enrollment	40,000
Total U.S. 9-12 enrollment	12,500,000
State share of U.S. total	0.32%
State public school enroll. rate	88.1%
Overall U.S. rate	91.6%
Rank among states	44

Enrollment figures (which include unclassified students) are rounded to nearest thousand pupils in fall term; kindergarten (K)-8 grade figures include some prekindergarten students. Enrollment rate is based on percentage of persons 5-17 years old. Rank is from highest to lowest.
Source: U.S. National Center for Education Statistics.

Public college finances, 1996

State FTE enrollment	25,200
Total U.S. FTE enrollment	8,268,800
State share of total U.S.	0.30%
Rank among states	46
State and local appropriations	$128,100,000
Total U.S. state and local appropriations	$39,699 mill.
State share of total U.S.	0.32%
Rank among states	45
State net tuition revenues	$108,900,000
Total U.S. net tuition	$18,348,100,000
State share of total U.S.	0.59%
Rank among states	40

FTE=Full-time equivalent; credit and noncredit enrollment including summer session in academic year ending in 1996.
Enrollments are rounded to nearest thousand students. Net tuition revenues exclude appropriation to students attending in-state public institutions. Rankings are from highest shares to lowest.
Source: Research Associates of Washington.

TRANSPORTATION AND TRAVEL

Highway mileage, 1996

Interstate	69
Other arterial	821
Collector roads	1,362
Local roads	4,254
Urban roads	4,641
Rural roads	1,360
Total state	6,001
U.S. total	3,933,985
State share	0.2%
Rank among states	48

Source: U.S. Federal Highway Administration.

Motor vehicle registrations and driver licenses, 1996

In thousands

Vehicle registrations	State	U.S.	Share	Rank
Autos, trucks, buses	696	206,365	0.34%	45
Autos only	508	128,439	0.40%	41
Motorcycles	17	3,832	0.44%	44
Driver licenses	669	179,539	0.37%	45

Figures do not include vehicles owned by military services.
Source: U.S. Federal Highway Administration; *Highway Statistics; Selected Highway Statistics and Charts.*

Domestic travel expenditures, 1995

Spending by U.S. residents on overnight trips and day trips of at least 100 miles

Total expenditures in state	$744 mill.
Total expenditures in U.S.	$360,314 mill.
State share of total U.S.	0.21%
Rank among states	50

Source: Travel Industry Association of America.

CRIME AND LAW ENFORCEMENT

State and local police officers, 1996

Local police	1,958
State police	193
Sheriffs	153
Total	2,422
Officers per 10,000 residents	24
U.S. average	25
Rank among states.	17

Figures cover full-time sworn officers; totals include special
police not shown separately.
Source: U.S. Bureau of Justice Statistics; *Census of State and
Local Law Enforcement Agencies, 1996.*

Crime rates, 1996

Rates per 100,000 resident population

Violent crimes	State	U.S.
Total violent	347	634
Murder	2.5	7.4
Forcible rape	29.0	36.1
Robbery	83	202
Aggravated assault	232	388
Property crimes		
Total property	3,646	4,445
Burglary	822	943
Larceny/theft	2,360	2,976
Motor vehicle theft	464	526
Totals	3,994	5,079

Source: U.S. Federal Bureau of Investigation; *Crime in the
United States,* annual.

State prison populations, 1980-1996

	State	U.S.	State share
1980	813	305,458	0.27%
1990	2,392	708,393	0.34%
1996	3,271	1,025,624	0.32%

Figures exclude prisoners in federal penitentiaries.
Source: U.S. Bureau of Justice Statistics.

South Carolina

Location: Southeast coast of continental United States

Area and rank: 30,111 square miles (77,988 square kilometers); 32,007 square miles (82,898 square kilometers) including water; fortieth largest state in area

Coastline: 187 miles (301 kilometers)

Shoreline: 2,876 miles (4,627 kilometers)

Population and rank: 3,760,181 (1997); twenty-sixth largest state in population

Capital: Columbia

Charleston's Battery district, located near Fort Sumter, is famed for its historic homes. (South Carolina Department of Parks, Recreation & Tourism)

Largest city: Columbia (110,840 people in 1998)

Entered Union and rank: May 23, 1788; eighth state

Present constitution adopted: 1895

Counties: 46

State name: South Carolina was named after Charles II of England

State nickname: Palmetto State

Mottos: *Animis opibusque parati* (Prepared in mind and resources); *Dum spiro spero* (While I breathe, I hope)

State flag: Blue field with palmetto tree and crescent moon

Highest point: Sassafras Mountain — 3,560 feet (1,085 meters)

Lowest point: Atlantic Ocean — sea level

Highest recorded temperature: 111 degrees Fahrenheit (44 degrees Celsius) — Camden, 1954

Lowest recorded temperature: −19 degrees Fahrenheit (−28 degrees Celsius) — Caesar's Head, 1985

State song: "Carolina"

State tree: Palmetto tree

State flower: Carolina yellow jessamine

State bird: Carolina wren

South Carolina History

South Carolina, known as the Palmetto State, is the smallest of the southeastern states and is one of the richest in history and enduring influence on national events and development. A blend of diverse cultures, including European, Native American, and African American, produced notable social, artistic, political, military, and cultural accomplishments. The state has been among the richest and the poorest in the United States and has known both victory and harsh defeat.

Early History. The first human inhabitants of what is now South Carolina arrived around 13,000 B.C.E. as hunters of the large animals, including elephants, that inhabited the region. During the period from 8000 to 1500 B.C.E., the area's climate changed, bringing hardwood trees and

more easily huntable animals such as deer, turkey, and squirrel. Many inhabitants became largely migratory, moving through the seasons to follow their prey. Along the coast, shellfish provided a major diet staple for more settled groups.

Around 1150 B.C.E. a new group, the Mississippians, moved into the area. They built large villages with earthen mounds for temples along river bluffs. These villages established a nation known as Cofitachequi, after its capital, located on the banks of the Wateree River in central South Carolina. In 1540 the Spanish explorer Hernando de Soto was greeted by the "queen" of Cofitachequi during his expedition across the Southeast.

At the time of the arrival of the Europeans, there were thirty to forty separate Native American na-

Reenactment of a Revolutionary War battle in Kings Mountain State Park, where Tennessee pioneers turned back a British force trying to occupy South Carolina in 1780. (South Carolina Department of Parks, Recreation & Tourism)

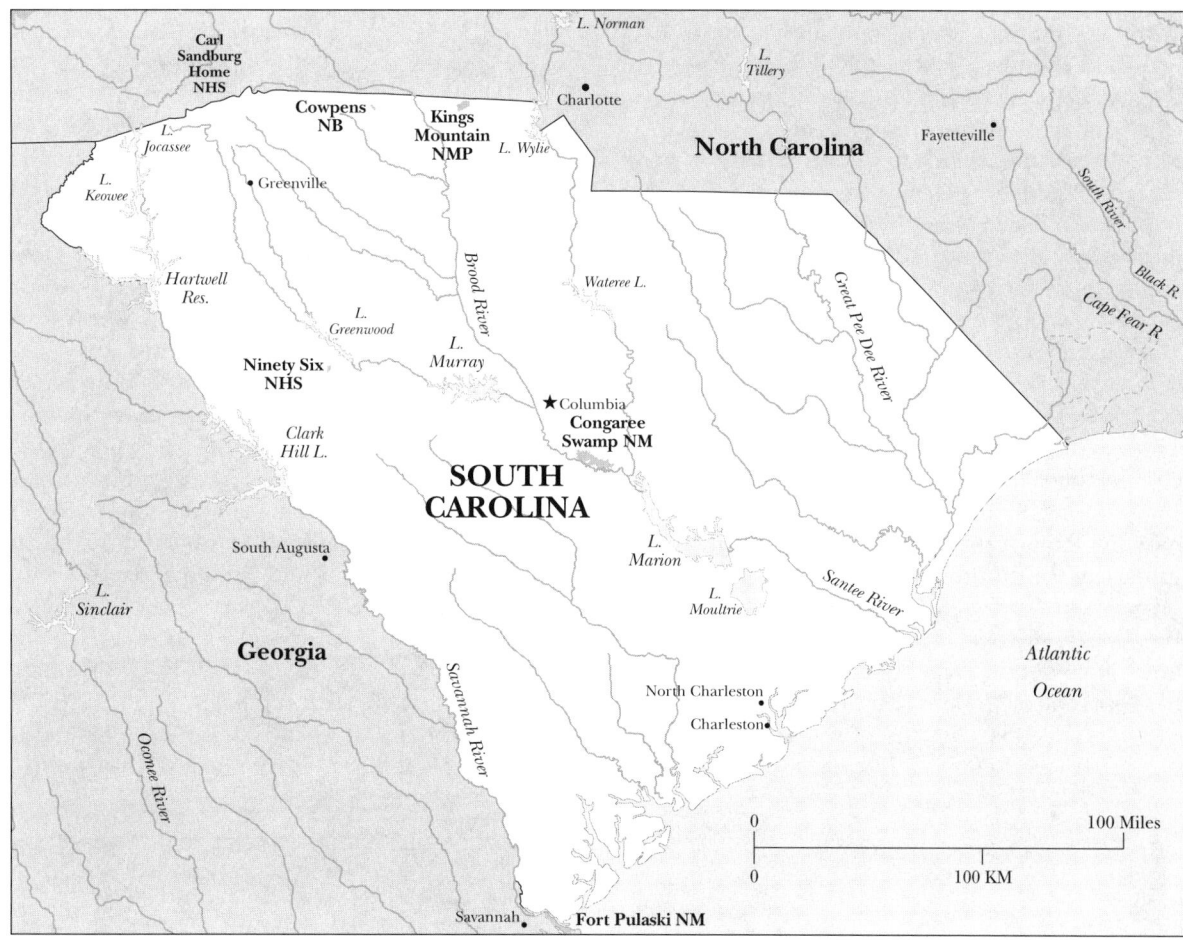

tions in the region, including Cherokee, Saluda, Catawba, Wateree, Congaree, Wando, Waccamaw, and Coosaw. All of these names, and many others, were preserved in place names in South Carolina.

Exploration and Colonization. By 1521 the Spanish had explored the Carolina coast, and on August 18, 1525, Saint Helena's feast day, they sighted and named an island and a sound in her honor; both would retain the name Saint Helena. Lucas Vásquez de Ayllón founded a short-lived Spanish settlement on Winyah Bay near modern Georgetown in 1526, and in 1562, the French under Jean Ribaut challenged the Spanish by establishing a small fort on an island in what they named Port Royal Sound.

The Spanish returned in 1566 and established Santa Elena, also on Port Royal Sound, which grew into a settlement of considerable size and was for a

time the capital of all Spanish colonies in North America. However, under increasing pressure from the Native Americans and the English, the Spanish abandoned Santa Elena in 1587 to consolidate their position at St. Augustine in northern Florida.

Colonization and Revolution. In 1663 King Charles II of England granted extensive lands, named "Carolina" after himself, to eight Lord Proprietors, chief among them Anthony Ashley Cooper, Earl of Shaftesbury. Cooper, along with English philosopher John Locke, drafted an elaborate Fundamental Constitution for the colony. In April, 1670, the first settlers arrived. Within ten years they had established the city of Charleston at the confluence of the Ashley and Cooper Rivers. Settled largely by English inhabitants of Barbados, the new colony prospered from the production of crops including rice, indigo, and cotton. The wealth of these crops, and the plantation systems they fostered, was gained only through the knowledge and labor of large numbers of African slaves. Long before the American Revolution, there were more blacks than whites in the colony. Along the South Carolina Sea Islands, they created their own distinctive culture, including the Gullah language, a mixture of African, Caribbean, and English languages.

Early threats to the colony included struggles with the Native Americans and raids by pirates such as the notorious Blackbeard (Edward Teach). These dangers were increased by proprietary incompetence, and in 1729 South Carolina became a royal colony. South Carolina was a leader in the move for American independence, and during the American Revolution more than 130 battles and skirmishes were fought in the state. In June, 1776, British naval forces were repulsed from Charleston but returned and captured the city in 1780. The battles of Kings Mountain in 1780 and Cowpens in 1781 helped turn the tide of the war in favor of the Americans. Partisan leaders such as Francis Marion, known as the Swamp Fox, played an essential role in the struggle for independence.

Civil War and Reconstruction. South Carolinians Charles Pinckney and John Rutledge were highly influential in drafting the U.S. Constitution, and they were instrumental in having it adopted by the state legislature in 1788. However, as with many others in the state and throughout the South, they wished to restrain the powers of the federal government, especially regarding the highly sensitive issue of slavery.

It was because of this concern that South Carolina, along with other southern states, increasingly insisted upon the doctrine of state's rights. Senator John C. Calhoun became the chief spokesperson for the South, and while he helped to fashion compromises that kept South Carolina in the Union, he also advocated nullification, the doctrine that a state could declare invalid within its borders an act of the national government. During the Nullification Crisis of 1832-1833 President Andrew Jackson ordered U.S. Navy ships to Charleston to enforce federal law. The election of President Abraham Lincoln in 1860 prompted

The Civil War is traditionally regarded as having begun on April 12, 1861, when Confederate troops fired on Union soldiers defending Fort Sumter in Charleston's harbor. (Corbis)

Tree-shaded entrance to one of South Carolina's great farm homes evokes the opulence of the state's nineteenth century plantation economy. (PhotoDisc)

South Carolina to become the first state to secede from the Union, on December 20, 1860.

On April 12, 1861, the Civil War began, when Confederate troops fired on Union-held Fort Sumter in Charleston harbor. During the war, Union troops quickly captured the sea islands around Port Royal Sound, liberating thousands of slaves and placing Charleston under a four-year siege. After General William T. Sherman's Union army completed its March to the Sea from Atlanta to Savannah, it "let South Carolina howl" as it swept through the state, forcing the Confederates to abandon Charleston and Columbia, the state capital. Sherman largely blamed South Carolina for the war because it was the first state to secede, and he punished it harshly.

South Carolina was readmitted to the Union in 1868, and a Reconstruction government mingled social and educational reforms with blatant corruption. In 1876, under the leadership of former Confederate general Wade Hampton, white South

Carolinians reclaimed their hold on the state. For almost a hundred years, the memory of the Civil War and Reconstruction ensured that South Carolina would remain a solidly Democratic state. It was only during the civil rights era of the 1960's, when the Democratic Party became closely associated with that effort, that many white South Carolinians turned to the Republican Party. Senator Strom Thurmond, who had run as a Dixiecrat in 1948 to protest the Democrats' civil rights platform, became a Republican in 1964. In 1974 James Edwards was the first Republican elected governor after Reconstruction.

A Modern Economy. After the Civil War, agriculture remained South Carolina's primary source of income. In the 1880's the textile industry greatly increased, due in large part to the hydroelectric power available upstate. Textile plants drew workers from the farms and rural areas to create a new and thriving industry, until the Great Depression brought economic disaster in the 1930's. The New

Deal of President Franklin Delano Roosevelt sought to remedy these problems in part by the creation of the Santee Cooper project, one of the largest hydroelectric and navigational efforts in North America, which helped advance South Carolina's economy into the twentieth century. During and after World War II, large military bases throughout the state provided additional economic benefits.

However, agriculture and textiles remained the state's major sources of income until the early 1970's, when modern industry and technology took hold, best exemplified by BMW's 1993 decision to locate its first car-manufacturing plant outside Germany in South Carolina. By that time, manufacturing had become the state's number-one industry in terms of employees and included more than two hundred international companies.

Tourism became a major source of income, with visitors flocking to South Carolina's two hundred miles of coastline and beaches; historic cities such as Camden, Charleston, and Beaufort; and three hundred golf courses, many of them world class and the site of prestigious tournaments.

Modernization in the economy brought increased attention to both an old problem and a new concern: the issue of resolving racial differences among the state's population and the need to protect the state's natural environment. South Carolina, with its long and often troubled history, and its abundant natural resources threatened by rapid development and population growth, faced the delicate task of balancing past, present, and future.

Michael Witkoski

South Carolina Time Line

1500-1600	Native American nation of Cofitachequi is powerful in Southeast.
1521	Spanish explore South Carolina coast.
1525	Spanish explore and name Saint Helena Island and Sound.
1526	Lucas Vásquez de Ayllón establishes Spanish settlement on Winyah Bay.
1540	Spanish explorer Hernando de Soto passes through area.
1562	Jean Ribaut establishes short-lived French colony on Port Royal Sound.
1566	Spanish establish Santa Elena on Port Royal Sound.
1587	Spanish abandon Santa Elena.
1663	King Charles II of England grants Carolina to eight Lord Proprietors.
Mar., 1670	English establish Charles Town (later Charleston) on Ashley River.
1670	First African slaves arrive from the West Indies.
1680	Charleston is moved to a peninsula between Ashley and Cooper Rivers.
1680	Rice introduced as a crop.
1715	War rages between English settlers and Yamasee Indians.
1718	Colonists end threat of pirates.
1729	Carolina becomes a royal colony.
1730	North and South Carolina become separate colonies.
1742	Indigo introduced as a crop.

1760	Cherokees defeated in conflicts with colonists.
1776	British defeated in attack on Charleston.
1778	South Carolina declares independence from Great Britain.
1780	British capture Charleston.
1786	State capital moved to Columbia.
May 23, 1788	South Carolina becomes eighth state to join the Union.
1801	University of South Carolina is established in Columbia.
1820	Cotton begins to replace rice and indigo as the major crop.
1822	Denmark Vesey leads abortive slave revolt in Charleston.
1832	Legislature passes Ordinance of Nullification.
1833	President Andrew Jackson orders U.S. Navy fleet to South Carolina to enforce federal laws.
Dec. 20, 1860	South Carolina becomes first state to secede from the Union, starting movement that leads to the Civil War.
1865	Union forces under General William T. Sherman march through state; Columbia is burned.
1866-1876	South Carolina undergoes Reconstruction.
June 25, 1868	South Carolina is readmitted to the Union.
1880	Textile industry begins rapid expansion.
1895	New state constitution is adopted.
1942	Santee Cooper hydroelectric project is completed.
1948	Governor Strom Thurmond runs for president as a Dixiecrat to protest civil rights plank in Democratic party platform.
1950	Site in Aiken and Barnwell counties selected for plutonium-making project known as the Savannah River Plant.
1952	U.S. Supreme Court upholds segregation in South Carolina.
1963	Integration of state's public school system begins in Charleston.
1964	U.S. Senator Strom Thurmond switches from Democratic to Republican party, beginning realignment of state's political structure.
1970	State begins to attract modern industrial and technological companies.
1974	James Edwards is first Republican elected governor after Reconstruction.
1989	Hurricane Hugo sweeps through state, leaving $6 billion in damage and twenty-nine dead.
1993	BMW locates its first manufacturing facility outside Germany in upstate South Carolina.

Notes for Further Study

Published Sources. South Carolina's most distinguished historian, Walter Edgar, wrote two excellent studies of the state. *South Carolina: A History* (1998) is the definitive state history presented in a cleanly written and engaging narrative. It is well illustrated and amply annotated. His *South Carolina in the Modern Age* (1992) is a study of the years following the Civil War, focusing on the transformation from an agricultural to a textile and then industrial economic base. *Mary Chestnut's Civil War* (1981), edited by C. Vann Woodward, is an acclaimed presentation of a key historical document, the wartime diary of Mary Chestnut of Charleston, which is fundamental to understanding the Civil War's impact on the state. Edward Miller's *Gullah Statesman: Robert Smalls, from Slavery to Congress, 1835-1915* (1995) is a comprehensive biography of the man who became one of the outstanding African American leaders of the post-Civil War era.

South Carolina Politics and Government (1994), by Cole Blease Graham, Jr., and William V. Moore, presents the intricate nature of South Carolina political life clearly and engagingly. Peter A. Coclanis's *The Shadow of a Dream: Economic Life and Death in the South Carolina Low Country, 1670-1920* (1989) is a review of economic developments throughout most of the state's history. It is especially valuable for its discussion of the major cash crops of the antebellum era.

Web Resources. The best place to begin a search for information on South Carolina, with links to state government sites, educational institutions, and other organizations, is the State of South Carolina Public Information Home Page (http://www.state.sc.us). This site can be supplemented with a visit to the home page of the South Carolina State Library (http://www.state.sc.us/scsl), which is valuable because the library provides extensive resources for those interested in all aspects of

South Carolina, from contemporary events to its earliest history. An excellent source for historical information is the South Carolina Department of Archives and History (http://www.state.sc.us/scdah/homepage.htm). As the holder of the state's official records, papers, and documents, the Department of Archives has a site that is very useful to any student of South Carolina and its history. Those in search of historical information should also visit the South Carolina Historical Society (http://www.schistory.org). The state's rich history has encouraged study by professional, independent, and amateur scholars; this site is an excellent place to sample their research and to find links to additional Web pages.

Those who are interested in more general and contemporary topics should visit South Carolina "A" to "Z" (http://www.s-carolina.com), which is a comprehensive source that gives users the opportunity to explore a wide range of topics and interests. Another excellent source for a variety of Web sites is SCIWay (South Carolina Information Highway) (http://www.sciway.net). This is a frequently updated site that directs users to Web resources of all sorts relating to South Carolina. The sites listed run the gamut from artistic to zoological. Finally, the most famous city in South Carolina has its own Web site, the Charleston Connection (http://www.aesiricom/charleston/welcome.html). This site is devoted to information on one of the most historic cities in South Carolina and the nation.

Counties

County	Sq. miles	1996 pop.	County	Sq. miles	1996 pop.
Abbeville	508.0	24,275	Dorchester	574.8	84,920
Aiken	1,073.1	133,130	Edgefield	501.9	19,051
Allendale	408.2	11,471	Fairfield	686.6	22,305
Anderson	718.0	156,558	Florence	799.2	123,365
Bamberg	393.3	16,702	Georgetown	814.9	51,555
Barnwell	548.5	21,640	Greenville	792.1	345,173
Beaufort	587.0	102,735	Greenwood	455.5	62,789
Berkeley	1,099.5	132,502	Hampton	559.9	19,098
Calhoun	380.3	13,724	Horry	1,133.7	163,856
Charleston	917.4	277,721	Jasper	654.3	16,365
Cherokee	392.7	48,003	Kershaw	726.3	47,279
Chester	580.6	33,488	Lancaster	549.0	57,164
Chesterfield	798.8	39,794	Laurens	713.2	61,614
Clarendon	607.2	29,406	Lee	410.3	18,537
Colleton	1,056.5	36,893	Lexington	700.8	195,606
Darlington	562.1	65,319	McCormick	359.6	9,432
Dillon	404.9	29,574	Marion	489.1	34,895

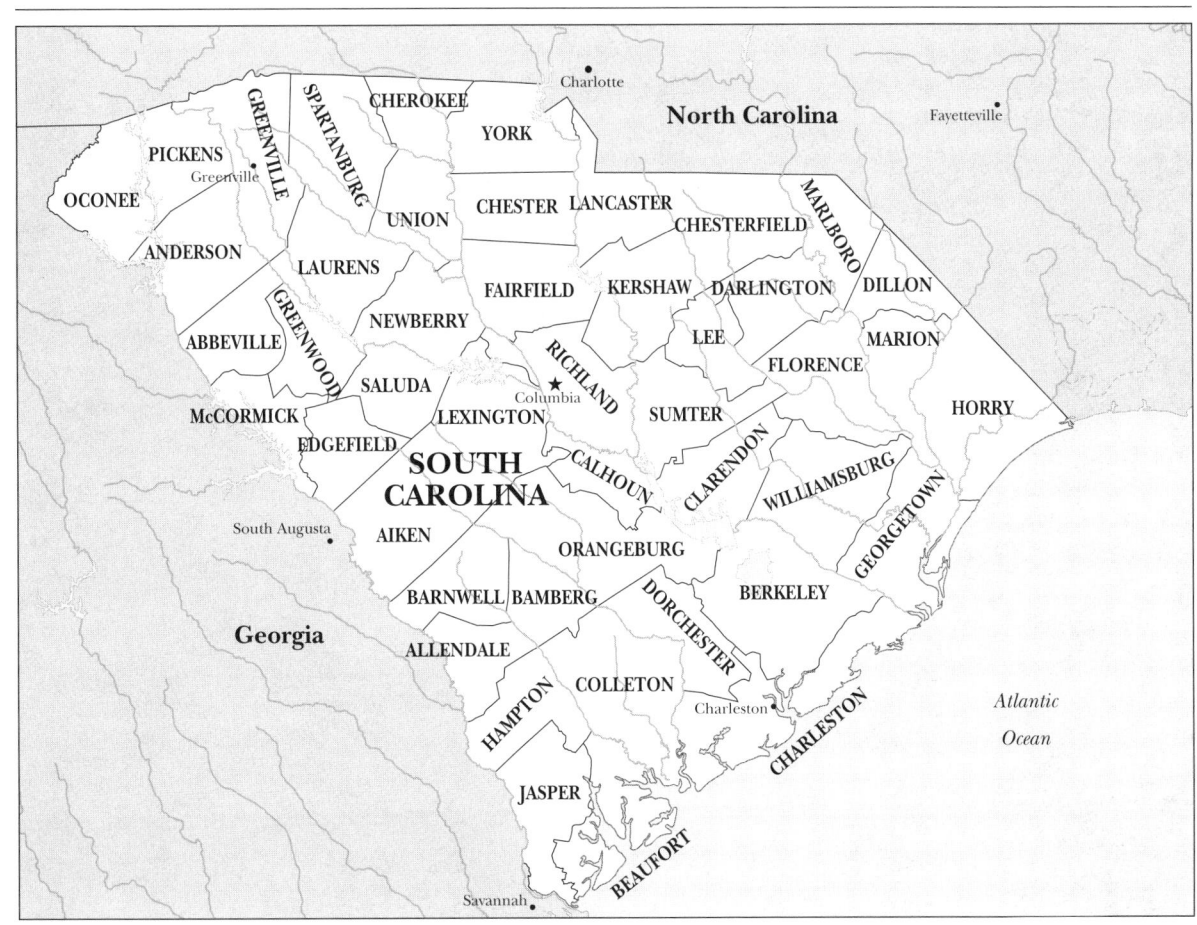

County	Sq. miles	1996 pop.
Marlboro	479.7	29,770
Newberry	630.8	34,268
Oconee	625.1	62,643
Orangeburg	1,106.0	87,324
Pickens	496.9	103,983
Richland	756.5	292,601
Saluda	451.4	16,843
Spartanburg	811.0	242,962

County	Sq. miles	1996 pop.
Sumter	665.5	107,161
Union	514.2	30,709
Williamsburg	934.0	37,244
York	682.5	147,299

Source: U.S. Bureau of the Census; National Association of Counties.

Cities

With 10,000 or more residents

Rank	City	Population
1	Columbia	110,840
2	Charleston	87,044

Rank	City	Population
3	North Charleston	68,072
4	Greenville	56,436

(continued)

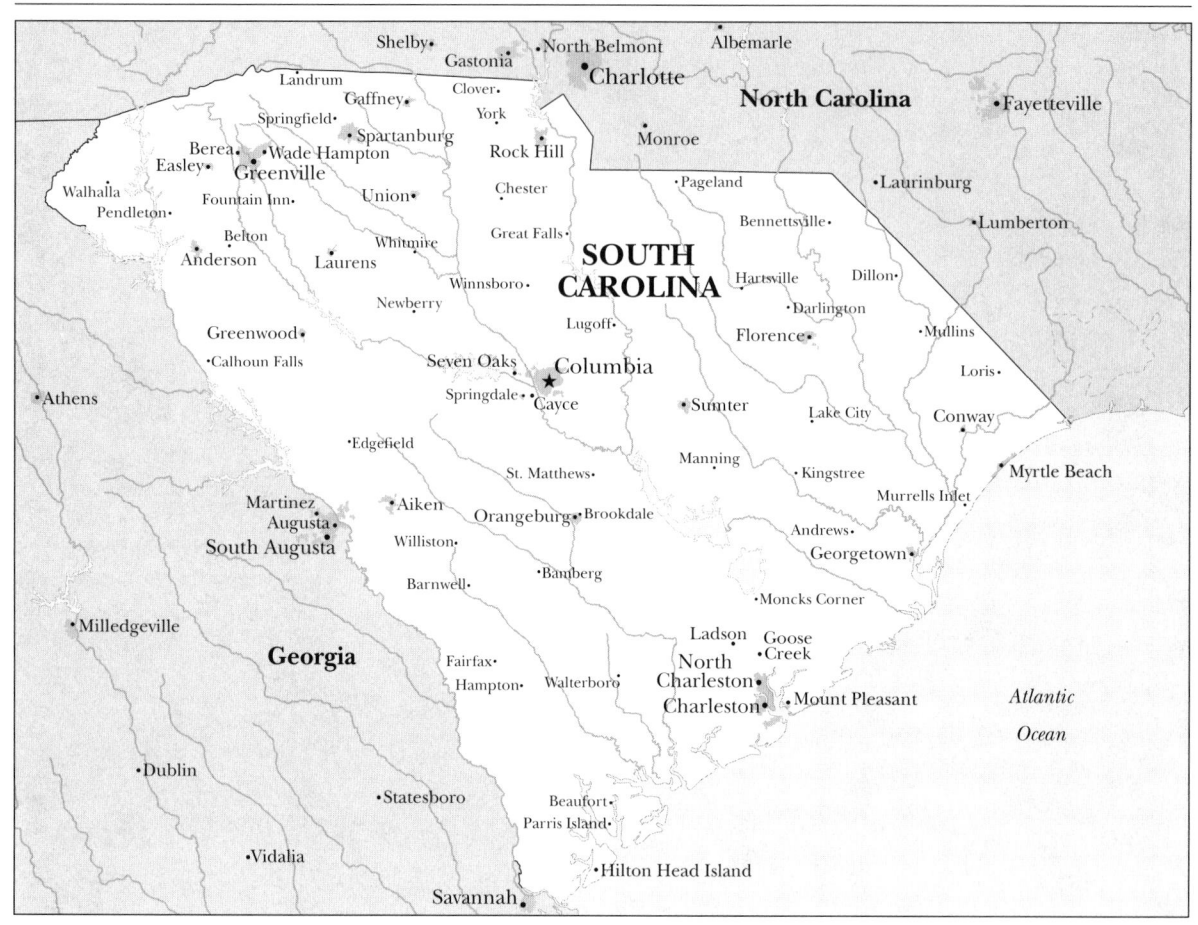

Rank	City	Population
5	Rock Hill	46,218
6	Mount Pleasant	41,330
7	Spartanburg	40,954
8	Sumter	40,518
9	Hilton Head Island	30,377
10	Florence	29,511
11	Goose Creek	26,673
12	Anderson	26,098
13	Myrtle Beach	25,284
14	Summerville	24,292
15	Aiken	22,861
16	Greenwood	19,536
17	Easley	17,703

Rank	City	Population
18	North Augusta	16,307
19	Mauldin	14,330
20	Gaffney	13,078
21	Hanahan	13,047
22	Greer	12,965
23	Orangeburg	12,733
24	Clemson	12,336
25	Cayce	11,936
26	Simpsonville	11,661
27	West Columbia	10,941
28	Irmo	10,850

Population figures are estimated for mid-1998.
Source: U.S. Bureau of the Census.

Index to Tables

NA = Reliable data are not available.

DEMOGRAPHICS

Resident state and national populations, 1970-1997

Population figures given in thousands

	State pop.	U.S. pop.	Share	Rank
1970	2,591	203,302	1.3%	26
1980	3,122	226,546	1.4%	24
1985	3,303	237,924	1.4%	24
1990	3,486	248,765	1.4%	25
1995	3,683	262,761	1.4%	26
1997	3,760	267,636	1.4%	26

Source: U.S. Bureau of the Census.

Resident population by age, 1997

Age group	Total population
Under 5 years	254,000
5 to 17 years	702,000
18 to 24 years	377,000
25 to 34 years	567,000
35 to 44 years	603,000
45 to 54 years	485,000
55 to 64 years	319,000
65 to 74 years	262,000
75 to 84 years	149,000
85 years and over	43,000
Portion of residents 65 and older	12.1%
National average	12.7%

Population figures are rounded to nearest thousand persons;
figures include armed forces personnel stationed in state.
Source: U.S. Bureau of the Census.

Resident population by race, Hispanic origin, 1997

	State pop.	Share	U.S.
All residents	3,760,000	100.0%	100.0%
Hispanic white	39,000	1.0%	10.0%
non-Hispanic white	2,550,000	67.8%	72.7%
African American	1,130,000	30.1%	12.7%
Native American	9,000	0.2%	0.9%
Asian, Pacific Islander	32,000	0.9%	3.8%

Source: U.S. Bureau of the Census.

Projections of state population, 2000-2025

	Model A Uses interstate migration observed from 1975-1994	Model B Uses Bureau of Economic Analysis employment projections
Year	Population	Population
2000	3,858,000	3,852,000
2005	4,033,000	4,015,000
2010	4,205,000	4,169,000
2015	4,369,000	4,318,000
2020	4,517,000	4,455,000
2025	4,645,000	4,574,000

All population projections, including those for 2000, were calculated in 1997.
Source: U.S. Bureau of the Census, Population Paper Listings PPL-47.

VITAL STATISTICS

Average lifetime in years by race, 1989-1991

	State	U.S.	Rank
All residents	73.51	75.37	47
White residents	75.33	76.13	39
Black residents	68.82	69.16	24

Ranks are from longest-lived to least longest-lived. Ranks exclude Alaska, for which reliable data are not available. Rank for black residents is based on the 32 states for which reliable data are available.
Source: U.S. National Center for Health Statistics.

Infant mortality rates, 1980 and 1995

	State	U.S.
All residents		
1980	15.6	12.6
1995	9.6	7.6
White residents		
1980	10.8	11.0
1995	6.7	6.3
Black residents		
1980	22.9	21.4
1995	14.6	15.1

Figures represent deaths per 1,000 live births of resident infants under 1 year old, exclusive of fetal deaths; all-residents figures include other races not listed separately.
Source: U.S. National Center for Health Statistics.

Marriages and divorces

Marriages in 1996.	43,100
Rate per 1,000 population, 1995	12.1
U.S. rate, 1995	8.9
Rank among all states.	7
Divorces in 1996	15,200
Rate per 1,000 population, 1995.	4.0
U.S. rate, 1995	4.4
Rank among all states	32

Rank is from highest to lowest in country.
Source: U.S. National Center for Health Statistics.

Death rates by leading causes, 1995
Deaths per 100,000 resident population

Cause	State	U.S.
Heart disease	277.6	280.7
Cancer	201.9	204.9
Cerebrovascular diseases	75.2	60.1
Accidents and adverse effects	44.5	35.5
Motor vehicle accidents	23.1	16.5
Chronic obstructive pulmonary diseases	38.4	39.2
Diabetes mellitus	27.4	22.6
HIV	15.2	NA
Suicide	11.9	11.9
Homicide	8.9	8.7
All causes	912.7	880.0
Rank in overall death rate among states		25

Figures exclude nonresidents who die in state. Causes of death follow International Classification of Diseases. Rank is from highest to lowest in country.
Source: U.S. National Center for Health Statistics.

ECONOMY

Gross state product, 1990-1996
In current dollars

	State product	Increase
1990	$65.4 billion	
1993	$75.2 billion	
1994	$80.7 billion	7.31%
1995	$85.3 billion	5.70%
1996	$89.5 billion	4.92%

Source: U.S. Bureau of Economic Analysis; *Survey of Current Business,* June, 1998.

Gross state product by industry, 1996
In billions

Farms, forestry, fisheries	$1.1
Construction	3.6
Manufacturing	23.4
Transportation, public utilities	6.7
Wholesale trade	4.9
Retail trade	8.9
Finance, insurance, real estate	10.3
Services	11.7
Government	11.9
State total	$82.7
Total U.S.	$6,923.8
State share	1.19%
Rank among states	27

Total figures include mining, not listed separately.
Source: U.S. Bureau of Economic Analysis; *Survey of Current Business,* June, 1998.

Personal income per capita, 1990 and 1997
In current dollars

	1990	1997
Per capita income	$15,448	$20,755
U.S. average	$19,188	$25,598
Rank among states	39	39

1997 data are preliminary.
Source: U.S. Bureau of Economic Analysis; *Survey of Current Business,* May, 1998.

Energy consumption, 1995
In trillions of British thermal units (BTU)

End-use sectors

Residential	275.5
Commercial	183.5
Industrial	617.9
Transportation	323.7

Sources of energy

Petroleum	435.5
Natural gas	156.0
Coal	314.5
Hydroelectric power	28.8
Nuclear electric power	524.1
Total state per capita consumption	382.0
Total U.S. per capita consumption	344.4
Rank among states	18
Total state energy consumption	1,400.7
Total U.S. energy consumption	90,547.4
State share of U.S. total	1.55%
Rank among states	23

Total figures include items not listed separately.
Source: U.S. Energy Information Administration; *State Energy Data Report.*

Nonfarm employment by sectors, 1997

Total	1,722,000
Construction	100,000
Manufacturing	362,000
Transportation, public utilities	75,000
Wholesale trade, retail trade	414,000
Finance, insurance, real estate	75,000
Services	395,000
Government	299,000

Figures are rounded to nearest thousand persons. Total includes mining, not listed separately.
Source: U.S. Bureau of Labor Statistics; *Employment and Earnings,* monthly.

Foreign exports, 1990-1997
In millions of dollars

Year	State	U.S.	State share
1990	3,116	394,045	0.79%
1996	6,698	624,767	1.07%
1997	7,517	688,896	1.09%

Source: U.S. Bureau of the Census; *U.S. Merchandise Trade,* series FT 900.

LAND USE

Federally owned land, 1996

	State	U.S.	State share
Total acres	19,374,000	2,271,343,000	0.85%
Federally owned	935,000	563,129,000	0.17%
Federal share	4.8%	24.8%	—

Areas are rounded to nearest thousand acres. Figures for
federally owned land do not include trust properties.
Source: U.S. General Services Administration; *Inventory Report
on Real Property Owned by the United States Throughout the
World,* annual.

Land use, 1992

In acres, rounded to nearest thousand

Total surface area	19,912,000
Federal land	1,156,000
Total nonfederal	17,961,000
Developed	1,856,000
Total rural	16,105,000
Cropland.	2,983,000
Pasture land	1,190,000
Range land	0
Forest land	10,922,000
Minor cover/use.	1,010,000

Total surface area figures include water area not shown
separately.
Source: U.S. Dept. of Agriculture; Soil Conservation Service;
Iowa State University, Statistical Laboratory; *Summary
Report, 1992 National Resources Inventory.*

Farms and crop acreage, 1997

	State	U.S.	Share	Rank
Farms (thousands)	22	2,058	1.07%	32
Acres (millions)	5	968	0.52%	38
Acres per farm	233	471	—	31
Acres planted	2,030	334,139	0.61%	32
Acres harvested	1,962	319,894	0.61%	32
Farm value (mill.)	$737	$108,805	0.68%	13

Numbers of farms are rounded to nearest thousand
Source: U.S. Dept. of Agriculture; National Agricultural
Statistics Service.

GOVERNMENT AND FINANCE

Units of local government, 1997

	State	Total U.S.	Rank
All local governments	716	87,453	35
Counties	46	3,043	31
Municipalities	269	19,372	29
Townships	0	16,629	—
School districts	91	13,726	35
Special districts	310	34,683	36

County ranks are based on the 48 states with county
governments; township ranks are based on the 20 states
with township governments; school district ranks are based
on the 46 states with such districts.
Source: U.S. Bureau of the Census; *1997 Census of Governments,
Government Organization,* Series GC97(1).

State government revenue, 1996

Total revenue	$12,602 mill.
General revenue	10,261 mill.
Per capita.	2,761
U.S. per capita average	2,910
Rank among states.	29
Intergovernmental revenue	
Total	$3,187 mill.
From federal government	3,062 mill.
From local government	125 mill.
Charges and Miscellaneous	
Total	$1,961 mill.
Current charges	1,414 mill.
Misc. general revenue	547 mill.
Taxes	
Total	$5,113 mill.
General sales	1,919 mill.
Selective sales.	684 mill.
License taxes	389 mill.
Individual income	1,813 mill.
Corporate income	251 mill.
Other.	56 mill.
Insurance trust revenue	1,697 mill.

Total revenue figures include items not listed separately.
Source: U.S. Bureau of the Census.

State government expenditures, 1996

General expenditures
Intergovernmental	$2,720 mill.
Direct expenditures	7,963 mill.
Total	10,683 mill.

Selected direct expenditures
Education	$3,832 mill.
Public welfare.	2,554 mill.
Health, hospital	1,308 mill.
Highways	616 mill.
Police	140 mill.
Corrections.	391 mill.
Natural resources.	171 mill.
Parks and recreation.	51 mill.
Government administration	221 mill.
Interest on debt	185 mill.

Other
State per capita expenditures	$2,874
U.S. per capita average	2,854
Rank among states.	23
Total state expenditures	12,400 mill.
Total U.S. expenditures	859,959 mill.

Totals include items not listed separately.
Source: U.S. Bureau of the Census.

POLITICS

Governors since statehood
D = Democrat; R = Republican; O = other;
(r) resigned; (d) died in office; (i) removed from office

John Rutledge.	(r) 1776-1777
Rawlins Lowndes	1777-1779
John Rutledge.	1779-1782
John Mathews.	1782-1783
Benjamin Guerand	1783-1785
William Moultrie	1785-1787
Thomas Pinckney.	1787-1789
Charles Pinckney	1789-1792
William Moultrie (O).	1792-1794
Arnoldus Vanderhorst (O)	1794-1796
Charles Pinckney (O)	1796-1798
Edward Rutledge (O) . . . . (d) 1798-1800
John Drayton (O).	1800-1802
James B. Richardson (O).	1802-1804
Paul Hamilton (O)	1804-1806
Charles Pinckney (O)	1806-1808
John Drayton (O).	1808-1810
Henry Middleton (O)	1810-1812

Joseph Alston (O)	1812-1814
David R. Williams (O)	1814-1816
Andrew Pickens (O)	1816-1818
John Geddes (O)	1818-1820
Thomas Bennett (O)	1820-1822
John L. Wilson (O)	1822-1824
Richard I. Manning (O)	1824-1826
John Taylor (O).	1826-1828
Stephen D. Miller (D)	1828-1830
James Hamilton, Jr. (D)	1830-1832
Robert Y. Hayne (D)	1832-1834
George McDuffie (D)	1834-1836
Pierce M. Butler (D)	1836-1838
Patrick Noble (D) . . . . (d) 1838-1840
Barnabas K. Henagan (D)	1840
John P. Richardson (D).	1840-1842
James H. Hammond (D)	1842-1844
William Aiken (D)	1844-1846
David Johnson (D)	1846-1848
Whitemarsh B. Seabrook (D)	1848-1850
John H. Means (D)	1850-1852
John L. Manning (D).	1852-1854
James H. Adams (D)	1854-1856
Robert F. W. Allston (D)	1856-1858
William W. Gist (D).	1858-1860
Francis W. Pickens (D)	1860-1862
Milledge L. Bonham (D).	1862-1864
Andrew G. Magrath (D) . . . . (i) 1864-1865
Benjamin F. Perry.	1865
James L. Orr	1865-1868
Robert K. Scott (R)	1868-1872
Franklin J. Moses, Jr. (R)	1872-1874
Daniel H. Chamberlain (R)	1874-1876
Wade Hampton (D) . . . . (r) 1876-1879
William D. Sampson (D) . . . . (r) 1879-1880
Thomas B. Jeter (D)	1880
Johnson Hagood (D).	1880-1882
Hugh S. Thompson (D) . . . . (r) 1882-1886
John C. Sheppard (D)	1886
John P. Richardson, Jr. (D)	1886-1890
Benjamin R. Tillman (D).	1890-1894
John G. Evans (D)	1894-1897
William H. Ellerbe (D). . . . . (d) 1897-1899
Miles B. McSweeney (D)	1899-1903
Duncan C. Heyward (D)	1903-1907
Martin F. Ansel (D)	1907-1911
Coleman L. Blease (D) . . . . (r) 1911-1915
Charles A. Smith (D)	1915
Richard I. Manning III (D).	1915-1919
Robert A. Cooper (D) . . . . (r) 1919-1922
William G. Harvey (D)	1922-1923
Thomas G. McLeod (D)	1923-1927
John G. Richards (D)	1927-1931
Ibra C. Blackwood (D)	1931-1935

(continued)

Olin D. T. Johnston (D) 1935-1939
Burnet R. Maybank (D) . . . . (r) 1939-1941
Joseph E. Harley (D) . . . . (d) 1941-1942
Richard M. Jeffries (D) 1942-1943
Olin D. T. Johnston (D) . . . . (r) 1943-1945
Ransome J. Williams (D) 1945-1947
J. Strom Thurmond (D) 1947-1951
James F. Byrnes (D) 1951-1955
George B. Timmerman, Jr. (D) 1955-1959
Ernest F. Hollings (D) 1959-1963
Donald S. Russell (D) . . . . (r) 1963-1965
Robert E. McNair (D) 1965-1971
John C. West (D) 1971-1975
James B. Edwards (R) 1975-1979
Richard W. Riley (D) 1979-1987
Carroll A. Campbell, Jr. (R) 1987-1995
David M. Beasley (R) 1995-1999
Jim Hodges (D) 1999-

Governors were called state presidents before 1778.

Composition of state legislature, 1990-1998

	Democrats	Republicans
State House (124 seats)		
1990	79	43
1992	71	52
1994	58	62
1996	53	70
1998	57	66
State Senate (46 seats)		
1990	33	13
1992	30	16
1994	29	17
1996	26	20
1998	24	22

Figures for total seats may include independents and minor
party members.

Source: Council of State Governments; *State Elective Officials and the Legislatures.*

Composition of congressional delegations, 1989-1999

	Dem	Rep	Total
House of Representatives			
101st Congress, 1989			
State delegates	4	2	6
Total U.S.	259	174	433

	Dem	Rep	Total
102d Congress, 1991			
State delegates	4	2	6
Total U.S.	267	167	434
103d Congress, 1993			
State delegates	3	3	6
Total U.S.	258	176	434
104th Congress, 1995			
State delegates	2	4	6
Total U.S.	197	236	433
105th Congress, 1997			
State delegates	2	4	6
Total U.S.	206	228	434
106th Congress, 1999			
State delegates	2	4	6
Total U.S.	211	222	433
Senate			
101st Congress, 1989			
State delegates	1	1	2
Total U.S.	55	45	100
102d Congress, 1991			
State delegates	1	1	2
Total U.S.	56	44	100
103d Congress, 1993			
State delegates	1	1	2
Total U.S.	57	43	100
104th Congress, 1995			
State delegates	1	1	2
Total U.S.	46	53	99
105th Congress, 1997			
State delegates	1	1	2
Total U.S.	45	55	100
106th Congress,[7] 1999			
State delegates	1	1	2
Total U.S.	45	54	99

Figures are for starts of first sessions. Figure for U.S. Representatives for 101st Congress does not include Alabama
and Indiana, which had vacancies. Figures for total U.S.
Representatives for 102d, 103d, and 106th Congresses do
not include Vermont, which had 1 Independent-Socialist.
Figure for U.S. Representatives for 104th Congress does
not include Vermont, which had 1 Independent-Socialist,
and California, which had 1 vacancy. Figure for U.S. Representatives for 105th Congress does not include New York,
which had 1 vacancy. Figure for U.S. Senators for 104th
Congress does not include Oregon, which had 1 vacancy.
Figure for U.S. Senators for 106th Congress does not
include New Hampshire, which had 1 Independent.

Source: U.S. Congress; *Congressional Directory,* biennial.

Voter participation in presidential elections, 1992 and 1996

	1992	1996
State voting age pop.	2,669,000	2,777,000
Total U.S. voting age pop.	189,524,000	196,509,000
State share of U.S. total	1.4%	1.4%
Rank among states	26	26
Percent of state casting vote	45.1	47.1
Percent of U.S. total voting	55.1	49.0
Rank among states	49	36

Source: U.S. Bureau of the Census.

HEALTH AND MEDICAL CARE

Medicare, 1997

	Recipients	Payments
State	533,000	$2,366 mill.
Total U.S.	37,514,000	$206,064 mill.
State share	1.42%	1.15%
Rank among states	25	27

Recipient figures are rounded to nearest thousand persons. Ranks are from highest to lowest.
Source: U.S. Health Care Financing Administration.

Medicaid, 1996

	Recipients	Payments
State	503,000	$1,523 mill.
Total U.S.	35,028,000	$121,419 mill.
State share	1.44%	1.25%
Rank among states	23	23

Recipient figures are rounded to nearest thousand persons. Payment figures for fiscal year reflect federal and state contribution payments. Ranks are from highest to lowest.
Source: U.S. Health Care Financing Administration.

Health insurance coverage, 1996

	State	U.S.
Total persons covered	3,077,000	225,070,000
Total persons not covered	634,000	41,716,000
Part not covered	17.1%	15.6%
Rank among states	10	—
Children not covered	199,000	10,554,000
Part not covered	20.7%	14.8%
Rank among states	4	—

Ranks are from most to fewest uninsured. Population figures are rounded to nearest thousand persons.
Source: U.S. Bureau of the Census.

AIDS, syphilis, tuberculosis, and measles cases, 1997

Cases	U.S.	State	Share
AIDS	58,443	779	1.33%
Syphilis	8,550	378	4.42%
Tuberculosis	18,534	293	1.58%
Measles	148,000	1,000	0.68%

Measles figures are rounded to nearest thousand cases.
Source: U.S. Centers for Disease Control and Prevention.

HOUSING

Homeownership rates, 1985-1997

	1985	1990	1997
State	72.0%	71.4%	74.1%
Total U.S.	63.9%	63.9%	65.7%
Rank among states	4	6	5

Source: U.S. Bureau of the Census.

Home sales, 1990 and 1997
In thousands of units

Existing home sales	1990	1997	Change
State sales	57.8	81.5	23.7
Total U.S. sales	3,560	4,730	1,170
State share of U.S. total	1.62%	1.72%	0.10%
Rank among states	23	22	—

Source: National Association of Realtors; *Real Estate Outlook: Market Trends and Insights.*

EDUCATION

Public school enrollment, 1995

State K-8 enrollment 463,000
Total U.S. K-8 enrollment 32,341,000
State share of total U.S. 1.43%
State 9-12 enrollment 182,000
Total U.S. 9-12 enrollment 12,500,000
State share of U.S. total 1.46%
State public school enroll. rate 94.9%
Overall U.S. rate. 91.6%
Rank among states. 11

Enrollment figures (which include unclassified students) are
    rounded to nearest thousand pupils in fall term;
    kindergarten (K)-8 grade figures include some
    prekindergarten students. Enrollment rate is based on
    percentage of persons 5-17 years old. Rank is from highest
    to lowest.
Source: U.S. National Center for Education Statistics.

Public college finances, 1996

State FTE enrollment 123,900
Total U.S. FTE enrollment 8,268,800
State share of total U.S. 1.50%
Rank among states. 24
State and local appropriations $490,800,000
Total U.S. state and local
    appropriations. . . . . $39,699 mill.
State share of total U.S. 1.24%
Rank among states. 26
State net tuition revenues. $352,700,000
Total U.S. net tuition $18,348,100,000
State share of total U.S. 1.92%
Rank among states. 20

FTE=Full-time equivalent; credit and noncredit enrollment
    including summer session in academic year ending in
    1996.
Enrollments are rounded to nearest thousand students. Net
    tuition revenues exclude appropriation to students
    attending in-state public institutions. Rankings are from
    highest shares to lowest.
Source: Research Associates of Washington.

TRANSPORTATION AND TRAVEL

Highway mileage, 1996

Interstate 829
Other arterial. 6,871
Collector roads 14,858
Local roads 43,267

Urban roads. 10,574
Rural roads 53,785

Total state 64,359
U.S. total 3,933,985
State share 1.6%
Rank among states. 31

Source: U.S. Federal Highway Administration.

Motor vehicle registrations and driver licenses, 1996

In thousands

Vehicle registrations	State	U.S.	Share	Rank
Autos, trucks, buses	2,791	206,365	1.35%	28
Autos only	1,754	128,439	1.37%	24
Motorcycles	39	3,832	1.02%	28
Driver licenses	2,575	179,539	1.43%	28

Figures do not include vehicles owned by military services.
Source: U.S. Federal Highway Administration; *Highway
    Statistics; Selected Highway Statistics and Charts.*

Domestic travel expenditures, 1995

Spending by U.S. residents on overnight trips and day
trips of at least 100 miles

Total expenditures in state . . . . $5,366 mill.
Total expenditures in U.S. . . . . $360,314 mill.
State share of total U.S. 1.49%
Rank among states. 23

Source: Travel Industry Association of America.

CRIME AND LAW ENFORCEMENT

State and local police officers, 1996

Local police	4,004
State police	892
Sheriffs	3,037
Total	8,675
Officers per 10,000 residents	23
U.S. average	25
Rank among states	21

Figures cover full-time sworn officers; totals include special
police not shown separately.
Source: U.S. Bureau of Justice Statistics; *Census of State and
Local Law Enforcement Agencies, 1996.*

Crime rates, 1996
Rates per 100,000 resident population

Violent crimes	State	U.S.
Total violent	997	634
Murder	9.0	7.4
Forcible rape	49.2	36.1
Robbery	172	202
Aggravated assault	767	388
Property crimes		
Total property	5,217	4,445
Burglary	1,284	943
Larceny/theft	3,505	2,976
Motor vehicle theft	429	526
Totals	6,214	5,079

Source: U.S. Federal Bureau of Investigation; *Crime in the
United States,* annual.

State prison populations, 1980-1996

	State	U.S.	State share
1980	7,862	305,458	2.57%
1990	17,319	708,393	2.44%
1996	20,446	1,025,624	1.99%

Figures exclude prisoners in federal penitentiaries.
Source: U.S. Bureau of Justice Statistics.

South Dakota

Location: Upper Midwest of continental United States

Area and rank: 75,898 square miles (196,575 square kilometers); 77,121 square miles (199,743 square kilometers) including water; sixteenth largest state in area

Population and rank: 737,973 (1997); forty-sixth largest state in population

Capital: Pierre

Largest city: Sioux Falls (116,762 people in 1998)

Became territory: March 2, 1861

Entered Union and rank: November 2, 1889; fortieth state

Present constitution adopted: 1889

Counties: 66 (64 county governments)

State name: "South Dakota" comes from a Sioux word meaning "allies"

State nicknames: Mount Rushmore State; Coyote State

Motto: Under God the people rule

State flag: Blue field with state seal and sunburst, with words "South Dakota" above and "The Mount Rushmore State" below

Highest point: Harney Peak — 7,242 feet (2,207 meters)

Lowest point: Big Stone Lake — 966 feet (294 meters)

Highest recorded temperature: 120 degrees Fahrenheit (49 degrees Celsius) — Gannvalley, 1936

Lowest recorded temperature: −58 degrees Fahrenheit (−50 degrees Celsius) — McIntosh, 1936

State song: "Hail! South Dakota"

State tree: Black Hills spruce

State flower: American pasqueflower

State bird: Ring-necked pheasant

State fish: Walleye

State animal: Coyote

National parks: Badlands, Wind Cave

State capitol building in Pierre. (South Dakota Tourism)

South Dakota History

One of the plains states in America's Midwest, South Dakota is bounded on the north by North Dakota, on the east by Iowa and Minnesota, on the south by Nebraska, and on the west by Montana and Wyoming. It stretches 360 miles from east to west and 240 miles from north to south. The state is the sixteenth largest of the United States but ranks forty-sixth in population. Its capital is Pierre (pronounced "Peer"). Temperatures in South Dakota are extreme—low in winter and high in summer—with minimal precipitation and low humidity.

South Dakota's terrain, with more than three hundred natural lakes and four huge reservoirs created by the damming of its rivers, has considerable variety. Sparsely wooded, it consists largely of rolling plains marked occasionally by buttes rising dramatically from the landscape. In the western part of the plains, well before the towering Black Hills, are the Badlands, with deep canyons and formations carved into the red rocks over eons by wind and water erosion.

Early History. Humans inhabited the Dakotas more than twenty-five thousand years ago. Forty million years ago, dinosaurs roamed the landscape. Dinosaur bones have been unearthed in South Dakota as well as shells of archela, the largest known turtles, which were ten feet long.

The earliest settlers hunted the abundant big game in the area. By 500 C.E., a society of seminomadic Mound Builders thrived in the area and remained for about three hundred years, leaving behind valuable artifacts.

The Arikara Indians moved north from Nebraska in the 1500's and settled along the eastern banks of the Missouri River, where they farmed and

The rugged canyons and mountains of western South Dakota's Badlands were carved through eons of powerful winds and erosion. (PhotoDisc)

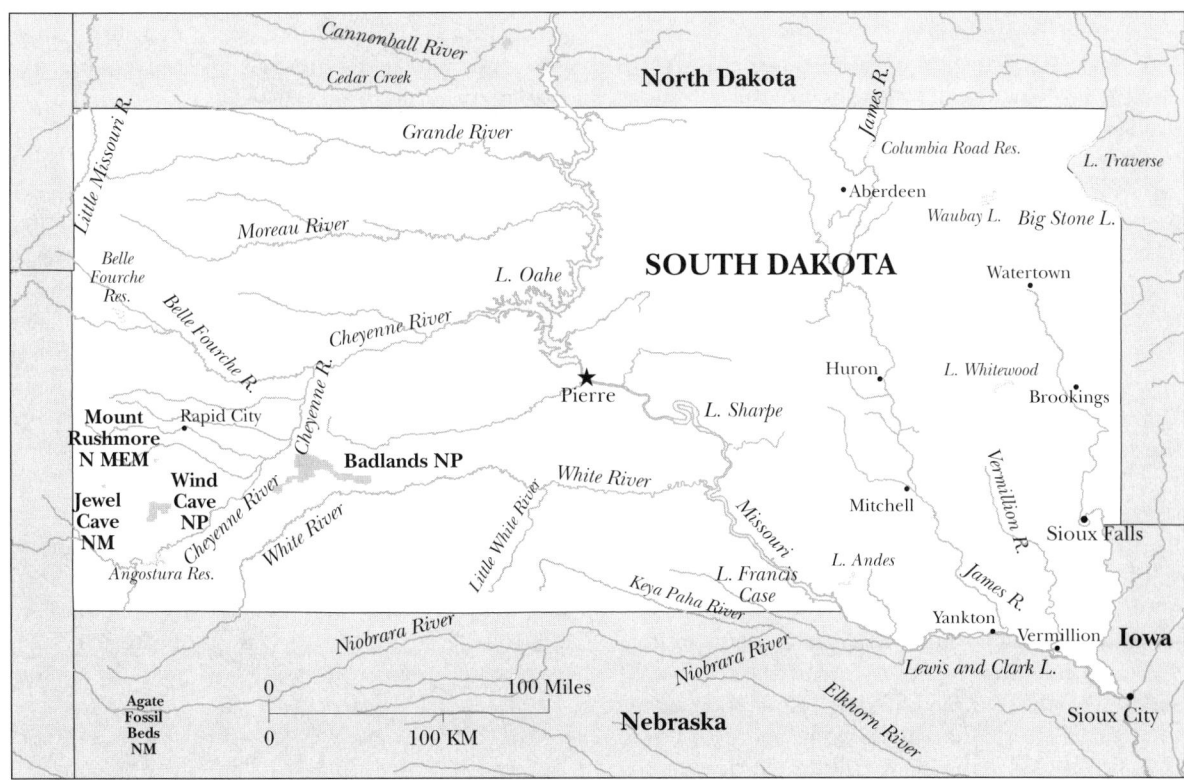

fished, prospering to the extent that, by the late 1700's, they had established thirty earth-lodge settlements. In the early nineteenth century, however, the Sioux, a powerful tribe that entered the area from the east, drove the Arikara away.

Exploration and Settlement. The Dakotas became part of France's vast Louisiana Territory in 1682. The first white explorers in the region were French Canadian brothers, François and Louis Joseph de La Vérendrye. While seeking a water route to the Pacific, they entered the area in 1743 and claimed it for France, burying a lead plate near Fort Pierre—the plate was found in 1913.

In 1762 France ceded all its land west of the Mississippi River to Spain, so when the French Canadian fur trader Pierre Dorion became the first permanent white resident in the Dakotas in 1775, the Spanish were in control. The Louisiana Territory was returned to France in 1800 and, in 1803 as a result of the Louisiana Purchase, became the property of the United States.

Explorers Meriwether Lewis and William Clark passed through the area in 1804, bound for the Pa-

cific Northwest, and again in 1806 on their return. A Spanish trader, Manuel Lisa, began trading with the American Indians along the Missouri River in 1809. In 1812 the entire area became part of the Missouri Territory. In the same year, the Sioux Indians, whose property rights were being severely infringed by the United States, sided with the British in the War of 1812.

Relations between the Native Americans and whites in the area were marked by peace treaties that the federal government, with its substantial economic stake in the lands of the Missouri Territory, soon broke. When the Missouri River proved navigable by steamboat in 1831, the commercial viability of the areas along the river became obvious.

Government Relations with the Sioux. In 1857 the modern-day city of Sioux Falls on the Missouri River was planned. Development began in the area, which in 1861 was declared the Dakota Territory, encompassing all of contemporary North and South Dakota, as well as parts of Wyoming and Montana. The southeastern town of Yankton became the territory's capital.

In 1862 the government, frequently warring with the Sioux, forced the Santee Sioux from Minnesota into the Dakota Territory. Strife between the Sioux and the federal government continued until 1890, when, at Wounded Knee, government forces massacred more than two hundred Sioux, including women and children who were attempting to surrender. As late as 1973, two hundred armed members of the American Indian Movement occupied Wounded Knee for seventy-one days demanding reparations.

In 1979 the U.S. Court of Claims ordered the U.S. government to pay the Sioux $100 million for the land it confiscated in 1877. The Sioux, however, refused to accept a monetary settlement, insisting instead on the return of their land, which has great spiritual significance to them.

Moving Toward Statehood. With the formation of the Montana Territory in 1864 and the Wyoming Territory in 1868, the Dakota Territory was downsized to what has become North and South Dakota. In 1872 railroad service began in the territory. In 1874, Lieutenant Colonel George Custer discovered gold in the Black Hills, triggering a gold rush. In 1876, when the Sioux attacked prospectors, trying to expel them from Sioux property in the Black Hills, the federal government intervened; in 1877, it confiscated the Black Hills from the Sioux.

Many easterners, eager to obtain land from the government under the Homestead Act of 1862, came to the Dakotas to obtain their allotted 160 acres, for which they filed claims. They cultivated the land and, after living on it for five years, it became theirs. With the discovery of gold, miners flocked into the Black Hills, swelling the population by 1879 to the point that the territory was large enough to warrant consideration for statehood.

The area was wracked by floods in 1881. The devastating blizzard of 1888 killed hundreds of Dakotans. Nevertheless, development continued with the establishment of Yankton College in 1881 and the University of South Dakota at Vermillion in the following year. In 1888 Republicans urged, as part of their platform, the admission of the Dakota Territory as two states.

In 1889 Congress voted to divide the Dakota Territory evenly into North and South Dakota and

The monumental relief of four U.S. presidents on Mount Rushmore, in southwestern South Dakota, took nearly fifteen years to carve in the early twentieth century. (PhotoDisc)

admitted them as the thirty-ninth and fortieth states in the Union. North Dakota was designated the thirty-ninth state because of its alphabetical preeminence.

South Dakota was plagued by the worst drought in its history for the next nine years. It was another half century before the federal government assisted the state in mounting a concerted effort to build dams to irrigate farms and provide hydroelectric power.

Political Progressivism and the Economy. South Dakota's voters consistently elected reform candidates from the Populist and Progressive Republican parties. In 1898 South Dakota became the first state to pass initiative and referendum laws, enabling voters to pass any law directly if they obtained enough signatures on petitions to put the matter on the ballot or to reject any laws passed by the legislature if 5 percent of the voters signed petitions requesting that their repeal be placed on the ballot and the repeal is supported by the electorate.

Agriculture and mining were the two most important industries in South Dakota during its early days. In 1909 the Morrell Company opened a large meat processing and packing plant in Sioux Falls, thereby launching an important industry in the state. South Dakota became a major national supplier of meat.

The state needed a dependable railway system to transport its cattle and produce to eastern markets. In 1917 Governor Peter Norbeck spearheaded a movement to end railroad monopolies and to stabilize rates. Under Norbeck's progressive leadership, the legislature voted to extend loans to farmers.

The droughts during the early years of the Great Depression ravaged South Dakota agriculture. Plagues of grasshoppers ate the few crops that survived the drought. The economic situation deteriorated so badly that, in 1932, voters for the first time elected Democratic candidates to every state office in what had long been a Republican state.

In 1954 the state's first productive oil well was drilled in western South Dakota, producing more

Seen here with a scale model of its design in the foreground, the Chief Crazy Horse monument begun south of Mount Rushmore in 1948 will ultimately be the world's largest sculpture. (South Dakota Tourism)

than two million barrels annually. Strip mining of bituminous coal contributes to the economy of western South Dakota, which also has a large gold-mining industry. Despite the mineral wealth of its western region, South Dakota's non-Native American peoples have settled largely in the eastern region, where manufacturing and service industries flourish.

The electronics industry brings considerable revenue into the state and employs many of its citizens. In 1982 Citicorp, the largest bank holding company in the United States, transferred its credit-card division to Sioux Falls, which underwent a substantial increase in population.

The Native American Population. In the 1990's, more than 7 percent of South Dakotans were Native Americans. Most of them lived on eight major reservations, the largest of them being the Rosebud, the Pine Ridge, the Cheyenne River, and the Standing Rock Indian Reservations in the central or western reaches of the state.

Life for South Dakota's Native Americans remains difficult. Stripped of much of their most fertile and mineral-rich land, they have often been forced during difficult economic times to sell the land remaining to them.

R. Baird Shuman

South Dakota Time Line

500 to 800 C.E.	Seminomadic Mound Builders flourish in South Dakota.
c. 1500	Arikara, the first native settlers of whom there are written records, arrive.
1682	René-Robert Cavalier, sieur de La Salle, claims area for France.
c. 1700	Sioux Indians move into South Dakota from the east.
1743	French Canadian brothers François and Louis Joseph de La Vérendrye claim area for France.
1762	France cedes land west of the Mississippi River to Spain.
1800	France regains possession of the Dakotas.
1803	United States acquires the area through the Louisiana Purchase.
1804	Meriwether Lewis and William Clark pass through South Dakota on journey to the Pacific Northwest.
1809	Spanish trader Manuel Lisa organizes St. Louis Fur Company to trade in Upper Missouri Valley.
1812	South Dakota region becomes part of the Missouri Territory.
1817	First permanent white settlement is established at Fort Pierre.
1831	Steamboat service begins to Upper Missouri Valley on the Missouri River.
Mar. 2, 1861	Congress creates Dakota Territory.
1868	Sioux are promised the Black Hills in Fort Laramie Treaty.
1872	First railroad service begins.
1874	George Custer discovers gold in the Black Hills; prospectors descend on territory.
1877	Gold rush intensifies, causing federal confiscation of the Black Hills from the Sioux.
1878	Homesteaders arrive during South Dakota land boom.
1888	Severe blizzard kills hundreds in South Dakota.
Nov. 2, 1889	South Dakota becomes fortieth state.
Dec. 29, 1890	Federal cavalry massacre Sioux at Wounded Knee Creek.
1897	South Dakota's nine-year drought ends.
1910	State capital is established at Pierre.
1927	Mount Rushmore National Memorial is begun by Gutzon Borglum; is completed in 1941.
1929-1939	Droughts and the Great Depression devastate South Dakota.
1944	Congress passes Flood Control Act to build dams.
1948	Korczak Ziolkowski begins work on Crazy Horse sculpture, the world's largest sculpture.
1972	Collapse of Rapid City Canyon Dam kills 236 people.
1973	American Indians occupy site of Wounded Knee for seventy-one days.
1979	U.S. Court of Claims orders U.S. government to pay Sioux $100 million for land seized in 1877.
1980	U.S. Supreme Court grants $22.5 million to Sioux for their confiscated lands; Sioux decline monetary settlement.

1982	Citicorp moves its credit-card operation to Sioux City.
1987	South Dakota establishes state lottery.
1988	Casino gambling legalized in South Dakota; National Indian Gaming Act legalizes tribal casinos.
1996	U.S. Supreme Court overturns South Dakota law requiring parental permission for teenage abortions.
1998	Tornado devastates Spencer, injuring more than three hundred.

Notes for Further Study

Published Sources. Catherine McNicol Stock's *Main Street in Crisis: The Great Depression and the Old Middle Class on the Northern Plains* (1992) and Paula Nelson's *The Prairie Winnows out Its Own: The West River Country of South Dakota in the Years of the Depression and Dust* (1996) focus on the Great Depression and the accompanying droughts in South Dakota during the 1930's. Native American-white relations are examined in *The Politics of the Hallowed Ground: Wounded Knee and the Struggle for Indian Sovereignty* (1999) by Mario Gonzalez and Elizabeth Cook-Lynn and in *Boarding School Seasons: American Indian Families, 1900-1940* (1998) by Brenda Child. Mikael Kurkiala focuses on the Pine Ridge Reservation in *Building the Nation Back Up: The Politics of Identity on the Pine Ridge Indian Reservation* (1997).

South Dakota (1991) by Emilie U. Lepthien is aimed at adolescent readers, whereas *South Dakota* (1995) by Dennis Brindell Fradin and Judith Bloom Fradin targets younger readers. *South Dakota: Every Town on the Map and More* (1998) by Vernell Johnson and Louise Johnson explores the variety of towns in the state.

Web Resources. The most complete Web site on South Dakota is the state government's site (http://www.state.sd.us), offering information about the state's history, economy, industries, and population. Those seeking tourist information should turn to various tourist Web sites, including those of the State Tourist Office (http://www.state.sd.us/tourism), Badlands (http://www.nps.gov/bdl), Big Stone Lake (http://www.bigstonelake.com), Black Hills Information (http://blackhills-info.com), Corn Palace (http://www.cornpalace.com), Dakota Dunes (http://www.dakotadunes.com), Missouri River (http://www.nps.gov/mnrr), Mount Rushmore (http://www.npa.gov/moru), and Wind Cave (http://www.nps.gov/wica).

South Dakota's communities maintain individual Web sites, among them Brookings (http://www.brookings.com), Deadwood (http://www.deadwood.net), Huron (http://www.huronsd.com), Rapid City (http://www.rapidcitycvb.com), Sioux Falls (http://www.siouxfalls.com), and Wygen (http://www.wygen.com). Each contains information about the community, listing attractions of interest to visitors. South Dakota's institutions of higher learning maintain informative Web sites. Among these are Augustana College (http://www.augie.edu), Black Hills University (http://www.bhsu.edu), Dakota State University (http://www.dsu.edu), Dakota Wesleyan University (http://www.dwu.edu), South Dakota University (http://www.sdstate.edu), the University of Sioux Falls (http://www.thecoo.edu), and the University of South Dakota (http://www.usd.edu).

Counties

County	Sq. miles	1996 pop.	County	Sq. miles	1996 pop.
Aurora	708.2	3,038	Bon Homme	563.4	7,032
Beadle	1,259.4	18,149	Brookings	794.5	26,394
Bennett	1,185.4	3,379	Brown	1,712.8	35,829

(continued)

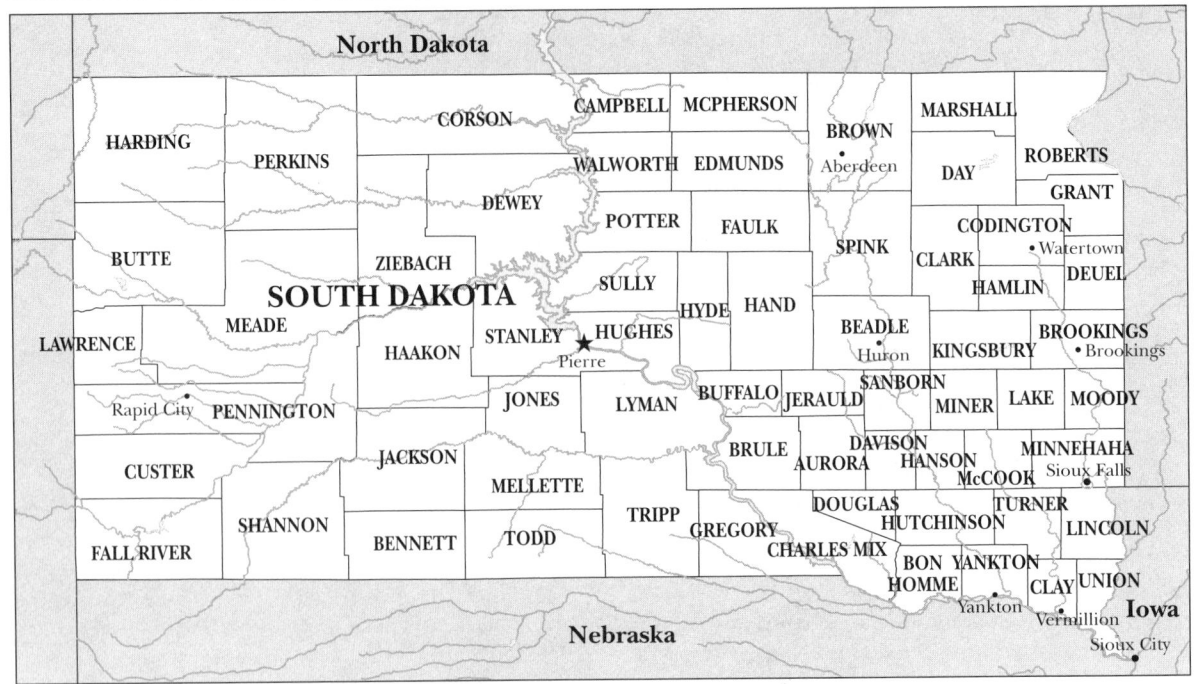

County	Sq. miles	1996 pop.	County	Sq. miles	1996 pop.
Brule	819.0	5,541	Hughes	741.0	15,531
Buffalo	470.6	1,805	Hutchinson	813.0	8,129
Butte	2,248.6	9,039	Hyde	861.1	1,648
Campbell	735.8	1,893	Jackson	1,869.3	2,909
Charles Mix	1,098.3	9,395	Jerauld	530.3	2,310
Clark	958.0	4,373	Jones	970.6	1,262
Clay	411.6	13,639	Kingsbury	838.4	5,877
Codington	687.8	25,099	Lake	563.3	10,656
Corson	2,473.1	4,269	Lawrence	800.1	22,371
Custer	1,557.8	6,828	Lincoln	578.1	18,377
Davison	435.5	17,769	Lyman	1,640.1	3,849
Day	1,028.6	6,567	McCook	574.6	5,808
Deuel	623.6	4,578	McPherson	1,137.0	2,950
Dewey	2,302.8	5,772	Marshall	838.9	4,699
Douglas	433.6	3,577	Meade	3,470.8	22,592
Edmunds	1,145.7	4,394	Mellette	1,306.6	2,023
Fall River	1,739.9	7,164	Miner	570.4	3,014
Faulk	1,000.2	2,581	Minnehaha	809.2	138,221
Grant	682.5	8,054	Moody	519.7	6,608
Gregory	1,016.0	5,125	Pennington	2,776.4	87,145
Haakon	1,813.1	2,514	Perkins	2,871.8	3,647
Hamlin	511.2	5,359	Potter	866.5	2,983
Hand	1,436.7	4,143	Roberts	1,101.3	9,857
Hanson	434.7	2,942	Sanborn	569.0	2,759
Harding	2,670.6	1,559	Shannon	2,094.0	11,837

County	Sq. miles	1996 pop.
Spink	1,504.0	7,746
Stanley	1,443.4	2,961
Sully	1,007.0	1,593
Todd	1,388.2	9,246
Tripp	1,613.6	6,861
Turner	616.9	8,630

County	Sq. miles	1996 pop.
Union	460.4	11,644
Walworth	707.8	5,784
Yankton	521.6	20,848
Ziebach	1,962.5	2,230

Source: U.S. Census Bureau; National Association of Counties.

Cities
With 10,000 or more residents

Rank	City	Population
1	Sioux Falls	116,762
2	Rapid City	57,513
3	Aberdeen	24,865
4	Watertown	19,909
5	Brookings	17,138
6	Mitchell	14,386

Rank	City	Population
7	Yankton	14,325
8	Pierre	13,267
9	Vermillion	11,967
10	Huron	11,778

Population figures are estimated for mid-1998.
Source: U.S. Bureau of the Census.

Index to Tables

NA = Reliable data are not available.

DEMOGRAPHICS

Resident state and national populations, 1970-1997

Population figures given in thousands

	State pop.	U.S. pop.	Share	Rank
1970	666	203,302	0.3%	44
1980	691	226,546	0.3%	45
1985	698	237,924	0.3%	45
1990	696	248,765	0.3%	45
1995	735	262,761	0.3%	45
1997	738	267,636	0.3%	45

Source: U.S. Bureau of the Census.

Resident population by age, 1997

Age group	Total population
Under 5 years	49,000
5 to 17 years	148,000
18 to 24 years	76,000
25 to 34 years	93,000
35 to 44 years	117,000
45 to 54 years	88,000
55 to 64 years	61,000
65 to 74 years	53,000
75 to 84 years	37,000
85 years and over	15,000
Portion of residents 65 and older	14.3%
National average	12.7%

Population figures are rounded to nearest thousand persons;
figures include armed forces personnel stationed in state.
Source: U.S. Bureau of the Census.

Resident population by race, Hispanic origin, 1997

	State pop.	Share	U.S.
All residents	738,000	100.0%	100.0%
Hispanic white	6,000	0.8%	10.0%
non-Hispanic white	664,000	90.0%	72.7%
African American	5,000	0.7%	12.7%
Native American	58,000	7.9%	0.9%
Asian, Pacific Islander	5,000	0.7%	3.8%

Source: U.S. Bureau of the Census.

Projections of state population, 2000-2025

	Model A Uses interstate migration observed from 1975-1994	Model B Uses Bureau of Economic Analysis employment projections
Year	Population	Population
2000	777,000	770,000
2005	810,000	811,000
2010	826,000	853,000
2015	840,000	893,000
2020	853,000	930,000
2025	866,000	962,000

All population projections, including those for 2000, were calculated in 1997.

Source: U.S. Bureau of the Census, Population Paper Listings PPL-47.

VITAL STATISTICS

Average lifetime in years by race, 1989-1991

	State	U.S.	Rank
All residents	76.91	75.37	8
White residents	77.91	76.13	4
Black residents	NA	69.16	NA

Ranks are from longest-lived to least longest-lived. Ranks exclude Alaska, for which reliable data are not available. Rank for black residents is based on the 32 states for which reliable data are available.

Source: U.S. National Center for Health Statistics.

Infant mortality rates, 1980 and 1995

	State	U.S.
All residents		
1980	10.9	12.6
1995	9.5	7.6
White residents		
1980	9.0	11.0
1995	7.9	6.3
Black residents		
1980	NA	21.4
1995	NA	15.1

Figures represent deaths per 1,000 live births of resident infants under 1 year old, exclusive of fetal deaths; all-residents figures include other races not listed separately.

Source: U.S. National Center for Health Statistics.

Marriages and divorces

Marriages in 1996 6,700
Rate per 1,000 population, 1995 . . . . 10.0
U.S. rate, 1995 . . . . 8.9
Rank among all states 14

Divorces in 1996 2,700
Rate per 1,000 population, 1995 . . . . 4.0
U.S. rate, 1995 . . . . 4.4
Rank among all states 32

Rank is from highest to lowest in country.
Source: U.S. National Center for Health Statistics.

Death rates by leading causes, 1995
Deaths per 100,000 resident population

Cause	State	U.S.
Heart disease	312.3	280.7
Cancer	214.5	204.9
Cerebrovascular diseases	73.2	60.1
Accidents and adverse effects	44.4	35.5
Motor vehicle accidents	22.1	16.5
Chronic obstructive pulmonary diseases	44.4	39.2
Diabetes mellitus	23.0	22.6
HIV	-	NA
Suicide	11.8	11.9
Homicide	-	8.7
All causes	948.5	880.0
Rank in overall death rate among states		14

Figures exclude nonresidents who die in state. Causes of death follow International Classification of Diseases. Rank is from highest to lowest in country.

Source: U.S. National Center for Health Statistics.

ECONOMY

Gross state product, 1990-1996
In current dollars

	State product	Increase
1990	$12.9 billion	
1993	$16.3 billion	
1994	$17.5 billion	7.36%
1995	$18.7 billion	6.86%
1996	$20.3 billion	8.56%

Source: U.S. Bureau of Economic Analysis; *Survey of Current Business,* June, 1998.

Gross state product by industry, 1996
In billions

Farms, forestry, fisheries	$1.7
Construction	0.6
Manufacturing	3.1
Transportation, public utilities	1.5
Wholesale trade	1.2
Retail trade	1.7
Finance, insurance, real estate	3.4
Services	2.7
Government	2.2
State total	$18.4
Total U.S.	$6,923.8
State share	0.27%
Rank among states	46

Total figures include mining, not listed separately.
Source: U.S. Bureau of Economic Analysis; *Survey of Current Business,* June, 1998.

Personal income per capita, 1990 and 1997
In current dollars

	1990	1997
Per capita income	$15,510	$21,447
U.S. average	$19,188	$25,598
Rank among states	38	37

1997 data are preliminary.
Source: U.S. Bureau of Economic Analysis; *Survey of Current Business,* May, 1998.

Energy consumption, 1995
In trillions of British thermal units (BTU)

End-use sectors

Residential	57.2
Commercial	39.3
Industrial	58.1
Transportation	81.2

Sources of energy

Petroleum	114.5
Natural gas	34.8
Coal	36.7
Hydroelectric power	61.9
Nuclear electric power	0
Total state per capita consumption	323.2
Total U.S. per capita consumption	344.4
Rank among states	32
Total state energy consumption	235.8
Total U.S. energy consumption	90,547.4
State share of U.S. total	0.26%
Rank among states	48

Total figures include items not listed separately.
Source: U.S. Energy Information Administration; *State Energy Data Report.*

Nonfarm employment by sectors, 1997

Total	354,000
Construction	15,000
Manufacturing	49,000
Transportation, public utilities	16,000
Wholesale trade, retail trade	88,000
Finance, insurance, real estate	21,000
Services	92,000
Government	70,000

Figures are rounded to nearest thousand persons. Total includes mining, not listed separately.
Source: U.S. Bureau of Labor Statistics; *Employment and Earnings,* monthly.

Foreign exports, 1990-1997
In millions of dollars

Year	State	U.S.	State share
1990	205	394,045	0.05%
1996	443	624,767	0.07%
1997	517	688,896	0.08%

Source: U.S. Bureau of the Census; *U.S. Merchandise Trade,* series FT 900.

LAND USE

Federally owned land, 1996

	State	U.S.	State share
Total acres	48,882,000	2,271,343,000	2.15%
Federally owned	2,577,000	563,129,000	0.46%
Federal share	5.3%	24.8%	—

Areas are rounded to nearest thousand acres. Figures for federally owned land do not include trust properties.
Source: U.S. General Services Administration; *Inventory Report on Real Property Owned by the United States Throughout the World,* annual.

Land use, 1992
In acres, rounded to nearest thousand

Total surface area	49,354,000
Federal land	2,907,000
Total nonfederal	45,459,000
Developed	1,135,000
Total rural	44,324,000
Cropland	16,436,000
Pasture land	2,158,000
Range land	21,933,000
Forest land	540,000
Minor cover/use	3,257,000

Total surface area figures include water area not shown separately.
Source: U.S. Dept. of Agriculture; Soil Conservation Service; Iowa State University, Statistical Laboratory; *Summary Report, 1992 National Resources Inventory.*

Farms and crop acreage, 1997

	State	U.S.	Share	Rank
Farms (thousands)	33	2,058	1.60%	27
Acres (millions)	44	968	4.55%	6
Acres per farm	1,354	471	—	7
Acres planted	17,535	334,139	5.25%	8
Acres harvested	16,545	319,894	5.17%	8
Farm value (mill.)	$2,681	$108,805	2.46%	29

Numbers of farms are rounded to nearest thousand.
Source: U.S. Dept. of Agriculture; National Agricultural Statistics Service.

GOVERNMENT AND FINANCE

Units of local government, 1997

	State	Total U.S.	Rank
All local governments	1,810	87,453	18
Counties	66	3,043	21
Municipalities	309	19,372	25
Townships	956	16,629	10
School districts	177	13,726	26
Special districts	302	34,683	38

County ranks are based on the 48 states with county governments; township ranks are based on the 20 states with township governments; school district ranks are based on the 46 states with such districts.
Source: U.S. Bureau of the Census; *1997 Census of Governments, Government Organization,* Series GC97(1).

State government revenue, 1996

Total revenue . . . . $2,284 mill.
General revenue . . . . 1,886 mill.
Per capita 2,557
U.S. per capita average 2,910
Rank among states 39

Intergovernmental revenue
Total . . . . $695 mill.
From federal government . . . . 687 mill.
From local government . . . . 8 mill.

Charges and Miscellaneous
Total . . . . $461 mill.
Current charges . . . . 181 mill.
Misc. general revenue . . . . 280 mill.

Taxes
Total . . . . $730 mill.
General sales . . . . 383 mill.
Selective sales . . . . 189 mill.
License taxes . . . . 90 mill.
Individual income . . . . NA
Corporate income . . . . 38 mill.
Other . . . . 29 mill.
Insurance trust revenue . . . . 397 mill.

Total revenue figures include items not listed separately.
Source: U.S. Bureau of the Census.

State government expenditures, 1996

General expenditures

Intergovernmental	$369 mill.
Direct expenditures	1,492 mill.
Total	1,861 mill.

Selected direct expenditures

Education	$529 mill.
Public welfare	393 mill.
Health, hospital	107 mill.
Highways	265 mill.
Police	20 mill.
Corrections	44 mill.
Natural resources	86 mill.
Parks and recreation	18 mill.
Government administration	79 mill.
Interest on debt	108 mill.

Other

State per capita expenditures	$2,523
U.S. per capita average	2,854
Rank among states	39
Total state expenditures	1,975 mill.
Total U.S. expenditures	859,959 mill.

Totals include items not listed separately.
Source: U.S. Bureau of the Census.

POLITICS

Governors since statehood

D = Democrat; R = Republican; O = other;
(r) resigned; (d) died in office; (i) removed from office

Arthur C. Mellette (R)	1889-1893
Charles H. Sheldon (R)	1893-1897
Andrew E. Lee (R)	1897-1901
Charles N. Herreid (R)	1901-1905
Samuel H. Elrod (R)	1905-1907
Coe (Corie I.) Crawford (R)	1907-1909
Robert S. Vessey (R)	1909-1913
Frank M. Byrne (R)	1913-1917
Peter Norbeck (R)	1917-1921
William H. McMaster (R)	1921-1925
Carl Gunderson (R)	1925-1927
William J. Bulow (D)	1927-1931
Warren E. Green (R)	1931-1933
Thomas M. Berry (D)	1933-1937

Leslie Jensen (R)	1937-1939
Harlan J. Bushfield (R)	1939-1943
Merrell Q. Sharpe (R)	1943-1947
George T. Mickelson (R)	1947-1951
Sigurd Anderson (R)	1951-1955
Joseph J. Foss, Jr. (R)	1955-1959
Ralph Herseth (D)	1959-1961
Archie M. Gubbrud (R)	1961-1965
Nils A. Boe (R)	1965-1969
Frank L. Farrar (R)	1969-1971
Richard F. Kneip (D)	1971-1979
William J. Janklow (R)	1979-1987
George S. Mickelson (R)	1987-1993
Walter Dale Miller (R)	1993-1995
William J. Janklow (R)	1995-

Composition of state legislature, 1990-1998

	Democrats	Republicans
State House (70 seats)		
1990	25	45
1992	28	42
1994	24	46
1996	23	47
1998	19	51
State Senate (35 seats)		
1990	17	18
1992	20	15
1994	16	19
1996	13	22
1998	13	22

Figures for total seats may include independents and minor
party members.
Source: Council of State Governments; *State Elective Officials
and the Legislatures.*

Composition of congressional delegations, 1989-1999

	Dem	Rep	Total
House of Representatives			
101st Congress, 1989			
State delegates	1	0	1
Total U.S.	259	174	433
102d Congress, 1991			
State delegates	1	0	1
Total U.S.	267	167	434

	Dem	Rep	Total
103d Congress, 1993			
State delegates	1	0	1
Total U.S.	258	176	434
104th Congress, 1995			
State delegates	0	1	1
Total U.S.	197	236	433
105th Congress, 1997			
State delegates	0	1	1
Total U.S.	206	228	434
106th Congress, 1999			
State delegates	0	1	1
Total U.S.	211	222	433

Senate

	Dem	Rep	Total
101st Congress, 1989			
State delegates	1	1	2
Total U.S.	55	45	100
102d Congress, 1991			
State delegates	1	1	2
Total U.S.	56	44	100
103d Congress, 1993			
State delegates	1	1	2
Total U.S.	57	43	100
104th Congress, 1995			
State delegates	2	0	2
Total U.S.	46	53	99
105th Congress, 1997			
State delegates	2	0	2
Total U.S.	45	55	100
106th Congress, 1999			
State delegates	2	0	2
Total U.S.	45	54	99

Figures are for starts of first sessions. Figure for U.S. Representatives for 101st Congress does not include Alabama and Indiana, which had vacancies. Figures for total U.S. Representatives for 102d, 103d, and 106th Congresses do not include Vermont, which had 1 Independent-Socialist. Figure for U.S. Representatives for 104th Congress does not include Vermont, which had 1 Independent-Socialist, and California, which had 1 vacancy. Figure for U.S. Representatives for 105th Congress does not include New York, which had 1 vacancy. Figure for U.S. Senators for 104th Congress does not include Oregon, which had 1 vacancy. Figure for U.S. Senators for 106th Congress does not include New Hampshire, which had 1 Independent.
Source: U.S. Congress; *Congressional Directory*, biennial.

Voter participation in presidential elections, 1992 and 1996

	1992	1996
State voting age pop.	505,000	530,000
Total U.S. voting age pop.	189,524,000	196,509,000
State share of U.S. total	0.3%	0.3%
Rank among states	46	46
Percent of state casting vote	66.6	47.7
Percent of U.S. total voting	55.1	49.0
Rank among states	7	32

Source: U.S. Bureau of the Census.

HEALTH AND MEDICAL CARE

Medicare, 1997

	Recipients	Payments
State	118,000	$476 mill.
Total U.S.	37,514,000	$206,064 mill.
State share	0.31%	0.23%
Rank among states	45	45

Recipient figures are rounded to nearest thousand persons. Ranks are from highest to lowest.
Source: U.S. Health Care Financing Administration.

Medicaid, 1996

	Recipients	Payments
State	77,000	$316 mill.
Total U.S.	35,028,000	$121,419 mill.
State share	0.22%	0.26%
Rank among states	46	43

Recipient figures are rounded to nearest thousand persons. Payment figures for fiscal year reflect federal and state contribution payments. Ranks are from highest to lowest.
Source: U.S. Health Care Financing Administration.

Health insurance coverage, 1996

	State	U.S.
Total persons covered	639,000	225,070,000
Total persons not covered	67,000	41,716,000
Part not covered	9.5%	15.6%
Rank among states	45	—
Children not covered	16,000	10,554,000
Part not covered	8.7%	14.8%
Rank among states	41	—

Ranks are from most to fewest uninsured. Population figures are rounded to nearest thousand persons.
Source: U.S. Bureau of the Census.

AIDS, syphilis, tuberculosis, and measles cases, 1997

Cases	U.S.	State	Share
AIDS	58,443	11	0.02%
Syphilis	8,550	1	0.01%
Tuberculosis	18,534	19	0.10%
Measles	148,000	8,000	5.41%

Measles figures are rounded to nearest thousand cases.
Source: U.S. Centers for Disease Control and Prevention.

HOUSING

Homeownership rates, 1985-1997

	1985	1990	1997
State	67.6%	66.2%	67.6%
Total U.S.	63.9%	63.9%	65.7%
Rank among states	28	30	29

Source: U.S. Bureau of the Census.

Home sales, 1990 and 1997
In thousands of units

Existing home sales	1990	1997	Change
State sales	11.6	15.2	3.6
Total U.S. sales	3,560	4,730	1,170
State share of U.S. total	0.33%	0.32%	NA
Rank among states	42	39	—

Source: National Association of Realtors; *Real Estate Outlook: Market Trends and Insights.*

EDUCATION

Public school enrollment, 1995

State K-8 enrollment	101,000
Total U.S. K-8 enrollment	32,341,000
State share of total U.S.	0.31%
State 9-12 enrollment	43,000
Total U.S. 9-12 enrollment	12,500,000
State share of U.S. total	0.34%
State public school enroll. rate	94.5%
Overall U.S. rate	91.6%
Rank among states	15

Enrollment figures (which include unclassified students) are rounded to nearest thousand pupils in fall term; kindergarten (K)-8 grade figures include some prekindergarten students. Enrollment rate is based on percentage of persons 5-17 years old. Rank is from highest to lowest.
Source: U.S. National Center for Education Statistics.

Public college finances, 1996

State FTE enrollment	21,900
Total U.S. FTE enrollment	8,268,800
State share of total U.S.	0.26%
Rank among states	47
State and local appropriations	$87,900,000
Total U.S. state and local appropriations	$39,699 mill.
State share of total U.S.	0.22%
Rank among states	48
State net tuition revenues	$61,600,000
Total U.S. net tuition	$18,348,100,000
State share of total U.S.	0.34%
Rank among states	45

FTE=Full-time equivalent; credit and noncredit enrollment including summer session in academic year ending in 1996.
Enrollments are rounded to nearest thousand students. Net tuition revenues exclude appropriation to students attending in-state public institutions. Rankings are from highest shares to lowest.
Source: Research Associates of Washington.

TRANSPORTATION AND TRAVEL

Highway mileage, 1996

Interstate	678
Other arterial	6,286
Collector roads	19,478
Local roads	57,132
Urban roads	1,940
Rural roads	81,435
Total state	83,375
U.S. total	3,933,985
State share	2.1%
Rank among states	23

Source: U.S. Federal Highway Administration.

Motor vehicle registrations and driver licenses, 1996
In thousands

Vehicle registrations	State	U.S.	Share	Rank
Autos, trucks, buses	751	206,365	0.36%	44
Autos only	366	128,439	0.29%	46
Motorcycles	25	3,832	0.65%	37
Driver licenses	519	179,539	0.29%	44

Figures do not include vehicles owned by military services.
Source: U.S. Federal Highway Administration; *Highway Statistics; Selected Highway Statistics and Charts.*

Domestic travel expenditures, 1995
Spending by U.S. residents on overnight trips and day trips of at least 100 miles

Total expenditures in state	$909 mill.
Total expenditures in U.S.	$360,314 mill.
State share of total U.S.	0.25%
Rank among states	47

Source: Travel Industry Association of America.

CRIME AND LAW ENFORCEMENT

State and local police officers, 1996

Local police	847
State police	155
Sheriffs	344
Total	1,464
Officers per 10,000 residents	20
U.S. average	25
Rank among states	36

Figures cover full-time sworn officers; totals include special police not shown separately.
Source: U.S. Bureau of Justice Statistics; *Census of State and Local Law Enforcement Agencies, 1996.*

Crime rates, 1996
Rates per 100,000 resident population

Violent crimes	State	U.S.
Total violent	177	634
Murder	1.2	7.4
Forcible rape	41.0	36.1
Robbery	19	202
Aggravated assault	116	388
Property crimes		
Total property	2,793	4,445
Burglary	557	943
Larceny/theft	2,122	2,976
Motor vehicle theft	114	526
Totals	2,970	5,079

Source: U.S. Federal Bureau of Investigation; *Crime in the United States,* annual.

State prison populations, 1980-1996

	State	U.S.	State share
1980	635	305,458	0.21%
1990	1,341	708,393	0.19%
1996	2,063	1,025,624	0.20%

Figures exclude prisoners in federal penitentiaries.
Source: U.S. Bureau of Justice Statistics.

Tennessee

Location: Southern continental United States

Area and rank: 41,220 square miles (106,759 square kilometers); 42,146 square miles (109,158 square kilometers) including water; thirty-fourth largest state in area

Population and rank: 5,368,198 (1997); seventeenth largest state in population

Capital: Nashville

Largest city: Memphis (603,507 people in 1998)

Tennessee's capital and second-largest city, Nashville. (Corbis)

Entered Union and rank: June 1, 1796; sixteenth state

Present constitution adopted: 1870; amended 1953, 1960, 1966, 1972, 1978

Counties: 95

State name: "Tennessee" is derived from a Cherokee word

State nickname: Volunteer State

Motto: Agriculture and Commerce

State flag: Red field with two vertical stripes of white and blue on the end, with blue circle in center containing three white stars

Highest point: Clingmans Dome — 6,643 feet (2,025 meters)

Lowest point: Mississippi River — 178 feet (54 meters)

Highest recorded temperature: 113 degrees Fahrenheit (45 degrees Celsius) — Perryville, 1930

Lowest recorded temperature: −32 degrees Fahrenheit (−36 degrees Celsius) — Mountain City, 1917

State songs: "Tennessee Waltz"; "My Homeland, Tennessee"; "When It's Iris Time in Tennessee"; "My Tennessee"; "Rocky Top"; "Tennessee"

State tree: Tulip poplar

State flower: Iris

State bird: Mockingbird

State animal: Raccoon

National park: Great Smoky Mountains

Tennessee History

Tennessee is one of the south central states, strategically located along the Mississippi River on the west and the Unaka range of the Appalachian Mountains on the east. To its north lie Kentucky and Virginia, to its south Georgia, Alabama, and Mississippi, to its east North Carolina, and to its west Arkansas and Missouri. The state, which runs 120 miles from north to south and 430 miles from east to west, has dense forests in the portions that lie within the Great Smoky Mountains. In its lower regions in the west are cypress swamps much like those found in parts of southern Georgia.

Early History. Ancient burial mounds and archaeological artifacts verify the presence of inhabitants in Tennessee prior to recorded history and long before European explorers made their ways into the area. Paleo-Indians are thought to have lived in this region as long as fifteen thousand years ago. These prehistoric inhabitants were followed by other early American Indians.

The early British and Spanish explorers in the area encountered several Indian tribes, notably the Cherokee, the Chickasaw, the Shawnee, the Creek, and the Yuchi. Of these, the Cherokee were the most sophisticated, living in their own well-developed enclaves in the southeastern part of Tennessee in the Appalachian Mountains. The Chickasaw lived to the west toward the Mississippi River and were considered a belligerent tribe.

By 1714 the Cherokee and the Chickasaw had driven the Shawnee out of the Cumberland Valley,

Site of a Civil War battlefield overlooking modern Chattanooga. (PhotoDisc)

which they inhabited, through the Kentucky area, to north of the Ohio River. At about the same time, these two dominant tribes drove the Creek and Yuchi Indians south to Georgia, leaving the area very much in their hands.

Exploration and Settlement. It is known that a group of explorers led by the Spanish explorer Hernando de Soto, presumably the first Europeans to enter the area, were in southeastern Tennessee in 1540. By the following year, this group had pushed west and had reached the Mississippi River. By 1566-1567, another Spanish group, led by Juan Pardo, had carried out two expeditions in the southeastern part of Tennessee and had erected a fortification near modern Chattanooga.

It was not until 1673 that both French and British explorers arrived, at almost the same time, in the area. Two Virginia traders of British descent, James Needham and Gabriel Arthur, made their way into eastern Tennessee at about this time. In the western extreme of the area, two Frenchmen, Father Jacques Marquette, a missionary, and Louis Jolliet, a fur trader, arrived, having sailed down the Mississippi from the north. A decade later, in 1682, another famous French explorer, René-Robert Cavalier, sieur de La Salle, and his band of followers constructed Fort Prud'Homme on the Natchez (Hatchie) River.

Early Tennessee. The territory into which many of the explorers pressed was a part of the large Cherokee nation in eastern Tennessee. The French and British competed for control of the Cherokee, with the French initially emerging as the victors. At the end of the French and Indian War, however, the Treaty of Paris, enacted in 1763, ceded the area to the British.

Daniel Boone explored this territory, and, in 1769, permanent settlement by whites began, with four parts of the state attracting residents. One settlement was in eastern Tennessee near the Virginia border, a town that eventually was to lie partly in Virginia and partly in Tennessee. Another settlement grew up along the Watauga River near Elizabethtown. West of the Holston River near Rogersville, a settlement was established, while a fourth settlement developed near Erwin along the banks of the Nolichuky River.

When it was discovered in 1771 that all the land on which the white inhabitants had settled except that north of the Holston River belonged legally to the Cherokee, the white settlers were forced to lease the land from them. These settlers finally bought it in 1775 under the Treaty of Sycamore Shoals.

The Revolutionary War. Although this area was remote from the major battlefields of the Revolutionary War, people from the Tennessee region engaged in some combat against the British and the Loyalists. In October, 1780, the Battle of King's Mountain marked the most severe British defeat in the South. Shortly before this battle, North Carolina annexed the eastern region of Tennessee into its western territory and held it until 1784, when it gave the territory over to the U.S. government.

The people in this territory established a separate state, called the state of Franklin, with John Sevier as governor. This state existed for four years. North Carolina, however, attempted to retrieve the territory and finally succeeded in 1789 but soon again ceded it to the United States. In 1790 it officially came to be known as the Territory South of the River Ohio; its governor was William Blount. By 1794 the Tennessee region became the first territory to achieve the representative-government stage under the recently enacted Northwest Ordinance. The first territory to have a delegate in the U.S. Congress, Tennessee, in 1796, became the sixteenth state to enter the Union.

Slavery and the Civil War. Tennessee had few of the sprawling plantations found in parts of the Deep South, although in its eastern lowlands and central area, where cotton was grown, there was considerable slave labor. In eastern Tennessee, however, the agricultural economy was on a small scale. Farmers raised their own food, hunted, and were essentially self-sufficient. What help they had usually came from their children and other family members.

Before the Civil War, significant road building took place in Tennessee. Turnpikes were constructed, railroad tracks were laid, and waterways were improved for river navigation. Some industry developed, mainly ironworks, but the chief occupation was farming.

Naturally, where slave labor was used, mainly in the western and middle parts of the State, people favored slavery, but in its eastern extremes, Tennesseans were resolutely antislavery. After South Carolina and other southern states left the Union, Tennessee refused to call a convention to consider secession. In April, 1861, however, Tennessee's governor refused to send troops to join the Union Army, and on June 8, Tennesseans voted to secede.

Aside from Virginia, Tennessee had more battles fought on its land than any other southern state—more than four hundred. Of its 145,000 soldiers, however, more than 30,000, mostly from eastern Tennessee, joined the Union Army. In 1865 Tennesseans voted to abolish slavery, although in 1870 they voted to ban interracial marriages and in 1875 enacted the first Jim Crow laws that strictly limited the freedom of African Americans.

Postwar Tennessee. Tennessee was readmitted to the Union on July 25, 1866. It was spared many of

During the 1930's the federal Resettlement Administration produced films such as The River *(1937) to win public support for the construction of the Tennessee Valley Authority, part of whose purpose was to combat flooding.* (Museum of Modern Art, Film Stills Archive)

Graceland, the Memphis home of rock and roll legend Elvis Presley, has become one of Tennessee's major tourist draws.
(©Kent Knudson/Weststock)

the punitive programs that Reconstruction imposed on other southern states. The war left Tennessee impoverished to the point that it was unable to meet its financial obligations and in 1883 settled with its lenders for fifty to eighty cents on the dollar. Farmers were extremely strained financially. In 1891 and 1892, coal miners, protesting the use of convicts leased to Tennessee's coal mines, revolted in the Coal Miner War.

Tennessee gained national attention in 1925, when charges were leveled against schoolteacher John Scopes for teaching the theory of evolution in his high school classes. The Scopes Trial, known as the Monkey Trial, focused attention on the state, and the outcome, which favored Tennessee's religious conservatives, was decried by much of the nation.

The Tennessee Valley Authority. Rich in natural resources, Tennessee did not profit significantly from its natural wealth until the years following 1933, when Congress established the Tennessee

Valley Authority (TVA) as a flood control and power project of President Franklin Roosevelt's New Deal. The TVA harnessed rivers and created lakes. It enhanced the power output that private industry had already begun to finance by building dams on the Little Tennessee, Ocoee, and Pigeon Rivers in the 1920's.

By the mid-1990's, Tennessee was generating some seventy-two billion kilowatt-hours of electricity annually. Besides serving its stated purposes, the TVA created attractive recreational areas in parts of the state. Moreover, the lakes created by the TVA, the Mississippi, Tennessee, and Cumberland Rivers combine to give Tennessee more than a thousand miles of inland waterways. These navigational routes are supplemented by more than 1,100 miles of interstate highways and 154,000 miles of public roads. With 155 airports, Tennessee has ample provision for air transport.

Other Commercial Enterprises. One of the longstanding commercial enterprises in Tennessee is lumbering. The forests of the Appalachian Mountains provide a great deal of hardwood, and the central area of the state is known for its red cedar.

Manufacturing is centered mostly in eastern Tennessee, which produces grain mill products, inorganic chemicals, drugs, and plastics. A major nuclear research facility at Oak Ridge has brought many scientists into the state, enhancing some of its manufacturing enterprises.

Rich in minerals, Tennessee produces a great deal of gravel, zinc, coal, and clay. It ranks first in the nation for its production of ball clay and gemstones. Although coal production dropped off significantly after 1980, two of the most important zinc-producing operations are in Mascot and Jefferson City, Tennessee.

R. Baird Shuman

Tennessee Time Line

1540	Spanish explorer Hernando de Soto comes to the Tennessee region.
1566	Juan Pardo and his men build a fort near Chattanooga.
1673	First British explorers, James Needham and Gabriel Arthur, arrive in eastern Tennessee.
1673	First French explorers, missionary Jacques Marquette and fur trader Louis Jolliet, travel down the Mississippi River to western Tennessee.
1682	French explorer René-Robert Cavalier, sieur de La Salle, and his men build Fort Prud'Homme on the Natchez (Hatchie) River.
1757	Fort Loudon, the westernmost fort of the British, is built by Loyalists from South Carolina.
1769	First permanent white settlement is established near the Watauga River.
1772	Early settlers establish the Watauga Association.
1779	Nashville is founded in Middle Tennessee.
1780	Tennesseans deliver a stunning defeat to the British in the Battle of King's Mountain.
Dec., 1784	Eastern Tennesseans create the state of Franklin.
1788	State of Franklin is disbanded.
May 26, 1790	Territory is officially designated "Territory South of the River Ohio," also called the Southwest Territory.
1794	Founding of Blount College, which eventually becomes the University of Tennessee at Knoxville.
June 1, 1796	Tennessee joins the Union as the sixteenth state.
1818	Jackson Purchase buys western Tennessee from the Chickasaw.
1829	Tennessean Andrew Jackson becomes seventh president of the United States.
1835	Charter of 1796 is replaced by new state constitution.
1838	Cherokee Indians involuntarily relocated to Oklahoma.
1843	Nashville becomes Tennessee's state capital.
1845	Tennessean James Knox Polk becomes seventeenth president of the United States.
1854	Railroad is completed to join Nashville and Chattanooga.
1860	Tennessee refuses to call convention to consider secession.
June 8, 1861	Tennessee secedes from the Union, joining the Confederacy.

1863	Eastern Tennessee cleared of Confederates.
1864	Andrew Johnson becomes vice president of the United States.
Jan. 9, 1865	Union Convention to restore civil government and abolish slavery meets in Nashville.
Feb. 22, 1865	Tennesseans vote to abolish slavery.
1865	Civil government restored and slavery abolished.
Apr. 15, 1865	Andrew Johnson becomes president of the United States the day after President Abraham Lincoln is assassinated.
July 25, 1866	Tennessee is readmitted to the Union.
1867	Tennesseans vote to extend the franchise to former slaves.
1870	New state constitution is written and adopted; interracial marriages banned.
1875	Tennessee passes the first Jim Crow laws, which limit the rights of blacks and deny them considerable public access.
1891	First Coal Miner War takes place.
1925	John Scopes tried and found guilty of teaching evolution in the famed Monkey Trial.
1926	Great Smoky Mountains National Park is established.
1933	Congress approves the Tennessee Valley Authority (TVA).
1942	Manhattan Project is established at Oak Ridge for nuclear and atomic research.
1954	State constitution of 1870 amended.
1960	Downtown lunch counters are integrated after "sit-ins."
1964	Tennessee Space Institute is established at Tullahoma.

Notes for Further Study

Published Sources. Two of the most accessible resources for Tennessee history, both by Wilma Dykeman, are *The French Broad* (1965) and *Tennessee: A Bicentennial History* (rev. ed. 1984). Aimed at juvenile readers, David A. Bice and Jessie Strickland's *Horizons of Tennessee* (1990), although brief, is illuminating and accessible. John Chimprich's *Slavery's End in Tennessee: Eighteen Sixty-One to Eighteen Sixty-Five* (1985) discusses in detail one of the most divisive questions in Tennessee history, a question that pitted eastern Tennessee against the middle and western parts of the state. Volume 2 of Donald Davidson's *The Tennessee,* entitled *The New River: Civil War to TVA* (1992) is a thoroughly researched and well-written account of Tennessee history from 1861 to 1940. Margaret E. Dick and Amy Lynch offer an informative study of the economic history of Nashville in *Nashville: Upbeat and down to Business* (1990).

Web Resources. Resources on the Web grow rapidly and change from day to day. Generally any one of the many resources on the Web will lead users to other Web sites and to expanded resources. Two virtually identical Web sites are those of the Tennessee Chamber of Commerce (http://www.tncoc.com) and (http://www.tncoc.org). They offer considerable information about the state and are both arranged under the major headings "Chambers," "Card File," "Domains," and "Info." Under these classifications, one can obtain a broad variety of demographic information about Tennessee as well as information about its political structure and people who occupy state and national offices, about most of its towns and cities, about its educational institutions and major businesses, and about many of its attractions. This resource, if one clicks on "Domain," cross-references other Web sites that contain relevant information about the state.

Another popular Web site provides information about lodging, golf, dining, entertainment, state parks, leisure activities, and tourist attractions within Tennessee. This Web site (http://www.tennessee.com) is sponsored by the state. It contains useful cross-references to other Web sites. It also has a list of cities about which specific information can be obtained by clicking on the name of the city. Some cities, such as Nashville, have their own Web sites (http://www.NashvilleDigest.com) that provide local information about various aspects of the city. The Nashville site is particularly strong in listing entertainment and tourist attractions. Among its features are news, chat rooms, forums, and polls. It also lists all the print media, numbering some sixteen publications, in Nashville as well as the city's six television stations. It refers one for additional information to other valuable Web sites (http://www.Nashlinks.com) and (http://www.NashvilleWebDirectoryCountry.com).

Counties

County	Sq. miles	1996 pop.
Anderson	337.5	71,587
Bedford	473.7	33,856
Benton	394.8	16,014
Bledsoe	406.3	10,386
Blount	558.6	99,010
Bradley	328.8	80,133
Campbell	480.1	37,340
Cannon	265.7	11,722
Carroll	599.1	28,836
Carter	341.1	53,193
Cheatham	302.7	33,175
Chester	288.5	14,099
Claiborne	434.3	28,828
Clay	236.1	7,323
Cocke	434.4	31,495
Coffee	428.9	44,780
Crockett	265.3	13,686

County	Sq. miles	1996 pop.
Cumberland	681.6	42,048
Davidson	502.3	535,036
Decatur	333.9	10,731
DeKalb	304.6	15,474
Dickson	489.9	39,666
Dyer	510.6	36,193
Fayette	704.5	28,309
Fentress	498.7	15,714
Franklin	553.1	36,850
Gibson	602.7	47,657
Giles	611.0	28,430
Grainger	280.4	19,107
Greene	621.8	58,613
Grundy	360.6	13,859
Hamblen	161.0	53,321
Hamilton	542.5	295,373
Hancock	222.3	6,879

County	Sq. miles	1996 pop.
Hardeman	667.6	24,228
Hardin	577.9	24,566
Hawkins	486.7	48,388
Haywood	533.2	19,764
Henderson	520.1	23,451
Henry	561.8	29,736
Hickman	612.7	19,430
Houston	200.2	7,782
Humphreys	532.2	16,675
Jackson	308.9	9,409
Jefferson	273.8	40,268
Johnson	298.5	16,485
Knox	508.5	364,566
Lake	163.4	8,331
Lauderdale	470.5	23,972
Lawrence	617.2	38,785
Lewis	282.1	10,548
Lincoln	570.3	28,756
Loudon	228.6	37,240
McMinn	430.3	45,706
McNairy	560.1	23,679
Macon	307.1	17,373
Madison	557.1	84,390
Marion	499.8	26,533
Marshall	375.4	25,173
Maury	612.9	66,683
Meigs	194.9	9,289
Monroe	635.2	33,289
Montgomery	539.2	120,923
Moore	129.2	5,241
Morgan	522.1	18,280

County	Sq. miles	1996 pop.
Obion	544.9	32,053
Overton	433.4	18,654
Perry	414.9	7,217
Pickett	162.9	4,633
Polk	435.1	14,421
Putnam	401.0	57,928
Rhea	315.9	27,214
Roane	361.0	49,859
Robertson	476.5	49,672
Rutherford	619.0	154,333
Scott	532.1	19,575
Sequatchie	265.9	9,994
Sevier	592.3	61,335
Shelby	754.9	867,409
Smith	314.4	15,663
Stewart	457.7	11,009
Sullivan	413.0	149,844
Sumner	529.4	119,675
Tipton	459.4	45,006
Trousdale	114.2	6,588
Unicoi	186.1	17,135
Union	223.6	15,539
Van Buren	273.5	5,046
Warren	432.7	35,556
Washington	326.2	100,265
Wayne	734.0	16,308
Weakley	580.3	32,568
White	376.7	21,872
Williamson	582.7	106,119
Wilson	570.6	79,502

Source: U.S. Census Bureau; National Association of Counties.

Cities
With 10,000 or more residents

Rank	City	Population
1	Memphis	603,507
2	Nashville-Davidson (remainder)	510,274
3	Knoxville	165,540
4	Chattanooga	147,790
5	Clarksville	97,978
6	Murfreesboro	58,430
7	Johnson City	57,079
8	Jackson	51,115
9	Kingsport	41,139
10	Hendersonville	38,625
11	Germantown	37,587
12	Cleveland	35,454
13	Bartlett	35,391
14	Columbia	31,865
15	Franklin	30,925
16	Oak Ridge	27,045
17	Cookeville	25,471
18	Collierville	23,720
19	Brentwood	23,331
20	Maryville	23,308
21	Bristol	23,109
22	Morristown	23,068
23	Smyrna	22,686
24	Gallatin	21,608

Rank	City	Population
25	East Ridge	19,885
26	Tullahoma	19,153
27	Millington	18,677
28	Lebanon	17,282
29	Farragut	16,805
30	Dyersburg	16,422
31	Shelbyville	16,149
32	La Vergne	15,072
33	Greeneville	13,973
34	Athens	13,486
35	Goodlettsville	13,325
36	Elizabethton	13,211
37	Springfield	12,952
38	McMinnville	12,319
39	Dickson	11,996
40	Red Bank	11,498
41	Lawrenceburg	11,107
42	Lewisburg	11,096
43	Sevierville	10,662
44	Union City	10,147
45	Brownsville	10,003

Population figures are estimated for mid-1998.
Source: U.S. Bureau of the Census.

Index to Tables

NA = Reliable data are not available.

DEMOGRAPHICS

Resident state and national populations, 1970-1997

Population figures given in thousands

	State pop.	U.S. pop.	Share	Rank
1970	3,926	203,302	1.9%	17
1980	4,591	226,546	2.0%	17
1985	4,715	237,924	2.0%	17
1990	4,877	248,765	2.0%	17
1995	5,235	262,761	2.0%	17
1997	5,368	267,636	2.0%	17

Source: U.S. Bureau of the Census.

Resident population by age, 1997

Age group	Total population
Under 5 years	362,000
5 to 17 years	963,000
18 to 24 years	509,000
25 to 34 years	798,000
35 to 44 years	875,000
45 to 54 years	712,000
55 to 64 years	480,000
65 to 74 years	371,000
75 to 84 years	225,000
85 years and over	75,000
Portion of residents 65 and older	12.5%
National average	12.7%

Population figures are rounded to nearest thousand persons;
figures include armed forces personnel stationed in state.
Source: U.S. Bureau of the Census.

Resident population by race, Hispanic origin, 1997

	State pop.	Share	U.S.
All residents	5,368,000	100.0%	100.0%
Hispanic white	49,000	0.9%	10.0%
non-Hispanic white	4,374,000	81.5%	72.7%
African American	884,000	16.5%	12.7%
Native American	12,000	0.2%	0.9%
Asian, Pacific Islander	49,000	0.9%	3.8%

Source: U.S. Bureau of the Census.

Projections of state population, 2000-2025

	Model A Uses interstate migration observed from 1975-1994	Model B Uses Bureau of Economic Analysis employment projections
Year	Population	Population
2000	5,657,000	5,668,000
2005	5,966,000	6,039,000
2010	6,180,000	6,385,000
2015	6,365,000	6,707,000
2020	6,529,000	6,998,000
2025	6,665,000	7,249,000

All population projections, including those for 2000, were calculated in 1997.
Source: U.S. Bureau of the Census, Population Paper Listings PPL-47.

VITAL STATISTICS

Average lifetime in years by race, 1989-1991

	State	U.S.	Rank
All residents	74.32	75.37	42
White residents	75.27	76.13	40
Black residents	68.97	69.16	22

Ranks are from longest-lived to least longest-lived. Ranks exclude Alaska, for which reliable data are not available. Rank for black residents is based on the 32 states for which reliable data are available.
Source: U.S. National Center for Health Statistics.

Infant mortality rates, 1980 and 1995

	State	U.S.
All residents		
1980	13.5	12.6
1995	9.3	7.6
White residents		
1980	11.9	11.0
1995	6.8	6.3
Black residents		
1980	19.3	21.4
1995	17.9	15.1

Figures represent deaths per 1,000 live births of resident infants under 1 year old, exclusive of fetal deaths; all-residents figures include other races not listed separately.
Source: U.S. National Center for Health Statistics.

Marriages and divorces

Marriages in 1996. 82,100
Rate per 1,000 population, 1995 . . . . 15.7
U.S. rate, 1995 . . . . 8.9
Rank among all states. 3

Divorces in 1996 34,400
Rate per 1,000 population, 1995. . . . . 6.3
U.S. rate, 1995 . . . . 4.4
Rank among all states. 7

Rank is from highest to lowest in country.
Source: U.S. National Center for Health Statistics.

Death rates by leading causes, 1995
Deaths per 100,000 resident population

Cause	State	U.S.
Heart disease	308.2	280.7
Cancer	220.9	204.9
Cerebrovascular diseases	79.8	60.1
Accidents and adverse effects	47.3	35.5
Motor vehicle accidents	24.5	16.5
Chronic obstructive pulmonary diseases	41.9	39.2
Diabetes mellitus	23.4	22.6
HIV	9.7	NA
Suicide	13.0	11.9
Homicide	11.1	8.7
All causes	976.1	880.0
Rank in overall death rate among states		10

Figures exclude nonresidents who die in state. Causes of death follow International Classification of Diseases. Rank is from highest to lowest in country.
Source: U.S. National Center for Health Statistics.

ECONOMY

Gross state product, 1990-1996
In current dollars

	State product	Increase
1990	$94.2 billion	
1993	$116.7 billion	
1994	$127.9 billion	9.60%
1995	$134.9 billion	5.47%
1996	$140.8 billion	4.37%

Source: U.S. Bureau of Economic Analysis; *Survey of Current Business,* June, 1998.

Gross state product by industry, 1996
In billions

Farms, forestry, fisheries	$1.4
Construction	4.8
Manufacturing	31.1
Transportation, public utilities	10.3
Wholesale trade	9.9
Retail trade	14.9
Finance, insurance, real estate	16.4
Services	24.0
Government	15.4
State total	$128.7
Total U.S.	$6,923.8
State share	1.86%
Rank among states	18

Total figures include mining, not listed separately.
Source: U.S. Bureau of Economic Analysis; *Survey of Current Business,* June, 1998.

Personal income per capita, 1990 and 1997
In current dollars

	1990	1997
Per capita income	$16,328	$23,018
U.S. average	$19,188	$25,598
Rank among states	36	33

1997 data are preliminary.
Source: U.S. Bureau of Economic Analysis; *Survey of Current Business,* May, 1998.

Energy consumption, 1995
In trillions of British thermal units (BTU)

End-use sectors

Residential	417.3
Commercial	127.6
Industrial	896.5
Transportation	533.8

Sources of energy

Petroleum	678.5
Natural gas	264.8
Coal	668.2
Hydroelectric power	92.9
Nuclear electric power	167.4
Total state per capita consumption	376.5
Total U.S. per capita consumption	344.4
Rank among states	19
Total state energy consumption	1,975.2
Total U.S. energy consumption	90,547.4
State share of U.S. total	2.18%
Rank among states	16

Total figures include items not listed separately.
Source: U.S. Energy Information Administration; *State Energy Data Report.*

Nonfarm employment by sectors, 1997

Total	2,582,000
Construction	116,000
Manufacturing	517,000
Transportation, public utilities	150,000
Wholesale trade, retail trade	609,000
Finance, insurance, real estate	120,000
Services	683,000
Government	383,000

Figures are rounded to nearest thousand persons. Total includes mining, not listed separately.
Source: U.S. Bureau of Labor Statistics; *Employment and Earnings,* monthly.

Foreign exports, 1990-1997
In millions of dollars

Year	State	U.S.	State share
1990	3,746	394,045	0.95%
1996	8,094	624,767	1.30%
1997	9,233	688,896	1.34%

Source: U.S. Bureau of the Census; *U.S. Merchandise Trade,* series FT 900.

LAND USE

Federally owned land, 1996

	State	U.S.	State share
Total acres	26,728,000	2,271,343,000	1.18%
Federally owned	1,576,000	563,129,000	0.28%
Federal share	5.9%	24.8%	—

Areas are rounded to nearest thousand acres. Figures for
federally owned land do not include trust properties.
Source: U.S. General Services Administration; *Inventory Report
on Real Property Owned by the United States Throughout the
World,* annual.

Land use, 1992
In acres, rounded to nearest thousand

Total surface area	26,972,000
Federal land	1,379,000
Total nonfederal	24,740,000
Developed	2,161,000
Total rural	22,579,000
Cropland	4,857,000
Pasture land	5,165,000
Range land	0
Forest land	11,580,000
Minor cover/use	977,000

Total surface area figures include water area not shown
separately.
Source: U.S. Dept. of Agriculture; Soil Conservation Service;
Iowa State University, Statistical Laboratory; *Summary
Report, 1992 National Resources Inventory.*

Farms and crop acreage, 1997

	State	U.S.	Share	Rank
Farms (thousands)	80	2,058	3.89%	7
Acres (millions)	12	968	1.24%	27
Acres per farm	148	471	—	46
Acres planted	4,925	334,139	1.47%	20
Acres harvested	4,673	319,894	1.46%	21
Farm value (mill.)	$1,260	$108,805	1.16%	5

Numbers of farms are rounded to nearest thousand.
Source: U.S. Dept. of Agriculture; National Agricultural
Statistics Service.

GOVERNMENT AND FINANCE

Units of local government, 1997

	State	Total U.S.	Rank
All local governments	940	87,453	30
Counties	93	3,043	10
Municipalities	343	19,372	23
Townships	0	16,629	—
School districts	14	13,726	44
Special districts	490	34,683	24

County ranks are based on the 48 states with county
governments; township ranks are based on the 20 states
with township governments; school district ranks are based
on the 46 states with such districts.
Source: U.S. Bureau of the Census; *1997 Census of Governments,
Government Organization,* Series GC97(1).

State government revenue, 1996

Total revenue	$14,749 mill.
General revenue	12,510 mill.
Per capita	2,357
U.S. per capita average	2,910
Rank among states	47
Intergovernmental revenue	
Total	$4,726 mill.
From federal government	4,689 mill.
From local government	38 mill.
Charges and Miscellaneous	
Total	$1,599 mill.
Current charges	1,133 mill.
Misc. general revenue	466 mill.
Taxes	
Total	$6,185 mill.
General sales	3,537 mill.
Selective sales	1,207 mill.
License taxes	610 mill.
Individual income	114 mill.
Corporate income	534 mill.
Other	182 mill.
Insurance trust revenue	2,239 mill.

Total revenue figures include items not listed separately.
Source: U.S. Bureau of the Census.

State government expenditures, 1996

General expenditures

Intergovernmental	$3,517 mill.
Direct expenditures	9,367 mill.
Total	12,885 mill.

Selected direct expenditures

Education	$4,383 mill.
Public welfare	3,958 mill.
Health, hospital	1,058 mill.
Highways	1,233 mill.
Police	87 mill.
Corrections	445 mill.
Natural resources	166 mill.
Parks and recreation	82 mill.
Government administration	284 mill.
Interest on debt	192 mill.

Other

State per capita expenditures	$2,428
U.S. per capita average	2,854
Rank among states	45
Total state expenditures	13,829 mill.
Total U.S. expenditures	859,959 mill.

Totals include items not listed separately.
Source: U.S. Bureau of the Census.

POLITICS

Governors since statehood

D = Democrat; R = Republican; O = other;
(r) resigned; (d) died in office; (i) removed from office

John Sevier (O)	1796-1801
Archibald Roane (O)	1801-1803
John Sevier (O)	1803-1809
Willie Blount (O)	1809-1815
Joseph McMinn (O)	1815-1821
William Carroll (O)	1821-1827
Sam Houston (O)	(r) 1827-1829
William Hall (O)	1829
William Carroll (D)	1829-1835
Newton Cannon (O)	1835-1839
James K. Polk (D)	1839-1841
James C. Jones (O)	1841-1845
Aaron V. Brown (D)	1845-1847
Neill S. Brown (O)	1847-1849
William Trousdale (D)	1849-1851
William B. Campbell (O)	1851-1853
Andrew Johnson (D)	1853-1857
Isham G. Harris* (D)	(i) 1857-1865
Andrew Johnson**	(r) 1862-1865
Edward H. East	1865
William G. Brownlow (R)	(r) 1865-1869
DeWitt C. Senter (R)	1869-1871
John C. Brown (D)	1871-1875
James D. Porter (D)	1875-1879
Albert S. Marks (D)	1879-1881
Alvin Hawkins (R)	1881-1883
William B. Bate (D)	1883-1887
Robert L. Taylor (D)	1887-1891
John P. Buchanan (D)	1891-1893
Peter Turney (D)	1893-1897
Robert L. Taylor (D)	1897-1899
Benton McMillin (D)	1899-1903
James B. Frazier (D)	(r) 1903-1905
John I. Cox (D)	1905-1907
Malcolm R. Patterson (D)	1907-1911
Benjamin W. Hooper (R)	1911-1915
Thomas C. Rye (D)	1915-1919
Albert H. Roberts (D)	1919-1921
Alfred A. Taylor (R)	1921-1923
Austin L. Peay (D)	(d) 1923-1927
Henry H. Horton (D)	1927-1933
Hill McAlister (D)	1933-1937
Gordon W. Browning (D)	1937-1939
Prentice Cooper (D)	1939-1945
James M. McCord (D)	1945-1949
Gordon W. Browning (D)	1949-1953
Frank G. Clement (D)	1953-1959
Buford Ellington (D)	1959-1963
Frank G. Clement (D)	1963-1967
Buford Ellington (D)	1967-1971
Winfield C. Dunn (R)	1971-1975
Leonard Ray Blanton (D)	1975-1979
Lamar Alexander (R)	1979-1987
Ned Ray McWherter (D)	1987-1995
Don Sundquist (R)	1995-

*Confederate governor
**Union governor

Composition of state legislature, 1990-1998

	Democrats	Republicans
State House (99 seats)		
1990	57	42
1992	63	36
1994	59	40
1996	61	38
1998	59	40
State Senate (33 seats)		
1990	20	13
1992	19	14
1994	18	15
1996	18	15
1998	18	15

Figures for total seats may include independents and minor party members.

Source: Council of State Governments; *State Elective Officials and the Legislatures.*

Composition of congressional delegations, 1989-1999

	Dem	Rep	Total
House of Representatives			
101st Congress, 1989			
State delegates	6	3	9
Total U.S.	259	174	433
102d Congress, 1991			
State delegates	6	3	9
Total U.S.	267	167	434
103d Congress, 1993			
State delegates	6	3	9
Total U.S.	258	176	434
104th Congress, 1995			
State delegates	4	5	9
Total U.S.	197	236	433
105th Congress, 1997			
State delegates	4	5	9
Total U.S.	206	228	434
106th Congress, 1999			
State delegates	4	5	9
Total U.S.	211	222	433

	Dem	Rep	Total
Senate			
101st Congress, 1989			
State delegates	2	0	2
Total U.S.	55	45	100
102d Congress, 1991			
State delegates	2	0	2
Total U.S.	56	44	100
103d Congress, 1993			
State delegates	2	0	2
Total U.S.	57	43	100
104th Congress, 1995			
State delegates	0	2	2
Total U.S.	46	53	99
105th Congress, 1997			
State delegates	0	2	2
Total U.S.	45	55	100
106th Congress, 1999			
State delegates	0	2	2
Total U.S.	45	54	99

Figures are for starts of first sessions. Figure for U.S. Representatives for 101st Congress does not include Alabama and Indiana, which had vacancies. Figures for total U.S. Representatives for 102d, 103d, and 106th Congresses do not include Vermont, which had 1 Independent-Socialist. Figure for U.S. Representatives for 104th Congress does not include Vermont, which had 1 Independent-Socialist, and California, which had 1 vacancy. Figure for U.S. Representatives for 105th Congress does not include New York, which had 1 vacancy. Figure for U.S. Senators for 104th Congress does not include Oregon, which had 1 vacancy. Figure for U.S. Senators for 106th Congress does not include New Hampshire, which had 1 Independent.

Source: U.S. Congress; *Congressional Directory,* biennial.

Voter participation in presidential elections, 1992 and 1996

	1992	1996
State voting age pop.	3,796,000	4,021,000
Total U.S. voting age pop.	189,524,000	196,509,000
State share of U.S. total	2.0%	2.1%
Rank among states	16	16
Percent of state casting vote	52.2	45.6
Percent of U.S. total voting	55.1	49.0
Rank among states	39	44

Source: U.S. Bureau of the Census.

HEALTH AND MEDICAL CARE

Medicare, 1997

	Recipients	Payments
State	794,000	$4,722 mill.
Total U.S.	37,514,000	$206,064 mill.
State share	2.12%	2.29%
Rank among states	16	13

Recipient figures are rounded to nearest thousand persons.
  Ranks are from highest to lowest.
Source: U.S. Health Care Financing Administration.

Medicaid, 1996

	Recipients	Payments
State	1,409,000	$2,886 mill.
Total U.S.	35,028,000	$121,419 mill.
State share	4.02%	2.38%
Rank among states	7	13

Recipient figures are rounded to nearest thousand persons.
  Payment figures for fiscal year reflect federal and state
  contribution payments. Ranks are from highest to lowest.
Source: U.S. Health Care Financing Administration.

Health insurance coverage, 1996

	State	U.S.
Total persons covered	4,702,000	225,070,000
Total persons not covered	841,000	41,716,000
Part not covered	15.2%	15.6%
Rank among states	20	—
Children not covered	281,000	10,554,000
Part not covered	18.7%	14.8%
Rank among states	8	—

Ranks are from most to fewest uninsured. Population figures
  are rounded to nearest thousand persons.
Source: U.S. Bureau of the Census.

AIDS, syphilis, tuberculosis, and measles cases, 1997

Cases	U.S.	State	Share
AIDS	58,443	784	1.34%
Syphilis	8,550	747	8.74%
Tuberculosis	18,534	358	1.93%
Measles	148,000	NA	NA

Measles figures are rounded to nearest thousand cases.
Source: U.S. Centers for Disease Control and Prevention.

HOUSING

Homeownership rates, 1985-1997

	1985	1990	1997
State	67.6%	68.3%	70.2%
Total U.S.	63.9%	63.9%	65.7%
Rank among states	29	20	17

Source: U.S. Bureau of the Census.

Home sales, 1990 and 1997
In thousands of units

Existing home sales	1990	1997	Change
State sales	92.7	149.9	57.2
Total U.S. sales	3,560	4,730	1,170
State share of U.S. total	2.60%	3.17%	0.57%
Rank among states	12	11	—

Source: National Association of Realtors; *Real Estate Outlook:
  Market Trends and Insights.*

EDUCATION

Public school enrollment, 1995

State K-8 enrollment	651,000
Total U.S. K-8 enrollment	32,341,000
State share of total U.S.	2.01%
State 9-12 enrollment	243,000
Total U.S. 9-12 enrollment	12,500,000
State share of U.S. total	1.94%
State public school enroll. rate	94.7%
Overall U.S. rate	91.6%
Rank among states	14

Enrollment figures (which include unclassified students) are rounded to nearest thousand pupils in fall term; kindergarten (K)-8 grade figures include some prekindergarten students. Enrollment rate is based on percentage of persons 5-17 years old. Rank is from highest to lowest.

Source: U.S. National Center for Education Statistics.

Public college finances, 1996

State FTE enrollment	153,400
Total U.S. FTE enrollment	8,268,800
State share of total U.S.	1.86%
Rank among states	20
State and local appropriations	$724,600,000
Total U.S. state and local appropriations	$39,699 mill.
State share of total U.S.	1.83%
Rank among states	18
State net tuition revenues	$302,500,000
Total U.S. net tuition	$18,348,100,000
State share of total U.S.	1.65%
Rank among states	25

FTE=Full-time equivalent; credit and noncredit enrollment including summer session in academic year ending in 1996.

Enrollments are rounded to nearest thousand students. Net tuition revenues exclude appropriation to students attending in-state public institutions. Rankings are from highest shares to lowest.

Source: Research Associates of Washington.

TRANSPORTATION AND TRAVEL

Highway mileage, 1996

Interstate	1,062
Other arterial	8,713
Collector roads	19,714
Local roads	57,940
Urban roads	17,277
Rural roads	68,518
Total state	85,795
U.S. total	3,933,985
State share	2.2%
Rank among states	21

Source: U.S. Federal Highway Administration.

Motor vehicle registrations and driver licenses, 1996
In thousands

Vehicle registrations	State	U.S.	Share	Rank
Autos, trucks, buses	4,830	206,365	2.34%	14
Autos only	2,975	128,439	2.32%	15
Motorcycles	79	3,832	2.06%	17
Driver licenses	3,806	179,539	2.12%	14

Figures do not include vehicles owned by military services.
Source: U.S. Federal Highway Administration; *Highway Statistics; Selected Highway Statistics and Charts.*

Domestic travel expenditures, 1995
Spending by U.S. residents on overnight trips and day trips of at least 100 miles

Total expenditures in state	$7,679 mill.
Total expenditures in U.S.	$360,314 mill.
State share of total U.S.	2.13%
Rank among states	15

Source: Travel Industry Association of America.

CRIME AND LAW ENFORCEMENT

State and local police officers, 1996

Local police	7,076
State police	768
Sheriffs	3,520
Total	12,152
Officers per 10,000 residents	23
U.S. average	25
Rank among states	21

Figures cover full-time sworn officers; totals include special police not shown separately.
Source: U.S. Bureau of Justice Statistics; *Census of State and Local Law Enforcement Agencies, 1996.*

Crime rates, 1996
Rates per 100,000 resident population

Violent crimes	State	U.S.
Total violent	774	634
Murder	9.5	7.4
Forcible rape	46.5	36.1
Robbery	224	202
Aggravated assault	494	388
Property crimes		
Total property	4,675	4,445
Burglary	1,164	943
Larceny/theft	2,865	2,976
Motor vehicle theft	647	526
Totals	5,449	5,079

Source: U.S. Federal Bureau of Investigation; *Crime in the United States,* annual.

State prison populations, 1980-1996

	State	U.S.	State share
1980	7,022	305,458	2.30%
1990	10,388	708,393	1.47%
1996	15,626	1,025,624	1.52%

Figures exclude prisoners in federal penitentiaries.
Source: U.S. Bureau of Justice Statistics.

Texas

Location: Southern continental United States

Area and rank: 261,914 square miles (678,358 square kilometers); 268,601 square miles (695,677 square kilometers) including water; second largest state in area

Coastline: 367 miles (591 kilometers)

Shoreline: 3,359 miles (5,405 kilometers)

Population and rank: 19,439,337 (1997); second largest state in population

Texas is the only state with three cities with populations of more than a million people; Houston, pictured above, is the largest. (PhotoDisc)

Capital: Austin

Largest city: Houston (1,786,691 people in 1998)

Became independent republic: 1836

Entered Union and rank: December 29, 1845; twenty-eighth state

Present constitution adopted: 1876

Counties: 254

State name: "Texas" comes from an Indian word meaning "friends"

State nickname: Lone Star State

Motto: Friendship

State flag: One-third (vertical) is blue with white star, other two-thirds (horizontal) red and white

Highest point: Guadalupe Peak — 8,749 feet (2,667 meters)

Lowest point: Gulf of Mexico — sea level

Highest recorded temperature: 120 degrees Fahrenheit (49 degrees Celsius) — Seymour, 1936

Lowest recorded temperature: −23 degrees Fahrenheit (−31 degrees Celsius) — Seminole, 1933

State song: "Texas, Our Texas"

State tree: Pecan

State flower: Bluebonnet

State bird: Mockingbird

State fish: Guadalupe bass

National parks: Big Bend, Guadalupe Mountains

Texas History

Until Alaska was admitted as the forty-ninth state in 1959, Texas was the largest of the United States and still is the largest of the contiguous forty-eight states, occupying one-twelfth of the entire American land mass. With a total area of more than a quarter of a million square miles, it stretches almost eight hundred miles from its eastern boundary in Arkansas and Louisiana to its western extremes at Mexico and New Mexico. On the south it is bordered by the Gulf of Mexico and Mexico. Its northern boundary, Oklahoma, lies 730 miles from its southern extreme.

Texas is the only state in the Union ruled under six flags: those of Spain, France, Mexico, the Republic of Texas, the Confederate States of America, and the United States. Early explorers found this vast area intimidating, but modern transportation and a wealth of natural resources, particularly oil and natural gas, helped Texas achieve the third largest population of the United States.

Early History. The earliest settlers in Texas were American Indians who dwelt there before 12,000 B.C.E. By 5000 B.C.E., the early residents were farming and hunting with bows and arrows. In far western Texas, remnants of Pueblo dwellings similar to those found in New Mexico have been unearthed. Indian mounds like those found in the western parts of Illinois, Tennessee, Louisiana, and Mississippi were discovered in east Texas.

Exploration and Colonization. The earliest explorations of Texas were made by Spaniards. In 1519 Alonso de Piñeda sailed along the Gulf of Mexico coastline from Florida to Mexico, establishing Spain's claim to the land that lay along it. By 1528 Alvar Núñez Cabeza de Vaca explored the interior. In the 1540's, Francisco Vásquez de

Late nineteenth century drawing of the Mexican siege of the Alamo in 1836. (Library of Congress)

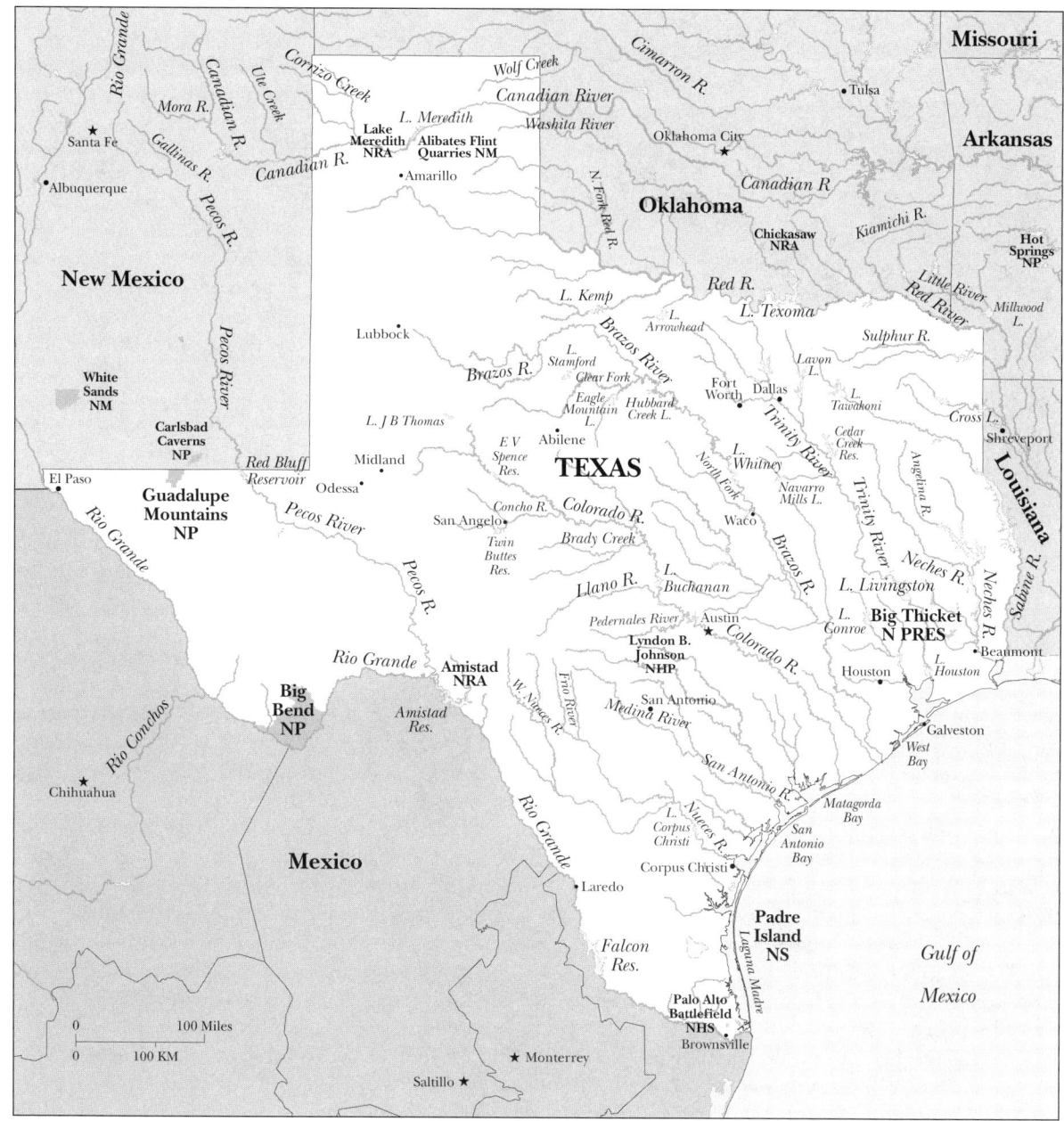

Coronado and Hernando de Soto both led expeditions into Texas, but their reports made the territory sound so forbidding that explorers avoided the area for the next half century.

It was not until 1682, after René-Robert Cavalier, sieur de La Salle, declared Texas a possession of France, that the Spaniards took a renewed interest in the area. The French were driven out by Native Americans, but in 1690 the Spanish renewed their claim by establishing two missions among the Indians in east Texas. By 1716 they had established five missions in east Texas.

The Native American population of the state ranged from Cherokees in the east, who had been displaced from their lands in other areas, to the Tonkawa, nomadic plains Indians in the central

Oil rig by the Gulf of Mexico, where the discovery of massive oil fields in 1901 triggered the transformation of Texas's economy. (PhotoDisc)

who were summarily executed. The following year, he stormed the Alamo, taking control from the few Texans remaining inside.

As Anglo-American immigrants flooded into the area, the United States sought to purchase Texas. The Mexican government, which held claims to the region, tried unsuccessfully to discourage American immigration. Tensions arose between the United States and Mexico, which objected to the presence of slavery in Texas. In 1836 Texas declared its independence as the Republic of Texas, a status it held until it was annexed as the twenty-eighth state of the United States in 1845.

part of the area, to the Coahuitecan and Karankawa tribes, the most primitive of the Native American dwellers, along the Gulf coast. The Lipan Apache, the Comanche, the Kiowa, and the Kiowa Apache inhabited the west.

The U.S. Claim to Texas. Louisiana was ceded to Spain in 1762. By 1800 Texas had established three permanent Spanish settlements, San Antonio, Goliad, and Nacogdoches. In 1800 France took the title to Louisiana, which was sold to the United States in 1803. The boundary between the Spanish and French claims in this area had never been established, so the United States now held a tenuous claim to Texas.

When Texas became part of the new nation of Mexico in 1821, colonization was encouraged. Moses Austin came from Missouri with three hundred families who were given land. Austin's son Stephen brought in more settlers after his father died. Land was plentiful, and land grants were generous and easily obtained.

By 1835 about twenty thousand settlers had arrived in east Texas, bringing with them more than four thousand slaves to work in the cotton fields, thereby establishing Texas as a slave state. In the same year, Mexican general Antonio López de Santa Anna waged war against the Texans during the Texas Revolution, taking about 350 prisoners,

Cotton, an important crop in eastern Texas during its early settlement, made slave labor attractive to those who raised cotton. With slavery as a part of the Texan economy, Texas joined the Confederate States of America in 1861, sixteen years after it had gained admission to the Union.

The Early Texas Economy. Agriculture became a major element in the early economy of Texas, some 85 percent of whose land consists of farms and ranches. Cattle and poultry production are significant in the state. Citrus fruit was grown early in the southern areas along the Gulf of Mexico and the Rio Grande. Industry was slow to develop in the nineteenth century, largely because Texas did not have sufficient hydroelectric power to drive mechanized industry.

Texas came into its own economically after 1901, when the great Spindletop oil field was discovered in southeastern Texas near Beaumont. This discovery triggered a rush to explore other parts of the state for oil, and it was soon found that Texas rested on a huge subterranean sea of oil that extended beyond its land mass into the Gulf of Mexico. Natural gas was also discovered in such quantities that Texas was the source of more than a third of the nation's supply.

The oil rush brought enormous revenues into Texas and created hundreds of millionaires almost overnight. The state's population grew from about three million in 1900 to almost four million in 1910, partly because of oil. By 1990, Texas had almost seventeen million residents, making it the third most populous of the United States. By 1998, it was home to slightly less than twenty million.

The sale of oil and natural gas was important to the Texas economy. The discovery of these two fuels spurred the growth of manufacturing industries in the state, which now had the reasonable and ready supply of energy it had previously lacked.

The Move to Manufacturing. Contemporary Texas is one of the ten most productive manufacturing states in the Union. Oil refining and petrochemical companies are among the largest manufacturing industries in the state, most of them centered around the Houston-Beaumont-Port Arthur area in the southeastern portion. In 1961 Houston was chosen as the location of the Manned Spacecraft Center, at which astronauts are trained. It is the control center for the U.S. government's manned space ventures. The establishment of this center brought into Texas considerable other industry that focuses on the manufacture of transportation equipment, including aircraft, automobile assembly plants, and mobile-home manufacturing.

Giant food processing plants grew up to process the livestock, poultry, and vegetables the state produces in abundance. Texas is also preeminent in the manufacturing of machinery, including the complex equipment used in oil exploration and drilling. A thriving mining industry exists, along with extensive textile, clothing, and timber operations.

Transportation. Because of its enormous size, Texas early developed a comprehensive transportation system that, in the early days, involved boat transportation along the Gulf of Mexico and on the state's rivers, as well as rail transportation served by fourteen thousand miles of track. As the highway system grew to the point that it was the largest in the United States, with sixty-five thousand miles of paved roads, Texans relied more on automobiles than on trains for transportation, so passenger service waned.

In the late twentieth century, Texas had splendid air transportation. The climate is good for fly-

Ultramodern skyline of Dallas, Texas's third-largest city. (PhotoDisc)

ing, and the distances make it the most reasonable means of rapid transport. In 1974, the opening of the Dallas-Fort Worth International Airport, the third largest airport in the world, established Texas as an important hub for many national and international airlines. This airport has the second greatest passenger volume in the United States.

Texas Politics. Texas represents an interesting mix of political conservatism and populism. Texans are staunch individualists, yet the state was essentially a one-party state until the election of George W. Bush as its Republican governor in 1994.

Realizing that Texas is a politically important state, with thirty-two electoral votes, national politicians have flocked to it looking for support. Among these was President John F. Kennedy, who went to Texas in November, 1963, to support Democrats running for public office and to help ensure his own victory there when he ran for reelection in 1964. Kennedy was assassinated in Dallas, Texas, by Lee Harvey Oswald. He was succeeded by his vice president, Texan Lyndon Baines Johnson, who remained in office until 1969.

Modern Population. Texas has always had a mix of cultures. In the southern areas along the Rio Grande live many people of Mexican descent, some of whose families have lived there for two hundred years. These people are technically American citizens, but their ties to Mexico remain strong. The Anglo-American population includes not only people of British extraction but also large numbers of Germans, in San Antonio, New Braunfels, Seguin, and other towns in central Texas. Eastern and southern Europeans are well represented in the state's population, as are people from the Middle Eastern countries, especially the major oil-producing ones.

In the late twentieth century, about one-third of all Texans were of African American or Hispanic lineage, particularly the latter. Spanish is a second language throughout much of Texas and is used along with English in most of its restaurants, hotels, and stores.

R. Baird Shuman

Texas Time Line

1519	Texas is claimed for Spain by Spanish explorer Alonso de Piñeda.
Nov. 6, 1528	Alvar Núñez Cabeza de Vaca explores interior Texas.
1541	Francisco Vásquez de Coronado explores west Texas.
1541	Hernando de Soto explores central Texas.
1682	René-Robert Cavalier, sieur de La Salle, claims Texas for France; Spaniards establish permanent settlement in Ysleta in west Texas.
1685	La Salle builds fort near Matagora Bay on the Gulf coast.
1690	Spanish establish missions in east Texas.
1691	Texas officially becomes a Spanish province.
1716	Spanish revitalize their mission settlements to thwart the French.
May 1, 1718	Alamo mission is established in what later becomes San Antonio.
1821	Texas becomes part of the new nation of Mexico.
1835	Twenty thousand southerners arrive in east Texas with four thousand slaves.
Oct. 2, 1835	Texas Revolution begins.
Mar. 6, 1836	Mexican general Santa Anna's troops capture the Alamo.
1836	Republic of Texas, independent of Mexico, is formed.

1837	United States recognizes Republic of Texas.
1839	Texas State Library is established in Austin.
1839	Education Act of 1839 promises a university system.
Dec. 29, 1845	Texas enters the Union as twenty-eighth state.
Feb. 1, 1861	Texas secedes from the Union, joining the Confederacy.
1865	Texas frees its slaves following the Civil War.
Mar. 30, 1870	Texas is readmitted to the United States.
1876	State constitution is adopted.
1883	University of Texas opens in Austin.
Sept. 8, 1900	Galveston is devastated by hurricane that kills six thousand.
1901	Spindletop oil field is discovered.
1915	Compulsory school attendance law passed.
1931	Discovery of the rich east Texas oil field.
1944	U.S. Supreme Court outlaws state's whites-only primary voting law.
1950	Supreme Court bans racial segregation at University of Texas Law School.
1953	Texas recovers offshore tidal oil fields from U.S. government.
1961	Houston is chosen for Manned Spacecraft Center.
Nov. 22, 1963	President John F. Kennedy is assassinated in Dallas; Texan Lyndon Baines Johnson becomes president of the United States.
1965	Reapportionment of state legislature ensures concept of one person, one vote.
1966	Federal courts ban payment of poll tax as a condition of voting.
1968	HemisFair '68 is held to mark San Antonio's 250th anniversary.
1969	Amistad Dam is completed on Rio Grande to serve United States and Mexico.
1970	Hurricane devastates Corpus Christi.
1974	Dallas-Fort Worth International Airport opens.
1988	Drought disaster is declared in Texas.
1988	Waxahachie is chosen as the site of the Superconductor Super Collider.
1990	Two barges and oil tanker collide near Galveston Bay, spilling 500,000 gallons of oil.
1994	Texas has 394 prisoners on death row, the most in the nation.
1994	George W. Bush is elected first Republican governor.
1999	Amoco announces billion-barrel oil discovery in Gulf of Mexico off Texas coast.

Notes for Further Study

Published Sources. One of the best overviews of Texas is found in James L. Haley's *Texas: From Spindletop Through World War II* (1993), which, in a series of short essays, captures a great deal of Texas history. Pete A. Y. Gunter and Max Oelschlager explore some of the nefarious land dealings in Texas in their somewhat specialized

Texas Land Ethics (1997). The question of capital punishment in Texas is well addressed in Ken Light's *Texas Death Row* (1997), which contains haunting illustrations and sometimes frightening commentary about the Texas justice system. W. Dirk Raat considers the clash of contrasting cultures in *Mexico and the United States: Ambivalent Cultures* (1996), which is nicely supplemented by the essays in Oscar J. Martinez, ed., *U.S.-Mexican Borderlands: Historical and Contemporary Perspective* (1996). T. Lindsay Baker's *Building the Lone Star State: An Illustrated Guide to Historic Sites* (1986) will prove useful to those planning to travel in the state. Jerry Thompson's *A Wild and Vivid Land: An Illustrated History of the Texas Border* (1997) offers excellent pictures and interesting commentary about south Texas.

William Curry Holden's *Alkalai Trails: Or, Social and Economic Movements of the Texas Frontier, 1846-1900* (1998) offers a detailed and lucid presentation of the economic growth of Texas from the time of the Mexican-American War to the beginning of the twentieth century. Among the issues dealt with during this period was the question of immigration, particularly from Mexico, which Kenneth L. Stewart and Arnold De Leon address fully in *Not Room Enough: Mexicans, Anglos, and Socio-economic Change in Texas, 1850-1900* (1993). Focusing on later times in the economic history of the state, the contributors to *The Depression in the Southwest* (1980), edited by Donald W. Whisenhunt, write about the effects on Texas of the great droughts of the 1930's and the economic upheaval throughout the United States.

Web Resources. Scores of Web sites relating to Texas exist. Many of them offer references to other Web sites, and most are frequently updated. Perhaps most generally useful of all the Web sites is Web Texas (http://www.utexas.edu/texas), which offers a comprehensive, searchable index for every Web site connected with the state. Web Texas offers an accessible interface. A useful Web site about Texas government (http://www.texas.gov) presents facts about Texans, future Texans, and visitors, as well as information about the Texas Electronic Library. It addresses frequently asked questions. Another Web site (http://www.texas.com) has useful home pages for various Texas sites.

Those interested in library sources and general information regarding the state should consult the Electronic Library Web site (http://link.tsl.texas.gov/s/subject index.html), whose facts-at-your-fingertips section provides extensive information. This site also offers complete texts of books, Library of Congress access, and a means of asking questions by electronic mail. Those interested in employment opportunities in the state or needing information about the state's economy should consult the state employment Web site (http://www.state.tx.us/#work). The state constitution can be accessed and questions asked about it on a Web site (http://capitol.tlc.state.tx.us./txconst/toc.html) that focuses on the interpretation of the constitution. The Web site of the Dallas Museum of Art (http://www.unt.edu/dfw/dma/www/dma.htm) lists the museum's holdings in ancient American, African, Indonesian, and contemporary art, as well American decorative arts, including pictures. The Texas Environmental Center's Web site (http://www.tech.org) provides access to environmental resources.

Counties

County	Sq. miles	1996 pop.	County	Sq. miles	1996 pop.
Anderson	1,070.9	52,174	Bexar	1,246.9	1,318,322
Andrews	1,500.7	14,087	Blanco	711.3	7,774
Angelina	801.6	76,069	Borden	898.9	807
Aransas	252.0	21,803	Bosque	989.3	16,756
Archer	909.8	8,247	Bowie	887.9	84,969
Armstrong	913.7	2,162	Brazoria	1,386.9	220,854
Atascosa	1,232.2	35,044	Brazos	585.8	131,904
Austin	652.6	22,768	Brewster	6,193.0	9,221
Bailey	826.7	6,789	Briscoe	900.3	1,917
Bandera	791.8	14,287	Brooks	943.3	8,493
Bastrop	888.5	46,819	Brown	944.0	36,746
Baylor	870.8	4,153	Burleson	665.6	15,288
Bee	880.2	27,833	Burnet	995.3	29,753
Bell	1,059.0	222,450	Caldwell	545.8	30,514

County	Sq. miles	1996 pop.	County	Sq. miles	1996 pop.
Calhoun	512.4	20,711	Frio	1,133.1	15,824
Callahan	898.7	12,580	Gaines	1,502.4	14,719
Cameron	905.6	315,015	Galveston	398.7	240,653
Camp	197.5	10,913	Garza	895.6	4,729
Carson	923.2	6,714	Gillespie	1,061.2	19,635
Cass	937.5	30,621	Glasscock	900.8	1,407
Castro	898.4	8,535	Goliad	853.6	6,586
Chambers	599.4	22,789	Gonzales	1,067.9	17,608
Cherokee	1,052.3	42,484	Gray	928.3	23,335
Childress	710.4	7,580	Grayson	933.7	100,589
Clay	1,097.9	10,450	Gregg	274.1	112,138
Cochran	775.2	4,083	Grimes	793.8	22,192
Coke	898.9	3,437	Guadalupe	711.2	75,235
Coleman	1,272.9	9,700	Hale	1,004.7	36,548
Collin	847.7	372,445	Hall	903.1	3,750
Collingsworth	918.8	3,269	Hamilton	835.8	7,570
Colorado	963.0	18,757	Hansford	919.9	5,372
Comal	561.5	67,687	Hardeman	695.4	4,808
Comanche	937.8	13,645	Hardin	894.4	47,574
Concho	991.5	3,186	Harris	1,729.0	3,126,966
Cooke	873.8	32,254	Harrison	898.8	59,685
Coryell	1,051.9	74,446	Hartley	1,462.4	5,210
Cottle	901.2	1,975	Haskell	903.0	6,247
Crane	785.6	4,514	Hays	677.9	81,744
Crockett	2,807.6	4,372	Hemphill	909.7	3,648
Crosby	899.6	7,349	Henderson	874.4	65,664
Culberson	3,812.7	3,210	Hidalgo	1,569.1	495,594
Dallam	1,504.8	6,269	Hill	962.4	29,698
Dallas	879.9	2,000,192	Hockley	908.3	23,931
Dawson	902.1	15,172	Hood	421.6	34,976
Deaf Smith	1,497.4	19,519	Hopkins	784.8	30,455
Delta	277.2	4,923	Houston	1,231.0	21,962
Denton	888.5	348,453	Howard	902.9	32,836
DeWitt	909.3	19,657	Hudspeth	4,571.3	3,265
Dickens	904.3	2,317	Hunt	841.2	67,906
Dimmit	1,331.0	10,475	Hutchinson	887.4	24,425
Donley	929.8	3,863	Irion	1,051.6	1,718
Duval	1,792.9	13,383	Jack	917.4	7,285
Eastland	926.1	18,064	Jackson	829.5	13,687
Ector	901.1	123,398	Jasper	937.5	32,954
Edwards	2,119.9	3,374	Jeff Davis	2,264.6	2,155
El Paso	1,013.1	684,446	Jefferson	903.6	243,733
Ellis	940.0	97,054	Jim Hogg	1,136.2	5,036
Erath	1,086.4	30,815	Jim Wells	864.7	39,725
Falls	769.1	17,727	Johnson	729.4	110,344
Fannin	891.6	27,614	Jones	931.1	18,692
Fayette	950.1	21,185	Karnes	750.4	12,567
Fisher	901.2	4,449	Kaufman	786.1	62,116
Floyd	992.3	8,334	Kendall	662.5	19,639
Foard	706.7	1,719	Kenedy	1,456.9	438
Fort Bend	875.0	306,832	Kent	902.4	864
Franklin	285.7	9,320	Kerr	1,106.3	41,406
Freestone	885.3	17,476	Kimble	1,250.8	4,215

(continued)

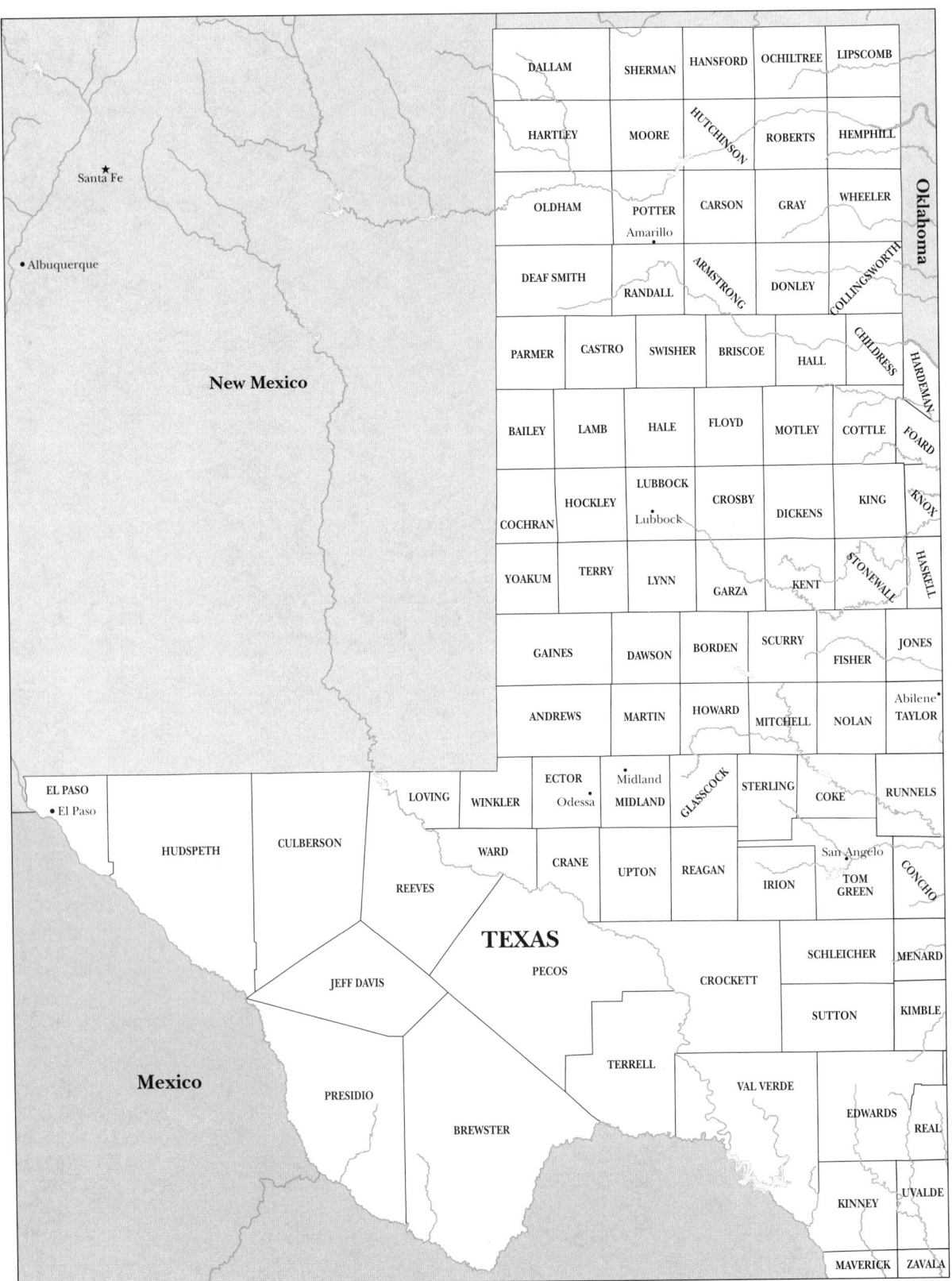

County	Sq. miles	1996 pop.	County	Sq. miles	1996 pop.
King	912.3	336	Potter	909.4	108,636
Kinney	1,363.5	3,402	Presidio	3,855.8	7,966
Kleberg	871.1	30,325	Rains	232.1	7,869
Knox	854.2	4,425	Randall	914.5	97,379
Lamar	917.1	45,255	Reagan	1,175.4	4,254
Lamb	1,016.3	14,989	Real	700.0	2,724
Lampasas	712.1	17,163	Red River	1,050.2	13,959
LaSalle	1,489.0	6,063	Reeves	2,636.1	14,993
Lavaca	970.0	18,872	Refugio	770.3	7,903
Lee	628.6	14,442	Roberts	924.1	988
Leon	1,072.1	14,190	Robertson	854.6	15,522
Liberty	1,159.8	63,294	Rockwall	128.8	34,153
Limestone	908.9	20,829	Runnels	1,054.5	11,410
Lipscomb	932.2	3,081	Rusk	923.6	45,596
Live Oak	1,036.4	10,195	Sabine	490.3	10,443
Llano	934.9	12,861	San Augustine	527.9	8,051
Loving	673.1	141	San Jacinto	570.7	19,957
Lubbock	899.6	232,035	San Patricio	691.8	68,334
Lynn	891.9	6,588	San Saba	1,134.5	6,024
McCulloch	1,069.4	8,694	Schleicher	1,310.7	3,088
McLennan	1,041.9	201,775	Scurry	902.6	18,248
McMullen	1,113.1	799	Shackelford	914.0	3,296
Madison	469.7	11,984	Shelby	794.2	22,677
Marion	381.2	10,430	Sherman	923.1	2,818
Martin	914.9	4,957	Smith	928.5	165,002
Mason	932.1	3,598	Somervell	187.2	5,986
Matagorda	1,114.5	38,192	Starr	1,223.1	53,974
Maverick	1,280.2	46,563	Stephens	894.7	9,798
Medina	1,327.9	35,363	Sterling	923.4	1,411
Menard	902.0	2,361	Stonewall	918.7	1,813
Midland	900.3	116,016	Sutton	1,453.9	4,449
Milam	1,016.8	23,972	Swisher	900.5	8,495
Mills	748.2	4,767	Tarrant	863.5	1,305,185
Mitchell	910.1	9,002	Taylor	915.7	122,130
Montague	930.7	18,030	Terrell	2,357.9	1,237
Montgomery	1,044.3	245,845	Terry	889.9	13,093
Moore	899.7	19,427	Throckmorton	912.4	1,797
Morris	254.5	13,262	Titus	410.6	24,909
Motley	989.4	1,330	Tom Green	1,522.2	102,580
Nacogdoches	946.8	56,533	Travis	989.4	683,967
Navarro	1,071.2	41,290	Trinity	692.9	12,454
Newton	932.8	14,259	Tyler	923.0	20,283
Nolan	912.1	16,370	Upshur	587.7	34,909
Nueces	835.9	315,722	Upton	1,241.8	3,816
Ochiltree	917.6	8,791	Uvalde	1,556.6	25,343
Oldham	1,500.7	2,270	Val Verde	3,170.7	43,131
Orange	356.4	84,488	Van Zandt	848.8	42,579
Palo Pinto	953.0	25,463	Victoria	882.6	81,541
Panola	801.0	22,899	Walker	787.5	54,417
Parker	903.6	76,073	Waller	513.6	26,195
Parmer	881.7	10,403	Ward	835.6	11,994
Pecos	4,764.0	16,349	Washington	609.3	28,610
Polk	1,057.4	44,906	Webb	3,357.0	176,792

County	Sq. miles	1996 pop.	County	Sq. miles	1996 pop.
Wharton	1,090.2	40,224	Wise	904.7	40,451
Wheeler	914.3	5,344	Wood	650.3	33,321
Wichita	627.7	128,064	Yoakum	799.8	8,325
Wilbarger	971.1	14,308	Young	922.4	17,528
Willacy	596.7	19,419	Zapata	996.8	11,100
Williamson	1,124.4	198,286	Zavala	1,298.6	12,322
Wilson	807.2	28,867			
Winkler	841.1	8,043			

Source: U.S. Census Bureau; National Association of Counties.

Cities

With 10,000 or more residents

Rank	City	Population	Rank	City	Population
1	Houston	1,786,691	37	Round Rock	60,686
2	San Antonio	1,114,130	38	College Station	59,742
3	Dallas	1,075,894	39	Galveston	59,567
4	El Paso	615,032	40	Bryan	58,763
5	Austin	552,434	41	Harlingen	58,210
6	Fort Worth	491,801	42	Port Arthur	56,827
7	Arlington	306,497	43	North Richland Hills	54,622
8	Corpus Christi	281,453	44	Sugar Land	51,725
9	Plano	219,486	45	Bedford	50,148
10	Garland	193,408	46	Temple	49,427
11	Lubbock	190,974	47	Euless	45,249
12	Irving	178,253	48	Flower Mound	44,338
13	Laredo	175,783	49	League City	43,633
14	Amarillo	171,207	50	Texas City	42,488
15	Brownsville	137,883	51	Pharr	42,318
16	Pasadena	133,964	52	Edinburg	40,579
17	Mesquite	114,632	53	McKinney	40,404
18	Grand Prairie	113,329	54	Grapevine	40,299
19	Beaumont	109,841	55	Mission	40,083
20	Waco	108,272	56	San Marcos	39,491
21	Abilene	108,257	57	Rowlett	39,030
22	McAllen	106,822	58	Allen	38,941
23	Carrollton	100,463	59	Hurst	37,266
24	Midland	99,621	60	Haltom City	37,061
25	Wichita Falls	99,236	61	New Braunfels	36,526
26	Odessa	91,572	62	Duncanville	36,160
27	San Angelo	88,233	63	De Soto	35,686
28	Richardson	86,020	64	Conroe	35,353
29	Tyler	83,908	65	Del Rio	34,990
30	Killeen	80,720	66	Sherman	34,044
31	Denton	76,933	67	Lufkin	33,253
32	Longview	75,576	68	La Porte	32,999
33	Lewisville	72,466	69	Huntsville	31,706
34	Baytown	68,588	70	Texarkana	31,485
35	Missouri City	62,371	71	Copperas Cove	30,946
36	Victoria	61,882	72	Nacogdoches	30,755

(continued)

Rank	City	Population
73	Deer Park	30,575
74	Pearland	29,164
75	Rosenberg	29,081
76	Coppell	28,940
77	Friendswood	28,897
78	Georgetown	28,790
79	Eagle Pass	28,713
80	Cedar Hill	28,248
81	Weslaco	27,630
82	The Colony	27,440
83	Socorro	27,085
84	Lake Jackson	26,394
85	Frisco	26,304
86	Farmers Branch	26,156
87	Paris	25,513
88	Kingsville	25,211
89	Greenville	25,051
90	Cleburne	25,033
91	Lancaster	24,216
92	Mansfield	23,567
93	Marshall	23,548
94	Keller	23,352
95	San Benito	23,317
96	Watauga	23,213
97	Corsicana	23,184
98	University Park	23,018
99	Plainview	22,697
100	Big Spring	22,382
101	Denison	22,170
102	Waxahachie	22,038
103	Benbrook	21,742
104	Seguin	21,719
105	Kerrville	21,031
106	Burleson	20,817
107	Alvin	20,797
108	Alice	20,532
109	Angleton	20,518
110	Colleyville	20,030
111	Brownwood	19,235
112	Palestine	18,931
113	Stafford	18,870
114	Pampa	18,704
115	Weatherford	18,572
116	Orange	18,524
117	Balch Springs	18,435
118	Bay City	18,386
119	Cedar Park	18,371
120	San Juan	18,157
121	Harker Heights	17,347
122	Nederland	16,774
123	Southlake	16,552
124	Groves	16,523
125	Schertz	16,521

Rank	City	Population
126	Uvalde	16,214
127	White Settlement	15,956
128	Ennis	15,902
129	Rockwall	15,668
130	Belton	15,639
131	Bellaire	15,506
132	Universal City	15,354
133	Stephenville	15,262
134	South Houston	15,240
135	Donna	15,193
136	Rio Grande City	14,886
137	Mineral Wells	14,825
138	Gainesville	14,760
139	La Marque	14,723
140	Taylor	14,690
141	Portland	14,682
142	Hereford	14,667
143	Sulphur Springs	14,616
144	Mercedes	14,531
145	Terrell	14,498
146	Borger	14,444
147	Richmond	14,307
148	West University Place	14,103
149	Dumas	13,821
150	Beeville	13,736
151	Brenham	13,661
152	Levelland	13,596
153	Canyon	13,346
154	Humble	13,341
155	Port Neches	13,225
156	Robstown	13,115
157	Mount Pleasant	13,037
158	Jacksonville	13,012
159	Dickinson	12,828
160	Addison	12,276
161	Highland Village	12,253
162	Forest Hill	12,040
163	Gatesville	12,003
164	Wylie	11,959
165	Port Lavaca	11,908
166	Sweetwater	11,862
167	Athens	11,822
168	Lockhart	11,602
169	Freeport	11,594
170	Snyder	11,502
171	Converse	11,415
172	Kilgore	11,363
173	Henderson	11,280
174	Saginaw	11,238
175	Roma	11,216
176	Hewitt	11,205
177	Alamo	11,078
178	Vidor	10,956

Rank	City	Population
179	Live Oak	10,807
180	Katy	10,792
181	Vernon	10,784
182	Pecos	10,757
183	Burkburnett	10,673
184	El Campo	10,643
185	Galena Park	10,409
186	Leon Valley	10,348

Rank	City	Population
187	Azle	10,345
188	Andrews	10,271
189	Ingleside	10,257
190	Lamesa	10,050

Population figures are estimated for mid-1998.
Source: U.S. Bureau of the Census.

Index to Tables

NA = Reliable data are not available.

DEMOGRAPHICS

Resident state and national populations, 1970-1997

Population figures given in thousands

	State pop.	U.S. pop.	Share	Rank
1970	11,199	203,302	5.5%	4
1980	14,229	226,546	6.3%	3
1985	16,273	237,924	6.8%	3
1990	16,986	248,765	6.8%	3
1995	18,738	262,761	7.1%	2
1997	19,439	267,636	7.3%	2

Source: U.S. Bureau of the Census.

Resident population by age, 1997

Age group	Total population
Under 5 years	1,609,000
5 to 17 years	3,969,000
18 to 24 years	1,993,000
25 to 34 years	2,882,000
35 to 44 years	3,188,000
45 to 54 years	2,353,000
55 to 64 years	1,486,000
65 to 74 years	1,106,000
75 to 84 years	638,000
85 years and over	216,000
Portion of residents 65 and older	10.1%
National average	12.7%

Population figures are rounded to nearest thousand persons;
figures include armed forces personnel stationed in state.
Source: U.S. Bureau of the Census.

Resident population by race, Hispanic origin, 1997

	State pop.	Share	U.S.
All residents	19,439,000	100.0%	100.0%
Hispanic white	5,515,000	28.4%	10.0%
non-Hispanic white	10,933,000	56.2%	72.7%
African American	2,374,000	12.2%	12.7%
Native American	93,000	0.5%	0.9%
Asian, Pacific Islander	524,000	2.7%	3.8%

Source: U.S. Bureau of the Census.

Projections of state population, 2000-2025

	Model A Uses interstate migration observed from 1975-1994	Model B Uses Bureau of Economic Analysis employment projections
Year	Population	Population
2000	20,119,000	20,178,000
2005	21,487,000	21,635,000
2010	22,857,000	23,158,000
2015	24,280,000	24,775,000
2020	25,729,000	26,453,000
2025	27,183,000	28,170,000

All population projections, including those for 2000, were calculated in 1997.
Source: U.S. Bureau of the Census, Population Paper Listings PPL-47.

VITAL STATISTICS

Average lifetime in years by race, 1989-1991

	State	U.S.	Rank
All residents	75.14	75.37	32
White residents	75.75	76.13	37
Black residents	69.79	69.16	13

Ranks are from longest-lived to least longest-lived. Ranks exclude Alaska, for which reliable data are not available. Rank for black residents is based on the 32 states for which reliable data are available.
Source: U.S. National Center for Health Statistics.

Infant mortality rates, 1980 and 1995

	State	U.S.
All residents		
1980	12.2	12.6
1995	6.5	7.6
White residents		
1980	11.2	11.0
1995	5.9	6.3
Black residents		
1980	18.8	21.4
1995	11.7	15.1

Figures represent deaths per 1,000 live births of resident infants under 1 year old, exclusive of fetal deaths; all-residents figures include other races not listed separately.
Source: U.S. National Center for Health Statistics.

Marriages and divorces

Marriages in 1996	179,700
Rate per 1,000 population, 1995	10.1
U.S. rate, 1995	8.9
Rank among all states	13
Divorces in 1996	NA
Rate per 1,000 population, 1995.	5.3
U.S. rate, 1995	4.4
Rank among all states	13

Rank is from highest to lowest in country.
Source: U.S. National Center for Health Statistics.

Death rates by leading causes, 1995
Deaths per 100,000 resident population

Cause	State	U.S.
Heart disease	222.9	280.7
Cancer	168.9	204.9
Cerebrovascular diseases	52.3	60.1
Accidents and adverse effects	34.3	35.5
Motor vehicle accidents	17.8	16.5
Chronic obstructive pulmonary diseases	33.3	39.2
Diabetes mellitus	24.4	22.6
HIV	14.8	NA
Suicide	11.9	11.9
Homicide	9.6	8.7
All causes	736.1	880.0
Rank in overall death rate among states		44

Figures exclude nonresidents who die in state. Causes of death follow International Classification of Diseases. Rank is from highest to lowest in country.
Source: U.S. National Center for Health Statistics.

ECONOMY

Gross state product, 1990-1996
In current dollars

	State product	Increase
1990	$388.9 billion	
1993	$453.0 billion	
1994	$484.1 billion	6.87%
1995	$514.2 billion	6.22%
1996	$551.8 billion	7.31%

Source: U.S. Bureau of Economic Analysis; *Survey of Current Business,* June, 1998.

Gross state product by industry, 1996
In billions

Farms, forestry, fisheries	$6.4
Construction	20.8
Manufacturing	90.8
Transportation, public utilities	55.4
Wholesale trade	38.4
Retail trade	46.6
Finance, insurance, real estate	66.6
Services	86.7
Government	57.9
State total	$502.9
Total U.S.	$6,923.8
State share	7.26%
Rank among states	3

Total figures include mining, not listed separately.
Source: U.S. Bureau of Economic Analysis; *Survey of Current Business,* June, 1998.

Personal income per capita, 1990 and 1997
In current dollars

	1990	1997
Per capita income	$17,310	$23,656
U.S. average	$19,188	$25,598
Rank among states	29	28

1997 data are preliminary.
Source: U.S. Bureau of Economic Analysis; *Survey of Current Business,* May, 1998.

Energy consumption, 1995
In trillions of British thermal units (BTU)

End-use sectors

Residential	1,220.0
Commercial	1,079.8
Industrial	6,032.9
Transportation	2,169.3

Sources of energy

Petroleum	4,746.3
Natural gas	3,943.2
Coal	1,361.7
Hydroelectric power	17.5
Nuclear electric power	385.3
Total state per capita consumption	559.1
Total U.S. per capita consumption	344.4
Rank among states	4
Total state energy consumption	10,511.5
Total U.S. energy consumption	90,547.4
State share of U.S. total	11.61%
Rank among states	1

Total figures include items not listed separately.
Source: U.S. Energy Information Administration; *State Energy Data Report.*

Nonfarm employment by sectors, 1997

Total	8,602,000
Construction	458,000
Manufacturing	1,081,000
Transportation, public utilities	514,000
Wholesale trade, retail trade	2,046,000
Finance, insurance, real estate	464,000
Services	2,392,000
Government	1,482,000

Figures are rounded to nearest thousand persons. Total includes mining, not listed separately.
Source: U.S. Bureau of Labor Statistics; *Employment and Earnings,* monthly.

Foreign exports, 1990-1997
In millions of dollars

Year	State	U.S.	State share
1990	32,931	394,045	8.36%
1996	66,862	624,767	10.70%
1997	76,184	688,896	11.06%

Source: U.S. Bureau of the Census; *U.S. Merchandise Trade,* series FT 900.

LAND USE

Federally owned land, 1996

	State	U.S.	State share
Total acres	168,218,000	2,271,343,000	7.41%
Federally owned	2,008,000	563,129,000	0.36%
Federal share	1.2%	24.8%	—

Areas are rounded to nearest thousand acres. Figures for federally owned land do not include trust properties.

Source: U.S. General Services Administration; *Inventory Report on Real Property Owned by the United States Throughout the World,* annual.

Land use, 1992
In acres, rounded to nearest thousand

Total surface area	170,756,000
Federal land	3,203,000
Total nonfederal	163,687,000
Developed	8,231,000
Total rural.	155,456,000
Cropland	28,261,000
Pasture land	16,710,000
Range land	94,155,000
Forest land.	9,960,000
Minor cover/use.	6,369,000

Total surface area figures include water area not shown separately.

Source: U.S. Dept. of Agriculture; Soil Conservation Service; Iowa State University, Statistical Laboratory; *Summary Report, 1992 National Resources Inventory.*

Farms and crop acreage, 1997

	State	U.S.	Share	Rank
Farms (thousands)	205	2,058	9.96%	1
Acres (millions)	129	968	13.3%	1
Acres per farm	629	471	—	13
Acres planted	23,389	334,139	7.00%	4
Acres harvested	19,979	319,894	6.25%	6
Farm value (mill.)	$5,038	$108,805	4.63%	39

Numbers of farms are rounded to nearest thousand.

Source: U.S. Dept. of Agriculture; National Agricultural Statistics Service.

GOVERNMENT AND FINANCE

Units of local government, 1997

	State	Total U.S.	Rank
All local governments	4,700	87,453	3
Counties	254	3,043	1
Municipalities	1,177	19,372	2
Townships	0	16,629	—
School districts	1,087	13,726	1
Special districts	2,182	34,683	3

County ranks are based on the 48 states with county governments; township ranks are based on the 20 states with township governments; school district ranks are based on the 46 states with such districts.

Source: U.S. Bureau of the Census; *1997 Census of Governments, Government Organization,* Series GC97(1).

State government revenue, 1996

Total revenue	$51,118 mill.
General revenue	42,616 mill.
Per capita.	2,232
U.S. per capita average	2,910
Rank among states.	50
Intergovernmental revenue	
Total	$13,077 mill.
From federal government	12,612 mill.
From local government	465 mill.
Charges and Miscellaneous	
Total	$8,268 mill.
Current charges	3,344 mill.
Misc. general revenue	4,924 mill.
Taxes	
Total	$21,271 mill.
General sales	10,811 mill.
Selective sales.	6,424 mill.
License taxes	3,048 mill.
Individual income	NA
Corporate income	NA
Other	988 mill.
Insurance trust revenue	8,502 mill.

Total revenue figures include items not listed separately.

Source: U.S. Bureau of the Census.

State government expenditures, 1996

General expenditures

Intergovernmental.	$12,364 mill.
Direct expenditures.	29,154 mill.
Total	41,519 mill.

Selected direct expenditures

Education	$17,049 mill.
Public welfare	10,636 mill.
Health, hospital	3,079 mill.
Highways	3,563 mill.
Police	292 mill.
Corrections	2,351 mill.
Natural resources.	643 mill.
Parks and recreation.	67 mill.
Government administration	932 mill.
Interest on debt	741 mill.

Other

State per capita expenditures	$2,175
U.S. per capita average	2,854
Rank among states.	50
Total state expenditures	46,082 mill.
Total U.S. expenditures	859,959 mill.

Totals include items not listed separately.
Source: U.S. Bureau of the Census.

POLITICS

Governors since statehood

D = Democrat; R = Republican; O = other;
(r) resigned; (d) died in office; (i) removed from office

James Pinckney Henderson (D)	1846-1847
George T. Wood (D)	1847-1849
Peter H. Bell (D)	(r) 1849-1853
James W. Henderson (D).	1853
Elisha M. Pease (D).	1853-1857
Hardin R. Runnels (D).	1857-1859
Sam Houston (D).	(r) 1859-1861
Edward Clark (D).	1861
Francis R. Lubbock (D)	1861-1863
Pendleton Murrah (D)	(r) 1863-1865
Fletcher S. Stockdale (D).	(i) 1865
Andrew J. Hamilton	1865-1866
James W. Throckmorton (D).	(i) 1866-1867
Elisha M. Pease	(r) 1867-1869
Edmund J. Davis (R)	1870-1874
Richard Coke (D).	(r) 1874-1876
Richard B. Hubbard (D)	1876-1879
Oran M. Roberts (D).	1879-1883

John Ireland (D)	1883-1887
Lawrence ("Sul") Ross (D)	1887-1891
James S. Hogg (D)	1891-1895
Charles A. Culberson (D)	1895-1899
Joseph D. Sayers (D)	1899-1903
Samuel W. T. Lanham (D)	1903-1907
Thomas M. Campbell (D)	1907-1911
Oscar B. Colquitt (D).	1911-1915
James E. Ferguson (D)	(i) 1915-1917
William P. Hobby (D).	1917-1921
Patrick M. Neff (D).	1921-1925
Miriam A. Ferguson (D)	1925-1927
Daniel Moody (D)	1927-1931
Ross S. Sterling (D).	1931-1933
Miriam A. Ferguson (D)	1933-1935
James V. Allred (D)	1935-1939
Wilbert Lee O'Daniel (D)	(r) 1939-1941
Coke R. Stevenson (D)	1941-1947
Beauford H. Jester (D).	(d) 1947-1949
Allan Shivers (D)	1949-1957
Price Daniel (D)	1957-1963
John B. Connally, Jr. (D)	1963-1969
Preston E. Smith (D)	1969-1973
Dolph Briscoe (D)	1973-1979
William P. Clements, Jr. (R)	1979-1983
Mark White (D).	1983-1987
William P. Clements, Jr. (R)	1987-1991
Ann Richards (D).	1991-1995
George W. Bush (R)	1995-

Composition of state legislature, 1990-1998

	Democrats	Republicans
State House (150 seats)		
1990	93	57
1992	91	58
1994	89	61
1996	82	68
1998	78	72
State Senate (31 seats)		
1990	22	9
1992	18	13
1994	17	14
1996	14	16
1998	15	16

Figures for total seats may include independents and minor party members.
Source: Council of State Governments; *State Elective Officials and the Legislatures.*

Composition of congressional delegations, 1989-1999

	Dem	Rep	Total
House of Representatives			
101st Congress, 1989			
State delegates	19	8	27
Total U.S.	259	174	433
102d Congress, 1991			
State delegates	19	8	27
Total U.S.	267	167	434
103d Congress, 1993			
State delegates	21	9	30
Total U.S.	258	176	434
104th Congress, 1995			
State delegates	17	13	30
Total U.S.	197	236	433
105th Congress, 1997			
State delegates	16	14	30
Total U.S.	206	228	434
106th Congress, 1999			
State delegates	17	13	30
Total U.S.	211	222	433
Senate			
101st Congress, 1989			
State delegates	1	1	2
Total U.S.	55	45	100
102d Congress, 1991			
State delegates	1	1	2
Total U.S.	56	44	100
103d Congress, 1993			
State delegates	1	1	2
Total U.S.	57	43	100
104th Congress, 1995			
State delegates	0	2	2
Total U.S.	46	53	99
105th Congress, 1997			
State delegates	0	2	2
Total U.S.	45	55	100
106th Congress, 1999			
State delegates	0	2	2
Total U.S.	45	54	99

Figures are for starts of first sessions. Figure for U.S. Representatives for 101st Congress does not include Alabama and Indiana, which had vacancies. Figures for total U.S. Representatives for 102d, 103d, and 106th Congresses do not include Vermont, which had 1 Independent-Socialist. Figure for U.S. Representatives for 104th Congress does not include Vermont, which had 1 Independent-Socialist, and California, which had 1 vacancy. Figure for U.S. Representatives for 105th Congress does not include New York, which had 1 vacancy. Figure for U.S. Senators for 104th Congress does not include Oregon, which had 1 vacancy. Figure for U.S. Senators for 106th Congress does not include New Hampshire, which had 1 Independent.
Source: U.S. Congress; *Congressional Directory*, biennial.

Voter participation in presidential elections, 1992 and 1996

	1992	1996
State voting age pop.	12,681,000	13,622,000
Total U.S. voting age pop.	189,524,000	196,509,000
State share of U.S. total	6.7%	6.9%
Rank among states	2	2
Percent of state casting vote	48.5	45.1
Percent of U.S. total voting	55.1	49.0
Rank among states	47	45

Source: U.S. Bureau of the Census.

HEALTH AND MEDICAL CARE

Medicare, 1997

	Recipients	Payments
State	2,153,000	$14,275 mill.
Total U.S.	37,514,000	$206,064 mill.
State share	5.74%	6.93%
Rank among states	4	4

Recipient figures are rounded to nearest thousand persons. Ranks are from highest to lowest.
Source: U.S. Health Care Financing Administration.

Medicaid, 1996

	Recipients	Payments
State	2,572,000	$6,871 mill.
Total U.S.	35,028,000	$121,419 mill.
State share	7.34%	5.66%
Rank among states	3	3

Recipient figures are rounded to nearest thousand persons. Payment figures for fiscal year reflect federal and state contribution payments. Ranks are from highest to lowest.
Source: U.S. Health Care Financing Administration.

Health insurance coverage, 1996

	State	U.S.
Total persons covered	14,557,000	225,070,000
Total persons not covered	4,680,000	41,716,000
Part not covered	24.3%	15.6%
Rank among states	1	—
Children not covered	1,367,000	10,554,000
Part not covered	24.5%	14.8%
Rank among states	2	—

Ranks are from most to fewest uninsured. Population figures are rounded to nearest thousand persons.
Source: U.S. Bureau of the Census.

AIDS, syphilis, tuberculosis, and measles cases, 1997

Cases	U.S.	State	Share
AIDS	58,443	4,718	8.07%
Syphilis	8,550	676	7.91%
Tuberculosis	18,534	1,817	9.80%
Measles	148,000	7,000	4.73%

Measles figures are rounded to nearest thousand cases.
Source: U.S. Centers for Disease Control and Prevention.

HOUSING

Homeownership rates, 1985-1997

	1985	1990	1997
State	60.5%	59.7%	61.5%
Total U.S.	63.9%	63.9%	65.7%
Rank among states	45	42	44

Source: U.S. Bureau of the Census.

Home sales, 1990 and 1997
In thousands of units

Existing home sales	1990	1997	Change
State sales	240.0	293.1	53.1
Total U.S. sales	3,560	4,730	1,170
State share of U.S. total	6.74%	6.20%	-0.55%
Rank among states	2	2	—

Source: National Association of Realtors; *Real Estate Outlook: Market Trends and Insights.*

EDUCATION

Public school enrollment, 1995

State K-8 enrollment	2,757,000
Total U.S. K-8 enrollment	32,341,000
State share of total U.S.	8.52%
State 9-12 enrollment	991,000
Total U.S. 9-12 enrollment	12,500,000
State share of U.S. total	7.93%
State public school enroll. rate	98.9%
Overall U.S. rate.	91.6%
Rank among states	1

Enrollment figures (which include unclassified students) are rounded to nearest thousand pupils in fall term; kindergarten (K)-8 grade figures include some prekindergarten students. Enrollment rate is based on percentage of persons 5-17 years old. Rank is from highest to lowest.
Source: U.S. National Center for Education Statistics.

Public college finances, 1996

State FTE enrollment	617,900
Total U.S. FTE enrollment	8,268,800
State share of total U.S.	7.47%
Rank among states	2
State and local appropriations	$2,955 mill.
Total U.S. state and local appropriations.	$39,699 mill.
State share of total U.S.	7.44%
Rank among states	2
State net tuition revenues.	$1,085,900,000
Total U.S. net tuition	$18,348,100,000
State share of total U.S.	5.92%
Rank among states	4

FTE=Full-time equivalent; credit and noncredit enrollment including summer session in academic year ending in 1996.
Enrollments are rounded to nearest thousand students. Net tuition revenues exclude appropriation to students attending in-state public institutions. Rankings are from highest shares to lowest.
Source: Research Associates of Washington.

TRANSPORTATION AND TRAVEL

Highway mileage, 1996

Interstate	3,234
Other arterial	29,355
Collector roads	72,163
Local roads	200,426
Urban roads	82,197
Rural roads	214,062
Total state	296,259
U.S. total	3,933,985
State share	7.5%
Rank among states	1

Source: U.S. Federal Highway Administration.

Motor vehicle registrations and driver licenses, 1996
In thousands

Vehicle registrations	State	U.S.	Share	Rank
Autos, trucks, buses	13,487	206,365	6.54%	2
Autos only	7,391	128,439	5.75%	3
Motorcycles	144	3,832	3.76%	8
Driver licenses	12,568	179,539	7.00%	2

Figures do not include vehicles owned by military services.
Source: U.S. Federal Highway Administration; *Highway Statistics; Selected Highway Statistics and Charts.*

Domestic travel expenditures, 1995
Spending by U.S. residents on overnight trips and day trips of at least 100 miles

Total expenditures in state	$22,562 mill.
Total expenditures in U.S.	$360,314 mill.
State share of total U.S.	6.26%
Rank among states	3

Source: Travel Industry Association of America.

CRIME AND LAW ENFORCEMENT

State and local police officers, 1996

Local police	28,269
State police	2,873
Sheriffs	11,326
Total	47,767
Officers per 10,000 residents	25
U.S. average	25
Rank among states	14

Figures cover full-time sworn officers; totals include special police not shown separately.
Source: U.S. Bureau of Justice Statistics; *Census of State and Local Law Enforcement Agencies, 1996.*

Crime rates, 1996
Rates per 100,000 resident population

Violent crimes	State	U.S.
Total violent	644	634
Murder	7.7	7.4
Forcible rape	43.8	36.1
Robbery	172	202
Aggravated assault	421	388
Property crimes		
Total property	5,065	4,445
Burglary	1,069	943
Larceny/theft	3,447	2,976
Motor vehicle theft	549	526
Totals	5,709	5,079

Source: U.S. Federal Bureau of Investigation; *Crime in the United States,* annual.

State prison populations, 1980-1996

	State	U.S.	State share
1980	29,892	305,458	9.79%
1990	50,042	708,393	7.06%
1996	132,383	1,025,624	12.91%

Figures exclude prisoners in federal penitentiaries.
Source: U.S. Bureau of Justice Statistics.

Utah

Location: Western continental United States

Area and rank: 82,168 square miles (212,816 square kilometers); 84,904 square miles (219,901 square kilometers) including water; twelfth largest state in area

Population and rank: 2,059,148 (1997); thirty-fourth largest state in population

Capital: Salt Lake City

Largest city: Salt Lake City (174,348 people in 1998)

Became territory: September 9, 1850

Entered Union and rank: January 4, 1896; forty-fifth state

Utah's capital, Salt Lake City, looking south, with the domed state capitol building visible at the left. (Corbis)

Present constitution adopted: 1896

Counties: 29

State name: "Utah" is derived from a Ute word meaning "people of the mountains"

State nickname: Beehive State

Motto: Industry

State flag: Blue field with variant of the state seal

Highest point: Kings Peak — 13,528 feet (4,123 meters)

Lowest point: Beaverdam Wash — 2,000 feet (610 meters)

Highest recorded temperature: 117 degrees Fahrenheit (47 degrees Celsius) — St. George, 1985

Lowest recorded temperature: −69 degrees Fahrenheit (−56 degrees Celsius) — Peter's Sink, 1985

State song: "Utah, We Love Thee"

State tree: Blue spruce

State flower: Sego lily

State bird: California gull

State fish: Bonneville cutthroat trout

State animal: Rocky Mountain elk

National parks: Arches, Bryce Canyon, Canyonlands, Capitol Reef, Zion

Utah History

Early History. As attested by archaeological evidence, Utah's territory has been continuously inhabited for the past eleven thousand years. The earliest indigenous peoples hunted with spears, used baskets to gather wild foods, and made stone tools. Later peoples, besides hunting and gathering, grew maize. Utes and Paiutes arrived about six hundred years ago, followed later by Navajos. When Anglo-Americans began settling the Utah region, these American Indians, together with the Shoshones and Bannocks, were most numerous.

The first non-American Indians to enter the region were Spaniards and Mexicans. Juan Maria Rivera made two expeditions to the area in 1765. In 1776 two priests of the Franciscan Order, Fathers Francisco Atanasio Domínguez and Francisco Silvestre Vélez de Escalante, led an expedition from Santa Fe, now in New Mexico, seeking passage to Monterey, California. No further expeditions were recorded until the early nineteenth century, when trade between Santa Fe and Indians of the Utah region became common. From then until the 1840's, numerous fur traders and other mountain men visited the area for varying lengths of time, and many pioneers and adventurers on their way to California traveled across it, but no permanent settlements were established. In 1824 the famous scout Jim Bridger came upon the Great Salt Lake and, tasting its briny water, believed it an ocean.

In its formative period, Utah's inhospitable terrain and geographically remote location far from both the populous east and the growing Pacific region were principal factors in its destiny. On one hand, its arid and mountainous landscape dissuaded early travelers from settling, but on the other, its remoteness attracted the people whose predominance most influenced its character from first settlement to the present day. Those were the Mormons, hearty, closely knit, deeply religious, hardworking folk who adapted well to Utah's harsh topography.

Arrival of the Mormons. Numbering about three million today, Mormons are formally members of the Church of Jesus Christ of Latter-day Saints. They take their name from the title of the

"This Is the Place Monument" marks the spot where Brigham Young led the first Mormon settlers in the Salt Lake Valley in 1847. (Utah Travel Council/Frank Jensen)

Book of Mormon, an important holy book along with the Bible. A principal belief is that Jesus appeared in the New World after His crucifixion. After their church was founded in 1830 by Joseph Smith in Fayette, New York, Mormons were persecuted wherever they settled. Non-Mormons feared their aloofness from society and what appeared as strange ways, such as their communal economy and theocratic organizational structure, in which religious and civic affairs were intertwined. What antagonized others most, however, was the Mormon belief in polygamy, families with several wives, a church doctrine that emerged in the 1850's. Leaving New York in 1831, Smith and his followers moved to Ohio, but trouble there led to expulsion in 1838-1839. Settling in the Illinois town of Nauvoo, by 1842 they had aroused deep resentment in that state. Arrested in 1844, Smith and his brother were murdered by a mob. Two years later, led by Brigham Young, a man of exceptional leadership qualities, the Mormons fled Illinois, venturing west into unsettled territory in search of secure autonomy. Young, traveling with an advance party, upon sighting the Great Salt Lake Valley in 1847, is said to have declared, "This is the place."

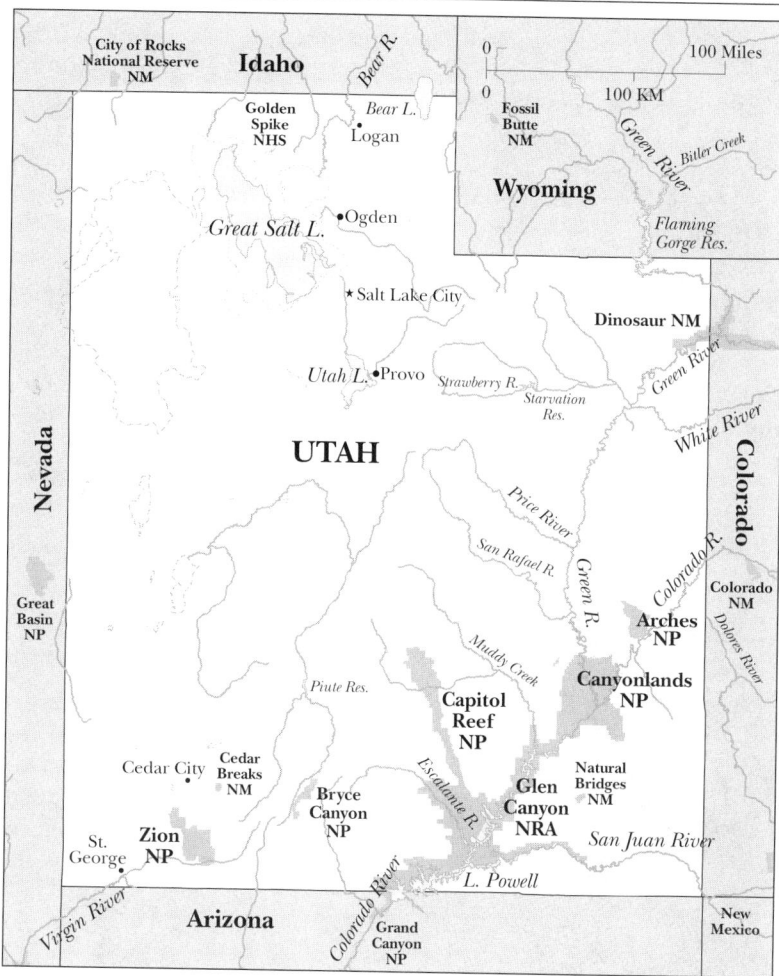

Since their beginnings the Mormons had sent missionaries to other states and western European countries to gain adherents. Now in their new desert home, they called their followers to join them, and Mormons began arriving in the thousands, especially from northern Europe. By 1850 a number of towns had been founded; within Brigham Young's lifetime, some 350 settlements were established. By 1900 the number had grown to 500 settlements in Utah and surrounding states, the result of the Mormon policy of colonization.

The towns, based on communal ownership, were planned communities of farmers and tradesmen.

Becoming a Territory. Meanwhile, after the Mexican-American War of 1846, the Mormon territory became part of the United States, and the community's autonomy was once more put in jeopardy. Mormons had participated in the war on the American side, sending a volunteer battalion on a famous march from Kansas to San Diego. In 1849-1850, Brigham Young declared the Mormon settlement a new state of Deseret, after the word for honeybee in the Book of Mormon. With Young as governor, church leaders filled all offices. Deseret encompassed an immense area extending to San Diego in Southern California, giving access to a port for Mormon immigration and trade. Congress, however, suspicious of the proposed state's huge size and theocratic polity, rejected it, setting up instead the smaller, but still large, territory of Utah, including Nevada, Wyoming, and parts of Colorado. Utah Territory's size was progressively pared, until 1868, when the future state's present borders were drawn. Brigham Young was the first territorial governor.

The Mormon Church did its utmost to populate its territory, issuing a call for members to gather there. In 1849 the Church set up a Perpetual Emigrating Fund, used to bring poor members from distant places. Mormons soon began arriving in the thousands from northern Europe, including many from the British Isles. In the end, the fund raised hundreds of thousands of dollars for Mormon emigration.

Conflicts with Non-Mormons. Relations between Mormons and non-Mormons were tense, and conflicts frequent. Outsiders were excluded from positions of power and influence, and mutual suspicion abounded. Mormons recalled persecution; non-Mormons questioned Mormon loyalty to American democracy. In 1857 rumors of Mormon rebellion against the United States led the administration of President James Buchanan to send some 2,500 troops to occupy Salt Lake City and its environs—events known as the Utah War. Mormon attacks on the troops' supply trains did little to relieve federal anxieties.

Later, the Church's official neutrality in the Civil War had a similar effect. Young was stripped of his office, and a non-Mormon was installed as governor by the U.S. government. Then, in the darkest chapter of Utah's history, Mormons slaughtered more than one hundred non-Mormon civilian men, women, and children traveling through southern Utah from Missouri and Arkansas. However, after some negotiation, peace was achieved in 1858, though further incidents recurred in the 1860's, when federal soldiers returned.

Besides trouble with non-Mormons and with Washington, D.C., the new territory also experienced conflicts with American Indians. At first Brigham Young's Indian policy was successful in securing peace. American Indian resentment over settler occupation of their lands soon led to hostilities, however. In 1852 the Walker War, named for a Ute chief, broke out, but it ended the next year when Young persuaded the Utes to lay down their arms. Bannock and Shoshone raids continued in northern Utah until 1863, when U.S. Army troops defeated them. Peace was restored in 1867, but raids continued until late 1872. More conflicts occurred in the twentieth century, but by the

The Kennecott Copper Mine was one of several new mining ventures that transformed Utah's economy in the early twentieth century. (Utah Travel Council/Frank Jensen)

With one of the largest concentrations of spectacular natural scenery, such as that in Arches National Park, Utah has five national parks. (PhotoDisc)

mid-1920's the Indians had receded. By century's end, however, Native Americans used the legal system to further their interests.

While these events were taking place, others occurred that would have far-reaching effects on Mormon-dominated Utah. Non-Mormons were arriving in significant numbers to work mines, after silver and lead were discovered in Bingham Canyon, near Salt Lake City. Mormons had previously made such discoveries but were discouraged from exploiting them for fear of attracting outsiders and losing labor needed to produce necessities. Other non-Mormons opened stores or other businesses.

At this time, the nation's communications were progressing. For a scant nineteen months in 1860-1861, the Pony Express road across Utah carried mail from St. Joseph, Missouri, to Sacramento, California. The arrival of the telegraph linking the nation from coast to coast and the completion of a transcontinental railroad in 1869 opened Utah's products to national markets, and a boom began in railroad feeder lines to transport them.

From Territory to State. As the territory progressed economically, it sought entrance to the Union as a state. This proved a formidable task, since distrust of Mormons was prevalent. In 1852 Brigham Young had publicly acknowledged Mormon polygamy. In the 1870's and 1880's, Congress passed acts prohibiting this practice. Utah petitioned for statehood seven times before it was successful. Opposition to statehood receded only after 1890, when Mormon leader Wilford Woodruff issued a manifesto renouncing polygamy. In 1895 a constitution was ratified outlawing this practice and separating church and state; the following year Utah became the nation's forty-fifth state.

Utah's new constitution called for several elected officials in the executive branch, some of whom cannot be reelected. In keeping with a tradition of strong leadership authority, governors have more power than those of nearby states. Most judges are elected, however, and the legislature is bicameral.

Into the American Mainstream. The old ways of the original Mormon settlers died hard. When the last survivor of the 1847 trek from Illinois died in Idaho in the 1920's, thousands of Mormons trooped north to pay their final respects. By then, Utah had begun decisive change that would transform it into a modern society. By World War I Utah was entering the American mainstream. The social landscape was increasingly urbanized, and the economy was developing. New ores, especially copper, were mined, and smelting became a large industry. Labor unions emerged, and with them labor conflict appeared. The Depression hit the state particularly hard, and severe droughts in 1931 and 1934 did not help matters. However, as elsewhere in the nation, the coming of World War II eased economic hardship, as federal defense dollars combined with conscription to lessen unemployment.

Postwar Developments. After World War II, Utah passed from being an agricultural and mining state to an industrial state. A Geneva steel plant opened in 1943, and federal investment in defense industries during the decades that followed spurred industrialization. Utah became a principal site of missile development, and other defense industries took root.

By the 1980's and 1990's a number of high-tech industries that were growing in importance were located in Utah. The state was becoming more politically and culturally sophisticated. Environmental politics entered the scene, and figures such as Utah senator Orrin Hatch became important in Washington politics. As the end of the century approached, Utah had moved from a predominantly industrial to a service economy, as tourism and other service industries expanded. While the position of the Mormon Church remained strong, barely more than a century of statehood had seen Utah move squarely into the modern world.

Charles F. Bahmueller

Utah Time Line

1776	Fathers Francisco Silvestre Vélez de Escalante and Francisco Atanasio Domínguez seek a new route from New Mexico to California and explore Utah.
1821	Utah's territory becomes part of Mexico.
1824	Trappers arrive in northern Utah; Jim Bridger discovers Great Salt Lake.
1825	Jedediah Smith passes through Utah in the first overland expedition to California.
1841	First wagon train of settlers crosses Utah en route to California.
1842	John C. Frémont and Kit Carson explore the Great Basin.
1843	Fort Buenaventura is established.
July 24, 1847	First party of Mormon pioneers arrives in the Salt Lake Valley.
1848	Utah is ceded to the United States after Mexican-American War.
Mar. 12, 1849	Constitutional convention declares the state of Deseret, which encompasses the entire Great Basin.
1850	Utah Territory is organized.
1852	Mormon Church publicly acknowledges doctrine of plural marriage; begins construction of Salt Lake Temple.
1852	Walker War with Ute Indians begins over slavery among the Indians.
1853	Grasshopper plagues endanger crops.
1857-1858	Federal government removes Governor Brigham Young from office as Utah War begins.
1862	Silver and lead are discovered in Bingham Canyon.

1865-1868	Black Hawk War with Utes is last major American Indian conflict in state.
May 10, 1869	Union Pacific and Central Pacific railroads meet at Promontory Point.
1869	First non-Mormon church building in Utah is constructed.
1869	John Wesley Powell explores the Colorado River.
1874	Poland Act passed in Congress, making it legal to prosecute Mormons for practicing polygamy.
1875	Holy Cross Sisters open Holy Cross Hospital, their first in the United States.
1879	First telephone service is established in Ogden.
1887	Edmunds Act is passed by Congress, outlawing cohabitation.
1890	Mormon Church president Wilford Woodruff issues a manifesto ending church-sanctioned polygamy.
1891	B'Nai Israel Temple is dedicated in Salt Lake City.
Jan. 4, 1896	Utah becomes the forty-fifth state.
1906	Open-pit copper mining begins in Bingham Canyon.
1911	Strawberry Reservoir is completed.
1914	Auto racing begins on the Bonneville Salt Flats near Great Salt Lake.
1919	Zion National Park is established.
1928	Bryce Canyon National Park is established.
1942-1945	Topaz, Japanese American Relocation Camp, operates near Delta during World War II.
1943	Geneva steel plant begins operation in Utah County.
1952	Six-mile Duchesne Tunnel carrying irrigation water is completed.
1956	Congress creates Colorado River Storage Project.
1964	Flaming Gorge Dam on the Green River is dedicated.
1964	Glen Canyon Dam in Arizona creates Lake Powell, nation's second largest artificial lake.
1965	Canyonlands National Park is opened.
1985	Utah's Jake Garn becomes first U.S. senator to fly in space.
1995	Salt Lake City is announced as the site for the 2002 Winter Olympics.

Notes for Further Study

Published Sources. For an overview of the state's history, see Thomas G. Alexander's *Utah, the Right Place: The Official Centennial History* (1995), Charles S. Peterson's *Utah: A Bicentennial History* (1984), and Dean L. May's *Utah: A People's History* (1987). Edward Leo Lyman wrote *Political Deliverance: The Mormon Quest for Utah Statehood* (1986) about the struggle to be recognized as a state. For an account of Utah's founding father, readers should see *Brigham Young and the Expanding American Frontier* (1995) by Newell G. Bringhurst.

A slice of the state's ethnic history is found in Juanita Brooks's *History of the Jews in Utah and Idaho, 1853-1950* (1973). For information on Utah's indigenous peoples, *Discover Native America: Arizona, Colorado, New Mexico, and Utah* (1995), by Tish Minear and Janet Limon, explores Indians of the state; *Cowboys & Cave Dwellers: Basketmaker Archaeology in Utah's Grand Gulch* (1997), by Fred M. Blackburn and Ray A. Williamson, examines ancient Indian artifacts; and *Sacred Images: A Vision of Native American Art* (1996), by Leslie G. Kelen et al., looks at early Utah art. On the state's geography, see David L. Petersen's *Zion National Park* (1993) and F. A. Barnes's *Utah Canyon Country* (1994).

Web Resources. For Web sites on Utah state government, one might begin with the state of Utah site (http://www.state.ut.us). This site has links to state agencies, services, education, travel, and other topics. There is also a Utah State Government Services page (http://utahreach.usu.edu/govt/state.htm), and Utah's governor maintains a site (http://governor.state.ut.us) that has links to numerous topics and documents in such areas as education, transportation, and technology. For information on Utah's colorful history, see A Thumbnail Sketch in Utah History (http://www.libutah.edu/spc/photo/photo2.html), which includes historical photos. One Utah site (http://www.ce.ex.state.ut.us/history) gives a summary of Utah's history and a chronology of the territory's complex struggle to become a state. A re-

markable compendium of Utah history found online is the Utah History Encyclopedia (http://eddy.media.utah.edu/medsol/UCME).

An enormous amount of detailed, often fascinating historical narrative is found in the History of the Church of Jesus Christ of Latter-day Saints (http://www.lds1.com/hc/hc5.html). Utah's indigenous peoples are discussed at Native Americans in Utah (http://eddy.media.utah.edu/medsol.UCME/n/NATIVEAMERICANS.html). The Utah Museum of Natural History maintains a site (http://www.cyberspacemuseum.com/umnh.html). Utah sources maintain the nation's most extensive genealogical databases. For information, see, for example, the Family History Library (http://www.utah.citysearch.com/E/V/SLCUT/0010) and Stevenson's Genealogy Center (http://www.ut-biz.com/stevensons genealogy).

Counties

County	Sq. miles	1996 pop.
Beaver	2,590.1	5,591
Box Elder	5,723.7	39,177
Cache	1,164.6	83,710
Carbon	1,478.6	20,437
Daggett	698.4	752
Davis	304.5	214,990
Duchesne	3,238.4	13,778
Emery	4,452.1	10,402
Garfield	5,174.5	4,076
Grand	3,681.8	7,826
Iron	3,298.5	26,875
Juab	3,391.9	6,845
Kane	3,992.2	5,751
Millard	6,589.6	12,019
Morgan	609.1	6,660
Piute	757.9	1,404
Rich	1,028.6	1,799
Salt Lake	737.4	827,818
San Juan	7,820.7	13,221
Sanpete	1,588.2	19,883
Sevier	1,910.4	17,156
Summit	1,871.2	23,988
Tooele	6,945.9	29,558
Uintah	4,477.3	24,472
Utah	1,998.4	319,694
Wasatch	1,180.9	12,046
Washington	2,427.2	73,161
Wayne	2,460.5	2,371
Weber	575.6	175,034

Source: U.S. Census Bureau; National Association of Counties.

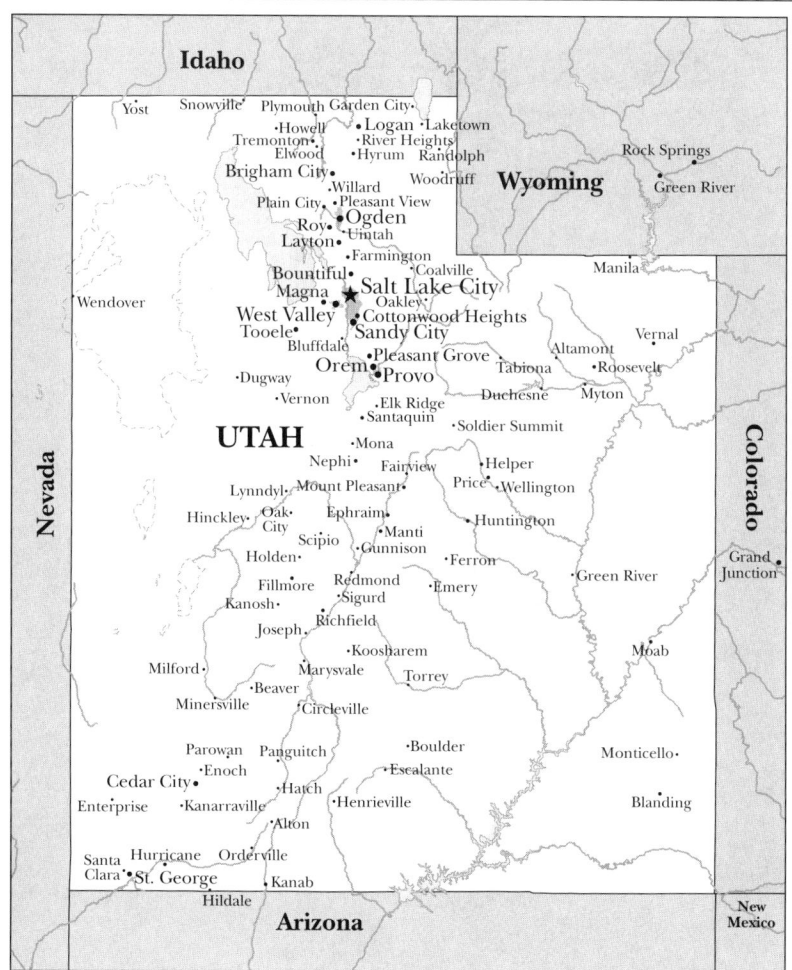

Cities

With 10,000 or more residents

Rank	City	Population
1	Salt Lake City	174,348
2	Provo	110,419
3	West Valley City	99,372
4	Sandy	99,186
5	Orem	78,937
6	Ogden	66,507
7	West Jordan	60,804
8	Taylorsville	56,753
9	Layton	55,112
10	St. George	46,186
11	Bountiful	40,427
12	Logan	40,272
13	Murray	33,167
14	Roy	31,441
15	South Jordan	26,414
16	Clearfield	25,877
17	Pleasant Grove	20,491
18	Riverton	20,410
19	American Fork	19,215
20	Draper	19,147
21	Kaysville	19,118
22	Cedar City	18,953
23	Brigham City	16,960
24	Tooele	16,748
25	Springville	15,944
26	Spanish Fork	15,555
27	Lehi	15,297
28	Centerville	14,811
29	North Ogden	14,811
30	South Ogden	14,671
31	Midvale	11,628
32	Clinton	11,514
33	Farmington	11,175
34	Payson	10,951

Population figures are estimated for mid-1998.

Source: U.S. Bureau of the Census.

Index to Tables

NA = Reliable data are not available.

DEMOGRAPHICS

Resident state and national populations, 1970-1997

Population figures given in thousands

	State pop.	U.S. pop.	Share	Rank
1970	1,059	203,302	0.5%	36
1980	1,461	226,546	0.6%	36
1985	1,643	237,924	0.7%	35
1990	1,723	248,765	0.7%	35
1995	1,974	262,761	0.8%	34
1997	2,059	267,636	0.8%	34

Source: U.S. Bureau of the Census.

Resident population by age, 1997

Age group	Total population
Under 5 years	196,000
5 to 17 years	492,000
18 to 24 years	278,000
25 to 34 years	294,000
35 to 44 years	282,000
45 to 54 years	207,000
55 to 64 years	131,000
65 to 74 years	98,000
75 to 84 years	62,000
85 years and over	20,000
Portion of residents 65 and older	8.7%
National average	12.7%

Population figures are rounded to nearest thousand persons;
figures include armed forces personnel stationed in state.
Source: U.S. Bureau of the Census.

Resident population by race, Hispanic origin, 1997

	State pop.	Share	U.S.
All residents	2,059,000	100.0%	100.0%
Hispanic white	123,000	6.0%	10.0%
non-Hispanic white	1,838,000	89.3%	72.7%
African American	18,000	0.9%	12.7%
Native American	29,000	1.4%	0.9%
Asian, Pacific Islander	51,000	2.5%	3.8%

Source: U.S. Bureau of the Census.

Projections of state population, 2000-2025

	Model A Uses interstate migration observed from 1975-1994	Model B Uses Bureau of Economic Analysis employment projections
Year	Population	Population
2000	2,207,000	2,216,000
2005	2,411,000	2,477,000
2010	2,551,000	2,738,000
2015	2,670,000	2,995,000
2020	2,781,000	3,246,000
2025	2,883,000	3,487,000

All population projections, including those for 2000, were calculated in 1997.
Source: U.S. Bureau of the Census, Population Paper Listings PPL-47.

VITAL STATISTICS

Average lifetime in years by race, 1989-1991

	State	U.S.	Rank
All residents	77.70	75.37	3
White residents	77.77	76.13	5
Black residents	NA	69.16	NA

Ranks are from longest-lived to least longest-lived. Ranks exclude Alaska, for which reliable data are not available. Rank for black residents is based on the 32 states for which reliable data are available.
Source: U.S. National Center for Health Statistics.

Infant mortality rates, 1980 and 1995

	State	U.S.
All residents		
1980	10.4	12.6
1995	5.4	7.6
White residents		
1980	10.5	11.0
1995	5.3	6.3
Black residents		
1980	27.3	21.4
1995	NA	15.1

Figures represent deaths per 1,000 live births of resident infants under 1 year old, exclusive of fetal deaths; all-residents figures include other races not listed separately.
Source: U.S. National Center for Health Statistics.

Marriages and divorces

Marriages in 1996.	22,000
Rate per 1,000 population, 1995	11.1
U.S. rate, 1995	8.9
Rank among all states.	8
Divorces in 1996	9,300
Rate per 1,000 population, 1995.	4.6
U.S. rate, 1995	4.4
Rank among all states	24

Rank is from highest to lowest in country.
Source: U.S. National Center for Health Statistics.

Death rates by leading causes, 1995
Deaths per 100,000 resident population

Cause	State	U.S.
Heart disease	148.1	280.7
Cancer	108.6	204.9
Cerebrovascular diseases	39.9	60.1
Accidents and adverse effects	32.4	35.5
Motor vehicle accidents	17.2	16.5
Chronic obstructive pulmonary diseases	24.1	39.2
Diabetes mellitus	21.3	22.6
HIV	4.8	NA
Suicide	14.8	11.9
Homicide	3.9	8.7
All causes	560.6	880.0
Rank in overall death rate among states		49

Figures exclude nonresidents who die in state. Causes of death follow International Classification of Diseases. Rank is from highest to lowest in country.
Source: U.S. National Center for Health Statistics.

ECONOMY

Gross state product, 1990-1996
In current dollars

	State product	Increase
1990	$31.1 billion	
1993	$38.1 billion	
1994	$42.0 billion	10.24%
1995	$45.6 billion	8.57%
1996	$50.4 billion	10.53%

Source: U.S. Bureau of Economic Analysis; *Survey of Current Business,* June, 1998.

Gross state product by industry, 1996
In billions

Farms, forestry, fisheries	$0.5
Construction	2.5
Manufacturing	6.8
Transportation, public utilities	4.2
Wholesale trade	3.0
Retail trade	5.0
Finance, insurance, real estate	7.1
Services	8.6
Government	6.7
State total	$45.9
Total U.S.	$6,923.8
State share	0.66%
Rank among states	35

Total figures include mining, not listed separately.
Source: U.S. Bureau of Economic Analysis; *Survey of Current Business,* June, 1998.

Personal income per capita, 1990 and 1997
In current dollars

	1990	1997
Per capita income	$14,231	$20,432
U.S. average	$19,188	$25,598
Rank among states	47	44

1997 data are preliminary.
Source: U.S. Bureau of Economic Analysis; *Survey of Current Business,* May, 1998.

Energy consumption, 1995
In trillions of British thermal units (BTU)

End-use sectors

Residential	110.4
Commercial	100.6
Industrial	245.8
Transportation	184.5

Sources of energy

Petroleum	234.2
Natural gas	166.7
Coal	357.2
Hydroelectric power	10.0
Nuclear electric power	0
Total state per capita consumption	326.0
Total U.S. per capita consumption	344.4
Rank among states	31
Total state energy consumption	638.4
Total U.S. energy consumption	90,547.4
State share of U.S. total	0.71%
Rank among states	36

Total figures include items not listed separately.
Source: U.S. Energy Information Administration; *State Energy Data Report.*

Nonfarm employment by sectors, 1997

Total	995,000
Construction	65,000
Manufacturing	133,000
Transportation, public utilities	56,000
Wholesale trade, retail trade	239,000
Finance, insurance, real estate	53,000
Services	270,000
Government	172,000

Figures are rounded to nearest thousand persons. Total includes mining, not listed separately.
Source: U.S. Bureau of Labor Statistics; *Employment and Earnings,* monthly.

Foreign exports, 1990-1997
In millions of dollars

Year	State	U.S.	State share
1990	1,596	394,045	0.41%
1996	3,296	624,767	0.53%
1997	3,239	688,896	0.47%

Source: U.S. Bureau of the Census; *U.S. Merchandise Trade,* series FT 900.

LAND USE

Federally owned land, 1996

	State	U.S.	State share
Total acres	52,697,000	2,271,343,000	2.32%
Federally owned	33,898,000	563,129,000	6.02%
Federal share	64.3%	24.8%	—

Areas are rounded to nearest thousand acres. Figures for federally owned land do not include trust properties.

Source: U.S. General Services Administration; *Inventory Report on Real Property Owned by the United States Throughout the World,* annual.

Land use, 1992

In acres, rounded to nearest thousand

Total surface area	54,336,000
Federal land	35,582,000
Total nonfederal	16,866,000
Developed	561,000
Total rural	16,305,000
Cropland.	1,815,000
Pasture land	665,000
Range land	10,050,000
Forest land.	1,626,000
Minor cover/use.	2,148,000

Total surface area figures include water area not shown separately.

Source: U.S. Dept. of Agriculture; Soil Conservation Service; Iowa State University, Statistical Laboratory; *Summary Report, 1992 National Resources Inventory.*

Farms and crop acreage, 1997

	State	U.S.	Share	Rank
Farms (thousands)	13	2,058	0.63%	36
Acres (millions)	11	968	1.14%	28
Acres per farm	821	471	—	11
Acres planted	1,126	334,139	0.34%	36
Acres harvested	1,068	319,894	0.33%	36
Farm value (mill.)	$315	$108,805	0.29%	46

Numbers of farms are rounded to nearest thousand.

Source: U.S. Dept. of Agriculture; National Agricultural Statistics Service.

GOVERNMENT AND FINANCE

Units of local government, 1997

	State	Total U.S.	Rank
All local governments	683	87,453	38
Counties	29	3,043	36
Municipalities	230	19,372	34
Townships	0	16,629	—
School districts	40	13,726	40
Special districts	384	34,683	32

County ranks are based on the 48 states with county governments; township ranks are based on the 20 states with township governments; school district ranks are based on the 46 states with such districts.

Source: U.S. Bureau of the Census; *1997 Census of Governments, Government Organization,* Series GC97(1).

State government revenue, 1996

Total revenue	$6,773 mill.
General revenue	5,831 mill.
Per capita.	2,890
U.S. per capita average	2,910
Rank among states.	23
Intergovernmental revenue	
Total	$1,757 mill.
From federal government	1,712 mill.
From local government	45 mill.
Charges and Miscellaneous	
Total	$1,160 mill.
Current charges	826 mill.
Misc. general revenue	335 mill.
Taxes	
Total	$2,914 mill.
General sales	1,170 mill.
Selective sales.	300 mill.
License taxes.	99 mill.
Individual income	1,139 mill.
Corporate income	177 mill.
Other.	29 mill.
Insurance trust revenue	854 mill.

Total revenue figures include items not listed separately.

Source: U.S. Bureau of the Census.

State government expenditures, 1996

General expenditures

Intergovernmental	$1,527 mill.
Direct expenditures	4,136 mill.
Total.	5,663 mill.

Selected direct expenditures

Education	$2,751 mill.
Public welfare.	952 mill.
Health, hospital	440 mill.
Highways	357 mill.
Police.	44 mill.
Corrections.	158 mill.
Natural resources.	133 mill.
Parks and recreation.	35 mill.
Government administration	235 mill.
Interest on debt	128 mill.

Other

State per capita expenditures	$2,807
U.S. per capita average	2,854
Rank among states.	25
Total state expenditures	6,172 mill.
Total U.S. expenditures	859,959 mill.

Totals include items not listed separately.
Source: U.S. Bureau of the Census.

POLITICS

Governors since statehood

D = Democrat; R = Republican; O = other;
(r) resigned; (d) died in office; (i) removed from office

Heber M. Wells (R)	1896-1905
John C. Cutler (R)	1905-1909
William Spry (R)	1909-1917
Simon Bamberger (D)	1917-1921
Charles R. Mabey (R).	1921-1925
George H. Dern (D)	1925-1933
Henry H. Blood (D)	1933-1941
Herbert B. Maw (D)	1941-1949
Joseph Bracken Lee (D)	1949-1957
George D. Clyde (R)	1957-1965
Calvin L. Rampton (D)	1965-1977
Scott M. Matheson (R)	1977-1985
Norman H. Bangerter (R)	1985-1993
Mike Leavitt (R)	1993-

Composition of state legislature, 1990-1998

	Democrats	Republicans
State House (75 seats)		
1990	31	44
1992	26	49
1994	20	55
1996	20	55
1998	21	54
State Senate (29 seats)		
1990	10	19
1992	11	18
1994	10	19
1996	9	20
1998	11	18

Figures for total seats may include independents and minor
party members.
Source: Council of State Governments; *State Elective Officials
and the Legislatures.*

Composition of congressional delegations, 1989-1999

	Dem	Rep	Total
House of Representatives			
101st Congress, 1989			
State delegates	1	2	3
Total U.S.	259	174	433
102d Congress, 1991			
State delegates	2	1	3
Total U.S.	267	167	434
103d Congress, 1993			
State delegates	2	1	3
Total U.S.	258	176	434
104th Congress, 1995			
State delegates	0	3	3
Total U.S.	197	236	433
105th Congress, 1997			
State delegates	0	3	3
Total U.S.	206	228	434
106th Congress, 1999			
State delegates	0	3	3
Total U.S.	211	222	433

	Dem	Rep	Total
Senate			
101st Congress, 1989			
State delegates	0	2	2
Total U.S.	55	45	100
102d Congress, 1991			
State delegates	0	2	2
Total U.S.	56	44	100
103d Congress, 1993			
State delegates	0	2	2
Total U.S.	57	43	100
104th Congress, 1995			
State delegates	0	2	2
Total U.S.	46	53	99
105th Congress, 1997			
State delegates	0	2	2
Total U.S.	45	55	100
106th Congress, 1999			
State delegates	0	2	2
Total U.S.	45	54	99

Figures are for starts of first sessions. Figure for U.S. Representatives for 101st Congress does not include Alabama and Indiana, which had vacancies. Figures for total U.S. Representatives for 102d, 103d, and 106th Congresses do not include Vermont, which had 1 Independent-Socialist. Figure for U.S. Representatives for 104th Congress does not include Vermont, which had 1 Independent-Socialist, and California, which had 1 vacancy. Figure for U.S. Representatives for 105th Congress does not include New York, which had 1 vacancy. Figure for U.S. Senators for 104th Congress does not include Oregon, which had 1 vacancy. Figure for U.S. Senators for 106th Congress does not include New Hampshire, which had 1 Independent.
Source: U.S. Congress; *Congressional Directory,* biennial.

HEALTH AND MEDICAL CARE

Medicare, 1997

	Recipients	Payments
State	195,000	$887 mill.
Total U.S.	37,514,000	$206,064 mill.
State share	0.52%	0.43%
Rank among states	39	38

Recipient figures are rounded to nearest thousand persons. Ranks are from highest to lowest.
Source: U.S. Health Care Financing Administration.

Medicaid, 1996

	Recipients	Payments
State	152,000	$422 mill.
Total U.S.	35,028,000	$121,419 mill.
State share	0.43%	0.35%
Rank among states	38	39

Recipient figures are rounded to nearest thousand persons. Payment figures for fiscal year reflect federal and state contribution payments. Ranks are from highest to lowest.
Source: U.S. Health Care Financing Administration.

Voter participation in presidential elections, 1992 and 1996

	1992	1996
State voting age pop.	1,169,000	1,323,000
Total U.S. voting age pop.	189,524,000	196,509,000
State share of U.S. total	0.6%	0.7%
Rank among states	35	35
Percent of state casting vote	63.6	47.5
Percent of U.S. total voting	55.1	49.0
Rank among states	14	33

Source: U.S. Bureau of the Census.

Health insurance coverage, 1996

	State	U.S.
Total persons covered	1,758,000	225,070,000
Total persons not covered	240,000	41,716,000
Part not covered	12.0%	15.6%
Rank among states	32	—
Children not covered	73,000	10,554,000
Part not covered	11.1%	14.8%
Rank among states	28	—

Ranks are from most to fewest uninsured. Population figures are rounded to nearest thousand persons.
Source: U.S. Bureau of the Census.

AIDS, syphilis, tuberculosis, and measles cases, 1997

Cases	U.S.	State	Share
AIDS	58,443	152	0.26%
Syphilis	8,550	5	0.06%
Tuberculosis	18,534	36	0.19%
Measles	148,000	1,000	0.68%

Measles figures are rounded to nearest thousand cases.
Source: U.S. Centers for Disease Control and Prevention.

HOUSING

Homeownership rates, 1985-1997

	1985	1990	1997
State	71.5%	70.1%	72.5%
Total U.S.	63.9%	63.9%	65.7%
Rank among states	6	9	11

Source: U.S. Bureau of the Census.

Home sales, 1990 and 1997

In thousands of units

Existing home sales	1990	1997	Change
State sales	22.1	30.0	7.9
Total U.S. sales	3,560	4,730	1,170
State share of U.S. total	0.62%	0.63%	0.01%
Rank among states	37	34	—

Source: National Association of Realtors; *Real Estate Outlook: Market Trends and Insights.*

EDUCATION

Public school enrollment, 1995

State K-8 enrollment 328,000
Total U.S. K-8 enrollment 32,341,000
State share of total U.S. 1.01%
State 9-12 enrollment 149,000
Total U.S. 9-12 enrollment 12,500,000
State share of U.S. total 1.19%
State public school enroll. rate 97.4%
Overall U.S. rate. 91.6%
Rank among states 2

Enrollment figures (which include unclassified students) are rounded to nearest thousand pupils in fall term; kindergarten (K)-8 grade figures include some prekindergarten students. Enrollment rate is based on percentage of persons 5-17 years old. Rank is from highest to lowest.
Source: U.S. National Center for Education Statistics.

Public college finances, 1996

State FTE enrollment. 81,600
Total U.S. FTE enrollment 8,268,800
State share of total U.S. 0.99%
Rank among states. 32
State and local appropriations $383,100,000
Total U.S. state and local
  appropriations. . . . . $39,699 mill.
State share of total U.S. 0.97%
Rank among states. 34
State net tuition revenues. $148,400,000
Total U.S. net tuition $18,348,100,000
State share of total U.S. 0.81%
Rank among states. 37

FTE=Full-time equivalent; credit and noncredit enrollment including summer session in academic year ending in 1996.
Enrollments are rounded to nearest thousand students. Net tuition revenues exclude appropriation to students attending in-state public institutions. Rankings are from highest shares to lowest.
Source: Research Associates of Washington.

TRANSPORTATION AND TRAVEL

Highway mileage, 1996

Interstate	940
Other arterial	3,332
Collector roads	8,368
Local roads	29,629
Urban roads	6,412
Rural roads	35,306
Total state	41,718
U.S. total	3,933,985
State share	1.1%
Rank among states	37

Source: U.S. Federal Highway Administration.

Motor vehicle registrations and driver licenses, 1996
In thousands

Vehicle registrations	State	U.S.	Share	Rank
Autos, trucks, buses	1,445	206,365	0.70%	36
Autos only	802	128,439	0.62%	34
Motorcycles	23	3,832	0.60%	39
Driver licenses	1,319	179,539	0.73%	36

Figures do not include vehicles owned by military services.
Source: U.S. Federal Highway Administration; *Highway Statistics; Selected Highway Statistics and Charts.*

Domestic travel expenditures, 1995
Spending by U.S. residents on overnight trips and day trips of at least 100 miles

Total expenditures in state	$3,046 mill.
Total expenditures in U.S.	$360,314 mill.
State share of total U.S.	0.85%
Rank among states	34

Source: Travel Industry Association of America.

CRIME AND LAW ENFORCEMENT

State and local police officers, 1996

Local police	1,882
State police	355
Sheriffs	1,198
Total	3,699
Officers per 10,000 residents	18
U.S. average	25
Rank among states	43

Figures cover full-time sworn officers; totals include special police not shown separately.
Source: U.S. Bureau of Justice Statistics; *Census of State and Local Law Enforcement Agencies, 1996.*

Crime rates, 1996
Rates per 100,000 resident population

Violent crimes	State	U.S.
Total violent	332	634
Murder	3.2	7.4
Forcible rape	41.8	36.1
Robbery	69	202
Aggravated assault	218	388
Property crimes		
Total property	5,654	4,445
Burglary	848	943
Larceny/theft	4,377	2,976
Motor vehicle theft	429	526
Totals	5,986	5,079

Source: U.S. Federal Bureau of Investigation; *Crime in the United States,* annual.

State prison populations, 1980-1996

	State	U.S.	State share
1980	932	305,458	0.31%
1990	2,496	708,393	0.35%
1996	3,972	1,025,624	0.39%

Figures exclude prisoners in federal penitentiaries.
Source: U.S. Bureau of Justice Statistics.

Vermont

Location: New England (northeastern continental United States)

Area and rank: 9,249 square miles (23,956 square kilometers); 9,615 square miles (24,903 square kilometers) including water; forty-third largest state in area

Population and rank: 588,978 (1997); forty-ninth largest state in population

Capital: Montpelier

Largest city: Burlington (38,453 people in 1998)

Entered Union and rank: March 4, 1791; fourteenth state

Present constitution adopted: 1793

Church Street in Vermont's largest city, Burlington. (Vermont Department of Tourism & Marketing)

Counties: 14

State name:
"Vermont" is taken
from the French
"vert mont," for
"green mountain"

State nickname:
Green Mountain
State

Motto: Vermont,
Freedom and Unity

State flag: Blue field
with state coat of
arms

Highest point: Mount Mansfield — 4,393 feet (1,339 meters)

Lowest point: Lake Champlain — 95 feet (29 meters)

Highest recorded temperature: 105 degrees Fahrenheit (41 degrees Celsius) — 1911

Lowest recorded temperature: −50 degrees Fahrenheit (−46 degrees Celsius) —
Bloomfield, 1933

State song: "Hail, Vermont!"

State tree: Sugar maple

State flower: Red clover

State bird: Hermit thrush

State animal: Morgan horse

Vermont History

Vermont is the eighth smallest state in area. The only New England state not bordered by the Atlantic Ocean, Vermont is bordered by New Hampshire in the east, New York on the west, Massachusetts in the south, and Quebec, Canada, in the north. Vermont owns more than half of Lake Champlain, which makes up half of the state's western border.

Vermont's terrain has a little of everything, from the Taconic Mountains, with good granite quarries, to the Champlain Valley, with the flattest land and best soil in the state, to the Green Mountains, which run through the middle of the state. There are about 430 lakes and ponds in Vermont, 420 named peaks, and forests on about 80 percent of the land. The waterways in the state provide trade routes to Canada and New York, and the forests produce hardwood, paper, and the nation's largest supply of maple syrup.

Native American Lands. Until the 1500's, Vermont land was inhabited by Abenaki, Mahican, and Pennacook Indians, all members of the Algonquian tribe. Then the land was overtaken by tribes of the powerful Iroquois Confederacy. When French settlers arrived in the 1600's, they allied themselves with the Algonquians, because they wanted to trade furs with them. The first permanent white settlement in Vermont was Fort Dummer in the southeast, built by the English to protect Massachusetts residents from French and American Indian raids.

At Vermont's Battle of Bennington in 1777, the Continental Army defeated a major British force. (Library of Congress)

There were never any major battles between Native Americans and Europeans over land, as there were in the rest of New England. Still, American Indians were made unwelcome in the state, and they made up less than 2 percent of Vermont's population in the late twentieth century.

Settlement of Vermont. After French explorer Samuel de Champlain settled Quebec and Montreal, he traveled south on the Richelieu River into the lake named for him. In 1609 he claimed the Vermont area for France, naming the mountains *Verd Mont* (green mountains). The French built a few military posts to protect their land and established a fur trade with the Algonquians, but Vermont, unlike the other New England states and New York, was not settled for a long time.

In 1724 Dutch newcomers moved into the southwest of the state, and in 1750 Vermont began to attract settlers. Benning Wentworth, the royal gov-

ernor of New Hampshire, sold pieces of land west of the Connecticut River to pay off his debts, though he had no claims to the region. Between 1750 and 1764, 138 towns on 3 million acres were established, and the area was called the New Hampshire Grants.

From 1754 to 1763, the French and Indian War raged because of land disputes between the French and British. Fighting in the Lake Champlain area ended with the British, with Iroquois allies, defeating the French and Algonquians. The 1763 Treaty of Paris, ending the war, gave control of Vermont to Great Britain.

The governor of New York, George Clinton, had also been making claims on the New Hampshire Grants. After he decreed that settlers in the Grants should pay New York for their land, the landowners in the Grants went to King George III of England with their cause. The king sided with

the Grants residents, ordering Clinton not to bother them or to issue any land grants for land that was not his. However, in 1769-1770 Clinton gave titles to 600,000 acres in the Grants and tried to evict those who lived there. Some Vermonters, called the Bennington Nine, fought New York's claims to the area and formed a regiment, the Green Mountain Boys, led by Ethan Allen. The group drove the New York settlers out of the region.

The American Revolution. The Green Mountain Boys were active in the American Revolution (1775-1783), capturing Fort Ticonderoga, a British military post, and a British ship in 1775. Even though they logically should have sided with the British for supporting their claims to the Vermont land, they were more interested in liberty for the United States. American Indians fought on the British side, hoping to be able to keep some of their rightful land, in vain. The only Revolutionary battle fought for Vermont took place in July of 1777 at the Battle of Bennington. Although the battle took place on New York land, the fight remains significant to Vermonters because Vermont won, leading to the defeat of the British at Saratoga, a turning point in the war.

Independence. In 1777 the residents of the New Hampshire Grants declared their independence from England and New York and called their state New Connecticut. Five months later, they changed the name to Vermont. In 1777 they drafted a constitution; the Bill of Rights from that year would be used for more than two hundred years. In 1778 Vermont declared itself independent of the Continental Congress, because the region believed the Congress was a danger to Vermont's liberty; the area made a separate peace treaty with Britain.

Although the Congress wanted to invade Vermont, General George Washington warned against it, but he advised Vermont governor Thomas Chittenden to relinquish his claims to thirty-five New Hampshire and fourteen New York towns. In 1790 Vermont paid New York thirty thousand dollars for disputed land. In 1791 it became the fourteenth state, but its people never forgot its tradition of independence and the fact that it was, unlike the rest of New England, never an English colony.

Industry. Vermont's early industry depended on water and timber, of which the state had plenty. Gristmills, sawmills, and paper mills were built on the state's fast streams. In 1805 Brattleboro became a printing center, and cities such as Brandon became iron-mining hubs. The first canal built in the United States was at Bellows Falls in the Connecti-

Like its neighbor New Hampshire, Vermont is rich in granite quarries. (Vermont Department of Tourism & Marketing)

Vermont is the nation's leading producer of maple syrup, which is made from a sugar extracted from maple trees.
(Vermont Department of Tourism & Marketing/Andre Jenny)

cut River in 1802, and steamboats began operating on Lake Champlain in 1808, carrying goods to and from Canada. The Embargo Act of 1807 mandated against trade between the United States and foreign countries, so Vermonters had to smuggle food and lumber into Canada in order to maintain their livelihoods.

A special breed of horse, the Justin Morgan, was bred to plow hilly farms in the state, and Spanish merino sheep were imported for the manufacture of wool, leading to the opening of tanneries, carding mills, and finally textile factories. In the 1870's-1880's industries and cities grew, but Vermont never became fully industrialized, like the rest of New England, with huge cities and numerous factories. The state stayed mostly rural. In fact, the Great Depression of the 1930's did not really affect Vermont because the state was so rural.

Economy. During the War of 1812 the economy boomed, because the production of wool was essential for troops fighting Britain. However, after the war, in 1814, trade with Britain resumed, lowering wool prices. By 1820 the economy was doing poorly, and thousands of people left the state. The construction of the Champlain-Hudson Canal in 1823 and the Erie Canal in 1825 helped trade, but by the 1840's Vermonters were leaving again because of cheaper land in the West and depleted resources and topsoil in the state. The residents who stayed behind turned to dairy farming, which would be Vermont's main industry for more than one hundred years.

Although during the 1820's-1850's the population was declining, more so-called summer people were visiting the state for the refreshing air and spring waters. Tourism became a big business, and Vermont was the first state to open a state publicity service to encourage tourism, in 1891. After the Civil War (1861-1865) agriculture stayed in decline, and more Vermonters took the federal government's offer of cheap land in the West. However, immigrants began flocking to the state, from Ireland, Scotland, Italy, Spain, and Sweden. In the late twentieth century most immigrants were from Quebec.

World War II. The Vermont General Assembly declared war on Germany in September of 1941, three months before Pearl Harbor was attacked. Because Vermont men in training for the war returned fire under attack at sea, they declared war. The state sent fifty thousand soldiers to the war. Vermont experienced a huge population growth after the 1940's, with people looking to return to a quieter, simpler way of life. The state was still two-thirds rural, with the highest proportion of rural residents in the country.

Independent Thinkers. Vermont never followed the religious movements of the rest of New England, such as the Puritan or Congregationalist faiths. For this they were deemed atheistic sinners by the surrounding communities.

Vermont was very antislavery, providing numerous stops on the Underground Railroad, the escape route for slaves out of the South. Vermonters were so antislavery that more than 75 percent voted for Abraham Lincoln in 1860 rather than for opponent Stephen Douglas, who was a native Vermonter. Vermont contributed more than $9 million and thirty-five thousand men to the Civil War effort on the Union side.

After the Civil War the state became notoriously Republican-minded, and it remained that way until 1958. During the 1950's and 1960's it became more liberal, electing a Democrat, William H. Meyer, to the House of Representatives for the first time in more than one hundred years. In 1974 Patrick Leahy became the first Democratic senator from Vermont since the inception of the Republican Party in 1854.

Environment and Industry. Soon after World War II, Vermont became a huge ski attraction, due to the invention of the mechanized rope tow to pull skiers up a mountain. The downside of this technology and influx of people is that the environment suffered. In 1970 the Environmental Control Law was passed to cut down on pollution and development. It stated that developers would have to prove their projects would have no adverse effects on the surrounding environment.

By the 1990's, the service industry was the largest in the state, accounting for 67 percent of the workforce and 62 percent of the gross state product (GSP), mostly in the tourism and leisure fields. Manufacturing accounted for 21 percent of the workers and 26 percent of the GSP, and agriculture only applied to 6 percent of the workers and 1 percent of the GSP. However, 40 percent of the dairy products in New England come from Vermont, and it is the leading producer of maple syrup in the United States.

Lauren M. Mitchell

Vermont Time Line

1500's	Algonquian tribes are overtaken by Iroquois tribes.
1609	Samuel de Champlain claims Vermont for France.
1666	First French settlement, Forte Sainte Anne, is built on Isle La Motte.
1690	First English trading post, Chimney Point Fort, is constructed.
1724	British found first permanent settlement, Fort Dummer, in southeast.

1752	First maple syrup is made by Europeans.
1754-1763	French and Indian War is fought in Lake Champlain region.
1763	Control of Vermont passes to Britain; New Hampshire and New York lay claims to the land.
1770	Green Mountain Boys regiment forms to protect Vermont from New York control.
1775	Green Mountain Boys capture Fort Ticonderoga during the Revolution.
Jan. 15, 1777	Vermont declares its independence from Britain and establishes republic.
July, 1777	State constitution is written; Vermont becomes first state to abolish slavery.
1785	First marble quarry in United States opens in Vermont.
1790	New York sells its land claims in Vermont for thirty thousand dollars.
1790	First U.S. patent is given to Samuel Hopkins of Pittsford for making potash out of wood ashes.
Mar. 4, 1791	Vermont becomes fourteenth state.
1791	University of Vermont is founded.
1793	First American copper mine opens at Strafford.
1800	Middlebury College is chartered.
1802	Bellows Falls canal is first in the country.
1805	Montpelier becomes state capital.
1814	First school of higher education for women opens at Middlebury.
1823	Champlain-Hudson canal opens.
1848	First railroad opens.
1861	Vermont is first state to offer troops to Union during Civil War.
Oct., 1864	Confederate soldiers raid Saint Albans, in northernmost Civil War confrontation.
1896	Vermont is first state to implement an absentee voting law.
Aug. 3, 1923	Calvin Coolidge is sworn in as U.S. president in Plymouth Notch, Vermont.
1931	First state income tax is instituted.
1933	First ski tow in the country opens at Woodstock, Vermont.
1938	Hurricane kills five, causes $12 million in damage.
Sept. 11, 1941	Vermont declares war on Germany.
1954	Vermont's Consuelo N. Bailey is first woman in country elected a lieutenant governor.
1958	William Meyer is first Vermont Democrat elected to Congress since 1854.
1964	Vermont votes Democratic in a presidential race for the first time in its history.
1970	Environmental Conservation Agency is established.

(continued)

1974	Patrick Leahy is first Democratic senator elected in Vermont since 1854.
Jan. 26, 1976	Vermont Nuclear Power Corporation closes as a safety precaution.
1976	Abenaki Indians are given official status to qualify for federal benefits; the next year the status is revoked by Governor Richard Snelling.
1985	Madeline Kunin becomes first elected female governor of Vermont.
Mar. 11, 1992	Ice floes dam Winooski River, flooding Montpelier.
June 17, 1992	Vermont supreme court denies a claim by Abenaki Indians to 150 square miles of land.

Notes for Further Study

Published Sources. *Vermont: A History* (1993), by Charles T. Morrissey, is a good place to learn the background of the state. Other good general history books include *The Story of Vermont* (1999), by Christopher McGrory Klyza and Stephen C. Trombulak, and *Tales of Vermont Ways and People* (1989) by Bertha Sanford Dodge. Excellent books for the traveler to Vermont are *The Beauty of Vermont* (1998) by Tom Slayton and Elizabeth Bassett's *Nature Walks in Northern Vermont and the Champlain Valley* (1998). For more specialized studies, readers should see *The Abenaki* (1996), by Elaine Landau, and *The Original Vermonters: Native Inhabitants, Past and Present* (1994), by William A. Haviland and Marjory W. Power. These books offer insights into the American Indians who lived in Vermont.

A good overview of early America is found in *Voyages and Explorations of Samuel de Champlain, Sixteen Four to Sixteen Sixteen* (1973), Champlain's own writings edited by Edward Gaylord Bourne. *The Great Warpath: British Military Sites from Albany to Crown Point* (1999), by David R. Starbuck, is an excellent report from an archaeologist detailing the lives of soldiers during the Revolution, including accounts from Fort Ticonderoga. Stewart H. Holbrook's *Ethan Allen* (1992) and Michael T. Hahn's *Ethan Allen: A Life of Adventure* (1994) chronicle the life of the Revolutionary soldier. Civil War history is recounted in *Full Duty: Vermonters in the Civil War* (1995) by Howard Coffin and *A War of the People: Vermont Civil War Letters* (1999) edited by Jeffrey D. Marshall. The latter contains correspondence written by Vermont soldiers in the 1860's.

Web Resources. The best place to start for Vermont information and links to other Web sites is the official state site (http://www.state.vt.us). Vermont Judiciary (http://www.state.vt.us/courts) has calendars and court schedules; Vermont Legislative Home Page (http://www.leg.state.vt.us) has fiscal facts, schedules, reports, and documents; and Vermont Democratic Party (http://homepages.together.net/~vtdems) contains information on that party, with links to party members. For tourist and travel information, Link Vermont (http://www.linkvermont.com) offers a calendar of events, rental listings, and more, from the Board of Tourism. Vermont.com (http://www.vermont.com) also offers lodging and entertainment updates. VDTM Explore Vermont History (http://www.travel-vermont.com/history.htm) is a virtual drive through the beautiful state.

Vermont History Web site (http://www.vermont.com) gives state historical events and biographies of important Vermont figures. Other good history Web sites include Samuel de Champlain (http://www.linkvermont.com) and The Life of Samuel de Champlain (http://www.cyber-north.com/public/champlain.htm), which give background about the explorer and his findings. About the Ethan Allen Homestead (http://www.uvm.edu/~vhnet/hertour/eallen/eahome.html) has good information about the Green Mountain Boys. The French and Indian War site (http://www.kidinfo.com/American_History/FrenchandIndianWar.html) has much information and many links to other resources, as does Digital History Ltd. (http://digitalhistory.org/ Digital History Ltd.). The Abenaki Home Page (http://millennianet.com/slmiller/abenaki) contains maps, history of the Native American tribe, and links. Also good is the Traditional Abenaki Web site (http://www.hmt.com/abenaki).

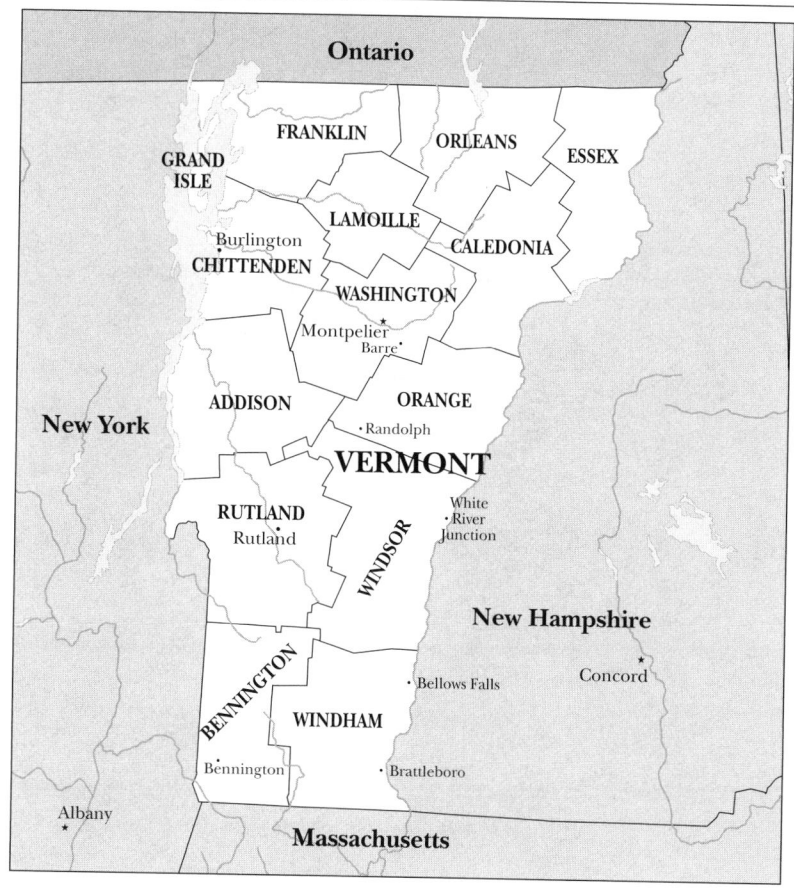

Counties

County	Sq. miles	1996 pop.
Addison	770.0	35,079
Bennington	676.3	36,357
Caledonia	651.0	28,800
Chittenden	539.0	141,115
Essex	665.3	6,511
Franklin	637.1	43,465
Grand Isle	82.6	5,968
Lamoille	460.6	21,373

County	Sq. miles	1996 pop.
Orange	688.7	27,562
Orleans	696.9	25,117
Rutland	932.2	62,757
Washington	689.6	56,437
Windham	788.8	42,923
Windsor	971.3	55,190

Source: U.S. Census Bureau; National Association of Counties.

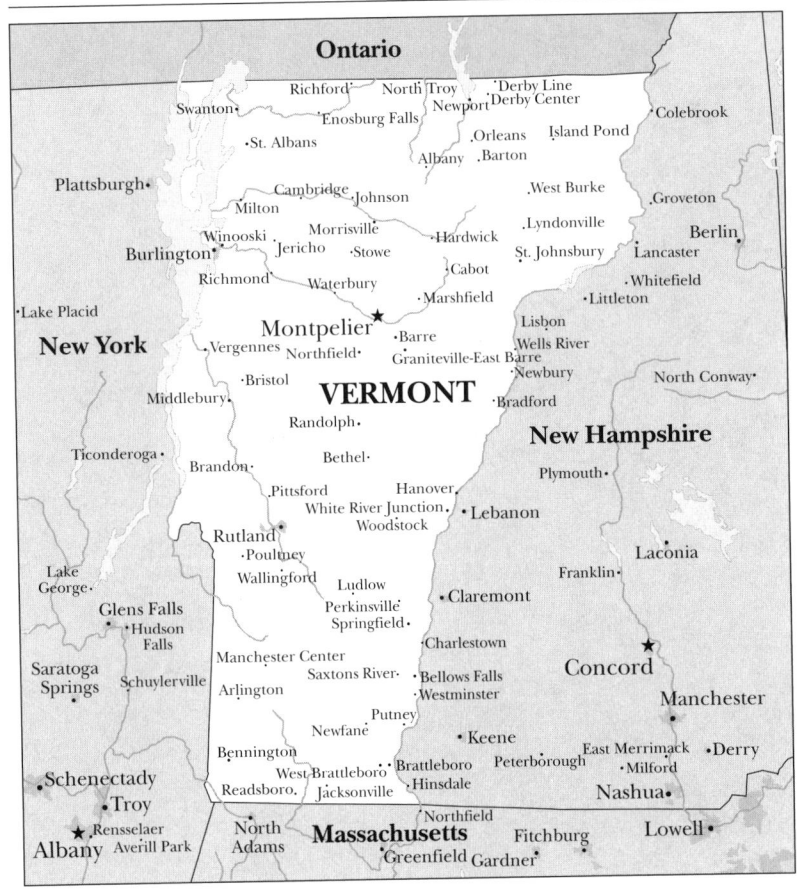

Cities
With 10,000 or more residents

Rank	City	Population
1	Burlington	38,453
2	Rutland	17,348
3	South Burlington	14,037

Population figures are estimated for mid-1998.
Source: U.S. Bureau of the Census.

Index to Tables

NA = Reliable data are not available.

DEMOGRAPHICS

Resident state and national populations, 1970-1997

Population figures given in thousands

	State pop.	U.S. pop.	Share	Rank
1970	445	203,302	0.2%	48
1980	511	226,546	0.2%	48
1985	530	237,924	0.2%	49
1990	563	248,765	0.2%	48
1995	583	262,761	0.2%	49
1997	589	267,636	0.2%	49

Source: U.S. Bureau of the Census.

Resident population by age, 1997

Age group	Total population
Under 5 years	35,000
5 to 17 years	111,000
18 to 24 years	51,000
25 to 34 years	86,000
35 to 44 years	104,000
45 to 54 years	83,000
55 to 64 years	47,000
65 to 74 years	39,000
75 to 84 years	24,000
85 years and over	9,000
Portion of residents 65 and older	12.3%
National average	12.7%

Population figures are rounded to nearest thousand persons;
figures include armed forces personnel stationed in state.
Source: U.S. Bureau of the Census.

Resident population by race, Hispanic origin, 1997

	State pop.	Share	U.S.
All residents	589,000	100.0%	100.0%
Hispanic white	5,000	0.8%	10.0%
non-Hispanic white	575,000	97.6%	72.7%
African American	3,000	0.5%	12.7%
Native American	2,000	0.3%	0.9%
Asian, Pacific Islander	5,000	0.8%	3.8%

Source: U.S. Bureau of the Census.

Projections of state population, 2000-2025

	Model A Uses interstate migration observed from 1975-1994	Model B Uses Bureau of Economic Analysis employment projections
Year	Population	Population
2000	617,000	607,000
2005	638,000	623,000
2010	651,000	636,000
2015	662,000	646,000
2020	671,000	655,000
2025	678,000	661,000

All population projections, including those for 2000, were calculated in 1997.
Source: U.S. Bureau of the Census, Population Paper Listings PPL-47.

VITAL STATISTICS

Average lifetime in years by race, 1989-1991

	State	U.S.	Rank
All residents	76.54	75.37	16
White residents	76.50	76.13	20
Black residents	NA	69.16	NA

Ranks are from longest-lived to least longest-lived. Ranks exclude Alaska, for which reliable data are not available. Rank for black residents is based on the 32 states for which reliable data are available.
Source: U.S. National Center for Health Statistics.

Infant mortality rates, 1980 and 1995

	State	U.S.
All residents		
1980	10.7	12.6
1995	6.0	7.6
White residents		
1980	10.7	11.0
1995	6.2	6.3
Black residents		
1980	NA	21.4
1995	NA	15.1

Figures represent deaths per 1,000 live births of resident infants under 1 year old, exclusive of fetal deaths; all-residents figures include other races not listed separately.
Source: U.S. National Center for Health Statistics.

Marriages and divorces

Marriages in 1996	5,900
Rate per 1,000 population, 1995	10.3
U.S. rate, 1995	8.9
Rank among all states	10
Divorces in 1996	2,500
Rate per 1,000 population, 1995	4.8
U.S. rate, 1995	4.4
Rank among all states	20

Rank is from highest to lowest in country.
Source: U.S. National Center for Health Statistics.

Death rates by leading causes, 1995

Deaths per 100,000 resident population

Cause	State	U.S.
Heart disease	278.2	280.7
Cancer	198.9	204.9
Cerebrovascular diseases	57.1	60.1
Accidents and adverse effects	32.8	35.5
Motor vehicle accidents	16.1	16.5
Chronic obstructive pulmonary diseases	41.2	39.2
Diabetes mellitus	24.5	22.6
HIV	4.6	NA
Suicide	13.0	11.9
Homicide	-	8.7
All causes	846.7	880.0
Rank in overall death rate among states		33

Figures exclude nonresidents who die in state. Causes of death follow International Classification of Diseases. Rank is from highest to lowest in country.
Source: U.S. National Center for Health Statistics.

ECONOMY

Gross state product, 1990-1996
In current dollars

	State product	Increase
1990	$11.6 billion	
1993	$13.0 billion	
1994	$13.6 billion	4.62%
1995	$13.9 billion	2.21%
1996	$14.6 billion	5.04%

Source: U.S. Bureau of Economic Analysis; *Survey of Current Business,* June, 1998.

Gross state product by industry, 1996
In billions

Farms, forestry, fisheries	$0.3
Construction	0.5
Manufacturing	2.7
Transportation, public utilities	1.2
Wholesale trade	0.9
Retail trade	1.4
Finance, insurance, real estate	2.3
Services	2.6
Government	1.6
State total	$13.5
Total U.S.	$6,923.8
State share	0.19%
Rank among states	50

Total figures include mining, not listed separately.
Source: U.S. Bureau of Economic Analysis; *Survey of Current Business,* June, 1998.

Personal income per capita, 1990 and 1997
In current dollars

	1990	1997
Per capita income	$17,721	$23,401
U.S. average	$19,188	$25,598
Rank among states	24	30

1997 data are preliminary.
Source: U.S. Bureau of Economic Analysis; *Survey of Current Business,* May, 1998.

Energy consumption, 1995
In trillions of British thermal units (BTU)

End-use sectors

Residential	44.1
Commercial	25.3
Industrial	34.7
Transportation	50.6

Sources of energy

Petroleum	80.5
Natural gas	7.2
Coal	0.1
Hydroelectric power	27.6
Nuclear electric power	41.1
Total state per capita consumption	256.3
Total U.S. per capita consumption	344.4
Rank among states	41
Total state energy consumption	149.9
Total U.S. energy consumption	90,547.4
State share of U.S. total	0.17%
Rank among states	50

Total figures include items not listed separately.
Source: U.S. Energy Information Administration; *State Energy Data Report.*

Nonfarm employment by sectors, 1997

Total	279,000
Construction	13,000
Manufacturing	47,000
Transportation, public utilities	12,000
Wholesale trade, retail trade	65,000
Finance, insurance, real estate	12,000
Services	84,000
Government	45,000

Figures are rounded to nearest thousand persons. Total includes mining, not listed separately.
Source: U.S. Bureau of Labor Statistics; *Employment and Earnings,* monthly.

Foreign exports, 1990-1997
In millions of dollars

Year	State	U.S.	State share
1990	1,154	394,045	0.29%
1996	3,302	624,767	0.53%
1997	3,811	688,896	0.55%

Source: U.S. Bureau of the Census; *U.S. Merchandise Trade,* series FT 900.

LAND USE

Federally owned land, 1996

	State	U.S.	State share
Total acres	5,937,000	2,271,343,000	0.26%
Federally owned	377,000	563,129,000	0.07%
Federal share	6.3%	24.8%	—

Areas are rounded to nearest thousand acres. Figures for federally owned land do not include trust properties.

Source: U.S. General Services Administration; *Inventory Report on Real Property Owned by the United States Throughout the World,* annual.

Land use, 1992
In acres, rounded to nearest thousand

Total surface area	6,153,000
Federal land	368,000
Total nonfederal.	5,521,000
Developed	324,000
Total rural	5,197,000
Cropland.	635,000
Pasture land	349,000
Range land	0
Forest land.	4,138,000
Minor cover/use	75,000

Total surface area figures include water area not shown separately.

Source: U.S. Dept. of Agriculture; Soil Conservation Service; Iowa State University, Statistical Laboratory; *Summary Report, 1992 National Resources Inventory.*

Farms and crop acreage, 1997

	State	U.S.	Share	Rank
Farms (thousands)	6	2,058	0.29%	43
Acres (millions)	1	968	0.10%	47
Acres per farm	225	471	—	32
Acres planted	365	334,139	0.11%	43
Acres harvested	358	319,894	0.11%	43
Farm value (mill.)	$82	$108,805	0.08%	32

Numbers of farms are rounded to nearest thousand.

Source: U.S. Dept. of Agriculture; National Agricultural Statistics Service.

GOVERNMENT AND FINANCE

Units of local government, 1997

	State	Total U.S.	Rank
All local governments	691	87,453	37
Counties	14	3,043	43
Municipalities	49	19,372	43
Townships	237	16,629	17
School districts	279	13,726	20
Special districts	112	34,683	46

County ranks are based on the 48 states with county governments; township ranks are based on the 20 states with township governments; school district ranks are based on the 46 states with such districts.

Township figures include "town" governments.

Source: U.S. Bureau of the Census; *1997 Census of Governments, Government Organization,* Series GC97(1).

State government revenue, 1996

Total revenue	$2,146 mill.
General revenue	1,950 mill.
Per capita.	3,325
U.S. per capita average	2,910
Rank among states.	13
Intergovernmental revenue	
Total	$650 mill.
From federal government	647 mill.
From local government.	4 mill.
Charges and Miscellaneous	
Total	$459 mill.
Current charges	286 mill.
Misc. general revenue	173 mill.
Taxes	
Total	$841 mill.
General sales	183 mill.
Selective sales.	221 mill.
License taxes.	72 mill.
Individual income	281 mill.
Corporate income	45 mill.
Other.	40 mill.
Insurance trust revenue	168 mill.

Total revenue figures include items not listed separately.

Source: U.S. Bureau of the Census.

State government expenditures, 1996

General expenditures
Intergovernmental . . . . $313 mill.
Direct expenditures . . . . 1,605 mill.
Total. . . . . 1,918 mill.

Selected direct expenditures
Education . . . . $623 mill.
Public welfare. . . . . 516 mill.
Health, hospital . . . . 60 mill.
Highways . . . . 189 mill.
Police. . . . . 34 mill.
Corrections . . . . 43 mill.
Natural resources . . . . 53 mill.
Parks and recreation . . . . 9 mill.
Government administration . . . . 85 mill.
Interest on debt . . . . 105 mill.

Other
State per capita expenditures $3,270
U.S. per capita average 2,854
Rank among states. 11
Total state expenditures . . . . 2,061 mill.
Total U.S. expenditures . . . . 859,959 mill.

Totals include items not listed separately.
Source: U.S. Bureau of the Census.

POLITICS

Governors since statehood
D = Democrat; R = Republican; O = other;
(r) resigned; (d) died in office; (i) removed from office

Thomas Chittenden . . . . (d) 1791-1797
Paul Brigham 1797
Isaac Tichenor (O) 1797-1807
Israel Smith (O) 1807-1808
Isaac Tichenor (O) 1808-1809
Jonas Galusha (O) 1809-1813
Martin Chittenden (O). 1813-1815
Jonas Galusha (O) 1815-1820
Richard Skinner (O) 1820-1823
Cornelius P. Van Ness (O) 1823-1826
Ezra Butler (O) 1826-1828
Samuel C. Crafts (O) 1828-1831
William A. Palmer (O) 1831-1835
Silas H. Jenison (O) 1835-1841
Charles Paine (O) 1841-1843
John Mattocks (O) 1843-1844
William Slade (O) 1844-1846
Horace Eaton (O) 1846-1848
Carlos Coolidge (O) 1848-1850

Charles K. Williams (O) 1850-1852
Erastus Fairbanks (O) 1852-1853
John S. Robinson (D). 1853-1854
Stephen Royce (O) 1854-1856
Ryland Fletcher (R) 1856-1858
Hiland Hall (R) 1858-1860
Erastus Fairbanks (R). 1860-1861
Frederick Holbrook (R) 1861-1863
John G. Smith (R) 1863-1865
Paul Dillingham (R) 1865-1867
John B. Page (R) 1867-1869
Peter T. Washburn (R) . . . . (d) 1869-1870
George W. Hendee (R). 1870
John W. Stewart (R) 1870-1872
Julius Converse (R) 1872-1874
Asahel Peck (R). 1874-1876
Horace Fairbanks (R) 1876-1878
Redfield Proctor (R) 1878-1880
Roswell Farnham (R) 1880-1882
John L. Barstow (R) 1882-1884
Samuel E. Pingree (R) 1884-1886
Ebenezer J. Ormsbee (R) 1886-1888
William P. Dillingbam (R) 1888-1890
Carroll S. Page (R) 1890-1892
Levi K. Fuller (R) 1892-1894
Urban A. Woodbury (R) 1894-1896
Josiah Grout (R) 1896-1898
Edward C. Smith (R) 1898-1900
William W. Stickney (R) 1900-1902
John G. McCullough (R) 1902-1904
Charles J. Bell (R) 1904-1906
Fletcher D. Proctor (R). 1906-1908
George H. Prouty (R) 1908-1910
John A. Mead (R). 1910-1912
Allen M. Fletcher (R). 1912-1915
Charles W. Gates (R) 1915-1917
Horace F. Graham (R) 1917-1919
Percival W. Clement (R) 1919-1921
James Hartness (R) 1921-1923
Redfield Proctor, Jr. (R) 1923-1925
Franklin S. Billings (R) 1925-1927
John E. Weeks (R) 1927-1931
Stanley C. Wilson (R) 1931-1935
Charles M. Smith (R) 1935-1937
George D. Aiken (R) 1937-1941
William H. Wills (R) 1941-1945
Mortimer R. Proctor (R) 1945-1947
Ernest W. Gibson, Jr. (R) . . . . (r) 1947-1950
Harold J. Arthur (R) 1950-1951
Lee E. Emerson (R) 1951-1955
Joseph B. Johnson (R) 1955-1959
Robert T. Stafford (R) 1959-1961
Frank Ray Keyser, Jr. (R) 1961-1963
Phillip H. Hoff (D) 1963-1969

(continued)

Deane C. Davis (R) 1969-1973
Thomas P. Salmon (D) 1973-1977
Richard A. Snelling (R) 1977-1985
Madeleine Kunin (D). 1985-1991
Richard A. Snelling (R) . . . . (d) 1991
Howard Dean (D) 1991-

Composition of state legislature, 1990-1998

	Democrats	Republicans
State House (148 seats)		
1990	73	75
1992	87	57
1994	86	61
1996	89	57
1998	79	67
State Senate (30 seats)		
1990	15	15
1992	14	16
1994	12	18
1996	17	13
1998	17	13

Figures for total seats may include independents and minor party members.

Source: Council of State Governments; *State Elective Officials and the Legislatures.*

Composition of congressional delegations, 1989-1999

	Dem	Rep	Total
House of Representatives			
101st Congress, 1989			
State delegates	0	1	1
Total U.S.	259	174	433
102d Congress, 1991			
State delegates	0	0	0
Total U.S.	267	167	434
103d Congress, 1993			
State delegates	0	0	0
Total U.S.	258	176	434
104th Congress, 1995			
State delegates	0	0	0
Total U.S.	197	236	433
105th Congress, 1997			
State delegates	0	0	0
Total U.S.	206	228	434

	Dem	Rep	Total
106th Congress, 1999			
State delegates	0	0	0
Total U.S.	211	222	433
Senate			
101st Congress, 1989			
State delegates	1	1	2
Total U.S.	55	45	100
102d Congress, 1991			
State delegates	1	1	2
Total U.S.	56	44	100
103d Congress, 1993			
State delegates	1	1	2
Total U.S.	57	43	100
104th Congress, 1995			
State delegates	1	1	2
Total U.S.	46	53	99
105th Congress, 1997			
State delegates	1	1	2
Total U.S.	45	55	100
106th Congress, 1999			
State delegates	1	1	2
Total U.S.	45	54	99

Figures are for starts of first sessions. Figure for U.S. Representatives for 101st Congress does not include Alabama and Indiana, which had vacancies. Figures for total U.S. Representatives for 102d, 103d, and 106th Congresses do not include Vermont, which had 1 Independent-Socialist. Figure for U.S. Representatives for 104th Congress does not include Vermont, which had 1 Independent-Socialist, and California, which had 1 vacancy. Figure for U.S. Representatives for 105th Congress does not include New York, which had 1 vacancy. Figure for U.S. Senators for 104th Congress does not include Oregon, which had 1 vacancy. Figure for U.S. Senators for 106th Congress does not include New Hampshire, which had 1 Independent.

Source: U.S. Congress; *Congressional Directory,* biennial.

Voter participation in presidential elections, 1992 and 1996

	1992	1996
State voting age pop.	429,000	441,000
Total U.S. voting age pop.	189,524,000	196,509,000
State share of U.S. total	0.2%	0.2%
Rank among states	48	48
Percent of state casting vote	67.5	56.9
Percent of U.S. total voting	55.1	49.0
Rank among states	5	10

Source: U.S. Bureau of the Census.

HEALTH AND MEDICAL CARE

Medicare, 1997

	Recipients	Payments
State	86,000	$328 mill.
Total U.S.	37,514,000	$206,064 mill.
State share	0.23%	0.16%
Rank among states	48	48

Recipient figures are rounded to nearest thousand persons.
  Ranks are from highest to lowest.
Source: U.S. Health Care Financing Administration.

Medicaid, 1996

	Recipients	Payments
State	102,000	$302 mill.
Total U.S.	35,028,000	$121,419 mill.
State share	0.29%	0.25%
Rank among states	42	45

Recipient figures are rounded to nearest thousand persons.
  Payment figures for fiscal year reflect federal and state
  contribution payments. Ranks are from highest to lowest.
Source: U.S. Health Care Financing Administration.

Health insurance coverage, 1996

	State	U.S.
Total persons covered	522,000	225,070,000
Total persons not covered	65,000	41,716,000
Part not covered	11.1%	15.6%
Rank among states	39	—
Children not covered	9,000	10,554,000
Part not covered	6.0%	14.8%
Rank among states	49	—

Ranks are from most to fewest uninsured. Population figures
  are rounded to nearest thousand persons.
Source: U.S. Bureau of the Census.

AIDS, syphilis, tuberculosis, and measles cases, 1997

Cases	U.S.	State	Share
AIDS	58,443	29	0.05%
Syphilis	8,550	NA	NA
Tuberculosis	18,534	6	0.03%
Measles	148,000	NA	NA

Measles figures are rounded to nearest thousand cases.
Source: U.S. Centers for Disease Control and Prevention.

HOUSING

Homeownership rates, 1985-1997

	1985	1990	1997
State	69.5%	72.6%	69.1%
Total U.S.	63.9%	63.9%	65.7%
Rank among states	17	3	21

Source: U.S. Bureau of the Census.

Home sales, 1990 and 1997
In thousands of units

Existing home sales	1990	1997	Change
State sales	6.1	8.1	2
Total U.S. sales	3,560	4,730	1,170
State share of U.S. total	0.17%	0.17%	NA
Rank among states	48	46	—

Source: National Association of Realtors; *Real Estate Outlook:
  Market Trends and Insights.*

EDUCATION

Public school enrollment, 1995

State K-8 enrollment	75,000
Total U.S. K-8 enrollment	32,341,000
State share of total U.S.	0.23%
State 9-12 enrollment.	30,000
Total U.S. 9-12 enrollment	12,500,000
State share of U.S. total	0.24%
State public school enroll. rate	95.9%
Overall U.S. rate.	91.6%
Rank among states	5

Enrollment figures (which include unclassified students) are
rounded to nearest thousand pupils in fall term;
kindergarten (K)-8 grade figures include some
prekindergarten students. Enrollment rate is based on
percentage of persons 5-17 years old. Rank is from highest
to lowest.

Source: U.S. National Center for Education Statistics.

Public college finances, 1996

State FTE enrollment.	15,300
Total U.S. FTE enrollment	8,268,800
State share of total U.S.	0.19%
Rank among states.	50
State and local appropriations	$36,700,000
Total U.S. state and local appropriations.	$39,699 mill.
State share of total U.S.	0.09%
Rank among states.	50
State net tuition revenues.	$132,600,000
Total U.S. net tuition	$18,348,100,000
State share of total U.S.	0.72%
Rank among states.	38

FTE=Full-time equivalent; credit and noncredit enrollment
including summer session in academic year ending in
1996.

Enrollments are rounded to nearest thousand students. Net
tuition revenues exclude appropriation to students
attending in-state public institutions. Rankings are from
highest shares to lowest.

Source: Research Associates of Washington.

TRANSPORTATION AND TRAVEL

Highway mileage, 1996

Interstate	320
Other arterial.	1,316
Collector roads	3,326
Local roads	9,441
Urban roads	1,334
Rural roads	12,858
Total state	14,192
U.S. total	3,933,985
State share	0.4%
Rank among states.	46

Source: U.S. Federal Highway Administration.

Motor vehicle registrations and driver licenses, 1996

In thousands

Vehicle registrations	State	U.S.	Share	Rank
Autos, trucks, buses	503	206,365	0.24%	50
Autos only	298	128,439	0.23%	48
Motorcycles	18	3,832	0.47%	42
Driver licenses	469	179,539	0.26%	50

Figures do not include vehicles owned by military services.
Source: U.S. Federal Highway Administration; *Highway
Statistics*; *Selected Highway Statistics and Charts.*

Domestic travel expenditures, 1995

Spending by U.S. residents on overnight trips and day
trips of at least 100 miles

Total expenditures in state	$1,136 mill.
Total expenditures in U.S.	$360,314 mill.
State share of total U.S.	0.32%
Rank among states.	46

Source: Travel Industry Association of America.

CRIME AND LAW ENFORCEMENT

State and local police officers, 1996

```
Local police  . . . . . . . . . . . . . . . . . . . . .  548
State police . . . . . . . . . . . . . . . . . . . . . .  290
Sheriffs . . . . . . . . . . . . . . . . . . . . . . . .   87
Total  . . . . . . . . . . . . . . . . . . . . . . . .   981
Officers per 10,000 residents . . . . . . . . . . . .   17
U.S. average  . . . . . . . . . . . . . . . . . . . .   25
Rank among states . . . . . . . . . . . . . . . . . .   46
```

Figures cover full-time sworn officers; totals include special
  police not shown separately.
Source: U.S. Bureau of Justice Statistics; *Census of State and
  Local Law Enforcement Agencies, 1996.*

Crime rates, 1996
Rates per 100,000 resident population

Violent crimes	State	U.S.
Total violent	121	634
Murder	1.9	7.4
Forcible rape	27.0	36.1
Robbery	15	202
Aggravated assault	77	388
Property crimes		
Total property	2,882	4,445
Burglary	673	943
Larceny/theft	2,058	2,976
Motor vehicle theft	150	526
Totals	3,003	5,079

Source: U.S. Federal Bureau of Investigation; *Crime in the
  United States,* annual.

State prison populations, 1980-1996

	State	U.S.	State share
1980	480	305,458	0.16%
1990	1,049	708,393	0.15%
1996	1,119	1,025,624	0.11%

Figures exclude prisoners in federal penitentiaries.
Source: U.S. Bureau of Justice Statistics.

Virginia

Location: East Coast of continental United States

Area and rank: 39,598 square miles (102,558 square kilometers); 42,769 square miles (110,772 square kilometers) including water; thirty-seventh largest state in area

Coastline: 112 miles (180 kilometers)

Shoreline: 3,315 miles (5,334 kilometers)

Population and rank: 6,733,996 (1997); twelfth largest state in population

Capital: Richmond

Largest city: Virginia Beach (432,380 people in 1998)

The neoclassical design of the state capitol building in Richmond was inspired by the architecture of Thomas Jefferson.
(Virginia Tourism Corporation)

Entered Union and rank: June 25, 1788; tenth state

Present constitution adopted: 1970

Counties: 95, as well as 39 independent cities

State name: Virginia was named after England's Queen Elizabeth I, who was known as the Virgin Queen

State nicknames: The Old Dominion; Mother of Presidents; Cavalier State

Motto: *Sic semper tyrannis* (Thus always to tyrants)

State flag: Dark blue field with state coat of arms in white border

Highest point: Mount Rogers — 5,729 feet (1,746 meters)

Lowest point: Atlantic Ocean — sea level

Highest recorded temperature: 110 degrees Fahrenheit (43 degrees Celsius) — Balcony Falls, 1954

Lowest recorded temperature: −30 degrees Fahrenheit (−34 degrees Celsius) — Mountain Lake Biological Station, 1985

State song: "Carry Me Back to Old Virginia"

State tree: American dogwood

State flower: American dogwood

State bird: Cardinal

National park: Shenandoah

Virginia History

One of the most historic of all the fifty United States, Virginia played pivotal roles during the colonial period, the American Revolution, and the Civil War. Following the adoption of the Constitution, Virginians had a major influence in shaping the direction and destiny of the early nation, and four of the first five American presidents, from George Washington through James Monroe, were from Virginia. In fact, a Virginian held the presidency for twenty-four out of the first twenty-eight years of the United States.

Early Inhabitants and European Settlement. Compared to other portions of the East Coast, Native Americans seem to have arrived fairly late in the Virginia area, settling there after 8000 B.C.E. In the Piedmont area to the west, the tribes of the Sioux language family included Manahoac,

Monacan, and Tutelo. In the southwestern portion were the Cherokee, while the Nottoway were found in the southeast; both of these were part of the Iroquoian language community. To the north, along the upper portions of Chesapeake Bay, the Susquehanna had migrated into the region from the area that is now Pennsylvania. These were also Iroquoian speakers. Along the lower portions of the Chesapeake Bay coast itself, including the area where the first English settlers arrived, the dominant Native Americans were the Algonquian speaking members of the group known as the "Powhatan Confederacy," named after its powerful chieftain.

In addition to hunting and fishing, especially along the bountiful coastal waters of the Chesapeake Bay, the tribes turned to agriculture, which flourished in the excellent soil and long, warm

Mount Vernon, the plantation home of George Washington, the first president of the United States. (Virginia Tourism Corporation)

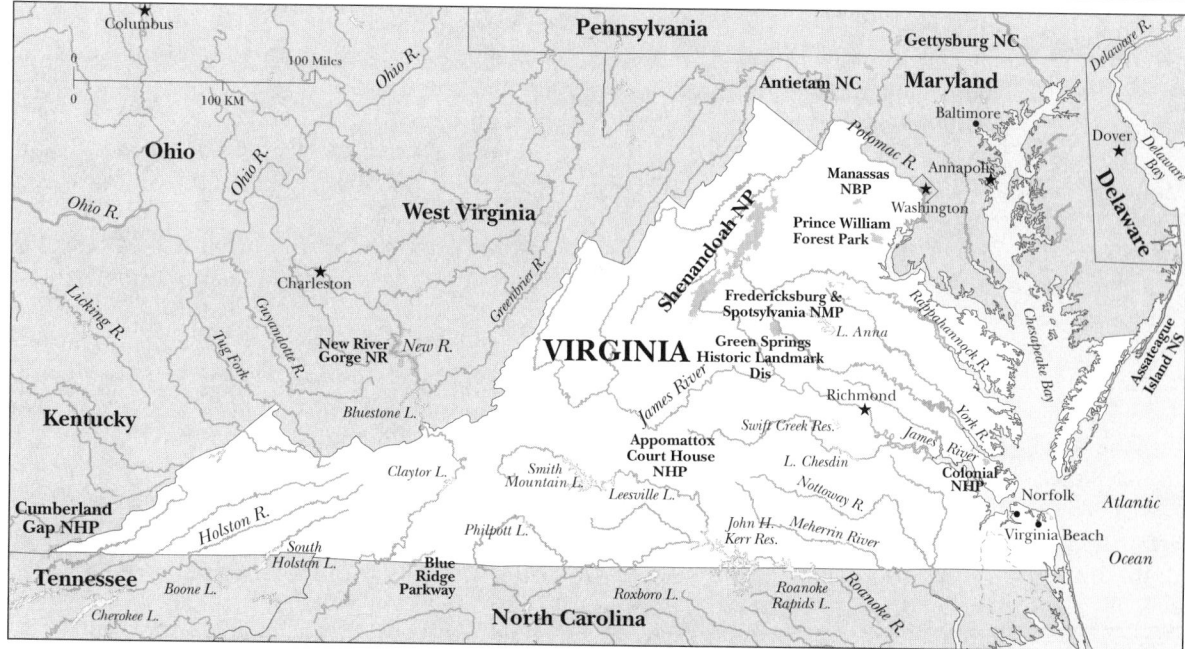

growing season of the area. One of their major innovations was the growth and cultivation of tobacco, which the Native Americans passed on to English settlers shortly after their arrival in 1607.

The English colony of Jamestown, founded on a peninsula jutting into the Chesapeake Bay, was part of a grandiose land grant from the English King James I which stretched from what is now southern Maine to California and included both the island of Bermuda and the modern Canadian province of Ontario. However, despite the imperial designs, during its early days Jamestown was hard pressed to simply survive and barely weathered internal division, attacks by the Native Americans, disease, and near starvation. Under the leadership of Captain John Smith, the new colony endured and by the 1620's was exporting tobacco to England as a cash crop. The cultivation of tobacco and other crops was transformed in 1619 when the first Africans arrived in the colony as indentured servants; by the 1630's slavery had been introduced and in 1661 it was legalized. Slavery was to remain an essential part of Virginia's plantation economy until the end of the American Civil War.

A Rich Colony Leads a Revolution. The first legislative assembly in the English colonies gathered in Jamestown in 1619. Even though Virginia became a royal colony in 1624, the House of Burgesses, as the assembly was known, remained a potent force in colonial affairs, including encouraging growth and development, including expansion beyond the Blue Ridge Mountains to the west. In eastern Virginia, especially along the rich lands of the tidewater, tobacco farming brought enormous wealth to planters, merchants and traders. By the middle of the 1700's, Virginia was among the richest of the American colonies.

It was also among the most independently minded. In 1676 Virginian Nathaniel Bacon led a popular revolt against despotic colonial governor Sir William Berkeley. As early as 1765 the Virginia House of Burgesses had officially opposed the Stamp Act, and in 1769 Virginia launched a boycott of all British goods to protest additional taxes which the colonists regarded as unfair and illegal. It was at the Virginia Convention of 1775 that Patrick Henry delivered the speech which included his famous words, "Give me liberty, or give me death." Henry's sentiment was given more practical form in June, 1776, when Virginia officially declared itself independent from Great Britain. On July 4, 1776, the Declaration of Independence, largely written by Virginian Thomas Jefferson, extended this freedom to all thirteen colonies.

Virginia provided both leaders and a battleground for the American Revolution. George Washington was named commander of the Continental Army, while other military leaders included George Rogers Clark, Daniel Morgan, and "Light-Horse Harry" Lee, father of Robert E. Lee. The founder of the American Navy, John Paul Jones, was a Virginian, although born in Scotland. The climactic battle of the Revolution came with the combined American and French defeat of British forces under Lord Cornwallis at the siege of Yorktown. This victory ensured final victory for the American cause.

A New Nation and Civil War. Virginians were active in the creation and growth of the new United States. The Constitution, which replaced the ineffective Articles of Confederation, was largely drafted by James Madison, who later became the fourth president of the United States. He shared that office with a number of others from his state, including George Washington, our first president; Thomas Jefferson, the third; and James Monroe, the fifth. In all, Virginians held the position of chief executive for twenty-four of the first twenty-eight years of the new nation. In addition, the most influential chief justice of the United States, John Marshall, was a Virginian. He served from 1801 through 1835 and established the independent judiciary as an essential branch of the American federal government.

Although a southern, slave-holding state, Virginia had not taken the radical position held by others such as South Carolina during the intense national debate over slavery. The seizure of the federal arsenal at Harpers Ferry in 1859 by abolitionist John Brown, who hoped to spark a slave revolt, was put down by Colonel Robert E. Lee of the U.S. Army. When the first seven states seceded from the Union after the election of Abraham Lincoln in 1860, Virginia refrained from action. It did not leave the Union until April, 1861, after Lincoln had called up volunteers to suppress the rebellion. When Richmond, less than a hundred miles from Washington, D.C., was named capital of the Confederacy, it ensured that the major battles of the Civil War would be fought in Virginia.

Colonial-era carriage rolling through Williamsburg, which was rebuilt to appear as it did in colonial times, when it was the capital of Virginia. (Virginia Tourism Corporation)

Over the next four years, Robert E. Lee and the Confederate Army of Northern Virginia repulsed repeated attacks by federal forces. Aided by generals such as "Jeb" Stuart and "Stonewall" Jackson, Lee defeated Union forces that greatly outnumbered his own. In his classic 1863 victory at Chancellorsville, however, Lee lost his best lieutenant when Stonewall Jackson was killed by his own troops, and later that summer Lee and his army were defeated at Gettysburg. During the bloody campaigns of 1864 Union general Ulysses S. Grant wore down Lee's troops and brought about the Confederate surrender at Appomattox Courthouse in April, 1865, effectively ending the Civil War.

A Modern State. During the Civil War Virginia had lost the western part of its territory when counties beyond the mountains loyal to the Union formed a new state, West Virginia, which entered the Union in 1863. Following the Civil War, Virginia went through the harsh period of Reconstruction imposed on the other states of the defeated Confederacy. During this time, Robert E. Lee lost his U.S. citizenship and Jefferson Davis was imprisoned at Fort Monroe on Chesapeake Bay. Virginia was readmitted to the Union on January 26, 1870.

Prior to the war, Virginia had been an industrial and manufacturing leader in the South. Its Tredegar Ironworks in Richmond, for example, was the Confederacy's most important supplier of metal and weapons. However, following the devastation brought by the war, Virginia reverted to a primarily agricultural economy, based largely on crops such as tobacco, cotton, peanuts, and forestry products. It was not until the early years of the twentieth century that the state began to recover its industrial and manufacturing capabilities. By the middle of the century, thanks in large part to the stimulus of production during World War II, these again had become important aspects of the state's economic base.

During the 1970's and 1980's Virginia, in cooperation with Maryland and other neighboring states, made a concentrated effort to clean up and restore Chesapeake Bay, whose environment had

A natural arch in the Blue Ridge Mountains. (PhotoDisc)

been severely damaged by decades of neglect and pollution. More than one hundred rivers flow into the bay, some of them originating as far away as New York and West Virginia but many of them rising in Virginia itself. Excess nutrients from agricultural fertilizer and organic chemicals have been two of the major elements damaging conditions in the bay. However, by 1992 efforts at environmental stewardship had reached the point where more than three-quarters of the bay (78 percent) was reported as being in "excellent" condition. This was good news for Virginia's seafood industry, in particular for the fishers who harvest world-famous Virginia oysters and blue crabs.

Fishing is indeed important to the state, but the modern Virginia economy is a diverse one. Agriculture, much of it located in the fertile Shenandoah Valley and in the southwestern portion of the state, remains a mainstay, with tobacco, corn and other grains as significant crops. Shipbuilding and ship repair remain important along the coast, especially in the Hampton-Norfolk-Portsmouth area, which also is the site of a major U.S. naval base. Manufacturing, including electronic equipment and other technologically sophisticated products, is important; Virginia is one of the nation's major producers of synthetic fibers. In northern Virginia many residents are employed by the federal government. Because of the state's great natural beauty and multitude of historical sites, Virginia's tourism industry is a key part of its economy. This economic diversity means that the state retains a position it has long held in its history—that of being one of the leading states in the nation.

Michael Witkoski

Virginia Time Line

1500's	Iroquois Indians flourish in the south and Algonquians in the north.
1606	King James I of England charters company to colonize Virginia.
May 13, 1607	Jamestown is founded; John Smith becomes leader of colony.
1612	John Rolfe begins cultivation of tobacco.
1619	Virginia creates House of Burgesses, the first representative assembly in New World.
1619	First black indentured servants arrive.
1622	War with Native Americans results in death of many colonists.
1624	Virginia Company's charter is revoked.
1635	First free school is established in Virginia.
1661	Virginia legalizes slavery.
1693	College of William and Mary is chartered at Williamsburg.
1699	Williamsburg becomes capital, replacing Jamestown.
1716	First theater in United States is built at Williamsburg.
1776	Virginia declares its independence from Great Britain.
1779	Richmond is named state capital.
Oct. 19, 1781	Lord Cornwallis surrenders to George Washington at Yorktown, effectively ending American Revolution.
1784	Virginia cedes its northwestern lands to United States.
June 26, 1788	Virginia ratifies U.S. Constitution, becoming tenth state to enter the Union.
Apr. 30, 1789	Virginia native George Washington becomes first president of United States.
1801	Thomas Jefferson becomes president of the United States; John Marshall becomes chief justice of the United States.
1819	Thomas Jefferson founds University of Virginia in Charlottesville.
1831	Nat Turner's slave rebellion suppressed.
Oct. 16, 1859	John Brown seizes arsenal at Harpers Ferry; later is captured, tried, and hanged for treason.

Apr. 17, 1861	Virginia secedes from Union.
July 21, 1861	Union army is routed at Bull Run (Manassas) in first major battle of the Civil War.
June 20, 1863	West Virginia becomes separate state.
Apr. 9, 1865	General Robert E. Lee surrenders to General Ulysses S. Grant at Appomattox Courthouse, ending Civil War.
Jan. 26, 1870	Virginia is readmitted to the Union.
1908	Staunton becomes first city in United States with a city-manager form of government.
1926	John D. Rockefeller, Jr., oil tycoon, restores colonial Williamsburg.
1964	Chesapeake Bay Bridge-Tunnel is completed.
1966	U.S. Supreme Court rules Virginia's poll tax unconstitutional, outlawing the tax in all states.
1970	New state constitution is adopted.
1985	Hurricane Juan brings devastating floods.
1990	Virginia's Douglas Wilder becomes first African American governor elected in the United States.
1992	Seventy-eight percent of Chesapeake Bay is in excellent environmental condition.

Notes for Further Study

Published Sources. Good history books on Virginia include Chiles Larson's *Virginia's Past Today* (1998), which examines the legacy and meaning of Virginia's historic past; Lovis Rubin's *Virginia: A History* (1984), a solid history with excellent discussions of colonial period, the Civil War and Reconstruction, and economic and cultural developments following 1900; and *The Edge of the South: Life in Nineteenth-Century Virginia* (1991), edited by Edward Ayers and John C. Willis, which provides a fascinating glimpse of Virginia during the period from the Revolution to the Civil War. The period between Reconstruction and the Civil Rights era is discussed in Parke Rouse's *We Happy WASPS: Virginia in the Days of Jim Crow and Harry Byrd* (1996).

Virginia is a state defined by the famous men and women who lived there. Lyon G. Tyler's *Encyclopedia of Virginia Biography* (1998) is an excellent source of information about that subject. *Virginia History and Government: 1850 to the Present* (1986), by Daniel Fleming, Paul Slayton, and Edgar Toppin, is a valuable survey of Virginia during some of its most turbulent and decisive periods.

Web Resources. Because of its many resources for history, tourism, industry, and agriculture, Virginia has a constantly expanding presence on the World Wide Web. An excellent place to begin is the official site, Virginia! Welcome to the Commonwealth (http://www.state.va .us), which offers a wealth of information and provides links to many other sites. Those interested in Virginia's history, including its rich heritage of colonial and Civil War materials, should consult the State Archival Resources (http://www.scv.org). Another site worth visiting for students who wish to learn about practically any aspect of Virginia life, history, and culture is The Library of Virginia (http://leo.usla.edu/lva). Virginia has long been recognized as one of the most naturally beautiful and varied of the southeastern states, and this aspect of the state is well presented on the Virginia Natural Heritage Program Homepage (http://www.state.va.us/~dcr/vaher.html).

Although designed primarily for high school students, the Thomas Jefferson High School Educational Links Page (http://www.mother.richmond.K12.va.us/schools/jefferson/various.html) is a valuable resource for college students, adults, and anyone in general who has an interest in Virginia and wishes to learn more about the state. The site is especially good at providing information about other sources of information. Finally, Virginia's leadership role, which began in colonial times, is aptly represented in a site that examines the entire South. Resources for Southern Culture (http://www .wsrv.clas.virginia.edu/~abhgh/sovesrc.html) helps explain what makes Virginia unique and how it has contributed to the development of both a region and a nation.

Counties

County	Sq. miles	1996 pop.
Accomack	454.6	32,065
Albemarle	722.8	74,189
Alleghany	445.9	12,586
Amelia	356.8	9,912
Amherst	475.3	30,065
Appomattox	333.7	12,879
Arlington	25.9	175,334
Augusta	971.7	59,515
Bath	531.9	4,959
Bedford	754.8	52,768
Bland	358.7	6,834
Botetourt	542.7	27,813
Brunswick	566.2	16,458
Buchanan	503.9	30,033
Buckingham	580.9	14,388
Campbell	504.5	48,946
Caroline	532.6	21,399
Carroll	476.5	27,703
Charles City	182.5	6,887
Charlotte	475.0	12,218
Chesterfield	425.7	242,686
Clarke	176.6	12,543
Craig	330.1	4,839
Culpeper	381.2	31,981
Cumberland	298.5	7,845
Dickenson	332.7	17,381
Dinwiddie	503.8	22,961
Essex	257.8	9,373
Fairfax	395.6	902,492
Fauquier	650.3	51,765
Floyd	381.5	12,832
Fluvanna	287.4	16,887
Franklin	692.1	43,574
Frederick	414.6	52,459

County	Sq. miles	1996 pop.
Giles	357.9	16,349
Gloucester	216.6	33,659
Goochland	284.5	16,586
Grayson	442.7	16,420
Greene	156.6	12,972
Greensville	295.5	10,954
Halifax	813.8	37,581
Hanover	472.8	76,781
Henrico	238.1	232,810
Henry	382.4	56,326
Highland	415.9	2,543
Isle of Wight	315.9	28,391
James City	142.9	41,370
King and Queen	316.3	6,390
King George	180.0	16,379
King William	275.4	12,333
Lancaster	133.2	11,418
Lee	437.2	24,257
Loudoun	519.9	123,333
Louisa	497.5	23,321
Lunenburg	431.8	11,104
Madison	321.5	12,405
Mathews	85.7	8,967
Mecklenburg	624.0	30,946
Middlesex	130.3	9,396
Montgomery	388.2	75,443
Nelson	472.4	13,529
New Kent	209.8	12,047
Northampton	207.4	12,908
Northumberland	192.3	11,226
Nottoway	314.7	15,230
Orange	341.7	24,512
Page	311.1	22,891
Patrick	483.2	18,075

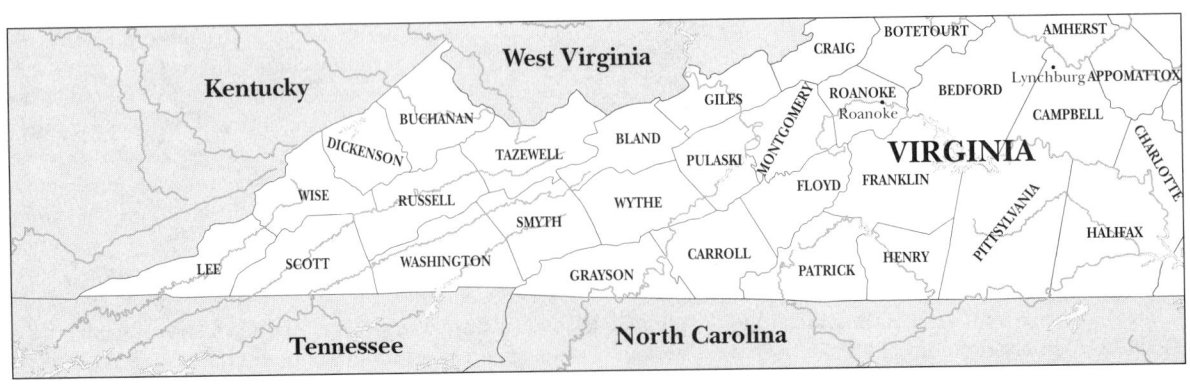

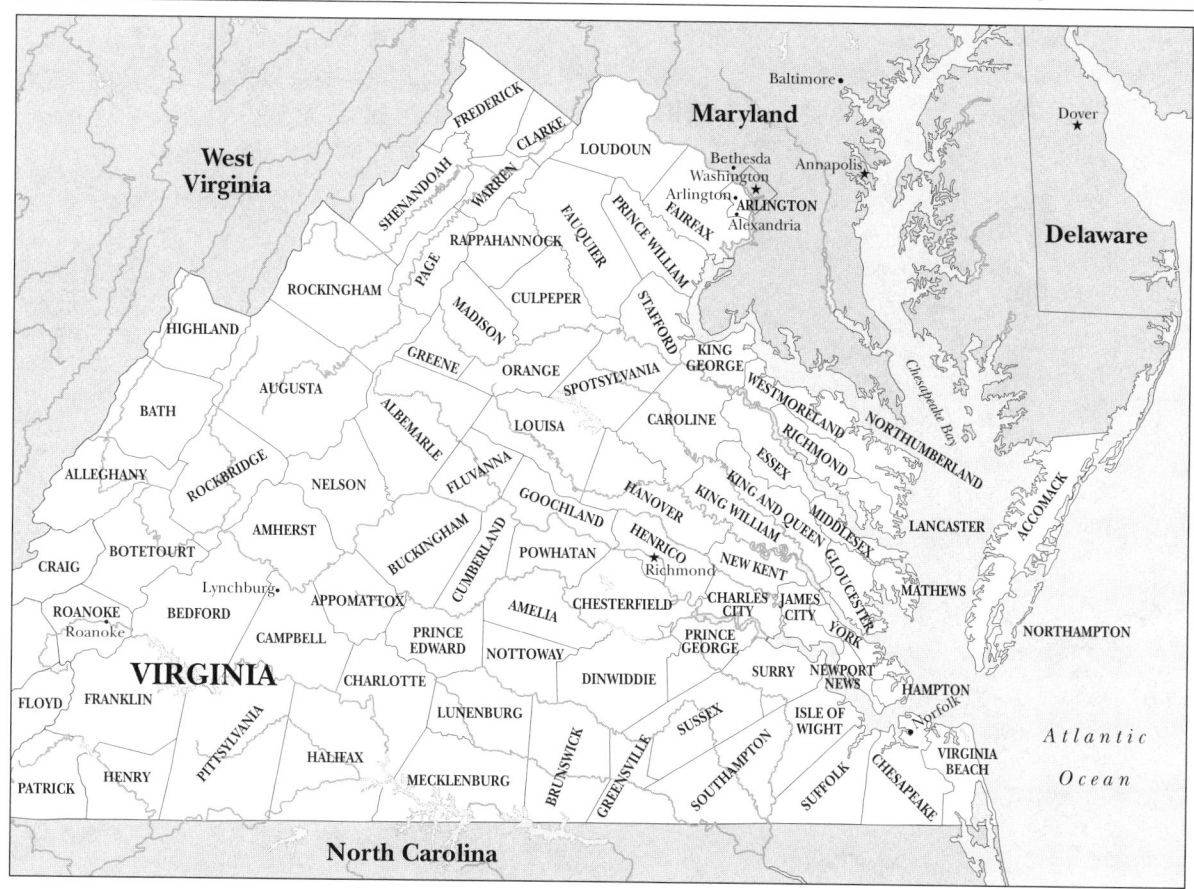

County	Sq. miles	1996 pop.	County	Sq. miles	1996 pop.
Pittsylvania	970.9	55,774	Sussex	490.8	10,088
Powhatan	261.3	19,794	Tazewell	519.8	47,070
Prince Edward	352.8	18,751	Warren	213.7	29,879
Prince George	265.6	28,401	Washington	564.2	48,498
Prince William	338.4	249,278	Westmoreland	229.2	16,549
Pulaski	320.6	34,290	Wise	403.4	39,494
Rappahannock	266.6	7,206	Wythe	463.3	26,357
Richmond	191.5	8,496	York	105.6	55,010
Roanoke	250.7	81,585			
Rockbridge	599.7	19,006			
Rockingham	851.2	62,432			
Russell	474.7	29,134			
Scott	536.6	22,949			
Shenandoah	512.2	33,612			
Smyth	452.1	33,076			
Southampton	600.3	17,682			
Spotsylvania	400.9	74,106			
Stafford	270.0	82,488			
Surry	279.1	6,406			

Virginia has 39 independent cities: Alexandria, Bristol, Buena Vista, Charlottesville, Chesapeake, Clifton Forge, Colonial Heights, Covington, Danville, Emporia, Fairfax, Falls Church, Franklin, Fredericksburg, Galax, Hampton, Harrisonburg, Hopewell, Lexington, Lynchburg, Manassas, Manassas Park, Martinsville, Newport News, Norfolk, Norton, Petersburg, Poquoson, Portsmouth, Radford, Richmond, Roanoke, Salem, South Boston, Staunton, Suffolk, Virginia Beach, Waynesboro, and Williamsburg.

Source: U.S. Census Bureau; National Association of Counties.

Cities

With 10,000 or more residents

Rank	City	Population
1	Virginia Beach	432,380
2	Norfolk	215,215
3	Chesapeake	199,564
4	Richmond	194,173
5	Newport News	178,615
6	Arlington	177,275
7	Hampton	136,968
8	Alexandria	118,300
9	Portsmouth	98,936
10	Roanoke	93,749
11	Lynchburg	65,473
12	Suffolk	62,703
13	Danville	50,868
14	Charlottesville	38,223
15	Manassas	35,336
16	Petersburg	34,724
17	Blacksburg	33,651
18	Harrisonburg	33,434
19	Leesburg	27,009
20	Salem	24,679

Rank	City	Population
21	Staunton	23,346
22	Winchester	22,659
23	Hopewell	22,529
24	Fredericksburg	21,686
25	Fairfax	20,697
26	Herndon	19,197
27	Waynesboro	18,561
28	Bristol	17,486
29	Colonial Heights	16,955
30	Vienna	16,867
31	Christiansburg	16,153
32	Radford	15,734
33	Martinsville	15,668
34	Front Royal	13,464
35	Williamsburg	11,971
36	Poquoson	11,455
37	Falls Church	10,042

Population figures are estimated for mid-1998.
Source: U.S. Bureau of the Census.

Index to Tables

NA = Reliable data are not available.

DEMOGRAPHICS

Resident state and national populations, 1970-1997

Population figures given in thousands

	State pop.	U.S. pop.	Share	Rank
1970	4,651	203,302	2.3%	14
1980	5,347	226,546	2.4%	14
1985	5,715	237,924	2.4%	13
1990	6,189	248,765	2.5%	12
1995	6,601	262,761	2.5%	12
1997	6,734	267,636	2.5%	12

Source: U.S. Bureau of the Census.

Resident population by age, 1997

Age group	Total population
Under 5 years	453,000
5 to 17 years	1,192,000
18 to 24 years	647,000
25 to 34 years	1,095,000
35 to 44 years	1,159,000
45 to 54 years	888,000
55 to 64 years	544,000
65 to 74 years	425,000
75 to 84 years	253,000
85 years and over	78,000
Portion of residents 65 and older	11.2%
National average	12.7%

Population figures are rounded to nearest thousand persons;
figures include armed forces personnel stationed in state.
Source: U.S. Bureau of the Census.

Resident population by race, Hispanic origin, 1997

	State pop.	Share	U.S.
All residents	6,734,000	100.0%	100.0%
Hispanic white	209,000	3.1%	10.0%
non-Hispanic white	4,930,000	73.2%	72.7%
African American	1,344,000	20.0%	12.7%
Native American	18,000	0.3%	0.9%
Asian, Pacific Islander	233,000	3.5%	3.8%

Source: U.S. Bureau of the Census.

Projections of state population, 2000-2025

	Model A Uses interstate migration observed from 1975-1994	Model B Uses Bureau of Economic Analysis employment projections
Year	Population	Population
2000	6,997,000	6,965,000
2005	7,324,000	7,234,000
2010	7,627,000	7,474,000
2015	7,921,000	7,708,000
2020	8,204,000	7,939,000
2025	8,466,000	8,165,000

All population projections, including those for 2000, were calculated in 1997.

Source: U.S. Bureau of the Census, Population Paper Listings PPL-47.

VITAL STATISTICS

Average lifetime in years by race, 1989-1991

	State	U.S.	Rank
All residents	75.22	75.37	31
White residents	76.34	76.13	24
Black residents	70.05	69.16	11

Ranks are from longest-lived to least longest-lived. Ranks exclude Alaska, for which reliable data are not available. Rank for black residents is based on the 32 states for which reliable data are available.

Source: U.S. National Center for Health Statistics.

Infant mortality rates, 1980 and 1995

	State	U.S.
All residents		
1980	13.6	12.6
1995	7.8	7.6
White residents		
1980	11.9	11.0
1995	5.7	6.3
Black residents		
1980	19.8	21.4
1995	15.3	15.1

Figures represent deaths per 1,000 live births of resident infants under 1 year old, exclusive of fetal deaths; all-residents figures include other races not listed separately.
Source: U.S. National Center for Health Statistics.

Marriages and divorces

Marriages in 1996.	65,400
Rate per 1,000 population, 1995	10.3
U.S. rate, 1995	8.9
Rank among all states	10
Divorces in 1996	28,600
Rate per 1,000 population, 1995	4.4
U.S. rate, 1995	4.4
Rank among all states	26

Rank is from highest to lowest in country.
Source: U.S. National Center for Health Statistics.

Death rates by leading causes, 1995
Deaths per 100,000 resident population

Cause	State	U.S.
Heart disease	240.2	280.7
Cancer	190.4	204.9
Cerebrovascular diseases	57.5	60.1
Accidents and adverse effects	33.4	35.5
Motor vehicle accidents	13.9	16.5
Chronic obstructive pulmonary diseases	34.1	39.2
Diabetes mellitus	17.6	22.6
HIV	12.6	NA
Suicide	12.5	11.9
Homicide	7.8	8.7
All causes	799.9	880.0
Rank in overall death rate among states		40

Figures exclude nonresidents who die in state. Causes of death follow International Classification of Diseases. Rank is from highest to lowest in country.
Source: U.S. National Center for Health Statistics.

ECONOMY

Gross state product, 1990-1996
In current dollars

	State product	Increase
1990	$148.1 billion	
1993	$170.0 billion	
1994	$178.8 billion	5.18%
1995	$187.0 billion	4.59%
1996	$197.8 billion	5.78%

Source: U.S. Bureau of Economic Analysis; *Survey of Current Business,* June, 1998.

Gross state product by industry, 1996
In billions

Farms, forestry, fisheries	$1.7
Construction	7.5
Manufacturing	30.3
Transportation, public utilities	16.1
Wholesale trade	10.6
Retail trade	15.7
Finance, insurance, real estate	31.2
Services	34.7
Government	34.3
State total	$183.2
Total U.S.	$6,923.8
State share	2.65%
Rank among states	13

Total figures include mining, not listed separately.

Source: U.S. Bureau of Economic Analysis; *Survey of Current Business,* June, 1998.

Personal income per capita, 1990 and 1997
In current dollars

	1990	1997
Per capita income	$20,054	$26,438
U.S. average	$19,188	$25,598
Rank among states	13	14

1997 data are preliminary.

Source: U.S. Bureau of Economic Analysis; *Survey of Current Business,* May, 1998.

Energy consumption, 1995
In trillions of British thermal units (BTU)

End-use sectors

Residential	489.8
Commercial	431.6
Industrial	530.3
Transportation	604.3

Sources of energy

Petroleum	771.9
Natural gas	254.9
Coal	342.2
Hydroelectric power	2.3
Nuclear electric power	267.9
Total state per capita consumption	310.8
Total U.S. per capita consumption	344.4
Rank among states	38
Total state energy consumption	2,056.0
Total U.S. energy consumption	90,547.4
State share of U.S. total	2.27%
Rank among states	15

Total figures include items not listed separately.

Source: U.S. Energy Information Administration; *State Energy Data Report.*

Nonfarm employment by sectors, 1997

Total	3,231,000
Construction	186,000
Manufacturing	404,000
Transportation, public utilities	168,000
Wholesale trade, retail trade	724,000
Finance, insurance, real estate	168,000
Services	974,000
Government	596,000

Figures are rounded to nearest thousand persons. Total includes mining, not listed separately.

Source: U.S. Bureau of Labor Statistics; *Employment and Earnings,* monthly.

Foreign exports, 1990-1997
In millions of dollars

Year	State	U.S.	State share
1990	9,333	394,045	2.37%
1996	12,215	624,767	1.96%
1997	12,755	688,896	1.85%

Source: U.S. Bureau of the Census; *U.S. Merchandise Trade,* series FT 900.

LAND USE

Federally owned land, 1996

	State	U.S.	State share
Total acres	25,496,000	2,271,343,000	1.12%
Federally owned	2,279,000	563,129,000	0.40%
Federal share	8.9%	24.8%	—

Areas are rounded to nearest thousand acres. Figures for federally owned land do not include trust properties.
Source: U.S. General Services Administration; *Inventory Report on Real Property Owned by the United States Throughout the World*, annual.

Land use, 1992
In acres, rounded to nearest thousand

Total surface area	26,091,000
Federal land	2,389,000
Total nonfederal	22,774,000
Developed	2,183,000
Total rural	20,591,000
Cropland	2,901,000
Pasture land	3,444,000
Range land	0
Forest land	13,539,000
Minor cover/use	707,000

Total surface area figures include water area not shown separately.
Source: U.S. Dept. of Agriculture; Soil Conservation Service; Iowa State University, Statistical Laboratory; *Summary Report, 1992 National Resources Inventory.*

Farms and crop acreage, 1997

	State	U.S.	Share	Rank
Farms (thousands)	47	2,058	2.28%	18
Acres (millions)	9	968	0.93%	32
Acres per farm	181	471	—	40
Acres planted	2,926	334,139	0.88%	29
Acres harvested	2,774	319,894	0.87%	29
Farm value (mill.)	$829	$108,805	0.76%	11

Numbers of farms are rounded to nearest thousand.
Source: U.S. Dept. of Agriculture; National Agricultural Statistics Service.

GOVERNMENT AND FINANCE

Units of local government, 1997

	State	Total U.S.	Rank
All local governments	483	87,453	43
Counties	95	3,043	9
Municipalities	231	19,372	33
Townships	0	16,629	—
School districts	1	13,726	46
Special districts	156	34,683	44

County ranks are based on the 48 states with county governments; township ranks are based on the 20 states with township governments; school district ranks are based on the 46 states with such districts.
Source: U.S. Bureau of the Census; *1997 Census of Governments, Government Organization*, Series GC97(1).

State government revenue, 1996

Total revenue	$20,072 mill.
General revenue	16,617 mill.
Per capita	2,493
U.S. per capita average	2,910
Rank among states	42
Intergovernmental revenue	
Total	$3,515 mill.
From federal government	3,377 mill.
From local government	138 mill.
Charges and Miscellaneous	
Total	$4,201 mill.
Current charges	2,483 mill.
Misc. general revenue	1,719 mill.
Taxes	
Total	$8,900 mill.
General sales	1,996 mill.
Selective sales	1,593 mill.
License taxes	419 mill.
Individual income	4,301 mill.
Corporate income	363 mill.
Other	229 mill.
Insurance trust revenue	3,206 mill.

Total revenue figures include items not listed separately.
Source: U.S. Bureau of the Census.

State government expenditures, 1996

General expenditures

Intergovernmental	$4,463 mill.
Direct expenditures	11,844 mill.
Total	16,307 mill.

Selected direct expenditures

Education	$6,430 mill.
Public welfare	2,916 mill.
Health, hospital	1,613 mill.
Highways	2,011 mill.
Police	313 mill.
Corrections	809 mill.
Natural resources	138 mill.
Parks and recreation	69 mill.
Government administration	678 mill.
Interest on debt	550 mill.

Other

State per capita expenditures	$2,446
U.S. per capita average	2,854
Rank among states	43
Total state expenditures	17,717 mill.
Total U.S. expenditures	859,959 mill.

Totals include items not listed separately.
Source: U.S. Bureau of the Census.

POLITICS

Governors since statehood

D = Democrat; R = Republican; O = other;
(r) resigned; (d) died in office; (i) removed from office

Patrick Henry	1776-1779
Thomas Jefferson	1779-1781
William Fleming	1781
Thomas Nelson	1781
Benjamin Harrison III	1781-1784
Patrick Henry	1784-1786
Edmund J. Randolph	1786-1788
Beverly Randolph	1788-1791
Henry Lee	1791-1794
Robert Brooke	1794-1796
James Wood (O)	1796-1799
James Monroe (O)	1799-1802
John Page (O)	1802-1805
William H. Cabell (O)	1805-1808
John Tyler III (O)	(r) 1808-1811
James Monroe (O)	(r) 1811
George W. Smith (O)	(d) 1811
Peyton Randolph (O)	1811-1812
James Barbour (O)	1812-1814
Wilson C. Nicholas (O)	1814-1816
James P. Preston (O)	1816-1819
Thomas Mann Randolph (O)	1819-1822
James Pleasants, Jr. (O)	1822-1825
John Tyler IV (O)	(r) 1825-1827
William B. Giles (D)	1827-1830
John Floyd (D)	1830-1834
Littleton W. Tazewell (D)	(r) 1834-1836
Wyndham Robertson (D)	1836-1837
David Campbell (D)	1837-1840
Thomas W. Gilmer (O)	(r) 1840-1841
James M. Patton (O)	1841
John Rutherford (O)	1841-1842
John M. Gregory (O)	1842-1843
James McDowell (O)	1843-1846
William Smith (D)	1846-1849
John B. Floyd (D)	1849-1852
Joseph Johnson (D)	1852-1856
Henry A. Wise (D)	1856-1860
John Letcher (D)	1860-1864
William Smith (D)	(i) 1864-1865
Francis H. Pierpoint (D)	(i) 1865-1868
Henry H. Wells	(i) 1868-1869
Gilbert C. Walker	1869-1874
James L. Kemper (D)	1874-1878
Frederick W. M. Holliday (D)	1878-1882
William E. Cameron (O)	1882-1886
Fitzhugh Lee (D)	1886-1890
Philip W. McKinney (D)	1890-1894
Charles T. O'Ferrall (D)	1894-1898
James Hoge Tyler (D)	1898-1902
Andrew J. Montague (D)	1902-1906
Claude A. Swanson (D)	1906-1910
William H. Mann (D)	1910-1914
Henry C. Stuart (D)	1914-1918
Westmoreland Davis (D)	1918-1922
Elbert Lee Trinkle (D)	1922-1926
Harry F. Byrd (D)	1926-1930
John G. Pollard (D)	1930-1934
George C. Perry (D)	1934-1938
James H. Price (D)	1938-1942
Colgate W. Darden, Jr. (D)	1942-1946
William M. Tuck (D)	1946-1950
John S. Battle (D)	1950-1954
Thomas B. Stanley (D)	1954-1958
James Lindsay Almond, Jr. (D)	1958-1962
Albertis S. Harrison, Jr. (D)	1962-1966
Mills E. Godwin, Jr. (D)	1966-1970
Abner Linwood Holton, Jr. (R)	1970-1974
Mills E. Godwin, Jr. (R)	1974-1978
John N. Dalton (R)	1978-1982
Charles S. Robb (D)	1982-1986
Gerald L. Baliles (D)	1986-1990
L. Douglas Wilder (D)	1990-1994
George F. Allen (R)	1994-1998
James S. Gilmore III (R)	1998-

Composition of state legislature, 1990-1998

	Democrats	Republicans
State House (99 seats)		
1990	58	41
1992	52	47
1994	52	47
1996	53	46
1998	50	49
State Senate (40 seats)		
1990	22	18
1992	22	18
1994	22	18
1996	20	20
1998	19	21

Figures for total seats may include independents and minor party members.

Source: Council of State Governments; *State Elective Officials and the Legislatures.*

Composition of congressional delegations, 1989-1999

	Dem	Rep	Total
House of Representatives			
101st Congress, 1989			
State delegates	5	5	10
Total U.S.	259	174	433
102d Congress, 1991			
State delegates	6	4	10
Total U.S.	267	167	434
103d Congress, 1993			
State delegates	7	4	11
Total U.S.	258	176	434
104th Congress, 1995			
State delegates	6	5	11
Total U.S.	197	236	433
105th Congress, 1997			
State delegates	6	5	11
Total U.S.	206	228	434
106th Congress, 1999			
State delegates	6	5	11
Total U.S.	211	222	433

	Dem	Rep	Total
Senate			
101st Congress, 1989			
State delegates	1	1	2
Total U.S.	55	45	100
102d Congress, 1991			
State delegates	1	1	2
Total U.S.	56	44	100
103d Congress, 1993			
State delegates	1	1	2
Total U.S.	57	43	100
104th Congress, 1995			
State delegates	1	1	2
Total U.S.	46	53	99
105th Congress, 1997			
State delegates	1	1	2
Total U.S.	45	55	100
106th Congress, 1999			
State delegates	1	1	2
Total U.S.	45	54	99

Figures are for starts of first sessions. Figure for U.S. Representatives for 101st Congress does not include Alabama and Indiana, which had vacancies. Figures for total U.S. Representatives for 102d, 103d, and 106th Congresses do not include Vermont, which had 1 Independent-Socialist. Figure for U.S. Representatives for 104th Congress does not include Vermont, which had 1 Independent-Socialist, and California, which had 1 vacancy. Figure for U.S. Representatives for 105th Congress does not include New York, which had 1 vacancy. Figure for U.S. Senators for 104th Congress does not include Oregon, which had 1 vacancy. Figure for U.S. Senators for 106th Congress does not include New Hampshire, which had 1 Independent.

Source: U.S. Congress; *Congressional Directory,* biennial.

Voter participation in presidential elections, 1992 and 1996

	1992	1996
State voting age pop.	4,855,000	5,089,000
Total U.S. voting age pop.	189,524,000	196,509,000
State share of U.S. total	2.6%	2.6%
Rank among states	12	12
Percent of state casting vote	52.7	49.9
Percent of U.S. total voting	55.1	49.0
Rank among states	37	25

Source: U.S. Bureau of the Census.

HEALTH AND MEDICAL CARE

Medicare, 1997

	Recipients	Payments
State	847,000	$3,636 mill.
Total U.S.	37,514,000	$206,064 mill.
State share	2.26%	1.76%
Rank among states	13	17

Recipient figures are rounded to nearest thousand persons.
Ranks are from highest to lowest.
Source: U.S. Health Care Financing Administration.

Medicaid, 1996

	Recipients	Payments
State	623,000	$1,776 mill.
Total U.S.	35,028,000	$121,419 mill.
State share	1.78%	1.46%
Rank among states	17	22

Recipient figures are rounded to nearest thousand persons.
Payment figures for fiscal year reflect federal and state
contribution payments. Ranks are from highest to lowest.
Source: U.S. Health Care Financing Administration.

Health insurance coverage, 1996

	State	U.S.
Total persons covered	5,680,000	225,070,000
Total persons not covered	811,000	41,716,000
Part not covered	12.5%	15.6%
Rank among states	29	—
Children not covered	160,000	10,554,000
Part not covered	10.9%	14.8%
Rank among states	31	—

Ranks are from most to fewest uninsured. Population figures
are rounded to nearest thousand persons.
Source: U.S. Bureau of the Census.

AIDS, syphilis, tuberculosis, and measles cases, 1997

Cases	U.S.	State	Share
AIDS	58,443	1,175	2.01%
Syphilis	8,550	236	2.76%
Tuberculosis	18,534	349	1.88%
Measles	148,000	1,000	0.68%

Measles figures are rounded to nearest thousand cases.
Source: U.S. Centers for Disease Control and Prevention.

HOUSING

Homeownership rates, 1985-1997

	1985	1990	1997
State	68.5%	69.8%	68.4%
Total U.S.	63.9%	63.9%	65.7%
Rank among states	20	10	24

Source: U.S. Bureau of the Census.

Home sales, 1990 and 1997
In thousands of units

Existing home sales	1990	1997	Change
State sales	96.9	98.5	1.6
Total U.S. sales	3,560	4,730	1,170
State share of U.S. total	2.72%	2.08%	-0.64%
Rank among states	11	17	—

Source: National Association of Realtors; *Real Estate Outlook: Market Trends and Insights.*

EDUCATION

Public school enrollment, 1995

State K-8 enrollment	788,000
Total U.S. K-8 enrollment	32,341,000
State share of total U.S..	2.44%
State 9-12 enrollment	292,000
Total U.S. 9-12 enrollment	12,500,000
State share of U.S. total	2.34%
State public school enroll. rate.	93.4%
Overall U.S. rate.	91.6%
Rank among states.	19

Enrollment figures (which include unclassified students) are rounded to nearest thousand pupils in fall term; kindergarten (K)-8 grade figures include some prekindergarten students. Enrollment rate is based on percentage of persons 5-17 years old. Rank is from highest to lowest.

Source: U.S. National Center for Education Statistics.

Public college finances, 1996

State FTE enrollment	219,000
Total U.S. FTE enrollment	8,268,800
State share of total U.S..	2.65%
Rank among states.	10
State and local appropriations	$818,100,000
Total U.S. state and local appropriations.	$39,699 mill.
State share of total U.S..	2.06%
Rank among states.	15
State net tuition revenues.	$664,800,000
Total U.S. net tuition	$18,348,100,000
State share of total U.S..	3.62%
Rank among states	7

FTE=Full-time equivalent; credit and noncredit enrollment including summer session in academic year ending in 1996.

Enrollments are rounded to nearest thousand students. Net tuition revenues exclude appropriation to students attending in-state public institutions. Rankings are from highest shares to lowest.

Source: Research Associates of Washington.

TRANSPORTATION AND TRAVEL

Highway mileage, 1996

Interstate	1,107
Other arterial.	8,304
Collector roads	16,157
Local roads	45,750
Urban roads.	18,530
Rural roads	50,854
Total state	69,384
U.S. total	3,933,985
State share	1.8%
Rank among states.	30

Source: U.S. Federal Highway Administration.

Motor vehicle registrations and driver licenses, 1996
In thousands

Vehicle registrations	State	U.S.	Share	Rank
Autos, trucks, buses	5,576	206,365	2.70%	12
Autos only	3,603	128,439	2.81%	11
Motorcycles	57	3,832	1.49%	23
Driver licenses	4,692	179,539	2.61%	12

Figures do not include vehicles owned by military services.
Source: U.S. Federal Highway Administration; *Highway Statistics*; *Selected Highway Statistics and Charts.*

Domestic travel expenditures, 1995
Spending by U.S. residents on overnight trips and day trips of at least 100 miles

Total expenditures in state	$9,996 mill.
Total expenditures in U.S..	$360,314 mill.
State share of total U.S..	2.77%
Rank among states.	10

Source: Travel Industry Association of America.

CRIME AND LAW ENFORCEMENT

State and local police officers, 1996

Local police	8,911
State police	1,662
Sheriffs	6,605
Total	18,448
Officers per 10,000 residents	28
U.S. average	25
Rank among states	7

Figures cover full-time sworn officers; totals include special police not shown separately.
Source: U.S. Bureau of Justice Statistics; *Census of State and Local Law Enforcement Agencies, 1996.*

Crime rates, 1996
Rates per 100,000 resident population

Violent crimes	State	U.S.
Total violent	341	634
Murder	7.5	7.4
Forcible rape	26.7	36.1
Robbery	123	202
Aggravated assault	185	388
Property crimes		
Total property	3,627	4,445
Burglary	588	943
Larceny/theft	2,760	2,976
Motor vehicle theft	279	526
Totals	3,968	5,079

Source: U.S. Federal Bureau of Investigation; *Crime in the United States,* annual.

State prison populations, 1980-1996

	State	U.S.	State share
1980	8,920	305,458	2.92%
1990	17,593	708,393	2.48%
1996	27,655	1,025,624	2.70%

Figures exclude prisoners in federal penitentiaries.
Source: U.S. Bureau of Justice Statistics.

Washington

Location: Northwest coast of continental United States

Area and rank: 66,582 square miles (172,447 square kilometers); 71,303 square miles (184,675 square kilometers) including water; twentieth largest state in area

Coastline: 157 miles (253 kilometers)

Shoreline: 3,026 miles (4,869 kilometers)

Population and rank: 5,610,362 (1997); fifteenth largest state in population

Capital: Olympia

State capitol building in Olympia. (State of Washington Tourism Development)

Largest city: Seattle (536,978 people in 1998)

Became territory: March 2, 1853

Entered Union and rank: November 11, 1889; forty-second state

Present constitution adopted: 1889

Counties: 39

State name: Washington was named for President George Washington

State nicknames: Evergreen State; Chinook State

Motto: *Al-Ki* (American Indian word meaning "by and by")

State flag: Dark green background with state seal

Highest point: Mount Rainier — 14,410 feet (4,392 meters)

Lowest point: Pacific Ocean — sea level

Highest recorded temperature: 118 degrees Fahrenheit (48 degrees Celsius) — Ice Harbor Dam, 1961

Lowest recorded temperature: −48 degrees Fahrenheit (−44 degrees Celsius) — Mazama and Winthrop, 1968

State song: "Washington, My Home"

State tree: Western hemlock

State flower: Coast rhododendron

State bird: Willow goldfinch

State fish: Steelhead trout

National parks: Mount Rainier, North Cascades, Olympic

Washington History

Like its southern neighbor Oregon, Washington is divided into two distinct geographical parts, a wet, forested western portion and a semi-arid east. Washington's forests made it one of the nation's great timber producers, while its dry eastern portion requires extensive irrigation for agricultural productivity. While it shares geographical features with Oregon and Idaho, making up the Pacific Northwest region, Washington has a social and political complexion with its own unique qualities. One reason is that unlike Oregon, Washington was not first settled by farmers.

After the earliest period, in which its white inhabitants were predominantly trappers, Washington's early history was dominated by extraction industries, such as gold mining and logging. Later, toward the end of the nineteenth century, large industry brought with it conflict between big business and big labor, which affected the state's social character. Later still, after the middle of the twentieth century, industries that prospered in the state on account of the Cold War left their own indelible imprint on the state's economy, society, and politics.

Early History. The early history of the area that became Washington was dominated by the struggle for control of the region by Great Britain, Russia, and Spain, followed by the United States. By 1775 Spain was sending expeditions up the Pacific coast, mainly to secure a buffer zone between Russian and British claims and its Mexican territory. Russia asserted claims far distant from Alaska,

Seattle, looking south toward Mount Rainier. The prominent Space Needle, at the left, was built for the 1962 world's fair. (State of Washington Tourism Development)

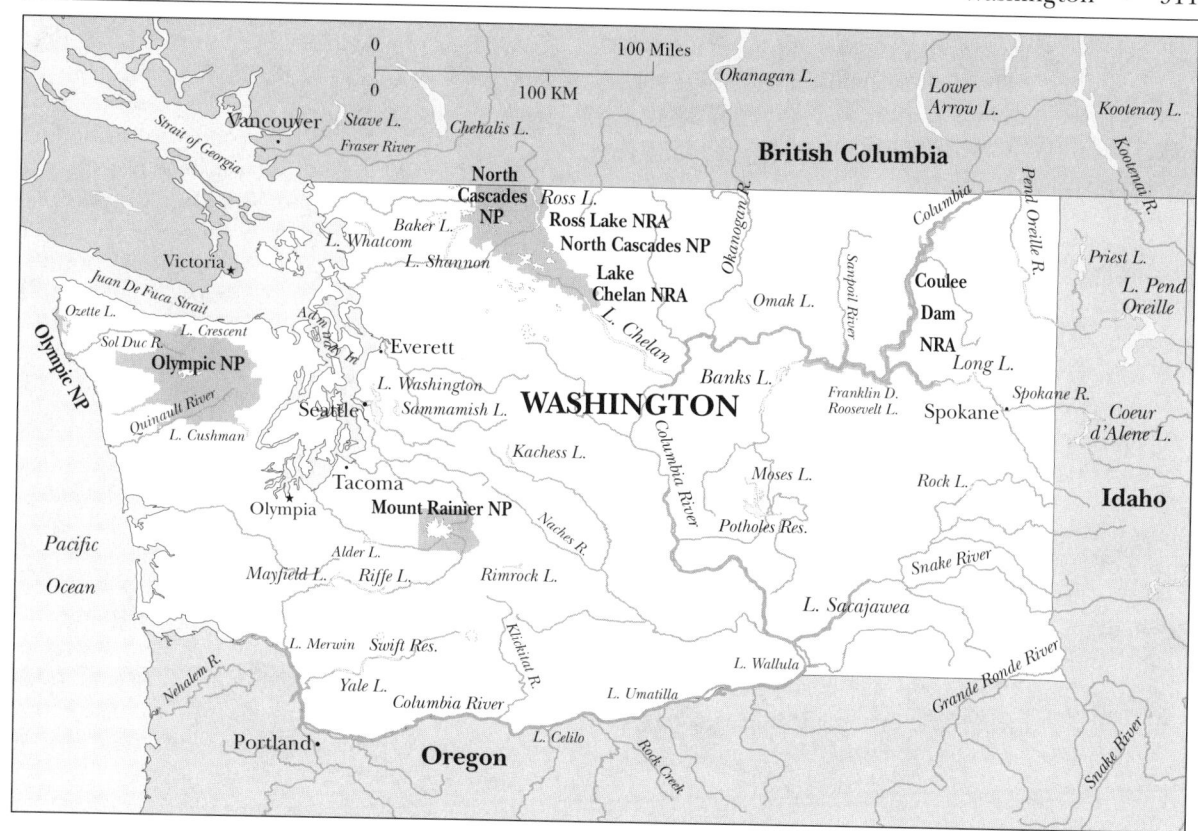

sending landing parties as far south as California. While Spain and Russia dropped out of the competition by the end of the eighteenth century, Britain opposed its former colonies, now a scrappy young republic. The Americans, for their part, strengthened their claims to the region when, after the 1803 Louisiana Purchase, the expedition of Meriwether Lewis and William Clark arrived and wintered by the Pacific at Fort Clatsop.

In 1792 the Americans sent Captain Robert Gray to the northwest, where he discovered the Columbia River and named it after his ship. In the same year, Britain sent an expedition led by George Vancouver to the region. Members of the expedition of British Captain James Cook had already discovered the value of sea otter pelts bought from American Indians and sold profitably in China. By 1818 the two nations agreed to share the region. The Pacific North West Company dominated the fur trade until 1821, when it merged with Hudson's Bay Company, which remained the most influential non-Indian power in the area until 1846.

Native American peoples occupied a key position in the fur trade, especially in the beginning, before white trappers appeared in any numbers and before Indian populations became depleted. Native Americans provided sea otter pelts and other furs to white traders in exchange for manufactured goods, especially those made of metal, unknown in Indian cultures. These included tools that added to the Native Americans' ability to produce goods for themselves. Indians benefited from material goods, but their contact with whites proved catastrophic, because they contracted smallpox and other diseases that decimated their numbers. It has been estimated that the population of Native American peoples on the northwest coast declined during the century following 1774 from about 200,000 to about 40,000, or some 80 percent. Moreover, by the 1820's sea otters were nearly extinct.

By 1810 a second phase of the fur trade began, increasingly dominated by Europeans and centered on beavers and similar mammals. This trade was focused on inland areas and required European trading companies to establish forts and interior avenues of transportation. News of the area finally took hold of the American imagination in the East and Midwest after the success of fur-trading companies illustrated the possibilities of internal development. The stage was set for the arrival of immigrants in large numbers.

The Anglo-American condominium begun in 1818 lasted into the 1840's. By then, however, the U.S. westward expansion, with its drive to possess the continent as its manifest destiny, brought hundreds, then thousands of American settlers to the region. In the early 1840's, Hudson's Bay Company, which was interested in commerce, not settlement, moved its base of operations northward, focusing on the area that became British Columbia. Although American nationalists sought lands north of the fifty-fourth parallel, the United States, negotiating in 1846 with far-stronger Britain, settled for the forty-eighth parallel as a boundary. Two years later Oregon Territory, including what became Washington, was established.

From Territory to State. After the establishment of Oregon Territory in 1848, the population north of the Columbia River grew rapidly. Accordingly, in 1853 the Territory of Washington was formed. A decade later, gold strikes in the eastern portion led to its breaking off to become separately organized as Idaho Territory. Except for adjustments in Puget Sound's San Juan Islands, Washington's boundaries were now fixed. Sentiment for statehood strengthened during the Civil War, and in 1867 territorial legislature urged Congress to admit a new state. Not until 1889, however, did Congress pass the required legislation for statehood, admitting Washington into the Union.

As it was growing toward statehood, Washington experienced an ugly social and moral pathology, in the form of anti-Chinese racism. When economic downturns arrived, labor unions made scapegoats of Chinese laborers, who arrived after 1840. Chinese were reviled for driving down wages, and serious incidents occurred, especially in the mid-1880's in Seattle, Tacoma, and other cities, when Chinese were driven out. As a result, the Chinese

Crater of Mount Saint Helens, viewed from the north, several years after its 1980 eruption. (PhotoDisc)

population in the Pacific Northwest dropped sharply.

If few Chinese could resist ill treatment, the same was not always true of the state's Native American peoples. Prophetic religious visions encouraging American Indians to live by their old customs were one form of resistance. Suing in the courts was another. Such attempts at peaceful resolution of disputes followed the armed conflicts that occurred, for example, between 1855 and 1859, when the influx of miners after gold strikes alarmed the Indians. Relations between settlers and Indians were complicated by the fact that there were different points of view not only among federal government, settlers, and the Indians, but within each group as well. Tribes or subtribal bands sometimes fought among themselves over policy toward white society.

Policy toward the American Indians reflected both idealism and self-interest, resulting in the reservation system. Reservations were designed both to separate tribal societies from the settlers and to "civilize" them, that is, to adapt them to the European ways, "detribalizing" and assimilating them to American society. Native American children were taken to boarding schools for this purpose. The treaty system that reflected this policy was unreliable, however, partly because the U.S. Senate frequently rejected treaties. Moreover, not all tribal members agreed with the treaties as negotiated, and discontent and confusion sometimes followed their signing. Treaties signed in 1854 and 1855 failed to prevent the conflicts of 1855-1858. Both wars and considerable crime broke out between American Indians and settlers between 1850 and 1880. Efforts were made to reform the reservation system and assimilation policy, to little effect. After the 1930's, however, the goal of assimilation was reconsidered. By the 1970's, Native Americans were having considerable success defending tribal rights in the courts.

1880's to 1945. Washington inaugurated its statehood with a government that reflected its past as a frontier society. As the frontier distrusted political power, especially executive power, so did the state. Accordingly, Washington's constitution called for a plural executive, with a number of elected offices, rather than a single, all-powerful governor. These included, besides governor and lieutenant governor, a secretary of state (chief elec-

tions officer), attorney general, treasurer, auditor, and others.

The state's politics in the next decades followed national trends as well as homegrown movements. Populism and radical parties and sects arose between 1880 and 1920, making a lasting impact. Reformers were influential because the state saw itself in a formative, malleable stage of collective life. The state's constitution showed strong Populist influence, distrusting big business by banning gifts or loans of public money and credit to private enterprise. The constitution's bill of rights protected individual rights even more than the federal Bill of Rights. Not surprisingly, the People's Party candidate for president received 22 percent of the vote in 1892.

The Progressive movement also deeply affected Washington, as it did its southern neighbor. Around the turn of the century, like Oregon, Washington voters gained the powers of initiative, referendum, and, later, recall elections. Municipal ownership of utilities and urban planning became public policy, and nature conservation, a recurring feature of the state's politics, appeared. In addition, radicalism and utopianism had some influence; the International Workers of the World (IWW), a Marxist party founded in Chicago in 1905, was active on the political fringes prior to and just after World War I.

By the Depression years of the 1930's, radicalism was a spent force, and, as elsewhere in the nation, federal policies attempted to come to the state's rescue. In building dams and in other projects, federal spending became an essential element in the state's economy, prefiguring what was to come. The most important single project was the Grand Coulee dam, but other dams were constructed. In addition, the Civilian Conservation Corps (CCC) was active in parks and forests; and there existed public housing and irrigation projects, among other federal programs.

Power generated from the Columbia River Basin was essential for the defense industries that sprang up during the war years. Among them were atomic development works at Hanford, where the plutonium for the nation's first atomic weapons was produced. Later it was discovered that the Hanford nuclear reactor also produced much radioactive waste that endangered both people and the natural world.

Rafters on Washington's White Salmon River in the Columbia River gorge. (State of Washington Tourism Development)

Postwar Economy and Politics. After World War II, many thought the state's economy would suffer badly from the nation's military stand down, but they were mistaken. The advent of the Cold War brought further defense spending to Washington, including additional development of the Hanford atomic facility. By the 1950's the Boeing Company near Seattle was receiving large contracts from the Pentagon. Federal spending also helped the state with the continuing development of hydroelectric power and crop-irrigation facilities through dam construction. Thanks to voter loyalty, the state was gaining influence in Washington, D.C., through the reelection of its senators Warren Magnuson and Henry "Scoop" Jackson, sometimes called "the senator from Boeing." Later, Representative Tom Foley became Speaker of the U.S. House of Representatives.

To celebrate the success of the state and its principal city, a world's fair was held in Seattle in 1962. Its futuristic freestanding tower, known as a space needle, became an icon of forward-thrusting technological prowess and self-confidence and was widely imitated around the world. As might be expected, the influence of the Boeing Company on the exposition was widely noticeable.

Later decades, however, saw a different side of Washington's success, as environmentally conscious activists sought to counterbalance the influence of timber and other industries. This was especially evident as the state's nuclear-power board defaulted on bonds used to build nuclear reactors, all but one of which were never completed. This was also evident as early as 1974, when Spokane opened Expo '74, the world's first environmental world's fair. By the end of the century, Washington was economically thriving on a balance of "high-tech" industries such as Boeing and Microsoft, tourism, and agriculture. Although anti-Asian sentiment was long outdated, civil rights issues for African Americans remained. Environmental problems, such as the decline of salmon, a state icon, also remained, and there was marked resistance to further economic development that would endanger the state's natural environment.

R. Baird Shuman

Washington Time Line

1500's	Spanish and English explorers sail off Washington coast.
1775	Spanish explorers Bruno Hecta and Juan Bidega y Quadra are first Europeans on Washington soil.
1778	English explorer Captain James Cook sights Washington coast.
1788-1794	Great Britain sends twenty-five fur-trading ships to Washington, compared to fifteen by United States.
1790	Spain and Britain sign Nootka Sound Convention, resolving claims to Northwest in British favor.
1792-1795	Explorer George Vancouver surveys Puget Sound and Georgia Gulf region.
1795-1814	U.S. sends ninety fur-trading ships to region, compared to twelve by Britain.
1805	Meriwether Lewis and William Clark lead their expedition down Columbia River to the Pacific Ocean.
1807-1811	Canadian explorer and geographer David Thompson travels down Columbia River to the Pacific Ocean.
1818	United States and Britain sign treaty allowing joint occupation of Oregon Country, including Washington.
1825	John McLoughlin of Britain's Hudson's Bay Company completes Fort Vancouver on Columbia River.
1840's	Americans trekking over the Oregon Trail settle in modern Washington.
1844	Election slogan Fifty-Four Forty or Fight adopted during presidential campaign of James K. Polk.
1846	United States and Britain sign treaty fixing northwest U.S. boundary at the forty-ninth parallel.
1848	Congress passes bill creating Oregon Territory, including Washington; General Joseph Lane is appointed territorial governor.
1852	Seattle is settled.
1853	Bill creating Washington Territory is signed into law; Isaac Ingalls Stevens is appointed first governor.
1855	Governor Stevens's efforts to move Indians to reservations lead to Indian wars.
1858-1859	Indian wars end, and treaties with the tribes are ratified.
1860	Gold strikes in nearby regions lead to increased migration to Washington.
1863	Washington receives present boundaries when neighboring lands become Idaho Territory.
1872	San Juan Islands in Puget Sound awarded to United States, ending dispute with Britain.
1883	Completion of transcontinental railroad leads to increased migration from the East.
Nov. 11, 1889	Washington becomes nation's forty-second state.
1900	Irrigation of arid Eastern Washington lands creates fertile farmland.
1897	Klondike gold rush brings boom as merchants provide supplies to miners.
1909	Alaska-Yukon-Pacific Exposition held in Seattle to celebrate port's growth.
1917	U.S. entrance into World War I proves a boon to Washington economy.

(continued)

1919	Nation's first general strike is held in Washington.
1930's	Great Depression brings economic hardship to state.
1930's	Construction on Bonneville and Grand Coulee dams helps ease economic ills.
1942-1945	World War II provides great stimulus to state's economy.
1942	Federal government establishes Hanford nuclear energy facility, which helps build first atomic bombs.
1950's-1960's	Postwar economy develops industrial, manufacturing sectors.
1960's	Hanford nuclear energy facility begins producing electricity.
1962	Seattle's World's Fair is signal success and stimulates tourist industry.
1964	United States and Canada approve plan for cooperative development of hydroelectric power.
1960's	Growth of Boeing Aircraft Company provides important economic expansion in the state.
1970's-1980's	State project to build five nuclear power plants incurs large cost-overruns; four are never completed.
1980	Mount Saint Helens, long-dormant volcano, erupts, causing billions of dollars in damage.
1983	State nuclear power agency defaults on $2.25 billion of municipal bonds; construction on the power plants ceases.
1980-1990's	Led by Microsoft and Boeing Corporations, high-tech firms provide significant economic strength to the state.
1999	One hundredth anniversary of Mount Rainier National Park.

Notes for Further Study

Published Sources. For Washington's history, see Robert Ficken and C. P. LeWarne's *Washington: A Centennial History* (1988), Mary W. Avery's *Washington: A History of the Evergreen State* (1965), and Norman Clark's *Washington: A Bicentennial History* (1976). A brief introduction to the study of local history is *Discovering Washington: A Guide to State and Local History* (1989) by Keith Petersen and Mary Reed. Resources on recreation include Ira Spring and Harvey Manning's *One Hundred Classic Hikes in Washington* (1998) and Archie Satterfield and Dale Swensson's *Natural Wonders of Washington: A Guide to Parks, Preserves, and Wild Places* (1996). For those touring the state or a locality, an excellent work is *A Traveler's History of Washington* (1996) by Bill Gulick. The state's geography is discussed in James Scott and R. L. Delorme's *Historical Atlas of Washington* (1988).

Web Resources. For government and public resources on the Web, the state of Washington home page is a good starting point (http://www.wa.gov). A Washington directory with government, entertainment, political, real estate, and other links is Silverlink (http://www.silverlink.net/washington.html). For state education, see the site of the Office of Superintendent of Public Education (http://www.ospi.wed.net.edu). For election information, see the home page of the Secretary of State (http://www.secstate.wa.gov.default.htm).

Information on state parks may be found at Parks (http://www.parks.wa.gov), and state documents are easily viewed at Washington Documents (http://www.foley.gonzaga.edu/govdocs/wadocs.html). For resources on the history of Native Americans, including Washington's tribes, on the Internet, users should consult the Hanksville site (http://www.hanksville.org/NAresources/indices/NAhistory/html).

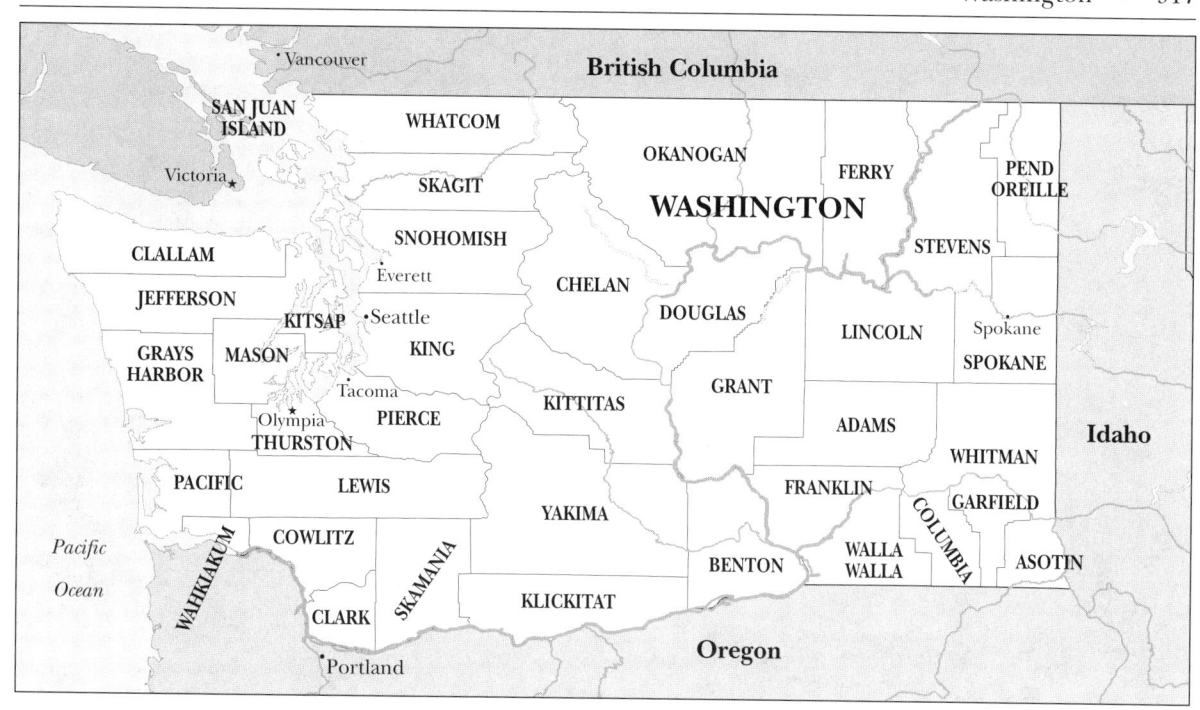

Counties

County	Sq. miles	1996 pop.
Adams	1,925.0	15,254
Asotin	635.9	20,761
Benton	1,703.1	134,359
Chelan	2,921.6	59,532
Clallam	1,745.2	63,419
Clark	627.9	305,171
Columbia	868.8	4,265
Cowlitz	1,138.7	89,984
Douglas	1,820.6	32,689
Ferry	2,204.0	7,195
Franklin	1,242.2	45,590
Garfield	710.5	2,306
Grant	2,676.4	67,597
Grays Harbor	1,917.3	67,923
Island	208.6	69,194
Jefferson	1,808.8	25,477
King	2,126.1	1,619,411
Kitsap	396.0	231,741
Kittitas	2,296.7	30,846
Klickitat	1,872.5	18,526

County	Sq. miles	1996 pop.
Lewis	2,407.8	66,848
Lincoln	2,311.2	9,594
Mason	961.1	48,577
Okanogan	5,268.3	38,005
Pacific	974.6	21,067
Pend Oreille	1,400.5	11,141
Pierce	1,675.5	657,272
San Juan	174.9	12,061
Skagit	1,735.3	95,543
Skamania	1,656.5	9,371
Snohomish	2,090.2	546,102
Spokane	1,763.8	404,920
Stevens	2,478.3	38,624
Thurston	727.1	197,109
Wahkiakum	264.3	3,775
Walla Walla	1,270.5	53,488
Whatcom	2,120.1	152,512
Whitman	2,159.4	39,456
Yakima	4,296.1	216,234

Source: U.S. Census Bureau; National Association of Counties.

Cities

With 10,000 or more residents

Rank	City	Population	Rank	City	Population
1	Seattle	536,978	22	Edmonds	33,086
2	Spokane	184,058	23	Lynnwood	32,942
3	Tacoma	179,814	24	University Place	32,219
4	Bellevue	104,052	25	Lacey	29,114
5	Everett	88,625	26	Puyallup	29,042
6	Federal Way	74,254	27	Walla Walla	28,721
7	Vancouver	73,526	28	Pasco	27,366
8	Lakewood	65,933	29	Burien	27,018
9	Yakima	64,967	30	Pullman	24,950
10	Bellingham	61,894	31	Wenatchee	23,918
11	Shoreline	52,116	32	Mount Vernon	22,688
12	Kennewick	50,316	33	Seatac	22,647
13	Renton	47,463	34	Des Moines	21,425
14	Kirkland	45,724	35	Mercer Island	21,351
15	Kent	45,066	36	Mountlake Terrace	20,879
16	Redmond	44,084	37	Oak Harbor	20,599
17	Bremerton	39,540	38	Port Angeles	18,769
18	Olympia	39,188	39	Marysville	18,702
19	Auburn	37,615	40	Bothell	18,062
20	Richland	37,291	41	Aberdeen	16,326
21	Longview	33,800	42	Anacortes	14,880

Rank	City	Population
43	Moses Lake	14,759
44	Mukilteo	14,620
45	Tukwila	14,572
46	Ellensburg	14,419
47	Centralia	13,176
48	Sunnyside	12,940
49	Kelso	12,246

Rank	City	Population
50	Tumwater	11,488
51	Camas	11,130
52	Edgewood	10,629
53	Issaquah	10,103

Population figures are estimated for mid-1998.
Source: U.S. Bureau of the Census.

Index to Tables

NA = Reliable data are not available.

DEMOGRAPHICS

Resident state and national populations, 1970-1997

Population figures given in thousands

	State pop.	U.S. pop.	Share	Rank
1970	3,413	203,302	1.7%	22
1980	4,132	226,546	1.8%	20
1985	4,400	237,924	1.9%	20
1990	4,867	248,765	2.0%	18
1995	5,436	262,761	2.1%	15
1997	5,610	267,636	2.1%	15

Source: U.S. Bureau of the Census.

Resident population by age, 1997

Age group	Total population
Under 5 years	386,000
5 to 17 years	1,068,000
18 to 24 years	522,000
25 to 34 years	819,000
35 to 44 years	983,000
45 to 54 years	752,000
55 to 64 years	433,000
65 to 74 years	343,000
75 to 84 years	230,000
85 years and over	75,000
Portion of residents 65 and older	11.5%
National average	12.7%

Population figures are rounded to nearest thousand persons;
figures include armed forces personnel stationed in state.
Source: U.S. Bureau of the Census.

Resident population by race, Hispanic origin, 1997

	State pop.	Share	U.S.
All residents	5,610,000	100.0%	100.0%
Hispanic white	302,000	5.4%	10.0%
non-Hispanic white	4,701,000	83.8%	72.7%
African American	196,000	3.5%	12.7%
Native American	100,000	1.8%	0.9%
Asian, Pacific Islander	311,000	5.5%	3.8%

Source: U.S. Bureau of the Census.

Projections of state population, 2000-2025

	Model A Uses interstate migration observed from 1975-1994	Model B Uses Bureau of Economic Analysis employment projections
Year	Population	Population
2000	5,858,000	5,829,000
2005	6,258,000	6,184,000
2010	6,658,000	6,524,000
2015	7,058,000	6,857,000
2020	7,446,000	7,179,000
2025	7,808,000	7,480,000

All population projections, including those for 2000, were calculated in 1997.
Source: U.S. Bureau of the Census, Population Paper Listings PPL-47.

VITAL STATISTICS

Average lifetime in years by race, 1989-1991

	State	U.S.	Rank
All residents	76.82	75.37	12
White residents	76.92	76.13	12
Black residents	71.34	69.16	3

Ranks are from longest-lived to least longest-lived. Ranks exclude Alaska, for which reliable data are not available. Rank for black residents is based on the 32 states for which reliable data are available.
Source: U.S. National Center for Health Statistics.

Infant mortality rates, 1980 and 1995

	State	U.S.
All residents		
1980	11.8	12.6
1995	5.9	7.6
White residents		
1980	11.5	11.0
1995	5.6	6.3
Black residents		
1980	16.4	21.4
1995	16.2	15.1

Figures represent deaths per 1,000 live births of resident infants under 1 year old, exclusive of fetal deaths; all-residents figures include other races not listed separately.
Source: U.S. National Center for Health Statistics.

Marriages and divorces

Marriages in 1996.	39,200
Rate per 1,000 population, 1995.	7.7
U.S. rate, 1995	8.9
Rank among all states	35
Divorces in 1996	26,500
Rate per 1,000 population, 1995.	5.5
U.S. rate, 1995	4.4
Rank among all states	12

Rank is from highest to lowest in country.
Source: U.S. National Center for Health Statistics.

Death rates by leading causes, 1995
Deaths per 100,000 resident population

Cause	State	U.S.
Heart disease	208.6	280.7
Cancer	183.0	204.9
Cerebrovascular diseases	60.7	60.1
Accidents and adverse effects	34.9	35.5
Motor vehicle accidents	13.7	16.5
Chronic obstructive pulmonary diseases	39.7	39.2
Diabetes mellitus	19.4	22.6
HIV	10.9	NA
Suicide	14.4	11.9
Homicide	5.5	8.7
All causes	751.0	880.0
Rank in overall death rate among states		42

Figures exclude nonresidents who die in state. Causes of death follow International Classification of Diseases. Rank is from highest to lowest in country.
Source: U.S. National Center for Health Statistics.

ECONOMY

Gross state product, 1990-1996
In current dollars

	State product	Increase
1990	$114.1 billion	
1993	$136.4 billion	
1994	$144.7 billion	6.09%
1995	$150.0 billion	3.66%
1996	$159.6 billion	6.40%

Source: U.S. Bureau of Economic Analysis; *Survey of Current Business,* June, 1998.

Gross state product by industry, 1996
In billions

Farms, forestry, fisheries	$4.0
Construction	6.6
Manufacturing	19.4
Transportation, public utilities	12.0
Wholesale trade	11.3
Retail trade	15.0
Finance, insurance, real estate	25.0
Services	28.8
Government	21.5
State total	$143.8
Total U.S.	$6,923.8
State share	2.08%
Rank among states	15

Total figures include mining, not listed separately.

Source: U.S. Bureau of Economic Analysis; *Survey of Current Business,* June, 1998.

Personal income per capita, 1990 and 1997
In current dollars

	1990	1997
Per capita income	$19,637	$26,718
U.S. average	$19,188	$25,598
Rank among states	15	12

1997 data are preliminary.

Source: U.S. Bureau of Economic Analysis; *Survey of Current Business,* May, 1998.

Energy consumption, 1995
In trillions of British thermal units (BTU)

End-use sectors

Residential	406.0
Commercial	304.3
Industrial	786.7
Transportation	635.5

Sources of energy

Petroleum	846.9
Natural gas	229.2
Coal	69.8
Hydroelectric power	833.2
Nuclear electric power	74.0
Total state per capita consumption	396.2
Total U.S. per capita consumption	344.4
Rank among states	15
Total state energy consumption	2,158.6
Total U.S. energy consumption	90,547.4
State share of U.S. total	2.38%
Rank among states	14

Total figures include items not listed separately.

Source: U.S. Energy Information Administration; *State Energy Data Report.*

Nonfarm employment by sectors, 1997

Total	2,512,000
Construction	136,000
Manufacturing	369,000
Transportation, public utilities	133,000
Wholesale trade, retail trade	607,000
Finance, insurance, real estate	128,000
Services	677,000
Government	458,000

Figures are rounded to nearest thousand persons. Total includes mining, not listed separately.

Source: U.S. Bureau of Labor Statistics; *Employment and Earnings,* monthly.

Foreign exports, 1990-1997
In millions of dollars

Year	State	U.S.	State share
1990	24,432	394,045	6.20%
1996	26,482	624,767	4.24%
1997	32,752	688,896	4.75%

Source: U.S. Bureau of the Census; *U.S. Merchandise Trade,* series FT 900.

LAND USE

Federally owned land, 1996

	State	U.S.	State share
Total acres	42,694,000	2,271,343,000	1.88%
Federally owned	11,939,000	563,129,000	2.12%
Federal share	28.0%	24.8%	—

Areas are rounded to nearest thousand acres. Figures for federally owned land do not include trust properties.
Source: U.S. General Services Administration; *Inventory Report on Real Property Owned by the United States Throughout the World,* annual.

Land use, 1992
In acres, rounded to nearest thousand

Total surface area	43,608,000
Federal land	12,479,000
Total nonfederal	29,931,000
Developed	1,851,000
Total rural	28,081,000
Cropland.	6,745,000
Pasture land	1,352,000
Range land.	5,476,000
Forest land	12,547,000
Minor cover/use.	1,960,000

Total surface area figures include water area not shown separately.
Source: U.S. Dept. of Agriculture; Soil Conservation Service; Iowa State University, Statistical Laboratory; *Summary Report, 1992 National Resources Inventory.*

Farms and crop acreage, 1997

	State	U.S.	Share	Rank
Farms (thousands)	36	2,058	1.75%	25
Acres (millions)	16	968	1.65%	19
Acres per farm	436	471	—	17
Acres planted	4,369	334,139	1.31%	25
Acres harvested	4,236	319,894	1.32%	24
Farm value (mill.)	$3,443	$108,805	3.16%	45

Numbers of farms are rounded to nearest thousand.
Source: U.S. Dept. of Agriculture; National Agricultural Statistics Service.

GOVERNMENT AND FINANCE

Units of local government, 1997

	State	Total U.S.	Rank
All local governments	1,812	87,453	17
Counties	39	3,043	33
Municipalities	275	19,372	28
Townships	0	16,629	—
School districts	296	13,726	18
Special districts	1,202	34,683	9

County ranks are based on the 48 states with county governments; township ranks are based on the 20 states with township governments; school district ranks are based on the 46 states with such districts.
Source: U.S. Bureau of the Census; *1997 Census of Governments, Government Organization,* Series GC97(1).

State government revenue, 1996

Total revenue	$24,790 mill.
General revenue	17,195 mill.
Per capita.	3,115
U.S. per capita average	2,910
Rank among states.	18
Intergovernmental revenue	
Total	$3,891 mill.
From federal government	3,834 mill.
From local government	56 mill.
Charges and Miscellaneous	
Total	$2,718 mill.
Current charges	1,685 mill.
Misc. general revenue	1,034 mill.
Taxes	
Total	$10,586 mill.
General sales	6,182 mill.
Selective sales.	1,685 mill.
License taxes	493 mill.
Individual income	NA
Corporate income	NA
Other	2,226 mill.
Insurance trust revenue	7,341 mill.

Total revenue figures include items not listed separately.
Source: U.S. Bureau of the Census.

State government expenditures, 1996

General expenditures

Intergovernmental	$5,430 mill.
Direct expenditures.	12,157 mill.
Total	17,587 mill.

Selected direct expenditures

Education	$7,475 mill.
Public welfare.	3,804 mill.
Health, hospital	1,405 mill.
Highways	1,435 mill.
Police	172 mill.
Corrections.	497 mill.
Natural resources.	438 mill.
Parks and recreation.	57 mill.
Government administration	406 mill.
Interest on debt	509 mill.

Other

State per capita expenditures	$3,186
U.S. per capita average	2,854
Rank among states.	14
Total state expenditures	21,086 mill.
Total U.S. expenditures	859,959 mill.

Totals include items not listed separately.
Source: U.S. Bureau of the Census.

POLITICS

Governors since statehood

D = Democrat; R = Republican; O = other;
(r) resigned; (d) died in office; (i) removed from office

Elisha P. Ferry (R)	1889-1893
John H. McGraw (R)	1893-1897
John R. Rogers (D). . . . . (d)	1897-1901
Henry McBride (R).	1901-1905
Albert E. Mead (R)	1905-1909
Samuel G. Cosgrove (R) . . . . (d)	1909
Marion E. Hay (R)	1909-1913
Ernest Lister (D) . . . . (d)	1913-1919
Louis F. Hart (R)	1919-1925
Roland H. Hartley (R)	1925-1933
Clarence D. Martin (D)	1933-1941
Arthur B. Langlie (R)	1941-1945
Monrad C. Wallgren (D)	1945-1949
Arthur B. Langlie (R)	1949-1957
Albert D. Rosellini (D)	1957-1965
Daniel J. Evans (R)	1965-1977
Dixie Lee Ray (D).	1977-1981
John Spellman (R)	1981-1985
Booth Gardner (D)	1985-1993

Mike Lowry (D)	1993-1997
Gary Locke (D)	1997-

Composition of state legislature, 1990-1998

	Democrats	Republicans
State House (98 seats)		
1990	58	40
1992	65	33
1994	38	60
1996	45	53
1998	49	49
State Senate (49 seats)		
1990	24	25
1992	28	21
1994	25	24
1996	23	26
1998	27	22

Figures for total seats may include independents and minor
party members.
Source: Council of State Governments; *State Elective Officials
and the Legislatures.*

Composition of congressional delegations, 1989-1999

	Dem	Rep	Total
House of Representatives			
101st Congress, 1989			
State delegates	5	3	8
Total U.S.	259	174	433
102d Congress, 1991			
State delegates	5	3	8
Total U.S.	267	167	434
103d Congress, 1993			
State delegates	8	1	9
Total U.S.	258	176	434
104th Congress, 1995			
State delegates	3	6	9
Total U.S.	197	236	433
105th Congress, 1997			
State delegates	5	4	9
Total U.S.	206	228	434
106th Congress, 1999			
State delegates	5	4	9
Total U.S.	211	222	433

	Dem	Rep	Total
Senate			
101st Congress, 1989			
State delegates	1	1	2
Total U.S.	55	45	100
102d Congress, 1991			
State delegates	1	1	2
Total U.S.	56	44	100
103d Congress, 1993			
State delegates	1	1	2
Total U.S.	57	43	100
104th Congress, 1995			
State delegates	1	1	2
Total U.S.	46	53	99
105th Congress, 1997			
State delegates	1	1	2
Total U.S.	45	55	100
106th Congress, 1999			
State delegates	1	1	2
Total U.S.	45	54	99

Figures are for starts of first sessions. Figure for U.S. Representatives for 101st Congress does not include Alabama and Indiana, which had vacancies. Figures for total U.S. Representatives for 102d, 103d, and 106th Congresses do not include Vermont, which had 1 Independent-Socialist. Figure for U.S. Representatives for 104th Congress does not include Vermont, which had 1 Independent-Socialist, and California, which had 1 vacancy. Figure for U.S. Representatives for 105th Congress does not include New York, which had 1 vacancy. Figure for U.S. Senators for 104th Congress does not include Oregon, which had 1 vacancy. Figure for U.S. Senators for 106th Congress does not include New Hampshire, which had 1 Independent.
Source: U.S. Congress; *Congressional Directory*, biennial.

HEALTH AND MEDICAL CARE

Medicare, 1997

	Recipients	Payments
State	707,000	$3,033 mill.
Total U.S.	37,514,000	$206,064 mill.
State share	1.88%	1.47%
Rank among states	18	23

Recipient figures are rounded to nearest thousand persons. Ranks are from highest to lowest.
Source: U.S. Health Care Financing Administration.

Medicaid, 1996

	Recipients	Payments
State	621,000	$1,393 mill.
Total U.S.	35,028,000	$121,419 mill.
State share	1.77%	1.15%
Rank among states	18	25

Recipient figures are rounded to nearest thousand persons. Payment figures for fiscal year reflect federal and state contribution payments. Ranks are from highest to lowest.
Source: U.S. Health Care Financing Administration.

Voter participation in presidential elections, 1992 and 1996

	1992	1996
State voting age pop.	3,812,000	4,122,000
Total U.S. voting age pop.	189,524,000	196,509,000
State share of U.S. total	2.0%	2.1%
Rank among states	15	15
Percent of state casting vote	60.0	41.2
Percent of U.S. total voting	55.1	49.0
Rank among states	23	50

Source: U.S. Bureau of the Census.

Health insurance coverage, 1996

	State	U.S.
Total persons covered	4,881,000	225,070,000
Total persons not covered	761,000	41,716,000
Part not covered	13.5%	15.6%
Rank among states	24	—
Children not covered	171,000	10,554,000
Part not covered	11.2%	14.8%
Rank among states	27	—

Ranks are from most to fewest uninsured. Population figures are rounded to nearest thousand persons.
Source: U.S. Bureau of the Census.

AIDS, syphilis, tuberculosis, and measles cases, 1997

Cases	U.S.	State	Share
AIDS	58,443	641	1.10%
Syphilis	8,550	17	0.20%
Tuberculosis	18,534	298	1.61%
Measles	148,000	2,000	1.35%

Measles figures are rounded to nearest thousand cases.
Source: U.S. Centers for Disease Control and Prevention.

EDUCATION

Public school enrollment, 1995

State K-8 enrollment 680,000
Total U.S. K-8 enrollment 32,341,000
State share of total U.S. 2.10%
State 9-12 enrollment 277,000
Total U.S. 9-12 enrollment 12,500,000
State share of U.S. total 2.22%
State public school enroll. rate 92.9%
Overall U.S. rate. 91.6%
Rank among states. 23

Enrollment figures (which include unclassified students) are rounded to nearest thousand pupils in fall term; kindergarten (K)-8 grade figures include some prekindergarten students. Enrollment rate is based on percentage of persons 5-17 years old. Rank is from highest to lowest.
Source: U.S. National Center for Education Statistics.

HOUSING

Homeownership rates, 1985-1997

	1985	1990	1997
State	66.8%	61.8%	62.9%
Total U.S.	63.9%	63.9%	65.7%
Rank among states	31	41	42

Source: U.S. Bureau of the Census.

Home sales, 1990 and 1997
In thousands of units

Existing home sales	1990	1997	Change
State sales	87.7	116.5	28.8
Total U.S. sales	3,560	4,730	1,170
State share of U.S. total	2.46%	2.46%	NA
Rank among states	13	13	—

Source: National Association of Realtors; *Real Estate Outlook: Market Trends and Insights.*

Public college finances, 1996

State FTE enrollment 192,400
Total U.S. FTE enrollment 8,268,800
State share of total U.S. 2.33%
Rank among states. 12
State and local appropriations $879,500,000
Total U.S. state and local
   appropriations. . . . . $39,699 mill.
State share of total U.S. 2.22%
Rank among states. 13
State net tuition revenues. $314,300,000
Total U.S. net tuition $18,348,100,000
State share of total U.S. 1.71%
Rank among states. 23

FTE=Full-time equivalent; credit and noncredit enrollment including summer session in academic year ending in 1996.
Enrollments are rounded to nearest thousand students. Net tuition revenues exclude appropriation to students attending in-state public institutions. Rankings are from highest shares to lowest.
Source: Research Associates of Washington.

TRANSPORTATION AND TRAVEL

Highway mileage, 1996

Interstate	763
Other arterial	7,614
Collector roads	18,829
Local roads	54,388
Urban roads	17,647
Rural roads	61,908
Total state	79,555
U.S. total	3,933,985
State share	2.0%
Rank among states	25

Source: U.S. Federal Highway Administration.

Motor vehicle registrations and driver licenses, 1996
In thousands

Vehicle registrations	State	U.S.	Share	Rank
Autos, trucks, buses	4,603	206,365	2.23%	16
Autos only	2,619	128,439	2.04%	16
Motorcycles	104	3,832	2.71%	12
Driver licenses	3,908	179,539	2.18%	16

Figures do not include vehicles owned by military services.
Source: U.S. Federal Highway Administration; *Highway Statistics; Selected Highway Statistics and Charts.*

Domestic travel expenditures, 1995
Spending by U.S. residents on overnight trips and day trips of at least 100 miles

Total expenditures in state	$6,060 mill.
Total expenditures in U.S.	$360,314 mill.
State share of total U.S.	1.68%
Rank among states	20

Source: Travel Industry Association of America.

CRIME AND LAW ENFORCEMENT

State and local police officers, 1996

Local police	5,430
State police	906
Sheriffs	2,553
Total	9,292
Officers per 10,000 residents	17
U.S. average	25
Rank among states	46

Figures cover full-time sworn officers; totals include special police not shown separately.
Source: U.S. Bureau of Justice Statistics; *Census of State and Local Law Enforcement Agencies, 1996.*

Crime rates, 1996
Rates per 100,000 resident population

Violent crimes	State	U.S.
Total violent	431	634
Murder	4.6	7.4
Forcible rape	51.1	36.1
Robbery	119	202
Aggravated assault	256	388
Property crimes		
Total property	5,478	4,445
Burglary	1,058	943
Larceny/theft	3,899	2,976
Motor vehicle theft	522	526
Totals	5,909	5,079

Source: U.S. Federal Bureau of Investigation; *Crime in the United States,* annual.

State prison populations, 1980-1996

	State	U.S.	State share
1980	4,399	305,458	1.44%
1990	7,995	708,393	1.13%
1996	12,527	1,025,624	1.22%

Figures exclude prisoners in federal penitentiaries.
Source: U.S. Bureau of Justice Statistics.

West Virginia

Location: Eastern continental United States

Area and rank: 24,087 square miles (62,384 square kilometers); 24,231 square miles (62,758 square kilometers) including water; forty-first largest state in area

Population and rank: 1,815,787 (1997); thirty-fifth largest state in population

Capital: Charleston

Largest city: Charleston (55,056 people in 1998)

Entered Union and rank: June 20, 1863; thirty-fifth state

Present constitution adopted: 1872

Suspension bridge at Wheeling, where delegates voted to secede from Virginia in 1861 and which later briefly served as state capital. (West Virginia Division of Tourism & Parks/Steve Shaluta, Jr.)

Counties: 55

State name: West Virginia takes its name from Virginia, from which it seceded during the Civil War

State nickname: Mountain State

Motto: *Montani semper liberi* (Mountaineers are always free)

State flag: State seal on a white field framed by blue border

Highest point: Spruce Knob — 4,861 feet (1,482 meters)

Lowest point: Potomac River — 240 feet (73 meters)

Highest recorded temperature: 112 degrees Fahrenheit (44 degrees Celsius) — Martinsburg, 1936

Lowest recorded temperature: −37 degrees Fahrenheit (−38 degrees Celsius) — Lewisburg, 1917

State songs: "West Virginia, My Home Sweet Home"; "The West Virginia Hills"; "This Is My West Virginia"

State tree: Sugar maple

State flower: Rhododendron

State bird: Cardinal

State fish: Brook trout

State animal: Black bear

West Virginia History

More than most states, West Virginia has been shaped in its development and its history by its geography. Although part of Virginia for almost a century, it was separated from the coastal and central portions of Virginia by the Allegheny Mountains and was thus removed from the sources of political and economic power and influence. Lying completely within the Appalachian Highlands, the state is mountainous and rugged, and although it is blessed with abundant mineral resources such as coal and natural gas, it has little land available for large-scale agriculture.

Travel and transportation have often been extremely difficult and even hazardous, fostering a sense of isolation in the state, which in turn fostered a high degree of independence expressed in the state's official motto, *Montani semper liberi* (mountaineers are always free).

Early Times. Although Native Americans entered the West Virginia area as early as fifteen thousand years ago, most of them regarded the territory as unfit for permanent settlement and good only as hunting and battle grounds. Later, when the Cherokee, Iroquois, and Shawnee arrived to establish

Detail from an imaginative mural painted by John Steuart Curry in the late 1930's, depicting John Brown leading his raid on Harpers Ferry. (National Archives)

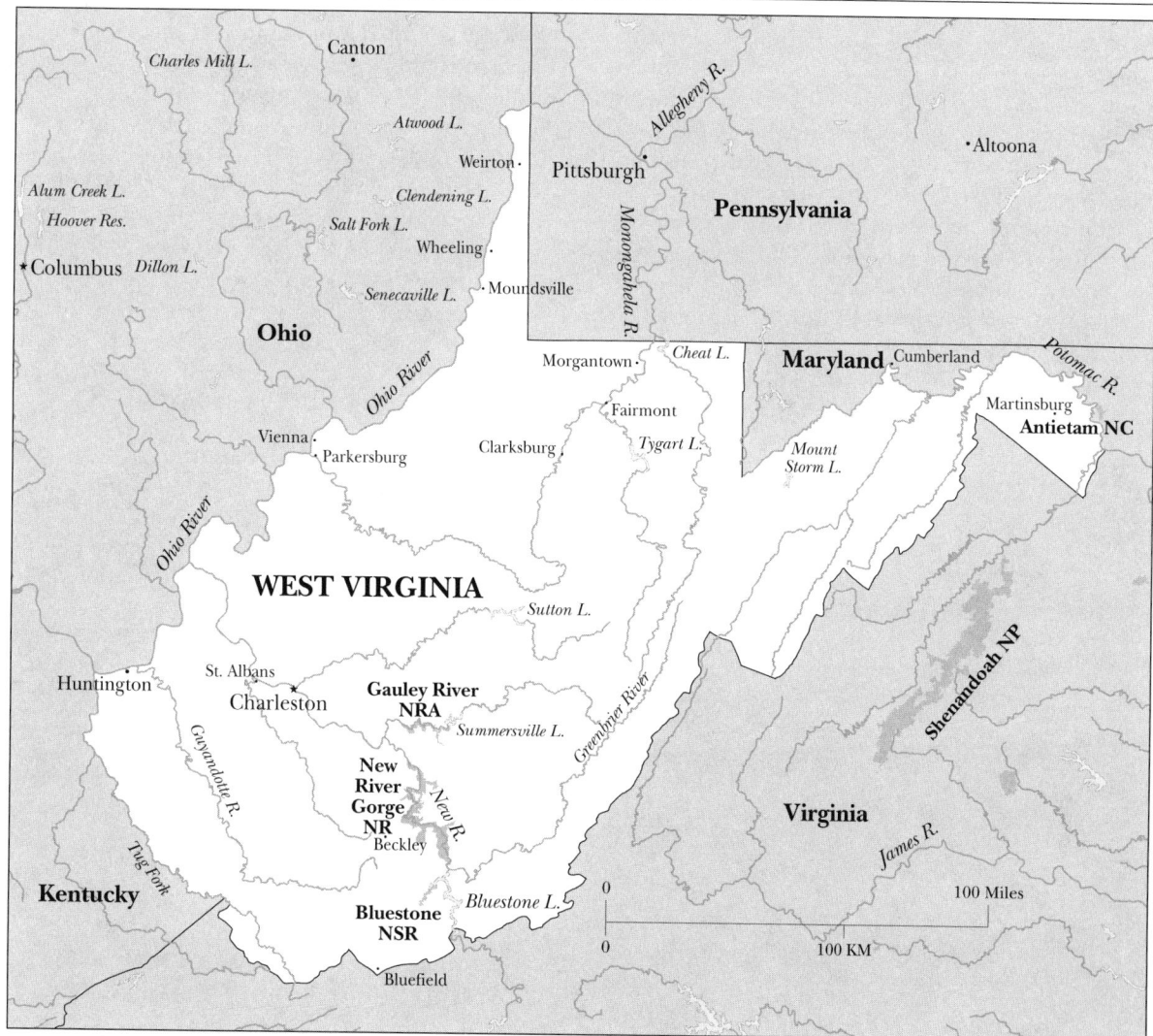

villages, they located them near the major rivers; instead of developing agriculture, they relied on hunting. The tradition of tribal warfare continued, including fights over the springs found throughout the area that were a source of valuable salt, used in food preservation and for trading.

Colonization. The original grant of Virginia by King James I of England included what is now West Virginia. The colonists first explored the western portion of their territory in 1669, when an expedition under John Lederer reached the Blue Ridge Mountains. Thomas Batts and Robert Fallam followed in 1671, striking along the New River and claiming the Ohio Valley for England, a claim that was disputed both by France and by Native Americans. Morgan Morgan, a Welshman, is traditionally considered the first European settler in the West Virginia area, having established Bunker Hill in 1726. Morgan was followed by other colonists, including Germans from Pennsylvania and Scotch Irish from northern Ireland. Although King George III prohibited American colonists from crossing the Allegheny Mountains, this ban was largely ignored, and during the period from 1722 through 1740, the Iroquois and Cherokee ceded their lands to advancing settlers.

The distance and physical barriers between the western settlements and the rest of Virginia began to cause difficulties. In addition, the planters and traders along the Virginia tidewater and eastern rivers exerted a monopoly on the state's political and economic life. Settlers beyond the Alleghenies grew restive, and by 1776, when the American colonies were ready to break with Great Britain, western Virginia was asking the Continental Congress for independence from Virginia. The necessities of the ensuing American Revolution put this request on hold, however. As part of Virginia, it joined the Union in 1788.

Independence and Civil War. Following American independence, political and economic power in Virginia shifted more than ever toward the tidewater and eastern section, where slaveholders were dominant. The west was unsuccessful in its requests for fairness during the revision of the state constitution in 1829, and it continued to suffer from neglect by the Richmond state government. Poor roads, inadequate schools, higher taxes, neglected economic development, and lack of representation in the state legislature were among the west's major complaints. Some, but not all, were addressed in a new state constitution adopted in 1851, but the movement toward separate statehood continued.

West Virginia takes its nickname, the "Mountain State," from its rugged terrain. (PhotoDisc)

Winery in Summers County. (West Virginia Division of Tourism & Parks/David E. Fattaleh)

In 1859 John Brown, a militant abolitionist from Kansas, seized the federal armory at Harpers Ferry as the first step in a revolt. He was soon captured, tried, and hanged for treason. Soon the nation was in the throes of the Civil War, and Virginia joined other southern states in seceding from the Union. The largely non-slave-holding and pro-Union western counties summoned a convention in Wheeling in August, 1861, and formed a government for a new state to be known as Kanawha. In November of that year a second convention at Wheeling adopted the name of West Virginia and began drafting a constitution. In December, 1862, President Abraham Lincoln approved an act admitting the new state.

In the aftermath of the Civil War arose one of the most famous feuds in American history, that of the Hatfields and the McCoys. Both families lived along both banks of the Tug River, which forms the border between Kentucky and West Virginia. The precise cause of the feud is unknown. Some have suggested the theft of a McCoy hog by a Hatfield; others, a forbidden romance between a McCoy girl and a Hatfield boy. Whatever the underlying reasons, the feud began in earnest during 1882, when a West Virginia Hatfield was killed by Kentucky McCoys. As the feud escalated, West Virginia authorities sought to suppress it by legal action, even taking their case to the U.S. Supreme Court. By the time the feud finally came to an end in the late 1880's, more than a dozen people had been killed.

Coal Mining and Coal Strikes. Following the Civil War, West Virginia advanced in exploitation of its major resources, primarily timber, coal, and natural gas. Coal had been discovered as early as 1742, but the deposits were not effectively mined until after the Civil War, primarily because of transportation difficulties. When these difficulties were solved by the spread of the railroads, West Virginia became the leading producer of bituminous, or soft, coal in North America. In addition to its abundance and relative ease of mining, the state's coal proved to be remarkably free from sulfur and other impurities, making it even more valuable.

Although coal was the chief source of West Virginia's revenues, it was also a major cause of internal problems. Coal mining was hard and dangerous work, and mine owners insisted on long hours and low pay for their workers. Deaths in mine disasters were frequent, and the toll was often high: in 1907, 537 persons died in mining accidents, 362 of them in one mine alone, the worst single mining disaster in U.S. history. Efforts to organize and unionize the miners to fight for better pay and working conditions were met with bitter hostility by mine owners, other businesses, and even the state and federal governments. Time and again, West Virginia governors declared martial law and called up the National Guard to put down strikes and other union-organizing efforts. The struggles reached a peak of violence in the years between the end of World War I and the Great Depression. In 1920 the Matewan Massacre led to the deaths of more than ten people during a confrontation between miners and their supporters in the community and mine owners and their forces. As a result, the United Mine Workers of America saw an increase in its membership, but its work toward better conditions was smothered when federal troops were ordered into the area. The strikes and conflicts continued until New Deal programs and the need for increased coal supplies for defense production in World War II brought better conditions to the mines.

Into the Future. The market for coal was often uncertain, and prices for the product could fall to low levels. Because of this and its isolation, poor economic base, and inadequate schools, West Virginia suffered from a high degree of poverty, which reached its depth during the Great Depression. As part of Appalachia, the mountainous region stretching from Pennsylvania to upper Alabama, West Virginia was among the prime targets for massive federal assistance, especially during the Great

Society's War on Poverty during the administration of President Lyndon Johnson. Funding was made available for roads, schools, retraining for workers, forest restoration, and the fight against rural poverty. Entire communities, especially in the more remote areas of the state, were aided by these efforts. In addition, the state's private sector began to revive.

Following World War II, coal production proved uncertain, largely because it was linked to the availability of other energy sources, such as oil, and to environmental concerns about matters such as strip mining. The timber industry, which had been a source of income for the area since the mid-1700's, expanded greatly after steam power replaced hydroelectric power in the late nineteenth century. Natural gas, which had been discovered in 1815, was also plentiful in the state. However, manufacturing became the major source of income for the state, ahead of mining and timbering combined. Chief products were first steel and later chemicals and allied products.

In 1960 West Virginia played a major role in U.S. presidential politics when its Democratic presidential primary pitted candidate John F. Kennedy against Hubert H. Humphrey. Kennedy's landslide victory over Humphrey (almost 61 percent of the vote) caused Humphrey to withdraw from the race and, more important, demonstrated that a Catholic such as Kennedy could have a chance at victory. In the November presidential election Kennedy won the presidency. Political analysts regarded the West Virginia primary as a turning point in Kennedy's campaign and its results among the most important in American politics.

As the twentieth century ended, West Virginia continued to diversify its economic base, adding to mining, forestry, and manufacturing and drawing increasingly on recreation and tourism. The completion of major interstate highways through the state made travel easier and faster and encouraged development of the southern portion of the state, where vast areas of largely untouched natural beauty lured visitors, campers, and nature enthusiasts. Once an isolated and difficult-to-reach territory, West Virginia was rapidly becoming a destination for a variety of travelers.

Michael Witkoski

West Virginia Time Line

1500's	Cherokee, Iroquois, and Shawnee tribes inhabit West Virginia area.
1609	English king James I grants area to Virginia colony.
1669	Explorer John Lederer becomes first European to see West Virginia.
1671	Thomas Batts and Robert Fallam explore New River valley and claim land for England.
1725	Fur traders enter area west of Appalachians.
1726	Morgan Morgan establishes first permanent English settlement in West Virginia near Bunker Hill.
1742	Peter Salley discovers coal on Coal River at Racine.
1749	Jacob Marlin and Stephen Sewell establish first recorded settlement west of Allegheny Mountains.
1768	Iroquois cede lands to British in Treaty of Fort Stanwix.
1774	Colonists defeat alliance of Native Americans at battle of Point Pleasant, in what is considered the first battle of the Revolution.
June 26, 1788	Virginia ratifies Constitution, becoming tenth state to enter the Union.
1790	First iron-ore furnace west of Allegheny Mountains opens on Kings Creek.
1794	"Mad Anthony" Wayne defeats Native Americans at Fallen Timbers.
1815	First gas well in United States is drilled near Charleston.
1818	Cumberland Road opens to Wheeling.
1819	State constitutional crisis grows over division between eastern and western portions of state.
1851	Virginia adopts new constitution with concessions to western portion of the state.
1853	Baltimore and Ohio Railroad reaches Wheeling.
Oct. 16, 1859	John Brown raids federal armory at Harpers Ferry; is later tried, convicted, and hanged for treason at Charles Town.
1861	Convention at Wheeling nullifies Virginia ordinance of secession and established loyal Union government.
June 20, 1863	West Virginia enters Union as thirty-fifth state.
1867	State university is chartered at Morgantown.
1870	State capital is moved to Charleston.
1872	West Virginia adopts new state constitution.
1875	State capital is moved to Wheeling.
1885	State capital is moved back to Charleston.
1896	State begins first rural free mail delivery in United States.
1907	Five mine disasters kill 537 people.
1920	Ten people are killed in Matewan Massacre during bitter coal strike.
1921	National Guard and U.S. Army troops put down coal strike.

(continued)

1938	Tygart Dam on Tygart River is completed.
1954	West Virginia Turnpike is completed.
1962	Green Bank movable radio telescope, world's largest, begins operations.
1965	Major gas field is found near Charleston.
1966	Summersville Dam on Gauley River is dedicated.
1967	Some forty people die in collapse of suspension bridge over Ohio River at Point Pleasant.
1972	Failure of dam on Buffalo Creek produces flash flood that kills more than one hundred people.
1977	Workers complete New River Gorge Bridge, world's longest single-arch steel span.
1988	Major oil spill pollutes Monongahela and Ohio Rivers, endangering water supplies.
1996	Charlotte Pritt becomes first woman nominated for governor by a major political party in West Virginia.
1996	West Virginia coal industry sets production record at 174 million tons.
1998	Marie Redd becomes first female African American elected to West Virginia state senate.

Notes for Further Study

Published Sources. Two good general studies of West Virginia are Otis K. Rice's *West Virginia: A History* (1985), an academic but well-written survey of the state's development that is objective, and John Alexander Williams's *West Virginia: A History* (1984), a very good overview of West Virginia from early days to more modern times. Well-paced and well-written, this volume provides useful information for the beginning student. *The Americanization of West Virginia: Creating a Modern Industrial State, 1916-1925* (1998), by John C. Hennen, is an excellent study of what is probably the major transition in West Virginia's history, which brought it into the modern world at a price that was sometimes terrible to individuals and communities. One of the states hardest hit by the Great Depression, West Virginia was in many ways a test case for President Franklin Roosevelt's New Deal. Jerry Bruce Thomas's *An Appalachian New Deal: West Virginia in the Great Depression* (1998) examines the plans, attempts, and consequences that resulted from the New Deal's implementation. *The 55 West Virginias: A Guide to the State's Counties* (1998), by E. Lee North, is an excellent introduction into the varieties of history, geography, and culture that compose West Virginia. The diverse state receives its due in this study of the Mountain State's individual counties.

Web Resources. An excellent starting point for material on history and current events is the state of West Virginia Main Page (http://www.state.wv.us). This has links to the many government agencies and departments that have statistics and connections to additional resources. The State Archival Resources (http://www.scv.org/uttowy.htm) provides access to a wide range of historical information about West Virginia and its development. Those specifically interested in history should also consult the West Virginia History Journal (http://www.wvlc.wvnet.edn/history/journal_wvh/journal_toc.html) and the West Virginia Culture and History Menu of the West Virginia Division of Culture and History (http://www.wvlc.wvnet.edu/culture/front.html). Both of these sites offer information and links to other pages.

For more generalized information, consult the Open Directory—West Virginia (http://www.dmoz.org/regional/US/west_virginia), which offers a unique perspective on the material available about the history and culture of the state and its people. Another good source for introductory and general information, as well as good links to other sites, is West Virginia Online (http://www.wvonline.com).

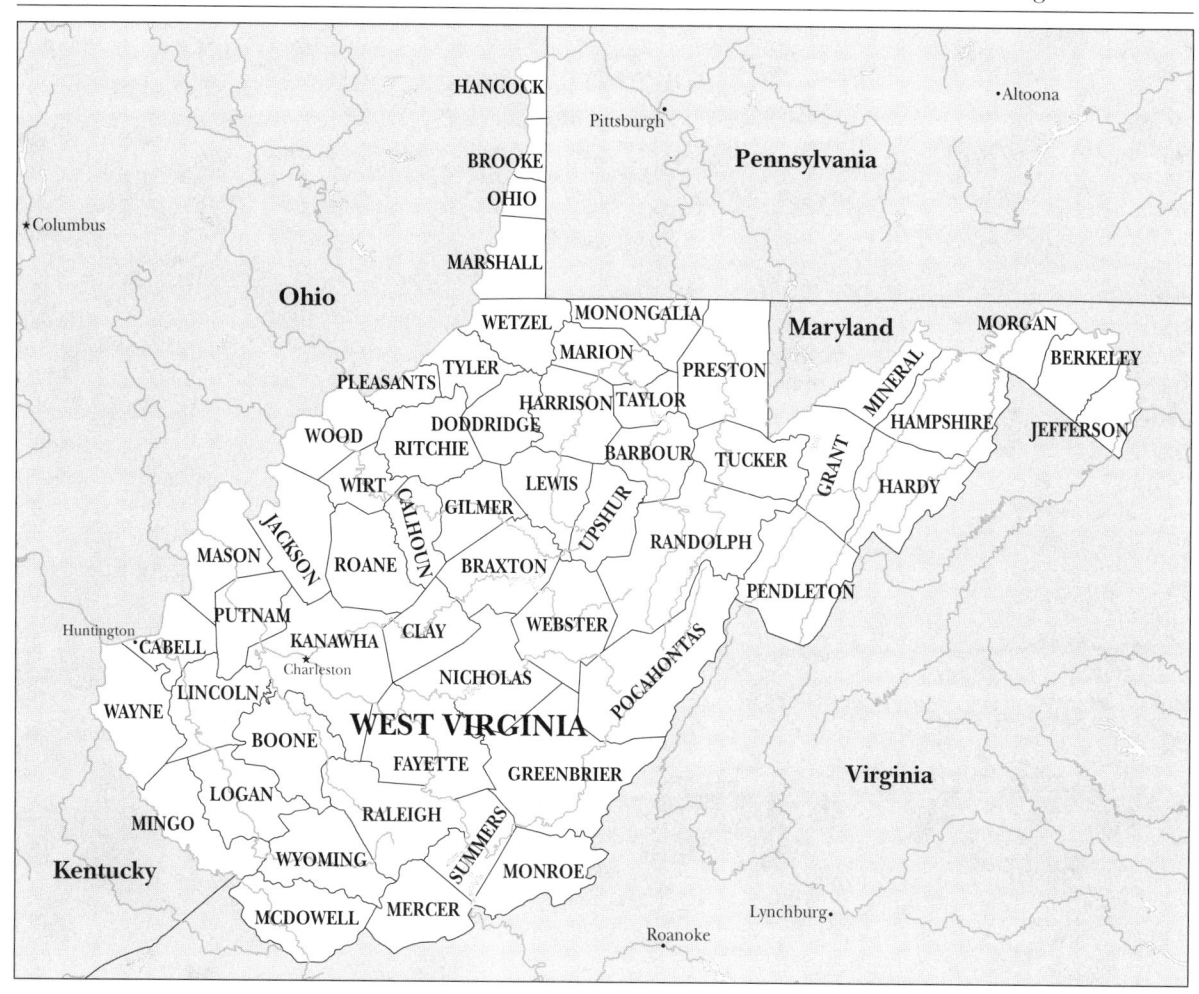

Counties

County	Sq. miles	1996 pop.	County	Sq. miles	1996 pop.
Barbour	340.8	16,360	Hancock	83.0	34,705
Berkeley	321.2	68,197	Hardy	583.4	11,723
Boone	503.0	26,403	Harrison	416.1	71,143
Braxton	513.5	13,449	Jackson	465.8	27,399
Brooke	88.9	26,573	Jefferson	209.6	39,979
Cabell	281.6	96,178	Kanawha	903.2	204,968
Calhoun	280.6	7,982	Lewis	388.8	17,642
Clay	342.4	10,412	Lincoln	437.5	22,150
Doddridge	320.5	7,235	Logan	454.2	41,839
Fayette	664.0	48,908	McDowell	534.8	31,524
Gilmer	340.1	7,184	Marion	309.7	57,571
Grant	477.2	11,172	Marshall	307.0	36,284
Greenbrier	1,021.3	35,734	Mason	431.9	25,838
Hampshire	641.8	18,808	Mercer	420.5	64,521

(continued)

County	Sq. miles	1996 pop.
Mineral	327.8	27,563
Mingo	422.6	32,986
Monongalia	361.2	78,234
Monroe	473.4	13,015
Morgan	229.0	13,520
Nicholas	648.7	27,604
Ohio	106.2	49,502
Pendleton	698.0	8,112
Pleasants	130.7	7,484
Pocahontas	940.3	9,086
Preston	648.4	29,903
Putnam	346.3	49,607
Raleigh	607.0	78,963
Randolph	1,039.8	28,999

County	Sq. miles	1996 pop.
Ritchie	453.5	10,286
Roane	483.6	15,400
Summers	361.2	13,909
Taylor	172.8	15,387
Tucker	418.9	7,787
Tyler	257.6	9,995
Upshur	354.8	23,640
Wayne	505.8	42,431
Webster	556.1	10,420
Wetzel	359.2	18,688
Wirt	233.0	5,589
Wood	367.4	87,770
Wyoming	500.9	27,993

Source: U.S. Census Bureau; National Association of Counties.

Cities
With 10,000 or more residents

Rank	City	Population		Rank	City	Population
1	Charleston	55,056		9	Clarksburg	17,011
2	Huntington	52,571		10	Martinsburg	15,049
3	Wheeling	32,541		11	South Charleston	13,148
4	Parkersburg	31,715		12	Bluefield	12,047
5	Morgantown	26,751		13	St. Albans	11,867
6	Weirton	21,206		14	Vienna	11,285
7	Fairmont	19,088				
8	Beckley	18,187				

Population figures are estimated for mid-1998.
Source: U.S. Bureau of the Census.

Index to Tables

NA = Reliable data are not available.

DEMOGRAPHICS

Resident state and national populations, 1970-1997

Population figures given in thousands

	State pop.	U.S. pop.	Share	Rank
1970	1,744	203,302	0.9%	34
1980	1,950	226,546	0.9%	34
1985	1,907	237,924	0.8%	34
1990	1,793	248,765	0.7%	34
1995	1,822	262,761	0.7%	35
1997	1,816	267,636	0.7%	35

Source: U.S. Bureau of the Census.

Resident population by age, 1997

Age group	Total population
Under 5 years	104,000
5 to 17 years	308,000
18 to 24 years	184,000
25 to 34 years	231,000
35 to 44 years	280,000
45 to 54 years	253,000
55 to 64 years	181,000
65 to 74 years	152,000
75 to 84 years	93,000
85 years and over	30,000
Portion of residents 65 and older	15.1%
National average	12.7%

Population figures are rounded to nearest thousand persons;
figures include armed forces personnel stationed in state.
Source: U.S. Bureau of the Census.

Resident population by race, Hispanic origin, 1997

	State pop.	Share	U.S.
All residents	1,816,000	100.0%	100.0%
Hispanic white	9,000	0.5%	10.0%
non-Hispanic white	1,738,000	95.7%	72.7%
African American	58,000	3.2%	12.7%
Native American	2,000	0.1%	0.9%
Asian, Pacific Islander	9,000	0.5%	3.8%

Source: U.S. Bureau of the Census.

Projections of state population, 2000-2025

	Model A Uses interstate migration observed from 1975-1994	Model B Uses Bureau of Economic Analysis employment projections
Year	Population	Population
2000	1,841,000	1,833,000
2005	1,849,000	1,842,000
2010	1,851,000	1,852,000
2015	1,851,000	1,861,000
2020	1,850,000	1,866,000
2025	1,845,000	1,864,000

All population projections, including those for 2000, were calculated in 1997.

Source: U.S. Bureau of the Census, Population Paper Listings PPL-47.

VITAL STATISTICS

Average lifetime in years by race, 1989-1991

	State	U.S.	Rank
All residents	74.26	75.37	43
White residents	74.37	76.13	49
Black residents	69.75	69.16	14

Ranks are from longest-lived to least longest-lived. Ranks exclude Alaska, for which reliable data are not available. Rank for black residents is based on the 32 states for which reliable data are available.

Source: U.S. National Center for Health Statistics.

Infant mortality rates, 1980 and 1995

	State	U.S.
All residents		
1980	11.8	12.6
1995	7.9	7.6
White residents		
1980	11.4	11.0
1995	7.6	6.3
Black residents		
1980	21.5	21.4
1995	NA	15.1

Figures represent deaths per 1,000 live births of resident infants under 1 year old, exclusive of fetal deaths; all-residents figures include other races not listed separately.

Source: U.S. National Center for Health Statistics.

Marriages and divorces

Marriages in 1996.	11,100
Rate per 1,000 population, 1995	6.1
U.S. rate, 1995	8.9
Rank among all states	50
Divorces in 1996	8,000
Rate per 1,000 population, 1995	5.1
U.S. rate, 1995	4.4
Rank among all states	15

Rank is from highest to lowest in country.

Source: U.S. National Center for Health Statistics.

Death rates by leading causes, 1995
Deaths per 100,000 resident population

Cause	State	U.S.
Heart disease	378.9	280.7
Cancer	259.4	204.9
Cerebrovascular diseases	67.9	60.1
Accidents and adverse effects	40.4	35.5
Motor vehicle accidents	21.2	16.5
Chronic obstructive pulmonary diseases	60.0	39.2
Diabetes mellitus	32.8	22.6
HIV	-	NA
Suicide	15.1	11.9
Homicide	5.5	8.7
All causes	1,107.0	880.0
Rank in overall death rate among states		1

Figures exclude nonresidents who die in state. Causes of death follow International Classification of Diseases. Rank is from highest to lowest in country.

Source: U.S. National Center for Health Statistics.

ECONOMY

Gross state product, 1990-1996
In current dollars

	State product	Increase
1990	$28.0 billion	
1993	$31.9 billion	
1994	$34.5 billion	8.15%
1995	$36.0 billion	4.35%
1996	$37.2 billion	3.33%

Source: U.S. Bureau of Economic Analysis; *Survey of Current Business,* June, 1998.

Gross state product by industry, 1996
In billions

Farms, forestry, fisheries	$0.2
Construction	1.5
Manufacturing	6.2
Transportation, public utilities.	4.8
Wholesale trade.	1.9
Retail trade	3.2
Finance, insurance, real estate	3.6
Services	5.3
Government.	4.6
State total.	$35.0
Total U.S.	$6,923.8
State share.	0.51%
Rank among states.	38

Total figures include mining, not listed separately.
Source: U.S. Bureau of Economic Analysis; *Survey of Current Business,* June, 1998.

Personal income per capita, 1990 and 1997
In current dollars

	1990	1997
Per capita income	$14,197	$18,957
U.S. average	$19,188	$25,598
Rank among states	48	49

1997 data are preliminary.
Source: U.S. Bureau of Economic Analysis; *Survey of Current Business,* May, 1998.

Energy consumption, 1995
In trillions of British thermal units (BTU)

End-use sectors

Residential	145.9
Commercial	93.6
Industrial	399.5
Transportation	179.9

Sources of energy

Petroleum	272.6
Natural gas	157.4
Coal.	860.3
Hydroelectric power.	12.4
Nuclear electric power	0
Total state per capita consumption	448.7
Total U.S. per capita consumption	344.4
Rank among states	8
Total state energy consumption.	818.9
Total U.S. energy consumption	90,547.4
State share of U.S. total.	0.90%
Rank among states.	33

Total figures include items not listed separately.
Source: U.S. Energy Information Administration; *State Energy Data Report.*

Nonfarm employment by sectors, 1997

Total	709,000
Construction	35,000
Manufacturing	82,000
Transportation, public utilities.	39,000
Wholesale trade, retail trade	162,000
Finance, insurance, real estate.	28,000
Services	199,000
Government	139,000

Figures are rounded to nearest thousand persons. Total includes mining, not listed separately.
Source: U.S. Bureau of Labor Statistics; *Employment and Earnings,* monthly.

Foreign exports, 1990-1997
In millions of dollars

Year	State	U.S.	State share
1990	1,550	394,045	0.39%
1996	2,169	624,767	0.35%
1997	2,276	688,896	0.33%

Source: U.S. Bureau of the Census; *U.S. Merchandise Trade,* series FT 900.

LAND USE

Federally owned land, 1996

	State	U.S.	State share
Total acres	15,411,000	2,271,343,000	0.68%
Federally owned	1,077,000	563,129,000	0.19%
Federal share	7.0%	24.8%	—

Areas are rounded to nearest thousand acres. Figures for federally owned land do not include trust properties.

Source: U.S. General Services Administration; *Inventory Report on Real Property Owned by the United States Throughout the World*, annual.

Land use, 1992

In acres, rounded to nearest thousand

Total surface area	15,508,000
Federal land	1,201,000
Total nonfederal	14,138,000
Developed	689,000
Total rural	13,449,000
Cropland.	915,000
Pasture land	1,609,000
Range land	0
Forest land	10,534,000
Minor cover/use.	391,000

Total surface area figures include water area not shown separately.

Source: U.S. Dept. of Agriculture; Soil Conservation Service; Iowa State University, Statistical Laboratory; *Summary Report, 1992 National Resources Inventory.*

Farms and crop acreage, 1997

	State	U.S.	Share	Rank
Farms (thousands)	20	2,058	0.97%	34
Acres (millions)	4	968	0.41%	39
Acres per farm	185	471	—	38
Acres planted	646	334,139	0.19%	39
Acres harvested	637	319,894	0.20%	39
Farm value (mill.)	$85	$108,805	0.08%	18

Numbers of farms are rounded to nearest thousand.

Source: U.S. Dept. of Agriculture; National Agricultural Statistics Service.

GOVERNMENT AND FINANCE

Units of local government, 1997

	State	Total U.S.	Rank
All local governments	704	87,453	36
Counties	55	3,043	28
Municipalities	232	19,372	32
Townships	0	16,629	—
School districts	55	13,726	39
Special districts	362	34,683	33

County ranks are based on the 48 states with county governments; township ranks are based on the 20 states with township governments; school district ranks are based on the 46 states with such districts.

Source: U.S. Bureau of the Census; *1997 Census of Governments, Government Organization*, Series GC97(1).

State government revenue, 1996

Total revenue	$6,866 mill.
General revenue	5,836 mill.
Per capita.	3,206
U.S. per capita average	2,910
Rank among states.	16
Intergovernmental revenue	
Total	$2,094 mill.
From federal government	2,079 mill.
From local government	15 mill.
Charges and Miscellaneous	
Total	$971 mill.
Current charges	555 mill.
Misc. general revenue	416 mill.
Taxes	
Total	$2,771 mill.
General sales	797 mill.
Selective sales.	655 mill.
License taxes	156 mill.
Individual income	751 mill.
Corporate income	235 mill.
Other	177 mill.
Insurance trust revenue	985 mill.

Total revenue figures include items not listed separately.

Source: U.S. Bureau of the Census.

State government expenditures, 1996

General expenditures

Intergovernmental	$1,325 mill.
Direct expenditures	4,297 mill.
Total	5,623 mill.

Selected direct expenditures

Education	$2,079 mill.
Public welfare	1,588 mill.
Health, hospital	203 mill.
Highways	705 mill.
Police	39 mill.
Corrections	82 mill.
Natural resources	140 mill.
Parks and recreation	40 mill.
Government administration	266 mill.
Interest on debt	163 mill.

Other

State per capita expenditures	$3,089
U.S. per capita average	2,854
Rank among states	17
Total state expenditures	6,970 mill.
Total U.S. expenditures	859,959 mill.

Totals include items not listed separately.
Source: U.S. Bureau of the Census.

Albert B. White (R)	1901-1905
William M. O. Dawson (R)	1905-1909
William E. Glasscock (R)	1909-1913
Henry D. Hatfield (R)	1913-1917
John J. Cornwell (D)	1917-1921
Ephriam F. Morgan (R)	1921-1925
Howard M. Gore (R)	1925-1929
William G. Conley (R)	1929-1933
Herman G. Kump (D)	1933-1937
Homer A. Holt (D)	1937-1941
Matthew M. Neely (D)	1941-1945
Clarence W. Meadows (D)	1945-1949
Okey L. Patteson (D)	1949-1953
William C. Marland (D)	1953-1957
Cecil H. Underwood (D)	1957-1961
William W. Barron (D)	1961-1965
Hulett C. Smith (D)	1965-1969
Arch A. Moore, Jr. (R)	1969-1977
John D. Rockefeller IV (D)	1977-1985
Arch A. Moore, Jr. (R)	1985-1989
Gaston Caperton (D)	1989-1997
Cecil H. Underwood (R)	1997-

POLITICS

Governors since statehood

D = Democrat; R = Republican; O = other;
(r) resigned; (d) died in office; (i) removed from office

Arthur I. Boreman (O)	(r) 1863-1869
Daniel D. T. Farnsworth (R)	1869
William E. Stevenson (R)	1869-1871
John J. Jacob (D)	1871-1877
Henry M. Mathews (D)	1877-1881
Jacob B. Jackson (D)	1881-1885
Emanuel Willis Wilson (D)	1885-1890
Aretas B. Fleming (D)	1890-1893
William A. MacCorkle (D)	1893-1897
George W. Atkinson (R)	1897-1901

Composition of state legislature, 1990-1998

	Democrats	Republicans
State House (100 seats)		
1990	74	26
1992	79	21
1994	69	30
1996	74	25
1998	75	25
State Senate (34 seats)		
1990	33	1
1992	32	2
1994	26	8
1996	25	9
1998	29	5

Figures for total seats may include independents and minor
party members.
Source: Council of State Governments; *State Elective Officials
and the Legislatures.*

Composition of congressional delegations, 1989-1999

	Dem	Rep	Total
House of Representatives			
101st Congress, 1989			
State delegates	4	0	4
Total U.S.	259	174	433
102d Congress, 1991			
State delegates	4	0	4
Total U.S.	267	167	434
103d Congress, 1993			
State delegates	3	0	3
Total U.S.	258	176	434
104th Congress, 1995			
State delegates	3	0	3
Total U.S.	197	236	433
105th Congress, 1997			
State delegates	3	0	3
Total U.S.	206	228	434
106th Congress, 1999			
State delegates	3	0	3
Total U.S.	211	222	433
Senate			
101st Congress, 1989			
State delegates	2	0	2
Total U.S.	55	45	100
102d Congress, 1991			
State delegates	2	0	2
Total U.S.	56	44	100
103d Congress, 1993			
State delegates	2	0	2
Total U.S.	57	43	100
104th Congress, 1995			
State delegates	2	0	2
Total U.S.	46	53	99
105th Congress, 1997			
State delegates	2	0	2
Total U.S.	45	55	100
106th Congress, 1999			
State delegates	2	0	2
Total U.S.	45	54	99

Figures are for starts of first sessions. Figure for U.S. Representatives for 101st Congress does not include Alabama and Indiana, which had vacancies. Figures for total U.S. Representatives for 102d, 103d, and 106th Congresses do not include Vermont, which had 1 Independent-Socialist. Figure for U.S. Representatives for 104th Congress does not include Vermont, which had 1 Independent-Socialist, and California, which had 1 vacancy. Figure for U.S. Representatives for 105th Congress does not include New York, which had 1 vacancy. Figure for U.S. Senators for 104th Congress does not include Oregon, which had 1 vacancy. Figure for U.S. Senators for 106th Congress does not include New Hampshire, which had 1 Independent.

Source: U.S. Congress; *Congressional Directory,* biennial.

Voter participation in presidential elections, 1992 and 1996

	1992	1996
State voting age pop.	1,376,000	1,414,000
Total U.S. voting age pop.	189,524,000	196,509,000
State share of U.S. total	0.7%	0.7%
Rank among states	34	34
Percent of state casting vote	49.7	47.0
Percent of U.S. total voting	55.1	49.0
Rank among states	45	38

Source: U.S. Bureau of the Census.

HEALTH AND MEDICAL CARE

Medicare, 1997

	Recipients	Payments
State	332,000	$1,504 mill.
Total U.S.	37,514,000	$206,064 mill.
State share	0.89%	0.73%
Rank among states	34	34

Recipient figures are rounded to nearest thousand persons. Ranks are from highest to lowest.

Source: U.S. Health Care Financing Administration.

Medicaid, 1996

	Recipients	Payments
State	395,000	$1,128 mill.
Total U.S.	35,028,000	$121,419 mill.
State share	1.13%	0.93%
Rank among states	28	29

Recipient figures are rounded to nearest thousand persons. Payment figures for fiscal year reflect federal and state contribution payments. Ranks are from highest to lowest.

Source: U.S. Health Care Financing Administration.

Health insurance coverage, 1996

	State	U.S.
Total persons covered	1,487,000	225,070,000
Total persons not covered	261,000	41,716,000
Part not covered	14.9%	15.6%
Rank among states	21	—
Children not covered	27,000	10,554,000
Part not covered	7.9%	14.8%
Rank among states	44	—

Ranks are from most to fewest uninsured. Population figures are rounded to nearest thousand persons.
Source: U.S. Bureau of the Census.

AIDS, syphilis, tuberculosis, and measles cases, 1997

Cases	U.S.	State	Share
AIDS	58,443	130	0.22%
Syphilis	8,550	1	0.01%
Tuberculosis	18,534	54	0.29%
Measles	148,000	1,000	0.68%

Measles figures are rounded to nearest thousand cases.
Source: U.S. Centers for Disease Control and Prevention.

HOUSING

Homeownership rates, 1985-1997

	1985	1990	1997
State	75.9%	72.0%	74.6%
Total U.S.	63.9%	63.9%	65.7%
Rank among states	1	5	4

Source: U.S. Bureau of the Census.

Home sales, 1990 and 1997
In thousands of units

Existing home sales	1990	1997	Change
State sales	42.0	45.2	3.2
Total U.S. sales	3,560	4,730	1,170
State share of U.S. total	1.18%	0.96%	-0.22%
Rank among states	30	33	—

Source: National Association of Realtors; *Real Estate Outlook: Market Trends and Insights.*

EDUCATION

Public school enrollment, 1995

State K-8 enrollment	211,000
Total U.S. K-8 enrollment	32,341,000
State share of total U.S.	0.65%
State 9-12 enrollment	96,000
Total U.S. 9-12 enrollment	12,500,000
State share of U.S. total	0.77%
State public school enroll. rate	96.6%
Overall U.S. rate	91.6%
Rank among states	4

Enrollment figures (which include unclassified students) are rounded to nearest thousand pupils in fall term; kindergarten (K)-8 grade figures include some prekindergarten students. Enrollment rate is based on percentage of persons 5-17 years old. Rank is from highest to lowest.
Source: U.S. National Center for Education Statistics.

Public college finances, 1996

State FTE enrollment	60,800
Total U.S. FTE enrollment	8,268,800
State share of total U.S.	0.74%
Rank among states	36
State and local appropriations	$198,300,000
Total U.S. state and local appropriations	$39,699 mill.
State share of total U.S.	0.50%
Rank among states	40
State net tuition revenues	$160,800,000
Total U.S. net tuition	$18,348,100,000
State share of total U.S.	0.88%
Rank among states	35

FTE = Full-time equivalent; credit and noncredit enrollment including summer session in academic year ending in 1996.
Enrollments are rounded to nearest thousand students. Net tuition revenues exclude appropriation to students attending in-state public institutions. Rankings are from highest shares to lowest.
Source: Research Associates of Washington.

TRANSPORTATION AND TRAVEL

Highway mileage, 1996

Interstate	550
Other arterial	3,248
Collector roads	9,240
Local roads	22,537
Urban roads	3,177
Rural roads	31,953
Total state	35,130
U.S. total	3,933,985
State share	0.9%
Rank among states	39

Source: U.S. Federal Highway Administration.

Motor vehicle registrations and driver licenses, 1996
In thousands

Vehicle registrations	State	U.S.	Share	Rank
Autos, trucks, buses	1,406	206,365	0.68%	37
Autos only	785	128,439	0.61%	36
Motorcycles	15	3,832	0.39%	47
Driver licenses	1,274	179,539	0.71%	37

Figures do not include vehicles owned by military services.
Source: U.S. Federal Highway Administration; *Highway Statistics; Selected Highway Statistics and Charts.*

Domestic travel expenditures, 1995
Spending by U.S. residents on overnight trips and day trips of at least 100 miles

Total expenditures in state	$1,467 mill.
Total expenditures in U.S.	$360,314 mill.
State share of total U.S.	0.41%
Rank among states	43

Source: Travel Industry Association of America.

CRIME AND LAW ENFORCEMENT

State and local police officers, 1996

Local police	1,416
State police	595
Sheriffs	726
Total	2,977
Officers per 10,000 residents	16
U.S. average	25
Rank among states	50

Figures cover full-time sworn officers; totals include special police not shown separately.
Source: U.S. Bureau of Justice Statistics; *Census of State and Local Law Enforcement Agencies, 1996.*

Crime rates, 1996
Rates per 100,000 resident population

Violent crimes	State	U.S.
Total violent	210	634
Murder	3.8	7.4
Forcible rape	19.6	36.1
Robbery	40	202
Aggravated assault	146	388
Property crimes		
Total property	2,273	4,445
Burglary	547	943
Larceny/theft	1,550	2,976
Motor vehicle theft	177	526
Totals	2,483	5,079

Source: U.S. Federal Bureau of Investigation; *Crime in the United States,* annual.

State prison populations, 1980-1996

	State	U.S.	State share
1980	1,257	305,458	0.41%
1990	1,565	708,393	0.22%
1996	2,749	1,025,624	0.27%

Figures exclude prisoners in federal penitentiaries.
Source: U.S. Bureau of Justice Statistics.

Wisconsin

Location: Upper Midwest of continental United States

Area and rank: 54,314 square miles (140,673 square kilometers); 65,503 square miles (169,653 square kilometers) including water; twenty-fifth largest state in area

Population and rank: 5,169,677 (1997); eighteenth largest state in population

Capital: Madison

Largest city: Milwaukee (578,364 people in 1998)

Became territory: July 4, 1836

Entered Union and rank: May 29, 1848; thirtieth state

Present constitution adopted: 1848

Counties: 72

State name: "Wisconsin" comes from a Chippewa word meaning "grassy place"

State nickname: Badger State

Motto: Forward

State flag: Field of royal blue with state coat of arms, state name in white above, "1848" below

Highest point: Timms Hill — 1,951 feet (595 meters)

Lowest point: Lake Michigan — 579 feet (176 meters)

Highest recorded temperature: 114 degrees Fahrenheit (46 degrees Celsius) — Wisconsin Dells, 1936

Lowest recorded temperature: −54 degrees Fahrenheit (−48 degrees Celsius) — Danbury, 1922

State song: "On, Wisconsin"

State tree: Sugar maple

State flower: Wood violet

State bird: Robin

State fish: Musky (Muskellunge)

State animal: Badger

State capitol building in Madison. (Wisconsin Department of Tourism/Bob Queen)

Wisconsin History

Influenced by a landscape shaped by ancient glaciers, Wisconsin developed into a state with three distinct regions. The southeast corner of Wisconsin, along the shore of Lake Michigan, is an urban, industrial area, dominated by Milwaukee, the state's largest city. The northern third of the state is a sparsely populated area of forests and lakes, primarily used for tourism and recreation. Between these two regions, the southern, western, and central areas of the state are productive agricultural lands, particularly in dairy farming.

Early History. During the last two million years, glaciers advanced and retreated over much of North America. The last major advance began about twenty-five thousand years ago and reached its greatest extent around fifteen thousand years ago. At this time, it covered nearly two-thirds of

Wisconsin. A smaller advance, about ten thousand years ago, covered only the northern part of the state. As a result of this glacial activity, this area now contains numerous streams and marshes, as well as more than fourteen thousand lakes. The areas of older glacial activity, which have been subjected to erosion, now contain flat plains and rolling hills. The southwest part of the state, which was not covered by glaciers, is an area of ridges and valleys carved by rivers.

The first humans to inhabit the area arrived about twelve thousand years ago, when much of northern Wisconsin was still covered with glaciers. These people, known as the Paleo-Indian culture, hunted bison and other large animals. About ten thousand years ago, as the climate warmed, the people of the Archaic culture hunted large and

Wisconsin's dairy farms have made the state the nation's leading producer of milk and cheese products. (PhotoDisc)

small animals and gathered wild plants for food. About three thousand years ago, the people of the Woodland culture used bows and arrows to hunt, made pottery, and built large mounds. About one thousand years ago, the people of the Mississippian culture lived in large, permanent villages and grew corn, beans, and squash.

In the early seventeenth century, just before Europeans arrived in the area, the major Native American peoples living in Wisconsin included the Santee Dakota in the northwest, the Menominee in the northeast, the Iowa in the southwest, and the Winnebago in the southeast. In addition to crops associated with the Mississippian culture, the peoples of northern Wisconsin also subsisted on wild rice growing in wetlands.

During the 1640's, the Iroquois, a powerful confederation of Native Americans living in the New York area, launched a series of wars against Native Americans living to the west. The Iroquois were enemies of the French, while the peoples living in the Great Lakes region were generally allied with the French and participated in the French fur trade. The wars drove many Native American peoples westward into Wisconsin, including the Potawatomi, the Ojibwa, the Sauk, the Fox, the Ottawa, the Huron, the Miami, the Mascouten, and the Kickapoo. Many of these peoples later moved farther west, but the Ojibwa, the Menominee, the Winnebago, and the Potawatomi remained in the state. Other Native American peoples moved westward into Wisconsin in the 1820's, including the Oneida, the Stockbridge, the Munsee, and the Brotherton. Most Native Americans in Wisconsin now live in reservations in the northern part of the state or in Milwaukee.

European Exploration and Settlement. The first European known to reach Wisconsin was the French explorer Jean Nicolet. In 1634 Nicolet journeyed from Lake Huron through the strait between the Upper and Lower Peninsulas of Michigan, becoming the first European to reach Lake Michigan. He then sailed into Green Bay, a narrow inlet of Lake Michigan, and reached Wisconsin. Here he negotiated a peace treaty with the Winnebago. In 1671 the French missionary Claude-Jean Allouez founded a mission at Green Bay. A fort was built on the site in 1717, and Green Bay served as the center of the fur trade in the area for one hundred years.

At the end of the French and Indian War, a struggle between France and Great Britain for control of North America, the area was acquired by the British. At the end of the American Revolution, twenty years later, the area was acquired by the United States. Wisconsin was part of the Northwest Territory from 1787 to 1800, part of the Indiana Territory from 1800 to 1809, part of the Illinois Territory from 1809 to 1818, and part of the Michigan Territory from 1818 to 1836. The Wisconsin Territory was created in 1836.

American settlement of the area began slowly. Although the future site of Milwaukee was settled as early as 1800, it did not develop into a town for thirty years. The United States built Fort Howard at Green Bay in 1816 and began building the town of

Locks on the upper Mississippi River, which forms part of Wisconsin's western border. (PhotoDisc)

With ports on Lake Superior, Lake Michigan, and the Mississippi River, Wisconsin has excellent access to world shipping. (Wisconsin Department of Tourism)

Green Bay in 1829. The opening of the Erie Canal in 1825, linking the Hudson River with Lake Erie, made travel between the heavily populated eastern states and the sparsely populated Great Lakes region much easier. The discovery of lead ores in southwestern Wisconsin in the 1820's also encouraged settlers. Mineral Point, established in the area of the lead mines in 1827, quickly became the most important settlement in the area and served as the first territorial capital.

Statehood and Economic Growth. At first, the Wisconsin Territory was settled mostly by Americans from eastern states. The lead mines brought immigrants from Cornwall, a region of southwestern England famous for mines, in the 1830's. These were soon followed by immigrants from Germany, Ireland, and Italy moving into southwestern Wisconsin. German immigrants also settled in Milwaukee in the 1840's. After losing a large part of its western lands to the newly created Iowa Territory in 1838, the Wisconsin Territory became the thirtieth state ten years later.

After statehood, settlers entered Wisconsin from eastern and southern states, Germany, Poland, Scandinavia, and the British Isles. As lead mining played a less important role in the state, dairy farming and other forms of agriculture came to dominate the economy. Several institutes of higher learning were founded in the late 1840's, and the nation's first kindergarten was opened in Watertown in 1856.

The national crisis over slavery led to the creation of the Republican Party of Wisconsin in Ripon in 1854. During the Civil War, Wisconsin was firmly on the side of the Union. The Republican Party continued to dominate state politics for a century. The war brought industrial development to Milwaukee, and the city went on to be an important center of labor-union activity.

In the 1870's, zinc ores were discovered in southwestern Wisconsin. Zinc mining remained an important industry in the state for more than one hundred years. The 1870's also saw the rise of the production of lumber in the northern part of the state. Lumber resources were nearly depleted by the 1920's, so the forestry industry turned from lumber to the production of woodpulp for paper-making. This would remain an important part of the economy. Iron mining developed in northern Wisconsin in the 1880's and continued into the 1960's.

The Twentieth Century. Wisconsin played an important role in the Progressive movement of the early twentieth century, as political reformers fought corruption and the influence of the railroads and other powerful business interests. A national leader in the Progressive movement, Wisconsin native Robert Marion La Follette, Sr., served as governor of the state from 1900 to 1906, and as a U.S. senator from 1906 until his death in 1925. The Progressive movement remained a faction within the Republican Party until 1934, when the Wisconsin Progressive Party was created. The party rejoined the Republicans in 1946, but many of its members joined the Democratic Party instead.

Influenced by the Progressive movement and labor unions, Milwaukee elected Socialist mayors in 1910, 1916, and 1948. Despite the state's reputation for reformist and radical politics, it also produced numerous conservative politicians. One of the most controversial was Wisconsin native Joseph Raymond McCarthy, who served as a U.S. senator from 1946 until his death in 1957. McCarthy drew national attention with accusations that a large number of Communists had infiltrated the government of the United States.

During the Great Depression of the 1930's, Wisconsin's economy, balanced between manufacturing and agriculture, suffered less than those of most states. Agriculture in particular remained remarkably stable, with Wisconsin leading the nation in dairy farming after 1920. Despite this stability, Wisconsin, like the rest of the nation, saw a shift in its population from farmlands to cities. In the 1920's about half of the state's residents lived in rural areas; by the 1980's, about two-thirds of the population lived in urban areas.

The need for military equipment during World War II greatly increased industrial production in the southeastern part of Wisconsin and made it one of the leading manufacturing states in the nation. The rise in the tourism industry in the second half of the twentieth century also greatly benefited the economy. Wisconsin's economy was slowed by a nationwide recession in the late 1980's, but to a lesser extent than most other states. During the 1990's, Wisconsin maintained a reputation for economic stability; an honest, efficient state government; and innovative, if controversial, public policies.

Rose Secrest

Wisconsin Time Line

1600's	Native Americans farm Wisconsin land.
1634	French explorer Jean Nicolet sails into Green Bay and becomes the first European to reach Wisconsin.
1640's	Iroquois begin a series of wars against other Native Americans, driving them west into Wisconsin.
1671	French missionary Claude-Jean Allouez founds a mission at Green Bay.
1717	French build a fort at Green Bay.
1763	End of the French and Indian War brings the area under British control.
1783	End of the American Revolution brings the area under the control of the United States.
1787	Wisconsin becomes part of the Northwest Territory.
1800	Future site of Milwaukee is settled.
1800	Wisconsin becomes part of the Indiana Territory.

1809	Wisconsin becomes part of the Illinois Territory.
1816	Americans build a fort at Green Bay.
Dec. 3, 1818	Wisconsin becomes part of the Michigan Territory.
1820's	Lead mining begins in Wisconsin.
1825	Opening of the Erie Canal improves transportation from eastern states to Wisconsin and other Great Lake states.
1827	Mineral Point is founded.
1830's	Cornish miners become the first major group of European immigrants to settle in the area.
1836	Wisconsin Territory is created, with the territorial capital at Mineral Point.
1837	Territorial capital is moved to Burlington.
1838	Newly formed settlement of Madison becomes the territorial capital.
1840's	Large numbers of German immigrants arrive.
1846	Beloit Colege in Beloit and Carroll College in Waukesha are founded.
1847	Carthage College in Kenosha and Lawrence University in Appleton are founded.
May 29, 1848	Wisconsin is admitted to the Union.
1849	University of Wisconsin is founded at Madison.
1854	Republican Party of Wisconsin is created at Ripon.
1856	Nation's first kindergarten is established at Watertown.
1857	Marquette University is founded in Milwaukee.
1863	Ripon College is founded in Ripon.
1870's	Zinc mining and lumber production begin in Wisconsin.
1875	Free high schools are established by state law.
1880's	Iron mining begins in the state.
1890's	Large numbers of Polish and Italian immigrants arrive.
1898	Saint Norbert College is founded in De Pere.
1900	Robert Marion La Follette, Sr., is elected governor.
1906	La Follette is elected a U.S. Senator.
1910	First Socialist mayor of Milwaukee is elected.
1920	For the first time, Wisconsin leads the nation in dairy farming.
1920's	Lumber production declines.
1936	University of Wisconsin hires painter John Steuart Curry as the nation's first artist-in-residence.
1946	Wisconsin's Joseph Raymond McCarthy is elected a U.S. senator.
1960's	Iron mining declines.
1970's	Zinc mining declines.
1971	University of Wisconsin merges with the Wisconsin State University system, creating one of the largest university systems in the nation.
1982	Community Options Program is created, allowing the elderly to be cared for in homelike settings.

(continued)

1983	Laws are passed allowing health maintenance organizations (HMOs) to exist in the state, greatly changing health care.
1990	Population reaches 4.9 million.
1997	Population reaches 5.2 million.
1999	BadgerCare, a state program designed to provide medical insurance for low-income families, is created.

Notes for Further Study

Published Sources. For the student new to the subject, a good starting place is *Wisconsin* (1998) by Jean F. Blashfield, which discusses the state's geography, history, natural resources, economy, culture, and people. To understand the political process in Wisconsin, a useful resource is Jack Stark's *The Wisconsin State Constitution: A Reference Guide* (1997). An excellent, often dramatic account of how laws are made in the state is found in *The Art of Legislative Politics* (1994) by Tom Loftus, which uses examples of political battles in Wisconsin over controversial topics such as abortion, gun control, and education. *Power to the People: An American State at Work* (1996), by Wisconsin governor Tommy G. Thompson, presents an interesting look at state politics from the inside. The economic changes in Wisconsin in the 1990's are discussed in *The End of the Line: Lost Jobs, New Lives in Postindustrial America* (1994) by Kathryn Marie Dudley, which deals with the closing of an automobile manufacturing plant in Racine and its aftereffects. A visual guide to the state's history is provided in *Wisconsin's Past and Present: A Historical Atlas* (1998) by members of the Wisconsin Cartographer's Guild. Frank L. Klement's *Wisconsin in the Civil War: The Home Front and the Battle Front, 1861-1865* (1997) provides a detailed account of a period often overlooked in Wisconsin history.

Web Resources. Several Web sites offer useful guides to the enormous variety of information about the state available on the Internet. A site with a long list of links to other Web sites is found at Wisconsin Information and Web sites (http://www.infomad.com/wisconsin). Another source of general information is Wisconline (http://www.wisconline.com), which also lists upcoming events in the state, provides detailed information on current weather conditions, and supplies an unusual star map displaying the constellations visible from Wisconsin at particular times. The state government's official Web site, State of Wisconsin Information Service (http://www.badger.state.wi.us) is a detailed source of information on the state, including national, state, and local governments. An excellent discussion of law and the lawmaking process is found at The Wisconsin Legislature (http://www.legis.state.wi.us). Statistical data can be found at Wisconsin (http://www.census.gov/cgi-bin/datamap/state?55), provided by the U.S. Bureau of the Census.

Travel in Wisconsin is the subject of Wisconsin Department of Tourism (http://www.travelwisconsin.com), which also provides maps of the state. Outstanding Web sites dedicated to the major cities in the state include Madison.com (http://www.madison.com), which also provides links to the city's newspapers, and Milwaukee Online (http://www.exeopc.com/~trilux), which also provides information for tourists. Official Web sites for the city governments can be found at City of Madison, Wisconsin (http://www.ci.madison.wi.us) and City of Milwaukee (http://www.ci.mil.us). Of the many sites dedicated to the state's history, a good place to start is The State Historical Society of Wisconsin (http://shsw.wisc/edu), which provides links to archives and historical libraries. Excellent information on many of the Native American peoples living in Wisconsin is provided by Great Lakes Intertribal Council Native Wisconsin Home Page (http://www.glitc.org/index.html).

Counties

County	Sq. miles	1996 pop.	County	Sq. miles	1996 pop.
Adams	647.8	17,836	Bayfield	1,476.4	15,059
Ashland	1,043.9	16,569	Brown	528.7	213,072
Barron	862.9	43,451	Buffalo	684.5	14,215

County	Sq. miles	1996 pop.	County	Sq. miles	1996 pop.
Burnett	821.5	14,383	Forest	1,014.1	9,588
Calumet	319.9	37,762	Grant	1,147.9	49,531
Chippewa	1,010.5	54,348	Green	584.0	32,755
Clark	1,215.7	32,866	Green Lake	354.3	19,414
Columbia	773.9	49,914	Iowa	762.7	21,862
Crawford	572.8	16,479	Iron	757.3	6,520
Dane	1,202.2	395,366	Jackson	987.3	17,325
Dodge	882.4	81,750	Jefferson	557.1	73,042
Door	482.7	26,934	Juneau	767.7	23,753
Douglas	1,309.3	43,051	Kenosha	272.8	141,646
Dunn	852.1	38,494	Kewaunee	342.7	19,661
Eau Claire	637.7	88,897	La Crosse	452.8	102,318
Florence	488.1	5,230	Lafayette	633.6	16,568
Fond du Lac	723.0	94,400	Langlade	872.7	20,535

(continued)

County	Sq. miles	1996 pop.
Lincoln	883.0	29,395
Manitowoc	591.6	82,588
Marathon	1,545.1	121,791
Marinette	1,402.0	42,751
Marquette	455.5	14,566
Menominee	358.0	4,609
Milwaukee	241.6	922,243
Monroe	900.9	39,044
Oconto	998.1	32,795
Oneida	1,124.7	35,516
Outagamie	640.4	153,099
Ozaukee	232.0	80,257
Pepin	232.3	7,130
Pierce	576.5	34,994
Polk	917.3	37,761
Portage	806.4	65,146
Price	1,252.7	15,910
Racine	333.1	185,003
Richland	586.3	17,958
Rock	720.5	150,584

County	Sq. miles	1996 pop.
Rusk	913.2	15,433
Saint Croix	722.0	56,137
Sauk	837.7	52,164
Sawyer	1,256.5	15,985
Shawano	892.6	38,487
Sheboygan	513.7	109,705
Taylor	975.0	19,264
Trempealeau	734.1	26,191
Vernon	795.0	27,279
Vilas	872.8	20,769
Walworth	555.4	83,355
Washburn	809.7	15,132
Washington	430.8	111,358
Waukesha	555.6	343,797
Waupaca	751.1	49,811
Waushara	626.1	21,272
Winnebago	438.6	149,703
Wood	792.9	76,219

Source: U.S. Census Bureau; National Association of Counties.

Cities
With 10,000 or more residents

Rank	City	Population
1	Milwaukee	578,364
2	Madison	209,306
3	Green Bay	97,789
4	Kenosha	87,849
5	Racine	81,095
6	Appleton	65,514
7	Waukesha	61,989
8	West Allis	59,974
9	Eau Claire	59,200
10	Janesville	59,149
11	Oshkosh	57,955
12	Sheboygan	49,377
13	La Crosse	49,075
14	Wauwatosa	45,850
15	Fond du Lac	39,724
16	Brookfield	37,747
17	New Berlin	37,230
18	Wausau	36,359
19	Beloit	35,157
20	Greenfield	34,497
21	Manitowoc	33,067
22	Menomonee Falls	31,386
23	West Bend	28,495

Rank	City	Population
24	Franklin	27,579
25	Oak Creek	27,219
26	Superior	27,142
27	Neenah	23,580
28	Stevens Point	22,196
29	Mequon	21,938
30	Muskego	21,589
31	Watertown	20,641
32	South Milwaukee	20,466
33	Sun Prairie	19,763
34	Marshfield	19,666
35	Fitchburg	19,500
36	De Pere	19,479
37	Wisconsin Rapids	18,475
38	Cudahy	18,108
39	Ashwaubenon	17,325
40	Germantown	17,269
41	Middleton	15,694
42	Menasha	15,412
43	Greendale	15,032
44	Onalaska	14,751
45	Menomonie	14,727
46	Pleasant Prairie	14,611

Rank	City	Population
47	Beaver Dam	14,603
48	Allouez	14,514
49	Glendale	13,533
50	Whitewater	13,251
51	Howard	13,228
52	Two Rivers	13,029
53	Whitefish Bay	12,978
54	Shorewood	12,777
55	Chippewa Falls	12,708
56	Kaukauna	12,150
57	Marinette	12,025
58	Brown Deer	11,999

Rank	City	Population
59	River Falls	11,726
60	Stoughton	11,542
61	Oconomowoc	11,385
62	Fort Atkinson	10,873
63	Monroe	10,762
64	Cedarburg	10,559
65	Port Washington	10,542
66	Plover	10,369
67	Merrill	10,298
68	Little Chute	10,236

Population figures are estimated for mid-1998.
Source: U.S. Bureau of the Census.

Index to Tables

NA = Reliable data are not available.

DEMOGRAPHICS

Resident state and national populations, 1970-1997

Population figures given in thousands

	State pop.	U.S. pop.	Share	Rank
1970	4,418	203,302	2.2%	16
1980	4,706	226,546	2.1%	16
1985	4,748	237,924	2.0%	16
1990	4,892	248,765	2.0%	16
1995	5,113	262,761	1.9%	18
1997	5,170	267,636	1.9%	18

Source: U.S. Bureau of the Census.

Resident population by age, 1997

Age group	Total population
Under 5 years	335,000
5 to 17 years	1,011,000
18 to 24 years	484,000
25 to 34 years	725,000
35 to 44 years	859,000
45 to 54 years	650,000
55 to 64 years	422,000
65 to 74 years	355,000
75 to 84 years	240,000
85 years and over	88,000
Portion of residents 65 and older	13.2%
National average	12.7%

Population figures are rounded to nearest thousand persons;
figures include armed forces personnel stationed in state.
Source: U.S. Bureau of the Census.

Resident population by race, Hispanic origin, 1997

	State pop.	Share	U.S.
All residents	5,170,000	100.0%	100.0%
Hispanic white	114,000	2.2%	10.0%
non-Hispanic white	4,646,000	89.9%	72.7%
African American	286,000	5.5%	12.7%
Native American	46,000	0.9%	0.9%
Asian, Pacific Islander	77,000	1.5%	3.8%

Source: U.S. Bureau of the Census.

Projections of state population, 2000-2025

	Model A Uses interstate migration observed from 1975-1994	Model B Uses Bureau of Economic Analysis employment projections
Year	Population	Population
2000	5,326,000	5,324,000
2005	5,479,000	5,502,000
2010	5,590,000	5,682,000
2015	5,693,000	5,864,000
2020	5,788,000	6,035,000
2025	5,867,000	6,185,000

All population projections, including those for 2000, were calculated in 1997.
Source: U.S. Bureau of the Census, Population Paper Listings PPL-47.

VITAL STATISTICS

Average lifetime in years by race, 1989-1991

	State	U.S.	Rank
All residents	76.87	75.37	11
White residents	77.18	76.13	9
Black residents	70.96	69.16	5

Ranks are from longest-lived to least longest-lived. Ranks exclude Alaska, for which reliable data are not available. Rank for black residents is based on the 32 states for which reliable data are available.
Source: U.S. National Center for Health Statistics.

Infant mortality rates, 1980 and 1995

	State	U.S.
All residents		
1980	10.3	12.6
1995	7.3	7.6
White residents		
1980	9.7	11.0
1995	6.3	6.3
Black residents		
1980	18.5	21.4
1995	18.6	15.1

Figures represent deaths per 1,000 live births of resident infants under 1 year old, exclusive of fetal deaths; all-residents figures include other races not listed separately.
Source: U.S. National Center for Health Statistics.

Marriages and divorces

Marriages in 1996. 36,200
Rate per 1,000 population, 1995. . . . . 7.1
U.S. rate, 1995 . . . . 8.9
Rank among all states 43

Divorces in 1996 17,300
Rate per 1,000 population, 1995. . . . . 3.4
U.S. rate, 1995 . . . . 4.4
Rank among all states 37

Rank is from highest to lowest in country.
Source: U.S. National Center for Health Statistics.

Death rates by leading causes, 1995
Deaths per 100,000 resident population

Cause	State	U.S.
Heart disease	281.4	280.7
Cancer	206.3	204.9
Cerebrovascular diseases	69.8	60.1
Accidents and adverse effects	35.6	35.5
Motor vehicle accidents	15.1	16.5
Chronic obstructive pulmonary diseases	36.7	39.2
Diabetes mellitus	21.6	22.6
HIV	-	NA
Suicide	12.1	11.9
Homicide	4.7	8.7
All causes	880.1	880.0
Rank in overall death rate among states		29

Figures exclude nonresidents who die in state. Causes of death follow International Classification of Diseases. Rank is from highest to lowest in country.
Source: U.S. National Center for Health Statistics.

ECONOMY

Gross state product, 1990-1996
In current dollars

	State product	Increase
1990	$99.2 billion	
1993	$117.7 billion	
1994	$125.8 billion	6.88%
1995	$132.7 billion	5.48%
1996	$139.2 billion	4.90%

Source: U.S. Bureau of Economic Analysis; *Survey of Current Business*, June, 1998.

Gross state product by industry, 1996
In billions

Farms, forestry, fisheries	$2.6
Construction	5.2
Manufacturing	38.3
Transportation, public utilities	9.2
Wholesale trade	8.4
Retail trade	11.7
Finance, insurance, real estate	19.7
Services	20.0
Government	13.5
State total	$128.7
Total U.S.	$6,923.8
State share	1.86%
Rank among states	18

Total figures include mining, not listed separately.
Source: U.S. Bureau of Economic Analysis; *Survey of Current Business*, June, 1998.

Personal income per capita, 1990 and 1997
In current dollars

	1990	1997
Per capita income	$17,722	$24,475
U.S. average	$19,188	$25,598
Rank among states	23	22

1997 data are preliminary.
Source: U.S. Bureau of Economic Analysis; *Survey of Current Business*, May, 1998.

Energy consumption, 1995
In trillions of British thermal units (BTU)

End-use sectors

Residential	387.4
Commercial	263.2
Industrial	720.8
Transportation	394.6

Sources of energy

Petroleum	535.7
Natural gas	384.7
Coal	443.0
Hydroelectric power	55.6
Nuclear electric power	116.9
Total state per capita consumption	341.5
Total U.S. per capita consumption	344.4
Rank among states	27
Total state energy consumption	1,749.1
Total U.S. energy consumption	90,547.4
State share of U.S. total	1.93%
Rank among states	19

Total figures include items not listed separately.
Source: U.S. Energy Information Administration; *State Energy Data Report*.

Nonfarm employment by sectors, 1997

Total	2,653,000
Construction	109,000
Manufacturing	609,000
Transportation, public utilities	123,000
Wholesale trade, retail trade	605,000
Finance, insurance, real estate	140,000
Services	678,000
Government	386,000

Figures are rounded to nearest thousand persons. Total includes mining, not listed separately.
Source: U.S. Bureau of Labor Statistics; *Employment and Earnings*, monthly.

Foreign exports, 1990-1997
In millions of dollars

Year	State	U.S.	State share
1990	5,158	394,045	1.31%
1996	9,504	624,767	1.52%
1997	10,125	688,896	1.47%

Source: U.S. Bureau of the Census; *U.S. Merchandise Trade*, series FT 900.

LAND USE

Federally owned land, 1996

	State	U.S.	State share
Total acres	35,011,000	2,271,343,000	1.54%
Federally owned	1,733,000	563,129,000	0.31%
Federal share	5.0%	24.8%	—

Areas are rounded to nearest thousand acres. Figures for federally owned land do not include trust properties.
Source: U.S. General Services Administration; *Inventory Report on Real Property Owned by the United States Throughout the World,* annual.

Land use, 1992
In acres, rounded to nearest thousand

Total surface area	35,938,000
Federal land	1,829,000
Total nonfederal	32,747,000
Developed	2,357,000
Total rural	30,390,000
Cropland	10,813,000
Pasture land	2,954,000
Range land	0
Forest land	13,410,000
Minor cover/use	3,212,000

Total surface area figures include water area not shown separately.
Source: U.S. Dept. of Agriculture; Soil Conservation Service; Iowa State University, Statistical Laboratory; *Summary Report, 1992 National Resources Inventory.*

Farms and crop acreage, 1997

	State	U.S.	Share	Rank
Farms (thousands)	79	2,058	3.84%	8
Acres (millions)	17	968	1.76%	18
Acres per farm	213	471	—	35
Acres planted	8,012	334,139	2.40%	15
Acres harvested	7,677	319,894	2.40%	15
Farm values (mill.)	$2,373	$108,805	2.18%	37

Numbers of farms are rounded to nearest thousand.
Source: U.S. Dept. of Agriculture; National Agricultural Statistics Service.

GOVERNMENT AND FINANCE

Units of local government, 1997

	State	Total U.S.	Rank
All local governments	3,059	87,453	11
Counties	72	3,043	19
Municipalities	583	19,372	11
Townships	1,266	16,629	7
School districts	442	13,726	12
Special districts	696	34,683	15

County ranks are based on the 48 states with county governments; township ranks are based on the 20 states with township governments; school district ranks are based on the 46 states with such districts.
Township figures include "town" governments.
Source: U.S. Bureau of the Census; *1997 Census of Governments, Government Organization,* Series GC97(1).

State government revenue, 1996

Total revenue	$24,365 mill.
General revenue	16,071 mill.
Per capita	3,123
U.S. per capita average	2,910
Rank among states	17
Intergovernmental revenue	
Total	$3,860 mill.
From federal government	3,578 mill.
From local government	282 mill.
Charges and Miscellaneous	
Total	$2,626 mill.
Current charges	1,505 mill.
Misc. general revenue	1,121 mill.
Taxes	
Total	$9,586 mill.
General sales	2,708 mill.
Selective sales	1,322 mill.
License taxes	614 mill.
Individual income	4,151 mill.
Corporate income	621 mill.
Other	170 mill.
Insurance trust revenue	8,294 mill.

Total revenue figures include items not listed separately.
Source: U.S. Bureau of the Census.

State government expenditures, 1996

General expenditures
Intergovernmental	$6,290 mill.
Direct expenditures	8,961 mill.
Total	15,251 mill.

Selected direct expenditures
Education	$5,324 mill.
Public welfare	3,193 mill.
Health, hospital	969 mill.
Highways	1,172 mill.
Police	61 mill.
Corrections	513 mill.
Natural resources	496 mill.
Parks and recreation	57 mill.
Government administration	427 mill.
Interest on debt	548 mill.

Other
State per capita expenditures	$2,964
U.S. per capita average	2,854
Rank among states	20
Total state expenditures	16,990 mill.
Total U.S. expenditures	859,959 mill.

Totals include items not listed separately.
Source: U.S. Bureau of the Census.

Edward Scofield (R)	1897-1901
Robert M. LaFollette (R)	(r) 1901-1906
James O. Davidson (R)	1906-1911
Francis E. McGovern (R)	1911-1915
Emanuel L. Philipp (R)	1915-1921
John J. Blaine (R)	1921-1927
Fred R. Zimmerman (R)	1927-1929
Walter J. Kohler (R)	1929-1931
Philip F. LaFollette (R)	1931-1933
Albert G. Schmedeman (D)	1933-1935
Philip F. LaFollette (O)	1935-1939
Julius P. Heil (R)	1939-1943
Walter S. Goodland (R)	(d) 1943-1947
Oscar Rennebohm (R)	1947-1951
Walter J. Kohler, Jr. (R)	1951-1957
Vernon W. Thomson (R)	1957-1959
Gaylord A. Nelson (D)	1959-1963
John W. Reynolds, Jr. (D)	1963-1965
Warren P. Knowles (R)	1965-1971
Patrick J. Lucey (D)	(r) 1971-1977
Martin Schreiber (D)	1977-1979
Lee S. Dreyfus (R)	1979-1983
Anthony S. Earl (D)	1983-1987
Tommy G. Thompson (R)	1987-

POLITICS

Governors since statehood
D = Democrat; R = Republican; O = other;
(r) resigned; (d) died in office; (i) removed from office

Nelson Dewey (D)	1848-1852
Leonard J. Farwell (O)	1852-1854
William A. Barstow (D)	(r) 1854-1856
Arthur MacArthur (D)	1856
Coles Bashford (R)	1856-1858
Alexander W. Randall (R)	1858-1862
Louis P. Harve(r)y (R)	1862
Edward Saloman (R)	1862-1864
James T. Lewis (R)	1864-1866
Lucius Fairchild (R)	1866-1872
Cadwallader C. Washburn (R)	1872-1874
William R. Taylor (D)	1874-1876
Harrison Ludington (D)	1876-1878
William E. Smith (D)	1878-1882
Jeremiah M. Rusk (D)	1882-1889
William D. Hoard (R)	1889-1891
George W. Peck (D)	1891-1895
William H. Upham (R)	1895-1897

Composition of state legislature, 1990-1998

	Democrats	Republicans
State Assembly (99 seats)		
1990	58	41
1992	51	47
1994	48	51
1996	47	52
1998	45	54
State Senate (33 seats)		
1990	19	14
1992	16	17
1994	16	17
1996	17	16
1998	17	16

Figures for total seats may include independents and minor
party members.
Source: Council of State Governments; *State Elective Officials
and the Legislatures.*

Composition of congressional delegations, 1989-1999

	Dem	Rep	Total
House of Representatives			
101st Congress, 1989			
State delegates	5	4	9
Total U.S.	259	174	433
102d Congress, 1991			
State delegates	4	5	9
Total U.S.	267	167	434
103d Congress, 1993			
State delegates	4	5	9
Total U.S.	258	176	434
104th Congress, 1995			
State delegates	5	4	9
Total U.S.	197	236	433
105th Congress, 1997			
State delegates	5	4	9
Total U.S.	206	228	434
106th Congress, 1999			
State delegates	5	4	9
Total U.S.	211	222	433
Senate			
101st Congress, 1989			
State delegates	1	1	2
Total U.S.	55	45	100
102d Congress, 1991			
State delegates	1	1	2
Total U.S.	56	44	100
103d Congress, 1993			
State delegates	2	0	2
Total U.S.	57	43	100
104th Congress, 1995			
State delegates	2	0	2
Total U.S.	46	53	99
105th Congress, 1997			
State delegates	2	0	2
Total U.S.	45	55	100
106th Congress, 1999			
State delegates	2	0	2
Total U.S.	45	54	99

Figures are for starts of first sessions. Figure for U.S. Representatives for 101st Congress does not include Alabama and Indiana, which had vacancies. Figures for total U.S. Representatives for 102d, 103d, and 106th Congresses do not include Vermont, which had 1 Independent-Socialist. Figure for U.S. Representatives for 104th Congress does not include Vermont, which had 1 Independent-Socialist, and California, which had 1 vacancy. Figure for U.S. Representatives for 105th Congress does not include New York, which had 1 vacancy. Figure for U.S. Senators for 104th Congress does not include Oregon, which had 1 vacancy. Figure for U.S. Senators for 106th Congress does not include New Hampshire, which had 1 Independent.

Source: U.S. Congress; *Congressional Directory*, biennial.

Voter participation in presidential elections, 1992 and 1996

	1992	1996
State voting age pop.	3,675,000	3,824,000
Total U.S. voting age pop.	189,524,000	196,509,000
State share of U.S. total	1.9%	2.0%
Rank among states	18	18
Percent of state casting vote	68.9	49.7
Percent of U.S. total voting	55.1	49.0
Rank among states	3	26

Source: U.S. Bureau of the Census.

HEALTH AND MEDICAL CARE

Medicare, 1997

	Recipients	Payments
State	770,000	$3,109 mill.
Total U.S.	37,514,000	$206,064 mill.
State share	2.05%	1.51%
Rank among states	17	21

Recipient figures are rounded to nearest thousand persons. Ranks are from highest to lowest.

Source: U.S. Health Care Financing Administration.

Medicaid, 1996

	Recipients	Payments
State	434,000	$1,904 mill.
Total U.S.	35,028,000	$121,419 mill.
State share	1.24%	1.57%
Rank among states	26	21

Recipient figures are rounded to nearest thousand persons. Payment figures for fiscal year reflect federal and state contribution payments. Ranks are from highest to lowest.

Source: U.S. Health Care Financing Administration.

Health insurance coverage, 1996

	State	U.S.
Total persons covered	4,781,000	225,070,000
Total persons not covered	438,000	41,716,000
Part not covered	8.4%	15.6%
Rank among states	50	—
Children not covered	90,000	10,554,000
Part not covered	6.2%	14.8%
Rank among states	48	—

Ranks are from most to fewest uninsured. Population figures are rounded to nearest thousand persons.
Source: U.S. Bureau of the Census.

AIDS, syphilis, tuberculosis, and measles cases, 1997

Cases	U.S.	State	Share
AIDS	58,443	255	0.44%
Syphilis	8,550	89	1.04%
Tuberculosis	18,534	130	0.70%
Measles	148,000	1,000	0.68%

Measles figures are rounded to nearest thousand cases.
Source: U.S. Centers for Disease Control and Prevention.

HOUSING

Homeownership rates, 1985-1997

	1985	1990	1997
State	63.8%	68.3%	68.3%
Total U.S.	63.9%	63.9%	65.7%
Rank among states	37	20	25

Source: U.S. Bureau of the Census.

Home sales, 1990 and 1997
In thousands of units

Existing home sales	1990	1997	Change
State sales	74.2	104.6	30.4
Total U.S. sales	3,560	4,730	1,170
State share of U.S. total	2.08%	2.21%	0.13%
Rank among states	17	16	—

Source: National Association of Realtors; *Real Estate Outlook: Market Trends and Insights.*

EDUCATION

Public school enrollment, 1995

State K-8 enrollment 603,000
Total U.S. K-8 enrollment 32,341,000
State share of total U.S. 1.86%
State 9-12 enrollment 267,000
Total U.S. 9-12 enrollment 12,500,000
State share of U.S. total 2.14%
State public school enroll. rate 87.0%
Overall U.S. rate 91.6%
Rank among states 47

Enrollment figures (which include unclassified students) are rounded to nearest thousand pupils in fall term; kindergarten (K)-8 grade figures include some prekindergarten students. Enrollment rate is based on percentage of persons 5-17 years old. Rank is from highest to lowest.
Source: U.S. National Center for Education Statistics.

Public college finances, 1996

State FTE enrollment 180,900
Total U.S. FTE enrollment 8,268,800
State share of total U.S. 2.19%
Rank among states 14
State and local appropriations $1,034,200,000
Total U.S. state and local appropriations . . . . $39,699 mill.
State share of total U.S. 2.61%
Rank among states 12
State net tuition revenues $425,100,000
Total U.S. net tuition $18,348,100,000
State share of total U.S. 2.32%
Rank among states 15

FTE=Full-time equivalent; credit and noncredit enrollment including summer session in academic year ending in 1996.
Enrollments are rounded to nearest thousand students. Net tuition revenues exclude appropriation to students attending in-state public institutions. Rankings are from highest shares to lowest.
Source: Research Associates of Washington.

TRANSPORTATION AND TRAVEL

Highway mileage, 1996

Interstate	745
Other arterial	11,857
Collector roads	22,931
Local roads	77,393
Urban roads	15,982
Rural roads	95,453
Total state	111,435
U.S. total	3,933,985
State share	2.8%
Rank among states	15

Source: U.S. Federal Highway Administration.

Motor vehicle registrations and driver licenses, 1996
In thousands

Vehicle registrations	State	U.S.	Share	Rank
Autos, trucks, buses	3,972	206,365	1.92%	18
Autos only	2,460	128,439	1.92%	19
Motorcycles	169	3,832	4.41%	6
Driver licenses	3,724	179,539	2.07%	18

Figures do not include vehicles owned by military services.
Source: U.S. Federal Highway Administration; *Highway Statistics; Selected Highway Statistics and Charts.*

Domestic travel expenditures, 1995
Spending by U.S. residents on overnight trips and day trips of at least 100 miles

Total expenditures in state	$4,809 mill.
Total expenditures in U.S.	$360,314 mill.
State share of total U.S.	1.33%
Rank among states	25

Source: Travel Industry Association of America.

CRIME AND LAW ENFORCEMENT

State and local police officers, 1996

Local police	7,640
State police	497
Sheriffs	3,886
Total	12,678
Officers per 10,000 residents	25
U.S. average	25
Rank among states	14

Figures cover full-time sworn officers; totals include special police not shown separately.
Source: U.S. Bureau of Justice Statistics; *Census of State and Local Law Enforcement Agencies, 1996.*

Crime rates, 1996
Rates per 100,000 resident population

Violent crimes	State	U.S.
Total violent	253	634
Murder	4.0	7.4
Forcible rape	21.0	36.1
Robbery	97	202
Aggravated assault	131	388
Property crimes		
Total property	3,569	4,445
Burglary	588	943
Larceny/theft	2,635	2,976
Motor vehicle theft	346	526
Totals	3,821	5,079

Source: U.S. Federal Bureau of Investigation; *Crime in the United States,* annual.

State prison populations, 1980-1996

	State	U.S.	State share
1980	3,980	305,458	1.30%
1990	7,465	708,393	1.05%
1996	12,991	1,025,624	1.27%

Figures exclude prisoners in federal penitentiaries.
Source: U.S. Bureau of Justice Statistics.

Wyoming

Location: Western continental United States

Area and rank: 97,105 square miles (251,501 square kilometers); 97,818 square miles (253,349 square kilometers) including water; ninth largest state in area

Population and rank: 479,743 (1997); fiftieth largest state in population

Capital: Cheyenne

Largest city: Cheyenne (53,640 people in 1998)

State capitol building in Cheyenne. (©James Blank/Weststock)

Became territory:
May 19, 1869

Entered Union and rank: July 10, 1890; forty-fourth state

Present constitution adopted: 1890

Counties: 23, as well as Yellowstone National Park

State name: "Wyoming" is derived from the Delaware Indian word meaning "mountains and valleys alternating"

State nickname: Equality State

Motto: Equal rights

State flag: Blue field with border of white and red with white silhouette of buffalo bearing the state seal in blue

Highest point: Gannett Peak — 13,804 feet (4,207 meters)

Lowest point: Belle Fourche River — 3,099 feet (945 meters)

Highest recorded temperature: 114 degrees Fahrenheit (46 degrees Celsius) — Basin, 1900

Lowest recorded temperature: −63 degrees Fahrenheit (−53 degrees Celsius) — Moran, 1933

State song: "Wyoming"

State tree: Cottonwood

State flower: Indian paintbrush

State bird: Meadowlark

National parks: Grand Teton, Yellowstone

Wyoming History

Wyoming is an expansive, arid land of high sweeping plains punctuated by series of mountain ranges. Its average elevation is some 6,700 feet above sea level. Travelers have frequently remarked on the state's austere beauty: "Nature has collected all of her beauties together," explorer John C. Frémont wrote of the region in 1842, "in one chosen place." Passing through the state's southern tier at night, travelers are mesmerized by multiple, simultaneous lightning storms illuminating vast plains, jagged mountains silhouetted in the background.

For all its magnificence, however, for much of its history Wyoming has been only the path to somewhere else. Today, Wyoming's immense emptiness supports fewer than half a million people, a diminishing portion of whom are destined to lead rugged lives employed in mining, livestock grazing, and agriculture. Memory of the state's colorful past is kept alive by frequent rodeos, roundups, and frontier celebrations. Each summer tourists flock to its spectacular scenery—to Jackson Hole, the Grand Tetons, and incomparable Yellowstone, the world's first national park.

Early History. According to archaeological evidence, the earliest immigrants to Wyoming arrived about eleven thousand years ago, leaving various traces. In 1965 two dwellings testifying to the habitation of the earliest peoples were discovered near Guernsey, on the North Platte River, southeast of Casper. For many years immense herds of buffalo roamed the midwestern plains. They attracted many migrating peoples from Asia who traversed the Bering Straits, many of them inhabiting the Wyoming region—tribes such as the Arapaho, Bannock, Crow, Cheyenne, Sioux, and Shoshone.

Yellowstone National Park's Old Faithful geyser is perhaps Wyoming's single most famous landmark. (PhotoDisc)

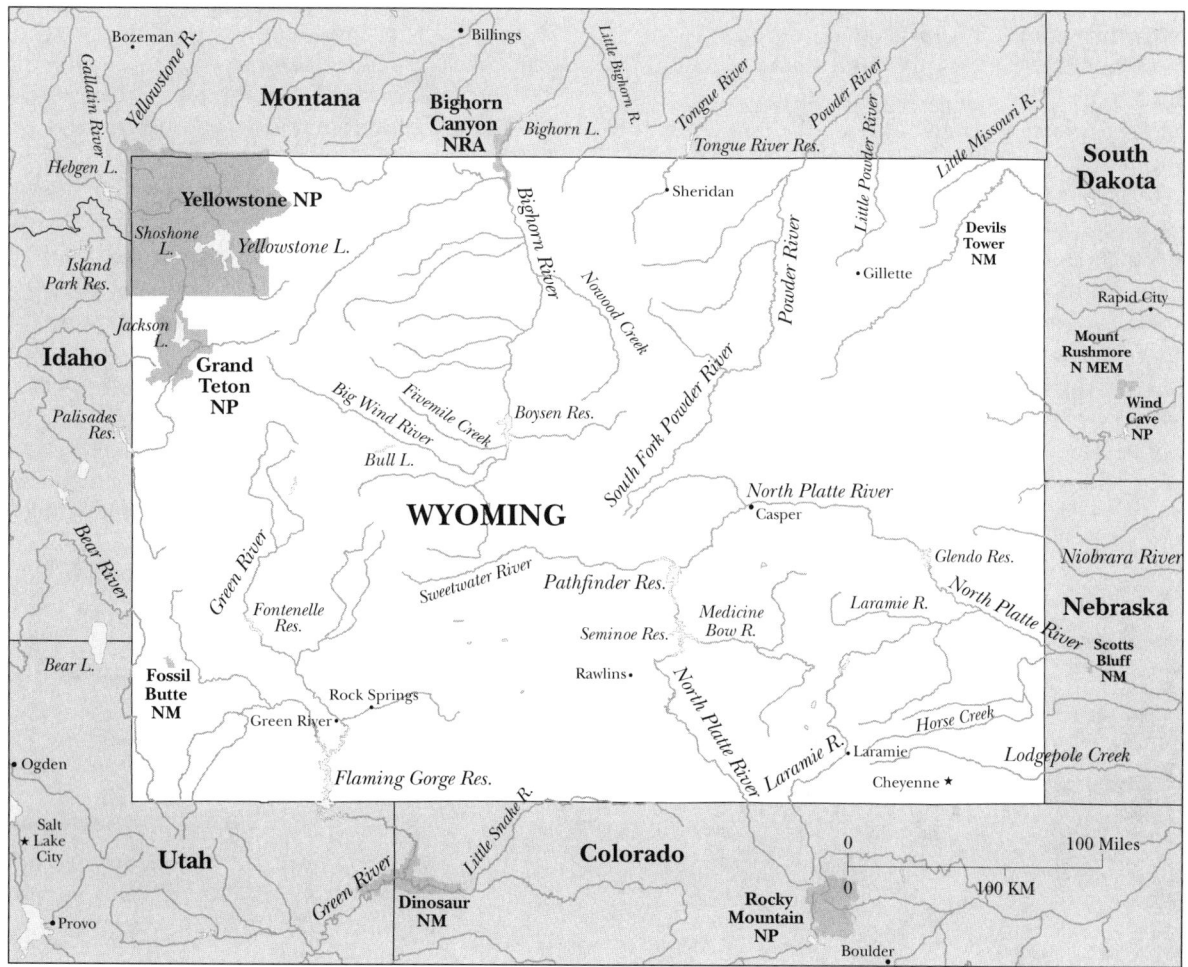

Earliest contact between these peoples and whites may have occurred in the mid-eighteenth century, when French trappers entered the area. Extensive exploration did not begin until the following century, however, after the United States concluded the Louisiana Purchase in 1803 and President Thomas Jefferson sent Meriwether Lewis and William Clark to chart what the nation had bought. By then, parts of Wyoming had been claimed by Spain, France, and Great Britain. It required several more acquisitions for Wyoming's modern territory to be completed. The 1819 Treaty with Spain, the partition of Texas after the Lone Star Republic joined the Union in 1845, the agreement with Britain over the Columbia River country in 1846, and the Treaty of Guadalupe Hidalgo in 1848 all included land within the state's modern borders.

Exploration. Fur trading was the initial stimulus to exploring Wyoming. The first American to do so was a former member of the Lewis and Clark Expedition, John Colter. In 1807 Colter traveled across the Yellowstone area, where he sighted its geothermal activity. Other fur traders crossed Wyoming going to and from Astoria, Oregon. In the 1820's more fur trappers and traders made their way west, many of them to Wyoming. In 1825 an annual gathering of these men, who included Indians, was inaugurated that lasted for fifteen years. In 1834 traders founded Fort Williams, later renamed Fort Laramie, which became the area's first permanent trading post. In 1843 famous scout Jim Bridger founded a second trading post near the western end of the state, east of Evanston.

At about the same time, John C. Frémont led a

party through the region guided by scout Kit Carson. Frémont's reports to Congress on his explorations spurred provision for protection of migrants on the Oregon Trail, and in 1849, the government purchased Fort Williams. Wyoming had become a pathway for tens of thousands of migrants and adventurers using several trails leading west, including the Oregon, California, and Mormon Trails. These trails traversed the South Pass through the Rocky Mountains, continued to Fort Bridger, then divided. The first Mormon party passed through in 1847. A Mormon colony established near the Utah border perished in a blizzard in 1856. A succession of outposts was established in the 1860's, including telegraph stations and state coach and freight line stops. In 1860-1861, Pony Express riders crossed Wyoming in their epic journey from Missouri to California.

From the late 1840's onward, Native Americans viewed these developments with suspicion. The opening of the Bozeman Trail in 1863-1865 after gold was discovered in Montana particularly alarmed them, as settlers streamed in. Native Americans and settlers made and broke treaties, and fighting continued throughout the decade. Settlers began to arrive in greater numbers when gold was discovered in the South Pass area in 1867 and later when coal was found. To keep the Bozeman Trail operating, the U.S. Army opened Fort Phil Kearney in 1866. The Sioux, led by Chief Red Cloud, detested the fort and determined to raze it. More than 150 white men were killed in its defense, including 81, led by Captain W. J. Fetterman, killed in a single battle. The army closed the fort in 1868 after concluding a treaty with the Sioux, who agreed not to oppose the building of a railroad in the south.

Becoming a Territory. The greatest influx of settlers occurred with railroads, beginning with the Union Pacific, which crossed Wyoming in 1868. Construction camps that sprang up became towns, such as Rawlins, Green River, and Rock Springs; more towns arose along the great trails. By 1870 Wyoming had more than nine thousand white inhabitants. Discovery of gold in the Black Hills of the Dakotas led to fierce Indian resistance, when thousands of settlers ignored treaty provisions and moved into territory the Sioux considered sacred. Bloody battles were fought with the U.S. Army. Peace was finally restored in 1876, when the last of the Indian fighters fled or surrendered and settled on reservations.

By then Wyoming had undergone development as a separate society. The coming of the railroad led to the formation of Wyoming Territory in 1869. Population jumped to more than twenty thousand in 1880 and to some sixty-two thousand in 1890. Mining was supplemented by cattle

Women voting in Cheyenne in 1888. Wyoming was one of the first states, or territories, to give women the vote—largely as an inducement to attract women to come to the predominantly male pioneer territory. (Library of Congress)

grazing and shipments of longhorns from Texas on their way to market. Sheep also made their appearance, setting the stage for protracted struggle between sheep- and cattlemen later immortalized in Hollywood films. Oil had been known to exist in the region since the 1830's, when it was used to grease wagon wheels. In 1883 the first well was drilled in the Dallas Field, in the Wind River region.

Politically, Wyoming Territory was growing up quickly. In 1869 it became the first territorial legislature to allow women to vote, serve on juries, and hold office. In 1924 it was first to elect a woman governor. However, in certain respects it remained primitive. The Wyoming Stock Growers Association, formed as a local association in 1873, grew powerful enough to enforce its own vigilante law in defense of its interests. In the 1890's matters deteriorated with the decline of the cattle industry and ruinous cattle rustling, by groups such as the notorious Hole-in-the Wall Gang. Homesteaders, who fenced off the open range, arrived. In 1892 the association decided to act, embarking on the Johnson County cattle war. Texas gunmen, hired to murder a list of enemies, killed two men before the law stepped in. Later in the 1890's more violence occurred with the influx of sheepherders, blamed for the inability of cattle to find sufficient food.

Statehood. These events aside, by the turn of the century Wyoming was fast becoming part of the nation. In 1889, without waiting for passage of a congressional enabling act, a proposed state constitution was drawn up. The following year Wyoming became the nation's forty-fourth state. It arrived into the Union with a progressive constitution that included a provision for women's suffrage. The constitution also included fulsome support for popular sovereignty and freedom of religion. Judges would be elected, not appointed, on a nonpartisan basis. The constitution was made difficult to amend.

The state's politics have been marked by both conservative and maverick tendencies. In the

In 1906 Devil's Tower became the first site in the United States to receive federal protection as a national monument. (PhotoDisc)

1980's one of its senators, Dick Cheney, was selected secretary of defense, and another, Alan Simpson, was widely admired by political opponents for his candor and civility. Wyoming has also been noted for its patriotism. Despite its small size, it contributed to the Spanish-American War of 1898, surpassing its quota of volunteers. It also sent twelve thousand men and women to World War I.

Economically, Wyoming was able to increase its agriculture after the turn of the century through irrigation, as homesteaders continued to arrive. In addition, tourism became more economically significant for the state, as better roads and railroad service made it easier for people to reach scenic areas such as Yellowstone. The Depression, however, hit the state hard, though an increase in oil production and New Deal projects helped hard-pressed wage earners.

World War II and Postwar Developments. World War II found Wyoming's patriotic spirit intact, as tens of thousands of men and hundreds of women went off to war. At home the economy bustled with government's demands for food and mineral deposits for the war effort. After the war, the state continued to prosper, when the Cold War brought more federal government spending. Atomic weapons production brought lucrative mining ventures when uranium was discovered in the state, and military spending increased when Wyoming was chosen as a primary site for testing of intercontinental missiles.

The state's population continued to grow, from 92,000 at the turn of the century to 290,000 in 1950 and 40,000 more a decade later. After that time, however, growth was uneven, advancing only 2,000 from 1960 to 1970 and actually losing ground from 1980 to 1990. By then, although it had grown to more than 450,000, comparatively little manufacturing in the state and the difficulty of agriculture still placed it at the bottom of the list of state populations. Economically, although services provide some 60 percent of the state's income, it is heavily dependent on the land, through mining, grazing, and construction. By the 1990's, the state was attempting to broaden its economic base, especially by developing tourism. Politically, the state was divided between those who favored economic development and those who looked to the conservation of the state's natural resources.

Charles F. Bahmueller

Antler arches form the entrances to a park in Jackson, located at the southern end of Grand Teton National Park. They recall the region's earlier history as a hunting and trapping ground. (McCrea Adams)

Wyoming Time Line

1742-1743	François de La Vérendrye enters Wyoming.
1807	John Colter is first white American to enter Wyoming.
1812	Returning party from Astoria builds first known cabin in Wyoming, on North Platte River near Bessemer Bend.
1825	Fur trade begins.
1832	First wagons travel through South Pass; Fort Bonneville, near modern Daniel, is established.
1834	Fort Laramie, first permanent trading post in Wyoming, is established.
1842	John C. Frémont enters Wyoming.
1843	Fort Bridger, second permanent settlement, is established by Jim Bridger and Louis Vasquez.
1849	U.S. government purchases Fort Laramie.
1852	First school opens, at Fort Laramie.
1852	Fort Supply, the first agricultural settlement, is established by Mormons near Fort Bridger; later deserted and burned.
1860	Pony Express mail service begins.
1862	F. Halleck is established on Overland Trail.
1863-1865	Bozeman Trail is opened.
1863	First newspaper in Wyoming, the *Daily Telegraph*, is established at Fort Bridger.
1863	Fort Reno is established.
1866	Fort Phil Kearney is established on Bozeman Trail.
1866	Cheyenne is founded; Union Pacific Railroad enters Wyoming.
1869	Wind River Reservation for Shoshone Indians is created.
May 19, 1869	Wyoming Territory is organized.
1873	Yellowstone Park, world's first national park, is created.
1876	Cheyenne-Black Hills stage line is launched.
1877	Agreement is made with Shoshone Indians to allow Arapahoes to move to Wind River Reservation.
1880	Electric lights are introduced in Cheyenne.
1885	Chinese Massacre takes place at Rock Springs.
1886	Northwestern Railroad reaches eastern boundary.
1887	University of Wyoming opens.
1888	Wyoming constitutional convention takes place.
July 10, 1890	Wyoming is admitted to Union as forty-fourth state.
1892	Johnson County Invasion occurs.
1893	Cort F. Meyer is elected state superintendent of public instruction, becoming the first woman in the country elected to a state office.

(continued)

1906	Devil's Tower National Monument opens, the first in the United States.
1918	Uranium is discovered near Lusk.
1922	Salt Creek Oil Field opens.
1925	Nellie Tayloe Ross becomes the first woman governor in the country.
1925	Teapot Dome scandal transpires.
1935	State sales tax is adopted.
1939	Trona, marketed as baking soda, is discovered in Sweetwater County.
1949	Severe blizzard paralyzes state.
1978	World's largest radio telescope is built on Jelm Mountain.
1990	Voters approve term limitation initiative.
1995	Wolves are reintroduced to Yellowstone National Park.

Notes for Further Study

Published Sources. Books on Wyoming government include Robert B. Keiter and Tim Newcomb's *The Wyoming Constitution* (1993), Oliver Walter's *Equality State: Government and Politics in Wyoming* (1988), and Lewis L. Gould's *Wyoming from Territory to Statehood* (1989). Historical accounts of the state include Taft A. Larson, *History of Wyoming* (1990); *Frontier Spirit: The Story of Wyoming* (1996), by Craig Sodaro and Randay Adams; and *Readings in Wyoming History* (1996), by Phil Roberts. Not to be overlooked is the New Deal's Federal Writers Project's American Guide series publication *Wyoming: A Guide to Its History, Highways, and People* (1941).

For Wyoming's Indian tribes, see Speaks Lightning's *Indians of Idaho, Montana, and Wyoming: A Winter Count* (1999), Joel C. Janetski's *The Indians of Yellowstone Park* (1987), and Bert Webber's *Indians Along the Oregon Trail: The Tribes of Nebraska, Wyoming, Idaho, Oregon, and Washington Identified* (1992). For an account of Indian wars, see *The Indian Wars of the West and Frontier Army Life, 1862-1898* (1998), edited by Robert Lester. An aspect of Native American artifacts is presented in Mary Helen Hendry's *Indian Rock Art in Wyoming* (1983). For the Chinese massacre at Rock Springs, see Craig Storti, *Incident at Bitter Creek: The Story of the Rock Creek Chinese Massacre* (1991). Yellowstone Park is examined from varying perspectives in *Yellowstone Ecology: A Road Guide* (1992), by Sharon Eversman et al. The state's geology is discussed more generally in Darwin R. Spearing and David R. Lageson, *Roadside Geology of Wyoming* (1988). For geography, see

Mae Bobb Urbanek's *Wyoming Place Names* (1988).

Web Resources. For information on Wyoming government, see the state's home page (http://ww.state .wy.us), which has numerous appropriate links, including to some county and city sites. The governor's home page at this site has a calendar of events of the state for each month. At the judicial branch site (http://courts .state.wy.us), Wyoming supreme court opinions, as well as other information on the judiciary, are given. For Wyoming well as state government, there is also the Library of Congress Internet Resource page (http://lcweb.loc .gov/global/state/wy-gov.html). An excellent "bibliography" of Internet sites of information can be found at the Wyoming state agencies site (http://www-wsl.state .wy.us/sis/agency.html). For election information, see The League of Women Voters of Wyoming (http://lariat .lariat.org/LWV).

The state's history can be accessed at the Campbell County School District's Wyoming History page (http:// www-cchs.ccsd.k12.wy.us/cchs_web/curriculum/ss/ Wyoming.html), which has numerous historical and related links . For the state's Native Americans, see, for example, the Arapaho nation's site (http://www.fotw .stm.it/flags/us-arapa.html); for the state's geography, a site that includes maps and helpful links is Geography (http://geography.mininggco.com/library/maps/ bluswy.htm). Yellowstone National Park can be accessed at The Total Yellowstone Page (http://www. yellowstone-natl-park.com/).

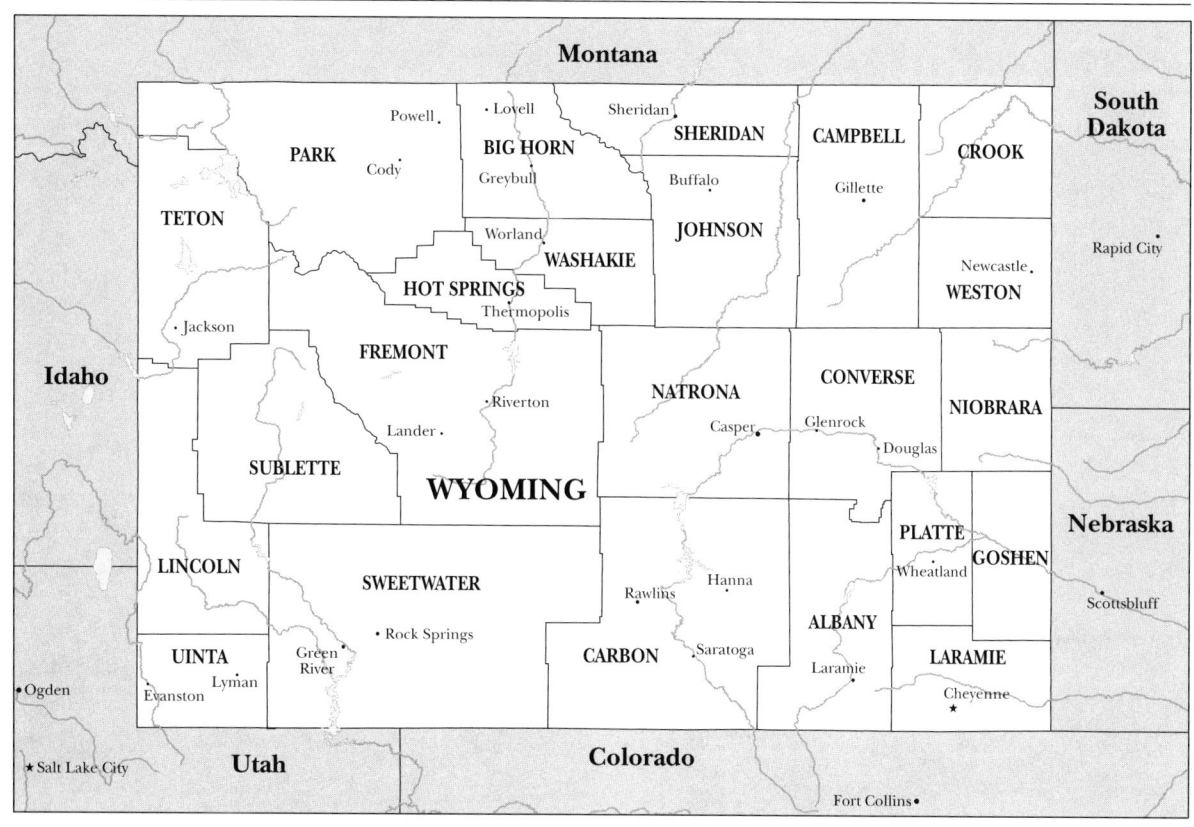

Counties

County	Sq. miles	1996 pop.	County	Sq. miles	1996 pop.
Albany	4,273.8	30,831	Natrona	5,340.1	63,875
Big Horn	3,137.1	11,276	Niobrara	2,625.9	2,637
Campbell	4,796.9	32,012	Park	6,942.7	25,373
Carbon	7,896.6	15,855	Platte	2,085.0	8,425
Converse	4,254.9	11,989	Sheridan	2,523.4	25,318
Crook	2,858.7	5,763	Sublette	4,881.6	5,577
Fremont	9,182.7	35,940	Sweetwater	10,425.9	40,322
Goshen	2,225.5	12,731	Teton	4,007.9	13,587
Hot Springs	2,004.0	4,627	Uinta	2,081.8	20,255
Johnson	4,166.4	6,690	Washakie	2,240.2	8,617
Laramie	2,686.2	79,175	Weston	2,397.9	6,554
Lincoln	4,069.3	13,971			

Source: U.S. Census Bureau; National Association of Counties.

Cities
With 10,000 or more residents

Rank	City	Population
1	Cheyenne	53,640

Population figures are estimated for mid-1998.
Source: U.S. Bureau of the Census.

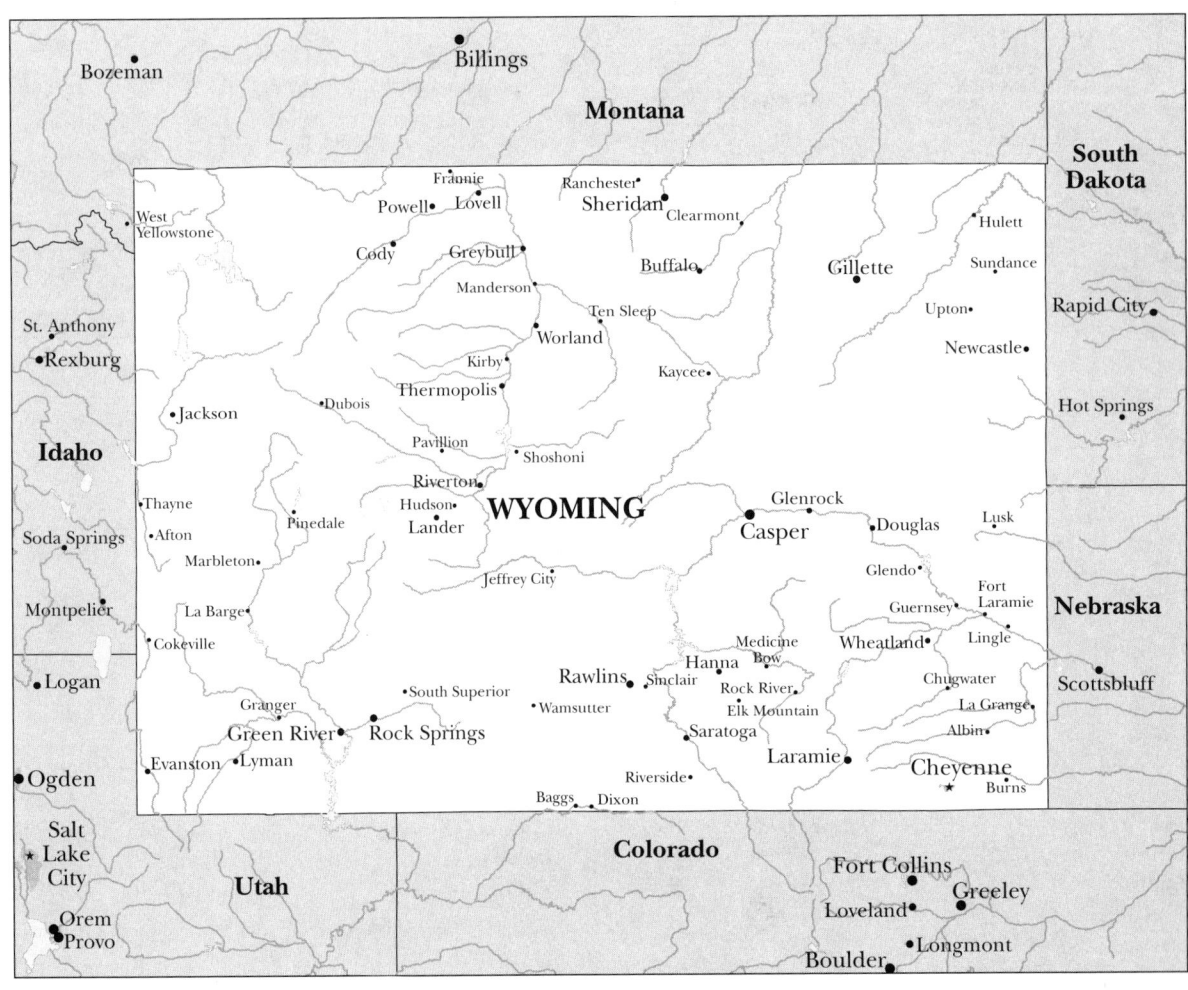

Index to Tables

NA = Reliable data are not available.

DEMOGRAPHICS

Resident state and national populations, 1970-1997

Population figures given in thousands

	State pop.	U.S. pop.	Share	Rank
1970	332	203,302	0.2%	49
1980	470	226,546	0.2%	49
1985	500	237,924	0.2%	50
1990	454	248,765	0.2%	50
1995	479	262,761	0.2%	50
1997	480	267,636	0.2%	50

Source: U.S. Bureau of the Census.

Resident population by age, 1997

Age group	Total population
Under 5 years	31,000
5 to 17 years	101,000
18 to 24 years	52,000
25 to 34 years	54,000
35 to 44 years	80,000
45 to 54 years	66,000
55 to 64 years	41,000
65 to 74 years	31,000
75 to 84 years	18,000
85 years and over	6,000
Portion of residents 65 and older	11.3%
National average	12.7%

Population figures are rounded to nearest thousand persons;
figures include armed forces personnel stationed in state.
Source: U.S. Bureau of the Census.

Resident population by race, Hispanic origin, 1997

	State pop.	Share	U.S.
All residents	480,000	100.0%	100.0%
Hispanic white	26,000	5.4%	10.0%
non-Hispanic white	435,000	90.6%	72.7%
African American	4,000	0.8%	12.7%
Native American	11,000	2.3%	0.9%
Asian, Pacific Islander	4,000	0.8%	3.8%

Source: U.S. Bureau of the Census.

Projections of state population, 2000-2025

	Model A Uses interstate migration observed from 1975-1994	Model B Uses Bureau of Economic Analysis employment projections
Year	Population	Population
2000	525,000	519,000
2005	568,000	559,000
2010	607,000	598,000
2015	641,000	636,000
2020	670,000	671,000
2025	694,000	702,000

All population projections, including those for 2000, were calculated in 1997.
Source: U.S. Bureau of the Census, Population Paper Listings PPL-47.

VITAL STATISTICS

Average lifetime in years by race, 1989-1991

	State	U.S.	Rank
All residents	76.21	75.37	21
White residents	76.34	76.13	24
Black residents	NA	69.16	NA

Ranks are from longest-lived to least longest-lived. Ranks exclude Alaska, for which reliable data are not available. Rank for black residents is based on the 32 states for which reliable data are available.
Source: U.S. National Center for Health Statistics.

Infant mortality rates, 1980 and 1995

	State	U.S.
All residents		
1980	9.8	12.6
1995	7.7	7.6
White residents		
1980	9.3	11.0
1995	6.8	6.3
Black residents		
1980	25.9	21.4
1995	NA	15.1

Figures represent deaths per 1,000 live births of resident infants under 1 year old, exclusive of fetal deaths; all-residents figures include other races not listed separately.
Source: U.S. National Center for Health Statistics.

Marriages and divorces

Marriages in 1996 4,900
Rate per 1,000 population, 1995 . . . . 10.7
U.S. rate, 1995 . . . . 8.9
Rank among all states. 9

Divorces in 1996 3,100
Rate per 1,000 population, 1995. . . . . 6.7
U.S. rate, 1995 . . . . 4.4
Rank among all states. 2

Rank is from highest to lowest in country.
Source: U.S. National Center for Health Statistics.

Death rates by leading causes, 1995
Deaths per 100,000 resident population

Cause	State	U.S.
Heart disease	203.3	280.7
Cancer	186.6	204.9
Cerebrovascular diseases	55.8	60.1
Accidents and adverse effects	50.0	35.5
Motor vehicle accidents	27.1	16.5
Chronic obstructive pulmonary diseases	55.4	39.2
Diabetes mellitus	22.1	22.6
HIV	-	NA
Suicide	17.1	11.9
Homicide	-	8.7
All causes	774.7	880.0
Rank in overall death rate among states		41

Figures exclude nonresidents who die in state. Causes of death follow International Classification of Diseases. Rank is from highest to lowest in country.
Source: U.S. National Center for Health Statistics.

ECONOMY

Gross state product, 1990-1996
In current dollars

	State product	Increase
1990	$13.5 billion	
1993	$14.6 billion	
1994	$14.9 billion	2.05%
1995	$15.8 billion	6.04%
1996	$16.8 billion	6.33%

Source: U.S. Bureau of Economic Analysis; *Survey of Current Business,* June, 1998.

Gross state product by industry, 1996
In billions

Farms, forestry, fisheries	$0.3
Construction	0.5
Manufacturing	0.9
Transportation, public utilities	2.5
Wholesale trade	0.5
Retail trade	1.1
Finance, insurance, real estate	1.6
Services	1.4
Government	2.0
State total	$15.8
Total U.S.	$6,923.8
State share	0.23%
Rank among states	48

Total figures include mining, not listed separately.
Source: U.S. Bureau of Economic Analysis; *Survey of Current Business,* June, 1998.

Personal income per capita, 1990 and 1997
In current dollars

	1990	1997
Per capita income	$17,213	$22,648
U.S. average	$19,188	$25,598
Rank among states	30	34

1997 data are preliminary.
Source: U.S. Bureau of Economic Analysis; *Survey of Current Business,* May, 1998.

Energy consumption, 1995
In trillions of British thermal units (BTU)

End-use sectors

Residential	37.8
Commercial	40.1
Industrial	227.2
Transportation	100.0

Sources of energy

Petroleum	136.8
Natural gas	103.9
Coal	461.9
Hydroelectric power	8.2
Nuclear electric power	0
Total state per capita consumption	845.6
Total U.S. per capita consumption	344.4
Rank among states	3
Total state energy consumption	405.2
Total U.S. energy consumption	90,547.4
State share of U.S. total	0.45
Rank among states	42

Total figures include items not listed separately.
Source: U.S. Energy Information Administration; *State Energy Data Report.*

Nonfarm employment by sectors, 1997

Total	224,000
Construction	15,000
Manufacturing	11,000
Transportation, public utilities	14,000
Wholesale trade, retail trade	53,000
Finance, insurance, real estate	8,000
Services	49,000
Government	58,000

Figures are rounded to nearest thousand persons. Total includes mining, not listed separately.
Source: U.S. Bureau of Labor Statistics; *Employment and Earnings,* monthly.

Foreign exports, 1990-1997
In millions of dollars

Year	State	U.S.	State share
1990	264	394,045	0.07%
1996	481	624,767	0.08%
1997	560	688,896	0.08%

Source: U.S. Bureau of the Census; *U.S. Merchandise Trade,* series FT 900.

LAND USE

Federally owned land, 1996

	State	U.S.	State share
Total acres	62,343,000	2,271,343,000	2.74%
Federally owned	30,878,000	563,129,000	5.48%
Federal share	49.5%	24.8%	—

Areas are rounded to nearest thousand acres. Figures for federally owned land do not include trust properties.

Source: U.S. General Services Administration; *Inventory Report on Real Property Owned by the United States Throughout the World,* annual.

Land use, 1992

In acres, rounded to nearest thousand

Total surface area	62,598,000
Federal land	30,020,000
Total nonfederal	32,012,000
Developed	541,000
Total rural	31,471,000
Cropland.	2,272,000
Pasture land	901,000
Range land	26,015,000
Forest land.	975,000
Minor cover/use.	1,309,000

Total surface area figures include water area not shown separately.

Source: U.S. Dept. of Agriculture; Soil Conservation Service; Iowa State University, Statistical Laboratory; *Summary Report, 1992 National Resources Inventory.*

Farms and crop acreage, 1997

	State	U.S.	Share	Rank
Farms (thousands)	9	2,058	0.44%	38
Acres (millions)	35	968	3.62%	9
Acres per farm	3,802	471	—	2
Acres planted	1,911	334,139	0.57%	33
Acres harvested	1,847	319,894	0.58%	33
Farm value (mill.)	$372	$108,805	0.34%	33

Numbers of farms are rounded to nearest thousand.

Source: U.S. Dept. of Agriculture; National Agricultural Statistics Service.

GOVERNMENT AND FINANCE

Units of local government, 1997

	State	Total U.S.	Rank
All local governments	654	87,453	39
Counties	23	3,043	37
Municipalities	97	19,372	40
Townships	0	16,629	—
School districts	56	13,726	38
Special districts	478	34,683	25

County ranks are based on the 48 states with county governments; township ranks are based on the 20 states with township governments; school district ranks are based on the 46 states with such districts.

Source: U.S. Bureau of the Census; *1997 Census of Governments, Government Organization,* Series GC97(1).

State government revenue, 1996

Total revenue	$2,348 mill.
General revenue	2,004 mill.
Per capita.	4,175
U.S. per capita average	2,910
Rank among states	4

Intergovernmental revenue

Total	$768 mill.
From federal government	753 mill.
From local government	15 mill.

Charges and Miscellaneous

Total	$610 mill.
Current charges	95 mill.
Misc. general revenue	515 mill.

Taxes

Total	$626 mill.
General sales	211 mill.
Selective sales	63 mill.
License taxes.	74 mill.
Individual income	NA
Corporate income	NA
Other	278 mill.
Insurance trust revenue	310 mill.

Total revenue figures include items not listed separately.

Source: U.S. Bureau of the Census.

State government expenditures, 1996

General expenditures

Intergovernmental	$687 mill.
Direct expenditures	1,120 mill.
Total.	1,807 mill.

Selected direct expenditures

Education	$659 mill.
Public welfare.	253 mill.
Health, hospital	118 mill.
Highways	270 mill.
Police.	12 mill.
Corrections	32 mill.
Natural resources	83 mill.
Parks and recreation.	16 mill.
Government administration	71 mill.
Interest on debt	54 mill.

Other

State per capita expenditures	$3,764
U.S. per capita average	2,854
Rank among states	5
Total state expenditures	2,062 mill.
Total U.S. expenditures	859,959 mill.

Totals include items not listed separately.
Source: U.S. Bureau of the Census.

POLITICS

Governors since statehood

D = Democrat; R = Republican; O = other;
(r) resigned; (d) died in office; (i) removed from office

Francis E. Warren (R)	(r) 1890
Amos W. Barber (R)	1890-1893
John E. Osborne (D)	1893-1895
William A. Richards (R)	1895-1899
DeForest Richards (R)	(d) 1899-1903
Fennimore Chatterton (R)	1903-1905
Bryant B. Brooks (R)	1905-1911
Joseph M. Carey (D)	1911-1915
John B. Kendrick (D)	(r) 1915-1917
Frank L. Houx (D)	1917-1919
Robert D. Carey (R)	1919-1923
William B. Ross (D)	(d) 1923-1924
Frank E. Lucas (R)	1924-1925
Nellie D. Ross (D)	1925-1927
Frank C. Emerson (R)	(d) 1927-1931
Alonzo M. Clark (R)	1931-1933
Leslie A. Miller (D)	1933-1939
Nels H. Smith (R).	1939-1943

Lester C. Hunt (D)	(r) 1943-1949
Arthur G. Crane (R)	1949-1951
Frank A. Barrett (R)	(r) 1951-1953
Clifford J. Rogers (R).	1953-1955
Milward L. Simpson (R)	1955-1959
John J. Hickey (D)	(r) 1959-1961
John R. Gage (D)	1961-1963
Clifford P. Hansen (R)	1963-1967
Stanley K. Hathaway (R)	1967-1975
Edgar J. Herschler (D)	1975-1987
Mike Sullivan (D).	1987-1995
Mike Geringer (R)	1995-

Composition of state legislature, 1990-1998

	Democrats	Republicans
State House (64 seats in 1990; 60 seats thereafter)		
1990	22	42
1992	19	41
1994	13	47
1996	17	43
1998	17	43
State Senate (30 seats)		
1990	10	20
1992	10	20
1994	10	20
1996	9	21
1998	10	20

Figures for total seats may include independents and minor
party members.
Source: Council of State Governments; *State Elective Officials
and the Legislatures.*

Voter participation in presidential elections, 1992 and 1996

	1992	1996
State voting age pop.	329,000	352,000
Total U.S. voting age pop.	189,524,000	196,509,000
State share of U.S. total	0.2%	0.2%
Rank among states	50	50
Percent of state casting vote	61.0	62.9
Percent of U.S. total voting	55.1	49.0
Rank among states	19	3

Source: U.S. Bureau of the Census.

Composition of congressional delegations, 1989-1999

	Dem	Rep	Total
House of Representatives			
101st Congress, 1989			
State delegates	0	1	1
Total U.S.	259	174	433
102d Congress, 1991			
State delegates	0	1	1
Total U.S.	267	167	434
103d Congress, 1993			
State delegates	0	1	1
Total U.S.	258	176	434
104th Congress, 1995			
State delegates	0	1	1
Total U.S.	197	236	433
105th Congress, 1997			
State delegates	0	1	1
Total U.S.	206	228	434
106th Congress, 1999			
State delegates	0	1	1
Total U.S.	211	222	433
Senate			
101st Congress, 1989			
State delegates	0	2	2
Total U.S.	55	45	100
102d Congress, 1991			
State delegates	0	2	2
Total U.S.	56	44	100
103d Congress, 1993			
State delegates	0	2	2
Total U.S.	57	43	100
104th Congress, 1995			
State delegates	0	2	2
Total U.S.	46	53	99
105th Congress, 1997			
State delegates	0	2	2
Total U.S.	45	55	100
106th Congress, 1999			
State delegates	0	2	2
Total U.S.	45	54	99

Figures are for starts of first sessions. Figure for U.S. Representatives for 101st Congress does not include Alabama and Indiana, which had vacancies. Figures for U.S. Representatives for 102d, 103d, and 106th Congresses do not include Vermont, which had 1 Independent-Socialist. Figure for U.S. Representatives for 104th Congress does not include Vermont, which had 1 Independent-Socialist, and California, which had 1 vacancy. Figure for U.S. Representatives for 105th Congress does not include New York, which had 1 vacancy. Figure for U.S. Senators for 104th Congress does not include Oregon, which had 1 vacancy. Figure for U.S. Senators for 106th Congress does not include New Hampshire, which had 1 Independent.

Source: U.S. Congress; *Congressional Directory,* biennial.

HEALTH AND MEDICAL CARE

Medicare, 1997

	Recipients	Payments
State	63,000	$216 mill.
Total U.S.	37,514,000	$206,064 mill.
State share	0.17%	0.10%
Rank among states	49	49

Recipient figures are rounded to nearest thousand persons. Ranks are from highest to lowest.

Source: U.S. Health Care Financing Administration.

Medicaid, 1996

	Recipients	Payments
State	51,000	$183 mill.
Total U.S.	35,028,000	$121,419 mill.
State share	0.15%	1.25%
Rank among states	49	50

Recipient figures are rounded to nearest thousand persons. Payment figures for fiscal year reflect federal and state contribution payments. Ranks are from highest to lowest.

Source: U.S. Health Care Financing Administration.

Health insurance coverage, 1996

	State	U.S.
Total persons covered	422,000	225,070,000
Total persons not covered	66,000	41,716,000
Part not covered	13.5%	15.6%
Rank among states	23	—
Children not covered	14,000	10,554,000
Part not covered	10.5%	14.8%
Rank among states	32	—

Ranks are from most to fewest uninsured. Population figures are rounded to nearest thousand persons.

Source: U.S. Bureau of the Census.

AIDS, syphilis, tuberculosis, and measles cases, 1997

Cases	U.S.	State	Share
AIDS	58,443	16	0.03%
Syphilis	8,550	NA	NA
Tuberculosis	18,534	2	0.01%
Measles	148,000	NA	NA

Measles figures are rounded to nearest thousand cases.
Source: U.S. Centers for Disease Control and Prevention.

HOUSING

Homeownership rates, 1985-1997

	1985	1990	1997
State	73.2%	68.9%	67.6%
Total U.S.	63.9%	63.9%	65.7%
Rank among states	3	16	29

Source: U.S. Bureau of the Census.

Home sales, 1990 and 1997
In thousands of units

Existing home sales	1990	1997	Change
State sales	7.4	9.5	2.1
Total U.S. sales	3,560	4,730	1,170
State share of U.S. total	0.21%	0.20%	-0.01%
Rank among states	47	45	—

Source: National Association of Realtors; *Real Estate Outlook: Market Trends and Insights.*

EDUCATION

Public school enrollment, 1995

State K-8 enrollment 69,000
Total U.S. K-8 enrollment 32,341,000
State share of total U.S. 0.21%
State 9-12 enrollment. 31,000
Total U.S. 9-12 enrollment 12,500,000
State share of U.S. total 0.25%
State public school enroll. rate 97.0%
Overall U.S. rate. 91.6%
Rank among states 3

Enrollment figures (which include unclassified students) are rounded to nearest thousand pupils in fall term; kindergarten (K)-8 grade figures include some prekindergarten students. Enrollment rate is based on percentage of persons 5-17 years old. Rank is from highest to lowest.
Source: U.S. National Center for Education Statistics.

Public college finances, 1996

State FTE enrollment. 21,300
Total U.S. FTE enrollment 8,268,800
State share of total U.S. 0.26%
Rank among states. 48
State and local appropriations $147,500,000
Total U.S. state and local
  appropriations. . . . . $39,699 mill.
State share of total U.S. 0.37%
Rank among states. 43
State net tuition revenues $39,700,000
Total U.S. net tuition $18,348,100,000
State share of total U.S. 0.22%
Rank among states. 48

FTE=Full-time equivalent; credit and noncredit enrollment including summer session in academic year ending in 1996.
Enrollments are rounded to nearest thousand students. Net tuition revenues exclude appropriation to students attending in-state public institutions. Rankings are from highest shares to lowest.
Source: Research Associates of Washington.

TRANSPORTATION AND TRAVEL

Highway mileage, 1996

Interstate	913
Other arterial	3,666
Collector roads	10,997
Local roads	19,011
Urban roads	2,321
Rural roads	31,794
Total state	34,115
U.S. total	3,933,985
State share	0.9%
Rank among states	41

Source: U.S. Federal Highway Administration.

Motor vehicle registrations and driver licenses, 1996
In thousands

Vehicle registrations	State	U.S.	Share	Rank
Autos, trucks, buses	562	206,365	0.27%	48
Autos only	227	128,439	0.18%	49
Motorcycles	15	3,832	0.39%	47
Driver licenses	343	179,539	0.19%	48

Figures do not include vehicles owned by military services.
Source: U.S. Federal Highway Administration; *Highway Statistics; Selected Highway Statistics and Charts.*

Domestic travel expenditures, 1995
Spending by U.S. residents on overnight trips and day trips of at least 100 miles

Total expenditures in state	$1,232 mill.
Total expenditures in U.S.	$360,314 mill.
State share of total U.S.	0.34%
Rank among states	44

Source: Travel Industry Association of America.

CRIME AND LAW ENFORCEMENT

State and local police officers, 1996

Local police	618
State police	151
Sheriffs	507
Total	1,377
Officers per 10,000 residents	29
U.S. average	25
Rank among states	5

Figures cover full-time sworn officers; totals include special police not shown separately.
Source: U.S. Bureau of Justice Statistics; *Census of State and Local Law Enforcement Agencies, 1996.*

Crime rates, 1996
Rates per 100,000 resident population

Violent crimes	State	U.S.
Total violent	250	634
Murder	3.3	7.4
Forcible rape	29.1	36.1
Robbery	20	202
Aggravated assault	197	388
Property crimes		
Total property	4,004	4,445
Burglary	662	943
Larceny/theft	3,203	2,976
Motor vehicle theft	139	526
Totals	4,254	5,079

Source: U.S. Federal Bureau of Investigation; *Crime in the United States,* annual.

State prison populations, 1980-1996

	State	U.S.	State share
1980	534	305,458	0.17%
1990	1,110	708,393	0.16%
1996	1,499	1,025,624	0.15%

Figures exclude prisoners in federal penitentiaries.
Source: U.S. Bureau of Justice Statistics.

Appendices

Order in which states entered the Union

Rank	State	Entered Union	Rank	State	Entered Union
1	Delaware	December 7, 1787	26	Michigan	January 26, 1837
2	Pennsylvania	December 12, 1787	27	Florida	March 3, 1845
3	New Jersey	December 18, 1787	28	Texas	December 29, 1845
4	Georgia	January 2, 1788	29	Iowa	December 28, 1846
5	Connecticut	January 9, 1788	30	Wisconsin	May 29, 1848
6	Massachusetts	February 6, 1788	31	California	September 9, 1850
7	Maryland	April 28, 1788	32	Minnesota	May 11, 1858
8	South Carolina	May 23, 1788	33	Oregon	February 14, 1859
9	New Hampshire	June 21, 1788	34	Kansas	January 29, 1861
10	Virginia	June 25, 1788	35	West Virginia	June 20, 1863
11	New York	July 26, 1788	36	Nevada	October 31, 1864
12	North Carolina	November 21, 1789	37	Nebraska	March 1, 1867
13	Rhode Island	May 29, 1790	38	Colorado	August 1, 1876
14	Vermont	March 4, 1791	39	North Dakota	November 2, 1889
15	Kentucky	June 1, 1792	40	South Dakota	November 2, 1889
16	Tennessee	June 1, 1796	41	Montana	November 8, 1889
17	Ohio	March 1, 1803	42	Washington	November 11, 1889
18	Louisiana	April 30, 1812	43	Idaho	July 3, 1890
19	Indiana	December 11, 1816	44	Wyoming	July 10, 1890
20	Mississippi	December 10, 1817	45	Utah	January 4, 1896
21	Illinois	December 3, 1818	46	Oklahoma	November 16, 1907
22	Alabama	December 14, 1819	47	New Mexico	January 6, 1912
23	Maine	March 15, 1820	48	Arizona	February 14, 1912
24	Missouri	August 10, 1821	49	Alaska	January 3, 1959
25	Arkansas	June 15, 1836	50	Hawaii	August 21, 1959

States ranked by area

Areas are given in square miles

Rank	State	Land area	Including water	Rank	State	Land area	Including water
1	Alaska	570,374	656,424	26	Florida	53,997	65,758
2	Texas	261,914	268,601	27	Arkansas	52,075	53,182
3	California	155,973	163,707	28	Alabama	50,750	52,423
4	Montana	145,556	147,046	29	North Carolina	48,718	53,821
5	New Mexico	121,365	121,598	30	New York	47,224	54,475
6	Arizona	114,000	114,006	31	Mississippi	46,914	48,434
7	Nevada	109,806	110,567	32	Pennsylvania	44,820	46,058
8	Colorado	103,730	104,100	33	Louisiana	43,566	51,843
9	Wyoming	97,105	97,818	34	Tennessee	41,220	42,146
10	Oregon	96,003	98,386	35	Ohio	40,953	44,828
11	Idaho	82,751	83,574	36	Kentucky	39,732	40,411
12	Utah	82,168	84,904	37	Virginia	39,598	42,769
13	Kansas	81,823	82,282	38	Indiana	35,870	36,420
14	Minnesota	79,617	86,943	39	Maine	30,865	35,387
15	Nebraska	76,644	77,358	40	South Carolina	30,111	32,007
16	South Dakota	75,898	77,121	41	West Virginia	24,087	24,231
17	North Dakota	68,994	70,704	42	Maryland	9,775	12,407
18	Missouri	68,898	69,709	43	Vermont	9,249	9,615
19	Oklahoma	68,679	69,903	44	New Hampshire	8,969	9,351
20	Washington	66,582	71,303	45	Massachusetts	7,838	10,555
21	Michigan	58,110	96,810	46	New Jersey	7,419	8,722
22	Georgia	57,919	59,441	47	Hawaii	6,423	10,932
23	Iowa	55,875	56,276	48	Connecticut	4,845	5,544
24	Illinois	55,593	57,918	49	Delaware	1,982	2,489
25	Wisconsin	54,314	65,503	50	Rhode Island	1,045	1,545

States are ranked by their land surfaces.
Source: U.S. Bureau of the Census.

States ranked by population

Estimated populations in 1997

Rank	State	Population	Rank	State	Population
1	California	32,268,301	26	South Carolina	3,760,181
2	Texas	19,439,337	27	Oklahoma	3,317,091
3	New York	18,137,226	28	Connecticut	3,269,858
4	Florida	14,653,945	29	Oregon	3,243,487
5	Pennsylvania	12,019,661	30	Iowa	2,852,423
6	Illinois	11,895,849	31	Mississippi	2,730,501
7	Ohio	11,186,331	32	Kansas	2,594,840
8	Michigan	9,773,892	33	Arkansas	2,522,819
9	New Jersey	8,052,849	34	Utah	2,059,148
10	Georgia	7,486,242	35	West Virginia	1,815,787
11	North Carolina	7,428,194	36	New Mexico	1,729,751
12	Virginia	6,733,996	37	Nevada	1,676,809
13	Massachusetts	6,117,520	38	Nebraska	1,656,870
14	Indiana	5,864,108	39	Maine	1,242,051
15	Washington	5,610,362	40	Idaho	1,210,232
16	Missouri	5,402,058	41	Hawaii	1,186,602
17	Tennessee	5,368,198	42	New Hampshire	1,172,709
18	Wisconsin	5,169,677	43	Rhode Island	987,429
19	Maryland	5,094,289	44	Montana	878,810
20	Minnesota	4,685,549	45	Delaware	739,337
21	Arizona	4,554,966	46	South Dakota	737,973
22	Louisiana	4,351,769	47	North Dakota	640,883
23	Alabama	4,319,154	48	Alaska	609,311
24	Kentucky	3,908,124	49	Vermont	588,978
25	Colorado	3,892,644	50	Wyoming	479,743

Source: U.S. Census Bureau.

States ranked by gross state product in 1996

Rank	State	GSP	Rank	State	GSP
1	California	880.1	26	Kentucky	89.3
2	New York	563.3	27	South Carolina	82.7
3	Texas	502.9	28	Oregon	79.4
4	Illinois	345.5	29	Iowa	70.3
5	Florida	326.1	30	Oklahoma	66.7
6	Pennsylvania	298.7	31	Kansas	62.0
7	Ohio	280.7	32	Mississippi	51.7
8	New Jersey	251.1	33	Arkansas	51.5
9	Michigan	241.0	34	Nevada	48.3
10	Georgia	197.1	35	Utah	45.9
11	Massachusetts	191.0	36	Nebraska	43.2
12	North Carolina	190.9	37	New Mexico	40.4
13	Virginia	183.2	38	West Virginia	35.0
14	Indiana	144.1	39	Hawaii	34.9
15	Washington	143.8	40	New Hampshire	31.7
16	Missouri	132.8	41	Delaware	28.9
17	Maryland	130.2	42	Maine	26.0
18	Minnesota	128.7	43	Idaho	25.9
19	Wisconsin	128.7	44	Rhode Island	23.3
20	Tennessee	128.7	45	Alaska	21.4
21	Connecticut	113.0	46	South Dakota	18.4
22	Louisiana	109.6	47	Montana	16.9
23	Colorado	106.8	48	Wyoming	15.8
24	Arizona	102.6	49	North Dakota	14.3
25	Alabama	90.7	50	Vermont	13.5
				United States	$6,948.7

In billions of dollars, measured in chained (1992) dollars.
Source: U.S Bureau of Economic Analysis, Survey of Current Business, June, 1998.

The 50 States

INDEX

Death rates

Debt, government. *See*
Expenditures, government

Diabetes. *See* **Death rates**

Disease. *See* **Acquired
immunodeficiency syndrome
(AIDS); Death rates; Measles;
Syphilis; Tuberculosis**

Divorces

Domestic travel. *See* **Travel,
domestic**

Driver licenses

Economy. *See* **Employment, nonfarm; Exports, foreign; Gross state product; Income, personal**

Education. *See* **Expenditures, government; Public college finances; School enrollment**

Elections. *See* **Congressional delegations, composition of; Legislatures, composition of; Presidential elections**

Employment, nonfarm

Energy consumption

Expenditures, government

Vital statistics. *See* **Death rates; Infant mortality; Lifetime, average**

Voter participation. *See* **Presidential elections**

Wholesale trade. *See* **Gross state product by industry**

Wholesale trade employment. *See* **Employment, nonfarm**